SIX YEARS THAT CHANGED THE WORLD

1939 - 1945

Intelligencer Journal
LANCASTER NEW ERA
SUNDAY NEWS

Lancaster, Pa.

WORLD WAR II - SIX YEARS THAT CHANGED THE WORLD...1939 -1945

Developed under agreement with **Historical Briefs, Inc.**, Box 629, Sixth Street & Madalyn Ave., Verplanck, NY 10596.

Printed by:
Monument Printers & Lithographer, Inc.
Sixth Street & Madalyn Ave., Verplanck, NY 10596

Foreword

Think about a newspaper and you think about today's news...headlines and information that are important right now. But a newspaper is much more. It is a history book in the making, and each day's edition is a new chapter.

That's what makes this book unique. You really can "live" through the Second World War. If you were in the Army, Navy, Air Force or Marines there will be memories aplenty. There was fear, panic, pain and death. And if you were on the "home front," you'll recall the rationing, recapped tires, savings bond drives and blackouts. But, there were good times, too. Our country was pulling together, fighting for freedom, making sacrifices and, finally, winning in Europe and in the Pacific.

Of course, many of us were not born yet. Even so, the history "lives" because you're reading newspaper pages. You not only have a sense of the immediacy of news from the front lines, but also the chance to see what was going on in the communities that make up Lancaster County, Pennsylvania and the rest of the world. Connie Mack was managing the Philadelphia Athletics and Lancastrians could root for the Phillies in the National League or the Athletics in the American. We could watch Joe DiMaggio and Ted Williams play when the New York Yankees and Boston Red Sox visited Philadelphia. Radio brought the latest news, but people also listened to Jack Benny, Burns and Allen, Edgar Bergen and Charlie McCarthy, Gangbusters, Fred Allen, Lowell Thomas and the NBC Symphony. Betty Grable had great legs and there were movie theaters almost everywhere. Tom Mix, Clark Gable, Jimmy Stewart, Shirley Temple, Roy Rogers and Trigger helped entertain us. So did Glenn Miller, Tommy Dorsey and Benny Goodman with their bands.

Franklin Delano Roosevelt was elected President four times before he died and Harry Truman took over. It was Truman, Winston Churchill, Joseph Stalin and others who negotiated the peace that ended the second World War. And it was through the pages of the *Intelligencer Journal, Lancaster New Era* and *Sunday News* that people of Lancaster City and County stayed abreast of the earth-shaking events and the everyday happenings that made up the lives of local residents in the 1940's.

Now, through the pages of the *Intell, New Era* and *Sunday News* you can live or re-live the history that affected the world as a whole and the lives of our parents, ourselves, our relatives and friends. As you read about the battles and the every day local events you will come to understand the war and its implications for the people of Lancaster County...people like you and me.

You'll discover that newspapers report, inform and entertain. But they do more. They mirror our existence and record our history as it happens. They make the world...even the universe...come alive for all of us.

John M. Buckwalter
President, Chief Executive Officer
Lancaster Newspapers, Inc.

SCENES FROM LANCASTER DURING WORLD WAR II

LANCASTER NEW ERA

Examiner Founded 1830.
New Era Founded 1877.

Published Every Evening Except Sunday by New Era Company.
Entered as Second Class Matter at Post Office, Lancaster, Pa.

LANCASTER, PA., TUESDAY, JANUARY 3, 1939

CITY EDITION

16 PAGES—128 COLUMNS—THREE CENTS

WEATHER

Cloudy, with slowly rising temperature tonight and Wednesday; light rain Wednesday and in north portion tonight. Details on page 3.

State Senate Is in Uproar Over Control

Democrats Defy Supreme Court in Successful Attempt to Seat Philadelphian Whose Election Is Contested; GOP, in Full Control of House, Elects Turner Speaker

HARRISBURG, Jan. 3—(A. P.)—A dramatic and successful attempt to seat Herbert S. Levin, Democrat, in the State Senate in defiance of a Supreme Court order, threw the ordinarily routine start of the new State legislative session into an uproar today.

Democrats, attempting to block Republican control of the Senate, held up convening of that body for an hour while the House convened and when they finally arrived, commotion ensued.

Levin, accompanied by two State Policemen, went to a Senate seat. The high court had ordered that he should not be seated until a challenge by his Republican opponent, in the November election, Samuel W. Salus, of Philadelphia, was settled.

Mutterings arose in Republican ranks.

Kennedy Interrupted At Once

Lieutenant Governor Thomas Kennedy convened the Senate and was interrupted immediately by Representative Robert S. Hamilton, Philadelphia Republican, who sought to serve a paper on him. It may have been the court order, some observers guessed.

Kennedy pounded his gavel, he shouted:

"I want to inform the gentleman on my left (Hamilton) that I am the presiding officer of the Senate. I have entire jurisdiction in this chamber and I refuse to accept this paper."

Democrats shouted: "Get the —— out of there."

The crowd ringing the Senate seats gaped.

Sergeants-at-arms clanged the heavy doors and locked them. Newspapermen could not get in or out. Kennedy sent to the Elections Bureau for the certification of Levin.

Eventually, order was restored, but the doors were kept locked.

Election Returns Read

Kennedy then ordered the returns read in each 1938 Senate race and questioned the election of one Republican — John G. Snowden of Lycoming county. A contest of Snowden's victory was dismissed by the courts.

Kennedy said "there has been an error."

This produced new protests from the Republican side. Kennedy said the certification showed Snowden's Democratic opponent received more votes.

Later, however, Kennedy ruled Snowden had been properly elected and the Republican member retained his seat.

Levin's was the first name read. G. Mason Owlett, Republican floor leader, opposed seating him. Kennedy asserted there had been no injunction served on the Senate, and added "and there could not be any."

He insisted the Senate made its own rules—not the courts.

Bard Upholds Levin

Levin later was seated officially after Attorney General Guy K. Bard ruled that the Senate was "the sole judge" of its members.

Said Bard: "There is nothing in the court's decree preventing the Senate from seating Levin. The Senate is the sole judge of its members. The Supreme Court has ruled that way. It declared that elections contests in courts were only to determine the number of legal votes."

G. O. P. Easily Rules House

In sharp contrast, the House convened at 12:03 P. M. and proceeded with the Republicans in undisputed control.

Ellwood Jackson Turner, Delaware Veteran, was chosen Speaker, as had been expected for weeks.

The Democrats nominated retiring Speaker Roy E. Furman, but it was only a gesture, as their party trails 129 to 79 in the chamber.

Robert E. Woodside, Dauphin county, took over the duties of Republican floor leader relinquished by Turner.

Herbert B. Cohen, York county, continued as Democratic leader.

The Republicans then elected William B. Ward, Jr., who resigned as mayor of Chester only today, as chief clerk at $7,500 a year. Democrats went through the motions again, putting up Thomas Callaghan, retiring clerk, as their candidate.

Turner Urges Harmony

Turner assumed the post of Speaker with an admonition to the Legislators for concerted action rather than individual effort to "seek the spotlight."

"I approach my task with humility." Turner said in his acceptance speech.

He reminded the legislators that Pennsylvania "is indeed fortunate to have elected a Governor who x x x has pledged the people to maintain

(See LEGISLATURE—Last Page)

The Scribbler

THE holidays put residents of the 400 block of State street in a dither.

Someone put a garbage can out early last Friday night, apparently in the belief that collections would be made early Saturday. Neighbors followed suit and by midnight, almost every home had a can out front.

The garbage was collected yesterday.

MRS. Fred Ashmead, of Nevin street, poured the cream into the sugar bowl while preparing dinner the other night. She later looked all over the kitchen and on the back porch, having forgotten where she put the cream. Members of the family discovered where it was.

MRS. B. P. Chodos, wife of the veterinarian, and her daughter, Betty, left their home the other night to attend two separate parties. They met again shortly after. The parties were both being held at the same tea room.

MRS. Lillian Gehman, of Ephrata, spent part of a recent afternoon looking for her bedroom slippers. After a thorough search she told her sister she was certain she had left the slippers in her clothes closet.

She found them later—on her feet.

EARLE SAYS HE "PAID OWN WAY"

Admits in Farewell Message That State Deficit Will Be $34,000,000.

HARRISBURG, Jan. 3—(A. P.)—Governor George H. Earle, retiring from the political scene in Pennsylvania, asserted today in his farewell message prepared for delivery before the General Assembly that his "Little New Deal" administration paid its own way in the past four years, though it wound up with a $34,000,000 deficit.

He said financing relief until the end of the biennium, May 31, would pile up a $40,000,000 debt. Against this, he said the state had unexpected balances of $6,000,000 assured.

Earle pointed out that his administration "inherited" a deficit of almost $36,000,000 from that of former Governor Pinchot, a Republican.

The outgoing Chief Executive referred briefly to the political charges which covered his final year in office, warned the newly Republican-controlled Legislature against acting in behalf "of the few," and levelled some parting criticism at the courts.

He declared "we had just barely begun to see daylight after the dark hours of national economic catastrophe" when he took office.

"In the past four years," he said, "the changes in our governmental structure have been more rapid than in the entire 40 years preceding. It was inevitable that we should suffer certain reverses and disappointments.

"It was inevitable because progress means readjustment, and readjustment is all too frequently painful."

Says Promises To People Kept

He said the Democratic platform had been fulfilled in the legislature and termed that "one fact" which stood out during his term.

"Our promises to the people have been kept," he said.

The Governor disclosed that his administration had appropriated $735,000,000, of which $343,000,000 was for relief of all kinds; $171,400,639 for subsidies; $30,193,000 for interest and the sinking fund; $154,467,763 for other governmental operations and $35,751,878, was the inherited deficiency.

He said the administrative costs for departments under the Governor had risen approximately $5,000,000 from the previous administration to $62,393,328, adding, however, that "this was counterbalanced by the new services of government," including the new labor and public assistance laws.

Earle asserted his administration, spending $46,425,927 to collect taxes, saved $4,235,924 over the Pinchot regime.

"When the required adjustments are made, the appropriations compare

(See EARLE—Last Page)

HULL UNDERGOES THROAT OPERATION

J. L. Huebener To Help Supervise P. P. & L. Here; John E. Malone Ill.

Ralph B. Hull, vice president of the Pennsylvania Power and Light Company in charge of the Lancaster division, is recuperating in the General Hospital from a throat operation, performed Saturday. He was reported today to be making "satisfactory progress."

Pending Mr. Hull's recovery, P. P. and L. officials at Allentown said today, James L. Huebener, district manager of the Bethlehem division of P. P. and L., will spend several days in Lancaster each week to supervise the company's affairs here. Mr. Huebener, a native of Lehigh county, has been associated with P. P. and L. since 1922 and after serving in all departments of the organization became manager of the Bethlehem division in 1926.

John E. Malone, president of the Lancaster Bar Association, is a patient in St. Joseph's Hospital, reported threatened with pneumonia. I. P. Hepler, real estate man, is in the same hospital with an infected leg.

Escape Ringleader

Frank Haines, convicted robber, who was described by a recaptured partner, as ringleader in the escape of five prisoners from the Ohio Criminal Insane Hospital at Lima, O. He said Haines was headed for Chicago "to kill his wife and a couple of cops."

(STORY ON LAST PAGE)

WALLY IS ANGRY WITH EX-KING

Duchess Peeved Because Edward Plans to Visit Ailing Mother Alone.

LONDON, Jan. 3.—(U. P.) — The Duke of Windsor is expected to arrive in England, alone, about Jan. 13 for a private visit to his mother, Dowager Queen Mary, a usually reliable informant said today.

The Duke's American born Duchess, for whom he gave up his throne, was alleged by the same informant to be most angry because he had agreed to return, even for the briefest visit, without her.

It was understood that the Duke had agreed to return only because his brother King George informed him in a personal message that the condition of Queen Mary's heart was causing some anxiety, and that she had wanted for many months to see him

This was the first intimation that Queen Mary's heart was giving trouble. Although she will be 72 next May 26 and has been saddened by the death of her husband and the abdication of her eldest son, the Dowager Queen has remained active and had been considered in robust health.

The informant asserted that the Duke of Gloucester, brother of King George VI and the Duke of Windsor, prepared the way for the visit when he visited the Duke several weeks ago. It was said that Gloucester took Windsor the personal message from the King.

A plan is being considered to send the King's own airplane to Cannes, on the French Riviera, so that the Duke can fly direct to Sandringham, the Royal country estate on the Norfolk coast; visit Queen Mary in privacy there, and fly back to France without even visiting London, it was understood.

The information coincided with publication today by the London News Chronicle of a poll taken by the British Institute of Public Opinion which stated that more than 60 per cent of the British public want the Duke and Duchess of Windsor to return and make their home in England.

(Copyright, 1939)

FIND AUTO USED BY SAFE ROBBERS

Police Continue Hunt For Strongbox Stolen At Bottling Plant.

City police reported today that they had recovered an automobile stolen from the G. F. Plitt Company bottling plant, 213-215 North Plum street, but had no trace of the 400-pound safe which had been loaded into the car and hauled away by the thieves early yesterday morning. The car was found last evening by State Motor Policemen Templeton and O'Boyle, of the Quarryville sub-station, on a dirt road near Hopkins mill, south of Quarryville.

The safe, according to police, contained $30 in cash.

CHRISTMAS DISPLAY VISITED BY 25,000

Filter Plant Decorations To Be Illuminated All This Week

Twenty-five thousand persons have vsited the Christmas display at the Filter plant of the City Water Works since it was opened to the public during the holiday season, Commissioner Donald M. Mylin reported today.

Last year approximately 10,000 visited the display.

Employes at the plant announced today that the display will remain open until next Sunday night.

Alspach Gets Seat in 4th Row Of House as Legislature Opens

Big Local Delegation in Harrisburg; Trout, Ill for Past Week, Attends the Session

HARRISBURG, Jan. 3—Because his name begins with "A" and comes fourth among the 208 on the House roll call, Rep. Alfred C. Alspach, of Lancaster, got a seat in the fourth row—which is near the front—of the House.

When the seats were doled out, Rep. Norman Wood, also of Lancaster, argued that Alspach, the new member of the delegation should sit where everything would be audible.

Those early on the roll call can have no one to guide them. Wood said. Alspach has seat 65, near the rest of the Lancaster delegation.

Trout At Session

Rep. Harry Trout, Manheim, who was confined to his home through the past week, came to Harrisburg today to take the oath. He missed the Republican caucus last night.

Among the Lancastrians with seats on the House floor when the four members took office were Mrs. Nancy Keiper Long, state committeewoman; Mrs. Henry J. Pierson. Mrs. Baker Royer, Rev. and Mrs. T. A. Alspach, parents of the new assemblyman, and Col. Daniel B. Strickler.

Those in the gallery included Miss Mary Helen Alspach, Miss Mary Frances Embree, St. Louis, Mo. Mr. and Mrs. A. G. Hoober, Mr. and Mrs. William G. Hassler, Esq., Adolph Koehler, Esq., Kendig Bare and Joseph Holzworth, Jr.

Others in the Capitol included County Chairman, G. Graybill Diehm,

(See ALSPACH—Last Page)

MAYOR URGES ANNEXATION, ZONING LAW

Modern Police Station Also Asked By Cary in Annual Message.

WANTS GRUBB HOME FOR COMMUNITY USE

ANNUAL REPORTS OF 7 CITY DEPARTMENTS ON BACK PAGE

Summaries of seven departmental reports presented to City Council today will be found on the last page of this edition. They cover 1938.

A program for study to build a "Greater Lancaster" was outlined by Dr. Dale E. Cary, the Mayor, in his annual message to City Council this morning. Seven departments also presented reports.

In presenting his program, the Mayor added a word of caution that "we know all these things cannot be accomplished in the year to come, but certainly they will be sometime."

His program includes:

—Enlarging of the city boundaries.

—A modern Zoning Ordinance and revision of the Building Code.

—A modern Police Station.

—Serious consideration of the use of parking meters in the business section.

—Acquiring of the home of the late Miss Daisy E. Grubb, Lime and Chestnut streets, for community use.

—An ordinance governing the disposal of city sewage.

In his message, the Mayor pointed out that Lancaster cannot hope to grow without enlarging its boundaries because practically all available land within the city has been utilized for building. He pointed out the achievements of the past year and called to the attention of Council that Lancaster entered 1939 "with all bills paid, the sinking fund up to date, no increase in bonded indebtedness and no floating debt."

The Mayor spoke as follows:

Mayor's Message

"To the Honorable Commissioners and other connected with our city government:

"With the opening of the fiscal year 1939, I have the honor to transmit my annual communication dealing with the affairs of the city in the year just closed and the year at hand.

"At the beginning of the year we stressed certain things which we hoped to accomplish:

"(1) Efficient, economical municipal government, without adding to the burden of taxation.

"(2) A reorganization of the Police Department and the Fire Department.

"(3) A constructive plan to control traffic and parking of automobiles.

"(4) A study of the water and sewage problem as it affects the suburban areas of Lancaster, to the end that our suburban neighbors shall pay an equitable share in supporting these systems.

"With the whole-hearted cooperation of all the city commissioners, we feel that we have been able to accomplish many of these objectives. I, therefore, want to take this opportunity to thank the city commissioners for the cooperation and commend them for the efficient manner the work in their various departments has been accomplished. This applies

(See MAYOR—Last Page)

HUSBAND, 54, SHOOTS HIMSELF AS WIFE PHONES FOR DOCTOR

C. J. Maier Was Ill Since June; Physician Hears Shot Over the Telephone

Christian J. Maier, fifty-four, 418 Rockland street, was reported in a critical condition at the General hospital after shooting himself shortly after 8 A. M. today, according to police. Hospital attendants said the bullet punctured his lung and Maier was immediately placed in an oxygen tent.

Police were told that Maier, a bookkeeper at Miller and Hartman, wholesale grocers, 23 West Chestnut street, had been ill since June and returned to work this morning for the first time since he was taken sick. He was stricken shortly after reporting for work and forced to return home.

His wife, Edith M., was telephoning to Dr. M. K. Hessen, the family physician, when Maier fired the shot into his body. Maier was seated in a chair nearby and Dr. Hessen, who heard the shot over the telephone, rushed to the Maier home. Mrs. Maier notified her son, Carl, also employed at the grocery firm, and he picked up Policeman John Wiebush at Duke and Mifflin streets while driving to the house. The revolver, a .32 caliber, had been kept in Maier's desk at the office and he apparently brought it along with him when he returned home.

GRAND JURY RESUMES PROBE OF CHARGES

H. H. Temple, Dismissed Chief Engineer, Appears "Voluntarily"

HARRISBURG, Jan. 3.—(A. P.)—H. H. Temple, dismissed chief engineer of the State Highways Department, took the witness stand today in the campaign charges Grand Jury investigation.

District Attorney Carl B. Shelley, conducting the inquiry, said that Temple, appeared "voluntarily" before the Grand Jury to tell his story of the Erie gravel case.

Temple and a District Highways engineer were dismissed by Governor Earle a year ago after a State Police investigation of charges of the use of sub-standard material on highways in the Erie district.

The Dauphin County Grand Jury, which started looking into the charges aimed at Governor Earle and other high Democrats on December 15, resumed its work after a recess over the New Year's holiday period.

Stanton C. Funk, an engineer of Hollidaysburg, was the first witness entering the Grand Jury room today.

Uncle Sam Chooses His Weapons—

★ ★ ★ ★ ★ ★

U. S. Warned Against Folly Of Too Great an Air Fleet

GEORGE FIELDING ELIOT

No. 1 concern of the new Congress and of the man in the street is: national defense. No. 1 expert on national defense is George Fielding Eliot, author of that widely hailed, recently published book, "The Ramparts We Watch". Today begins the first of six new articles—written by Major Eliot exclusively for NEA Service and The New Era—outlining the problem of protecting America.

By GEORGE FIELDING ELIOT

(Copyright, 1939, NEA Service, Inc.)

THE airplane has captured the imagination of the American people, including American congressmen.

Many people appear to think that the primary need of national defense is a great increase in our military and naval air forces—an air force second to none.

Rumors that Germany was able to put 10,000 combat planes in the air (highly exaggerated rumors, by the way) found instant response in demands for an American air force of similar size.

But the fact is that when present plans are complete, we will have an air force adequate to our own peculiar necessities; and we do not need, and ought not to create, a vast air armada beyond the reasonable requirements of our strategical situation. That way lies waste, extravagance—and inevitable retrenchment.

The life of any airplane is not very long. The useful life of a military plane, considering the factor of rapid obsolescence as science moves swiftly forward is short indeed.

It is a mistake to pile up great quantities of expensive planes which will become quickly obsolete. The French did that in 1930-1933 and today their air force ranks fifth in Europe.

The proper method of building an air force is to determine how many planes you will need at the outset of any war, considering your geographical location with respect to dangerous enemies, then allow a reasonable percentage for reserve, and prepare an annual replacement program to keep the force thus determined upon up-to-date in all respects.

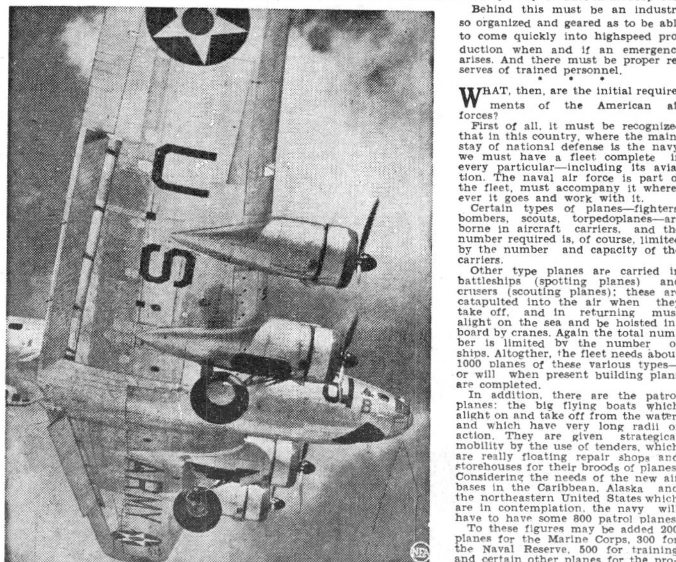

A view from below of a "flying fortress," a giant of the U. S. Army Air corps.

Behind this must be an industry so organized and geared as to be able to come quickly into highspeed production when and if an emergency arises. And there must be proper reserves of trained personnel.

* * *

WHAT, then, are the initial requirements of the American air forces?

First of all, it must be recognized that in this country, where the mainstay of national defense is the navy, we must have a fleet complete in every particular—including its aviation. The naval air force is part of the fleet, must accompany it wherever it goes and work with it.

Certain types of planes—fighters, bombers, scouts, torpedoplanes—are borne in aircraft carriers, and the number required is, of course, limited by the number and capacity of the carriers.

Other type planes are carried in battleships (spotting planes) and crusers (scouting planes); these are catapulted into the air when they take off, and in returning must alight on the sea and be hoisted inboard by cranes. Again the total number is limited by the number of ships. Altogther, the fleet needs about 1000 planes of these various types—or will when present building plans are completed.

In addition, there are the patrol planes: the big flying boats which alight on and take off from the water, and which have very long radii of action. They are given strategical mobility by the use of tenders, which are really floating repair shops and storehouses for their broods of planes. Considering the needs of the new air bases in the Caribbean, Alaska and the northeastern United States which are in contemplation, the navy will have to have some 800 patrol planes.

To these figures may be added 200 planes for the Marine Corps, 300 for the Naval Reserve, 500 for training and certain other planes for the projected Tactical School, and for miscellaneous service on the naval dis-

(See AIR FLEET—Page 11)

SUPREME COURT TO TEST AAA

Agrees to Review Validity of Act; Upholds Liquor Ban By 2 States.

WASHINGTON, Jan. 3—(U. P.)—The Supreme Court, meeting in its first session of 1939, today agreed to hear its first challenge of constitutionality of the Administration's new AAA program. It was the first time that the quesion of validity of the Farm program, designed to replace the original AAA which was invalidated by the Supreme Court, had reached the High Court.

The Court also gave broad power today to states to prevent the sale of intoxicating liquor.

It sustained Michigan and Missouri statutes barring the importation of alcoholic beverages from other States which enact discriminatory legislation.

Justice Brandeis, who delivered the decisions, said that "the substantive power of the state to prevent the sale of intoxicating liquor is undoubted." No dissent was announced.

NLRB Case Decided

Chief Justice Hughes delivered the next decision, holding that the National Labor Relations Board had the right to withdraw from a Circuit Court litigation involving validity of an order against the Ford Motor company.

The Hughes decision affirmed a ruling by the Federal Circuit Court at Covington, Ky., permitting withdrawal. The Labor Board sought the withdrawal after deciding upon new procedure in the light of a Supreme Court decision on April 25 condemning procedure employed by Secretary Wallace in ordering a reduction of charges permitted commission merchants at Kansas City stockyards.

The Labor Board had directed the Ford company to reinstate 29 employes and to cease interference with the self-organization of workmen. The Ford company contended the order was invalid because no opportunity had been given the concern

(See SUPREME COURT—Last Page)

BUCKIUS IS NAMED NEW CITY ASSESSOR

Deputy Finance Commissioner Succeeds the Late F. J. Vaux.

Walter A. Buckius, 211 West Orange street, today was named city assessor by Mayor Cary. The appointment was approved by City Council.

Buckius succeeds the late Frederick John Vaux, who died last month.

The new assessor has been Deputy Commissioner of Finance for nearly a year. Previous to that he was in the United States Department of Revenue and a property assessor in the First Ward.

NAVY URGES THIRTY NEW AIR, SUB BASES

Special Board Asks Projects to Meet "Normal Operations" of Fleet.

WASHINGTON, Jan. 3.—(A. P.)—The Navy Department told Congress today it was in urgent need of 30 new air, submarine, destroyer and mine bases in the United States and its outlying possessions to meet the "normal operations" of the fleet.

Secretary Swanson transmitted to Speaker Bankhead a 90-page report of a special Naval board which surveyed the base requirements of the fleet.

Listing 30 separate projects as the ultimate need, the board, headed by Rear Admiral Arthur J. Hepburn, said it had no hesitation in naming nine for the mid-Pacific, Alaskan and Puerto Rican areas which it regarded as "necessary of accomplishment at the earliest practicable date" without regard to the expansion contemplated by the big Navy act passed last year.

LABOR BUREAU HIT AS RED AID

Dies Committee Scores Failure to Enforce Deportation Laws.

WASHINGTON, Jan. 3—(A. P.)—The Dies committee placed responsibility on the Labor Department today for "a large part" of subversive espionage, activities and propaganda in the United States.

Reporting to the House on a five-months inquiry of un-American activities, the committee accused the department of failure to enforce the deportation laws.

Cites Convincing Proof

"The laxity with which the Department of Labor deals with alien agitators would be unbelievable if we did not have before us the most convincing proof," the report said.

"Due to limited time and funds, we were unable to go into this question as fully as it deserves, but we are convinced that a large part of the espionage and un-American activities carried on in this country can be directly traced to the failure of the Labor Department to enforce the deportation laws of the land."

The committee was composed of Representatives Dies (D-Tex), as chairman; Mosier (D-Ohio), Starnes (D-Ala), Dempsey (D-NM), Healey (D-Mass), Thomas (R-NJ), and Mason R-Ill), all of whom signed the report.

The committee expressed a belief that the National Relations Board

(See DIES—Page 14)

COERCION FOUND ON PENNA. WPA

Senate Committee Upholds Charges That Workers Were Maced.

WASHINGTON, Jan. 3—(A. P.)—The report of the Senate Campaign Expenditures Committee today sustained several charges of WPA coercion in Pennsylvania.

The State Highway Department received "undue financial advantages as against the Federal government in the matter of its contributions to road projects," the report said, declaring that the "department was generally active politically."

Hershey Rally Covered

How WPA workers were rounded up for the Democratic rally held at Hershey on August 27 was revealed in the following excerpt from the report:

"There was evidence presented to the committee that a Democratic rally was held at Hershey, Pa., on or about August 27, for which tickets were sold at $1 each; that a Mr. Halloran, a director for the fifth WPA district of Pennsylvania, turned over to Charles H. Spangler, chief payroll examiner of this district, 5,000 of these tickets; that Mr. Spangler distributed for sale approximately 4,500 of the 5,000 tickets to administrative workers, supervisory persons in the field, and to WPA relief workers."

School Children on WPA

Declaring school children had been employed on WPA projects in the state before the November election, the committee said:

"Work cards on the State Highway were being handed out to children under 16 and 17 years of age who were in high schools. Their names were taken and placed on WPA or

(See COERCION—Page 14)

$4,000 FIRE RAZES PARADISE TWP. BARN

Four Fire Companies Save Farm House, Woods

Fire, of undetermined origin destroyed a one and one-half story barn on the farm of James Simpson, of Paradise township, with an estimated loss of $4,000 at 9 A. M. today.

Fire companies from Strasburg, Quarryville, Gordonville and Paradise saved the farm house and a nearby woods. They also extinguished a blaze in the wagon shed, although one side of the building was damaged. A quantity of hay and tobacco, several pieces of farm equipment, an automobile and a new wheat driller were destroyed.

Quarryville firemen believe the fire might have resulted from an overheated stove in the tobacco cellar, as the blaze started in the roof near the smoke stack.

The barn, 40 feet by 60 feet, is one and one-half miles north of Mt. Pleasant.

REJUVENATED GOP MINORITY PLEDGES CUT IN U.S. COSTS

New Members of Both Houses Sworn in as Congress Convenes; Bankhead Re-elected.

F. D.'S MESSAGE WILL BE GIVEN TOMORROW

WASHINGTON, Jan. 3 — (A. P.)—Congress, its Republican minority membership heavily bolstered by recent elections, assembled today to tackle national defense, relief and scores of other debate-laden problems affecting the nation's welfare.

Amid the holiday atmosphere that usually marks the opening day—this is the first session of the 76th—gavels banged down at noon sharp in both Senate and House, calling members to their seats.

Senate Republicans, meeting separately before the general Senate session, agreed to "cooperate with any group" to reduce government expenditures "without doing injury to those in distress."

"We did not discuss legislation beyond that," said Senator McNary (R-Ore.), who was renamed the Republicans' leader.

Vice President Garner quickly obtained order in the Senate, where galleries filled a half hour before the session began. The larger and noisier House took minutes to subside after South Trimble, its clerk, called for the members to be silent for the prayer.

After a few preliminaries, the Senate swore in its new members. House members took their oaths in a body.

Soon thereafter, Representative Bankhead, of Alabama, was re-elected Speaker of the House. He defeated his Republican opponent, Representative Martin of Massachusetts, 250 to 167.

Representatives Hull and Gehrmann, Wisconsin Progressives, voted for one another in the contest. Representative Marcantonio of New York, only American Labor Party member, cast his for Martin, while the only Farmer-Laborite, Buckler of Minnesota, favored Bankhead.

F. D.'s Message Tomorrow

Both branches will meet together tomorrow to hear President Roosevelt's message, which is given added significance because it will be delivered in person.

Before the session today, Senator Smith (D-SC), who some Roosevelt leaders hoped would be defeated in last Summer's primary, announced to newsmen that he would seek complete revision of the administration's farm program.

Chairman of the Senate agriculture committee, Smith said he would offer

(See CONGRESS—Last Page)

KINZER TAKES OATH FOR HIS 6TH TERM

Local Congressman In Suite 1213 In House Office Building

(Special to The New Era)

WASHINGTON, D. C., Jan. 3. — J. Roland Kinzer of Lancaster, took the oath of office for his sixth consecutive term as representative from Pennsylvania's 10th Congressional District at noon today.

Kinzer has again been assigned to the two-roomed Suite 1213 in the new House Office building.

Mrs. Kinzer was in the Capitol chamber when the Congressman took the oath. Members were alloted only one ticket for a guest to witness the ceremony.

BOY IS REPRIMANDED FOR TAMPERING WITH LAMP

A West Junior High pupil, accused by city police of tampering with the arc light at Chestnut and Charlotte streets Tuesday night, was dismissed with a reprimand from Alderman Broome in police court Wednesday afternoon.

Lewis Gibble, 40 East Vine street, and Daniel Arnold, 133 Prospect street, charged with drunkenness and disorderly conduct, also were dismissed in police court.

YOUTH INJURES ANKLE IN BASKETBALL GAME

Charles Adams, sixteen, 626 N. Queen st., was treated in the Lancaster General hospital Wednesday for an injury to his left ankle suffered while playing basketball.

Bathtub exports from the United States last year totaled $518,000. Electric fans valued at $622,000 were shipped to foreign markets in the same period.

IMMENSE CROWDS ATTEND OPENING OF WATT & SHAND'S 61st ANNIVERSARY SALE

Parade and Window Unveiling Bring Biggest Turn-Out In Store's History

If there was any doubt regarding the interest the people of Lancaster take in a Watt & Shand Anniversary Sale that doubt was certainly dispelled Wednesday. The immense crowds that filled Center Square to see the opening ceremonies jammed into the store when the doors opened rushing to every part of the store for the items they had come for. The first and second floors were especially crowded, for here are the apparel and accessories wanted for Spring—and for Easter—which is but 4 weeks away.

PARADE ATTRACTS THOUSANDS

The parade, headed by the Veterans of Foreign Wars Junior Drum Corps carried out its pre-determined line of march to the minute, arriving back at the store at 12:45 with "Miss Yesterday" and "Miss Tomorrow"—who proceeded to officially signal the unveiling of each of the store's 23 display windows, accompanied by martial drum corps music and the firing of 6 aerial bombs from the roof of the store.

The old Jackson car with its comically costumed driver and "Miss Yesterday" proved to be as unique as it was advertised, and "Miss Tomorrow," driven in a new LaSalle convertible coupe, made a very smart appearance. The store's 10 delivery trucks wound up the parade and were dramatic proof of the number of patrons this store serves in this community.

OLD EMPLOYEES OPENED DOORS

Four of Watt & Shand's retired employees officially opened the doors for the start of the sale. Those who took part in this were Miss Alice Kauffman, Miss Nellie Shultz, Jacob Hartle and Frank Brooks. They were about the store during the remainder of the afternoon greeting old friends and acting as honorary hosts and hostesses.

FIRST PRIZES DRAWN AT 5:20

The first drawing of names of those who deposited slips in the box provided for this purpose on the main floor near the package desk took place at 5:20 Wednesday with the result that each of the following 10 persons will receive a prize: Miss Leta B. Ferree, 528 W. Walnut St.; Mrs. F. K. Landis, 31 N. Lime St.; Mrs. Wm. Seibel, R. D. No. 2; Mrs. Nathan Wappenstein, 129 Green St.; Miss Mabel Crouthamel, 1129 Louise Ave.; Mrs. Sarah Klouse, 41 S. Water St.; Miss Isabelle S. Todd, 202 E. New St.; Mrs. H. C. Bixler, 521 Dauphin St.; Miss Kathryn Kepner, 324 W. Lemon St., and Miss Margaret McGowan, 120 S. Duke St.

ORDERS FOR PRIZES IN MAIL

Letters addressed to each of the 10 lucky winners were mailed Wednesday at 5:30, advising them that they had won a prize and that by presenting their letter to Watt & Shand's main office, 3rd Floor, they will each be given $1.00 in cash.

Each winner must wait until they receive their official notice thru the mail, which they must bring in person to the Main Office, 3rd floor, to receive their $1 in cash. This is done to prevent anyone receiving a prize who is not entitled to it.

Cash prizes will be awarded each day's visitors. In fact those who visit the store each morning and each afternoon of the sale increase their chances of winning a cash prize. No purchases are required to participate in the prize drawing, the only restrictions being that only one slip may be deposited each morning and only one slip may be deposited each afternoon by any individual; only adults are permitted to deposit slips and no employees of Watt & Shand's or any member of their immediate families are eligible for prizes.

Prize entry slips will be issued to all eligible adults on the main floor near the package desk. Each slip provides space for a name and address and it can then be deposited in the box provided for that purpose.

Each noon, five slips will be drawn and the box emptied. At 5:20 each afternoon five more slips will be drawn and the box emptied. Each slip drawn entitles the lucky person to $1 in cash. Each day's lucky winners will be announced in the next day's papers. It is not necessary to be present at the drawings to win a prize . . . In addition a grand prize of $50 in cash will be awarded the 61st slip drawn at the end of the sale for all slips deposited during the sale. Thus those who deposit a slip both morning and afternoon each day of the sale have the best chances to win one of the one hundred $1.00 cash prizes and the $50 grand cash prize.

SALE VALUES REAL ATTRACTION

Regardless of all the unusual and entertaining features arranged for the opening of the sale—the real attractions are the unusual values offered in new Spring and Easter apparel for men, women and children and the hundreds of remarkable values in furniture, rugs and other home needs of every new type and description.

Every department in the store participates in this great event with a host of offers not to be obtained at any other time of the year—and judging from past attendance and sales records—the public knows this and each year finds more and more shoppers turning out to attend this great Anniversary event.

Wednesday from 1 to 5:30 P. M. was called Opening Day — and Thursday will be Pennsylvania Day—dedicated to the prosperity of all Pennsylvania enterprises. Each following day will have special value attractions that will induce thousands of people to attend the sale each day.—Adv.

MUSIC FESTIVAL PLANS ANNOUNCED

Expect 580 Pupils To Participate In Annual Event March 18

A total of 580 pupils from 21 county school districts are expected to participate in the annual Music Festival of the Lancaster county schools on Saturday, March 18, in the Manheim township high school. A public concert will be held in the evening.

Rehearsals for the various music groups will be held throughout the day with the bands scheduled at 9:30 A. M., orchestras at 10:30 A. M. and chorus at 3 P. M.

The band will number 135 pieces, the orchestra will have 125 pieces and the chorus will have 300 voices.

Districts represented in all three events will be Mount Joy, Manheim, Terre Hill, Manor Township, Manheim Township, New Holland, Ephrata, Paradise, Lititz and West Lampeter Township. Districts entering the orchestra and chorus will be East Hempfield and Upper Leacock. East Cocalico will enter the band and chorus. Fulton, Drumore and Little Britian will enter orchestra only. Akron, Adamstown, Salisbury, Warwick and Christiana will enter chorus only.

Supervisors in charge will be the following: Miss Isabel Cox, Mount Joy; Mrs. Evelyn H. Cramer, East Hempfield; Miss Elizabeth Slotter, Akron, Adamstown, Terre Hill and East Cocalico; Marlin O'Neal, Fulton, Drumore and Little Britain; Miss Helen Cassel, Manheim Boro; John Enck, Manheim Boro and Upper Leacock; Miss Kathryn Sheaffer, Salisbury township; Earl B. Landis, Warwick Township; Miss Dorothy Hauck, Upper Leacock; Paul Eshelman and Charles Henrie, Manor Township; Harry Baughey and George Landry, Manheim Township; William Burley, New Holland; Miss Mildred Cressman, Ephrata; Miss Grace Hornberger, Christiana; Samuel Harnish, Paradise; Joseph Sheckard, Lititz; Miss Kathryn Shriver and William Torchia, West Lampeter.

The festival is in charge of the following: George Landry, orchestra; John Enck, chairman, with William Burley and Miss Mary Belle Nissley, Lancaster Township, band; Harry Baughey, Miss Kathryn Shriver and Samuel Harnish, chorus.

The sanderling, a little two-ounce Atlantic coast bird, flies at a speed of 43 miles an hour with occasional sprints at 46 to 47 miles an hour.

The rare silversword plant, with foliage gleaming like polished silver and a mass of purple blossoms, grows within the crater of a volcano in Hawaii.

Letting some of the air from the tires will aid in getting traction, but it is harmful to the tires. The sidewalls are weakened by driving with the tires under-inflated.

LANCASTER NEW ERA

WEATHER
Generally fair tonight and Saturday; little change in temperature.

New Era Founded 1877.
Examiner Founded 1830

Published Every Evening Except Sunday by New Era Company.
Entered as Second Class Matter at Post Office, Lancaster, Pa.

LANCASTER, PA., FRIDAY, SEPTEMBER 1, 1939 — CITY EDITION — 22 PAGES—176 COLUMNS—THREE CENTS

GERMANY INVADES POLAND

Britain and France Prepare to Fight; Italy Refuses; Hitler Hurls Troops, Planes and Tanks Into Poland

Warsaw Bombed, Women and Children Killed as 3 German Armies Push Way into Poland

POLES CLAIM 7 NAZI PLANES SHOT DOWN

Many Cities Reported Bombed; Casualties Unknown; Poles Calm.

WARSAW PUTS WAR GUILT ON GERMANY

(By LLOYD LEHRBRAS)

WARSAW, Sept. 1—(5:35 P. M., 12:35 P. M., E. D. T.) — (A. P.) — German warplanes swooped over Warsaw his afternoon in an air attack in advance of three German armies invading this country.

A communique at 5:30 P. M. (1:30 P. M. EDT) asserted the Poles had brought down four German airplanes near Gdynia, port of the Baltic sea, and three others near Krakow.

Reports have started reaching here of German air attacks elsewhere in Poland.

A large number of women and children were killed, a government communique said, when German planes bombed a refugee train from Poznan at the Kutno station, 70 miles west of Warsaw.

I am telephoning this dispatch to Budapest with the phone in one hand and a gas mask in the other.

From where I am I can hear the wail of power-diving fighting ships and can see 14 German bombers steadily following the course of the Vistula river, Poland's outlet to the sea.

Apparently they are attempting to destroy all bridges.

The raid began at about 4:30 P. M. (11:30 A. M., E. D. T.) and is still continuing more than an hour later.

The German air raiders now

(See WARSAW—Page 19)

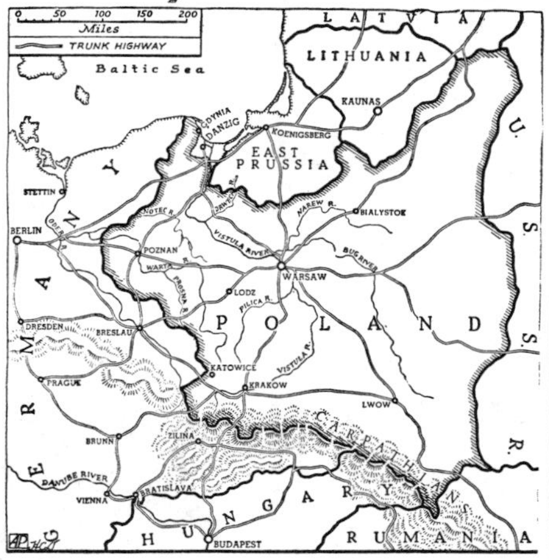

Where Germany invaded Poland.

WILSON RESIGNS POST AT BERLIN

F. D. Makes Announcement, Believes U. S. Can Keep Out of War.

WASHINGTON, Sept. 1—(A. P.)—President Roosevelt told reporters today that he believed the United States could stay out of the European conflict and the administration would make every effort to keep this country out.

In response to a press conference question about whether America could keep from being involved the President authorized a direct quotation that "I not only sincerely hope so, but I believe we can and that every effort will be made by the administration so to do."

Wilson Resigns Post

Mr. Roosevelt announced at the conference that Hugh Wilson, ambassador to Germany, had submitted his resignation this morning, that it had been accepted, and that Wilson was being assigned to special duty in the State department.

Wilson has been in this country for months.

The chief executive asserted that he would not be able to answer a question of whether anyone was under consideration to take the ambassadorship in Berlin.

Mr. Roosevelt said also he was not ready to announce what Wilson's duties at the State Department would be.

Developments abroad today and those that may be expected tomorrow, Mr. Roosevelt declared, would have an important bearing on what the administration would do about invoking the neutrality act and sum-

(See ROOSEVELT—Page 17)

ITALY DECIDES TO STAND PAT

Cabinet States Nation Will Not Open Military Operations.

ROME, Sept. 1.—(A. P.)—The Italian cabinet announced today that Italy would refrain from starting any military operations.

The ministers had met with Premier Mussolini at 3:50 P. M. (10:50 A. M., E. D. T.) to decide Italy's course of action as an ally of Germany.

They met knowing of French mobilization and that Hitler had declared Italy's aid would not be solicited in the German hostilities with Poland for the time being.

(In London, King George VI signed an order in council for full British Army, Navy and Air force mobilization.)

Before the cabinet met at Viminale Palace, where Il Duce has an office as Minister of Interior, British Ambassador Sir Percy Loraine had sought an interview with Italian Foreign Minister Count Galeazzo Ciano to learn Italy's intentions.

The cabinet session lasted less than an hour. It was announced officially that the cabinet approved the precautionary military measures already taken together with "the necessary economic and social measures" which accompanied them.

However, it was asserted that Italy would "not take any initiative of military operations" as a result of the war between Germany and Poland.

The official announcement said the cabinet had examined the situation which had arisen in Poland as the result of the German-Polish conflict, "the origin of which goes back to the Versailles treaty."

FUEHRER SAYS HE WILL LEAD ARMY HIMSELF

Names Goering as First Choice to Succeed Him If He Is Killed.

REICHSTAG PLEDGES UNSWERVING LOYALTY

BERLIN, Sept. 1—(A. P.)—Official announcement that an undeclared war, between Germany and Poland was on, was made today, shortly after Fuehrer Hitler had told a cheering Reichstag that he would enforce a Polish settlement of the Danzig situation or die fighting in the Army gray uniform he wore.

The army high command issued a communique at 5:45 P. M. 11:45 A. M. (EST) which said the German army which advanced on Poland from East Prussia is "deep in Polish territory" and that the airforce is "controlling Polish air."

The communique said advances of German troops and airforce which started from Pomerania, Silesia and East Prussia this morning were well under way toward their objectives.

The communique said the troops reached the Netze river near Nakel in the Polish corridor and that a battle was raging near Grudziacz.

Authorized sources insisted there was no war—but merely that a counterblow had been struck in retaliation for last night's alleged Polish attack on Gleiwitz and for border incidents which have been occurring for weeks.

German land forces, the announcement said, were determined to break all resistance.

Does Not Count On Italy

In his passionate 36-minute Reichstag speech the Fuehrer declared significantly that Germany does not count on Italian help. On the other hand he pictured Soviet Russia as Germany's eternal friend. He inferred that the Rome-Berlin axis had been smashed.

(In Moscow, rumors abroad of a possibility that Russia and Germany will follow up their nonaggression pact with a military agreement met with extreme skepticism in informed circles today.)

Hitler spoke as if war already were under way, but he did not go through the old-fashioned procedure of formally declaring war.

The supreme Nazi leader declared to his nation and the world that Germany would fight until the Polish government yields or is supplanted by a government that will yield.

He threatened to answer "bomb with bomb and gas with gas"—depending on the sort of warfare Poland wages.

He told the German nation he would achieve the return of Danzig and Pomorze (Polish Corridor) and halt Polish attacks on Germans or die fighting.

Hitler Designates Successors

As a sign of his determination to "live henceforth more than ever for Germany alone," the Fuehrer and his adjutants appeared at the momentous session of the Reichstag in grey army uniforms.

"I am putting on the uniform and I shall take it off only in victory or death," Hitler vowed in his speech.

The Fuehrer dramatically disclosed his wishes as to his successors in the leadership of the Reich.—Field Marshal Hermann Goering and Rudolf Hess, Hitler's deputy, were first and second choices respectively.

After Goering and Hess, Hitler said, the nation would be led by men

(See BERLIN—Page 8)

'1st Soldier of Reich'

Adolf Hitler, who gave himself the title quoted above in today's address to the Reichstag.

FRANCE ORDERS STATE OF SIEGE

Every Able-Bodied Man Called to Colors; Parliament Summoned.

PARIS, Sept. 1—(A. P.)—France today ordered general mobilization, decreed a stage of siege and summoned Parliament to meet tomorrow in quick reaction to Germany's invasion of Poland.

The mobilization means that every able-bodied Frenchman is called for military service and experts estimated it would put a total of 8,000,000 men under arms. Mobilization date is tomorrow.

The state of siege was proclaimed throughout France and Algeria by an emergency cabinet meeting.

France acted immediately on reports that Hitler's troops were on the march in Poland and that his warplanes were bombing Polish cities.

Confers With Gamelin

Premier Daladier, after the cabinet meeting at Elysee Palace, went into conference with Generalissimo Gustave Maurice Gamelin at the War Ministry.

Naval Minister Cesar Campinchi was called in, as was Admiral Jean Darlan, commander-in-chief of the French Navy.

Hitler's swift move in the face of repeated British and French statements that they would go to the aid of Poland in the event she finds it necessary to fight left the next fateful move up to those two countries.

Blames Germany

The French government, in a communication broadcast to the nation,

(See FRANCE—Page 17)

STOP OR WE'LL FIGHT, SAYS CHAMBERLAIN

George Signs Mobilization; Men Between 18 and 41 to Be Called.

ACT AFTER POLAND INVOKES NEW TREATY

LONDON, Sept. 1—(A. P.)—(Passed through British censorship) — Prime Minister Chamberlain declared tonight that unless Germany would suspend aggressive action and withdraw her forces from Poland, Britain would unhesitatingly fulfill her obligations to Poland.

Chamberlain made the statement at an extraordinary session of Parliament.

If the reply to this last British warning is not favorable, he said, the British Ambassador to Berlin, Sir Nevile Henderson will be instructed to ask for his passport.

The Prime Minister's statement came a few hours after Poland had called on Great Britain for help against Germany and after King George had signed an order for complete mobilization of the British army, navy and air force.

The Prime Minister said a bill would be introduced making the ages for military service between 18 and 41 years.

Duce 'Doing Best'

"Mussolini has been doing his best," Chamberlain declared.

He began addressing the Commons at 6:04 P. M. (1:04 P. M., E. D. T.) and finished at 6:30 P. M. (1:30 P. M., E. D. T.)

The Prime Minister said he did not suggest that the German reply "is likely to be otherwise" than unfavorable.

News of the German air raid on Warsaw came as he spoke.

Chamberlain declared: "We shall stand at the bar of history knowing that the responsibility for this terrible catastrophe rests on the shoulders of one man—the German Chancellor!"

The momentous Polish step in invoking the British-Polish mutual assistance treaty was made on the grounds of Ger-

(See BRITAIN—Page 8)

England Rushes to Fulfill Obligations Of Warsaw Treaty

Hitler Seizes Danzig, Then Launches "Counter-attack" on Poles But War So Far Is Undeclared; Roosevelt Asks That Unfortified Cities Be Spared from Bombing

(By The Associated Press)

German troops and warplanes have invaded Poland in force.

Poland has called for aid from Britain and France, invoking her treaties with them.

Prime Minister Chamberlain, in a fateful statement to Parliament in emergency session, said unless Germany withdraws from Poland Britain will fulfill her obligations to Poland.

He said he did not expect Germany would withdraw.

He said all men between 18 and 41 would be called.

There were authoritative indications that Britain will fight.

King George VI signed an order in Council for complete British army, navy and airforce mobilization.

France has ordered general mobilization.

Official sources in Warsaw said Polish cities had been bombed, German troops were moving in heavy concentrations toward Poland's frontier from East Prussia and the border elsewhere had been violated.

Berlin announced that German armies had penetrated deep into Poland.

German bombers were systematically sailing throughout Poland.

The Italian cabinet announced Italy will refrain from starting any military operations.

So far war is undeclared.

Adolf Hitler this morning spoke to a hurried session of the Reichstag.

Previously, Danzig's Nazi leader, Albert Forster, declared the Free City a part of Germany. Hitler accepted Danzig into the Reich.

The Fuehrer said:

"I am putting on the uniform and I shall take it off only in death or victory."

Dramatically, he named Field Marshal Hermann Wilhelm Goering his first choice as his successor if he should be killed.

The German advance was described in Berlin as a "counterattack" in retaliation for Polish border violations.

But a declaration in London, which passed through British censorship, said if "as it would seem x x x Germany has declared war on Poland," Britain and France will be in it.

President Roosevelt appealed to Britain, France, Ger-

(See EUROPE—Page 8)

The Scribbler

"YOU get cards from far and near but here's one from Trinidad to talk about in your want ad," is the message on a post card sent us by Knobby Gross, U. S. N., now on the U. S. S. St. Louis. The stamp, incidentally, was claimed by the first person who saw it.

Ragged and with dirty faces, a pair of urchins slipped into a local clothing store the other day and climbed the steps to the men's wear department. The boy was about seven, the girl, six. Seriously, they began feeling the texture of men's suits.

"Something I can do for you?" asked the floor manager, in his best floor manager manner.

"We want to buy a suit for pop," said the boy. "We're going to save our movie money any week now. I get twenty cents a week and sis gets ten cents." Sis nodded in confirmation.

"That's fine," the floor manager said. "In a few years you'll be able to get a fine suit. I'm a little busy today you come back again and we'll look them over." Away went the little couple, promising to return.

THE BOYS: Max Mattke, Armstrong corker, took his first trip to Atlantic City with his father, and after traipsing up and down the boardwalk, asked where the diving board was . . . Eph Eshelman, mail carrier, while on an outing was sent for pretzels and came back with a live duck . . . Clement Ganse, of Marshall street, appeared recently in an overcoat and felt hat, explaining that friends had warned a cold wave was coming.

GERMANY WARNS U. S. ON AIR FLIGHTS

Planes Are Not To Go Over Danzig And Poland

WASHINGTON, Sept. 1—(A. P.)—The United States received, as a neutral, today its first warning from the German government not to violate neutrality in the air over Danzig and Poland.

The warning, forwarded to the State Department by the American Charge D'Affaires at Berlin, Alexander C. Kirk, referred to neutral aircraft which are "warned in their own interest against flying over the territories mentioned."

Hitler Answers F. D.'s Peace Appeal

WASHINGTON, Sept. 1.—(A. P.) — Adolf Hitler sent President Roosevelt today his reply to the President's appeal for peace last week.

The German Embassy forwarded it to the State Department this morning.

A well-informed person described the reply as being "very positive."

London Sadly Sends Children To Safety in the Country

Mothers Weep as 1,000,000 Youngsters Are Evacuated in Fear of Bombs; 3,000,000 Persons to Be Moved from Key Cities

By DREW MIDDLETON

LONDON, Sept. 1—(A. P.)—(Passed through British censorship)—London sent away its children and turned its face to the grim prospect of war today as more than a million youngsters, beginning at dawn, left the metropolis for safety in the English countryside.

Within the next few days more than 3,000,000 persons will have been sent from the various key cities. Today's withdrawal jammed surface traffic throughout London's business section and touched the busy "City" streets with sadness.

At the Liverpool street and London Bridge railroad stations, in the heart of London's poorer sections, children were in line, with their mothers near by, from early morning.

School teachers lined them up: kids of four and five, scared by the roar and bustle of the big station; older boys yanking the girls' hair; big girls with a toddler clinging to each hand.

3,000 At London Bridge

There were 3,000 children in one line at London Bridge, which gave its name to a children's game.

Each had a gas mask slung over his shoulder and even the smallest among them clutched a big canvas duffel bag containing blankets and clothes. From the tops of some bags dolls peered out. One boy dropped his bag and a box of lead soldiers spilled out onto the platform.

These children were poor. But even the poorest had a bag of candy or

(See EVACUATION—Page 17)

LATE WAR BULLETINS

AIR RAID SIRENS SCATTER BERLIN POPULACE

Berlin, Sept. 1—(A. P.)—Warning air raid sirens howled through Berlin tonight, announcing the advance of enemy warplanes. The populace immediately rushed to cellars and other protective shelters.

REPORT GDYNIA SHELLED BY NAZI

Helsinki, Finland, Sept. 1—(A. P.)—(Passed through British censorship)—Unconfirmed reports were received here today that the German fleet had bombarded Gdynia, Poland's port on the Baltic Sea.

GERMANS SAY WARSAW AIRPORT BOMBED

Berlin, Sept. 1—(A. P.)—The Berlin radio station today announced the first "successful air raid" of a German bombing squadron on Warsaw's military airdrome, Radom. It was asserted no Polish anti-aircraft guns went into action. Returning home, the report said, the airmen observed Polish troop movements on a "Polish railroad station," which also was successfully bombed.

N.Y. STOCK EXCHANGE TOLD TO STAY OPEN

No Restrictions On Price Movements Adopted Despite War

WASHINGTON, Sept. 1.—(A. P.) — A securities commission spokesman said this morning, a half hour before the regular time for opening the New York Stock Exchange that the "big board" would open and stay open in spite of the war, barring unforeseen actions.

The official added that, as far as he knew, no restrictions on minimum or maximum price movements had been adopted.

20 DIE AS BRIDGE COLLAPSES

STOCKHOLM, Sweden, Sept. 1 — (A. P.)—Twenty workers were killed and 20 injured today in the collapse of a large concrete bridge under construction at Sando, 20 miles from Hernos.

Smart Girls Prefer Simplicity in Style

In saying "No fuss. I like simple, tailored clothes," Deanna Durbin has voiced the fashion wish of school girls from coast to coast.

This term's dresses, particularly follow the "no fuss" formula, whether they are developed in washable cottons, practical wools, spun rayons, or velvets and silks for dressier occasions.

Predominant in girl's dresses are checks and plaids, with the swing skirt the favored silhouette, whether achieved with gores or pleats. And jacket dresses have unanimous approval, in even the smaller size ranges, because of their semblance to the jacket and skirt "uniform" worn by older girls.

Usually, the jacket and skirt contrast, and the attached blouse introduces yet a third tone or color. Jackets are developed in youthful bellhop, flattering windbreaker, or straight and boxy styling.

One piece dresses favor new odd color and prefer patterned to plain treatment. In addition to popular checks, plaids and stripes, much novelty is seen in a group of crown spun rayon back-to-school fabrics, whose patterns were designed by Eleanor Roosevelt II. These small, quaint prints are perfectly adapted to the challis texture in which they have been woven for sport frocks, matching shirts and skirts, and softly detailed dresses as suitable for classroom as date and party wear.

Already long an arbiter of juvenile chic, Deanna Durbin has showed a preference for velveteen party dresses' and some of this season's most popular will be in princess silhouette with heart shaped or squared necklines and dainty lingerie or lace edging. Dear to the heart of every girl, will be the party dress with suggestion of a very grownup bustle in a bow which is removable, or in a peplum. Taffeta and crepe join velvet as party-going fabrics.

Practically all school girl dresses appear with short sleeves, simply puffed with self-cuff, or occasional contrasting edging.

"Youth will be served" and served well, seems to be the dictum of fashion this season, because a greater variety is offered in girls' frocks, in silhouette, fabrics, and colors than ever before.

Buying wisely to outfit a school daughter, is a matter of having a preconceived notion of what to buy; so that the family budget can distinguish between momentary fads, and all-term styles (even if some of these seem freakish to the older generation.) With this page in hand, the family expense account in mind, and well stocked stores to shop in, every school girl can be sent back to school in the best of style.

U. S. SPEEDING MAIL TO NATIONS AT WAR

Service To Orient, South America, Continues As Usual

The United States Postoffice Department is using every means available to speed the handling of mail to countries at war, according to an announcement received by Postmaster Charles M. Howell today.

Steamer service to England and France is not as frequent as in peace times but the department is taking advantage of every available means to send mail to those countries. Mail for Poland and Germany is being sent to other countries and then forwarded to its destination.

Mail to the Orient, South Pacific, South Africa and South American countries is moving as usual.

Daytime Girl Evolves As Evening Butterfly

A pair of class-conscious casuals! Left—in rich shetland, smooth as a Princeton senior: Right—in nubby tweed with a British look. Both are Nancy Jane Junior Campus Leaders, eager to go to high school and college.

Furs Cast a Spell of Luxury Over Fall Scene

Most interesting feature in the new furs is their highly detailed handling. It is hard to believe their could be any improvement over last season, but the advance models of the 1939-1940 season are manipulated so there is as much fluidity as in coats of softest woolen or evening wraps of supple silk. This conquers every challenge of women who've demanded artistry in fur silhouettes, for even the bulky furs are built with insets of crepe and chiffon to give flattering figure lines.

Jackets are good as ever, but a new-looking stole effect has been inspired by Molyneux. Collarless, the stole slithers down the front, backed with silk, rather than another thickness of the fur. This style is good in every kind of fur.

There is a great deal of "hoopiness" around the sleeves of jackets . . . that is to say . . . a spiral effect. Capes look like jackets, and jackets look like capes, which makes the wearing of them a more secure business. The Hollywood-born fad of casually tossing fur coats over slacks, play clothes, (and even bathing suits) is further fostered by the most amazing coats of Kaola bear and Guanaco for this express purpose, Bulky-shouldered, straight-hanging, this group caused gasps a-plenty at their first showing in New York, which was attended by almost every mogul one could name from the fashion world.

But as ever, nothing surpasses mink in favor. Selection of skins by customers is taking place much earlier than usual this season, at many smart furriers and these fresh bundles of skins are being made up in every conceivable style . . . from floor length evening wraps, to sports coats.

All the "brown furs" are outstanding, and bear out early predictions of their popularity. The smooth-surfaced ones, such as nutria and beaver, are exceptionally smart. Cut on dressmaker lines, they are being received enthusiastically. The fur in one nutria beauty is handled to give the effect of seaming to flare the skirt. Patch pockets make the effect a hundred percent jaunty.

Fox is dyed in every conceivable shade. The cinnamon foxes are strangely exciting, and are proving very popular, even with ultra-conservative women.

A spectacular creation is a full-length cape of Russian lynx . . . dramatic in the extreme. Ermine also fashions a full-length evening wrap that's pulled to a tiny waist with a velvet sash.

Stone Age Women Had Good Light

Light Meter Tells Amount Needed Today

Women would do well to consider the ways of their primitive ancestors when it comes to the matter of lighting, says Rita Otway, lecturer on lighting for the Consolidated Edison Company of New York. The women of the Stone Age may not have had bathtubs or vaccum cleaners, but they did have good light—natural sunlight that measures 5,000 to 10,000 foot candles, with at least 500 foot candles under a shady tree, as recorded by the light meter, a handy little instrument that measures light and tells the amount required for various seeing tasks.

Eye Protection

When man moved indoors, he did himself a great favor in the way of comfort, but put a far greater strain on his eyes. Today, although most people spend at least one-third of their home life under artificial light, nine homes out of ten are improperly illuminated, Miss Otway says. It is up to the homemaker, she adds, to bridge the gap between outdoor and indoor illumination with lighting equipment of sufficient intensity and proper quality to protect the eyes of her family, as well as bring out the best points of her home.

Right Ingredients

Good home lighting involves both quantity and quality. The amount varies according to the visual tasks to be performed under various lamps. The most accurate way to determine lighting requirements is through the light meter, which most local electric utilities have available for customers' use, along with the lighting expert's free advice.

In general, engineers recommend for home lighting 5 to 10 foot candles for general illumination in a room; 10 to 20 foot candles for casual reading, card playing and kitchen work; 25 to 50 foot candles for closer prolonged tasks, such as studying, sewing, knitting or reading small type; and 50 to 100 foot candles for exacting tasks, such as sewing on dark materials, close work at a drafting board or over account books.

Local lighting should be supplemented by general light throughout the room, lighting experts say, to avoid too great contrasts and harsh black shadows. Other considerations for correct lighting listed by Miss Otway are elimination of glare, diffusion of light, sufficient lamps to provide for family members' needs at the same time and decorative fitness.

Drape-ways

Draped detail has its way in daytime and evening fashions. Many of the newest dresses in crown rayon favor the bustle, draped sleeve, and bodice or skirt fulness indicated in these sketches—to help the smart shopper recognize draping that is fashion-right.

College Wear Sets Pattern for the Smart Junior

For those special evenings—a bustle dress in black silk taffeta, with low square back decolletage and long fitted sleeves. sleeves.

Something to write about! A new eight gore skirt fashioned of naphthalated wool gabardine, and worn with a contrasting shade angora sweater.

Ease Found in Sports Clothes

Today, sportswear is just as important a part of a man's wardrobe as a business suit. For driving, country walks and just plain lounging, sportswear's the keynote of the day, equally as important in these varied uses as in actual spectator wear.

The men's ensemble suit of slacks and inner-outer shirt, which has been so widely seen this last summer with certain variations, will be carried over into fall in heavier fabrics.

Sweaters will be offered in both pullover and coat models with the latter—because of their more general usefulness—holding the lead in popularity. One coat sweater which has been seen has a talon slide fastener front applied in the surcoat manner; that is, the slide fastener ends at the waistline in a pair of tabs which make it easy to put the separating components of the fastener together.

Dress Adds A Jacket

Looking for a dressy ensemble from which she can get the most wearability, this fall's lady of fashion will determine that the costume suit —in one of its many variations—best answers her wardrobe problem.

With a modest clothes budget, she will probably buy the fitted, hip length jacket and dress, untrimmed. But a more generous allowance will permit the smart trimming of one of the new brown furs favoring mink and sable dyes, fox or skunk, sheared beaver, mouton, caracul, kidskin or Persian.

The bolero costume suit is another of fashion's favorite children, very young in feeling, whether the jacket be waist or hip length. When jackets do not match, they contrast by means of allover braid embroidery if not woven pattern. Fur bands outlining the bolero closing are very dressy, and the separate fur bolero can be independently worn over other dresses.

Eminently practical is the costume suit with long, fitted coat finely detailed in dressmaker handling, and also wearable over other dresses whether it be self trimmed or encrusted with fur.

Wearable by every figure, is the boxy costume suit which appears sportsy as well as dressy, depending on the fabric of which it is made. In the boxy jacketed ensemble fur brilliantly appears casually styled in wrist-length garments which can be worn over an entire wardrobe of daytime and evening dresses.

LANCASTER NEW ERA

New Era Founded 1877.
Examiner Founded 1830.

Published Every Evening Except Sunday by New Era Company.
Entered as Second Class Matter at Post Office, Lancaster, Pa.

LANCASTER, PA., WEDNESDAY, OCTOBER 11, 1939 — CITY EDITION — 20 PAGES—160 COLUMNS—THREE CENTS

WEATHER

Fair and cooler tonight; Thursday partly cloudy. (Details on page 3.)

Moscow Opens Conference to Give Its "Protection" to Unwilling Finns

A warship of the small but efficient Finnish Navy which was mobilized today in fear of "impossible demands" from the Russian government.

3 PUPILS DIE, 62 HURT IN CRASH OF BUS

School Vehicle Plunges Over 75-Foot Bank in West Virginia.

MACHINE BROKEN TO BITS ON R. R. TRACKS

WAR, W. Va., Oct. 11—(A. P.)—A disabled school bus careened from a highway and plunged down a 75-foot embankment today, killing three pupils and injuring 62 others, some critically.

The big, 70-passenger machine, carrying 64 students and the driver to Big Creek High school here, fell on the Norfolk and Western Railway tracks and smashed to bits.

The dead were identified as Maxine Beavers of Bartley, 18-year-old High School senior, crushed under the wreckage; Lucille Mullins of Raysal, who died in Stevens Clinic at Welch; and seventeen-year-old Ernest Wood of Bartley, who succumbed in Grace hospital at Welch.

Fear Heavy Toll

Physicians held little hope for several others who were badly hurt.

The accident occurred at 8 A. M. (EST) on a hill a half mile from the school, which draws students from a dozen nearby mining villages.

The three hospitals at Welch, in the heart of the rich southwestern West Virginia coal fields, were jammed with screaming and frightened injured. Physicians were called from a half-dozen mine communities to aid overtaxed hospital staffs. The injured were rushed to the hospitals in automobiles, trucks and ambulances.

Driver Says Axle Broke

The bus driver, H. L. Belcher of War, who was badly hurt and may lose a foot, said of the wreck:

"A spindle on the front axle gave way just as we started around the turn. The bus began to slip and I could not control it on the narrow road.

"The next thing we were tumbling

(See 3 DEAD—Page 15)

Farley Sets New Mark as Handshaker

Postmaster General Greets 4000 Persons Within 3 Hours

WASHINGTON, Oct. 11—(A. P.)—Postmaster General Farley has set what is believed to be a new American record for the standing handshake.

Working in the hottest October weather which the Capital ever experienced, he pressed the moist palms of more than 4,000 persons yesterday within the space of three hours.

Those who got grasped were delegates to the 39th annual convention of the National Association of Postmasters, and unto the last man the report was that the handshake remained firm.

Statisticians of the shake said the beaming Postmaster General went through the throng at the rate of 22.22 handshakes a minute.

The .22 stands for the few small boys who muscled into the shoving line of parents and shook the hand of the man who helped papa get his job.

At one point postmasters came at Farley from six directions. He managed to shake their hands without turning his back on anyone, which is some tricq.

In most cases he beat the shakee to the grip, which is considered the ultimate in timing.

On several postmasters, the General used two hands. Hundreds got a slap on the back with the left hand as well as a palm-press with the right.

And—when Farley left the delegates, he raised his hands above his head and shook hands with himself!

SUSQUEHANNA RIVER LOWEST IN 9 YEARS

Flow For Past 5 Months Equals Record In 1930

"The flow of the Susquehanna river in the past five months has been lower than at any other period since 1930, H. W. Lowry, hydrographic engineer at the Holtwood dam said today.

The flow in the past few days has averaged about 6,000 cubic feet per second, he said, but at some times in the summer it was as low as 2,000 c. f. per sec. In the flood period of 1936 it reached 787,000, an all-time recorded high, exceeding even that of 1889, the Johnstown flood year.

"The Susquehanna is a 'flashy' river" Lowy said, "as is shown by the fact that it has nearly 400 times as much volume at some times as in others." The low flow necessitates more generation of power by steam instead of water power, Lowy added.

The Scribbler

John H. Myers, and Ed Matterer, the insurance man, were seen in New York listening to a fellow giving a sermon from a soap box.

A down-town department store is running a Baby special on photographs. With the advertisement in the window is a lovely portait of a well know local gent who, incidentally, rebels vociferously every time he has to face a camera. The portrait is a brand new likeness of Daniel Coulter, city clerk.

H. James Highberger, of a local dairy, drove with his daughter Ann to see a movie at Lititz last night. It was only on their trip home that he learned the same movie was playing at the theater on Manor street, not far from his home.

Mrs. Lillian Painter, of the Columbia pike, has been roasting so many turkeys lately that she woke up the other night, thinking she detected the odor of burning bird. It was only a nightmare.

Betty Is Divorced

Betty Grable, shown above with Jackie Coogan, was granted a divorce from "The Kid" today. The uncontested divorce was granted in Los Angeles on the grounds of extreme cruelty. Miss Grable was accompanied to court by her mother, Mrs. Lillian Grable. Young Coogan did not appear.

SEN. CLARK RAPS "WAR" SPEECH

Charges Johnson With Arousing War Spirit; Hits Arms Bill.

WASHINGTON, Oct. 11—Sen. Bennett C. Clark (D-Mo), today accused Assistant Secretary of War Louis Johnson of making an "idiotic, moronic and unpatriotic" attempt to inflame the public with a war spirit.

Clark, opposing the administration neutrality bill on the Senate floor, referred to a speech yesterday at White Sulphur Springs, W. Va., in which Johnson said that we should draw a defense lesson from the German conquest of Poland.

"In my judgment," Clark said, "no more idiotic, moronic, unpatriotic remark has ever been made by a man in a high public position.

"To compare the situation of the United States, located between Canada and Mexico, with 3,000 miles of ocean between us and any possible adversary on one side and 7,000 miles of sea between us and any possible adversary on the other, with a superb navy and magnificient air force, with the situation of Poland caught in a nutcracker, surrounded on three sides by Germany and the other side by Russia, is an attempt to alarm and

(See NEUTRALITY—Page 15)

MAN IS REFUSED DIVORCE BY JURY

Claimed Wife Locked Him Out of Home; 2 Sons Testify For Mother.

A jury in the county court this afternoon refused to grant a divorce to Guy D. Schroll, forty-three, 224 West Liberty street, from his wife, Anna Brown Schroll, forty-four, Highspire. The case went to the jury of 12 men at 11:45 A. M.

Mrs. Schroll who opposed the divorce wept when she heard the verdict. She had testified that she would be willing to return to live with him, if he would treat her properly. The couple was married in June, 1915, and separated on December 31, 1937.

Mrs. Schroll, who was sued for divorce on grounds of cruel and barbarous treatment and indignities, said the only money her husband gave her was $5 a week for food, necessities for the house and her own clothing.

2 Sons Testify For Mother

The couple's two sons, Elwood, twenty-three, and Joseph, twenty-one, both testified on behalf of their mother.

Schroll accused his wife of saying she "hated me," locking him out of the home he had built in Highspire, asking him "a dozen times to leave," and threatening him with a butcher knife and a plate. He said he left his

(See COURT—Page 17)

MILK FOR CHILDREN OF RELIEF FAMILIES

1,500 Boys and Girls Now Getting Pint Daily Under State Plan

An estimated 1,500 local children of families on relief are receiving a pint of milk a day under the new State law requiring milk as a part of the relief grant.

Distribution is made through normal milk-marketing channels by cards distributed to relief clients by the Department of Public Assistance, and the cost of the milk is subtracted from the amount of relief money which the family would otherwise receive.

Miss Myrtle Brands, acting assistance head here during the incapacity of Edgar Hare, Jr., said the certification of children under 16 for milk cards was not fully completed. The State pays 12 cents a quart and seven cents a pint for milk in the city and suburbs, and 11 cents a quart and six cents a pint, elsewhere in the county.

JAPANESE HOLD U. S. MARINE

TIENTSIN, Oct. 11—(A. P.)—Marcell Szymansky, a private in the United States Marines, was held by Japanese police tonight after an altercation in which a railway policeman was reported wounded in the thigh after having drawn a sword. Japanese authorities said the wounded man was Japanese.

BLAME STALIN FOR 35,000 ARMY DEATHS

Gen. Krivitsky Says Red Leader Sent Millions to Concentration Camps.

CLAIMS BEST OFFICERS DIED IN "PURGE"

WASHINGTON, Oct. 11—(A. P.)—General Walter G. Krivitsky, who said he was in the Soviet Military Intelligence for 17 years, told the Dies committee today that the 1936-37 purge in Russia resulted in the deaths of 35,000 members of the Red Army officers' corps.

In addition, Krivitsky related to the House committee investigating un-American activities that Josef Stalin sent from 300,000 to 400,000 persons to imprisonment or exile and "millions of the population to concentration camps."

Says Germans Were Shot

Krivitsky told the committee that Communist Party leaders in Germany, Poland and Hungary were recalled to Moscow and shot even though they were not Russian citizens. The reason was that Joseph Stalin "distrusted" them, he said.

Some were former members of the German Reichstag.

"Were these people citizens of Germany?" the witness was asked.

Yes," he replied.

Kritvitsk asserted that "the most important Hungarian Communist party leader" who met death in this way was Bela Kun.

"He was arrested in May, 1937, and shot in the same year," the witness asserted.

Krivitsky, a small slight man of 40 with greying brown hair and hazel eyes, said that he broke with Stalin over the purge.

The witness testified through the aid of an interpreter. The purge, he said, reached its climax in 1936 and 1937.

"In this climatic period one could not remain in the party without taking part in the purge himself," he continued.

"Stalin demanded that I take an active part in the purge. This I refused to do and I broke with Stalin."

That was in 1937, Krivitsky said.

Born Samuel Ginsberg in the Russian Ukraine in 1899, he testified, his "official, legal Soviet government name" had been Krivitsky since 1919.

Entering the Military Intelligence in 1920, he said that from 1921 to 1923 he worked in the third bureau of the red army general staff.

Was Sent To Germany

Answering questions by Rhea Whitley, Committee counsel, about his various connections with the Soviet government, Krivitsky said that in 1923 he was sent to Germany "to organize the German revolution and prepare the manpower for the German Red army."

Holding various positions in the intervening years, he said he became director of the War Industries Institute and then in 1934 returned to General Staff intelligence work. In 1936-37 he was chief of soviet military intelligence for western Eur-

(See EX-AIDE—Page 18)

LOU GEHRIG GETS $6,000 N. Y. JOB

Mayor Appoints Ailing Ball Star to City Parole Post.

NEW YORK, Oct. 11—(A. P.)—Mayor LaGuardia today appointed Lou Gehrig, former New York Yankee star first baseman incapacitated by a subtle form of paralysis, a city parole commissioner.

The appointment, for a term of slightly more than 10 years, carries a salary of $6,000, less a current 5 per cent pay cut.

LOU GEHRIG

The commission is a five-man board headed by the police and correction commissioners, ex officio, with three members appointed by the Mayor.

"The matter has been under advisement for over four months," the Mayor said in making the announcement at the summer City Hall in Queens.

"In the meantime, Mr. Gehrig has read about all the reports on parole that have been published and several works on the subject. I have had several conferences with him, and the final decision was made a few days ago.

"I believe he will not only be an able, intelligent commissioner, but that he himself will be an inspiration and a hope to many of the younger boys who have gotten into trouble,"

"Surely," the Mayor said, "the misfortune of some of the young men will compare as trivial with what Mr. Gehrig has so cheerfully and courageously faced. He expects to devote his life to the public service."

Since June, when Gehrig was found to have an ailment which precluded much strenuous activity, he has remained as the captain of the Yankees on the "active" player list, although doing little except walk out occasionally with the day's batting order.

His future after the expiration of his baseball contract this winter had been indefinite, although there had been talk of his possibly taking up executive baseball work, or radio on which he at one time had a commercial contract.

OPEN AIR COURT

Judge Accommodates Plaintiff In Wheel Chair

SOUTH BEND, Ind., Oct. 11—(A. P.)—Judge Dan Pyle held court on steps outside the court house for Joseph B. Lyvers, 23, crippled peddler who goes around in a wheelchair.

Lyvers sued Joseph Badura, whose automobile struck him, for $5,000. He won judgment for $1,500.

158,000 BRITONS NOW IN FRANCE

25,000 Army Vehicles, Including Tanks, Sent Across Channel.

LONDON, Oct. 11. — War Secretary Leslie Hore-Belisha told the House of Commons today that Britain had sent an expeditionary force of 158,000 men to France during the first five weeks of the war.

Just before Hore-Belisha spoke, Winston Churchill, First Lord of the Admiralty, declared the balance now was in Britain's favor in the war on merchant shipping.

"From September 24 to October 9 we have lost by U-boat action 5,809 tons and we have taken from the enemy 13,615 tons, leaving a balance in our favor of 7,806 tons," Churchill said.

There have been no British shipping losses since October 9, Churchill said, so the figures actually cover 16 days. During this period 50,000 tons of new merchant ships prepared before the war for such an emergency have entered trade, so "we are 58,000 tons better off," he said.

Hore-Belisha declared "we have fulfilled and more than fulfilled our undertaking, recently given to France, to dispatch to that country in event of war an expeditionary force if specified dimension within a specified time.

"Nor are the contingents at present across the channel the last that will arrive," he said.

There has not been a single casualty

(See LONDON—Page 18)

"LESS-THAN-COST" SALES APPROVED

Reno Rules Invalidation of State Law Permits Merchants To Advertise

HARRISBURG, Oct. 11—(A. P.)—With failure of the Commonwealth's second attempt to legislate out of existence the sale of merchandise at less than cost, Attorney General Claude T. Reno asserted today there is nothing to prevent merchants from advertising such sales.

"So-called loss leaders are entirely okay," the State's highest law officer announced in response to queries.

Pennsylvania merchants had been reported as uncertain whether, with the State Superior Court's invalidation of the 1937 "fair sales" law yesterday, they could advertise "leaders"—well-known products—at less than cost to draw customers who might buy other products at the same time.

Reno said no Pennsylvania law was left on the statuate boks to restrict sales.

MRS. ROOSEVELT IS 55 YEARS OLD TODAY

Busy First Lady's Activities Not Interrupted; Two Sons At Home

WASHINGTON, Oct.. 11—(A. P.)—Mrs. Franklin D. Roosevelt had a birthday anniversary today—her fifty-fifth—but the busy First Lady's activities went on as usual.

Two of her four sons, James and Elliott, "just happened" to be in town on business, Mrs. Roosevelt explained, an hence could see her cut a birthday cake with 21 candles—the maximum at family parties.

Otherwise there was nothing in the way of celebration. Three diplomatic wives were coming to call. Madame Vegrova, author of a book on the wife of Czecho-Slovakia's late President Masaryk, was to be received. A White House luncheon was to honor Madame Peter, wife of the retiring Swiss Minister.

5TH NAZI EXECUTED AS SPY

BERLIN, Oct. 11—(A. P.)—Guenter Haupt, convicted of spying on German defense works for an unnamed foreign country, was beheaded today. He was the fifth spy executed here this week.

Bomb Berlin or Make Peace, Shaw Advises Chamberlain

Declares If Britain Won't Go the Whole Way, She Had Better Table Her Grievances

LONDON, Oct. 11. — (A. P.)—George Bernard Shaw says it's up to Prime Minister Chamberlain to declare whether he is willing to pursue the war by bombing Berlin and if not the sooner a peace conference is held the better.

"Our pledge . . . . to Poland was explicit," Shaw wrote in a letter to the Manchester Guardian. "We were to come to her aid with all our resources, which meant that when the first German soldier crossed the Polish frontier, the R. A. F. would bomb Berlin; for in no other way could we help Poland, being unable to put a British soldier into Poland or a British ship into the Baltic before Poland was conquered.

"On the strength of that pledge, Poland put up desperate resistance . . . . Now bombing Berlin meant the beginning of a series of retaliations in which our cities and German cities would be changed into rubbish heaps. And when it came to this point Mr. Chamberlain found simply that he could not bring himself to do it. Now this was only one instance of what was happening all around.

"The Berlin-Rome axis was to have annihilated us, but when Signor Mussolini realized what he was letting Italy in for at the hands of the French and British (air) aces and the Mediterranean fleet, he backed out. The Anti-Comintern pact was to have rallied all capitalist Europe against the U. S. S. R., with the Fuehrer and Il Duce as saviours of the world from Communism; but what actually happened was that when all capitalist Europe, with Japan in the bargain, realized that the Red army held the military balance they all sought an alliance with Russia.

"Stalin just pushed them out of the way and took what he wanted of Poland . . . . Herr Hitler, seeing that the Anti-Comitern pact had gone 'phut' quickly decided to claim Stalin as an ally and share the spoils with him.

"When we and the French attacked Hitler on his western front . . . . and it was his business to raid London with his famous air force, he too recoiled from starting that ruinous game . . . .

"What Minister Chamberlain has to declare now is whether he is going to bomb Berlin or not. If he does the consequences will go far beyond our maddest intentions and be different from anything either we or Herr Hitler contemplate. If not, the sooner we stop the war and arrange for tabling of our respective grievances and those of the little states we have destroyed, the better . . . .

URGE LOCAL FISH WARDEN

3,500 Sign Petition Asking Appointment to Improve Angling Here.

Appointment of a Lancaster man, as Fish Warden, charged exclusively with the protection of fish in Lancaster county streams and the Susquehanna river, is being asked of the State Fish Commission by 3,500 local sportsmen.

Petitions which point out the reasonableness of the request in view of the lengthy local stream mileage and the $25,000 or more paid into the commission by 10,500 local licensees and the Conowingo and Safe Harbor companies, will be forwarded to the commission this week end.

See Streams Improved

Sportsmen's associations from throughout the city and county took the initiative in the movement, and it was pointed out that no particular individual is urged for the position, but it is asked only that the warden be a resident of Lancaster county.

"Unless Lancaster County stream conditions are improved which we believe will come through appointing a county fish warden," a spokesman for the sportsmen said, "we stand to lose about 3,000 licensed

(See WARDEN—Page 18)

MERCURY IS IN 60'S AFTER 91 YESTERDAY

Unseasonable Heat Broken, Cooler Weather Forecast

Cloudy and cooler weather today brought the unseasonable heat wave that shattered all-time temperature records for this time of the year in many sections of the state.

Early this afternoon the temperature was at 68 degrees in Lancaster, 21 degrees lower than the temperature at the corresponding hour yesterday. The temperature rose to 91 degrees yesterday, within two degrees of the all-time high for October recorded in 1900. Last night the temperature dropped to 59 degrees.

Fair and cooler weather have been forecast by the U. S. Weather Bureau.

MANY SEEKING ELLIOTT'S JOB

West Grove Man Says Pay Sufficient to Overcome Aversion.

NEW YORK, Oct. 11—(A. P.)—Gaunt Robert Elliott, who began his career at 52 and executed some 400 persons in 13 years, appears destined to go into history as America's most successful legal practitioner of the fine art of putting his fellow man to death.

Apparently no one man will be chosen as successor to the slim gray tired-faced disbeliever in capital punishment who served six eastern states as official executioner with unparalleled skill.

Hundreds of persons throughout the nation have applied for the posts vacated yesterday by Elliott's death from heart disease, but prison officials in the six states—New York, Massachusetts, New Jersey, Connecticut, Pennsylvania and Vermont — have

(See ELLIOTT—Page 18)

BRITAIN AND RUSSIA SIGN TRADE PACT

Commercial Agreement Expected To Have "Important" Political Significance

LONDON, Oct. 11 —(A. P.)— The British Ministry of Supply and a Soviet trade delegation today concluded an agreement in London for the exchange of Russian timber for British rubber and tin.

The barter agreement was called a commercial arrangement, but the authoritative Press Association declared it was expected to "have important political as well as trade impacts."

The amounts of timber, rubber and tin involved were not disclosed. It was said, however, they would be about the same as involved in normal peacetime trade between the two nations.

The agreement was reached in an effort to facilitate exchange of products before White Sea ports, Russia's Arctic outlets, freeze over, preventing export of timber.

FINNS PREPARE 'SUICIDE' STAND

Little Navy in Position, Thousands Evacuate the Cities.

HELSINGFORS, (Helsinki), Finland, Oct. 11—(U. P.)—Finland's little navy massed off the southwest coast today, troops mounted machine guns in streets and on public buildings, and scores of thousands of non-combatants evacuated the principal cities as a Finnish mission arrived in Moscow to receive Russian "friendship" demands.

It was realized that a fight by Finland, with 3,800,000 people, against the Soviet Union with 160,000,000 would be suicidal. But Finland's leaders, as they prepared to resist any threat to the nation's independence, said they and their countrymen would rather die free men than live as Russia's slaves.

The population was grim and calm.

Blackout Test Last Night

The country held the first air raid blackout test in its history last night. Naval units mobilized at Abo, on the southwest coast, ready to take troops and war materials to the Aaland Islands, 75 miles out at the juncture of the gulfs of Bothnia and Finland.

Trucks were mobilized for troops. Soldiers mounted machine guns on roof-tops. The post office and telegraph buildings were heavily guarded. Anti-aircraft searchlight batteries were installed.

Scores of thousands of women and children, ill and aged, fled into the country from the big cities—Helsingfors (293,000 people), Tammersfors

(See FINNS—Page 15)

SOVIET "LIQUIDATED" PRIESTS IN POLAND

Atheist Organ Charges Clergyman Conducted Espionage

MOSCOW, Oct. 11.—(A. P.)—The Moscow newspaper Bezbozhnik (The Godless), organ of the anti-religious movement, indicated today a large number of Roman Catholic and Greek Orthodox priests were "liquidated" when Soviet Russian troops marched into White Russia and the western Ukraine in partitioned Poland.

The newspaper asserted that many priests barricaded themselves "with capitalists and Polish officers in Catholic churches and met the Red army with machine-gun fire."

Bitter articles, assailing both Catholic and Orthodox priests in the region, accused them of espionage and being in the pay of the Polish government.

The paper praised a Red army soldier who, it said, threw several hand grenades into a group of priests and Polish officers who refused to surrender, killing all of them.

NAZI PLANES RENEW ATTACK ON FLEET

Berlin Orders Raids on British Warships Be Continued

BERLIN, Oct. 11 —(A. P.)— The German air force today was ordered to continue its attacks on British warships blockading the North Sea. Official quarters called the order one of the most important German announcements since the war on Poland ended with Warsaw's capitulation.

Aerial cooperation with seacraft in fighting the British North Sea fleet was launched Oct. 7 and authorities said success of the first three days brought the new order to continue joint sea and air operations.

Germany reported six hits on British vessels during an attack on British ships, Monday. Two German planes made forced landings in Denmark.

(The British Admiralty declared, however, that the German air raiders were driven off without inflicting damage.)

THREE BALTIC NATIONS NOW IN RED ORBIT

Northern Countries Reported Appealing to Allies to Stop Russia.

MOSCOW, Oct. 11—(A. P.)—Russia turned today to "political and economic" talks with Finland in the drive to regain the Baltic dominance she enjoyed in the heyday of the Czars.

Against a background of troops massed on Finland's border and concentrations of men, warplanes and warships elsewhere in the Baltic region, the Kremlin stage was set for reception of the Finnish delegation, which arrived in Moscow today by train.

As the Finns arrived it was reported unofficially here that the northern European countries, especially Sweden and Finland, were urging Britain and France to end their war with Germany so as to aid in efforts to halt Russia's military and diplomatic expansion.

The northern states, said reports in usually well-informed circles, believe that if Germany were at peace in the west she could prevent the Soviets from dominating eastern Europe.

The Soviet Union has just concluded a series of military alliances with Estonia, Latvia and Lithuania, three former segments of the Russian empire which broke away following the World War. They became, in effect, Soviet protectorates. The pact with Lithuania was concluded last night.

Finland, also once a part of the Czarist empire, appeared next in line for this "protection."

(But the Finns were making feverish military preparations and seemed determined to defend their independence to the death).

Russia gained bases for the garrisoning of thousands of troops and bases for warships and warplanes as well as trade and transport concessions through her bargains with the three little states to the south of Finland.

Finnish Mission Greeted At Station

The Finnish mission, headed by Dr. Juho Kusti Paasikivi, one-time Premier and now Minister to Sweden, was greeted at the railway station by the Chief of Protocol of the Moscow Foreign Office and the Finnish and Scandinavian Ministers to Russia.

Concurrently with the coming of the Finns the Communist Party newspaper Pravda declared editorially that Russia's policy of "peace, good neighborly relations and friendship with nations scores one success after another."

The newspaper said that by the treaty with Lithuania—as with the Estonian and Latvian pacts—"the Soviet Union assures the security of its frontiers and further consolidates its defense.

"The Soviet Union removes the menace on the part of imperialist powers toward the weakly defended states neighboring with the U. S. S. R.

"Thus an iron belt of Soviet defense is being erected throughout the Baltic. Thus stable peace is being created in eastern Europe.

"The peoples of our country will greet with tremendous satisfaction the conclusion of the new treaty (with Lithuania) consolidating the power of the Soviet Union and creating a new barrier against all imperialist intrigues.

The third of the Baltic pacts, that with Lithuania, was concluded last night. Aside from its military features, it provided for return to Lithuania of her historic capital, Wilno (Vilna), and the Wilno region, seized Oct. 9, 1920, by a "rebel" Polish general.

The Lithuanians never have ceased to regard Wilno as their capital. The Russian army captured it after a two-

(See RUSSIA—Page 15)

WEATHER
Eastern Pennsylvania: Fair With Slowly Rising Temperature Wednesday; Thursday Fair And Warmer.
Intell Journal Stormograph Reading: Fair And Warmer Wednesday.

Intelligencer Journal.

The Leading Newspaper in the Garden Spot of America, Home Owned for Home Folks Since 1794

Football
Stevens Trade School loses three players for violation of training rules.
For details turn to Page 8.

VOLUME LXXVI.—NO. 56. CITY The Intelligencer Founded 1799 The Journal Founded 1794 LANCASTER, PA., WEDNESDAY MORNING, NOVEMBER 15, 1939 Entered at Post Office at Lancaster, Pa. as second class mail matter 14 PAGES, 112 COLUMNS.—THREE CENTS.

QUAKE ROCKS PHILA., FELT IN COUNTY

4 States Shaken With No Serious Damage Reported

Windows, Dishes And Furniture Rattled In Southern End Townships As Maryland, Delaware, New Jersey And Other Pennsylvania Points Report Quake; Tremors Last For Ten Seconds

An earthquake of considerable intensity, apparently centering in Southern New Jersey, shook a four-state area Tuesday night.

Southern Lancaster and Chester counties were apparently on the fringe of the earthquake area. Residents in those sections reported feeling a tremor shortly before 10 p. m., but the shock was not noticed as far north as Quarryville or Coatesville.

Windows, dishes and furniture were rattled in Fulton, Drumore, Colerain and Little Britain townships, and throughout the southern tip of Chester county. The quake was also felt in Northern Maryland as far west as Conowingo.

Farther east, in the Philadelphia area and New Jersey, the shocks were more severe, but no serious damage was reported.

LAST EARTHQUAKE HERE OCCURRED 4 YEARS AGO

The last earthquake of any intensity in Pennsylvania occurred about 1 a. m. on November 1, 1935, when shocks traveled over the northeastern section of the United States from Canada to Washington.

Windows were violently rattled in the brewery at Walnut and Water streets, and houses in Mount Joy were shaken.

Seismologists at that time said the earthquake had no connection with the series of tremors which shook Helena, Montana, from October 12 to the early part of November, causing heavy damage.

The Franklin Institute in Philadelphia said its seismograph showed the tremors began at 9:45 p. m. and lasted for approximately ten seconds.

CENTER NOT LOCATED

An institute spokesman said the 'quake was the most severe registered in this area in recent years. Reports from several seismographs will be necessary, he said, to locate the exact center of the disturbance.

The tremors were felt as far South as Bridgeton, N. J., as far West as Baltimore, and northward to Allentown, Pa., and Trenton, Riverton and Palmyra, N. J. Wilmington, Del., also reported a severe shaking.

A deep rumbling that resembled distant thunder accompanied the rocking and rattling of buildings.

FEARED POWDER PLANT BLAST

Resident of Southern New Jersey and Delaware, where many powder plants are located, at first feared there had been an explosion.

Police in Philadelphia were reported to be on the lookout for fires that might start from swinging lamps and overturned stoves.

A Philadelphian, dozing on a sofa at the time, declared:

"It felt just like two fellows picked up the davenport and shook it back and forth like a baby's cradle."

Sergeant William R. Hall, of the Salem, N. J., police said he heard "a

More of QUAKE on Page 7

EDGERLY AND GOLL GET NEW STATE POSTS

Hwy. Supt. Becomes Chief Sanitary Engineer; Assistant To Compensation Post

OLD POST FOR HORST

Appointments of a number of Lancastrians to posts in the state government were announced Tuesday by C. Maurice Hershey, register of wills.

Edward Edgerly, superintendent of highways in the county, will become chief sanitary engineer in the Health department.

Henry S. Horst, former superintendent of highways, is to succeed Edgerly, it was reported although Mr. Hershey would not confirm or deny the report.

George H. Goll, of the Lititz pike, who was named assistant superintendent of highways, but never took the post because of illness, is to become senior claim adjuster for the State Workmen's Compensation fund.

DR. R. G. LeFEVRE GETS POST

Dr. Robert G. Lefevre, of Lancaster, was named an assistant director in the Health department at a salary of $4,000. According to Mr. Hershey he will be assigned to the Hospital for Crippled Children at Elizabethtown.

Dr. Lefevre is a brother of Dr. W. Hess Lefevre, 234 N. Duke st. He moved to this city and opened an office ten days ago having formerly had an office in Chambersburg.

Edgerly is expected to assume his new duties on December 1. His salary to start will be $3,600, it was announced, with the maximum salary being $4,000. His salary as superintendent of the highways is $3,000.

Hershey and Horst were in Harrisburg Tuesday conferring with State Highway department officials. Horst was superintendent of the state highways in Lancaster county for a period of eighteen years, and served as an assistant for one year during the Earle administration. Then he returned to his private business as road builder and contracter.

EDGERLY'S WORK COMMENDED

According to reports from the State Highway department at Harrisburg, Edgerly was declared to be one of the best superintendents of highways in the state.

Goll, after his appointment as an assistant to Edgerly, was stricken ill and never was able to serve in that position. During his illness, the county was divided into different highway zones than in previous years, and as a result of this division, Goll probably would not have had a section of the county in which to serve. However, he never reported for work because of his illness. The new ap-

More of POSTS on Page 7

"We Lead All the Rest"
FARM CORNER
By
The Farm Editor

URGE TOBACCO BEDS BE STEAMED IN FALL

Experts Recommend Practice As Better Than Spring Steaming To Kill Weed Seeds

Fall steaming of tobacco beds is recommended as better than steaming in the spring, the usual practice in order to kill weed seeds in the soil. In recent years more tobacco growers are adopting the plan of sterilizing their beds in the fall instead of waiting until spring. This point is only a short time remains to do it this year as the ground is generally frozen by early December. Tobacco experts cite the case in favor of fall steaming as follows:

"Fall steaming of beds appears superior to spring steaming, as normal condition in respect to moisture-holding properties may be reestablished before seeding."

When beds are steamed in the spring in order to kill weed seeds, some soils, especially the heavier types of soil, appear to lose their moisture-holding properties.

In order to overcome this condition, most growers water their beds and plants frequently. The experts say this has an unfortunate result because "considerable nutrient material is leached from the upper soil layers and the development of the root system is seriously impeded—conditions resulting in a disturbance of the mineral balance." Therefore, fall sterilization of beds is recommended.

TREES AS A FARM ASSET

Although not so important as they were at one time, trees continue to hold a vital position in the program

More of FARM CORNER on Page 7

Intelligencer Journal
Weather Calendar

COMPARATIVE TEMPERATURES

Station	High	Low
Intell Journal	46	31
Water Works	47	31
Ephrata	46	32
Last Year (Ephrata)	56	40
Character of Day		Clear

HOURLY TEMPERATURES

Tuesday			
		9 p. m.	37
8 a. m.	36	10 p. m.	36
11 a. m.	39	11 p. m.	35
2 p. m.	42	Midnight	34
5 p. m.	42	Wednesday	
6 p. m.	41	1 a. m.	33
7 p. m.	39	2 a. m.	31
8 p. m.	38	3 a. m.	30

HUMIDITY
8 a. m.—53; 11 a. m.—43; 2 p. m.—39; 5 p. m.—39; 8 p. m.—43; 11 p. m.—45
Average humidity—44
Dew point, 11 p. m.—28

More of WEATHER on Page 7

Allied Generals At Front

Viscount Gort (left), head of the British Expeditionary Force, and Gen. Maurice Gamelin, head of the French army, shown on the western front in what the British war office describes as their first picture together in France. General Gamelin also is supreme commander of the allied land forces, which continued to play a waiting game behind the well-protected Maginot line.

724 Members Are Enrolled In Welfare Seven P. C. Club

Second Report Meeting Of Campaign Will Be Held At Brunswick Hotel Today

With the addition of 288 members in the Welfare "Seven Percent Plus" club, the membership list now totals 724, it was announced at headquarters Tuesday.

The second report meeting for the campaign is scheduled for noon Wednesday (today) at the Hotel Brunswick, when Rev. Robert Batchelder, rector of St. James Episcopal church, will be the speaker. Rev. George W. Brown, rector of St. Mary's Catholic church, will be the speaker at Friday's report meeting.

NEW 7 PERCENT MEMBERS

New "Seven Percent Plus" club members announced Tuesday include: Mrs. K. A. Brown, Mr. and Mrs. J. Carl Bleacher, Alberta Herr, Rovert Maxwell, Mildred Carpenter, Miss Sadie L. Fritz, Rev. and Mrs. George A. Laughead, H. W. Fegley, Dr. A. E. Kegerreis, Mrs. Sara K. Mitchell, Mrs. W. E. Zecher, Rev. C. P. Kichline, Albert Myers, Miss Mary C. Knodel, Mrs. Charles D. Rhoads, Mrs. I. K. Witmer, Mrs. Joseph Wacker, Abraham Snyder, Siebers' Optical parlors, Mrs. Emily Heller, Mrs. Anne H. Wohlsen, M. J. Hershey, Mrs. Flora Martin, Mrs. L. T. Lampe, Mrs. J. H. Gardner, Miss Ruth Rogers, Mrs. Mary S. Bender, Mrs. Robert Suter, John W. Lefever, Mr. and Mrs. I. F. Davis, Mr. and Mrs. B. Elliot, Mrs. L. M. Kamm, Mrs. Paul B. Eshelman, Mr. and Mrs. Philip Swain, Hubert A. Fulk, John Martin, Mrs. H. J. Heidelbaugh, John Kolb, Frank H. Dougherty, Verne's Potato Chips, Howard H. Herr, Howard H. Herr, Jr., Beatrice

More of WELFARE on Page 7

I KNOW ONE THING- THERE'D BE A LOT O' MOTHERS A LOT LESS GRAY IF EVERYBODY WOULD GIVE TO THE RELIEF FUND

Contributed to the Lancaster Welfare drive by The Intelligencer Journal and J. R. Williams, who draws "Out Our Way."

Thieves Are Foiled On Third Visit To Store In Two Weeks

Raymond Cohen, who operates a grocery store at Christian and Chester streets, reported to city police Tuesday that the store was entered and robbed twice within the past two weeks and a third attempted entry was made Monday night.

Two weeks ago, police were told, someone broke into the store and stole a dollar bill from the cash register. Last Thursday night, police said, $6 in cash was stolen from a box behind a counter.

Investigation, police said, showed the thieves entered by way of a cellar window on the north side of the building. After these two thefts, Cohen told police, he locked a door leading from the cellar into the store.

Monday night, according to detectives, someone kicked in boards which Cohen had nailed across the cellar window, but apparently failed to gain entrance, however, they added.

LOCAL COMMITTEE FOR "GIVE-A-JOB" CAMPAIGN MEETS

Plans For Drive And Naming Sub-Committee Discussed At First Session

The first meeting of the Lancaster county committee of the "give-a-job" campaign was held Tuesday in the Unemployment Compensation and Employment Service offices on North Duke street.

Those present were George B. Blaisdell, of Hamilton road, chairman; Robert Zecher, president of the Lancaster County National Bank; George J. Kamm, president of the Central Labor Union, and E. C. Hertzler, of the Lancaster Wholesale Grocery company. They were appointed by Governor Arthur H. James, who also named

More of COMMITTEE on Page 7

WAR COST SEEN AS $100,000,000 A DAY IN CASH

Additional Costs In Property Arms And Revenue Not Computed

FIGURE NOT OFFICIAL

Washington—(AP)— Europe's war is costing the belligerents possibly 100 million—a tenth of a billion—dollars a day in current cash outlay alone. Additional costs in losses of property, arms and commercial revenue cannot be computed now.

The 100 million is neither an official nor exact figure. It is merely an estimate made from the best information available here—and the best is none too good.

The estimate may be far too high. On the other hand, war costs may rise even further, if and when wholesale destruction of men, guns, fortifications and ships begins.

However, data from several sources indicates that Germany, heading the list, may have spent $12,000,000,000 for war by the end of her fiscal year next March; Great Britain, her dominions and colonies, at least $5,262,000,000, and France, using a calendar year fiscal period, at least $2,194,758,000 by the end of 1939.

The 100 million-dollar figure was computed like this: By the end of March, Germany and the British Empire supposedly will have spent $17,262,000,000 for a war that began 211 days earlier on Sept. 2, or $81,800,000 a day. By the end of December, 120 days after the start of hostilities, France will have spent $2,194,758,081 or $18,200,000 a day. The total is $100,000,000 a day.

That figure does not take into account the billions that were spent in years prior to the German-British fiscal period of 1939-40 and the French year of 1939 for arms and ammunition now being expended on the western front.

Hitler Balks At Mediation; Sea Warfare Intensified

(By The Associated Press)

Adolf Hitler politely but firmly turned his back on peace mediation efforts by little Netherlands and Belgium Tuesday. Simultaneously there was a revival of the bitter sea warfare between Britain and Germany.

The Fuehrer's foreign minister, Joachim Von Ribbentrop, made known Hitler's decision to say "no" in a polite manner to Queen Wilhelmina of The Netherlands, and King Leopold of The Belgians, who extended their good offices for peace on Nov. 7.

NO CHANCE OF PEACE

Hitler was described as considering the possibility of peace non-existent at the present time since Britain and

More of WAR on Page 7

AYRES LISTS THREE WAYS TO KEEP BOOM IN INDUSTRY GOING

War Orders, Pump Priming, Increase In New Capital Issues Listed

Cleveland—(AP)—There is no room for doubt "about the genuineness of this industrial revival," Col. Leonard P. Ayres said Tuesday night, "but there is real doubt about the possibilities of keeping it going."

"Apparently there are only three sources from which it could receive enought motive power to sustain its upward progress for any considerable number of months," The Cleveland statistician observed in his monthly business review for the Cleveland Trust Co.

LISTS THREE SOURCES

He listed these sources as "genuinely big war orders, increased large-scale pump-priming" and "an important increase in the volume of new capital issues."

He said it "seems unlikely" that warring nations will order here in volumes comparable to those of 1915-16. Pump-priming expenditures probably will decrease and new capital issues depend "on such improved relations between government and business as will enhance the prospects for profits," Ayres asserted.

Blames Bowers For Failure

Without her aviator husband, who still is held captive by Franco's forces in Spain, Mrs. Edith Rogers Dahl, violinist and singer, is shown as she arrived at Boston. Mrs. Dahl said she held former U. S. Ambassador Claude Bowers partly to blame for the continued imprisonment in Spain of her husband. Mrs. Dahl referred to statements she said Bowers made last March, while still ambassador to Spain, concerning her sending her photograph to General Franco, with a plea for her husband.

ELECTION BOARD COMPLIMENTED BY JUDGE SCHAEFFER

Recount In Columbia's Fifth Ward Doesn't Change Result; Resume Count Today

The recount of the votes cast in the Fifth ward of Columbia Tuesday showed no material changes. Judge Oliver S. Schaeffer, sitting as the sole member of the Lancaster County Return board, with five assistants, complimented the Fifth ward election board after the recount stating that there was no evidence of fraud or irregularities.

In the day's recount on the county commissionership, County Commissioner Albert H. Fritz lost one vote and Fred W. Wagner lost fourteen. Wagner, however, more than overcame this loss by picking up twenty-nine votes in East Lampeter township, making his total gain for the day fifteen votes over the unofficial count announced by the newspapers.

15 BALLOTS RULED VOID

The official count of the Fifth ward gave Fritz 80 votes instead of 81 as unofficially reported, and listed Wagner as receiving 265 votes rather than the unofficial report of 279. However, this was accounted for when Judge Schaeffer ruled as void fifteen ballots on which eraser marks were discovered after the names of candidates.

As for the count of County Commissioner G. Graybill Diehm, he was listed as running ahead of the ticket with 310 votes. County Commissioner H. R. Metzler received 221 votes. The unofficial count for Diehm was 322 and for Metzler, 224.

The recount of the votes of the Fifth ward started at 11 a. m. and was completed at 7:15 p. m.

OTHER BOARDS APPEAR

The assistants to Judge Schaeffer were not requested to count the votes for the First, Second and Ninth wards of Columbia but the election boards of those wards explained just how the votes were tabulated and this explanation met with the approval of

More of COUNT on Page 7

Lancaster Newspapers Win Prize At P. N. P. A. "Classified Clinic"

Judges Find Local Want-Ad Pages Had Best Business-Building Idea Of The Year

Harrisburg — (AP) — Awards for advertising sections of newspapers were announced Tuesday at the close of the Pennsylvania Newspaper Publishers Association's two-day "classified clinic."

The awards:

Philadelphia Record—Best real estate-selling idea submitted during the past year.

Charleroi Mail—Classified department showing the greatest percentage of ad count gain in any month of the past year, as compared with the corresponding month a year ago.

Lancaster Newspapers, Inc.—Best classified business-building idea, during the past year.

Greensburg Tribune—Best used car-selling idea.

Awards for the best classified pages were:

Papers under 10,000 circulation—First, Valley Daily News, Tarentum; second, Washington Reporter; 10,000 to 25,000 circulation—First, Chester Times; second, Norristown Times; over 25,000—First, Philadelphia Bulletin; second, Erie Dispatch; weekly or semi-weekly, first, New Wilmington Globe; second, Royersford Advertiser.

FIRE DESTROYS TOWN ON STILTS, 500 MISSING

Flames Spread Quickly Over Oil-Covered Lake In Venezuela

RECOVER 100 BODIES

Caracas, Venezuela — (AP) — The oil town of Lagunillas, built on stilts on the edge of Lake Maracaibo and one of the major oil terminals in Venezuela, was destroyed Monday night by a fire in which more than 500 persons were reported dead or missing. Some estimates of the dead ranged as high as 800.

The flames were assumed to have spread quickly over the oil film on the lake in which hundreds of oil derricks stand. The fire roared through some 200 wooden shacks which had been built out over the water as homes of the oil workers of the Great Lake Maracaibo field.

The town of 2,500 population, believed to be all native, was virtually wiped out by the high-shooting flames before any attempt could be made to fight the fire or send for help.

The stilt village, through which was shipped much of the oil sent to Great Britain from Venezuela's fields, burned like tinder, and trapped hundreds in the houses.

Within four hours nothing was left of the town but floating debris and smouldering piles.

Although oil continually covers the water about the village persons who arrived on the scene shortly after the fire was over said the flames did not spread across the lake, which is 60 miles wide.

RELIEF FUND RAISED

A relief fund totaling 355,000 bolivars ($110,050) was quickly raised by President Eleazar Lopez Contreras and the Venezuelan government.

There were conflicting versions of the start of the fire, which first was seen Monday night about 9 p. m.

One report to the government said the fire started after a warehouse explosion, but another stated the explosion of a kerosene lamp in a bar had touched off the conflagration.

An indication of the rush of the flames over the oil-scummed water was seen in the report that a rescue launch, which had sighted the blaze and rushed to the stricken town, sank with all aboard, presumably burned by the wave of flames.

Three cabinet ministers were sent to coordinate relief work and investigate the fire. Doctors and nurses were rushed to the town by airplane and automobile.

100 BODIES RECOVERED

Relief work was extremely difficult and Tuesday night but 100 bodies had been recovered. It was believed by authorities many hundreds of bodies were yet under the smouldering, floating ruins.

INTRUDER STEALS PURSE FROM ROOM AS MAN SLEEPS

Albert Oram, Aroused By Thief's Blunder, Sees Man Leave By Front Door

A daring thief late Tuesday afternoon entered the home of Albert Oram, 409 E. Strawberry st., as the latter was sleeping in the dining room and stole Mrs. Oram's purse from a buffet.

Oram told city police he was awakened by a noise and saw a man leaving by way of the front door. Oram followed but when he reached the street could not see the thief.

The thief, who entered by way of the unlocked front door, knocked the lid of a jar as he picked up the purse. It contained $3 in cash and some papers.

PURSE RECOVERED

Police said the purse later was found in a lot at Christian and Locust streets. The money had been removed and the papers were strewn about the ground, they added.

June Hapner, 332 S. Queen st., who was visiting at 411 E. Strawberry st., gave police a description of the thief. She told them she saw a man looking in a window at the Oram home shortly before the theft occurred.

MARIETTA ASSESSOR NAMED

Earl E. Carver has been appointed assessor for the Second ward of Marietta to fill the unexpired term of E. A. Child, it was announced Tuesday by County Commissioner G. Graybill Diehm. Carver was elected as assessor on November 7. Diehm gave no reason for Child's resignation.

de Peyster Statue Loses Bright Hues Following Protest

The statue of Gen. de Peyster on the Franklin and Marshall college campus has resumed its sombre hue again, after having been painted in brilliant colors by unidentified persons. Removal of paint is an annual problem at the school.

Painting the statue as a traditional stunt by college students was criticized last week by A. H. Rothermel, of Reading, a member of the Board of Trustees. He termed it an act of vandalism.

ANNENBERG MOVES TO DISSOLVE RACE NEWS SERVICES

Will Quit Supplying "Race Information Over Wires To Gamblers And Bookies"

Chicago—(AP)—M. L. Annenberg's Nationwide Racing News Service, a continent-spanning wire network linking race tracks to thousands of betting rooms, was doomed to dissolution Tuesday.

U. S. District Attorney William J. Campbell announced that Weymouth Kirkland, counsel for Annenberg and the system, had informed him that his clients had decided "immediately to dissolve Nationwide News Service, Inc., and definitely and forever quit the business of providing race information over wires to gamblers and bookies." The prosecutor added:

"Dissolution of Nationwide News Service, Inc., will affect not only every state in the union but the dominion of Canada and Cuba."

TO CUT OFF ALL FACILITIES

Annenberg's attorneys reported that the facilities used for transmitting race entries, odds, results and payoff prices from the tracks to horse playing parlors would be cut off Wednesday or not later than Thursday noon.

"Counsel has stated that his clients will voluntarily cancel contracts with the A. T. and T. company and the

More of RACE NEWS on Page 7

MARGIOTTI URGED GRAVEL CONTRACTS COLEGROVE SAYS

Testifies Author Of Corruption Charges Recommended Awards On Six Occasions

Harrisburg—(AP)—The author of corruption charges against high Democrats in Pennsylvania was represented in court Tuesday as having been one of the first to urge gravel contract awards, now the basis for the blackmail-conspiracy trial of Democratic State Chairman David L. Lawrence.

The testimony was drawn by prosecution attorneys from Arthur Colegrove, self-styled "country newspaper publisher" who served as secretary of property and supplies in the Demo-

More of TRIAL on Page 7

DENY JOBLESS RELIEF DURING WAITING TIME FOR COMPENSATION

New Ruling of James Administration Is In Operation Here, Assistance Board Head Announces

Unemployed persons in Lancaster are being denied direct relief during the waiting periods required before they can receive unemployment compensation under a recent ruling of the James administration.

According to Edgar Hare, Jr., executive director for the Lancaster County Assistance board, if a person becomes unemployed and files a claim for unemployment compensation, direct relief can not be given to that person during his waiting period for his unemployment compensation checks because of a new ruling issued by Howard L. Russell, State Secretary of Public Assistance.

During the Democratic administration of former Governor George H. Earle and for the first eight months of the James administration, a person who lost his job and was able to show that he had no other source of income was entitled to receive relief during the waiting period before he received his first unemployment compensation check. Now he must wait at least three weeks for his first unemployment compensation check.

However, exceptions are made in cases of persons receiving unemployment compensation for the second time following a long period on relief. The persons in this class will continue to receive direct aid until their checks come through for their second unemployment compensation.

ROBBERS MAKE HAUL AT JET D. SHEETZ'S APARTMENT IN CITY

Several Thousand Dollars And Considerable Amount of Jewelry Stolen; Detectives Investigate

City detectives are investigating a robbery which occurred recently at the apartment of Jet D. Sheetz, 121 N. Queen st., it was learned Tuesday.

Several thousand dollars and a considerable amount of jewelry were taken. Some of the jewelry, it is reported, was recovered in a pawn shop.

Police refused to discuss the case, except to admit that they were investigating.

EDITORS PLAN "EVIL OLD MAN'S DINNER"

"Vile Occasion Dedicated To Sin And Corruption" By Garner's Friends, Announcement States

Dallas, Tex.—(AP)—An "evil old man's dinner" will be given here Thursday night by the Texas Editorial Association.

The program announced "this vile occasion is given and dedicated to sin and corruption by the friends of John N. Garner, vice president of the United States."

Specific mention of John L. Lewis, C. I. O. labor chief, will be made at the dinner, it was announced. Lewis once referred to Vice-President Garner as a "poker playing, whiskey drinking, evil old man."

WHAT THE DECADE HAS DONE TO THE MAP

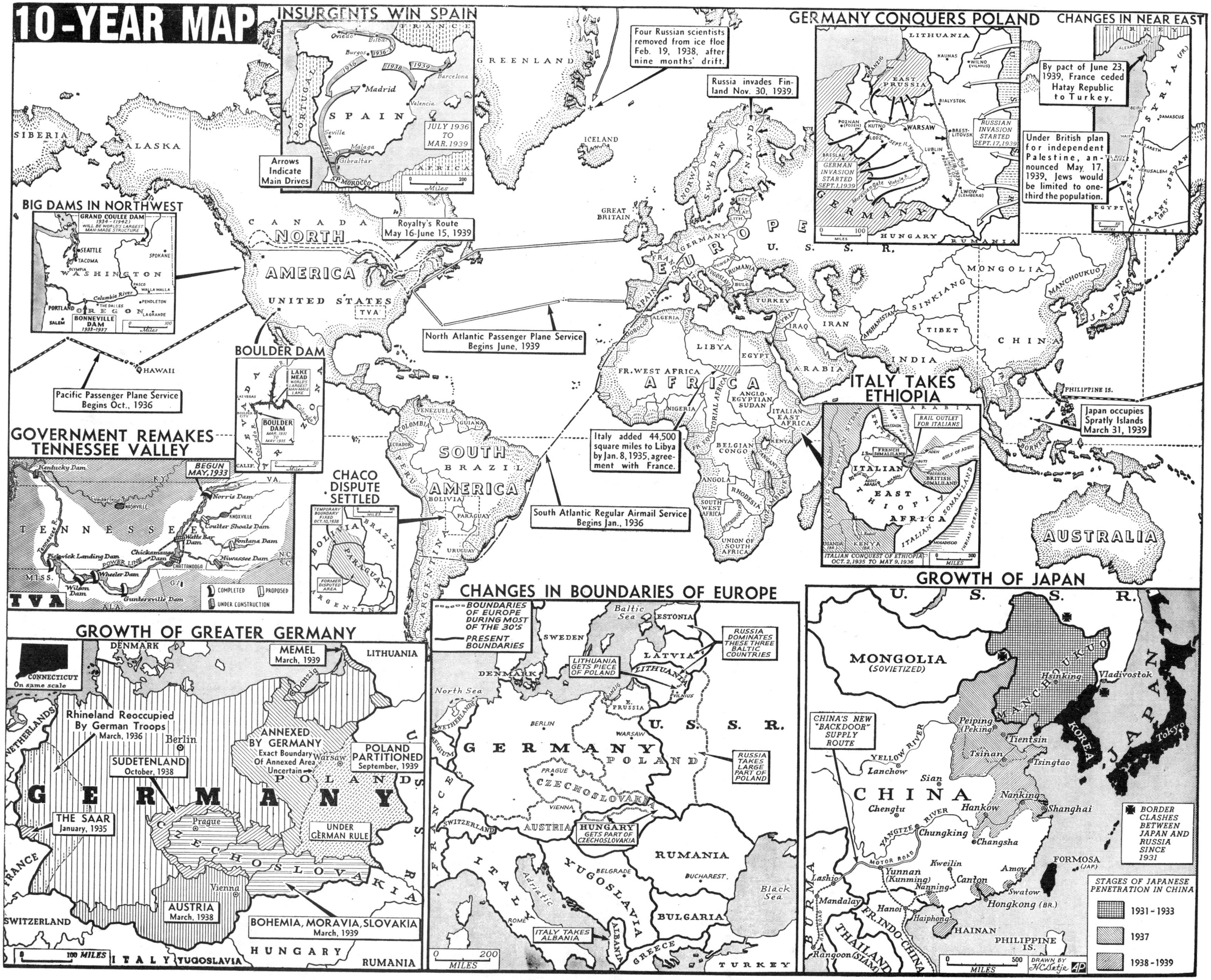

Louis Tiffany invented favrite, a variety of iridescent enameled glass, in 1894.

EXCEPTIONS TO RULING IN GROFF CASE ARGUED

Exceptions to the ruling which dismissed the suit of Mrs. Ida B. Groff against the estate of her husband, the late Fred F. Groff, local undertaker, were argued in Orphans Court Monday. Mrs. Groff is seeking a larger share of her husband's estate than the $50,000 trust fund left to her under an agreement made before their marriage.

Alfred C. Alspach, one of the widow's counsel, quoted from a letter written to Mrs. Groff by the undertaker before his second marriage in an effort to prove that the local man did not tell her his true financial status.

The attorney said that in 1933 when that letter was written Groff had an annual income of $22,500; paid premiums on $68,000 worth of life insurance and owned real estate valued at $73,500 and his gross wealth valued at $316,000.

Alspach told the court that according to the will, Mrs. Groff is to receive approximately $1,900 net per year from the $50,000 trust fund.

Judge C. E. Charles reserved his decision.

Two adjudications were filed during the day. One distributed $22,254.11 in the estate of James P. Marsh, late of Salisbury township, and the other $1,601.05 in the estate of Edward H. Phillips, late of Lancaster.

TARGET TOSSER LOSES EYE

Kutztown, Pa. — (AP) — Oliver Schlegel, 37, of Fleetwod, lost his left eye Monday when he was struck by a blast of shot-gun pellets at a target range of the Walnut Rod and Gun Club. He was tossing up wooden targets. There were 15 gunners on the range.

PHILA. PAY TAX UPHELD BY COURT

Counsel For Worker Attacking 1½ Per Cent Levy Will Carry Fight Higher

Philadelphia—(AP)—The Pennsylvania Supreme Court upheld Monday the right of Philadelphia to impose a 1 1-2 per cent tax on wages and earned income, but failed to end a fight which labor groups have waged against the levy since its inception.

Counsel for a $10-a-week widowed shirt factory worker, whose attack on the validity of the tax was dismissed, anounced they would carry their battle to the U. S. Supreme Court on the ground the Federal Constitution was violated.

The tax—an important pillar in the city's 1940 "pay-as-you-go" financial program—became effective January 1 for one year as an "emergency" measure. It is expected to yield $18,000,000.

Every person earning a living in Philadelphia, from scullery maids to the highest executive, is affected. Even non-residents must pay if they work in the city.

In a suit supported by CIO unions, Mrs. Jennie Dole, 51-year old mill worker, contended the levy was not uniform and was discriminatory. The Supreme Court made no comment on her contentions, merely affirming a lower court ruling which dismissed her suit.

Her counsel, Gilbert J. Braus, said the fight in the U. S. Supreme Court would be made on the ground the tax violated the 14th amendment to the Federal Constitution prohibiting the taking of property "without due process of law."

2,000 VOTERS "UNKNOWN" AT LISTED ADDRESSES

Approximately 2,000 of the letters sent to persons who have not voted for two years have been returned to the registration office in the Court House because they do not reside at the listed addresses, it was announced Monday by Miss Mabel M. Hartman. In most cases the letters were marked "unknown" by the postal authorities, she explained.

The commission sent out 8,600 letters to persons who have not voted for the past two years, asking them to notify the commission if they are living at the same place and want to remain registered. Hundreds have replied, according to Miss Mabel Hartman, clerk in charge.

Those who have not replied and wish to remain on the books should reply before Thursday. The easiest way, Miss Hartman said, is to write "I want to remain on the registration books" on the bottom of the letter sent by the commission, and return it to the commission at the Court House.

STATE BAKERS HEAR ADDRESS BY BROWN

Pittsburgh—(AP)—The State Department of Commerce joined hands Monday with Pennsylvania bakers to attain their motto "forward with Pennsylvania."

Addressing the convention of the State Bakers Association, Secretary Richard P. Brown stressed that the motto was the purpose for which the department was created by the 1939 legislature.

"Attainment of our objective," Brown said in a prepared speech "means greater purchasing power, which means more people can buy and pay for more baked goods. That means bigger sales and larger payrolls for your plants, which in turn add to the general prosperity of our people."

JUDGE BARD APPOINTS RECEIVER FOR BROKERS

Philadelphia—(AP)—The brokerage firm of McMillan, Rapp and Company of Philadelphia was placed Monday under control of a Federal receiver by Federal Judge Guy K. Bard.

He named as receiver Irving L. Stone, a member of the brokerage of Newburger, Loeb and Company.

..ge Bard acted on a petition for receivership by three customers who said the firm "misappropriated, misapplied and converted to its own use" their securities.

PLAN EARLIER FAIR

Clearfield, Pa.—(AP)—To avoid the chilly nights of late autumn, officials of the Clearfield County Fair have moved the fair dates up 10 days. Instead of late September, the 1940 exposition will be held Sept. 10-14, the earliest fair in the history of the event.

WEATHER

Eastern Pennsylvania: Generally Fair Thursday, Except Light Snow In North Portion Thursday Morning; Not Quite So Cold Thursday Afternoon; Friday Increasing Cloudiness With Rising Temperature.
Intell Journal Stormograph Reading: Clearing With High Winds Thursday.

Intelligencer Journal.

The Leading Newspaper in the Garden Spot of America, Home Owned for Home Folks Since 1794

Boxing
Earl Frederick decisions Billy Donley in eight-round bout at Armory.
For details turn to Page 12.

VOLUME LXXVI.—NO. 135. CITY The Intelligencer Founded 1799 The Journal Founded 1794 LANCASTER, PA., THURSDAY MORNING, FEBRUARY 15, 1940 Entered at Post Office at Lancaster, Pa. as second class mail matter 18 PAGES, 144 COLUMNS.—THREE CENTS.

LANCASTER COUNTY IS SNOWBOUND AS BLIZZARD HITS EASTERN U. S.

Finns To Fight 'To The Last Man', President Avers

Has No Choice But To Fight On, "Alternative Is Extinction," Kallio Says; More Men Called To Colors As Mannerheim Line Still Holds Against Ferocious Assaults; Viipuri Bombed Again By Reds

Helsinki—(AP)—Finland, calling more men to the colors and still holding an unbroken Mannerheim line against the greatest assaults since the World war, has no choice but to fight on regardless of how the battle goes, President Kyosti Kallio declared Wednesday night.

"Everyone knows we are outnumbered fifty to one," the veteran chief executive told news correspondents in an informal chat at the presidential residence.

"But the issues at stake are clear. We appreciate the sympathy shown us by Americans in our struggle to be free—indeed to live at all—but we really hope our cause might stir onlookers abroad to offer us material help.

"For after all we are defending the interests common to all civilized peoples.

"If, however, such help does not arrive we cannot change our course. Regardless of the overwhelming odds we would still carry on our fight—if 't must be alone.

"The alternative is extinction for our nation.

"If the world ignores us in our need, we have no choice but to fight to the last man."

Before the President spoke to the newspaper men, Viipuri, Finland's Karelian city, was bombed repeatedly Wednesday by Soviet Russian planes, which also raided other Finnish civilian centers—Hamina, Lapeenranta, among them.

Numerous buildings were burned in all three towns.

Russian gains in the Karelian snows—tossed up into dirty red by the steady churning of concentrated Russian artillery fire and stained by

More of FINNS on Page 16

"We Lead All the Rest"

FARM CORNER

By

The Farm Editor

FARM ACCOUNT BOOKS CONTEST IS PLANNED

Event Is Limited To Vocational Students In High Schools Of Three Counties

In an effort to stimulate interest in the keeping of proper farm account records, the Lancaster Production Credit Association will conduct a tri-county contest this year and award cash prizes for the best books presented, Carl B. Thomas, secretary-treasurer, announced Wednesday.

The contest is limited to vocational students in high schools of Lancaster, Lebanon and Dauphin, the three counties served by the association. Three prizes of five dollars each will be presented for the "best set of farm records kept by a vocational student on operations of his father's farm during the year ending Dec. 31. 1940", in the three counties. A grand prize will be awarded the best book of the three, which will entitle the winner to a free trip, all expenses paid, on a visit to the Farm Credit Administration headquarters in Baltimore.

Endorsement of the contest has been given by the State Department of Education. The records must be presented in the farm account books used by the State College agricultural extension service.

Wayne B. Rentschler, agricultural supervisor at the West Lampeter High school, has already entered five of his students in the contest. Other schools eligible in the county are the East Donegal, East Cocalico, Quarryville, Manor and Manheim high schools.

The purpose, according to Mr. Tho-

More of FARM CORNER on Page 9

Intelligencer Journal Weather Calendar

COMPARATIVE TEMPERATURES

Station	High	Low
Intell Journal	35	20
Water Works	45	24
Ephrata	37	24
Last Year (Ephrata)	51	28
Official High for Year, Feb. 12		55
Official Low for Year, Jan. 20		2
Character of Day		Cloudy

HOURLY TEMPERATURES

(Wednesday)			
8 a. m.	32	9 p. m.	20
11 a. m.	29	10 p. m.	20
2 p. m.	26	11 p. m.	20
5 p. m.	24	Midnight	20
6 p. m.	23	(Thursday) 1 a. m.	21
7 p. m.	22	2 a. m.	21
8 p. m.	21	3 a. m.	21

SUN

Rises—6:54 a. m. Sets—5:35 p. m.

More of WEATHER on Page 16

3 BOYS SELECTED FOR TRY-OUTS FOR YOUTH ORCHESTRA

R. W. Getz, Terre Hill; R. E. Laushey And Sylvan Stein, This City, to Have Auditions

Three youths—one from Terre Hill and two from Lancaster—were selected Wednesday by the Citizens' Committee as the local applicants for the All-American Youth Orchestra which is scheduled to tour South and Central America under the leadership of Leopold Stokowski.

The trio, Richard W. Getz, eighteen, of Terre Hill, who plays a trumpet; Sylvan Stein, twenty, of 602 East End ave., who plays a French horn, and Robert E. Laushey, twenty, of 507 Ruby st., a trombone player, will be given auditions at the National Youth Administration headquarters in Harrisburg. They will be notified direct from the NYA headquarters when the auditions are to be given.

The boys were selected on their qualifications, it was announced by Jacques Conrad, chairman of the committee. The application list closed Saturday.

Other members of the committee are City Commissioner E. W. Bowman, Harry Metzgar, Jacob Steinbaecher, Amandus Stetler, Puzant Barsumian, Harry Ilgenfritz, Gerald Scully, Leigh Wittel and E. W. Ford.

PENNA. R. R. APPEALS TWO ASSESSMENTS

Asks Reduction Of Valuation On Arch Street Lots, North Queen Street Property

Two appeals from the triennial assessment were filed by special permission with the county commissioners Wednesday by the Pennsylvania Railroad company, it was announced by County Commissioner G. Graybill Diehm.

Diehm said the firm termed the $800 assessment placed on the vacant lots at 413 and 415 Arch street by Assessor William Howard, of the Ninth ward, is too high and asked a reduction of $300. The company also appealed from the $2,500 assessment placed on a small property at 344 North Queen street, and asked that the sum be reduced to $1,500 on the grounds that the building cost only $540.

Howard had refused to reduce the assessments and the company was granted special permission to file the appeals. The appeal days ended Monday.

The commissioners have not acted so far on any of the appeals filed, Diehm said.

YOUTH KNOCKED OUT BY BUTT OF TREE

Willard Tomlinson, Mount Nebo, Suffers Jaw Injury While Cutting Timber In Woods

Willard Tomlinson, about eighteen, of Mount Nebo, was injured Tuesday afternoon when the butt of a tree hit him on the jaw. Tomlinson, who was cutting timber in the woods of Mount Nebo, was knocked unconscious and was found by Frank Hershey, of Mount Nebo, who was working with him. He was treated at his home for a cracked jaw, and also had four front teeth cracked. He is the son of Mrs. Ella Tomlinson, of Mount Nebo.

FILING OF ESTATE LETTER SETS RECORD

Fourteen Here In Single Day Is Highest In Eighteen Years, Reflects Increased Winter Death Rate

Reflecting an increased death rate during the outbreak of winter ills, the number of letters of administration filed Wednesday at the court house broke an eighteen-year record.

Deputy Register of Wills John D. Tripple reported letters in fourteen estates filed—more than has been filed in a single day for that period. He said the average daily number is six.

DOZEN STATES FEEL BRUNT OF SEVERE STORM

Previous Record Of Fifteen Inches Of Snowfall Exceeded At Pittsburgh

WIND HITS 100 M.P.H.

(By The Associated Press)

One of the worst blizzards of the twentieth century held the greater part of the Keystone State firmly in its grasp Thursday.

Snow, which fell steadily throughout most of Wednesday, blanketed the ground from six to 20 inches deep. The previous record of 15 inches established in Pittsburgh in 1902 was exceeded by about five inches.

The storm, screaming up from the south and funneling as it spread reached a 100-mile an-hour crescendo atop the Empire State building in New York and dropped a burden of deepening snow and ice over a dozen states of the Atlantic seaboard...

Deaths of half a dozen persons in Pennsylvania were charged to the storm, either directly or indirectly. Hundreds of thousands of school children took or were given holidays, which in numerous instances will extend until next Monday. All traffic was tied up.

Most of the eastern section of the state had a foot of snow, with 12-foot drifts reported in Susquehanna county and eight-foot ones in Lackawanna. Villages were isolated except for telephones.

The freezing gale winds, strongest since the 1938 hurricane ripped a $500,000,000 path of destruction across Long Island and New England, left a trail of traffic deaths and wrecked power lines and harried shipping. The storm grounded commercial air traffic from Ohio to Boston.

Hundreds were hurt in storm accidents. In New York city, faced with the possibility of its most serious traffic tieup in years, emergency police details were kept busy caring for more than 100 injured. A wind gust swept one man to his death from a fourth floor scaffolding on the Criminal Courts building. A woman, blown against a building in the fi-

More of STORM on Page 9

FARLEY SCOFFS AT DICTATORSHIP TALK IN THE U. S.

Asserts Only Mortgage Party In Power Has On Control Is "Confidence Of People"

Memphis, Tenn. —(AP)—James A. Farley termed "all moonshine" here Wednesday night "constant talk of a regime to perpetuate itself" in the United States.

Without elaborating on whether he referred to a third term for President Roosevelt, the Postmaster General spoke on "Americanism" at a gathering under Junior Chamber of Commerce auspices.

"After all, the only mortgage that the party in power has on the control of our national affairs is the confidence of the people," he said. "So long as the administration gives good government, so long is it kept in power. x x x No administration can survive a majority disapproval."

The Democratic cabinet officer said the balance of power was held by "a group numbering perhaps ten mission voters, who have either no party affiliation or whose allegiance is so slight and tenuous that it is shifted one way or the other as the conflicting policies and opposition candidates please or displease the individuals in this group."

Farley asserted empires and civilizations of the past all fell because they lacked "liberty."

"We have grown into the most powerful of all nations," he said, by Americanism, which he defined as "tolerance."

"Down South they still refer to us Northerners as dam Yankees. We of the North flatter ourselves that we have the better of our Southern citizens in aggressive enterprise. Our Easterners cherish to themselves the comforting belief that they are superior to our Westerners in culture and polite arts. They in the West deign to assume that they have almost a monopoly of independence and breezy courage. But all of us, regardless of the points of the compass, are quite satisfied that even those at the opposite end of the country are of immensely better type than those unfortunate enough to be nationals of foreign states, which, after all, is a happy conceit."

Farley planned to leave Wednesday night for a vacation in Miami, Fla.

MIDDLETOWN MAN HIT BY TREE LIMB, DIES

Edward Laverty Injured While Removing Limbs From Tree Near Home, Had Skull Fractured

Harrisburg—(AP)—His skull fractured by a falling tree limb, Edward Laverty, 35, of Middletown, died Wednesday in a hospital. Laverty and a friend were removing limbs from a tree at his home when one fell unexpectedly.

Snow Adds Finnish Touch To Square

Lancaster took on a Finnish appearance as the full fury of Wednesday's blizzard struck. With the ground buried under the thickening blanket of white, pedestrian's clothing became covered so quickly with snow that they appeared to be wearing white mantles. Typical of the scenes is the one above snapped at the Penn Square monument—where only the hardy ones braved the storm while awaiting buses or trolley cars. (Intell Photo)

One of the early casualties of Wednesday's raging snow storm is shown above—an automobile crushed under a fallen pole it had snapped off after skidding in Mountville. Richard Degregoria and Neil Stamo, of Philadelphia, enroute to Hanover to repair an ambulance, escaped serious injury. (Intell Photo)

Hero Of Rescue At Ephrata Returns To Claim Reward

Man Who Pulled Seven-Year-Old Robert Snader From Creek Gets Food, Cash And Clothing And "Run" Of Lock-up; Tells Police He Can't Swim

Ephrata borough's hero, George B. Smith, thirty-five, a wanderer, returned to Ephrata Wednesday to claim his reward of "a warm bed, warm clothing and food."

Where he came from or where he may go, is a mystery, for Smith will not tell anything about himself—except his name.

Smith leaped into the ice-covered Cocalico creek near the Ephrata electric light plant and saved the life of Robert Snader, seven, son of Mr. and Mrs. Ralph Snader last Tuesday after the boy had fallen into the stream while at play.

Now he has the run of the borough lock-up for sleeping purposes until the weather conditions permit him to be on his way.

After saving the boy's life, Smith, spent the night at the electric light plant and left the next morning without anyone finding out who he was. Chief Burgess John M. Royer heard about the rescue and expressed his desire to reward the man.

Smith returned Wednesday and went to Chief of Police Harry Doremus who gave him his first reward—a big meal. Burgess Royer then gave Smith several dollars and later took a collection which netted several more. Ralph Snader, father of the rescued boy added new clothing as his share of the reward.

Smith told officials that he was walking along the railroad when he heard the screams of the Snader boy's companion, Robert Simmons, also

More of HERO on Page 9

STUDENT FLIER KILLED

Pittsburgh, Kas.—(AP)—Sam Von Schriltz, 20, student flier in the government's pilot-training program at Pittsburgh Teachers College, was injured fatally late Wednesday. The light training plane he had taken aloft for a solo flight crashed after one wing crumpled during a dive.

Stranded Phone Men Roll Down Drifts To Save Energy

Two Columbia Telephone company employes put the old rule of "whatever goes up must come down" to good use in battling two and one-half miles of snow drifts Wednesday evening.

Stranded near Maytown when their truck stalled, Howard Hanlen, of Marietta, and Joseph Finnegan, of Columbia, began to walk toward Marietta. They found the going tough until—they discovered it took just about half that much energy to clamber to the top of drifts that were three feet deep or better—then roll down the other side.

BUSES, TROLLEYS TIED UP; TRAINS ARE RUNNING LATE

Transportation Units Fail As Big Blizzard Hits And Closes Nearly All County Roads

Buses and trolley cars of the Conestoga Transportation company were paralyzed by the blizzard Wednesday night.

At midnight Wednesday, officials reported, there were buses stranded on every one of the lines. Two buses were stalled on the Harrisburg pike, near Elizabethtown, the Quarryville ou^ was able to proceed only as far as Willow Street after 8 p. m., buses were stranded on the Strasburg pike, the Lincoln highway near Leaman Place, and the Millersville pike. Buses traveling between Manheim and Lititz and this city were running more than an hour behind schedule. A Columbia bus was disabled along the Columbia pike, about four miles west of this city, and was brought to the city early Thursday (today).

Company officials said they had issued orders to all drivers who were on these buses to attempt to bring them back to the city and then discontinue service for the night. The Ephrata trolley car was running more than an hour behind schedule.

In the city trolley cars and buses were stalled innumerable times during the night by the icy streets and drifts. Four Duke street trolleys became stalled at Duke and James streets about 11 p. m. and the passengers were transferred to buses that were pressed into service. Company workmen freed the cars and removed them to the car barn. The Laurel stree trolleys were also delayed and their passengers transferred to buses late Wednesday night.

Every available workman was called out to work Wednesday night to keep trolley tracks free of snow Officials said trucks and plows were

More of BUSES on Page 16

AWNING BLOWN AWAY

Mishap In Downtown Section In City's Only Wind Damage

Despite high winds which swept the city Wednesday night, city police said they had only one report of any damage. An awning was blown away at the Whalen Drug store, located on the northeast corner of Queen and Orange streets, they said.

Sixty-Mile Gale Drifts Snow And Strands Travelers

All But Few Of Principal Roads Are Closed; Trains, Trolleys And Buses Fall Behind Schedules In Battle With Storm; Only Minor Damage Reported

Lancaster county is snowbound.

That, briefly, tells the story of the blizzard of St. Valentine's day, 1940, a blizzard that weathermen say compared with the famous storms of 1858, 1888, 1928 and 1932. To go into details would require a book, for everywhere, from Lebanon county to the Mason-Dixon line and from the Susquehanna river to the Chester county line, the countryside is paralyzed.

Lincoln Highway, Parts of Route 222 and Harrisburg Pike Only Roads Open

The Lincoln highway, east and west; Route 222, from Lancaster to Quarryville, and from Brownstown to Ephrata, and the Harrisburg pike, were the only roads open in the county at midnight. A plow was stuck on the Lititz pike and one-way traffic was the rule on small sections of other principal highways. The State Highway department had 35 plows and 100 men at work, trying to keep open the roads not already closed and trying to open other principal roads that were blocked.

A gale that swept out of the northeast, at times reaching a velocity of 60 miles an hour, drifted the snow that measured from six to 10 inches. All but a few of the principal highways were closed at midnight and the wind was still blowing hard. Secondary and township roads were hopelessly blocked and it was believed that several days' work will be required to reopen them.

A barometer reading of 29.40 was recorded during the storm. It was one of the lowest readings ever recorded here and showed well the intensity of the storm.

The weatherman predicted generally fair weather for Thursday (today) and rising temperatures Thursday afternoon. The mercury was at the 20 mark at midnight having dropped from 32 at 8 a. m. Wednesday when the storm really let go. A sleet storm preceded the snow and followed a rainy day. The storm, which abated about 10:30 p. m., is expected to move out to sea Thursday.

TRANSPORTATION UNITS FAIL

Nearly all forms of transportation failed Wednesday night. City and county buses and trolley cars stalled or were delayed until service was barely maintained. Trains were running late and through buses were far off schedule. Trucks and autos were abandoned in snow drifts and the occupants sought shelter at nearby homes and farmhouses. Some school buses were stalled for a time but all the occupants were accounted for late Wednesday night, a check showed.

Many schools were closed early Wednesday to enable the children to reach their homes, and some industries eliminated the night shifts because their workers were unable to reach the plants.

Communication lines held up well, but only because the sleet storm ended when it did, officials said.

Power lines failed in some sections but repairmen braved the storm to restore service.

Despite the fury of the storm, little damage was reported. There were numerous minor motor accidents but the worst trouble seemed to be starting motor vehicles either because of drifts or mechanical troubles brought on by the cold snap. Garagemen did a rushing business.

SCHOOL GIRLS STRANDED

Miss Margaret Carter and Miss Pauline Burkins, both of Drumore

More of BLIZZARD on Page 16

COUNTY SCHOOLS CLOSE EARLY TO PROTECT PUPILS

Many Will Not Resume Classes Today; Buses Have Difficulty; Few Children Stranded

The blizzard Wednesday hampered operation of some of the school buses in the county, and many schools dismissed early so the pupils could be gotten home safely.

LIST OF SCHOOLS WHICH WILL BE CLOSED TODAY

Schools in the following townships will be closed Thursday (today), officials announced Wednesday night:

Manheim, Manor (except Millersville Training school), East Lampeter, Warwick, East Hempfield, Gap Consolidated school, Salisbury Township High school, White Horse, Drumore, East Cocalico and Ephrata.

City schools ran on schedule and expect to open as usual Thursday (today), but if the snow and wind do not abate, the schools may have to close, according to Superintendent of Schools, Dr. Harvey A. Smith.

Likewise the storm caused little inconvenience at the Catholic High school, which ran on schedule and will reopen Thursday (today) Father Anthony J Kane, principal said. The parochial schools also will reopen as usual.

The Manheim township schools will

More of SCHOOLS on Page 16

CHARGE MAN CREATED RUMPUS AT STATION

Roy Owen, York, Arrested By P.R.R. Police, Pays Cost On Disorderly Conduct Charge

Roy Owen, forty-five, of York, charged with disorderly conduct by Sergeant J. J. Duersmith, of the Pennsylvania Railroad police, pleaded guilty before Justice of the Peace C. H. Martin, Manheim township, Wednesday and was released upon payment of the costs. He was arrested Tuesday by State Motor Policeman D. M. Rabenold after allegedly creating a disturbance at the local railroad station.

MRS. T. WALLACE REILLY ILL

Mrs. T. Wallace Reilly, 38 N. Lime st., was admitted to St. Joseph's hospital early Thursday (today) as a medical patient.

Lost & Found

FOX TERRIER, male. All white, black, brown head. Reward 5968.

YOU MAY phone your lost ad to us for publication in this evening's paper as late as 12 o'clock noon today. Please phone 5252.

WGAL Will Broadcast School Schedules And Road Conditions

Radio Station WGAL will go on the air at 6:30 a. m. Thursday (today) to give the latest information on road conditions and school schedules.

Officials of the school districts are invited to communicate with the radio station (Phone Lancaster 5259) advising whether or not their schools will be open, and the information will be broadcast immediately.

Road conditions will be determined by checking with the State Highway department and the Pennsylvania Motor Police.

HIT-RUN CHARGE DROPPED

A hit and run charge against Harold L. Frank, New Holland, has been withdrawn by Earl L. Palmer, the prosecutor, it was announced today by Justice of the Peace Harold Overly. Frank was prosecuted and arrested by Chief of Police K. C. Sharp, New Holland, after a parked automobile owned by Palmer had been struck and damaged.

RAIL HISTORIAN TO ADDRESS CLUB

Leon R. Franks, president of the Railway Historical society, will speak at a luncheon meeting of the Lancaster Exchange club at the Hotel Weber next Wednesday.

Clyde T. Bishoff, of Allentown, gave a hand-writing analysis demonstration and talk at the dinner meeting Wednesday evening.

SPECTACLE—"The Grapes of Wrath," based on John Steinbeck's much-discussed novel opened in the Colonial theatre yesterday. Hailed as one of the most fearless films of all times the picture is being received with much interest by local theatre-goers. John Ford directed. Henry Fonda has the role of Tom Joad and Jane Darrell is Ma Joad. John Carradine is the crusading minister. Others in the cast are: Charley Grapewin, Dorris Bowdon, Russel Simpson, O. Z. Whitehead, John Qualen, Eddie Quillan and Zeffie Tilbury. The Colonial will open Saturday morning at 9 o'clock. The screen play was written by Nunnally Johnson.

LITITZ THEATRE—Brings to the screen Margaret Mitchell's "Gone With The Wind," starring Clark Gable as Rhett Butler and Vivien Leigh as Scarlett O'Hara. Opens today for 6-day showing.

MYSTERY—Boris Karloff as Mr. Wong and Grant Withers as Captain Street examine a clue in "Mr. Wong in Chinatown," the exciting new mystery thriller playing at the Fulton.

WESTERN DRAMA — "Saga of Death Valley," the latest of the Roy Rogers series, comes to the Hamilton Theatre, tomorrow only.

NEW ROLE—Carole Lombard stars in "Vigil In The Night" at the Grand theatre today. Carole plays the role of a nurse. Co-starred with Miss Lombard are Brian Aherne and Anne Shirley. The story is by A. J. Cronin, author of "The Citadel."

DANCING STARS—Fred Astaire and Eleanor Powell, stars of "Broadway Melody of 1940" at the Auditorium Theatre, Manheim, tomorrow only.

IN NEW COMEDY—Opening today at the Strand theatre are Joel McCrea and Nancy Kelly, co-starred in 20th Century-Fox's "He Married His Wife."

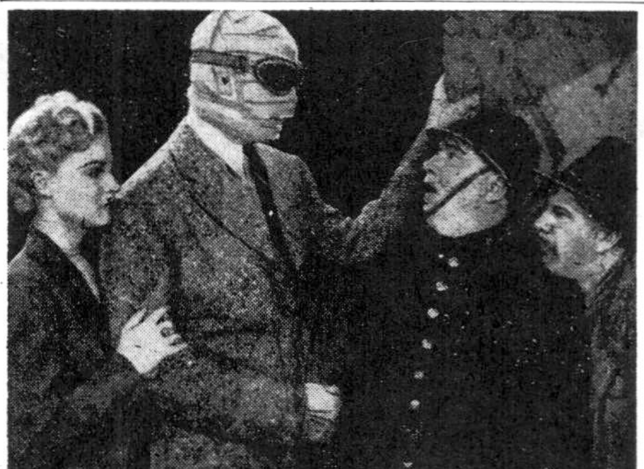

CREEPY—"The Invisible Man Returns" to the Capitol theatre tomorrow. The cast is headed by Vincent Price, Sir Cedric Harwicke, Nan Grey and John Sutton. Saturday only there will be a stage show. Another added feature on Saturday will be the WGAL Kiddie Show which will be broadcast from the stage from 12:30 to 1:00. "Green Hell," starring Douglas Fairbanks, Jr., Joan Bennett, George Bancroft, George Sanders, John Howard and Alan Hale is showing today for the last times.

AUTO IS RECOVERED

An auto owned by Paul Peel, 45 West Chestnut street, reported stolen from a parking space in the 600 block of East Orange street at 10 P. M. yesterday, was recovered by city police in the 400 block of Poplar street an hour later.

WEATHER
Eastern Pennsylvania: Cloudy With Light Snow In North And Light Rain In South Portion Thursday; Friday Cloudy Followed By Occasional Rain; Not Much Change In Temperature.
Intell Journal Stormograph Reading: Cloudy Thursday.

Intelligencer Journal.

The Leading Newspaper in the Garden Spot of America, Home Owned for Home Folks Since 1794

Boxing
Earl Frederick gains technical kayo over Billy Donley in fifth round of pro windup at State Armory.
For details turn to Page 13.

VOLUME LXXVI.—NO. 171. CITY The Intelligencer Founded 1799 The Journal Founded 1794 LANCASTER, PA., THURSDAY MORNING, MARCH 28, 1940 Entered at Post Office at Lancaster, Pa. as second class mail matter 18 PAGES, 144 COLUMNS.—THREE CENTS.

Fierce Blaze Rages In Nazi Military Supply Plant; Sub Sinks Ship In British Port

Powder Stores Believed Burning; Police Shroud Blaze In Secrecy

BLAST ON FRENCH SHIP

British Hold Soviet Freighter From U. S. At Port Of Hongkong

Berlin, (Thursday) — (AP) — A fiercely blazing fire in a closely guarded military supply plant reddened the skies of the thinly inhabited outskirts of North Berlin yet early today.

Starting late last night in a wooden warehouse of an industrial plant at Wilhelmsruh, six miles from the center of Berlin, the blaze persisted this morning though apparently confined by a great mobilization of fire fighting apparatus tc the one building.

BELIEVE POWDER BURNING

DNB, official German news agency, in reporting the blaze, did not mention the name of the plant. Observers, however, said it was the Bergmann Electricity Works, which is understood to have been converted to manufacture of war materials.

The intense red reflection of the blaze against the clouds and the manner in which it flared up fiercely from time to time caused observers to believe powder stores were burning.

Police secrecy intensified this belief.

DNB, without confirming reports that the plant made machine-gun ammunition, only said the fire started in "highly inflammable material."

NO SOUND OF BLASTS

The rapid rise and fall of the flames caused early reports to be circulated that frequent explosions were occurring, but there were no sounds of loud blasts.

Reporters were refused details by a cordon of tight-lipped military police.

Stringent wartime laws against the reporting of news of any military value likewise hampered efforts to obtain information.

Reporters driving through blacked-out streets to the fire found the last half mile a mass of fire equipment.

Police cordoned the area, and army guards halted newspapermen at the walls of the plant with the abrupt explanation: "No information available."

Unofficial information was to the effect that the plant made only small arms ammunition.

There was no evidence of casualties.

Warfare On Seas And In Air Blazes In New Fury

(By The Associated Press)

Warfare on the high seas and in the air blazed into new fury Thursday with mounting accounts of sinkings and air fights, an explosion aboard a French destroyer and a tangle of incidents issuing out of the tightening tension of the British blockade.

The British tallied sundry losses and fumed over the report that a German undersea raider had penetrated the big, closely guarded blockade base of Kirkwall in the Orkney Islands, there to sink the

More of INTERNATIONAL Page 9

R. A. F. Plane Sinks U-Boat

These two pictures, made from a British bomber, record the sinking of a German submarine. Top, the 500-ton U-boat is taken unawares, her hatch closed ready for diving. The plane dropped four 250-pound bombs and (lower) the sub sinks in a swirl of oily foam.

13-INCH SNOW FALLS IN UPPER PENNSYLVANIA

Average Of 12 Inches Reported Throughout Venango County

FOLLOWED BY RAINFALL

Southern Tier Of Counties Report Temperatures More Springlike

(By The Associated Press)

Snow ranging up to thirteen inches covered northern Pennsylvania Wednesday as winter paid spring a visit. Along the southern tier of counties, however, temperatures jumped as high as 60 degrees although skies were overcast and rain predicted.

SPRING WEATHER HERE!

Spring weather prevailed here Wednesday as other sections of the state were shoveling out from under a snowfall eight inches deep in some places.

The official high temperature for the day was 53 degrees at the U. S. Weather station at Ephrata. The low was 28. Unofficial temperatures were recorded as high as 60 degrees. The temperature stood at 40 degrees at the Intelligencer Journal weather station at 1 a. m. Thursday (today).

Light rain is forecast for this section Thursday (today) with Friday cloudy followed by occasional rain. Not much change in temperature is expected.

In northern Venango county the snowfall was reported at 13 inches with an average of 12 inches for the county. The weather observer reported eight inches at Franklin. Rain Wednesday night followed the 12 hour fall.

7 INCHES AT MEADVILLE

Meadville, in the northwest section of the state, had seven inches of snow. The Highway Department reported a fall of five to eight inches in Clinton, Cameron, Elk and Columbia counties.

In Forest and Venango counties there was 5 to 7 inches of snow. Two to three inches were reported in Erie, Mercer, Warren and Crawford counties; two to five in Luzerne county; two to four in Centre, Clearfield, McKean, Potter, Lycoming, Sullivan, and Tioga; and one to two inches in Bradford, Lackawanna, Pike, Susquehanna, Wayne and Wyoming counties.

Cinder crews were ordered out to keep the highways open—especially U. S. route 6—the Roosevelt high-

More of SNOW on Page 9

Snow Shoveler Still Has Long Way To Go

Even as new snow was falling in some sections, Al Shumaker started digging out his car, buried by 20-foot drifts on route 238 near Warsaw, N. Y. The black frame is the top of Shumaker's car, and he still has a long way to go.

N.Y.A. AND C.C.C. FUND INCREASE VOTED BY HOUSE

Adds $67,450,000 To Next Year's Appropriations For Two Agencies

WARNING IS IGNORED

Committee Limit On Funds For Wage-Hour Administration Upheld

Washington — (AP) — Despite cries of "how are you going to pay the bill," the House Wednesday added $67,450,000 to next year's appropriations for the CCC and the NYA.

Subject to final confirmation Thursday, the members ran roughshod over economy forces, adding $50,000,000 to President Roosevelt's request for $230,000,000 for Civilian Conservation Camps and upping by $17,450,000 his request for $85,000,000 for the National Youth Administration.

"TRAGIC THING" OCCURS

Both increases, their sponsors said, would insure continuance of the 1941 NYA and CCC programs at their present levels. The President had asked for a flat $15,000,000 slash in NYA funds and elimination of 273 of the 1,500 CCC camps.

Immediately after the CCC increase was approved tentatively by a 134 to 100 vote, Rep. Woodrum, Dem., Va., leader of the House Economy bloc, told an attentive membership that a "tragic thing" had just occurred.

Asserting that the House had reversed its previous policy of attempting to "live within budget estimates," Woodrum shouted:

"If we are now going to go ahead, pell mell, and appropriate, then I submit to you that it is honest to decide somewhere how are you going to pay the bill? Are you going to have a tax bill or are you going to raise the debt limit and borrow the money?

"You know as well as I know that the Congress has no idea of doing either one at this session. x x x much more important than keepint the CCC camp in my district is to try to protect the economic foundations of this country, and today they are in danger."

CALLS AMOUNT "TRIFLE"

Rep. Scrugham, Dem., Nev., replied that Congress passed "very lightly" appropriations of $50,000,000 or $100,000,000 to purchase "instrumentalities of destruction and death" but opposed strenuously another $50,000,000, "comparatively a trifle," to help young men.

Whereupon the House voted, 144 to 133, to increase the NYA fund at the request of Rep. Johnson, Dem., Okla., and a host of others who argued that the pro-

More of HOUSE on Page 9

DR. G. P. ROWLAND DIES IN 65TH YEAR AT HOME OF SON

Retired Presbyterian Minister Was Father Of Assistant Pastor Of First Church

The Rev. George P. Rowland, D. D., sixty-four, a retired Presbyterian minister, died at 3:30 p. m. Wednesday at the home of his son, Rev. John B. Rowland, 226 E. Orange st., after an illness of three weeks.

DR. GEORGE P. ROWLAND

He was born in Grafton, W. Va., a son of the late Josephus and Frances King Rowland and graduated from Washington and Jefferson college, class of 1900, and the Western Theological seminary, Pittsburgh, in 1903. He served pastorates in Steubensville, Ohio, and Aspinwall, Pa., and was granted the degree of Doctor of Divinity by Washington and Jefferson college in 1931.

The Rev. Rowland retired from the ministry in 1939, his last charge having been the First Presbyterian church at Aspinwall. He was a resident of this city for the past four months, residing with his son, who is assistant pastor of the First Presbyterian church.

Beside Rev. John B. Rowland, he is survived by his widow, the former Mary Beacom, and another son, Dr. George P. Rowland, Jr., of Akron, Ohio. A brother, W. J. Rowland, Grafton, W. Va., and a sister, Sarah E., wife of Ross Timms, of Pittsburgh, also survive.

REPORTS TOOLS STOLEN

Clifford Kreider, janitor at the R. K. Buehrle school, reported to city police Wednesday, the theft of several tools and a pair of glasses from the basement of the building sometime within the past week.

Supreme Court Orders New Trial For Herman Petrillo

Rule Evidence Used In Conviction For Murder Violated Constitutional Rights

Pittsburgh—(AP)—A 41-year-old convicted Philadelphia slayer whose arrest last year brought disclosure of a far-flung murder-insurance syndicate, won a new trial from the State Supreme Court Wednesday on grounds some of the evidence admitted had violated his constitutional rights.

The defendant, Herman Petrillo, spaghetti salesman, and three others were sentenced to death during the commonwealth's prosecution of the ring, which it charged was responsible for as many as 100 deaths in which "hexing", the "evil eye" and "magic love potions" were involved. Thirteen persons have pleaded guilty.

HERMAN PETRILLO

CONVICTED YEAR AGO

Petrillo was convicted March 23, 1939 of first degree murder for the poisoning of Ferdinand Alfonsi, who died October 27, 1938. Alfonsi's widow was acquitted on a similar charge. Alfonsi's $2,000 insurance policy has lasped 27 days before his death, leaving him but a $400 lodge policy in force.

Month of investigation brought the arrest of a score of persons as police pieced together the picture of the "slay for pay" syndicate. Most of the victims lived in Philadelphia's Latin quarter and believed in witch craft, "hexes" and "love concoctions." Some of those killed were husbands of disgruntled wives.

CHALLENGES TESTIMONY

Justice George W. Maxey's opinion in the case challenged the testimony of the "commonwealth's chief witness, George Myer, who on cross examination said his real name was Newmyer, and that in 1927 he had served eight months and ten days of a 10 months jail

More of PETRILLO on Page 16

Ben Parmer Pays $6.55 For Freedom, Enjoys It 7 Hours

Seven hours after he pleaded guilty, paid $6.55 costs and was released from police headquarters on charges of drunkenness and disorderly conduct, Ben Parmer, sixty, no home, was back in a cell Wednesday, charged with drunkenness and disorderly conduct again.

Parmer paid costs on the first charge at 8 a. m. Wednesday and was released. At 3 p. m. he was rearrested by Policeman Ross Brubaker. He is being held for a hearing in police court Thursday.

DENY ATTEMPTS TO FORCE PAYMENTS TO POLITICAL FUND

Indiana County Democratic Leaders Assert There Was No Coercion Practiced

Harrisburg —(AP)— The prosecution called Indiana and Jefferson county Democratic leaders to the stand Wednesday in the trial of State Chairman David L. Lawrence and seven other Democrats to explain their part in building up the party's fiances by a system of payroll percentage contributions.

The Indiana county witnesses, Chairman Howard R. Spicher and Vice Chairman Grace Lahr, both denied any conspiracy on their own or the eight defendants' part, to force collections—the charge on which the eight are being tried.

CORROBORATE TAYLOR

In that respect they corroborated the testimony of Frank E. Taylor, 23-year-old cashier of the Democratic State Committee, who declared he never heard of any appointments, dismissals, promotions or raises being contingent upon payments by state workers.

Taylor testified that the total "quotas" assigned to the 67 counties, based on a percentage of the salaries of state employes from each county, was $901,257, of

More of TRIAL on Page 9

HOUSE COMMITTEE VOICES APPROVAL OF PLANE POLICY

U. S. Builders Prepare To Handle $1,000,000,000 Worth Of Prospective Allied Orders

Washington—(AP)—The administration's new policy of releasing late model warplanes for export won the general approval of an inquiring House committee, Wednesday, and American manufacturers immediately prepared to handle prospective Allied orders totalling $1,000,000,000.

Secretary of War Woodring, explaining and defending the policy before the House Military Committee, asserted it had been formulated by the War Department "without coercion or pressure from anyone."

"As long as I am Secretary of War, I am not going to be pushed around," he assured the committee bluntly, in denying he had had any "friction" with Secretary of the Treasury Morgenthau over sale of planes to the Allies.

After hearing Woodring, Louis Johnson, Assistant Secretary of War, and Gen. George C. Marshall, Army Chief of Staff, endorse the revamped policy unqualifiedly, committee members generally expressed satisfaction with it, although no vote was taken.

Meanwhile, members of the House Military Appropriations sub-committee disclosed they had completed work on the Army's supply bill for the coming fiscal year and had trimmed more than $60,000,000 from the amount recommended by President Roosevelt. They said $27,000,000 of the cut was made possible when the War Department agreed to elimination of the major portion of 496 planes originally designed to be held in the air corps' rotating reserve.

Woodring testified the reduction was possible because the tremendous increase in the nation's aircraft productive capacity resulting from foreign orders had made a large reserve of planes unnecessary.

Germans Fed Up With Hitler, Fuehrer's Nephew Tells Elks

Says Majority Would Like To See Him Ousted, But Fear His Power

Hitler's regime is definitely unpopular now with the German people, William Patrick Hitler, British subject, and nephew of the German fuehrer, told members of Lancaster lodge, No. 134, B.P.O. Elks, at their fifty-first annual banquet held in the lodge home Wednesday night.

WILLIAM PATRICK HITLER

The speaker, son of an Austrian who is a half half-brother of Adolf Hitler, and an Irish mother, was in Germany from 1932 to 1939, and like many others in Germany, he said, thought at first that the ideas of the Nazi party and Hitler himself were "top-flight." However, he said, due to the suppression of minorities, speech, the press, the church, religion, Jews, he became alienated.

"The people now feel that Hitler and his close associates have put the country in a condition from which it will never recover," he said. Hitler owes his rise, he declared, to the belief of the people that he was one person who could prevent the spread of communism, but now they feel that it is only a question of time before it arrives. The majority would like to see him ousted, but they don't know how to do it because of his immense power, the speaker said.

The War has been foisted on the people, they believe, but they have entered it because there is nothing else for them to do, according to the speaker.

John L. Hamaker, retiring exalted ruler, was presented with a pen and pencil desk set by the drill team, while the Round Table luncheon club gave him a desk clock and pad.

K. L. Shirk, past exalted ruler and past district deputy, was toastmaster, and Christian Dutten-

More of GERMANS on Page 9

CITY HALTED FROM COLLECTING SEWER LEVY IN SUBURBS

Public Utility Order Is Effective For Six Months, More Information Asked

The city has been stopped in an order handed down Wednesday by the Public Utilities Commission from collecting the new sewer charge on properties outside the city. The order is effective for six months, ending October 1.

City Solicitor Bernard M. Zimmerman expressed surprise at the order, which he said came "without warning." He said that for the present the city will have to return to the plan of collecting $2.50 per front foot for sewage connection on all properties outside the city. This charge, he explained, is made only once, when the property is first connected to the sewer lines. After that, there is no further charge for sewage disposal, just as there was none in the city before the new sewage disposal ordinance went into effect.

NOT EFFECTIVE IN CITY

The order does not affect the collection of the tax inside the city limits, Zimmerman said.

A notice of the order was received by city officials Wednesday with the explanation that additional information would be filed later.

The secretary of the P. U. C. said at Harrisburg that city officials had been asked for more information about the rates and that a hearing may be held later.

The new sewage disposal rate which became effective January 1, this year, was levied on the basis of the front footage of each property receiving city sewage disposal service. At the same time the city eliminated the "stand-by" charge on water.

SOCIETY WOMAN DIES

Palm Beach, Fla. —(Thursday) — (AP) — The household of Mrs. Madeline Force Astor Fiermonte stated early today that the society woman was dead.

LEBANON LEGION POST LOSES LIQUOR LICENSE

State Control Board Suspends Permit Of William H. Bollman Unit For Forty Days

Harrisburg —(AP)— The Pennsylvania Liquor Control Board announced Wednesday the suspension of two licenses and the revocation of three others.

Suspensions included: William H. Bollman Post 158, American Legion, Lebanon, 40 days.

"We Lead All the Rest"

FARM CORNER

By *The Farm Editor*

WARM DAY BRINGS 1ST SPRING PLANTING

Goshen Farmer Seeds Four Acres In Peas, Mascot Man Plows Alfalfa Field

Streams may still be lined with ice but unmistakable signs of Spring appeared in the county on Wednesday when warmer weather lured a few hardy farmers to the fields.

Four acres were seeded in peas by Ross Ulrich, who owns a farm at Goshen in Fulton township, the first planting of the season in that community. He grows peas under contract for the Phillips Packing company. The ground was plowed last fall, the fertilizer was disced in on Tuesday and he seeded the crop on Wednesday. Because of the delayed Spring, it was not expected any peas would be planted in the Lower End during the month of March. Farmers predict there will be a considerable increase in the acreage of canning crops this year.

Enos H. Nolt, of Mascot, plowed an acre of alfalfa sod Wednesday afternoon. These were the first furrows turned in his district to date in 1940.

SELLS TOBACCO AT 16-10-5

Aaron M. Yake, of Millersville, Wednesday reported the sale of his 6-acre crop of tobacco to Bayuk Cigars, Inc. The price was 16-10-5. All but a few hundred lath have been stripped. The crop will be delivered to the Mountville warehouse.

Landis Buchen, Bayuk representative, this week opened the Jacob Martin warehouse at Farmersville. Delivery the opening day totaled 12,500 pounds of leaf.

Intelligencer Journal Weather Calendar

COMPARATIVE TEMPERATURES

Station	High	Low
Intell Journal	60	30
Water Works	55	24
Ephrata	53	28
Last Year (Ephrata)	70	53
Official High for Year, Mar. 20		57
Official Low for Year, Jan. 20		2
Character of Day		Clear

HOURLY TEMPERATURES

(Wednesday)			
8 a. m.	34	10 p. m.	43
11 a. m.	43	11 p. m.	41
2 p. m.	53	Midnight	40
5 p. m.	54	(Thursday)	
6 p. m.	52	1 a. m.	40
7 p. m.	50	2 a. m.	39
8 p. m.	48	3 a. m.	39
		9 p. m.	45

SUN

Rises—5:52 a. m. Sets—6:19 p. m.

More of WEATHER on Page 16

Columbia 'Judge' Jails Nephew As Suspect In Robbery Case

Man Accused Of Beating Wrightsville Boy After Stealing His Pocketbook; Found On Road

Martin Hasselbach, thirty-five, Pottstown, was committed to jail Wednesday by his uncle, Justice of the Peace Harry E. Hasselbach, for a further hearing on a charge of robbery.

Hasselbach, who formerly lived in Columbia, was arrested in Pottstown Wednesday after Edward Musser, Wrightsville, preferred the charge in behalf of his son, Stephen, twenty-one, who, he said, was beaten and robbed by Hasselbach.

Musser charged that Hasselbach threw his son out of his auto at 1 a. m. Sunday near the farm of George Fry, Washington Boro, after taking from him his pocketbook containing $14. Musser said that his son attempted to climb on the running board as Hasselbach started to drive away and that he beat him unconscious with the crank handle.

The injured boy was found unconscious at 9 a. m., according to the complaint, by Earl Caswell and his son-in-law. He was taken to his home and treated for frost bite, bruises and lacerations, his father said.

Chief of Police Eugene McManus and Policeman Christian Schwerdt arrested Hasselbach. State Motor Policeman Harry E. Fitzgerald took part in the investigation. The magistrate said the prisoner admitted stealing $7 but denied beating Musser.

MAN BURNS TO DEATH FIGHTING GRASS FIRE

York County Farmer, Overcome By Smoke While Battling Flames In Hollow

York, Pa. — (AP) — Byron P. Hughes, 49, a farmer at Delta near the Mason and Dixon Line, was burned to death while fighting a grass fire on the farm of a neighbor Wednesday. Coroner L. U. Zech said the man suffered first, second and third degree burns and that he was overcome by the smoke while battling the flames in a hollow.

ROBBED OF $28

Clair Mylin, about thirty, 105 Howard ave., reported to city police early Thursday (today) that he was robbed of his bill fold, containing $28 in cash, by two Negroes in the southern section of the city about 1 a. m. today. The men grabbed him as he approached his auto, parked on, Chester street, between Duke and Christian streets, he said, and dragged him about three or four blocks before snatching his billfold.

BRENEMAN BUILDING WILL BE IMPROVED

Permit For Work Issued To John H. Wickersham, Cost Estimated At $1,200

A building permit was issued Wednesday to John H. Wickersham to make interior alterations at the Breneman building, 53 North Duke street, for the Farmer's Trust company, at a cost of $1,200. The work will include miscellaneous improvements.

Is Federally-Paid Minister's Prayer A Hatch-Act Sin?

Des Moines, Ia.—(AP)—Is it a Hatch-act sin for a minister on the federal payroll to pray in public for "continued divine blessings upon the Democratic party, its principles, policies, platform and candidates?"

Iowa Democratic Chairman E. H. Birmingham has asked Attorney General Robert H. Jackson for a ruling on that question.

"At our 1938 State convention," Birmingham wrote, "we were glad to avail ourselves of the fervor and eloquence of Rev. D. Gwilym Roberts, a Presbyterian minister employed as a watchman upon an NYA project.

"I hestitate to invite Dr. Roberts to open our 1940 convention with prayer, if this is illegal. Could he be punished under the law for praying upon such an occason?"

WEATHER
Eastern Pennsylvania: Partly Cloudy Tuesday; Wednesday Increasing Cloudiness; Slightly Warmer Followed By Rain In Afternoon Or At Night.
Intell Journal Stormograph Reading: Cloudy Tuesday.

Intelligencer Journal

The Leading Newspaper in the Garden Spot of America, Home Owned for Home Folks Since 1794

Bowling
The Knights of Malta five-man team rolled a 2629 score in the American Bowling Congress competition in Detroit.
For details turn to Page Ten.

VOLUME LXXVI.—NO. 175. CITY The Intelligencer Founded 1799 The Journal Founded 1794 LANCASTER, PA., TUESDAY MORNING, APRIL 2, 1940. Entered at Post Office at Lancaster, Pa. as second class mail matter 16 PAGES, 128 COLUMNS.—THREE CENTS.

FLOOD NEAR CREST AT WILKES-BARRE

River Still Rising At Sunbury; Six Dead, Thousands Homeless

GERMAN GUNS POUND FRENCH IN SAAR AREA

France And Britain Seen Ready To Cut Ore Supply Route

BRITISH CURB ALIENS

(By the Associated Press)

German guns, following up a series of aerial battles between French and Nazi planes along the western front, pounded the French lines in the valleys of the Saar river sector Monday but military dispatches failed to report any change in the stalemated lines.

The French communique said the artillery fire was "particularly heavy." The French also said several air fights took place Sunday but that all French planes returned safely to their fields.

AIR REPORTS DIFFER

German and French reports on Sunday's aerial battling differed. The Nazi command said seven French planes were downed. The French acknowledged the loss of only two.

On the much-wider economic front, France and Britain were reported nearly ready to strike against the sea route down Norways' coast by which Germany imports Swedish iron ore.

Informed British sources said the Allies are discussing technical points connected with the plan and this was taken to mean everything has been settled except details. It was asserted the Allies did not intend to police neutral waters, nor would they attempt to establish a naval base on the Norwegian coast.

CHAMBERLAIN TO SPEAK

The British Parliament, meeting today (Tuesday) after its Easter recess, is expected to hear from Prime Minister Chamberlain a brief outline of steps taken to throttle Germany's ore supplies.

The French Chamber of Deputies also meets Tuesday. In preparation for what may prove a critical session for his new government, France's Premier Paul Reynaud, told his cabinet the Allied decisions reached at the Supreme War Council meeting in London March 28. It was at that session that the Allies are reported to have decided to take more energetic

More of WAR on Page 4

"We Lead All the Rest"
FARM CORNER
By
The Farm Editor

99 P. C. OF TOBACCO CROP REPORTED SOLD

Three Growers Report Sales At 16½ And 5 Cents At Meeting Of County Association

Ninety-nine per cent of the 1939 crop has been marketed, with only a few scattered crops totaling possibly 300 acres known to be unsold, it was estimated Monday night at the Lancaster County Tobacco Growers' association meeting. Three of the growers present reported they sold their tobacco recently at 16½ and 5 cents.

Ammon G. Huber, treasurer, reported receipt of $21.92 from the sale of 137 pounds of Harrisburg show tobacco at 16 cents a pound. H. C. Meyers, Lancaster R. D. 6, who cared for the samples since January and sold them along with his crop, was given a vote of thanks.

The State Farm Show commission was asked, in a resolution, to eliminate the stogie wrapper class from the next premium list and substitute a class of "farm fillers." The growers also suggested that the dividing line in the two divisions of the present binder and filler classes be changed from 24 to 26 inches; that is, "26 inches and under," for one length of leaves, and "over 26 inches" for the other. The long tobacco has been predominating at the exhibit.

A committee of three was authorized to cooperate with Dr. O. E. Street, director of the Lancaster Tobacco experiment station, and other authorities, in a move to have a laboratory added to the facilities of the local station. H. K. Mar-

More of FARM CORNER on Page 4

Intelligencer Journal Weather Calendar

COMPARATIVE TEMPERATURES

Station	High	Low
Intell Journal	49	40
Water Works	66	52
Ephrata	56	36
Last Year (Ephrata)	54	33
Official High for Year, Mar. 31		67
Official Low for Year, Jan. 20		2
Character of Day		Clear

HOURLY TEMPERATURES

(MONDAY)			
8 a. m.	41	10 p. m.	42
1 a. m.	44	11 p. m.	41
2 p. m.	48	Midnight	40
5 p. m.	48	(Tuesday)	
6 p. m.	47	1 a. m.	39
7 p. m.	46	2 a. m.	39
8 p. m.	45	3 a. m.	39
		9 p. m.	44

SUN
Rises—5:46 a. m. Sets—6:24 p. m.

More of WEATHER on Page 4

Pal Of Slayers

EVELYN MITTLEMAN

"KISS OF DEATH" GIRL IS DETAINED IN MURDER, INC.

Evelyn Mittleman Under $50,000 Bail; Three Former Swains Were Killed

New York —(AP)— Evelyn Mittleman, 25, dark and slender, was held Monday night as a material witness in District Attorney William O'Dwyer's investigation of Brooklyn's dollar - a - death ring, Murder, Inc.

"She has given the kiss of death to three people already." Assistant District Attorney Burton Turkus told the court when she was ordered held in $50,000 bail.

Turkus said that in the order of their appearance in her life—and disappearance from earth — her slain former swains were Hymie Miller, Robert Furer and Solomon Goldstein.

Miller went to his death in a quarrel over her affections, Turkus said, when the girl was only 17. Goldstein dispatched Furer and was himself done to death and his body weighted down in Loch Sheldrake, Sullivan county, N. Y., where the gang held summer sessions, the prosecutor added.

Turkus said Goldstein's successor to the affections of the dark-haired young woman was Harry (Pittsburgh Phil) Strauss, who is held as an accused member of the rubout syndicate.

CENSUS BEGINS, FIGHT GOES ON OVER "PRIVACY"

Sen. Tobey Offers Bill To Repeal Jail Penalty, Raps Hopkins

COUNT STARTS TODAY

Washington—(AP)—With 120,000 canvassers ready to begin the 1940 census Tuesday, Senator Tobey, Rep., N. H., continued his fight Monday against the income question, accusing Secretary of Commerce Hopkins of resorting to a "subtle trick" in his plan to allow answers to this question to be mailed in sealed envelopes.

REFUSES TO LIST CENSUS ENUMERATORS

The names of the 163 census enumerators who are scheduled to start work in Lancaster county Tuesday (today) will never be announced, C. Allen DePugh, the director, said Monday night. He would not give his reason.

Tobey introduced in the Senate a bill to repeal the possible 60-day jail penalty for persons refusing to answer census questions. He had objected that inquiries about wage and salary income were improper and that the answers might be misused for political purposes.

BROADCASTS ATTACK

His attack on Hopkins was made in a broadcast Monday night, in which he reiterated his previous stand that any person would be justified in refusing to answer any of the questions which he felt violated his constitutional right of privacy.

He criticized the plan for mailing in answers to the income query as not actually providing anonymity, since key letters on the blank containing the answers to this query correspond to letters on the regular census report, which gives the questioned citizen's name.

"What hypocrisy! What deceit! What a fraud upon the American people, telling you in a press statement that you do not need to sign your name on the income blank x x x and then through a subtle system of earmarking your identity learning the amount of your income by deception x x x."

AUSTIN RETORTS

Hopkins' plan for mailing in the income information was announced after Tobey had objected that persons questioned verbally might in some cases have to reveal private information to census enumerators who were neighbors.

Meanwhile, Census Director William L. Austin, who said he could not recall in a lifetime of work for the agency that anyone ever had been jailed for refusing to talk to enumerators, played a counter card. He issued a statement saying that Francis P. Murphy, Republican Governor of Tobey's state, had urged public cooperation with the census.

The census began technically at 12:01 Monday morning. Although the enumerators won't ring doorbells until Tuesday, they will base their count exclusively on who was alive at the official zero hour. Thus, babies born Monday won't count, while adults who died Monday still will be listed.

TOM MOONEY UNDER KNIFE

San Francisco—(AP)—An ulcer that has been troubling Tom Mooney for 16 years was removed Monday by Dr. Leo Eloesser.

Total Tax Bill For Local Government During Past Year

This is the first of three articles on the "Total Tax Bill for Local Government" prepared by the Lancaster County Committee of the Pennsylvania Economy League, Inc.

Do you know that the total tax bill for local government in Lancaster County for the year 1939 amounted to $4,430,888?

This sum of money was used for running the business of your County, City, Borough, Township and School Governments, over the entire county, according to the following breakdown of taxes levied in these units:

County Government:		
Taxes levied on Real Estate	$311,325	
Taxes levied on Personal Property (county)	221,414	$ 532,739
City Government (Lancaster):		
Taxes levied on Real Estate	540,511	
Water Rents*	410,000	950,511
School District of Lancaster:		
Taxes levied on Real Estate (school purposes)	945,894	
Per Capita Tax Levy	100,517	1,046,411
Borough Government (18 units):		
Borough Taxes levied	199,650	
School Taxes levied	384,095	
Per Capita Tax levied (schools)	67,135	650,880
Township Governments (41 units):		
Township Road Taxes levied	312,464	
Township School Taxes levied	793,103	
Per Capita Tax levied (schools)	144,780	1,250,347
Combined Total Taxes levied (1939) (Lancaster County—all units of government)		$4,430,888

* City Water Rents are considered as taxes in above tabulations.

COUNTY GOVERNMENT TRENDS:

Total County Government Expenditures, excluding payments (bonds, interest and taxes) on Inter-County Bridge Bonds, computed on the Per Capita expenditure basis.

1931	1932	1933	1934	1935	1936	1937	1938	1939	1940
$6.36	$4.95	$4.40	$4.43	$4.57	$4.31	$5.03	$4.46	$4.43	
COUNTY TAX RATES (MILLS):									
3	3	3	3	3	3	3	2½	2¼	1.9

The 1940 County Tax rate of 1.9 mills is distributed as follows:
1.5 mills for County Institution District purposes (Co. Home & Hospital)
.4 mills for County Government purposes (Operations & Maintenance)

ROAD FLOODED

Road From Colemanville To Pequea Closed; Little Damage Here

BUNGALOWS FLOODED

The Susquehanna flood waters lapped the Lancaster county shores Monday night but veteran observers did not expect much trouble, even though the crest is not expected until late Tuesday night or Wednesday.

Backwater in creeks was responsible for nearly all of the trouble Monday night, the Pequea creek backing up over the road between Colemanville and Pequea, and causing traffic in and out of the rivertown to detour. The Chickies also was over its banks.

TROUBLE AT MIDDLETOWN

At Middletown, flood waters from the river and the Swatara creek, rose to the first floor level of a dozen homes. Some water seeped into the flying field at the U. S. Army Air Corps depot. The river, which was short of a 20-foot flood stage, would inundate the field if it goes beyond 21 feet, authorities said.

Fire Chief James Myers, of Middletown, and two youths scoured the river in a motor boat searching for two youths who were reported to have embarked on the river at Harrisburg in a frail canoe. They planned to resume the search Tuesday morning.

The Conowingo-Port Deposit road was still under water Monday night.

EXPECT CREST TODAY

At the Safe Harbor dam, the flow was reported as 470,000 cubic feet per second at midnight. Eleven gates were open and more will be opened as the flow increases. There are thirty-two gates. The flow is expected to reach 515,000 at noon Tuesday, far below the 900,000 odd cubic feet recorded during the 1936 flood.

The flow over the Holtwood dam Monday night was 13 3-4 feet. It was 17 feet during the crest of the 1936 flood.

At the Conowingo dam, the flow at midnight was 458,000 cubic feet per second. In 1936 the peak was 875,000. The peak Tuesday is expected to be 475,000 feet.

ISLANDS UNDER WATER

Islands were underwater everywhere but in the vicinity of Fishing creek. A number of bungalows

More of ROAD on Page 4

SAY YOUTH BROKE INTO GARAGE AND STOLE AUTOMOBILE

Suspect In Manheim Robbery To Be Charged With Burglary, Police Say

John R. Nissley, nineteen, Manheim R. D. 3, was arrested by State Motor Police Monday and accused of breaking into a garage owned by M. W. Reichenbach, Wolf and Mill sts., Manheim, last Wednesday night and stealing the latter's car. Police said they will lodge a charge of burglary against Nissley Tuesday (today). Another suspect in the case was picked up and held at the local police station for further investigation.

According to State Motor Policemen T. W. Dooner and Roy W. Radcliffe, Nissley and a companion were occupants of the stolen car last Friday night and fled from the Stumpf gas station, Fruitville and Manheim pikes, without paying for a dollar's worth of gasoline.

Private Dooner said the car was recovered in Columbia Saturday by Chief of Police Eugene H. McManus after being abandoned on South Fifth street, near Locust street. Chief McManus and Officer Harold Shortlidge aided State Motor Police in the investigation.

Court House Doors Get Numbers, Too, At Request Of P. O.

The Court House will have numbers on its front doors, like all other buildings, very shortly because the Post Office department, has requested it.

Workmen Monday began placing 43-55 on the front doors and are expected to complete the job this week.

Office employes hurried to the front of the building to see the numbers after the April Fool cries throughout the building brought "no foolin'" answers.

Streets became canals in South Plymouth, Pa., when the Susquehanna river burst its dikes and flooded the Wyoming Valley. In circle above, a Coast Guard lifeboat is evacuating marooned residents from their homes.

Aviators seeking to use the airport at Wilkes-Barre, Pa., needed seaplanes after the spring floods got through with it. Above, the airport after the Susquehanna river smashed through dikes. High waters caused fatalities and made 10,000 homeless through the Wyoming Valley.

BUILDING PERMITS WORTH $102,875 ISSUED IN 2 DAYS

March Total Of $160,290 Is Almost Four Times Value In March, 1939

Building permits for construction work in Lancaster city, estimated to cost $102,875, have been issued in the past two days, J. Herbert Shartle, city building inspector, announced Monday.

Shartle also announced that building operations during the past month were nearly four times as great as during the same period last year. Although twenty-three permits were taken out in each period, estimated costs for construction work planned last month totaled $160,290 as compared to $41,200 during March of last year.

Heading the list of permits for March was one issued Saturday to D. S. Warfel for a fifty by ninety foot, four-story addition and alterations at 15½-17 South Queen street for Watt and Shand department store at an estimated cost of $90,000.

D. S. Seiple took out a permit to construct a fifteen by forty-eight foot brick building for Domenick Paparo at 722 North Queen street at an estimated cost of $5,000. A permit to make a twenty-four by fifteen foot addition and alterations to four apartments at 449 East Mifflin street, at an estimated cost of $3,000, was issued to B. Warren Henwood.

J. Frank Herdlauf took out a permit to build a twenty-six by

More of BUILDING on Page 4

CITY OFFICIALS, PUC TO CONFER WEDNESDAY

City's Sewage Disposal Rates For Suburban Area To Be Discussed Informally At Meeting

City Solicitor B. M. Zimmerman, City Commissioner Daniel W. Coulter and City Engineer J. Haines Shertzer will appear before the Bureau of Rates of the Public Utility commission in Harrisburg at 10 a. m. Wednesday to discuss informally Lancaster city's sewage disposal rates for properties in the areas adjacent to the city.

The Public Utility commission last week suspended the city's new sewage disposal rates for properties in the suburban areas for a period of six months.

Court 'Doubts' Countian's Claim Man Can Live 150 Yrs.

Elam G. Hess, Manheim, Placed On Probation On Charge Of Using Mails To Defraud; Judge Says He "Overstated Value" Of Pills

Philadelphia—(AP)—The question of whether human beings can live to be 150 years old was seriously debated in federal court Monday—and left open for further discussion.

But U. S. District Judge George A. Welsh, placing Elam G. Hess on probation on the latter's plea of no defense to a charge of using the mails to defraud in selling "concentrated" tablets accompanied by "longevity" diets, warned:

"Watch your step hereafter, and when you make statements of the value of your products, make them in the interest of science instead of for money."

Hess, 63, a dignified, former school teacher from Manheim, Pa., refused to budge, however, from his contention that life up to a century and a half is possible.

"Why," he exclaimed, "I have in my files the cases of a number of persons who have lived a century and a half. . . . And further the year-book of the United States Department of Agriculture, 1939, supports my thesis that proper diet aids longevity."

Postal inspectors testified Hess sold nearly $20,000 worth of his tablets in 1937 and 1938, accompanying the tablets, the inspectors added, was a pamphlet on "secrets of how to live 150 years," calling primarily for a strict diet of products in the raw.

"We don't want to discourage men who have scientific vision, or men who work in laboratories hoping to push back the barrier of death," remarked Judge Welsh, "but I feel Professor Hess has gone beyond the bounds of professional and scientific enthusiasm and overstated the value of his products."

Motorist With Restricted License Nabbed Again On Speeding Charge

David S. Beiler Who Had License Suspended On First Charge Is Accused Of Driving At 65 M.P.H.

David S. Beiler, Elverson R. D. 2, displayed a "restricted license" after being nabbed Monday for speeding at 65 miles per hour by State Motor Policeman J. J. Boyle on the Harrisburg pike near Salunga. Beiler is driving under a 90-day "restriction" after being nabbed previously for speeding, police said.

Boyle said he had to chase Beiler

More of MOTORIST on Page 4

NO SPEEDERS HEARD IN SPEEDERS' COURT

Not a single speeder was brought before Inspector Ralph W. Cummings in speeders' court Monday, the first time since Cummings has assumed his duties as inspector that he has passed by a scheduled court session without hearing a single case.

RAIN IN NORTH

Weather Expert Predicts Only Slight Rises At Sunbury And Harrisburg

RELIEF IN FULL SWING

(By The Associated Press)

Sleepless riverfront towns over a 100-mile stretch suspiciously watched the rain-gorged Susquehanna Monday night as it stood stationary at Wilkes-Barre nine feet above flood level after driving thousands from their homes.

Expressing a hope the Wilkes-Barre crest had been reached, Weather Bureau spokesmen warned, however, that in the catastrophic flood of 1936 the unpredictable river began to fall, only later to move up an additional five feet. It was raining to the north near the New York state line.

RISING AT SUNBURY

Downstream at Sunbury, at the confluence of the Susquehanna's north and west branches, a steady rise was reported.

Excepting slight rises expected at Sunbury and Harrisburg, "stationary or falling stages will prevail throughout the Susquehanna river system," Leslie F. Conover, chief of the U. S. Weather Bureau at Harrisburg, announced at midnight.

Conover predicted a final crest at Wilkes-Barre as 31.5 to 32 feet Monday night and at Sunbury 21 feet Tuesday night.

HARRISBURG FEARS EBB

Harrisburg flood fears ebbed downstream with the cocoa-colored Susquehanna Monday night. The rise of the river slowed to less than five-hundredths of a foot an hour before midnight to 19.7 feet and was expected to crest at 21 feet Tuesday night or Wednesday morning.

A few streets were flooded, some by backed-up sewers, but inconvenience was slight except to a few families in low-lying areas.

Floating fire on the surface of the stream added to the hazards of high water in one section as a half-million gallon gasoline tank broke loose at Edwardsville, collided with another, and both exploded.

Within ten minutes two more tanks blew up with a boom heard for miles in the Wyoming valley. Sheets of flame billowing from the

More of FLOODS on Page 4

APRIL 1 RUSH BOOMED BY BETTER BUSINESS

Recorder Of Deeds Office Kept Busy As Real Estate Men Report Increase In Property Sales

Because business is reported slightly better now than it was a year ago, the annual "April 1 Settlement Day" rush at the office of the Recorder of Deeds is topping the 1939 figure. The "rush", which began about ten days ago, is expected to continue this week.

The Lancaster Real Estate Board said that a ten per cent increase in property sales was noted during the first three months of this year over the same period last year. March sales were a "bit" over those of 1939, members stated.

HOUSE PASSES BILLS AUTHORIZING BRIDGES

Senate Gets Measures Permitting Construction Of Spans At Millersburg And Middletown

Washington —(AP)— The House passed and sent to the Senate Monday a bill authorizing construction of a toll bridge across the Susquehanna river at or near Millersburg, Pa., and a bill authorizing the General State Authority of Pennsylvania or the Pennsylvania Bridge and Tunnel Commission to construct and operate a toll bridge across the Susquehanna river near Middletown.

WEATHER
Eastern Pennsylvania: Rain In North And Cloudy Preceded By Rain In South Portion Tuesday; Slightly Cooler Tuesday Night; Wednesday Generally Fair.
Intell Journal Stormograph Reading: Cloudy Tuesday.

Intelligencer Journal.

Baseball
Ten teams will compete in the City and County Baseball League this season.
For details turn to Page 14.

The Leading Newspaper in the Garden Spot of America. Home Owned for Home Folks Since 1794

VOLUME LXXVI.—NO. 181. CITY The Intelligencer Founded 1799 The Journal Founded 1794 LANCASTER, PA., TUESDAY MORNING, APRIL 9, 1940 Entered at Post Office at Lancaster, Pa. as second class mail matter 20 PAGES, 160 COLUMNS.—THREE CENTS.

GERMAN ARMY INVADES NORWAY DENMARK

COPENHAGEN SEIZED; OSLO ABANDONED

RAINS FLOOD SUSQUEHANNA RIVER AGAIN

Water Passes 16-Foot Level At Towanda, Wilkes-Barre Expects 22.5 Feet

AWAIT TODAY'S CREST

Harrisburg—(AP)—The Federal-State Flood forecasting service Monday night said that the Susquehanna river, swelling from Monday's rain, would exceed the 16-foot flood stage at Towanda by three feet by noon Tuesday (today).

At 11 p. m. the river was already two-tenths of a foot above the flood mark there.

The service said the only other Pennsylvania community where the Susquehanna would rise above flood stage by Tuesday noon is Wilkes-Barre. The stage predicted for then is 22.5 feet, the flood mark being 22. The 11 p. m. stage was 20.3.

E. A. Hoffman, Red Cross flood consultant, predicted at 12:30 a. m. the river at Wilkes-Barre would reach a crest of about 25 feet by 6 p. m., Tuesday.

OVER AT BINGHAMTON

The river was already over 14-foot flood levels at Binghamton and Vestal, N. Y. The stage at Binghamton at 10:30 p. m., was 15.4. At Vestal at 9 p. m. it was 21.7.

"There is a little rise in the upper watershed at Binghamton," the flood forecasting office said. "It will take until Tuesday to know what really will happen."

Williamsport, with a flood stage of 20 feet, reported 14.5 feet at 11 p. m. and 18 was predicted there for noon Tuesday. Sunbury, whose flood stage is 16 feet, had 12.2 at 11 p. m. and Tuesday's forecast was 14.5.

RENEW 24-HOUR SERVICE

Flood emergency headquarters at the Capitol went on 24-hour duty again Monday, after reports

More of FLOOD on Page 6

"We Lead All the Rest"

FARM CORNER

By *The Farm Editor*

MEETING TO BE HELD BY FARMERS' GUILD

Committee Reports To Be Given At Session Wednesday At Farm Of John Lehman

A meeting of the Farmers' Guild of Lancaster County is scheduled to be held at the farm of John Lehman, a half mile west of Mountville along the Lincoln highway, on Wednesday evening at 8 o'clock. A number of committee reports will be given during the business session. S. S. Boshnaugle, president, and Morris H. Kauffman, secretary, will conduct the program.

TO DISCUSS MILK REFERENDUM

Approximately 600 producers in Lancaster county whose milk is marketed in the metropolitan New York area are eligible to vote in the mail referendum on an amended order to change producer milk prices and revise administrative provisions now regulating the handling of milk in the New York market.

To acquaint local shippers to the New York market with details of the amended Federal-State milk marketing order issued by Secretary Wallace and for general discussion of the referendum vote, Charles E. Cowan, Lancaster Inter-State Milk Market manager, announced three meetings will be held this week, as follows:

Fire Company Hall at Lititz on Wednesday; High School building at Quarryville on Thursday; and

More of FARM CORNER on Page 6

Intelligencer Journal Weather Calendar

COMPARATIVE TEMPERATURES

Station	High	Low
Intell Journal	54	40
Water Works	58	43
Ephrata	56	35
Last Year (Ephrata)	49	28
Official High for Year, April 4		70
Official Low for Year, Jan. 20		2
Character of Day		Cloudy

HOURLY TEMPERATURES

(Monday)			
8 a. m.	48	10 p. m.	52
11 a. m.	50	11 p. m.	52
2 p. m.	50	Midnight	51
5 p. m.	52	(Tuesday)	
6 p. m.	52	1 a. m.	51
7 p. m.	52	2 a. m.	50
8 p. m.	52	3 a. m.	50
9 p. m.	52		

SUN
Rises—5:33 a. m. Sets—6:31 p. m.

More of WEATHER on Page 6

DARBY CREEK FLOODS PHILADELPHIA STREETS

Philadelphia—(AP) — Swollen by an all-day rain, Darby creek overflowed into the low-lying Eastwick section of southwest Philadelphia Monday night, rising curb-deep in some streets and draining into cellars.

The Schuylkill river, meantime, was rising steadily, but was still within its banks. At Reading, however, C. S. Ling, weather bureau observer, reported nearly two inches of rain in the upper Schuylkill valley. He predicted a sharp rise in the stream during the night.

CREEKS OVERFLOW, CLOSING SEVERAL ROADS IN COUNTY

Two And One-Half Inches Of Rain Falls Here, More Is Forecast

Several roads were closed to traffic Monday night when creeks overflowed their banks following Monday's heavy rains.

A total of two and one-half inches of rainfall was measured at the Water Works, while precipitation at the U. S. Weather station, at Ephrata was 2.27 inches up to 6 p. m. Monday. Fog was reported at night after the rainfall stopped.

Highway officials said Route 222 was barricaded and high water signs posted between Talmage and Brownstown when the Conestoga overflowed its banks, and on the same highway about one mile north of Ephrata by water from the Cocalico creek.

CONEWAGO OVERFLOWS

Water up to the running boards of automobiles was reported covering the road from Elizabethtown to Hershey, about two miles north of Elizabethtown, late Monday night, after the Conewago creek went over its banks.

Ephrata park was flooded by the swollen Cocalico creek and many fields were inundated in other sections.

Creeks in the southern section of the county were reported running bankfull.

More rain is forecast for Tuesday (today) with cooler weather expected at night. Wednesday is to be fair.

The high temperature for the day at Ephrata was 56 degrees. The low was 35.

PLANE FORCED DOWN

The storm twice forced the pick-up airmail plane of All-American Aviation, Inc., down at the Lancaster Municipal airport, Monday. The first time, Holgar Horris, the pilot, landed at 11 a. m., after picking up a sack at the Old Lancaster airpolt. At 3:30 p. m., Horris took

More of CREEKS on Page 6

BURNED BY CAP PISTOL

Grace Hershey, Twelve, 309 S. Prince St., Injures Leg

Grace Hershey, twelve, 309 S. Prince st., was treated at St. Joseph's hospital Monday for a powder burn of her left leg inflicted by a cap pistol.

JUDGE ATLEE IMPROVED

The condition of Judge Benjamin C. Atlee, of Millersville, who has been ill for some time, was reported as "much improved" at his home Monday night. Judge Atlee underwent an operation at the Lancaster General hospital in January.

PARIS ARCHBISHOP DIES

Paris, (Tuesday) —(AP)— Jean Cardinal Verdier, archbishop of Paris, died today.

Norway Declares War As Nazi Warships Attack; Berlin Radio Announces "Protective" Invasion

Forts Hold Fjord

Battle Follows Movement Of German Fleet Into Skagerrak; British Sub Sinks Troop Ship

Washington—(AP)—Mrs. J. Borden Harriman, American Minister to Norway, notified the State department Monday night that the Norwegian foreign minister had informed her that Norway is at war with Germany.

The State department issued the following statement:

"The American Minister to Oslo, Mrs. J. Borden Harriman, telegraphed to the Department of State tonight that the foreign minister has informed her that the Norwegians fired on four German warships coming up Oslo Fjord and that Norway is at war with Germany.

"In response to a request by the British minister to Norway, the American legation at Oslo has been authorized to take over British interests in Norway."

The Norwegian minister to the United States, Wilhelm De Morgenstierne, was in conversation with the State Department shortly before midnight.

STATE DEPT. ACTIVE

The department, where a night watch has been maintained constantly since the outbreak of the European war, stirred quickly to activity. Officials there hurried to their offices.

Across the street, lights burned in the White House executive offices although President Roosevelt was at his Hyde Park home.

There was no comment from officials here as to whether the President would take immediate steps to issue a proclamation under the Neutrality act adding Norway to the list of belligerents.

Such action undoubtedly would be coupled with a proclamation forbidding American ships to enter Norwegian waters. The present "combat zone" from which these vessels now are banned ends just south of Bergen, Norway.

When the State Department issued its dispatch from Mrs. Har-

More of WASHINGTON on Page 6

PRESIDENT TALKS WITH STATE DEPT.

Hyde Park—(Tuesday)—(AP)—President Roosevelt communicated with the State Department by telephone early today over the northern European crisis.

Aides awakened him with the news shortly before 4 a. m. (EST) and he immediately got in touch with Washington. Meanwhile, a secretary set about making arrangements, if feasible, to have a special train rushed here to return the President to the capital as soon as possible.

OSLO BATTLE

(By The Associated Press)

Breaking Norway's traditional neutrality with a sudden attack, four foreign warships early today (Tuesday) attempted to enter Oslo Fjord, the water gateway of the Norwegian capital, but were driven off by the heavy fire of coastal defense batteries.

The brief battle was confirmed in Stockholm by high authoritative quarters but the nationality of the warships was not determined.

Presumably the attack was from a German fleet, which earlier was reported steaming through the Kattegat, near Denmark, from the Baltic in a northerly direction. However, British naval units also were numerous off Norwegian shores yesterday.

Amid heavy burst of canon fire from the warships, one of which was reported to be a heavy cruiser, an air battle was reported to have taken place between Norwegian planes and foreign fighting aircraft above the dark gorge of Oslo Fjord.

OSLO BLACKED OUT

Oslo itself was blacked out, the city's communication with all Norway having been cut by censorship, the country's radio stations silenced, and the lighthouses darkened.

Oslo, however, was reported to have experienced an air raid alarm for an hour at the time of the naval cannonade.

The Exchange Telegraph Agency at London reported that an air raid alarm was sounded at 2 a. m. (8 p. m., Monday, E. S. T.) in Oslo, and that no all clear signal had been given three hours later.

Although the nationality of the attacking ships was not ascertained in the darkness, both British and German warships have been reported off the Norwegian coast for the past 24 hours.

Earlier, an armada of 125 German ships, including one pocket battleship, was reported concentrated in the Kattegat off the Danish coast and 100 miles directly south of the Norwegian capital across the waterway.

Reliable sources in Oslo, which was astonished yesterday (Monday) when the Allies sowed mines within Norwegian waters, said the German warships were off the Danish island of Lesoe in the Kattegat and apparently were headed for the

More of NORWAY on Page 6

FIRST IVY POISON CASE

Lorraine Zahm, Eleven, Treated At St. Joseph's Hospital

The first ivy poison case of the season was reported Monday at St. Joseph's hospital. The victim, Lorraine Zahm, eleven, 665 Union st., had her right knee treated.

Over 500 Tickets Sold For Annual Dutch "Volkes Fescht" On April 19

Lebanon, Berks And Lehigh County Groups To Attend Event In Moose Hall, Committee Reports

More than 500 tickets have already been sold for the second annual "vokes fescht" to be held in the Moose hall at 6:30 p. m. on April 19, it was reported at a meeting of the committee Monday night.

It was also announced at the meeting that members of similar groups from Lebanon, Berks and Lehigh counties will attend the local banquet this year. Special favors are being provided for diners while arrangements have been completed for the "little Deitsch band" of eight pieces from Denver to play.

Members of the committee, who are handling tickets for the dinner, are Rev. T. A. Alspach, John L. Bowman, Dr. Peter M. Harbold, Dr. Edwin M. Hartman, Forrest V. Heckman, John G. Keplinger, Joseph B. Wissler and Prof. Colsin R. Shelly, all of this city; Silas E. Bard, Rev. W. S. Brandle and Rev. Wallace R. Knerr, all of Denver; Ammon H. Bucher, of Manheim R. D. 2; Horace Martin and Harry F. Ruhl, Jr., of Manheim; Alvin B. Eberly, Dr. John F. Mentzer and Samuel Y. Wissler, of Ephrata; Roy S. Forney, of East Petersburg; W. E. Glasmire, of Bareville; Prof. Daniel W. Geist, of Blue Ball; Dr. John L. Hertz, Rev. Byron K. Horne and Victor Wagner, of Lititz; Henry K. Landis, of Landis Valley; Amos B. Musser, of Bowmansville; Dr. Adam V. Walter, of Brownstown; Dr. Henry Walter, of Rothsville, and George F. Weidler, of Akron.

New Theatre Of War

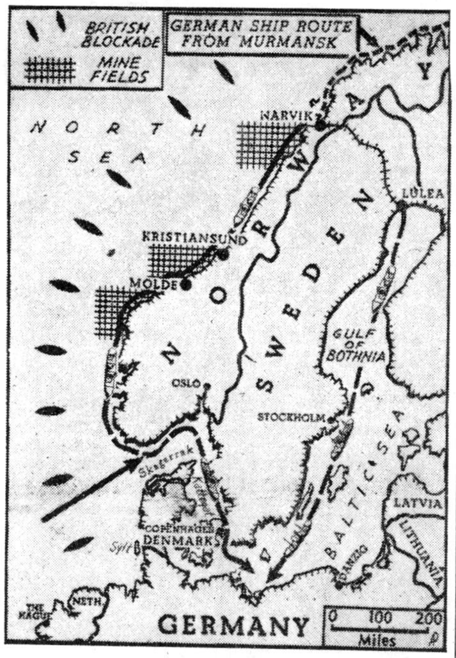

The theatre of war moved into Denmark and the adjoining Skagerrak and Kattegat straits Monday night and early Tuesday (today), with German troops reported occupying Copenhagen and other parts of Denmark, and an unsuccessful attempt by four unidentified warships to enter the fjord leading to Oslo, capital of Norway. An armada of 125 German ships was seen at the northern tip of Denmark, headed toward the Norweigian coast where a British submarine torpedoed a German troop ship.

Germans Bomb Scapa Flow For Third Time In Month

London—(Tuesday)—(AP)— German warplanes dropped incendiary and high explosive bombs in their third raid within a month Monday night on Britain's Scapa Flow Naval base, the Air Ministry reported early today. At least two German planes were shot down, the British said, and a third was believed brought down before the attack ended.

The raid, which came while the Allies stood fast in their defiant mine-laying in Norwegian territorial waters despite vigorous Norwegian protests, resulted in no damage to shipping, the British added.

CIVILIAN BURIED, UNHURT

A civilian was buried under the debris caused by a high explosive bomb, a communique added, but suffered no injury beyond shock.

The statement issued by the Air Ministry and the ministry of Home Security said:

"During a raid on Scapa flow yesterday (Monday) evening a number of incendiary and high explosive bombs were dropped. No damage was caused to warships or other shipping.

"A civilian was buried under debris by a high explosive bomb but sustained no injury beyond shock. There were no other casualties.

SMALL FIRES STARTED

"Small fires were started in the heather by the incendiary bombs which fell on the Moorland and the roof of an outlying farmhouse was damaged by the fire of high explosive bombs which fell near. No other damage to property was caused.

"It is now known that two of the enemy aircraft which took part in the raid were shot down by the Royal Air Force fighter aircraft and it is believed that a third which was severely damaged by machine gunfire and was last seen diving towards the sea met with the same fate."

(In Berlin, the official German news agency, DNB, said that the

More of SCAPA FLOW on Page 6

Skagerrak Scene Of Jutland Battle During World War

(By The Associated Press)

The Skagerrak, scene of the attack by foreign warships upon Oslo, capital of Norway, where a German troopship was sunk Monday by the British, is the scene of the World War's most famous naval engagement, the Battle of Jutland.

The Skagerrak is a strategic arm of the North Sea between Norway and Denmark. Leading from the North Sea, the narrow stretch of water becomes known as the Kattegat, as it threads the narrow expanse and islands between Denmark and Sweden into the Baltic Sea.

Thus the Skagerrak is the key to the Baltic Sea. To the Germans, the Battle of Jutland is known as the Battlè of the Skagerrak.

The Battle of Jueland took place at the western mouth of the Skagerrak on May 31, 1916. The engagement between the British grand fleet under Admiral Sir J. R. Jellicoe and the German high seas fleet under Admiral Reinhard Scheer was the only one in which the rival fleets met in force.

After Jutland the British fleet was undisputed master of the German navy, which remained bottled up in the Baltic.

Ports Are Seized

Bergen And Trondheim Occupied By German Forces; Danish Frontier Crossed By Troops

London—(Tuesday)—(AP)—A special announcement of the German radio intercepted today by Reuters, British news agency, said German troops had invaded Denmark and Norway.

The agency only shortly before carried a dispatch from Paris saying that the radio at Oslo, Norway's capital, had announced the landing of German troops at Norwegian ports at 3 a. m. (9 p. m., Monday, E. S. T.)

OFFICIAL ANNOUNCEMENT MADE

Reuters said that the following announcement was made by the German radio:

"The high command of the German army announces that in order to counteract the actions against Denmark and Norway (apparently the Allied minelaying along the Norwegian coast) and to prevent a possible hostile attack against these countries, the German army has taken these two countries under its protection.

"The strong forces of the German army have therefore invaded these countries this morning."

The intercepted Oslo radio report said that the Norwegian government had abandoned its capital and was moving to Hamar.

German forces were said to have occupied Bergen and Trondheim.

Hamar, reported as the new seat of the Norwegian government is in central Norway, about 60 miles north of Oslo.

SUBMISSION DEMAND REFUSED

Reuters said that before the Norwegian government left Oslo Foreign Minister Halvdan Koht announced that the German minister had demanded that Norway should not oppose the German occupation.

The demands, said to have been delivered both orally and in writing at about 5 a. m. (11 p. m. EST, Monday), also asked that Norway place herself under German military administration.

The Norwegian government, Reuters said, decided that Norway would not submit to the German demands on the ground they constituted an infringement of Norway's sovereignty.

More of SCANDINAVIA on Page 6

Rumania Alarmed By British Acts; Dynamite Is Seized

Bucharest—(AP)—Detention of a fleet of dynamite-laden British barges, charged by Germans with being designed to blow up a narrow Danube gateway and block a German supply line, Monday electrified southeastern Europe with the fear war soon might spread to this quarter of the world.

Rumanian police, acting on a tip said to have been supplied by the pro-Nazi Iron Guard, halted the fleet near Giurgiu, Danube river port whence Germany ships much needed Rumanian oil supplies.

Aboard were tons of dynamite.

CHARGE BLOCKADE PLAN

Germans alleged the British planned to blockade the spot in the Danube known as the Iron Gate by sinking the barges and wrecking the narrow channel where the

More of RUMANIA on Page 6

"GLASS SNAKES" ARE LIZARDS

So-called "glass snakes" really are lizards, belonging to the Genus Ophisaurus. Covered in hard, shingle-like plates, their habit of breaking to pieces is limited to separating themselves from their tails, a custom common among other lizards.

EARTHQUAKES AND SUNSPOTS

Much remains to be learned as to why earthquakes occur more frequently during certain periods of the year than during others, but there seems to be sufficient data on hand to prove that most quakes occur in years when sunspots are fewer.

Churchill Charges Fleet To Clear Baltic Gateway

Britain's Military Strategist Acclaims Sea Forces As Destroyer Of More Than 18 Nazi Vessels And Upwards Of 5000 German Lives

London —(AP)— The somber shapes of Britain's fleet, acclaimed already as the destroyers of more than 18 Nazi vessels and perhaps upward of 5,000 Nazi lives, tossed and fought in prolonged battle Thursday, charged by Winston Churchill with the task of sinking every German ship in the gateways to the Baltic.

The "first crunch of war", set off by German invasion of Denmark and Norway, raged on in the stormy northern seas, and the Royal navy was bidding for total destruction of Hitler's seapower.

To Churchill, First Lord of the Admiralty and director of strategy of all the British armed services, the navy's feats of the last two days "are worthy of any in our history" and have put the Allies on the high road to "victory." This he pugnaciously proclaimed to a wildly excited House of Commons Thursday.

This rejoicing nation, comparing the heavy German sea losses with a total of four sunken British destroyers, was willing to believe him.

Vast crowds milled about Whitehall while Churchill spoke and the House of Commons was packed. First of the diplomats to arrive in the galleries was United States Ambassador Joseph P. Kennedy.

FIRST "CRUNCH OF WAR"

Churchill saw the Nazi campaign against Norway as possibly a prelude to "far larger events" and he said dramatically:

"We have probably arrived at the first crunch of the war."

Four German cruisers, a number of destroyers, a number of submarines have been destroyed since Sunday, he said, and "nearly a dozen ships, some of large tonnage, have been sunk or captured." The 26,000-ton battleship Scharnhorst was damaged.

British losses, he said, included the destroyer Glowworm, sunk by two German destroyers, the destroyer Gurkha, sunk by aerial bombs, injury of seven men when the battleship Rodney was hit and piercing of the battle cruiser Renown by two German shells.

These were in addition to the loss of two British destroyers yesterday at Narvik and the damaging of two others.

The conflict still is raging in the North Sea, Churchill said, but he refused to "lift the veil."

He further told the House that he found no reason "to deter us from entering on further perils and promised that the Navy would sink remaining German ships in the Skagerrak and the Kattegat.

TELLS OF RENOWN BATTLE

Britons, who dearly love a fight, got plenty of thrills as Churchill with gusto told how the 32,000-ton Renown, one of Britain's sleek battle cruisers, engaged the 26,000-ton battleship Scharnhorst.

He lauded the action of Captain Warburton Lee and the destroyer Flotilla which attempted to take Narvik, saying their action was "as worthy as any in British naval history."

The destroyers Hunter and Hardy were lost at Narvik while the Gurkha went down when hard hit during five unsuccessful bombing attacks on the cruiser Aurora. The Glowworm was sunk by German destroyers when she turned back from her squadron to pick up a seaman who had gone overboard.

DISCOUNTS AIR ATTACKS

The First Lord discounted feared German air atatcks on he home fleet, pointing out that the flagship Rodney's deck armor resisted the explosion of a heavy German bomb.

Sir Archibald Sinclair, leader of the Liberals in the House, followed Churchill with a warning that the possibility that the attack on Norway was only a fake could not be discounted.

He contended that when Britain's attention was distracted, the main German blow might fall elsewhere.

KING'S VISIT DISCLOSED

It was disclosed Thursday night that King George VI visited the Admiralty on Tuesday while various actions were in progress.

Churchill looked comparatively fresh when he entered the House, considering that he spent three days in a virtually sleepless vigil in the Admiralty map room where wireles reports on the naval actions were received.

After commenting on Germany's being "deeply mutilated" in the cruiser element, Churchill said, "a number of German destroyers together with some U-boats have been destroyed—all since Sunday."

British submarines are "by no means asleep" Churchill said, for they "have taken a heavy toll" of German transport troop ships crossing to Scandinavia.

"We are not going to let the enemy supply their troops along those waters with impunity," he said.

SAY GERMANS ERRED

Speaking "for myself," the First Lord said he considered Germany's Norwegian occupation "as great a strategic and political error as that which was committed by Napoleon in 1808 when he invaded Spain."

"I cannot see any counter advantage which he (Hitler) has gained except the satisfaction of another exercise of brutal lust, of unbridled power," he said.

As the House cheered, Churchill observed "we certainly find no reason to deter us from entering on any further perils that might lie before us."

"We feel ready to encounter the utmost malice of the enemy and to achieve a ready victory in what is a world cause."

Churchill said the Norwegians "in their wild and mountainous country" should be able to maintain "vigorous and prolonged resistance" against the German invaders.

WON'T LIFT VEIL

"I have been asked in some quarters what is the (British) Navy doing," the First Lord of the Admiralty said, "but the House will not expect me to lift the veil at this juncture."

"If the Norwegian government had not been so very strict and severe in enforcing her neutrality against us," he said, "it would have been very easy to give them more timely and more support than is now posible," he went on.

He charged that German invasion had been "long and elaborately prepared" against a number of small countries and it was only in

More of CHURCHILL on Page 19

"I'M READY TO GRADUATE NOW!"

LANCASTER NEW ERA

WEATHER
Fair tonight; Saturday cloudy followed by light showers; slightly cooler in west and north portions. (Details on Page 3.)

Examiner Founded 1830.
New Era Founded 1877.

Published Every Evening Except Sunday by New Era Company.
Entered as Second Class Matter at Post Office, Lancaster, Pa.

LANCASTER, PA., FRIDAY, MAY 10, 1940 — CITY EDITION — 26 PAGES—208 COLUMNS—THREE CENTS

GERMAN TROOPS ARE REPORTED HALTED JUST INSIDE BELGIAN-DUTCH BORDERS

Late War Bulletins

Churchill Is New British Premier

London, May 10—(U. P.)—Prime Minister Neville Chamberlain is expected to broadcast to the nation tonight at 9:15 P. M., (4:15 P. M., E. D. T.), announcing his resignation and appealing to all factions to unite behind a government headed by Winston Churchill.

Winston Churchill

Chamberlain was granted an audience just before 6 P. M. tonight by King George at Buckingham palace at which it was thought probable he submitted his resignation and suggested that Churchill be called in to form a cabinet.

Immediately after Chamberlain returned to No. 10 Downing Street Churchill appeared at Buckingham Palace, presumably to receive the formal request from the King.

The speed with which the British political transition was occurring in the face of the great war crisis came as a surprise. It had been expected that Chamberlain would continue on an interim basis for at least a few days while the preliminaries of constructing a national unity cabinet were being dealt with.

Dutch Down 70 Nazi Planes; Blow Up Troop Train

Amsterdam, May 10—(A. P.)—The Netherlands officially announced today that her defense forces had shot down at least 70 German planes, blown up a German armored train at Venlo and were offering strong resistance just inside the eastern border with Germany.

The armored train, described as one of four "successfully attacked," was reported blown up while attempting to cross the Maas River bridge at Venlo, on the border between the province of Limburg and Germany.

The announcement said Netherlands troops offered strong resistance to the invaders on the Ijssel and Maas rivers, a short distance within The Netherlands, and maintained positions at Delfzijl.

Allied High Commander Sees "Big Battle of All Times"

Paris, May 10—(A. P.)—General Maurice Gustave Gamelin, Commander-In-Chief of the British and French armies, proclaimed to his forces today that Germany has begun "a fight to the death against us."

In his order of the day to the Allied troops he said: "The attack which we have foreseen since last October was launched this morning.

"Germany has begun a fight to the death against us.

"The orders are, for France and her allies: Courage, energy, confidence."

A British-French army was authoritatively reported moving rapidly across the Belgian border today to meet German legions which had entered from the east and a Paris military spokesman said the "most gigantic battle of all times" may be near at hand.

The spokesman said that the Germans must have one of two military purposes in mind!

1. An operation to gain control of a long strip of coastline facing England, or

2. "A vast strategical movement of invasion comparable to and infinitely larger than that carried out by the German troops across Belgium in 1914."

In the latter case, he said, "we are at the beginning of the most gigantic battle of all time."

NAZIS DRIVEN BACK AT ROTTERDAM

Rotterdam, The Netherlands, May 10—(A. P.)—Germany's plane and parachute troops, attempting to fight their way through Rotterdam, were driven back into a

(See BULLETINS—Page 12)

Belgium troops, like these shown above, are reported to have stopped Hitler's Blitzkrieg within a few hundred yards at the frontier. Lower left is a section of Belgium's "Little Maginot Line" designed to hold the Germans until the Allied forces get there. These plans were worked out by Lieut.-Gen. Vandenbergen, King Leopold and General Denis,

Hitler's 'Chute Troops Fight for Key Cities Along West Coast

(By The Associated Press)

Adolf Hitler's armed forces struck in the direction of England today with a pre-dawn "Blitzkrieg" invasion of the "low countries" — Belgium, Holland and Luxembourg — apparently to obtain a close base to attack the British Isles.

Britain and France themselves were raided by the German air force in bombing forays over both countries.

The Belgian foreign ministry announced that the Nazi invaders had been stopped cold a few hundred yards inside the frontier. The German thrust, it was said, crumpled against the Belgian "demolition zone."

Detailed map of "The Low Countries" is on the last page.

Allied troops went to the defense of the imperilled small nations, which are able to muster a combined military strength of 1,000,000 men.

British, French Cross Into Belgium

A French-British army was reported to have swiftly crossed the Belgium frontier to check the German onslaught, while the Belgian army—re-enacting the tragic history of 26 years ago—fought desperately to stave off the initial rush.

The hour of the long-waited "total war" in the west had apparently arrived.

Holland opened her flood-gates and dikes, blew up bridges and threw her army into action, holding the Germans near Arnheim.

Nazi bombers blasted Antwerp and Brussels and the French cities of Nancy, Lille and Calais, and Chilham, in England, also were bombed.

Berlin claimed tiny Luxembourg had been overrun in the early hours of the pre-dawn invasion and, shortly after 8 A. M., E. S. T., the Berlin radio asserted Nazi troops had occupied The Hague, the capital of the Netherlands. However, dispatches received four hours later directly from Amsterdam, 30 miles from The Hague, did not mention its fall.

A Paris military spokesman declared "the most gigantic battle of all time" appeared imminent.

Nazi Armored Train Blown Up

Holland officially announced her defense forces had shot down at least 70 German planes, blown up a German armored train and were offering "strong resistance."

In London, the Ministry of Home Security issued a general warning to all England to "be prepared"—presumably for a land invasion of the British isles by Germany.

At Doorn, Holland, the aged Kaiser Wilhelm clung to his haven while the troops he once commanded poured into his host country.

'Chute Troops Rained Down In Dark

Nazi parachute invaders rained down in the darkness, striking at vital airports and strategic centers, while the German land steamroller rumbled across the three frontiers.

General Maurice Gustave Gamelin, Commander-In-Chief of the French and British armies, declared Germany has begun "a fight to the death against us."

A Paris military spokesman said "the most gigantic battle of all time" was apparently imminent.

Within a few hours, the Berlin radio announced the fall of The Hague, capital of The Netherlands.

Rotterdam Airport Is Seized

Nazi troops dropped from the skies seized the airport at Rotterdam after a heavy bombardment that destroyed the flying field and hangars.

Queen Wilhelmina of The Netherlands issued a "flaming protest" against the invasion, and spurred her troops into a last-ditch defense.

Balkan capitals viewed the German trust in western Europe as a "reprieve" to the Mediterranean area.

With Nazi planes striking for the heart of England and France in a series of lightning bombing raids, the French and British announced they would retaliate if Germany attempted to bomb civilian centers of population.

"The fight beginning today decides the fate of the German nation for the next 1,000 years. Do your duty now!" commanded the Nazi Fuehrer in an order to his legions already overrunning Europe.

Eyes Turn on Mussolini

World eyes turned anxiously toward Italy, expecting this might be the moment for Premier Mussolini to take the jump

(See EUROPE—Page 12)

BRITISH LABOR WANTS CHANGE

London Hints Churchill to Succeed Chamberlain as Prime Minister.

LONDON, May 10.—(A. P.)—Winston Churchill was received in audience by King George tonight shortly after Prime Minister Chamberlain had been received in connection with Britain's cabinet crisis.

The action was interpreted immediately as indicating that Chamberlain had resigned and Churchill was being asked to form a new government.

Shortly after Churchill's audience with the King, it was announced that Chamberlain will broadcast a message to the nation at 9 P. M. (3 P. M. EST) tonight.

A broadcast from him had been expected generally throughout a day of anxiety over Germany's invasion of the lowland neutrals.

The Labor executive committee announced the Laborite opposition in Parliament would join the British cabinet "under a new Prime Minister."

Its statement, issued in Bournemouth where the Labor party is holding a regular conference, came shortly after Prime Minister Chamberlain—center of controversy over the Allied failure in Norway—left for an audience with King George.

"The national executive of the Labor party," it said, "has unanimously decided to take their share of responsibility as a full partner in a new government under a new Prime Minister who would command the confidence of the nation."

War Cabinet Meets 3 Times

Immediately after the decision was announced, Clement R. Attlee, leader of the opposition in the House of Commons, and Arthur Greenwood, his deputy, who conferred last night and today with Chamberlain, returned to London for a further conference with the Prime Minister.

The war cabinet met this afternoon, for the third time at Chamberlain's office. Chiefs of staff and Sir John Anderson, Home Secretary and Minister of Home Security also were present.

Parliament, in recess until May 21, was expected to be recalled, perhaps next Tuesday; Whitsuntide holidays were cancelled.

Britain promised full Allied help to the invaded neutrals and announced her "protective" occupation of Iceland, North Atlantic island tied through the Danish throne with Denmark, to prevent German seizure.

Iceland Is Occupied

The island will be under British protection only until the "conclusion of hostilities," it was announced.

It was not believed that the Brit-

(See BRITISH—Last Page)

Here's How German Invaders Operated

Nazi Chute Troops Hop Land Barriers to Capture Strategic Coast Towns of Netherlands

By FRED VANDERSCHMIDT

Associated Press Staff Writer

The German invasion of the low countries is essentially the forerunner to frontal assault on England.

This time, however, Adolf Hitler did not find the British and French unprepared.

Race To Albert Canal

Thousands of Allied troops, probably most if not all British, have crossed into Belgium from their 16-mile line on the French-Belgium frontier, where they have been waiting for months. Their long-range plan is to race the Germans to the Albert canal, where the Belgian army is mobilized, and fight there.

But besides assaulting the Dutch and Belgian eastern frontiers, the Nazis, by an amazing feat of aerial transport, actually have circumvented in a matter of hours the elaborate flood water and land defenses of the Netherlands. They have landed troops by parachute and seaplane in Rotterdam itself, western seaport of 600,000 people which is a little more than a hundred miles to England by air line.

Depended On Water Defenses

Now the Dutch water-line defenses were built to keep the Germans from reaching the rich sec-

(See INVASION—Last Page)

BELGIUM SAYS SHE IS ABLE TO HALT NAZIS

Declares Nation Can Not Be Vanquished; King Leopold at Front.

BRUSSELS, May 10—(A. P.)—The German land forces have been stopped within a few hundred yards of the frontier after entering Belgium as part of Adolf Hitler's blitzkrieg against the low countries, the Foreign Ministry announced today.

Defense Minister General Henri Denis told the Chamber of Deputies that, at noon, the Germans were halted everywhere on the Belgian defensive lines. He said he was "convinced the Germans failed to obtain their first objective and failed to gain the initial success they expected."

Premier Hubert Pierlot told the House that King Leopold III had expected to make an address, but had taken his place as Commnader-in-Chief with the army in the front lines.

Belgium met the German invasion by full mobilization and her King, Leopold III, assumed command of the nation's forces, as his father, Albert, did more than 25 years ago.

French and British liaison officers reached Brussels for contacts with the Belgian General staff six hours after Belgium had asked her old allies of 1914 for aid against the new German invasion.

Brussels Bombed 3 Times

Brussels was bombed this morning and had three air raid alarms in the early afternoon.

While the first wave of Nazi bombers took a toll of at least seven killed and 80 wounded throughout the country, the Foreign Ministry said the German land forces had been stopped no more than a few hundred yards over the Belgian frontier.

They were halted by Belgian troops entrenched behind the "demolition line," a first defense area of destroyed bridges and roads and other barriers.

At the same time Foreign Minister Paul Henri Spaak, in a note to the German Ambassador, announced "Belgium will defend herself with all means and can not be vanquished."

Warns of Nazi Power.

After the first bombing of Brussels, German Ambassador Von Bulow-Schwantz delivered to Foreign Minister Spaak a note saying a "tremendous" German army was marching into Belgium and neighboring Holland and Luxembourg to forestall an Allied attack.

The note asked the Belgians not to resist and promised to preserve their country.

Even before the Ambassador spoke, Spaak reported "the answer is negative," and handed him a note

(See BELGIUM—Last Page)

NO CHANGE IN U. S. STATUS

F. D. "In Sympathy" With Holland Proclamation; Studying Many Factors.

WASHINGTON, May 10.—(A. P.)—President Roosevelt said today he saw no change with respect to the possibilities of the United States keeping out of Europe's war.

At a press conference he told reporters who crowded his office to the walls that there was not much he could say about the situation abroad now and that it spoke for itself.

"I think I can say personally," he declared, authorizing direct quotation, "I am in full sympathy with the very excellent statement that was given out, the proclamation by the Queen of The Netherlands, and let it go at that. It is worth reading."

(In her proclamation read to the Dutch people over the radio, the Queen also addressed "a flaming protest against this unexampled violation of good faith and what is considered decent between civilized nations.")

With reference to possible effects of Germany's invasion of Holland, Belgium and Luxembourg on this country, the President asserted a great many things were being studied. He did not give details.

Probe Bombing of Cities

But in response to a question, he said that a German pledge, at the outbreak of the current war, not to bomb "open," unfortified towns was being considered in the light of reports of the bombing of such cities.

A reporter asked him whether there was "anything you can say at this time as to what you think the chances are that we can keep out of the war."

That, he said, would be speculative. Then he hastened to add an

(See WASHINGTON—Page 12)

GERMANS DROP ON ROTTERDAM

Heavy Fighting in City; Nazi Planes Hurdle Dutch Defenses.

ROTTERDAM, THE NETHERLANDS, May 10.—(A. P.)—A German "army of the air" spanned the strong land and water defenses of The Netherlands today and, landing by parachute and in huge seaplane transports at the western side of the nation, fought its way into part of this seaport city.

The troops occupied Rotterdam's Waalhaven Airport, after first leveling it with a tremendous aerial bombardment, alighted on the Nieuwe Maas River in the center of Rotterdam, occupied a big bridge across the river and captured the Maas railway station in the city.

Heavy fighting was going on in Rotterdam itself, with the Dutch troops clinging tenaciously to the right bank of the Nieuwe Maas, which bisects the city.

On the other side of Holland, across the main water line now fed by wide-open dykes, Netherlands' first line defenders were resisting a German land army which entered the country along the Rhine and swarmed ahead some 15 miles to the vicinity of the Ijssel River, near Arnhem.

Queen Rallies Her People

Doughty Queen Wilhelmina uttered a "flaming protest" against Germany, urged her nation to its duty and sought strong assistance from the British-French Allies.

They said they would help, and quickly. British and French planes were over the country long before noon, seeking the enemy. Allied troops and naval forces were confidently expected.

It all was part of a vast, combined German offensive against Belgium, The Netherlands, and Luxembourg, combined with aerial

(See ROTTERDAM—Page 12)

The SCRIBBLER

MAY DAY, 1940 STYLE

THE May Queen, wiping an icicle off her nose, buttons up her fur coat and enters with her court.

Ladies-in-waiting, wearing three sweaters each under their finery, skate onto the stage to the tune of "Jingle Bells."

A fellow wearing hood and ear-muffs, Admiral Byrd style, drags a bobsled in and has an escort of penguins, who march double file and appear very solemn.

Some other possible features for these chilly May Day celebrations might be:

Eskimo dance.

Parade of highway department snow plows.

Serving of coffee and hot soup by the second-alarmers.

Distribution of mustard plasters, cold remedies, and the like.

CLEM Hoover, Gordonville, feed and lumberman, left business for the day informing his wife not to bother with dinner that evening as he was going to Paradise Lions Club dinner.

Arriving at the designated place, Clem discovered he had the wrong date in his notebook.

Neighbors say Clem should have his wife pack lunch for such occasions in the future.

ROOSEVELT SPEECH ON WGAL TONIGHT

WGAL will broadcast an address by President Roosevelt before the 8th American Scientific Congress, from Constitution Hall, Washington, at 10:30 o'clock tonight. The address will be a coast to coast broadcast and will reach Lancaster county listeners through WGAL from the Red Network of the National Broadcasting Company.

EX-KAISER STAYS AT DOORN ESTATE

BERLIN, May 10—(A. P.)—Aged ex-Kaiser Wilhelm II remained at his Dutch estate in Doorn today while legions of the army he once commanded poured into the Netherlands which has given him refuge since Germany went down to defeat in the last European war.

CUDAHY FORETOLD GERMAN INVASION

WASHINGTON, May 10—(A. P.)—John Cudahy, American Ambassador at Brussels, "broke the news" about Germany's invasion of Belgium, Holland and Luxembourg several hours before it happened.

Brigadier General Edwin M. Watson, secretary to President Roosevelt, told reporters today that Cudahy telephoned him at his home between 8:30 and 9 P. M. EST, last night, after he had failed to get the President, who was still at dinner.

"Cudahy hit it exactly," Watson said. "The remarkable thing about it is that he said 'it's going to be Belgium, Holland and Luxembourg'."

Newest Countries Engulfed in Europe's Total War

DUTCH COUNT ON FAMED "WATER LINE"—German blitzkriegers faced this intricate system of defenses when they invaded Holland. A fortified line runs along the border, but the invaders' biggest obstacle was Holland's famed "water line." This the Dutch had bolsted by scattering light fortifications on "islands" through the floodable areas.

Convinced that she could not hold out long in the northeast or southeast, Holland counted on the water line to protect the rich area near the coast—including Rotterdam, Amsterdam and The Hague. But the invaders hurdled the central defenses by air yesterday and landed parachute troops at Rotterdam and elsewhere. Meanwhile ground forces struck into Holland near the Rhine river and advanced in the direction of Arnhem.

NAZIS STRUCK HERE—Amsterdam, historic capital of The Netherlands, lashed by the Nazi blitzkrieg.

THEY STAND TOGETHER—Queen Wilhelmina of The Netherlands and King Leopold of Belgium, whose countries were withstanding the Nazi invasion today. They are shown during a recent meeting in Brussels.

DUTCH MACHINE GUNS SWEEP ROADS—Dutch army's twin defense strategy was inundation of flat, low-lying areas to bar mechanized transport and covering of important roads with cross-angled machine-gun fire. Picture shows highway in Netherlands frontier town blocked by Dutch machine-gun nest during recent pre-invasion practice.

HOW NAZIS DROP STREAMLINED BATTALIONS FROM THE SKY—These dramatic scenes, photographed at recent German maneuvers, were repeated when Nazis catapulted hundreds of parachute troops into Belgium and Holland in lightning invasion. Above, soldiers previously parachuted to earth rush after miniature arsenal (in container), dropped from plane after them. Minutes later (right), machine guns and sighting instruments assembled, they're ready for action—a formidable field unit.

SAYS BELGIUM WILL FIGHT to the end—Paul Spaak, Belgian Foreign Minister, who said that Belgium would fight to the end.

GERMANS BOMB FRENCH CITIES—A view of Nancy, one of the cities bombed by the Germans as they opened a bombing offensive over many French industrial and rail centers.

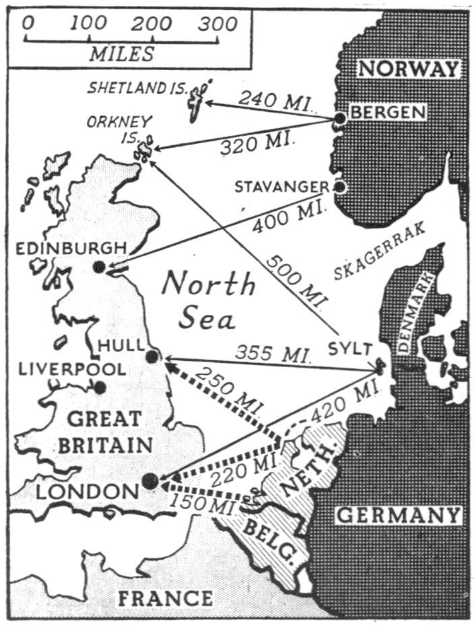

NAZI INVASION OF LOWLANDS—A successful German invasion of the Low Countries would add to the circle Germany started drawing around the British Isles when she invaded Denmark and Norway. Scandinavia gives her bases closer to England; conquest of the lowlands would give her bases still closer—might enable her to blast the British blockade of the English Channel.

NAZIS BOMB FRENCH CHANNEL PORTS—A view of the railroad station at this Calais channel port. The Nazis bombed this port and also Dunkerque, according to a telephone message from U. S. Ambassador William C. Bullitt to Washington.

DUTCH AIRPORT REPORTED BOMBED BY NAZIS—A scene at the Welschaf airdrome near Eindhoven which was reported bombed by six German planes.

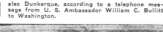

INVADED BY GERMANS—A view of the city of Luxembourg, capital of this tiny country which has now become a battleground as France rushes troops to stem a Nazi invasion.

NAMED TO HAVERFORD POST

Philadelphia — (AP) — Dr. Benjamin Gerig, former member of the secretariat of the League of Nations, has been appointed associate professor of government at Haverford college.

OUT OUR WAY

By WILLIAMS

JAILED 30 DAYS

Charged with drunkenness and disorderly conduct, Albert Nickon, Hillsboro, Wis., was jailed for 30 days following a hearing before Alderman Miller in police court Saturday.

TODAY'S HIGHLIGHTS

FROM NBC NETWORK CENTRES — NEWS ON EUROPEAN SITUATION, 8:00 A. M., 8:55 A. M., 7:15 P. M.

FROM MUTUAL—WAR NEWS FROM PARIS, 2:00 P. M. RAYMOND GRAM SWING, FOREIGN NEWS ANALYST, 10:00 P. M.

FROM NBC RED NETWORK — THE TELEPHONE HOUR: JAMES MELTON, TENOR; FRANCIA WHITE, SOPRANO; MIXED CHORUS OF 14 VOICES WITH DONALD VOORHEES 57 PIECE BELL SYMPHONY ORCHESTRA, 8:00 P. M.

FROM NBC RED NETWORK — ALEC TEMPLETON TIME, PRESENTED BY ALKA-SELTZER, 9:30 P. M.

7:00—WGAL—War News
7:05—WGAL—Wake Up and Sing
8:00— NBC—News Here and Abroad
8:15— NBC—Wife Saver
8:30— NBC—Ray Perkins
8:45— NBC—Harvey and Dell
8:55— NBC—Associated Press News
9:00— NBC—Breakfast Club
10:00—WGAL—Devotions, Rev. Canon
10:30— MBS—Keep Fit to Music
10:45—WGAL—Julia Blake, Armstrong
11:00— NBC—David Harum, Sketch
11:15—WGAL—Woman's Corner
11:30—WGAL—Melody Ranch Show
12:00—WGAL—Luncheon Club
12:15—WGAL—Dolly Madison News
12:30— NBC—Farm and Home Hour
1:15— NBC—Ted Malone
1:30— NBC—Jordon Conservatory Choir
1:45— NBC—Maurice Spitalny's Orch.
2:00— MBS—War News from Paris
2:30—WGAL—Melody Matinee
3:00— ABN—Phillies vs. Pittsburgh, The Atlantic Refining Co.
5:30—WGAL—Shoppers Guide
6:00—WGAL—Home Store Transradio News
6:05— NBC—Herman Middleman's Orch.
6:15— NBC—Norsemen Quartet
6:30—WGAL—Fleet-Wing Sports Parade
6:45—WGAL—Wiggin's Chevrolet World Wide Transradio News
7:00— NBC—Fred Waring in Pleasure Time
7:15— NBC—European Situation
7:30—WGAL—Radio Forum: Rabbi Davis
7:45— NBC—Rhumba Band
8:00— NBC—The Telephone Hour
8:30—WGAL—Catholic Hour
9:00— MBS—Mrs. Franklin D. Roosevelt
9:30— NBC—Alec Templeton Time
10:00— MBS—Raymond Gram Swing
10:15—WGAL—War News—Dance Parade
10:30— NBC—Gallant American Women
11:00—WGAL—Transradio News
11:05— NBC—Ben Cutler's Orch.
11:30— NBC—National Radio Forum
12:00—WGAL—War News—Sign Off—Adv.

Radio Program

MONDAY, MAY 20

MORNING

6:00—WOR—Farmers Digest
6:25—WABC—Program Review
6:30—WEAF—News; Recorded Program; WJZ—News; Recorded Program
6:35—WABC—Larry Elliott
6:50—WOR—Outdoor Guide
7:00—WOR—Music; Weather; WABC — Music; Phil Cook
7:15—WOR—Musical Clock
7:30—WEAF—News; Don Goddard
7:45—WABC—News
7:55—WJZ—News; European Comments
8:00—WOR—News; Gospel Singer; WABC —News of Europe
8:03—WEAF—News; Variety
8:15—WJZ—Wife Saver; WABC—Music and News
8:30—WEAF—Gene and Glen; WOR—Kitty Keane; WJZ—Ray Perkins; WABC —Phil Cook
8:45—WOR—The Goldbergs; WJZ—Harvey and Dell; WABC—Hollywood Music
8:55—WJZ—News; Woman of Tomorrow
9:00—WEAF—New!; Happy Jack; WOR—Arthur Godfrey; WABC—Woman of Courage
9:15—WEAF—Miller Orch.; WOR—Heart of Julia Blake; WABC—Richard Maxwell
9:25—WABC—War Reports
9:30—WEAF—Escorts and Betty; WOR—Exercises to Music; WJZ—Breakfast Club; WABC—Talk—Adelaide Hawley
9:45—WEAF—Edward MacHugh; WOR — Beauty, Nell Vinick; WABC—Bachelor's Children
10:00—WEAF—Man I Married; WJZ — Painted Dreams; WOR—Food Hour WABC—Pretty Kitty Kelly
10:15—WEAF—Midstream; WJZ—Vic and Sade; WABC—Myrt and Marge
10:30—WEAF—Ellen Randolph; WJZ — Mary Marlin; WABC—Hilltop House
10:45—WEAF—Woman in White; WJZ—Pepper Young Family; WABC—Stepmother
11:00—WEAF—David Harum; WOR—News; WJZ—Linda Dale; WABC—Short Story
11:15—WEAF—Road of Life; WOR—Martha Deane; WJZ—Clark Dennis; WABC —Life Begins
11:30—WEAF—Against the Storm; WJZ—Jack Berch; WABC—Big Sister
11:45—WEAF—Guiding Light; WJZ—Affairs of Anthony; WABC—Aunt Jenny

AFTERNOON

12:00—WEAF—Friendship Circle; WOR—Talk—Victor Lindlahr; WJZ—What Foreign Trade Means to Average New Yorker—Mayor La Guardia; WABC—Kate Smith
12:15—WEAF—The O'Neills; WABC—When a Girl Marries
12:20—WJZ—Kidoodlers
12:25—WJZ—News; Farm and Home Hour
12:30—WEAF—Talk—Dr. R. S. Meadowcroft; WOR—News; Quiz Club; WABC —Helen Trent
12:45—WEAF—News; Market; WABC—Our Gal Sunday
1:00—WEAF—Bartal Orch.; WOR—Voice of Experience; WABC—The Goldbergs
1:15—WEAF—Ben Bernie Orch.; WOR—Ed Fitzgerald; WJZ—Poetry—Ted Malone; WABC—Life Can Be Beautiful
1:30—WEAF—H. V. Kaltenborn; WOR—Carters of Elm Street; WJZ—Jordan Conservatory Choir; WABC—Right to Happiness
1:45—WEAF—Hollywood News Girl; WOR —Health Drama; WJZ—M. Spitalny Orch.; WABC—Road of Life
2:00—WEAF—Biblical Drama; WOR — Alice Blair; WJZ—Adventures in Reading; WABC—Young Dr. Malone
2:15—WEAF—Arnold Grimm's Daughter; WOR—Meet Miss Julia; WABC—Joyce Jordan
2:30—WEAF—Valiant Lady; WOR—Garden Club; WJZ—Secretary of Agriculture Wallace, Rabbi David de Sala Pool; WABC—Fletcher Wiley
2:45—WEAF—Hymns; WOR—News; Baseball: Dodgers-Cubs, Ebbets Field; WABC—My Son and I
3:00—WEAF—Mary Marlin; WJZ—Orphans of Divorce; WABC—Society Girl
3:15—WEAF—Ma Perkins; WJZ—Honeymoon Hill; WABC—Baseball: Giants-Cardinals
3:30—WEAF—Pepper Young's Family; WJZ—John's Other Wife
3:45—WEAF—Vic and Sade; WJZ—Just Plain Bill
4:00—WEAF—Backstage Wife; WJZ — Club Matinee
4:15—EAF—Stella Dallas; WJZ—Fashion Stakes, Belmont
4:30—WEAF—Lorenzo Jones; WJZ—Matinee Club Variety
4:45—WEAF—Young Widder Brown
4:50—WJZ—Variety Program
4:55—WJZ—News; James Orch.
5:00—WEAF—Girl Alone
5:15—WEAF—Life Can Be Beautiful; WOR—Sports—Waite Hoyt
5:30—WEAF—Jack Armstrong; WOR — McFarland Orch.; WJZ—Ireene Wicker
5:45—WEAF—The O'Neills; WOR—Little Orphan Annie; WJZ—Bud Barton; WABC—Scattergood Baines

EVENING

6:00—WEAF—Li'l Abner; WOR—Uncle Don; WJZ—News; Middleman Orch.; WABC—News; Talk—Edwin C. Hill
6:15—WEAF—News; Jingles—Ed East; WJZ—Sports—Bill Stern; WABC — Hollywood—Hedda Hopper
6:30—WEAF—Stamps—Tim Healy; WOR —News; Superman; WJZ—Whispering Rhythm; WABC—Paul Sullivan
6:45—WEAF—Sports—Paul Douglas; WJZ —Lowell Thomas; WABC—The World Today
7:00—WEAF—Fred Waring Orch.; WOR—Sports—Stan Lomax; WJZ—Stabile Orch.; WABC—Amos 'n' Andy
7:15—WEAF—H. V. Kaltenborn; WOR—Wythe Williams; WJZ—Youth in the Toils; WABC—Lanny Ross
7:50—EAF—Kay Orch.; WOR—Lone Ranger; WJZ—One of the Finest; WABC —Blondie
8:00—WEAF—James Melton; WOR—Play Broadcast; WJZ—Hollywood Variety; WABC—Tony Martin
8:30—WEAF—Symphony Orch.; WOR — Let's Go to Work; WJZ—True or False; WABC—Howard and Shelton
8:55—WABC—Elmer Davis
9:00—WEAF—Doctor I. Q.; WOR—Gabriel Heatter; WJZ—The Green Hornet; WABC—Play: Midnight
9:15—WOR—Miller Orch. (Recording)
9:30—WEAF—Alec Templeton; WOR — Mrs. Franklin D. Roosevelt; WJZ—Land and the People
10:00—WEAF—Opal Cavern; WOR—Raymond Swing; WJZ—John Gunther; WABC—Guy Lombardo
10:15—WOR—Who Knows? WJZ—Dance Music
10:30—WEAF—Winton Orch.; WOR — Rhythm Music; WJZ—Drama: American Women; WABC—Concert Orch.
11:00—WEAF—News; Dance Music; WOR —News; WABC—News; Dance
11:15—WOR—Campaign Talk—State Sen. Hendrickson of N. J.;
11:30—WOR—Campaign Talk — Former Gov. Hoffman of N. J.; WJZ—Preparedness and America's National Defense Needs—Rep. Andrew J. May
11:45—WOR—Dance Music;
12:00—WEAF—Petroleum Exposition, Tulsa
12:30—WEAF—Dance Music; WJZ—Dance Music (To 1)
1:30—WOR—News; Music (Off at 2)
1:55—WABC—News (Sign Off at 2:03)

INJURED BY FISH HOOKS

Two boys were treated at St. Joseph's hospital Sunday for injuries of the hands inflicted by fish hooks. They were Eugene Clark, ten, New Providence R. D. 1, who caught a hook in his left middle finger, and William Chester Barton, nine, 618 High st., caught a hook in his right hand.

SCHOOL TO CLOSE

Bareville—The closing session of the Fire School for firemen of this vicinity being held in the Bareville Fire company hall, will be held Monday (this) evening. The teacher is J. Royer Miller, of Bareville. This is one of the four fire schools being conducted in the county sponsored by the Lancaster County Firemen's association.

The word "ornery" is a corruption of "ordinary."

EPHRATA RED CROSS RELIEF FUND UNDER WAY

Ephrata — The drive of the Ephrata branch of the Lancaster Chapter of the Red Cross for the borough quota of $1,450 for the European relief fund, is well organized and under way, according to Mrs. I. G. Wagner, president of the local group. A number of organizations have already contributed sums to the fund. Donations will be received at the churches and receptacles for contributions have been placed at the theaters.

A general committee of citizens has been named which includes: Burgess John M. Royer, John L. Hamaker, D. Lyman Hamaker, W. D. Leed, Mrs. Samuel Mohler, Mrs. A. W. Hacker, Ira E. Fasnacht, W. E. Burkholder, D. Alvin Esslinger, E. A. Lewis, W. Fred Smith, I. L. Sprecher, H. E. Rohrbach, Dr. I. G. Wagner, L. H. Hackman, Fred R. Janda, Dr. J. F. Mentzer, Walter W. Moyer, J. Harry Hibshman, C. P. Wenger, S. Millo Herr, J. Kreider Kurtz, H. M. Gerhart and Joseph S. Harris.

The female oyster is said to be fatter than the male.

EUROPEAN NEWS MAP

This map is another in the series prepared to enable you to follow European events as reported by United Press. It shows the vital resources, economic and military objectives throughout central Europe, the Mediterranean area and the Near East. American trained correspondents of the United Press are placed in key positions to report all developments for you. Read their dispatches daily in

LANCASTER NEW ERA

LANCASTER NEW ERA

Examiner Founded 1830.
New Era Founded 1877.

Published Every Evening Except Sunday by New Era Company.
Entered as Second Class Matter at Post Office, Lancaster, Pa.

LANCASTER, PA., MONDAY, JUNE 10, 1940 | CITY EDITION | 16 PAGES—128 COLUMNS—THREE CENTS

WEATHER

Occasional light rains tonight; Tuesday partly cloudy and warmer, followed by thunder showers in late afternoon. (Details on Page 3.)

Italy Joins Hitler in War Upon Allies, Duce's Troops Cross French Border; Nazis Hurl 1,800,000 Against French

AUTOIST TRIED AS "ZIG-ZAG," SECOND FINED

Pequea Driver Arrested After Crash; City Motorist Pleads Guilty.

DOCTOR CRITICISES DRUNKENNESS TESTS

O. C. Manning, Pequea R. D. 1, charged with drunken driving, went on trial before Judge Schaeffer this morning at the opening of the June term of Quarter Sessions Court.

Motor Policeman O'Boyle, the prosecutor, testified he arrested Manning on December 21 after his car ran into a ditch between Smithville and Rawlinsville. O'Boyle said Manning was intoxicated and that he found a bottle of whiskey in the car.

Auto Ran Into Ditch

Edmund Lefever, of near Smithville, said he saw the car in the ditch near his home and found it was damaged. He testified he told Manning to turn off his motor after determining it was impossible to pull it out of the ditch. Lefever said he thought Manning was intoxicated.

Other Commonwealth witnesses included: Lefever's wife, Hattie, and his son, Ben, this city; Paul Herr, 240 North Mary street; and Dr. H. C. Eggley, Quarryville.

Dr. Eggley said Manning gave his name as "William Mann of 233 North Queen street," when brought by police to his office for examination. The doctor testified Manning told him he "had taken a sleeping tablet the night before." Dr. Eggley said he examined Manning and found him to be intoxicated.

Manning denied he was intoxi-

(See COURT—Page 13)

ARMSTRONG CANNOT START ON ORDER FOR SHELLS UNTIL JAN.

WASHINGTON, D. C., June 10.—The public contracts division, U. S. Department of Labor, today announced approval under the terms of the Walsh-Healey Act, of the following award: Armstrong Cork Company, Lancaster, machined shell for the Army Ordnance Department, $81,311.34.

Work on the $81,311 "educational order" for the production of 5,000 shells of the 75 mm type for the War Department cannot be started until the middle of next January, officials of the company said today. Because of the crowded condition of the machine tool industry, certain important units cannot be delivered until late in December, it was said. This situation has been called to the attention of the War Department. Officials said that once the machinery is installed the order can be filled within three or four weeks.

The Scribbler

BOYS who live on Ruby street in the vicinity of Fifth and Sixth, kept telling their fathers how good they were at baseball and challenged the elders to a game, which was played last week after long negotiations.

The fathers pulled a surprise and won, 14-13, in a contest replete with thrills. The game was originally scheduled for seven innings, but when the kids found they were trailing at the end of that time, they insisted on the regulation nine frames. They lost anyway.

One of the big events of the game was John Miller's home run for the proud papas, in which he lost a shoe while circling the bases. Melvin Hughes, another oldtimer, sprained his wrist. The winners' battery was John Licht and George Dorwart.

JOHN C. Truxal, of the Lancaster County National, bent over Saturday morning and ripped the seam in the seat of his last summer's pants. He sat down immediately to cover the rip, was doubly embarrassed because he couldn't rise to greet customers. Presently he slipped into the directors' room, where he stayed for ten minutes while an associate hurried to the men's store across the street to get him a new pair of trousers.

MISS Violet Weber, teacher at the Haupt school, just naturally courteous. While shopping for summer frocks at a department store, she accidentally knocked down a dress form.

"Oh, pardon me!" exclaimed Miss Weber.

Quite a Feat

It's well known that the Marine Corps is no place for the effete. And when Recruiting Sergeant William F. Black, above, lands, "the situation is well in hand"—plus. Those size 12-F's he's displaying in his Philadelphia office, are the largest allowed in the Corps.

F. D. TO SPEAK ON WAR TODAY

Talk at Virginia U. Will Be Broadcast Abroad; Army Increase Voted.

WASHINGTON, June 10.—(A. P.)—Italy's entry into the war was expected to bring from President Roosevelt in an address at Charlottesville, Va., tonight a new appraisal of the place of "democracy" in a growing world conflict.

This hint was given by Stephen Early, Presidential secretary, who told reporters Mr. Roosevelt had received word of Premier Mussolini's declaration of war against Britain and France in a telephone call from Ambassador William C. Bullitt in Paris at 11:53 A. M. E. S. T.

Early noted that the President was speaking at the University of Virginia which Thomas Jefferson, third president of the United States, was instrumental in founding.

Jefferson, Early said, was certainly "one of the first and one of the greatest advocates of democracy." He added that "democracy today seems to be the issue over which a good bit of the world is clashing."

Vote For Army Of 400,000

The House Military committee approved legislation increasing the authorized strength of the regular army from 280,000 to 400,000.

The measure also would permit the President to call out the National Guard, during the recess of Congress, for "use or training" within the United States or its possessions.

Before voting, 16 to 8, to approve the National Guard permit, the committee defeated, 14 to 10, an amendment which would have permitted use of the guard anywhere within the Western Hemisphere. The vote on increasing the strength of the Regular Army was said to have been unanimous.

As now drafted, the Guard measure would provide that the troops "shall not be ordered beyond the Continental United States, its island possessions and the Panama Canal Zone."

The Presidential authority, is limited to the period between the adjournment of the present Congress and the convening of the next Congress in January.

Awaited Il Duce's Address

Mr. Roosevelt had awaited Mussolini's scheduled address which became a declaration of war, before

(See DEFENSE—Page 13)

ROOSEVELT'S SPEECH ON WGAL TONIGHT

The President's message on the European situation will be broadcast at 7:15 o'clock this evening by Radio Station WGAL through the facilities of the Red Network of the National Broadcasting Company.

Red Cross Relief Fund Is at $15,665

The Red Cross War relief fund totalled $15,665.90 today, with contributions over the week-end totalling $224.68.

Included in the branch reports today are Neffsville, $262.01, and Churchtown, $381.45, to date.

Contributions may be made at the Red Cross office, 129 East Orange street, or at any of the thirteen booths open in banks, theatres, department stores, hotels and the Post Office.

GOVERNMENT MAY BE MOVED FROM PARIS

Germans Drive Armored Wedge to Within 35 Miles of Capital.

SUSPEND TRADING ON FAMOUS BOURSE

PARIS, June 10—(A. P.)—Trading was suspended on the world-famous Paris Bourse today, and there were indications that the government might remove from the Capital as the Germans, nearly two million strong, hammered at the defenses guarding the city from the north.

"From the sea to the Argonne the battle continues more and more violently," said the High Command's morning communique while more than 100 German divisions, some 1,800,000 men, tried to wrest victory from the stubborn Poilus.

At one place they had driven an armored wedge into the lines within 35 miles of Paris.

The French were resisting powerfully all along the front as the battle went through its sixth day.

In the titanic struggle to save their homeland against the biggest German offensive of the war, the French had dropped back yesterday to a main line along the heavily wooded Bresle river, which empties into the sea at Eu,—a line extending through the Oise valley to the Marne plains south of the Aisne.

Center Still Falling Back

Today the center of the Weygand line was still falling back to meet the threat to its left flank from the mighty German tank column which broke through the Seine.

But the right flank was reported striking back around the Argonne.

The Germans were using not only masses of infantry and their force of armored vehicles, but were drawing on their strength to the full with big guns and dive bombers and parachute troops trying to smash the French lines with all the ferocity and skill at their command.

Strengthening indications of a possible withdrawal of part of the government it was Premier Reynaud's cancelation of a cabinet meeting scheduled for tonight in Paris.

However, this morning the Ministries still were functioning in Paris.

Some Files And Papers Moved

Some important files and papers of the government have already been moved out of the city.

The usual morning military press conference at the War Ministry was omitted today, and only orderlies remained at the Ministry.

In the last war the government moved to Bordeaux for a few months late in 1914 when the Germans threatened Paris.

The order to suspend trading on the Bourse was issued by the Board of Governors, and it could not be learned immediately whether the exchange would be moved outside the city.

The order annulled the latest

(See FRENCH—Page 4)

WIFE HURT IN ROW WITH HER HUSBAND

Mrs. Rea Terry, twenty-four, 451 North Prince street, was treated at St. Joseph's hospital early yesterday morning for a laceration of the head.

Motor Policeman Gerhard said the case was first reported as an auto accident but investigation disclosed that Mrs. Terry received the injury in Columbia when struck by her husband during an argument.

Terry started to drive his wife and son, Donald, seven, home but abandoned the car near Mountville when he became frightened at the blood from his wife's wound, the policeman said. A passing motorist conveyed her to the hospital.

AMERICAN BOY, 8, KILLED IN GERMANY

PHILADELPHIA, June 10—(A. P.)—Eight-year-old Paul Ritter, reported killed June 4 in an air bombing attack at Klingenstein near Ulm, Germany, formerly lived with an aunt, Mrs. Lillie Schneider, at nearby Collingdale, Pa.

A telegram announcing the boy's death was received from the state department today by the aunt who forwarded it to his mother, Mrs. Marie Ritter, now living in New York City. The child's father died in 1936.

Bulletins

BRITAIN RESENTS TREACHERY

LONDON, June 10.—(A. P.)—Authoritative sources described the Italian entry into the war tonight as a "treacherous blow" and declared that now that the Italians are in the conflict "they must expect to be treated by us in exactly the same way as the Germans."

TURKEY TO FULFILL PROMISE

ISTANBUL, June 10.—(A. P.)—Turkey's resolve to fulfill her mutual assistance pact with France and Britain was voiced by Turkish officials in first reaction to Italy's announcement of her declarations of war on the Allies.

ROME FRONTIER CLOSED

ROME, June 10.—(A. P.)—The Italian-French frontier was reported closed today and telephone communications with France were cut.

HITLER FORESEES VICTORY

BERLIN, June 10.—(A. P.)—Adolf Hitler telegraphed King Vittorio Emanuele of Italy tonight his conviction that "the tremendous power of Italy and Germany will gain victory over the enemy."

"Providence has willed that we defend the freedom and future of our nations in battle against England and France against our own intentions," Hitler told the King.

ALLIES SAY THEY ARE READY

LONDON, June 10.—(A. P.)—Preparations of the Allies with regard to Italy are complete, the Ministry of Information declared tonight, and Britain and France will "know how to meet the sword with the sword."

REYNAUD ASSAILS ITALY

PARIS, June 10.—(A. P. via Radio)—Premier Paul Reynaud in a radio address to the French nation today said "our armies have retreated slowly, and only after destroying all points they have relinquished." "And this is the moment that Mussolini chooses to declare war on us. France has nothing to say.

"Posterity will be able to judge."

6 MILLION FARMERS UNDER AAA CONTROL

WASHINGTON, June 10—(A. P.)—The Agricultural Adjustment Administration reported today that a record total of 6,020,400 farmers, operating 82 per cent of the nation's cropland, were cooperating with Federal Crop Control programs this year.

Last year's 5,764,200 cooperators operated 80 per cent of the cropland.

Benefit payments totaling about $775,000,000 will be distributed among the cooperating farmers.

BERLIN HEARS ITALY ON MOVE INTO RIVIERA

Ribbentrop Declares Nazis Are Jubilant Over Il Duce's Aid.

GERMAN FORCES CLAIM MAGINOT LINE PERILED

BERLIN, June 10.—(A. P.)—Italian forces marched into French territory through the Riviera at approximately 6:30 P. M. tonight (12:30 P. M., Lancaster Time).

This information was given reporters by authorized sources at a conference at the Berlin Foreign Office called by Foreign Minister Joachim Von Ribbentrop.

Information concerning the Italian invasion of France was given out before a statement by Von Ribbentrop.

Germany Is Elated

The Foreign Minister declared all Germany was "filled with jubilant enthusiasm" over Italy's intervention and said Nazi and Fascist forces would fight shoulder-to-shoulder until "the rulers of England and France are ready to respect the vital rights of both our nations."

He read this statement, which was broadcast throughout Germany:

"The Reich government and the entire German nation is deeply moved to have just heard the words of Il Duce of Italy.

"All Germany at this historic hour is filled with jubilant enthusiasm that Fascist Italy, of its own free will, is coming to Germany's side in the fight against the common enemy, England and France.

"German and Italian soldiers will now fight shoulder-to-shoulder until the rulers of England and France are ready to respect the vital interests of our two nations.

"Only after this victory of young National Socialist Germany and young Fascist Italy will it be possible to secure also for our peoples a happy future.

"The guarantors of victory are: the uncontrollable power of the German and Italian peoples and the unalterable friendship of our two great leaders, Adolf Hitler and Benito Mussolini.

The foreign office conference

(See GERMANY—Last Page)

Army of 9,000,000 Called by Mussolini; Balkans Warned

ROME, June 10. — (A. P.) — Italy joined the war tonight at the side of German Nazi legions which are pressing down perilously on France and Paris itself.

(In Berlin it was announced that Italian troops already had entered France through the Riviera.)

Notice of the plunge into hostilities, after months of teetering on the brink, was made in a wildly cheered, bombastic speech by Premier Mussolini from the balcony of the Palazzo Venezia.

The announcement hurled Mussolini's "9,000,000 bayonets" into the titanic struggle.

MUSSOLINI

His announced war aims called chiefly for recovered control of the Mediterranean.

Declares for Peace in Balkans

He declared for preservation of peace in the Balkans and in Turkey and Egypt, all factors in Mediterranean control.

"Our will," he said, "is that Italy does not intend to bring other people into the conflict.

"Yugoslavia, Greece, Turkey and Egypt will take notice of this fact." He also mentioned Switzerland in this connection.

Speaking from the balcony to Fascist blackshirts crowded by the thousands in the square below and in other squares throughout the kingdom where loudspeakers were rigged up at his urgent behest to "listen!" the Premier declared:

"We are descending to battlefields against plutocratic reactionary democracies."

Where Italy would strike its first blow he did not say, but it long has been said in Fascist circles that the first act of war would be a surprise, sprung probably before the actual declaration of war.

Mediterranean Nations Warned

Mussolini warned the Balkans and the Mediterranean nations that any breach of neutrality would spread the war to them.

His pronouncement affecting Egypt and Turkey was seen as an attempt to divert them from pledges to assist the Allies.

Overtures to Egypt were made by the Italian press last week but were generally rejected.

Italians have attempted to break up the mutual assistance pact the Allies have with Turkey, a vital point in the control of the Eastern Mediterranean.

With Turkey favorable or acquiescent to the Axis aims, Italy might open up for itself the British controlled gateway to the rewards of its conquest of Ethiopia.

Hope to Get Control of Gibraltar

At the other end, the Axis powers hope to wrest control of Gibraltar from England, with Spain as the nominal overseer of the great fortified rock.

Word Handed To Allies

Italy's declaration of war, Mussolini said, had been handed to the Ambassadors of France and England.

The fateful step was made after weeks—even months—of hesitation to weld into actual hostilities the ends of the long existant axis between Berlin and Rome.

Before making his definite announcement of war on the Allies, Mussolini called upon "combatants on land, sea and in the air, blackshirts of the revolution and of the legion, men and women of Italy, of the Empire and the Kingdom of Albania"—to listen.

"I wish to declare," he said, "that Italy does not wish to drag into the conflict other people—neighboring and friendly people. The neutrality of these nations will be severely respected."

Cites Move for Peace

He said Italy had tried in vain for peace.

After every sentence, the gesticulating Premier was cheered by demonstrators who long have asked for war and have menaced Allied nationals lingering on in Rome in the face of certain war.

He declared that "the Allies should have accepted the proposals of Hitler before the Polish campaign" which began the war last Sept. 1, two days before the actual declaration of open histilities by the Allies.

Clears Up Meeting At Pass

The declaration by Italy today clears up the verdict reached in the historic meeting of Hitler and Mussolini at the Brenner Pass, a highway now linking the common war interests of Italy and Germany.

"A great people is ready to face its destiny and mark its own history in the future," the Premier exhorted his cheering multitudes.

"We want to break the chains that suffocate us in the Mediterranean."

Mussolini's war aims, it long has been known, call for the recovery of mastery over "Mare Nostrum," our sea to the Italians, and this involves the removal of British controls at Gibraltar and the eastern outlet.

"It is a struggle," he said, "between young and progressive people as against the decadent people, the struggle of one century as against another century."

"The dies are now cast!"

Voice Rises To Breaking Point

Mussolini's voice rose at times to the breaking point as he drove his points home.

"In a memorable meeting at Milan I declared that friends will always help each other," he said, apparently referring to the Rome-Berlin Axis.

His words evoked fresh explosive cries.

"In this great historic event, we turn our thoughts to the King-Emperor."

Again there was a long interruption as the masses roared.

"The King of Italy has always interpreted the soul of Italy as wanting to join her soul with that of Germany," he said.

"Totalitarian and Fascist history for the third time is on its feet ready to strike.

"The order of the day binds all to the same cause," he cried.

"We will give a new era of peace to Italy, to Europe and to the world."

"People of Italy run to your arms!"

Fresh waves of applause swept

(See ITALY—Last Page)

BRITISH LOSE BIG WARSHIP

Admit Aircraft Carrier, 3 Other Vessels, Sunk; Send Fresh Troops.

LONDON, June 10.—(A. P.)—Britain announced today the sinking of the 22,500-ton aircraft carrier Glorious, the 19,840-ton transport Orama and the presumable loss of the destroyers Acasta and Ardent and the tanker Oil Pioneer.

The Orama formerly was a liner in Britain's service to the Far East and was the namesake of another auxiliary British war vessel sunk by the Germans in the World War.

Two destroyers, Acasta and Ardent, presumably were lost along with the tanker Oil Pioneer.

All the ships were in company of the Glorious in northern waters.

The Germans announced yesterday that the Glorious, sister ship of the aircraft carrier Courageous which was torpedoed Sept. 17 by a Nazi submarine, had been sunk June 8 in the North Sea.

The Glorious carried a normal complement of 1,216 men, including Royal Air Force pilots. Her actual crew normally was 748 men.

The Admiralty announcement failed to say how many men were lost in the sinkings.

Promise More Aid

"Further extensive reinforcements" of the B. E. F. will be available shortly, Prime Minister Winston Churchill informed French Premier Reynaud, assuring him of Britain's "maximum possible support."

Churchill's message and official announcement of the Allied withdrawal from northern Norway came as British military circles acknowledged that the situation in France is of "increasing difficulty."

A spokesman warned against undue optimism and said German tanks had reached the Seine. British troops, fighting shoulder to shoulder with the French on the left end of the line, he said, are in the thick of some of the fiercest fighting.

Of three main German thrusts—toward Rouen to the south of Soissons and a new drive on both sides of Rethel—he said the most advanced and apparently the most menacing was the one to Rouen.

King Haakon In England

King Haakon of Norway and his government, which capitulated last midnight after just two months of resistance against overwhelming Nazi power, already have arrived in England.

The monarch arrived on a British warship and was received by High

(See BRITISH—Page 4)

WAR AT A GLANCE

(By The Associated Press)

Italy plunged into the European war at the side of Germany against England and France today, and Berlin reported that Mussolini's Fascist legions began to march into French territory through the Riviera at 12:30 P. M., Lancaster Time.

Warns Neighbors To Be Neutral

Announcing the double-barreled declaration of war, Mussolini hurled his vaunted "9,000,000 bayonets" into the titanic struggle of nations with a pointed notice that he would respect the neutrality of "neighboring and friendly people." If they observed neutrality.

He mentioned in this connection Yugoslavia, Greece, Switzerland, Turkey and Egypt.

Turkey has a mutual assistance pact with Britain and France, effective in the event of an act of aggression leading to war in the Mediterranean. Greece has received one-sided guarantees of protection from the Allies. Egypt is Allied with Britain.

Egypt Distributes Free Gas Masks

The Egyptian government immediately ordered free distribution of gas masks to the civilian population. Egypt's Suez Canal, vital "life line" between England and her Far East dominions, may become an early target of attack in Mussolini's war plans.

Three huge Italian trans-Atlantic liners, the Rex, Conte Di Savoia and Augustus, were reported "missing" from Italian ports and presumably were being used as troopships.

Britain Sends Fresh Troops To France

Britain rushed fresh troops to France in her darkening 11th hour as 1,800,000 tank-led German troops plunged forward to new successes on the 200-mile Western Front and reached two points within 35 miles of Paris.

Hitler's High Command said German troops were moving toward the Lower Seine—apparently in a sharp circling movement in the Rouen-Gisors sector on the Western road to Paris—and toward the historic Marne in the Soisson-Reims area, northeast of Paris.

Norway Surrenders To Germans

Almost overshadowed by the din of death on the Western Front, Norway gave up her struggle against the German invaders Sunday at midnight after two months of conflict with the aid of British and French forces.

King Haakon and his government fled to England.

Moscow announced that the Italian and Soviet Russian Ambassadors were returning to duty.

Russia also announced the patching up of a quarrel of long standing with an agreement with Japan on the Manchouku outer Mongolia border, scene of many a fight.

Carrier Graduates!

HIGH SCHOOL CLASSES 1940

Mr. EMPLOYER! *Do You Need a Bright Young Man in Your Business?*

Newspaper Carrier Graduates Have School Diplomas ***PLUS . . .***
ACTUAL EXPERIENCE AND TRAINING IN . . .

Punctuality — Regularity — Salesmanship
Self Reliance — Courtesy — Tact — Thrift
Discipline — Meeting the Public
Collecting Money — Honesty
Learning the Value of Earned Dollars

THEY LEARNED TO DO BY DOING!

School work coupled with route work gives a boy that PLUS VALUE, putting him AHEAD of boys without similar training.

Boys are required to do their school work, but those boys who are AMBITIOUS, who have that DESIRE TO ACHIEVE, have VOLUNTARILY become newspaper-boys. That's why they are worthy of your first interviews when seeking new employees.

If you have an opening for a "young business man" of this caliber, phone or write the Circulation Department of the Lancaster Newspapers. We will gladly refer one or more desirable applicants to you.

BLAKE DULANEY
447 W. Chestnut St., Lancaster
McCaskey High School

ROBERT E. BRICKER
553 Howard Ave., Lancaster
McCaskey High School

NELSON P. REYNOLDS
1021 S. Duke St., Lancaster
McCaskey High School

FRANKLIN CLARK
1133 Maple Ave., Lancaster
McCaskey High School

PAUL F. HARPLE
511 W. Walnut St., Lancaster
McCaskey High School

LUTHER L. LINTNER
1017 S. Duke St., Lancaster
McCaskey High School

DONALD YOUNG
.017 N. Lime St., Lancaster
Catholic High School

ROBERT M. BYERLY
312 E. New St., Lancaster
McCaskey High School

VICTOR GARMAN
25 N. 5th St., Lebanon
Lebanon High School

JACQUE R. CREAMER
252 E. Clay St., Lancaster
McCaskey High School

BENJ. F. DAVIS, JR.
142 E. Vine St., Lancaster
McCaskey High School

HENRY R. DILLER
439 W. Orange St., Lancaster
McCaskey High School

ROBERT A. ZIEGLER
450 High St., Lancaster
Catholic High School

LEROY LEFEVER
R. D. 6, Lancaster, Bausman
Manor Twp. High School

STANLEY FRIEDMAN
717 S. Lime St., Lancaster
McCaskey High School

HARRY B. DOERR
544 High St., Lancaster
McCaskey High School

ROBERT ROBINSON
R. D. No. 4, Lancaster
E. Lampeter H. School

JAMES R. PHELAN
243 Jackson St., Lancaster
Manheim Twp. H. School

WALLACE HEISEY
111 Mill St., Manheim
Manheim High School

RUSSEL W. HAUS
433 East End Ave., Lancaster
McCaskey High School

VINCENT W. HABEL
R. D. 1, Columbia, Klinesville
Columbia High School

GRANT H. RICHWINE
223 N. Pine St., Lancaster
McCaskey High School

CARL SAMMET
119 W. Orange St., Lititz
Lititz High School

MAHLON KILHEFFER
601 Pearl St., Lancaster
Catholic High School

RAYMOND HACKER
S. State St., Ephrata
Ephrata High School

Congratulations

BOTH IN YOUR school work and on your newspaper routes, you have demonstrated the spirit exemplified by our Carrier Salesmen Organization. Punctuality, faithfulness, integrity, and courtesy have characterized your service.

You have now attained an important milestone along the path toward successful manhood and citizenship.

We're proud of you. We anticipate successful accomplishment in your chosen field of life's work. We covet your friendship in the years ahead, and hope you will always look back with fond memories on your days as a newspaperboy . . . your first experience in the business world.

ROBERT L. PIPKIN
585 Pershing Ave., Lancaster
McCaskey High School

JACK H. ARNOLD
309 Green St., Lancaster
McCaskey High School

RODNEY RAILING
Mount Nebo
Manor Twp. High School

JOSEPH A. STOKES
835 Manor St., Lancaster
McCaskey High School

PAUL G. YESSLER
730 Columbia Ave., Lancaster
McCaskey High School

ROBERT B. SHARLEY
818 N. Shippen St., Lancaster
McCaskey High School

MARK R. EABY
528 N. Duke St., Lancaster
McCaskey High School

EDWARD H. EMMERT
40 Green St., Lancaster
McCaskey High School

CHAS. E. FLICK
250 E. Clay St., Lancaster
McCaskey High School

KENNETH A. LONG
507 Woodward St., Lancaster
Catholic High School

RAY V. BOETTNER
508 W. Chestnut St., Lancaster
McCaskey High School

PANFILO DiFONZO
371 Jefferson Ave., Downingtown
Downingtown H. School

HARRY WOOLGER
Box 212, Ephrata
Ephrata High School

R. PAUL WEAGLEY
60[illegible] S. Lime St., Lancaster
McCaskey High School

JAMES V. McMINAME
612 Columbia Ave., Lancaster
McCaskey High School

JOHN MOHLER
R. D. No. 2, Ephrata
Ephrata High School

DONALD SWEIGART
Kinzer Ave., New Holland
New Holland H. School

HAROLD EBERSOLE
212 S. Mt. Joy St., Elizabethtown
Elizabethtown H. School

EUGENE SWEIGART
R. D. No. 2, Ephrata
Ephrata High School

JAMES K. EAGER
216 N. Shippen St., Lancaster
McCaskey High School

LANCASTER NEW ERA

WEATHER
Fair and continued cool tonight; Saturday partly cloudy and warmer, followed by local showers Saturday night or Sunday. (Details on Page 3.)

Examiner Founded 1830. New Era Founded 1877.
Published Every Evening Except Sunday by New Era Company. Entered as Second Class Matter at Post Office, Lancaster, Pa.
LANCASTER, PA., FRIDAY, JUNE 14, 1940 — CITY EDITION — 24 PAGES—192 COLUMNS—THREE CENTS

PARIS FALLS TO GERMAN ARMY

Nazis Also Report Capture of Key Maginot Fort and Harbor of Le Havre

French Government Fleeing; Its Army Near Collapse

(By The Associated Press)

Hitler's armies marched into the streets of Paris today, captured the vital French port of Le Havre on the English Channel and in their hour of triumph — bitter defeat for France—launched a bold frontal attack on the great Maginot line itself.

The Nazis' tempestuous 9-day conquest of the French capital spurred Great Britain late today to unleash all the vast wealth of her war chest for the purchase of American supplies.

Rapidly swarming German mechanized columns poured behind the main Maginot fortifications between Paris and Montmedy to imperil from the rear the 1,000,000 French Poilus manning the steel-and-concrete line.

In case of an assault from behind, it was not believed that the French could turn their Maginot guns around.

"Pursuit of the enemy until final destruction, has now begun," the Nazi High Command declared exultantly as Hitler's armies swept on past fallen Paris late today, striking 30 miles south of the Marne to Romilly.

The French government was reported fleeing from Tours, presumably to take refuge in Bordeaux, on France's southwest coast.

Maginot Line Attack Centers in the Saar

The frontal attack on the Maginot line centered in the Saar region.

Destruction of eight Allied transports off Le Havre and damage to six others was reported by the Nazi High Command, indicating heavy losses to British troops rushing to support their beleaguered French Allies.

Madrid announced that Spanish troops have occupied the international zone of Tangier in the name of the Sultan of Morocco "to safeguard the independence and neutrality of the city"—which lies opposite the British stronghold of Gibraltar, guardian rock of the Mediterranean.

May Put Spain Into War

It was not immediately apparent whether this action heralded the entrance of Spain into the fast-widening European conflict.

Hitler's legions began marching into Paris yesterday afternoon.

Frenchmen Weep As They March

As they marched, Frenchmen wept. And the outside world wondered whether the French defense was in reality shattered—as the German High Command asserted—or whether they would rally below Paris to fight "to the last corner of France" as Premier Reynaud recently vowed.

Paris itself, the fifth largest metropolis in the world, was a dead city. Only a skeleton remnant of the once gay capital's normal 3,000,000 population remained—mostly behind shutter-drawn windows—while the rest streamed south over refugee-choked roads.

Premier Reynaud's urgent appeal to the United States for immediate help and "clouds of planes" elicited from President Roosevelt a statement to the effect that "we are already sending all possible help."

British Drop Plan For Long War

London reported that the desperate plight of France has caused Britain to drop plans for a long war and go "all out" with her resources, releasing huge sums for purchase of American war materials.

The Nazi High command said Montmedy, vital northern anchor of the Maginot line, has been captured and declared there has been "complete collapse" of the French all along the 200-mile Western Front.

France's High Command, however, insisted the French retreat was being carried out "in the greatest order."

It was the first time since Bismarck's troops took Paris in 1871 that Germany's goose-stepping warriors have marched into the beautiful old French capital.

British Rush Troops Into France

In France's blackest hour, Britain rushed new reinforcements of British Tommies behind Paris to bolster the morale and fighting strength of the desperately driven French.

Weakening French resistance was indicated in a heavily-censored dispatch from Tours stating that a new French

(See BERLIN—Page 20)

CITY FORMS EMERGENCY DEFENSE UNIT

Council of 10 Named to Unite Drive Against Un-American Activities.

WILL HELP GET DATA ON "5TH COLUMNISTS"

Mayor Cary today announced the appointment of an Emergency Defense Council for Lancaster. Its duties, he explained, will be:

To immediately co-ordinate the efforts of all citizens or groups of citizens seeking to curb un-American activities in Lancaster city;

To cooperate with city police, the sheriff and State Motor Police in the gathering of information concerning fifth-column activities.

To notify the Adjutant General of Pennsylvania, commanding officers of the Pennsylvania National Guard that an organization is ready to cooperate in any national defense program they launch.

To cooperate with such state and federal agencies as may be launched later in any national emergency.

Mayor Cary said that the names of members of the Council will not be made public.

10 Leading Men On Council

"The Council," the Mayor said, "is made up of ten representative citizens; men long familiar with Lancaster whose service to the nation and community have made them outstanding through the years.

"We believe that by keeping the names of the Emergency Council members secret that they will be able to function more efficiently."

Tentative machinery has been set up to carry out the program, the Mayor said.

"For the present," the Mayor said, "any citizen, any group of citizens or the representatives of any group of citizens who believe they have information about activities of disloyal citizens or fifth column activities should report to Commissioner of Police Carlson at Police headquarters. However, if any citizen

(See CITY—Page 21)

F. D. Implies U. S. Can't Trust Hitler

WASHINGTON, June 14.—(A. P.)—President Roosevelt repeated today that all possible help was being extended to the Allies and pointed to Hitler's record in response to a report that the German Chancellor had said invasion of the Western Hemisphere was grotesque.

Mr. Roosevelt was told at a press conference that Hitler had called the possibility of German invasion of the Americas "grotesque" in an interview with a newspaperman.

Asked for comment, the Chief Executive said he could give none except to say "that it brings up recollections."

He authorized direct quotation.

He added that his remark could be enlarged on with dates and nations, going back over quite a period of years.

JAILED 3 TO 6 YRS. FOR ROBBERY

Indiana Man Sentenced, Woman Is in Prison; Open Arson Trial.

Arnold Jines, twenty-six, Indiana, who pleaded guilty to charges of felonious entry and larceny in connection with a $500 robbery at the home of Walter S. Kreider, Zook's Corner, on June 9, 1938, was sentenced to 3 to 6 years in the Eastern Penitentiary by Judge Schaeffer this morning. A fine of $100 and costs also were imposed.

Jines changed his plea to guilty after his accomplice, Mary Tennis, took the stand and testified he accompanied her during the robbery. Miss Tennis previously pleaded guilty after she was returned from Lansing, Mich., and was sentenced to 3 to 6 years in the county prison.

Jailed 2 to 4 Years On Bad Check Charge

Robert Clauser, alias Y. Yocum, Sinking Springs, who pleaded guilty to charges of passing fraudulent checks, was fined $25 and costs and jailed for 2 to 4 years. He ad-

(See COURT—Page 21)

OCTAVIA DUPONT UNHURT AS PLANE IS FORCED DOWN HERE

Miss Octavia duPont, daughter of Irenee duPont, Granogue, Del., made a forced landing in her airplane in a tobacco field on the farm of Elmer Gantz, Safe Harbor, shortly before 11 o'clock this morning.

Miss duPont was not hurt and her plane, according to reports, was not damaged.

Mechanical failure of the engine is believed to have made the emergency landing necessary. Miss duPont was enroute from the duPont airport to Harrisburg.

"Total War" at Once, Use of All Resources Pledged by Britain

Plight of France Brings Resolve to Speed Up Purchases of Arms in U. S.; Loss of Armed Liner Is Admitted

LONDON, June 14. — (A. P.) — The plight of France has caused Great Britain to drop her plans for a long war and go "all out" with her resources, sources close to the government said today.

This releases a fund of money and credit for purchase in America of anything which will convey or fire explosives. The fund originally was allocated for future years.

As a result of the change in policy, these sources said, Britain is giving the United States a blank check, in effect, for any kind of useable war material she can provide.

Everything already found purchasable in America in arsenals, National Guard units and elsewhere is being sent.

This speed-up was indicated following disclosure in British military circles that Britain had sent reinforcements to France to join the Allied forces fighting behind Paris.

German Battleship Hit

At the same time, the Admiralty announced that the 17,046-ton liner Caledonia, fitted as an auxiliary armed cruiser and renamed the Scotstown, had been sunk yesterday by a submarine. On the credit side, the Admiralty reported at least one heavy bomb hit, perhaps two, on the 26,000-ton German battleship Scharnhorst in Trondheim fjord yesterday.

The communique said:

"Aircraft of the fleet air arm caried out an attack on German Naval units in Trondheim Fjord early yesterday morning.

"Information has now been received that one hit abaft the funnel was obtained with a heavy bomb on the battleship Scharnhorst. It is also reported that possibly a second hit was registered on the same ship."

The Scotstoun, formerly the anchor liner Caledonia was popular in the New York-Glasgow run as a passenger liner. She was a sister ship of the Transylvania and was famed among Americans for several world cruises. But she sank with all guns firing and with the crew still at stations, waist deep in water.

No program aimed at later production will be permitted to stand in the way of the fullest possible effort now, these British sources declared.

This is partly the result of the loss of Allied resources because of the widening Nazi hold on France.

From 75 to 80 per cent of France's steel producing plants now are in German hands, these sources said, and the same is true of many factories producing war material.

But, they added, fortunately for the Allies, most of the French factories producing ammunition are in the south.

Want U. S. Materials

The government is not so much concerned momentarily about the United States' production capacity as about the material there already manufactured, they said.

For instance, they explained, the

(See BRITAIN—Page 8)

Nazis Hold Bullitt

WILLIAM C. BULLITT

NAZIS 'PROTECT' U.S. AIDE IN PARIS

Against What or Whom? Asks F. D. as Word Is Received.

BERLIN, June 14.—(A. P.)—Trustworthy sources reported today that United States Ambassador William C. Bullitt had been placed in protective custody in Paris by German military authorities.

Bullitt had remained in Paris during the German occupation with the approval of Washington, it was understood.

It was he who, yesterday, informed the German government of France's decision to make no defense in Paris itself.

AGAINST WHAT? ASKS F. D.

WASHINGTON, June 14.—(A. P.)—Informed today of Berlin reports that Ambassador William J. Bullitt was in "protective custody" in Paris, where earlier he had sent the word that German troops were "inside the gates," President Roosevelt posed this question:

Could the Ambassador be protected against what and whom?

The exchange was at the President's press conference, some 10 hours after the State Department received Bullitt's laconic message which, while saying "the city was

(See BULLITT—Page 20)

FAY GATES SLAYING "SOLVED", NEIGHBOR CONFESSES CRIME

HARRISBURG, June 14.—(A. P.)—Commissioner Lynn G. Adams of the State Police announced today the "solution" of the slaying of Fay Gates, 27-year-old Centre county girl, with the arrest of Richard Millinder, 25-year-old WPA worker, who lived about 200 feet from Miss Gates' home at Mt. Eagle.

The girl was killed with a rock the night of May 5 on a lonely road near her home, Adams said Millinder admitted the slaying.

"There appears to be no connection" between this case and the previous slaying of Rachel Taylor, 17-year-old student at Pennsylvania State College, Adams said. Miss Taylor's mutilated body was found near the school a short time before the Gates killing.

The Commissioner said Millinder is married and the father of a ten-months-old child. Miss Gates was motoring to her home the night of the killing and apparently stopped to pick up Millinder, Adams said. She knew him well and frequently did this, Adams said. He declined further details.

FRENCHMEN PURSUED AS THEY RETREAT

Tired Army Awaits Word Whether Battle of France Is to Go On.

MILLION IN MAGINOT LINE ALSO PERILED

TOURS, France, June 14—(A. P.) — Beating a retreat from Paris, the tired French army withdrew southward tonight, assailed by the mightiest forces of the German Reich and awaiting word as to how or even whether the battle of France is to go on.

Germans Close Around City

The latest word here was that German divisions, preceded by slashing columns of tanks and armored cars, had closed around the French Capital. (The Germans announced Paris had been occupied.)

Some rumors put the German advance guard on the west (five words censored). It was officially confirmed that to the east and slightly south of Paris they had reached Romilly, 65 miles southeast of Paris, well down the road to Dijon.

Whether the war is to go on or end for the French seemed to hinge on President Roosevelt's answer to Premier Reynaud's "last appeal" for aid from the United States. The appeal was mentioned in a Reynaud broadcast last night.

(In Washington, it was said that the "last appeal" had not yet been received).

Up to nightfall no definite word had been made public. Both optimistic and pessimistic opinions could be heard.

The advance to Romilly placed the Germans 30 miles south of the Marne, and about 100 miles northwest of Dijon.

Officials Quit Tours

With the German sweep in mind, the French worked at removal of officials and press services from Tours throughout the day. Tours, which has been one of the seats of government, is about 120 miles southeast of Paris.

By nightfall almost all persons connected with the government and the press had left. (Here one line was censored.)

The German drive deep into France between Paris and the Maginot line threatened the fortified line from the rear. It was said that the great fortifications were fast being "turned" from Montmedy, their northern anchor.

(This would indicate a grave threat to the 1,000,000-odd French troops defending the line.)

If the fight goes on, the Loire river line running through Tours and Orleans would be the next really strong natural barrier behind which the French could defend themselves.

(Editor's Note: This dispatch was heavily censored. The phrase "If

(See FRENCH—Page 8)

U. S. DRAFT PLAN BEING SOUGHT

Demand Is Growing For Program to Use Manpower in Emergency.

Defense developments today are:

A proposal that Congress set up machinery immediately for drafting manpower in a national emergency is being advanced in various circles.

President Roosevelt announced that he is establishing a national defense research commission of technical experts to speed up rearmament.

Plans to produce 10,600 trained men a year, including 7,000 pilots, to staff the expanding Army air force, were announced by War Secretary Woodring.

WASHINGTON, June 14—(A. P.)—A proposal that Congress set up machinery immediately for drafting manpower in a national emergency, but that it retain the right to say when this machinery should be placed in operation, is being advanced in various military and Congressional circles.

Advocates said that the plan would cut a month from the time required to mobilize large numbers of men in any situation which Congress deemed to warrant such action.

If a selective service law were

(See DEFENSE—Page 8)

Hitler Moving Many Thousands Of New Troops into War Zone

England's Turn Next, It Is Hinted, as Fuehrer's Mouthpiece Rejects Peace Talk and Declares Sole Aim Is to Conquer

(Louis P. Lochner in his third trip to the front with the German forces, sent the following dispatch by special courier to Cologne, from an unidentified point behind the German front line, and thence by telephone to Berlin.)

By LOUIS P. LOCHNER

WITH THE GERMAN ARMY ENROUTE TO PARIS, June 13—(Delayed)—(A. P.)—Countless thousands of fresh German troops were being speeded into the zone of operations today as Dr. Otto Dietrich, personal press chief of Adolf Hitler, rejected all talk of peace and said Germany's only aim now is to win the war.

Declares Nazis Unbeatable

Addressing foreign journalists Dietrich said:

"Germany is simply unbeatable no matter what may yet come. The Fuehrer towers high above all our enemies. Nothing can avert their defeat and disaster."

Ridiculing earlier assertions by the leaders of Great Britain and France that Germany would be forced to her knees, Dietrich pointed to Germany's present military position and said that complete victory was the goal.

He said that peace might have been had before the war started at the price of the Polish Corridor and of a plebiscite in the regions of Poland which the Nazi government claimed as German.

Just Came From Hitler

Dietrich had just come from Hitler's general headquarters, at a secret place on the front. As he talked the new troops marched, looking fresh and confident and accompanied by the most modern equipment.

It seemed as though all city buses for miles along the German-Dutch and German-Belgian borders had been requisitioned to move them speedily.

While questions concerning ex-

(See LOCHNER—Page 20)

Late News Bulletins

CLAIM FRENCH PRESIDENT WANTS PEACE

Rome, June 14 — (U. P.) — The newspaper Lavoro Fascista in a dispatch from Geneva reported today grave dissension between President Albert Lebrun and Premier Paul Reynaud of France. The Geneva dispatch said Le Brun wishes to conclude a separate peace with Germany and Italy to save France from destruction. The newspaper said that Lebrun had been conferring with former Premier Pierre Laval and that Reynaud's position as Premier fast was becoming untenable as several members of the cabinet agreed with Lebrun's stand.

BRITAIN PLANS WAR TO THE END

London, June 14—(A. P.)—Authoritative British sources said today that Great Britain's attitude toward a separate French peace was expressed by Prime Minister Churchill June 4 and in the British government's message to France last night.

"We shall go on to the end," Churchill told the House of Commons June 4. "We shall fight in France. We shall fight on the seas and oceans . . . we shall never surrender . . ."

UNIDENTIFIED BOY KILLED BY TRUCK

An unidentified boy was struck by a truck in the 400 block of North Market street at 3:30 o'clock this afternoon. He was removed to the General Hospital where surgeons reported him dead. Police sent a radio cruiser to the scene.

The Scribbler

AN ABSORBED group of spectators stood about the sewer adjacent to the Court House on Duke street near King yesterday, to watch George Brunner and Raymond Smith, Street department employes, hunting a key ring belonging to E. O. Ullman, Larchmont, N. Y., salesman.

Ullman, who calls on local department stores selling linens, dropped the keys while standing at the corner, and they fell through the grating before he could grab them. The rescuers worked for about an hour, bringing up several bottles (all empty) and a lot of other material. But they finally found the keys.

From Art Pontz, chief clerk in the department, we learned that about two dozen calls of this type come in yearly. The percentage of recoveries is pretty high. Jewelry and wallets are often the objects of seach, although a package of baby socks was among the recent assignments.

LILA MAY KIRK, of 142 North Plum street, recently bought dress goods at a department store, but when she arrived home she exercised her woman's privilege and changed her mind. She decided to return the goods for a pattern she might like more, grabbed a package and headed back to the store. When she wanted to extract the goods to show the clerk, she found—banana skins.

MIKE KLIMECK, of 1 North Mulberry street, bought a new gas stove and read the instructions on the canning of asparagus. He tried to follow through, and the stove and parts of the kitchen were decorated with a sickly shade of green. Mike now could give lessons on how NOT to can the vegetable.

Censorship

Readers again are reminded that dispatches from Europe, regardless of sources and media, are subject to censorship at the source.

Red Cross Fund Is Up to $20,254

The Red Cross has a total of $20,254.42 in the War Relief fund, it was reported today.

Contributions this morning totalled $178.10.

Contributions of cash or check may be taken or mailed to the Red Cross office, 129 East Orange street.

Use Our Personal Shopping Service
When you find it inconvenient to shop for yourself, gifts or prizes, call or write our personal shopper who will give the smallest order her most careful attention.

WATT & SHAND

Special Treats For The Week-End!
Asst. Cellophane Wrapped Hard Candy, **22c lb.**
Assorted Gum Drops .... **15c lb.**
Crisp Peanut Crunch .... **18c lb.**
Asher's Chocolates, **45c lb.; 60c or 2 lbs. for $1**

Everything For Your Summer Vacation

Chic Coats
for Chilly Weather

$10.95 : 16.75

There will be many cool days this summer that you will welcome the smart comfort of one of these navy or black sheer crepe coats. Worn over a smart summer frock, they make a perfect ensemble. Sizes 16 to 44.

Other Coats, $3.50 Up

Dark Sheers
A Vacation "Must"

$10.95 : 16.75

For a cool, well dressed appearance you can always depend on a dark sheer to do its bit . . . Black and navy as well as dots and stripes on dark grounds in sizes 12 to 44 . . . Ideal for town and travel.

Half Size Dresses
for Hard To Fit Women

$7.95

A boon to the woman of somewhat shorter stature. Sheer Bembergs, chiffons and sheer crepes, skillfully designed to flatter the figure with little or no alterations. Sizes 16½ to 26½.

Cool Cottons
Many Made To Sell Up To $5.95 3.95

Every woman appreciates the practical features of chambray and seersucker dresses. They're smart for any daytime occasion with the added advantage of being easily laundered. Stripes and solid shades in sizes from 12 to 44.

ECONOMY ☐ SHOP

Save Now On Corsetries
Usual $2.50 Values $1.89

Corsettes of voile, mesh and novelty brocades in various styles and all sizes up to 52 with inner belts. Side hook and stepin girdles in summer weights as well as brocade and rayon satin. All sizes.

SECOND ☐ FLOOR

So Many Uses!
KLEENEX
Package of 500
2 for 55c

Make sure you have plenty of these soft, absorbent tissues. In white, peach, green or orchid. One box is priced 28c.

STREET ☐ FLOOR

All $1 Bags
All Summer Styles!

84c

There's no reason to be without a white handbag this summer! A mere 84c buys either a white simulated leather or a striped fabric bag in a copy of higher priced models.

STREET ☐ FLOOR

79c Gloves
White Hand Crocheted

49c

Buy two pairs of these cool gloves so that you will always have a fresh pair. You'll wear them with all of your sheer summer frocks. Several styles.

STREET ☐ FLOOR

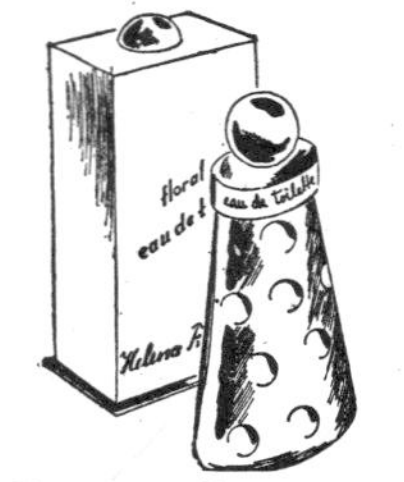

Sweet Scents
Cologne & Toilet Water

$1 to 3.50

Colognes and toilet waters made especially for summer use . . . Rubinstein's Apple Blossom; Dorothy Gray's hot weather cologne; others by Lucien Lelong, Lentheric, Coty and Hudnut.

STREET ☐ FLOOR

For Sunburn
50c : 1.00

Protect your skin with one of these sunburn requisites:

Lentheric Sun Oil 50c up
Coty's Sun Cream . . . $1
Dorothy Gray Sun Cream $1

STREET ☐ FLOOR

DU-PARC
Toilet Soap
In Various Shapes and Attractively Boxed

$1.00 Box 59c

A big special purchase of fine toilet soap in all the popular odeurs and several attractive shapes. Supply your bathroom with fine soap for your summer guests and family.

STREET ☐ FLOOR

Stunning Summer Hats
That Are Really Remarkable Values! $1.98

The style and quality of these hats, you'll agree, are worthy of a higher price tag. You can select turbans, berets, sport and large dress brims from this group, in white and colors.

WATT & SHAND ☐ SECOND FLOOR

★ ★ ★ ★ ★ ★ ★ ★

America's Finest Bathing Suits
★ JANTZEN
★ CATALINA
★ BRADLEY
★ SACONY

$1.95 to $12

Whether you get in the swim or simply bask in the sun on the shores, you'll make a pretty picture in a suit selected from our extensive stock. Every new version is here in the smartest materials. Plain and printed.

SECOND ☐ FLOOR

★ ★ ★ ★ ★ ★ ★ ★

Cool Play Togs
for Girls 7 to 16

50c to $2.95

Watt & Shand's is headquarters for girls' play togs. The newest styles in shorts, shirts, slacks and play suits are gay, cool and infinitely comfortable.

SECOND ☐ FLOOR

★ ★ ★ ★ ★ ★ ★ ★

Colorful Play Shoes
In A Variety of New Styles

1.95 to 3.95

Kedettes' Dutchboy shoe of colorful beachrobe fabric, mounted on springy tractor tread. For all sports occasions, $2.95.

Saddle oxfords — the sportiest, most practical and popular shoes for active and spectator sports. Brown and white, $3.95.

Beach Sandals of fancy woven cotton; and plain and vari-colored chenille. $1.95 and $2.45.

Kedettes in moccasin and other sporty styles. Cool cotton — easily washable, $1.95.

White leather moccasins with rubber soles, $2.95.

SHOE STORE

★ ★ ★ ★ ★ ★ ★ ★

All Our 25c Dress Fabrics
Go On Sale Friday!

19c

DIMITIES	STRIPES
BATISTES	FLORALS
LAWNS	POLKA DOTS
VOILES	ALL FAST
FLAXONS	COLOR
BROADCLOTHS	36 AND 39 INCHES WIDE

Buy Now! You'll Save!

STREET ☐ FLOOR

Colorful Beach Umbrellas
$2.95

Made of heavy striped canvas with long jointed hard wood pole, pointed to stick into the earth . . In a large assortment of gay colors.

THIRD ☐ FLOOR

New Luggage
At Popular Prices!

Gladstone Bags
$6.50 Values Special! 4.92

Durable split cowhide bags shown in black and brown.

Week-End Bags
3.95 To 14.50
Striped canvas, imitation leather and real leather bags in 18 inch size.

Ladies' Wardrobes
7.95 To 18.95
Lightweight wardrobe cases of striped canvas in various sizes.

BASE ☐ MENT

PHOENIX
Vita Bloom Processed
SILK HOSE
79c

For practical economy wear Phoenix hose—the hose that are specially treated to make them wear longer.

STREET ☐ FLOOR

July Portrait ★ Special $1
Large 8 X 10 Inch Size
With Choice of 4 Proofs!
STUDIO ☐ 4TH FLOOR

The Suits With 1600 Windows

TAILORED BY GOODALL
Palm Beach
FROM THE GENUINE CLOTH

$16.75

1600 Little Windows are in every square inch of cloth and they're all wide open, to let your body breathe. But what will win your heart is the quick fit and superb style in these greatest of all washable suits. Darker tones in pin stripes and solid shades for business . . distinctive summer colors for sports and all outdoors.

Palm Beach Slacks . . $5.00
Evening Formals . . $18.50

STREET ☐ FLOOR

★ ★ ★ ★ ★ ★ ★ ★

Sport Ensembles
Are Featured Special!

$3.95 To $5 Values 2.95

Men are fast realizing the importance of a sports outfit that is cool, comfortable and easily laundered. Here it is—and for the small sum of $2.95. In-and-outer styles in gabardine, poplin and calvary twill. Sizes up to 42 inch waist.

STREET ☐ FLOOR

★ ★ ★ ★ ★ ★ ★ ★

All Straws Reduced
1/3

Every straw hat in this season's newest models is reduced 1/3 less regular price. All styles.

Arrow Shirts
For Cool Smartness

$2

Come in today and get your white Arrow shirt—a Trump, Drew or Hitt—the shirts with good fitting collars. They stay crisp all day long.

New Arrow Silk Ties, $1

STREET ☐ FLOOR

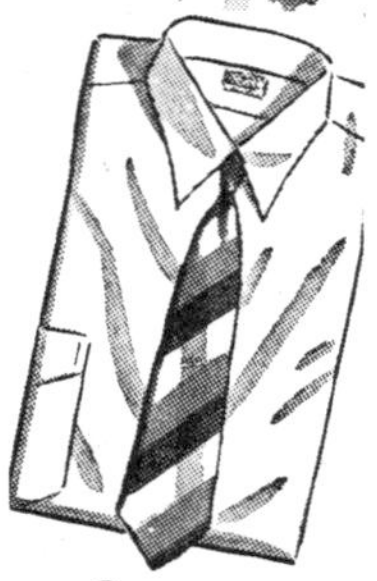

Cool Keds
for Men & Boys

$1.25 To 2.50

White, blue and brown canvas with rubber soles, as shown.

Men's Kedsman of canvas combined with mesh weave. All white, brown, and white with blue or black trim, $2.50.

SHOE ☐ STORE

★ ★ ★ ★ ★ ★ ★ ★

July Sale of Gliders!

$26.50 Gliders Now Only 19.95

$29.50 Gliders For Only 24.50

METAL SPRING CHAIRS TO MATCH $6.95

$3.95 Metal Chairs, Special, $2.25

WATT & SHAND ☐ THIRD FLOOR

Costume and Doll Shows Spur Competition At City Playgrounds

Arthur Ott, five, won the prize for the most comic costume yesterday at East Junior playground by wearing his father's baseball uniform.

Thelma Barrett, ten, in a boot-black's costume, shines the shoes of Marion Patton, eight, who, dressed in a Danish costume, took the prize for the most colorful at the East Junior playground costume show yesterday afternoon.

These two pretty little girls brought their dolls to the doll show at the Hamilton Park playground yesterday afternoon and one walked away with a prize. Patricia O'Day, ten, (left,) won the prize for the prettiest doll while Frances Graybill, eight, (right) doubtless still thinks her ice-skater doll is just as nice.

Gilbert Bair, four, brought his yellow-haired doll to Hamilton Park and put some of the girls to shame by winning a prize. It took first place as the most comic.

Shirley Evans, eight, doesn't seem to have enough room in the coach for her four big dolls. Shirley won a prize for having the most dolls at the show. Three other little girls also had four dolls each and won duplicate prizes.

THE DAY'S LOG

The New Era barometer shows the following forecast for the next twelve hours:

Generally fair weather.

The United States Weather Bureau forecast at 11 A. M. today was:

EASTERN PENNSYLVANIA: Fair and slightly warmer tonight. Sunday increasing cloudiness. Slightly warmer in north portion. Monday showers.

NEW JERSEY, DELAWARE and MARYLAND: Fair and slightly warmer tonight. Sunday increasing cloudiness. Monday showers.

SANDY HOOK to HATTERAS: Gentle to moderate northeast winds, increasing somewhat Sunday and fair weather tonight becoming overcast Sunday.

WESTERN PENNSYLVANIA: Fair and slightly warmer tonight, Sunday increasing cloudiness and slightly warmer; Monday showers.

WASHINGTON, July 6—(U. P.)—Weekly weather forecasts:

North and Middle Atlantic: General showers Monday and Tuesday. Generally fair middle of week, and local showers Friday and Saturday, temperature will average near normal.

Ohio Valley and Tennessee: General showers beginning of week and local showers latter part. Generally fair middle of week, temperature normal or slightly below beginning of week. Mostly normal or slightly above, remainder of week.

The Sun rose at 5:37 A. M. and sets at 8:32 P. M.

The Moon sets at 9:34 P. M. First Quarter—July 12.

The morning stars are Venus, Jupiter and Saturn.

The evening star is Mars.

The conditions in Lancaster and vicinity yesterday were as follows: Character of day, clear; prevailing winds, west and north.

The lowest and highest temperatures yesterday and last night as recorded at the New Era Weather Station on top of the New Era Building, City Water Works and the Ephrata Weather Stations were:

	Low	High
New Era	50	80
City Water Works	49	84
Ephrata	52	85

The temperature variations today, as recorded at the New Era Weather Station on top of the New Era Building were:

	Low	High
8 A. M.	68	68
8 A. M. to Noon	68	79

The relative humidity, as recorded today at the New Era Weather Station on top of the New Era Building was:

	Per Cent
8 A. M.	55
Noon	63

Hourly temperatures today, as shown on the recording thermometer in front of the New Era Building were:

Saturday, July 6.

A. M.

1	2	3	4	5	6	7	8	9	10	11	12
64	63	60	60	60	59	59	66	65	67	70	72

DEATHS

Adam C. Peters, fifty-three, Wyomissing.

Mrs. Mary C. Acker, eighty-three, Hinkletown.

Miss Florella Samson, ninety, this city.

John Leonard, Royalton.

William J. Klinefelter, sixty-two, Washington, D. C.

Dr. David C. Posey, sixty, Christiana.

Mrs. Horace W. Weaver, sixty-four, Ephrata.

MARRIAGE LICENSES

Applicatons

Evart Olsie Fink and Theda Marie Kellenberger, both of Lancaster.

Charles G. Snyder and Florence S. Hall, both of Lancaster.

James Howard Rogers, Harrisburg, and Frances Grissinger, Mt. Joy.

Franklin Zecher, Lancaster, and Evelyn Snyder, Millersburg.

Granted

John William Montague, Yeadon, and Margaret E. Welch, Mt. Airy.

Anthony Edward Discavage, Shenandoah, and Susanne Theresa Sanudoski, Coatesville.

BIRTHS

Boys

Mr. and Mrs. Benjamin Greenberg, 528 Woodward street, at the General hospital, yesterday.

Mr. and Mrs. J. Greenawalt, 432

OTHER LOG NEWS ON PAGE 10

OBITUARY

Time and Place of Services will be found under Funeral Invitations ON PAGE 14, COLUMN 5

DR. DAVID C. POSEY DIES IN CHRISTIANA

Dr. David C. Posey, sixty, of 11 Gay street, Christiana, died at 6:15 o'clock this morning at his home, of coronary thrombosis following a long illness.

He was born in York county, a son of the late Mordecai A., and Rebecca Posey, and came to Christiana in 1921. He was a member of Latta Memorial Presbyterian church and was a graduate of the University of Maryland School of Medicine. He was a member of the American Medical association, Pennsylvania State Medical association and the Lancaster County Medical society.

Besides his wife, the former Margaret Morton before marriage, he is survived by two sons: Harry C. Posey, Downingtown, and Dale M. Posey, at home; also two brothers: Daniel H. Posey and B. Frank Posey, both of York, and two sisters: Mrs. Mary Brooks and Mrs. Ralph Gilgore, both of Delta, York county.

ADAM C. PETERS

Adam C. Peters, fifty-three, 1303 Reading blvd., Wyomissing, Pa., died suddenly at 6:15 P. M. Thursday in Ocean City, N. J., where he and his wife had been living for the past week with a Reading family who employed them. He was born in Monterey, a son of Adam and the late Wilhelmina Muehleizen Peters Levanight. He was formerly a resident of Lancaster and Reading. He was a member of St. Andrew's Evangelical and Reformed church, this city. Besides his widow, Ethel Cox Peters, and his father, he is survived by the following half-brothers and half-sisters: Norton Steinmetz, Ella, wife of Harrison Harmess; Alice, wife of Arthur Frey; Arthur, Walter, Amos and Christian Steinmetz, and Mabel, wife of Martin Harmess, all of Lancaster.

MRS. MARY C. ACKER

Mrs. Mary C. Acker, eighty-three, widow of William R. Acker, died at 1 P. M. yesterday, at her home in Hinkletown, after an illness of about six months. She was a member of the Bergstrasse Lutheran church. Surviving her are a son, Cloyd W. Acker, of Reading, and a sister, Mrs. Annie Widman, Hinkletown.

MISS FLORELLA SAMSON

Miss Florella Samson, ninety, died at 2 P. M. yesterday at the home of Mrs. Ada Shuman, in this city, with whom she resided. She was a daughter of the late Joseph and Mary Hoffman Samson and was the last of her family. She was the oldest member of the First M. E. church, this city.

JOHN LEONARD

John Leonard, of Royalton, Pa., died at 1:30 A. M., today at St. Joseph's hospital. Attendants said he underwent an operation at the hospital about a week ago.

WILLIAM J. KLINEFELTER

William J. Klinefelter, sixty-two, brother of George Klinefelter, Ephrata, died recently in Washington, D. C. He was formerly of York.

MRS. HORACE W. WEAVER

Mrs. Mame Miller Weaver, sixty-four, wife of Horace W. Weaver, 332 North State street, Ephrata, died last evening, at her home, at 11:30 o'clock, of a complication of diseases, after an illness of two weeks.

She is survived by her husband and three sons, Clyde W., at home; Roy M. and Carl M., both of Ephrata; two grandchildren.

She was a daughter of the late L. E. and Sally Miller, formerly of Lincoln and a member of the Ephrata United Brethren church.

'COON DRAWS CROWD AT COURT HOUSE

"Smoky," a twelve-weeks-old 'coon, stopped pedestrian traffice on East King street in front of the Court House this morning.

The grey 'coon was bought by Deputy Game Protector Milton Dietrich, of Millersville, for his four-year-old son, Jimmy. Dietrich parked in front of the Court House when he came to the city to do some banking. Jimmy and the 'coon were soon the center of an interested crowd.

PAROLED YOUTH KILLS 2 OF KIN

Hammers Brother and Sister to Death as They Slept.

BUFFALO, N. Y., July 6.—(A. P.)—A 19-year-old undertaker's assistant on parole for the 1937 ax slaying of a brother confessed today, acting assistant detective chief Richard Mack said, to hammering to death last night another brother and sister as they slept.

Mack asserted Frank Swiontek claimed his step-father, Peter Miziolek, goaded him into slaying Gordon Swiontek, 9, and Teresa, 12. Miziolek, appearing on verge of collapse, denied the charge.

Police found the children in the same bed, their heads battered and the bed clothes covered with blood, after Swiontek walked into a police station and reported he had discovered the two bodies. The boy met instant death and the girl died several hours later. Their mother and step-father were at a movie. A blood-covered hammer was found in a fruit basket in the kitchen.

Swiontek, who the police official said would be charged with first degree murder, was on parole from Elmira reformatory where he was sent in 1938 for fatally attacking his 17-year-old brother Leo. Frank made a statement later that he committed the crime because of Leo's failure to do any work around the house.

Annual Picnic For Blind On July 16

The blind of Lancaster city and county will be entertained at their annual picnic, all day Tuesday, July 16, at Long park.

Plans for the event were made by members of the picnic committee, meeting yesterday at the headquarters. Milton Michaelis, the chairman, was in charge, and others present were Mrs. Michaelis, Mrs. Fred J. Hausch, Miss Ida Lind, Miss Eliza B. Paine and Dr. J. B. McCaskey.

A dinner and supper will be served at the park, and there will be a special program of games, under the direction of the Blind Women's club and the Blind men's club.

The program of entertainment will be given by various blind persons from the city and county. All who can sing, play musical instruments or entertain in any other way will be invited to participate, the committee said.

Members of the Lions' club will furnish transportation to and from the picnic. Cars will leave the association headquarters at Walnut and Mary streets at 10 o'clock.

2 WOMEN START SUITS FOR DIVORCE

Two women started suits for divorce here yesterday, both on grounds of desertion.

Elizabeth B. Eckman, 42 East Chestnut street, asks divorce from Richard E. Eckman, 226 East New street. They were married May 16, 1936, and separted February 16, 1938.

Elsie Huber, 210 North Mulberry street, seeks divorce from Frank E. Huber, 608 South Queen street. They were married December 10, 1924, and lived together until March, 1936.

MILK BOTTLE HURLED THROUGH WINDOW

Saul L. Solomon, 523 North President avenue, reported to city police that someone hurled a milk bottle through the kitchen window at his home at 10:20 P. M. yesterday. Solomon was seated in the living room at the time when he heard the glass crash.

Police searched the neighborhood but could not find anyone.

BURNS HAND WITH CAP PISTOL

Dorothy Rineer, three, 308 Filbert street, was a belated Fourth of July victim today. She burned her hand with a cap pistol and was treated in St. Joseph's hospital.

50 Dolls Of All Kinds Shown At Hamilton Park Playground

Announce Winners of Costume Shows At City Centers; Paddle Tennis and Volley Ball Games

Fifty dolls were entered in the doll show held yesterday afternoon at Hamilton Park.

Awards were made to the following: Margaret Jones, smallest doll, about one inch; Arlene Coffin, largest; Patricia O'Day, prettiest; Louis Ann Bair, oldest doll, fifty-three years old; Joan Seitz, most original doll made of pecans; Gilbert Bair, funniest; and Rosanne Schanerberger; Shirley Evans, Doris Walick and Marie Herington, the most dolls.

Miss Esther Kiehl, of the WPA was the supervisor in charge and the judges included: Mrs. Edward Ranck, Miss Dorothy Kiphorn and Mrs. Charles Cooper.

Prize winners of the costume shows held yesterday at the various playgrounds were as follows:

Franklin, Paul Snyder, cleverest costume; Alma Derring, prettiest; Rosemary Snyder, youngest contestant Donald Edwards, funniest; Mary Whitcomb and Patsy Bare, cutest couple. The judges were Miss Hazel Lefever, Paul Tomlinson, Miss Dorothy Barley, Miss Elizabeth Wertz and Miss Anne Frey, supervisor.

Rodney park: Donna Carnish, prettiest Mary Bair, funniest; James Dennis, most original; Jane Souders, most exotic; Corinne Kirchner, most daring Ruth Duke, neatest; Shirley Fritsch and Betty Bachman, best looking couple and Mary James, most old-fashioned. The judges were Gloria Gunzenhauser, Teddy Nolan and June Watson.

Edward Hand: Arthur Ott, cleverest; Jane Herr, most unique; Nancy Ott, prettiest; Marion Patton, most colorful; Lorraine Phillips, smallest contestant James Paton, most colorful boy's costume; Doris Marie Bushong, most authentic; James Patton, best character representation; and honorable mention was given to Nancy Landis, Barbara Watts and Thelma Barrett. The judges were Miss Nancy Houck and Peter White. The supervisors in charge were Miss Breneisen and Arthur Ott of the Playground association and Samuel Parks of the WPA.

Muhlenberg: Two brothers, Robert and William Williams won prizes for the cutest costume and best impersonator. Wendell Means won the prize for the most original costume. The judges were Mrs. Walter Hyson and Miss Elizabeth Craig.

Rockland and Green: Leah Cohen, dressed as "Miss Lancaster, prettiest; Charles Stewart, funniest; Joan Flory, most grotesque, Ray and Fay Sherman, dressed as twins, most original; Jack Baker and Barbara Baker, best characterizations; Beatrice Leapman, and Dolores De Gregoril, best impersonations. The judges were Mrs. E. Trimble, Mrs. J. V. Sterrett, Miss Bertha Neff, Miss Leona Cooper, and Mrs. Ruby N. Payne, supervisors.

The Rodney volley ball team defeated Buchanan two out of three games in a match played yesterday at Rodney. Playing for the winning team were Shirley Rittenhouse, captain; Betty Goodhart, Gloria Gunzenhauser, Teddy Nolan, Esther Souders, Sis Fritsch and June Watson. The Buchanan team included Effie Martin, captain; Rosemary Sprout, Pat Martin, Dorothy Barber, and Jane Cunningham.

Miss Marian Skeen and Joseph Wesley supervised the activities.

Charles Long was winner of a paddle tennis tournament held Friday at the Reigart playground, with Frank Geraci as runner-up.

Others participating were John Kreider, Arline Rankin, Frank Williams, Albert Sauerbaugh, Edwin Ewell, Thelma Book, Dorothy Book, and Chester Waters.

Salvatore Vangari was referee and Pauline Rankin was scorekeeper.

Miss Marie Vatter and J. Nevin Rentz are the supervisors.

The Muhlenberg volley ball team defeated the Rockland team by a score of 15-3, 15-6 in a match played on the winning team's ground yesterday.

The Rockland team included Jacqueline Hoehn, Mildred Cooper, Anna May Brown, Betty Vollrath, Veta Lewis, Gloria Manning, and Amanda Troop, substitute.

Playing for Muhlenberg were Gladys Waters, captain; Ella Waters, Evelyn Jason, Bernice Gant, Gloria Wilson, and Florence Williams.

Miss Bertha Neff, supervisor at Rockland, was referee. Miss Anna Mary Smith and James Elliott are in charge of activities at Muhlenberg.

Thirty-five girls of the Buchanan park playground organized the "Happy Hour Club" recently and elected the following officers: Nancy Brubaker, president; Gloria Gunzenhauser, vice president; Doris Yarnall, secretary; Rosemary Sprought, assistant secretary, and Jane Cunningham, general manager.

"The Twilight Singing Group," also was organized. at the play center and includes boys and girls of all ages and meets at the playground each evening from 7 to 8 o'clock to sing old time, modern and folk songs.

CALENDAR OF EVENTS

TONIGHT

Boy Scout Council, Chiquetan Day, band concert and Indian pageant; Camp Chiqueton, afternoon and evening.

Women's Fellowship of Methodist churches, performance of "Golgotha," talking motion picture; Y. M. C. A., continuous afternoon and evening.

Meadia Heights club, semiformal dance; club house, 10 P. M.

Lancaster County Industrial Council, card party; 38 South Queen street, 8:30 P. M.

TOMORROW

Eighth Ward Republican club, picnic; Pequea, meet at Fairview and Vine strets, 10 A. M.

Lancaster Catholic High school, class of 1937, doggie roast; Williamson park, meet at 602 South Queen street, 1:30 P. M.

St. Paul's Methodist church, repeat performance of "The Lost Church;" church, 7:30 P. M.

Workers' Alliance, Local G-581, picnic Williamson park, Pavilion No. 3, 11 A. M.

MONDAY (Until 7 P. M.)

Women's Auxiliary of the Men's Democratic club of Lancaster county, picnic; Wililamson park, afternoon.

WOMAN HURT IN FALL

Mrs. Helen Kauffman, seventy-eight, 144 East Vine street, was injured when she fell at her home at 11:20 P. M. yesterday, city police reported. Dr. H. F. Myers attended her.

RED CROSS AIDED BY PARTIES

Relief Materials Made Here Arrive in Spain.

The American Red Cross war relief supplies, which included shipments of materials produced by local volunteers as well as supplies purchased with funds raised locally, have arrived at Bilbao, Spain, for distribution among the refugees and evacuees from the war zones, according to cables received by National headquarters and word forwarded to the local chapter.

The national war relief fund has now reached $17,810,552, it was announced today. The local chapter is seeking $52,000 in the national $20,000,000 war relief drive.

Among the contributions given Lancaster chapter this week is an allocation from the $22,000 gift given the national headquarters by the Standard Oil company.

The benefit polo game at Overlook on Thursday netted $30 for the fund. A group of Pleasure Road children contributed $5 raised in a show given by Robert and Dickie Campbell, Michael Martin, Suzanna and Dickie Schneebeli, Billy Andes, Peter Ireys, Billy Sawyer, Joan Sabo and Mary Jane Crouthamel.

A group of children in the 300 block of East Orange street held a carnival last evening at the home of Mr. and Mrs. Jack Zook, 352 East Orange street, and raised $43.50, the largest amount raised to date in a children's benefit. The group included Dickie Zellers, Spencer Raezer, Nancy Raezer, Ellen Brinton, Peter and Jakie Zook, Tony and Hay Brown; Doris Hopf, Gilbert Lyons and Victor Brenner.

ONLY 42 MARRIAGE LICENSES IN JUNE

Marriage licenses applications in June totalled 42, a drop of 178 from the 1939 figure of 220, it was announced today at the office of Register of Wills A. Z. Moore.

The big decrease for the month was caused by the new state law, which required that applicants file affidavits showing freedom from contagious syphilis for licenses granted on and after May 17, it was said. May became the leading month for applications as an unusually large number of couples made their applications before the deadline.

"EXPLOSION" TRACED TO R. R. BLASTING

Blasting of a rock fall on the Pennsylvania railroad tracks close to the Susquehanna river is believed responsible for the "earth shivers" felt in Washington borough and at Long Level, on the York side of the river, about 10:25 o'clock last night.

A strong east wind carried the echo of the blast over a wide area and many believed there was an explosion in the vicinity of Millersville.

Engineers said that minor rock falls are frequently dynamited for quick removal.

Claims Refined Sugar Is Chief Cause of Decay In Teeth

Dr. L. M. Waugh, Who Made 10-year Study of Effects On Eskimo's Molars Advises Sweets With Natural Sugar

CHICAGO, July 6—(A. P.)—Tooth decay, one of mankind's most common diseases, is caused chiefly by refined sugar, an eminent health authority has concluded.

Dr. L. M. Waugh, professor of Dentistry at Columbia University, based his judgment upon 10 years of research among the primitive Eskimos, long considered by science to have the best teeth of any race.

Reporting his findings in the current issue of the Journal of the American Dental Association, Dr. Waugh asserted:

"An unsweetened tooth cannot decay. Refined sugar, in any form, is the essential factor in decay."

Dr. Waugh started his researches in Labrador in 1929 and established the first bacteriological field laboratory in Eskimo territory in 1935. After noting increases of as high as 600 per cent in tooth decay among Eskimos when sweets were introduced into their diet, Dr. Waugh said, he devised an actual laboratory test to measure the effects.

The scientist said that Alaskan Eskimos, ranging in age from 12 years to advanced age, were divided into two groups. Their mouths were free of tooth decay and their saliva had no germs of tooth decay.

One group received, daily, in addition to the native diet, a fixed quantity of refined sugar in the form of candy and cube sugar. The other group was given natural sugar, such as that formed in dried raisins, figs, dates and prunes.

"In two weeks," Dr. Waugh reported, "88 per cent of the first group showed the presence of bacteria of dental caries and at the end of five and one-half weeks, every mouth showed tooth decay with an average of 3.6 cavities per mouth.

"In the parallel experiment with the second group, not one person developed any tooth decay."

Summarizing his report, Dr. Waugh suggested the substitution of natural sugars for refined sweets whenever possible, recommended that sweets be eaten immediately after meals and said, "the sooner the mouth is cleansed after eating sweets, the less the danger."

Dr. Waugh, whose previous findings on the diets of the Eskimos have been given wide scientific recognition, is reserve dental director of the United States Public Health Service and dental consultant of the Indian Service.

CENTURY-OLD DEEDS ARE RECORDED HERE

Three deeds, all more than 100 years old and in excellent state of preservation, were brought to the office of Recorder of Deeds Christ B. Mylin yesterday for recording.

The deeds cover a farm of 101 acres in Warwick township, successively owned by Peter Becker, Sr., Peter Becker, Jr., and wife, Christian Longenecker and wife, and Peter Longenecker. The first two deeds, dated 1823 and 1824, are on white sheepskin. Seals and ribbons are in good condition. The third is dated 1839.

AUTO STOLEN AT QUARRYVILLE

An auto, belonging to Harry S. Kirk, Nottingham R. D. 1, bearing license tags JD-681, was stolen last night from a parking space in Quarryville, Motor Police announced today.

MERCANTILE LIST IN NEW ERA TODAY

MERCHANTS URGED TO REPORT RETAILERS NOT LISTED TO COUNTY APPRAISER

The Mercantile Appraiser's list for 1940 appears in today's issue of the New Era, with the names of persons or firms engaged in retail trade in Lancaster city and county.

Merchants and residents are asked to check the list to find whether any retailer is evading the tax. Reports should be made to Appraiser August A. Krimmel, Jr.

The appeal date has been set for July 9, 1940, after which prosecution will be brought for collection of license taxes.

Love without Music

by Helen Welshimer

WRITTEN FOR AND RELEASED BY CENTRAL PRESS ASSOCIATION

SYNOPSIS

THE CHARACTERS:

LINDA AVERY, receptionist at a New York models' agency, starts to rebuild her romance with

RONALD STAFFORD, her childhood sweetheart, who has "swung his way to fame on a trumpet," but

SARAH MARKLEY, wealthy glamor girl, is trying to capture Ronald for herself. Meanwhile

ROBERT BARTON, young engineer, strikes up a friendship with Linda. He introduces her to

TERRY ADAMS, publicity man, and Terry's sweetheart,

CAROLINE PICKARD, who has been unable to find work. Life is complicated by

MINA NEVINS, a famous actress, who is determined to marry Robert. She believes Linda is romancing with the young engineer.

* * *

YESTERDAY: Ronnie asks Linda to marry him right away and promises to call her later that night after rehearsal. Sitting in her apartment, Linda picks up a newspaper.

CHAPTER TEN

The news story was not long. It did not need to be. To Linda, reading it as he waited for Ronnie to finish rehearsal and call her, the words held double meaning.

The i'em explained that all members of the band and cast of the Markley company were being asked to sign a contract that they would not marry, unless already married, until the completion of the show.

So this was Sarah's way of erecting a blockade. Linda let the paper fall to the floor. She knew that Ronnie had not been informed of the decision yet, when she rode through the park such a brief while before. Of course he knew by now. And what would he do?

Leave the show to do as he pleased, she supposed. And she knew that she could not let him do that. If love was real, if it endured, if it suffered all things, bore all things, believed all things, hoped all things, then it could wait and not grow tarnished in the waiting. If it did, then it was not real. No, Linda told herself in the amazed moments that followed the reading of the feature, she had no reason for fear. In a certain sense she was relieved. That was odd. It was cowardly, she reflected. Loving Ronnie as she did, even a little while ago she had been afraid to interfere with the web the fates were spinning.

But she put all philosophy aside as the real knowledge came home. Ronnie was bound to a job and the job put her out for a long time.

When the telephone call came her voice was light and casual, though.

"I've read the news in the morning papers. Good going, isn't it?"

"There are other spots for a trumpet player, honey. Don't let that upset our plans. We're going straight ahead." His voice meant it, too. She knew that stern quality from old. He would have his way unless she prevented.

"We're taking a detour. Listen, nut, do you think I would let you slave to get a certain height and then destroy your billing? Anyway, I wanted to marry a trumpet man whose scales were on the up-and-up!"

It worked. And the man's relief was almost humble, as it came across the midnight city.

When he had hung up at last, still not sure that the delay was right, but grateful that Linda understood, she turned to Caroline and explained.

"We run in the same track," the other girl said. "Last night I refused because pity prompted the grand gesture and tonight it's thumbs down for you because a man's work should come before a man's love. But you're right. My father gave up a medical education for my mother and went to work in her father's bank. And he never forgot or quite forgave. Oh, he thought he did. But she knew better and so did I."

"How is Terry today?" Linda asked, storing away this new bit of comfort for her actions.

"Fine. He called at noon." She lifted her eyes to meet Linda's. "But he is awfully busy this week—is lining up a new radio program for his company, so I'm to stay on call for free moments. I know about that. He won't have any this week and then next week he'll want to celebrate nightly if the contract brings a raise. Only—maybe I will, and maybe I won't, be included. But he'll come back. He always does. Preceded by orchids and bon-bons."

Her voice was a little bitter. She stood up. "May I have some more milk? I want to put on weight and get a job in a hurry."

The next two weeks went so swiftly that they might have been torn from the calendar, Linda reflected one night near the end of April. The show opened. It was a hit. The critics were approving and enthusiastic. They were special notices for Ronnie, and his face appeared in theater sections.

Linda cut them out, and put the notices and pictures away. She even bought a scrapbook and began to paste up the stories. There were parties following the theater several nights and she went with Ronnie. She bought two new evening gowns. One was a white lace frock, rivuleted with white organdy ruffles, and the other was a yellow crepe, printed with white kangaroos, full and low over the bust, and smooth fitting at the hips, after which it billowed into yards and yards of unneeded material. Her slippers for it were yellow, and she knew that it was more sophisticated than the other more feminine one.

It was a little difficult to go partying so many nights, and yet be alert and eager at her desk the next day. Now and then she found her eyes closing and lectured severely to herself. Finally, one day, she declined a party date with Ronnie.

"I'd adore it," she murmured into the white ivory telephone on her desk, "but I have to work until nine tonight, and honestly, I'm too dead to go home and dress. Count me out just this once, won't you, honey?"

And count yourself out, too, she wanted to add. After all, none of the others went to every merry-making—that is, the stars didn't. Ronnie would wear out at this pace. And Sarah would adore it if his horn grew rusty. Only she, Linda, couldn't tell him.

But Ronnie sensed her thought. "I've been overdoing it this week. There's a halt called now. One milk-shake after performances, a walk or ride, a brief one, and home. Like that better?"

"Much. Except on Saturday nights. Sunday you are free—"

"Oh, by the way, I'm going out of town this week-end. A party the Markleys are throwing until Monday noon. Since I stayed put I'm in for it. But I'll hurry back. I may get Sarah to invite you. She knows I want it, and she's doing a peaches and cream act lately. Maybe she needed to be taken down a few pegs—have the glamor spanked out of her."

That's what you think, Linda mused, when the telephone was back in its cradle. But I know the girl, and she's waiting, waiting!

Caroline had been engaged at the agency and she continued to live with Linda. It was nice to have someone with whom to share the rent, she had decided, especially since frocks like the kind she was choosing weren't found on $19.95 racks.

Rob, busy with plans for some city engineering, came by once in a while to drag both girls out to dinner, amused at Linda's insistence that she escape to dress on

More of STORY on Page 5

DAILY CROSSWORD

ACROSS

1. Pierce
5. Mists
9. Wire rope
11. Shout aloud
12. Metallic compound
13. Motto
14. Seesaws
16. To be in debt
17. Fine-grained rock
19. Part of a play
22. Boat used on ice
26. Abusive speech
28. Stripped
29. Snares
30. Length measure
31. Highest point
32. Military students
33. Mends
35. Born
36. Nautical miles
38. Turkish measure
41. Chirp
45. Proverb
47. Coerce
48. Capital of Delaware
49. To toy
50. Bang
51. Ostrich-like birds

DOWN

1. A tax
2. A story
3. Capable
4. Stains
5. Crafty animal
6. Hodgepodge
7. To shine
8. Any
10. Covers over eyes
11. Swiftness
15. To rush
18. Subsided
19. Oil of roses
20. A sorceress
21. To hike
23. Made of oats
24. Rugged mountain crest
25. Concise
27. In a vertical line (naut.)
30. A dog
32. Black bird
34. Bury
37. Neckpiece
38. Cushions
39. Heathen deity
40. Beverage
42. To lop off
43. Beige
44. Soaks flax
46. Jewel

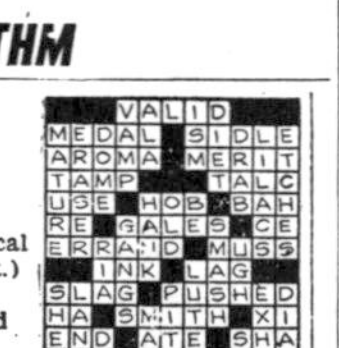

Yesterday's Answer

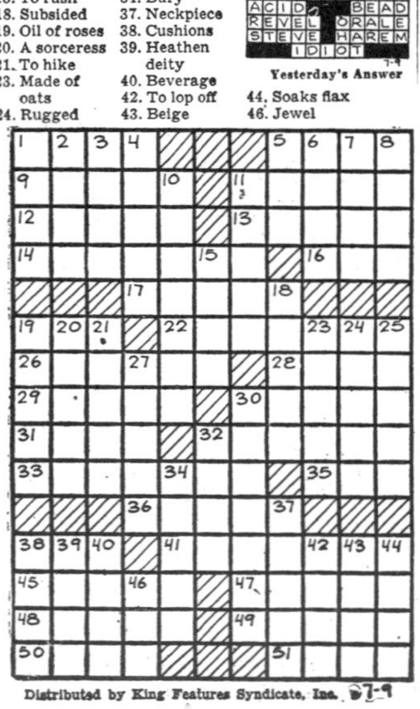

Distributed by King Features Syndicate, Inc.

ALLEY OOP (You'll Find "Alley Oop" In The Sunday News) By Hamlin

BRICK BRADFORD By William Ritt and Clarence Gray

INSPECTOR WADE By Edgar Wallace

BIG SISTER By Les Forgrave

POLLY AND HER PALS (Follow "Polly and Her Pals" In The Sunday News) By Cliff Sterrett

TILLIE THE TOILER By Westover

BRINGING UP FATHER ("Maggie and Jiggs" appear in The Sunday News, Too) By George McManus

MUGGS McGINNIS By Wally Bishop

FRECKLES AND HIS FRIENDS By Blosser

G. O. P. Board Meets Monday To Plan Party

Plans for the annual Garden Party of the Women's Republican club of Lancaster county to be held August 1, on the grounds at the home of Mr. and Mrs. Charles B. Long, 708 North Duke street, will be discussed at a meeting of the club executive board, Monday afternoon. Mrs. Albert M. Herr is general chairman.

Mrs. Charles B. Long will be hostess to the Board, at her home, Monday, and after the business session, supper will be served on the lawn. Mrs. Edward E. Stehman will preside.

Members of the Board who expect to attend the meeting are: Mrs. Clair Rice, Mrs. William Sahm, Mrs. H. Clifford Kreisle, Mrs. Daisy K. Lingenfelter, Mrs. John W. Weaver, Mrs. Paul M. Hess, Mrs. Paul B. Souder, Mrs. W. E. Burkholder, Mrs. Lloyd C. Ritchie, Mrs. H. E. Hendren, Mrs. Albert M. Herr, Mrs. C. Blaine Parker, Miss Bess Gilfillan, Mrs. A. H. Powden, Mrs. Charles L. Marshall, Miss Elizabeth Getz, Mrs. Milton H. Bertram, Mrs. Marvin E. Bushong, Mrs. W. N. Appel, Mrs. W. C. Marshall, Miss Agnes Lantz, Miss Emma Smaling, Mrs. T. Warren Metzger, Miss Ada M. Forry, Mrs. W. L. Bomberger, Miss Mary Shank, Mrs. Edgar Dunlap, Mrs. C. B. Keller, Mrs. Paul R. Richer and Mrs. Chester M. Reed.

Mt. Joy Girl Is Married to James Rogers

Miss Mary Frances Grissinger, daughter of Mrs. Sue R. Grissinger, 128 East Main street, Mount Joy, and James H. Rogers, of Harrisburg, were married this morning at 10 o'clock in the garden of the bride's mother's home in the presence of the immediate families.

The ceremony was performed by Rev. Ezra H. Ranck, pastor of St. Mark's United Brethren church, of Mount Joy.

The bride, who was given in marriage by her brother, Earl Grissinger, of Lancaster, wore a powder blue gown and a corsage of orchids. The bride's mother wore dark blue sheer crepe and wore a corsage of roses. There were no attendants.

Mrs. George Broske, of Mount Joy, played the wedding music and Miss Myrtle Grissinger, of Lancaster, sister of the bride, sang "I Love You Truly" and "Because".

A wedding breakfast for the immediate families was served at Hostetter's, Mount Joy, immediately after the ceremony.

The bride attended Mount Joy High School and Lancaster Business College and is employed as accountant for George Brown's Sons cotton and woolen mill in Mount Joy. The bridegroom is a graduate of Trinidad, Colorado, High School, and attended the University of Pennsylvania where he was a member of the Sigma Pi fraternity. He is sales manager for Remington Rand, Inc., of Harrisburg.

Following a two weeks' wedding trip to Mount Rushmore, South Dakota, and Denver, Colorado, the couple will be at home after August 1 at 128 East Main street, Mount Joy.

Miss Susan Houser Engaged to Wed

Mr. and Mrs. D. Reah Houser, of Palisade, N. J., announce the engagement of their daughter, Miss Susan Elizabeth Houser, to William Richard Schubart, son of Mr. and Mrs. William Schubart, of Kew Gardens, Queens, N. Y.

The Houser family is formerly from this city and Miss Houser was born in Lancaster. She is a niece of Miss Mabel Houser, of North West End avenue, and is a frequent visitor here.

The bride-elect was graduated from Mount Holyoke college in 1938. She has been studying for an M. A' degree in philosophy at Columbia University.

Mr. Schubart was graduated from Dartmouth college in 1938 and is taking a Ph. D., in philosophy at Columbia. He is a member of Phi Delta Theta, the Dartmouth Outing Club of New York, the Eastern Ski association and the Ocean Club of Forest Hills, Queens.

Fete Bride-Elect At Bridge Party

Mrs. William L. Troop, of 733 East End avenue, entertained at a bridge party last evening for Miss Margaret Aukamp, of Howard avenue, whose marriage to Arthur Ulrich, of Manheim, will take place in the near future.

Prizes were won by Mrs. Abram Heistand, Mrs. J. Bowman and Mrs. George Werner. Other guests were Mrs. George Kunzler, Mrs. Les Haldeman, Mrs. Wililam Sahm and Mrs. Gervase Long.

OTHER SOCIAL NEWS PAGE 7

Will Enter University of Pennsylvania

Miss Betty Blake, daughter of Mr. and Mrs. H. L. Blake, of 656 West Chestnut street, who will enter the University of Pennsylvania this fall for a Liberal Arts course. She is a graduate of McCaskey High school class of 1940.

Recent Bride

Mrs. Richard J. Diehl, the former Miss Justiena Mae Slick, daughter of Mr. and Mrs. Robert M. Slick, of 24 East New street, whose marriage took place last Saturday in the rectory of St. Joseph's Catholic church.

Maid of Honor

Miss Sarah Hanley, of Poplar street, who will be maid of honor at the wedding of Miss Iva Musselman, of Poplar street, and Richard E. Metz, of West King street, on July 27, at 9 o'clock at St. Joseph's Catholic church.

Bride of Henry Ford, 2nd

Miss Anne McDonnell is pictured as she was married to Henry Ford, 2nd, son of Mr. and Mrs. Edsel Bryant Ford, of Grosse Pointe Shores, Mich., and grandson of motor magnate Henry Ford, at the Church of the Sacred Hearts of Jesus and Mary, Southampton, L. I. The bride is the daughter of Mr. and Mrs. James F. McDonnell, New York and Southampton.

Anne McDonnell Is Married To Manufacturer's Grandson

SOUTHAMPTON, N. Y., July 13—(A. P.)—Twenty-year-old Anne Mcdonnell and Henry Ford, 2nd, grandson of the automobile manufacturer, were married today in a pageant-like ceremony of the Roman Catholic church.

As they stood at the flower-banked altar of the church of the Sacred Hearts of Jesus and Mary, Monsignor Fulton J. Sheen gave a discourse on the power of love.

"Rings can be broken and lost," he said, "but love is undying."

The pretty blonde bride was smiling as she went to the altar, with her long white veil trailing behind her.

The 22-year-old son of Mr. and Mrs. Edsel Ford was baptized into the Catholic faith, the faith of his bride, by Monsignor Sheen late yesterday in the presence of his parents, his bride-to-be and her parents.

Long before the marriage ceremony, hundreds of villagers had gathered across the street from the little church to view the notables and to applaud such personages as former New York Governor Alfred E. Smith, Henry Ford, Sr., and William S. Knudsen, head of the nation's defense production program.

The bride's 13 brothers and sisters and her 100 first cousins, uncles and aunts formed a cheery family background for her wedding today to Henry Ford, 2nd, grandson of the automobile manufacturer.

Their camaraderie broke the ice that might have surrounded a social event of first rank, and was an informal note in a scene thronged with fashionable guests and industrial leaders.

The silver-haired elder Ford and his wife, who have been married 52 years, came by private car for the ceremony at noon in the Roman Catholic Church of the Sacred Hearts of Jesus and Mary.

Young Ford's baptism into the faith of his bride took place shortly before the wdeding which was performed by Msgr. Fulton John Sheen of the Catholic University of America.

Among the 700 guests who crowded the gray stone church was James Farrell, the steel manufacturer. Kathleen Kennedy, daughter of Joseph P. Kennedy, U. S. Ambassador to England, was one of Anne's bridesmaids.

Special police were on duty, but no more, said the village police chief, than ordinarily handle the crowds and traffic at a big wedding here.

A program of liturgical music by organist Pietro Yon and choir-singers from St. Patrick's Cathedral in New York, preceded the half-hour service in the lily-decorated sanctuary.

Twenty-year-old Anne, daughter of James Francis McDonnell, a Wall Street broker, and granddaughter of the late inventor, Thomas E. Murray, wore a billowing white tulle gown and carried white orchids.

For the reception and wedding breakfast afterward, a pavilion was erected on the lawn of her home, a huge half-timbered house overlooking the Atlantic Ocean.

There was to be dancing on a specially built floor. Two rooms of the house were nearly full of wedding presents.

Mr. and Mrs. Edsel Ford, parents of Henry, 2nd, remained before the wedding aboard their yacht anchored off Southampton.

Among the ushers was Harry Quinn, of Lebanon, Pa.

PLAN CONCERT

The Hickory Grove band will present a sacred concert in the grove at Middle Octorara Presbyterian church on Sunday evening, July 21.

PRESBYTERY TO MEET

Donegal Presbytery will meet at Middle Octorara Presbyterian church on Tuesday, opening at 9:30 A. M.

Personals

Mrs. Howard J. Eshelman, of Eden, returned recently from a week's visit with her son-in-law and daughter, Mr. and Mrs. Harry M. Bitner, Jr., and family, in Indianapolis, Ind.

Miss Mary Jane Taylor, of Bluefield, W. Va., is the guest of Miss Lois Barnes, of Hamilton Road. Miss Taylor and Miss Barnes graduated from the University of North Carolina last month. Miss Barnes, Miss Taylor, Miss Constance Barnes, Miss Emily Detwiler, of Marietta avenue; Miss Maryanne Wickersham, of the Lincoln Highway East; the Misses Nancy and Phyllis Auten, of the Lititz Road, and Miss Barbara Miller, of Wheatland avenue, are spending the week-end at the summer cottage of Miss Miller's parents, Mr. and Mrs. Charles L. Miller, at Avalon, N. J.

Miss Henrietta Reist, daughter of Mr. and Mrs. John L. Reist, of the Lititz Road; Miss Josephine Eshelman, daughter of Mr. and Mrs. H. Roy Eshelman, and Miss Phyllis Eshelman, daughter of Mr. and Mrs. Howard J. Eshelman, both of Eden, have returned from Ocean City, N. J., where they spent several days.

Miss Hildegarde Pilgram, of Germantown, and Miss Gurney Naile, of Chestnut Hill, are spending the week-end with the former's parents, the Rev. and Mrs. Robert J. Pilgram of State street.

Mrs. Pierce Lesher and Mrs. William Lee will be hostesses to the Ladies' Auxiliary of the Knights Templar, No. 13, at their summer home, near Reamstown, on Tuesday afternoon.

Dr. and Mrs. F. P. Auten and daughters, Nancy and Phyllis, of the Lititz Road, spent several days recently in Ocean City, N. J.

Mr. and Mrs. J. Clark Houghton, of 20 West King street, have returned from a two weeks' trip to the New England states.

Mrs. Ralph E. Hetherton, of South West End avenue, has returned from a ten-day visit with friends in Georgetown, Del., and Salisbury, Md.

Rabbi and Mrs. Daniel L. Davis and son, Baruch, of Woods avenue, have gone to their summer home, "Chimney Acres," in the Berkshire Mts., Ghent, N. Y.

Dr. and Mrs. James F. Miller, of Altoona, are spending some time with the former's mother, Mrs. John Miller, of College avenue.

Miss Marguerite Ault, daughter of Mr. and Mrs. Victor E. Ault, of Elm avenue, is spending some time with Miss Gladys Woodwell, in Brookline.

Miss Betty Young, of Mount Joy, and Miss Estelle Flammand, of East End avenue, will spend next week at the North Woods Dude ranch, Lake George, N. Y.

Miss Ruby Detwiler, of Atkins avenue, and Miss Rose Herzon, of South Duke street, are spending the week-end in New York City.

Mrs. Augustus Daescher and her sister, Mrs. Joseph Kohler, of High street, are expected home tomorrow from a week's visit with friends in Philadelphia, Newark, N. J., and New York City.

Mr. and Mrs. H. F. Winters and son, Wayne, of Ruby street, and Miss Betty Jo McComsey, of East End avenue, are spending the week-end as the guests of Mr. and Mrs. H. H. Wiggins and daughter, Arlene, of Marietta avenue, on their yacht, "Lady Alberta," on the Chesapeake Bay.

Mrs. John A. Ford and sons, John and William, of College avenue, are spending a week with Mrs. Ford's parents, Dr. and Mrs. William Shrike, of Phoenixville.

Mr. and Mrs. Louis Fisher, of Lancaster avenue, have returned from a week's trip to Atlantic City.

Mr. and Mrs. Harry Mull and son, Billy, of Dauphin street, Russell Snyder, Misses Helen Aster and June Graham, all of Green street, will leave tomorrow for Ocean City, Md., to spend a week.

Mrs. Madeline Reynolds, of Conestoga, has returned from a month's visit in Bloomsburg. While there she attended the reunion of the Bardo family in Paradise Valley, Madison township.

WAKEFIELD REUNION

The Wakefield reunion will be held at Germany Valley church on Saturday, July 20. Charles O. Wakefield is president and Ethel Wakefield, Huntingdon, is secretary. The program will include worship service, business and music at 2 P. M., and games and races at 2:30 o'clock.

MAKES CHOICE CHURCH LINENS

COPR. 1938, NEEDLECRAFT SERVICE, INC.

CHURCH LINENS PATTERN 2603

These motifs in simplest embroidery, are a handsome decoration on religious lines for home as well as church. Pattern 2603 contains a transfer pattern of 34 motifs ranging from 6½ x 7 inches to 1 x 1 inch; directions and charts for edgings; materials required; illustrations of stitches.

Send ten cents in coin for this pattern to New Era, Needlecraft Dept., 8 West King street, Lancaster, Pa. Write plainly PATTERN NUMBER, your NAME and ADDRESS.

Conventional Rules Are Not Required at One's Own Table

By EMILY POST

The distinction that must be made between conventional requirements of good usage and what we may choose to do in our own houses, is illustrated in a letter which asks if it is also wrong to serve salad **on a separate plate** with meat if vegetables are not included. This letter says further, "It is very hard to go without vegetables, because some of us do not like meat without vegetables, while one of us likes to eat the salad and the meat together."

Emily Post

To this the answer is that hot vegetables eaten at the same time as salad (according to formal usage) is almost as wrong as serving cream soup and ice cream at the same time. Some one **might** like this, and in her own house there is no reason why she may not have what she or her family likes. I cite this example merely to make my point, knowing very well of course that more people like salad and vegetables than could possibly like the soup and ice cream combination. I must of course repeat that when salad is served with meat it correctly takes the place of vegetables. Otherwise, it should be served as a separate course.

But I must also add that if in a house of limited service, it is easier to prepare the salad on individual plates ahead of time and to put these at each place at table, to be eaten when each one prefers, this is a compromise that (even though not correct) might in such cases be quite sensible to make.

* * *

WHO EATS FIRST?

Dear Mrs. Post: At a very big public dinner where there is a speakers' table and smaller tables, when does a guest begin eating? Must the people at the small tables wait for some one at the speakers' table—perhaps the chairman—to begin eating, or how is this determined? At an ordinary dinner I know of course that people would wait for the hostess to begin.

Answer; You pay no attention whatever to the head table. That is, the first one served at your table may begin eating when two or three others have been served. This is exactly the same rule that is followed, according to best convention, at every dinner. The hostess, who is properly served last, should not expect any one to wait for her to begin—unless a foreigner from a distant land is not sure about the use of table implements.

* * *

THE BRIDESMAIDS' AND USHERS' PARENTS

Dear Mrs. Post: Please tell me why those parents of the bridesmaids and ushers whom we don't even know personally have to be invited to the wedding reception.

Answer: Because they naturally have an especial interest in the wedding of those who are very intimate friends of their children. They are not asked if it is a very small party of relatives and intimate friends and they do not belong in either category. But if any outsiders are invited they should be among the first, and of course they should be invited to the ceremony in church.

Will Matriculate at Penn State

Miss Marguerite Waddell, daughter of Mr. and Mrs. Robert Waddell, of 173 South President avenue, who will enter Penn State college this fall for a Liberal Arts course. She is a graduate of McCaskey High school class of 1940.

Recent Bride

Mrs. Richard R. Reardon, the former Miss Dorothy Shay, daughter of Mr. and Mrs. Harold Shay, whose marriage to Mr. Reardon, son of Mr. and Mrs. James B. Reardon, took place last Saturday at Warrenton, Va., with Rev. Joseph S. Johnston officiating.

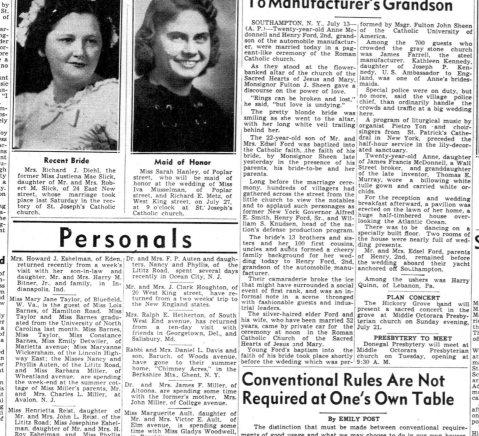

Bridesmaid

Miss Phyllis Tully, of Lewistown, who will be a bridesmaid at the wedding of Miss Mary E. Krushinski, of Poplar street, and Theodore G. Kendig, of North Queen street, on July 27 at 8 o'clock in St. Joseph's Catholic church.

Sarah Stahle Is Bride of M. L. Mathiot

Miss Sarah J. Stahle, daughter of Mrs. G. Harry Stahle, of York, and M. Luther Mathiot, son of Henry Mathiot, of this city, are being married this afternoon at 4 o'clock in the Union Lutheran church, York. The pastor, the Rev. Carl Simon, officiates.

The bride, given in marriage by William Grove of Harrisburg, is attended by Mrs. A. E. Uhler, as matron of honor, and Miss Loraine Stahle, as maid of honor. S. E. Scott is best man and the ushers are Dr. J. P. Adams and A. E. Uhler. Adam Hamme plays the wedding marches and Donald Worley is vocal soloist.

A reception follows at "Julius," after which the couple will leave on a trip to Skyline Drive and points south.

The bride is a graduate of York High school and studied organ at Peabody Conservatory of Music, Baltimore. She is organist of the Union Lutheran church, York, and is a member of the Musical Matinee club and the Yorktowne chapter, D. A. M.

Mr. Mathiot is associated with the Mason-Dixon Radio group.

WILL BE WED JULY 26

Miss Mary Elizabeth Shoemaker, daughter of Mr. and Mrs. Clifford Shoemaker, of Lancaster R. D. 6, and Richard W. Henry, son of Mr. and Mrs. Richard L. Henry, of Chestnut Level, will be married Friday, July 26, at 7 P. M., at the home of the bride's parents.

The Rev. G. Aubrey Young, pastor of the Chestnut Level Presbyterian church, will officiate.

Miss Muriel Shoemaker will attend her sister as maid of honor. The bridesmaids will be Miss Mary Henry, sister of the bridegroom, and Miss Sara Myers, of this city. David Henry, brother of the bridegroom, will serve as best man. The ushers will be Charles Shoemaker, brother of the bride, and Eugene Carrigan, of Liberty Square.

The wedding marches and incidental music will be played by Miss Florence Shaffner, harpist. Mrs. Kersey Bradley will be soloist.

A reception will follow the ceremony at the home of the bride.

Republican Club Lists Winners

The Seventh Ward Republican club will hold another in its series of card parties next Friday evening at 8:30 o'clock in the rooms, 134 Locust street.

Prizes at the party last evening were won by the following: Mrs. R. Eshelman, Jesse Brown, Mrs. Charles Schlinkman, Mrs. A. D. Kemp, I. Leicey, Elsie Forrest, Mrs. Kempfle, Laura Asper, Robert Slick, M. Miller, Mrs. Buller, Mrs. Edward Garnet, G. B. Ammon, George Miller, W. J. Bradshaw, Mrs. Reuben Weaver, H. W. Maurer, Mrs. A. D. Evans, Mrs. Llyod Beach, Carl Luneke, Mrs. Philip Olt, Mrs. Mary Bare, Mrs. W. S. Deen, Arthur Myers, Mrs. Irene Bauer, Mrs. M. Sheely, Goldenaire Yarrodd, Jacob Bowman, Mrs. Annie Oakley, Mary Jacoby, Mrs. Mary Stigelman, W. Gast,

Weddings

STOOPS—SCHROEDER

The marriage of Miss Janet Schroeder, daughter of Mr. and Mrs. J. Walter Schroeder, 138 Lancaster avenue, Columbia, and Harry M. Stoops, of Waynesboro, R. D. 2, took place this morning at Hagerstown, Md.

The couple was attended by Miss Jane Bigler, of Columbia, Mr. and Mrs. Chester Bair, of Waynesboro.

The bride was attired in a dark blue triple sheer dress with white accessories and wore a corsage of white rosebuds. Miss Bigler was dressed in a rose pink crepe dress with white accessories and she wore a corsage of pink rosebuds. Mrs. Bair was dressed in a dress of powder blue with white accessories and she wore a corsage of pink rosebuds.

A reception will be held at the home of the bride's parents at 5 P. M. for the bridal party, immediate families and friends, after which they will leave on a short wedding trip.

Mrs. Stoops is a graduate of the Columbia High School, class of 1937, and is employed as bookkeeper at Schroeder Auto Company. Mr. Stoops is a graduate of Quincy High School, Waynesboro, class of 1937, and is an employee of the Waynesboro Knitting Company.

HOROSCOPE

Exceptional success and good fortune will be the portion of those whose birthdays are today. They will benefit in various unexpected ways, and their undertakings will prosper. A stern and unyielding character is predicted for the child born on this date. Such a one will be somewhat morose, sarcastic and hard to understand, ever on the defensive and ready to resort to force. A great deal of latent power and unusual critical abilities are indicated, however.

HOROSCOPE FOR SUNDAY

The business prospects during the next year for today's birthday celebrants are of the very best. Some deception on the part of a relative threatens them, however, but they should make the most of their opportunities. The nature of the child born on this date will be firm and strong, brave to the point of recklessness, and admirably suited to a nautical career.

OTHER SOCIAL NEWS PAGE 7

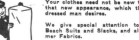

"Equal Rights" Urged as Plank At Convention

BY RUTH COWAN

CHICAGO, July 13.—(A. P.)—Helen Hunt West, youthful Jacksonville, Fla., attorney with large dark eyes, urged the Democratic platform committee to endorse an equal rights for women plank, declaring:

"Women are people and not angels in need of special legislative protection."

She turned a routine committee meeting into such a question-and-answer session yesterday that Senator Wagner of New York, chairman, adjourned the gathering because "the members are visiting as though they had a date."

Admittedly nervous but determined, Mrs. West, a former newspaper woman and the wife of a Jacksonville newspaper man, said: "I represent the National Association of Women Lawyers. What we want is equal legal rights with men as people.

"We have been protected a little like Norway for our own good—and we've suffered for it."

Senator Wagner and Committeeman Thomas Kennedy of Pennsylvania, cited instances of legislation to prevent women from working in dangerous occupations.

"I don't think legislators ever kept house," answered Mrs. West. "Furthermore, you don't favor protective legislation for weak men, do you? A man who isn't very strong doesn't take a miner's job. He becomes a bookkeeper, for example."

The Republican platform, she added, contains an equal rights plank.

Randolph Carpenter, the Kansas member of the committee, wanted to know how under the proposal women would be affected in case of conscription.

"If a nation decides to conscript its natural resources—well, women are part of those resources," said Mrs. West. "In time of war every nation becomes a dictatorship—and then all rules are off."

"Maybe," said Senator Pepper of Florida, "legislators in passing protective legislation were going on the assumption that women are angels and need protection."

"If they are acting on that assumption, I want to tell you they are making a mistake," shot back Mrs. West, breaking up the meeting.

"Speak Softly"

From her experience as dean of the Democratic National committeewomen, Mrs. James J. Billington of Jersey City, N. J., recommended today that the best way for a woman to get a man to agree with her is to "speak softly."

Here for her sixth National Democratic convention, Mrs. Billington, a pioneer suffrage worker, said women make a big mistake in campaigning in a loud voice and decorating themselves with badges when they are trying to enlist men in their cause.

Speak softly, wear feminine clothes and don't challenge men with arguments, but reason gently "in a motherly manner," and, according to Mrs. Billington, it is easy to win men over.

Mrs. Billington, who headed a group of women which called on President Wilson to urge him to come out for suffrage—and the next day he did!—ought to know.

Looking back on the 20 years that women have had the vote—which she helped them get—Mrs. Billington, now gray-haired and slow of step, was confident women have accomplished much good with the vote for themselves and for men.

One good thing women have done with the vote has been to clean up the voter, she said. Thanks to the feminine influence, voting now has dignity.

"Why, before women started going to the polls men used to vote anywhere—saloon backrooms, barns, just any old shack. Furthermore men were careless about how they looked when they went to vote. They didn't bother to get dressed up or put on a collar."

But that is changed now. Polls are usually set up in school houses or other public places, and when John Citizen comes to cast his ballot he usually has his neck and ears washed, for when men go where women are they want to make a good appearance, she said.

MARRIAGE ANNOUNCED

Miss Dorothy Shay, daughter of Mr. and Mrs. Harold Shay, and Richard R. Reardon, son of Mr. and Mrs. James B. Reardon, both of this city, were married on Saturday, July 6, at Warrenton, Va., with the Rev. Joseph S. Johnston officiating. The bride is a graduate of McCaskey High school, class of mid-1940, and was employed with F. W. Woolworth Co. Mr. Reardon is a graduate of McCaskey high school, class of mid-1938, and is associated with his father in business.

PLAN PARTY

A benefit card party will be held by the Lancaster County Industrial Council Union, this evening, at 8:30 o'clock, at 38 South Queen streeet.

You're Paying For An Electrical Refrigerator Whether You Own One or Not!

The Electric Refrigerator

Health Protection . . . Economy . . . Convenience

Of all the luxuries which Electricity has brought to man, none is more valuable than the Electric Refrigerator.

To the family who owns one, it brings an unvarying and absolute protection of those perishable foods upon which man depends for nourishment. By steadily maintaining a temperature below 50°, it prevents the growth of dangerous bacteria that may cause illness, even death.

It means greater convenience and more ease to the woman who prepares meals. Frozen desserts and chilled salads add richness to any meal and their preparation is simple with an Electric Refrigerator. Left-overs may be stored in safety until they're used. Perishable greens acquire new crispness . . . new life. And ice cubes abound for the quick and easy preparation of the cold drinks that are so welcome at all times.

Its operation is entirely automatic and without the need of any human attention. Night and day, regardless of outside temperature, the food compartment is maintained at a constant degree of cold that never varies beyond the limits of safety.

It is famous for economy. It allows the smart buyer to purchase perishables in quantity at bargain prices and store them until they're needed. And a great part of that spoiled food that is wasted every month by the family without adequate refrigeration could be kept fresh and good until needed.

Best of all, it is available to everyone. The rich man can buy no better refrigeration service than that which is easily accessible to nearly every other income group. Each gets the same health protection, the same dependability, automatic operation, convenience and freedom from worry.

WEATHER
Eastern Pennsylvania: Generally Fair And Not Quite So Warm Except For Scattered Afternoon Thundershowers In South Portion Wednesday; Slightly Cooler Wednesday Night; Thursday Fair.
Intell Journal Stormograph Reading: Fair Wednesday.

Intelligencer Journal

The Leading Newspaper in the Garden Spot of America. Home Owned for Home Folks Since 1794

Horse Racing
Eight Thirty won the Wilson Stakes at Saratoga track.
For details turn to Page 8.

VOLUME LXXVI.—NO. 278. CITY The Intelligencer Founded 1799 The Journal Founded 1794 LANCASTER, PA., WEDNESDAY MORNING, JULY 31, 1940. Entered at Post Office at Lancaster, Pa. as second class mail matter 14 PAGES, 112 COLUMNS.—THREE CENTS.

ITALIAN, NAZI 'BLITZ' FORCES MASSED

68 BUILDINGS RAZED IN CAMDEN FIRE

FEAR 10 DEAD AS FLAMES SWEEP 4-BLOCK AREA

500 National Guardsmen Patrol Section To Prevent Looting

300 MADE HOMELESS

Camden, N. J.—(AP)—Flames touched off by a series of explosions in a paint factory swept four city blocks of central Camden Tuesday, killing at least one factory employe, hiding the fate of seven others, and destroying the million-dollar plant, 67 adjoining homes and small business places.

Raymond Harter, 40, an employe of the extensive R. M. Hollingshead Company Paint and Chemical factory, where the blaze started at noon (EST), succumbed to burns in a hospital—first known fatality of a disaster officials feared might have caused ten or more deaths.

150 INJURED

At least seven workers in the plant were officially reported missing after the fire had been brought under control Tuesday night. Some 150 other persons, including firemen, were injured, two of them so seriously that physicians said they might die of burns.

So fierce and widespread was the blaze, described by police as "by far the worst" in Camden's history, that Mayor George E. Brunner decreed a state of emergency and 500 National Guardsmen patrolled the area with rifles as a protection against looting of homes and business establishments.

One suspected looter was menaced by a crowd as police sought to take him to headquarters for questioning.

1000 FLEE HOMES

More than a thousand men, women and children fled into the streets as explosion after explosion soundled throughout the densely-populated industrial and residential section.

Some of them were able to return

More of FIRE on Page 9

"We Lead All the Rest"
FARM CORNER
By
The Farm Editor

HONEY PRODUCERS PLAN DISTRICT TOUR

Local Group Will Attend Meeting At Sachs Apiary Near Biglerville Saturday

Officials of the local Honey Producers' association are planning an organized tour to a district meeting of beekeepers of Adams, Franklin, Cumberland, York and Lancaster counties, which is scheduled to be held at the apiary of E. H. Sachs, at Biglerville, Adams county, on Saturday afternoon, August 3, County Agent F. S. Bucher announced Tuesday.

The program arranged will include discussions and demonstrations conducted by prominent bee authorities of the state, with special attention to be given to the marketing phase of bee products.

The Lancaster group will assemble on the 400 block of W. Chestnut street, this city, at 10 o'clock (S.T.) Saturday morning, headed west. Those who go on the trip should carry a basket lunch.

SOME WHEAT CUT "TOO GREEN"

Great judgment is needed to determine when grain is dry enough to be combined and stored safely, and the machines have to be very carefully adjusted and operated to

More of FARM CORNER on Page 9

Intelligencer Journal Weather Calendar

COMPARATIVE TEMPERATURES

Station	High	Low
Intell Journal	95	72
Water Works	98	70
Ephrata	101	73
Last Year (Ephrata)	93	72
Official High for Year, July 26		102.5
Official Low for Year, Jan. 20		2
Character of Day		Clear

HOURLY TEMPERATURES

(Tuesday)			
8 a. m.	77	9 p. m.	77
11 a. m.	84	10 p. m.	77
2 p. m.	92	11 p. m.	77
5 p. m.	94	Midnight	75
		(Wednesday)	
6 p. m.	79	1 a. m.	74
7 p. m.	78	2 a. m.	74
8 p. m.	79	3 a. m.	74

HUMIDITY

8 a. m.—84 11 a. m.—64 2 p. m.—50
5 p. m.—54 8 p. m.—79 11 p. m.—79
Average Humidity 69
Dew Point, 11 p. m. 71

More of WEATHER on Page 7

DAYLIGHT TIME IN INTELL

All time mentioned in The Intelligencer Journal is Daylight Time unless otherwise noted.

Fire, Explosions Destroy Camden Factory

This is an aerial view made as fire and explosions destroyed the R. M. Hollingshead company paint plant in Camden, N. J. Loss was expected to reach millions. One employe was dead, seven were reported missing and hospital officials said at least 27 were so critically burned they might die. Fortunately half of the plant's 300 employes were at lunch when the first explosions shook the entire city of Camden.

116 STORES READY FOR SEMI-ANNUAL SALES DAY TODAY

Hour More Of Shopping To Be Provided At 37th Such Event

This is Lancaster Sales Day, the semi-annual event eagerly waited by thousands of consumers in the Lancaster trade area.

After thirty-six such sales, experienced shoppers need no assurance that this sale, the thirty-seventh, will be well worth while. Those who plan to visit Lancaster for the first time Wednesday (today) are sure to be delighted with the great assortment of merchandise from which they can select bargains.

STORES OPEN EARLY

One hundred and sixteen participating stores are ready to open at 8:30 a. m. a half hour earlier than usual. Stores will remain open an extra half-hour in the afternoon—until 5:30—thus giving buyers an extra hour for shopping.

Each of the 116 stores has made careful preparation for the event. Windows have been newly decorated (and incidentally, in the window of each participating store is a large, green and white sales day banner as a means of identification); stocks have been replenished; extra salespeople have been employed to take care of the expected crowds. Merchandise values and services will be excellent, making this an event worth planning to attend. Those who have not already made plans to come to Lancaster Wednesday may still do so to take advantage of this opportunity to fill personal and household needs at the reductions in effect for this one day only. Bargains will be available to the late afternoon shopper as well as to those who are on hand early in the morning.

AID TO ALLIES DRIVE LITERATURE ARRIVES

Local Unit of Committee To Defend America Also Has Buttons To Distribute At Headquarters

Buttons and literature relative to the newly organized Women's Division of the Committee to Defend America by Aiding the Allies are available at the local committee's headquarters, 117 East King street, it was announced Tuesday by Mrs. John F. Steinman, chairman of the local committee. The committee members are busy circulating petitions which are being sent to President Franklin D. Roosevelt and Congress asking them to aid those who are fighting against dictators of Europe. These buttons and literature are free and may be obtained at the headquarters.

Remember Last Year's Vacation

After the novelty of the first day or two wore off you felt lonesome and you wanted to hear from home, didn't you?

Arrange now to have the Intelligencer Journal mailed to you at your vacation address. No change in rates to regular subscribers for papers mailed to their vacation address, anywhere in the United States.

Simply notify your carrier boy or phone the newspaper office. 5252.

INTELLIGENCER JOURNAL

Heavy Storm Causes Damage, Fails To Crack Heat Wave

Wind Lashes Mount Joy-Florin Area, Lightning Fires Barn At Milton Grove; Two Killed By Bolts In Dauphin County; Temperature Here Hits 101

A violent wind and electrical storm caused substantial damage in the northwestern part of Lancaster county late Tuesday afternoon, but the twelve-day-old heat wave was unabated by scattered showers throughout this area.

Temperatures again went over 100 degrees—101 at Ephrata.

In nearby Dauphin county, two men were killed by lightning. One was Harold Nerozzi, thirty-two, of Hershey, struck while working near the Hershey Country club, and the other John Russell Livingston, twenty-two, killed by a bolt as he swam in the Susquehanna river near Rockville, five miles north of Harrisburg.

Another lightning bolt fired the barn of Clayton Gibble, at Milton Grove, destroying it.

Most wind damage occurred in Florin and Mount Joy. A chimney was blown down at the Rollman Manufacturing company plant in Mount Joy, and the rear door of the Mount Joy township school in Florin was blown from its hinges.

The sheet iron roof was blown from two garages in a row owned by William Weidman, near the railroad station in Florin, and a chimney was damaged at the home of Mrs. Selina Shires, Church street, Florin.

WIRES KNOCKED DOWN

Limbs from trees were scattered on the streets throughout the two towns. One limb, falling in front of Forney's store in Florin, tore down

More of STORM on Page 9

RUMANIA SEEKING TO KEEP CLAIMS 'WITHIN LIMITS'

Foreign Minister Threatens To Use Force To Scale Down Territorial Demands

Bucharest —(Wednesday)—(AP)—Foreign Minister Mihail Manoilescu expressed today the Rumanian government's determination to keep Hungarian and Bulgarian territorial claims "within certain limits"—by the use of force if necessary.

In a declaration after a cabinet meeting which had discussed Adolf Hitler's talks with Manoilescu and Premier Gigurtu in Salzburg, the foreign minister said Rumania was determined not to permit further loss of this country's territory in the manner by which Soviet Russia took Bessarabia and Northern Bucovina.

HARD BARGAIN SOUGHT

His remarks were interpreted in diplomatic quarters as meaning that the government was determined to drive with Hungary and Bulgaria a hard bargain in the forthcoming negotiations with those countries—negotiations to be held at Hitler's orders.

The foreign minister declared "we want peace but with justice for Rumania. We want the people of the interior and ever more those outside to know that the situation which happened a short time ago under unique circumstances (the Russian occupation of Bessarabia and Northern Bucovina) will not be repeated.

"It is necessary to maintain peace but if certain limits are exceeded, the Rumanians must use other ways."

Manoilescu said "Rumania means to grant greater minority rights and suggest an exchange of populations. Rumania recognizes she

More of RUMANIA on Page 9

ROOSEVELT CALLS FOR COOPERATION IN ECONOMIC FIELD

Rejects Idea U. S. Defeated In Efforts To Maintain Liberal Trade Principles

San Francisco —(AP)— President Roosevelt Tuesday night rejected the idea that the United States had been defeated in its efforts to maintain "liberal trade principles" and asserted that if it adopted "totalitarian control" over foreign trade it would be taking a step toward economic dictatorship.

He called for "the closest possible economic cooperation with other countries, particularly with those of the western hemisphere," but said that course would safeguard the progress made under the trade agreement program.

SENDS MESSAGE

In a message to the National Foreign Trade Convention, the Chief Executive wrote that it had been "suggested or implied by a few faint-hearted defeatists in re-

More of ROOSEVELT on Page 9

Last Chance to Order Anniversary Edition

Extra copies of Lancaster's 200th anniversary edition must be ordered before 9 o'clock tonight.

Orders can be placed at the Newspaper Office or by calling 5252 and asking for Circulation Department. Mail orders, postmarked tonight, will be accepted. A special order blank will be found on Page 19 of today's New Era.

Newsprint restrictions make it necessary to print just enough papers to supply regular subscribers and extra orders on file.

The Anniversary edition will tell the story of Lancaster past and present in pictures and

WORKMAN KILLED BY LIGHTNING AT HERSHEY; 4 HURT

Bolt Hits Group Near Country Clubhouse As They Put Their Tools Away

Hershey—Harold Nerozzi, thirty-two, of 40 W. Areba st., was instantly killed and four other men were injured when lightning struck a tree near a group of workmen at the Hershey Country club at 4 p. m. Tuesday.

Nerozzi and the others had been working on an addition to the clubhouse, and were putting away their tools as the storm arose suddenly. The bolt shattered the large tree near them, damaged an electric light pole nearby, and felled the five men. Nerozzi's hat was torn from his head and ripped into two pieces.

TAKEN TO HOSPITAL

The injured, suffering from minor burns and shock, were taken by ambulance to the Hershey hospital. Charles Jameson, forty-five, of Campbelltown, most seriously injured, remained at the hospital overnight. Part of his clothing was torn off by the bolt.

Others injured, released from the hospital after treatment, were Riley Placket, thirty-nine, Swatara; George Rey, sixty, Hershey, and Russell Putt, forty-six, Hershey.

Dr. H. H. Hostetter, Dauphin county deputy coroner, issued a certificate of death from lightning shock in the case of Nerozzi.

EMPLOYED BY HERSHEY ESTATES

Nerbzzi was employed by the Hershey Estates for several years. He is survived by his wife, Mary; his parents, Mr. and Mrs. Guido Nerozzi, Philadelphia; a brother, Peter, Philadelphia, and six sisters: Mrs. Joseph Braun, Philadelphia; Mrs. Benney Cagnoli, Hershey; Mrs. Francis Monzoni, Miss Pearl Nerozzi and Mrs. Matthew Ballerino, Philadelphia, and Mrs. Sylvester Weidler, Hershey.

BOY SWALLOWS KEROSENE

Robert Gerlitzki, fourteen months old, 2 Breneman Court, was admitted to the Lancaster General hospital Tuesday evening after he swallowed a quantity of kerosene at his home. Attendants said his condition was fair.

SENATE GROUP OKAYS PLAN TO CALL OUT GUARD

Gen. Marshall Says Training Proposal Necessary, Endorses Conscription

LATTER BOGS DOWN

Washington — (AP) — President Roosevelt's appeal for power to call out the National Guard and Officers Reserve Corps for training—a proposal backed unstintedly by the Army—received Tuesday the quick approval of the Senate Military Committee.

Its action came shortly after it had heard General George C. Marshall, the chief of staff, describe such an authorization as urgently necessary and add a strong endorsement of selective conscription—a proposal apparently bogged down in congressional controversy.

DECLINES TO BE DRAWN OUT

On the latter subject, President Roosevelt declined to be drawn out at a press conference—although the committee earlier had engaged in an acrimonious dispute over a Republican demand that he make his views known.

When a reporter asked his attitude toward the pending Burke-Wadsworth Bill—requiring all men 18 to 64 inclusive, to register for possible selective training—he said he did not care to go into details. To this, he added the statement that a lot of machines without men to run them were worthless, and many men without machines were equally valueless.

This led some to the conclusion that the President favored conscription, but at no more rapid a rate than the men called up could be provided with equipment for their training.

Chairman Sheppard, Dem., Texas, of the Senate Military Commit-

More of DEFENSE on Page 9

LOCAL GUARDSMEN ARE INCLUDED IN TRAINING PROGRAM

Two Units Of 213th Regiment, Located Here, Would Get Year's Training

Two units of Lancaster guardsmen will be among the first to be called for a year's active training service if the bill now in Congress is passed. They are Battery E and Second Battalion Headquarters Combat company, 213th Regiment, anti-aircraft, Coast Artillery.

Battery E is commanded by Captain David J. Evans and the Headquarters company is commanded by Lieutenant C. Stauffer. Battery E has three officers and 111 men and the headquarters company is composed of two officers and 35 men. Both units are now at full peacetime strength.

TWO UNITS AT LEBANON

Two units of the 213th are located at Lebanon. They are Battery H, commanded by Captain George Tucker, and First Battalion Headquarters Combat company, Captain R. O. Bowman, commander.

Colonel Charles C. Curtis, of Allentown, regimental commander, has been advised the regiment will train at Virginia Beach, Va., should legislation urged by General George C. Marshall, army chief of staff, receive Congressional approval.

The 213th is Pennsylvania's only regiment included in the call. Other units are stationed at Allentown, Reading, Bethlehem, Easton and Pottsville.

MEN READY TO GO

Colonel Curtis said Tuesday night:

"Our men are ready to go. If the President sees fit to call us into

More of GUARDSMEN on Page 9

Eight Nations, In Signing Havana Document, Make Reservations

But Secretary Hull Sails For Home With Expressed Feeling That Much Has Been Accomplished

Havana — (AP) — The historic conference of Havana, which bolstered the Monroe Doctrine with new bars against war dangers from Europe—despite the last-minute qualifications and reservations of Argentina and seven other of the 21 American republics — ended Tuesday night with a flurry of cheers, speech-making and document-signing.

Argentine delegate Leopold Melo argued against the "conjectural hypothesis" of need of action concerning European colonies in the Western Hemisphere, and contended that setting up machinery to occupy them was like calling in a specialist for a disease not yet suffered.

He made the reservation that the convention creating such machinery would require Argentine congressional ratification before participation. Mexico, Chile, Bolivia, Colombia, Venezuela, Peru and Uruguay also made eleventh-hour reservations.

Nevertheless, U. S. Secretary of

More of CONFERENCE on Page 7

Troops, Equipment Reported Ready In Bases Near Britain

COMMUNAL FEEDING PROPOSED IN BRITAIN

London—(AP)—Home cooking soon may be forbidden in Britain, to be replaced by communal feeding for the populace—rich and poor alike sharing simple fare in government-controlled "mass-production dining halls in an effort to strengthen the war effort by economizing on food supplies.

Whitehall circles disclosed that the groundwork is being laid for possible introduction of such a far-reaching project, but said that details have not been worked out.

Labor quarters are described as especially enthusiastic about the proposal, since they see it as the solution to their protest against "luxury dining-out" by persons who can pay the price.

Hitler Limits Italian Participation In Drive To "Token" Forces

CLOSES SWISS BORDER

Bern, Switzerland — (Wednesday) — Italian fighting planes and German-trained Italian troops were reported today to be massed alongside Nazi blitzkrieg forces for a part in the invasion of England.

Italian sources in Switzerland said that plane-load after plane-load of parachute troops, veterans of battles in Ethiopia and Spain, have flown across France to take-off bases from the Bay of Biscay to the low countries facing the English Channel and North Sea.

Reports have been current in foreign diplomatic circles that Premier Benito Mussolini specifically asked Adolf Hitler to let the Italians share the job of bringing Britain to her knees.

Il Duce was said to have wanted a strong part for his troops in a direct invasion of the shores where Caesar's legions landed almost 2,000 years ago.

Hitler was said to have agreed —but to have limited Italy's part in invasion to "token" land and parachute forces, plus large air squadrons for bombing and ferrying troops.

Reports from France, Germany, Italy and Spain all indicated that Germany is making her last minute preparations for the blow.

German and Italian travelers from Spain said the Nationalist government there appeared to be preparing to try to grab Gibraltar—a move which it long has been reported may coincide with a German attack on England across the channel.

These sources said troops in small armed boats carrying artillery were concentrated near La Linea, Spain, behind Gibraltar.

Reports from France said the Italians were concentrating bombing planes at their Sardinian bases for an air attack on Gibraltar—another move expected in a coordinated German attempt to invade Britain.

'POCKET' SUBS DELIVERED

Italian informants reported that the last of the Italian-made "pocket" submarines—about 36 feet long—had passed through the Brenner Pass in sections on railway flat cars. These little submarines are expected to be one of the main protecting arms of the expected German channel attempt.

(In Germany Tuesday it was stated that any speculation that the movements of Nazi troops in German-occupied parts of France were for specific purposes would come under the head of military secrets.)

CLOSE SWISS BORDER

All rail and road frontier posts on the Swiss-German frontier, except that at Saint Margarethen in Austria, were closed Tuesday by the Germans, apparently to ensure secrecy of troops movements through

More of TROOPS on Page 9

BRITAIN EXTENDS BLOCKADE TO RING SPAIN, PORTUGAL

Every Ship At Sea Liable To Seizure Unless Navicert Is Carried, Under New Rule

London —(AP)— A vast extension of the British blockade designed to close every possible avenue to Germany and Italy and especially to ring Spain and Portugal lest war supplies be trans-shipped there was announced in Commons Tuesday.

CLAIM HARBORS PARALYZED BY REPEATED AIR RAIDS

Berlin, (Wednesday) — (AP) —Repeated air raids have virtually paralyzed England's south and east coast harbors, informed German sources claimed today, driving sea-borne commerce to the west coast where ports are inadequately equipped to handle the increased traffic.

Hugh Dalton, Minister of Economic Warfare, disclosed the innovation of a new and sweeping policy under which:

1. Every ship in the Atlantic ocean will be subject to seizure by the Royal navy unless its master can produce a navicert—British-approved certificates of clearance—for its entire cargo.

2. Spanish and Portuguese imports will be limited strictly to their own needs, supplies to be permitted to reach such neutrals in "imports adequate for domestic consumption, but not for re-export."

It was explained authoritatively that with the broadening of the navicert requirement, Britain hoped

More of BLOCKADE on Page 9

SWIMMERS HURT

John Kast, fourteen, 751 Fremont st., was treated at St. Joseph's hospital Tuesday for a lacerated right foot, suffered while swimming. Fred White, Jr., fourteen, 603 E. Madison st., was treated at the Lancaster General hospital Tuesday for a lacerated scalp, suffered when he struck a rock while diving.

Thieves Throw Cash Register Into Dam Near Lexington

An electric cash register, valued at $400, stolen from the hardware and general store operated by M. N. Zimmerman in Martindale, early Saturday, was recovered in Zortman's dam on Hammer creek near Lexington, Tuesday afternoon.

Corporal F. X. Kelly, of the Ephrata sub-station, who is investigating, said Charles Zortman, owner of a mill at that place, discovered the drawer of the cash register floating in the mill race. He notified police who found the cash register about a half-mile upstream, protruding from the water.

The cash drawer had been smashed before it was removed, Corporal Kelly said, but the register was in good condition otherwise and was returned to Zimmerman. Four one dollar bills and twelve dollars in silver were taken from the machine. The store robbery also netted the thieves 2 guns, twenty-eight pocket watches, three wrist watches and three safety razors.

LANCASTER NEW ERA

WEATHER
Fair and continued cool tonight and Sunday. (Details on Page 3.)

Examiner Founded 1830. New Era Founded 1877. Published Every Evening Except Sunday by New Era Company. Entered as Second Class Matter at Post Office, Lancaster, Pa.

LANCASTER, PA., SATURDAY, AUGUST 10, 1940 POSTSCRIPT EDITION 14 PAGES—112 COLUMNS—THREE CENTS

COMPROMISE ON DRAFT IS TURNED DOWN

Barkley Says Compulsory and Volunteer Plans Can Not Be Linked.

CONSCRIPTION DELAY TO JAN. 1 SUGGESTED

WASHINGTON, Aug. 10—(A. P.)—Administration leaders turned a cold shoulder today to talk of a compromise in the Senate fight over conscription.

Senator Barkley of Kentucky, the Democratic floor leader, expressed the opinion to reporters that conscription and voluntary enlistments could not be linked successfully in such a system as that offered by Senator Maloney (D-Conn), as a substitute for the Burke-Wadsworth bill.

Maloney would require the registration of all men from 21 through 30, as would the Burke-Wadsworth bill, but he would delay the draft until January 1 while

SEN. BARKLEY SEES FIGHT ON DRAFT ALREADY WON

WASHINGTON, Aug. 10 — (U. P.)—Senate Majority Leader Alben W. Barkley said today that the administration's fight for the first peace-time conscription law already is won though the debate in the Senate will continue for weeks.

He expressed himself as "well-pleased" with the first day's debate on the controversial legislation, on the Burke-Wadsworth compulsory military training bill, and predicted that conscription opponents would fail to muster more than 25 votes.

Members of the anti-conscription bloc, he said, have admitted to him that their opposition cannot continue for more than a week. He added, however, that lengthy debate on other controversial issues in the past may signify that the debate will continue for at least two weeks.

voluntary enlistments were sought. If these enlistments did not fill the Army's quota, conscription would be ordered.

(Army enlistments totaled 23,442 in June and 31,958 in July, a peacetime record. The Army's strength was 270,183 on July 31, and will be brought to 322,922 as quickly as possible.)

Proposal Gets Support

Maloney said his proposal appeared to be attracting increasing support, despite administration opposition and the reluctance of conscription opponents to agree that the draft might be needed while the nation was at peace.

One of the latter group, Senator Nye (R-ND), said he was willing to have men from 21 through 30 registered in order to have the draft machinery ready if war came, but could see no reason for abandoning the traditional American peacetime policy of voluntary enlistments.

He predicted that supporters would find it necessary to compromise the Burke-Wadsworth bill before they could obtain Senate approval.

This view was echoed in private by one administration strategist, who said he had no doubt that some sort of conscription bill would be voted by the chamber. He said it was "touch and go," however, whether the Maloney proposal or

(See DRAFT—Page 9)

FRANCE IS AGAINST TOTAL PROHIBITION

VICHY, France, Aug. 10—(A. P.)—The new French government is determined to do something to restrict the use of alcohol, but will not "make the same mistake the United States made through total prohibition," the French press declared today.

The newspapers said manufacturers would be permitted to continue making wines, cider, beer and alcohol distilled from hops and grape juices.

The Scribbler

MRS. ALBERT H. HOSTETTER, of 901 Manor street, was given a car other than the one she usually drives when she called at her husband's garage the other evening.

After a few blocks, mostly downgrade, the car gave a "whoof" and stopped dead. Mrs. Hostetter got it going again, but after a short run it gave up for good. She fussed around for quite a while, gave up, and finally called the garage to "come and tour this old wreck back!"

She had been given a car that had been undergoing repairs. The gas tank had been removed. Her trip lasted, apparently, only until the gas line was cleared.

A READER is aroused by poor spelling on the Lincoln Highway East. He tells us a market just across the bridge at Bridgeport advertises VEGATABLES for sale.

FOLKS YOU KNOW: We hear from Strasburg that Mrs. Clifford Bair could not understand why she couldn't start her car the other evening, until she discovered she was using the wrong key. . . . Miss Ann Maley, department store millinery expert, was seen bouncing a rubber ball when business was quiet. . . . Bob Ditzler, the barber, was trusted to watch a roast of meat, but let it burn.

More Local Guardsmen Off to War Games

Top: Young soldiers eager for field training are these members of Headquarters Company and Combat Train, 213th Coast Artillery, gathered at the Armory this morning just before leaving at 4:25 for the war games in New York State.

Left: Six-year-old Joseph Evans says goodbye to his daddy, Sergeant Abram Evans.

Right: "Don't forget the pennon—we usually forget something," Lieutenant Carryl E. Stauffer, left, tells Private First Class Cornelius Heipler, battery clerk.

F. D. INSPECTING MORE DEFENSES

Begins Week-End Tour at Portsmouth, N. H.; Heads For Boston.

PORTSMOUTH, N. H., Aug. 10—(A. P.)—President Roosevelt began a week-end inspection of New England sea and land defenses today by observing conditions at the Portsmouth Navy Yard where five submarines costing $27,500,000 were being built and plans for several others were being drafted.

Accompanied by Secretary of the Navy Frank Knox, the Chief Executive arrived by train at 8:59 A. M. (Lancaster time) from Hyde Park, N. Y., and went immediately to the yard. Francis P. Murphy, Republican Governor of New Hampshire, joined the Presidential party at the railroad station.

New Hampshire and Maine State Police combined with secret service men in closely guarding the President as he was driven under a scorching sun to the yard over a route from which traffic had been cleared.

The commandant of the year, Rear Admiral John D. Wainwright, also joined the President at the station and rode with him to the base.

Driving about the plant, the President saw where facilities were being expanded as rapidly as possible.

(See F. D.—Page 11)

N. Y. WRITER LEAPS TO HIS DEATH

NEW YORK, Aug. 10—(A. P.)—Shouting a warning to pedestrians below, Harlan C. McIntosh, 32-year-old writer, plunged to his death last night from the roof of a five-story apartment in Greenwich Village.

Police listed the death as suicide. They said McIntosh handed several notes to Frank Ferraro, a taxi driver who had delivered him to his apartment a few minutes before.

One note, addressed to "Darling Jane" said: "Can't go on without you. God bless you."

A letter signed "Mom," which was left with Ferraro, was written on stationery of the Department of Journalism, Oregon State College, Corvallis, Ore. Its contents were not disclosed.

EXPENSIVE RESCUES, PAIR LOSE WALLETS

OCEAN CITY, Md., Aug. 10—(A. P.)—Elmer Perdue and Louis Joseph found it costly business rescuing two girls from possible drowning.

Perdue, who plunged into the waves fully clothed, watched his pocketbook float away during the rescue.

Joseph, who had taken off his trousers and shoes, returned to shore to find "some beachcomber had made off with my wallet."

2 GO FISHING, CATCH A DEER

EASTPORT, Me., Aug. 10—(A. P.)—Here's a fish story—about two men who went deep sea fishing and caught a deer.

William Conley and Remington Whelpley of Eastport, spotted the animal swimming around as they neared the fishing grounds several miles off that town.

The deer was almost exhausted so they hauled it into their boat, carried it ashore and freed it in the woods.

HOODED BANDIT KIDNAPS GIRL

Forces Her Escort From Auto and Drives Her to Her Home.

BADEN, Pa., Aug. 10—(A. P.)—A masked gunman kidnaped a 19-year-old Baden girl early today after forcing her escort from their automobile near this Beaver county community.

Colleen Hetherington told Corp. Paul Rittlemann of the State Motor Police the hooded man drove her over country roads for more than an hour and then left her in the machine near her home.

The girl related, Rittlemann said, that the man forced her escort, John Johnson, 22, to drive into the country after entering the car parked on a lane two blocks from her home about 1:15 A. M.

Johnson was put out of the machine a mile east of Baden and told by the masked man to walk

(See BANDIT—Page 9)

WHEN YOU PACK YOUR BAG

When you have packed your bag and before you make final checkup to leave on your vacation, just pick up your telephone and call 5252. Circulation Department. Tell us to have the New Era sent to you, and then your vacation will be complete. There is no extra charge to regular subscribers. You cannot afford to take the chance of spoiling your vacation for the small sum of 18c per week.

TWO FUGITIVES HELD IN DEATH

Toss Body of Woman From Auto; Wound Oklahoma Cop.

OILTON, Okla., Aug. 10—(A. P.)—Two prison fugitives who hurled the shot-torn body of a woman clad in red from their speeding automobile, wounded Oilton's police chief and kidnaped a farmer, were held today as officers hunted a motive for the woman's death.

The gunmen, Bill Hall, 25, and Joe Lovelace, 24, surrendered to highway patrolmen west of here last night after a running gunfight. Hall had been shot five times.

Bill Glimp of Drumright, the farmer hostage, had a flesh wound in one leg. Patrolmen mistook him for one of the fugitives.

Sheriff L. L. Fisher said Lovelace declared the slain woman, whom he identified as Jeanne Culp, 30, Asher, Okla., was thrown from the car because "she seemed to be dead" and Hall complained that her body interfered with his driving.

As they drove through Oilton following a pistol-shotgun duel in which Police Chief Ben D. Clark was critically wounded, Lovelace said he noticed the woman was badly hit. He contended, Fisher said, that he did not know who shot her, nor did he account for her presence in the car.

Clark and Constable C. L. Irwin, hunting three men who robbed an Oilton restaurant earlier in the day, halted a black sedan in which Hall, Lovelace, the woman and a Negro were riding.

Police Chief Wounded

The officers leaped to the running boards. A point-blank shotgun charge knocked Clark to the

(See FUGITIVES—Page 9)

LAST UNITS OFF FOR N. Y. TODAY

Headquarters Co. on Way, Battery E Entrains For Camp Tonight.

Just before dawn today another unit of local National Guardsmen—the Headquarters Company and Combat Train of the 213th Coast Artillery—left the armory for the war games in northern New York state.

Lieutenant Carryl E. Stauffer, in a regulation station wagon, led the unit, traveling in five trucks, away from the armory at 4:25 A. M. The company includes another officer, Second Lieutenant William S. Renkin, and 35 men.

The last local outfit to leave for the maneuvers, Battery E, 213th Coast Artillery, commanded by Capt. David J. Evans, entrains at the Pennsylvania Railroad station at 11:08 o'clock tonight.

Most members of the headquarters company stayed up all night to be on time for the trip. While

(See GUARDS—Page 9)

Pinchot at 75 Favors Draft, Deplores Delay by Congress

Ex-Governor Refrains from Comment on Political Outlook

MILFORD, Pa., Aug. 10—(U. P.)—Former Governor Gifford Pinchot, feeling "fit as a fiddle" on the eve of his 75th birthday anniversary, today supported the proposed conscription bill and urged this country to aid Great Britain by selling her destroyers.

"I am emphatically in favor of the selective draft," said the tall forester who served two terms as Chief Executive of Pennsylvania. He will observe his birthday anniversary tomorrow at Gray Towers, his Pike county home, with a "half dozen or so" friends who are stopping for lunch.

"I am opposed to the inexcusable waste of time in experimenting

(See PINCHOT—Page 9)

GIFFORD PINCHOT

FARLEY TAKES POSITION WITH EXPORT FIRM

Postmaster General Heads Coca Cola's Foreign Sales Branch.

HE ALSO PREPARES TO HEAD N. Y. YANKEES

WILMINGTON, Del., Aug. 10—(A. P.)—James A. Farley, retiring Postmaster General and Democratic National chairman, today was appointed chairman of the Coca-Cola Export corporation.

Robert W. Woodruff, chairman of the Coca-Cola Company's board of directors, announced Farley had accepted a position "in charge of all export business and particularly of the expansion of our business in foreign countries."

Farley's resignation as Democratic chairman becomes effective Aug. 17 and he leaves the cabinet Aug. 31.

Woodruff indicated the retiring Postmaster General would report here after a vacation and said his headquarters would be in Wilmington.

A company spokesman said Farley has been "acquainted for years" with Woodruff and that his appointment climaxes discussion between the two "over a considerable period."

It is up to Farley, the spokesman added, to say whether he will disclose his salary and when he will start his new job.

Reports have been current that the retiring Democratic leader, who bowed out of politics after his party's recent National convention, would head a syndicate to purchase the New York Yankees American League baseball club.

A Coca-Cola company official said he did not believe Farley's position as head foreign salesman for the soft drink would interfere with any plans he might have about the baseball team. He added, however, that Farley must make this decision himself.

May Also Head Yankees

In New York, a close friend of Farley said the Postmaster General's new position with the Coca-Cola corporation in no way would interfere with his negotiations to buy the New York Yankee baseball property.

He added, in fact, that the transaction probably would be completed next week.

with the Yankees and there are only a few matters to be ironed out," the friend said. "There is nothing serious in the way of completing the purchase."

Farley and a group of unidentified associates have been reported to have offered approximately $4,000,000 for the club.

Farley has refused comment on all questions concerning the Yankee position would be his only business deal. Friends said his coca-cola connection in private life, except for the Yankee matter.

Farley said in a statement he would take at least a month's vacation before assuming his new duties.

Forley Says He's Fortunate

The statement said:

"For a long time I have indicated my desire to retire to private life for reasons that I have frequently given. I consider myself extremely fortunate, therefore, to be associated with the Coca-Cola company, which is one of the outstanding business concerns in the world.

"My duties will be in connection with their export business. I know I am going to be very happy in my new work. I have had no vacation for a long time and I shall take at

(See FARLEY—Page 11)

ADJUST TAXES ON CRAMP SHIPYARD

PHILADELPHIA, Aug. 10—(A. P.)—Reopening of the long-closed Cramp shipyards moved a step nearer today with approval by City Council and the Board of Education of a compromise on $1,300,000 delinquent taxes.

The city agreed to settle its claim for $100,000 and the Board of Education decided to accept $35,000 from that amount plus about $50,000 guaranteed for 1940.

Mayor Robert E. Lamperton said, however, that the firm, controlled by the Harriman interests of New York, must bank $2,500,000 of the $5,000,000 estimated necessary for rehabilitation or the proposed purchase plan through sheriff's sale September 16 will be cancelled.

Stukas Raid Balloons Over British Convoy

Whistling Shells Rained on British Coast in "Terror" Attacks; Fascists Bomb Berbera, Claim Gains in Africa

By The Associated Press

German bombers, power-diving at 400 miles an hour, unloaded explosives in mass attacks today on British ships protected by balloon barrages and rained whistling bombs on coastal Britain in heavy "terror" raids.

The Germans attacking the balloon-protected ships off the southeast coast were reported to have been driven off without hitting their targets by anti-aircraft fire.

The Nazi High Command claimed destruction of the 12 of the big balloons, anchored to the ships by long cables, in Thursday's heavy air fighting over the English Channel.

Drop Dozen Whistling Bombs

Aiming one of the biggest assaults of the war that the northwest coast has experienced, the Nazis dropped a dozen whistling bombs, whose ear-splitting screeching frightens as well as does damage.

Heavy explosive bombs showered on another sector in that area killed four persons, injured two and damaged residential property but missed military objectives.

Two men were killed and a number injured in a raid on a northeast coastal town.

In a second raid on shipping off the southeast coast, German bombers ran into heavy anti-aircraft fire, hurriedly deposited three bombs which missed their mark and scurried back toward France.

The raid on the balloons came as the belligerent powers settled down to a punishing war of air power and the United Kingdom, the European continent and Africa felt and heard the crash of bombs, the thunder of anti-aircraft fire and chattering of machinegun fire in growing volume.

Italy Claims Further Gains

Italy claimed further gains in her land drive into British Somaliland and all the belligerents issued communiques telling of aerial exploits.

THE GERMANS SAID:

Their methodical bombers, working "on schedule," blasted British airplane and munitions plants, causing great fires and explosions; destroyed an airport runway north of Bristol and blasted shipyards; German anti-aircraft batteries brought down two British planes, bringing their total bag for the war to 1,500 "enemy" planes.

THE ITALIANS SAID:

Their columns, pushing into Somaliland, have passed Adueins, east of Hargeisa; their planes bombed Berbera, main seaport of British Somaliland; their warplanes hit British objectives along the Egyptian coast; British battleship Resolution and a destroyer were damaged seriously by bombs Aug. 1.

THE BRITISH SAID:

Their aircraft bombed an Italian vessel in Tobruk Harbor,

(See AIR RAIDS—Page 11)

NAZI ACE TELLS OF BALLOON RAID

Miles of Steel Cable Fall With Much Damage, He Declares.

BERLIN, Aug. 10—(A. P.)—A Nazi pilot who participated in Thursday's first air attack on a balloon barrage-protected British convoy told in a German broadcast today watching six of the big rubber balls crash in blue and red flames.

The pilot was identified as aviator-reporter Hans Theodor Wagner.

"Six went down," he said, "leaving long sheets of smoke behind them. Those miles of steel cables must have caused confusion and damage when they crashed down.

"A number of the barrier balloons were plainly visible near Dover. They were at a height of 2,000 meters (6,560 feet), just below the cloud ceiling.

"When our first Heinkels reached the balloons, volleys from their machine-guns tore up the well-rounded envelopes and a moment later billowed flames quivered from within them.

"While the first balloon was quickly enveloped in flames and descended, British crews below at motor winches tried in vain to pull down the others or to release them so they could ascend into the clouds out of our view.

"But we were too fast and volley after volley penetrated the balloons."

POLICE RESTRAIN BOY, 12, ON LEDGE

NEW YORK, Aug. 10—(A. P.)—It took a police emergency call to quell 12-year-old David Hershkowitz' tantrum over his mother's request that he take a bath.

David really put on a show. Folks from all around his East Side neighborhood came to watch the spectacle of a husky lad standing perilously close to the edge of a third-floor fire escape and shouting to his mother:

"If you won't leave me alone, I'll take a jump."

Somebody called the cops. Two patrol cars answered, and out of one stepped patrolman Edward Stack. David yielded at the sight of the uniform—and took his bath.

15 FROM HERE GOING TO ELWOOD

Fifteen Lancastrians have notified Walter Foust, chairman of the committee on arrangements, that they intend to go to Elwood, Indiana, next week-end to hear Wendell Willkie make his speech of acceptance of the Republican Presidential nomination.

The party will travel by special train which will carry Pennsylvanians to the ceremonies. They leave here next Friday night and return Sunday evening. Foust said there are accommodations for a few more in the all-Lancaster car, and invites anyone interested to consult him before tomorrow night.

CHILD IS CRITICALLY INJURED BY AUTO

WEST CHESTER, Aug. 10—Patricia Chandler, four, daughter of Mr. and Mrs. Ross Chandler, West Chester, was in a critical condition at the Homeopathic Hospital from head injuries suffered when struck by a car operated by John W. Owens, seventy-three, Jeffersonville, Montgomery county, last night.

The girl was playing with other children near her home when she darted into the path of the auto, police said. Owens was held in $500 bail on a technical charge of assault and battery by auto.

IT'S SKOKIE NOW, NOT NILES CENTER

NILES CENTER, Ill., — After wrangling for two years about it, this Chicago suburb has finally agreed to change its name.

A committee of village trustees and civic leaders decided the community should henceforth be known as Skokie (pronounced Skokee, accent on the first syllable).

Citizens clamoring for a new name said Niles Center made the suburb sound like a hick town. Opponents said Oshkosh, Wis., and Kalamazoo, Mich., were doing all right despite their names.

Skokie is an Indian name. The village is in the Skokie Valley.

FOOD STAMP PLAN FOR PHILADELPHIA

HARRISBURG, Aug. 10—(A. P.)—Extension of the stamp plan of food distribution to families on relief in the Philadelphia area has been approved by the Federal Government, Howard L. Russell, Secretary of Public Assistance, announced today.

Russell said he was notified by Henry A. Wallace, Secretary of Agriculture, that an agreement between the Assistance Department, the city, and the Federal Surplus Marketing Administration has been approved, making surplus foods available free to 50,000 families on relief rolls in the city.

Under the plan, Relief families or those on WPA purchase orange stamps good for any foods, and receive free blue stamps which entitle them to foods designated as surplus commodities. The plan allows one free blue stamp for each two orange stamps purchased.

WEATHER

Eastern Pennsylvania: Fair Wednesday And Thursday; Little Change In Temperature.
Intell Journal Stormograph Reading: Fair Wednesday.

Intelligencer Journal

The Leading Newspaper in the Garden Spot of America, Home Owned for Home Folks Since 1794

VOLUME LXXVI.—NO. 308. CITY The Intelligencer Founded 1799 The Journal Founded 1794 LANCASTER, PA., WEDNESDAY MORNING, SEPTEMBER 4, 1940 Entered at Post Office at Lancaster, Pa. as second class mail matter 16 PAGES, 128 COLUMNS.—THREE CENTS.

Football

Thirty-six gridders report to Coach Alan Holman at Franklin and Marshall College. Mike Kenny fails to report.
For details turn to Page 10.

BRITISH REJOICE AS U. S. EXCHANGES 50 DESTROYERS FOR NAVAL AND AIR BASES

RUMANIAN GUNMEN TRY TO SLAY KING CAROL

ARMY CRUSHES PLOT TO PLACE SON ON THRONE

Iron Guard Blamed For Attack On Palace, Radio And 'Phone Centers

AIM AT KING'S WINDOW

Bucharest, (Wednesday) — Gunmen attempted in vain to assassinate King Carol last night in an alleged Iron Guardist plot to seize power and place Prince Mihai on the throne.

While the would-be assassins broke through the palace guard and fired seven shots at a lighted window in Carol's palace, other groups of Iron Guardists attacked the Bucharest radio station and the American-owned telephone company's central office.

Similar coups were attempted at Brasov and Constanza but were quickly crushed.

TWO REPORTED WOUNDED

One Iron Guardist and one palace guard were reported shot in the assassins' attempt to storm the palace here, but neither was wounded fatally.

Many shots were fired in the palace grounds before the attackers were overcome and hustled away by soldiers in the car in which they had arrived at the palace.

Several men entered the telephone exchange and wrecked some of the switchboards with hatchets. Most local lines were put out of order. The radio station went off the air after a group of men in uniform burst in and tried to destroy the equipment. All were arrested.

The fact that a coup had been attempted was acknowledged in an official communique, but the

More of GUNMEN On Page 14

First Recruit Sworn In Here In P. N. G. Enlistment Drive

The drive to recruit Lancaster's two units of the 213th Coast Artillery to full strength before they move out for a year's training got off to a flying start Tuesday night. The first sworn in by Captain David J. Evans, commander of Battery E, was Garland W. Lambert (right), a native—of all places—of War, W. Va. Administering the oath to Lambert is Captain Evans, with Paul C. Long, battery clerk, in the background. Lambert, who resides at 335 N. Queen st., came here three months ago as a furniture buyer for his brother, T. E. Lambert, who operates stores in West Virginia. (Intell photo)

British Also Pledge Not To Sink Or Surrender Fleet To Nazis In Return For 'Over-Age' Craft From The U. S.

ADMIT NEED

Admiralty Head Says Fleet Will Be Of "Inestimable Value"

TOO LATE, SAY NAZIS

London—(AP)—The British rejoiced Tuesday night wherever they gathered from Cheapside pubs to the austere and misty corridors of the foreign office, over the news that fifty over-age U. S. destroyers will fill the gaps of the royal navy in the total German siege of these islands.

First Lord of the Admiralty A. V. Alexander in a statement greeted "with the utmost pleasure and satisfaction" the transfer of destroyers. He added: "They come at a time when the strain upon our destroyer fleet has been very great and will be of inestimable value to us not only for escorting convoys but also for protecting our coasts from the threat of invasion."

Moreover, he added, "this event will strengthen the feeling of goodwill and friendship between our two great peoples."

The official reaction from a foreign office spokesman was that "successful conclusion of this agreement (for delivery to Britain of the destroyers; for lease to the United States of North and South Atlantic air and naval bases) is greeted with the greatest possible satisfaction by His Majesty's government and the peoples of the British Empire and Commonwealth of Nations."

SPOKESMAN ENTHUSIASTIC

The traditionally careful spokesman could not restrain his personal enthusiasm. He greeted reporters with the words: "For once I've got some good news for you."

On the street the little man read

More of REACTION On Page 14

Map shows location of proposed chain of naval and air bases for defending the eastern seaboard, rights to which have been obtained from Great Britain in exchange for 50 over-age U. S. destroyers. President Roosevelt announced he had arranged the deal after assurance from Attorney General Jackson that he possessed legal authority, and informed Congress of what he had done.

CONGRESS TOLD

President Says Bases Will Help Keep Overseas Enemy From America

DELIVERY BY FRIDAY

Washington—(AP)—To an accompanying chorus of Congressional approval and protest, President Roosevelt disclosed Tuesday that he was turning over 50 "over-age" American destroyers to Great Britain to bulwark that beleaguered country against the onslaught of Nazi Germany.

The United States is to receive, in turn, the right to construct a string of outlying naval and air bases extending from Newfoundland to South America. Their chief value, the President declared, would be in keeping an overseas enemy away from America's front door.

The State Department announced that it had received also a British pledge that in no event would the British fleet be sunk or surrendered to Germany. If driven out of European waters, it was said, the English ships of war would be sent abroad for the "defense of other parts of the empire."

The whole transaction, which Attorney General Jackson ruled did not require Congressional action, was described by President Roosevelt, in a brief message notifying Congress of what was being done, as "an epochal and far-reaching act of preparation for continental defense in the face of grave danger."

"This is the most important action in the reinforcement of our national defense that has been taken since the Louisiana Purchase," Mr. Roosevelt added.

CONGRESS' REACTION VARIED

The Congressional bloc which has supported the President's policy of helping England went on record swiftly and enthusiastically as approving the exchange.

But with the group that has urged strict aloofness from the European conflict, it was a different matter. Its members denounced the transaction as an "act of war," which, some said, would justify Adolf Hitler in declaring war on the United States.

Members of this group contended that Congress should have been given the opportunity to pass upon the transaction. They called it the act of a "dictator," and asserted that the transfer of the destroyers was forbidden by law.

JACKSON'S OPINION

On the latter point, Mr. Roosevelt attached to his Congressional message the opinion by Attorney General Jackson holding that no

More of DESTROYERS On Page 14

CRASH VICTIM DIES

West Chester, Pa.—(Wednesday)—Dorothy Young, seventeen, Washington, D. C., died early today in a hospital from injuries suffered Monday in a motorcycle accident. Two young men who also were injured when their motorcycles ran off the road near here are improving, the hospital said.

Bridge Tolls Hit New Peak, $57,415 Collected In Month

August Income Is More Than $5,000 Higher Than Any Previous Monthly Income, Labor Day Week-End Traffic Sets New Record

A new record for toll collections was established at the Inter-County bridge in August, when motorists paid a total of $57,415.10 at the Columbia and Wrightsville ends of the span over the Susquehanna river.

This was more than $5,000 higher than the revenue for August, 1937, when toll receipts reached a peak of $51,755.90—highest until now—since the bridge was opened in October, 1930.

Traffic, always heaviest in August, increased in spite of the cold and rainy weather of the last week, members of the Bridge commission noted at their meeting in Wrightsville Tuesday.

Another record was set in the Labor Day week-end, it was re-

More of TOLLS On Page 14

BURNING OLD BOOKS CAUSES FIRE SCARE

Neffsville Firemen Called To Brecht School, Find Discarded Texts Smoldering In Furnace

Smoke from burning discarded school books in the furnace of the Milton J. Brecht school, in Manheim township, caused a fire scare at 7 p. m. Tuesday.

Clarence Weaver, Lancaster R. D. 3, janitor of the school, said persons residing on the Lititz pike near the school saw smoke issuing from the basement windows and summoned the Neffsville Fire company.

Weaver said he had placed a number of discarded books in the furnace Tuesday afternoon. Apparently they were not completely consumed, and began to smolder. Firemen said there may be slight smoke damage.

Just a year ago the Brecht school was damaged by an incendiary fire which was started in a store of school supplies in the gymnasium. The flames spread to the stage before firemen could check them and the loss was estimated at more than $5,000. A week later Charles B. Miller, Jr., sixteen, 134 S. Water st., was arrested in Altoona and brought to this city where police said he admitted he started the fire after taking a quantity of supplies from the cartons piled in the gymnasium.

EIGHT INJURED IN TRAFFIC ACCIDENTS IN CITY, COUNTY

Motorist Waves To Friend, Auto Hits Trolley; Two Bicyclists Hurt

Eight persons were injured in automobile accidents Tuesday. One was the victim of an auto-trolley crash in Leacock and two were bicyclists. In addition, a man applied Tuesday for hospital treatment of injuries suffered in a mishap last Friday.

AUTO HITS TROLLEY

Henry Brenneman, about twenty-eight, of Landisville, suffered a fractured right leg, lacerations of the right knee and chin and bruises of the body when his auto crashed head-on with an Ephrata trolley car in Leacock at 6:55 a. m. Tuesday.

Dr. J. M. Ranck, of Leola, who treated the victim, said he was told Brenneman was traveling east on the New Holland pike, enroute to Girvin's greenhouses, where he is employed. He was passing another car, operated by a fellow employe and waved to him, Dr. Ranck said. As he did so his car and the trolley crashed.

Officials of the Conestoga Transportation company said the trolley, operated by D. Claire Lefever, 544 E. Orange st., was stopped to take on a passenger. Seeing the approaching car, the motorman ran to the rear of the car and escaped injury, they said. No other passengers on the car were injured, they added.

Brenneman, who boards in Leacock, was taken to St. Joseph's hospital from Dr. Ranck's office

More of ACCIDENTS On Page 14

NINE MEN ENLIST AS 213TH LAUNCHES RECRUITING DRIVE

Six Join Battery E, Three Sworn Into Headquarters Unit Here

Nine men enlisted in the two local units of the 213th Coast Artillery, Pennsylvania National Guard, Tuesday night as the recruiting campaign got underway here.

These men enlisted in Battery E, commanded by Captain David J. Evans: Richard Heidig, 141 Grofftown road; his brother, Robert, same address; Garland Lambert, 335 N. Queen st.; James R. Wilson, 1013 Lititz ave.; B. Bernard Barr, 134 E. Lemon st., and Harry N. Haar, Jr., 241 Ruby st.

Three men enlisted in the Second Battalion Headquarters battery, commanded by Lieutenant Carryl Stauffer. They are Robert Daugherty, 212 E. New st.; Dean Robinson, of Maytown, and William McGarvey, of Florin.

MORE APPLICATIONS

Although only nine were accept-

More of 213TH On Page 14

AUTOMOBILE STOLEN

An auto owned by Elizabeth Sharp, of New Holland, was stolen in the borough between 3 a. m. and 3 p. m. Tuesday, State Motor Police reported. Police said the car is a gray sedan bearing license F9725.

HOUSE COMMITTEE MODIFIES PLAN TO DRAFT INDUSTRY

Would Allow Government To Take Over Plants On Rental Basis; Debate Conscription

Washington—(AP)—A modified plan to conscript industries under certain circumstances won approval of the House Military committee Tuesday, and the House itself then began debate on the Burke-Wadsworth Conscription bill.

That measure, providing for peace-time drafting of the nation's young manhood for military training, was denounced on the House floor as a step toward "Hitlerism" and praised as the democratic way to strengthen the army.

MAY HAS AMENDMENT

Chairman May, Dem., Ky., announced that on behalf of the

More of HOUSE On Page 9

Dr. Smith Stresses Ways To Teach Value Of Democracy To Children

Urges Teachers To Help Eradicate "Apparent Inferiority Complex" Regarding Form Of Government

Eight ways in which the value of democracy can be taught to children and make them good citizens of city, state and nation, were outlined by Dr. Harvey A. Smith, superintendent of schools, at a meeting of the 350 local teachers in the administration building Tuesday. The meeting preceded the opening of classes Wednesday.

Pointing out that there is an "apparent inferiority complex with regard to democracy" on the part of some people, Dr. Smith urged, that children should understand, "First, that the citizens of the United States have a higher standard of living and enjoy material comforts far in excess of any other people. The comparatively poor person today enjoys comforts and advantages superior to those of the average middle-class family forty years ago.

"Second, there is no marked class distinction in the United States.

"Third, there is freedom of speech, press, assembly and religion.

"Fourth, this is still the land of oportunity, and any man or woman who is willing to work and

More of DR. SMITH On Page 9

Enemy Planes Over Berlin, British Repel Nazi Raiders

Bombs Dropped In German Areas But Officials Say Capital Escaped

Berlin— (AP) —(Wednesday)—The British, trying to mislead the night-long attacks of the German air force, set great fires in open places, authorized German spokesmen charged today in describing the unremitting aerial assaults on England which ushered in the second year of war.

Implying that the ruse failed, the Germans said the fires started by Tuesday's titanic bombardments led the overnight raiders to their objectives without the aid of maps.

Bombs of the heaviest caliber were dropped on southern England through the night, the sources declared.

At the same time, British bombers droned over Berlin early today. One plane was reported shot down over the Elbe river as heavy anti-aircraft fire met the enemy.

Reports that the bomber crashed after striking a barrage balloon near Magdeburg were not verified.

(The British originated the barrage balloon idea and have described

More of BERLIN On Page 9

Heavy Curtain Of Defensive Fire Thrown Up About England's Vital City

London—(AP)— (Wednesday) — German raiding planes in great waves beat in vain yesterday at a curtain of defensive fire thrown up about London and were driven off a third time late last night after a 14-minute engagement at the city's outskirts.

Other night bombers, however, attacked the industrial midlands; northwest, northeast, southeast and southwest England and areas in Wales and Scotland. Bombs fell in at least one southeast town. At least 13 cities reported raiders overhead.

The day's third raid on London came at 11:35 p. m. (6:35 p. m., Lancaster time). It was the shortest on record for the London area.

The RAF continued at night its raids on the French coast. Observers in England saw anti-aircraft shells and bombs bursting in the Calais region.

The Nazis' daylight attacks on

More of BRITISH On Page 14

DISCONTINUE BAND CONCERTS FOR YEAR

Members of Commission Decide On Action Because of Probability of Cool Nights

There will be no more public band concerts this year, members of the Band Concert commission decided at their final meeting Tuesday. One was scheduled last week but was not held because of rain.

They agreed to discontinue the concerts because of uncertain weather, damp ground, probability of cool nights, and the fact that schools are opening. However, they expressed hope that with favorable conditions the concerts can be resumed next summer.

The seven concerts held during the summer had an attendance of approximately 22,000, Walter N. Foust, chairman of the commission, said. The concerts were given by the City Band, B. Frank Streaker, director; Malta Band, Floyd Reddig, director; Military Band, Fred Zellers, director, and the 103rd Medical Regiment Band, directed by Warrant Officer Fred S. Bear.

NAZIS HIT SWISS "LAME NEUTRALITY"

German News Commentary Says British Flights Over Switzerland "Of Systematic Character"

Berlin—(AP)—The news commentary Dienst Aus Deutschland, which is close to the foreign office, said Tuesday night that Germans were "increasingly astonished" because Switzerland had replied to violation of Swiss territory by British planes "merely with weak and completely ineffective protests."

It spoke of "lame neutrality." The same charges frequently were made against the Netherlands prior to last spring's German invasion.

The commentary said the "systematic character" of British flights over Switzerland, mainly to Italy, "is taken especially seriously in Berlin."

REINFORCES DEFENSES

Bern, Switzerland— (AP) — Switzerland was reported Tuesday to be reinforcing her anti-aircraft defenses in an effort to halt British flights across Swiss territory on bombing raids to Italy and southern Germany.

Heavy caliber batteries were said to have been erected on high Alpine peaks.

"We Lead All the Rest" FARM CORNER

By *The Farm Editor*

FARM SHOW SEASON OPENS NEXT WEEK

First Fair To Be Held At Black Barren Springs Next Thursday, Friday and Saturday

A dozen communities in Lancaster county are planning to hold local farm fairs this fall. The annual community farm show season here will open September 11 with the exhibit by the Black Barren Springs Fair association and will continue with one or more fairs in different communities each week until late October. The schedule to date, as listed with the Lancaster County Agricultural Extension association through which judges of the various home and farm products are secured, is as follows:

Sept. 11, 12 and 13—Black Barren Springs Fair, at Black Barren Park, Fulton township.

Sept. 18, 19 and 20—West Lampeter High School Community Fair, at Lampeter.

Sept. 26, 27 and 28—Manor Township Farm Show, at Millersville; and the Manheim Community Show, at Manheim.

Oct. 3, 4 and 5—New Holland Farmers' Day, at New Holland.

Oct. 9, 10, 11 and 12—Ephrata Farmers' Day, at Ephrata.

Oct. 17, 18 and 19—Lititz and Mount Joy Community Farm Shows in the two boroughs.

Four additional communities held

More of FARM CORNER On Page 14

Intelligencer Journal Weather Calendar

COMPARATIVE TEMPERATURES

Station	High	Low
Intell Journal	82	61
Water Works	83	55
Ephrata	82	56
Last Year (Ephrata)	88	63
Official High for Year, July 26		102.5
Official Low for Year, Jan. 20		2
Character of Day		Clear

HOURLY TEMPERATURES

Tuesday			
8 a. m.	62	9 p. m.	70
11 a. m.	69	10 p. m.	69
2 p. m.	76	11 p. m.	68
5 p. m.	78	Midnight	66
		Wednesday	
6 p. m.	77	1 a. m.	66
7 p. m.	76	2 a. m.	65
8 p. m.	74	3 a. m.	64

HUMIDITY

8 a. m.—61; 11 a. m.—58; 2 p. m.—62; 5 p. m.—53; 8 p. m.—58; 11 p. m.—90
Average Humidity—64
Dew point, 11 p. m.—60

More of WEATHER On Page 9

DAYLIGHT TIME IN INTELL

All time mentioned in The Intelligencer Journal is Daylight Time unless otherwise noted.

Sports Revue

F. & M. Grid Chances Depend Largely on Farkas and Manotti.

by GEORGE W. KIRCHNER

NOT even Coach Alan Holman, himself, will deny that the success or failure of his 1940 Franklin and Marshall College football team will depend largely on the way two of its players, Big Bill Farkas, the fullback and Billy Manotti, the fleet-footed runner come through.

As a matter of fact, it was Holman who first pointed this out the other day when discussing his team, its terrific schedule and its chances for turning in a season that will be better than that of last year which, everything considered, wasn't such a bad one, at that.

Bill Farkas

For Farkas this will be his first campaign on the Diplomat varsity, while for Manotti it marks a return after a year's absence. The fact that both boys are experienced ball players, capable to the nth degree, goes a long way to make the situation encouraging.

Holman Wants More Proof

BUT this must still be proved and until it is, Holman is not willing to go out on the limb and make any bright prediction. So far—(meaning in the practice sessions, including the two warm-up games) — the pair who hail from Windber have come through nobly. If they continue once the season gets underway and the chips go down, F. & M. has a better than even chance of doing some good this year.

Holman has quite a few new faces around this year, but of all the additions to last year's regulars, who are back again, Farkas and Manotti are the most outstanding. Farkas is a terrific blocker and tackler and Manotti is one of the cleverest and fastest open field runners around these parts.

Give Team Offensive Spark

TOGETHER, they give the Diplomats two grand offensive spark plugs with both being able to toss better than average passes, while Farkas, whose duty it will be to do most of the kicking, is a pretty fair booter.

Considering the individual ability of each player you can appreciate why Holman is counting so heavily on the two of them. Of course, he has other players to send in to fill their places, but if Farkas and Manotti fail to live up to expectations, put it down as a blow to the team, as a whole, and one that, as Holman has pointed out, may just mean the difference between a successful season and a dismal one.

All of this may go down as putting quite a burden on the shoulders of these boys, but if I know Farkas and Manotti they are more than equal to such a task. From here they look like the kind who can come through, and who are most likely to do so when the pressure is on and the best is demanded.

BASEBALL STANDINGS

American League

	W.	L.	P.C.	*G.B.
Cleveland	84	61	.579	——
Detroit	83	61	.576	½
New York	79	64	.552	4
Chicago	79	66	.545	5
Boston	75	68	.524	8
St. Louis	62	83	.428	22
Washington ..	60	84	.417	23½
ATHLETICS ..	53	88	.376	29

National League

	W.	L.	P.C.	*G.B.
Cincinnati	93	47	.664	——
Brooklyn	83	61	.576	12
St. Louis	75	65	.536	18
Pittsburgh	73	68	.518	20½
Chicago	70	73	.490	24½
New York	66	75	.468	27½
Boston	61	82	.427	33½
PHILLIES	46	96	.324	48

*G.B.—Games behind leader.

TOMORROW'S GAMES

American League

Cleveland at Detroit.
Chicago at St. Louis.

National League

New York at Boston.
Philadelphia at Brooklyn.

YESTERDAY'S RESULTS

National League

Cincinnati 4, Philadelphia 3 (13 innings).
Boston 4, Pittsburgh 1.
St. Louis 14, Brooklyn 7.
Chicago 6, New York 4.

American League

Detroit 14, Philadelphia 0 (1st).
Philadelphia 13, Detroit 6 (2nd).
Cleveland 3, Washington 1 (1st).
Cleveland 2, Washington 1 (2nd).
Chicago 6, New York 3 (1st).
New York 9, Chicago 8 (2nd).
St. Louis 11, Boston 2.

International League Playoffs

Newark 3, Jersey City 1.
Rochester 4, Baltimore 1.
Both night games.

WILDCATS WIN, 13 TO 0

The Sacred Heart Wildcats defeated the Virginians by a 13 to 0 score in a football encounter played Wednesday afternoon at Buchanan Park.

These Tornado Boys Are Raring to Go Saturday

Harvey Rooker has his McCaskey High gridders ready for their opening game with Middletown Saturday at McCaskey Stadium.

At the top Al Ruth, an end, shows how to hold on to the ball after a pass; Larry Braner is the dependable tackle and captain of the team, and that fellow charging into the camera is Dick Reese, a hard-running back.

At the bottom, Don Schneider gives you an idea of how he'll stiff-arm those would-be tacklers, while Jim Walker is getting off a nifty boot.

Reds' Official Wants Detroit To Win Flag

PHILADELPHIA, Sept. 19—(A. P.)—The champions of the National League — the Cincinnati Reds — don't care what team wins the American League pennant, but general manager Warren Giles hopes it's Detroit.

Giles watched his club clinch their second straight flag by coming from behind yesterday to beat the Phillies, 4 to 3, in 13 innings as Brooklyn lost to St. Louis.

"We'd probably draw more in dollars and cents if we played Cleveland," Giles said. "But on the other hand we might not. There might be 80,000 in the Cleveland Stadium one day and then drop off. Then that dissension sort of takes the bang out of it.

"In spite of what a lot of people might think, ball clubs consider more things than money. I don't care who wins the American League pennant —we'll beat whoever it is—but I think we'd do better with Detroit than any other team."

The Reds whooped it up in their dressing room after southpaw Johnny Vander Meer scored the winning run in the 13th, but the big celebration was reserved for tonight. The boys want Paul Derringer to win his 20th game against the Phils today.

"We'll celebrate tonight," explained Manager Deacon Bill McKechnie. "We have a day off tomorrow. Today we play ball. The boys deserve a celebration."

McKechnie had heaps of praise for Jimmie Wilson, 40-year-old coach who returned to active duty behind the bat after Ernie Lombardi was hurt.

"I don't believe any one realizes what Jimmy has meant to this team," the Deacon said. "When we were in that Brooklyn series and every game was a money game it was Jimmy who pulled us through. It was Jimmy who caught the rest of the game when Lombardi sprained his ankle and it was Jimmy who caught the next two wins over the Dodgers. It was Jimmy who really put us over the top."

Cincinnati Calm As Reds Triumph

CINCINNATI, Sept. 19.—(A. P.)—A year ago next week, followers of the national sport in this town were whooping themselves hoarse, kissing perfect strangers, doing handsprings across the suspension bridge, and acting in general as if somebody had just gone the length of Vine street tossing negotiable bonds out of a barrel.

Today there is a strange calm, as dead as the geometric center of a vacuum, spread over the queen city. Solid citizens are going about their beer and skittles as if nothing had happened.

Last year the Reds won their first pennant in 20 years and this year they won their second in 21. But for all the excitement, you'd think the Red fans were New Yorkers, who have had pennants in one league or the other for a good part of those two decades.

2 Golfers Tie For Honors

Twenty-five members of the Women's Golf Association of the Lancaster Country Club participated in the poker-hand tournament held by the women Wednesday afternoon. In the first division, Mrs. Kendig H. Bare and Miss Josephine Eshelman tied for first prize for the eighteen hole golfers and Mrs. Bare won the draw. Miss Eshelman received second prize. In the second division, Mrs. E. Kearney Smith won first prize and Mrs. Amos Herr second.

Others taking part for the eighteen hole players were Mrs. Penrose H. Ruhl, Mrs. Charles S. Gaige, Mrs. J. Maurice Westerman, Mrs. Frank Herr, Mrs. J. H. C. Whiting, Mrs. H. F. Schell, Miss Elizabeth Atlee, Mrs. D. M. Warren, Mrs. H. J. Pierson, Mrs. Charles S. Foltz, Miss Sydney Sides, Mrs. Elizabeth S. Ludgate, Mrs. Donald Brown, Mrs. Paul M. Hess, Mrs. Gerald H. Effing and Mrs. Claire C. Simeral.

The nine hole golfers also played a poker hand tourney, and Miss Elizabeth Fritchey won first prize and Mrs. Fred P. Auten second. Others participating were Mrs. O. S. Schaeffer, Mrs. J. Clifton Ryan and Mrs. S. W. Miller.

In a recently played to par tournament, Mrs. Frank Herr was awarded first prize which was given by Mrs. Donald Brown. Mrs. Ludgate, Mrs. Amos Herr and Mrs. Ruhl tied for second, and the draw was won by Mrs. Ludgate.

The next weekly tournament will be held at 1:15 o'clock Wednesday afternoon, September 25, and will be an alibi tourney.

Columbia Day at Meadia Heights

The eighth annual "Columbia Day" was observed at Meadia Heights yesterday with 20 members of the club, residents of Columbia, entertaining at golf and dinner.

A blind bogey tournament was held and prizes awarded to F. X. Kasel, S. S. Christ, C. A. Etzweiler, C. W. Knipe and Donald Livingston. Etzweiler was chairman of the party.

Reds Clinch Pennant; A. L. Lead Changes 6 Times in 10 Days

By JUDSON BAILEY

Associated Press Sports Writer

While the American League has been muddling around for two weeks like so many rabbits in a pen, the Cincinnati Reds have copped their second straight National League pennant with an impressive display of decision and dispatch.

Their 4-3 triumph in 13 innings over the Phillies yesterday was their 16th victory in 18 games. A blistering finish, that may have an important bearing on the world series.

It used to be the other way around. The American Leaguers would show up early with a great show of invincibility and pounce upon their prey when the National League delegate finally arrived all out of breath. The Reds didn't stave off the rush of the St. Louis Cardinals last year until September 28, three days before the season closed, and they practically collapsed into the pit the Yankees had waiting.

It's Different Now

But now, it is the American League that is locked in a death struggle. The Cleveland Indians were so desperate yesterday they called out Bobby Feller with two days' rest to face the seventh-place Washington Senators. The strategy worked, and the tribe triumphed in both ends of a doubleheader, 3-1 and 2-1, to regain first place. But it might boomerang when the Indians open a three-game series with Detroit tomorrow.

The Philadelphia Athletics, the same tag-alongs who knocked Cleveland off the top perch Tuesday, scored nine runs in the second game of their double bill at Detroit yesterday to get a split and force the Tigers out of the lead. With the New York Yankees and Chicago White Sox dividing their double feature, the standings are:

Club	Won	Lost	Pct.	G. B.	G. T. P.
Cleveland	84	61	.579		9
Detroit	83	61	.576	½	10
New York	79	64	.552	4	11
Chicago	79	66	.545	5	9

Cincinnati hardly could be blamed for snickering at that sort of a spectacle, with the lead changing hands six times in ten days. As far as their own race is concerned, the Reds have been in first place continuously since July 7 and never worse than third any time this year.

Vander Meer Stars

The honor of clinching the flag fell to Johnny Vander Meer, as a bit of added drama. The no-hit king showed signs of his old self as he kept eight hits scattered and struck out ten. Then, in the 13th, he led off with a double and scored the winning run.

The St. Louis Cardinals, of all clubs, gave the Reds an assist by crushing the Brooklyn Dodgers, 14-7, with a 17-hit bombardment that included four singles by Johnny Mize good for six runs. This left Brooklyn 12 games behind with ten to play. The Reds have 13 to go and could lose them all without harm.

In the two other National League games, Jim Tobin held his old Pirate teammates to five hits as the Boston Bees beat Pittsburgh, 4-1, and Stan Hack hit two homers and a single to help the Chicago Cubs hand the New York Giants their tenth straight setback, 6-4.

Allen Wins First

Cleveland's opening victory over Washington was credited to the six-hit pitching of Johnny Allen, but Lefty Ken Chase of the Senators forced in all three of the Indians' runs with walks to help. Feller was practically untouchable with five-hit hurling in the nightcap.

The tragedy of the Tigers was that they won their first game from the A's, 14-0, and weren't able to save any of this margin for the second session. In the first game, Tommy Bridges went so well he was pulled out in the seventh to rest for Cleveland. Hank Greenberg hit two homers, one with the bases loaded. Then, in the nightcap, Detroit got a 6-4 lead on homers by Greenberg and Rudy York and collapsed in the ninth, giving nine runs. Bob Johnson hit a three-run homer in this frame. Benny McCoy had done the same in the fourth.

Chicago came close to passing over the Yanks into third place, and 37,000 ardent southsiders were present for the kill. Lefty Thornton Lee pitched six-hit ball as the Sox won the first game, 6-3. In the second game, the Yanks led off with four runs in the first, but Chicago came right back with five and added three more in the fourth. Then Twink Selkirk homered with two on in the seventh; the Yanks got two more in the eighth, and darkness closed the show before Chicago could do anything about it.

The St. Louis Browns squelched the Boston Red Sox, 11-2, with a 14-hit offensive.

WEATHER

Eastern Pennsylvania: Cloudy, Continued Cool, Light Rain Southeast And Extreme East Portions Early Wednesday; Thursday Fair And Slightly Warmer.
Intell Journal Stormograph Reading: Cloudy Wednesday.

Intelligencer Journal

Baseball

The 1940 world series between Detroit and Cincinnati will start this Wednesday. For details turn to Page 10.

The Leading Newspaper in the Garden Spot of America, Home Owned for Home Folks Since 1794

VOLUME LXXVII.—NO. 18. CITY The Intelligencer Founded 1799 The Journal Founded 1794 LANCASTER, PA., WEDNESDAY MORNING, OCTOBER 2, 1940. Entered at Post Office at Lancaster, Pa. as second class mail matter 18 PAGES, 144 COLUMNS.—THREE CENTS.

BRITISH TAKE AIR OFFENSIVE AGAIN

ROOSEVELT HITS "ASSAULTS" ON WILLKIE PARTY

Throwing Of Eggs, Other Incidents Condemned As Thoroughly Reprehensible

TAKES STERN TONE

Washington — (AP) — Two incidents which occurred during Wendell Willkie's tour of Michigan—the dropping of a basket from a high window in Detroit and the throwing of eggs in Pontiac—were condemned by President Roosevelt Tuesday as thoroughly reprehensible.

Talking to reporters at his press conference, Mr. Roosevelt said he imagined that laws of most states classified such deeds as assaults and crimes.

A reporter had asked the President whether he had read in newspapers that a "presidential candidate had been subjected to harsh treatment in Michigan."

The President obviously had expected the question and answered in stern tones. He said he had heard of the incidents through a secretary, Stephen Early, who had told him an RFC employe was involved in the wastebasket affair. He added that she should forfeit her position.

Detroit dispatches said police had arrested Doris Larue, 31, who, they said, admitted dropping the basket from an 18th floor hotel window shortly after Willkie had entered the building Monday. Miss Larue was identified as an RFC worker. Betty Wilson, a 19-year-old girl who was in the crowd near Willkie was struck on the head and seriously injured.

In Pontiac, an egg thrown from the crowd, spattered Mrs. Willkie as she and her husband drove away from a platform where the Re-

More of ROOSEVELT on Page 4

Here Friday

WENDELL L. WILLKIE

WILLKIE TO SPEAK AT P. R. R. STATION DURING VISIT HERE

Special Train Carrying Republican Nominee And Party To Arrive At 12:25 P. M.

Wendell L. Willkie, Republican nominee for president, will deliver a short talk from a stand in front of the Pennsylvania Railroad station during his twenty-minute visit to Lancaster Friday.

The special train, carrying Mr. Willkie, Senator Charles L. McNary, nominee for vice president, and Republican National Chairman Joseph W. Martin, will arrive in Lancaster at 12:25 p. m. During the time the party is here, the station will be closed to the public, George W. Good, station agent, announced.

Lancaster County Chairman G. Graybill Diehm is planning to join the group at Harrisburg. While here, the Republican nominee will receive from Miss Mary Hostetter, a scroll prepared by the First Voters League of Lancaster county.

Mayor D. E. Cary, who is planning to greet Mr. Willkie, said that Police Commissioner Albert Carlson hsa made arrangements for a detachment of police to be on hand at the station.

After speaking here, Mr. Willkie is scheduled to stop at Coatesville at 1:05 p. m., while enroute to Philadelphia.

Increased Production To Boost Unemployment Urged

Grand Rapids, Mich. — (AP) — Wendell L. Willkie, declaring that "the road to prosperity is paved with jobs," Tuesday placed increased production at the top of a threefold program to increase employment.

Speaking before a crowd estimated by police at 30,000, the Republican presidential nominee said he also wanted to revamp the tax structure to encourage new enter-

More of WILLKIE on Page 4

EXCESS PROFITS TAX BILL IS SENT TO WHITE HOUSE

Estimate $525,000,000 Yield On 1940 Income From New Levies

TO SPEED DEFENSE PLAN

Washington — (AP) — Congress sent a compromise excess profits tax bill to the White House Tuesday amid forecasts in both House and Senate that still further taxes would be levied early next year.

The bill's draftsmen estimated that it would yield $525,000,000 on 1940 income, including $230,000,000 from an increase in the normal corporation tax, and from $900,000,00 to $1,000,000,000 on 1941 income.

TO SPEED UP DEFENSE

In addition to the tax provisions, the legislation also contained clauses designed to speed up the defense program. These would suspend existing profits limitations on government contracts for construction of warships and airplanes and permit corporations to charge off against earnings over a five-year period the cost of new defense manufacturing facilities completed after June 10, 1940.

Included also was a section under which conscripts and other members of the armed forces may obtain low-rate government life insurance.

Designed originally to hold in check the profits that might accrue to industries engaged in the sale of national defense items, the completed legislation also would depend for a substatial part of its revenue upon a flat addition of 3.1 per cent to the normal corporation income tax of concerns earning more than $25,000 a year. This change would increase the rate for these corporations to 24 per cent.

A tax of from 25 to 50 per cent would be levied on profits defined in the bill as exceeding normal.

REPRESENTS COMPROMISE

As it went to President Roosevelt the bill represented a compromise of House and Senate bills as worked out by a conference committee of

More of CONGRESS on Page 16

956 ENROLLED AT F. & M., HIGHEST IN SCHOOL'S HISTORY

Total Exceeds By 22 Number Of Students At Opening Of Institution Last Year

Final enrollment figures at Franklin and Marshall college stand at 956, highest in the 153 years of tl college's history, Dr. John A. Schaeffer, president, announced Tuesday. There are 22 more students than last year at the opening of the institution.

There are 344 Freshmen, 258 Sophomores, 201 Juniors and 153 Seniors enrolled.

Dr. Schaeffer pointed out that F. and M.'s large enrollment this year is unusual, since the great majority of the colleges are showing a decrease.

Dr. Schaeffer will attend the ceremonies next Tuesday, Wednesday and Thursday for the inauguration of Dr. George N. Shuster as president of Hunter college, New York city. This Wednesday he will go to New York to meet several of the trustees of F. and M., and on Friday he and Rev. R. J. Pilgram, alumni secretary, will attend the meeting of the Boston Alumni club. They will attend the F. and M.-Dartmouth football game at Hanover, N. H., on Saturday, and F. and M. Day at the World's Fair Sunday.

Weds Cabby

Florence Thornton, socially prominent Baltimore girl, telephones her parents following her marriage to Gilman Milliken, Bar Harbor, Me., taxi driver. Their romance reportedly began in "a mutual interest in the great out-of-doors."

BRITAIN DECLARES WARPLANES OF U. S. CHEERING NATION

"Renewed Confidence In Triumphant Conclusion" Of Air Battle Seen By Beaverbrook

Washington —(AP)— Great Britain, in a formal statement issued here Tuesday night. declared "that the flow of airplanes from the United States of America gives us renewed confidence in the triumphant conclusion of our long battle in the air."

The statement, by Lord Beaverbrook, in charge of aircraft procurement for the British, was sent to the British Purchasing commission here and made public by that agency.

"The Brewster fighting squadron is in use," it said. "It is earning the praise of our finest pilots. The Douglas D.B.7 is also in action and the new Curtiss has arrived. These three aircraft are equal to our best machines."

Meantime, President Roosevelt said, in response to questions at a press conference, that he had made no recommendations and expected to make none, for repeal or modification of the Johnson act, which bars American loans to Great Britain and other nations in default on debts to this country.

Senator King, Dem., Utah, introduced legislation Monday which would permit credits to Great Britain, but Senator Barkley, Dem., Ky., the majority leader, said it would be impossible to act on the legislation at this session of Congress because it would "provoke a lot of debate."

The view of a number of officials here appeared to be that material help in the form of planes and other supplies was a more urgent matter

More of AID on Page 16

REPORT STOLEN TRUCK SEEN IN LANCASTER

Big Tractor-Trailer Type Vehicle Was Stolen At Petersburg, Va., September 20

City and State Motor Police are searching for a large tractor-trailer type truck, stolen September 20 at Petersburg, Va., which was reported seen in this city several days ago.

Police said the truck is owned by J. C. Fretwell, Tavares, Fla., and bears Florida registration plates 4GK425. The trailer registration number is 12L36.

WORK STARTED HERE TO SET UP DRAFT BOARDS

Advisory Committee Holds First Meeting; Election Officials Are Notified

PLAN EIGHT BOARDS

Machinery to set up eight draft boards for Lancaster city and county was put in motion Tuesday at the first meeting of the Lancaster County Advisory Conscription committee.

Possible make-up of those boards was discussed by Judge Oliver S. Schaeffer, County Superintendent of Schools Arthur P. Mylin and County Commissioners G. Graybill Diehm, Fred W. Wagner and Harry R. Metzler, but no selections were made.

The group, serving in an advisory capacity to Governor Arthur H. James, will select twenty-four men, three for each of the eight boards, and recommend their appointment. Actual appointment is made by the President on the recommendation of the Governor of the state in which they are to serve.

They will select citizens who have shown an interest in military affairs over a period of years, by contacts with leading citizens in the various communities, Chambers of Commerce, medical and legal groups, and through civil and military training corps committees and those who have volunteered their services.

ELECTION OFFICIALS NOTIFIED

Meanwhile, notices were prepared Tuesday for mailing to county election boards, asking members to serve without pay for the registration on October 16 of men eligible for the draft. Individuals are asked to notify the Lancaster County Election board whether they will serve.

All polling places used for elections will be open for draft registration, the election board announced. There will be three draft

More of DRAFT on Page 4

MINIMUM PRICES FOR CONSIGNMENT MILK UP IN COURT

State Asks Board's Ruling May Be Upheld To Avert "Breakdown" In Mill Industry

Pittsburgh—(AP)—The commonwealth Tuesday asked the Pennsylvania Supreme Court to avert a "breakdown of the milk industry" by upholding minimum wholesale prices for milk shipped by producers on consignment to dealers.

In an appeal from a Dauphin county court decision, the state declared that unless dealers were compelled to pay producers the minimum prices set by the Milk Control Commission for consigned milk "chaos" would return to the industry.

APPEAL LOWER COURT DECISION

The lower court upheld 19 Pennsylvania dealers who claimed the milk commission was not empowered under the milk control law to fix prices on consigned milk. At the same time, Judge William Hargest of Dauphin county, granted the dealers an injunction restraining the commission from proceedings with criminal action for alleged violation of the law.

Under the consignment system producers ship milk to dealers at an unspecified price. The dealer then attempts to sell the milk at the most favorable figure, retaining a commission on the sale.

Another phase of the case involving an injunction to prevent the commission from denying the Harrisburg Dairies, Inc., a dealers'

More of MILK on Page 16

Nabbed At Pier

Dr. Frederick Ernest Auhagen, (above) former professor of languages at Columbia University, will be brought to New York City from Los Angeles to testify concerning reported organization of an American Nazi party, Dies committee investigators announced. Dr. Auhagen, a German citizen, was arrested as he prepared to sail. (Story Page 3).

Hit At Nazi-Held Bases Along Coast, Then Roar Inland

Berliners Flee Homes For Dugouts As London Is Spared Extensive Damage In Night Raid; British Capital's Residents Prepare For Winter Expected To Be Worst In 20 Centuries

(By The Associated Press)

The Royal Air force, on the offensive again, struck at Nazi-held bases on the French coast Tuesday night and early Wednesday and roared inland against Germany proper.

Berliners fled their homes for raid dugouts as Londoners have done for 25 straight nights and expect to do most of the coming winter.

Following the Berlin alarm, Nazi spokesmen said bomb damage was not noteworthy. They made the same statement for the previous night's attack in contrast to British statements that docks, depots, and railways throughout northern and western Germany were rocked by "great explosions and great fires."

Radio stations in Hamburg, Bremen and other German stations fell silent, without explanation, before the usual hour of sign-off, and it thus appeared that British raiders were over many areas of the Reich.

An authoritative British statement on the British counter-offensive last night against Germany reported attacks on Berlin, communications and oil supplies elsewhere, and "the invasion ports."

London, which had 13,000 casualties from Nazi raids in September, underwent another routine overnight assault with Nazi raiders bombing the east end slum and factory district. While bombs also fell in northern suburban areas, London was spared from extensive damage.

The German air force, avowedly extending itself to keep the British capital from "catching its breath," maintained the seemingly interminable rain of bombs to which the city has been subjected for 25 successive nights.

As a nip in the air foretold the cold which Nazi bombs will make more horrible, a "dictator" was named to make London's air raid shelters warm and impregnable; emergency feeding centers were established for the city's homeless; removal of mothers and children was extended to cover 14 boroughs; and development of a new and stronger defense system was officially assured.

NAZIS LIST AIMS

The Germans, keeping up their air siege in good weather and bad, told of new attacks intended to make London groggy, and listed as other primary aims interference with British war production and blockading of the nation's essential imports.

In that last connection, the British acknowledged that in the past week German U-boats had destroyed 159,288 tons of merchant shipping—three times the weekly average—but said British warehouses were filled to overflowing with the necessities.

Speculating on this sudden spurt, informed British sources said it might be pure luck or the use of French and Italian submarines as commerce raiders.

On their own account, the British continued to strew aerial bombs on German territory, concentrating afresh on the Nazi big guns emplacements along the ominously-near French coast.

SHELL SHIPS NEAR DOVER

The Germans said their big guns continued to shell ships around Dover, England with "visible success."

But the shudder of the earth beneath their feet and the flare of bombs and anti-aircraft shells in France told watchers in Dover that their air force was at work.

Britain announced also farflung raids on Germany's greatest industrial areas, concentrating on Berlin Monday night and Tuesday morning in what was apparently one of the

More of WAR on Page 4

Children See Newspaper Made—Ask Many Questions

Five Senior And Junior High School Groups Tour Lancaster Newspapers Plant As Part Of Observance Of National Newspaper Week, See Old Papers On Display

Five groups of senior and junior high school pupils from the county visited the plant of the Lancaster Newspapers, Inc., Tuesday as part of the observance of National Newspaper week.

Other similar student groups will be taken through the plant during the week and the remainder of the month, until all have been given an opportunity to do so.

The groups were first taken to the General Engraving plant on the fifth floor, then visited the studios of Radio Station WGAL, the editorial rooms of the Intelligencer Journal, New Era and Sunday News, the composing rooms, the job printing department, the advertising and business departments, the press room, mailing and storage rooms and the circulation and want ad departments.

On display in the editorial rooms are copies of newspapers covering a period of 150 years, from George Washington's day up until the present time. The papers are opened to pages "covering" the War of 1812, Civil War, Spanish American War, World War and the present European War.

Most of the questions asked by the pupils were regarding general

More of PUPILS on Page 4

PROPOSED SEWAGE RENTAL APPEALED

Phila. Taxpayer Claims Charge Would Be Merely "Subterfuge" For Tax

Pittsburgh—(AP)—In a case before the Pennsylvania Supreme Court which may effect municipal financing in Pennsylvania, a Philadelphia taxpayer Tuesday appealed a sewage rental proposed by the city to finance extension of its sewage system.

Philadelphia's city council proposed a $42,000,000 bond issue to construct the extension and was upheld by the Philadelphia common pleas court. Revenue would be gained through a rental charge of 40 cents per each $100 of assessed property valuation.

Counsel for the taxpayer, John Hamilton, argued that the rental charge was merely a "subterfuge" for a tax and that the proposed bond issue would increase the city's indebtedness beyond constitutional limits.

Justice Horace Stern declared "what is there to stop the city of Philadelphia from building fire engine houses and police stations and charging property owners rent for them simply because they are available to all?"

Chief Justice Schaffer said "this is a case of vital importance, not only to the city of Philadelphia, but to many other municipalities in the state as well."

WGAL TO BROADCAST WORLD SERIES GAMES

WGAL will bring local listeners complete coverage of the World Series games. Initial broadcast is at 1:15 p. m. Wednesday. Red Barber and Bob Elson, veteran baseball play-by-play announcers, will do the description for the Mutual Broadcasting system.

FIREBUG BLAMED FOR FIVE BLAZES IN ATGLEN AREA

Fire Company Hall And Feed Warehouse Fired Sunday Night; Kerosene Found

A kerosene sprinkling "fire-bug" was blamed Tuesday by State Motor Police for setting at least five fires in Atglen and vicinity during the past five weeks.

Attempts late Sunday night to burn down both the Atglen Fire company hall and the Brown and Rea feed warehouse spurred officials to redouble efforts to catch the arsonist.

CHURCH DAMAGED

Corporal S. H. Smith, of the Coatesville sub-station, said it was the second attempt at the fire house, and that the same person—as yet unknown—is suspected of having fired the Maple Grove Mennonite church on August 25, and the warehouse near the Lechler and Rutter fireworks plant on Zion Hill, just west of Atglen, on September 22.

Damage of about $500 resulted from the fire in the church, attributed at the time to a short circuit. The Zion Hill fire caused damage of $6,000 or more, as the building, an old barn, contained a large stock of paper boxes.

FIRE HALL DAMAGED

Late Sunday night a fire was discovered in the fire hall, causing minor damage to the ladder on the new fire truck and to the steps leading to the borough council chamber upstairs. Early Monday morning fire was found smoldering in grain at the Brown and Rea warehouse, but damage was negligible.

Corporal Smith said kerosene had been sprinkled around liberally in both places. The warehouse fire, he said, was probably set before the one in the fire house, but failed to

More of FIREBUG on Page 4

16 ENROLL IN SECOND DEFENSE SHOP COURSE

Remainder Of Those Accepted For Classes Are Expected To Enroll Today

Sixteen men enrolled Tuesday night in the second course in machine shop practice sponsored by the state and the city school district in the interests of National Defense.

Ten were enrolled at the McCaskey High school, where the instructor is Eugene Ziegler, and six at the Thaddeus Stevens Industrial school, Enos Kreider, instructor. The remainder of the thirty-nine men who have been accepted for the course are expected to enroll Wednesday. Of the entire group, twenty will be taking the course at McCaskey H. S. and nineteen at Stevens Trade.

"We Lead All the Rest"

FARM CORNER

By

The Farm Editor

HOLSTEIN CLUBS WILL MEET HERE

Federation To Name Officers And Directors At Session On October 23

Officers and a board of directors to serve during 1941 will be elected at the annual meeting of the Pennsylvania Federation of Holstein Clubs to be held at the Stevens House, this city, on October 23, at 10 a. m., Earl L. Groff, Strasburg R. D. 1, a state director, announced Tuesday night.

Seventy-five animals from leading Holstein herds in ten Pennsylvania counties, including 13 head from Lancaster breeders, will be entered in the annual consignment sale sponsored by the State Federation of Holstein clubs. This will be staged at the Mt. Vernon Inn, along the Lincoln Highway, near Gap, beginning at noon Tuesday, Oct. 22.

A tour of the Garden Spot for the benefit of out-of-county visitors is being arranged for Tuesday morning, prior to the sale, and the first day program will end with the annual banquet of the organization at the Stevens House in the evening.

The committee arranging the tour, sale and banquet consists of Mr. Groff, chairman; Aaron Glick, Harry Griffith, H. Roy Eshelman, John Shirk, Harry L. Zook, Clarence Lyons, Ira Eby, Naaman Stoltzfus, Harry Ranck, D. C. Martin and Harold Book.

LOCAL COWS IN NATIONAL SHOW

Forty-eight head of cattle representing three of the major breeds have been entered by Lancaster and nearby breeders for exhibit in

More of FARM CORNER on Page 4

CANDY SALES RACKET WORKED HERE AGAIN

Mrs. Elwood Gring, 234 N. Shippen St., Tells Police Boy Got 30 Cents At Her Home

Mrs. Elwood Gring, 234 N. Shippen st., reported to city police that a boy, about fourteen years old, worked a candy order racket at her home Tuesday afternoon, obtaining thirty cents from her daughter.

Mrs. Gring said the boy arrived during her absence and said she had ordered three bags of candy. The boy said he was to collect the money for it, and her daughter who had answered the doorbell, paid him thirty cents.

Police said they believe the boy is the same one who tricked residents of the 1300 block of Rose avenue into buying candy Saturday afternoon.

Tragedy Strikes Adjoining Homes Within Five Days

Tragedy struck twice in five days at two adjoining homes in the 800 block of Race avenue.

Last Friday Clarence B. Grosh, thirty-two, and his wife, Louise Austin Grosh, twenty-four, 26 S. Duke st., son and daughter-in-law of Mr. and Mrs. Clarence W. Grosh, 804 Race ave., died of injuries suffered in a head-on auto collision on the Lincoln highway, east of Mountville.

Tuesday John G. Gormley, nineteen, son of Mr. and Mrs. James J. Gormley, 802 Race ave., was killed when an airplane he was piloting crashed near Washington, D. C. (Story on Page 16).

A brother of the victim, James J. Gormley, sixteen, was fatally injured when struck by a light truck on New Holland avenue, near Liberty street, on July 2, 1934.

DRIVER ARRESTED IN HIT-RUN CRASH

Robert Graybill, Refton, Posts Bail For Hearing Before Magistrate At Quarryville

Robert Graybill, of Refton, was arrested Saturday night by State Motor Policeman H. R. Diem, of the Quarryville sub-station, on a charge of failing to stop after an accident. He posted bail for a hearing before Justice of the Peace Samuel Gall, of Quarryville.

The officer said a car operated by Graybill is alleged to have sideswiped a car operated by Joseph C. Rineer, Quarryville R. D. 3, on a road a half mile east of Willow Street. Graybill failed to stop, Rineer told the officer. Rineer said he and several friends searched the vicinity and finally located Graybill's auto at Refton. Police said Graybill admitted to Rineer that he was driving the car at the time of the accident.

VAIL GIVEN APPOINTMENT

Harrisburg — (AP) — Robert M. Vail, of Kingston, retired major general of the Pennsylvania National Guard, Tuesday was appointed deputy adjutant general in charge of veterans' affairs. The post was created by the 1939 legislature.

To Start Building Cantonment At Indiantown Gap Within 10 Days

Deadline For Construction Of 700 More Buildings, Other Facilities To Train Troops, Set For Jan. 1

Pittsburgh — (AP) — Work of converting the National Guard encampment at Indiantown Gap into a vast cantonment capable of housing 30,000 conscripted soldiers will start within 10 days, contractors reported Tuesday.

Reminiscent of the speed with which military preparations were pushed in 1917, the deadline for construction of 700 additional buildings, several miles of roads, heating plants and sewerage system has been set for Jan. 1—less than three months away.

TO USE 3000 LABORERS

To attain that goal, three construction firms who shared the $5,500,000 contract for the expansion will throw 3,000 laborers into the work.

W. F. Trimble, Jr., of the W. F. Trimble and Son company, one of the contractors, declared there was "nothing around here to compare with the size of this job."

"We'll probably have to work day and night," he said. "We have men down there already preparing to get things moving at top speed."

The encampment, between Lebanon and Harrisburg, has been used for several years for summer

More of CAMP on Page 16

Intelligencer Journal Weather Calendar

COMPARATIVE TEMPERATURES

Station	High	Low
Intell Journal	68	41
Water Works	67	46
Ephrata	67	46
Last Year (Ephrata)	66	51
Official High for Year, July 26		102.5
Official Low for Year, Jan. 20		2
Character of Day		Partly Cloudy

HOURLY TEMPERATURES

Tuesday			
8 a. m.	50	9 p. m.	56
11 a. m.	58	10 p. m.	55
2 p. m.	66	11 p. m.	55
5 p. m.	62	Midnight	54
		Wednesday	
6 p. m.	58	1 a. m.	54
7 p. m.	57	2 a. m.	54
8 p. m.	56	3 a. m.	54

HUMIDITY

8 a. m.—46; 11 a. m.—41; 2 p. m.—41; 5 p. m.—59; 8 p. m.—84; 11 p. m.—100
Average humidity—62
Dew Point 11 p. m.—52

More of WEATHER on Page 16

Cincinnati Takes Seventh Game, 2-1 To Win 1940 Series

Derringer's Twisters Again Prove Too Much For Detroit Batsmen

National League's First World Series Championship Since 1934; Werber's Wild Throw Allows Detroit To Score Only Run

Crosley Field, Cincinnati—(AP)—The heroic Cincinnati Reds surged from behind in the seventh inning Tuesday to tame the Detroit Tigers 2 to 1 and win the 1940 world's championship of baseball behind the dead-game hurling of lion-hearted Paul Derringer.

The National League's first triumph since 1934 was a throbbing struggle that stirred the blood of everyone of the 26,769 spectators at the seventh and deciding game of the World Series.

Derringer and bulging Buck Newsom, each of whom had worked in two previous series installments, waged as tight a battle as two capable and courageous hurlers ever could throw at each other and for some time it seemed that the outcome might hinge on one error by an outstanding fielder of the series.

In the third inning Bill Werber, the Reds' valiant third baseman made a wild throw to first and let in the Tigers' only run—an unearned tally that kept the Reds stewing until they finally burst their bonds in the seventh for the winning runs.

The home town fans, hoping anxiously for their first world championship since 1919 when the Chicago "Black Sox" sold out to gamblers, stood up to stretch in the seventh and were still standing and shouting encouragement when Frank (Buck) McCormick bounced a terrific liner against the high green wall in left field, 380 feet from the plate.

Then red-headed, freckled Jimmy Ripple shot the first pitch against the screen in front of the right field bleachers, 370 feet away, and McCormick crossed the plate with the tying run.

No team is any better at getting home one vital run than the Reds, and Manager Bill McKechnie maneuvered the winning tally with as much care as he ever exercised.

He had catcher Jim Wilson lay down a sacrifice bunt to bring Ripple to third. He put in big Ernie Lombardi to pinch hit for Eddie Joost and, when Manager Del Baker rushed out of the dugout and ordered Lombardi intentionally walked, Lonnie Frey was sent in to run for "Schnozzle."

Little Billy Myers waited out a 3 and 1 count and then lifted a tremendous fly that Barney McCosky caught with his back against the center field fence, 385 feet away, Ripple racing home after the catch with the crucial score.

$1,000,000 SERIES

That broke the tension of the series' tightest game and one of the most memorable in many years. It was the perfect climax to the first million dollar series since 1937 and the first to go seven games since the St. Louis Cardinals beat these same Detroit Tigers in 1934.

Once ahead the Reds were impregnable. Derringer was nicked for a single by Charley Gehringer at the start of the eighth, but he retired the next six batters in order and in the last inning, while McKechnie had both Bucky Walters and Joe Beggs warming up in the bull pen. Derringer didn't let the Tigers hit the ball out of the infield.

He should have won a shutout, but the early part of the game was packed with unusual plays and situations and one of them unravelled from the wrong end for the Reds.

Billy Sullivan, the Detroit catcher, started the trouble in the third inning by beating out a grounder along the first base line ahead of Frank McCormick's throw to Derringer. Newsom sacrificed him to second and, after Dick Bartell popped up, McCosky walked.

Then Gehringer smacked a sizzling grounder toward third and Werber just knocked it down. He threw badly to first and before McCormick could recover the ball, Sullivan raced home and easily beat the belated throw.

Each pitcher permitted seven hits, but until the seventh frame old Bobo actually had out-hurled his rival and was well along to becoming the first man to acquire three World Series victories since Stanley Coveleskie did it for Cleveland in 1920.

Newsom struck out six batters and his lone walk was intentional, to Lombardi in the seventh. In the first six frames Newsom allowed only four hits, all in separate innings, and faced only 21 batters.

The blows that he gave were a single by Wilson with two out in the second, a single by Wilson to lead off the fifth when he was quickly erased in a double play, a single by Myers to lead off the third and a double by Mike McCormick with two out in the sixth.

This last shot apparently was the signal that Newsom was tiring. He took the clinching assignment with one day's rest after shutting out the Reds on three hits in Detroit Sunday.

Even so, he finished strong, striking out two of Cincinnati's top batters in the eighth and giving up only one other hit, a drag bunt that Mike McCormick beat out.

The first run against Newsom might have been cut off by a little more alertness on the part of Dick Bartell. It looked for a moment like Bruce Campbell might snare Ripple's drive in the seventh and Frank McCormick hovered near second until he saw the ball fall safe. He was only half way from third to the plate when Bartell took the throw-in, but the fiery little shortstop had his back to McCormick and was watching Ripple slide into second.

Derringer struck out only one batter and walked three, one intentionally, but he pitched his own kind of a ball game and with the help of fine fielding by his teammates came through flying.

He was in trouble in the second, fourth and sixth frames in addition to the third.

Hank Greenberg led off with a single in the second, went to second on an infield out but was trapped and run down when Derringer snagged Campbell's grounder.

With two out in the fourth Higgins smashed a hopper at Werber, who just managed to deflect the ball against the railing of the left field stands and Higgins scurried to second. Sullivan was purposely passed and then Newsom socked a liner that struck Higgins in the stomach as he ran for third. It was an automatic out.

In the sixth Greenberg again singled, went to second as Campbell waited out a walk and moved to third as Higgins forced Campbell on a sparkling play by Myers.

But that was the end of the party for the Tigers, who got only ten men to the plate in the final three innings.

Derringer's single strikeout was a vital one, a high fast ball over the inside corner against Greenberg to end the inning in which the Tigers tallied.

"Big Paul"

DETROIT (A. L.)

	AB	R	H	O	A	E
Bartell ss	4	0	0	3	2	0
McCosky cf	3	0	0	3	0	0
Gehringer 2b	4	0	2	3	2	0
Greenberg lf	4	0	2	1	0	0
York 1b	4	0	0	5	0	0
Campbell rf	3	0	0	2	0	0
Higgins 3b	4	0	1	0	4	0
Sullivan c	3	1	1	6	0	0
Newsom p	2	0	1	1	0	0
x-Averill	1	0	0	0	0	0
Totals	32	1	7	24	8	0

Note—Sullivan scored in third on Werber's error.
x—Batted for Newsom in 9th.

CINCINNATI (N. L.)

	AB	R	H	O	A	E
Werber 3b	4	0	0	1	3	1
M. McCormick cf	4	0	2	4	0	0
Goodman rf	4	0	0	3	0	0
F. McCormick 1b	4	1	1	6	1	0
Ripple lf	3	1	1	1	0	0
Wilson c	2	0	2	2	0	0
Frey 2b	0	0	0	0	1	0
Myers ss	3	0	1	5	1	0
Derringer p	3	0	0	0	1	0
x-Lombardi	0	0	0	0	0	0
Totals	29	2	7	27	8	1

x—Batted for Joost in 7th.

DETROIT	001 000 000—1
CINCINNATI	000 000 20x—2

Runs batted in: Ripple, Myers. Two base hits: Higgins, M. McCormick, F. McCormick, Ripple. Stolen base: Wilson. Sacrifices: Newsom, Wilson. Left on bases: Detroit 8, Cincinnati 5. Bases on balls: Off Newsom 1, Derringer 3. Struck out: By Newsom 6, Derringer 1. Double play: Gehringer, Bartell, York. Winning pitcher: Derringer. Losing pitcher: Newsom.

Umpires: Ballanfant (N), plate; Basil (A), first; Klem (N), second; Ormsby (A), third. Time—1:47.

MacFAYDEN RELEASED

Pittsburgh — (AP) — Danny MacFayden, veteran right-hand hurler, has been given his unconditional release, the Pittsburgh Pirates announced.

The Pirate office said that Danny, now 34-years-old and with 15 major league seasons behind him, "did not fit in with the policy of Manager Frankie Frisch to rebuild the Pittsburgh club with young men."

MacFayden, who has pitched in both major leagues, was traded to the Bucs by the Boston Bees last winter.

Cincinnati, National League Champs, Capture World Series Flag

National League champions, the Cincinnati Reds, who won the World Series championship Tuesday, pose for a group picture. Front row, left to right, are Lew Riggs, Mike McCormick, Bill Myers, Jim Ripple, Coach Jimmy Wilson, Manager Bill McKechnie, Coach Hank Gowdy, Bill Werber, Morrie Arnovich and Trainer Rhode. Second row, left to right, Traveling Secretary Gabe Paul, Witt Guise, John Hutchings, Gene Thompson, Joe Beggs, Eddie Joost, Bill Baker, Frank McCormick, Dick West and Paul Derringer. Back row, left to right, Lonnie Frey, Elmer Riddle, Ival Goodman, Johnny Vander Meer, Harry Craft, Milburn Shoffner, Bucky Walters, Lloyd Moore, Jim Turner. Bat boy is Joe Hurst. Ernie Lombardi was absent when this photograph was taken.

FINAL FIGURES

(By The Associated Press)

Final standings:

	W.	L.
CINCINNATI (N. L.)	4	3
DETROIT (A. L.)	3	4

First game (at Cincinnati):

	R.	H.	E.
DETROIT (A. L.)	7	10	1
CINCINNATI (N. L.)	2	8	3

Batteries: Newsom and Sullivan; Derringer, Moore, Riddle, and Wilson, Baker
Attendance—31,793.

Second game (at Cincinnati):

	R.	H.	E.
DETROIT (A. L.)	3	3	1
CINCINNATI (N. L.)	5	9	0

Batteries: Rowe, Gorsica and Tebbetts; Walters and Wilson.
Attendance—30,640.

Third game (at Detroit):

	R.	H.	E.
CINCINNATI (N. L.)	4	10	1
DETROIT (A. L.)	7	13	1

Batteries: Turner, Moore, Beggs, and Lombardi, Baker; Bridges and Tebbetts.
Attendance—52,877.

Fourth game (at Detroit):

	R.	H.	E.
CINCINNATI (N. L.)	5	11	1
DETROIT (A. L.)	2	5	1

Batteries: Derringer and Wilson; Trout Smith, McKain, and Sullivan.
Attendance—54,093.

Fifth game (at Detroit):

	R.	H.	E.
CINCINNATI (N. L.)	0	3	0
DETROIT (A. L.)	8	13	0

Batteries: Newsom and Sullivan; Thompson, Moore, Vander Meer, Hutchings and Wilson.
Attendance—55,189.

Sixth game (at Cincinnati):

	R.	H.	E.
DETROIT (A. L.)	0	5	0
CINCINNATI (N. L.)	4	10	2

Batteries: Rowe, Gorsica, Hutchinson and Tebbetts; Walters and Wilson.
Attendance—30,481.

Seventh game (at Cincinnati):

	R.	H.	E.
DETROIT (A. L.)	1	6	0
CINCINNATI (N. L.)	2	7	1

Batteries: Newsom and Sullivan; Derringer and Wilson.
Attendance—26,769.

Seventh game attendance and financial figures:
Attendance—26,769.
Receipts $120,794.75.
Advisory Council $18,119.21.
Clubs and leagues' share $102,675.54.

Total attendance and financial figures, seven games:
Attendance 281,842.
Receipts $1,221,817.84.
Players' pool (first four games only) (x) $373,830.56.
Advisory Council (x) $183,273.07.
Clubs and leagues' share (x) $664,714.61.
(x) Does not include share in $100,000 broadcast rights.

EACH CINCI REDS' PLAYER GETS $2,000 MORE BY WIN

Cincinnati—(AP)—Winning the World Series Tuesday was worth $5,782 to each of the Cincinnati Reds, approximately $2,000 more than if they had lost.

The Detroit Tigers will receive $3,519 for each of their individual shares.

The players received a share of the receipts of only the first four games and a proportionate part of the sale of radio rights.

The Reds voted before the Series to divide their swag in 28 3-4 shares after taking $3,000 off the top for cash bonuses.

DIEHL LOST TO M-VILLE

Frankie Diehl, hard running back for Millersville State Teachers college, has been admitted to the Lancaster General hospital, suffering from a leg infection. Diehl's home is in Harrisburg, Pa. Diehl will be unable to play against Montclair Teachers at Millersville, Saturday.

. . . Details Of Seventh World Series Game . . .

FIRST INNING

TIGERS—Bartell lined the first pitch directly at Myers. McCosky lifted a high fly to M. McCormick in deep center. Gehringer lifted a fly in short left and Ripple came rushing in to make a great catch. No runs, no hits, no errors, none left.

REDS—Werber lined to Greenberg deep in left. M. McCormick struck out on four pitches. Goodman grounded to Bartell. No runs, no hits, no errors, none left.

SECOND INNING

TIGERS—Greenberg sent a sharp grounder which Myers was able to knock down but unable to throw and it was scored as a single. York topped the ball toward third base, Werber rushing in for a gloved-hand pickup and throwing to first just in time to nip the runner in a spectacular play. Campbell grounded to Derringer, who wheeled and saw Greenberg streaking for third and ran toward him setting up a trap, in which Greenberg was run down, Derringer to Myers to Werber to Joost, Campbell going to second. Higgins was thrown out, Joost to F. McCormick. No runs, one hit, no errors, one left.

REDS—F. McCormick grounded to Higgins on the grass in front of third. Ripple struck out on five pitches. Wilson hit the first pitch into left field for a single. Wilson stole second, getting half way there before Newsom's pitch reached the catcher. Joost grounded out, Gehringer to York. No runs, one hit, no errors, one left.

THIRD INNING

TIGERS—Sullivan sent a grounder along the first base line and beat F. McCormick's throw to Derringer for a single. Newsom laid down a sacrifice bunt, F. McCormick to Joost who covered first. Bartell raised a high pop fly to Joost. McCosky walked on five pitches. Gehringer sent a sharp grounder to Werber who stopped the ball but had to pick it up and threw wild to first, the ball getting past F. McCormick and Sullivan coming home. The play was scored as a basehit and an error for Werber. Greenberg fanned. One run, two hits, one error, two left.

REDS—Myers looped a single into short left. Derringer, attempting to bunt on the first pitch, popped directly into Newsom's glove. Werber knocked the first pitch straight at Higgins who threw to Gehringer, forcing Myers at second. M. McCormick struck out. No runs, one hit, no errors, one left.

FOURTH INNING

TIGERS—York lifted a pop foul to Wilson in front of the Tigers' dugout. Campbell raised a high fly to Goodman. Higgins hit a hot grounder that Werber deflected against the railing in front of the left field stands and had to run down, Higgins getting a double. Sullivan was walked intentionally. Newsom hit a grounder that struck Higgins in the stomach as he was running toward third, making an automatic out, with Newsom getting credit for a single and Myers a putout. No runs, two hits, no errors, two left.

REDS—Goodman struck out. F. McCormick raised a high fly to McCosky. Ripple grounded out to York, unassisted. No runs, no hits, no errors, none left.

FIFTH INNING

TIGERS—Bartell lined the first pitch to M. McCormick, who took it without moving. McCosky flied to Goodman. Gehringer lifted a pop fly to Myers. No runs, no hits, no errors, none left.

REDS—Wilson lined a single into right center. Al Benton, a right-hander, warmed up in the Tigers' bull pen. Joost grounded into a double play, Gehringer to Bartell to York. Myers raised a long fly to Campbell. No runs, one hit, no errors, none left.

SIXTH INNING

TIGERS—Greenberg drove a hard single into left center. York lifted a high pop to Joost. Campbell walked. Myers came over back of second to make a fancy stop of Higgins' grounder and stepped on second, forcing Campbell, but Higgins beat his throw to first, and Greenberg reached third unmolested. F. McCormick, crouching on his knees, stopped Sullivan's grounder and walked to first for the putout. No runs, one hit, no errors, two left.

REDS—Derringer raised a high fly to Campbell. Werber popped to Bartell. M. McCormick hit a clean double into right center. Goodman lined the first pitch at McCosky, who started in and then backed up to make the catch. No runs, one hit, no errors, one left.

SEVENTH INNING

TIGERS—Newsom raised a short fly to right field which Joost took on an easy run. Bartell lined the first pitch to Werber. McCosky lifted a fly to M. McCormick in deep center. No runs, no hits, no errors, none left.

REDS—F. McCormick drove the first pitch on one bounce against the fence in left field, 380 feet from home plate, for a double. Ripple picked out the first pitch and slammed it against the screen in front of the bleachers in right field for two bases and brought F. McCormick in with the tying run. Fans threw cushions and paper onto the field and Newsom huddled with his infielders while the playing field was getting cleared. Both Benton and Tommy Bridges began warming up in Detroit's bull pen. Wilson sacrificed Ripple to third, Higgins to Gehringer. Ernie Lombardi, the Reds' injured catcher and a right handed hitter, batted for Joost. Manager Del Baker of the Tigers came out of the dugout and ordered an intentional walk for Lombardi. Linus Frey, who had been kept out of action by a broken toe, ran for Lombardi. Myers lifted a high fly which McCosky took against the center field wall, Ripple scoring after the catch and Frey holding first. Derringer sent a grounder to Higgins who threw to Gehringer forcing Frey at second. Two runs, two hits, no errors, one left.

EIGHTH INNING

TIGERS—Frey went to second base for the Reds. Gehringer knocked a ground single into right field. Greenberg lined directly at Myers, but Gehringer scrambled back to first to prevent a double play. York lifted a high fly which M. McCormick took after a run in right center. Campbell hit a high fly to Goodman in right field. No runs, one hit, no errors, one left.

REDS—Werber was called out on a third pitch. M. McCormick laid down a drag bunt along the third base line for a single. Goodman struck out. F. McCormick raised a high pop to Bartell. No runs, one hit, no errors, one left.

NINTH INNING

TIGERS—Bucky Walters and Joe Beggs went to work in the Reds' bull pen before Derringer ever got to the mound. Higgins grounded out, Werber to F. McCormick. F. McCormick took Sullivan's grounder and beat him to the bag. Earl Averill, a left-handed batter, pinch hit for Newsom, and grounded out, Frey to F. McCormick. No runs, no hits, no errors, none left.

STEVE BELLOISE KAYOES HARKINS IN THIRD ROUND

White Plains, N. Y.—(AP)—Steve Belloise, New York contender for the middleweight title, knocked out Wicky Harkins, of Philadelphia, in 2:42 of the third round of their eight round bout at the West-Chester Country center Tuesday night.

Belloise almost flattened his rival with a barrage of punches to the head in the first round and sent him down for a short count in the second.

The bout was Belloise's tune-up for a title shot against Ken Overlin next month.

Belloise weighed 155, Harkins 157 1-2.

EXPORT SPORTS FOLLOWERS PAY TRIBUTE TO RIPPLE

Export, Pa.— (AP) —This little western Pennsylvania town toasted its native son-hero, Jimmy Ripple, of the Cincinnati Reds.

He batted in the tying run and scored the winning tally himself as the Reds beat the Detroit Tigers to win the World Series Tuesday.

All over town the sole topic was "Jimmy" who will be 31 years old October 14. A committee got to work to give the Red outfielder a victory dinner October 15 at the Greensburg Country Club.

DORMAN SIGNS CONTRACT TO MANAGE SUNBURY CLUB

Sunbury, Pa. — (AP) — Fred (Dutch) Dorman signed a contract Tuesday to manage the Sunbury Indians of the Interstate Baseball League next season at what owner Oren Sterling said was a substantial increase over his 1940 salary. The amount was not disclosed.

Sterling said there was a possibility that the Indians would become a major league farm in 1941.

Reds Nose Out Tigers To Win Deciding Series Game

Hank Greenberg, Detroit Tiger outfielder, was trapped and run down between second and third in this play of the seventh and deciding World Series game with the Cincinnati Reds, which the Reds took 2 to 1. Joost is tagging Greenberg, while Myers watches with interest from the right. At left is Paul Derringer, who made one unsuccessful effort to halt the Tigers but scored his second triumph in the final game.

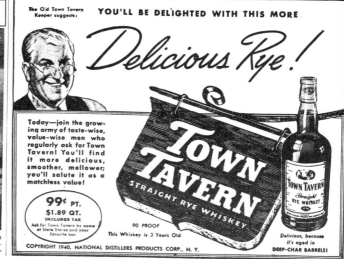

. . . Composite Box Score . . .

Cincinnati—(AP)—Following is the composite box score of the seven games in the 1940 World Series:

DETROIT

	G	AB	R	H	2B	3B	HR	RBI	BB	SO	PCT.	PO	A	E	PCT.
Bartell, ss	7	26	2	7	2	0	0	3	3	3	.269	13	12	1	.962
Croucher, ss	1	0	0	0	0	0	0	0	0	0	.000	0	0	0	.000
Fox (x)	1	1	0	0	0	0	0	0	0	0	.000	0	0	0	.000
McCoskey, cf	7	23	5	7	1	0	0	1	7	0	.304	19	0	0	1.000
Gehringer, 2b	7	28	3	6	0	0	0	1	2	0	.214	17	20	0	1.000
Greenberg, lf	7	28	5	10	2	1	1	6	2	5	.357	12	0	0	1.000
York, 1b	7	26	3	6	0	1	1	2	4	7	.231	60	2	0	1.000
Campbell, rf	7	25	4	9	1	0	1	5	4	4	.360	17	0	0	1.000
Higgins, 3b	7	24	2	8	3	1	1	6	3	3	.333	4	30	2	.944
Sullivan, c (zz)	5	13	3	2	0	0	0	0	5	2	.154	23	2	0	1.000
Tebbetts, c (y)	4	11	0	0	0	0	0	0	0	0	.000	13	3	1	.941
Newsom, p	3	10	1	1	0	0	0	0	0	1	.100	2	0	0	1.000
Rowe, p	2	1	0	0	0	0	0	0	0	1	.000	0	1	0	1.000
Gorsica, p	2	4	0	0	0	0	0	0	0	2	.000	0	6	0	1.000
Bridges, p	1	3	0	0	0	0	0	0	0	1	.000	0	1	0	1.000
Trout, p	1	1	0	0	0	0	0	0	0	0	.000	0	1	0	1.000
Smith, p	1	1	0	0	0	0	0	0	0	1	.000	0	1	0	1.000
Averill (z)	3	3	0	0	0	0	0	0	0	0	.000	0	0	0	.000
McKain, p	1	0	0	0	0	0	0	0	0	0	000	0	1	0	1.000
Hutchinson, p	1	0	0	0	0	0	0	0	0	0	.000	0	0	0	.000
Totals	7	228	28	56	9	3	4	24	30	30	.246	180	80	4	.985

(x)—Batted for Bartell 9th inning 4th game.
(y)—Batted for McKain 9th inning 4th game.
(z)—Batted for Smith 6th inning 4th game and for Gorsica 8th inning 6th game and Newsom 9th inning 7th game.
(zz)—Batted for Bartell 8th inning 6th game.

CINCINNATI

	G	AB	R	H	2B	3B	HR	RBI	BB	SO	PCT.	PO	A	E	PCT.
Werber, 3b	7	27	5	10	4	0	0	2	4	2	.370	9	16	2	.926
M. McCormick, cf	7	29	2	9	3	0	0	2	1	6	.310	24	1	1	.962
Goodman, rf	7	29	5	8	2	0	0	5	0	3	.276	10	0	0	1.000
F. McCormick, 1b	7	28	2	6	1	0	0	0	1	1	.214	58	4	1	.984
Ripple, lf	7	21	3	7	2	0	1	6	4	2	.333	14	0	0	1.000
Arnovich, lf	1	1	0	0	0	0	0	0	0	0	.000	2	0	0	1.000
Wilson, c	6	17	1	6	0	0	0	0	1	2	.353	26	2	0	1.000
Riggs (a)	3	3	1	0	0	0	0	0	0	2	.000	0	0	0	.000
Baker, c	3	4	1	1	0	0	0	0	0	1	.250	7	0	1	.875
Lombardi, c (e)	2	3	0	1	1	0	0	0	1	0	.333	4	0	0	1.000
Joost, 2b	7	25	0	5	0	0	0	2	1	2	.200	15	12	0	1.000
Myers, ss	7	23	0	3	0	0	0	2	2	5	.130	14	17	3	.912
Derringer, p	3	7	0	0	0	0	0	0	0	1	.000	0	5	0	1.000
Moore, p	3	2	0	0	0	0	0	0	0	1	.000	0	1	0	1.000
Craft (b)	1	1	0	0	0	0	0	0	0	0	.000	0	0	0	.000
Riddle, p	1	0	0	0	0	0	0	0	0	0	.000	0	0	0	.000
Walters, p	2	7	2	2	1	0	1	2	0	1	.286	0	4	0	1.000
Turner, p	1	2	0	0	0	0	0	0	0	0	.000	0	1	0	1.000
Beggs p	1	0	0	0	0	0	0	0	0	0	.000	0	0	0	.000
Frey, 2b (d)	3	2	0	0	0	0	0	0	0	0	.000	0	1	0	1.000
Thompson, p	1	1	0	0	0	0	0	0	0	1	.000	0	1	0	1.000
Vander Meer, p	1	0	0	0	0	0	0	0	0	0	.000	0	0	0	.000
Hutchings, p	1	0	0	0	0	0	0	0	0	0	.000	0	1	0	1.000
Totals	7	232	22	58	14	0	2	21	15	30	.250	183	66	8	.969

(a)—Batted for Wilson seventh inning first game; for Moore 8th inning third game, for Vander Meer 8th inning 5th game.
(b)—Batted for Moore 8th inning, 1st game.
(d)—Batted for Beggs 9th inning 3rd game; for Moore 5th inning 5th game; ran for Lombardi 7th inning 7th game.
(e)—Batted for Joost 7th inning 7th game.

COMPOSITE SCORE BY INNINGS

Cincinnati (NL)	5	2	3	3	0	1	2	4	2—22
Detroit (AL)	2	5	5	5	2	2	4	3	0—28

Earned runs—Cincinnati (NL) 20, Detroit (AL) 27. Stolen bases—Wilson. Sacrifices—Campbell and Newsom (2), Detroit; Arnovich, M. McCormick, Goodman and Wilson, Cincinnati. Double plays—Cincinnati (9), Wilson and Joost; Werber, Joost and F. McCormick (3); Myers, F. McCormick and Baker; Joost, Myers and F. McCormick (2); Derringer, Myers and F. McCormick; F. McCormick, Myers and F. McCormick; Detroit (4), Higgins, Gehringer and York; Bartell, Gehringer and York; Gorsica, Tebbets and York; Gehringer, Bartell and York. Left on bases—Cincinnati 49, Detroit 50. Umpires—Klem and Ballanfant (NL), Ormsby and Basil (AL). Times of games—First, 2:09; second, 1:54; third, 2:08; fourth, 2:06; fifth, 2:26; sixth, 2:01; seventh, 1:47. Attendance by games—First, 31,793 (at Cincinnati); second, 30,640 (at Cincinnati); third, 52,877 (at Detroit); fourth, 54,093 (at Detroit), fifth, 55,189 (at Detroit); sixth, 30,481 (at Cincinnati); seventh, 26,769 (at Cincinnati).

PITCHING RECORDS

Cincinnati	G	CG	IP	H	R	ER	BB	SO	WP	HB	W	L	PCT.	ERA
Walters	2	2	18	8	3	3	6	6	0	0	2	0	1.000	1.50
Derringer	3	2	19⅓	17	8	7	10	6	0	0	2	1	.667	3.26
Turner	1	0	6	8	5	5	0	4	0	0	0	1	.000	7.50
Thompson	1	0	3⅓	8	6	6	4	2	0	0	0	1	.000	13.50
Moore	3	0	8⅓	8	3	3	6	7	0	0	0	0	.000	3.24
Riddle	1	0	1	0	0	0	0	2	0	0	0	0	.000	0.00
Beggs	1	0	1	3	2	2	0	1	0	0	0	0	.000	18.00
Vander Meer	1	0	3	2	0	0	3	2	0	0	0	0	.000	0.00
Hutchings	1	0	1	2	1	1	1	0	1	0	0	0	.000	9.00

Detroit	G	CG	IP	H	R	ER	BB	SO	WP	HB	W	L	PCT.	ERA
Bridges	1	1	9	10	4	3	1	5	0	0	1	0	1.000	3.00
Newsom	3	3	26	18	4	4	4	17	0	0	2	1	.667	1.38
Rowe	2	0	3⅔	12	7	7	1	1	0	0	0	2	.000	17.18
Trout	1	0	2	6	3	2	1	1	0	0	0	1	.000	18.00
Gorsica	2	0	11⅓	6	1	1	4	4	0	0	0	0	.000	0.79
Smith	1	0	4	1	1	1	3	1	0	0	0	0	.000	2.25
McKain	1	0	3	4	1	1	0	0	1	0	0	0	.000	3.00
Hutchinson	1	0	1	1	1	1	1	1	0	0	0	0	.000	9.00

. . . Club House Notes . . .

Cincinnati—(AP)—William (Deacon) McKechnie, kindly, bespectacled 56-year-old manager of the victorious Cincinnati Reds, was the happiest man in baseball Tuesday night.

His triumphant players shared his joy.

Gloom flooded the dressing room of the vanquished Detroit Tigers, but they had no alibis.

Twenty-one years of accumulated steam blew the safety valve as the victorious Reds clattered past each other up the steel stairs to their clubhouse.

Noise ballooned out of the windows, shouts and shrieks, yipping and songs.

Del Baker, Detroit Tigers manager, defeated but gallant, came up the stairs with the Reds, was lost in a seething crowd and had to be steered to Manager McKechnie.

"We lost to a great team, Bill," Baker said, clasping McKechnie's hand.

"We won from a great one, Del," the Deacon smiled.

McKechnie said: "It was the cleanest and hardest world's series I ever saw in my 35 years of baseball. I extend my regards to manager Briggs of the Tigers, the players and the Detroit fans. It was a pleasure to play the Tigers."

Paul Derringer, unshaven, worn and wanting only to sit down, trudged up the stairs. As he entered, a tremendous howl cut loose. He sat down beside catcher Jimmy Wilson, 40-year-old hero of heroes, grabbed Wilson by the hair and gave him a kindly pat on the head and grinned.

Wilson, with tape all over his bruised body and legs, was supremely happy. There was a day's growth of whiskers upon his face, too.

"We gave them hell, didn't we kid?" he beamed at Derringer. Paul just smiled.

McKechnie came over to shake hands.

"I feel just great," the Deacon said. "I'm ready to go out and play those guys again right now."

"Not for me," yelled the worn-out Wilson. "I'm through. No more catching for me. The hell with it. Give it back to the Indians."

Wrinkled Hank Gowdy, the Reds' coach, said he never saw any better catching in a world's series than Wilson's performance.

Warren Giles, general manager of the Reds, hugged and kissed McKechnie. Wilson kissed Gowdy. Some wild-eyed fan aimed for Powel Crosley, Jr., owner of the Reds, and kissed a cop.

Slowly Derringer got his strength back. Somebody hit him on the back so hard that he swallowed his gum.

McKechnie climbed on a folding seat and told the boys to keep their uniforms and jackets — "compliments of the club."

And Ford Frick, president of the National League, held up three fingers and chortled:

"Two all-star games and the world series in the same year." The Tigers, without their manager, gloomy trooped into their dressing room and began slamming their clothes into trunks. Barney McCosky dropped exhausted into a chair and blurted: "Well, those guys knew they were in a ball game, anyway, didn't they?"

Bobo Newsom praised Derringer's

More of CLUB HOUSE On Page 13

MIRTH AND MELODY—Reign at the Colonial theatre where Mickey Rooney, Judy Garland and a group of clever youngsters, many of them seen with the youthful stars in "Babes In Arms," are regaling audiences with harmonies and comicalities. Mickey and Judy organize a high school band in the story and that's when things begin to happen. Paul Whiteman has announced a radio contest for high school bands. They set out to raise funds for the trip to Chicago. They stage a travesty on old-time melodrama, with the buzz saw, heroine tied to the railroad tracks, and such ancient ditties as "Heaven Will Protect a Working Girl." When Paul Whiteman appears in their town they borrow his orchestra's instruments during an intermission and give him an audition he never expected. They raise money for the trip, then one of the youngsters becomes ill and must be flown to a great surgeon. They sacrifice the money for the trip to save him but fate in the person of the town millionaire provides the train fare and they win the prize in a grand musical climax embellished by their comical specialties. Mickey masters the drums and is irresistibly funny. He also does some appealing "Straight" drama with Ann Shoemaker, playing his mother. Judy sings the catchy "Our Love Affair" and "Nobody," and burlesques such old-time numbers as "The Curse of An Aching Heart" fetchingly. She rises to comedy heights in the melodrama number. June Preisser, amazing little dancer, also imitates Anna Held singing "I Just Can't Make My Eyes Behave." Paul Whiteman not only conducts an orchestra but proves himself a very capable actor in his scenes with the youngsters.

The clever juvenile group includes William Tracy of "Shop Around the Corner" fame, Larry Nunn from the Irene Rich radio show, and Margaret Early, the little Southern girl of "Forty Little Mothers." The broadcast climax featuring Gershwin's "Strike Up the Band," and a musical medley including Mickey's strenuous drum solo, brings the mirth to a close in a blaze of harmony. There will be a morning show Saturday at 10 A. M.

GAY MUSIC—Deanna Durbin with some of her supporting players in "Spring Parade," which comes to the Grand theatre today for a week's engagement. Left to right Robert Cummings, Mischa Auer, S. Z. Sakall, Anne Gwynne and Butch and Buddy.

ROMANTIC DRAMA—Cary Grant and Martha Scott star in "The Howards of Virginia," which opens tomorrow at the Capitol. The supporting cast includes: Richard Carlson, Alan Marshall and Sir Cedric Hardwick. The story is based on Elizabeth Page's "The Tree Of Liberty." "Dance, Girl, Dance," starring Maureen O'Hara, Louis Hayward, Lucille Ball and Ralph Bellamy is showing today for the last times.

BRIDGE REOPENED AT MIDDLETOWN

The Harrisburg Pike bridge over Swatara Creek at the entrance to Middletown is open to traffic again.

The old bridge collapsed several weeks ago. Plans are being made for a new bridge to be built down stream from the present span.

WESTERN DRAMA ON STRAND SCREEN

Filmed in spectacular Technicolor the exciting and stirring climax to the daring exploits of the world's most famous outlaws came to the screen of the Strand Theatre Wednesday in the 20th Century-Fox production, "The Return of Frank James."

The millions of moviegoers who thrilled to last year's "Jesse James" will find this new Darryl F. Zanuck production even more colorful and action-packed. These same millions will also find many familiar faces in the cast, for "Jesse James" players fill most of the important roles.

Henry Fonda, who created the part of Frank James, Jesse's grim older brother, is cast in the title role. Others appearing in the production, who were also featured in "Jesse James," include Henry Hull, John Carradine, J. Edward Bromberg, Donald Meek, Ernest Whitman, Charles Tannen and George Chandler.

The cast is completed by Gene Tierney and Jackie Cooper, who are featured, and such popular favorites as Eddie Collins and George Barbier.

The story of "The Return of Frank James" is the story of Frank's determination to avenge the cowardly murder of his brother Jesse, shot in the back by the traitorous Ford brothers.

LANCASTER NEW ERA

WEATHER
Fair and continued cold with frost tonight; Thursday fair with slowly rising temperature. (Details on Page 3).

Examiner Founded 1830. New Era Founded 1877.

Published Every Evening Except Sunday by New Era Company. Entered as Second Class Matter at Post Office, Lancaster, Pa.

LANCASTER, PA., WEDNESDAY, OCTOBER 16, 1940 — CITY EDITION — 16 PAGES—128 COLUMNS—THREE CENTS

16,404,000 REGISTER FOR ARMY DRAFT

London Raked By 1,000 Tons Of Air Bombs

Nazis Report Fires 48 to 60 Miles Wide Started, Threaten to Triple Force of Raids to 'Typhoon Stage;' 300 Killed or Wounded as Dive Bomber Attacks Troop Train

(By The Associated Press)

Nazi quarters in Berlin threatened a triple-force "typhoon stage" in the aerial siege of Britain today after an armada of 1,000 German bombers reportedly dropped 1,000 tons of bombs on London during the night and left the British capital a scene of "indescribable chaos."

Even that terrific assault was only a "zephyr" compared to the storm ahead, the Germans said.

London dispatches said diving Nazi warplanes machine-gunned the streets and dropped the biggest explosives yet rained on the empire capital, but estimated that 250 tons of bombs were dropped by from 200 to 250 planes.

German airmen returning from the dusk-to-dawn assault told of "deafening detonations . . . terrific concussions . . . skies reddened by great fires . . ."

Nazi fliers said they observed fires raging throughout an area 48 to 60 miles wide, and they described London as "a great sea of flames."

300 Killed On Train

Informed German sources said that at least 300 persons had been killed or injured when a German dive bomber attacked an English transport train today.

The locomotive and the first six cars of the train went over an embankment and the rest of the train was torn apart, these informants said.

The London Ministry of Information admitted the night raids were "of a heavy nature," but said the damage was "not as great as that done in raids in early September" raids which took a daily death toll of 300 to 400 victims.

Many Killed In School House

Many were feared killed and wounded in the smashing of a 2-story London schoolhouse used as an air-raid shelter. The building, hit squarely by two huge bombs, was levelled.

Fire and oil bombs, known as "Goering cocktails," started countless fires throughout the metropolitan area, and Germans said the havoc recalled the wreckage of Warsaw, Roterdam and Dunkerque.

Hitler's High Command, complaining angrily that British RAF bombers were "planelessly" attacking non-military targets "and thus primarily against the German civilian population," said retaliatory attacks on London "therefore were considerably increased."

"Big fires following strong explosions in the city's heart, the Thames Bend, as well as the Victoria docks, were visible from the Channel coast on the return flight," the German communique asserted.

Short Alarm At Berlin

Berlin had a short midnight alarm but no planes appeared over the city.

The British Air Ministry reported raids by the RAF on a naval dockyard in Northern Germany, the Channel ports, and industrial and communication targets in Western and Central Germany.

London office buildings and homes crumbled under heavy German bombs, and workers still were digging into the debris for bodies after a dawn renewal of the attack. Parts of the Midlands and Southeastern England were reported to have had their longest, most intense raids of recent weeks.

Delayed explosion bombs increased the horror in London. One time bomb, the largest yet dropped on London, fell near a famous building. German planes strafed streets with machine-gun fire.

At one place where the dead and dying could be brought out they

(See WAR—Page 11)

DEFENSE UNITS FORMED HERE

Thirty Groups Totaling 360 Men Are on Call, Council Reports.

Some 360 men, most of them qualified by previous military experience and all of them equipped and vested with full authority, have been organized to combat espionage and fifth-column activities in Lancaster city and county, and to be available, further, for any emergency which may develop.

This was announced today by Col. J. Hale Steinman, chairman of the Defense Council for Lancaster, following a meeting of the Council.

Organization of the Council's defense unit, he added, is the first phase of a comprehensive program on which the Council is engaged. For the second phase of its effort, he added, the Council will concern itself with co-ordinating and cooperating with local agencies and organizations in any movement intended to strengthen the nation's defenses.

This is in keeping with official requests from Washington and Harrisburg that local committees be organized for that purpose. Col. Steinman's statement follows:

"Effective emergency defense measures for Lancaster city and county have now been completed.

"Major Frederick S. Foltz, in charge of the Council's emergency defense activities, reports that thirty units of twelve men each, strategically located throughout the county, have been organized.

"These selected groups are comprised largely of men with past military service all of whom are completely equipped and officered. In them has been vested full authority by duly-constituted law-enforcement authorities and their duties have been carefully outlined.

"They will function at the call of these authorities in any emergency growing out of sabotage or fifth-column activities until the arrival of federal or state militia.

"The Defense Council also heard reports of progress in several other of its activities whose objective is to weld the citizens of city and county into a smooth-working, effective and patriotic whole."

HIGH-FLYING PLANES BOMB GIBRALTAR

ALGECIRAS, Spain, Oct. 16 — (A. P.)—High flying planes raided Gibraltar at mid-day today in the heaviest attack since French airmen bombed the British Rock September 24 and 25.

The anti-aircraft guns of the British stronghold went "all out" against the raiders.

Observers here and at nearby La Linea, Spain, were unable to determine the nationality or the strength of the raiders because of the clouds.

BRITISH WAR FUND ADDS 4 BILLIONS

LONDON, Oct. 16—(A. P.)—The House of Commons voted today to make another £1,000,000,000 (about $4,000,000,000) war credit available to the government to cover heavy war expenditures between now and March. This constituted approval of the credit which the government announced yesterday.

Sir Kingsley Wood said the war is costing Britain £9,000,000 ($36,-000,000) a day.

CANADA GOVERNOR TO BE F. D.'S GUEST

QUEBEC, Oct. 16—(A. P.)—Authorities at the citadel announced today that the Earl of Athlone, Governor-General of Canada, and Princess Alice will spend the week-end of Oct. 19-21 at Hyde Park, N. Y., as guests of President Roosevelt.

The Scribbler

DRAFT NOTE: The committee planning the dance to be held by the high school class of 1931 on the night after Thanksgiving is making a special concession for members subject to conscription, in line with action taken by local stores. Any member who buys a ticket and is drafted may have his money back and attend the dance free.

DICK HERR, the mattress salesman, committed a remarkable shot while golfing with two customers recently at Galen Hall. He drove off from the tee of the third hole, later found his ball in the water bucket on the eleventh.

GEORGE SCHLOTZHAUER, bakery foreman, dashed downtown to cash a check yesterday, but when he arrived at the bank, found he had brought a check made out to another employe. He had to hurry back for his own.

GLADYS KEIPER, Ephrata nurse in training at Jefferson Hospital, Philadelphia, should have no excuse for not writing home. She collects pencils, and now has several hundred from all over the United States.

WILLKIE SEES STRENGTH IN PROSPERITY

Asserts Nation Must Be Sound Economically to Defend Itself.

DEMANDS F. D. TELL PEOPLE HIS PLANS

ABOARD WILLKIE TRAIN EN-ROUTE TO CINCINNATI, Oct. 16—(A. P.)—Wendell L. Willkie, declaring that America must be strong in the economic as well as military field, said today he wanted to bring about prosperity through the cooperation of labor, industry and agriculture.

"There is no conflict of American groups," he told a trainside audience at Marion, O., home of the late President Harding. "Whatever brings prosperity to one group leads to the prosperity of all."

"My object is to preserve for labor every social gain it has made. No man in the country will fight more for that goal than Wendell Willkie will.

"But I want to give much more than that to labor. I want to give an expanding economy that will bring jobs and a rising standard of living."

As he told an earlier gathering at Mansfield, Willkie asserted that America has but touched the borders of her achievement.

"In the home town of a former President I say this: Join with me and the other Republican candidates in a program of more jobs, a defense so impregnable that we will not become involved in war with anyone.

Unity—Not Discord

"Join me in cooperation with all the elements of the people so that we will have unity in America, not discord."

The only things the opposition has to offer, Willkie reiterated, are "smears, silence, imaginary military inspection trips, and the pressure of billions of dollars."

The Republican Presidential nominee asked the audience how it helped defense for President Roosevelt to spend 21 minutes in a steel mill "when he knows nothing about producing steel and never will."

Gov. John W. Bricker of Ohio and Mayor Harold H. Burton, of Cleveland, Republican candidate for U. S. Senator, were aboard Willkie's train as it moved southwest through the state.

During the Marion speech, someone in the audience called, "I want to be a captain."

Not "Right Family"

"You don't belong in the right family," the candidate replied.

Elliott Roosevelt, the President's second son, recently commissioned a captain in the Air Corps Reserves

(See WILLKIE—Page 13)

FINAL TRIBUTE PAID TOM MIX

HOLLYWOOD, Oct. 16.—(U. P.)—Hundreds of actor friends and former army buddies crowded silently into the Little Church of the Flowers today to pay final tribute to Tom Mix, dashing cowboy, soldier, actor and showman.

A Masonic ritual was read by Monte Blue, film player and close friend of the greatest of all the western horse and gun artists, and the service was conducted by the Rev. J. Whitcomb Brougher.

The ceremony for Mix, killed last Saturday when his automobile overturned at 80 miles an hour near Florence, Ariz., was in true, but restrained, Hollywood fashion, with orchestra leader Rudy Vallee singing Mix's favorite song, "Empty Saddles."

He will be buried under the pines of Forest Lawn Memorial Park.

YOUNG HUNTER KILLED IN JERSEY

TRENTON, N. J., Oct. 16.—(A. P.)—George S. Ziegler, 17, of Lawrence Township, was killed by a shotgun blast at 7:30 A. M. today as he crouched in a duck blind on the Delaware river with a companion. The youths had gone out at the opening of New Jersey's waterfowl hunting season at sunrise.

Hamilton Township police said Ziegler was shot in the head when his mate's gun went off accidentally. No charge was immediately made against Ziegler's 19-year-old companion.

Ziegler and three other boys were hunting on Bleak Duck Island, several miles below Trenton, they separated in pairs and Ziegler and another boy set up their blind in a canoe.

MERCURY IS AT 42, FROST IS FORECAST

The mercury toppled 42 degrees in less than twelve hours and touched a new seasonal low of 33 degrees at the City Water Works early today.

More cold weather and frost have been forecast by the United States Weather Bureau for the next twelve hours.

The mercury touched a high mark of 75 degrees yesterday afternoon and dropped sharply in the wake of a chilly north wind. Early this afternoon the temperature hovered around the 50's.

Without Regard to Color, Race or Creed . . .

Alfred C. Alspach, Lancaster city's representative in the Legislature, being registered by Miss Mary Kreider at the First Methodist Church at Duke and Walnut streets.

Gideon Fisher, Ronks, a member of the Amish faith, registering at the Intercourse Fire Hall. Charles M. Slack is the registration officer.

Even the blind had to register. Here Edward R. Henry, of 588 N. Plum St., accompanied by his Seeing Eye guide dog, is giving the necessary information to Walter Fickes at the Unitarian Church, Chestnut and Pine Streets.

Stanley Holmes, of Philadelphia, captain of the Franklin and Marshall football team, is getting on the conscription list at St. Peter's Reformed Church, College and Buchanan Avenues. Ralph H. Patterson is the registration clerk.

Frank Johnson, Negro, of 516 Rockland Street, is being registered by John W. Shertz at the Rockland Playground.

F. D. IN CONTROL OF ALL EXPORTS

Orders Requisitioning of All Materials Needed For Defense.

WASHINGTON, Oct. 16—(A. P.)—President Roosevelt today assumed full control over the sale or export of raw and manufactured products vital to the National Defense program, after invoking the government's power to requisition any equipment, munitions, machinery, tools, materials or supplies needed to prepare the nation for any emergency.

In an executive order the President ordered the Army and Navy Munitions Board to make an immediate survey to determine the necessity for requisitioning any of the items deemed necessary for National Defense purposes.

The Board was authorized at the same time to determine whether it is in the public interest to sell, or otherwise dispose of, any of the articles or materials requisitioned.

The President's action was considered very far reaching and significant. Defense experts said that under that authority the United States could regain possession of many war materials, equipment and supplies already sold but not

(See ROOSEVELT—Page 11)

MRS. TOMPKINS NEW DAR HEAD

Succeeds Mrs. Forney as State Regent; Defense Arms Urged.

Mrs. William H. Tompkins, Wilkes-Barre, was elected regent of the Pennsylvania State Society of the Daughters of the American Revolution at the forty-fourth annual state conference in Hotel Brunswick today. Approximately 500 delegates and members attended the sessions.

Mrs. Tompkins succeeds Mrs. Joseph G. Forney, this city. Mrs. Forney is slated for a national office next year.

Other state officers elected today are:

Vice-regent, Mrs. Clinton D. Higee, Erie; chaplain, Mrs. John G. Love, Bellefonte; recording secretary, Mrs. Ralph J. Miller, Shenandoah; corresponding secretary, Mrs. William C. Langston, York; treasurer, Mrs. J. Markley Freed, Germantown; registrar, Mrs. John C. Hartman, Wilkinsburg; historian, Mrs. Arthur G. Schautz, Scranton; Librarian, Miss Louise M. Hook, Waynesburg; directors, Eastern district, Miss Emily Schall, Reading; Central district, Mrs. R. H. Van Or-

(See D. A. R.—Page 11)

Early Rush to Register Here; 25,000 Expected to Be Enrolled

Crowds Wait in Line at Many of the 143 Places as Volunteers Aid Election Officials; All Must Report by 9 O'clock Tonight

With apparent good humor and a desire to have it done early, more than 14,500 young men registered their availability for national defense at the county's 143 registration places in the first eight hours today.

Some were on hand even before the places opened at 7 A. M., and county officials predicted that the early rush—particularly in the first two hours—had taken care of a sizeable share of the total, estimated at no more than 25,000. The places close at 9 P. M., or as soon thereafter as everyone is registered.

An estimated 5,300 registered at the city's 32 places by 3 P. M., lining up for as much as a half-block in front of some of them. There was a rush over the noon hour.

"They joke about it" one chief registrar said. "Everyone is taking it good-naturedly." The average registration time here is from 10 to 12 minutes, it was estimated. No arguments or disputes were reported to the court house, and most of the persons telephoning there wanted to know where to go to register.

Teachers and volunteers augmented the election boards in some districts.

• • •

A thoughtful Columbia merchant rigged up a loud-speaker system and played "The Star-Spangled Banner" at 7 A. M., after which prayer was offered over the amplifier by the Rev. J. W. Reed, Episcopal rector who leaves November 1 for a year's service as chaplain. Patriotic airs were played on the device throughout the morning and other business places in the vicinity put their flags out. Nearby a picket marched back and forth in front of a chain store, closed due to a strike.

• • •

Members of the plain sects, from all reports, were registering without objection. Conscientious objectors may list their sentiments on blanks which the draft boards will send out in the next few weeks. Ministers and divinity students also register, although they can claim exemption under the draft law.

* * *

Most of the men registering at Clay spoke Pennsylvania Dutch.

(See LOCAL DRAFT—Last Page)

ALL CLASSES, RACES ENROLL

1,107,000 N. Y. Men Register; Movie Stars, Notables, on List.

NEW YORK, Oct. 16—(A. P.)—In grimy overalls, tailored business suits and immaculate evening clothes, New York's youth rose to the top of this great new world melting pot today and flowed off to be counted and recorded for the defense of the nation.

From squalid tenements and gilded apartments they came, all races, creeds and colors.

Some were heavy-muscled and clear-eyed; others were anemic and pasty of face. But they came, many of them long before dawn, and lined up in front of 712 registration places throughout the five boroughs.

Within 14 hours, Uncle Sam will have the names of more than 1,107,000 New York men who will be available for the defense of the country.

They were a motley sight as they assembled in the chill dawn.

(See SIDELIGHTS—Last Page)

ANTHONY EDEN ARRIVES IN EGYPT

LONDON, Oct. 16 — (A. P.) — Anthony Eden, Secretary for War, has arrived in Egypt for consultations with Lieut.-Gen. Sir Archibald P. Wavell, commanding Britain's near eastern armies, it was announced here tonight.

5 MILLION MEN TO BE CALLED IN $4\frac{1}{2}$ YEARS

High Officials Included in 21-36 Age Bracket; A. E. F. Vets Enroll.

PRESIDENT, WILLKIE PRAISE REGISTRANTS

(By the Associated Press)

For the second time in the life of most Americans, the young manhood of the nation registered in mass today for military service.

"It is a day of deep and purposeful meaning in the lives of all of us," President Roosevelt said in a brief, early-morning address, as registration places across the country were opening for a 14-hour day.

Millions of men who answered the same call 23 years ago last June 5 saw their sons step into line for registration at election precincts and schools.

Even some veterans of the A. E. F.—those who lied about their ages then and enlisted at 12 or 13—retraced their steps after nearly a quarter of a century to enroll again.

1,250,000 An Hour

The men signed up for possible service in the nation's first peacetime draft army at an estimated rate of 1,250,000 an hour.

Reports going into Washington from state capitals, which in turn had gathered them from every city, town and rural district, prompted selective service headquarters to announce that the whole vast registration machinery was "clipping along smoothly."

In fact, officials said that if registrations continued all day at their estimate of 1,250,000 hourly the expected national total of 16,-404,000 registrants of ages 21 through 35 would be reached before the closing hour of 9 o'clock (local time) tonight.

Foe Of Bill Signs

Senator Rush Holt of West Virginia, who fought the conschiption bill in Congress, registered in his office where a registrar visited him. He issued a statement that "to call this a draft for peace is not only to state an untruth but to be hypocritical. It is a draft for war."

Rep. Lindley Beckworth of Texas, the youngest member of Congress at 27, made his way through Washington's wet streets in early morning to register at an old red school house near the Capitol.

Dr. Clarence A. Dykstra, recently-appointed selective service administrator, telegraphed headquarters at Washington that he would arrive in the Capital tomorrow to start work. The Wisconsin University president was expected to leave Chicago this afternoon.

His will be the job of arranging the lottery to be held next week to determine the order of calling men for service. He must prepare, too,

(See U. S.—Last Page)

ODDS IN ELECTION BETTING NARROW

NEW YORK, Oct. 16—Narrowing of the betting odds on the election was reported by the betting commission house of S. Woodruff Valentine Co. today. They quoted the national election at 8 to 5 Roosevelt as against a recent 12 to 5 quotation.

The firm quotes New York and New Jersey at even money. It quotes Pennsylvania, Massachusetts, Connecticut and Wisconsin, Willkie 7 to 5. Even money also is slated for Illinois, Indiana and Iowa. In California, the statement of Senator Hiram Johnson that he will oppose a third term, was said to be responsible for a narrowing of odds for Roosevelt to carry that state to 8 to 5.

WEATHER
Eastern Pennsylvania: Mostly Cloudy And Much Colder, Occasional Rain In The Mountains Wednesday; Thursday Fair.
Intell Journal Stormograph Reading: Cloudy And Colder.

Intelligencer Journal

The Leading Newspaper in the Garden Spot of America, Home Owned for Home Folks Since 1794.

Ice Hockey
Hershey Bears will open home season in American League with Pittsburgh at sports arena Thursday night.
For details turn to Page Twelve.

VOLUME LXXVII.—NO. 48. CITY The Intelligencer Founded 1799 The Journal Founded 1794 LANCASTER, PA., WEDNESDAY MORNING, NOVEMBER 6, 1940. Entered at Post Office at Lancaster, Pa. as second class mail matter 18 PAGES, 144 COLUMNS.—THREE CENTS.

ROOSEVELT WINS HIS THIRD TERM

CARRIES LANCASTER CITY AND PENNA. AGAIN

President's Lead In State Over 225,000; County Goes G.O.P.

Marshall M. Cohen Unseats Alfred C. Alspach As Other Republican Candidates Win

President Roosevelt carried Lancaster city for the third time Tuesday while the Republicans polled their traditional majority in the county. The vote in the city was 13,759 for Roosevelt and 13,085 for Willkie.

Jubilant Democrats organized a victory parade about 1 a. m., touring the city in a long motorcade with horns blaring. Local Democratic leaders and a brass band led the procession which circled the city continuously for an hour or more.

Light rain which fell late in the evening failed to dampen the enthusiasm of the crowds, many of whom stayed out until the early morning hours.

Marshall M. Cohen, former deputy State Attorney General, was elected the city's Representative in the General Assembly, polling 13,129 votes to 12,974 for his Republican opponent, Alfred C. Alspach, incumbent.

G.O.P. CARRIES COUNTY

The remainder of the Democratic ticket carried the city by majorities ranging from 450 to 750, but this slight lead was quickly erased by top-heavy Republican pluralities in the county districts.

Congressman J. Roland Kinzer was re-elected in the Tenth Pennsylvania district, with a majority of around 8,000 in Lancaster county and about 6,000 in Chester county. He defeated George M. May, Lancaster Democrat.

The three Republican State Assemblymen from the county, Baker Royer, Norman Wood and Harry E. Trout, were also re-elected, togeth-

More of LANCASTER on Page 7

Jay Cooke Concedes Defeat By Guffey; Wagner, Ross Lead

Philadelphia (Wednesday)—(AP)—President Roosevelt, piling up a steadily growing margin, led Wendell L. Willkie by over a quarter of million votes in Pennsylvania early today with election returns complete from three-fourths of the state.

Republican State Chairman James F. Torrance conceded the Keystone State and its 36 electoral votes—the nation's second largest state bloc—to Roosevelt.

Senator Joseph F. Guffey, running somewhat behind Roosevelt, was conceded re-election by Jay Cooke, his opponent and the Republican city chairman of Philadelphia, at 1:30 a. m.

Democratic candidates for State Treasurer and Auditor General—the only statewide elective offices held by Democrats at Harrisburg—also built up mounting leads over Republican opponents.

Returns from 7,132 of the 8,118 precincts in Pennsylvania gave Roosevelt (D) for President 1,912,401; Willkie (R) 1,670,032. Included are 1,314 of the 1,316 Philadelphia precincts and 804 of the 988 in Allegheny county (Pittsburgh).

Returns from 7,018 of the 8,118 precincts in Pennsylvania gave Guffey (D) for senator 1,796,618; Cooke (R) 1,649,669. Included are 1,314 of the 1,316 Philadelphia precincts and 766 of the 988 in Allegheny county (Pittsburgh).

Returns from 6,858 of the 8,118 precincts in Pennsylvania gave Wagner (D) for state treasurer 1,760,217; Malone (R) 1,591,422. Included are 1,314 of the 1,316 Philadelphia precincts and 646 of the 988 in Allegheny county (Pittsburgh).

Returns from 6,854 of the 8,118 precincts in Pennsylvania gave Ross (D) for auditor general 1,772,360; Gelder (R) 1,574,746. Included are 1,314 of the 1316 Philadelphia precincts and 646 of the 988 in Allegheny county (Pittsburgh).

In tabulations at 2 a. m., Willkie led, however, in Adams, Armstrong, Bedford, Blair, Bradford, Bucks, Butler, Cameron, Center, Chester, Clarion, Crawford, Dauphin (Harrisburg), Erie, Delaware, Forest, Franklin, Fulton, Huntington, Indiana, Jefferson, Lancaster, Lebanon, Lycoming, McKean, Mercer, Montgomery, Perry, Pike, Potter, Snyder, Somerset, Sullivan, Susquehanna, Tioga, Union, Venango, Warren, Wayne, Wyoming.

Pike county is the home of former Republican Governor Gifford Pinchot, who campaigned for Roosevelt.

Some Democratic gains were indicated in the Pennsylvania legislature, threatening hopes of Republicans for a working majority. Democratic gains were in prospect also among the Pennsylvania delegation in Congress.

CARRIES PHILADELPHIA

President Roosevelt carried Philadelphia by upwards of 170,000 votes and Allegheny county (Pittsburgh) by more than 75,000. He led in the five counties of the anthracite region—as in 1936—and in the principal soft coal counties of southeastern Pennsylvania. Somerset county gave Willkie an early lead.

Shortly after 11 p. m. The Philadelphia Inquirer, said President Roosevelt "seemed" to have been reelected—but did not at that time concede a Democratic victory in Pennsylvania.

President Roosevelt carried Pennsylvania in 1936—after having lost to Herbert Hoover in '32—by a

More of STATE on Page 8

"We Lead All the Rest"

FARM CORNER
By
The Farm Editor

FARM CONSERVATION MEETINGS PLANNED

Organization of Farmers To Administer 1941 Program Will Be Formed Series At Sessions

An organization of farmers to administer the 1941 Agricultural Conservation Program here will be formed at a series of 17 community meetings to be held in Lancaster county next week.

In each of the 17 districts into which the county has been divided for administrative purpose, the farmers residing therein will meet to discuss the main features of the 1941 farm program and elect the following: A chairman and two additional members of a "community committee," together with two alternate members; also a delegate to attend the County Convention which will be held later.

A County Conservation Committee will be elected by the delegates at the convention. They, together with the members of the 17 community committees, will handle the local administration of the farm program next year.

Those eligible to vote at the meetings are farmers who own or have an interest in a farm in the county and who have participated in an AAA program or signify their intention to participate in 1941. They have "a responsibility to attend the district meeting and help in the selection of local leaders for next year," according to John S. Shenk, chairman, of the County Conservation Committee.

The schedule of meetings, all to

More of FARM CORNER on Page 8

Intelligencer Journal Weather Calendar

COMPARATIVE TEMPERATURES

Station	High	Low
Intell Journal	76	41
Water Works	75	41
Ephrata	66	44
Last Year (Ephrata)	42	37
Official High for Year, July 26		102.5
Official Low for Year, Jan. 20		2
Character of Day		Partly Cloudy

HOURLY TEMPERATURES

(Tuesday)			
8 a. m.	52	9 p. m.	65
11 a. m.	59	10 p. m.	63
2 p. m.	65	11 p. m.	62
5 p. m.	67	Midnight	61
		(Wednesday)	
6 p. m.	67	1 a. m.	60
7 p. m.	66	2 a. m.	59
8 p. m.	66	3 a. m.	59

HUMIDITY

8 a. m.—65 11 a. m.—61 2 p. m.—55
5 p. m.—66 8 p. m.—70 11 p. m.—78
Average Humidity ... 66
Dew Point, 11 p. m. ... 51

More of WEATHER on Page 8

City Vote
(32 Dists. Complete)

PRESIDENT	
Roosevelt	13759
Willkie	13085
SENATOR	
Guffey	13285
Cooke	12815
STATE TREASURER	
Wagner	13240
Malone	12796
AUDITOR GENERAL	
Ross	13362
Gelder	12733
CONGRESSMAN	
May	13446
Kinzer	12728
STATE SENATOR (13th)	
Lightner	13542
Homsher	12790
ASSEMBLYMAN	
Cohen	13129
Alspach	12974

Chief Executives Of The U. S. A.

FRANKLIN DELANO ROOSEVELT

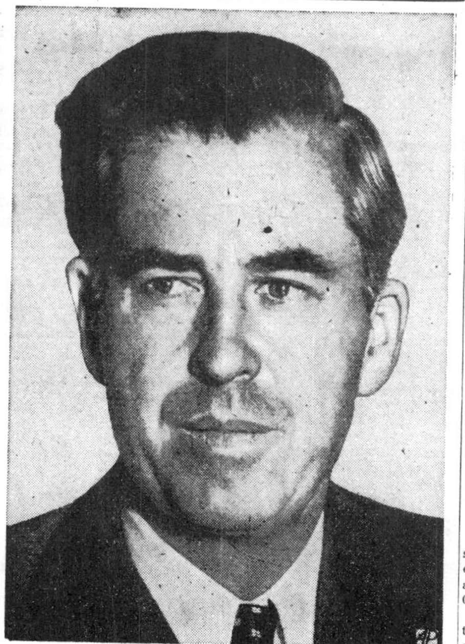

HENRY A. WALLACE

WILLIS G. KENDIG, VETERAN LAWYER, DIES IN HOSPITAL

Admitted To Bar In 1901, He Also Served On Board Of Viewers

Willis G. Kendig, sixty-six, 1022 Marietta ave., a member of the Lancaster County Bar, died at 3:40 p. m. Tuesday at the Lancaster General hospital after a lingering illness.

WILLIS G. KENDIG

A practicing attorney in this city since he was admitted to the bar in 1901, Mr. Kendig also served for the past twenty-two years as a member of the Board of Viewers of Lancaster county. He was also a

More of KENDIG on Page 7

GUARDSMEN AT CAMP FAVOR ROOSEVELT

Local Men Stationed At Virginia Beach Vote 50 To 17 In Favor Of President

National Guardsmen from Lancaster stationed at Virginia Beach, Va., voted 50 to 17 in favor of President Roosevelt over Wendell Willkie, according to absentee ballots received late Tuesday night at the Court House. Those from the city, however, voted 21 for Alspach to 16 for Cohen for Assemblyman.

Other candidates received votes as follows from the Guardsmen: Guffey 46, Cooke 21; Wagner 45, Malone 23; Ross 45; Gelder 22; May 32, Kinzer 18; Lightner 34, Homsher 14; Light 2, Becker 0; Kauffman 1, Dietrich 0, Pannell 0, Trout 1, Wood 0, Royer 1.

More votes are expected from other training centers where Lancaster men are stationed. Col. Daniel B. Strickler, county solicitor, said about 150 National Guardsmen from the county are absent in service at present, but William Paes clerk to the County Commissioners, said only 100 ballots were sent to Harrisburg for distribution to men in camps.

SUNDAY MOVIES WIN IN CITY BUT LOSE IN COUNTY

Columbia, Ephrata And Manheim Township Vote For Sabbath Observance

(Tables on Pages 6 and 7)

Sunday movies were approved in Lancaster city Tuesday, but Manheim township, Columbia and Ephrata voted against permitting theatres to show pictures on Sundays.

The Lancaster city vote was 11,103 to 8,602, with 22 of the 32 precincts in favor of Sunday movies. Five years ago the same question lost by a margin of 1,675 votes.

The entire Fifth ward, the third and fourth precincts of the Sixth, the sixth of the Seventh, the fourth of the Eighth, and the third, fourth and fifth of the Ninth, turned in "No" majorities, but the "Yes" vote was preponderant in the others.

A spirited campaign was held here by both sides.

In Manheim township the majority against Sunday movies was 319, with 1512 opposed and 1193 for. The vote by districts:

	Yes	No
Northern	207	366
Southern	986	1146

The worst defeat for Sunday movies was administered in Columbia, where the vote was 3,390 against to 1,934 in favor, a plurality of 1,456.

Ephrata, too, turned thumbs down on this form of Sabbath entertainment. The vote was 1,331 to 900 in the four wards.

COLUMBIA FAVORS VOTING MACHINES

Voters Decide On Paper Ballots By A Vote Of 2,808 To 2,372

(Table On Page 6)

Columbia voters used paper ballots Tuesday to declare their preference for voting machines, which they will have at the next election. The vote was 2,808 for and 2,372 against, a plurality of 436.

Casts Ballot After Being Hit By Truck On Way To Polls

Christ Shirk, fifty-nine, 106½ E. Donegal st., Mount Joy, who left his home for the first time Tuesday after being ill for three weeks, was injured when struck by a truck, while on his way to vote. The accident happened at Barbara and Main streets, Mount Joy.

According to Chief of Police Elmer Zerphey, of Mount Joy, Mrs. Dora E. Krodel, Florin, driver of the truck was making a left turn from Barbara street into Main street at the time.

Shirk, who suffered a fracture of the left arm and cuts of both knees and mouth, cast his vote after receiving treatment.

NOMINEE WILLKIE GOES TO BED, WON'T CONCEDE DEFEAT

Says He'll Have Statement At 9 A. M., Tells Workers "Never Quit"

New York—(Wednesday)—(AP)—Wendell L. Willkie retired at 1:30 a. m. (EST) today after announcing that he would have no further statement on the election until he awakened.

The Republican presidential nominee gave up his vigil at the radio and his study of newspaper election returns after telling a group of cheering supporters at the Commodore hotel: "Don't be afraid; never quit."

He said he would have a statement to make at 9 a. m. (EST).

Willkie appeared tired, but he still was smiling as he sent word to reporters that he would withhold comment until morning. That announcement came shortly after Republican Chairman Joseph W. Martin made a similar statement from his home at North Attleboro, Mass.

Shortly after midnight, Willkie went to the hotel ball room and was loudly cheered when he asserted that the principles for which he had fought would prevail, "as truth always prevails."

The candidate, who conducted a strenuous ooast-to-coast campaign which took him into 34 states, said

More of WILLKIE on Page 7

KNOX SAYS ELECTION BACKS UP DEFENSE

Sees Choice Is Mandate To Continue "Firm Foreign Policy," In The U. S.

Chicago—(AP)—Secretary of the Navy Frank Knox said Tuesday night that the nation had reelected President Roosevelt "by a considerable margin," and that this constituted "an unmistakable mandate" to "continue a firm foreign policy" and "an accelerated program of national defense."

Secretary Knox, who is publisher of the Chicago Daily News, turned over active direction of the paper to a committee when he accepted the cabinet post. The News supported Wendell Willkie in the campaign.

29 PA. COMMUNITIES FAVOR SUNDAY MOVIES

Fifty Others Reject Proposal, 3 Communities Vote To Halt Shows Now Legal

Harrisburg—(AP)—The Sunday movies movement gained ground in Pennsylvania in Tuesday's voting.

At least 29 communities where Sabbath showings had been prohibited, lifted the ban, but at least 50 others refused to lower the bars.

The tide turned the other way in three communities which voted to shut off their Sunday shows, but five towns retained the "open" Sabbath.

MOTHER, SON DIE OF HEART ATTACKS WITHIN 5 MINUTES

Shock Of Death Of William Henry Brown, Norwood, Is Fatal To Mrs. Mary S. Brown

The shock of the sudden death at 3:35 p. m. Tuesday of William Henry Brown, Jr., forty-three, in his home at Norwood, took the life five minutes later of his mother, Mrs. Mary Sweigart Brown.

Mrs. Mary Brown

W. H. Brown, Jr.

Dr. Edward C. Kottcamp, Jr., deputy coroner of Marietta, said death in each case was caused by coronary occlusion.

The son was stricken about 2:30 p. m., the deputy coroner said, while running up a hill for a shot at a pheasant while on a hunting trip near his home. He managed to reach home and Dr. Charles G. Hill, of Columbia, was called. Shortly after the physician left, Brown was walking through a hallway when he collapsed and died, the deputy

More of MOTHER on Page 8

WEST CHESTER YOUTH DIES FROM WOUNDS

Raymond B. McGrogan, 18, Captain of High School Football Team, Injured While Hunting

West Chester—Raymond B. McGrogan, eighteen, captain of the West Chester High school football team, died at 8:40 p. m. Tuesday from gunshot wounds of the abdomen suffered by the accidental discharge of his shotgun while hunting.

His father, Hugh, gave him a blood transfusion in Chester County hospital and six of his teammates volunteered their blood.

URGES HOLDING OF "UNITY MEETINGS"

Public Bonfires To Destroy All Campaign Literature Asked By W. A. White

New York —(Wednesday)—(AP)—Public bonfires to destroy all campaign literature and buttons were suggested by William Allen White today as a means of "healing partisan bitterness."

The Emporia, Kas., editor also urged "unity mass meetings" in a statement issued as National Chairman of the Committee to Defend America By Aiding the Allies. It was sent to the group's 717 chapters.

McNary Concedes Defeat; Willkie Doggedly Refuses

Democratic Nominee, On Basis Of Still Incomplete Returns, Ahead In 37 States With 433 Electoral Votes; GOP Vice-Presidential Candidate Says "We Are A United Country"

(By The Associated Press)

In a national election without precedent in the history of the republic, Franklin D. Roosevelt amassed such a lead for a third term in the White House today that many leading supporters of Wendell L. Willkie, including his running mate, conceded the President's re-election.

Roosevelt, on the basis of still incomplete returns, was ahead in 37 states with 433 electoral votes while the Republican nominee, who had battled him up and down the land in one of the most strenuous campaigns on record, could show a lead in only 11 states having 98 electoral votes.

The President carried his home state, New York, sweeping its 47 electoral tallies into his column by a plurality of approximately 200,000 votes.

"Things look perfectly fine," he told neighbors who marched in an old-time torchlight procession to salute him at his portico in Hyde Park, N. Y. Then, with the plaudits still echoing over the Hudson river country-side, he went to bed for the night.

Willkie, too, retired. He had spent the evening and part of the small hours of today listening to returns through a blaring loudspeaker in his New York hotel. At first expressing optimism, he later grew more silent.

The Republican candidate did not concede defeat. Reserving any formal statement until later in the day, he contented himself with telling a cheering crowd of his followers that the principles for which he fought would prevail, "as truth always prevails."

But Senator Charles L. McNary, the Republican vice-presidential nominee, acknowledged that the 1940 struggle had ended in defeat for his ticket. In his rural home in Oregon, he issued a statement congratulating President Roosevelt and Henry Wallace, second man on the Democratic ticket, and said:

"We are a united country. The two-party system is secure. We shall try to afford Mr. Roosevelt and his associates a worthy and vigilant opposition."

Besides definitely carrying New York, Connecticut and Rhode Island, Mr. Roosevelt held leads in such states as Pennsylvania, Illinois, Ohio and many others with important weight in the electoral college.

One of the more exhilarating races was in Willkie's native Indiana. Hoosier-land was giving a slim margin to Willkie with less than two-thirds of the returns counted.

The tabulators of little Vermont were the first to complete their count and go off to bed. Sticking to the Republican tradition which it refused to break even in the mammoth Roosevelt landslide of 1936, the green mountain state gave 78,355 votes to Willkie, 64,244 to Roosevelt.

Soon afterward Connecticut and Rhode Island finished their counting jobs. Connecticut showed 417,858 for Roosevelt; 361,869 for

More of NATIONAL on Page 7

County Vote
(143 Dists. Complete)

PRESIDENT	
Roosevelt	32,170
Willkie	44,913
SENATOR	
Guffey	31,299
Cooke	44,608
STATE TREASURER	
Wagner	31,104
Malone	44,543
AUDITOR GENERAL	
Ross	31,511
Gelder	44,363
CONGRESSMAN	
May	32,222
Kinzer	44,061
STATE SENATOR (13th)	
Lightner	24,622
Homsher	29,218
STATE SENATOR (17th)	
Light	9,893
Becker	15,489
ASSEMBLYMEN	
Kauffman	18,121
Dietrich	17,972
Pannell	17,643
Trout	31,879
Wood	31,763
Royer	31,846

ROOSEVELT TELLS NEIGHBORS THAT 'IT LOOKS ALL RIGHT'

Says They'll Find Him The "Same Roosevelt You've Known Many Years"

Hyde Park, N. Y. —(Wednesday)—(AP)—With "full returns" still lacking, President Roosevelt told a jamboree of his Hyde Park neighbors early today that "it looks all right" and that he thought in the future they would find him "just the same Franklin Roosevelt you've known a great many years."

The Chief Executive spoke from the portico of his country home to hundreds of persons who had staged a torchlight parade from Hyde Park village. Elmer Van Wagner, Hyde Park supervisor, said it was a "victory" parade.

"We, of course, face difficult days in this country," Mr. Roosevelt asserted. "But I think you will find me in the future just the same Franklin Roosevelt you have known a great many years."

In a jocular mood, grinning and waving at the crowd, the President remarked that "we haven't got the full returns yet—there's nothing

More of ROOSEVELT on Page 7

FARLEY BROADCASTS APPEAL FOR UNITY

Expresses Hope That "Losers Will Pitch In Like Loyal Citizens They Are"

New York—(AP)—Former Democratic National Chairman James A. Farley said early Wednesday in a nation-wide radio broadcast from Democratic headquarters that "now, perhaps more than ever before in history, the United States has need for national unity."

Farley expressed hope that the "victors will be moderate and considerate" and that the "losers will overcome their disappointment and pitch in like the loyal citizens that they are."

The Weather
Eastern Pennsylvania — Cloudy, snow flurries in west and north, preceded by light rain in southeast. Monday generally fair and colder.

SUNDAY NEWS

3 A. M. Edition
The Sunday News carries the full report of two world wide news services—LATEST NEWS by Associated Press, International News Service. And Complete Local News.

VOL. 18—NO. 13 | Entered at Post Office at Lancaster, Pa. as second class mail matter | LANCASTER, PA., SUNDAY, DECEMBER 1, 1940 | 52 PAGES, 288 COLUMNS—FIVE CENTS

Revolution Breaks Out In Bessarabia

U. S. To Lend 100 Millions To China

ANTI-JAPAN REGIME IS RECOGNIZED

Credit Announced After Puppet President Signs Peace Pact With Tokyo's Envoy

Washington, Nov. 30.—(AP)—The United States pointedly made clear its attitude toward the Tokyo-Nanking "peace" treaty today by reaffirming its recognition of Chiang Kai-Shek's anti-Japanese government and announcing a $100,000,000 credit to it.

With the ink hardly dry on the pact signed at Nanking by Japanese Ambassador General Nobuyuki Abe and Wang Ching Wei, recognized by the Japanese as president of a national government of China, there were these developments here:

Still Recognize Chiang

First, Secretary of State Hull said at his press conference that of course the United States continued to recognize Chiang Kai-Shek's Chungking administration as the government of China.

Secondly, President Roosevelt announced that two $50,000,000 credits to Chungking were "contemplated." One, to be made by the Export-Import Bank and to be repaid in shipments of strategic materials, will be for the Chiang Kai-Shek's administration's "general purposes" such as keeping its army of 2,500,000 in the field.

The other allocation will be from the Treasury's $2,000,000,000 stabilization fund. The President said this sum was "for purposes of monetary protection and management as between American and Chinese currencies." Presumably, it will be used to bolster the sagging Chinese currency.

Plan Metal Purchases

Along with his statement, the Chief Executive made public a letter to him from Jesse Jones, federal loan administrator.

Jones said that in connection with repayment of the loans, the Metals Reserve company, a subsidiary of the Reconstruction Finance Corporation was arranging for additional purchases of wolframite, antimony and tin from China to the value of $60,000,000. Jones added that China is "up to her schedule" in deliveries of wood oil and tin to this country in repayment of previous loans amounting to $25,000,000.

The White House statement made no reference to the Tokyo-Nanking treaty.

At Hull's meeting with newsmen the pact was brought up by a reporter's request for comment. The Secretary of State in reply referred to what he described as a basic statement he made last March 30 when the Nanking regime was set up.

Attitude Unchanged

That statement said that "the attitude of the United States toward use of armed force as an instrument of national policy is well known" and stated belief that the Chungking administration "has the allegiance and support of the great majority of the Chinese people."

"The government of the United States of course continues to recognize that government as the government of China," Hull added.

The President's statement said

CHINA—Page 17

REWARD PLACED ON WANG'S HEAD

National Chinese Govt. Offers $6,000 For "Usurper" Who Signed Treaty

Chungking, China, Nov. 30.—(AP)—The National Government of China offered a reward of 100,000 Chinese dollars ($6,000) today for Wang Ching-Wei, head of the Japanese-recognized Nanking government, "for usurping the presidency and signing with the enemy a treaty detrimental to China's sovereignty."

Foreign Minister Wang Ching-Hui threatened cessation of normal relations with any foreign powers recognizing the Wang regime.

INDEPENDENCE THREATENED

Nanking, China, Nov. 30.—(AP)—A "peace" treaty signed today by Wang Ching-Wei and the Japanese overlords who recognize him as president of a National government of China threatens to end China's existence as an independent nation if it ever can be carried into practical effect, informed foreigners said tonight.

They asserted it was tantamount to complete surrender to domination by Japan—which, however, has yet to crush the government and armies of Chiang Kai-Shek (which both Britain and the United States will continue to recognize.)

Wang and Japanese Ambassador General Nobuyuki Abe signed the

REWARD—Page 11

Christmas Shopping Starts With Rush

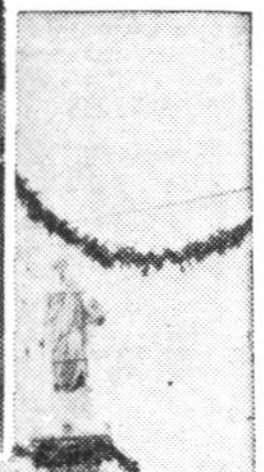

Santa's hand was weary but still in order at 9 p. m. on his first working day, Saturday, in Lancaster stores. Pictures here shown caught the thick streams of shoppers in the central area buying or getting their first survey of the brilliant things readied on the counters and in the windows for Dec. 25.

Stores all reported heavy traffic inside and out as the crowds moved up and down the decorated shopping district almost without cessation from the time the stores opened Saturday morning until they closed Saturday night.

MEXICO FOILS PLOT TO START UPRISING TODAY

2 Killed, 21 Wounded In Fight Between Reds And Police On Inauguration Eve

Mexico City, Nov. 30 —(INS)—Mexico City bristled with guns tonight while the government hastily organized protective measures against a Communist plot to start an insurrection during the inauguration tomorrow morning of President-elect Manuel Avila Comacho.

Two persons were killed, 21 wounded and nearly 100 arrests in gun fights between Communists and police when the plot was nipped in the bud this morning in a spectacular raid on the party's headquarters, and in a clash in a suburb of Mexico City.

Armed Peasants Arrive

Aroused by the threat to the man they elected president for the next six years in the hectic campaign last fall, an estimated 20,000 peasants swept into Mexico City

MEXICO—Page 11

Throngs Open Xmas Buying Rush In City

Greeting the Yuletide shopping season with customary glitter, Lancaster's stores remained open until nine o'clock Saturday evening and were visited by old-fashioned crowds which some merchants said were larger than any of those on corresponding week-ends in other years.

Heaviest buying, merchants said, was in the small gifts departments. There'll be plenty of stockings, men's furnishings, toilet articles and toys around the tree Christmas morning, it is plainly evident. As for the "big gifts," they'll be bought later.

One store varied the Santa idea by furnishing a "Mrs. Santa," too, much to the wide-eyed awe of the pigtail and short-pants trade. Another hired Captain Stanley Holmes of the F. and M. team to give his autograph, with the result that it was a nip-and-tuck race between Mr. Claus and Mr. Holmes for popularity.

2 Planets And Comet To Join In Yule Show

New York, Nov. 30—(AP)—A rare heavenly conjunction of two planets and a newly-discovered comet—which astronomers believe may be one explanation of the Star of Bethlehem—will shine in the Christmas skies this year.

Prof. William H. Barton, Jr., executive curator of the Hayden planetarium, said today the Cunningham comet and the planets Jupiter and Saturn will be in visible conjunction by Christmas.

It will be the first time since 1683 that the two planets have been in conjunction, Barton said.

"The great astronomer Kepler was so impressed by a conjunction of Saturn and Jupiter that he figured back and found that in the year generally accepted as the Nativity these two planets were not only close together as they are at the present, but had been joined by the planet Mars, to form an extraordinary sight in the sky," Barton said, "perhaps that was the 'Star' the Wise men followed to Bethlehem."

Leland E. Cunningham of Harvard College observatory staff discovered the comet Sept. 18.

DIES CHARGES PLOT TO HALT HIS SPY FIGHT

Head Of Committee Will Appeal For New Method Of Combating Sabotage

Washington, Nov. 30—(INS)—Rep. Martin Dies, Dem., Tex., tonight disclosed he is preparing an urgent appeal for "radical revision" of this nation's methods of combatting spies and saboteurs, which he will lay before the American public in a nationwide radio address Monday night.

Dies, chairman of the House Committee Investigating un-American Activities, declared in an exclusive interview that sabotage in this country is shielded by present laws, and that a "complete change is imperative."

Authority Expires Jan. 3

He charged that forces "both inside and outside the government" are combining in a plot to "scuttle" his committee's investigation when its authority expires Jan. 3 next.

The Texan, predicting a "last-ditch fight," said he will bare the plans of his "foes" and will carry directly to the people his campaign for a two-year continuation of his committee's work, which he termed to be "imperative in these perilous times."

Promising to produce a climax in his major controversy with the

DIES—Page 17

All-Community Christmas Fete

An all-community Christmas program will be held under the sponsorship of the Lancaster Junior Chamber of Commerce at the McCaskey High School auditorium at 7:45 p. m., Tuesday, December 17, it was announced Saturday.

Various church groups are cooperating and a program will be announced soon, Richard Diller, chairman of the committee in charge, said. William Krantz is president of the organization.

AUTO KILLS COLUMBIA PEDESTRIAN

Philip Schlossman, 84, Fatally Hurt; Dr. A. V. Walter Reported Resting Comfortably

Philip Schlossman, eighty-four, 1224 Manor street, Columbia, a retired Conestoga Transportation company worker, was fatally injured when struck by an automobile in Columbia late Saturday night, police reported. This fatality brought the city and county accident death toll to 49 thus far this year.

Schlossman, Columbia police reported, was struck by a car operated by Vernon Shultz, seventeen, 706 Manor street, Columbia, west of the intersection of 12th and Manor streets, at 10:15 p. m.

Dr. J. P. Taylor, of Columbia, deputy coroner, who investigated, along with Officer Harrison Dietz, of the Columbia police, and Private Morgan, of the State Motor Police, said death was caused by shock, and fractures of the chest, arms, and legs. Dr. Taylor said the man apparently died enroute to the Columbia hospital in the automobile of Philip Funk, Washington Boro.

Shultz told the officers he was driving south on Manor street and the aged man stepped from behind a parked car directly into the path of his car. Shultz said the victim was struck by the right side of the automobile.

Members of the victim's family told police he was enroute to the home of a daughter, Miss Elizabeth Schlossman, with whom he resided, after a visit with a relative, when he was fatally injured.

Dr. A. V. Walter "Resting Well"

Dr. A. V. Walter, County Coroner who was injured in an automobile collision Saturday morning, was reported to be resting comfortably at the Lancaster General hospital at midnight.

Although the 71-year-old physician had suffered numerous bruises of the face and head and several fractured ribs, attendants said the extent of his internal injuries and skull fracture, if any would not be known until x-rays were taken today. He regained consciousness several hours after the accident.

Coroner for the county for the past six years, Dr. Walter recently sold his Brownstown home and abandoned his practice there so that he could move to 338 North West End avenue, Lancaster, and handle city deaths next year in the expected absence of Dr. H. K. Hogg on National Guard duty.

Reports To Continue

Paul G. Murray, Dr. Walter's son-in-law, said Saturday night that Dr. Hogg presumably would continue to handle city cases until his departure, by which time it would be known whether Dr. Walter was sufficiently recovered to do the work. A bookkeeper will receive the reports of the 40-odd deputy coroners over the county and make State reports as a matter of routine.

Dr. Walter was moving from the country, where he practiced more than 40 years, this week. He also figured prominently in the news last week-end when he discovered

ACCIDENTS—Page 11

ORPHANS' COURT PROVISION ASKED

Moore Requests Chief Justice To Name Appel Or Schaeffer To Preside

Register of Wills A. Z. Moore said Saturday he has asked Chief Justice William A. Schaffer, of the State Supreme court, to authorize a local Common Pleas Judge to handle Orphans' court work pending the appointment of a successor to the late Judge C. E. Charles.

Moore wrote Justice Schaffer at Philadelphia, asking that either Judge O. S. Schaeffer or Judge T. Roberts Appel, or both, be authorized to sit in Orphans' court. Two hearings and the regular Thursday session are scheduled for next week.

It was explained that while an Orphans' Court Judge is ill he may designate a Common Pleas Judge to preside in his place, but that the law provides that if an Orphans' Court Judge dies no one may preside in it unless designated by the Chief Justice. Moore said he expected an early reply.

The funeral of Judge Charles, who died Friday after five months' illness, will be held at 2:30 p. m. Monday in the Millersville Mennonite church. The Court House will close Monday at noon.

Judge Schaeffer or Judge Appel will preside only until Governor James appoints a successor to Judge Charles, it is understood.

Report 30 Prison Killers Have 'Committed Suicide'

Duce's Nemesis

GENERAL PAPAGOS

Rout Of Italy Breeds New Greek Hero

Gen. Papagos Takes Spotlight Beside Leonidar As Military Genius

By MERRILL MUELLER

London, Nov. 30—(INS)—In the freezing mud of Albania, under a roaring canopy of bursting shells and crashing aerial bombs, a new military genius has been born.

Outnumbered by the hosts of Fascism, poorly equipped, in a relative sense, and generally conceeded to have little chance against the armored divisions of Benito Mussolini, the Greeks have hurled the invader out of their land and sent him fleeing in wild panic through the storm swept valleys of his own Albania.

The man who worked this modern military miracle is Lieutenant General Alexander Papagos, slender, sinewy, handsome chief of staff of the ballet-skirted Evzones and the hard-bitten, fiercely determined Highlanders of the Pindus mountains.

Busted "Blitz"

At 54, General Papagos has completely upset the new theory of "blitzkrieg." By crushing the heavy tanks, motorized artillery and auto-borne infantry of the Fascist army he has demonstrated that the theory of warfare sprung from the fertile minds of the German general staff is not always a juggernaut.

By smashing them at first orderly retreat of the Italians into disgraceful, headlong flight, Papagos has further demonstrated that military genius not only can halt motorized advance, but can turn its best efforts at defense into pitiable rout.

The story behind the Greek army's amazing victories, according to qualified military observers, is one of the will to win plus a sound foundation in the science of war.

General Papagos is a veteran professional soldier who received his military education in the famous French Ecole de Guerre (war college), which graduated Foch and Petain, Weygand and Mangin,

ROUT—Page 17

NO AMERICANS ALLOWED

Rome, Nov. 30.—(INS)—Fifteen foreign correspondents — but no American journalists—tonight were invited to visit the Italian fleet to confirm the Italian version that little damage was suffered in the battle with a British fleet off Sardinia this week.

100,000 Iron Guards To Stage Demonstration For Return of Transylvania; State Funeral Held For Martyred Chief

(By The Associated Press)

Bucharest, Nov. 30 — In a macabre climax to elaborate funeral services over the gold casket of Corneliu Zelea Codreanu, the Iron Guard's "martyred captain," every one of the 30 Iron Guardists who participated in the prison assassinations of 64 persons high in King Carol's former regime were reported reliably tonight to have "committed suicide."

At the same time, a diplomatic communication reaching strife-torn Bucharest said revolution had broken out among the 4,000,000 inhabitants of Bessarabia, the territory Rumania ceded to Russia last June 27. Widespread deaths and injuries were reported there.

Details were lacking immediately on the reported suicide of the Iron Guards, who broke into Jilava prison early this week and began their revenge blood purge against those whom they held responsible for Codreanu's death two years ago today.

Comparatively calm reigned all day throughout Rumania, but nearly 100,000 Iron Guards headed tonight for Alba-Julia, ancient seat of Rumanian kings, where a demonstration for the return of northern Transylvania from Hungary is planned for tomorrow.

Premier To Speak

Premier General Ion Antonescu will speak before the Alba-Julia meeting, which coincides with the anniversary of Rumania's acquisition of Transylvania after the World War.

An official announcement said he would address the gathering in the role of "chief of the Iron Guard." Heretofore he has been known as "the conductor of the movement" or as "spiritual adviser."

Under Iron Guard rules, no one can hold Codreanu's title of "captain."

The chief of state was reported to have told Iron Guard leaders at a private audience that peace for Rumania is the thing nearest his heart and that he would take any step to achieve that goal.

(Reports reaching the Hungarian frontier said the Iron Guard may be at the beginning of bloody "total revenge" for the slaying of Codreanu. These dispatches said the country was on the verge of civil war.)

Solemn Rites Held

The tramp of marching feet echoed through Bucharest from dawn until far in the night as almost the entire Iron Guard membership turned out to bury Codreanu and his 13 slain lieutenants.

At the grave they gathered around the ornate gold coffin and promised solemnly "never to forget" the killing of their party's founder.

Iron Guard officials estimated some 150,000 green-shirted men and women were in the procession, led by Premier General Ion Antonescu, Vice-Premier Horia Sima, and the German, Italian and Spanish ministers.

Although King Mihai was represented only by an army officer, Adolf Hitler and Benito Mussolini sent two dignitaries each. (Mihai was reported in border dispatches to have fled Bucharest as a result of the week's disorders.)

ARMY BEING MOBILIZED

Bucharest, Nov. 30.—(INS)—General mobilization of the Rumanian army was understood to be in progress tonight with fighting between the Iron Guard and army flaring into civil war in the Ploesti area and fresh outbursts expected in Bucharest following the funeral of Corneliu Codreanu and 13 companion Iron Guard "martyrs."

WITMER B. ROHRER DIES

Witmer B. Rohrer, sixty-eight, local real estate and insurance man, died suddenly of a heart attack at his home, 1010 North Duke street, city, shortly after midnight, early today.

GREEKS SMASH ITALIAN FRONT, SINK SUBMARINE

High Command Reports Pogradetz Taken And First Victory At Sea

(By The Associated Press)

Athens, Nov. 30 — Greek forces smashed stubbornly resisting Italians at many points along the Albanian front today and made gains of "considerable depth," the high command reported tonight, while at sea the Destroyer Aetos was reported to have sunk an Italian submarine for Greece's first naval victory of the war.

On the northern wing of the front, the high command said, Greek soldiers occupying Pogradetz, 20 miles above the captured Italian invasion base of Koritza, seized 15 Fascist officers and more than 200 enlisted men, along with six guns, 50 machine-guns and "a considerable number" of Howitzers.

From Pogradetz on southward to the Adriatic coast tonight's communique said, the Greeks were on the offensive, but that they were meeting with stiff Italian opposition.

A brief communique said the 1,013-ton, British-built Aetos destroyed the Italian ship with depth charges after the latter fired two torpedoes at the convoy and missed.

Nazis Set Fires In Southampton

Berlin, Dec. 1—(Sunday)—(INS)—A "sea of flames" visible 120 miles away rolled over Southampton today as the German Luftwaffe, after a day of powerful assaults on London, concentrated its attacks on the big south English trans-Atlantic port, German authorities said.

Observers returning from the attack reported that 20 huge conflagrations and innumerable smaller ones swept the already badly-battered port.

The flames, the Nazi flyers said, were visible from the Island of

GREEKS—Page 11

EPHRATA BINGO GAMES ENDED

District Attorney K. L. Shirk said Saturday that officials of Ephrata organizations which sponsored "bingo" parties had assured County Detective Jacob Weller they planned to conduct no such other affairs for the public. Games scheduled for Saturday night were cancelled.

"Democratic Simplicity" To Keynote Inauguration

Washington —(AP)— President Roosevelt's third inauguration on January 20 may be marked by participation of the nation's citizenry as a whole, Joseph E. Davies, inaugural chairman, indicated today after a talk with the Chief Executive.

Davies said the Washington ceremony would be on a smaller scale than the two previous Roosevelt inaugurals, with fewer troops being used for the traditional parade.

"It is the President's desire," he said, "to have an inaugural ceremony marked by extreme democratic simplicity."

Regarding the possibility of having citizens throughout the country participate, Davies would not go into detail, but said Dorothy Thompson, the columnist, would be chairman of this undertaking.

Inaugurals to date have been strictly a Washington affair. There have been suggestions from several sources recently, however, that since it was a national occasion, the public as a whole should be given an opportunity to celebrate the day.

"The idea," Davies told reporters, "is to make the voice of the country articulate in these ceremonies."

Although some proposals have been made that the 1941 inaugural be spread over two or three days, Davies said it would be a "one-day affair."

MUSIC SUPERVISORS MEET

The Lancaster County Music Supervisors met Wednesday night in the Brownstown school building. C. N. McHose, in West Earl township, was in charge. Refreshments were served by Mrs. Annie Daugherty, Helen Daugherty, Margaret Weber and Martha Kling.

EAGLES WILL HOLD INITIATION SUNDAY

A class of candidates will be initiated Sunday by the Lancaster Aerie, No. 84, Fraternal Order of Eagles at 2 P. M., in charge of the drill and ritual teams.

The sixty-ninth birthday anniversary of Conrad H. Mann, of Kansas City, national organizer, also will be observed. A program of entertainment will follow the initiation.

"GONE WITH THE WIND" in technicolor, starring Clark Gable, Vivien Leigh, Leslie Howard, Olivia De Havilland and a cast of thousands opens tomorrow at the Capitol theatre for one week. The policy for this engagement will be continuous showings daily and the picture will be in full length, running three hours and forty minutes, exactly as previously shown. There will be nothing cut but the price. Saturday patrons can come anytime from 9 A. M. to 9:15 P. M. and see a complete performance. Saturday doors open at 9. A. M. with features at 9:30 A. M., 1:30, 5:30 and 9:15 P. M. Sunday doors open at 2 P. M. and features are at 3:15 and 8:30. Weekdays doors open at 11:45 A. M. and features are at 12:20, 4:20 and 8:30 P. M.

IT'S A FEUD—Jack Benny and Fred Allen as they appear in "Love Thy Neighbor" at the Ephrata Main today and tomorrow.

ROMERO GETS THE GIRL—"Love is fun and life is short," thinks pretty Virginia Gilmore, because even though dashing Cesar Romero is King of the Rackets, he is smooth ... gay ... exciting ... and he's "Tall, Dark and Handsome." Milton Berle and Charlotte Greenwood are also featured in the 20th Century-Fox hit which is now entertaining movie-goers at the Colonial theatre with its blend of laughter, thrills and music.

AIR DRAMA—Walter Pidgeon, Robert Taylor and Ruth Hussey in Taylor's new starring picture, "Flight Command," drama of the U. S. Naval Air Service, which comes to the Joy screen today. Frank Borzage directed.

BOLD ADVENTURE, daring heroism and thrilling romance dominate the action-filled scenes in "The Son of Monte Cristo," the sweeping spectacle drama which is slated for its premiere at the Grand theatre today, with Joan Bennett, Louis Hayward and George Sanders in the starring roles.

AN IRISH LASS—In "Little Nellie Kelly," opening today at the Strand theatre, Judy Garland gets a kiss from both Douglas McPhail and George Murphy. The new picture, based on the George M. Cohan musical drama, presents Miss Garland in her first solo starring role and gives her her first "grown up" love affair.

SAUCY CHORINE — Some smooth work by Lucille Ball, lands Louis Hayward in the matrimonial net in "Dance, Girl, Dance," dramatic romance of back-stage life, playing at The Fulton. Maureen O'Hara is co-starred with them.

11 GET COMMISSIONS AS NOTARIES PUBLIC

Commissions of five men and six women as notaries public were received today at the office of Recorder of Deeds Christ B. Mylin.

Those commissioned are as follows: David R. Forbes, Quarryville; J. K. Miller and Paul Keller, Manheim; Mrs. Ida E. Graybill, Strasburg township; Miss Arlene B. Young, Manheim township; Henry L. Gise, Elizabethtown; George F. Weidler, Akron; Miss Amy Gresser, Columbia, and Miss Nellie C. Shay, Miss Irene E. Henry and Miss Clara E. Roop, all of Lancaster.

4 FREIGHT CARS DERAILED

Four cars of a freight train were derailed on the low grade line of the Pennsylvania Railroad at Turkey Hill, between Washington Boro and Safe Harbor last night. The local wreck crew was summoned at 9:30 P. M.

GRAND TO SHOW NEW FILM HIT

Alfred Hitchcock, maker of many film hits, has done it again.

This time, it is "Mr. and Mrs. Smith." A bright sparkling comedy, a bit spicy but not offensive. The film opens in the Grand theatre February 7 after a preview for newspapermen recently in Philadelphia.

The film is a relief from the recent epidemic of heavy dramas.

Carole Lombard and Robert Montgomery show skill in comedy rolls. Gene Raymond lends excellent support. Although a little early in the year to pick the "Best of 1941," Hitchcock's new show should be well out in front at the finish.

NORRISTOWN AUTOIST FINED

Merrill Fisher, Norristown, charged with reckless driving by State Motor Police, was fined $10 and costs when he pleaded guilty before Justice of the Peace Martin, Manheim township, last night.

STRICKEN AT POLICE STATION

Frank Sload, twenty-five, 218 East Marion street, was stricken with an epileptic attack while making a call at city police headquarters this morning. Police conveyed him to his home.

TWO BOYS ADMIT HELPING IN THEFT

Two sixteen-year-olds boys, picked up yesterday by Motor Policemen Fitzgerald and Wilhere, admitted they accompanied Frank Zangari, twenty-three, Lancaster R. D. 3, when they were surprised by police while stealing gasoline from the American Oil Company bulk plant, Manheim pike, Monday night. Both will be petitioned into Juvenile Court.

One of the boys also admitted, police said, to breaking into the American Oil Company office on November 3. Nothing was stolen but several desks were ransacked.

The Average American

His Family Lives on $22 a Week

(Third of a series on the average American.)

By MORGAN M. BEATTY
AP Feature Service Writer

PLYMOUTH, Ind., Feb. 13.—The average American family can live pretty well on $22 a week!

I didn't believe it possible, but that was before I lived for a day with Mr. Average American—Ralph C. Suter of Plymouth—and his family.

I discovered a 56-cent dress for a child can look smart. A practical school dress can be made for 15 cents, if mother uses one of her old skirts for a pleated jumper.

I saw a family of four eating as well as the President eats and I've eaten at his house, too) for $4 to $5 a week.

Ralph brought out the figures and receipts. Together we figured out the annual Suter budget. Here it is:

Food, clothing, doctors, charity, gas, incidentals	$512.19
Rent ($16 mo.) and fuel ($45 a year)	237.00
Car notes ($15 mo.) plus insurance	193.30
Personal insurance	90.72
Utilities (approx. $6.28 mo.)	75.27
Direct taxes	35.81
Magazines, newspapers	15.00
TOTAL	$1,159.29

The difference between the Suters' spending and other average American family spending is a difference in living habits. The Suters bear down on tithing and insurance. Other people might accent drinks, smokes, amusements.

They Have No Furnace

The Suters forego furnace heat. They live in the winter with a single coal stove, supplemented by a small wood-stove water heater for baths.

They lay aside little cash (also an average American habit) but one of Ralph's two insurance policies matures in an endowment of $340 in three years. He considers that savings.

The Suters rent their six-room house for $16. Small bedroom, living room, dining room, kitchen and bath downstairs. A bedroom and a den upstairs.

The upstairs is without heating facilities. Mr. and Mrs. Suter manage by giving the children the downstairs bedroom just off the living room and the big coal stove, and take the upstairs bedroom themselves.

The Suter's one other inconvenience is the absence of a telephone. That's by choice, of course, and is not average.

The Suters have radio, electric lights and gas. Erma Suter has a vacuum cleaner, an electric washer, an electric iron, and a latest model cooking range.

These things make it possible for one woman to bring up two children, keep house, and still have time on her hands for the things she really likes. In her case it is church work and neighborhood gatherings of women.

TOMORROW: Mr. Average American felt the depression.

Mrs. Ralph Suter bakes apple pies so good that Morgan Beatty didn't end his interview until he had the recipe.

Mrs. Suter sat Morgan Beatty down to this meal:

Pork loin roast, gravy, potatoes, baked beans, lettuce salad, coffee and apple pie.

Beatty liked the pie, begged the recipe:

Crust—2½ cups flour, 1 teaspoon salt, ¾ cup shortening, 5 tablespoons cold water. Sift flour and salt together. Cut in shortening to fine mixture. Sprinkle water in and work into ball with fork. Roll.

Fill with thin apple slices and cover with mixture of 1 cup sugar, 1 teaspoon cinnamon, ½ teaspoon nutmeg, ⅛ teaspoon salt, 1 teaspoon lemon juice. Dot with 1 teaspoon butter. Place top crust dough, bake 30-40 minutes at 425 degrees.

60-DAY WAITING PERIOD URGED

State of Washington Plans Rigid Tests For Marriage.

OLYMPIA, Wash., Feb. 13.—(A. P.)—Love took a ribbing as the State Senate approved, 38 to 5, a bill to require medical examinations before marriage.

"Two years ago," declared Sen. A. E. Edwards, "we passed the 'gin marriage' law which saved the male of the species from being misled by the female. No longer does a man recover from a hangover and find himself married.

"Now we're going to require a medical examination not more than 60 days prior to marriage. This gives the male a lot of time to think marriage over. I predict if the bill passes that marriages in Washington will decrease 90 per cent. After all love is a mild form of insanity and it doesn't last over 30 days."

The act would forbid marriage of persons shown by Wasserman tests to have syphilis. It goes to the House today.

DR. KIRBY PAGE HERE FEB. 24

3 Addresses Will Be Given During Forum at St. Peter's Church.

Three addresses, with open discussions, will be given by Dr. Kirby Page, of La Habra, California, during a forum meeting on February 24, at St. Peter's Evangelical and Reformed church. The meetings are sponsored by the American Friends Service committee and a local committee.

The program will be as follows: 4 P. M., address on "Religion's Answer to Totalitarianism"; 6 P. M., dinner meeting and address on "The Place of Religion in a World at War"; and 8 P. M., address, "How Can We Defend American Democracy?"

Committee Members

Prof. Paul L. Whitely, of Franklin and Marshall college, heads the local committee which includes: the Rev. M. J. Weaver, pastor of the Church of the Brethren; Benjamin Bushong, Columbia; Miss Dorothea Wieand, Mrs. J. T. McNinch; the Rev. James E. Wagner, pastor of the host church; John McCandless, J. Richard Cogley and David S. Noss, students at Franklin and Marshall college; William Wimer, student at the Lancaster Theological seminary.

Also Mrs. H. Persifor Smith, Mrs. E. M. Hartman, Samuel C. Clark, of Franklin and Marshall academy; Prof. O. S. Frantz and Nevin C. Harner, of the Theological seminary; J. H. Breitigan, Lititz; Miss Mary Alice Thomas, of the Y. W. C. A.; the Rev. C. W. Clodfelter, pastor of the Church of the New Jerusalem; and Miss Ruth Weikert, of First Evangelical and Reformed church.

Author And Lecturer

Dr. Page, an ordained minister of the Disciples of Christ, has spoken in Lancaster before, at Franklin and Marshall college and academy, and at the Y. W. C. A., under the auspices of the Lancaster Peace council. He is the author of 19 books and sixteen pamphlets, has spoken in more than 300 colleges and universities, and more than a million copies of his books have been sold. He has crossed the ocean twenty times and visited in thirty-five countries of the world.

4th F. and M. "Stunt Night" On March 14

The fourth annual "Stunt Night" at Franklin and Marshall College, sponsored by the Alpha Delta Sigma national honorary advertising fraternity, will be held in Hensel Hall on March 14, it was announced by Robert G. Shaffer, Altoona, president of ADS.

With Shober Barr again acting as master of ceremonies, the eleven fraternities and numerous individual students, both organized and unorganized, will present skits, monologues and other bits of comic entertainment. Fraternities will vie for a twenty-inch loving cup. An eleven-inch cup will go to the second place chapter. First and second place medals will be awarded for individual acts.

The following committees have been appointed to arrange for Stunt Night: Albert Selenkow, contracts; Richard Price and Blaine Harrington, publicity; Paul Seltzer and Stanley Frank, posters; Harry Grove, tickets; Robert Haun, orchestra; Dr. Noel P. Laird, act arrangement; Pierce Hunter, Stanley Holmes and Robert Shaffer, program. Dr. Noel P. Laird, faculty adviser to ADS, will pass judgment on the stunts before they may be admitted to Stunt Night.

8 Men, 2 Women Are Elected Directors of Farm Association

H. R. Metzler Explains Democracy Days' Celebration; "Farm Family" Discussed by Dr. Benson

A board of directors consisting of eight men and two women was elected at the 28th annual meeting of the Lancaster County Agricultural Extension association yesterday at the Y. W. C. A. building.

The new board members will meet next month to elect officers. They are:

Northeast district: Simon R. Snyder, Ephrata RD1, and H. K. Martin, Goodville; Southeast district: Harry R. Metzler, Paradise RD1, and Earl L. Groff, Strasburg RD1; Northwest district: Ammon H. Bucher, Manheim RD2, and David C. Witmer, Mount Joy RD; Southwest district: D. L. Shellenberger, Columbia RD2, and Clyde K. Eshleman, Washington Boro RD1. Mrs. Arthur Eshleman, Paradise, and Mrs. Harrison S. Nolt, Columbia RD1, were named directors at large.

Officers Give Reports

Brief resumes of the association activities during the past year were given by members of the extension staff: County Agent F. S. Bucher and assistants, H. S. Sloat and M. M. Smith; and Miss Anne Forbes, home economics representative. Annual reports were presented by the officers.

Miss Martha Leighton, assistant state club leader, and H. G. Nissley, assistant director of extension, both of Penn State College; and Dr. Oscar H. Benson, Adams county farmer, were afternoon speakers.

County Superintendent of Schools Arthur P. Mylin and J. Edward Mack, president, Lancaster Chamber of Commerce, were special guests at the luncheon. The noon hour was enlivened with group singing, led by Mrs. Roy Forney, East Petersburg; and entertainment by the Farm Women Society. Members of the board and representative farmers from various districts were introduced and responded with brief remarks. Earl L. Groff, Strasburg RD1, served as toastmaster.

H. R. Metzler Speaks

County Commissioner H. R. Metzler, a member of the board was requested by S. R. Snyder, president of the association, to explain the purpose of the Democracy Day celebration. He warned against the "complacent attitude" and "dilatory" action of many farmers.

"This celebration is to call to the attention of all of us, to make us conscious of, the blessings and privileges we enjoy and also the responsibilities we have in maintaining this as a free country," he said. "It is necessary that people be educated and enlightened as to their duties. Democracy starts with the individual in his home." He saw danger "in going too far" in certain government activities, depending on the state instead of emphasizing individual responsibility.

As an example of "complacency," Mr. Metzler cited the fact that only 50 stockholders out of several hundred "who had a financial interest in the organization" showed up for the annual meeting recently. "They are satisfied," he said, adding "we have more to fear within a group than from outside." Pointing to juvenile delinquency and the degradation of morals, he predicted "we have more to fear within the county than any attack from the other side. In times like these, it behooves us to think things through and then act accordingly."

Warns Against Propaganda

Prof. Nissley urged a sound education in fundamentals of both juniors and adults. "Don't be swayed by propaganda, and we will come through this crisis as our country has in the past," he said.

Miss Leighton complimented local leaders for the growth of enrollment in 4-H clubs in Lancaster county. One out of every fourteen farm boys and girls between the ages of 10 to 20 years in the county is now engaged in some 4-H project, she reported. One of the main objectives is to "help them make up their minds what they want to do in life and develop the rural youth to be better future citizens."

In his address on "The Farm Family and America," Dr. Benson drew on a rich field of experience from his work as farmer, teacher, superintendent of schools, lecturer, and official, for a wealth of illustrations. For 15 years he was a national official of the Boy Scouts and served as national director of 4-H club work with the U. S. Dept. of Agriculture.

He characterized the family as the "great American unit of Democracy, where it begins and will end, if it does end." There was never a time in history when it was so important for parents and all good citizens to learn how "to replant the family circle," he said.

The speaker scored talk of "no more opportunities." He said he knew of plenty of $10 acre land that could be $100 acre land if properly developed; that there is opportunity to develop marketing systems to make all farm crops profitable; that the "best of all things remain to be done by your children." He closed with a plea for vision and courage; "dare to do like our forebearers did who made this country great."

PROSECUTE LINCOLN DRIVER

Donald L. Stonesifer, Lincoln, charged with using dealer's license plates illegally on a truck, was prosecuted by Motor Policeman Farra before Justice of the Peace Burkholder, Ephrata, yesterday.

INJURED AT SCHOOL

William Forrest, fifteen, 36 Seymour street, who injured his right ribs while wrestling at school, was treated yesterday at the General hospital.

Local Guardsmen Settle Down at Indiantown Gap

Here's one of the beds that make old timers shake their heads and say "What's this man's army coming to anyhow?" Springs, soft mattress and warm bed clothing. John Kautz gets ready for some real sleep.

Lancaster troops unload supplies to furnish their barracks. Sergeants Charles Shenk and William Schulz provide the direction. William Gable, Earl Reese and Jerry Jacobs provide the man power.

Radios are popular in the barracks where Lancaster troops established their home at Indiantown Gap yesterday. R. L. Webber and Leon Hershey are tinkering with the receiving set. Mearn Kuhns is in the background while Earl Elser and Sergeant Elwood Killian look on.

It takes a lot of spuds for a hungry army. Tony DeGemmoro and George Bunker, of the Lancaster company, do their share of kitchen duty at Indiantown Gap.

Sergeant George W. Hastings, sixty, veteran of the Mexican border and World war, member of the 103rd Medical Regiment band, and one of the oldest non-coms at Indiantown Gap.

U. S. Industry Now Has $15,000,000,000 In Arms Contracts

With Huge Awards to Come, "Business as Usual" Is Expected to Suffer; Output of Autos Certain to Drop

WASHINGTON, Feb. 26—(A. P.)—The gigantic size of America's arms production job was emphasized today by a survey indicating that contracts already placed totaled about $15,000,000,000—more than six times the estimated value of the automobile industry's entire output for 1939.

This figure represented formal awards both by the British government and United States defense agencies.

Nearly $6,000,000,000 of authorized American orders have yet to be placed under contract, although the government already has given manufacturers an informal but binding "go ahead" on much of this business. Moreover, additional billions in orders are in prospect, both for this country and probably for Britain under the pending lease-lend bill.

Crimp In Business Seen

In the light of these fiscal facts, many officials believed that arms production eventually would put a deeper crimp into "business as usual" than most of the country realized.

The opinion was advanced in well informed quarters that the automobile industry would be required to divert its attention increasingly from passenger car output to the manufacture of airplane engines, sub-assemblies for aircraft and perhaps ultimately complete planes.

Many defense industries still were in the process of "tooling up," and no large-scale rounded deliveries of munitions appeared in prospect before next fall. Peak production in some lines was scheduled well along in 1942, in others still later.

Plane deliveries during January totaled 1,026, better than the figure predicted officially a month before. William S. Knudsen, director general of the office of production management, was encouraged to forecast an output of 18,000 planes this year. Experts in the industry estimated that President Roosevelt's goal—the capacity to produce 50,000 planes a year—would not be reached, under programs announced thus far, until the end of 1944.

4 Light Tanks A Day

As to the 9,200 tanks which Knudsen said this country would produce, the latest official information was that light tanks were being produced at the rate of four a day and that medium tanks would be rolling from a number of plants by mid-summer. Progress on the Army's new heavy tanks of 55 tons or more was kept secret.

Officials said naval construction had reached the point where a new ship was joining the fleet every 12 days. They reported that the 35,000-ton battleship Washington would be placed in commission May 15, six and one-half months ahead of schedule.

There was little expectation that the two-ocean Navy would be completed before 1946, and naval builders were still wrestling with the problem of speeding up construction of escort vessels like destroyers and subchasers, which British and U. S. Navies want in large numbers.

War Department officials maintained silence regarding the current output of most types of arms, on the ground that this would be information of value to foreign powers. They did report, however, that production of the Garand semi-automatic rifle had reached 3,000 a week.

Machine Tools Are "Bottleneck"

Machine tools to equip arms-making factories continued to be a principal "bottleneck" delaying the day of greatly increased defense deliveries, although the machine tool industry had already expanded tremendously last year and pledged another great expansion in 1941.

The ultimate size of the arms production program was expected generally to be the peak which the country could produce without cutting into production deemed essential for the civilian population.

The probable proportions were indicated by Knudsen in a speech last December before the National Association of Manufacturers.

He listed the equipment in demand at that time as 50,000 airplanes, 130,000 engines, 17,000 heavy guns, 25,000 light guns, 13,000 trench mortars, 33,000,000 shells loaded, 9,200 tanks, 300,000 machine guns and ammunition, 400,000 automatic rifles and ammunition, 1,300,000 regular rifles and ammunition, 380 Navy ships, 200 mercantile ships, 210 camps and cantonments, 40 government factories, clothing and other equipment for 1,200,000 U. S. troops.

U. S. Program Compiled

The United States' own defense program and contract awards, as of Feb. 1, have been compiled officially as follows:

Purpose	Program	Awards
Naval vessels	$6,070,000,000	$4,370,000,000
Airplanes	3,210,000,000	2,240,000,000
Ammunition and explosives	1,780,000,000	1,000,000,000
Industrial facilities	1,630,000,000	1,130,000,000
Artillery and small arms	1,440,000,000	580,000,000
Posts, depots, fortifications	1,270,000,000	860,000,000
Clothing, equippage, subsistence	660,000,000	440,000,000
Tanks and combat vehicles	360,000,000	300,000,000
Transportation equipment	290,000,000	210,000,000
Miscellaneous Army and Navy	430,000,000	300,000,000
Stock pile	480,000,000	290,000,000
Emergency merchant fleet	350,000,000	—
Defense workers' housing	320,000,000	120,000,000
TOTALS	18,290,000,000	11,840,000,000

Since February 1, $33,374,500 of the merchant fleet orders have been placed. Prior to the time when President Roosevelt proposed this $350,000,000 "emergency" program to build 200 ships, the government was already well along on a program begun in 1938 to bolster the merchant marine with 196 other vessels. Of these, officials said, 66 had actually been delivered.

Additional contracts also have been awarded since February 1 in virtually all categories of defense equipment.

The extent of British orders in this country is not known exactly. However, Secretary Morgenthau has told Congress that the British paid $1,380,000,000 on government orders in the United States last year. Furthermore, he said last month, Britain owed American manufacturers an additional $1,400,000,000 on orders already placed.

GUARDS

(Continued From Page One)

snorted and the spinning wheels sent a shower of yellow clay into the air.

Band Last To Arrive

The 103rd Medical Regiment band, another Lancaster unit, was the last to reach camp. With that unit came Sergeant George W. Hastings, sixty, one of the oldest non-commissioned officers in the cantonment. The sergeant is a veteran of the Mexican border where he helped provide martial airs for Uncle Sam's troops. Again, in the World War, he played in bands at Camp Hancock and Jacksonville, Fla.

Barracks are complete with all the comforts of home — Comfortable beds and quarters, heated wash and shower rooms and plenty of good food.

Company H., Reading, was in charge of the mess hall on the first day. Mountains of spuds, sizzling steaks and onions, vegetables and fruits were required to satisfy the appetities of men who arrived in camp during the day.

No Local Men Ill

At midnight, cantonment headquarters announced there were 239 officers, two warrant officers and 3,465 enlisted men in camp. Twenty-one enlisted men were moved at once to the hospital. One man suffered a broken wrist while enroute to camp. The other twenty had minor colds. There was no illness among the Lancaster men.

Commanding officers said that by midnight March 1 there will be 11,700 men in camp. By April 15 the population will increase to 15,000 and by June 15 the arrival of Selective Service men will bring the camp to its maximum strength of 21,400.

Rush Recreation Centers

Work is now being pushed on the recreation centers. When the buildings are finished, work will start on the company streets. Main roads through the camp are hard-surfaced and built to withstand the heavy military traffic. Company streets, however, are just as nature made them. At night they are frozen hard but with the coming of the sun they quickly turn to yellow mud.

General H. Conger Pratt, commander of the Second Army Corps, inspected the camp yesterday and described it as one of the best in the country.

Troops rolled into camp yesterday from many sections of the state.

Among the arrivals were the artillerymen with their big six-wheeled trucks towing 75 mm cannon and heavy 155 mm Howitzers, mainstays of destruction in any man's army. The mud that seemed to annoy the infantry meant nothing to the hardy youngsters with the caissons.

The Headquarters Battery of the 53rd Field Artillery Brigade, commanded by Brigadier General Eric Fisher Wood, detrained before reveille at 6 A. M. The 48 men had been on the train all night from Coraopolis, and General Wood was at camp to welcome them and supervise movement of his regiments, the 107th, 108th and 109th — into camp.

All morning the trucks of the 107th, from Pittsburgh; the 108th from Philadelphia and the 109th from Wilkes-Barre rolled into camp, state and local police facilitating their travel with special traffic arrangements. In the camp area, military police gave them the right of way so they could go to barracks immediately. Hot dinner awaited them.

They took over 34 barracks—accommodating 63 men each — and 14 mess halls at the west end of the reservation ready for them was a new theater, with seats for more than 500. Movie programs have been arranged. There also is a stage for impromptu theatricals.

Cavalrymen Arrive

Following close on the heels of the artillery were advance detachments of the 104th Cavalry. The main body of the regiment is due in camp this week-end. The first unit of 126 enlisted men and five officers reported to organize their area, on the camp's highest elevation—the east end.

From Philadelphia came the first of thousands of Infantrymen, who start rolling into camp tomorrow. Troop trains are scheduled for every half hour, the climax of the soldier travel that has been going on all week.

Material and ground crews of the 103rd Observation Squadron of Philadelphia came by rail to New Cumberland, adjoining Harrisburg, 28 miles west of the encampment here. The outfit will be based at the Harrisburg Airport, coordinating its training with the Indiantown maneuvers.

INDIANTOWN

(Continued From Page One)

This is to cover supervision and checkup on the construction contractors' work. The percentage of the fee to the estimated cost was given as .56 per cent.

Brigadier General Brehon B. Somervell, acting chief of the Construction Division, Quartermaster General's office, told the House subcommittee that cost estimates were submitted originally without any concrete plans. "If," he said, referring to the nationwide cantonment program, "we could have had a small sum for plans prior to this time, I think I can say conservatively that we would have saved $100,000,000."

Somervell cited about a dozen factors which caused the increase in the Indiantown Gap costs over the original estimates. Some of these were: In addition to the original estimate, 36 buildings were required; the cost of lumber increased approximately 50 per cent; the estimate was based on a 40-hour week. Actually the working time required to complete the camp in time to meet desired troop arrivals was 54 hours per week, or 30.5 per cent overtime in hours for the crafts involved and 52.5 per cent increase in the normal 40-hour weekly wage.

Also added to the original estimate for special buildings were 50 buildings for the 104th Cavalry and 103d Observation Squadron. To provide adequate sewage disposal, 21 miles of line were required. A heavy shale formation was encountered and special trenching equipment was required to make cuts as much as 18 feet deep.

The Army also asked additional sums to complete other projects in Pennsylvania, as follows: Carlisle Barracks, $245,750, making a project total of $519,220; New Cumberland, $157,000, making a project total of $565,587; Middletown Air Depot, $48,504, making a project total of $260,000.

The Navy informed the committee of contracts it desired to make for plant expansion but on which no action had been taken. One of these expansion projects was listed for York where $600,000 would be spent on machine tools and equipment to produce gun mounts and gun slides.

LOOSE TRIAL DUE IN MARCH

Former Brownstown Bank Employee Indicted By U. S. Grand Jury.

PHILADELPHIA, Feb. 26—Elmer Gerhart Loose, thirty-one, former assistant cashier of the Brownstown National Bank, was indicted on embezzlement charges by a Federal Grand Jury here yesterday. His case is expected to be called for trial at the March term.

The twenty-three counts in the indictment charge that Loose made false entries to hide thefts of amounts between $100 and $300 from July, 1939, to November 23, 1940, the date he was arrested. When Loose was arraigned before U. S. Commissioner John L. Bowman at Lancaster early this month, the exact amount of the shortage was announced as $12,925.39. Loose sold his home for $8,000 and made restitution in other ways which, combined with funds paid by his bonding company, had cut the bank's loss to less than $300, it was said.

Loose is now a prisoner in the Philadelphia county jail in default of bail.

Indicted with Loose yesterday were two Philadelphia bank employes, charged with conspiracy and embezzlement of $887.55, and a Conshohocken post office clerk, charged with converting $301 in cash and stamps to his own use.

WOMAN IS KILLED NEAR W. CHESTER

WEST CHESTER, Feb. 26—(A. P.)—Mrs. Edna McKee, 38, wife of a farmer, was killed instantly last night when a station wagon driven by her 18-year-old daughter, Frances, hit a tree and plunged into a fence.

The daughter, who escaped with minor cuts, said the car struck a soft shoulder and struck a tree. She said her mother then grasped the wheel and the machine plunged 50 yards into the fence before turning over.

FINDS ALL BUT 19 OF 5,500 NICKELS

MALDEN, Mass., Feb. 26—(A. P.)—Speaking of coin collecting . . .

A bank messenger's bag broke open in the business section yesterday and sent 5,500 nickels rolling among passing high school students and automobiles.

Students, motorists and police turned coin collectors in a mad scramble to round up the $275—and did a good job.

All but 19 nickels were recovered.

RED ROSE CIRCLE EATS FASNACHTS

Red Rose Circle, No. 273, Protected Home Circle held a meeting and fasnacht social last evening at P. O. S. of A. hall.

Prize winners at cards were Charles Druck, Helen Shaub, Howard Best, Harry Wagner, Ira Eckman, Mrs. Martin Hertzler, George Blank, and Anna Slaugh. The next meeting will be held Tuesday evening, March 11.

CHARGED WITH SPEEDING

G. L. Droz, 1048 Elwood avenue, charged with speeding over intersections on West Chestnut street, was prosecuted today by city police before Alderman Wetzel.

March Draft Quotas to Take Men from Varied Occupations

Fence Builder, Cocoa Bean Roaster and Grinder in Hollowware Plant Among Those Going to Army Next Month

A fence builder, a cocoa bean roaster and a grinder in a hollowware plant will be among the March conscriptees to leave Lancaster under the Selective Service system, a survey of the occupations of the tentative contingents showed today.

The hat factories of the Adamstown-Ephrata-Denver section will lose a handful of employees, the linoleum plant and watch factory here, and the asbestos plant at Manheim will lose others.

The draft also will lift some farmers' sons and hired men from the farms—causing what some say will be a shortage at a time of the year when they are most needed.

Among the draftees in unusual occupations is Walter B. Greiner, Manheim R. 2, who builds fences for a living. Jay M. Kendig, Marietta, R. 1, roasts cocoa beans at the Klein chocolate plant at Elizabethtown. George Herchelroth, Marietta, a volunteer, is a grinder.

R. R. Mail Clerk To Go

Uncle Sam will have one less railway mail clerk in view of Board No. 5's refusal of deferment to Clyde Z. Myer, Ephrata. Others which it held had insufficient grounds for deferment are Ralph Weber, of Terre Hill, assistant treasurer of a chain of stores, with headquarters in Reading, and James Henry Geyer, of Mohnton, shoe factory employee.

The hat-making industry will lose Frank Weinhold, Denver R. 1, Harry Deibler, Ephrata, and Howard Hornberger, Ephrata, who are high on the list for next month, and it is considered likely that deferments or rejections may send John Richard Wise, Ephrata R. 3, and Ralph W. Sites, Denver R. 2.

County District No. 4, embracing the eastern end of the county, probably embraces the largest variety of occupations. The group includes this assortment.

George Lee Morrison, Jr., mechanics' helper at the Lukens Steel company, Coatesville; Arthur Eugene Hollinger, textile worker; Thomas Guest Supplee, farmer; Ira Samuel Shirk, plumber; George Willard Eager, electrician; William Deckman, greenhouse worker; Joseph Graham Reese, farmer laborer; Bernard J. Myers, Jr., attorney; Robert D. Esbenscheid, garage mechanic; Robert Franklin Weatherby, waiter.

The next three men in line, in case of rejections, are Raymond Salada, farm laborer, Arthur A. Denlinger, silk weaver, and Raymond Frank Jenks, farm laborer.

Other countians apparently selected and their occupations are:

Amos Hahn, Lancaster malleable castings company employee; Walter Shiffer and William Rudolph Sweigart, shoe company employes; John B. Steffy, farmer; Miles Gress, knitting mill employee; and Alfred Keller, watch company employee; Bradford Coker, salesman; Martin Camp, shoe cutter; Clyde Gerberich, Jr., shoe plant employee; Clarence Burris and Charles Neideigh, farm laborers; Carl D. Sheaffer, inspector at the asbestos plant; and Paul Brinser, shoe worker.

One-Third From Farms

County Boards 2 and 3 combined estimated today that about one-third of the men they have sent to camp thus far have come from the farms of Lancaster county. Employes of the Armstrong Cork Company and Columbia Casting company predominate among the Selective Service men called from industry.

County Board No. 5 last night refused to grant requests for reclassifications of three men placed in Class IA and are available for immediate military service.

James Henry Geyer, Mohnton, married since he registered, was refused re-classification. The board ruled his wife is not wholly dependent upon him.

Clarence Z. Myer, Ephrata, claimed he is the support of his mother. The Board ruled two other brothers can support her.

Ralph Weber, formerly of Terre Hill, claimed he is married and a conscientious objector. Board ruled his "conscientious objections not strong enough."

The Board granted re-classification to Charles Gable, Rothsville, who proved he is sole support of mother. He is now in Class 3.

List Men To Go

Three Boards today revised the list of men who will be sent to Harrisburg next month. They are:

County Board 2—William Gould, Columbia, volunteer; Harry H. Kline, Columbia, volunteer; Charles Roosevelt Reamer, Columbia, volunteer; Myer E. Diamond, 218 Chester street, volunteer; Harvey E. Shearer, 430 North Queen street; Harold R. McQueeny, Rohrerstown; Raymond Chester Haldeman, Lancaster R. D. 1; Lester Baker Fuhrman, Lancaster R. D. 1; Samuel Melvin Durham, Columbia, and James E. Riegel, Columbia.

County Board 3 — Abram H. Frey, Conestoga R. D. 2; Frank M. Bortzfield, Conestoga R. D. 1; William H. Rhodes, Holtwood; John Eshleman Hess, Washington borough; Clayton Edward Charles, Lancaster R. D. 2; Howard McFadden Weller, 1075 Columbia avenue; Clayton H. Brenneman, Millersville, and Charles Lewis Baily, Oxford R. D. 2.

City Board No. 3 — Walter E. Smith, 213½ North Mulberry street, volunteer; George E. Hawk, 130 Nevin street, volunteer; Paul V. Houghton, 625 Fifth street; Jack H. Miller, 837 Fourth street; Herman L. Walzl, Jr., 834 Marietta avenue; Samuel C. Wawhauser, Jr., 427 High street and Michael J. Conti, 623 Poplar street. The replacement men are Jack A. Frey, 242 North Mary street, and Thomas R. Lefever, 446 West Orange street.

City Board No. 2 last night announced the classification of additional men. They are as follows:

Class 1

R. E. Gordon Scheid, 914 Buchanan ave.
Robert DuBois Leman, 408 W. James st.
John Richard Schoenberger, 220 E. New st.
Edward Myers Wiley, 21 E. Ross st.
Lloyd Eugene Bergstresser, 819 N. Shippen st.
Robert Ambrose Richey, 429 Charlotte st.
John McGuire Melsom, 808 N. Plum st.
Archie Foster Myers, 420 N. Duke st.
Theodore Winthrop Pettit, 709 N. Lime st.
Elvin Rehm, 410 N. Water st.
Elwood Billett Hipple, 410 E. Ross st.
Richard Habecker, 124 E. Ross st.
Leland Samuel Benton, Jr., 525 N. Lime st.
Robert James Bell, 139 E. Chestnut st.
Robert Samuel Maurer, 221 W. James st.
Kenneth M. Wurster, 424 New Holland ave.
Robert Montgomery Rittenhouse, 524 Spruce st.
Daniel Benjamin Hartman, 519 W. Lemon st.
Martin Whittington Carlfield, 130 E. Lemon st.
William Walter Witmer, 427 Reynolds ave
Paul Elwood Warner, Jr., 256 E. Lemon st.
Herbert Harry Kemmerly, 525 N. Christian st.
Hugh Joseph Devenney, 36 W. Liberty st.
Samuel Joseph Stauffer, 752 N. Pine st.

CLASS 3

William Mowery Brinkman, 263 New Holland ave.
Frank Dreyer Sills, 238 N. Duke st.
Edward Paterson, 519 E. Walnut st.
Charles Edward Sener, 310 W. James st.
Raymond Wastle Roark, 152 E. Ross st.
John McCartney, 527 N. Duke st.
Ronald Chamberlain Hoover, 341 E. New st.
Elvin Victor Myers, 436 N. Charlotte st.
Charles Albert Regar, 724 Reservoir st.
John Carl Cook, 247 N. Lime st.
George Raymond Pew, 536 W. James st.
Robert Schuler DeMora, 126 E. Lemon st.
Leo Halpern, 758 Hamilton st.
Morris Shear, 29 E. Lemon st.
John Franklin Ferich, 826 N Plum st.
Martin Mowery Barley, 430 N. Lime st.
Warren Wiker Aument, 308 Ice ave.
Robert Browning Gibbel, 734 Lehigh ave.
William Milton Smith, 237 E. New st.
Harry M-rtin Cochran, 918 N. Plum st.
John Henry Eby, 921 N. Queen st.
Roy W Adams, 626 E. Fulton st.
Donald Francis Rote, 49 W. Frederick st
Melvin David Ruth, 606 N. Mary st.
Lloyd Engroff Herr, 312 Ice ave
Herman Rossman, 543 Burrows ave.
Robert L. Stauffer, 548 New Holland ave.
Edwin Nathaniel Horn, Jr., 327 E. Chestnut st.
Frederick Joseph Kuder, 626 N. Pine st.
Charles Diehl Coleman, 216 E. Liberty st
Louis Law, 609 N President ave.
Theodore Bart Finefrock, 134 E. James st
Arthur William Moore, 467 New Dorwart st.
John William Brown, 556 Reynolds ave.
Otis Raymond Shultz, 219 E. Frederick st
William Charles Hubert, 326 N. Mary st.
Richard Edward Hull, 859 N. Queen st.
Guy Frank Tallarico, 321 E. Chestnut st.
Henry Quinby Wilson, 241 N. Lime st.
Robert William Owens, 801 N. Shippen st.
Charles Ellis Duncan, 551 W. Lemon st.
Paul Lichty Martin, 348 E. New st
Walter Albert McDermott, 628 N. Franklin st.
Park Albert Caldwell, 614 Lehigh ave
John Michael Ganse, Jr., 413 W. Walnut st.
Clyde Gilbert Beazley, 693 New Holland ave.
Samuel Mark Evans, 809 N. Duke st.
Benjamin Lester Robinson, 593 N. Plum st.
Elwood Greider Brian, 320 W. James st.
Raleigh James See, 24 E. Frederick st
Harry Clayton Lynes, 32 E. James st.
William McKay Rhoads, 602 N. Marshall st.
Clyde William McClarigan, 222 E. New st
Clarence Elsworth Schaeffer, 332 E. New st.
Lester Graybille Eager, 523 E. New st.
Raleigh Showers Nies, 619 E. Frederick st
Charles Deane Kittinger, 336 E Ross st.
John Stolarz, 317 E. New st.
Leo Shopf, 610 Park ave.
Louis Herman, 556 W. Lemon st.
Lewis F. Owen, 742 Lehigh ave.
Harry Walter Enck, 17 E. Lemon st
Paul Herbert Kantz, 5809 Narcissus ave., Baltimore, Md.
Earl Clifford Wolf, 220 W. James st.
Nicholas George Wolf, 241 W. Lemon st.
William Schroeder, 705 E. Walnut st.
Richard Spencer Walker, 218 N Duke st
Charles Leonard Fisher, 1135 E Poplar st., York, Pa.
Edward Curtis Maloney, 319 N Marshall st.
Harold Cloyd Schoener, 596 N. Plum st.
William Bernard McVey, 426 W. Lemon st.
Abram Lewis Witmer, 646 Park ave.
William Elvin Reidenbach, 726 E. Chestnut st.
Alfred Charles Alspach, 127 E. Walnut st.
William Ralph Gamber, 350 E. New st.
Homer Ernest Rieker, 432 Charlotte st.
J. Robert DeHaven, 639 N. Pine st.
Benjamin Andrew Davish, 222 W. James st
Henry Beaver Tollaksen, 131 E. Walnut st.
Marice Willis Brady, 718 N. Queen st.
Richard Carrigan Kiehl, 303 Tenth st.
Augustus Valentine Brown, 29 E James st.
Osborne Thomas Hotchkiss, Pequea, R. D. 1
Elvin Elwood Boas, 721 N. Queen st.
Kenneth Hulbert Decker, 21 E Ross st.
Charles Howard Benfer, 508 W. Lemon st.
William Howard Carmitchell, 313 Reservoir st.
Park Elwood Yeager, 529 N. Queen st.
Harry Elmer Zwalley, 821 Reservoir st.
Russell Saylor Fink, Lancaster, R. D. 3
Earl Miller Stoudt, 470 S Dorwart st.

CLASS 4-C

Fernando Everto Alfonso, 607 State st.

CLASS 4-F

Albert Leroy Reynolds, 410 N. Mulberry st.

Objectors' Camps Are Discussed

Representatives of non-combatant sects met with War Department officials in Washington, D. C., yesterday to discuss matters relative to the camps for conscientious objectors, Samuel S. Wenger, local attorney, said today.

The War Department will furnish beds, cots, stoves, pans and other equipment to the camps provided the denominations assume liability for their return.

The matter of obtaining workmen's compensation protection for the objectors who work on government reforestation, soil conservation, and the like, was also discussed. No conclusion was reached but it is likely the denominations will make some provisions for it, Wenger said.

Heavyweight Boxers Again Feature Amateur Fight Bill

BURTON FIGHTS FELIX WAGNER AT ST. JOE CLUB

Eight Bouts On Program Should Furnish Fans Plenty Thrills

A mittfest which will result in a swingfest featuring heavyweights is booked for the St. Joseph Catholic Club this Monday night as Coach John Houck has rounded up some of the best amateurs in these parts to put in their appearance. The first bout starts at 8:30 o'clock.

Richard Danz, president of the club, and Coach Johnny Houck have left nothing unfinished to make this Monday night's card just as attractive as the last one.

The feature bout will find two heavyweights in action. Big fellows seem to be the magnet of the boxing fans eyes. The Hill officials always try to satisfy their patrons and they will have Felix Wagner Central Pennsylvania amateur heavyweight king meeting the dusky Charley Burton, of Harrisburg.

Wagner is a stable mate of Ted Camillio who made such a hit at the last show. Wagner is a steel worker and depends upon his ruggedness to gain him victory. He is not a finished boxer like his teammate Camillio. What he lacks in the finer points of the game, he makes up in durability as he keeps punching the entire time he is in the ring.

Willie Green, the State Police boxing instructor sends word Wagner is fit and will show the St. Joseph fans some real action.

Burton, Wagner's opponent is a big husky fellow and has been a consistent winner.

Buddy Knight, the Harrisburg trainer, feels sure that his boy will capture the fans eyes with his willingness to battle.

It looks as though the fans are in to see a titanic struggle when these two big boys start throwing punches.

Another bout that the fans are looking forward to is the one between Anthony Stoe, St. Joseph's popular youngster and Joe Smith, of the West Lancaster A. A. These two welterweights hammered, clawed and punched their way through a terrific three round bout that left the fans weak from excitement. The St. Joseph boy won the verdict. Smith still thought he could beat Stoe and immediately wanted a return bout. The St. Joseph boy gladly consented. The fans left out a deafening roar of approval when it was announced that these boys would again meet this Monday night.

It looks as though it will be a night for the Irish. Patrick Duffy, trainer and handler and athletic director of the 48th Ward Boys Club of Philadelphia, will present Jimmy Healey who will be pitted against little Charley McCullough, St. Joseph's gamester. This bout should prove a corker.

Another descendent from the land of the Green who will be swapping punches will be Tim Hallahan, a fighter from York. This wild Irishman is ever lasting throwing punches while in the ring.

Other boys who will be in action are: Soldier Harry Kurl, now of Indiantown Gap. "Bob" Mummert, Tony Piro, and Charley Meisenheter, of York. "Bob" Steward, and probably Art Mahon, of the 48th Ward Boys' Club, Philadelphia. The other St. Joseph boys who will be: Howard Berger, Zinzie Gaspri, Lou Scheuchenzuber, and Ray Kichner.

There will be eight bouts on the program.

STEELTON HI UNDEFEATED IN DISTRICT WRESTLING

DISTRICT NO. 3 P. I. A. A. STANDING

Teams	W.	T.	L.	Pts.
Steelton	7	0	0	14
Hershey	5	0	2	10
West York	5	0	2	10
Lancaster	4	0	3	8
Manheim	3	0	4	6
Hanover	2	0	5	4
Lebanon	2	0	5	4
Waynesboro	0	0	7	0

Steelton with seven victories and no losses is undefeated in the District No. 3 P. I. A. A. wrestling conference according to the statistics released for publication Friday by Palmer E. Poff, secretary.

The results of the matches are as follows:

Manheim 7, at West York 40.
Lebanon 0, at Hershey 48.
Lancaster 16, at Steelton 28.
West York 34, at Hanover 10.
Manheim 28, at Waynesboro 18.
Lebanon 3, at Lancaster 23.
Steelton 26, at Hanover 13.
Hershey 36, at Manheim 6.
Waynesboro 8, at West York 36.
Hanover 38, at Lebanon 10.
Hershey 22½, at Lancaster 15½.
Waynesboro 8, at Steelton 40.
Hershey 16, at West York 22.
Lancaster 21, at Manheim 23.
Hanover 9, at Hershey 31.
Waynesboro 21, at Lebanon 22.
West York 19, at Steelton 21.
Manheim 11, at Steelton 35.
Hanover 19, at Lancaster 21.
Lebanon 8, at West York 38.
Hershey 35, at Waynesboro 11.
Lancaster 28, at Waynesboro 15.
Steelton 32, at Lebanon 8.
Hanover 18, at Manheim 21.
Manheim 21, at Lebanon 23.
Waynesboro 19, at Hanover 25.
Steelton 19, at Hershey 15.
West York at Lancaster 21.

CARD ROOKIE ONLY 18

St. Louis — Max Surkont, Cardinal rookie pitcher who won 19 and lost five with Decatur last season, is only 18 years old.

New Grid Mentor

TOM DAVIES

Tom Davies, (above), has been appointed head grid coach at Western Reserve University, Cleveland, O., succeeding Bill Edwards who resigned recently to coach the professional Detroit Lions. Davies was a former star at the University of Pittsburgh.

NEWARK SWIMMERS HERE ON SATURDAY

New Jersey Team Will Meet Lancaster Lassies In Fackenthal Pool

In an effort to avenge a duel meet reversal suffered at the hands of the Lancaster Women's Swimming Association team about a month ago, the Newark Women's Athletic club swimming outfit will meet the locals in a return engagement in the Fackenthal Pool on Saturday night at 8 o'clock.

The New Jersey team will come here padded to the hilts with outstanding female stars. Topping the team's roster is Miss Patsy McWhorter, the 16 year old star who won the recent women's Junior National backstroke title held in this same Fackenthal Pool.

Patsy, a high school student in Jersey, will compete in two events, the 100 yard freestyle and the 100 yard backstroke. In both these numbers she will have sterling competition from Miss Mary Catherine Heckel, the 13 year old Lancaster freestyler, and Miss Charlotte Book, one of the up and coming backstrokers of the East.

But Patsy isn't the only big name on Miss Kitty Meyer's Newark aquatic outfit. Miss Berenice Lapp, a member of the Women's United States Olympic swimming team in 1936, will also be here. Miss Lapp, who is a great freestyler, will double in her Lancaster appearance, swimming in the 50 and 200 freestyle events.

Miss Lapp was not on hand the afternoon the Lancaster team beat Newark by a score of 36-26. But even with Miss Lapp and Miss McWhorter leading the Jersey combine it will still take a mighty fine group of swimmers to offset the brilliant local outfit.

Paul Gantz has his Lancaster lassies in top notch condition for this meet. And he reports that Miss Heckel, Book, Hoar, and Colon are turning in some remarkable performances in their practice sessions.

Belloise Battles Mauriello, Friday

New York—(AP)—Steve Belloise and Tami Mauriello, New York rival contenders for the middleweight crown, feature this week's national boxing program.

Belloise, who has met Ken Overlin for the title twice and lost close decisions on both occasions, takes on Mauriello in a 10-rounder at Madison Square Garden, Friday night. Mauriello has lost only one bout since he turned pro, and that came after 24 consecutive victories. The defeat was the hands of Billy Soose, clever boxer from Farrell, Pa., who has defeated both Overlin and Tony Zale, N. B. A. champion.

Overlin goes in a 10-round non-title bout against Mose Brown, of McKeesport, Pa., at Pittsburgh this Monday night.

MONDAY—At New York—Carmelo Fenoy, Bayargue, Spain vs. Tony Saraullo, Philadelphia, lightweights (8). At Pittsburgh—Ken Overlin, Washington, D. C. (middleweight champion) vs. Mose Brown, McKeesport, Pa. (10-non-title); Lee Q Murray, Norwalk, Conn. vs. Howard Stormy Williams, Detroit, heavyweights (10). At Philadelphia—Bobby Green, Philadelphia vs. Frank Donato, Philadelphia, featherweights (8). At Newark, N. J.—Al Roth, New York vs. Norman Rubio, Albany, N. Y., welterweights (10). At San Francisco—Pat Valentino, San Francisco vs. Solly Kreiger, New York, light-heavyweights (10). At Washington, D. C.—Tommy Forte, Philadelphia vs. Vic Corchado, Pureto Rico, bantamweights (10).

TUESDAY—At New York—Morris (Curley) Nichols, New York, vs. Joey Iannotti, New Haven, Conn., featherweights (8); Aaron Seltzer, New York vs. Joe Amico, Philadelphia, featherweights (8); Lenny (Boom Boom) Mancini, New York vs. Chief Crazy Horse, Pasadena, Calif., lightweights (8). At New Haven, Conn.—Al Gainer, New Haven, Conn., vs. Billy Nichy, Buffalo, N. Y., light-heavyweights (8).

WEDNESDAY—At Perth Amboy, N. J.—Young Terry, Trenton, N. J. vs. Tony Reno, Chicago, middleweights (8).

THURSDAY—At Philadelphia—Mike Evans, Philadelphia vs. Tommy Cross, Philadelphia, lightweights (8). At Chester, Pa.—Gus Dorazio, Philadelphia vs. Charley Robinson, Pennsgrove, N. J., heavyweights (8).

FRIDAY—At New York—Steve Belloise, New York vs. Tami Mauriello, New York, middleweights (10); Danny Bartfield, New York vs. Joey Fontana, New York lightweights (6); Charlie (Lulu) Constantino, New York vs. Tommy (Curley) St. Angelo, New York, featherweights (6).

"SOFTIES" NAME OFFICERS

Reading—Harry Dierolf, of Reading, was re-elected president of the Tri-State Softball league, here at the West Shore Club house of the Carpenter Athletic Association. John Wise, of Lancaster, was named vice president, while Carl A. Siegfried, of Reading, was selected as the secretary-treasurer for the sixth term.

LIBERATE 88 PHEASANTS

Members of the Strasburg Sportsmen's Association liberated 88 pheasants in that vicinity Thursday. The sportsmen urge all persons in that vicinity to feed the birds during this snowy period.

Van Lingle Mungo Fined And Banished From Camp

Havana — (AP) — Van Lingle Mungo, the unpredictable pitcher who was going to win 25 games for Brooklyn this season, was fined $200 and banished from the Dodgers training camp for drinking.

The fiery fireballer was given transportation to Macon, Ga., and told that if he wanted to return to the good graces of the Dodgers he would have to do it at the camp of their Montreal (International League) farm which begins training there next Saturday.

The latest upheaval in Mungo's long and turbulent relationship with the Dodgers occurred at Brooklyn headquarters in the Hotel National. After dinner he appeared at the bar in high spirits and offered to buy all the boys a drink. Two of the boys at the other end of the bar happened to be Manager Leo Durocher and Coach Chuck Dressen.

When the best known citizen of Pageland, S. C., arrived at La Tropical stadium for the Dodgers' doubleheader with the Cleveland Indians he was handed a note by club secretary John McDonald that his stay with Brooklyn was ended at least temporarily.

"You are being furnished transportation from Havana to Macon," the note said. "You are to leave the Dodgers camp tonight."

Thus ended the latest of Mungo's good intention campaigns. He had had many other adventures with the club, but last fall announced he was turning over a new leaf. He was carried on the club's coaching staff part of the season and supervised movies made by the club for training purposes in September. He has been a model of deportment up to now in camp and at his own request was assigned Whitlow Wyatt, a quiet, serious pitcher, for a roommate. He frequently and proudly declared he "hadn't had a drink since October."

In the past Mungo has always been the chief problem child of Brooklyn managers. In 1938 he jumped the club in Pittsburgh and was next heard from at his South Carolina home. Another time he and a couple of teammates got into a fist fight at a St. Louis hotel and he once rammed his fist through a train window while travelling with the club.

San Diego, Calif —(AP)— Jack Knott, Chubby Dean and Bill Beckman hurled the Athletics to a three-hit 3 to 2 victory over the San Diego Padres.

Knott, obtained from the Chicago White Sox, gave up a single and a homer, the latter to Mel Mazzera, a former Phillie player, in the first frame. Dean held the Padres hitless during his three innings, and Beckman was touched for a double in the eighth.

Two hits, two walks and an error gave the A's their three runs in the seventh.

Philadelphia (A) . 000 000 300—3 9 1
San Diego (PCL) 200 000 000—2 3 3
Knott, Dean (4), Beckman (7) and Wagner; Thomas, Olsen (6), Herbert (8) and Salkeld.

Miami Beach, Fla. —(AP)— The Sea Gulls defeated the Sand Dabs 11 to 7 in the Phillies' first intra-squad baseball game.

Charley Frye, who worked two innings for the Gulls, saw the roughest action, giving up eight hits and getting rid of a wild pitch, the Dabs got seven runs off Frye in the sixth.

Pitcher Paul Masterson, his Sand Dabs battery mate, Ben Warren, and Danny Litwhiler, the Gulls' rightfielder, connected for homers.

Pasadena, Calif. —(AP)— A home run in the ninth inning by Dario Lodigiani gave the Chicago White Sox a 10 to 9 victory over the Pittsburgh Pirates in an exhibition baseball game.

Ralph Kiner and Frank Kalin, Pirate rookies, and Larry Rosenthal also hit for the circuit.

The Pirates used three hurlers, Butcher, Klinger and Lanahan. Together they yielded 16 safeties, while the four Sox slabmen—Lyons, Dietrich, Lee and Humphries—held the National Leaguers to a dozen hits.

Contract troubles for the Pirates ended when Alfred Anderson, the holdout rookie from the Atlantic club of the Southern Association, walked into club headquarters at San Bernardino, Calif., and signed.

Pittsburgh (N) . 025 001 010— 9 12 1
CHICAGO (A) .. 103 201 201—10 16 1
Butcher, Klinger (5), Lanahan (7) and Davis, Schultz (9); Lyons, Dietrich (2), Lee (5), Humphries (8) and Turner, Dickey (8).

St. Petersburg, Fla. —(AP)— The New York Yankees looked like the team fans used to call the Bronx Bombers, scoring all their runs in one tremendous inning to wallop the St. Louis Cardinals 7 to 2 in an exhibition game.

The uprising came in the fourth against Harry Brecheen and Ira Hutchinson and the seven hits included homers by Tom Henrich and Mike Chartak and a couple of doubles, one by Gerry Priddy with the bases loaded.

Three Yankee pitchers allowed only one hit apiece, but the one Spud Chandler gave in the fifth was a home run by Martin Marion. The Cards' other run came on a pair of errors, a walk and an infield out in the sixth.

New York (A) ... 000 700 000—7 11 2
St. Louis (N) .. 000 011 000—2 3 0
Breuer, Chandler (4), Ardizoia (7) and Rosar; Warneke, Brecheen (4), Hutchinson (4), Cooper (6) Krist (8) and Cooper, Mancuso (7).

Miami, Fla. —(AP)— The hapless New York Giants felt the brunt of the Boston Red Sox' well-known power as the Sox ripped off three home runs and a 4 to 2 exhibition victory.

Each of New York's three pitchers gave up one of the Boston round-trippers—Lou Finney getting the first off Bob Bowman in the initial inning, Jim Tabor tabbing another with one runner on base against Harry Gumbert in the sixth and Pete Fox adding the last off Bump Hadley in the seventh.

The Giants, who haven't won a game yet, were held to five hits by Mike Ryba, Mickey Harris and Leslie Fleming. Hank Danning played left field for six innings and struck out three times. The only fielding chance he had was a bounding single, which he fumbled.

Boston (A) ..... 100 002 100—4 8 1
New York (N) ... 000 001 010—2 5 1
Ryba, Harris (4), Fleming (7) and Pytlak, Peacock (6); Bowman, Gumbert (4), Hadley (7) and Hartnett, O'Dea (6).

San Antonio, Tex.—(AP)—The St. Louis Browns succumbed to Boston power as Casey Stengel's Bees pounded out an 11 to 5 victory with a 14-hit attack led by Eddie Miller.

Miller showed no partiality in collecting four hits and a walk in five times at bat against the three Brownie pitchers, Bob Muncrief, Emil Bildilli and Maurice Newlin.

One of his blows was a home run over the left field wall at the 380 foot marker. There were two other homers, by Max West and Chet Laabs.

The Browns, who downed Boston in the exhibition opener Saturday, were held to six hits by a trio of Bee hurlers, Nich Strincevich, Al Piechota and Frank Lamanna.

St. Louis (A) .. 101 030 000— 5 6 2
Boston (N) ... 020 441 00x—11 14 1
Muncrief, Bildilli (4), Newlin (6) and Swift; Strincevich, Piechota (4), Lamanna (6) and Masi.

Havana —(AP)— The Cleveland Indians stopped the cocky Brooklyn Dodgers' winning streak 8 to 4 in the first game of a double-header, but the Flatbush Flashes retaliated by winning the 4 1-2 inning second game 3 to 0.

The Dodgers raked Bob Feller for three runs in the third inning of the opener while Kirby Higbe was holding the Indians scoreless for three frames. But in the fifth the Tribe teed off on Lee Grissom for five runs and that was the ball game.

The second contest was abbreviated to let the Indians catch their boat back to Florida, but before it ended Don Ross hit a two-run homer and Cleveland never threatened.

A crowd of 10,000 was on hand.

(First Game)
Cleveland (A) .. 000 050 300—8 11 1
Brooklyn (N) .. 003 100 000—4 9 1
Feller, Milnar (4), Bagby (7) and Hemsley; Higbe, Grissom (4), Hamlin (5), Swift (8) and Franks, Owen (7).

(Second Game)
Cleveland (A) .... 000 00—0 2 1
Brooklyn (N) .... 010 2x—3 5 2
Adkins, Smith (4) and Desautels; Head, Flowers (4) and Owen.
(Game called 4½ innings to enable Cleveland to catch boat).

Tampa, Fla.—(AP)—The Cincinnati Reds tasted a 6-5 defeat, the Washington Senators serving the medicine in an exhibition game before a topcoated crowd of 2,261 including Ford Frick, National League president.

Washington pounded Johnny Vander Meer for three runs in the fifth and clouted Joe Beggs for the winning tally in another three-marker rally in the eighth.

The Reds left 15 men stranded on base and blew chances to score the winning run in the eighth and ninth. In each instance the Reds got a run on four straight walks, then, with the bases loaded, Frank McCormick hit into a double play in the eighth and Pep Young forced a runner at second in the ninth.

Washington (A) 000 030 030—6 9 0
Cincinnati (N) .. 101 010 011—5 11 1
Materson, Cunningham (4), Mayer (7), Zukowski (8) and Evans, Early (5), Hahn (7); Thompson, Vander Meer (4), Beggs (6), Pearson (9) and West.

Lakeland, Fla.—(AP)—Big Hank Greenberg arrived in the Detroit Tigers' training camp and said he looked forward to "another good year."

But whether the American League's "most valuable" player will spend that year in the outfield or in Uncle Sam's army is a question yet to be decided by selective service officials. Greenberg holds a low order number, and draft officials in Detroit have classified him as immediately available for service.

All hands were accounted for at the workout, including Eris "Boob"

More of BASEBALL On Page 13

Kauffman-Gall Rematch For Maple Grove Mar. 17

Silent Abie Kauffman, the New York lightweight who meets Patsy Gall, of Hazleton, here Monday night, March 17 at the Maple Grove Field House in a return eight-rounder, is a quiet little guy, whose innate modesty is a strange characteristic, indeed, to come upon in the slightly boisterous profession in which he plys his trade.

When Abie says more than three or four words hand-running, he is practically bragging.

After his first fight here with Gall, about four weeks ago in which he registered the most startling upset of the indoor season, when he shaded the Hazleton Windmill, Kauffman said he had two bad hands before the fight. He bruised them in a fight with Tony Roman in Brooklyn several days before.

The New York youngster was implying that perhaps with two good hands the next time, he might do better with Gall. When put under the third degree with one of those rubber things, the dicks laughingly refer to as a persuader, Kauffman avered that he might even knock Patsy out the next time they meet.

That was practically par for the course for Abe. Unlike the majority of his ring kin who would have used the hand injuries as grounds for some such outburst as this: "Geez, I was lame in both maulies, or I'd a murdered the mug. Next time I'll knock 'im out in two heats," Kauffman merely said, apologetically, that he thought he would do better this next fight with two good hands.

The likes of Kauffman is something of a rarity in the fight profession, and very refreshing indeed. Besides being quiet, he is quite a fighter too. Unsung and unknown when he came here for the first fight with Gall, Kauffman was expected to be a stepping stone for the Hazleton favorite.

But Abe completely upset the dope with a grand display of prizefighting, and his return here Monday night, March 17 will be welcomed with open arms by the gallery gods. Especially since Abie has whispered that he might knock Gall out this time.

Injured In Spill

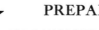

TEDDY ATKINSON

Jockey Teddy Atkinson, was painfully injured in spill during race at Tropical Park, Miami, Fla. The accident occurred when horse ridden by Wendell Eads tripped and fell in front of Atkinson's mount. Atkinson suffered deep gashes on his face. Eads suffered a fractured skull and internal injuries.

BUFFALO-HERSHEY IN 2-2 DEADLOCK

Tie Contest Keeps Bisons In Running For Playoff Position

Buffalo, N. Y. —(AP)— The Buffalo Bisons came from behind twice Sunday night to play a 2-2 overtime tie with the Hershey Bears before 7,735 spectators and remain in the running for an American Hockey League playoff position.

The visitors opened the scoring in the third minute of play when Bill Beveridge, attempting to clear Hank Lauzon's shot, knocked the puck into the net. Morey Rimstad equalized for the Bisons later in the period.

Harry Frost sent the Bears ahead again in the second period, but the Bisons came back at 6.26 of the third on Maxie Bennett's score while Lauzon was serving time for tripping. Hershey played defensive hockey thereafter with Nick Damore starring in goal.

The Bisons have lost only five of their last 21 games.

Bob Gracie, Buffalo left winger, took the ice despite a sudden illness to play his 587th successive regularly scheduled game in 11 seasons of professional hockey.

Hershey (2)		Buffalo (2)
Damore	G.	Beveridge
Lauzon	L. D.	McInenly
Jenkins	R. D.	Shannon
Pettinger	C.	Toupin
Bruce	L. W.	Klein
McReavy	R. W.	Bennett

Hershey alternates—Shewchuk, Frost, Kilrea, Sorrell, Roulston, Germann, Hamill.

Buffalo alternates—Mercer, Drouillard, Goldsworthy, Blake, Gracie, Hemmerling, Rimstad, Cunningham, Doran.

Referee, Clarence Campbell; linesman, Tiny Teasdale.

First period scoring: 1—Hershey, Lauzon (unassisted) 2:14; 2—Buffalo, Rimstad (Cunningham, Shannon) 12:28. Penalties—Shannon, McInenly, Sorrell.

Second period scoring: 3—Hershey, Frost (Lauzon, Sorrell) 5:15. Penalties—Germann, Blake.

Third period scoring: 4—Buffalo, Bennett (McInenly, Klein) 6:26. Penalty—Lauzon.

Overtime period: No scoring; no penalties.

Paul Runyan Leads West Coast Event

Belleair, Fla. — (AP) — Paul Runyan, former P. G. A. champion from White Plains, N. Y., clipped four strokes from par for a 67 to take a one-stroke lead on the opening round of the 54-hole West Coast Open here Sunday.

Ben Hogan, the leading money-winner of the season from Hershey, Pa., and Gene Sarazen, with whom Hogan teamed to win the Miami four-ball last week, did not enter.

Paul Runyan, White Plains, N. Y.	32-35—67
Joe Zarnhardt, Norristown, Pa.	34-34—68
Craig Wood, Mamaroneck, N. Y.	34-35—69
Willie Goggin, Miami, Fla.	34-35—69
Henry Picard, Oklahoma City	37-33—70
Chick Harbert, Battle Creek, Mich.	34-36—70
Sam Snead, Hot Springs, Va.	35-35—70
x-Skee Reigel, Glendale, Calif.	36-35—71
Reggie Myles, St. Petersburg	37-34—71
Lloyd Mangrum, Oak Park, Ill.	34-37—71
Ray Mangrum, Pittsburgh, Pa.	36-35—71
Jimmy Thompson, Chicopee, Mass.	35-36—71
Ted Turner, Pine Valley, N. J.	34-37—71
Herman Barron, White Plains, N. Y.	35-36—71
Ky Laffoon, Chicago	37-34—71
Lloyd Sparrow, Tampa, Fla.	36-35—71
Horton Smith, Oak Park, Ill.	36-35—71
Chandler Harper, Portsmouth, Va.	36-36—72
Bob Stupple, Glencoe, Ill.	35-37—72
Byron Nelson, Toledo, Ohio	35-37—72

MORRIS D. LEITZEL TOPS 50 GUNNERS AT READING

(Special to Intelligencer Journal)

Reading—Shattering 49 out of 50 clays, from 16 yards rise, Morris D. Leitzel, of Reading, topped field of 50 gunners facing the Lorane traps here Sunday afternoon, in the fourth and final shoot of the South End Gun Club's winter series of prize events. Seven knotted on 48 breaks each, to divide the runner-up honors.

In the class awards, Lewis system, Ray Behney, the Mt. Aetna wingshot won the second class donation, after a shoot off with Paul Schell, of Reading, on 45 breaks. The third group, with five tied on 40 targets each, was won by Charles Manske, of Reading, who shattered 24 out of his 25 additional "rocks."

The scores of Lancaster and vicinity follow:

George M. Leed, Fivepointville	44
William Crouse, Denver	39
George Stieff, Ephrata	38
Alton Eberly, Ephrata	46
John Martin, Terre Hill	44
C. W. Good, Lancaster	42
Morris Kern, Terre Hill	37
Charles Oberholtzer, Geigertown	47
Al Mittower, Denver	46
Ray Behney, Mt. Aetna	45
Frank Louser, Mt. Aetna	48
Joseph Angstadt, Fritztown	45
Raymond Brubaker, Reinholds	40
Warren Martin, Terre Hill	44
Joseph Fredericks, Harrisburg	38
Daniel Diffenderfer, Gibraltar	46
Webb Muhlenburg, Morgantown	48
Paul Sweigart, Churchtown	37
William Gift, Reinholds	37
Edward James, Lancaster	40
Charles Meister, Lancaster	40

ABC TRUNDLERS BEGIN ACTION THURSDAY NITE

30,000 Pin Busters From All Sections Will Compete In Tourney

St. Paul, Minn.—(AP)—Modern civilization's version of the ancient game of ten pins will be unfolded here in a mighty display for a 55 day period starting next Thursday night.

The event is the 41st annual American Bowling Congress which will attract in excess of 30,000 pin busters from 39 states in the United States and four Canadian provinces all seeking a share of the $230,000 which will be awarded in prizes.

The first shift of 40 teams will compete in the regular division of the tournament and will be followed by two forty team shifts in the booster section. Teams from outside of Minnesota total 3,356.

Outside teams participating on the first shift will come from Flin Flon, Manitoba; Dubuque and Sioux City, Ia; Marquette and Neguanee, Mich.; Williamsport, Pa.; Milwaukee, Washburn, Ashland, Wisconsin Rapids, La Crosse and Madison, Wis.; East Chicago and Mishawaka, Ind.

The Monarck team, of Chicago, won the team event with a 3,047 total in the tournament at Detroit last year, taking top prize of $1,500 and medals signifying the world championship. Two Chicago bowlers, Herbert Freitag and Joe Sinke also won the doubles first prize of $600 with a 1,346 total, while the singles title went to Ray Brown, of Terre Haute, Ind., with 742 pins. Top singles prize is $300.

Tropical Park Entries

Post 2:00 EST.

FIRST: $1,000, claiming, 3 yrs., 6 furlongs: chute (18): x-Dragon Lady 103, Subura 108, Interrupt 105, Long Legs 105, Sasnak 113, Bond Hill 110, Sun Wiggle 113, Lady Jaffa 108, Old Smoothy 113, x-Grimpish 108, Patricia A. 108, Dolinvar 110, x-Cherriko 113, x-Orcus 113, Rest Awhile 113, Charming Sudie 105, Shore Leave 108, Tee Cee 113.

SECOND: $1,000, claiming, 4 up 6 furlongs: chute (18): Hunting Home 116, x-Sir Quest 108, x-Symphon 111, x-Dusky Girl 104, Smilin Jack 111, x-Arched 108, Ethel Blume 106, Jaw Breaker 116, Judfry 111, Johnny Q. 111, Maecaro 111, Madison 113, Boy Baby 111, Sun Antioch 116, Ghost Flyer 113, Bobs Squad 111, x-Valdina Jack 108, Indian Penny 111.

THIRD: $1,000, claiming, 3 yrs., 6 furlongs: chute (18): Obisbo 113, x-Head Sea 100, Penny Arcade 105, Cadet Bob 113, Vesuvius 113, Red Metal 110, Boat Cover 108, Jota 108, Chance Run 113, x-Hadamoon 103, Wise T. 110, Notforme 113, x-Ever Time 105, x-Blushing Bride 103, Joe Pete 113, x-Wee Scot 106, Wise Dean 108, Villa Platte 113.

FOURTH: $1,000, claiming, 4 up, 6 furlongs: chute (15): Try Sak 111, x-The Thrust 108, x-Darby Dean 108, Happy Lark 111, Kleig Light 111, Red Meadow 108, War Declared 111, You Alone 106, Taxes 116, Mighty Miss 108, x-Big Brands Son 108, Indian Lodge 113, x-Best Quality 109, Gallant Stroke 113, Aristocracy 106.

FIFTH: $1,200, allowances, 4 years 1 1-16 miles (11). Harp Weaver 113; Nightland 110; Ringie 118; Croydon 110; Toree 115; Shot Put 120; Plowshare 113; Miss Quiz 108; Detroit Bull 118; Sickle T 120; Rex Flag 112.

SIXTH: $1,000, claiming, 3 years, 1 1-16 miles (15). He Man 115; Air Post 113; x-Red Burr 110; Bay Fox 115; Chorus 115; Lady Lyonors 110; Claypille 115; Banker Jim 115; x-Shaun G 110; Meritorious 115; Bonified 115; x-Blumere 105; x-Brooklandville 110; Octobre Onze 118; x-Flood II 110.

SEVENTH: $1,000, claiming, 4 up, 1⅛ miles (8). Wedding Morn 108; Snow 113; Charlotte Girl 108; Cherry Trifle 111; Rahanee 106; Big Rover 111; x-Jaybeedee 109; Bonzar 114.

EIGHTH: $1,000, claiming, 4 up; 1 1-16 miles (18) x-Transday 108; Wooden Indian 116; x-Wantarun 108; Gaspar De Salo 113, For Romance 108; Vollee II 111; Panjab 111; x-Upset Dove 106; Alca 109; x-Dunfrese 108; Sir Brookside 114; Mill River 113; x-Sweet Showno 103; x-Dizzy B. 111; x-Geo Krehbiel 106; Redrock Canyon 116; Easter Holiday 113; Cynic King 114.

x-AAC. Clear and muddy.

Oaklawn Park Entries

Post 3:15 EST.

FIRST: $600 claiming, 4 up, 6 furlongs: chute (12): Prince Placide 116, x-King Bee 111, Mount Kala 111, x-Peggy Byrd 106, Schnozzle 116, Charmette 111, Lookout Below 116, The Spotter 116, x-Pleasing Color 111, x-Carlade 106, x-Military Miss 106, Johnnie Dear 116.

SECOND: $600 claiming, 4 up, 6 furlongs chute (12); Broiler 112, Sherab Jr. 112, Onugo 112, x-Well Flight 102, x-Norman Sloat 113, Carrying Time 112, x-Martin Boy 107, Big Steel 112, Jimmie Tom 112, Some Good 112, Bully Time 110, Last Rose 113.

THIRD: $600 claiming, 3 yrs., 6 furlongs; chute (12); Skidad 112, x-Mr. Serajevo 107, x-Ripping Sun 107, Codoll 110, x-Fairy Ball 105, Madame Dever 107, x-Tervette 107, x-Bequest 105, x-Grand Court 108, x-Fittspool 110, Lady Memphis 107, x-Pilots Gal 102.

FOURTH: $700 claiming, 4 up, 6 furlongs; chute (6); x-Ottos Choice 110, x-Scandalous 107, Lazarus 112, x-Walter Light 107, x-Half Time 110, x-Moselem 101.

FIFTH: $600 claiming, 4 up, 1¼ miles (12). x-Sign Up 102; x-Azafran 102; x-Snobeedo 113; Lonely Road 112; x-Norma H. 102; x-King Joy 110; x-Bold General 107; x-Easiest Way 112; Soon 112; Willie J. 112; Fandan 118; x-Serbian Rose 108.

SIXTH: $700 claiming, 4 up, 1 1-16 miles (9). x-Jack Vennie 101; x-Little Abner 107; x-Adoress 108; x-Harebell 102; x-Whistling Dick 101; Molasses Bill 112; Knee Deep 115; Transbye 110; x-Vinum 107.

SEVENTH: $600 claiming, 4 up, 1 mile 70 yards (10). x-Pecks Bad Boy 105; Conville 116; Bachelors Bower 110; x-Geologist 105; Mistletoe 111; Waringa 110; x-Gay Sallie 100; Ho 110; x-Radio Wave 106; x-Self Starter 106.

EIGHTH: $600 claiming, 4 up, 1 mile 70 yards (12). Good Memory 112 x-Frank C. 110; x-Quick Quick 102; x-Moonish 108; Kiev Singer 113; Colonel Martis 115; x-Nan Stein 108; x-Calanta 97; Sangstee 112; x-Lincoln J 107; x-Bon Mint 110; Repercussion 110.

NINTH (sub) $600 claiming, 4 up, 1 mile 70 yards (12). x-Daisy May 97; x-Linkville 110; Parlor Trick 107; Playline 112; x-Alrose 107; Baby Lamb 113; x-Rabdol 107; Pipers Tune 110; x-Spanish Jewel 107; x-Speedy Booger 102; Extended 112; Respha 107.

x-AAC. Clear and slow.

. . . Bowling Scores . . .

ELKS WIN

Ironmen				
Bauer	126	171	180	477
Hohenadel	...	134	134	268
Brubaker	198	167	144	509
Weber	108	184	159	451
Hess	121	...	116	237
Miller	169	139	...	308
	722	795	733	2250

Elks				
Steman	121	131	...	252
Brackbill	119	117	...	236
Hess	187	183	134	504
Hambright	147	186	135	468
Eckert	136	165	...	301
Snyder	...	...	155	155
Deal	...	...	159	159
Ulmer	...	...	148	148
	710	782	731	2223

ELKS DUCK PIN LEAGUE

Bro. Love				
Bowman	111	128	109	348
Leaman	137	...	118	255
Fawber	...	126	106	232
Groff	...	124	112	236
Reese	116	...	118	234
Will, G.	159	104	...	263
Snyder	176	136	...	312
	699	618	563	1880

Deer				
Klump	117	153	121	391
Lurio	...	...	121	121
Imhoff	122	...	106	228
Tomlinson	137	136	...	273
Ulmer	168	97	146	411
J.Mellinger	...	158	...	158
Steman	170	110	148	428
	714	654	642	2010

Antlers				
J.Miller	141	160	107	408
Shindle	106	134	..	240
Blumenst'k	113	125	128	366
Shaub	...	...	106	106
Dowd	132	141	130	403
Hambright	166	126	125	417
	658	686	596	1940

Cubs				
Mowrer	...	111	138	249
Weaver	118	...	129	247
Keller	...	116	...	116
Barley	102	113	137	352
Diehl	120	111	...	231
Batdorf	...	...	145	145
Quackenb'h	108	...	152	260
Freitag	142	125	...	267
	590	576	701	1867

Bears				
Case	...	92	...	92
E Wolf	148	110	108	366
Miller	137	...	173	310
Sahm	133	188	125	446
Small	130	121	127	378
N.Bair	139	119	116	374
	687	630	649	1966

Leopards				
Detery	92	119	136	347
Landis	...	...	135	135
Shirk	100	133	...	233
Book	101	167	104	372
Clark	172	186	111	469
P.Hess	203	143	163	509
	668	748x	649	2065

x-Won roll-off

Lions				
Kolp	86	135	116	337
H.Mohn	100	...	...	100
Forrest	...	119	118	237
Stauffer	73	127	113	313
Herr	98	126	126	350
Kegel	129	147	147	423
	486	654	620	1760

Justice				
Lovett	154	175	141	470
J.Will	137	121	115	373
P.Snavely	112	150	112	374
Kahley	181	153	137	471
Doe	73	119	113	305
	657	718	618	1993

Wildcats				
Carpenter	122	...	...	122
Hoober	96	126	141	363
Marks	..	164	...	164
Maley	103	138	146	387
Kirchner	117	.	122	239
Powderly	...	136	110	246
I.Miller	136	139	149	424
	574	703	668	1945

Badgers				
Leeking	90	109	117	316
Rhoads	105	89	88	282
O.Mohn	125	83	104	312
Dirks	79	...	...	79
Doe	96	136	110	342
Doe	...	126	122	248
	495	543	541	1579

Comers				
Hess	...	166	112	278
Anderson	106	119	119	344
Brenner	118	...	...	118
Drach	117	124	111	352
Manbeck	116	128	144	388
Boothman	147	194	170	511
	604	731	656	1991

Wolves				
Brachten'f	121	131	109	361
Long	98	99	130	327
R.Mellinger	144	...	...	144
Hottenstein	96	117	108	321
Algard	162	121	168	451
Demuth	...	164	145	309
	621	632	660	1913

RAINBOW LEAGUE

Blue				
Edwards	133	91	90	314
Mowery	141	128	102	371
Shertz	95	79	153	327
Stoner	149	89	144	382
Wagner	137	122	133	392
	655	509	622	1786

Yellow				
McNerney	96	96	90	282
Huston	87	137	117	341
Ziegler	117	108	121	346
Otstot	160	127	117	404
Doe	95	79	90	264
	555	547	535	1637

Red				
Shenk	117	135	180	432
Bruce	119	111	121	351
Shilling	130	105	118	353
Farmer	119	121	125	365
E. Otstot	122	140	143	405
	607	612	687	1906

Green				
Bauman	121	131	110	362
K. Otstot	92	100	73	265
M. Shaub	137	127	98	362
DiGocomo	143	157	146	446
E. Shaub	167	120	157	444
	660	635	584	1879

COLUMBIA GIRLS WIN

Columbia Jrs.				
Sam	155	161	114	430
Smith	193	162	188	543
Lew	155	137	135	427
Fred	166	151	120	437
Smeeze	...	209	151	360
John	162	...	...	162
	831	820	708	2359

Columbia Girls				
Frey	195	120	165	480
Gilbert	114	...	...	114
Depew	162	160	161	483
Stover	166	121	137	424
Hogen'er	...	140	127	267
Michal	152	198	246	596
	789	745	936	2470

BROAD STREET WOMEN'S LEAGUE

Jeepers				
Yarnell	114	109	137	360
Neiss	96	133	71	300
Snyder	128	152	126	406
Shreiner	181	92	166	439
Phillips	114	132	96	342
	633	618	596	1847

Kreepers				
Yarnall	145	102	122	369
Hogarth	128	137	106	371
Aungst	97	84	100	281
Caulwell	100	97	94	291
McMonigal	126	86	114	326
	596	506	536	1638

Hawks				
Washburn	155	163	136	454
Gregg	150	170	136	456
Shissler	155	176	197	528
E.Shreiner	193	166	182	541
Doe	125	124	132	381
	778	799	793	2360

Doves				
R.Miller	183	156	202	541
Yarnall	125	124	161	410
Hunchell	204	138	182	524
Aungst	137	168	132	437
Flick	193	143	193	529
	842	729	870	2441

Eagles				
Hogarth	156	218	148	522
Sacks	152	113	198	463
DeFrank	135	107	156	398
Brown	167	156	149	472
Phillips	164	191	137	492
	774	785	788	2347

Wrens				
I.Shreiner	186	161	171	518
Eckman	153	147	151	451
Singley	100	129	122	351
Bowers	119	150	...	269
C.Snyder	166	212	174	552
E.Snyder	166	212	174	552
	724	799	785	2308

Crows				
Goodwin	181	150	140	471
Whitaker	134	150	...	284
Seiple	151	149	143	443
Zim'erman	...	169	165	334
Neiss	203	...	128	331
Shreiner	176	190	164	530
	845	808	740	2393

Robins				
Martin	115	158	138	411
Lafferty	155	128	131	414
Worley	...	140	135	275
Kendig	140	...	...	140
Smith	135	137	144	416
Chandler	133	127	125	385
	678	690	673	2041

PRESBYTERIAN SEWING (DUCK) LEAGUE

Snaps				
Parmer	103	106	85	294
Pickell	54	86	66	206
Laudenslager	89	60	49	198
Lichty	67	74	77	218
	313	326	277	916

Scissors				
Diehm	86	64	83	233
E. Pickell	99	99	63	261
Herr	57	44	60	161
Lyons	73	78	73	224
	315	285	279	879

Thimbles				
Weiler	75	103	63	241
Keefe	55	64	82	201
Shindle	84	99	79	262
Jackson	...	73	...	73
Eshelman	111	...	66	177
Rogers	76	71	87	234
	401	410	377	1188

Needles				
Alexander	68	90	84	242
Totten	109	62	96	267
Hershberger	58	73	...	131
Shimp	68	74	77	219
McNiss	88	74	84	246
Snavely	...	...	66	66
	391	373	407	1171

CIGAR LEAGUE

Havana				
F Bruce	84	117	88	289
Urban	76	99	118	293
Barnes	125	95	112	332
Dornes	88	107	79	274
H.Bruce	163	113	86	362
	536	531	483	1550

Shade				
Hershey	153	125	107	385
Sheaffer	101	112	83	296
Zecher	91	112	110	313
Wiker	131	101	98	330
Doe	76	95	79	250
	552	545	477	1574

Sumatra				
Shanberger	75	80	78	233
Pierson	80	89	80	249
Keene	118	123	114	355
Otstot	146	141	135	422
Doe	97	89	111	287
	516	522	518	1546

Florida				
Walters	99	108	112	319
Funk	124	112	112	348
Fisher	97	126	115	338
Zecher	112	116	111	339
Boyd	103	89	136	328
	535	551	586	1672

HYDRO LADIES' LEAGUE

Alleys				
L.Lefever	78	137	76	291
Dunkle	75	58	77	210
Weaver	108	77	73	258
Parrott	124	80	103	307
Doe	45	42	60	147
	430	394	389	1213

Spares				
McVey	64	87	78	229
Sheaffer	96	99	85	280
Becker	83	63	75	221
Cook	81	64	77	222
Groff	124	101	99	324
	448	414	414	1276

Balls				
Lesher	84	94	77	255
Stively	69	83	67	219
Farmer	82	114	105	301
Steman	53	53	51	157
Bair	110	110	128	348
	398	454	428	1280

Strikes				
E.Lefever	91	111	112	314
Mellinger	67	86	87	240
Cox	83	75	86	244
Patton	105	107	81	293
Pelanis	140	83	98	321
	486	462	464	1412

Gutters				
Born	91	71	95	257
E.Herr	...	74	...	74
Feifer	87	102	98	287
Poisal	69	70	96	235
Adams	107	...	97	204
C.Sechrist	74	87	102	263
	428	404	488	1320

Pins				
Snyder	...	...	85	85
M.Herr	72	109	107	288
Shultz	69	81	86	236
Weiler	65	78	...	143
Miller	74	76	71	221
C Kauffman	102	108	107	317
	382	452	456	1290

HOME LEAGUE

Curtains				
Barnes	190	155	149	494
Hurst	113	108	97	318
McConnell	166	148	139	453
Weaver	177	121	170	468
Hambleton	154	177	157	488
	800	709	712	2221

Lamps				
Witmer	171	190	207	568
Sneath	149	149	149	447
Bischoff	205	187	198	590
H.Flawd	149	169	174	492
Waters	160	149	194	503
	834	844	922	2600

Chairs				
McFarland	165	122	146	433
E.M.Wallick	171	192	166	529
Newcomer	167	167	150	484
Mull	130	167	160	457
Huss	165	173	152	490
	798	821	774	2393

Stools				
Bostrum	218	185	180	583
Tomkin	160	160	160	480
Gibble	149	137	181	467
Haefner	189	213	173	575
L.Flawd	173	166	195	534
	889	861	889	2639

Pictures				
Parker	139	188	168	495
Evans	207	163	143	513
Rohm	172	222	139	533
Long	178	206	196	580
E.Schwartz	201	214	193	608
	897	993	839	2729

Radios				
Doe	162	162	162	486
Mowrer	144	155	131	430
Shenk Jr	132	147	170	449
Kauffman	181	156	196	533
W.Schwartz	211	200	174	585
	830	820	833	2483

Desks				
R.Graeff	178	213	220	611
Doe	150	150	150	450
Brandt	186	172	188	546
Dornbaugh	124	122	241	487
Buckwalter	158	160	162	480
	796	817	961	2574

Beds				
L. Graeff	200	151	165	516
Hershock	194	160	140	494
Hudy	168	172	188	528
Quinn	138	172	183	493
Wehner	169	174	163	506
	869	829	839	2537

Drapes				
Thomas	141	166	166	473
Shoemaker	157	133	202	492
Goss	199	186	148	533
Bare	179	158	182	519
Rittenhouse	178	197	169	544
	854	840	867	2561

Rugs				
Hatton	148	168	179	495
Miller	134	165	181	480
Dorwart	167	143	150	460
Snyder	165	203	231	599
McKendrick	208	158	178	544
	822	837	919	2578

Tables				
Knaisch	183	178	181	542
Doe	160	160	160	480
Collins	173	151	179	503
Shenk	154	132	151	437
P.Severino	192	167	222	581
	862	788	893	2543

Shades				
H.E.Coble	159	134	138	431
F.Serevino	144	123	133	400
H.R.Coble	172	161	166	499
Wallick	137	163	172	472
Wendler	140	173	158	471
	752	754	767	2273

EXHIBITION MATCHES

Elizabethtown				
Stucky	170	185	191	556
Tronio	191	189	169	549
Coble	170	182	247	599
Alwine	182	190	150	522
Heck	181	228	181	590
	894	974	938	2816

Overlook				
Mensenber'r	187	184	223	594
Bauer	137	190	202	529
Welsh	189	176	226	591
Smith	192	145	195	532
Gilgore	180	178	152	510
	885	873	998	2756

Ephrata Girls				
Miller	166	147	178	491
Reilly	114	139	131	384
Wingen'th	118	138	130	386
Granger	114	154	134	402
Mohlen	144	147	141	432
	656	725	734	2095

Lancaster Girls				
Caccamo	153	180	192	525
McElligott	175	156	172	503
Connell	163	145	120	428
Morrison	175	119	162	456
Ashmead	145	158	179	48[illegible]
	811	758	825	2494

Overlook House				
Winter'rg	178	151	170	499
Brust	205	181	189	575
Smith	171	179	216	566
Artigiani	169	220	198	587
Eckert	178	200	175	533
	901	931	948	2780

Mount Joy Travelers				
Barnhart	161	161	168	490
Young	153	168	171	491
Mateer	164	188	220	572
Max	212	148	167	527
Derr	192	170	155	517
	881	835	881	2597

LINO LEAGUE

Corks				
Geesey	187	183	174	544
Gerhart	161	128	124	413
Kniep	161	156	217	534
Snyder	155	133	185	473
Doe	133	136	122	391
	797	736	822	2355

Stencils				
Rannels	133	177	167	477
Myers	166	159	143	468
Wike	134	136	153	423
Smith	176	156	122	454
Snyder	135	177	130	442
	744	805	715	2264

MOOSE PINMEN WIN

Pottstown Eagles				
Sell	203	194	184	581
Wenger	234	180	165	579
Moore	192	210	169	571
Hoffman	...	182	182	364
Strom	167	...	...	167
Volz	224	199	221	644
	1020	965	921	2906

Moose Specials				
Keen	177	...	194	371
Bauer	223	215	189	627
J.Keen	185	214	...	399
Ambler	225	189	182	596
Pyfer	169	202	192	563
Brubaker	...	188	200	388
	979	1008	957	2944

HIGH COURT DENIES TAX CASE REVIEW

12 States Sought Ruling On Collection Of Idle Compensation Levies

Washington — (AP) — Twelve states failed Monday to obtain a Supreme Court ruling as to the legality of their procedure in collecting unemployment compensation taxes.

At issue was a decision by the Indiana Supreme Court holding unconstitutional a state law which permitted small companies under the same ownership, which would not be subject to the unemployment tax individually, to be grouped together and subjected collectively to the assessment.

The Indiana tribunal had reversed a judgment of a lower court and returned the case to the lower court for final disposition. The Supreme Court refused a review "for want of a final judgment."

In addition to Indiana, the state seeking a Supreme Court ruling were Virginia, Oklahoma, New Mexico, North Carolina, Florida, Maine, Louisiana, Missouri, Mississippi, Illinois and North Dakota. Their petition said a score of other states also had similar legislation.

The court handed down no opinions Monday but upheld rulings by federal agencies in two other cases which had been appealed.

Deaf Couple Wed In Silent Service By Sign Language

Black Lick, Pa.—(AP)—A silent service united George I. Kuhns and Anna Strojan of Pittsburgh, in marriage at a ceremony in this Indiana county community.

Kuhns mother, Justice of the Peace Mary E. Kuhns, first read the wedding service, but neither the bridegroom nor the bride heard the words because both are deaf.

Then, Mrs. Kuhns repeated the service in sign language and the couple made their vows in the same manner. The two attendants also were deaf.

An illness of mumps as a child cost Kuhns his hearing and his bride became deaf after a bomb explosion in her native Russia several years ago.

MINERS TO MAKE DEMANDS TODAY

Lewis And 150 Coal Union Leaders To Meet With Bituminous Operators

New York —(AP)— The nation's soft coal industry—growing more vital daily to this country's defense—will bring management and labor together Tuesday in a joint effort to determine future conditions under which nearly a half million miners will work.

President John L. Lewis of the United Mine Workers of America (CIO) and 150 union leaders will present their already determined demands upon mine operators in the eight-state Appalachian bituminous area at the opening conference.

Although Lewis kept secret just what his "specific demands" would be, an earlier UMWA statement said higher wages and shorter hours would be asked in negotiations to replace the two-year contract which expires March 31.

Both groups met briefly Monday to organize their negotiating machinery and adjourned without making any official statements.

One question seemed to be uppermost in pre-conference conversations: How long will negotiations continue?

Two years ago, the eventful conference began March 14 and continued until May 12. Negotiations were marked by bitter sessions, a general strike in the coal fields after the old contract expired, a resultant coal shortage throughout the east, and ultimate federal intervention.

Approximately 450,000 men in the bituminous mines will be affected by the forthcoming negotiations. They dig almost 70 percent of the country's soft coal, a fuel widely used by defense industries.

When Man Jilts Girl His Right To Ring Is Lost, Judge Declares

Ex-Suitor Sues After Ardor Cools, But Loses Circlet And $65 Court Costs

Pittsburgh — (AP) — A woman judge ruled Monday that if a man jilts a girl, he hasn't any right to their engagement ring.

John A. Kish, 31, gave an engagement ring to Betty Bodnar, 26-year-old attractive brunette, in February, 1940. Then, he testified, he became "skeptical" of marriage and asked for the return of the ring. She refused to give it back and he filed suit.

In directing a verdict for Miss Bodnar, Judge Sara M. Soffel said:

"An engagement ring is a symbol of marriage and when it is given, there is an implied condition.

"Now if that condition is not fulfilled—by death, by physical incapacitation, by mutual agreement or by the girl, herself, refusing to marry—then the man is entitled to have his ring back."

But, Judge Soffel decided, Kish failed to show that any of those conditions existed.

Kish lost $65 in court costs in addition to the ring.

As far as Miss Bodnar was concerned, "it wasn't the ring—it was the principle of the thing."

PLEADS GUILTY TO DEATH OF WAITRESS LAST NOV.

Philadelphia — (AP) — Russell Wolfenden, 38, Chester dishwasher, pleaded guilty before three judges Monday to a murder charge in the slaying last November 12 of Mrs. Ella Parker, 56-year-old waitress.

The judges took the case under advisement after hearing Wolfenden tell of meeting the woman in a taproom and of beating her with a metal candlestick later at her home.

JAMES ROOSEVELT MAKES DIVORCE DECREE FINAL

Los Angeles — (AP) — James Roosevelt, son of the President, Monday made final the divorce which his wife, Betsey Cushing Roosevelt, obtained a year ago.

His attorneys, who entered the necessary decree in Superior cpurt, explained that since Mrs. Roosevelt was in the east it was considered more convenient for Roosevelt to enter the decree.

FARMERS CHARGE STATE OFFICIAL REFUSED AID IN SOIL SAVING PLAN

Harrisburg —(AP)— A group of Indiana county farmers told a House committee Monday that the director of the Agricultural Extension Service of the Pennsylvania State College refused to cooperate in establishing a soil conservation district.

John H. Stephens, Jr., secretary of the Black Lick Soil Conservation Board of Indiana, described a trip the group made to State College for a conference with M. S. McDowell, the Extension Service director.

"We found him absolutely not in sympathy with the program and he gave us no consideration," Stephens told the committee. "He stated that inasmuch as it was a federal government proposition rather than the state government, he was opposed to it."

The committee, headed by Rep. Clayton E. Moul, Dem., York, was created to determine the use made by the college of a $10,000 appropriation for soil erosion work, in cooperative with a federal government program.

Stephens said the group went to State College because they felt that the "Agricultural Extension Service was down there to help the farmer" but that McDowell told them:

"You're off on the wrong foot, and getting into something you don't know anything about."

Stephens said about 285,000 acres was represented in the soil erosion district and that after McDowell refused to cooperate they "went over his head" to the federal government to get the work started.

YOUTH CONGRESS CALLS FOR STUDENT STRIKE

New York —(AP)— The National Cabinet of the American Youth Congress called upon American students Monday to strike at 11 a. m. April 23 in a demonstration "against those who would muzzle education in order to mislead us deeper into the European war."

The Congress appealed to the students to demonstrate to "uphold the bill of rights on the campus, stop the blackout of democratic education, strike against war and dictatorship."

LEAVES FOR MARINE BASE
Robert Frailey, of 329 East New street, left Monday morning for Paris Island, S. C., where he will begin a four-year enlistment with the U. S. Marines.

"THE WINNAH"—REPRESENTING THE GOLD TEAM

TEAM RIVALRY MOUNTS IN WATT & SHAND SALE

One of the amusing team stunts given at Watt & Shand's 63rd Anniversary Sale banquet is pictured above, depicting the Gold team as the winner over the rival Red and Blue teams. And, to date, the act has made good its predictions as the Gold team is actually leading in sales over the Red and Blue teams. The photograph shows from left to right, Frank Spader, towel swinger, Paul Liller, the Gold team champ, dressed in Gold trunks and Elmer Kipphorn, so called referee.

Snow Storm No Match For The Sale Values

In spite of the mess of snow that fell Friday and Saturday—the attendance over the week-end proved that folks will go thru most anything to attend a Watt & Shand Anniversary sale and share in the savings offered. And it is well to remember that this is the last week to outfit the family for Easter and secure new things for the home at Anniversary prices. In fact, with a scarcity already showing in merchandise in some lines this may be the last opportunity to secure such offerings until the armament race is over.

Today Is Founders' Day; Wednesday Is Red Rose Day

The offerings for today, Founders' Day, are for today only—and what values they are! And tomorrow is Red Rose Day—another day of grand savings—in fact the only way to take full advantage of this great sale is to come every day.

$120 Prize Contests Continue

The three free window guessing contests continue to attract new interest each day—and many are taking advantage of the opportunity of making a guess on each contest each day. The more guesses you drop in the contest boxes—the better chance you have to win one of the prizes. Anyone may enter a guess each day of the sale for each contest but no individual will receive more than one prize, and no Watt & Shand employe or members of their immediate family are eligible to enter the contests.

A giant pillow, a printed dress and a huge cone of ball curtain fringe may be seen in different windows throughout the sale. The public is invited to guess the weight of the pillow, the number of figures on the printed dress, and the number of balls on the curtain fringe. $40 in prizes is offered for the 3 closest guesses for each contest, as follows: $25 first prize, $10 second prize, $5 third prize—a total of $120 in cash prizes for the 3 contests.

The blanks for the pillow contest, and the box in which to deposit guesses will be found in the pillow department, 1st floor; the blanks for the dress contest will be in the dress department on the 2nd floor, and the blanks for the curtain fringe contest will be in the drapery department on the 4th floor.—Adv.

Can Hitler Invade England This Year—and Will He?

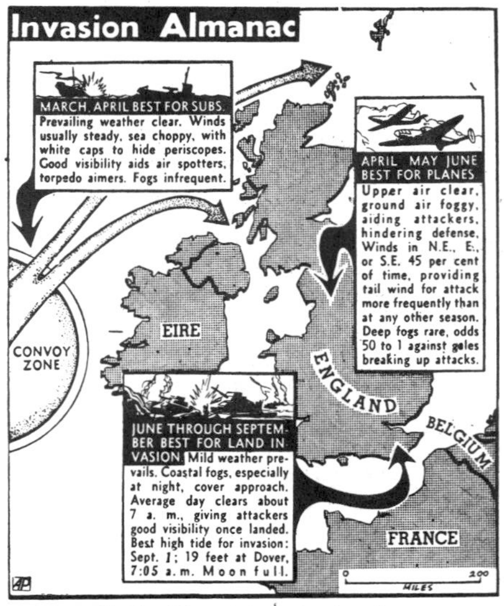

Invasion Almanac
MARCH, APRIL BEST FOR SUBS. Prevailing weather clear. Winds usually steady, sea choppy, with white caps to hide periscopes. Good visibility aids air spotters, torpedo aimers. Fogs infrequent.
APRIL MAY JUNE BEST FOR PLANES Upper air clear, ground air foggy, aiding attackers, hindering defense. Winds in N.E., E., or S.E. 45 per cent of time, providing tail wind for attack more frequently than at any other season. Deep fogs rare, odds 50 to 1 against gales breaking up attacks.
JUNE THROUGH SEPTEMBER BEST FOR LAND INVASION. Mild weather prevails. Coastal fogs, especially at night, cover approach. Average day clears about 7 a. m., giving attackers good visibility once landed. Best high tide for invasion: Sept. 1; 19 feet at Dover, 7:05 a. m. Moon full.
CONVOY ZONE
BRITISH DESTROYERS AWAIT MERCHANTMEN
THIS LINE separates heart of England (London) from its industrial support. Main German objective in invasion would be to cut through here.
NAZI E BOATS, SUBS AND MINES GUARD CHANNEL AT BOTH ENDS
EIRE
ENGLAND
BELGIUM
ZONE CLEARED FOR INVASION (22 MI., DEEP)
FRANCE
COASTAL DEFENSE (HEAVIEST ON EAST)
HOME GUARD DEFENSES
HEAVILY BOMBED AREAS
0 200 MILES
AP

Weather data suggest an order of events . . .

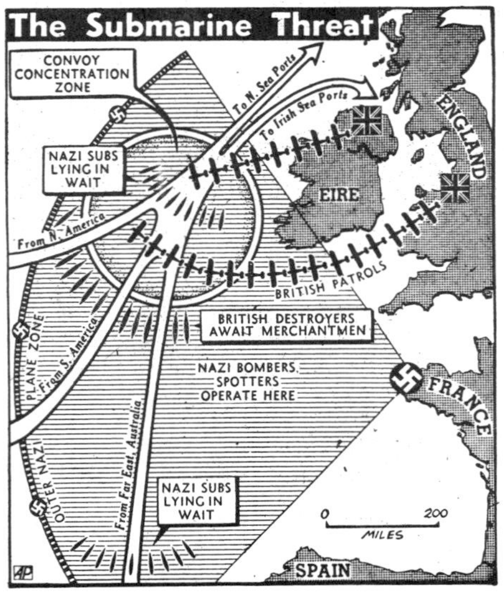

1. Early spring is ideal for attacks on shipping.

The Air Threat

STAVANGER

2. Flying conditions improve as the season advances.

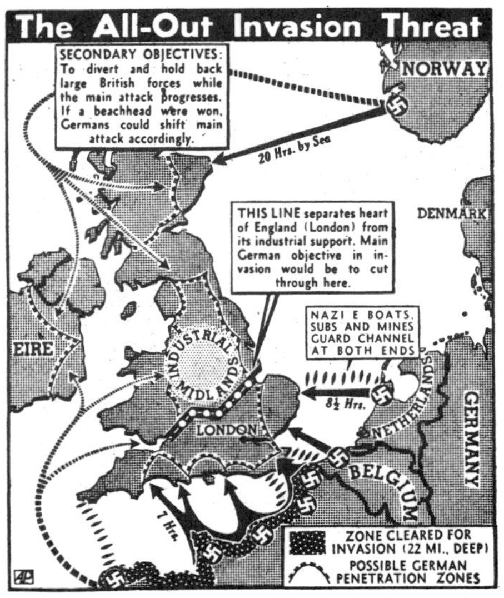

SECONDARY OBJECTIVES: To divert and hold back large British forces while the main attack progresses. If a beachhead were won, Germans could shift main attack accordingly.

3. Finally, the best conditions for invasion.

By MORGAN M. BEATTY

AP Feature Service Writer

WASHINGTON—Canvass the best military, economic and diplomatic opinion on this side of the Atlantic and you get a picture of Germany attempting an all-out invasion of the British isles along a fairly definite pattern. And you also find odds about 3 to 2 against an all-out attempt this year.

If the Germans should try it, however, the first week in September affords the most auspicious combination of advantages from their point of view.

The odds as reckoned here are a little higher than 2 to 1 that the invasion attempt would fail.

Most experts accept the general thesis that the Germans will first loose their submarines and planes on the British. In fact the battle of the Atlantic already has started, and the stepped-up air Battle of Britain should begin about mid-April. Meanwhile, the Nazis use axis diplomacy and force along the British lifelines to divert as much empire strength as possible to those danger points.

In the opinion of observers here—

If the submarines and their helping plane eyes threaten the British isles with strangulation, AND

If air attack shows signs of breaking British morale, AND

If thrusts at empire lifelines succeed,

Then—and only then—should a prudent German high command consider all-out invasion.

But nevertheless, Hitler should be prepared for the odds, and have a huge army ready to spring from the invasion coast of France anytime between April 1 and September 30.

* * *

ON the other hand there are three stark, compelling reasons why the Nazis might throw caution to the winds and attack this summer.

1. Germany must feed several hundred millions of people in conquered Europe. Diet deficiency among these people already ranges close to 50 per cent by official Nazi reports. The Germans must break the blockade soon.

2. American aid is mounting fast.

3. Except for war industry, economic stagnation is admittedly general over Europe. Peacetime work must be resumed before people can receive money for work and afford the necessities of life.

The weather should go a long way to dictate the timing of the German attack. It has always been a major factor with German military leaders.

The battle of the Atlantic, in line with this weather factor theory, was launched about March 1. Prevailing weather is clear, white caps hide periscopes, torpedo wakes. Spring air attacks should start in April as land storms subside and generally milder conditions prevail.

The ideal period for land invasion is the first week in September. It's usually extremely mild, storms almost never occur, and night fogs, lifting with the sunrise, are the rule.

If and when invasion comes, the pattern of attack is foreshadowed by the known training methods of the modern German army and navy, and their equipment.

The Germans are training huge forces in embarkation and landing from all types of large and small air and sea craft.

They're concentrating on the art of loading the big freight of war—tanks, ambulances, staff cars, medium-sized guns, etc.—in both air transports and huge motorless gliders.

* * *

ALL this adds up to this kind of attack:

While subs and bombers are striking at England's transport, the convoy lanes, and her industrial centers, some 30-odd sudden attacks by air infantry might be launched. Relays of planes carrying complete miniature armies would continue to supply these points of penetration until they had succeeded—or failed—to establish defensible positions.

All along the countryside between the penetration points, thousands of parachute pioneers would drop, undermine defense, spread panic. This should make it easier for the penetration points to join forces, and lop off chunks of the English coast (beachheads).

Finally, huge forces would cross the channel for the frontal assault.

All this sounds fairly easy, but nobody knows better than the German naval command the extreme military risk the invaders must run to hold a perch on the hostile shores of England. Besides the initial risk, the Germans have little naval strength to convoy and protect invasion troops.

Artist Previews Battle for Beachhead

This artist's conception of an all-out attack on the English coast is based on reports of actual preparations—of the Germans for the attack and of the British for the defense. The Germans are training huge forces in embarkation and landing and in transporting by air and by sea all the heavy equipment of an invading army. The British have ringed their beach areas with guns for throwing large drums of gasoline that will explode and spread flames among approaching craft or set up a curtain of fire along the shore. Barbed wire and tank traps also are important in the beach defenses, while farther back are big guns and the fields from which aircraft will take off to meet the invaders. The drawing depicts the battle for air supremacy as a part of the assault on the beachhead, a situation which observers agree must be expected unless the Germans knock out the Royal Air Force before they try to land troops. In the background is the city of Hastings, where William the conqueror won a battle in 1066.

Offense Vs Defense

By Land—

Parachutists.

Parashooters.

By Sea—

Secret Barges (Artist's version)

Sea Forts (Actual photograph)

By Air—

New Bomber.

Anti-Aircraft Gun.

Conquerors and Dreams of Conquerors Have Harassed England Through Centuries

Roman soldiers are depicted here in the first invasion of England. The legions of Julius Caesar landed in 55 B. C., subjugated the native Britons. The Romans ruled till 410, then withdrew. The Romans gone, Picts and Scots came down from the north, and the Britons called for aid from the Teutonic Angles, Saxons and Jutes, who ended up with control of most of the country.

Danish raiders, shown here, came across the sea to harass the Anglo-Saxon kings and eventually to establish a line of Danish kings, of which the first was the Canute of legendary fame. The Danish and Anglo-Saxon elements gradually blended and in 1042 the Saxon line of kings was restored. Hero of wars with the Danes was Alfred the Great (871-901).

Second in the second line of Saxon kings was Harold, whose death in 1066 at the Battle of Hastings, pictured above, was followed by successful conquest by William the Conqueror and his Normans. William and his son and grandson became complete masters of the country, remodeled the church, made Norman-French the official language, compiled the first English census and survey.

Napoleon considered conquest of the island vitally important to his plans, and in the summer of 1805 he had his army poised at Boulogne ready for a dash across the channel. Failure of one of his admirals to carry out instructions forced abandonment of the plan and the emperor turned to other conquests. Defeat of the Spanish Armada was the frustration of another attempt on the isle.

THAWS OUT PIPES, SETS FIRE TO HOME

Neffsville firemen were called to extinguish a blaze at the home of Noah Shiflet, Dillerville road, in sub-freezing temperatures at 6:15 A. M. today. According to Acting-Chief L. W. Nissley, of the Neffsville Fire company, Shiflet was thawing out frozen pipes in the kitchen when he set fire to the woodwork. The damage was slight.

The Ephrata Fire company responded to an alarm at the home of Frank Flory, 110 Lincoln avenue, Ephrata, about 6 o'clock last evening. Smoke from an overheated pipe caused a fire scare.

A chimney fire in the home of Jacob Hollinger, West High street, Manheim, was extinguished about 7 o'clock last evening by the Manheim Fire company. Fire Chief Paul Z. Knier said there was no serious damage.

Quebec's 1939 yield of provincial hay and clover was valued at $46,968,000.

COUNTY YOUTH, 19, HAS MENINGITIS

Stanley Brown, nineteen, Peach Bottom R. D. 1, has meningitis, Dr. A. J. Greenleaf, county medical director, reported last night. Brown has been a patient in the General hospital for the past ten days.

Other cases reported include: chicken pox 106, German measles 8, measles 9, mumps 10, pneumonia 2, scarlet fever 12, and whooping cough 60. Dr. Greenleaf said the 12 scarlet fever cases are scattered in the northeastern part of the county.

Thirty-five new cases of chicken pox were reported to the City Board of Health last week, according to the weekly bulletin issued Monday. There were nine new cases of whooping cough, four of measles, three of mumps, two of German measles and one of scarlet fever.

Current cases are as follows: whooping cough, fifty; chicken pox, forty-six; measles, six; scarlet fever, three; mumps, two

POWER ENGINEERS SEE MOVIE FILM

Motion pictures on boiler work and water treatment will be shown at the meeting of Lancaster chapter, National Association of Power Engineers, on April 7. A group from the chapter will attend the 40th annual banquet of the Frankford association at Philadelphia on Saturday.

Movies of the manufacture of wrought iron and allied products were shown at the meeting last evening at 32 South Queen sreet.

George Zink, of Mount Joy, was admitted as a member of the chapter. Thirty-five members were present.

PLAN FUTURE EVENTS

At a meeting of Sacred Heart Sodality last night, it was decided to hold a card party in April and a spring dance in May. The Sodality voted a $50 contribution to the new church fund. A short address was given by the new spiritual director, the Rev.

EX-LOCAL MAN ASKS TO CHANGE NAME

YORK, March 18—The York county court has been asked to change the name of Marshall Doubts, 266 W. Jackson street, York, to Marshall D. Carr. Born at Paperville, Chester county, a son of George and Cora Doubts, he was reared by Mr. and Mrs. Joseph Carr, 865 Manor street, Lancaster, after the death of his parents in 1919. The petitioner told the court he is

POULTRY MEETING AT MAYTOWN HIGH

Selection and management of pullets and laying hens is the topic for discussion at the eleventh weekly agricultural class meeting to be held at the East Donegal High School at Maytown this evening, starting at 7:30 o'clock. S. F. Simmons, supervisor of agriculture, will be in charge. Film slides illustrating the subject will be shown. Attendance is free to all persons in-

Sports Revue

Interest In Fight. Credit For Matmen. Other Sports Notes.

by GEORGE W. KIRCHNER

STRICTLY OFF THE CUFF . . . After watching Ken Overlin outpoint Harvey Massey here, local boxing fans feel sure that his fight with Billy Soose, with the middleweight title at stake, ought to be an exhibition worth seeing . . . At least, from the boxing standpoint . . . And many from here are planning on seeing the tiff, slated for Madison Square Garden on May 23rd . . . Including, among others, Joe McFadden, Leo Houck, Dr. Newton E. Bitzer, Promoter Ed Mellinger, Matchmaker Scotty Hemphill and quite a few others . . . Joey Welchans, the well-known m. c., is another candidate for the job of announcing at the local fights . . . Joe's had enough experience and nobody ever questioned his vocal chords . . .

Nat Hager saw the recent National A. A. U. wrestling matches in New York and returned with the information that F. & M.'s Al Schacheman came within inches of tossing the highly-touted Billy Arndt, of Oklahoma, in their match . . . But he missed and Al lost the decision . . . However, Nat says he was given a tremendous hand by the crowd and the match, he adds, was one of the best of the many staged during the two-day contest . . . He also said that Monk Hamsher was given a big hand for his work in finishing second in the 134 pound class . . .

Dan Parker told the New York fans that Bill Wagner, the F. & M. cage star, is among the cagers who received absolutely no financial aid from the college for his playing ability . . . But you knew that all along . . . Fred Jeffries is already making plans to see the World Series next year regardless of where it will be played . . . He went all the way to Cincinnati last season . . . Ever since he had that score of over 100 in the Elks Duck Pin League, Babe Guyer has been afraid to roll again for fear of spoiling it . . .

Biddie DeManicor, the Roses' first-sacker who was in a hitting slump last year, feels he's due for a comeback this season and made a special trip to this city just to order two powerful-looking bats at a local sporting goods store . . . He's much heavier and says he's in grand shape . . .

Ralph Hankinson will be back with automobile races at the Reading Fair Grounds on Sunday, April 20 . . . Dick Madison's basketball team at Lafayette finished the season with eight wins and ten losses, but because the boys again won the Middle Three title the year was called successful . . . And all of Dick's friends here will be glad to know it . . . Speaking of Lafayette, Skinny Chalmers, the Maroon coach, who used to be the ace swimmer at F. & M., had a great year with his team winning seven out of eight meets . . . Nice going, Skinny . . .

The State Amateur Softball Association, which once banned Mike Shipley, wants him to come back with the understanding that "all is forgotten" . . . But Mike isn't too much interested right now . . . In fact, he says he's too busy getting his City and County League in shape for a big season . . .

The next time Vic Hoover, the clerk at Shenk's, meets up with a certain salesman, he says he's going to run . . . but fast . . . and in the other direction . . . Their last meeting put Hoover in the well-known "dog-house" for a week . . . How am I doing, Mrs. Hoover? . . . That building which will "front" Ed. Stumpf's baseball park is on the way up and construction of the new third-base-line bleachers is underway . . .

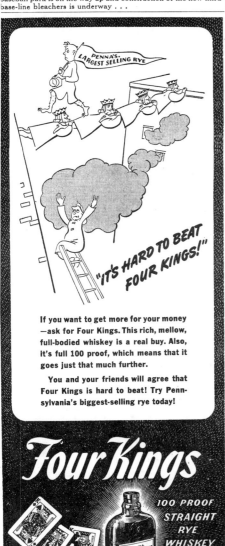

RECEIVERS—The Philadelphia Athletics' catching brigade includes, left to right, Earl Brucker, Frank Hayes, Hal Wagner.

Conn 6-1 Favorite In Fight

But Barlund Is Promised Louis' Tiff If He Wins Friday

BY TOM SILER.

CHICAGO, April 2.—(A. P.)—Gunnar Barlund, durable Finnish heavyweight, will be eligible for membership in the "bum-of-the-month club" if he can upset Pittsburgh Billy Conn Friday night in Chicago Stadium.

Such a triumph would qualify him to follow Gus Dorazio, Abe Simon, Tony Musto, et al, to the Joe Louis chopping block.

The 195-pound Finn, an in-and-outer for several years, is given almost no chance to get by the fancy-punching Conn despite a 15-pound weight advantage. The betting fraternity on Randolph street has set the miniature heavyweight up as a 6 to 1 choice over Barlund.

"Where do they get those kind of odds," asked Paul Damski, Barlund's loquacious manager. "I'd like some of that myself.

"This boy of mine is going to fool a lot of people. He was never in better shape than right now and he's ready to give Conn a real fight. Conn has never fought a heavyweight as experienced and smart as Barlund. And don't forget Conn will be giving away between 15 and 20 pounds."

Conn's Last Tune-up

This fight is slated as Conn's last before his June bout with the heavyweight champion. A defeat by the Finn would doubtless eliminate the Pittsburgh fighter from the title picture for several months.

Was Damski interested in throwing Barlund in against Louis in case he wins Friday?

"Say, I never make a match for a fighter of mine if he hasn't got a chance to win," Damski explained. "Three times I have turned down a chance to match Barlund with Joe Louis. I know he has the physical requirements to give Louis a battle, but he never has been ready up here." He pointed to his head.

"Maybe he'll be ready after the fight with Conn. I don't know."

The two fighters have met only one mutual opponent—Henry Cooper. Barlund knocked him out in seven rounds last July. Conn outpointed him in 12 rounds in November.

This will be Conn's first meeting with a seasoned heavyweight since he forsook the ranks of the light heavyweights in quest of Louis' crown. Barlund, now 28, has been fighting professionally for seven years.

McCoy Trade Reports Denied by Mack

HOLLYWOOD, Calif., April 2—(A. P.)—Reports that second baseman Benny McCoy might be traded to the White Sox were only a gag to Connie Mack of the Philadelphia Athletics. "It's pure bunk," he said. "It would take a handsome offer to make me even consider a trade for McCoy. His showing the other day (when he got four hits) was most encouraging, and I am sure he will play even better."

DeMolay Five Ahead

The Lancaster DeMolay quintet advanced in the Eastern Regional DeMolay Basketball tournament Tuesday night when they walloped the Reading DeMolay contingent by the score of 72 to 34 on the Biesecker court, at Franklin and Marshall college.

Lancaster will play Philadelphia in another playoff tilt within the next week.

Reading DeMolay	G	F	Tl	Lanc. DeMolay	G	F	Tl
Yeich F	1	0	2	Landis F	1	1	3
Liddicoat F	3	0	6	Eshleman F	15	0	30
Corkran C	3	0	6	Charles C	2	0	4
Liddicoat G	2	0	4	Lenhardt G	2	0	4
Shugar G	5	2	12	Drumm G	12	1	25
Gieder	1	0	2	Buckwalter	3	0	6
Buckle	1	0	2				
Simmons	0	0	0	Totals ..	35	2	72
Totals ..	16	2	34				

Score by Periods:

READING	6	8	8	12—34
LANCASTER	12	18	14	28—72

Referee, Newswanger.

Sasse at P. M. C.

CHESTER, Pa., April 2.—(A. P.)—Lieut.-Col. Ralph I. Sasse, former football coach at the United States Military Academy, has been appointed director of athletics and assistant to the president of the Pennsylvania Military College it was announced today.

Scene, Favorites in Masters' Golf

Jimmy Demaret — View of the Augusta course — Sammy Snead — Bobby Jones — Ben Hogan

With defending champion, Jimmy Demaret, and the former king, Bobby Jones, in the field, the Augusta, Ga., Masters' golf tourney gets under way tomorrow on Jones' home course. Favorite for the tourney is Ben Hogan. the par-busting Texan who has been collecting most of the money in the winter tourneys. Sammy Snead is highly regarded, also.

'41 Aquacado Opens 3-Day Stand at F. & M.

Beginning a three-day stand at Franklin and Marshall's Fackenthal Pool tomorrow night, the 1941 Aquacado brings to Lancaster outstanding swimmers and divers from the Eastern part of the United States, features seven new songs written especially for the show, along with an all-girl ballet. Proceeds from the four performances, which include a Saturday matinee, go to the Committee to Defend America by Aiding the Allies.

2 National Champs

Heading the guest performers are two national champions, Gloria Callen of New York and John Macionis, former Yale star. Miss Callen is the holder of five national titles and has been named "Eleanor Holm's Successor." Other Eastern stars include Audrey and Janet Druhmel, hits of last year's show, Mary Francis Cunningham and "Whitey" Hart, two youngsters already acclaimed by swimming experts, and Rutgers' collegiate diving champion, Ormand McClave.

Comedy will be handled by the diving team of Jack Keelen and George Newton and a comedy diving quintet, the Aquazanies, from Astoria Pool, New York. Returning again this year are the University of Pittsburgh quartet and two outstanding local swimmers, Marilyn Globisch and Lester Kachel, president of the Blue Key society at F. and M., which sponsors the annual Aquacado.

Local Girls In Ballet

Another Lancaster contribution to the show is the girls' ballet, made up of local girls who have been practicing together for the past several months. This group will be featured in two special numbers.

Musical background for the show will be provided by John Peifer's orchestra, and vocals will be handled by Don Richards. Accompanying him in the choruses will be the college Glee Club.

Fourteen different acts are listed and action will swing back and forth from the diving boards to the draped stage at the other end of the pool. Climaxing the action is a fire dive from the rafters of the building. Special underwater lights are being installed, and vari-colored spotlights will follow the performers.

NELSON'S PUTTING OFF

Ace Looks Good Otherwise as He Tunes Up for Start of Masters Tomorrow

AUGUSTA, Ga., April 2—(A. P.)—You can get 7 to 1 odds on Byron Nelson as a probable winner of the 1941 Augusta Masters tournament. But take it from Byron Nelson, he's no bargain at the price. The reason? He's missing two-foot putts.

PGA champion and winner of the recent Greensboro open, the big Toledo pro won the Masters crown in 1937 and was third last year, five strokes behind winner Jimmy Demaret. Yesterday, in practice over the incredibly smooth Augusta National course, he was the hottest thing in sight from tee to green. And there he folded.

"I took 37 putts," Nelson confessed gloomily after the disastrous round. "And you don't win tournaments that way. I was missing two to six-foot putts. And regularly. I never played better in my life up to the greens. And I never putted worse. It was horrible."

Still, no one is going to bank top money in this $5,000 event until Nelson's final score is posted Sunday night. Despite his 37 strokes on the greens, he turned in par 72 for the round—proof that he wasn't hitting the ball with a potato sack elsewhere on the course.

30 Putts Per Round

Nelson, voted by fellow pros last week as most likely to win the tournament this year, estimates you can't take more than 30 putts on 18 holes and expect to pay off the butcher, baker and your landlord. Thirty putts and average luck the rest of the way, he figures, would add up to a 69—entirely satisfactory if you can keep it up four days in a row. You could even indulge in a bobble now and then, because in Nelson's book 280 will win this year's Master championship, and likely the winner won't have less than 282 or 283.

Demaret won with 280 a year ago—and four strokes to spare. Ralph Guldahl did it in 1939 with 279, a record, while Nelson's win in 1937, came on 283.

Picard Missing

All former champions except Henry Picard, 1938 victim, were on deck today for final practice before Thursday's opening round. Horton Smith, only two-time winner, had a moderate 75 yesterday. Gene Sarazen and Guldahl spent most of their time on the practice green. Best score was posted by U. S. Open champion Lawson Little, who rounded the course in 68.

Highlight of today's program was a re-play of the old Master's match—Bobby Jones and Tommy Armour, the unbeaten duo of previous years, against Sarazen and Walter Hagen. Jones and Armour won, 3 and 2, at Nassau recently in a Red Cross benefit match.

PARALLEL CAREERS

Both Koverly and Stein Figured in Other Sports Before They Started Rasslin'

George (K. O.) Koverly, and Sammy Stein have had parallel careers in professional wrestling in all ways, except one.

The two big men who meet in the one-fall-to-a-finish feature of Danny Templeton's next professional show at Maple Grove Park next Monday night have had varied, successful careers in many other undertakings, and both have been unusually rewarded in the pro mat sport. But each has achieved this eminence in his own way.

They have done other things similarly.

Stein was an outstanding professional football player with the New York Giants. Koverly was an outstanding prize-fighter, having met such ringmen as Max Baer, George Godfrey, etc.

Both George and Sammy sustained injuries in their early specialties that forced them to quit their favorite pastimes.

They both went into the movies. Stein became a leading man with Boris Karloff, Edward G. Robinson and other stars, while Koverly appeared in all of Mae West's cinemas.

Next they turned their courses toward the wrestling championship, and both have climbed to the top rung. But Sam has climbed a different road than Koverly.

Sammy is the perfect hero. Koverly is the villian. There is nothing that Koverly will not employ in the ring, and by his tactics he is known today as the Mad Greek.

TEXANS TALLEST CAGERS

Canyon, Tex.—West Texas State College had the tallest basketball team in the country in the season just closed. The players averaged 6 feet 6 1-4 inches.

Pro Football League Planning to Operate On "Baseball Basis"

Layden Will Be Inducted as Commissioner and Owners Likely to Pass Petition Bringing American Loop Under His Supervision

By EARL HILLIGAN

CHICAGO, April 2—(A. P.)—The National Pro Football League likely will remodel its structure on a "baseball basis" this week-end.

Circuit club owners, at an annual session opening tomorrow and running through Sunday, formally will induct Elmer Layden as the league's first commissioner. And the owners probably will act favorably on a petition which would bring the American Pro League under Layden's supervision and give professional football a setup similar to that under which Kenesaw Mountain Landis rules organized baseball.

Layden No. 1 Man

The league, at its executive session Friday, may abolish the office of president, filled for the past two seasons by Carl Storck. Regardless of what action is taken on this question, however, it is reliably reported that even should Storck be retained, Layden will be the No. 1 man in the pro picture.

The American Association, made up of clubs at Newark, Paterson, Jersey City, N. J., Providence, R. I., Wilmington, Del., and Long Island, N. Y., has asked to be taken into the National League setup under Layden's supervision. Should this be done, the National League may work out plans whereby those minor league clubs would receive player and monetary support from the National League teams. The American Association president is Joseph Rosentover, Clifton, N. J.

There is no chance now that the American League will affiliate with the National League for the reason that the circuits are at odds over territorial rights.

Battle Looms Ahead

The retention or abolition of Storck's position, the term for which expires this week-end, may result in a battle, for his regime has been stormy. Some months ago he did not attend a meeting here to select a league commissioner, a post which Layden accepted on a five-year contract calling for $100,000.

Tomorrow the league's rules committee will consider several recommendations, including: Revision of the substitution rule to permit six men to return once during the final quarter; enforcement of a penalty from the spot of the previous down for a foul occurring during a kick; and installation of the honor system among coaches in regard to the number of substitutions so as to lighten the duties of the umpire.

George Halas, owner-coach of the Chicago Bears, heads the rules body. Action taken on the regulations must be approved by all club owners.

LITITZ HIGH WANTS GAME

The Lititz High baseball team would like to book a non-League opponent for tomorrow or Friday, the games to be played away from home. Coach Eugene Deckert can be reached by calling Lititz 281-J.

The Weather
Eastern Pennsylvania — Partly cloudy Sunday and Monday with continued mild temperature.

SUNDAY NEWS

3 A. M. Edition
The Sunday News carries the full report of two world wide news services—
LATEST NEWS by Associated Press, International News Service And Complete Local News.

VOL 18.—NO. 32 | Entered at Post Office at Lancaster, Pa. as second class mail matter | LANCASTER, PA., SUNDAY, APRIL 13, 1941 | 52 PAGES, 288 COLUMNS—FIVE CENTS

Greeks And British Halt Nazi Advance; Hungary Draws Sharp Russian Rebuke

ATTACK ON YUGOSLAVIA CONDEMNED

Moscow Warns Hungary, Too, May One Day Be Invaded; Presence Of Minorities Cited

Moscow, April 12—(AP)—Soviet Russia, asked by Hungary to endorse the Hungarian invasion of Yugoslavia, has replied with her disapproval and a reminder that Hungary, too, might one day be "torn to bits", TASS, official Soviet news agency, disclosed tonight.

"It is not difficult to realize what would be the position of Hungary should she herself get into trouble and be torn to bits, since it is known that there are national minorities in Hungary, too," was the word sent back to Budapest, TASS said.

Nazi Envoy Called Home

The German Ambassador, Count Friedrich Werner Von Der Schulenberg, meanwhile was summoned to Berlin.

At the same time, Joseph Stalin received Yosuke Matsuoka, Japan's travelling foreign minister, to bid him farewell before his departure for Japan after visits to Berlin and Rome and two stops in this capital.

Stalin was accompanied to the Kremlin by Russian Premier and Foreign Commissar Vyacheslaff Molotoff. The Japanese minister, who has prolonged his stay here to discuss Soviet-Japanese relations, offered thanks for Russian facilities provided for his travel.

Asked Recognition

Hungarian Minister Joseph Kristoffy called on Andrei Y. Vishinsky, Soviet vice commissar of foreign affairs, explained why Hungary had sent troops into Yugoslavia and expressed hope that Russia would recognize the action as just, TASS said.

Vishinsky, it continued, replied: "If this statement was made in order to invite the Soviet government to express its opinion, I must state that the Soviet government cannot approve such a step on the part of Hungary. A particularly bad impression is produced upon the Soviet government by the fact that Hungary commenced war against Yugoslavia but four months after she concluded with the latter a pact of eternal friendship.

"It is not difficult to realize what would be the position of Hungary should she herself get into trouble and be torn to bits, since it is known that there are national minorities in Hungary, too."

Kristoffy, TASS said, promised "to convey this statement of the government of the U. S. S. R. to his government."

4TH UTTERANCE FROM MOSCOW

Soviet Russia's rebuke to Hungary for her invasion of Yugoslavia on the heels of the German legions smashing that Balkan kingdom was the fourth time Moscow has spoken out since Germany began treading on her sphere of influence in the southeastern Europe.

Russia's latest official frown came as a German radio broadcast, heard in Bern, Switzerland, said General Dusan Simovic, premier of Yugoslavia, had left on a mission presumably taking him to Moscow.

Russia and Germany have been linked since Aug. 23, 1939, in a pact of friendship and non-aggression, however, and if there is any real crack in that accord as a result of Germany's advances to the Black and Aegean seas, the Kremlin has not been disposed to show it.

There was no elaboration of what Vishinsky may have implied in his reference to Hungary's own minorities but one of them, at least, is related to Russia.

Ukrainians In Hungary

In the break-up of Czecho-Slovakia Hungary acquired the Carpatho-Ukraine region of the dissolved republic, peopled by Ukrainians who are allied to the Ukrainian population of Russia.

This acquisition, also, gave

RUSSIA—Page 6

Bicycle Hits Auto, Boy Hurts Finger

William McCrae, sixteen, 129 North Mary street, was treated at the Lancaster General hospital Saturday afternoon for a laceration of the finger when he ran into an open door of a parked automobile while riding his bicycle, according to city police reports.

John Huber, West Willow, owner of the car, reported to police, that he had parked his car and was opening the door when the boy ran into it and was knocked to the street.

WOMAN'S FACE BURNED

Mrs. Mary Oster, twenty-two, 466 Beaver street, suffered first and second degree burns of the face Saturday when flames from a freshly started fire in a coal range shot up and struck her in the face. She was treated at the Lancaster General hospital.

Wave Of The Future—1,500 Easter Egg Hunters

High tide swept over John Farnum field Saturday, engulfing everything in its path as Lancaster's first public egg hunt got underway with 1500 shouting, laughing children tumbling over each other in the race for coveted prizes. (See other pictures on page two and back page.)

Lancaster Marks Easter — In Peace

Easter, anniversary of the Resurrection, is being observed here today in religious services, family reunions and promenading, with weather that has been predicted as the "most pleasant" in possibly ten years.

The holiday, celebrated in America in joyous manner contrasting strongly with the bitter grief and chaos in much of the rest of the Christian world, was opened at dawn with special services. The Lititz Moravians held their 182nd recorded observance at 5:15 A. M., with the accompaniment of the famed Trombone Choir.

Nests, Egg Hunts Expand Easter In Xmas Style

An Easter Bunny with a beard turned Lancaster's Easter into something more like Christmas with gifts of candy and colored eggs bringing joy to some 3,000 children. And the fun wasn't hurt a bit because some of the kids had to hunt for their eggs.

It was a combination of the traditional Easter basket distribution by Policewoman Agnes Ferriter, and the first community egg hunt at John Farnum playground. There some 1,500 youngsters lined up like something out of a Western movie, manhandled a troop of Boy Scouts put there to keep them back of the starting line, and then rushed out in search of hidden Eastern eggs.

Some were carefully togged out in the oldest clothes they owned. At least one wore a football helmet. They heaved up heavy planks on the off-chance that the Easter Bunny was up on his weight-lifting. They fell over each other and enjoyed themselves thoroughly.

There were more children than eggs at the fete held at Farnum playground, for although the committee had 1,200 hardboiled eggs, more than 1,500 little boys and girls came to take part. An additional 1,000 adults came to watch the fun. Some children picked up half a dozen eggs, while others found none.

Charles Wright, 47 North Water street, won first prize. Second prize was taken by Harold Roy Hershey,

EASTER—Page 6

Choirs Schedule Special Music; Traffic Is Heavy

The day brought to a close two weeks of preparations, with Saturday's fair weather bringing out shoppers in a closing rush to end their holiday buying. Merchants in general reported that business was "very good," and larger than last year's.

The mild weather will continue today, according to the forecast. The sun may be obscured at times by clouds both today and tomorrow, but there should be little change in temperature.

Many students are home from schools and colleges, and other Lancastrians who reside elsewhere have returned to be with their families.

Business Better

Merchants were able to take a well-deserved rest today, after the hectic last-minute seige on their stocks, which were well depleted by the time doors were closed. Women, most of them having bought their dresses, suits and coats during the week, concentrated Saturday on niceties such

CHURCHES—Page 6

IT'S A GIRL

Philadelphia, April 12—(AP)—For 14 years Big Boy has been pointed out as a fine example of a male Australian cassowary, a turkey-like bird, at the Philadelphia zoo.

Today "he" laid an egg.

'Git Along, 7th Ward,' Is Adieu To Old Trolley

With a quartet of bellsnickels moaning out "The Last Roundup," the Seventh Ward trolley made the closing run of its long career at midnight Saturday.

Just a twenty-minute ride from Penn Square around the route once and back to the Square, and it was all over.

Today at 7:50 a. m. the new Dauphin street bus line began operating, and at 8:02 a. m. the Seventh Ward bus line started carrying passengers. Where there was one trolley line, two buses now run.

As all "last events" are sad, so this last trip had its touch of melancholy too. The quartet enlivened the ride with the strains of "Get Along, Seventh Ward, get along," "Little Brown Jug" and "Roll Out the Barrel," as the one-man trolley bumped along over its old familiar path.

Makes Change Easily

Willard Styer, 610 East Fulton street, conductor who's been on the line for eighteen years, took the change philosophically. He took time out

TROLLEY—Page 6

Aeronautics Group Names Klein V. P.

New York, April 12.—(AP)—Prof. Frederic S. Klein, of Franklin and Marshall college, Lancaster, Pa., was elected vice president of Civil Aeronautics Authority administrators in Region 1 at an organization meeting today.

Purpose of the organization is to step up activities in aiding the Army and Navy find candidates for the Air Corps. Fifty representatives of eastern colleges participating in the Civil Pilot Training program attended the two-day conference. B. Herbert Brown, Jr., of the University of Baltimore, was elected president, and M. Daugherty, University of Delaware, secretary-treasurer.

Bitolj Lost To Less Than Six Nazi Tanks

By DANIEL DE LUCE

With Greek Forces On The North Albanian Front, April 11—(Delayed)—(AP)—Three haggard, stubble-bearded Yugoslav officers told me today that only one division, composed mostly of Croat Reservists, was stationed on the crucial southeastern frontier when the Germans, dropping parachutists, broke through from Bulgaria and sealed Yugoslavia's back door.

(The German stroke, on the second day of the Nazi offensive against Yugoslavia and Greece, broke the hinge between the Greek and Yugoslav lines, separating the allied armies and endangering the Greek left flank.)

The officers were among 200 who have arrived inside the Greek lines.

Few German Tanks

They said fewer than half a dozen German tanks took the Yugoslav town of Bitolj (Monastir) and that unsupported Yugoslav forces were unable to contact their headquarters for air support and were overwhelmed piecemeal.

The Greeks, with icy calm, are holding fast to their mountain positions against German attempts to swing around behind them.

BITOLJ—Page 6

DANISH ENVOY DEFIES RECALL

DeKauffmann Ordered Home Vią Berlin After Giving U. S. Bases In Greenland

Washington, April 12 —(AP)—The Danish foreign office in Copenhagen today recalled Henrik de Kauffmann as minister to the United States but the envoy, who signed the Greenland and the ship sale agreements with this country, has determined to disregard the order.

De Kauffman did not advise his government of the action by which the United States obtains air bases designed to protect Greenland from possible German agression, until after the formal announcement was made here at noon Thursday. Then he sent a lengthy cable which included the text of the agreement and his exchange of notes with Secretary Hull.

Order Via Berlin

He received a bare acknowledgement of the receipt of his report from Copenhagen only today and this was followed immediately by the order for his recall. The legation spokesman pointed out that all communications to and from Copenhagen go by way of Berlin.

De Kauffmann plans to notify Hull of the recall order "as a matter of form," the spokesman said, but it is expected that the United States will continue to recognize him as the official representative of his country.

DANISH—Page 6

Nazis Withdrawn From Turk Border

Istanbul, April 12. —(INS)—A formal and vigorous demand by Turkey has resulted in the withdrawal of more than 400,000 German and Bulgarian troops from the northwest Turkish frontier, it was learned tonight.

While Britain began evacuating her Nationals from Turkish territory now menaced with war as the result of Germany's conquest of Grecian Thrace, it was ascertained that some 27 divisions of the German and Bulgarian armies had been removed to points averaging about 20 miles back of the Turko-Bulgarian border.

This withdrawal was carried out after the Turkish governmene at Ankara demanded it in sharp notes to the German and Bulgarian governments.

Panzers Hurled Back On 12-Mile Front In Florina Area

(By International News Service)

Greek and British troops claimed to have shattered the armored vanguard of Hitler's Panzer divisions plunging southward toward the strategically important road junction town of Florina early Sunday as the main bodies of both armies locked in battle along the principal Greco-British defense line.

A midnight broadcast in Athens stated that the Nazi masses were now in contact with the organized central front held by the main British and Greek forces and that the battle which may decide the fate of southeastern Europe was on.

The initial setback inflicted by the Greek troops sent the Nazi vanguard reeling back in defeat along a 12-mile front from Florina to Vanitsa (Vevi), the Greeks claimed.

Battle West of Salonika

At the same time, British and Anzac armored troops were reported destroying German tanks and imposing heavy casualties on the invaders in a battle raging on the Yanitza Plain, about 28 miles west of Salonika, captured by the Germans a few days ago.

While this battle raged, Soviet Russia took an ominous step which held a threat of forthcoming action by the Red army and an extension of the conflict.

Moscow issued a sharp rebuke to Hungary for attacking Yugoslavia while that nation was being invaded by Germany and Italy. But, more important, the Kremlin added what must be taken as a veiled threat of forthcoming action in a stern warning that the same thing might happen to Hungary.

The German-dominated government of Denmark Saturday night recalled its American minister, Henrick De Kauffman, to Copenhagen as a result of the new agreement concluded between the minister and the United States government, extending an American military protectorate over the Danish Arctic possession.

RAF Wrecks 100 Axis Tanks And Trucks In Libya

(By the Associated Press)

Cairo, Egypt, April 12—Far-ranging British and German-Italian armored patrols clashed today in a wide area west and southwest of Tobruk while the RAF announced it wrecked nearly 100 Axis tanks and motor vehicles in a single heavy swoop on the road from Ain El Gazala to Tobruch.

Twenty-five Axis planes also were destroyed in a sharp series of fights, 21 of them being hit on or over Derna airport Thursday night, the RAF added.

Reports from the Libyan desert said the contact between ground forces had not yet developed into a battle, but implied that this might come in defense of Tobruch, which the British hold and which the Germans are striving to bomb.

Nearness of the advancing Germans and Italians was indicated by the RAF exploit on the road from Ain El Gazala, which is only [illegible] miles west of Tobruch, (and which the Italians said they had captured.)

Press Ethiopia Cleanup

The South African air force meanwhile pressed the cleanup of Ethiopia, announcing it destroyed six Italian planes on the ground at Gimna airport and shot down two of the planes which came up to

AFRICA—Page 6

British, German Armored Columns Clash In Battle

Bern, Switzerland, April 13.—(Sunday)—(AP)— British and German armored columns were reported early today to have met in a "violent" battle on the plain between Bitolj (Monastir) and Phlorina.

Fast moving columns, supported by dive bombers and fighter planes, said dispatches reaching here from Sofia, engaged in a fierce struggle—one of the first of its kind in this war between completely armored forces maneuvering on a flat plain.

The battle came as Great Britain's Balkan army tested its strength by patrol activities and other maneuvers.

Claim Nazi Unit Destroyed

Earlier British dispatches reaching here said armored car patrols scouting in the Bitolj region had destroyed a motorized German infantry unit without loss to themselves.

Yugoslav resistance, the dispatches from Sofia said, continued bitterly north of Zagreb, Croatian capital, south of Nis in the east, in the region near the Rumanian frontier and in mountains northwest of Tetovo.

(The Greeks Saturday night said their soldiers repulsed a heavy German force on a 12-mile front of the Allied left flank in a battle Friday. Saturday's communique from Athens indicated the Germans had attempted no main lunge at the line since then.

(However, the dispatches from Sofia indicate preliminary engagements of the tremendous battle may already be under way. These reports did not show the trend of the fighting.)

The British were reported throwing many planes into Greece Saturday, bombing and machine-gunning bridges, roads and tunnels along the line of march by which Germany must bring up men for

GREEK—Page 6

COTTAGE BURNED IN WOODS FIRE

Five Brush And Grass Fires Put Out In This Area; 15 Acres Of Trees Destroyed

Burning of fifteen acres of woodland in the river hills, destroying a cottage, led a march of flame over various sections of this area Saturday with minor damage.

The forest blaze singed off the sides of a large area between Fishing Creek and Benton and for a time threatened cottages in that section. It started Friday, was put down by railroad workers, but started again Saturday morning. About fifty fishermen and farmers finally put it out Saturday afternoon. Cottage burned was owned by Sylvester Smoker. Four other fires were reported.

Firemen Use Brooms

Shovels and brooms had to be used by Ephrata firemen Saturday afternoon to extinguish a grass fire at Point Lookout on Ephrata mountain, near the borough. The flames spread from a rubbish fire.

FIRES—Page 6

BRITISH FORT CAPTURED

New York, April 12.—(INS)—A Rome radio broadcast picked up in New York tonight by the National Broadcasting company claimed that pro-Nazi Iraq troops captured the British fort at Ruiga guarding the main line of communications between Bagdad and Damascus.

GANGWAY!

SEE PAGE 13

BABY CLINIC HELD AT ATTUCKS CENTER

Five new registrants were enrolled by Crispus Attucks Well Baby clinic at the session yesterday afternoon. Twenty-five babies attended.

The new enrollments are the following: Joanne Wilson, 339 Locust street; Helen Witts, 447 South Duke street; Christine Evans, 220 Howard avenue; Joseph Doutrich, 744 Union street, and Gertrude Lewis, 455 Rockland street.

Miss Lena Cooper was the hostess and Dr. J. V. Sterrett and Miss Mildred Musselman were in professional charge.

A number of visitors attended the clinic, as part of the "Come and See Tours" arranged by the Welfare Federation.

CITY BAND GIVES ANNUAL CONCERT

The City Band presented its annual benefit concert last evening under the direction of B. Frank Streaker, in the Malta Temple, before a capacity audience.

Featured on the program was a cornet solo by H. I. Musser and a xylophone solo by Miss Marguerite Way. Several encores were also played by the band in response to the audience.

Someday I'll Find You

BY MARGARET WIDDEMER

YESTERDAY: Eileen Gardner has at last made the great decision. She has had a success singing on a little Colorado radio station, but staying with that job means enduring the importunities of Jordan Estill, who wants to marry her. And going east with Molly Flanagan means taking a big chance for a big job—and the possibility of finding Martin, whom she has met only once, and would give everything she has to meet again. So she will go.

Chapter 13
New York

The interview with Jordan, which she had tried to escape, was hard.

"You're hard. You're unfeeling. You care for nothing but climbing to the top," he accused her; his ordinary, rather shy calm broken to tatters. "You love me—but you love career more. You'd rather trample down all your own human feelings and stand and sing into a little piece of tin and have applause, than have anything real—wifehood, motherhood, normal human contacts.".

She stared at him. She had somehow supposed that her real reason for going to New York was written across her forehead in gilt letters. And here was Jordan lecturing her for being a hard career girl! She wanted to laugh— and then she felt like crying, a little. So she did neither one.

She said, more sharply than she meant, "You're like all the rest of the men in the world. You think because I want to do something else more than marry you, that it applies to all the other men there are."

He looked at her for a moment as if she were speaking in a strange language.

"You mean—you mean you want to find somebody who has more than I have—who can give you more than I can give you?"

There was no way of explaining. Nevertheless she tried once more.

"No, Jordon. It's just that, while I don't love you enough to marry you, I might love home other man enough."

"You do love me," he said. "You love me, only you don't know it, you have some crazy idea in your head from the movies. We've gone round together and been good friends, we've been close, we've been congenial, and you've known I've loved you. I've seen your attitude to me. You couldn't have been my pal—my girl—all this time without really loving me. You think you're the kind that can bave some impossilbe emotion, go off the deep end. You're not. You aren't that kind, I tell you, you're a career woman."

He had, she saw, an image of her in his mind that no amount of argument on her part would turn into a truer one. He wanted her like that—cool to him because she could not be anything else to anyone else.

She tried once more.

"But I think I am, Jordan, it is the same as if it were true. You'll have to let me find out for myself."

Unfortunately he snapped at this. "That means there's a good

(See SERIAL STORY—Page 16)

ATTENDING CONFERENCE

Mrs. Ruby M. Payne, director of the Crispus Attucks Community Center, is in Louisville, Kentucky, this week, attending a conference on recreational work. She will return this week-end.

OFFICERS NOMINATED BY TRAFFIC CLUB; ELECTION ON MAY 26

Samuel Seaber was nominated as a candidate for president of the Traffic Club of the Manufacturers' Association without opposition at a dinner meeting of the organization held in the Elks' club last evening. The election will be held May 26.

Other candidates nominated are: Vice-president, R. P. Garrett; secretary-treasurer, Howard Gabriel; Board of Governors, E. George Siedle, R. E. Good, Charles B. Weise, J. J. Eshelman and B. G. Herr.

Louis F. Klein spoke on the history of the American Merchant Marine.

3,500 ACRES PEAS TO BE GROWN HERE

Lancaster county farmers have contracted to grow 3,500 acres of peas this season, an increase of 16 2-3 per cent over last year, according to H. S. Sloat, assistant county farm agent.

Six concerns have contracted to buy the peas at prices ranging from $50 per ton to $75 per ton for fancy pickings. Last year the crop yielded 1,300 to 4,200 pounds of hulled peas to the acre. The average for the state last year was 2,592 pounds to the acre.

Vineries to hull the peas were first built in the Lower end but have recently spread to other parts of the county and one or more are now located in 15 districts: Kirkwood, Mechanics Grove, Drumore Center, Little Britain, Christiana, Intercourse, New Holland, Honey Brook, Hinkletown, Reamstown, Neffsville, Mount Joy, Bainbridge, Lampeter and Oxford.

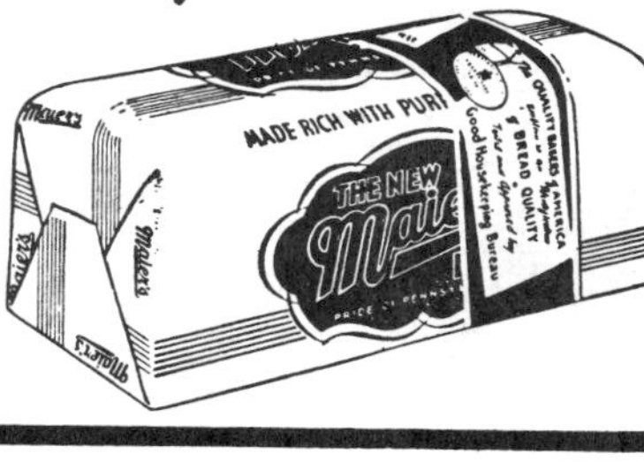

WEATHER

Eastern Pennsylvania: Generally Fair But With Some Cloudiness Thursday And Friday; Little Change In Temperature.

Intell Journal Stormograph Reading: Unsettled Weather. Increasing Winds And Warmer Thursday.

Intelligencer Journal

The Leading Newspaper in the Garden Spot of America, Home Owned for Home Folks Since 1794

Track

McCaskey High school wins 19th straight dual meet by topping York 79 to 54.

For details turn to Page Eleven.

VOLUME LXXVII.—NO. 19. | CITY | The Intelligencer Founded 1799 The Journal Founded 1794 | LANCASTER, PA., THURSDAY MORNING, MAY 1, 1941. | Entered at Post Office at Lancaster, Pa. as second class mail matter | 18 PAGES, 144 COLUMNS.—THREE CENTS.

PRESIDENT CALLS FOR CARGO SHIPS

ROSES BEAT WILMINGTON 4-3 TO OPEN SEASON

2-RUN RALLY IN 8TH FRAME DECIDES FRAY

4,500 Fans Turn Out For Opener Under Lights Of Stumpf Field

WHEATON HITS HARD

They may have been a little short in hitting during training camp time, but the Lancaster Red Roses packed wallop in their opening Inter-State Baseball league game Wednesday night when they nosed out the Wilmington Blue Rocks 4 to 3 on the Stumpf diamond. Approximately 4,500 fans were on hand for the 1941 debut of last year's champions.

Leading the powerhouse for Lancaster was centerfielder Woody Wheaton, who pounded out three doubles and a single to aid in scoring the first two Roses' runs.

The Roses topped their Delaware rivals in hits ten to seven. Wheaton had four, don Kellett two, Frank DeManicor two, and Bill Long and Jim John one each.

SCORE IN FIRST

Lancaster started things off in their first trip to the plate when Don Kellett, Ursinus baseball coach who joined the locals Wednesday afternoon, singled to center and Wheaton doubled the first pitched ball to center scoring Kellett.

Although they went down one, two, three in the first and second innings, Wilmington found itself in the third when Tom Lloyd singled to right, Lou McCollum walked, Emil Kreshka sacrificed and Paul Swobada singled to center scoring Lloyd and McCollum and putting the visitors ahead 2 to 1.

ROSES TIE SCORE

Coming right back in the same inning Manager Billy Rogell's Red Roses tied the count at 2-2 when Pitcher Norm Hibbs walked, Kellett singled for the second time and

More of ROSES on Page 10

Mayor Tosses Out First Ball To Open Roses' Season

Mayor D. E. Cary was "in there pitching" Wednesday night to formally open the Inter-State Baseball league season in Lancaster. After the mayor tossed out the first ball, about 4,500 fans saw the Red Roses battle the Wilmington Blue Rocks through nine thrill-packed innings—and, most important of all, score a 4 to 3 victory. That's Billy Rogell, the new manager of the Roses at the right of the photo, and Tom Oliver, Wilmington manager (left), watching as Mayor Cary lets fly with the ball. (Intell photo)

REVEAL 80 P. C. OF BRITISH IN GREECE SAVED

Successful Withdrawal Of 48,000 Men Attributed To Grim Rear-Guard Action

TURKS SCOLD BRITISH

(By The Associated Press)

Withdrawal of units of the British rear guard from Greece continued today (Thursday) as an official announcement in London declared that 80 per cent—approximately 48,000 men—of the 60,000-man British Expeditionary Force in Greece had been saved from the German-conquered nation.

To grim rear-guard fighting by a comparative handful of British soldiers, many of whom still were considered hopelessly trapped, was attributed the success of the difficult evacuation.

The withdrawal, a British middle east command communique said, was undertaken "when it became obvious that the resistance of the Greek army to the German invasion was at an end and the government of Greece requested that the empire contingent which had been sent to its help should be withdrawn from Greece."

The Axis troops, "by employment of greatly superior numbers," had obtained "complete command of the land and air by repeated attacks and had made unusable the one available good port, Piraeus, at Athens," the communique asserted.

REEMBARKED FROM BEACHES

The necessity of reembarkation from open beaches under a steady hail of gunfire, the command said, meant that the withdrawal of large numbers of troops could be accomplished only "at the cost of heavy losses of vehicles and equipment, while rearguards which cover its withdrawal may have to sacrifice themselves to secure the reembarkation of others."

The individual troops retained their personal fighting equipment

More of WAR on Page 6

President Appeals For Investments In Defense Stamps

Says Program Offers Chance To "Demonstrate Your Faith In America"

BUYS FIRST ISSUES

Washington —(AP)— President Roosevelt bought the first Defense Savings Bond and Stamp Wednesday night and appealed to his fellow Americans, through similar investments, to "demonstrate again your faith in America."

The Defense Savings program, he said, offers an opportunity "to share in the defense of all the things we cherish against the threat that is made against them." That threat must be fought wherever it appears, he said, "and it can be found at the threshold of every home in America."

OPENS NATIONAL CAMPAIGN

The Chief Executive spoke from the White House over all major radio networks in a program officially opening a campaign to bring billions of dollars into the Treasury through the public sale of Defense Savings Bonds and Defense Postal Savings stamps.

Secretary Morgenthau and Postmaster General Walker also took part in the program.

Mr. Roosevelt said the first Defense Saving Bond was being made out with Mrs. Roosevelt as beneficiary, and that he was buying "not one but 10 Defense Savings stamps to go into little books" for each of his ten grandchildren. White House officials said Mrs. Roosevelt's Bond would be of $500 denomination and that the grandchildren would each receive ten 25-cent stamps.

In purchasing the first securities, the President said it was fitting that he should do so as the symbol of a determination of all the peo-

More of SECURITIES on Page 6

Tells Of Work

WARREN R. ROBERTS

ROBERTS REVEALS PA. DISBURSEMENTS HALF BILLION A YR.

Retiring Auditor General Says Job "An Exacting If Not Exciting Experience"

Harrisburg —(AP)— Warren R. Roberts, retiring next Tuesday as auditor general of Pennsylvania, gave an accounting of his administration Wednesday night and said the job of disbursing one billion dollars each two years was "an exacting if not exciting experience."

Roberts, who will return to private life when he turns the auditor general's office over to his successor, F. Clair Ross, now state treasurer, summed up the work of his department in an address at a testimonial dinner in his honor attended by several hundred employes.

"It will no doubt surprise you when I tell you that, for the first time in the history of the Commonwealth, the disbursements from all the state funds have exceeded one billion dollars in a single biennial period," Roberts said.

Such a disbursement, he added, requires upwards of 100,000 requisitions a day at an average expenditure of $1,500,000 daily.

"To authorize the payment of so

More of ROBERTS on Page 4

WILL USE CRAFT TO CARRY AID TO DEMOCRACIES

Asks Maritime Comm. To Secure "At Least 2,000,000 Tons" Of Shipping

MAY MEAN SACRIFICES

Washington—(AP)—President Roosevelt asked the Maritime commission Wednesday night to obtain service of "at least 2,000,000 tons of merchant shipping" to be used to supply "all out aid to the democracies."

In a letter to the commission's chairman, Rear-Admiral Emory S. Land, the President indicated that cargo vessels of all types might be taken from their existing or proposed trade routes to haul vital war supplies and food across the seas.

He said also that the American merchant fleet must be expanded faster than was planned "so that ships and more ships will be available to carry the food and the munitions of war to the democracies of the world."

The President's action was another in a chain of steps designed to help insure that weapons of war produced in American factories shall arrive on the other side of the Atlantic.

Already Mr. Roosevelt has said that American naval vessels may range the seven seas, even into combat zones, to be on the lookout for craft that might prove a threat to the Western Hemisphere. These naval patrols are expected to be of help to Britain by spotting Axis warcraft and giving warning of their presence.

SHELVE ANTI-CONVOY MOVES

Mr. Roosevelt has said the government has no idea of using American naval vessels for convoy purposes, however, Wednesday, with administration forces arguing that he would not resort to convoys without asking the consent of Congress, the Senate Foreign Relations committee defeated a half dozen attempts to force anti-convoy resolutions to the Senate floor for debate.

The 2,000,000 tons of cargo shipping which Mr. Roosevelt called for would help remedy some of the depredations of Adolf Hitler's submarines, surface raiders and planes. Only Wednesday Admiral Land disclosed that British shipping losses

More of SHIPS on Page 6

C. T. CARPENTER DIES SUDDENLY IN PHILADELPHIA

Served On State Milk Control Board During Term Of Governor Earle

Philadelphia — Charles T. Carpenter, sixty-five, a member of the State Milk Control Board during the administration of Governor Earle, died Wednesday at the Penn A. C.

CHARLES T. CARPENTER

Carpenter, who lived at Donomore Farms, Chester county, was just entering a Turkish bath when he collapsed. He was a leader in dairy and horticultural circles and was one of the organizers of the Allied Dairy Farmers Association.

Charles T. Carpenter, was the Democratic congressional candidate

More of CARPENTER on Page 6

New Army Examination Plan For Draftees Praised Here

Officials, Young Men And Parents Say Experiment Deserves Worthy Try-out; Plan Would Prevent Severing Of Ties Before Selectee Knows He Is To Be Inducted

Praise for the new experimental plan of giving Selective Service men their Army examinations prior to the time they report to camps for induction into service was heard from many sources Wednesday.

Draft board clerks, the young men involved and parents, all agreed that the plan, devised to prevent men from severing their personal ties and then being rejected for service ,merited a worthy try-out.

TEST IN STATE

The U. S. Army is using Pennsylvania as a testing ground for the project and national Selective Service officials said the plan would be adopted nationally if it is satisfactory in this state.

Under the plan, details of which have not yet been received by local boards, Army examination centers would be set up in Philadelphia, Pittsburgh, Altoona, Harrisburg and Wilkes-Barre.

A man selected by his local draft board will be sent to one of these centers and given an Army medical test. He will have another thirty days after that to quit his job and sever other civil pursuits in preparation for a year's military training.

7 OBJECTORS TO REPORT

Meanwhile at Harrisburg, Governor James announced that seven men classified as conscientious objectors will report May 15, at Patapsco Camp, near Baltimore, operated by the American Friends' Service Committee, to do work of "national importance" under civilian direction. None of the men are

More of DRAFT on Page 6

SOLDIER FINED FOR SPEEDING

Daniel Rosenfield, a soldier stationed at the United States Army's Chanute Field, Ill., was prosecuted early Thursday (today) by State Motor Policeman D. L. Gibbons, of the Columbia sub-station, on a charge of speeding. Given an immediate hearing before Justice of the Peace E. L. Bertram, Kreadyville, he was fined $10 and costs. The officer said Rosenfield was driving west on the Lincoln highway, near Mountville, at a speed of 75 miles per hour.

24 OF 26 LOCAL SELECTEES PASS U. S. ARMY TESTS

Lancaster Man Who Was Married Tuesday Is Among Group Inducted

Twenty-four of the twenty-six young men sent to Harrisburg Wednesday from three city and one county draft boards were inducted for a year's service in the Army.

Lewis G. Keil, of New Holland, held over for examination Wednesday, was also accepted.

A newlywed, a man who traveled from Johannesburg, South Africa, to volunteer, and an F. and M. honor graduate and former track star were among those accepted Wednesday.

WED ON TUESDAY

Harold R. Beam, 111 Pearl st., was the newlywed. He was married Tuesday to Miss Mae Thomas, Lincoln Highway east, at Winchester, Va.

Lambert G. Snow, territorial representative for the Armstrong Cork company, returned to the United States a few weeks ago and immediately registered and volunteered.

The athlete and honor student was Charles Lecrone, 330 College ave., winner of the Williamson medal at F. and M. last year, and a quarter-miler and 220-yard dash man on the track team.

GROUP INDUCTED

Inducted Wednesday were:

City Board No. 1—Lambert G. Snow, 548 W. James st.; Harlan E. Kilgore, 441 E. Orange st.; Frank

More of SELECTEES on Page 6

PROBE ACTIVITIES OF 'BABY SELLING' RING

Detroit Police Say Unwed Mothers Received $50 Each For Children, Who Were Later Sold

Detroit — (AP) — Police disclosed Wednesday that they were investigating activities of a group of persons suspected of "buying and selling" babies of unmarried mothers.

A 47-year-old grandmother was arrested on a tentative charge of conspiracy to violate the state adoption laws and another woman was reported sought for questioning.

Lieut. Nell Coolidge of the Women's Police Division said that unwed, expectant mothers apparently were given hospital care and sums of money in exchange for their babies, who then were "sold" to childless couples for amounts as high as $1,000.

The mothers, Lieut. Coolidge said, received an average of $50 for their babies.

4 NAZI AVIATORS TAKEN OFF U. S. SHIP BY THE BRITISH

Canadian Auxiliary Cruiser Stops American Craft Near Honolulu

Honolulu—(AP) — The Canadian auxiliary cruiser Prince Robert stopped the American President lines vessel President Garfield on the high seas on Tuesday and removed four German aviators, Capt. John E. Murphy of the U. S. ship, radioed Wednesday.

The four flyers took passage at San Francisco and were en route to their homeland via the Orient.

A terse report of the incident was given by Captain Murphy to the ship's agents a few hours before the President Garfield put into port.

DELAYED LESS THAN HOUR

A naval party from the Prince Robert boarded the American ship, examined the passenger list and removed the four Germans, the report stated. The American ship was delayed less than an hour.

The quartet taken off were Edward Flesch, 34, Werner Naumar, Hans Sandkamm and Guenther Katzke, 41.

They were taken in custody by the immigration service on their arrival in the United States last August from Colombia, where they had been employed by a commercial air service.

The Japanese steamship line, Nippon Yushen Kaisha, had refused to transport them across the Pacific.

(Japanese steamship lines have refused to carry German Nationals

More of AVIATORS on Page 6

TWO POLICEMEN IN LOCAL TROOP WIN PROMOTIONS

Templeton Made Corporal; Corporal Smith Is Advanced To Rank Of Sergeant

The promotion of First Class Private William B. Templeton, assigned to the Lancaster headquarters of Troop B of the State Motor Police, to corporal was announced Wednesday night by Lieutenant F. G. McCartney, troop commander.

WILLIAM B. TEMPLETON

At the same time Lieutenant McCartney also announced the promotion of Corporal Stiles Smith, of the Coatesville sub-station, to sergeant. The promotions become effective Thursday (today).

Corporal Templeton, whose home is in Lititz, entered the Pennsylvania Highway Patrol training school at Harrisburg on May 16, 1929, and on August 1, 1929, was assigned to the Collegeville sub-sta-

More of POLICEMEN on Page 6

FIRE SCARE AT LAUNDRY

City firemen were called to the Lancaster Laundry, rear of 152 E. King st., at 10:45 p. m. Wednesday when two sprinkler heads opened in the basement of the building, Fire Chief Harry Miller reported. An overheated boiler may have been the cause, he said, adding that there was no damage. Engine Company No. 6 and Assistant Chief Frank Deen also responded to the call.

GIRL WHO UNDERWENT HEART OPERATION DIES

Jeanette Elaine Ginder, Nine, Manheim R. D. 3, Succumbs In Lancaster General Hospital

Jeanette Elaine Ginder, nine-year-old daughter of Mr. and Mrs. Jacob H. Ginder, of Manheim R. D. 3, who underwent a rare heart operation at the Lancaster General hospital April 4, died at that institution at 8:10 a. m. Wednesday.

The child, attendants said, recently suffered an attack of pneumonia effecting both lungs. A pus formation developed in the sac surrounding the heart. The attending physician performed the operation by inserting a drain into the sac to remove the pus.

Besides her parents, she is survived by her paternal grandparents, Mr. and Mrs. Jacob S. Ginder, her maternal grandparents, Mr. aand Mrs. C. R. Young, her maternal great grandmother, Mrs. Samuel Young, and her paternal great grandmather, Mrs. Benjamin Ruhl, all of Manheim R. D. 3. Two brothers, Mervin and J. Wilbur, and a sister, Melba Jean, all at home, also survive.

'SALESMAN' VICTIMIZES F. AND M. STUDENTS

Collects Down Payment On Shirt Order, Query To Company Reveals Fraud

City police reported Wednesday that a flim-flam artist, posing as a shirt salesman, had fleeced several Franklin and Marshall college students. The "salesman" took orders for the shirts and collected a down payment for which he gave a receipt signed J. J. Burns. When the shirts did not arrive, Paul Hawk, 423 W. James st., wrote to the company the man claimed he represented and learned that he was a fake.

BOY SHOOTS HIMSELF WHILE HUNTING RATS

Bullet Enters Left Leg Of Robert Fox, East Earl R. D. 1; Admitted To Hospital

Robert Fox, seventeen, East Earl R. D. 1, son of Mr. and Mrs. Ivan Fox, was admitted to the Lancaster General hospital Wednesday afternoon suffering a bullet wound of the left leg.

According to Dr. J. M. Wenger, of Terre Hill, the youth was walking in a field at Silver Hill, near Terre Hill, about 11 a. m. Wednesday, carrying a .22 calibre rifle when it accidentally discharged, the bullet striking him in the leg.

Continuing across the field after the accident, Dr. Wenger said, the youth enlisted the aid of a man who happened by and he took him to his office. Dr. Wenger said the youth's father told him his son had borrowed the gun from a neighbor.

At the hospital, Fox told attendants he was shooting rats when the accdient happened.

Lancaster Among Ten U. S. Cities Where Business Improvement Has Recently Been Outstanding

Lancaster is included in the list of ten cities in which business improvement has recently been outstanding, says Forbes Magazine, May 1, 1941.

The other nine cities are: Philadelphia, Pa.; New Orleans, La.; Indianapolis, Ind.; Portland, Ore.; Omaha, Nebr.; Montgomery, Ala.; Decatur, Ill.; Hamilton, Ohio; Superior, Wisc.

Forbes Business Pictograph, a business map which scientifically and accurately reports changes in business conditions throughout the country, is regularly used by thousands of leading business organizations, advertisers, distributors, and sales managers to guide them in concentrating their efforts in the right place at the right time. Each issue of the map names ten cities outstanding for recent gains and on this occasion one of the ten included in the roll of honor is Lancaster.

Specifically, in the cities named, business is said to compare more favorably with the same time last year than any previous occasion since April 1, 1940.

"We Lead All The Rest"

FARM CORNER

By *The Farm Editor*

TOBACCO SELLING AT 5 TO 13 CENTS

Number Of Crops Left In Southern Section Of County; Leaf Heating, Losing Weight

A number of scattered tobacco crops which remained in farmers' hands following the general buying wave in March have been picked up recently at prices ranging from five to thirteen cents a pound. Some of the growers never had a buyer till now, while others refused bids earlier and were left, stuck with their crops.

A 12-acre crop, believed to be the last in Donegal township, was reported sold this week at 13-11 cents for wrappers and five cents for fillers. During the big buying wave, 15 and 5 was the general price offered in that district; 16 and 5 for some crops.

What tobacco remains unsold appears to be south of Lancaster. Horace Sheaffer, AAA committeeman at New Providence, said Wednesday there may be several hundred of acres still held by farmers in that district. The crops are heating, losing weight, and several dealers have been trying to buy at bargain prices, it was reported.

Robert S. Posey, supervisor of the

More of FARM CORNER on Page 6

Intelligencer Journal Weather Calendar

COMPARATIVE TEMPERATURES

Station	High	Low
Intell Journal	82	51
Water Works	87	40
Ephrata	87	45
Last Year (Ephrata)	77	41
Official High for Year, April 20		93
Official Low for Year, January 14		11
Character of Day		Clear

HOURLY TEMPERATURES

(Wednesday)			
3 a. m.	58	4 p. m.	82
4 a. m.	55	5 p. m.	82
5 a. m.	54	6 p. m.	82
6 a. m.	52	7 p. m.	81
7 a. m.	52	8 p. m.	77
8 a. m.	57	9 p. m.	74
9 a. m.	61	10 p. m.	70
10 a. m.	67	11 p. m.	68
11 a. m.	74	Midnight	66
Noon	78	(Thursday)	
1 p. m.	79	1 a. m.	64
2 p. m.	80	2 a. m.	61
3 p. m.	81	3 a. m.	61

SUN

Rises—5:06 a. m. (EST)

Sets—6:57 p. m. (EST)

More of WEATHER on Page 6

DAYLIGHT TIME IN INTELL

All time mentioned in the Intelligencer Journal is Daylight Time unless otherwise noted.

'Cryptoquotes,' New Brain Teaser, Starts Today In Intell

"Cryptoquotes"—a new kind of brain teaser—is being added to the Intelligencer Journal's daily crossword puzzle. The first one appears in this issue on Page 13.

Here's how it works. Hidden in a cipher that looks just like a jumbled mess of letters, or a line of type pied by the printer, is a quotation of a famous person. A substitute character has replaced the original letter. For instance, an "R" may substitute for the original "E" throughout the entire "Cryptoquote," or a "BB" may replace an "LL." After the key to Cipher is found, the solution is easy.

Wheaton, Hero in Roses' Win, Headed for Big Leagues

Sports Revue

A Great Opening Tiff. Kellett Signed Only Yesterday Afternoon.

—by GEORGE W. KIRCHNER—

AS THE ROSES OPENED THE SEASON . . . The consensus of opinion among the more than 4,000 fans who gathered at Stumpf field was that everything worked out perfectly. The crowd was large; the game close and exciting and to top it all off our Roses came through with flying colors.

As one fan remarked going out of the ball park, the town last night really belonged to Woody Wheaton. Any guy that can bat four-for-four, including three doubles, knock in two runs and score one himself deserves some recognition. Wheaton got it and that's as it should be.

Concerning Don Kellett, the shortstop. Big Jim Peterson, one of the owners, took Kellett, who is football coach at Ursinus, right off the football field yesterday afternoon and put him into a baseball uniform.

Somebody told Peterson that Manager Billy Rogell was a bit worried about shortstop, so Jim lost no time and went right to Collegeville and signed up Kellett.

It was well that he did, too, for Don batted an even .500 for the evening, getting two solid singles in four trips . . . He had two put-outs . . .

So Kellett, who trained as he coached his Bears through spring football, will be with the Roses from now on . . . However, he'll have to miss tonight's game because he must complete arrangements at Ursinus, but he'll be on hand again on Friday and from then on in . . .

Despite the fact that he fanned four times in as many trips to the plate, Manager Rogell is not yet ready to give up on Bill Ford, his left-fielder.

"I don't know what's the matter with the boy," Rogell said, "but I certainly won't give up on him on one game. He fielded well and I only hope he can start hitting."

Ford had two nifty throws to the plate that cut off runs, but he was powerless at the plate.

It was pleasing for many of last year's rooters to see Frank (Biddy) DeManicor come through with a pair of hits, one of them a long-distance triple . . . Frank, however, caused some amazement when he dropped Norm Hibbs' toss-out in the fifth inning, but, fortunately, it did not lead to a run, Ford tossing out Kreshka at the plate with Billy Long assisting . . .

The Wilmington boys didn't particularly care for the way Jimmy John, the catcher, was tagging them out at home, but Jim's only explanation was that he was just making sure they were tagged.

Altogether the Roses collected ten bingles off Lou McCollum, the right hander, and they managed to put enough of them together to score runs. And that's what really counts.

Tonight the boys go at it again, weather permitting, but regardless of what happens nobody can take any glory out of that glorious opening. It was such a game that will long be remembered and the whole town, from Mayor Çary, last night's honor guest, right on down, is hoping the boys can keep it up.

Led by Wheaton, the Roses Bloom in Opening Game

WOODY WHEATON

Woody did the batting—getting 4 for 4—and Norm did the pitching and your Red Roses hopped off to a flying start with a 4-3 win over Wilmington here last night.

NORM HIBBS

Led by the perfect batting of Woody Wheaton, and the fine pitching of Norm Hibbs, your Red Roses, pictured above, hopped off to a grand start

At the left are our heroes, while those in the group picture are, left to right, back row: Bill Ford, Jack Lindstrom, Bill Witz, Dick Busby, Norm Hibbs, Ben Culp and Wheaton.

Second row: Ben Eckert, Frank DeManicor, Wayne Moffett, the Brownstown outfielder, Pat Graziani, Billy Morrison and Nick Scalla.

Front row: Mike Koons, Billy Long, Manager Bill Rogell, Bud Williams, Jim John and Johnny Tulacz.

Manager Is Trying To Sell Ace Fielder To Detroit Tigers

Rogell Says He Hates to Lose Player Who Batted 1.000 in Last Night's 4-3 Win, But Feels He Deserves Major Loop Chance

By GEORGE W. KIRCHNER

WOODY Wheaton, who stood out head and shoulders as the hero in last night's 4 to 3 victory which the Red Roses scored over Wilmington in the opening game of the Inter-State League season here, is headed for the Major Leagues.

You can take this from Manager Bill Rogell who admitted that he has already wired officials of the Detroit Tigers with regards to the popular centerfielder. Because Hank Greenberg, the Tigers' slugging fielder, will soon be drafted into the Army, Rogell feels that Wheaton has a better than even chance of getting a call.

"So far as our ball club is concerned," Rogell said after last night's glorious opening, "I'm going to be sorry to see Wheaton go, but I think the boy deserves that chance. If ever I saw a Major League ball player Wheaton is the guy. I thought that of him the first time I saw him in spring training and his performance last night only makes me doubly sure.

"However, I want to say here and now that if the Tigers decide to take Wheaton, they'll have to come across with a good outfielder to replace him. That much I'll demand and in the exchange I know the Tigers will be getting a break regardless of whom they send here. That boy sure can play ball and he certainly has no business out of the Big Leagues."

Fans Hail Woody

Rogell's opinion was shared by the rest of the 4,000 fans for Wheaton was the outstanding hero.

He came to bat four times and when it was all over and the Roses had tucked away their first victory, Wheaton was batting a perfect 1,000. Included in his list were three doubles and a single and once—in the eighth inning—he cracked out a double after the umpire called his first attempt foul on a close decision along the left field foul-line.

And that's how Wheaton, who batted in two of the Roses' four

(See RED ROSES—Page 25)

HOW THEY STAND

National League

Teams	W.	L.	P. C.
St. Louis	10	3	.769
Brooklyn	13	4	.765
New York	8	6	.571
Cincinnati	7	8	.467
Chicago	5	7	.417
Boston	6	9	.400
Philadelphia	5	10	.333
Pittsburgh	3	10	.231

American League

Teams	W.	L.	P. C.
Cleveland	11	4	.733
Chicago	9	4	.692
New York	10	6	.625
Boston	7	6	.538
Detroit	6	7	.462
Philadelphia	4	9	.308
Washington	4	10	.286
St. Louis	3	8	.273

INTER-STATE STANDINGS

Teams	W.	L.	P.C.
LANCASTER	1	0	1.000
Reading	1	0	1.000
Bridgeport	1	0	1.000
Harrisburg	1	0	1.000
Wilmington	0	1	.000
Trenton	0	1	.000
Hagerstown	0	1	.000
Allentown	0	1	.000

YESTERDAY'S RESULTS

National League

Philadelphia 8, Pittsburgh 4.
Brooklyn 4, Cincinnati 3.
Chicago 9, Boston 4.
St. Louis 6, New York 4.

American League

Cleveland 6, Philadelphia 5.
Detroit 12, Boston 8.
Chicago 5, Washington 1.
New York 7, St. Louis 1.

International League

No games scheduled.

Inter State League

Lancaster 4, Wilmington, Del. 3 (night).
Bridgeport 12, Trenton 7.
Reading 10, Allentown 2.
Harrisburg 3, Hagerstown 2 (11 innings).

Eastern League

Binghamton 20, Springfield 6.
Hartford 12, Albany 2.
Wilkes-Barre 6, Elmira 3.
Williamsport 4, Scranton 2.

American Association

No games scheduled.

Southern Association

Atlanta 14, Little Rock 2.
Nashville 8, New Orleans 1.
Memphis 8, Chattanoogo 8 (called 9th, darkness).
Knoxville 9, Birmingham 5.

BOBBY JONES' SON, 14, TAKES UP GOLF

CHATTANOOGA, Tenn., May 1—(A. P.)—Bobby Jones, 3rd, made his bow to competitive golf today with Robert Tyre Jones, Jr., hoping he would be accepted as a 14-year-old youngster out for the fun with no idea of a tournament golf career.

"I do not want to see him become a tournament golfer," said the father who retired in 1930 without new golfing worlds to conquer. "I hope he becomes good enough to get a lot of pleasure out of the game."

"Little Bobby," a student at Marist College in Atlanta, was among a field of 100 in the sixth annual Southern prep and high school tournament. His father predicted anything from 95 to 105 for the lad's first 18 holes in the 54 of medal play.

"King Bobby" said nothing as yet stamps his son as a promising golfer.

"He lacks experience," the father explained, "for he only recently took up the game. He gets the distance on the drives but that is about all."

High Trackmen Win Dual Meet From Yorkers

The Red and Black track warriors of McCaskey high school won their 19th straight dual meet victory by downing York 79 to 54 in York yesterday afternoon.

Coach Abe Herr's McCaskey track and field team has yet to lose a match since he took over the tutoring reigns, and the Red and Black track outfits are thus far undefeated in dual affairs for the fifth straight season.

The victors scored very heavily in the field events, taking all three places in the shot put and all the honors in the pole vault.

One record was set in the meet when Tom Smith, speedy McCaskey high hurdler, ran the 120-yard high hurdles in the good time of 16 seconds.

The complete results are as follows:

One mile run—Won by Kenneth Deckman, McCaskey; 2, Henry Saylor, York; 3, William Kauffman, York. Time, 5:00.4.

440-yard run—Won by Robert Gentzler, York; 2, George Weigle, York; 3, Richard Herr, McCaskey. Time, 53.2 seconds.

120-yard high hurdles—Won by Tom Smith, McCaskey; 2, George Hedrick, York; 3, Richard Reese, McCaskey. Time, 16 seconds (new school record).

100-yard dash—Won by Robert Gentzler, York; 2, Leonard Wilson, McCaskey; 3, George Weigle, York. Time, 10.2 seconds.

200-yard low hurdles—Won by George Hedrick, York; 2, William Edwards, McCaskey; 3, James Weimer, McCaskey. Time, 24.1 seconds.

880-yard run—Won by Richard Herr, McCaskey; 2, Wayne Sherman, York; 3, Paul Gerhart, McCaskey. Time, 2:08.5.

220-yard dash—Won by Robert Gentzler, York; 2, Richard Smith, McCaskey; 3, Allen Ruth, McCaskey. Time, 23.4 seconds.

Shot put—Won by Allen Ruth, McCaskey; 2, Richard Reese, McCaskey; 3, Jay Clymer, McCaskey. Distance, 46' 10 1-2 inches.

High jump—Won by Tom Smith, McCaskey; 2, George Smith, York; 3, William Edwards, McCaskey. Height, 5' 8".

Javelin throw—Won by Harold Hofnagle, York; 2, James Griffiths, McCaskey; 3, Richard Reese, McCaskey. Distance, 146' 6".

Discus throw—Won by William Strayer, McCaskey; 2, Richard Reese, McCaskey; 3, Robert Owens. Distance, 132' 2"

Pole vault—Tie for first place between William Edwards, Tom Smith, Richard Stockton and John Valentino, all of McCaskey. Height, 9'.

Broad jump—Won by Leonard Wilson, McCaskey; 2, George Smith, York; 3, George Weigle, York. Distance, 20' 9 1-2".

880-yard relay—Won by York (Ralph Lauer, Joseph Stees, Gordon Smith and Edward Tschop); 2, McCaskey (Leonard Wilson, Nelson Polite, James Sener and Ralph Smith.) Time, 1:36.3.

Mile relay—Won by McCaskey (Thomas Mannel, James Sener, William Leonard, and Raymond Maxwell); 2, York (George Hedrick, Ralph Lauer, George Wilson and Joseph Stees). Time, 3:48.7.

Veteran Jockeys For Derby

LOUISVILLE, Ky., May 1.—(A. P.)—Jockey society's "upper crust" will do most of the riding in Saturday's 67th Kentucky Derby, but a couple of youngsters could prove mighty embarrassing before the afternoon is over.

Nine of the 11 riders assigned to handle the hopefuls in the chase after the $75,000 rainbow are veteran standouts of the turf wars, steady under fire when the big money is on the line. Three of them have ridden derby winners—Eddie Arcaro in 1938, Carroll Bierman last year and Don Meade in 1933.

But this year in Conn McCreary, the St. Louis streak who is piloting the favored Our Boots and has been "hotter than forty dollars" all year, there's the chance that the Meades, the Arcaros and the Woolfs, might have to chase him home. And if it's a long-shot's year, it might be Herb Lemmons, who will ride the rank outsider, Valdina Paul.

Here's the list:

Conn McCreary (Our Boots); Eddie Arcaro (Whirlaway); Leon "Buddy" Haas (Porter's Cap); Carroll Bierman (Dispose); Basil James (Blue Pair); Harry Richards (Robert Morris); Irving Anderson (Market Wise); Don Meade (Little Beans); Georgie Woolf (Staretor); Herb Lemmons (Valdina Paul); and Johnny Gilbert (Swain).

Derr Aiming At Rematch

Not the least among the punchers who will be paraded before the fight fans Monday night at Maple Grove in Ed Mellinger's palace of swat, is Stanley (Choo-Choo) Derr of Allentown, who meets Buddy Holmes of Philadelphia in the six-round semi-windup.

(Choo-Choo), who got his name because he is always going forward in the ring, is a fine puncher with both his left and right hand, and against Rocky Luciano through the first three rounds he was winning with a fast "one-two."

"I thought I was winning that fight handily, until the fourth round, when Luciano hurt me with an unexpected solar-plexus punch," said Derr. "I am willing to meet Luciano again, and will bet my purse against his end that I can lick him."

Derr, however, first has to take care of Buddy Holmes, his foe this Monday night.

WEATHER
Eastern Pennsylvania: Fair And Rather Cool Tuesday; Wednesday, Partly Cloudy And Warmer.
Intell Journal Stormograph Reading: Fair Tuesday.

Intelligencer Journal.

BASEBALL
Phillies 12
Lancaster 1
Details Page 10.

The Leading Newspaper in the Garden Spot of America, Home Owned for Home Folks Since 1794

VOLUME LXXVII.—NO. 209. CITY The Intelligencer Founded 1799 The Journal Founded 1794 LANCASTER, PA., TUESDAY MORNING, MAY 13, 1941 Entered at Post Office at Lancaster, Pa. as second class mail matter 26 PAGES, 208 COLUMNS.—THREE CENTS.

HESS LANDS BY 'CHUTE IN BRITAIN; DESERTION FROM HITLER SUGGESTED

No. 3 Nazi Flies To Scotland In Forbidden Plane; Germans Report Him Lost, Hint Insanity

Fuehrer's Political Heir Suffered From "Hallucinations," Berlin Reports; Landed Saturday Night On Farm, Taken To Glasgow Hospital With Broken Ankle; Carried Photos To Identify Himself

(By the Associated Press)

London—(Tuesday)—Rudolf Hess, head of the German Nazi party and one of the oldest and closest confidantes of Adolf Hitler, has landed by parachute in Britain under circumstances suggesting the most profoundly important desertion in all history.

The British government announced from the home of Prime Minister Churchill at No. 10 Downing street that Hess was in a Glasgow hospital under treatment for a broken ankle suffered in floating down from a German Messerschmitt fighter plane near there.

CIRCUMSTANCES POINT TO ESCAPE

While the British statement did not specifically say that he had deserted, it made three observations of seeming inescapable significance:

That Hess had brought along photographs taken at varying years in his life to establish his identity if it were questioned.

That he had arrived in a plane which could not possibly have had enough gasoline for a return to Germany—and thus, inferentially, that his trip was clearly not a one-man offensive but a one-way flight.

That the Messerschmitt's guns were empty.

(Moreover, the British radio in a broadcast heard in the United States referred to Hess as "the only idealist" in the Nazi high command.)

BERLIN HAS FIRST WORD

This most extraordinary flight of this or any other war was disclosed in London a few hours after the Germans in Berlin had announced that Hess—Hitler's political heir but once removed—was missing, that he presumably had taken a forbidden plane flight and had cracked up; that he appeared to have been suffering "hallucinations" and had "left behind a confused letter."

The implication was that he was mentally unbalanced and had been deranged for some time; for it was stated that Hitler personally had directed that he not be permitted to use any plane.

(Early today German informants in Berlin insisted that they knew nothing beyond the Reich's announcement of Hess' disappearance.)

WAS POLITICAL HEIR

Hess from the beginning of National Socialism had stood at Hitler's right hand and in the Reich's councils of war he had held an inner place—the possessor of the deepest of military secrets and one of the most influential of all Nazis.

At the war's outset Hitler publicly gave him an extraordinary accolade by announcing that should he himself fall, Reichmarshal Herman Wilhelm Goering should be considered the new Fuehrer and the dour and earnest Hess Goering's heir apparent.

The story of Hess' strange and lonely flight to England, as told in the govrenment's announcement from Downing street, showed that he first crossed the Scottish coast on last Saturday night (and that was the date given by the Germans for his disappearance.)

He flew on in the direction of Glascow and later—just when was not disclosed—his Messerschmitt crashed. He bailed out. Taken to the Glasgow hospital he first identified himself as "Horn," but later by his correct name.

His photographs were examined,

More of HESS on Page 6, Second Section

Deserter?

RUDOLF HESS

HESS' AIDES PUT UNDER ARREST FOR LETTING HIM FLY

Germans Told He Crashed; Letter Showing "Mental Disorder" Reported

(By The Associated Press)

Berlin, (Tuesday)—Rudolf Hess, one of Germany's "Big Three," was reported missing today, presumably lost on an airplane flight while the victim of "hallucinations."

The Fuehrer had ordered his deputy in party affairs not to make airplane flights for some time past, and Hess' adjutants—whose number was not specified—have been arrested for permitting this and other trips, the announcement said.

(As heard in London, a Berlin radio broadcast said Hess was believed either to have crashed or fallen from the machine.)

LEFT AUGSBURG SATURDAY

The 47-year-old Hess, who was designated by Hitler at the outbreak of the war as his political heir after Reichsmarshal Hermann Goering, left Augsburg in Bavaria about 6 p. m. Saturday, piloting his own machine, and has not been heard from since, it was said. No plane wreckage has been reported found.

Hess left behind a letter showing "in its confusion traces of mental disorder which led to fears that party fellow member Hess was a victim of hallucinations," the party statement added.

The complete announcement said:

"FAILING HEALTH" CITED

"Party fellow member Hess, who because of his failing health, for years has been strictly forbidden

More of BERLIN on Page 14

COUNTY VOTES NOT TO ABATE TAX PENALTIES

Diehm Says New State Law Would "Teach" People Not To Pay Levies

TREASURER NOTIFIED

An Act of the General Assembly of Pennsylvania, signed by Governor Arthur H. James on May 1, which would abate all penalties and interest imposed on delinquent county, poor district and institutional district taxes, has been rejected by the Lancaster county commissioners, and notice of this rejection has been posted in the office of the counyt treasurer as provided under the law.

G. Graybill Diehm, president of the Lancaster County Board of Commissioners, said that by a majority vote Saturday, the commissioners decided to reject this act and notice has been served on the county treasurer to this effect.

REASONS FOR ACTION

The act would "teach the people not to pay their taxes," commented Commissioner Diehm. "The county, anticipating taxes to meet the budget requirements, probably would be forced to borrow the money to meet the expenses, whereas the taxpayers, if permitted to pay their delinquent taxes without penalties, just wouldn't pay until the last minute. Their money would not include interest, whereas the county would be forced to pay interest on money it borrowed to replace the unpaid tax money."

This act not only includes permission to county officials to abate the penalties for delinquent taxes, but also officials of any borough, town, township or school district. Commissioner Diehm said he has no knowledge as to what any of the boroughs in the county, or Lancaster city or any of the towns or townships might do about this

More of TAX on Page 14

President's Speech To S. A. Envoys Off; Radio Chat May 27

No "World-Shaking" Pronouncement Wednesday Despite Foreign Reports

"FINE" AFTER ILLNESS

Washington — (AP) — President Roosevelt was feeling "fine" Monday night, but a speech he was to have delivered Wednesday before the envoys of Latin America's 20 republics was called off and a "Fireside Chat" on May 27 substituted for it.

"So, despite the reports from abroad," said Stephen Early, presidential press secretary, "there will be no world-shaking pronouncement from the President on Wednesday evening, as this office has told you right along."

Mr. Roosevelt was to have spoken at a reception at the Pan-American union Wednesday night which Latin American diplomats had arranged in his honor. The President has had a gastro-intestinal ailment for a week, and, while Early said he was "feeling perfectly fine" once more, the envoys suggested in a resolution that the affair be postponed.

Although Early had asserted repeatedly that Mr. Roosevelt had been unable to begin drafting the address, it had been billed in some quarters as one which would be of extremely great significance in the fields of foreign policy and hemispheric defense.

There had been such a volume of speculation about Wednesday's speech that one responsible official

More of PRESIDENT on Page 14

Local OPM Chief

CALVIN M. KENDIG

CALVIN M. KENDIG TO BE IN CHARGE OF OPM OFFICE

Named At Meeting Of Board Of Directors Of Manufacturers' Association

Calvin M. Kendig, president of the Hamilton Watch company, will have charge of the office to be established in Lancaster by the Office of Production Management, Washington, D. C., it was announced following a meeting of the board of directors of the Manufacturers association Monday noon at the Hotel Brunswick.

Just when or where the office will be opened has not been definitely settled, it was said, but the association hopes to have it adjacent to its

More of KENDIG on Page 6, Second Section

ALICE FAYE WEDS

San Diego, Calif.—(AP)—Phil Harris, orchestra leader, and Alice Faye, film star, married Monday morning in Ensenada, Mex., they disclosed on arriving here Monday night.

Heads Board

CLIFFORD C. AUMENT

Clifford C. Aument, of Quarryville, was elected president of the newly appointed board of trustees of the Thaddeus Stevens Industrial school at a meeting Monday night. Louis B. Bond, of Christiana, was chosen vice-president; Theodore Schwalm, of Lancaster, secretary, and William A. Brock, of Lancaster, treasurer. Schwalm served as temporary chairman during the reorganization. Regular meetings of the board will be held on the second Thursday of each month.

$500,000,000 SHIP PROGRAM DELAYED FOR LABOR TROUBLE

Strike Called For Today In Hudson Plant; Green Scores Machinists' Strike

(By The Associated Press)

A new upsurge of labor difficulties halted work Monday on $500,000,000 of warship construction and other defense contracts in west coast shipyards, and on a $3,000,000 Naval drydock project in Boston.

In addition:

A strike was called for 11 a. m. (EST) today in the Hudson Motor Company in Detroit, great Michigan industrial center already in the throes of a teamsters' strike and faced with the threat of a walkout in many General Motors plants on Thursday.

A walkout of 200 employes of the Smoot Sand & Gravel Corporation, building supply concern, threatened to delay emergency construction in Washington, including new buildings for the War

More of STRIKES on Page 6, Second Section

DOCTOR SHORTAGE FEARED IN PENNA. RURAL DISTRICTS

State Defense Council Plans Survey To Distribute Supply Evenly

Harrisburg — (AP) — An impending "shortage" of doctors and nurses in Pennsylvania prompted the State Council of Defense Monday to undertake a survey aimed at "distributing" the medical profession so rural areas "would not be denuded" of competent medical care.

The announcement was made by Dr. Arnaud C. Marts, director of the State Council, who acted on suggestions made by Dr. Thomas B. Parran, surgeon general of the United States.

"The supply of doctors and nurses will be inadequate; there is a very decided shortage," Dr. Marts said. "The aim of the council is to make an even distribution of the available supply."

ONE FOR EVERY 2,500

He added that the aim was to have one doctor for every 2,500 population. Selective Service has drained this and other states of the supply, Dr. Marts pointed out, citing that the U. S. Navy had called for from 4,000 to 5,000 doctors whereas in the World War it needed only 2,000. This was accounted for by the expansion of the Navy and the creation of numerous additional bases.

LYNCHERS WOUND PRISONER

Quincy, Fla. (Tuesday)—(AP)—Sheriff M. P. Luten said early today that a Negro taken from the Gadsden county jail by four white men Monday night had been found alive but badly wounded about a mile and a half from here.

APPROPRIATION BILLS SOON TO MOVE IN HOUSE

Democrats Counter Gov. James' Warning Of Payless Payday Thru Delay

BIENNIUM NEARS END

Harrisburg — (AP) — Governor James warned Monday the state government faces a payless payday because of delay over tax bills in the Legislature and the Democratic spokesman for the House asserted immediately the general appropriation measure would be passed and sent to the Senate "in plenty of time."

James said he would be unable to authorize capitol paychecks after May 31 unless the assembly had approved his tax program and passed the enabling appropriations.

ACHTERMAN REPLIES

Rep. Leo A. Achterman, Dem., Monroe, majority House leader, retorted:

"The general appropriation bill will be out in sufficient time for the government to continue functioning as inefficiently as it has in the past two years."

Appropriation committee members said they planned to release approximately 50 bills providing sums for schools, hospitals and other institutions after a meeting on Wednesday.

The House has passed only two of the eight tax bills which constitute the financial program for the next two years.

Achterman had prepared several weeks ago a resolution authorizing continued government expenditures if the budget was not enacted by the end of this month, which is the end of the biennium. Governor James declared however there was some question about the legality of such a resolution.

HOUSE PASSES BILLS

Meanwhile the House:

Passed and sent to the Senate a bill permitting persons on relief to supplement their grants by obtaining odd jobs.

Received a dozen new bills, including one to study economic changes brought about by the National Defense Program with a view to reemployment when the emergency ends.

Approved and sent to the Senate a bill to bring milk sold on consignment under the jurisdiction of the Milk Control Commission. A similar measure, intended to plug a loophole in the present law, also was passed by the Senate recently and sent to the House.

CITY EXTENDS TIME OF TRAFFIC LIGHTS

Devices In Operation Until 1 A. M. Daily, Police Say Change Caused By Traffic Conditions

Traffic lights in the downtown section of the city are now being kept in operation until 1 a. m. daily instead of midnight.

City police said the lights are being kept in use an hour longer each day because traffic conditions warrant it. Traffic lights in Penn Square, which formerly went into operation at 8 a. m. now are placed in service from 6:30 a. m. until 11:30 p. m.

SOCIALITES FOUND DEAD IN WRECKED PLANE ON HILLTOP

Mr. And Mrs. Benjamin Brewster, Missing Four Days, Victims Of Crash

Lewistown, Pa.—(AP)—Mr. and Mrs. Benjamin Brewster, New York socialties missing four days on a cross country pleasure flight, were found dead Monday night in the charerd wreckage of their airplane atop a heavily wooded central Pennsylvania mountain.

The bodies were identified by Whitney Stone, a brother-in-law of Brewster, who accompanied searching parties to the top of Shade Mountain, 25 miles south of here, soon after the wreckage was sighted by an airmail pilot.

PLOWED UP GROUND

State police said the ship had struck the top of the 1800-foot mountain, plowing up nearly 100 feet of ground, snapping off tree tops and finally bursting into flames.

Stones and Edward Brewster, a brother of the pilot, flew from Dubois to Lewistown, when they heard the wreckage had been located. State police drove them by automobile to Shade mountain.

"There is no doubt about the identity of the bodies," Stone said.

Frank Martin, of Philadelphia, a private pilot who had been aiding in the search, said he visited the scene and that Mrs. Brewster's body was found in the fuselage of the

More of PLANE on Page 14

NEFFSVILLE DETOUR IN EFFECT TODAY

Traffic To Be Diverted From Lititz Pike South Of Village Square During Road Work

A detour will be established in the Neffsville area Tuesday (this) morning to divert traffic from the portion of the Lititz pike in the southern section of the village during reconstruction work. H. Lester Worst, county superintendent of highways, explained that traffic will use the Oregon pike and a crossroad leading to the square in Neffsville. When that section is completed, a detour will be established around the northern portion, and work will proceed there, Worst said.

"We Lead All The Rest" FARM CORNER By *The Farm Editor*

PLANTING OF TOMATO CROP STARTED HERE

Over 2½ Million Plants Distributed To Growers Of Lancaster, Neighboring Counties

Planting of the commercial tomato crop was started generally throughout Lancaster, Lebanon and Chester counties on Monday.

Approximately 2,560,000 seedling plants were distributed to growers of the three counties at Lancaster throughout the day, representing "the biggest shipment of tomato plants at any one time to this area," officials said.

Five solid carloads of plants made up Monday's consignment for growers in this district. The seedlings were pulled from the nurseries of the Campbell company at Tipton and Cairo, Georgia, on Saturday, packed in baskets, loaded at night, and shipped northward over the week-end.

Local growers came with trucks, automobiles and trailers to the Harrisburg pike yards of the Pennsylvania railroad, beginning at 8 a. m. and until late in the evening, to receive their plants.

Campbell officials said they have contracted for a total of 3,500 acres of tomatoes to be grown in the three counties, an increase of about 1,000 acres over last year. AAA authorities have urged commercial canneries to increase their output as a defense measure.

Intelligencer Journal Weather Calendar

COMPARATIVE TEMPERATURES

Station	High	Low
Intell Journal	62	44
Water Works	70	32
Ephrata	66	36
Last Year (Ephrata)	69	38
Official High for Year, April 20		93
Official Low for Year, January 14		11
Character of Day		Clear

HOURLY TEMPERATURES (Monday)

3 a m	49	4 p m	61
4 a m	47	5 p m	61
5 a m	47	6 p m	61
6 a m	45	7 p m	61
7 a m	45	8 p m	59
8 a m	48	9 p m	57
9 a m	50	10 p m	55
10 a m	52	11 p m	53
11 a m	55	Midnight	51
Noon	57	(Tuesday)	
1 p m	60	1 a m	50
2 p m	60	2 a m	49
3 p m	61	3 a m	48

SUN
Rises—4:52 a m (EST)
Sets—7:09 p m (EST)

More of WEATHER on Page 14

DAYLIGHT TIME IN INTELL

All time mentioned in the Intelligencer Journal is Daylight Time unless otherwise noted.

What Is It? A Tomato Field, Of Course

Not snow, despite the cold weather, but row on row of "hot caps," conical white paper coverings, to protect from being frost bitten 17,000 early tomato plants being grown on the farm of Frank M. Gamber, Washington Boro R. D. 1. Mr. Gamber grew 40 acres of tomatoes last year, the largest acreage in Lancaster county, but is reducing his crop to around 25 acres this season, due to the acute shortage of farm help. The 17,000 plants in the above scene which were capped singly by hand are of the very early staked variety marketed through the Washington Boro Tomato Growers' association. Most of his crop, later, goes to the Campbell Soup company. (Intell Photo)

Special Section Lists Bargains For May Day Sale Wednesday

Sale Offers Exceptional Opportunity To Fill Many Needs At Real Savings

This edition of the Intelligencer Journal carries a special section filled with the advertisements of about fifty downtown Lancaster stores which are participating in the May Day Sale Wednesday. Thrifty shoppers will find all kinds of merchandise advertised at unusually low prices and from this section will be able to make a list of their personal and household needs.

The unseasonal weather has prevented most people from buying spring and early summer merchandise. This sale offers an exceptional opportunity to fill needs at real savings. In addition, since National Cotton Week begins on May 16, many downtown merchants are taking this opportunity to promote cotton in this May Day sale. The wise shopper is going to welcome an opportunity to buy the most wanted summer fabrics at a saving.

GREEN, WHITE BANNERS

Such sales prove once again that

More of MAY SALE on Page 14

Senior Ball For M. S. T. C. To Be May 23

The Senior Ball of Millersville State Teachers' college will be held at Moose ballroom, next Friday evening, May 23. Dress will be formal.

The committee includes: Miron Hywiak, of Chester, chairman, Marion Dennis, Carrie Belle Jacobs, Robert Kunkel, Fern Everhart, Leon Billow, Paul Monkaitis, Charles Rettew, Ann Buckwalter and Dorothy Brubaker.

James Ebbert is president of the class; Ann Buckwalter, vice president; Annette Evans, secretary and Edwin Summers, treasurer. Miss Daisy Hoffmeier and Dr. Arthur R. Gerhart are class deans.

Chaperons will be: Dr. and Mrs. Milton H. Steinhauer, Dr. and Mrs. Lynwood S. Lingenfelter and Mr. and Mrs. John B. Shenk. Guests of honor will include: Talbot A. Hoover, Miss Marion Spencer, Miss Carolyn Howard, Miss Marion C. Terry, Miss Jane E. Rothe, Miss Edna M. Caton, Miss May Adams, Miss Mildred C. Simerson, Dr. and Mrs. Landis Tanger, Miss Dorothy G. Lee and Delbert P. Nave.

ENGAGED

Walters—Keller

Mrs. C. B. Keller, of Mount Joy, announced the engagement of her daughter, Miss Margurite Keller, to Harry G. Walters, son of Harry G. Walter, Sr., of Mount Joy, at a party at her home this week. The announcement was hidden in the favors, which were baskets of flowers and tea cups.

The decorations were in green and yellow with the table centered with a small imitation of a lake on which floated sail boats, flowers and swans, with yellow roses at either end.

Guests were: Dr. and Mrs. Theodore Gabel, of Lancaster; Miss Merriel Jean Nissley of Florin; Harold Backenstow, Miss Barbara Ann Waltrs, of Mount Joy; George Condash, of Harrisburg; Mr. and Mrs. Rittenhouse, of New Danville; Mr. and Mrs. Paris Hostetter, of Mt. Joy. Prizes were won by Dr. Gable, Mr. Backenstow and Mr. and Mrs. Rittenhouse.

Miss Keller attended Temple University and is a graduate of the Shoemaker School of Speech and Drama, class of 1939. Mr. Walters is a graduate of the University of Pennsylvania, class of 1939, and is manager of the Lititz Auto Supply store, at Lititz.

Mildred Miller Wed To Rev. M. R. Shaull

Miss Mildred B. Miller, daughter of Mr. and Mrs. Levi L. Miller, of Ephrata, and Rev. M. Richard Shaull, son of Mr. and Mrs. Millard Shaull, of Felton, were married this morning at 9 o'clock in Bethany Evangelical and Reformed church, Ephrata. Dr. Joseph Hromodka, a member of the faculty of Princeton Seminary officiated.

The bride wore white French embroidered organdy with a long veil falling from a tiara of seed pearls. She carried a shower bouquet of lilies of the valley and white rosebuds.

Miss Betty Miller, sister of the bride, was maid of honor. Her gown was yellow embroidered organdy trimmed in aqua velvet.

The bridesmaids, Miss Pauline Miller, another sister of the bride, and Miss Ruth Wolle, wore gowns of aqua organdy with cream rosebuds in their hair and carried cream rosebuds and forget-me-nots.

The Rev. Jan Pauli Dony, of Princeton, was best man and the ushers were Rev. Robert Sherill, of Knoxville, Tenn.; the Rev. Bruce Evans, of Elizabeth, N. J.; the Rev. J. Herbert Miller, of Hershey and John Keesey, of Red Lion. Richard Doremus, of Reading, was organist and Robert Adams, of Philadelphia, soloist.

A breakfast was served at the church. The couple will spend the summer at El Paso, Texas.

Supper to Precede Shippen School Prom

Miss Polly Barr, of North West End avenue, will entertain at a supper party, at her home, this evening, preceding the Senior Prom of Shippen School for Girls, at the Iris club.

Her guests will be members of her class and their escorts. The guest list includes: Misses Barbara Bell, Sally Schell, Jeanne Stevens, Jeanne Haverstick, Martha Griest, Barbara Smith, Cynthia Draper, Nancy Demuth, Kathryn Hambright, Harriet Ann Shand, Nan Barr and Nancy Strickler.

Also, Ken Stoudt, James Holdsworth, Nat Esten, Jerry Lacy, William Merrill, Sam Sardo, Walter Aierstock, Frank McCorkle, Bob Landis, Charles Erisman, Tom Flotte, Dick Landis, Bob Rossell and Dick Barr.

Entertains

Miss M. Elizabeth Sauer who is entertaining at a bridge luncheon at the Stevens House today in honor of Mrs. Henry C. Dobbs.

Miss Sauer Gives Party for Mrs. Dobbs

Miss M. Elizabeth Sauer, of 136 Juniata street, entertained this afternoon at a bridge luncheon at the Stevens House in honor of Mrs. Henry C. Dobbs, formerly Miss Jeanette Kreider. Decorations were in spring flowers and individual pond-lily candles.

Other guests were Mrs. Richard Oblender, Mrs. A. N. Gingrich, Mrs. Garfield Fellman, Mrs. Mabel S. Lehman, Mrs. Miriam Cope, Mrs. Baker Royer, of Ephrata, Mrs. John R. Leaman, of Philadelphia, and Misses Marion E. Everett, Helen M. Lamparter, Sara Leaman, Thelma Binkele, Dorothy I. McQuate and Miriam E. Good.

Homecoming Banquet Is Held by Nurses

The Nurses' Alumnae association of the Lancaster General Hospital held its annual Homecoming banquet, last evening at the General Sutter hotel, Lititz. Approximately 225 graduate nurses of the Hospital attended.

Decorations were in pink and white, with a centerpiece of pink and white carnations and snapdragons.

Miss Minnie White, the guest of honor, who was the first nurse graduated from the hospital in 1905, was presented with an orchid corsage. She was introduced to the guests by Miss Mae Brenner.

Miss Edna Schreiber gave a short history of the Hospital. Miss Vesta Miller was toastmistress. Letters congratulating the association were read from graduates who were unable to attend. A phone call was received from Anna Reist Baird, who arrived in Berkeley, Calif., Friday from Korea, and who flew from Berkeley to Lancaster.

Steed-Jones Wedding To Take Place June 5

The marriage of Miss Mildred Louise Jones, daughter of Mrs. Frew Jones, of Paradise, and G. Hubert Steed, Jr., son of the Rev. and Mrs. G. H. Steed, of New York City, will take place on Thursday afternoon, June 5, at 4 o'clock in the Leacock Presbyterian church, Paradise. The bridegroom's father will officiate.

Given in marriage by her grandfather, Harry S. Frew, of Paradise, the bride will be attended by her sister, Miss Mary E. Jones, as maid of honor; and Miss Mary Scott, of Paradise, and Miss Betty Jones, another sister, as bridesmaids.

John Davenport, of Westfield, N. J., will be the best man, and the ushers are Joseph Zettler, of Washington Crossing, Pa.; Joseph Pritts, and Wallace Bishop, both of Somerset, Pa. Mrs. Willis Herr will be organist.

A reception will be held at the bride's home. They will reside in New York City.

Mumper and Shenk Nuptials at Grace

The marriage of Miss Frances E. Shenk, daughter of Mr. and Mrs. T. R. Shenk, of Lancaster R. D. 3, and Levi D. Mumper, son of Mrs. Cleo Mumper, of 965 East King street, took place last evening at 6 o'clock, in Grace Lutheran church. The Rev. Allen L. Benner, D. D., officiated.

The bride, given in marriage by her father, wore white silk marquisette, with a lace bodice. Her elbow length veil fell from a Juliet cap of shirred tulle. She carried a bouquet of gardenias and lilies of the valley.

Miss Edith Thompson was the bride's only attendant. She wore a gown of heavenly blue marquisette, with a large natural straw hat and carried yellow daisies. Harry Dayhoff, of Harrisburg, was best man. Miss Josephine Kirkland was organist.

A reception was held at the Buchanan Tea room. After a cruise to Havana, they will reside at 965 East King street.

HEAVE TO AND GET STARTED!

SAILOR TOWELS PATTERN 2728

Just as much fun to embroider as to dry dishes with, these sailor towels make top-notch work for summer days. And how quickly the cross stitch and other easy stitches go! Pattern 2728 contains a transfer pattern of 7 motifs averaging 5 x 8 inches; color schemes; illustrations of stitches; materials required.

Write plainly pattern number, your name and address.

Send ten cents in coin for this pattern to Needlecraft Dept., Lancaster New Era, 82 Eighth avenue, New York, N. Y.

Engaged

Miss Marguerite Keller, of Mount Joy, whose engagement to Harry G. Walters of Mount Joy, has been announced.

Personals

Major and Mrs. W. Sanderson Detwiler, of Marietta avenue and School Lane, are attending the Bach Festival at Bethlehem today.

Mrs. Robert W. Troup, of Wheatland avenue, and Mrs. Benjamin W. Shaub, of College avenue, spent yesterday in Philadelphia, attending the Hey Day activities at the University of Pennsylvania.

Mrs. A. R. Stamy, of North Lime street, is spending the week-end with Miss Emily Stamy, in Shippensburg.

Mrs. J. Harlan Landes, of College avenue, has returned from Pittsburgh where she attended a convention of the Pennsylvania League of Women Voters.

Mr. and Mrs. Russell G. Shelly, of South President avenue, will have as week-end guests, Mr. and Mrs. Emmert Herr, of Elizabethtown.

Mr. and Mrs. George H. Kroeger, of North President avenue, have as week-end guests, Miss Emily Tea and Mrs. Clare Gallagher, of Larchmont, N. Y.

Mr. and Mrs. Harold F. Herr, of Miami, Fla., are coming today to spend some time with the former's sisters, the Misses Herr, of West Chestnut street.

Mr. and Mrs. Elvin S. Sheaffer, of Haskell Drive, and Mr. and Mrs. Paul Dissler and daughter, Floy, of Ephrata, have returned after spending several days in Pittsburgh.

Miss Frances Prutzman, a student at Lebanon Valley College is spending the week-end with her parents, Mr. and Mrs. Paul W. Prutzman, of Maple avenue.

Miss Louise Schaffner, of New York City, is spending the week-end with her mother, Mrs. Paul F. Schaffner, of North Lime street.

Theodore Hoskins, a student at the University of Pennsylvania, is spending the week-end with his parents, Mr. and Mrs. F. E. Hoskins, of Columbia avenue.

A shower was given by girls of the Bell Telephone Company in honor of Mrs. John Krantz, the former Miss Catherine Kirchner, at the home of her parents, 668 West Vine street. Those present were: Mrs. Carl Schaller, Mrs. Strickler, Mrs. Charles Krantz, Misses Kathryn B. Wendel, Adeline McCaughey, Alda Thompson, Mary LeFever, Eva Fasnacht, Agnes Long, Margaret Eggensberger, Gertrude Ganse, Miriam Rosenbaum, Mary Kempf, Bertie Frederick, Jeanette Gensemer, Jane Gehman, Sara Bergstresser, Bertha Huegel, Betty Weidman, Mary, Margaret, Rose and Patricia Kirchner and Mrs. A. G. Kirchner.

Mr. and Mrs. Park C. Devonshire, of Mountville, entertained this week in honor of their daughter, Gloria Jean, who celebrated her first birthday anniversary. Those present were: Mr. and Mrs. Levi A. C. Devonshire and children, Elizabeth, William and Glenn, of Soudersburg; Miss Elizabeth Shissler, Mr. and Mrs. Herman S. Good, Mr. and Mrs. William C. Good and daughters, Helen and Ruth, all of Lancaster.

The Village Book Club, of Millersville, held the annual banquet Wednesday evening at "The Trees." The following attended: Mr. and Mrs. George Kittridge, Mr. and Mrs. Edward Lingle, Rev. and Mrs. E. A. Lebo, Mr. and Mrs. Milton Steinhauer, Mr. and Mrs. Raymond Hovis and Dr. and Mrs. L. C. Rees.

Mrs. James E. Downes, of Summit, N. J., is spending the week-end with her uncle and aunt, Mr. and Mrs. L. G. McNeal, of Princeton avenue. She is a graduate nurse of the Lancaster General Hospital and attended the reunion banquet last evening at the General Sutter hotel.

Perry Kendig, a member of the faculty of Muhlenberg college, Allentown, is spending the week-end at his home in Mountville.

Mrs. George Kain, of York, entertained at a dessert bridge party at her home, yesterday for Miss Elizabeth Suter, of Wheatland avenue, whose marriage to Lawrence H. Dunlap, takes place on June 2. A number of local girls attended. Mrs. Kain is the former Miss Sally Ruth, of this city.

Miss Betty Chodos, daughter of Dr. and Mrs. B. P. Chodos, of West Chestnut street, is spending the week-end with her brother, Robert, a student at the Medical School of the University of Pennsylvania.

Mr. and Mrs. Charles Smithgall and daughters, Mary, Sara and Ann, of Race avenue, will spend tomorrow in Reading, visiting Mr. and Mrs. Harry Goodhart.

Mrs. Augustine R. Hoenninger, of West Vine street, entertained at a miscellaneous shower, at her home, this week for Miss Mary Burger, of St. Joseph street, whose marriage to Joseph Crnkovich will take place on May 27. Decorations were in white, with a centerpiece of bridal wreath and white tapers. Those present were Mrs. Philip Burger, Mrs. Robert Crnkovich, Mrs. Joseph Gardner, Mrs. Vincent Klos, Mrs. Earl Keggel, Mrs. Paul Checkley, Mrs. Vincent Keller, Mrs. George Kuhns, Mrs. Richard Danz, Mrs. Donald Wireback, Mrs. Clement Burger, Mrs. Edwin Schultz, Mrs. Anna Kieffer, Mrs. John Matt, Mrs. Anna Kieffer, Mrs. Frank Butzer. Also, Misses Magdalene Klos, Sophie Burger, Mary Billmyer, Emma Springman, Theresa Long, Carmelita and Geraldine Burger.

M. S. T. C. Garden Party Chairman

Miss Ruth Warfel, who has been president of the Womens Day Student Organization of M. S. T. C. for the past year, is general chairman of the garden party for all High school seniors, today on the college campus.

Engaged

Miss Viola Lawrence, daughter of Mr. and Mrs. George Lawrence, of East Marion street, whose engagement to Robert McCaslin, of 252 Elm street, has been announced.

Will Be Bride

Miss Mary Ellen Hurst, of North Lime street, whose marriage to Ray D. Andrews will take place on June 4.

Miss McCreary Entertained at Drop-in Tea

Mrs. Harry W. McCreary and daughter, Esther, of Lititz, are having a drop-in tea at their home this afternoon from 3 to 6 o'clock in honor of Miss Lillian McCreary, whose marriage to William Gates, son of Dr. and Mrs. Paul Gates, of Lebanon, will take place in the near future. Mrs. J. C. H. Light and Mrs. Frank Spickler presided at the tea urns, and pink snapdragons, yellow daisies and tall yellow candles formed a centerpiece for the tea tables.

Guests are: Mrs. Paul Gates, Lebanon; Mrs. Henry Kreider, Annville; Mrs. Arlene Kline, Mrs. Linneaus Roth, Mrs. Chester Ruth, Mrs. Henry Neff, Mrs. Tobias Erline, Mrs. William Oehme, Mrs. Irene Keenan, Mrs. Gilbert Keener, Mrs. Howard Keener, Mrs. Calvin Weitzel, Mrs. Eugene Stauffer, Mrs. Robert Batdorf, Mrs. Paul Meiskey, Mrs. Paul Spickler, Mrs. Robert Myers, Mrs. Wilbur Wolfe, Mrs. Vernon Dillman, Mrs. Donald Hyde, Mrs. Mahlon Frey, Mrs. Ellis Spickler, all of Lititz.

Misses Fay Musser, Evelyn Irwin, Helen Oehme, Jane Miller, Mary Sturgis, Mary Ellen Howard, Rhoda Nagle, Annabelle Minnich, Beatrice Batdorf, Sara Weidman, Edith Wertsch, Mildred Gangwer, Winifred Shaeffer, Marian Rosenberg, Irene Whitcraft, Mary Dengate, Margaret Longenecker, Arlyne Demmy, Dorothy Spickler, Helen Farrand, Teresa Klunk, Anna and Amelia Miller, all of Lititz.

Mrs. George Mason, Mrs. Barton Kent, Oxford; Mrs. Verla Williams, Mrs. Mary Brewster, Mrs. James O'Connell, Manheim.

Mrs. Edwin Leeking, Mrs. Phares Hollinger, Mrs. Lloyd Neff, Mrs. John Esslinger, Mrs. Adam Eckert, Mrs. Roy Rutt, Mrs. Henry Zook, Mrs. Harry Adams, Mrs. Elmer Ehrhart, Mrs. Eugene Deckert, Mrs. Frank Martin, Lititz.

Mrs. William Brossman, Mrs. William Hibshman, Ephrata; Miss Sue Schock, Mt. Joy; Mrs. Robert Adams, Jonestown; Mrs. Raymond Gundal, Manchester; Mrs. Alma Sheetz, Rothsville; Misses Dorothy and Emma McCreary, Rothsville; Mrs. Frank McCreary, Durlach; Mrs. Clair Weber, New Holland; Miss Evelyn Farrand, Philadelphia; Mrs. Virginia Enck, Miss Maybelle Stark, Lancaster; Mrs. Harry Rutt, Hinkletown; Mrs. Earl Reist, Trenton, N. J.

TRINITY MISSION SOCIETY

Trinity Lutheran Missionary society will meet Monday evening at 7:45 o'clock in the chapel. Mrs. M. Ray Adams will be in charge of the topic, "I Was a Stranger and Ye Took Me In." Devotions will be led by Mrs. A. B. MacIntosh.

Miss Hurst Announces Her Wedding Plans

Invitations have been issued for the marriage of Miss Mary Ellen Hurst, daughter of Mr. and Mrs. Leman S. Hurst, of 31 North Lime street and Roy David Andrews, son of Mr. and Mrs. Roy Andrews, of Lancaster.

The wedding will take place on Wednesday evening, June 4, at 6 o'clock in the Covenant United Brethren church, the Rev. O. T. Ehrhart officiating at the double ring ceremony.

She will be given in marriage by her father and will be attended by Miss Charlotte Fanelli as maid-of-honor. Miss Kathryn Folkman and Miss Jane Olt will be bridesmaids. Miss Emma Anne Hurst, sister of the bride, will be Junior bridesmaid. The best man will be Rictor Auman. The ushers will be Elvin J. Groff and Charles Weitkamp.

Preceding the ceremony, a short organ recital will be given by Miss Ruth Coble, who will also play the wedding marches and incidental music. Miss Jane Weaver will be soloist.

Both Miss Hurst and Mr. Andrews were graduated from McCaskey High school, class of 1939. Miss Hurst is employed at the Armstrong Linoleum plant and Mr. Andrews is in business with his father.

Linden Hall Senior Prom This Evening

Linden Hall Junior College will hold its annual Senior Prom, this evening, from 9 to 12 o'clock at the General Sutter hotel, Lititz. Music will be furnished by a local orchestra.

Among the local girls attending will be Miss Violet Delp, Miss Nancy Sheaffer, Miss Betty Jane Mellinger, Miss Helen Peiper, Miss Jane Lamparter, Miss Dorothy Kranich, Miss Minna Lestz, all of Lancaster; Miss Helen Posey, Miss Mary Sue Brubaker, Miss Jean Eberly and Miss Mary Hammond, all of Lititz.

The annual May Day Pageant and Horse Show will be held on Memorial Day, Friday, May 30. The Horse Show is scheduled for 9 A. M. and the pageant for 2 P. M.

Miss Louise Wallravon is directing the pageant, assisted by Miss Natalie Levy.

Student committees are: Publicity, Miss Violet Delp, chairman, Miss Jeannette Hoskins; program, Miss Janet Tombonson, chairman, Miss Patsy Seip; music, Miss Mary Hammond, chairman, Miss Mary Jane Francis, Miss Mary Sue Brubaker.

Properties, Miss Ruth Goldman, chairman, Miss Helen Housel; costumes, Miss Betty Edmondson, chairman, Miss Francoise Weinmann, Miss Mary Ryman.

Wed Today

Mrs. William H. Ehemann, who before her marriage this morning in St. Mary's rectory was Miss Jane B. Finegan, daughter of George W. Finegan, of this city.

Married Today

Mrs. Ira Herr Kauffman who before her marriage today was Miss Mildred Minerva Bomberger, of West James street.

WEDDINGS

Jane Finegan Wed To William Ehemann

The marriage of Miss Jane B. Finegan, daughter of George W. Finegan, and William H. Ehemann, son of William A. Ehemann, of this city, took place this morning, at 10:30 o'clock in the rectory of St. Mary's church. The Rev. George W. Brown, rector, officiated.

Mr. and Mrs. Ehemann will be home at 14 East Walnut street, after June 10.

The bride is a graduate of Parkesburg High school and Lancaster Business college. She is employed in the Advertising department of Watt and Shand. Mr. Ehemann was graduated from Lancaster High school and is employed at Armstrong Cork company.

MYLLY—PRUTZMAN

Miss Julia M. Prutzman, daughter of Mr. and Mrs. Paul W. Prutzman of 1196 Maple avenue, became the bride of W. John Mylly of this city, son of Mr. and Mrs. John Mylly, of Gloucester, Mass., this morning, at 10 o'clock in Covenant United Brethren church. Dr. O. T. Ehrhart officiated.

Given in marriage by her father, the bride wore white chiffon, with a fingertip length veil. She carried a bouquet of mixed white flowers.

Miss Charlotte Prutzman, sister of the bride, was maid of honor. Her gown was light blue chiffon. She wore a tiara of flowers and carried mixed flowers.

Russell Walters, of Baltimore, a cousin of the bride, was best man. Mrs. Mildred Huss Wissler was organist and Mrs. William Sneddon, of Tamaqua, soloist. Miss Frances Prutzman accompanied the latter.

A reception was held at Kauffman's near Manheim. After a trip, the couple will reside at 837 Columbia avenue.

HERR—GOCHENAUR

The marriage of Miss Ruth M. Gochenaur, daughter of Mr. and Mrs. Albert Gochenaur, of 25 South Broad street, Lititz, and Raymond G. Herr, son of Mr. and Mrs. Henry R. Herr, of Willow Street, R. D. 1, took place this afternoon, at 3 o'clock in the Moravian church, Lititz. The Rev. Byron K. Horne officiated.

Mr. and Mrs. Harry M. Herr, brother and sister-in-law of the bridegroom, were the attendants.

The bride wore a beige suit with brown accessories and a corsage of orchids. The matron of honor wore a navy sheer suit with navy and white accessories and a corsage of gardenias.

After a trip through the New England states, they will reside at Willow Street.

The bride is a graduate of the Lancaster General Hospital Training School for Nurses.

Letter Writina Easy If You Know Rules

The Paper Bigger Each Minute!

How huge a little sheet of notepaper can look when you've written "We're all well here"—and haven't another idea!

Letters stump some very clever people, so don't be discouraged. But do learn the interesting yet simple ways to write them or friends will lose interest in you.

A friendly letter is really easy. Gossip, talk about the weather, the book you read, the movie you saw! No matter how tiny the tit-bit your friend loves to read it because it's from you.

Then ask what he's doing. How does he like his new job, his new town? If he's spoken of at home, tell him so! "Mrs. Taylor told us she met you in Boomtown—lucky woman!"

Don't let your letters sound rushed. To sign "In haste, Mary" is really insulting. Write "Sincerely yours" or "Affectionately yours." And, in writing to Mrs. James Burt, take care not to address her wrongly as "Mrs. Ruth Burt"—even if she is a widow.

Thank-you letters? Sympathy notes? Our 32-page booklet helps you write them, gives sample letters including invitations, job applications, many other types. Tip on grammar, correct form.

Send 10c in coin for your copy of GOOD LETTER-WRITING MADE EASY to Home Service, Lancaster New Era, 635 Sixth Ave., New York, N. Y. Be sure to write plainly your NAME, ADDRESS, and the NAME of booklet.

Miss Bomberger Wed in Virginia

Mr. and Mrs. George D. Kilberry, of 336 West James street, announce the marriage of their daughter, Mildred Minerva Bomberger, and Ira Herr Kauffman, son of Mr. and Mrs. Harry M. Kauffman, of Lancaster, R. D. 2, which took place today at noon at Norfolk, Va. The ceremony was performed in the Freemason Street Baptist church by the Rev. Sparks W. Melton, D. D.

They were attended by Mr. and Mrs. Guy K. Herr, of Norfolk.

The bride wore blue silk sheer with blue and white accessories and a corsage of gardenias. Her attendant wore soldier blue with navy accessories and a corsage of pink carnations and blue delphinium.

After a short wedding trip they will reside in Rohrerstown. The bride is employed at the Watt and Shand store and Mr. Kauffman has a farm implement store and garage at Mountville.

Miss Gelwix Betrothed To Lieut R. B. Bare

Dr. and Mrs. John Montgomery Gelwix, of 51 South Second street, Chambersburg, announce the engagement of their daughter, Miss Mary Virginia Gelwix, to Lieut. Richard Breneman Bare, son of Mr. and Mrs. Ira H. Bare, of West Orange street, this city.

Miss Gelwix is a graduate of Wilson College, Chambersburg, and is known here through her former connection with the Community Service Association. Lieut. Bare is a graduate of Franklin and Marshall College and was associated with a local brokerage firm until called to service at Indiantown Gap, as a member of the Pennsylvania National Guard.

Helen Hersh Is Wed Today to K. I. Witmer

The marriage of Miss Helen Hersh, daughter of Mr. and Mrs. J. B. Hersh, of South Marshall street and Kenenth I. Witmer, son of Mr. and Mrs. I. M. Witmer, of East King street, takes place this afternoon, at 4 o'clock, in Memorial Presbyterian church. The Rev. C. A. Underwood officiates.

Given in marriage by her father, the bride is wearing a gown of white chiffon, with inserts of lace in the bodice and midriff. Her full skirt falls into a long train. She is wearing a finger-tip length veil caught to a coronet of orange blossoms and she is carrying a shower bouquet of white snapdragons, roses, lilies-of-the-valley and daisies.

The attendants are Mrs. Norman Johnson and Mrs. Clement Rohrer. Their gowns are made similar to the bride's; Mrs. Johnson in yellow chiffon and Mrs. Rohrer in aqua chiffon. They are wearing matching flowers in their hair and are carrying mixed spring flowers.

J. Brame Witmer is best man for his brother and the ushers are John Bell and J. Kenneth Hersh, brother of the bride. Leslie Harnley is organist and Miss Bettie Kile, soloist.

A reception for the immediate families and a few friends will be held at the bridegroom's home, following the ceremony.

Mrs. Hersh, mother of the bride, is wearing a blue and white printed dress with a corsage of pink rosebuds. Mrs. Witmer, mother of the bridegroom, is wearing a blue and pink printed dress with a corsage of pink rosebuds.

For going away, the bride will wear a pink gabardine suit, with brown and white accessories and a corsage of talisman roses. After a trip to New York, they will reside at 455 South Shippen street.

Mr. and Mrs. Clement Rohrer entertained members of the bridal party, at their home, Lancaster, R. D. 5, on Thursday evening, following the nuptial rehearsal. Mrs. Norman Johnson, of East Walnut street, gave a shower for the bride, at the home of her mother, Mrs. Charles Kile, of South Queen street, recently.

HOROSCOPE

The next year will prove an eventful one for those celebrating birthdays today. It will be one long remembered, as there will be some gain, but also upheavals, trouble in love, domestic and business affairs, it is foreseen. They should safeguard their health. Born on this date a child will also experience disappointment or trouble in love, and have sudden losses and unexpected changes to contend with. There will also be a predisposition to accidents.

HINTS ON ETIQUETTE

It is not good manners to boast to strangers of your sophistication; it also leads them to think you are naive rather than sophisticated.

Socially, a Woman Is No Longer "Miss" Once She Is Married

By EMILY POST

In the following example I think the friend referred to is being unnecessarily cavilling (or perhaps a better word would be stubborn!) to refuse to call a once-married woman Miss Mary Blank. An explanation of details from Miss Mary Blank is this: "I was married only a few months and then left my husband. In due course I was divorced. As I had been a teacher and had been married so short a time, I went back to teaching under my maiden name and again called myself Miss Mary Blank. I have used that name ever since at all times. A man I know refuses to write me, introduce me or even ask for me on the telephone as Miss. He merely uses my two names—Mary Blank—without any title. I think he is considerably more impolite than I am wrong. He says he is right and that he is merely following your advice."

EMILY POST

Your friend is right about my advice so far as this: Socially and personally a woman who has once been married is no longer "Miss." Professionally and impersonally she may be "Miss" if she chooses. But this piece of advice concerns you and not him, and in my opinion he is unexcusably wrong in refusing to call you whatever you may choose to call yourself. That you are putting yourself in a false situation by using the maiden prefix in your personal and social life, is another story.

* * *

LOSING SOMEONE ELSE'S MONEY

Dear Mrs. Post: When I visited my cousin not long ago we went to the circus. I had a small purse in my handbag with twenty-five dollars in it and I mentioned that I was afraid I might lose this. So he put the small purse in his inside pocket for safekeeping. In some way it wasn't safe and he lost it. This really means a good deal to me but I don't think he should feel that it is up to him to give me the money. He thinks it is and worries about it. What do you think?

Answer: I think, if your cousin persuaded you to give the purse to him for safekeeping, that the responsibility of making up the money is his. But if you asked him to take it, then I think with you that he should not be permitted to stand the loss.

* * *

A WOMAN LIVING ALONE

Dear Mrs. Post: I live alone in a small apartment for the first time in my life—which is almost thirty years long. When a man calls to take me out, is it proper for me to invite him up to the apartment for a short while the way I used to do at home, or must I always meet my men friends, when they come singly, downstairs?

Answer: It is quite all right for a friend to come up but not when he brings you home if it is late. The only question is that it might be more convenient for you to meet downstairs and let him come to see you some other evening at an early hour, when he can stay longer.

Bismarck Carried 2,400 Including 400 Young Cadets

NAZI SURVIVOR TELLS OF SINKING

British Quote German Sailor Of Final Battle As Saying "It Was Hell"

(By EDDY GILMORE)

A British Port—(AP)—The Battleship Bismarck, pride of the German navy, was crowded with 2,400 officers and men, 400 of them cadets under 20 years of age, when she sank under the blows of the British navy, a German survivor of the Bismarck was quoted Friday as saying to his British rescuers.

"That seems like an awful lot," declared one of the officers aboard a British ship which has just returned from helping sink the Nazi conqueror of the British battle cruiser Hood.

The British have reported approximately 100 officers and men were rescued from the Bismarck, whose normal complement was estimated at about 1,500 in previous accounts.

It was a case of "remember the Hood," the British officers said, and a German survivor gave a brief but dramatic story of how well they avenged the biggest ship in the world.

"'It was hell'," the British quoted this prisoner as saying.

"'Great holes burst out in us and flames spread around every direction.

"'We'd run this way and then something else would hit.

"'It was hideous'."

GREATEST THRILL

The British officer who pulled the trigger that spelled the final doom to the 35,000-ton German battleship Bismarck lounged against a table, balanced a tea cup delicately and said calmly that the event had been the greatest thrill in his life.

"When we came up the Bismarck seemed to be having the time of her life with some of our other ships," he said after his arrival in port.

"I pressed my finger on the trigger," he said, when the Captain told him to fire.

"What was your feeling?" I asked him.

"Well," he laughed, "I kept thinking what a bloody fool the fellows back at school would say I was if I missed."

But he didn't miss.

"From where I was standing," another officer said, "it looked as if clouds of dust were rising from the Bismarck. Oh, he didn't miss."

"We got around to the side of her and let her have a third shot," the gunnery officer continued.

The Bismarck then turned slowly over on her side, he said, adding "it was the most amazing sight of my life. She was really lovely."

"We could see her main mast hanging like a mass of vines and her turrets were spinning around. Her guns lay about in a mess."

Another officer took up the description.

THREW ROPES TO SURVIVORS

The sea was a mass of Nazi sailors, he said.

"Every available man was throwing ropes over to them and we must have lost thousands of fathoms of rope as we dragged them up."

"One German," the officer said, "had his arm almost blown off. I saw another between two of our men being dragged along the deck and then they dropped him. I came up and asked them why."

He said that the men had replied that the German sailor was dead.

"Two of us got to work on him," the officer continued, "and giving him first aid brought him around. He was told to speak English and he told plenty about what happened on the Bismarck."

Here, another officer broke in with "You've got to say this for her though, she never struck her ensign. She kept it up for the whole time and stuck to her guns the best she was able."

"Yes," said the first officer. "Another prisoner told me he was amazed at how accurate our fire was.

"You know I'm no gunner so I can talk about it. The sea that day was blowing up in a furious gale and it was very cold. It is a great tribute to our marksmanship."

"Just because it was what we've wanted," said another officer, "we kept remembering the Hood."

How The Bismarck Was Trapped By British Fire

This is an artist's conception of "Finis" in the saga of Germany's great battleship, Bismarck, sunk in the Atlantic by one of the largest naval forces ever assembled for a single fight. The drawing is based on the British Admiralty's incomplete story of a long running sea fight that ended when more than a dozen warships closed in on the Bismarck, 400 miles off Brest, France.

The British cruiser Dorsetshire, in the foreground, is shown delivering the final torpedo blow to the Bismarck, crippled by blows to its steering and propelling mechanism. Ringing the proud German vessel, already listing in the water with its forecastle afire, are British destroyers and, in the distance, other ships; above is one of the planes responsible for spotting the ship and striking the first blows.

Hundreds Of German Seamen Floated In Sea With No Rafts To Cling To

British Petty Officer Says 40 Salvos From Guns And Three "Steel Fish" Finished The Bismarck

An English Port—(AP)—Hundreds of German seamen floundered helplessly in the sea with no life rafts to cling to after 40 British salvos and three "steel fish" sent the 35,000-ton battleship Bismarck, pride of the German navy, to the bottom last Tuesday, the chief petty officer of a British warship said Friday.

The warship arrived here with approximately 100 German officers and men who survived the Bismarck.

In the words of the petty officer, the Rodney and another British battleship "banged hell out of her," and two British torpedoes lifted her bodily out of the water before the third sent the new dreadnaught to the bottom in revenge for destruction of Britain's 42,100-ton battle cruiser Hood.

"There were a lot of Jerries in the water," said Chief Petty Officer L. R. Crocker, "and there was nothing for them to hold on to, not even a raft, although some of them were wearing Japanese lifebelts."

(The exact complement of the Bismarck was not known, but a ship of her size normally would carry from 1,000 to 1,300 men. The latter was the number aboard the Hood, and only three survived.)

Crocker said rescue efforts were halted by attacks of German submarines and aircraft on British ships attempting to pick up the survivors and he quoted one Nazi officer as saying: "'It is a bad policy to pick up survivors in wartime.'"

"I couldn't understand a ship of the type of the Bismarck not having rafts," Crocker continued. "The biggest thing I saw afloat was a piece of timber about six feet long."

EYE-WITNESS STORY

Crocker gave the following eye-witness account of the Bismarck's last bitter hours:

"We sighted the Bismarck about 9 a. m. Tuesday. She was then engaged and doing barely ten knots.

"She fired a number of salvoes which came over the top. We gave her three salvoes for'ard. The Bismarck had to be destroyed and we were out to do it.

"I could see explosions bursting aboard the German, which was concentrating her fire mainly on the Rodney (British battleship). I guess the Nazis were surprised to see us. It's my belief, anyway, that they didn't spot us until our salvoes crashed into them.

"Now the Bismarck was afire, but her guns were still roaring.

"At the end of an hour's action, the Bismarck stopped moving altogether. The Rodney and another British battleship were banging hell out of her."

One of the returning British craft had 24 German seamen aboard, none of them officers. All were grimly silent. The first German down the gangplank had to be carried on the back of a medical corps private; his head was swathed in bandages.

Many of the survivors wore no shoes, indicating that they had been in the water for some time before being picked up.

Continuing his story, Crocker declared:

"As we went in closer to do our stuff, I saw our shells knock the brains out of the Bismarck. We smashed her after-control and the fire aboard her was spreading.

But the Nazis had guts.

"The Rodney knocked her after-turrent clean out until it was hanging over the side. The Bismarck was now ablaze from stem to stern, and her guns at last were silent.

"The order came to sink the Bismarck, and we banged her like the devil with our guns giving her roughly 40 salvoes.

"After that, we put two steel fish into the starboard side. I saw many of the Nazis waving coats as the Bismarck's stern was awash. The weather was blowing hard by this time and visibility was low. That's how we'd surprised her.

"The torpedoes lifted her bodily out of the water. What a sight! Then a cruiser from port side slammed a third torpedo into her, and that finished her off. It was the last shot fired.

"The Bismarck stood up for a few seconds and gradually keeled over towards the port side.

"Then she turned right over, showing her keel, and slid back. As she disappeared she seemed to break up.

"There were a lot of Jerries in the water and there was nothing for them to hold onto—not even a raft—although some of them were wearing Japanese lifebelts.

"If they had had rafts or boats more of them would have been saved.

"We steamed up to the survivors and started picking them up.

"There were roughly about eight (in one group) and they were punch drunk with gunfire and didn't know whether they were coming or going.

"German submarines and aircraft were reported and this caused rescue work to be stopped. We beat it.

"There were no casualties on our ship.

"On the runback to this country one of the survivors died and was buried at sea.

"We didn't have the Nazi ensign to use at the burial so an old German imperial ensign was used.

"All Nazi officers and men on deck gave the Nazi salute as the remains went over the side. Full naval honors were carried out by the British officers and men.

"Actually the Nazis were glad to be aboard our ship after the terrific hammering they received. Their attitude was pretty good and they showed no signs of truculence.

"One of the officers told me he and the crew were convinced that the Bismarck was unsinkable. Well, they learned differently.

"A British officer told me some of the survivors gave the Hitler salute to the British ensign on being pulled aboard.

"A former Nazi naval attache in London who was one of those saved gave short thanks to the British officers. He said, 'It is a bad policy to pick up any survivors in wartime.' That Nazi seemed very indifferent whether he was rescued or not.

"After recovering, some of the prisoners played the piano in our recreation room and sang the 'Blue Danube'. Then they received a plate of soup with bread. They were under the impression it was the whole meal. Roast beef and vegetables followed. That gave them a shock. When pudding was served they seemed flabbergasted."

BISMARCK A 50,000-TON VESSEL, BRITISH SAY

London—(AP)—The Bismarck was a 50,000-ton vessel instead of the 35,000 carried in official registers, a British naval officer who participated in the German battleship's destruction declared Friday night.

Such a tonnage would have made the Bismarck the world's largest warship. The 42,100-ton battle cruiser Hood, which the Bismarck destroyed, had long been classed as the world's largest.

"The Bismarck was undoubtedly far above anything we had thought of," said the officer.

GRIN AND BEAR IT — By. Lichty

"This is the time of the year when Ed takes out the straw hat he packed away so neatly and carefully last autumn and decides to buy a new one!"

Parts Of Hood's Hull Fly Hundreds Of Feet In Air In Last Fatal Blast

Eye-Wtiness To "Battle Of Giants" Says British Ship Went Down Within Few Minutes Of Terrific Explosion

(By J. R. N. NIXON)
(Reuters Special Correspondent With the Royal Navy)

London—I watched the "battle of giants" which culminated in the sinking of the 35,000-ton German battleship Bismarck.

Standing on the bridge of one of His Majesty's ships I saw the 42,100-ton HMS Hood, long the world's largest warship, go down only 200 or 300 yards away with her guns still firing.

The end of the mighty Hood was an almost unbelievable nightmare. Shortly after the engagement began shells hit the 21-year-old battle cruiser.

There was a bright sheet of flame and she blew up.

PARTS OF HULL THROWN UP

Parts of her great hull were thrown hundreds of feet into the air and in a few minutes all that remained was a patch of smoke on the water and some small bits of wreckage.

The battleship Prince of Wales was hit soon afterward by a 15-inch naval shell but the damage was slight.

The "battle of the giants" was the climax of a chase by the Hood and Prince of Wales and their accompanying destroyers at top speed to prevent the Bismarck from breaking out into the Atlantic to attack convoys.

Pursuit began off Iceland and continued hour after hour in the eerie half-light of an Arctic night.

The cruisers Suffolk and Norfolk, which had been shadowing the Bismarck since the big vessel left Bergen, Norway, kept the Hood and the Prince of Wales informed of her movements and thus helped find the quarry.

It did not get completely dark at any time that night.

We sighted the enemy at 6 a. m. when a curtain of snow suddenly lifted.

For some minutes our ships sped on toward the Germans to shorten the range.

'OPEN FIRE' SIGNAL

They too (the Germans) turned in toward their pursuers and the world's biggest warships were thundering toward each other at a combined speed of probably more than 60 miles an hour.

The tension of waiting for the battle to begin became acute.

The "open fire" order was given by signal.

Almost simultaneously, orange-gold flame burst with a roar from the Hood's forward guns. Within three seconds puffs of black smoke shot out from the Bismarck as she opened fire.

The Prince of Wales' guns then began firing. Dense clouds of yellow cordite smoke enveloped her bridge. She was to the left of the Hood, two or three hundred yards away, and still surging forward on a parallel course.

Fountains of water shot up in her wake—first about 100 yards behind her and then only 50 yards astern.

The Hood thundered on and then, suddenly, she was hit.

A shell, or shells, appeared to fall just forward of one of her after 15-inch gun turrets and great flames and heavy black smoke burst from her.

END OF THE HOOD

The Hood continued to fire and still raced forward.

What happened next was a strangling, sickening sight. There was a terrific explosion and the whole of a vast ship was enveloped in a flash of flame and smoke which rose high into the air in the shape of a giant mushroom.

Sections of funnels, masts and other parts of the ship hurtled hundreds of feet into the air and some of them fell on our ship.

The Hood's bow tilted vertically into the air and within three or four minutes she was gone entirely.

A destroyer was diverted to rescue work and managed to pick up three of the ship's company—two seamen and a midshipman.

All this time the Prince of Wales continued pouring shells at the Bismarck. More than once spurts of water showed she was straddled.

Again shells from the Bismarck crashed near the Prince of Wales, but she came out of the battle with little damage.

Then the Bismarck turned away to be pursued all that day and night and the next day over the Atlantic at top speed.

Twice during the night the Prince of Wales fired salvos and aircraft made attacks.

Finally there came the dramatic message that the cruiser Dorsetshire had torpedoed the Bismarck.

Japan Has Not Swerved From Axis Pact, Matsuoka Asserts

Foreign Minister Warns Nation May Have To Reconsider Peaceful Policy Towards South Seas

Tokyo—(AP)—Japan has not swerved an inch from the Axis tripartite pact, Foreign Minister Yosuke Matsuoka said Friday, and may—if world developments are deemed untoward,—even have to reconsider her peaceful policy toward the South Seas.

The Foreign Minister was speaking to Japanese newspapermen, replying to reports in some United States newspapers that Japan was cooling toward the Axis and seeking a loophole in the Tri-Partite Treaty, which binds Germany, Italy and Japan to come to each other's aid if one of the signatories is attacked by a power not now at war with them. (At the time this section of the treaty was interpreted as directed at either the United States or Russia, or both.)

His reference to the South Seas was interpreted as a warning to The Netherlands East Indies, with which Japan is deadlocked in economic negotiations. The Japanese are demanding that the N. E. I. come to terms.

Matsuoka said, of the Axis:

"It is absolutely impossible to imagine that Japan should fail in the slightest degree to carry out faithfully her obligations to Germany under the Tri-Partite pact. . . . There is no question whatever as to the fact that the Tri-Partite pact constitutes the immutable basis of Japanese foreign policy. . . . I can hardly believe that United States authorities are entertaining such a misunderstanding (as to think Japan would try to get out of the pact). . . There has of course been not the slightest deviation from this course of policy."

Of the South Seas, he said:

"As has frequently been affirmed, Japan's policy toward the South Seas is peaceful. Should, however, untoward international developments render the execution of such a policy impossible, it is a possibility that Japan might have to reconsider her attitude in the light of the changed situation."

At Friday's foreign press conference, Koh Ishii, the official spokesman, said further that the oil and rubber which Japan wants from the N. E. I. will be used internally and not be sent to Germany.

It is no secret that the Dutch delay in the negotiations is based on their suspicion that such supplies will reach the conqueror of their homeland.

(In Saigon, French Indo-China, travelers from Thailand reported increasing Japanese penetration in all departments of the Thai government, along with the removal or muzzling of all pro-British local officials).

U. S. PUBLIC POWER PROGRAM IS URGED

Senator Norris Advocates Multi-Billion Dollar Development To Meet Shortage

Washington — (AP) — Senator Norris, Ind., Nebraska, suggested Friday that the government undertake a multi-billion-dollar national power development to meet a "serious shortage" of electricity needed for the defense program.

Norris, legislative father of the Tennessee Valley Authority, told a press conference that such a program should provide for the establishment of regional power authorities throughout the country and should make possible a coast-to-coast network of transmission lines. The cost would be "several billion dollars," he said.

"Of course," he added, "the opponents of public power will argue that the program couldn't be finished in time to aid the national defense. But if we followed that theory, there would be no use building battleships or other armament that takes a long time in construction. If we believed in that theory, we might as well not ever do anything.

"If we had undertaken such a power program several years ago, we now could be giving Great Britain all the planes she needs. Even 500,000 more kilowatts of power would give a wonderful impetus to our defense effort.

"The dams that would be built and the flood-control work that would be undertaken would justify the project even if it never created a single kilowatt of power. It would save millions of dollars that now are lost every year by erosion and floods."

Norris said the TVA had demonstrated its value in the defense program, and added that when the development first was suggested opponents had argued it would never be of any real benefit to national defense.

"The assistance it has given to aluminum production, through the sale of power to the Aluminum Company of America, has been almost beyond imagination," the Senator declared. "If it had not been for the TVA the company would have been so crippled that the country would have practically no aluminum for defense needs."

Other development bearing on defense was a report from authoritative quarters that President Roosevelt had ordered creation of a new office of transportation, designed to coordinate various means of transportation, including railroads, buses, trucks, pipelines, ships, airlines and barges.

LICENSED AS UNDERTAKER

Edward T. Nicklaus, 13 E. Lemon st., has received word that he has passed the examination given by the Pennsylvania State Board of Undertakers held early this month in Pittsburgh and is now licensed as an undertaker. He is a graduate of Eckels College of Embalming, Philadelphia, class of 1940, and is a member of the Lambda Zeta Nu fraternity.

LABOR SERVICE PLANNED FOR CANADIAN OBJECTORS

Ottawa, Ont. — (AP)—Conscientious objectors, Mennonites and Doukhobors in the 21-year old class will be required to perform labor service in lieu of military service, War Services Minister J. G. Gardiner has announced.

"The 21-year old class now is being called out for military training," said Gardiner.

Arrangements have been made with the Mines department to open camps in national parks and in Ontario where Mennonites and conscientious objectors will be sent for labor service. They will be supplied with board and lodging and paid fifty cents a day. They must supply their own clothing.

CAN YOU SOLVE THIS PUZZLE?

What 3-Letter Word Does This Puzzle Represen

Rebus puzzles are lots of fun and you should have no difficulty solving this one. The comic characters on either side give you helpful hints, if you need them.

Now wouldn't you like the fun of solving more of these amusing Rebus puzzles? It can be very profitable fun, too, because . . .

The above Rebus is official puzzle No. 1 in the Philadelphia Record's fascinating new Rebus Contest, with $12,500.00 in cash prizes to be awarded. First prize is $7,500.00; second prize, $2,000.00; third prize, $1,000.00, with 97 other generous cash prizes; and a prize for every qualified contestant, regardless of score!

The first 21 puzzles in thi $12,500.00 Rebus Game reprinted in Sunday's phia Record, with every need to enter this f contest.

Sunday's Philadelp may be worth $7,500 Need we say more?

The Weather
Eastern Pennsylvania — Mostly cloudy and slightly cooler Sunday with local showers. Monday mostly cloudy and cooler.

SUNDAY NEWS

3 A. M. Edition
The Sunday News carries the full report of two world wide news services—
LATEST NEWS by Associated Press, International News Service. And Complete Local News.

VOL. 18—NO. 41 | Entered at Post Office at Lancaster, Pa. as second class mail matter | LANCASTER, PA., SUNDAY, JUNE 15, 1941 | 52 PAGES, 288 COLUMNS—FIVE CENTS

PRESIDENT FREEZES AXIS CREDITS

Red Army Opposes Stalin's Appeasement Of Hitler

UKRAINE IS OBJECT OF NERVE WAR

Developments Expected As Roads to Bessarabia Are Closed; Nazi Troops Leave Bulgaria

THE WAR TODAY

(By The Associated Press)

Helsinki diplomatic circles hear reports that Joseph Stalin is facing army opposition to his plan to "appease" Hitler—Turkish sources say roads between Rumania and Soviet-occupied Bessarabia closed and mined in anticipation of imminent developments.

French warships and planes attack British Mediterranean fleet as British continue systematic shelling of Lebanese coast—Vichy flatly denies French fleet has left Toulon—British and Free French still apparently stalled before Damascus and Beirut.

Japan sends new, undisclosed instructions to her economic negotiator in Netherlands East Indies. Foreign Minister Matsuoka congratulates Mussolini on his Tuesday speech in which Il Duce said Japan would not "remain indifferent in the face of American aggression against the Axis."

SOVIET TROOPS MOVED

New York, June 14.—(AP)—A Hungarian broadcast said tonight that "according to reports from Istanbul the Soviets are understood to have withdrawn the contrations of troops lined up along the Turkish frontier and to have launched moves of divisions to other fields." The broadcast was heard here by CBS.

RUSSIAN RIFT REPORTED

London, June 14.—(AP)—A rift has developed in Soviet Russia with Premier Joseph Stalin decided upon bending to the will of

UKRAINE—Page 11

MAN KILLED BY READING TRAIN IS UNIDENTIFIED

Fatally Injured Near Lititz After Earlier Train Stopped To Warn Him

An unidentified elderly man, believed a transient, was fatally injured when struck by a passenger train of the Reading railroad at Lime Rock, one and one-half miles south of Lititz, at 3:50 p. m. Saturday, according to State Motor Police.

The man, according to Motor Policeman A. Savanski and Dr. A. V. Walter, of this city, county coroner, who are investigating, died in the Lancaster General hospital two hours after he was admitted. Death was caused by a fractured skull, fractured legs, and a fractured arm. The investigation will be continued today.

Authorities said they were unable to contact members of the train crew for their version of the fatality. However, they reported that James Campbell, of Reading, an engineer of a freight train for the Reading company, stated that he had to stop his train and chase the man off the tracks a short time before the time of the accident. It is believed that the man failed to heed the warning and returned to walking on the tracks.

Members of a passenger train crew picked up the man and took him to the Lititz station where he was treated by Dr. Joseph Grosh, Lititz, and then removed to the hospital.

He was described as being about 60 years old, five feet four inches tall, and weighing about 130 pounds. He was wearing a green shirt, blue trousers with a purple stripe, and a white tie with a purple stripe.

Rules One Employe Can Sue For All

Chattanooga, Tenn., June 14 — (AP)—Federal Judge Leslie R. Darr ruled today in United States District Court that a single employe has the right to sue under the wage-hour law and obtain judgment "for all other employes" in the case, Judge Darr issued his ruling in a suit against the Cudahy Packing company brought by an employe, J. H. Tolliver, and 23 other employes, alleging the company failed to pay the minimum legal wage and overtime at the legal rate. The total amount they seek to recover is $20,000.

Judge Darr denied a petition of the Cudahy company which asked for dismissal of the case on the grounds Tolliver had no right to represent all the workers in the case.

Lancaster Was Shipshape For Flag Day

For a time Saturday evening it looked as if the town was to see its first launching, but the sun came out and changed this dreadnaught into a land schooner. City Street Department employes made it. It is almost entirely a cardboard creation, with a plain truck beneath. Below — Col. Stahr, chief marshal, heads the line with General Martin, left.

PROPERTY BILL UP TO CONGRESS

President To Leave Details Of Seizure Powers To Legislators

Washington, June 15 — (AP)—President Roosevelt will ask Congress, informed legislators said today, to write its own version of legislation permitting the government to requisition private property for defense purposes.

These legislators said the president was expected soon to address letters to the chairmen of the Senate and House Military Affairs committees setting forth the objectives the government wished to accomplish and suggesting that congress phrase a bill as it sees fit.

A property seizure bill submitted to congress last week by the War Department aroused a storm of controversy because of its sweeping nature. It proposed to authorize the president to requisition "temporarily or permanently" any property, tangible or intangible, which he decided was needed for defense.

The president would decide the value of the property and, if the owners thought his figure was too low, they would be paid 75 per ent of his price and could sue for any additional sum they thought was due.

Some legislators charged that the powers sought were so comprehensive that the president could take over private property where its use would be only remotely connected with the defense program.

Senator Byrnes, Dem., S. C., acting majority leader, told reporters that revisions would have to be made in the bill to define more clearly the powers to be exercised.

Spotty Weather To Feature Final Spring Week-End

One-third of an inch of rain fell in Lancaster Saturday, nearly all of it early in the evening.

The Weather Bureau held forth scant hope for sunny weather on this last week-end of spring (summer begins next Saturday) for it foresaw cloudy and cooler weather this afternoon, and cooler and light showers Monday morning.

Cherries were ripening on trees here, several weeks ahead of schedule, due to the rainy weather recently. The pea harvest in southern Lancaster county was in full swing.

Although the City Pumping station recorded .33 inches of rain Saturday, Official Weather Recorder Ira Keath of Ephrata had only .04 of an inch on his gauge—indicating the spottiness of the fall. The temperature, according to Keath, ranged between 63 and 84 degrees.

Truck Driver Dies, Helper Badly Hurt

Reading, Pa., June 14.—(AP)—Abner Styer, 55, of Hamburg, driver of an ice cream delivery truck, was fatally injured tonight when the vehicle crashed into an embankment at the foot of a Hamburg street and overturned.

Eugene Wanner, 18, Hamburg high school student, who was a helper on the truck, was taken to a hospital in a serious condition.

STORE THEFT REPORTED

Ruth Groff, Kinzer, reported to city police that her pocketbook containing between $7 and $8 was stolen while she was in a local store Saturday afternoon.

SPENT 23 DAYS IN OPEN BOAT

Survivors Of Sunken Britannia Tell Of Futile Fight With Nazi Raider

New York, June 14—(AP)—A grim story of 23 days in an open boat during which 44 men died and sharks fought for their bodies as they were thrown into the sea by the living was related today by 26 survivors of the sunken British liner Britannia.

William Mac Vicar, third officer of the Britannia and a member of the party which arrived on the Brazilian liner Cayru, declined to discuss the sinking, but the others, who included Lascar seamen and Hindu and Moslem merchants, told the story:

On March 27, en route to Bombay from Liverpool, the 8799-ton Britannia sighted a German raider eight miles away.

Although the Britannia had only a four inch gun against the raider's six-inch guns, the Britannia's captain, (believed to have been Captain Alexander Collie) decided to fight it out.

The Britannia shot 12 ineffectual rounds before she was mortally wounded by 70 shots from the raider. Three hundred passengers and 100 crew men crowded into four

SURVIVORS—Page 11

22 JOIN "DOLLAR CLUB"

Coatesville, June 14.—Twenty-two people joined Coatesville's "Dollar Club" over the week-end. According to Capt. Ralph E. Williams, of the city police, eight paid their dollar fines for minor traffic infractions Saturday, and fourteen more will be fined in police court by Monday.

THOUSANDS SEE BIGGEST PARADE FOR FLAG DAY

Floats Add Color As Procession Marches In Last-Minute Sunshine

Their spirits, colors and music undamped by rain which stopped only a half-hour short of the event, several thousand paraders honored their nation's emblem here Saturday night in the biggest Flag Day parade of the city's history.

Soldiers, civilians, women, Boy Scouts, pupils, high school bands, veterans, and selectees kept step jauntily for the 12-square line of march, and required 50 minutes to pass. A half-dozen floats added color, and patriotic tunes enlivened the event.

Spectators stood six-deep, and deeper, along the entire route. Anyone imaginable was there, from the kid with a busted arm in a sling to the folks from the country with six children, including two in arms. Penn Square was swarmed, and traffic was re-routed.

Police Head Parade

Twelve State Motor policemen from the Hershey training school, marching abreast, headed the parade, followed by white-gloved City policemen, and City officials, headed by Mayor D. E. Cary. In the startlingly simple summer khaki of the army, Col. Charles P. Stahr, chief marshal, and General Edward Martin, of Indiantown Gap, honorary chief marshal, marched side-by-side.

Rounds of applause greeted each band ,drum corps, or group of massed flags, and drum majors whose twirling showed individual skill got a hand. Firing of a gun from the Forty and Eight locomotive-box car truck brought squeals from the juvenile fans.

A float made to resemble a bat-

PARADE—Page 11

Parade Traffic Tangle Causes Crash, 2 Hurt

Two youths were slightly injured when the automobile in which they were riding crashed into the rear of another machine on Lime street between Lemon and James streets at 7:30 p. m. Saturday, city police reported.

The injured are: Howard Chalfont, sixteen, 252 Reservoir street, and Charles Dorsey, sixteen, 215 North Marshall street. Both were treated at the Lancaster General hospital for minor lacerations.

According to police reports, the youths were riding in a car driven by Marvin M. Musser, 642 East Walnut street, who had been driving north on Lime street and when another car, operated by H. L. Herr, 246 East Lemon street, stopped because of the heavy traffic in the vicinity of the start of the Flag Day parade. Musser was unable to stop and crashed into the rear of the Herr machine. Police said Herr's car in turn crashed into the rear of a third driven by E. C. Martin, 145 North Broad street.

NO-STRIKE PACT GIVEN SHIPYARDS

2-Year Agreement for Eastern Yards Would Stabilize Employment, Fix Base Pay

(By The Associated Press)

The government asked 55 eastern shipyards at work on defense orders Saturday to approve a two-year agreement designed to avoid strikes, stabilize employment, and prevent needless migration of workers.

The agreement was drafted at Washington by a shipbuilding stabilization committee set up by the labor division of the Office of Production Management and composed of representatives of employers, the Navy, the Maritime Commission, the CIO and the AFL.

It would be a counterpart of master contracts already established on the Pacific coast and projected for the Gulf and Great Lakes areas.

A conference was scheduled in the capital for next Friday for final action on the proposal.

Secretary of the Navy Knox, Chairman Emory S. Land of the Maritime Commission and William S. Knudsen and Sidney Hillman of the Office of Production Management wrote each of the yards asking prompt consideration of the proposals.

Ban On Lockouts

The agreement proposes a basic wage rate of $1.12 an hour for first-class skilled mechanics and a ban on lockouts by employers or suspension of work by employes during the tenrure of the pact.

The agreement, if adopted, would eliminate the differential which has existed heretofore in east and west coast shipyard wages. The western wages have averaged higher by "several cents" an hour, OPM officials said.

One of the big west coast yards did not sign the master agreement and a strike developed in which the defense mediation board yesterday said it had been unable to bring about an accord. Board officials said a panel had failed to bring representatives of the Bethlehem Steel company's shipbuilding division and the Bay Cities Metal Workers Council (AFL) into agreement and therefore the board would take its final step and draft recommendations for settlement.

The principal issue in the dispute was the demand for a union shop. A strike call on May 10 involved about 5,000 workers, but since then all but 800 have returned to their jobs.

Production was resumed at the Cleveland plant of the Lamson and Sessions company after a four-day walkout by CIO-United Automobile workers. The company, employing about 500, makes small parts for aircraft. A picket line was established and production at the plant slowed on Tuesday in what union officials said was a protest against the "refusal by company officials

SHIPYARDS—Page 11

Merchant Vessels Being Turned Into Airplane Carriers

Newport News, Va.—(AP)—United States shipbuilders were disclosed today to be turning merchant vessels into "escort" airplane carriers with only 90 days' work in an urgent drive to put more anti-submarine fire power into service.

First of the new fleet of carriers equipped for convoy work—the U. S. S. Long Island—was completed recently and already is at sea. The Long Island, formerly the merchant ship Mormacmail, was turned into a carrier in three months at the yards of the Newport News Shipbuilding and Drydock Company.

Italy May Seize U. S. Property In Swift Reprisal

Washington Predicts Arming of Merchant Vessels As Result of Robin Moor Sinking; Welles Defies German "Bluster and Threats"

(By The Associated Press)

Italy was reported ready Saturday night to seize American property in Italy in quick reprisal for President Roosevelt's order freezing German and Italian assets in the United States.

Some Fascists in Rome branded the Roosevelt move as "another example of gangsterism" following American "piracy" in previously seizing Axis ships in United States port.

President Roosevelt's freezing of the American finances of Axis-conquered or occupied countries of Europe, as well as those of Germany and Italy, was the highlight of the international situation.

Congressional circles in Washington expected the United States to start arming merchant vessels as a result of the Robin Moor sinking and Undersecretary Welles said the United States would not be bluffed off the seas by German "bluster and threats."

Arming of Merchant Vessels Predicted; Nazi Threat Defied

Washington, June 14 — (AP)—Arming of American merchant vessels was predicted in well-informed Congressional circles today after Sumner Welles, undersecretary of state, declared the United States would maintain its insistence on freedom of the seas despite German "bluster and threats."

One legislator, unwilling to be quoted by name but high in administration confidence, said that in view of the circumstances of the sinking of the freighter Robin Moor "the President is going to have to arm our merchant ships and tell them to protect themselves."

Welles commented at a press conference on a German spokesman's assertion that every ship carrying contraband to England would be sunk.

"Throughout the history of the United States," Welles asserted, "the American people have never been impressed by what they regarded as bluster and threats."

Welles also repeated this country's contention that the torpedoeing of the Robin Moor on May 21 by a Nazi submarine was in flagrant violation of every law of humanity and international morality as well as of German treaty obligations.

Await Survivors' Stories

The undersecretary made his observations with the reservation that he would not make a final statement on the sinking of the Robin Moor until the depositions of the 11 survivors—due here by Clipper on Monday—have been carefully studied.

It was believed that any such steps as the arming of American merchant men would be deferred until Germany replies to a stern diplomatic protest against the sinking of the Robin Moor.

This protest, it has been learned authoritatively, will be dispatched as quickly as the full facts are established. At the same time, it was predicted in informed quarters that Secretary Hull would demand restitution for the American lives and property loss and guarantees by Germany of the safety in the future of American ships on the high seas.

Says Facts Are Clear

What the American people want to do in a very quiet and dispas-

VESSELS—Page 11

Transactions With Soviet Put Under Strict Supervision

Washington, June 14—(AP)— At President Roosevelt's direction, the Treasury today froze the American assets of Germany and Italy and simultaneously imposed a strict supervision upon all financial transactions with Soviet Russia or its citizens.

In a complementary action, the Justice Department announced creation of an Alien Property Bureau to receive and study reports on transactions in alien property. A similar unit operated during the World War when much alien property was seized.

How much the freezing order might accomplish was brought into question, however, by those who recalled that Secretary of the Treasury Morgenthau recently said the Axis powers, acting in anticipation of such a move, had already withdrawn sizeable portions of their American funds.

"The barn is empty," was Morgenthau's comment.

Nevertheless, to determine the extent of whatever German and Italian holdings remain, and to acquire information of general usefulness in the present situation, the President also ordered an immediate census of all foreign-owned property in the United States.

Japan Not Included

In view of the sweeping geographical nature of the order and of the fact that Japan is an Axis partner, some surprise was ex-

ROOSEVELT—Page 11

Vichy Denies Fleet Sailed From Toulon

Vichy, June 14—(INS)—The government of Marshal Henri Philippe Petain tonight officially and emphatically denied through a spokesman a Vichy dispatch, carried by the German news agency DNB, which said the French battle fleet had sailed out of its base at Toulon into the Mediterranean.

The official Nazi agency's dispatch cited "well-informed" Vichy sources, but the government spokesman in the French provisional capital said the report was without foundation.

Indians Picket P. O. Declare Mural "Stinks"

Watonga, Okla., June 14.—(AP)—Cheyenne Indians withdrew from their picket path tonight after officials agreed to do what they could to remedy alleged indignities heaped upon them by the post-office's new mural.

Chief Red Bird, 71-year-old leader of the tribe, agreed to call off his 1941-style uprising after a peace pipe conference with the postmaster.

His objection to the mural, painted by Art Professor Edith Mahier of the University of Oklahoma, was laconic:

"It stinks," grunted Red Bird through Joe Yellow Eyes, his college-educated interpreter.

Red Bird was incensed particularly over the protrayal of his predecessor, Chief Henry Roman Nose, who, he grumbled, was made to look like a Navajo.

Red Bird doesn't like Navajos. Squinting at the mural, he observed:

"Chief should wear feathers farther back on head, and not tied on with store-bought string. Breech clout too short, look like Navajo."

Ponies in the picture also came in for criticism.

"Look like hobby horses with swan necks. Cheyennes like spotted ponies. No good. It stinks."

Red Bird's original band of pickets was augmented during the day by several other braves including Whiteface Bull and James Walking Coyote.

Postmaster Clarence Knappenberger, who appealed in vain to Mayor A. E. Goerke to have the pickets removed, was freshly aroused when the tepee was planted on the post office lawn. But after a peace pipe conference, he agreed to transmit their protest to the proper authorities in Washington.

WEATHER

Eastern Pennsylvania: Mostly Cloudy With Moderate Temperature, Scattered Afternoon Showers Monday; Tuesday Partly Cloudy.
Intell Journal Stormograph Reading: Unsettled Weather Monday.

Intelligencer Journal

The Leading Newspaper in the Garden Spot of America, Home Owned for Home Folks Since 1794

Baseball

Lancaster won the first game 6 to 3 and Hagerstown took the nightcap, 5 to 4.
Details Page 10.

VOLUME LXXVII.—NO. 238. CITY The Intelligencer Founded 1799 The Journal Founded 1794 LANCASTER, PA., MONDAY MORNING, JUNE 16, 1941 Entered at Post Office at Lancaster, Pa. as second class mail matter 16 PAGES, 128 COLUMNS.—THREE CENTS.

30 INCHES OF HAIL PILE UP IN FIELDS NEAR MONTEREY; LIGHTNING FIRES BARN

Nature Turns Lancaster County Field Into Winter Scene With Huge Piles Of Hailstones

A field on the farm of Titus M. Hess, Bareville R. D. 1, Sunday afternoon following a terrific hailstorm that swept the Monterey section of the county. A three-inch fall of hail, washed together by heavy rains, produced these drifts which at some places measured thirty inches. The size of the drifts can be readily comprehended by comparing them to Hess who stands surveying the oddity of nature, which beat down potato and tomato crops and leveled grain fields. (Intell photo)

Residents Shovel Walks And Roads Following Storm

Garden Crops Ruined By Freakish Storm, Torrential Rains Wash Several Inches Of Hail Into Huge Drifts; Homes Near City And In New Holland Damaged By Lightning Bolts; Quarryville Streets Flooded

Freakish thunder storms zig-zagged across Lancaster county Sunday, climaxing in a terrific fall of hail that slashed through the Monterey section at 3 p. m., leaving piles of hailstones thirty inches deep in low spots.

Lightning and floods from small streams that overran their banks added considerably to the damage caused by the hail.

Fire from lightning totally destroyed a barn, hog stables, four pigs and 140 chickens near New Holland with an estimated $8,000 loss. Two homes in widely scattered sections were damaged. Another bolt fired a barley shock in a field.

The hail storm in the Monterey section was so deep that residents were forced to use shovels to clear walks and roads. Garden crops in the section were completely destroyed.

Torrential rains that followed, washed the hail—the size of large marbles—into piles that resembled huge snow drifts.

Terrifying black clouds that heralded the approach of the storm in the Monterey section, were visible for miles around. Towards the center of the mass was a large reddish-tinged cloud.

The low mass of clouds cut visibility in the storm area to several feet. The storm broke with a sudden savage fury and the hailstones rattled like machine gun bullets.

HAIL IN OTHER AREAS

Hail, in lesser quantities also fell at Quarryville, and in the Bareville and Martindale sections. A small amount was also reported at Mount Joy and Terre Hill.

The hail, rain and thunder storms which plagued the county were confined to small sections. They struck at different times throughout the day. While some sections reported rains of cloudburst proportions, other sections reported mere sprinkles.

The spottiness of the rainfall was shown in a comparison of the rainfall records at the Lancaster Water Works and the United States Weather station at Ephrata.

Ira Keath at Ephrata reported only .09 of an inch of rainfall Saturday and Sunday, while the water works had .33 of an inch for Saturday evening alone.

Q-VILLE STREETS FLOODED

A small cloudburst struck Quarryville at 1:45 p. m. Sunday. Water was six to eight inches deep on the streets. Quarryville firemen were forced to use hose to flush States street of several inches of mud.

Small streams in numerous sections of the county went over their banks flooding lowlands. Near Hinkletown, Route 322 was impassable for a short time when a small stream overflowed. Fields in this area were badly washed. The New Holland bus was delayed twenty minutes by high water on the road near Bareville.

BARN HIT BY LIGHTNING

A 40 by 60 feet barn, silo and hog stable on the farm owned by Harry Fox, tenanted by his son, Martin Fox, about one and one-half miles northwest of New Holland, were destroyed by fire after being struck by lightning about 3:15 p. m. Sunday.

Firemen said four shoats and 130

More of STORM on Page 11

ITALY ORDERS U. S. PROPERTY REGISTERED

Announces Retaliatory Action To Blocking Of Axis Credits In America

MAY PRESAGE BREAK

Rome—(AP)—The Italian government announced Sunday that it had taken suitably retaliatory measures, including the ordering of a registration of United States property in Italy, following President Roosevelt's blocking of Italian and German credits in America.

Some observers pointed out that the Italian action might even be the prelude to a diplomatic break in relations with the United States which at least one Rome newspaper seemed to suggest.

Although the official communique referred only to registration of United States property in Italy, it was thought in American circles that this would be interpreted to mean the property of all American citizens. The only United States government property in Italy is the embassy which enjoys extraterritorial privileges.

The communique said, "following the blocking of Italian and German funds and the registration of all foreign property by the President of the United States, the Fascist government besides ordering suitable measures in reply, has ordered immediate registration of all property belonging to the United States and existing in Italy."

(Washington dispatches said American assets in Italy were estimated at $142,000,000.)

LITTLE DIFFERENCE

American quarters said their first reaction to this retaliation was that it would make little difference in the situation already existing.

Large American credits in Italy have been entirely blocked by the Italian government since 1935.

American firms already have millions of lire effectively tied up here because of the Fascists' re-

More of ITALY on Page 14

"We Lead All The Rest"
FARM CORNER
By
The Farm Editor

POSEY RESIGNS POST AS F. F. S. DIRECTOR

Lititz Man To Take Farm Loan Job For 3 Counties Under Federal Land Bank

Robert S. Posey, Lititz, director of the Federal Farm Security Administration in Lancaster and Lebanon counties since August, 1939, has resigned his post, effective Monday (today).

He resigned to accept a position with the Federal Land Bank of Baltimore. Following several weeks of instruction and training at the Baltimore office, Mr. Posey will become the acting secretary and treasurer of the National Farm Loan associations of Lancaster, Lebanon and Dauphin counties. Central headquarters of the three counties will be located at 36 E. Chestnut st., this city.

Claude H. Myers, of the Norristown FSA office, will succeed him as Farm Security administrator of

More of FARM CORNER on Page 14

Intelligencer Journal Weather Calendar

HOURLY TEMPERATURES

Sunday			
3 a. m.	64	4 p. m.	74
4 a. m.	62	5 p. m.	76
5 a. m.	61	6 p. m.	73
6 a. m.	60	7 p. m.	72
7 a. m.	62	8 p. m.	69
8 a. m.	64	9 p. m.	68
9 a. m.	66	10 p. m.	63
10 a. m.	68	11 p. m.	62
11 a. m.	72	Midnight	62
Noon	73	**Monday**	
1 p. m.	75	1 a. m.	61
2 p. m.	78	2 a. m.	61
3 p. m.	71	3 a. m.	61

COMPARATIVE TEMPERATURES

Station	High	Low
Intell Journal	78	60
Water Works	80	56
Ephrata	79	56
Last Year (Ephrata)	89	70
Official High for Year, May 22		97
Official Low for Year, Jan. 14		11
Character of Day		Partly Cloudy

SUN

Rises	4:30 a. m. (EST)
Sets	7:30 p. m. (EST)

More of WEATHER on Page 14

DAYLIGHT TIME IN INTELL
All time mentioned in the Intelligencer Journal is Daylight Time unless otherwise noted.

London Sees Russian Crisis Reports As Nazi-Inspired

Some Quarters Believed Stories Of Troop Movements Designed As Screen For Surprise Move, Probably Against Britain

London—(AP)—The status of German-Soviet Russian relations was still in the forefront of diplomatic conjecture Sunday night but there was an inclination in some quarters to regard reports of German troop movements as "obviously" Nazi-inspired—a screen for a surpise move, probably against Britain.

By this reasoning the most authoritative report of German troop movements, that is, concentrations in eastern and northeastern Germany facing Russia, which was circulated by Russia's official news agency, Tass, would represent propaganda collaboration between Moscow and Berlin.

Proponents of the screen theory recalled that the German propaganda campaign against Russia continued nearly up to the time Moscow and Berlin sprang their nonaggression pact upon a startled world before the start of the war.

BRITISH ENVOY UNLIKELY TO RETURN TO RUSSIA

London — (Monday)—(AP)—Sir Stafford Cripps, British ambassador home from Soviet Russia, was reported today unlikely to return to his post at Moscow. Some sources said he had expressed dissasisfaction over the results of his efforts there to improve British-Soviet relations.

Sir Stafford was reported to have said that while in Moscow he found it difficult to establish regular contact with members of the Soviet government and thus had been unable to carry out his work satisfactorily.

Some sources refused to speculate further on what Adolf Hitler might be up to.

"We've conjectured upon every possible phase of German-Russian relations," said one informant. "We think Hitler is up to something

More of NAZI-SOVIET on Page 14

BRITISH AND FREE FRENCH CLOSE IN ON DAMASCUS, BEIRUT

Syrian Capital's Key Defenses At Kissoue Taken Despite More Axis Support

London—(AP)—British and Free French took the key defenses of Damascus at Kissoue Sunday and in an encircling movement advanced to within five miles on two sides of the Syrian capital, British reports from the Levant stated Sunday night.

At the same time a column advancing up the central front captured Jezzine and forced French troops in the coastal city of Sidon, 10 miles to the west, to fall back to within 12 miles of Beirut, the Lebanon capital and chief port.

The advances were made despite reports indicating the Axis is attempting to throw both sea and air forces into the battle to support the faltering French.

The capture of Sidon, Jezzine and Kissoue, all key defenses to Beirut and Damascus, meant the British had straightened out their line of penetration to a uniform depth of about 50 miles all the way from the coast to Damascus and apparently meant that the fall of the two capitals could not be long delayed.

After taking Kissoue, 10 miles south of Damascus, where the French made a stand of several days, the British and Free French rushed on to Nahta and crossed the Aswad river to within five

More of MIDDLE EAST on Page 11

Man Found In City While Searchers Go Through Woods

While searching parties scoured woods and fields around Denver and Adamstown for him, John Schlater, seventy, of Denver R. D. 1, was found Sunday afternoon visiting friends in Lancaster. City police located the man, who was returned home by State Motor Police of the Ephrata sub-station.

Schlater's niece, Mrs. Melva McGarvey, reported him missing Saturday night when he did not return home after leaving the house at 7 a. m. police said. He was reported to get a haircut in Denver, seen later in the day at Adamstown, then disappeared until Sunday when found in Lancaster.

SENATOR HARRISON ENTERS HOSPITAL

Mississippian To Undergo Major Operation Today at Washington Institution

Washington—(AP)—Senator Pat Harrison, of Mississippi, was taken to Emergency hospital Sunday night to undergo a major operation Monday. Physicians said the 59-year-old Senator was suffering from an intestinal obstruction.

Harrison, president pro tempore of the Senate and chairman of its finance committee, has been in poor health for about two years.

VOTE TO CONTINUE STRIKE IN 11 WEST COAST SHIPYARDS

CIO Unionists Ratify Two-Year Agreement To Avert Atlantic Coast Strike

(By The Associated Press)

CIO unionists Sunday ratified a government proposal for a two-year agreement designed to avert labor strife in Atlantic coast shipyards while machinists of the San Francisco area voted to continue their strike against 11 shipyards there.

The Atlantic coast agreement, approved overwhelmingly by delegates from 33 locals of the Industrial Union of Marine and Shipbuilding Workers, provides for a basic $1.12 wage for skilled mechanics, adjustment with changes in the cost of living, premiums for night work and clauses for no strikes or lockouts.

Continuation of the San Francisco strike was approved 585 to 400 by AFL unionists while the vote of the CIO members was 359 to 56.

Meanwhile the Defense Mediation Board, which abandoned efforts to bring together the strikers and the management of Bethlehem Steel's shipbuilding division, prepared to put the case before the public in the

More of STRIKES on Page 12

SANDOE WINS HONORS IN PISTOL CONTEST

City Policeman Takes 3 Medals And Cash Award At Washington Tournament

Policeman Herman Sandoe, won three medals and a cash award in individual competition Sunday at the 12th Precinct Pistol Club Tournament in Washington, D. C.

Sandoe took first honors in the Marksmanship class with the .22 and .38 calibre pistols and had high aggregate score.

The police pistol team, competing in Class A, finished ninth with a score of 1,081. Sergeant Chester Dommel, captain, was high scorer for the team. Other members were Policemen Sandoe, Paul Glick and Albert Farkas.

Choir Rooms In 4 Churches Are Looted During Services

$38 In Cash, Purses, Keys And Other Articles Taken; Strange Man Wearing Brown Hat Seen By Sexton At One Church

Cash totaling approximately $38 and other articles were reported stolen from choir rooms of four city churches while services were being held between 11 a. m. and noon Sunday, city police reported.

The only clue, police said, was a report that a strange man was seen in the rest room of one of the four churches and that he was wearing a dark brown hat.

The largest theft, police said, took place at the First Presbyterian church on East Orange street, where approximately $17 in cash was taken.

Rev. Henry B. Strock, pastor of the church, reported the following thefts from the choir room, police said:

LOSERS LISTED

A wallet belonging to Beatrice Weaver, of 1187 Elm ave., containing fifteen cents; a wallet containing door keys and auto cards belonging to Jane Hampton, of 916 Pleasure Road; a change purse containing thirty-two cents which belonged to Dorothy Renninger of Woods ave.; a change purse containing between $5 and $10 belonging to Mary Stauffer, 348 S. Ann st.; a wallet containing a $5 bill, driver's license and a change purse containing change and a door key belonging to Betty Lefever, of 55 N. West End ave.; a wallet containing $1, a pass to the Lemoyne Army Depot and a house key belonging to Muriel McCalmont of Lemoyne, who is employed at the Depot there; and a wallet containing eighty cents which belonged to Paul Brosey, of 422 Poplar st.

$14 AT ST. JOHN'S

At St. John's Episcopal church at West Chestnut and Mulberry streets, police reported thefts of approximately $14 in cash.

Rev. Heber W. Becker, rector of the church reported the following theft from the church, police said:

Jean Falk, of 435 Lancaster ave.,

More of ROBBERIES on Page 11

SIX DANISH SHIPS ORDERED TO ACTIVE DUTY WITH THE U. S.

First Among 84 Foreign Ships Taken Over To Go Into Service

Washington—(AP) — The Maritime Commission announced Sunday that six Danish ships would be placed in active service of the United States merchant fleet Monday. They are among 84 foreign vessels tied up in American waters which were taken into protective custody some time ago.

The six vessels, which will become the property of the commission, are the motorship Nora and the steamships Marna and Jonna, tied up in New York; the steamships, Rita Maersk and Herta Maersk, in Boston; and the steamship Jutta, in Portland, Me. All are freighters.

The commission said that notices would be posted on each vessel at 9 a. m. Eastern Standard Time, informing the owners that the commission had taken title. The names of the owners were not announced pending completion of

More of SHIPS On Page 11

WILL CHANGE "STOP" SIGNS AT STRASBURG

Traffic On Route 741 East of Borough To Be Stopped At Intersection With Route 896

Harrisburg—The Department of Highways has announced its intention of changing location of the "stop" signs at the intersection of Routes 896 and 741 east of Strasburg Borough, Lancaster county. The change in the location of the sign at this intersection, the Department said, is necessary due to the change in the movements of traffic at this location.

Instructions have been given to the District Engineer to have the change made by June 23.

The sign which is in place stopping traffic on Route 896 will be removed and erected so as to require traffic on Route 741 coming to a stop before entering at this intersection.

Route 741 connects Strasburg and Gap, and Route 896 leads from Strasburg to Georgetown and Russellville.

Maytown Honors Dr. G. A. Harter, Practicing Physician 50 Years

Tribute To Doctor And Civic Leader Paid At Fathers' Day Service In Lutheran Church

Dr. G. A. Harter, of Maytown, who will observe fifty years as a practicing physician in the community Monday, was honored at a Fathers' Day service Sunday morning in St. John's Lutheran church, Maytown.

The pastor of the church, the Rev. Kirby Yingst, in speaking of Dr. Harter said that fifty years ago a man came to Maytown whose life was consecrated to the service of his community. He said he has "fathered many of you" and has been good to the persons of the community and to his church without any tangible evidence of appreciation.

Dr. Harter was presented with a vase of flowers by members of the congregation of which he has been a member for fifty years.

Dr. Harter, who is active in all civic affairs, is also a director of the Maytown National bank and president of the Maytown Fire company.

He came from Center county and settled in Maytown following his graduation from Jefferson Medical college.

LANCASTER YOUTH SUFFERS FRACTURE OF BACK IN CRASH

William A. Schaeffer And 2 Others Injured; Train Kills Unidentified Man

A Lancaster youth's back was broken in an automobile crash near Cornwall early Sunday morning, and an unidentified man was killed by a Reading company passenger train near Lititz Saturday afternoon.

Seven other persons were injured in week-end accidents on Lancaster county highways and city streets.

3 HURT IN CRASH

Three persons were injured at 1:25 a. m. Sunday in an auto collision on Route 72 in Cornwall.

William A. Schaeffer, twenty-one, son of Dr. and Mrs. J. Nevin Schaeffer, 503 N. President ave., was admitted to the Lancaster General hospital suffering two fractured vertebrae. Clayton White, Quentin, was admitted to the institution suffering a fractured rib and lacerated chin. June Kurtz, twenty, 399 S. State st., Ephrata, was treated at the hospital for a bruised foot and brush burns of the chin.

According to Constable John Stauffer, of Cornwall, Schaeffer and Miss Kurtz were riding in an auto operated by Charles Frey, Jr., twenty-three, of the Lititz pike. The Frey auto was going south while the other car, operated by White, was going north when the collision occurred, he said.

WOMAN INJURED

Dorothy Flood, twenty-seven, 233 Church st., was treated at St. Joseph's hospital for a lacerated hip following an auto accident at King and Mulberry streets at 10:05 p. m. Sunday.

City police said the woman was riding in an auto operated by Francis X. Kirchner, 415 High st., going south on Mulberry street, when it was struck by a car operated by Lloyd Troutman, Lambertville, N. J., going east on King street. Police said the Troutman auto went through a red traffic light.

2 HURT IN CRASH

Two youths were slightly injured when the automobile in which they

More of ACCIDENTS on Page 11

1,500,000 OF STATE'S AUTOS INSPECTED

Secretary Of Revenue Says Figure 100,000 Ahead Of Similar Inspection Period A Year Ago

Harrisburg—(AP)—New "Liberty Bell" stickers have been affixed to windshields of 1,500,000 Pennsylvania automobiles and the current motor vehicle inspection is about half concluded, William J. Hamilton, Jr., secretary of revenue, announced Sunday.

The figure is 100,000 above that of a corresponding figure a year ago and Hamilton predicted that before the period ends July 31, 2,500,000 automobiles will carry the new stickers.

"It is gratifying to find that more motorists than ever before are having their cars inspected early," he said. "That is the safe thing to do. It not only avoids the last-minute rush but gives the advantage of driving a car kept in good mechanical condition at all times."

Officials of the Bureau of Motor Vehicles pointed out that during the past inspection period, approximately 60,000 automobiles were ordered "junked" because they could not pass inspection. This was an increase of 11,000 over the previous inspection period.

SEEK HIT-RUN DRIVER

City police were searching early Monday (today) for a motorist who failed to stop after his auto struck another auto, operated by Martin Bressler, Narvon R. D. 1, at Franklin and Chestnut streets at 10:45 p. m. Sunday. Police said Bressler was going north on Franklin street when the other car, going east on Chestnut street, went through a stop sign.

WEATHER

Eastern Pennsylvania: Fair And Slightly Warmer Friday; Saturday Mostly Cloudy And Warm.

Intell Journal Stormograph Reading: Friday Cloudy And Warmer Followed By Unsettled Weather.

Intelligencer Journal

Baseball

The Red Roses defeat Reading, 5 to 3. Details Page 26.

The Leading Newspaper in the Garden Spot of America, Home Owned for Home Folks Since 1794

VOLUME LXXVII.—NO. 248. CITY The Intelligencer Founded 1799 The Journal Founded 1794 LANCASTER, PA., FRIDAY MORNING, JUNE 27, 1941 Entered at Post Office at Lancaster, Pa. as second class mail matter 34 PAGES, 272 COLUMNS.—THREE CENTS.

BIG TANK BATTLE RAGING IN POLAND

ANKARA SAYS ITALIAN SUB SANK STEAMER

Turkish Capital Hears Reliable Report Of Identity Of Attacker

20 SURVIVORS LANDED

Ankara, Turkey (Delayed)—(AP)—The Turkish steamer Refah, sunk in the Mediterranean with a loss of 160 lives out of 180 passengers and crew members, was reliably reported Thursday to have been sent down by an Italian submarine.

The 2,500-ton steamer carried Turkish naval personnel assigned to bring back from England several warships built there for the Turkish navy.

SURVIVORS LANDED

Some of the twenty survivors were reported to have landed in Palestine, others at the British Mediterranean island of Cyprus.

It was understood here that all the belligerent powers, had been notified before the vessel sailed three days ago.

Previous reports from survivors had not identified the attacking submarine's nationality.

BRIGHTLY LIGHTED

They said the ship, brightly lighted and with the Turkish colors painted on her sides, was torpedoed Monday night, sinking in two hours. The torpedo disabled the radio, so no distress call could be sent.

Only three officers and 26 men were known to have been saved, some landing at Karatas and Burum on the Turkish coast and others on the British island of Cyprus.

FILES PETITION

Paul W. Schriver, 1411 E. King st., salesman, filed his petition as a candidate for justice of the peace. Schriver's petition contained the signature of Aaron H. Palmer, superintendent of the Lancaster County Home; Willis Rohrer, veteran Lancaster township politician, and Edythe T. Bachman, committeewoman.

"We Lead All The Rest"

FARM CORNER

By

The Farm Editor

OPPOSES GROWING MARYLAND TYPE OF TOBACCO LOCALLY

Technologist Says Farmers Here Better Off Than Those Below Line

Lancaster county tobacco growers, at 13 and 4 cents, have more money per acre, than Maryland growers selling their crop at a top price of 45 cents per pound, according to E. G. Beinhart, senior tobacco technologist, of the U. S. Eastern Region Research Laboratory for the utilization of farm products, near Philadelphia.

Apparently alarmed over the possibility that local farmers might turn to the growing of Maryland type tobacco, following publication of a news story of top prices being paid for the Maryland crop, and an editorial, "The War and Tobacco," in the June 21 issue of the Intelligencer Jour-

More of FARM CORNER on Page 12

Intelligencer Journal Weather Calendar

COMPARATIVE TEMPERATURES

Station	High	Low
Intell Journal	86	62
Water Works	87	56
Ephrata	90	56
Last Year (Ephrata)	77	57
Official High for Year, May 22, June 22		97
Official Low for Year, January 14		11
Character of Day		Clear

HOURLY TEMPERATURES

Thursday			
3 a. m.	64	4 p. m.	86
4 a. m.	63	5 p. m.	85
5 a. m.	62	6 p. m.	85
6 a. m.	62	7 p. m.	82
7 a. m.	63	8 p. m.	78
8 a. m.	68	9 p. m.	75
9 a. m.	71	10 p. m.	74
10 a. m.	78	11 p. m.	72
11 a. m.	80	Midnight	71
Noon	83	Friday	
1 p. m.	84	1 a. m.	71
2 p. m.	85	2 a. m.	70
3 p. m.	86	3 a. m.	70

HUMIDITY

8 a. m.—72; Noon—63; 2 p. m.—52; 4 p. m.—56; Midnight—68

Average Humidity—62

Dew Point 11 p. m.—59

More of WEATHER on Page 21

DAYLIGHT TIME IN INTELL

All time mentioned in the Intelligencer Journal is Daylight Time unless otherwise noted.

Home Defenders Sign Up At Armory

Captain James Z. Appel, commander of the Lancaster company of the Pennsylvania Reserve Defense Corps, at the Armory, interviews Earl Leibley, 738 S. Lime st., who volunteered Thursday night, along with seventy-eight others, to join the outfit which replaces the National Guard, now in federal training. (Intell Photo).

Part of the large crowd of men from all walks of life who jammed the Armory corridor waiting their turn to offer their services as members of the Lancaster unit of the Reserve Defense company (Intell Photo).

79 MEN ANSWER CALL FOR GUARDS IN DEFENSE CORPS

Captain Appel Interviews Applicants; Minors And Man Over Age Limit Apply

Seventy-nine men responded Thursday evening to the call of Captain James Z. Appel for volunteers to Lancaster's Company H, of the Pennsylvania Reserve Defense Corps.

The men, representing nearly a score of trades and occupations, jammed the first floor corridor of the Armory and stood patiently in line for interviews after filling out application blanks.

Although the ranks of the company are open only to men between the ages of twenty-one and fifty, several minors made their appearance as did one man past the sixty mark.

A number of former National Guardsmen and World War veterans were among the applicants. Captain Appel said the average age of the applicants would be around thirty-five years.

The men who applied will be notified by Captain Appel when to report for physical examinations and formal enlistment. Additional applications will be received, the company commander said, next Tuesday night. The personnel of the company is limited to a captain, two lieutenants, and sixty enlisted men.

Assisting Captain Appel in work Thursday evening were Sergeants Earl Colson, Harry Hosan, George Althoff and George Sterneman.

MAN IS PINNED BETWEEN TRUCKS

Harry H. Barr Suffers Brush Burns In Accident On South Prince Street

Harry H. Barr, fifty-one, 125 E. Lemon st., suffered brush burns of the left arm and back at 9:45 a. m. Thursday when he was pinned between two trucks on South Prince street between Andrew and Hazel streets.

According to city police Barr was walking around the rear of his parked truck to enter it from the left side when another truck operated by Harry Kuski, of Manheim, attempted to pass. Barr was caught between the two vehicles. He was treated by a physician.

RAF Called Master Of Western Skies, Continues Attack

Look Now For Fighter With Longer Range Or Bases On The Continent

London —(AP)— The Royal Air Force, having gained mastery of the skies over the western front by relentless 'round the clock offensives, Thursday night plunged into its 16th successive night of blasting German targets without sign of slackening the thundering tempo.

During the day the RAF repeatedly raided the invasion coast and Nazi-occupied Northern France and reported destruction of nine German fighters. Three British fighters did not return.

CLAIM 161 NAZI PLANES

In the 10 days ended June 25, the British officially claimed the destruction of 161 German warplanes against a British loss of 66, while in the past six days the Germans lost 108, and the RAF 19 planes, 16 pilots.

With the Royal Air Force reporting its greatest 24-hour offensive—a rolling assault in which 400 to 500 planes were said to have taken part—British observers were studying new means of striking at the Luftwaffe.

The authoritative magazine Aeroplane said the recent RAF initiative was a "valuable element" in lowering morale in the Luftwaffe.

"To force back to the defensive an air force which has known nothing but offensives in war," the magazine said, "is to impose upon it, first, doubts as to its effectiveness and ultimately, by heavy repeated losses, to persuade it of its inferiority."

ESTABLISHES SUPREMACY

The article asserted that the RAF has established its supremacy over the French coast up to the present limit of its fighter capacity and "for anything beyond that must look either to new fighters of equal performance and greater range—and some of these are crossing the Atlantic—or to seizure for its use of advanced bases by successful military enterprise."

Developing the theme of British

More of RAF on Page 22

HITLER DEMANDS ALL EUROPE SEND HIM TOKEN FORCE

Each Country Told To Furnish Units For Fight Against Communism

Madrid, Spain—(AP)—Adolf Hitler has demanded from each country forming a part of the "new Europe" a token force to fight against Communism, but what part Spain will take in this connection has not yet been announced.

(Here three lines of this dispatch were deleted by censor). It was the first indication that Hitler had made such demands upon countries

More of HITLER on Page 22

FALANGIST PARTY OPENS RECRUITING HEADQUARTERS

Madrid—(AP)—The Falangist party early Friday (today) announced the opening of recruiting offices to enlist Spanish volunteers to fight against Russia.

The decision of the Spanish group was disclosed in a proclamation by Jose Luis De Arrese Magraz, secretary general of the Falange party. The proclamation did not indicate how many Spanish volunteers would be sent to fight beside the Germans.

Dies

SEN. A. J. HOUSTON

ANDREW HOUSTON DIES, OLDEST MAN TO ENTER SENATE

Son Of Famous Sam Houston Succumbs Following Stomach Operation

Washington, June 26—(AP)—Senator Andrew Jackson Houston Dem., Tex., 87-year-old son of the famous Sam Houston, died Thursday at Johns Hopkins hospital in Baltimore after an operation for a stomach ailment, his secretary, D. R. Potter,, announced here Thursday night.

Potter said physicians had called him from John Hopkins hospital saying that Houston had died at approximately 8 p. m.

With the Senator at the time of his death were his two daughters, Ariadne and Marguriete.

Oldest man ever to enter the United States Senate, Houston was appointed recently by Governor W. Lee O'Daniel of Texas to succeed the late Senator Morris Sheppard, who died April 9.

Houston was to serve only until

More of HOUSTON on Page 22

4 JOIN U. S. NAVY AT LOCAL STATION

Lancaster Youth Among Quartet Signing For Service; Lebanon Boy Also Enlists

Four enlistments in the United States Navy were reported Thursday by Chief William R. Leonard, of the Naval Recruiting station in the post office building.

The youths accepted were: Carl Kelley Walters, seventeen, 570 N. Plum st.; Emil Mervin Eyler, seventeen, 1137 N. Duke st., York; James Nicholas Smith, twenty-nine, 518 Chestnut st., Lebanon, and Carl Stanley Siegfried, seventeen, 527 N. Eleventh st., Reading.

All were sent to the Naval Training station at Newport, R. I.

REDS BATTLING GERMAN THRUST TOWARD MINSK

Moscow Claims "Manifest Advantage," Soviets Bomb Oil Fields

FIGHTING IS FIERCE

(By The Associated Press)

Red army troops fighting on the plains of old Poland were reported successfully battling a great German tank thrust aimed Friday (today) at Minsk, White Russian capital 160 miles inside Soviet territory.

An undisclosed number of German tanks Thursday broke through advance Soviet lines in the north and a war bulletin issued in Moscow said fighting there still was in progress.

REDS TAUNT ABOUT "BAFFLING" REVELATIONS

New York—(AP)—The Russian radio challenged Germany with heavy sarcasm Thursday night to come forth with its "baffling revelations which the Berlin radio has promised to the world repeatedly for the last two days."

The Russian announcer said in a broadcast heard here by NBC that the Germans had not announced anything but generalities because there "were no miracles to be reported x x x."

In central Poland "violent large scale engagements of tank troops" also occurred in the direction of Luck. This German thrust apparently was aimed at the Ukraine, and the communique said "fighting continued throughout the day with a manifest advantage for our troops."

The Russians were said to have thrown thousands of men and tanks against reputedly the most powerful army in the world with the aim of cutting off and ripping apart the main German thrusts at White Russia (Byelo Russia).

The Russian communique was a tale of success from the Polish front to the Black Sea; of parachute troops killed as they landed by charging cavalry, of successful raids into German and Rumanian lines, and of fierce bombing attacks on Bucharest, the port of Constanta and the rich Ploesti oil fields of Germany's Rumanian ally.

Far to the south along the Prut river boundary between Rumania and Russia the Red army also was declared to have stemmed repeated avalanches of attacking Germans and Rumanians, inflicting "heavy losses" and even counter-attacking across the river to capture men and guns.

Soviet bombers heavily attacked the oil fields where Adolf Hitler draws much of his strength for a continuing war in the east, it was said.

Another fierce land action was being fought by the Germans in central Poland toward Luck, about

More of WAR on Page 21

GOVERNMENT QUITS RUMANIAN CAPITAL

Leaves Bucharest Following Soviet Air Attacks, According To Reports From Ankara

New York—(AP)—The Rumanian government has left Bucharest following Soviet air attacks on that Capital, it was reported Thursday night from Ankara.

Government To Fix Tire Prices At June 16 Levels

Washington—(AP)—The government moved Thursday to fix automobile tire prices at the June 16 level, and there were new indications that efforts would be made to set up some sort of mandatory price controls applying to American industry generally.

Leon Henderson, price administrator, made known that a price schedule applying both to tires and tubes would be issued, probability next week after conferences with representatives of manufacturers. He said he was announcing the impending move in advance so that the trade would know what to expect and would avoid price increases before the schedule is issued.

NOT ALL SUCCESSFUL

Some of Henderson's price curbing efforts have not been successful, notably in the case of the Chrysler corporation and part of the furniture industry.

Concerning his power to enforce price schedules in general, his aides said that several methods are available under the Selective Service Act, a transportation act passed during the World War, and other legislation.

CHRYSLER CORP. ANSWERS

Detroit — (AP) — Recent retail price increases were necessitated by rising labor and material costs, Chrysler corporation asserted

More of PRICES on Page 22

MAN AND WIFE HURT IN CRASH AT MT. JOY

Mr. and Mrs. Willis Linn, Newcastle, Del., Admitted to General Hospital After Auto Runs Into Truck

Willis Linn, Newcastle, Del., suffered a fracture of the nose and lacerations and his wife suffered several rib fractures and lacerations when the automobile in which they were riding collided with a parked truck on Main street, Mount Joy, about 2 a. m. Thursday, according to Chief of Police Elmer Zerphey, of Mount Joy.

The officer said Mrs. Linn, who was driving, fell asleep at the wheel.

Following treatment by a physician the couple was admitted to the Lancaster General hospital.

DRAFT BOARDS ARE NOTIFIED OF CLASS 2 CHANGE

State Selective Service headquarters at Harrisburg notified the eight local draft boards Thursday that draft classification 2, "a man necessary in his civilian duty," has been broken down into A and B classes.

In Class 2-A, says the order, "shall be placed any registrant found to be a necessary man in any industry, business, employment, agricultural pursuit, governmental service x x x or in training therefor, the maintenance of which is necessary to the national health, safety or interest in the sense that it is useful or productive and contributes. to the employment of well-being of the community or the nation."

In Class 2-B will be placed registrants engaged in similar work, but deferment shall be granted "in the sense that a serious interruption or delay in such activity is likely to impede the national defense program."

The length of deferment for 2-A men shall not be for a period longer than six months. Additional deferments may be granted. Deferment in Class 2-B is not limited to a particular time.

Seven city and county boards

More of DRAFT on Page 22

"Bobby" Troup To Wed Main Line Deb

ROBERT W. TROUP, JR.

Young Composer's Fiancee Is Philadelphia Night Club Entertainer

Ever since Robert W. Troup, Jr., son of Mrs. Robert W. Troup, of 1140 Wheatland ave., could walk, he's been running up and down musical scales.

Now, twenty-three years later, "Bobby" is striking it rich as the composer of the song, "Daddy"... a song that's the hit of the hour!

He's winning laurels as a songwriter even while he managed to make the word love rhyme not only with stars above, but also rhyme with Hare and Troup.

Because Thursday "Bobby" announced he would wed Miss Cynthia Hare, vivacious Philadelphia Main Line society deb

More of TROUP on Page 22

CYNTHIA HARE

Around the Clock With a Lancaster Soldier at 'Gap

(Continued from Page 1)

7. Martin hikes to the summer colony at Lake Strausse during his off hour and indulges in some fishing—in vain. On warm nights the men often are taken to the lake in trucks for fishing. Many of the cottages at the lake are occupied by the families of men stationed at Indiantown Gap.

8. Back at the ambulance station in the mountains, the local boys face the serious aspects of warfare as a gas mask drill is staged. The Man-From-Mars mask that Martin is wearing has non-fogging eye glasses and protects the eyes, nose and lungs from most gases.

9. Here's a ticklish job. Martin (left) is called upon to put an arm bandage on Sergeant William Schulz, also of Lancaster, who was theoretically wounded while bringing an injured man in from the battlefield. Martin considers this the most important thing he has learned in the army. He knows that his knowledge may save lives in peace or war.

10. Ready to break their temporary camp in the mountains, the men police the grounds, leaving it as spic and span as when they arrived. Martin gathers up pieces of paper, cigarette butts, the photographer's flashlight bulbs, etc.

11. Back at 'Gap, Martin is assigned to a short trick at guard duty. The medical units, which once carried only side arms, also have been issued rifles and are being instructed in their use. German medical units also are reported using offensive weapens.

12. Dismissed for the day, supper eaten, Martin now is free to do more or less as he pleases until lights out at 10 P. M. In front of the barracks he meets a group of Lancaster girls who were having some trouble with their camera, and he shows them how to work it. The girls had dates with several of Martin's buddies.

13. With half of the company out of camp on passes, Martin sits on the company's cornerstone and ponders what to do next, with several free hours still before him. The stone, with the insignia "Lancaster G-Co." was painted and set in place by the local boys, and they are very proud of it.

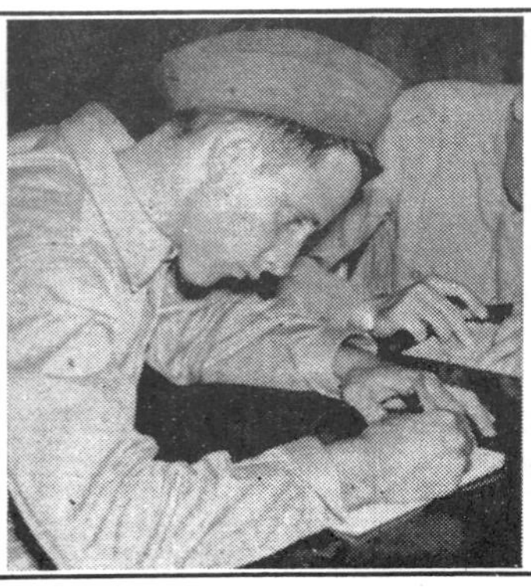

14. Martin decided to go over to the company recreation hall. Here he writes a letter home as an electric phonograph provides a musical background. He also tarries awhile to read a magazine, and play some ping-pong with Corporal Paul Musser.

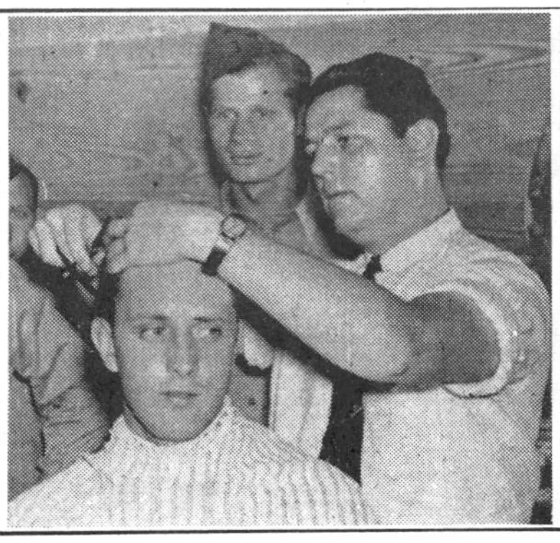

15. Expecting a week-end leave to be used for a trip to Lancaster, Martin then goes to the barber shop for a haircut. The chair and accessories are the same as in any city shop, but the setting is the pine boards of an army camp. The men await their turn on rough board benches, a familiar piece of army furniture.

16. Martin tops off his day with a bottle of beer in the post exchange. He stands up at the bar and "has one" with Corporal Musser. The tables in the place are crowded with men entertaining visitors from home, and a juke box grinds out the latest popular songs. In the center of the room stands a military policeman, his hands on his hips.

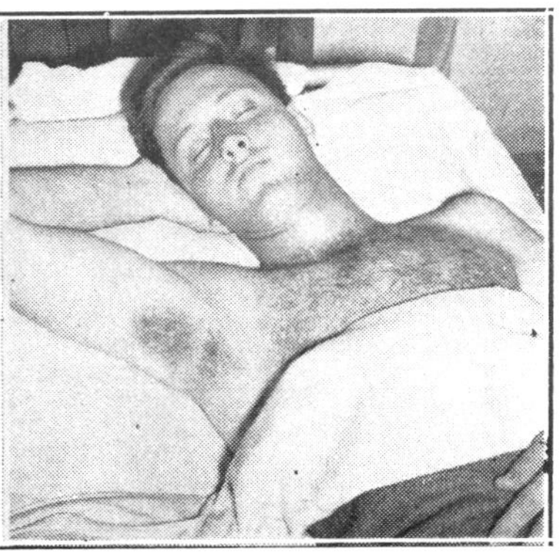

17. Just before 10 P. M. Martin climbs up the steps to his cot on the second floor of the barracks and soon is asleep. Even on the hottest days the men find the blankets comfortable for sleeping as the mountains release their cool night breezes. Thus ends a typical day in the army for a typical Lancaster soldier.

BATTERY E GETS USED TO HIKES

Enjoys Party After 15-Mile Jaunt Under Blazing Georgia Sun.

(Special to The New Era)

CAMP STEWART, GA., July 11—Hikes for Battery E, the Lancaster unit of the 213th Coast Artillery, Anti-Aircraft, in Federalized training here, are growing longer and more frequent but the boys seem to mind them less and less as the hardening process continues.

One 15-mile hike this week started at 3 A. M. But despite the day's grind under the blazing Georgia sun, the Battery was still chipper enough in the evening to enjoy a party given by Captain David J. Evans in honor of First Lieutenant John D. Peterson, who is going to school at Fort Eustis.

Col C. C. Curtis, commander of the 213th; Lt. Col. Atwood, and Major Brubaker were guests. The entertainment included numbers by "Battery E's Eight Voices of Harmony"; a "rubber legs" number by Sgt. Art Myers; radio-phonograph music courtesy of Cpl. John Colins, and movies by Cpl. Harry N. Harr.

On another hike this week, the Battery travelled over terrain so thick and rough that in some places the troops had to crawl on their stomachs.

Man Overcome After Firing Building Trying to Burn Wasp's Nest

Leo Hess, 527 Walnut street, Columbia, set his apartment afire, was overcome by smoke and taken to the Columbia hospital and routed his neighbors from the building when he tried to burn a wasp's nest in the attic late yesterday afternoon. The nest remained intact today.

Hess entered the attic with a blazing torch to burn the nest but a current of air carried sparks beneath the roof and started a fire. Columbia firemen responded and for two hours fought the blaze. In his efforts to help the firemen, Hess remained in the attic and was overcome. He was removed to the Columbia Hospital.

Edward Moore and his family who occupy the first floor of the building, removed most of the furniture when water began trickling from the attic to the lower floors. The front part of the second floor of the building was damaged and last night a large section of the ceiling collapsed. The Moore apartment on the first floor was not damaged seriously.

BRITISH CAPTURE GERMAN SHIP

LONDON, July 11. — (A. P.)—British Naval forces have intercepted the 7,209-ton German ship Hermes enroute from Rio de Janeiro to Hamburg, the Admiralty announced today.

A communique said:

"The German ship Hermes has been intercepted. Her captain, officers and crew have been taken prisoner. The Herms left Rio de Janeiro June 28 in an attempt to reach Hamburg."

The Hermes arrived in Rio de Janeiro April 9 after a 29-day voyage from Bordeaux, occupied France, with a cargo of pharmaceutical supplies and a plane.

MANNERHEIM URGES "GREATER FINLAND"

HELSINKI, Finland, July 11 —(A. P.)—Field Marshal Baron Mannerheim, commander of the Finnish Army, in an order of the day declared anew today his purpose to win for a "Greater Finland" all of Karelia, an area which spreads for approximately 100 miles east of Finland's present borders.

For 23 years Viena and Aunus (East Karelia), he said, had awaited fulfillment of his promise, made in Finland's war of independence of 1918, that he would not put away his sword "until Finland and East Karelia were free."

"Warriors of the war of independence, famed men of our winter war (1939-40), my brave soldiers," his order said, "the new day is dawned. Karelia arises, her own battalions march in our ranks. Karelian freedom and greater Finland gleam ahead of us in the mighty avalanche of world events. May the Providence that watches over nations, grant the Finnish army fulfillmet of my promise to the entire Karelian people."

LORD HALIFAX HOPES TO RETURN

WASHINGTON, July 11—(A. P.)—Lord Halifax, British Ambassador, hopes to return to London for a short visit some time in August.

The ambassador told newspapermen his purpose would be to discuss the international situation with his Foreign office. Answering questions, he said that his plans were to return to the United States after perhaps three weeks in London.

MISS LANDIS WILL SPEAK AT RALLY

HARRISBURG, July 11.—(A. P.)—Miss Alice E. Landis, Elizabethtown missionary who was aboard the Zamzam when it was sunk by a German submarine, will tell of her experiences at a Calvary youth rally here tomorrow.

Miss Landis was enroute to Africa when the Zamzam was sunk. With other passengers she was taken to Nazi-occupied France.

"Their Majesties" at 'Gap

Sergeant Robert G. Jones of Philadelphia and Miss Frances Phillips of Harrisburg reigned as king and queen of the 109th Field Artillery dance at Indiantown Gap, military reservation. The fact that Jones, of the 103rd Medical Regiment, rather than a 109th Artilleryman, won the crown proved embarrassing to the host company.

U. S. RED PARTY DEMANDS AID

Madison Square Garden Crowd of 19,000 Urges More U. S. Output.

NEW YORK, July 11—(A. P.)—In the Communist Party's first mass meeting since the beginning of the Russo-German war, a capacity crowd at Madison Square Garden last night adopted a resolution calling upon President Roosevelt "fully and completely to implement" his pledge of assistance to the U. S. S. R.

Robert Minor, acting secretary of the party during the imprisonment of Earl Browder, told the crowd, estimated by police at 19,000, that it is "the sacred obligation" of American workers to produce every tank, gun, plane and ship at greatest possible speed for war on all fronts against Hitler.

The resolution held that "the criminal aggression against the peoples of the Soviet Union and all progressive humanity clearly demonstrates that the peace, freedom and security of our people demands the crushing military defeat of Hitler."

The resolution called also for "the defeat of his friends in the United States, the Lindberghs, Hoovers, Wheelers, Norman Thomases and all other appeasing Munich-men."

Minor labeled a slander on working men and Communists alike that the strikes in aircraft and other industries were Communist conspiracies and asserted that the real conspirators were "the profiteering corporations and trusts."

Minor approved the landing of American forces in Iceland.

JUDGE A. M. LUMPKIN SUCCEEDS BYRNES

COLUMBIA, S. C., July 11—(A. P.)—Governor Burnet R. Maybank has appointed Alva Moore Lumpkin, of Columbia, 55-year-old Federal district judge, to fill the seat in the U. S. Senate vacated by James F. Byrnes, now a Supreme Court Justice.

Governor Maybank, in announcing appointment declined to say how long it was for. The law limits it to si x months. The Governor said, however, he planned to call a special election for Aug. 26 to fill the rest of the unexpired term. The term does not expire until January, 1943.

DECLARE GERMAN MORALE WEAKENING

NEW YORK, July 11—(A. P.)—Reports of lowered morale among German civilians reach Stockholm daily, Bernard Valery, Stockholm correspondent of the Columbia Broadcasting System, said today.

He said the German press yesterday carried an appeal to moviegoers to show more enthusiasm for military newsreels and declared that leaving the theater at once after the reels are shown (meaning apparently no pause for applause) shows "either thoughtlessness or something worse."

According to Valery's version of the press appeal, it said this attitude of moviegoers would not be tolerated.

ASKS $50 DAMAGES

Eugene W. Hayes, 524 East Grant street, is asking $50 from Florine B. Dochter, Christiana, R. D. 1, for automobile damages reputedly suffered in an accident January 21 on the Lincoln highway. The statement of claim, filed this week by A. C. Alspach, attorney for Hayes, asserts that Miss Dochter drove her car directly into the path of Hayes' car.

DRIVE TO HALT GOODS TO NAZIS

U. S. Studies Plan to List All Purchasing Agents For Germany.

WASHINGTON, July 11.—(A. P.)—United States defense officials, determined to end leakage of American goods to Germany, were reported giving serious consideration today to the compilation of a world-wide list of firms which serve as Nazi purchasing agents.

The British are known to have a "blacklist," as such listings are called when prepared by belligerent governments, and presumably this information has been made available to American officials for such use as they desire.

Other sources of information understood to be at the disposal of Brig.-Gen. Russell L. Maxwell, export control chief, include an inventory being made by the treasury of foreign assets frozen in this country and data on Nazi activities in South America gathered by the office of commercial and cultural relations between the American republics.

The extent to which American manufactured supplies and raw materials—steel, oil and the like—may now be reaching Germany was not ascertainable. Several factors, however, lead officials to believe that the flow has been greatly curtailed.

In the first place, the hostilities between the Reich and Russia has had the effect of closing the Siberian back-door route for supplies to Germany. Furthermore, the United States has imposed export restrictions on most militarily valuable supplies in recent months, and simultaneously has been waging virtual economic warfare on suspected Axis agents in South America.

If any further leaks are to be plugged, the next step was believed to be the preparation of a master list, which would provide a guide for all interested government departments, and also give exporters an index enabling them to determine what firms to deal with.

JUDGE WOULD WHIP DRUNKEN DRIVERS

DULUTH, Minn., July 11—(A. P.)—Punish drunken drivers at the whipping post, says Municipal Judge William P. Murphy of Crookston. Judge Murphy advocated such treatment yesterday during a heated discussion on traffic laws at the Minnesota Municipal Judges Association annual meeting here.

"Putting a man in jail or fining him only penalizes his family," said Judge Murphy. "As for society, it fails to profit by his incarceration. If I had my way I would advocate use of the whipping post. Then the one who deserves punishment would receive."

NAZI PROFESSOR CONVICTED BY U. S.

WASHINGTON, July 11—(A. P.)—Dr. Friedrich Ernst Auhagen of New York was convicted in Federal District Court today of charges of failing to register with the State Department as an agent of the German government and of distributing foreign propaganda in the United States.

Auhagen is a former college professor and lecturer. The guilty verdict carries with it a possible sentence of two years in jail and a $1,000 fine.

Tests Show N. Y. Harbor Traffic Safe From Air Raiders At Night

Ships Operate With Ease In Semi-Blackout of Buoy Lights in Channel; Searchlights At Army Bases Easily Trace Test Plane

NEW YORK, July 11.—(A. P.) — Air and water forces of the Coast Guard today totaled up results of surprise tests made during the night and decided that channels leading to the world's greatest harbor are safe from any enemy raiders at night.

Without advising the powerful ring of Army bases surrounding the vital waterway of the plans, a Coast Guard plane droned for hours over Ambrose channel, whose buoy lights had been dimmed sufficiently to permit merchant marine traffic. The modified blackout was effective at a fraction of the distance from which the lights normally become invisible.

The problem has been worked over by Treasury Department and naval experts for the past six months in an effort to determine whether New York might have to follow the custom now established in closing many belligerent ports between sunset and sunrise and facing the inevitable and devastating consequences of pre-dawn raiders preying upon merchant ships clustered at channel mouths.

The experiment barely had begun before surrounding forts sent out long fingers of lights seeking the identity of the Coast Guard plane. The beams played on the plane as it flew at high and low altitudes. Eventually, Lieut. Watson Burton, the pilot, requested the Army by wireless to turn off the searchlights so he could complete the tests.

From the plane, the channel lights — dimmed from 390 candlepower to 10 by removing reflectors and substituting green and red glass —seemed to go on and off as the amphibian lost of gained altitude. Climbing as little as 100 feet at times, it appeared as though some great breath had blown out the candles on a birthday cake.

Three Coast Guard vessels patrolled the 10-mile-long channel. Capt. Ralph Dempwolf, Coast Guard commandant, said they and merchant ships operated with ease in the semi-blackout.

Treasury officials said the test was of particular importance here, because the vast commerce through the port of New York would be vital to the nation at war as well as in peace. In normal times, about 100,000 vessels enter New York each year — about three times the number stopping at London, the world's second port.

Plays Tragic Role

A tragic role was the last one played by exotic, 27-year-old Tamara Charle, above, Russian-born Broadway singer. Found dead in an Albany, N. Y., hotel, police said "domestic difficulties" had driven her to kill her five-year-old daughter, Dorothy, and, 12 hours later, kill herself. (Photo by Bruno of Hollywood, from NEA)

DOOMED SLAYER GIVEN RESPITE

Gov. James Stays Execution of Hitch-Hiker Who Killed Lumber Dealer.

HARRISBURG, July 11—(A. P.)—Governor James today granted a respite to Harold Frisbie, 33, under death sentence in Sullivan county for murder, staying his execution until the week beginning October 20.

The respite was allowed to permit the Board of Pardons now in summer recess, to review Frisbie's case. He had been sentenced to die the week beginning July 28 for the slaying of Edward Lee, 60, wealthy lumber man last October 14.

Frisbie, a resident of Bucks county, pleaded guilty to shooting Lee while attempting to steal his automobile and was sentenced to death after the Sullivan County Court heard testimony to determine the degree of guilt. The sentence was affirmed recently by the State Supreme Court.

Lee's body was found stuffed under a small bridge five miles from Forksville, October 17, three days after he disappeared while enroute to Towanda to pay taxes.

Traced to his home near Doylestown, Pa., where the lumber man's car was found in the yard, Frisbie admitted shooting Lee seven times. On the witness stand, Frisbie said:

"I started firing. I don't know why. I just wanted the car. I didn't figure on shooting or anything."

He explained he had "hitched" a ride with Lee intending to take the car to commit a holdup in Sullivan County.

HUNT FOR BODIES OF UNIDENTIFIED MAN AND BOY, 7, IN RIVER

Police today were seeking the body of an unidentified man, about forty-five years old, who disappeared while swimming in the Susquehanna at the foot of Union street, Columbia, at 8:50 P. M. yesterday. Search also is being continued for the body of Eugene Henry Shenk, seven, Marietta, who drowned in the river near his home on June 21 when he toppled from a boat.

Harry Creek, 270 South Fifth street; Arthur Jones, 648 Furnace avenue, and Martha Jones, 313 Third street, Columbia, told police the man was swimming about 25 yards from the shore last evening when he began moaning, threw up his hands and went down. The trio spread an alarm and a party led by Motor Policemen Philip Gerhard and Frank Leventhal made a futile attempt to recover the body.

The victim's hat, coat, shoes and shirt was found on the river bank but there was no identification in the clothing. Police expressed the belief that the victim was a transient, who went swimming to cool off.

FLASH DENTISTRY FOR PATROLMAN

JEFFERSON CITY, Mo., July 11—(A. P.)—Patrolman Claude Short showed up for work with two chipped front teeth and this story:

"A storm came up while I was squirrel hunting. Lightning hit a tree in front of me, forked up out of the ground and into the end of my gun barrel. "My head shook so hard it broke these two front teeth."

City's Got Something To Tie To On Gasless Sundays

LEFT AT THE POST—In county towns the "carriage trade" hitches up its teams to plumber-style posts that have replaced old wooden ones that Dobbin could chew while he waited. Scene at right in New Holland. (Photo by Charles S. Rice)

BRIDLE BITER was the classic Federal eagle hitching post in 200 block of East King street. Post at right, in first block of South Lime street, dares you to try it.

FORGOTTEN BUT NOT GONE are the dozens of old hitching posts that wait in vain for a horse along the busy curbs of Lancaster city, crowded by shiny fenders or quarantined beneath "No Parking" signs. Maybe it will take a "gasless Sunday" to bring them back to their old-time usefulness.

HITCH SOMEWHERE?—Most of the city's remaining hitching posts are iron, a few wood, but this one, in 500 block of East King street, is made of concrete. That's Charles Kendig gnawing the apple.

THEN . . . AND . . . NOW
Photos three-quarters of a century apart, taken from the same spot along the North side of East King street just off the square, give you some inkling of why so many hitching posts still rear their iron heads around the town.

MORE HORSES than the iron hitching post at Farnum and Queen streets saw in its lifetime linger under the hood of the car parked beside it. Wooden post at right provides just that proper touch for cowboy games indulged in by Ronnie Herr at corner of Conestoga and Queen streets.

SCHOOL DAYS, COOL DAYS—Hoping low temperatures will yield high grades, these three Summer school students at MSTC cop a couple of cones between classes. They're Anna Mary Smith, Mary Smith, and Maribelle Brubaker, in the usual order.

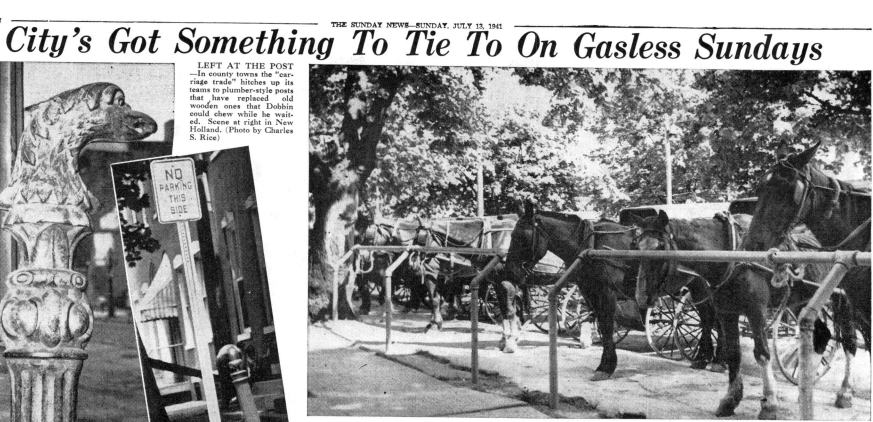

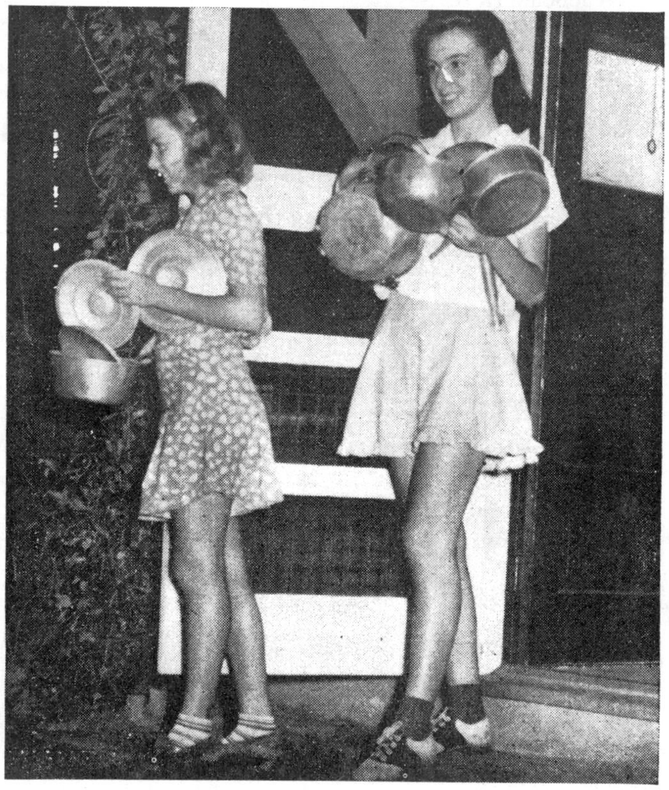

TO ARMS!—The call for all Lancaster's unused aluminum pots and pans to be converted into armament is answered by Ethel, eleven, and Marian, fourteen, daughters of Mrs. A. F. Chesly, of West Lancaster, who's going to contribute the kitchenware they're carrying, to the drive scheduled for July 23.

WEATHER
Eastern Pennsylvania: Fair And Slightly Warmer Wednesday; Thursday Increasing Cloudiness And Continued Warm.
Intell Journal Stormograph Reading: Cloudy And Warmer, Followed By Unsettled Weather Wednesday.

Intelligencer Journal.

The Leading Newspaper in the Garden Spot of America, Home Owned for Home Folks Since 1794

Baseball
Lancaster 7
Wilmington ... 2
Details Page 11.

VOLUME LXXVII.—NO. 270. CITY The Intelligencer Founded 1799 The Journal Founded 1794 LANCASTER, PA., WEDNESDAY MORNING, JULY 23, 1941. Entered at Post Office at Lancaster, Pa. as second class mail matter 16 PAGES, 128 COLUMNS.—THREE CENTS.

JAP DRIVE ON INDO-CHINA HINTED

WELLES GIVES OUTLINE FOR LASTING PEACE

Disarmament, Equal Economic Opportunities Urged As Post-War Aims

THRU STRONG LEAGUE

Washington — (AP) — Sumner Welles, acting Secretary of State, said Tuesday night that a post war association of nations, strong enough to guarantee disarmament and equal economic opportunities, was the ideal for which "peoples of good will" should strive as a foundation of permanent peace.

In an address at a cornerstone laying of a new wing of the Norwegian legation, Welles declared that free governments and peace loving people should now be preparing for "the better day" that would come with "the crushing defeat of those who are sacrificing mankind to their own lust for power and for loot."

Welles' speech constituted the most specific pronouncement yet given by a high administration official on the post war aims of the American government.

The League of Nations, as President Wilson conceived it, Welles said, "failed in part because of the blind selfishness of men here in the United States, as well as in other parts of the world."

(The United States Senate blocked American entry into the League in 1920.)

It failed also, he continued, "because of its utilization by certain powers primarily to advance their own political and commercial ambitions."

WHY LEAGUE FAILED

But he declared with emphasis that the League "failed chiefly because of the fact that it was forced to operate, by those who dominated its councils, as a means of maintaining the status quo."

"It was never enabled to operate," Welles said, as its chief spokesman had intended, as an elastic and impartial instrument in bringing about peaceful and equitable adjustments between nations as time and circumstances proved necessary."

Welles said that "some instrumentality must unquestionably be found to achieve such adjustments when the nations of the earth again undertake the task of restor-

More of PEACE on Page 9

"We Lead All The Rest"
FARM CORNER
By
The Farm Editor

LOCAL BOYS WIN JUDGING PRIZES

Melvin Rohrer, First With $8.00 In Prize Money At Percheron Conference

Melvin Rohrer, Lancaster R. D. 4, was awarded eight dollars in cash prizes at the National Percheron Judging conference held Monday and Tuesday at Frederick, Md. Rohrer was judged high boy from Lancaster county in the boys and girls contest, and was placed in the blue ribbon group of both the stallions and mares classes. Rohrer was one of 63 entrants, and scored approximately 500 points out of 600.

William Risser, Bainbridge R. D. 1, was also placed in the blue ribbon group for judging Percheron mares. Prizes were also won by Richard Lefever, Lancaster R. D. 4, Herbert Royer, Lancaster R. D. 3, and Dale Kreiner, Elizabethtown R. D. 3. The five boys totaled winnings of twenty-two dollars.

Fourteen states were represented from the east and mid-west United States.

Intelligencer Journal Weather Calendar

COMPARATIVE TEMPERATURE

Station	High	Low
Intell Journal	84	60
Water Works	81	54
Ephrata	87	54
Last Year (Ephrata)	98	72
Official High for Year, July 1		98
Official Low for Year, January 14		11
Character of Day		Clear

HOURLY TEMPERATURES (Tuesday)

3 a. m.	64	4 p. m.	84
4 a. m.	63	5 p. m.	83
5 a. m.	61	6 p. m.	81
6 a. m.	60	7 p. m.	80
7 a. m.	62	8 p. m.	78
8 a. m.	63	9 p. m.	73
9 a. m.	69	10 p. m.	72
10 a. m.	74	11 p. m.	70
11 a. m.	78	Midnight	70
Noon	81	(Wednesday)	
1 p. m.	83	1 a. m.	69
2 p. m.	84	2 a. m.	69
3 p. m.	84	3 a. m.	69

HUMIDITY
8 a. m.—72; Noon—55; 2 p. m.—42; 4 p. m.—46; Midnight—72
Average Humidity—58
Dew Point Midnight—61

More of WEATHER on Page 14

DAYLIGHT TIME IN INTELL
All time mentioned in the Intelligencer Journal is Daylight Time unless otherwise noted.

First Volunteer

RICHARD FLOWERS SHULTZ

MANHEIM YOUTH FIRST 21-YEAR-OLD SLATED FOR ARMY

Richard Flowers Shultz Volunteers; Will Be Examined On August 6

To Richard Flowers Shultz, 14 N. Charlotte st., Manheim, goes the honor of being the first twenty-one-year old registered July 1 with Country Board No. 1 at Mount Joy, who volunteered for the United States Army. His serial number is S-61.

Shultz, who was twenty-one in June, volunteered Monday. A son of Mary Ressler, he will go to Harrisburg August 6 for his final physical examination.

The youth, a former resident of Mount Joy, is employed at the Noggles Garment company, Manheim. He is a member of the Friendship Fire company at Mount Joy.

BOARD 5 GETS CALL FOR 3 OBJECTORS

Trio To Go To New Pennsylvania Camp On August 5; Two To Go Tomorrow

A second contingent of conscientious objectors from Lancaster county will leave August 5 for the new work camp which will be opened Thursday at Red Bridge, nine miles from Kane in the Allegheny National forest. The camp is operated by the Brethren church.

County Board No. 5 at Ephrata announced Tuesday that it had received orders for three conscientious objectors to report. Designated were, Abram W. Bollinger, Lititz R. D. 1; Samuel S. Fasnacht, Stevens R. D., and Earl F. Minnich, Lititz R. D.

The Lancaster county youths are scheduled to leave Thursday in the initial group of eighteen. They are: John H. Andes, Ephrata R. D. 3, and Richard Buckwalter, Bareville R. D. 1. They are enrolled with County Draft Board No. 4 at Strasburg.

The eight local draft boards were awaiting master lists of the numbers drawn in the National lottery Thursday for newly enrolled twenty-one-year-olds so that they could figure out order numbers. Delay in issuing the master lists, clerks point out, is holding up the mailing of questionnaires.

TALMAGE MAN LOSES LEG IN QUARRY GEARS

Chester Hoover, 35, Injured In Accident On Stone Grader At Stoltzfus Quarry

Chester Hoover, thirty-five, of Talmage, was seriously injured early Tuesday morning when working on the elevator at the D. M. Stoltzfus stone quarry, near Oregon. While adjusting the grader he fell and caught his right leg in the gears which turn the huge cylindrical sieve, and his foot and ankle were mangled.

Morris Stoltzfus, son of Hoover's employer, was working with Hoover and had to descend about 35 feet to the bottom of the crusher to stop the machinery. He and other employes then had to lower the injured man from the top, and rushed him to St. Joseph's hospital where Hoover's leg was amputated below the knee. His condition was reported as fair Tuesday evening.

COLUMBIANS NABBED FOR SHOPLIFTING

Girls Arrested In York; Police Say They Had Four Stolen Dresses

Two young Columbia women were arrested in York Monday on shoplifting charges after they were alleged to have stolen four dresses from one store, and attempted to walk out of another with four more dresses not paid for.

Goldie Heisey, twenty-one, of North Front street, Columbia, was committed to the York county prison for a hearing Friday before Alderman W. F. Owen, and her companion, aged fifteen, was committed to a home.

Mayor Cary Makes Last-Minute Plea For Aluminum

Collections Of "Pots And Pans For Airplanes" Starts At 2 P. M.

PLANS ARE COMPLETED

The deep throated roar of factory whistles and the pealing of bells at 2 p. m. Wednesday (today) will signal the start of the collection of unused aluminum "pots and pans for airplanes."

The actual collection of the metal for defense has been worked out with the precision of an Army maneuver by the Lancaster chapter of DeMolay, in charge of the drive, Clarence C. Newcomer, chairman.

NEW HOLLAND RESIDENTS CONTRIBUTE 220 POUNDS

New Holland—A total of 220 pounds of aluminum was collected in New Holland on Monday. Collection was made by the Boy Scout troop of the borough, and John Ruoss drove the truck.

At 1 p. m. hundreds of Boy Scouts under the direction of Scout Executive W. C. Armstrong will gather at the Old Boys High school. There each Scout will be assigned to one of the 124 trucks donated by local business concerns to collect the metal.

Quietly the Scouts will report for their transport vehicle and as the whistles and the bells sound, the trucks will roar out to cover the city. Each driver will have a map with the section he will cover outlined.

TAGS TO BE DISPLAYED

At each house where a brightly colored tag is hanging from the door—handed to each housewife who promised a contribution in the pre-collection canvass Monday and Tuesday—the truck will stop and the uniformed Scouts will get the aluminum. As the trucks are loaded the metal will be dumped at the

More of ALUMINUM on Page 9

MAYOR D. E. CARY

EXTEND USO FUND DRIVE AS TOTAL REACHES $11,500.43

Few County Reports In; Campaign May Be Continued Until August 1

A total of $11,500.43 has been raised to date in the city-county campaign for the United Service Organization, it was announced by Col. C. P. Stahr, chairman at a report meeting Tuesday night in the Y. W. C. A.

Of the total, $3,281.33 was reported Tuesday night, and the remainder previously. Few of the county districts have reported as yet, Col. Stahr said, commenting that the campaign will be extended to Saturday and if necessary, to August 1, until the total of $29,000 has been reached.

TUESDAY'S REPORTS

The detailed reports Tuesday night, which are in addition to amounts previously reported, are as follows: Second ward, city, $176.78; Third ward, $68.79; Fourth ward, $67; Fifth ward, $82.01; Sixth ward, $177.73; Seventh ward, $128; Eighth ward, $128.01; Ninth ward, $218.92; miscellaneous, including proceeds from benefit dance last Saturday, $34.84; clubs and organizations, $26; booths, $113.18; Mercantile division, $132.37; Industrial division, $51.11; Bausman, $5; Strasburg, $169.35; Churchtown, $70; West Lampeter, $32.11; Lincoln Highway East, $120; area west of Lancaster, $170.30;

More of U. S. O. on Page 9

SENATE APPROVES SPECIAL POLICE UNIT FOR THE NAVY

Sen. Walsh Reveals Some Serious Damage Suffered Due To Saboteurs

Washington —(AP)— Overriding protests that the legislation would create an American gestapo, the Senate Tuesday passed a bill setting up a special police force to investigate sabotage and espionage in Navy yards and stations. The vote was 41 to 14.

The measure, already passed by the House, goes back to that chamber for consideration of Senate amendments.

CLAIMS SABOTAGE

Chairman Walsh, Dem., Mass., of the Senate Naval committee said such an investigative force was necessary because some naval establishments had suffered serious damage at the hands of saboteurs, and because the Navy lacked information concerning the number of Communists and Nazis employed in its expanding centers.

Senator Norris, Ind., Neb., and Senator Johnson, Rep., Calif., spoke out critically in oposition. Norris said the investigating force would be patterned after the secret police of European totalitarian nations, and Johnson charged that the bill would provide $1,000,000 a year for a "private army for Frank Knox," Secretary of the Navy.

Johnson attacked Knox as "irresponsible." Walsh replied that while he had differed with Knox on foreign policies he believed the Secretary had done good work by putting "pep" in the Navy and cutting away red tape.

Explaining the pending bill,

More of NAVAL POLICE on Page 14

LIST PROGRAM FOR TONIGHT'S CONCERT

The Malta band, under the direction of William H. Price, will present the third in the series of public band concerts at Buchanan park at 7:30 o'clock this Wednesday evening.

The program will be: Fanfare, Trumpeter's Carnival, (Losey); Malta Band Theme song; overture, Poet and Peasant, (Suppe); Waltz, L'Estudiantina, (Waldteufel); overture, King of Diamonds, (Lavallee); Medley, Yankee Hash, (Miller); We're All Americans, (Mangan); March, The Invincible Eagle, (Sousa); overture, Adonis, (St. Clair); Waltz, Barcarole, (Roberts); Hot Trombone, (Filmore); The Old Army Game, (army marching song, Yoder); God Bless America, (Berlin); Star Spangled Banner, (Key).

34 REGISTER FOR FALL ELECTIONS

Registrars Will Sit Today In Akron, Elizabethtown, Columbia And Quarryville

Thirty-four persons registered to vote at the first of several special registration days held in the county Tuesday.

At Adamstown, three Democrats registered. At Strasburg, six Republicans and one Democrat registered and seven removal notices were filed. At Ephrata, 21 Republicans, one Democrat and one Independent registered; 16 removal notices were filed and two changed their registration from Democrats to Republicans and one from Independent to Republican.

Wednesday registrars will sit at Akron, Columbia, Elizabethtown and Quarryville. The additional registrars will be Monroe Duckworth, Rep., and Christ Rudy, Dem.

The special days were established as a convenience for voters who might find it impractical to get to the court house to register before the September primary.

BOYS BLAMED FOR BLAZE AT COLUMBIA

Bonfire Ignites Garage And Small Shed, Owner Says; Automobile Is Saved

Fire destroyed a two-story garage and a small adjoining shed on the property of John A. Gipe, 632 Walnut st., Columbia, shortly after 4 p. m. Tuesday. A general alarm brought out all equipment of the borough fire department.

Gipe told firemen the fire was started by a group of boys who built a bonfire at one corner of the building. He was able to enter the garage and drive out his automobile, but articles stored on the second floor were consumed. He said he could not estimate the damage.

REV. MUSSELMAN IMPROVED

The condition of Rev. J. H. Musselman, pastor of St. John's Lutheran church, was reported as improved Tuesday night by attendants at the Lancaster General hospital, where he is a medical patient.

NAZI PLANES BOMB MOSCOW SECOND NIGHT

Scores Killed And Wounded As Homes And A Hospital Are Hit

FIRES EXTINGUISHED

(By The Associated Press)

German bombers attacked Moscow for the second night in succession Tuesday night but the Russian communique declared stubborn defenses prevented the main body of the 150 attacking planes from reaching the Red capital.

"Only isolated planes broke through to the city," said the communique. It reported that several fires which broke out in dwellings were extinguished by fire brigades.

Earlier a German broadcast heard in London reported that many airmen were over Moscow "dropping bombs and causing more fires and destruction."

Moscow reported scores killed and wounded and several homes and a hospital damaged severely. For the second successive night a Russian communique said only a relative few of the attacking planes actually broke through the city's defenses—night fighter patrols and heavy anti-aircraft barrages.

The Russians declared at least 15 raiders downed.

The German radio, heard in London, announced early Wednesday (today) that 20 big fires were started in the district east of the Kremlin governmental headquarters during Tuesday night's Nazi attack on the Soviet capital.

These fires set in the second straight night raid were "apart from numerous direct hits in the Kremlin area," the announcer said in a broadcast heard here.

The German announcer added that Moscow's anti-aircraft defenses "hardly bothered the German airplanes at all."

A reactivated German-Finnish drive on the Karelian Isthmus apparently designed to cut the Murmansk-Leningrad railway was acknowledged by the Soviet com-

More of WAR on Page 9

COPPER MAGNATE LEAVES ESTATE TO FOUR SHOW GIRLS

William Guggenheim's Will Leaves Nothing To Widow Or Son

New York — (AP) — The Daily News said Tuesday night that four show-girls were to inherit the entire estate of William Guggenheim, copper millionaire who turned to song writing at 71, under the terms of his will soon to be filed in Probate court.

The will of the former philanthropist, who died June 27, left nothing to Mrs. Guggenheim or to his son, William, the News reported.

The widow's attorney, Abraham L. Bienstock, said that under New York law Mrs. Guggenheim could claim one-third of the estate, regardless of the will. He said he did not know what action Mrs. Guggenheim would take.

WORTH OVER $1,000,000

The News said the girls, identified as Mildred Borst, Mary Alice Rice, and Florence Sullivan, all of New York city, and Lilyan Andrus of Hollywood, were to "share and

More of WILL on Page 9

PROF. CHARLES UNIMPROVED

The condition of Professor Rollin E. Charles, of Franklin and Marshall college, was reported as unchanged Tuesday, by attendants at St. Joseph's hospital, where he is a medical patient.

New Librarian

CLIFFORD BUELL WIGHTMAN of Grand Rapids, Mich., recently appointed as librarian of the Lancaster Free Public Library, who will assume his duties on September 1.

4 U. S. Nurses Tell Story Of 12 Days In Open Boat At Sea

Survivors Of Torpedoed British Ship Landed By Navy Transport At Norfolk After Being Rescued By U. S. Destroyer

Norfolk, Va.— (AP) — The story of 12 days and 11 nights in an open boat in the North Atlantic after their ship, en route to England, had been torpedoed, was told Tuesday night by survivors landed here by a U. S. Navy transport.

Four were American Red Cross nurses and the fifth a Marine Corporal who were picked up by an American destroyer July 5 and taken to Reykjavik, Iceland, for medical care.

Put ashore at the Norfolk Navy Yard, the group was removed to the Portsmouth Naval hospital. Naval officers said at the time they were taken aboard the destroyer they were suffering of nervous exhaustion and some of gangrene.

REPORTED SAFE JULY 9

The four nurses, members of a party of ten who sailed as the only passengers aboard the 7,000-ton vessel from New Orleans, La., June 5, were reported safe July 9.

The nurses, listed as Marion Blissett of Detroit, Mich., Victoria Pelc, of Auburn, N. Y., Rachel St. Pierre, of Boston, and Lilian M. Pesnicak, of Albany, N. Y., were taken in a Navy ambulance to the Portsmouth Naval hospital.

The Marine, Corporal E. H. MacAllister, also was removed to the hospital.

In a statement made to Capt. Clarence Gulbranson of the Navy transport, the four nurses said the torpedo attack occurred at 7:15 a. m. June 24 without warning. Two minutes after the first torpedo struck the port side, another ripped into the vessel and the ship sank six to eight minutes later.

SUB CAME TO SURFACE

While watching the debris float by, the nurses said a submarine came to the surface, the conning tower opened and an officer, speaking perfect English, asked the name of the ship, the port from which it sailed, its cargo and destination.

After a conference among the submarine officers, the nurses said officers of the torpedoed ship rejected a proposal that the women be taken aboard the submersible and the submarine disappeared with a promise to "send a ship to pick you up."

Shortly after the sinking of the ship, six men and the four girls were transferred to the captain's boat, which then carried 14 per-

More of NURSES on Page 14

STOLEN AUTOMOBILE DESTROYED BY FIRE

Ruins of Car Taken From Garage Near Marietta Found In York County Woods

An automobile stolen on July 2 from A. H. Engle, Marietta R. D. 1, was found consumed by fire in the woods near York Haven by State Motor Police of the York substation, Columbia police were notified Tuesday.

Mr. Engle said the car was taken from his garage at night.

Appropriations Committee Group Studies Indiantown Gap's Needs

Need For Landscaping, Chapels, Plane Landing Field Seen On Congressional Inspection Tour

Indiantown Gap, Pa.—(AP)—A special group of the House Appropriations Committee of Congress made a study of the 28th Division's post here Tuesday to determine "what is needed to make this camp 100 per cent equipped."

Ten members of a sub-committee, headed by U. S. Rep. J. Buell Snyder of Fayette county made the inspection tour.

"Our specific mission here is to see just what has been accomplished in the way of material construction for the moneys we have given to Indiantown Gap," Snyder said.

Accompanying Snyder were U. S. Reps. J. P. McGranary, Francis J. Myers, Frank Smith, J. E. Sheridan and M. J. Bradley, of Philadelphia, James Wright and Samuel A. Weiss of Allegheny county, and Judge N. P. Carr, of North Carolina.

REVIEW TROOPS

The visiting officials arrived at the entrance to the reservation at 10:30 a. m. and were met by an escort comprised of the 104th Cavalry. As they approached the 28th Division headquarters they were accorded a 17-gun salute by Battery F, 107th Field Artillery, commanded by First Lt. Robert W. Ward, Pittsburgh.

The 2[illegible] Division's 14,000 troops and 1,9[illegible] motorized units then passed in an hour-long review before the official party and Major

More of INDIANTOWN on Page 9

Roosevelt Reveals Jap Censorship On Radio And Cables

Reports From Many Capitols Pieced Together To Indicate Possible Nipponese Drive Southward; President Hints New Action May Be Taken To Battle Nazi Infiltration Of Latin America

Washington—(AP) — President Roosevelt went out of his way Tuesday to announce that a radio and cable censorship had been imposed in Japan, and his action in conjunction with reports from other capitals prompted speculation as to whether the big Japanese push to the south was about to begin.

From Vichy in unoccupied France, came reports that negotiations on French-Indo China were in progress with the Tokyo government, inducing a general belief that the latter had presented sweeping demands for economic and military concessions.

At the same time, the Paris newspaper Les Nouveaux, spokesman for supporters of French collaboration with Germany, urged that France work with Japan for the protection of Indo-China, lest France lose that territory altogether.

TOKYO REPORTS SCANNED

In Tokyo the newspapers started a furore over Indo-China and Thailand (Siam) and the Dutch East Indies as well. They charged that British, Free French and Chinese forces were preparing to invade Indo-China. All three countries mentioned have been included in the Japanese "great Asia" program.

A Japanese army spokesman in Shanghai acknowledged that Japanese reservists living in China had been called for duty, but he said the move was merely for training.

A British radio broadcast heard in New York said reports of large scale mobilization throughout Japan and requistioning of horses and motor trucks indicated "big developments are imminent."

In London an authorized British source said reports that Japan was making demands on Indo-China were disturbing, noting that assurances given Britain last month that Japan had no territorial demands on Indo-China were rendered by Foreign Minister Yosuke Matsuoka, who since has been removed from the government.

British sources in Singapore, expressing surprise over Japanese reports that the British were preparing to invade Indo-China, said the reports "possibly are being circulated to pave the way for Japanese action."

"An attempt may be made to justify Japanese demands on Indo-China by the bogey of British intervention," these sources said.

Piecing the puzzle together, observers here pictured Japan obtaining both military and economic concessions of a major character in Indo-China and Thailand.

This would carry the Japanese within striking distance of British Malaya and the English stronghold at Singapore, with the Dutch East Indies and their great raw material resources lying just beyond.

A naval dispatch concerning the Japanese censorship was presented to the President late in the day just before his press conference.

More of DEFENSE on Page 14

SENATE PROBERS TOLD OF SURVEY FOR DEFENSE HERE

Firms Got Navy Yard Contracts By Cooperating Witness Tells Committee

Washington, D. C.—Lancaster county, Pa., manufacturers were able to get some orders from the Philadelphia Navy yard as the result of the formation of the Manufacturers' Cooperative Defense Committee of Lancaster county, the Senate Defense Investigating committee was told Tuesday by Pierce Williams, of the WPA labor staff.

Williams, formerly with the Labor division of the OPM, advocated pool production facilities on a local basis and simplification of procurement procedure through negotiated contracts.

Edward R. Stettinius, director of priorities for OPM, called for a clearer definition of the relationship between the priorities division of the Office of Production Management and the Office of Price Administration and Civilian Supply, which is headed by Leon Henderson.

Stettinius, chief of the Priorities Division, said that until the relationship was clarified the problem of small businesses unable to get raw materials because of priorities could not be solved satisfactorily.

Chairman Truman asked Stettinius if it was necessary that some-

More of SENATE on Page 9

RURAL CARRIERS NOMINATE OFFICERS

Park F. Esbenshade One of Two Seeking Presidency of State Association

Gettysburg, Pa.—(AP)—Park E. Esbenshade, of Bird-in-Hand, Lancaster county, and James E. Bratton, of Clearfield county, were nominated Tuesday for the presidency of the Pennsylvania Rural Letters Carriers Association at its 39th annual convention here.

Esbenshade

Mrs. John Kerr, Mercer county, was nominated without opposition for re-election as president of the Women's Auxiliary.

The convention ends Wednesday with election of officers and choice of the 1942 convention city. Delegates toured the battlefield Tuesday and attended a banquet Tuesday night, at which U. S. Senator James Mead of New York, Congressman Harry L. Haines, Red Lion, and the third assistant postmaster, General Ramsey Black, of Washington, were scheduled to speak.

PEANUT TAKEN FROM DENVER BABY'S LUNG

John Martin, 16-Months-Old, Undergoes Operation At Bronchoscopic Clinic In Philadelphia

Philadelphia — (AP) — A peanut was removed from the lung of sixteen-months-old John Martin of Denver R. D. 2, at the Jefferson hospital bronschoscope clinic Monday night. The clinic described his condition as excellent.

The boy is a son of Mr. and Mrs. John M. Martin, and was sent to Philadelphia from the Ephrata Community hospital Monday.

WEATHER
Eastern Pennsylvania: Generally Fair In Morning And Local Thundershowers In Afternoon Saturday; Slightly Cooler Saturday Night; Sunday Probable Scattered Thundershowers.
Intell Journal Stormograph Reading: Unsettled, Increasing Winds And Warmer Saturday.

Intelligencer Journal

The Leading Newspaper in the Garden Spot of America, Home Owned for Home Folks Since 1794

HALL OF FAME
Robert Moses Grove registered his 300th baseball pitching victory.
Details Page 10.

VOLUME LXXVII.—NO. 273. CITY The Intelligencer Founded 1799 The Journal Founded 1794 LANCASTER, PA., SATURDAY MORNING, JULY 26, 1941 Entered at Post Office at Lancaster, Pa. as second class mail matter 16 PAGES, 128 COLUMNS.—THREE CENTS.

U. S., BRITAIN FREEZE JAPAN'S ASSETS

N. J. POLITICAL LEADER GUILTY ON TAX CHARGES

Enoch L. (Nucky) Johnson Convicted Of Evading Income Levies

PLANS TO APPEAL

Camden, N. J.—(AP)—A federal jury convicted Enoch L. (Nucky) Johnson late Friday of two counts of an indictment charging the fifty-eight-year-old Atlantic City Republican leader with income tax evasion. He was acquitted of a third count.

The jury found that the Atlantic county treasurer evaded taxes on an income of $124,800 which the government contended came as protection money from numbers operators at the shore resort in 1936 and 1937.

ACQUITTED ON ONE COUNT

The third count on which Johnson was acquitted accused him of evading taxes on an income of $74,400 for 1935. This included $28,000 which the government asserted was unreported profit from the construction contract on Atlantic City's Union railroad terminal, and $46,400 from numbers operators.

Johnson reported an income of $87,076 for the three years.

Conviction carries a maximum penalty of 5 years imprisonment and $10,000 fine on each count of the indictment which government investigators considered the climax of a lengthy investigation of vice and gambling in the shore resort.

INCREASES BAIL

Judge Albert B. Maris announced he would impose sentence Friday at 9 a. m. (E.S.T.). The jurist increased the Atlantic City politician's bail from $5,000 to $25,000.

The Republican leader, who had admitted collecting $158,000 from the million dollar numbers business at Atlantic City during the three years, told newsmen after the verdict was announced that "I am shocked. I expected acquittal on all three counts."

He added he "most certainly" would appeal the case.

During the 10-day trial, Johnson, for 30 years Republican leader at the resort, testified he paid taxes on $79,875 he kept for himself out of the $158,500 he received from numbers operators. But he denied

More of JOHNSON on Page 14

House Overboard

Movers faced a tough job after this house fell off the timbers on which it was being hauled by trailer-truck from one location to another at White Plains, N. Y. The mishap occurred just a block from the structure's destination.

OBJECTORS' CAMP MAY BE SET UP IN LANCASTER COUNTY

Approval Of Federal Authorities Asked For Church-Sponsored Project

A request has been made to the federal authorities for the establishment of a camp for conscientious objectors in Lancaster county, it was learned Friday.

There are now 19 camps in the nation, largely in the east, which has about 600 conscientious objectors on induction lists.

A request for establishment of a camp in Franklin county is also before the authorities.

To receive federal approval, the camps selected by sponsoring churches must have work projects classed as "of national importance." Locally, it is understood, the project would be soil conservation, now being carried on by members of the CCC camp at the Water Works.

Latest of the camps to open was at Kane, Pa. There, Friday, 15 young men donned old clothes and set about preparing their civilian service camp for start of work August 1.

Thirteen Pennsylvanians, two from Lancaster county, and two men from Maryland, they were the initial contingent to arrive at the state's first camp for non-combatants. Twenty-two more are expected from Grottoes, Va., Sunday and others will arrive in groups until the camp's population numbers about 150.

The government pays their transportation and lodges them in five big wooden barracks at Red Bridge in the half-million acre Allegheny National Forest. The barracks formerly housed CCC workers, and the Civilian Service workers will continue their reforestation projects. They'll work without pay on a 44-hour week. Their board is paid by the churches with which they are affiliated.

Director L. L. Zeigler, said that while the camp is primarily for Pennsylvania members of the Church of the Brethren, members of other churches also opposed to war may be sent there.

Women Prisoners Whipped, Ala. Warden Loses Post

Five Offered To Take Lashings Instead Of Losing Privileges After Prison Beauty Parlor Riot; Governor Takes Action

Montgomery, Ala.—(AP)—Five white women prisoners accepted an offer to take whippings instead of losing privileges for participating in a Wetumpka State Prison beauty parlor riot and provoked an incident which resulted in the warden's resignation.

Governor Frank Dixon said Friday that seven lashes were administered by Warden J. Curtis Weldon, Sr., to each woman following a free-for-all fight that developed when an inmate was denied a manicure Saturday in the newly-installed prison beauty shop that was designed to improve morale and teach a trade.

SAYS WOMEN UNINJURED

The Governor declared the women were not injured by the whippings. "But we just don't use those methods in our prisons," he asserted.

A poker was wielded, hair pulled, faces slapped and scratched in the beauty parlor row, Dixon disclosed. From another authoritative source it was learned that the five leaders had been offered the alternative of the whipping or being deprived of prison privileges for sixty days.

Permission of the Department of Corrections and Institutions was not asked before the lashes were administered, the Governor said. Dixon emphasized that while prisoner floggings were permitted under Alabama law, regulations required that a permit be obtained from the department, that a physician examine the prisoner to determine if health would be impaired and witness the execution of such punishment.

WARDEN OFFERS RESIGNATION

Dixon said he learned of the affair Tuesday when he returned from Asheville, N. C., and called Weldon in immediately. Weldon's resignation was in his office Thursday, the Governor said.

Weldon declined comment. The Governor refused to reveal names of the women, pointing out it might retard rehabilitation efforts. "They have been treated badly, we recognize, and the warden is out," he said.

Mack Freeman was named acting warden at Wetumpka, where about 300 women are imprisoned, 30 per cent of them white.

The Governor said only one whipping had been administered during his administration at Atmore prison, which has 1,000 males, adding: "We have found other methods far more effective." He said that he now considered the incident closed.

MEXICO EXPELS NAZI FOR PLOT IN NICARAGUA

Report Exile Asked German Envoy For Planes To Start Revolution

TURNED OVER TO U. S.

Mexico City— (AP) —Informed diplomatic sources said Friday night that Mexico had expelled a Nicaraguan political exile because he had urged the German minister here to provide him with planes for a revolution in Nicaragua.

The ministry of the interior was said to have turned over the Nicaraguan, General Roberto Hurtado, to United States authorities at Laredo, Texas, where he was imprisoned pending final disposition of the case.

General Hurtado, a member of Nicaragua's Nazi party, was said to have written German Minister Rudt Von Collenberg that, "I have enough arms, but I need planes" for a coup against the Managua regime that exiled him several years ago.

RUMOR PLANES DELIVERED

One usually well-informed source said there were persistent rumors that crated Messerschmitt fighters had arrived recently in the Carribean area and it was believed Hurtado referred to these. The rumors of the arrival of the Messerschmitts, reported stored on out-of-the-way islands, have not been confirmed.

The General's request for assistance was said by the diplomatic sources to have been contained in a letter to Von Collenburg, a copy of which was obtained in a raid on Hurtado's home and turned over to the ministry of interior.

An official of the ministry, who acknowledged that Hurtado had been expelled, said he had been deported because "he was carrying on activities here contrary to Mexico's international policy."

U. S. Again Urges End Of Peru-Ecuador Clashes

Washington—(AP)—The United States sent a new appeal to Peru and Ecuador Friday night to end frontier clashes of their armed

More of PLOT on Page 11

RAF ATTACKS BERLIN FIRST TIME IN 53 DAYS

American - Made Flying Fortresses Used In Long Distance Raids

NAZIS SAY 4 DOWNED

Berlin —(Saturday)—(AP)— Berlin experienced another air raid last night after sleeping undisturbed for 53 consecutive nights. Authorized sources said no bombs were dropped within the city limits.

The RAF also attacked various points in northern Germany where explosive and incendiary bombs were said to have killed and wounded an unstated number of civilians and damaged or destroyed apartment buildings.

Military targets were undamaged, it was said, and five British planes were shot down.

German military circles claimed the British air offensive intended to relieve the Luftwaffe's pressure on Russia was a failure and said that German fighters and anti-aircraft artillery brought down 87 British planes in 30 hours on July 23-24.

Among these were nine American four-motored bombers described as "flying fortresses," they said.

(London said the raids were made with huge American-made Boeing "flying fortresses").

Moscow Says Lines Holding In Smolensk Sector

(By The Associated Press)

German efforts to smash through the Smolensk sector 230 miles west of Moscow were held for the tenth consecutive day Friday, and there were "no substantial changes" elsewhere on the long Baltic-Black Sea front, the Soviet information bureau announced early today (Saturday).

Fighting raged on into this, the eleventh day, in this vital area, and in the Porkhov, Polotsk-Nevel and Zhitomir sectors. The Germans were reported by Moscow to be still stalled 100 miles south of Leningrad in their northern push,

More of WAR on Page 11

Sweeping Economic Move Taken By Japs' 2 Largest Customers

Action Also Calls For Holding All Nipponese Ships; Netherlands Considers Similar Action; China's Assets Frozen Too, Upon Request, To Prevent Leakage To Japan; Nazis Encourage Axis Partners

(By the Associated Press)

The United States and the British empire took parallel counter-action against Japanese military moves into Indo-China today (Saturday), freezing all Japanese assets and holding all Japanese ships under their control.

The sweeping economic move by Japan's two largest customers was announced in separate statements by President Roosevelt in Hyde Park and the British in London.

The London statement said action to correspond with that of the British government in the United Kingdom was "being arranged in other parts of the Empire."

Informed sources said the British action was the first of its kind by Britain against "a country which neither is a declared enemy nor occupied or controlled by a declared enemy."

Earlier Prime Minister Mackenzie King had announced Canada's action in freezing Japanese assets and holding Japanese ships.

In London the Netherland government said it was in consultation with authorities of the Netherlands East Indies on measures "in connection with the British and American action."

China's assets also were frozen, at the specific request of Generalissimo Chiang Kai-Shek, apparently to make sure that Japan could not realize on property of the occupied part of China.

Foreign Secretary Anthony Eden told the House of Commons in London that "certain defense measures" had been taken in British Malaya and added that British and United States governments were in close communication over the situation.

The Vichy French government, meanwhile, announced definite conclusion of a "mutual defense agreement" with Japan on Indo-China—presumably giving Japan the right to occupy bases in the southern part of that French possession.

As the crisis thus rose, Germany offered more and more open encouragement to her Japanese partner in the Axis, indicating a greater interest in this Far-Eastern drama

More of JAPANESE on Page 9

U. S. ACTION MAY MEAN STOPPAGE OF OIL SHIPMENTS

Cash, Ships, Silk And Other Assets Included In President Roosevelt's Order

Washington —(AP)— President Roosevelt struck back Friday night against Japan for her push in French Indo-China by clamping a sweeping control over all economic intercourse between the United States and Japan, including cash, oil, ships, silk and other assets.

At the same time, at the request of China, he tied up Chinese assets in this country so that no one but the beleaguered government of Generalissimo Chiang Kai-Shek can use them.

Hereafter, a treasury license will be needed to take any Japanese assets outside the country or to send anything to Japan. This meant, according to a treasury spokesman, that oil can be kept from Japan's war machine by refusal of or even failure to act upon requests for permission to ship oil.

Whether such an embargo actually would be clamped down, however, remained to be seen. The asset "freezing" order put the treasury in a position to turn the economic screws on Japan. Just how hard they will be applied may depend, to some extent, on future events in the Far East.

The sweeping Presidential order, besides its ramifications in the field of high international policy, may have a marked effect on common folk both in the United States and Japan.

For example, it may eventually mean that American women will have to do without silk stockings, except for substitutes like nylon, the supply of which is inadequate. It may affect the Japanese curio

More of ROOSEVELT on Page 14

"We Lead All The Rest" FARM CORNER By *The Farm Editor*

PLAN SERIES OF FIELD MEETINGS FOR TOMATO GROWERS

J. M. Huffington, extension vegetable specialist of State College, has been engaged by the local Agricultural Extension Service to speak at a series of field meetings of tomato growers next week on plans for harvesting the coming crop. Seven meetings in all are planned.

Growers under contract with canning concerns are invited to bring their force of pickers to the sessions since points to be stressed at the field meetings are "what" kind of fruit to pick, "when" to pick, and "what to leave" on the field for further ripening.

Tomatoes used for fruit juice should be picked when "red ripe;" in the last four days of its ripening period the tomato normally adds from 15 to 20 per cent to its weight, so there is a gain in both grade and weight by leaving the fruit to reach the "red ripe" stage, it was announced. Last year the heaviest pickings came early in the month of August but from present

More of FARM CORNER on Page 9

U. S. O. CAMPAIGN EXCEEDS $15,000, MORE COMING IN

Many County Districts Yet To Be Heard From, Drive To Continue A Week

The Lancaster city and county campaign to raise funds for the United Service Organizations has gone over the $15,000 mark, it was announced by Col. Charles P. Stahr, general chairman, at a report meeting of the Steering Committee Friday night.

A total of $3,231.65 additional was turned in Friday night, which, added to the previous amount reported, brings the total to $15,127.91.

FINAL MEETING FRIDAY

Col. Stahr announced that the campaign in the county, where many districts are yet to be heard from, will continue all next week, and that the city drive will continue until the final report meeting next Friday night. The city districts will be thrown open to all workers, regardless of the district to which they have been assigned.

The new reports by divisions are as follows: First ward, $14.47; Second ward, $60.37; Fourth ward, $47.15; Fifth ward, $63.31; Sixth ward, $30.72; Eighth ward, $64.71; Ninth ward, $52.43; West Lancaster, $230; Big Gifts, $368; Clubs and organizations, $30; booths, $51.59; mercantile, $250.33; School Lane Hills, $66.25; Hamilton park and Lancaster township, $145.45; Industrial, $135.11; Rohrerstown, $104.57; Blue Ball, $100; Safe Harbor, $37.75; Christiana, $159.40; East Petersburg, $163.65; Strasburg,

More of U. S. O. on Page 14

TYPING BLOOD OF 15,000 MEMBERS OF THE 28TH DIVISION

Precautionary Move Intended To Insure Quick Aid For Wounded Men

Indiantown Gap, Pa.—(AP)—The 28th Division Friday began blood-typing approximately 15,000 officers and men in a precautionary move designed to insure quick aid for wounded men.

Knowledge of a soldier's blood type, a hospital attache pointed out, would be invaluable on a battlefield where immediate transfusions were needed to save lives.

Officers and enlisted men of the special troop, commanded by Lt. Col. Charles H. Middleton, Philadelphia, had their blood typed Friday and attaches said other units will be typed as quickly as possible. The time table calls for blood records of the entire 28th to be completed by August 13.

The blood type of each man will be inscribed on his personal identification disc, which is worn around his neck for the duration of his active service.

Six medical technicians Friday handled the mass typing operations for the special troop at the rate of three minutes per man.

GOV. JAMES SIGNS MEASURE CREATING 'LITTLE WPA' IN PA.

Appoints Harry R. Davidson Administrator, To Start Program At Once

Harrisburg — (AP) — Governor James Friday signed the bill creating a "little WPA" in Pennsylvania and appointed Harry R. Davidson as the administrator with instructions to inaugurate the program "at once."

Davidson has been a $5,000-a-year executive in the Highway Department handling Federal work relief angles of road construction. His salary remains the same and will be tapped from the Governor's payroll.

The bill authorized the state to set up its own work relief program with relief funds to be used to help local communities finance projects.

The Governor, before signing the measure, conferred with Howard L. Russell, Secretary of Assistance; I. Lamont Hughes, Secretary of Highways, Budget Secretary Edward B. Logan and Davidson.

TO START IMMEDIATELY

It was decided to initiate the WRP—Work Relief Program—immediately with "a great number of highway projects that either fell through or were abandoned entirely because the Federal WPA indicated it had not sufficient funds to go ahead with them," James said in a statement.

The measure provides the state "with something comparable to in-

More of LITTLE WPA on Page 9

BLOOD POISONING CLAIMS 2ND VICTIM

Jacob Myers, 56, Columbia, Dies From Tetanus As Result Of Fall; Gap Boy Died Thursday

Jacob Myers, fifty-six, 294 S. Fifth st., Columbia, died at 12:30 p. m. Friday of tetanus in the Columbia hospital, according to Dr. G. P. Taylor, deputy coroner, of Columbia. He was the second to die in the county in two days of blood poisoning. Robert H. Montgomery, thirteen, Gap R. D. 1, died Thursday of blood poisoning after a boil on his ankle became infected.

Mr. Myers suffered a head injury in a fall about two weeks ago, but had not believed the injury serious enough to seek medical attention. He was admitted to the hospital at 11 p. m. Thursday by ambulance.

He was a member of the Lutheran church at Middletown, where he was born, a son of the late George and Belinda Flowers Myers. Besides his wife, Annie Kathryn Myers, he is survived by the folowing children, Paul, William, George, Kathryn, wife of Lewis Laudenberger, Margaret, wife of Cleon Hilliar, and Elizabeth, wife of Russel Hilliar, all of Columbia; and Minnie R., wife of John Channels, of Pequea R. D. 1. He is also survived by two brothers, George Myers, of Columbia, and Henry Myers, of Chester; and one step-brother, John Gipe, of Columbia. Twelve grandchildren also survive.

DENVER REGISTRATION LARGEST THUS FAR

64 Qualify To Vote At Fall Elections; Registrars Sit In 30 Other Districts

A total of 64 persons registered Friday at Denver, the largest number to qualify in one day at the special registration places designated by the county election board.

Of this number, 42 were Republicans, 17 were Democrats and five were no-party. Twenty-three removal notices were filed and one no-party changed his registration to Republican.

Twenty-two registered at Marietta, eleven Democrats and eleven Republicans. Twelve removal notices were filed and one Republican changed to Democrat and four Democrats changed to Republicans.

At Intercourse, five Republicans registered and six removal notices were filed. At Wakefield, eight Republicans registered; four removal notices were filed and two Democrats changed to Republicans.

The registrars will not sit Saturday (today) but on Monday they will be at Lititz (fire company hall); New Holland (borough building) and Conestoga Center (community building).

E. T. HAGER APPOINTED ADJUTANT OF 316TH

First Lieutenant Edward T. Hager, 1130 Columbia ave., has been named regimental adjutant of the 316th Infantry, U. S. Army Reserves, it was announced Friday.

SAYS ROBBER BEAT HIM

Frank Rummel, fifty, Millersville, found injured in the 200 block of West King street at midnight, told police he was beaten up by a man who attempted to rob him. He was treated at the Lancaster General hospital for a laceration of the scalp and then removed to police station, where he was locked up for a hearing on charges of drunkenness and disorderly conduct.

Police Probing Accident Find Missing Girl, 3

Police investigating an accident case at 8 p. m. Friday found Connie Atland, three, 231 W. James st., who was reported missing from her home since 10:30 a. m. She had walked against an auto operated by Herbert Dunkle, 631 Rockland st., at Prince and Orange streets, but escaped injury, an examination at St. Joseph's hospital showed.

Police said her nurse, Mrs. Agnes Maley, 730 E. Chestnut st., was with her when the accident occurred.

Mrs. Atland reported the child and nurse missing at 6:30 p. m.

SWIMMER TAKEN ILL, SAVED BY ANOTHER

Donald Warfel Rescued From Lake Grubb By William Hess, Revived By Respiration

A sixteen-year-old Lancaster youth, who became ill while swimming across Lake Grubb with four companions, was rescued by another swimmer, William Hess, of 607 Union st., Columbia, who was nearby.

Hess said he saw Donald Warfel, of Locust st., sink beneath the surface, and called to three girls in a boat. Then he swam to the boy and grabbed him and started toward the boat.

With the aid of the girls, Janet and Arlene Schopf and Dorothy Greenawalt, all of Mountville, the youth was pulled into the craft and taken ashore where artifical respiration was applied by Hess and Tuffield Olena, Jr., of Columbia, and the youth responded in about fifteen minutes.

He was later taken to his home by Sergeant Charles Righter, of Camp Bragg, N. C., and Philip Wagley, of Columbia.

CAPT. HOOVER TRANSFERRED

Captain Carl H. Hoover, of Lancaster, has been relieved from duty with the 103rd Medical Regiment and attached to the 103rd Quartermaster Regiment, it was announced Friday at 28th Division headquarters, Indiantown Gap.

TOT BITTEN BY RAT

Ronald Martin, twenty-two-month-old, Lancaster R. D. 6, was treated at the Lancaster General hospital Friday for a wound of the little finger of his left hand suffered when he was bitten by a rat. He was given an injection of tetanus anti-toxin.

EVENTS POSTPONED ON PLAYGROUNDS BECAUSE OF HEAT

It was too hot even for play Friday, and a number of the city playgrounds cancelled or postponed scheduled events. The mercury rose to a high of 91 degrees in Lancaster and touched 94 at the Ephrata weather station.

Thundershowers Saturday (this) afternoon are expected to bring slightly cooler weather by evening, according to the forecast, and more scattered showers are predicted for Sunday.

WRIST AND ANKLE FRACTURED IN FALL

Anthony Steckel, Jr., 13, Injured In 10-Foot Tumble From Barn Ramp To Cement Runway

Anthony Steckel, Jr., thirteen, of 45 W. Vine st., was admitted to St. Joseph's hospital with a fracture of the left wrist and the right ankle suffered in a fall. His condition was reported as good by attendants. The boy, attendants said, fell ten feet from the barn ramp to a cement runway on the farm of his grandparents, Mr. and Mrs. H. A. Baker, on the Lincoln Highway west, with whom he was visiting. He was throwing stones at the time, attendants said, and lost his balance.

Intelligencer Journal Weather Calendar

COMPARATIVE TEMPERATURES

Station	High	Low
Intell Journal	91	66
Water Works	90	60
Ephrata	94	64
Last Year (Ephrata)	100	73
Official High for Year, July 1		98
Official Low for Year, January 14		11
Character of Day		Clear

HOURLY TEMPERATURES (Friday)

3 a. m.	70	4 p. m.	90
4 a. m.	69	5 p. m.	89
5 a. m.	67	6 p. m.	88
6 a. m.	66	7 p. m.	87
7 a. m.	67	8 p. m.	83
8 a. m.	68	9 p. m.	81
9 a. m.	72	10 p. m.	79
10 a. m.	78	11 p. m.	79
11 a. m.	81	Midnight	79
Noon	85	(Saturday)	
1 p. m.	87	1 a. m.	79
2 p. m.	89	2 a. m.	78
3 p. m.	90	3 a. m.	78

HUMIDITY

8 a. m.—82; Noon—57; 2 p. m.—52
4 p. m.—58; Midnight—75
Average Humidity—65
Dew Point Midnight—72

More of WEATHER on Page 9

DAYLIGHT TIME IN INTELL

All time mentioned in the Intelligencer Journal is Daylight Time unless otherwise noted.

G.B.S. (He's 85 Today) Predicts American, British, Soviet Victory

British Author And Playwright Also Declares Peace Terms This Time Won't Be So Simple As At Versailles

London—(AP)—George Bernard Shaw, who will be 85 years old tomorrow (quote: "I am trying to die but I simply cannot do it") marked his birthday eve with an interview in which he said that victory in the war "will be a joint affair of Britain, the United States and the U. S. S. R."

The oracle, celebrated for his plays, his wit and his whiskers, declared that "as Russia is now in the front line and likely to be a decisive factor, the peace terms will not be so simple as they were at Versailles where, although America had finished the job, France and Britain were not prevented by President Wilson from going all out for the disablement of Germany under cover of a League of Nations which was carefully reduced to impotence beforehand by giving every power represented on it a veto."

SAYS STALIN WILL CALL TUNE

As if to balance that long sentence as well as explain President Wilson's position, Shaw added:

"Wilson could do nothing because America was not at his back and turned him down.

"But Stalin has the U. S. S. R. at his back; and the U. S. S. R.,

More of SHAW on Page 14

FIND INJURED MAN LYING ON HIGHWAY

Found lying on the Pequea road at 1:30 a. m. Saturday (today), William N. Hogarth, twenty-three, 927 E. Orange st., was admitted to the Lancaster General hospital suffering a possible fracture of the skull and a severe laceration of the head.

City police, who took him to the hospital, said that William Hecker, 645 E. Walnut st., saw Hogarth lying on the road near his wrecked machine, and drove to this city to inform them. They went to the scene.

Police believe that Hogarth was alone at the time and that his car left the road and hit an embankment.

The Weather

Eastern Pennsylvania—Mostly clear with moderate daytime temperature Sunday and Monday, slightly cooler at night.

SUNDAY NEWS

3 A. M. Edition

The Sunday News carries the full report of two world wide news services—

LATEST NEWS by Associated Press, International News Service. And Complete Local News.

VOL. 18—NO. 48 | Entered at Post Office at Lancaster, Pa. as second class mail matter | LANCASTER, PA., SUNDAY, AUGUST 3, 1941 | 54 PAGES, 304 COLUMNS—FIVE CENTS

U. S. Warns Vichy Not To Yield Empire

New German Offensive Aimed At Kiev

Motorists Rush To Fill Tanks Before Gasoline Curfew Begins

Ban On Sales From 7 P. M. To 7 A. M. Is Effective Tonight; Many Take Big Cans Along On Trips For Reserves

New York, Aug. 2—(AP)—Gasoline stations along the eastern seaboard pumped steadily tonight as motorists rushed up for a final filling before the regional gasoline sales curfew becomes effective tomorrow night.

In many cases weekend-bound motorists lugged big cans along to use for reserve supplies in case their machines ran dry during the dusk-to-dawn moratorium.

This was the first popular reaction to Secretary of the Interior Harold L. Ickes' recommendation that gasoline stations lock their pumps from 7 p. m. to 7 a. m. in an effort to conserve supplies and counteract the effect of a shortage of tanker ships, principal method of transporting gasoline to the Eastern states.

Commercial Cars Exempt

In New York city, hundreds of worried tax cab drivers brightened when word came from John W. Frey, Director of Marketing in the office of the Petroleum coordinator in Washington, that gasoline could be sold to commercial vehicles, including taxis and trucks.

IT'S 7 TO 7—G.S.T.

Boonton, N. J., Aug. 2—(AP)—Charles Fisher posted this sign on his three automobile service stations today:

"Closed from 7 p. m. to 7 a. m. —G.S.T."

The G.S.T., of course, stands for "gasoline saving time."

Fisher said it was a customer's idea.

The metropolitan area reported a quick spurt in gasoline sales, and similar reports came from other seaboard areas.

New Jersey planned to revoke licenses if stations did not comply with the Ickes recommendation, but three hundred of the state's 12,000 stations, however, were designated for emergency service. In New York state a legislative investigation of the closing was urged by an assemblyman who asserted the state stood to lose $20,000,000 in tax revenue.

In Queens, one of New York city's boroughs, residents were advised to ignore the curfew by Borough President George U. Harvey.

He contended the plan would not conserve gasoline, would injure small business men and create unemployment.

Another protest came from the gasoline station and parking attendants union (AFL) whose officers announced that 50 unions had offered aid in the protest against a possible loss of jobs.

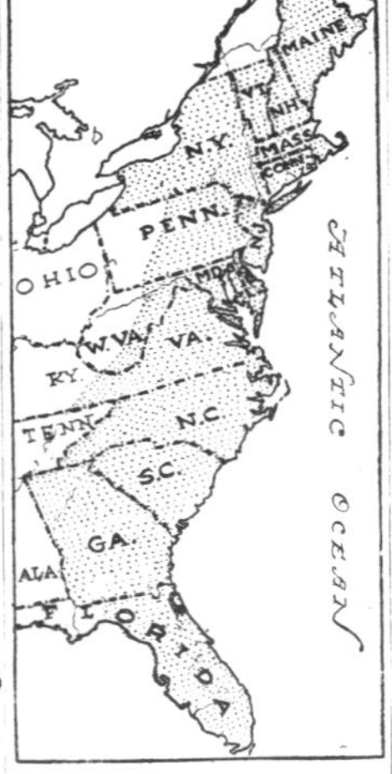

The shaded area on this map shows the approximate zone where Secretary of the Interior Harold L. Ickes, in his capacity as oil administrator, ordered no gasoline should be sold from 7 p. m. to 7 a. m. each night.

"GAS QUARANTINE" SIGN GOES UP

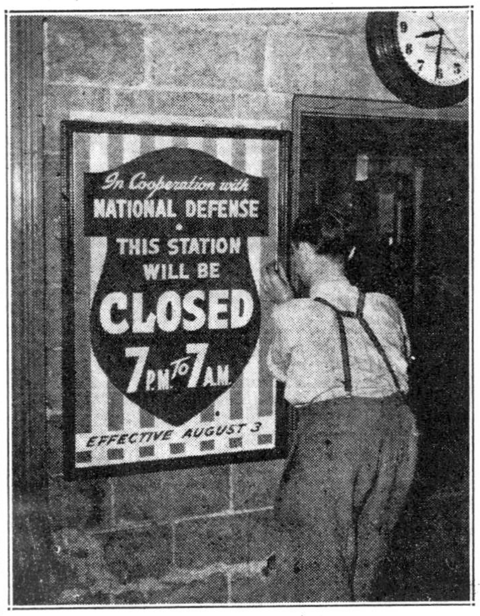

A manager of a local gas station on the Harrisburg pike is shown putting the finishing touches on a "gasoline quarantine" poster which spells an increase in weary pedestrian traffic after tonight. Most local dealers predict that the gasoline blackout, which lasts from 7 p. m. to 7 a. m., will not decrease gasoline consumption, but rather increase the daily output. Some will transfer their night men to the day schedule to take care of the last-minute rush expected today. None developed Saturday night.

POLICE LIST 11 FOR VIOLATIONS OF AUTO LAWS

Nine Prosecuted For Uninspected Cars; One Taken As Zig-Zag After Crash

Eleven motorists, including one woman, who was charged with drunken driving, were prosecuted by State and city police Saturday night. Nine were charged with operating uninspected vehicles, and the other alleged violator was charged with driving too fast for conditions.

Myrtle Trostle, 326 Jackson street, New Holland, was arrested on a charge of operating a motor vehicle while under the influence of liquor after her car allegedly crashed into two other machines at Shippen and Chestnut streets. She is being held for a hearing before Alderman Wetzel.

According to police reports, Miss Trostle pulled away from a parking space and crashed into cars owned by Paul R. Weaver, Landisville, and Annette and Mrs. Ray B. Miller, 138 Nevin street. Bessie Mattern, 222 West Vine street, who was riding with Miss Trostle was charged with drunkenness and disorderly conduct and she is being held for a hearing in police court.

Uninspected Cars

Those charged with driving uninspected cars are:—George Barefoot, Columbia R. D. 1; Henry Ottavaines, Phoenixville; Victor R. Kertickler, Minersville; J. Paul Reese, Karthaus, Clearfield county; William Noyes, 314 Atkins avenue; Clay T. Bradley, Downingtown; E. H. Finefrock, 135 South Queen street; Michael Tesoro, Upper Darby; and William J. Grillo, 522 North Duke street.

Loraine H. Scott, 27 Lee street, was prosecuted on a charge of driving too fast for conditions.

British En Masse Ignore Gas-Saving Stay-At-Home Plea

London, Aug. 2—(AP)—The British ignored en masse today an urgent government request to stay at home this week-end—the August Bank Holiday week-end—so that gasoline could be saved and so that railroads could be kept clear for important freight and coal traffic vital to Britain's war effort.

By the thousands they poured out of populous centers everywhere to spend today, tomorrow and Monday in the traditional peace-time manner at country and seaside resorts, defying the government despite the possibility they might be

2-Cent Gas Price Increase Forecast

New York, Aug. 2—(AP)—An increase of 2 cents a gallon in the service station price of gasoline and imposition of government priorities in the deliveries of petroleum and its products was forecast for the eastern seaboard tonight by authoritative oil men.

Virtually every citizen in the Atlantic states, from Florida to Maine, would be affected.

The price rise and government control are expected before cold weather arrives—perhaps within the month.

These drastic steps have been agreed to, in principle at least, by government officials and leaders of the oil industry. They are intended to keep defense industries operating and homes heated this winter.

"We are facing the worst supply

GAS—Page 7

2 Injured When Struck By Autos; Trolley Hits Girl

Three persons were slightly injured when struck by automobiles and a trolley car in the city Saturday.

Dr. K. Aznavorian, fifty-four, 245 West Chestnut street, was treated at the Lancaster General hospital for a back injury suffered when struck by a car operated by F. H. Frey, Lancaster R. D. 4, at Prince and Chestnut streets, according to hospital reports.

Reba Miller, twenty-two, Bird-in-Hand, suffered brush burns of the left arm when struck by a trolley car in the first block of East King street, according to reports at the General hospital where she was treated and discharged.

Theresa Abbott, six, 334 East Fulton street, was treated at the General hospital for an injury of the back suffered when struck by a car operated by Leon McLaughlin, 329 East Chestnut street, near her

RUN ON HOSIERY COUNTERS TAXES STORE SUPPLIES

Women Rush To Lay In Reserves Before Silk Freezing Brings Rations

(By The Associated Press)

The nation's biggest silk stocking run was under way Saturday as women stormed hosiery counters to lay in reserves before the government's order freezing silk supplies led to rationing.

RAYON MAKERS ORDERED TO HELP SILK INDUSTRY

Washington, Aug. 2—(INS)—The Office of Price Administration tonight announced an emergency program forcing rayon yarn producers to deliver partial output to silk mills so that hosiery production can be continued in the United States.

Moving swiftly to avert complete dislocation of the silk hosiery and silk weaving industry through the freezing order affecting 175,000 workers, the defense agency said that mills must immediately set aside an amount equal to one-tenth of their total daily output and a like amount of yarn stocks on hand.

It will be allocated among the maufacturers of hosiery and other products made largely or wholly of silk.

From Chicago, Philadelphia, San Francisco, Los Angeles and other cities across the continent came reports of tremendous increases in sales and limitations on purchases.

Stores disclosed varying stocks on hand, with some areas having reserves sufficient only for a few days and others prepared for months ahead.

The rise in New York city hosiery sales began Tuesday and reached a peak Friday night, just before the large stores closed for the week-end. Managers of 12 selected stores declared stocking orders had increased 200 to 500 per cent.

Popular Styles Depleted

Merchants estimated that if the pace continued the 4-month reserves normally maintained would be exhausted within 10 days to two weeks. The heavy buying had depleted most of the popular colors

SILK—Page 7

SHOT WHILE HUNTING

Mahlon Leidy, Jr., thirty, 339 North Marshall street, was admitted to St. Joseph's hospital Saturday night suffering gunshot wounds of the left side sustained when shot by a fellow companion while hunting groundhogs. His condition was reported as good.

"FLOOR" UNDER PRICES OF FARM PRODUCTS ASKED

Senate Agriculture Committee Opposed To Price Fixing Without Safeguard

Washington, Aug. 2—(AP)—The administration's price control bill was countered today by a demand from some farm State Senators that a "floor" be placed under farm prices if a "ceiling" was imposed by the legislation.

Chairman Smith, Dem., S. C., said that the Senate Agriculture committee "was unanimously opposed to any price fixing that did not fix a floor as well as a ceiling."

Others, including Capper, Rep., Kan., Gillette, Dem., Ia., Thomas, Dem., Okla., and Stewart, Dem., Tenn., said they agreed that if Congress was to fix a maximum price limit on things the farmer sells, it also should protect him by a minimum.

No Wage Control Given

The price fixing bill, introduced yesterday in both branches of Congress, would authorize the President to establish maximum prices for commodities and for rents in defense areas, but, in existing form, would give no control over wages or utility rates. Under its terms he could require licenses for engaging in transactions coming within the scope of the proposed law, but such licenses would

FLOOR—Page 7

PRESIDENT REBUFFED ON TAXES

His Request For Three Changes In Bill Turned Down Flatly By House Committee

Washington, Aug. 2—(AP)—President Roosevelt's request for three changes in the $3,529,200,000 tax bill were turned down today by the House Ways and Means committee by "decisive majorities" and Chairman Doughton, Dem., N. C., told the Executive he was "very greatly surprised" by his criticism of the measure.

Mr. Roosevelt asked Congress to lower income tax exemptions, impose stiffer excess profits levies on wealthy corporations and modify the requirement of joint returns from married persons as contained in the measure.

Suggested $750 Base

Expressing belief that some way should be found to cut present income tax exemptions for single persons from $800 to $750 and for married persons from $2,000 to $1,500, the President said "most Americans who are in the lowest income brackets are willing and proud to chip in directly" to the defense program "even if their individual contributions are very small in terms of dollars."

Addressing Doughton as "My Dear Bob," Mr. Roosevelt said he was "convinced that the overwhelming majority of our citizens want to contribute something directly to our defense and that most of them would rather do it with their eyes open than to do it through a general sales tax or through a multiplication of what we have known as 'nuisance taxes'."

In reference to the excess profits tax, Mr. Roosevelt said the levy approved by the committee was "clearly a discrimination" in favor of certain types of corporations which he said might be making "20 or 30 or 50 per cent" on their equity capital and still would not have to pay any more than last year.

"It is my definite opinion that they ought to contribute to the cost of our great defense program," the President wrote, "far more heavily this year than last year or the year before. But just because they happened to have made equally large profits in recent years, they are called on to contribute no more to the National Defense under the proposed bill than they did before."

Agrees On Joint Returns

Discussing the joint return provision, a storm center in the House, the President said he concurred heartily in the treasury opposition to joint returns unless "substantial relief" was granted to the earned income of both husband and wife.

The President, who attached a letter from Secretary Morgenthau setting forth the treasury's position on each item, also suggested that the committee might consider it worthwhile to study the desirability of permitting the filing of low income returns through local postoffices.

Doughton said in his letter to the President that the committee had devoted three months of study to the bill and that all the mat-

TAX—Page 7

Temperatures Range Between 70 And 90

The Lancaster temperature chart Saturday was a perfect circle. At no time did the recorder move below the 70 mark or above the 90 mark. At midnight it had returned to within ten degrees of the starting point. From 9 a. m. to 9 p. m. the mercury stayed within the 80 to 90 gradation in a gradual rise and fall.

Soviet, Nazis Claim Gains

Germany Seen Facing Serious Threats In Norway, With Declaration Of Martial Law; Reds Admit Enemy Nearing Kiev

(By International News Service)

A powerful new German offensive aimed at the Ukraine capital of Kiev ushered in the seventh week of the Russo-German conflict tonight while both Berlin and Moscow claimed successes on other parts of the 1,500-mile fighting front.

At the same time, a stern American warning went out to France against further pacts giving Axis powers military bases within the French empire, and repeated warnings that Japan will not permit American war aid to reach Soviet Russia via Pacific ports threatened imminent extension of the European war to the rest of the world.

To add to the dark outlook, Nazi Germany appeared to be facing serious threats in occupied Norway, where increasing resentment among the conquered populace caused Hitler's generals to take drastic defense steps, among them declaration of martial law.

Berlin's claims that Nazi "speed troops" were slashing deep into the Ukraine in pursuit of fleeing Red army rear guards in a gigantic battle raging south of Kiev was confirmed by the Moscow night communique which acknowledged that a new Nazi offensive had swept to within 45 miles of the Ukraine capital.

Counter-Attacks Reported

However, the Red army command claimed that Nazi troops aiming at capture of the northern industrial center of Leningrad and the Soviet capital of Moscow had been hurled back in several sectors by fierce Soviet counter attacks.

Moscow placed the scene of the new Ukraine battle at Byelaya-Tserkov, 45 miles south and west of Kiev, indicating that the Germans had managed to penetrate the southern section of the Ushomir line defending the Ukraine metropolis.

The Nazis apparently also had broken through Red army lines near Zhitomir, the Moscow communique mentioning heavy fighting at Korosten (Korotishev) about 15 miles beyond Zhitomir on the road to Kiev.

It also appeared that the Nazi had renewed their thus far vain attempts to hack their way across the narrow Estonian Isthmus north of Lake Peipus, the communique mentioning fighting in the Prokov and Estonian areas, southwest and west of Leningrad, respectively.

Smolensk Battle Continues

In the crucial Smolensk battlefield, on the central front, a bloody battle of pocketed troops which has

SOVIET—Page 7

PROPOSE CIVIL AIR RESERVE

Members Of Flying Club Here Will Ask State Defense Council For Authority

That a Civil Air Reserve of private pilots may soon be formed in this locality was announced Saturday by Prof. Frederic S. Klein, coordinator of civil pilot training.

A proposal for authority to proceed with details of the organization will be laid before the State Defense Council within the next week.

Similar to the plan now in operation in New Jersey the project would enlist all civilian pilots who desire training in military flying in cooperation with the natural guard or regular army units.

The flying club plan used by the Sensenich Brothers Flying Club Inc., makes possible the best basis on which to build the type of or-

AIR—Page 7

PETAIN RESISTS NAZI PRESSURE FOR DAKAR USE

Cabinet Believed Holding To Limits Of Present Agreement With Reich

Vichy, Unoccupied France, Aug. 2 (AP)—Chief of State Petain was reported tonight to have insisted before a lengthy cabinet meeting that France stay within the limits of her present agreements for collaboration with Germany, despite pressure for a military accord with the Reich which would extend to the African port of Dakar.

As a result, informed sources believed there would be no immediate change in the composition or policy of the French government.

There was no official announcement to this effect, a communique saying merely that the cabinet had adopted a project for payment of indemnities to civil victims of the war, conducted other routine business and discussed "current affairs."

For days the press in the German-occupied capital, Paris, has been waging a campaign for collaboration with Germany which, among other things, would include a military pact with the Reich for the defense of Dakar and other French possessions against possible American occupation.

(The British radio said the Germans were trying to induce Vichy to hand over the French fleet and the African ports of Dakar, Casablanca and Algiers).

The old Marshal, it was indicated, handled the situation calmly in his stand before the cabinet.

Woman Rolls Off Balcony Cot, Dies

Mrs. Robert Wickenheiser, sixty-one, of 536 South Ninth street, Columbia, was fatally injured at 11:30 p. m. Saturday when she fell from a second-story balcony at her home to the ground.

At the Columbia hospital, it was said Mrs. Wickenheiser died of head and internal injuries.

Members of the family explained Mrs. Wickenheiser was sleeping on a cot on the balcony. As she shifted her body, the cot tilted, and she rolled off against the balcony rail which gave way, precipitating her to the ground.

She is survived by her husband and these children: Anthony, Richard, Fred and Vincent, of Columbia; Robert, of Lancaster; Mrs. Eleanor Smallhofer, Catherine, wife of William Smith, Mrs. Anna Lease, and Helen, wife of John Smith, all of Columbia; and twenty-one grandchildren.

She was a member of Holy Trinity Catholic church, the Altar Rosary Sodality, the Women of the Moose, the Knights of Columbus Auxiliary, and the Holy Trinity Mothers' club.

Ask News Blackout On F.DR.'s Cruise

Washington, Aug. 2—(INS)—President Roosevelt will leave Washington Sunday for an Atlantic vacation cruise, which for the first time since he entered the White House will be enshrouded in complete secrecy.

Both Secretary of the Navy Frank Knox and Presidential Secretary Stephen T. Early today appealed to the nation's press and radio to observe a strict "blackout" of news reports on the President's whereabouts.

"From the time the President boards the Potomac until he returns, the movement of the ship will be a 'confidential naval operation,'" said Early, "and it is particularly requested that the press, radio and other media for dissemination of information so regard the movement of the Potomac."

WAY PAVED FOR TAKING DAKAR BASE

Action Threatened Against French Colonies If Axis Tries To Get Further Bases

Washington, Aug. 2—(INS)—The American government, in a blistering denunciation of France's action in giving Japan military control of Indo-China, today grimly warned Vichy that unless it defends its colonial empire against the Axis the United States may be forced in self-defense to take action against the colonies wherever their control by the Axis powers menaces U. S. security.

The American warning, which put Franco-American relations under their severest strain, clearly paved the way for U. S. occupation of Dakar and French Morocco, if those two vital strategic African bases are further threatened by Germany.

Guard Against Jap Move

Simultaneously Washington stepped up the tempo of pressure on Japan to deter any new move southward.

Diplomatic representatives of the United States, Great Britain, Australia and the Union of South Africa conferred at the State Department on joint action in the event Japan moves into Thailand or launches an attack on British or Dutch possessions in the Far Pacific.

The conference was presided over by Acting Secretary of State Sumner Welles and was attended by the British ambassador, Lord Halifax, Australian Minister Richard G. Casy, and South African Minister Ralph Close.

The blast at Vichy was issued by Welles with the approval of President Roosevelt. Welles made the note public at a press conference.

Baers On U. S. Security

He informed the pro-Nazi authorities of the Vichy government that its action in delivering Indo-China into Japanese hands has disclosed a policy which bears directly on American security.

"The turning over of bases for military operations and of the territorial rights under the pretext of 'common defense' to a power whose territorial aspirations are apparent here presents a situation which has a direct bearing upon the vital problem of American security," Welles asserted in his note.

"In its relations with the French government at Vichy and with the local French authorities in French territories, the United States will be governed by the manifest effectiveness with which these authorities endeavor to protect these territories from domination and control by those powers which are seeking to extend their rule by force and conquest or by the threat thereof."

This warning was taken to mean: If Vichy permits Germany to gain control of Dakar, strategic West African advanced base for invasion of the western hemisphere, the United States may be forced to take action against Dakar in its own defense.

Or, if the French forces in Morocco under command of Gen. Maxime Weygand, resist seizure attempts by the Axis, the United States will aid them in this resistance.

"Assurances" Cited

Welles reminded the French government that it had given the United States "repeated assurances" that it would not cooperate with the Axis powers beyond

WARNS—Page 7

Moscow Rail Yards Bombed By Germans

New York, Aug. 2—(INS)—Important railway yards in Moscow, capital of Soviet Russia, were bombed by the German Luftwaffe Saturday night and early Sunday, according to a Berlin radio broadcast picked up tonight by NBC.

Gary Cooper Best Paid In '40

Film Actor Received $482,820, Treasury Dept. Reveals

Washington, Aug. 2—(AP)—Film actor Gary Cooper, with a paycheck of $482,820, led the nation's industrial big-wigs and the motion picture colony as well, in a compilation of 1939 corporation salaries made public today by the Treasury.

The list did not include three of the leading Hollywood studios (Metro-Goldwyn-Mayer, Universal, Columbia), however, and corporate reports on file with the Securities commission indicated that Louis B. Mayer, head of MGM, remained on top of the salary list with $697,048, as he has for several years. Other actors may have topped Cooper, too.

As far as the Treasury list went, however, the first 10 salaries (in-

COOPER—Page 7

GARY COOPER

Prentis And Murrie Listed Among Pa. High Incomes

Washington, Aug. 2—(AP)—Forty persons in Pennsylvania received annual incomes totalling $75,000 or more during the calendar year 1939 or fiscal year ending in 1940, the Treasury announced today.

The names were made public under a law passed in 1939 requiring compilation of the list annually from reports submitted by corporations for income tax purposes.

Of the 40 Pennsylvanians with incomes above $75,000, a total of 18 received $100,000 or more. One Pennsylvanian, E. G. Grace of the Bethlehem Steel company, received a total of $271,224.

The Pennsylvanians:

Aluminum Company of America, Arthur V. Davis, salary $112,650;

MONEY—Page 7

LANCASTER NEW ERA

WEATHER

Cloudy and somewhat warmer tonight and Friday with scattered showers Friday afternoon. (Details on Page 3).

Examiner Founded 1830
New Era Founded 1877

Published Every Evening Except Sunday by New Era Company. Entered as Second Class Matter at Post Office, Lancaster, Pa.

LANCASTER, PA., THURSDAY, AUGUST 14, 1941 — CITY EDITION — 24 PAGES—192 COLUMNS—THREE CENTS

Roosevelt and Churchill, Meeting at Sea, Pledge "Destruction of Nazism"

22 OUT OF 47 21-YR.-OLDS FAIL EXAMS

High Percentage of Army Rejections Disappoints Draft Officials.

96 OUT OF 212 SAY THEY ARE OBJECTORS

COUNTY CALLED UPON TO SEND 69 FOR INDUCTION ON AUG. 25

Lancaster county was called upon today to furnish 69 selectees for induction at New Cumberland on August 25, it was announced at Harrisburg.

The number to be furnished by the respective boards are: City No. 1, 6; No. 2, 7 Whites and one Negro (the Negro to report at Ft. George Meade, Md., tomorrow); No. 3, 6. County No. 1, 8; No. 2, 9; No. 3, 9; No. 4, 11; No. 5, 12.

All those to be sent must already have passed their final physical exams at Harrisburg.

County Selective Service Board No. 4, at Strasburg, announced today that 25 passed and 22 failed in its first set of physical examinations for 21-year-old selectees.

It was the first mass examination of men in the new age group by any of the eight local draft districts, and clerks expressed disappointment that the percentage of those qualifying for the Army was not higher.

"They failed for the same reasons as the older men," one clerk said, "teeth, especially, and flat feet, heart disease, mental diseases, and whatnot. It failed to bear out the prediction of Washington officials that 60 per cent or more of the 21-year-olds would be fit."

96 of 212 Are Objectors

The same board announced a classification today, consisting principally of 21-year-olds. Clerks said that out of 212 men of that age in the district, 96 had conscientious objections to combatant service and 47 were married.

About 40 or more men of the last registration are not yet classified because the draft board is seeking more information.

The status of the 21-year-olds, who registered July 1, was said by the other boards to be as follows:

City Board No. 1, no examination of 21-year-olds yet.

City Board No. 2, planned to classify the first 21-year-olds at a meeting this afternoon.

City Board No. 3, none classified yet.

County Board No. 1, Mount Joy, plans to classify 21-year-olds at

(See LOCAL DRAFT—Page 22)

SEEK 1,200 SKILLED MEN FOR JOBS ON MARIETTA PROJECT

Through the depression years, Mark N. Wickert, head of the Lancaster Employment office, has been striving to find jobs for the city's and county's unemployed. Now he has a staggering order from Marietta, where work is starting on a $6,000,000 Army Supply Depot.

Representatives of six labor unions and the U. S. Department of Labor visited Wickert's office and asked for:

500 carpenters.
400 bricklayers.
150 truck drivers.
150 electricians.
Unskilled labor "in quantity."

Many are wanted for Monday morning.

Wickert said that he has two bricklayers listed for jobs and he's not sure whether they are still unemployed, and carpenters are a "rarity." He expressed the opinion that much of his common labor, now enrolled for jobs, will be absorbed quickly.

The Scribbler

HENRY PYZANOWSKI, agent in Coatesville for the New Era before he joined the Army, is stationed at Fort Knox, Kentucky. Longing for Pennsylvania, he asked to be transferred to a "place nearer home."

He was. The transfer was to the other side of the camp—one mile nearer Coatesville.

BETTY LAUDENBERGER, 542 East Orange street, went to Atlantic City recently. When she prepared to change to her swim suit she found that she had left the keys to her bag at home. The lock is now broken.

PERRY ADAMS, Millway, seems in hot water most of the time. Last summer he stepped in a bowl of snapper soup while doing a dance at a corn roast. True to tradition this year, he stepped into a pan filled with steaming corn.

Placing Placards

B. F. Charles, city health officer, shown placarding one of the 55 homes in Lancaster and suburbs placed under observation quarantine today in an effort to stop the spread of infantile paralysis.

QUARANTINE DUE TO PARALYSIS

55 Homes Here Placarded After Camper Contracts Disease.

Forty homes in Lancaster city and fifteen in the county were placed under observation quarantines today in one of a series of quick moves by health authorities to prevent a spread of infantile paralysis.

The plan of quick action was agreed upon late yesterday when Robert Gregg, sixteen, 557 Hamilton street, was admitted to the General Hospital with a case of acute paralysis. The boy had attended Camp Shand, conducted by the Y. M. C. A. at Cold Spring, Lebanon county, between July 26 and August 9.

71 Boys Were In Camp

There were seventy-one boys in Camp during the period Gregg participated in the activities there. Forty of those seventy-one boys reside in homes quarantined by city authorities today. The other thirty-one boys reside outside of the city. Fifteen names of those residing in the county were turned over today to Dr. A. J. Greenleaf, county medical director, and those residing outside the county will be reported at once to the State Department of Health.

City health authorities said that all children residing in the homes

(See PARALYSIS—Page 21)

TO CURB CARRIER OF TYPHOID

Dr. Greenleaf Says Steps Will Be Taken to Incarcerate Woman.

Steps will be taken under the Public Health laws to incarcerate a recognized typhoid "carrier' who lived in the household of Harry N. Greenawalt, Mt. Joy R. 2, who died Saturday of typhoid, Dr. Arthur J. Greenleaf, county medical director, said today.

She is Anna Faus, identified as a "carrier" on State Health records for some years, Dr. Greenleaf said.

Until three months ago she was making the necessary reports to the State Health Department and there was no official reason to believe she was failing to abide by regulations which forebade her from preparing food or doing other work which would jeopardize susceptible persons, he said.

A sister of Mrs. Greenawalt, she had lived in the household for some time and had previously been warned by health officials that she was an unwitting menace to those with whom she came into contact.

The investigation now being made by Dr. Greenleaf and by Dr. W. D. Schrack, Jr., of the State Department of Epidemiology, at Harrisburg, indicate that she has

(See TYPHOID—Page 22)

COOL SPELL IS DUE TO END TOMORROW

"Canadian weather," which sent local housewives scurrying for stored blankets is expected to break its three-day seige tomorrow as the weather man predicts fair and warmer weather.

Lancaster people still shivered today from the polar breezes which dropped the temperature to 45 degrees at 5 o'clock this morning, the lowest mark registered this summer at the Ephrata weather bureau station.

At 3 P. M., today the temperature was 78 degrees on the New Era roof. Yesterday atfernoon, the mercury stayed in the 60's.

5 ALUMINUM PLANTS FACE STRIKE THREAT

20,000 Alcoa Workers Involved; Telephone Dispute Is Cloudy.

PROPELLOR COMPANY WALKOUT IS ENDED

(By The Associated Press)

Strike threats in the telephone and aluminum industries added today to the anxieties of national defense officials, while a labor dispute in a New Jersey propellor factory was ended when striking workers voted to return to work after the issue was turned over to the Mediation Board.

War Department officials already had expressed grave concern over a sharp increase in work stoppages. As of last Tuesday, they said, 30 strikes were holding up production of Army equipment, and 23,400 workers were idle, compared with an average of 14,000 idle since early June.

The CIO Aluminum Workers Union told Secretary of Labor Perkins last night that 20,000 workers would strike at five key plants of the Aluminum Company of America (ALCOA) to support demands for elimination of North-South wage differentials, unless the government intervened in the dispute. No date was set for the projected walkout.

ALCOA recently granted a blanket wage increase of 10 cents an hour, bringing the minimum scale at its Badin, N. C., and Alcoa, Tenn., plants to 55 cents, which the company said was as good or better than prevailing wages there. ALCOA workers at New Kensington, Pa., receive a minimum of 73 cents an hour and those at Detroit, Mich., and Edgewater, N. J., 75 cents.

Conferences on the union's demand for elimination of the differentials recently ended without agreement.

'Phone Dispute May Spread

The telephone labor dispute at present involves only the installation department of the huge Bell system, but if a strike is called and other employes decided not to cross picket lines, union leaders pointed out that a complete tie-up of the Bell system was conceivable.

The Association of Equipment Workers, which is affiliated with the National Federation of Telephone Workers, an independent

(See STRIKES—Page 21)

PRICE OF MILK TO BE RAISED

Producers Say Increase Is Necessary to Cover Advance in Costs.

HARRISBURG, Aug. 14.—(A. P.)—Representatives of milk producers in Pennsylvania's smaller marketing areas declared today that prices received for their product must be increased to meet rising production costs.

"Dairy farmers of the state are facing one of the most critical periods since the World War," said F. B. Willets, representative of the Interstate Milk Producers Cooperative, and farmers in the Lancaster, Huntingdon and Altoona areas.

Willets, testifying before the Milk Control Commission as it opened hearings on producer wholesale and retail prices, said much of the increased production cost was caused by the existing national emergency.

Farm labor has been depleted through the draft and demands of defense industries, he said.

Before the hearing opened, Edwin H. Ridgeway, secretary of the commission predicted there would be a state-wide increase in retail milk prices.

RISE IN FOOD COSTS IS SMALLEST HERE

HARRISBURG, Aug. 14—(A. P.)—The cost of living in Pennsylvania rose this summer to the highest level since September, 1937, the Department of Labor and Industry said today. A further increase was predicted.

"During the quarter from mid-March to mid-June, the impact of the National Defense program scored decisively on retail prices and the cost of living for the first time," the Department reported.

In the six cities covered by the Department's survey food costs averaged 8.2 per cent higher in the middle of June, with Lancaster showing a 5 per cent boost, Johnstown 9.1 and Pittsburgh 9.5. In Connellsville, Philadelphia and Scranton the increase ranged from 7.1 to 7.7 per cent.

President Roosevelt and Prime Minister Churchill, who held a momentous meeting at sea recently to map the "destruction of Nazism," shown in a composite photograph.

Text of Agreement and Plan For Rehabilitation After War

WASHINGTON, Aug. 14—(A. P.)—The text of the announcement on the meeting of President Roosevelt and Prime Minister Winston Churchill of Great Britain follows:

The President of the United States and the Prime Minister, Mr. Churchill, representing His Majesty's government in the United Kingdom, have met at sea.

They have been accompanied by officials of their two governments, including high ranking officers of their military, naval and air services.

The whole problem of the supply of munitions of war, as provided by the lease-lend act, for the armed forces of the United States and for those countries actively engaged in resisting aggression has been further examined.

Lord Beaverbrook, the minister of supply of the British government, has joined in these conferences. He is going to proceed to Washington to discuss further details with appropriate officials of the United States government. These conferences will also cover the supply problems of the Soviet Union.

The President and the Prime Minister have had several conferences. They have considered the dangers to world civilization arising from the policies of military domination by conquest upon which the Hitlerite government of Germany and other governments associated therewith have embarked, and have made clear the stress (as received here by radio the text said "stress" but Stephen Early, White House secretary, said it might have been garbled and that the word possibly was "steps") which their countries are respectively taking for their safety in the face of these dangers.

Joint Declaration

They have agreed upon the following joint declaration:

Joint declaration of the President of the United States of America and the Prime Minister, Mr. Churchill, representing His Majesty's government in the United Kingdom, being met together, deem it right to make known certain common principles in the national policies of their respective countries on which they base their hopes for a better future for the world.

First, their countries seek no aggrandizement, territorial or other;

Second, they desire to see no territorial changes that do not accord with the freely expressed wishes of the peoples concerned;

Third, they respect the right of all peoples to choose the form of government under which they will live; and they wish to see sovereign rights and self government restored to those who have been forcibly deprived of them;

Fourth, they will endeavor, with due respect for their existing obligations, to further the enjoyment by all states, great or small, victor or vanquished, of access, on equal terms, to the trade and to the raw materials of the world which are needed for their economic prosperity;

Fifth, they desire to bring about the fullest collaboration between all nations in the economic field with the object of securing, for all, improved labor standards, economic advancement and social security;

Sixth, after the final destruction of the Nazi tyranny, they hope to see established a peace which will afford to all nations the means of dwelling in safety within their own boundaries, and which will afford assurance that all the men in all the lands may live out their lives in freedom from fear and want;

Seventh, such a peace should enable all men to traverse the high seas and oceans without hindrance;

Eighth, they believe that all of the nations of the world, for realistic as well as spiritual reasons must come to the abandonment of the use of force. Since no future peace can be maintained if land, sea or air armaments continue to be employed by nations which threaten, or may threaten, aggression outside of their frontiers, they believe, pending the establishment of a wider and permanent system of general security, that the disarmament of such nations is essential. They will likewise aid and encourage all other practicable measures which will lighten for peace-loving peoples the crushing burden of armaments.

(Signed) Franklin D. Roosevelt
(Signed) Winston S. Churchill

Bulletin

SENATE SENDS DRAFT BILL TO PRESIDENT

WASHINGTON, Aug. 14.—(A. P.)—Final Senate approval sent to President Roosevelt today legislation extending the service periods of all army enlisted personnel for 18 months. The vote was 35 to 19.

The measure, passed by the single vote margin of 203 to 202 in the House Tuesday, would authorize the President to retain selectees, National Guardsmen and reservists for a total of two and a half years. Regular enlisted men, who signed up for a three-year period, could be held for four and a half years.

The legislation gives all men who had served 12 months a $10 monthly pay increase.

NAZIS SAY MINE AREA CAPTURED

Declare Odessa Is Circled But Reds Report Offensive Bogged Down.

(By The Associated Press)

Adolf Hitler's field headquarters issued a special communique today reporting that Nazi Schnell Truppen ("Speed Troop"), slashing southward across the heart of the Ukraine had captured the big mining center of Krivoi Rog, in the Southern Dnieper River basin, about 80 miles from Dnepropetrovsk.

Germans said that the region produced 19,000,000 tons of iron ore annually and that with its loss the Russians lost 61 per cent of their ore production.

While the Germans pictured the Red Armies as reeling in retreat, Soviet war dispatches reported that

(See RUSSIAN WAR—Page 6)

SEE NO SHORTAGE OF FUEL OIL HERE

Lancaster home owners with oil burners need have little fear of going through a heatless winter, distributors here said today.

The supply of petroleum for heating purposes should be adequate to meet the demands of consumers throughout the winter, officials of the Petroleum Transport Company said

The present price of fuel oil, which varies between seven and eight cents a gallon, is expected to remain fairly constant. No price rise is expected unless the industry has to revert to rail transportation more than is expected, it was said.

UMPIRE "SATISFACTORY"

The condition of Roland Mackie, Inter-State League umpire, a patient in St. Joseph's Hospital, was reported today as "satisfactory." Mackie, struck on the head by a bottle thrown during a baseball game here Tuesday night, is suffering a brain concussion, hospital attendants said.

London Thinks They Agreed on When and How to Fight Japan

Mutual Use of British Naval Bases in Pacific and Opening of New Front in East by Russia Believed Included in Plans

(By the Associated Press)

President Roosevelt and Prime Minister Churchill, dramatically meeting somewhere at sea, have joined in a pledge to achieve "the final destruction of the Nazi tyranny" and agreed on an eight-point declaration of common national aims after the war, it was disclosed today.

Informed quarters in London, commenting on the secret rendezvous, declared that the United States now was enlisted in the task of reconstruction of post-war Europe and in support of the Russian-British cause on every front.

A Japanese diplomat in London said omission of reference to Japan in the eight-point policy "implies that Japan was one of the main points of discussion."

A British informant said the meeting was held at President Roosevelt's invitation.

High-ranking United States and British military, naval and air experts attended the conference, which was said to have lasted two or three days.

2 Weeks of Mystery

Climaxing two weeks of mystery, since Mr. Roosevelt sailed aboard the Presidential yacht Potomac Aug. 3, ostensibly on a "fishing cruise" in North Atlantic waters, the office of the Canadian Prime Minister in Ottawa revealed that the two Anglo-American leaders had met at an undisclosed point at sea.

Simultaneously, a White House announcement in Washington said Mr. Roosevelt and Mr. Churchill had joined in a declaration of general war aims and a determination to achieve "the final destruction of Nazi tyranny."

Covered 3 Topics

Disarmament of aggressor nations was said to be one of the paramount aims of the joint declaration, pending the establishment of "a wider and permanent system of general security."

Speculation on the topics discussed at the supposed meeting centered on:

1. **The Vichy French government's new policy of stronger collaboration with Germany.**
2. **Japan's threat to British and American interests in the Pacific.**
3. **The Axis program for a new world order.**
4. **Acceleration of U. S. lease-lend aid to Britain.**

To Deal With Japan

Competent London observers expressed belief that, although the eight points dealt mainly with general phrases, Mr. Roosevelt and Mr. Churchill also probably agreed on:

1. **The precise moment when the British and American governments would discard passive resistance for action against Japan.**
2. **Mutual use of British and United States bases in the South Pacific—presumably Singapore, Manila and others.**
3. **A request to Soviet Premier Joseph Stalin to open a northern front in the Far East with a Siberian army of 1,000,000 men if war should break out in the South Pacific.**

A synchronized London account of the meeting said the two leaders in addition to agreeing on measures to stiffen the war against Adolf Hitler's Reich, had decided on joint peace aims embodying disarmament and post-war economic collaboration.

It was further disclosed that Lord Beaverbrook, British Minister of Supply, attended the conference and that he would arrive in the United States to discuss "the whole problem of supply of munitions" for the "armed forces of the United States and for those countries actively engaged in resisting aggression."

It was said that the presence of

(See CONFERENCE—Page 21)

British Find Key in What Was Not Said

See United States Now Pledged to Aid Britain "On Every Front"

LONDON, Aug. 14.—(A. P.)—The United States is now pledged to the reconstruction of post-war Europe and the support of the Russian-British cause on every front, informed British sources said today in reviewing the jointly-issued Roosevelt-Churchill statement.

Things left unsaid in the statement are regarded as fully as important as those of the eight-point joint declaration.

Omission of reference to Japan "implies that Japan was one of the main points of discussion," a Japanese diplomat admitted.

British informant said the meeting was at Mr. Roosevelt's invitation.

The Japanese source said that the tempo of the Japanese advance in South Asia was slowed even as rumors of the historic meeting between the British and American leaders sped around the warring world.

Lasted 2 Or 3 Days

The Roosevelt-Churchill conferences, which were attended by ranking officials and military naval and air experts of both countries, were reliably reported to have lasted at least two or three days..

But neither the time nor the place of the meeting was disclosed here immediately.

Now there would be no surprise in London if a further announcement were made that Roosevelt and Churchill had sent personal assurances to Joseph Stalin and the Russian people that Britain and the United States will give the U. S. S. R. the fullest industrial cooperation in arming and supplying the Red Army, air force and navy.

News of the meeting was broadcast by radio to Britain by Lord Privy Seal Clement Attlee, who has been acting as Churchill's deputy in his absence.

Workers in factories and workshops throughout the country heard

(See BRITISH—Page 6)

PARLEY LAUDED AND CENSURED

F. D. Adherents See Principles as "Noble"; Foes Rap Agreements.

WASHINGTON, Aug. 14—(A. P.)—High praise came today from Administration supporters for the meeting and declaration of policy by President Roosevelt and Prime Minister Winston Churchill but Rep. Short (R-Mo), said it was "quite apparent that some sort of alliance has been formed."

"I don't like these secret, undercover agreements," Short told newsmen. "The President has no authority to form such an alliance. He shouldn't gamble with the destiny of 130,000,000 people and keep them in the dark about it."

Administration lieutenants, on the other hand, called the prin-

(See COMMENTS—Page 6)

WEATHER
Eastern Pennsylvania: A Few Scattered Showers Ending Early Saturday Morning Followed By Clearing Saturday Afternoon; Cooler Saturday Night; Sunday Fair And Somewhat Cooler.
Intell Journal Stormograph Reading: Unsettled Weather, Increasing Winds And Warmer.

Intelligencer Journal

The Leading Newspaper in the Garden Spot of America, Home Owned for Home Folks Since 1794

Swimming
Nancy Merki set a new American record for 1500 meters in National AAU swim meet.
Details Page 10.

VOLUME LXXVII.—NO. 291. | CITY | The Intelligencer Founded 1799 The Journal Founded 1794 | LANCASTER, PA., SATURDAY MORNING, AUGUST 16, 1941. | Entered at Post Office at Lancaster, Pa. as second class mail matter | 16 PAGES, 128 COLUMNS.—THREE CENTS.

GASOLINE RATIONING EFFECTIVE TODAY

Roosevelt, Churchill Invite Stalin To Join Parley On Soviet War Needs; Nazis Hurl Fourth Drive At Leningrad

PRAISE SOVIET DEFENSES

Russian Premier Told U. S. And Britain "Cooperating To Provide You The Very Maximum Of Supplies That You Urgently Need"; Say Long Term Policy Necessary To Avoid Wasting "Efforts And Sacrifices"

Washington — (AP) — President Roosevelt and Prime Minister Churchill followed up their historic sea-conference Friday night with a joint proposal to Premier Joseph Stalin that high British and American representatives meet with him in Moscow to discuss allocation of war supplies to the Soviet Union.

The message made public here Friday night was delivered to Stalin by the American and British ambassadors in Moscow during the afternoon.

The two leaders of the Western powers praised the "splendid defense" of the Soviet Union "against the Nazi attack" and asserted that the United States and Britain were "cooperating to provide you the very maximum of supplies that you urgently need."

"Already many shiploads have left our shores and more will leave in the immediate future," the message said.

The President and Prime Minister told Premier Stalin that it was necessary to consider a long-term policy because "there is still a long and hard path to be traversed before there can be won that complete victory without which our efforts and sacrifices would be wasted."

They said the war raged now upon many fronts and before it was over "further fighting fronts" may be developed.

It therefore became a question as to where and when the immense American and British resources "can best be used to further the greatest extent our common effort" and this, they asserted, applied equally to manufactured war supplies and raw materials.

"The needs and demands of your

More of CONFERENCE on Page 7

STALIN TO PUSH PLANS FOR PROPOSED PARLEY

Moscow, (Saturday)—(AP)—Premier Joseph Stalin told the United States and British ambassadors today he is ready to "take all necessary steps" for the conference in Moscow proposed by President Roosevelt and Prime Minister Churchill.

The Premier expressed to them the thanks of the Soviet government for the offer of "maximum aid" contained in the note and said he would expedite arrangements for the proposed conversations.

AIR ATTACKS

Unofficial Moscow Quarters Imply German Thrust In Ukraine Checked

FINNS CLAIM GAINS

(By The Associated Press)

The Germans appeared Friday night to have loosed a fourth grand offensive centered on the southern, western and northern approaches to Leningrad, while the available evidence indicated that their thrusts into the Ukraine were for the time being at least producing no spectacular results.

Berlin itself had little word to give to general operations in the south other than to repeat the standing claim of some days that pressure was being increased upon the Black Sea ports of Odessa and Nikolaev and that the Red retreat was being hampered by violent bombing attack.

UKRAINE THREAT CHECKED

Unofficial quarters in Moscow implied that the current Nazi thrust in that theater had been checked.

The Soviet command itself in its communique for Friday afternoon did not even mention the Ukraine—where Russian withdrawals from Kirovograd and Pervomaisk, lying 100 to 115 miles above Nikolaev, had been earlier admitted.

Early Saturday (this) morning, the Red command's official bulletin omitted mention of any specific sector, merely reporting fierce fighting "along the whole front."

TRADE AIR ATTACKS

The Soviet and German air forces attacked each other's capitals Friday night. The Soviets said a small number of Nazi planes failed to penetrate Moscow's defenses.

Dispatches from Berlin said residents there and in northeastern and eastern Germany were forced into air-raid shelters when the Red airmen attacked.

Finnish dispatches said German and Finnish troops destroyed three encircled Soviet battalions, about 3,000 men, at Tolvajarvi and Aglajarvi north of Lake Ladoga.

The British estimate of the situation took the middle of the road and was this:

The Russians apparently were re-

More of WAR on Page 7

PROPOSE 18 MO. INSTALLMENT CREDIT LIMIT

Federal Reserve Suggests Restrictions On Minimum Down Payments

TO MAKE REVISIONS

Washington—(AP)—As a first and tentative step in combatting inflation by tightening up on credit, the Federal Reserve Board proposed Friday that the maximum spread on numerous characteristic installment payments be fixed at 18 months.

This would include cash loans of less than $1,000, and purchases of such items as automobiles, both used and new, radios, airplanes, power-driven boats, outboard motors, motorcycles, refrigerators, washing machines, ironers, vacuum cleaners, stoves, and ranges, dishwashers, air conditioning units, radios, oil burners, furnaces, water heaters, plumbing and sanitary fixtures, and small residential repair contracts.

To supplement this restriction, it suggested, too, that a minimum down payment of one third be exacted on automobiles, airplanes, boats and motorcycles, 20 percent on radios, refrigerators, and similar household appliances and 15 percent on plumbing and air conditioning units.

The board's chairman, Marriner S. Eccles explained that these restrictions were intended for discussion purposes, as the board swings into the new inflation control assignment given it early this week by President Roosevelt.

The purpose is two-fold: To keep prices down by eliminating a portion of the present installment buying and thus reducing the volume of purchasing power; and to curb the manufacture of products which eat up materials needed for the production of defense equipment.

"It is proposed," Eccles said, "in the initial regulations covering only a limited number of articles and applying only moderate terms to lay a basis for such subsequent coverage and adjustment of terms as experience in this field and economic development may indicate to be necessary."

EXPECT TO MAKE REVISIONS

The proposal was presented during the day to a meeting of dealers, bankers, and other interested businessmen for their approval and discussion. On the basis of their suggestions and further conversations within the board it is expected that a revised draft and

More of CREDIT on Page 7

New Name?

Attired in a rose-colored hat and gown, Edward Price Richards, 29, is shown in Los Angeles court as he (or she) asked to have the name legally changed to Barbara Ann Richards. The case was continued when the court was told Richards' transformation from man to woman might not be permanent. Last November, before the change, Richards was wed to Lorraine Wilcox.

System Means Cut Of About 20% For Non-Essential Use

Unprecedented Peacetime Action Calls For 10 Per Cent Slash In Supplies Delivered To Service Stations Along Eastern Seaboard; Say More Curtailments May Be Necessary In Future

Washington — (AP) — A sweeping gasoline rationing system for the east, which means a cut of about 20 per cent in the fuel available for autos used for pleasure or "non-essential" purposes, was set up Friday by the Office of Price Administration and Civilian Supply, effective immediately.

The action, unprecedented in peace-time, did not involve the issuance of ration cards to individual automobile operators, but slashed by ten per cent the supplies delivered to service stations.

However, it was estimated the cut would be about twenty per cent as applied to "non-essential" motor cars because it was announced that the supplies for fire department vehicles, ambulances, commercial and agricultural activities and other essential services would not be reduced at all.

The announcement said "it is expected that more service curtailments will be necessary in the future."

Operators of filling stations were invested with responsibility to distribute the gasoline equitably among some 10,000,000 customers. Officials would not say what plans had been made for enforcing the order, but expected that oil companies would comply with it.

CURFEW TO CONTINUE

The 7 p. m. curfew on gasoline sales in the east will continue in effect, at least for the time, it was indicated.

Secretary of Interior Ickes, who recommended the action to OPACS, said the threatened eastern fuel shortage was due to "Mr. Hitler, and Mr. Hitler alone." The shortage was caused by the transfer of coast-wise tankers to the service of the British.

"Our planes and those of England must be kept in the air so long as those of Nazi Germany fly," the cabinet member said. "Our ships and those of England must be kept on the seas so long as a submarine carrying the swastika prowls the deep; our defense industries and those of England must be kept going full blast so long as Hitler remains a menace."

MAY FEEL PINCH ELSEWHERE

Ickes indicated that the middle west and the Pacific coast might face a "gasoline pinch," saying: "We must call upon the middle west to get along with less than its normal supply of gasoline by giving us some of its tank cars. We are asking the Pacific coast to get along with less than its normal supply of gasoline by giving us some of its tankers."

A definite conservation plan for those areas was not specified, however.

States affected by the action would include Maine, New Hampshire, Vermont, Massachusetts, Connecticut, Rhode Island, New York, Pennsylvania, New Jersey, Delaware, Maryland, Virginia, West Virginia, North Carolina, South Carolina, Georgia, the District of Columbia and a portion of Florida.

The action was taken, the announcement said, as an emergency measure to bring consumption of gasoline in this area into line with transport facilities. These facilities have been reduced by transfer of petroleum-carrying ships from the coastwise service to the British.

PROCLAIMED BY HENDERSON

The action was proclaimed by Leon Henderson, head of the Office of Price Administration and Civilian Supply, at the request of Secretary of Interior Ickes, who is defense petroleum coordinator.

The program was announced as follows:

1. Allocation of motor fuel—no supplier of motor fuel shall directly or indirectly deliver or cause to

More of RATIONING on Page 9

ROOSEVELT TO LAND THIS AFTERNOON AT ROCKLAND, MAINE

Will Complete Cruise During Which He Held Conference With Churchill

Swampscott, Mass.—(AP)—President Roosevelt will land at Rockland, Me., sometime Saturday afternoon, completing a cruise during which he held historic conferences with Winston Churchill, Prime Minister of Great Britain.

This disclosure gave rise to the possibility that in a press conference the President might define for the nation the bounds of America's part in the eight-point program agreed upon at the Roosevelt-Churchill meeting, a program which spoke of the 'final destruction of the Nazi tyranny."

Little is known of the high seas conference beyond the eight principles upon which the leaders of the two greatest Democracies based their "hopes for a better future for the world."

White House sources declined any comment and would not even promise that a press conference would be held.

MESSAGE FROM YACHT

William D. Hassett, of the Presidential Secretarial Staff, disclosed the time and place of Mr. Roosevelt's debarkation to White House newsmen gathered in this resort town for the past several days waiting word of the President's whereabouts.

Late Friday night, Hassett said he had received the following message from the President, who is aboard his yacht Potomac:

"Potomac is anchored near Deer Island, Maine, and has on board Hopkins, Watson, Berdall, McIntyre and myself. We land tomorrow (Saturday) and take train to Washington, arriving sometime Sunday morning. All well."

This was the first time since the Potomac sailed from New London, Conn., nearly a fortnight ago that Mr. Roosevelt had disclosed his exact whereabouts or the location of the yacht.

The companions he mentioned

More of ROOSEVELT on Page 7

DR. PHILIP KLEIN TO TEACH HISTORY AT STATE COLLEGE

Member Of Franklin And Marshall Faculty Since 1938 Accepts New Post

Dr. Philip S. Klein, of 540 N. President ave., has accepted an appointment as assistant professor of American history in the School of Liberal Arts at Pennsylvania State college. He will teach United States history and Pennsylvania history, and do research work in the latter field.

DR. PHILIP S. KLEIN

Dr. Klein, who received his Bachelor of Arts degree from Franklin and Marshall college in 1929, was a member of the history department of the college from 1938 to the present time. His father, Dr. H. M. J. Klein, acting president of Franklin and Marshall college, is head of

More of KLEIN on Page 7

SENATE RESTORES $750,000,000 TO DEFENSE MEASURE

Acts After Stimson Explains Need For Tank Equipment Anti-Aircraft Guns

Washington —(AP)— Heeding a plea of Secretary of War Stimson, the Senate partially reversed its recent action in striking $1,347,000,000 from a defense appropriation bill.

It restored $750,000,000 of that amount to the measure, and the House having previously acquiesced, Congressional action on the measure was completed. The bill went to the White House carrying a total of $7,586,895,000.

The amount which the Senate originally slashed from the bill had been intended for the purchase of special ordnance items, — tanks, tank equipment and anti-aircraft guns. Part of the material was intended, not for immediate use, but to provide a reserve supply.

STIMSON EXPLAINS

After the Senate cut, Stimson wrote to Chairman Glass, Dem., Va., of the Senate Appropriations committee saying that the money was needed to provide gyrostabilizers for tanks and to manufacture late type anti-aircraft guns.

Without the stabilizers, he said, a tank must come to a complete

More of SENATE on Page 7

RATIONING TASK LEFT SQUARELY UP TO STATION MEN

Officials Admit Blend Of Solomon's Wisdom And Job's Patience Will Be Needed

Washington — (AP) — The oil-stained gas station attendant assumed a new importance in the life of eastern seaboard motorists Friday night when the Government put squarely on his shoulders the task of doleing out a restricted supply of fuel.

Officials frankly acknowledged that the task called for a blend of Solomon's wisdom and Job's patience, but they expressed confidence that the gas station man was "a smart guy" and could perform satisfactorily.

Effective right away, the supply of gasoline delivered to the service stations is being cut 10 per cent. The operators of the stations are under mandate to see that ambulances, fire apparatus, doctors' cars, commercial vehicles, farm tractors, government autos and other "essential" cars get all the gas it takes to keep them moving.

THIS ONE'S EASY

Thus, if an ambulance rolls up to the pump and the driver says "Fill 'er up" the station man's decision is easy. He fills 'er up.

But if a man in a sedan drives in and says he is a traveling salesman whose livelihood depends on his car, it's something else again. The attendant apparently must determine whether the man is telling the truth.

As for those who go for a spin just for the fun of it, the station man's problems get harder and harder. The order issued Friday night says that he mustn't discriminate between different autoists or different classes of trade; that he shall spread the necessary cuts in the supply proportionately among the customers.

ANOTHER PROBLEM

Another tough problem posed for the attendant is the rule that he must distribute his sales of gas "proportionately throughout the day," asked just how he would do that and the other things called for in the order, one official said Friday night "how he does it is his job."

Privately, some officials envisioned a "first-come, first-served scramble" at some stations. They

More of ATTENDANTS on Page 9

PARACHUTIST CHIEF KILLED

Berlin— (AP) —Lieut. General Suessmann, German parachute troop commander, was killed May 20 during the German campaign in Crete, it was learned here Friday.

"We Lead All The Rest"
FARM CORNER
By
The Farm Editor

GUERNSEY FIELD DAY IN YORK CO. AUG. 20

Lancaster County Breeders Invited To Meeting Wednesday Near Dallastown

Lancaster county Guernsey breeders have been invited to attend a York county Guernsey Field day to be held Wednesday, August 20, at Taylor's Grove, two miles west of Dallastown. The affair is being sponsored by the York County Guernsey Bull association, Farm Agent F. S. Bucher said Friday.

The program is scheduled to begin at 9:30 a. m. with the judging of cow classes and will end with a woman's milking contest at 3 p. m. Invitations to local breeders were mailed Friday.

Dairy cattle will be judged on the basis of height and records of production. This new type of judging merit in dairy animals has been worked out by the Department of Animal Industry of the U. S. Department of Agriculture.

This is the first time this new system of judging will be put into

More of FARM CORNER on Page 7

NAZIS HAVE PLAN TO AID R.A.F. AVIATOR

Offer To Allow British To Drop Pair Of Artificial Legs By Chute For Legless Pilot

London—(AP) — The Germans have offered to allow an RAF plane to fly a new pair of artificial legs across the channel for Wing Commander Douglas R. Bader, legless RAF pilot who broke those he was wearing when he was forced down in occupied territory, it was reported unofficially Friday night.

The German offer was sent through the International Red Cross. If accepted, it was said here the new metal legs would be dropped by parachute.

TWO PERSONS HURT BY HIT-RUN CAR

Pedestrians Struck by Machine as They Were Walking Along Denver-Stevens Road

Two persons, identified by State Motor Police as Alice Wayne Netzley, of Schoeneck, and Fred Piefer, of 307 S. Fourth st., Denver, were injured late Friday night when struck and knocked down by a hit-run car while walking along the Denver-Stevens highway near Denver.

Motor Police said Harrison Hanley, of Denver R. D. 2, was taken into custody by Patrolman M. P. McGeary, of the Ephrata sub-station of State Motor Police, in Denver, as the alleged driver of the car.

Piefer, according to police suffered a concussion of the brain while his companion escaped with lacerations of the face.

CHILD STRICKEN WITH PARALYSIS NEAR ANNVILLE

James Morris, Of Miller's Quarry, Suffering From Mild Attack

Annville—James Morris, three and one-half years old, son of Mr. and Mrs. John Morris, of Miller's quarry, about one and one-quarter miles west of Annville, was stricken with infantile paralysis Friday, it was reported by Dr. James Monteith.

Dr. Monteith said the child is suffering from a mild attack, and that in its early stages he is unable to state just what parts of the child may be effected. The child is confined to his home.

Health authorities announced there are four other mild cases of the disease under quarantine in Lebanon county at the present time.

NO NEW CASES HERE

No new cases of infantile paralysis were reported here Friday as city health officials expressed gratification at the co-operation of residents in the measures taken to

More of PARALYSIS on Page 7

WORKERS LINE UP AT STATE OFFICE FOR MARIETTA JOB

Hundreds Register Here, Will Be Furnished To Unions On Demand

The threatened labor shortage at the new $6,000,000 Army Supply depot at Marietta may be eased considerably through a rush of skilled and unskilled workmen to register Friday at the state employment office on North Duke street.

Hundreds filed their names and qualifications during the day, according to Mark N. Wickert, manager of the office, who said those qualified would be furnished to the labor unions when they ask for workers.

In the meantime, representatives of construction trade unions were at the site of the new depot to contact skilled workers who applied there for jobs. Unemployed union men are also registering for work at the Central Labor Union headquarters, 677 Manor st.

FOUR YOUTHS HELD AS ARMY DESERTERS

One Suspect Surrenders When Police Pickup Fellow Workman In Shoe Shine Parlor

City police added an extra man to their catch of alleged army deserters Friday night when one voluntarily surrendered as police were taking his companion into custody. As the result police are holding four youths for military authorities.

Sergeant Ray Charles and Policeman A. J. Daecher walked into a shoe shine parlor at 10 p. m. and took into custody Robert E. Duncan, of 327 Howard ave., who was working at the place. When they finished telling him he was wanted for desertion, Paul Carter, of 430 North street, another employe, approached police and said "might just as well take me, too, I deserted in May from Fort Belvoire, Va."

Besides Duncan and Carter, police are also holding Leonard D. Cooper, of 324 North st., and Charles F. Stewart, of 354 Howard ave., as deserters from Camp Lee, Va. All are Negroes.

Intelligencer Journal
Weather Calendar

COMPARATIVE TEMPERATURES

Station	High	Low
Intell Journal	71	63
Water Works	79	57
Ephrata	78	61
Last Year (Ephrata)	85	64
Official High for Year, July 28		102
Official Low for Year, January 14		11
Character of Day		Cloudy

HOURLY TEMPERATURES
(Friday)

3 a m	63	4 p m	67
4 a m	63	5 p m	70
5 a m	64	6 p m	71
6 a m	64	7 p m	70
7 a m	65	8 p m	70
8 a m	65	9 p m	69
9 a m	68	10 p m	69
10 a m	70	11 p m	69
11 a m	70	Midnight	69
Noon	70	(Saturday)	
1 p m	69	1 a m	68
2 p m	65	2 a m	68
3 p m	66	3 a m	68

HUMIDITY
8 a m—72 Noon—57 2 p m—100
4 p m—96 Midnight—90
Average Humidity—83
Dew Point, Midnight—65

More of WEATHER on Page 7

DAYLIGHT TIME IN INTELL
All time mentioned in the Intelligencer Journal is Daylight Time unless otherwise noted.

SWALLOWS LEAVING FROM CAPISTRANO

But Mission Pastor Says Famed Birds Are Getting Irregular Habits

San Juan Capistrano, Calif.—(AP)—Irregularity is becoming a habit with the swallows of San Juan Capistrano Mission.

The swallows, legend had it, arrived each year March 19, St. Joseph's Day, and departed October 23, San Juan Day.

Father Arthur J. Hutchinson, pastor of the mission, says most of the swallows have headed south. They have been scattering early for the last four years.

AUTO THEFT FOILED

Emory Hummer, of 451 E. Orange st., reported to police an attempt to steal his coupe from in front of his home at 1:15 a. m. Saturday (today). The thieves had pushed the automobile down Ann street in an effort to get it started, abandoning their efforts when the car reached Fulton street.

Heavy Showers Break Three-Week Drouth Here, More Rain Forecast

Nearly An Eighth Of An Inch Of Rain Falls, Record Rain Floods Pittsburgh Streets

Heavy showers Friday broke a three-week drouth in this area and helped badly-parched crops and dwindling water supplies. Ephrata recorded .8 of an inch of rain.

The forecast for Saturday calls for scattered showers in the mornings followed by clear weather in the afternoon and cooler at night. Fair and moderate weather is forecast for Sunday.

The high temperature for the day was 78 degrees.

FLOOD AT PITTSBURGH

At Pittsburgh, scores of motorists were marooned and a dozen persons had narrow escapes from drowning Friday as a record rain deluged city streets.

U. S. Weatherman W. S. Brotzman reported that the torrential downpour was the heaviest two-hour rainfall in the 70-year history of the Weather Bureau here. Almost two inches of rain was recorded.

Some sections, notably Washington boulevard and the New Bigelow boulevard, were turned into virtual rivers during the height of the rain.

Mrs. Thomas Slane, 27, driving

More of SHOWERS on Page 9

SPEAKER RAYBURN TO TAKE VACATION

House Names Rep. Woodrum, Virginia, As Speaker Pro Tem While Texan Is Away

Washington — (AP) — Speaker Rayburn, homesick and desirous of "sniffing another atmosphere," told the House Friday he was going to the end of the narrowest road he knows about and take a vacation where there is no telephone.

A moment later the House elected Rep. Woodrum, Dem., Va., to act as Speaker Pro Tem while Rayburn is away. The House started a series of three-day recesses Friday afternoon which will extend until September 15. No controversial business is to be considered until September 22 unless an emergency arises.

Expressing hope that his colleagues would enjoy their vacation, Rayburn said that he himself was going to a Texas ranch.

"When I start to the ranch," he said, "the road gets narrower and narrower every mile I go. At the end of the narrowest road I know, there's the gate, and there's no telephone out there."

Stimson Says Army Being Trained To Defend Nation From Any Attack

Describes Present Area Of Greatest Danger As Being Central And South America In Talk To Soldiers

Washington—(AP) — Secretary of War Stimson declared Friday that the Army was being trained to defend the United States at any point from which an attack might be launched, and he described the present area of greatest danger as being Central and South America.

"If, by combining an air attack with a Fifth Column revolution," he said in an address prepared for broadcast, "an Axis power should succeed in making a lodgement upon the coast of South America, we should have a real task indeed; for it would not be difficult for an enemy lodged there to get within easy bombing distance of the Panama Canal."

SYMPTOMS DISCERNIBLE

Already, he said, some of the most significant symptoms which "invariably forecast the coming of an Axis attack" are discernible in South America. He mentioned "unrest and excitement" in various Latin Republics "which are being attributed by the governments of those Republics to the machinations of foreign secret agents." With these developments he linked the fact that Germany might take

More of STIMSON on Page 7

New York Yankees Win 1941 World Series Championship

"Big Ernie" Bonham Hurls Four Hit Ball To Tab Brooklyn, 3-1

Whitlow Wyatt And Joe DiMaggio Almost Come To Blows In Fifth Game Before 34,072 Fans; Tommy Henrich Homers In Fifth Inning

(Continued From Page One)

park during the game, to add to the confusion. One of these was on the roof back of a temporary press box and the other was a piece of bunting hanging on the railing of the second deck of the leftfield stands. It blazed up like a giant torch and fell downward, barely missing spectators in the boxes below.

Through all of these stormy scenes and the excitement of the fans, old, whitehaired Commissioner K. M. Landis just sat in stony silence, his broad-brimmed felt hat pulled low over his shaggy forehead and his chin resting on the railing in front of his box.

And, as though impelled by the force of his grim visage, the opposing clubs finally settled back into some sort of order to finish their struggle.

YANKS SCORE FIRST

The fun and fighting was largely a sideshow for the more sane observers, anyway, for the mighty Yankees took the lead and held it from the second stanza on as Bonham pitched a masterful game.

They were out to get, and did get, their eighth championship in the eight World Series they have reached since 1927. Over that stretch they captured 32 out of 36 games and they were just about as unbeatable Monday as they ever were.

Wyatt was wild at the start, walking five men in the first four innings, and the nervousness of catcher Mickey Owen, whose failure to hold a third strike on Tom Henrich in the ninth inning Sunday cost Brooklyn a victory, was no help to the National League ace who won 22 times during the regular season.

In the second inning he had a full count of 3 and 2 on Charley Keller and the slugger tipped a foul third strike which Owen was unable to hold. Then Wyatt served a wide ball which Owen let get through him and Keller not only got to first base, but made a gesture at turning toward second.

Tommy Henrich

Bill Dickey followed with a ringing single to right and Keller slid into third. Then with a one and one count on Gordon, Wyatt sailed a wild pitch high over Owen's outstretched glove and Keller loped home while Dickey ran to second. Gordon came through, then, with a scorching single off second baseman Pete Coscarart's glove and, as the ball rolled on into rightfield, Dickey scored.

This was all the margin that Bonham needed, but Henrich hammered a home run over the 40-foot fence in rightfield on the first pitch given him in the fifth inning. That was just for good measure and afterward the Yanks never bothered Wyatt—except with their continuous bench jockeying.

WYATT STARTS RALLY

Wyatt himself set off the rally that brought Brooklyn its only run in the third inning. He opened with a hard double into the leftfield corner. After Dixie Walker had flied out, Lew Riggs blasted a low liner that struck Bonham on the right leg below the knee and caromed toward the third base line for a single putting Wyatt on third. The pitcher raced home a few minutes later after Pete Reiser had flied to right.

Official Score

NEW YORK

	AB	R	H	O	A	E
Sturm 1b	4	0	1	9	0	0
Rolfe 3b	3	0	0	3	0	0
Henrich rf	3	1	1	1	0	0
DiMaggio cf	4	0	1	6	0	0
Keller lf	3	1	0	4	0	0
Dickey c	4	1	1	2	0	0
Gordon 2b	3	0	1	0	3	0
Rizzuto ss	3	0	1	2	2	0
Bonham p	4	0	0	0	1	0
Totals	31	3	6	27	6	0

BROOKLYN

	AB	R	H	O	A	E
Walker rf	3	0	1	0	0	0
Riggs 3b	4	0	1	1	3	0
Reiser cf	4	0	1	2	0	0
Camilli 1b	4	0	0	9	1	0
Medwick lf	3	0	0	0	0	0
Reese ss	3	0	0	2	3	1
Wasdell zz	1	0	0	0	0	0
Owen c	3	0	0	9	1	0
Coscarart 2b	2	0	0	3	3	0
Galan z	1	0	0	0	0	0
Herman 2b	0	0	0	0	2	0
Wyatt p	3	1	1	1	1	0
Totals	31	1	4	27	14	1

z—Batted for Coscarart in 7th.
zz—Batted for Reese in 9th.

NEW YORK .. 020 010 000—3
BROOKLYN .. 001 000 000—1

Runs batted in—Gordon, Reiser, Henrich. Two base hit—Wyatt. Three base hit—Reiser. Home run—Henrich. Double plays—Owen and Riggs; Reese, Coscarart and Camilli; Herman, Reese and Camilli. Earned runs—New York 3, Brooklyn 1. Left on bases—New York 6, Brooklyn 5. Bases on balls—Off Wyatt 5 (Henrich, Keller, Rolfe, Gordon, Rizzuto); off Bonham 2 Medwick, Walker). Struck out—By Wyatt 9 (DiMaggio 2, Bonham 4, Henrich. Keller, Rizzuto); by Bonham 2 (Camilli, Reiser). Wild pitch—Wyatt.

Umpires—McGowan (AL) plate; Pinelli (NL) 1b; Grieve (AL) 2b; Goetz (NL) 3b. Time—2:15.

Except for a tremendous triple by Reiser after two were out in the first inning, this was the only real threat the Dodgers made all afternoon.

Bonham fanned Dolph Camilli to end Brooklyn's rally in the third and he didn't give another hit until the eighth, when Walker wafted a single into right. This time he made Riggs pop foul to first baseman Johnny Sturm and struck out Reiser, and he finished strong by setting down the Dodgers in order in the ninth.

It was the first appearance the 220-pound righthander called "Tiny" ever had made in a World Series and he matched the four-hit hurling of his teammate, lefty Marius Russo, for the best pitched game of the 1941 classic.

Wyatt gave six hits, three less than he had allowed last Thursday and once over his early wildness he was as hot as the weather, which had many fans sittng peeled to their undershirts for the third straight day.

He struck out nine men, including Bonham on every one of the four times he came to bat, and DiMaggio the first two times that he came to the plate.

Sturm nipped him for a single to lead off the first inning, but after he was forced by Rolfe and Henrich walked (the fourth ball also getting away from Owen this time and rolling into the Yankee dugout) DiMaggio waited out a 3 and 2 count and then fanned. Owen caught this strike and threw to Riggs in time to get Rolfe sliding into third base for the first of three double plays the Dodgers pulled off during the contest.

After Wyatt walked Rolfe in the third he again struck out DiMaggio, loosening up the Yankee star once with a head-high pitch on the inside. It was after he had made DiMaggio drop with another similar pitch in the fifth, and DiMaggio had flied deep to centerfield, that they nearly came to blows.

Wyatt walked Gordon and Rizzuto in succession in the fourth. He had a 3 and 2 count on Gordon and it was Umpire McGowan's calling the fourth ball that precipitated the day's most violent argument with the umps.

When it was over, and Wyatt had retrieved his glove and the ball, he threw three straight balls to Rizzuto and finally walked him on five pitches.

This brought Bonham to bat and when McGowan called a strike on him as he drew back from a wide pitch after getting set to bunt, it was the Yankees' turn to holler and even Manager Joe McCarthy made one of his rare sorties from the dugout to protest.

He had come out for the first time in the series in the first inning when catcher Bill Dickey was struck in the groin by a foul tip off Riggs' bat. The lanky catcher fell sprawling to the ground in obvious pain, but after a few minutes rest was able to continue.

HERMAN IN LINEUP

The Dodgers used a pinchhitter, Augie Galan, for Coscarart in the seventh, unsuccessfully, and surprised the fans by bringing the injured Billy Herman back into the lineup to play second base for the last two frames.

He was called upon to handle two grounders in the eighth and on the first one initiated a fast double play and on the second easily threw out Dickey.

Wyatt finished strong, striking out Rizzuto and Bonham in succession to end the Yankees' half of the ninth.

$5,917 FOR EACH YANK

Brooklyn — (AP) — The World Series which ended Monday was worth $5,917.31 to each member of the victorious New York Yankees and $4,808.00 to the regulars of the Brooklyn Dodgers.

"Bill" Dickey Injured By Foul From Riggs' Bat

Catcher "Bill" Dickey, of the New York Yankees kneels in pain after being struck by a foul tip from the bat of Riggs (right), Brooklyn Dodger third baseman, in the fifth World Series game Monday at Ebbets Field, Brooklyn. Dickey was able to resume play after a few moments. Bending over Dickey is Rosar, Yankee backstop. The umpire is McGowan.

Play By Play Fifth Series Game

FIRST INNING

YANKEES—After working the count to two balls and one strike, Sturm opened with a single to left center and now has hit safely in every game of the series. With the count two strikes and one ball, Rolfe grounded to Reese who threw to Coscarart forcing Sturm, but the relay to Camilli was slow and wide preventing a double play. Henrich, who had struck out yesterday for what would have been the final out of the ball game except that Owen failed to catch the ball, waited out a base on balls in his first trip at bat and Owen missed the fourth ball which rolled into the Yankee dugout almost duplicating the dramatic situation yesterday. After waiting out a full count, DiMaggio fanned and Owen threw to Riggs to catch Rolfe sliding into third for a double play. No runs, one hit, no errors, one left.

DODGERS—Walker flied to Keller. On the first pitch Riggs tipped the ball foul and it struck Dickey, who fell to the ground in obvious pain while Manager McCarthy and the Yankee players crowded around him. He apparently had been hit in the groin. After laying on the ground a few minutes, Dickey was helped to his feet by his teammates, tightened up his chest protector, donned his mask and play was resumed. Riggs shot a hot grounder to Gordon and was thrown out. After getting the count to two and two, Reiser tripled against the wall in front of the centerfield bleachers, running into third base standing up. Camilli raised a high fly to Rizzuto. No runs, one hit, no errors, one left.

SECOND INNING

YANKEES—Keller drew a walk, the ball again getting away from Owen and rolling several yards back of the plate but he retrieved it in plenty of time to keep Keller from taking an extra base. Dickey single sharply along the ground into right center and Keller, running at full speed, slid safely into third. With the count one and one on Gordon, Wyatt made a wild pitch far over Owen's outstretched glove and Keller easily scored while Dickey went to second. Gordon drove a single off Coscarart's glove and Dickey scored as the ball continued into deep right. Rizzuto bounced the first pitch to Riggs who tossed to Coscarart forcing Gordon. Bonham struck out. Sturm bunted, but was thrown out by Riggs to Camilli. Two runs, two hits, no errors, one left.

DODGERS—After getting three straight balls, Medwick fouled off three pitches and finally walked. Reese picked out a two and two pitch and flied high to DiMaggio. Owen received another tremendous ovation from the crowd as he came to bat. With the count three balls and one strike on Owen, Bonham gave him what looked like a high pitch and Owen tossed aside his bat and ran halfway to first base before the umpire waved him back and informed him it was a strike. Manager Durocher protested briefly but Owen returned to the box and raised a high fly to Keller. Coscarart bounced to Bonham who threw to Sturm for the out. No runs, no hits, no errors, one left.

THIRD INNING

YANKEES—Rolfe walked on five pitches. Wyatt walked clear in behind the plate to protest to Umpire McGowan on the called ball and was joined by Durocher but the pitcher returned to the mound and Durocher to the dugout. Henrich flied deep to Reiser and Rolfe held first. DiMaggio fanned on four pitches. It was his second straight strikeout. On the first pitch Keller grounded to Coscarart and was thrown out. No runs, no hits, no errors, one left.

DODGERS—After fouling the first pitch back into the press box, Wyatt lined a double into the left field corner. With the count one and one, Walker lined to DiMaggio, Wyatt holding second. Riggs belted a liner that struck Bonham on the right leg below the knee and caromed off toward the third base line for a single, Wyatt reaching third. On the first pitch, Reiser drove a high fly which Henrich took a few feet from the scoreboard in right field, Wyatt scoring after the catch. After getting the count to three and two, Camilli struck out. One run two hits, no errors, one left.

FOURTH INNING

YANKEES—Dickey knocked the first pitch back at Wyatt, the ball hitting him on the shins, but he picked it up and threw to Camilli for the out. He apparently was not hurt. After getting the count to three and two Gordon walked, and Wyatt came running in from the mound waving his glove and shouting in protest. In a heated argument with Umpire McGowan, Wyatt threw his glove on the ground and stamped and yelled. Durocher joined in the dispute, kicked the dirt and gestured with his arms while standing chin to chin with the umpire. The Dodger infielders came up close but after several minutes of debate Durocher returned to the dugout. As Wyatt walked back to the mound, he threw the ball high in the air and let it lie on the dirt. Then he started digging a hole in the mound by kicking his cleated right foot. Finally he picked up the ball and started to pitch. He threw three straight balls to Rizzuto before the umpire called a strike. Then Rizzuto walked on the next pitch. When Bonham, after taking one strike, tried to bunt and checked himself as the ball went wide, McGowan first appeared to signal a ball and then waved a strike. This brought Manager McCarthy running from the Yankee dugout and also Coach Art Fletcher from the third base coaching box to make a brief protest. Bonham fanned on the next pitch. After getting the count to two and two Sturm grounded out to Camilli unassisted. No runs, no hits, no errors, two left.

DODGERS—On the second pitch, Medwick lined to DiMaggio in left center. Reese smashed a liner which Keller caught on the run in left center. Owen lifted a high foul to Rolfe between the third base coaching box and the field seats. No runs, no hits, no errors, none left.

FIFTH INNING

YANKEES—Rolfe knocked a roller to Camilli back of first and he threw to Wyatt for the putout. Henrich picked out the first pitch and shot a home run over the right field fence, 40 feet high and 300 feet from the plate. It was his first of the series. DiMaggio drove a high fly to Reiser in deep center. DiMaggio made a big turn for second base on the fly and as he headed back to the dugout he exchanged heated words with Wyatt, who on his previous time at bat had thrown a high inside pitch which made DiMaggio drop almost to the dirt. The two started for each other and almost every member of the two teams and the umpires raced to keep them apart. Peace was restored with nothing except conversation being exchanged and the field cleared for resumption of the game. Keller struck out after getting the count to three and two. One run, one hit, no errors, none left.

DODGERS—The crowd booed the Yankees as they took the field. With the count two strikes and one ball Coscarart raised a high fly to DiMaggio in left center and the crowd booed and hooted as he caught it. The jeers turned to cheers as Wyatt came to bat. Wyatt again fouled off a ball back into the stands, and then flied to DiMaggio. Walker was passed on four pitches. Riggs raised a high foul which Rolfe came in to take in front of the Yankee dugout. No runs, no hits, no errors, one left.

SIXTH INNING

YANKEES—Dickey grounded to

More of PLAY On Page 11

Composite Box Score

New York—(AP)—Following is the composite box score of the five games of the 1941 World Series:

NEW YORK	G	AB	R	H	2B	3B	HR	RBI	BB	SO	Pct.	PO	A	E	Pct.
Sturm, 1b	5	21	0	6	0	0	0	2	0	2	.286	48	1	0	1.000
Rolfe, 3b	5	20	2	6	0	0	0	0	2	1	.300	7	8	0	1.000
Henrich, rf	5	18	4	3	1	0	1	1	3	3	.167	6	0	0	1.000
DiMaggio, cf	5	19	1	5	0	0	0	1	2	2	.263	19	0	0	1.000
Keller, cf	5	18	5	7	2	0	0	5	3	1	.389	12	0	0	1.000
Dickey, c	5	18	3	3	1	0	0	1	3	1	.167	24	2	0	1.000
Bordagaray z	1	0	0	0	0	0	0	0	0	0	.000	0	0	0	.000
Rosar, c	1	0	0	0	0	0	0	0	0	0	.000	0	0	0	.000
Gordon, 2b	5	14	2	7	1	1	1	5	7	0	.500	6	19	1	.962
Rizzuto, ss	5	18	0	2	0	0	0	0	3	1	.111	12	18	1	.968
Ruffing, p	1	3	0	0	0	0	0	0	0	0	.000	0	0	0	.000
Chandler, p	1	2	0	1	0	0	0	1	0	0	.500	0	0	0	.000
Murphy, p	2	2	0	0	0	0	0	0	0	1	.000	1	0	0	1.000
Selkirk, zz	2	2	0	1	0	0	0	0	0	0	.500	0	0	0	.000
Russo, p	1	4	0	0	0	0	0	0	0	1	.000	0	4	0	1.000
Donald, p	1	2	0	0	0	0	0	0	0	1	.000	0	1	0	1.000
Breuer, p	1	1	0	0	0	0	0	0	0	0	.000	0	1	0	1.000
Bonham, p	1	4	0	0	0	0	0	0	0	4	.000	0	1	0	1.000
Totals		166	17	41	5	1	2	16	23	18	.247	135	55	2	.900

z—Ran for Dickey eighth inning, second game.
zz—Batted for Murphy 9th inning second game, for Breuer 8th inning fourth game.

BROOKLYN	G	AB	R	H	2B	3B	HR	RBI	BB	SO	Pct.	PO	A	E	Pct.
Walker, rf	5	18	3	4	2	0	0	0	2	1	.222	14	0	0	1.000
Herman, 2b	4	8	0	1	0	0	0	0	2	0	.125	4	13	0	1.000
Coscarart, 2b	3	7	1	0	0	0	0	0	1	2	.000	7	8	0	1.000
Reiser, cf	5	20	1	4	1	1	1	3	1	6	.200	14	1	0	1.000
Camilli, 1b	5	18	1	3	1	0	0	1	1	6	.167	45	5	0	1.000
Medwick, lf	5	17	1	4	1	0	0	0	1	2	.235	8	0	0	1.000
Lavagetto, 3b	3	10	1	1	0	0	0	0	2	0	.100	2	1	0	1.000
Reese, ss	5	20	1	4	0	0	0	2	0	0	.200	13	14	3	.900
Owen, c	5	12	1	2	0	1	0	2	3	0	.167	20	4	1	.960
Riggs x-3b	3	8	0	2	0	0	0	1	1	1	.250	1	5	0	1.000
Franks, c	1	1	0	0	0	0	0	0	0	0	.000	0	1	0	1.000
Davis, p	1	2	0	0	0	0	0	0	0	0	.000	1	0	0	1.000
Casey, p	3	2	0	1	0	0	0	0	0	1	.500	0	3	0	1.000
Wasdell, xx-lf	3	5	0	1	1	0	0	2	0	0	.200	2	0	0	1.000
Allen, p	3	0	0	0	0	0	0	0	0	0	.000	0	0	0	.000
Wyatt, p	2	6	1	1	1	0	0	0	0	1	.167	1	2	0	1.000
Fitzsim'ons, p	1	2	0	0	0	0	0	0	0	0	.000	0	2	0	1.000
French, p	2	0	0	0	0	0	0	0	0	0	.000	0	0	0	.000
Galan, xxx	2	2	0	0	0	0	0	0	0	1	.000	0	0	0	.000
Higbe, p	1	1	0	1	0	0	0	0	0	0	1.000	0	1	0	1.000
Totals		159	11	29	7	2	1	11	14	21	.182	132	60	4	.980

x—Batted for Owen seventh inning, first game.
xx—Batted for Casey 7th inning first game; for Reese 9th inning fifth game.
xxx—Batted for French 8th inning third game; for Coscarart 7th inning 5th game.

PITCHING RECORDS

PITCHER	G	CG	IP	H	R	ER	BB	SO	WP	HB	W	L	Pct.	ERA
New York														
Ruffing	1	1	9	6	2	1	3	5	0	0	1	0	1.000	1.00
Russo	1	1	9	4	1	1	2	5	0	0	1	0	1.000	1.00
Bonham	1	1	9	4	1	1	2	2	0	0	1	0	1.000	1.00
Murphy	2	0	6	2	0	0	1	3	0	0	1	0	1.000	0.00
Chandler	1	0	5	4	3	2	2	2	0	0	0	1	.000	3.60
Donald	1	0	4	6	4	4	3	2	0	0	0	0	.000	9.00
Breuer	1	0	3	3	0	0	1	2	0	0	0	0	.000	0.00
Brooklyn														
Wyatt	2	2	18	15	5	5	10	14	1	0	1	1	.500	2.50
Davis	1	0	5 1/3	6	3	3	3	1	0	0	0	1	.000	5.40
Casey	3	0	5 1/3	9	6	2	2	1	0	0	0	2	.000	3.60
Fitzsimmons	1	0	7	4	0	0	3	1	0	0	0	0	.000	0.00
Allen	3	0	3 2/3	1	0	0	3	0	0	2	0	0	.000	0.00
French	2	0	1	0	0	0	0	0	0	0	0	0	.000	0.00
Higbe	1	0	3 2/3	6	3	3	2	1	0	0	0	0	.000	6.75

COMPOSITE SCORE BY INNINGS

New York (A.L.)	1	4	1	3	1	1	0	2	4	—17
Brooklyn (N.L.)	0	0	1	2	5	1	1	1	0	—11

Earned runs—New York 13, Brooklyn 9. Stolen bases—Sturm, Rizzuto. Sacrifices—None. Double plays—Brooklyn (5): Reese, Herman and Camilli; Reese and Camilli; Owen and Riggs; Reese, Coscarart and Camilli; Herman, Reese and Camilli; New York (7): Gordon, Rizzuto and Sturm (4); Dickey and Gordon; Rolfe and Rizzuto; Rizzuto and Sturm. Left on bases—Brooklyn, 27; New York, 42. Hit by pitcher—By Allen 2 (Sturm, Henrich). Umpires—McGowan and Grieve (A.L.), Pinelli and Goetz (N.L.). Times of games—First, 2:08; second, 2:31; third, 2:22; fourth, 2:54; fifth, 2:13. Attendance by games—First, 68,540; second, 66,248; third, 33,100; fourth, 33,813; fifth, 34,092.

Manager Joe McCarthy Wins Sixth World's Championship

By CHARLES DUNKLEY

Ebbets Field, Brooklyn—(AP)—Joseph Vincent McCarthy, kindly 54-year-old leader of the victorious New York Yankees, was the happiest man in the baseball world Monday night.

Leo (The Lip) Durocher, foreman of the vanquished Dodgers, was the most disappointed one.

McCarthy proudly admitted he was happy over the achievement of his mighty Yanks in beating the Dodgers three straight right in their own backyard and presenting him with his sixth world championship in the eleven years that he has managed the club.

The triumphant Yankees burst out in a tremendous wild demonstration the instant they hit their dressing room. Greying Art Fletcher, grizzled veteran coach, jumped on a trunk, pulled off his cap, and burst out with the familiar old "On the Sidewalks of New York."

In booming basses, baritones and tenors the Yankees joined him, singing at the top of their voices.

Fletcher directed them like a dressing room Stokowski, waving his cap in place of a baton.

Manager Joe McCarthy

While the joyous Yanks were singing, McCarthy entered the room to embrace Pitcher Ernie (Tiny) Bonham, who held the Dodgers to four hits. McCarthy threw his arms around Bonham and then whispered into his ear. Bonham grinned in response, and grabbed McCarthy's hand. Then McCarthy jumped on the 220-pound pitcher's back, and rode around the room for a few seconds.

Bonham's suit was drenched with perspiration and he was tired but happy over winning his first World Series game.

By this time the room was crowded to overflowing with milling well-wishers, reporters and photographers. Huge floodlights had been set up to make movies, and the stuffy room was sweltering hot.

CONGRATULATIONS IN ORDER

William Harridge, president of the American League, shouldered his way through to congratulate McCarthy. Durocher, minus his pants, came in from his own dressing room, which adjoins that of the Yanks, to offer his congratulations. Then in came Edward Barrow, president of the Yanks, making his first dressing-room appearance of the season.

"I couldn't have lost to a better guy," said Leo The Lip.

McCarthy's Irish brown eyes twinkled with happiness.

"I am very happy to be the manager of a great ball club. The Yanks are a game club and I think we beat a good, game team."

Fletcher, still standing on the trunk and sucking on a cold bottle of beer, bellowed out:

"Say that again, Mac."

To which McCarthy replied:

"I will like h---."

Fletcher hadn't had enough of singing, so he screamed to the crowd:

"Where's them singers at?"

Joseph DiMaggio

Coach Earle Combs, Charley Keller, Tom Henrich, Pitcher Johnny Murphy, and Red Rolfe joined Fletcher and they broke out into "The Beer-Barrel Polka," their victory song of two years ago, when they beat the Cincinnati Reds.

After the singing, McCarthy sat down on a bench in front of his locker and was joined by Fletcher.

"I'm glad it's over, and I'm glad we won," he said. "I never went into any series that I didn't expect to win in four straight—nuts to those fifth and sixth games."

Johnny Sturm, the Yankees' sparkling first baseman, revealed that he was doubly happy. He is going to get married to his schooldays sweetheart Florence Knobbe, in St. Louis, Oct. 18.

"Holy cow!" he yelled.

AND THEY HAD WORDS

Joe DiMaggio, the Yankees' hitting star, said he had meant no offense in his attempt to needle Whitlow Wyatt, the Dodger pitcher, after DiMag had flied out to center field in the fifth. As he passed Wyatt on his return to the bench, Joe said he remarked facetiously:

"Well, boy, this series isn't over yet."

To which Wyatt took very deep exception, and what he said to DiMaggio in return cannot be printed in a family newspaper.

Asked specifically if he thought Wyatt was attempting to dust him off with his pitches, DiMaggio replied:

"Well, what do you think it looked like?"

Over in the Dodger dressing room, the Dodgers didn't know whether to be broken-hearted at losing or overjoyed at the chance to go home after one of the toughest pennant campaigns and battle-to-the-last-ditch World Series.

"We were great during the season and we were great in the series," Manager Durocher complimented them. "We were just beaten, that's all. But we gave them one h--- of a fight, didn't we?"

There were smiles and handshakes all over the place, but every man in the room was disappointed, not only for himself, but for the fact that they couldn't do a better job of hitting.

Whitlow Wyatt

"You pitched a great game, boy." Ducky Medwick said as he patted Wyatt on the back. "It's too bad we couldn't get you some runs. But you can pitch for me any time. You've got it in here (pointing to his heart)."

DISPUTE ALL SETTLED

Wyatt had a different version of his fifth inning row with DiMaggio. He said that as DiMaggio walked across the infield back to the Yankee dugout he mumbled "something I couldn't hear."

"I figured he was putting up a beef about a duster ball which sent him back from the plate," Wyatt went on. "So I guess I got hotheaded and hollered to him, 'if you can't take it why the h--- don't you get out of the game.' That's all there was to it. It was all settled as soon as it broke up. There's no hard feeling on my part."

Most of the players did a rush job of changing into street clothes and packing to make a quick getaway for their homes.

"It's back to the farm for me," Wyatt told the boys. "Twelve hours from now I'll be in Georgia."

Billy Herman was a pain-wracked figure. The pulled muscle in his side ached from his fielding efforts after he was called to second base duty for Pete Coscarart in the eighth inning.

"I had just one good throw in me," he said, "and I was lucky enough to come up with a double play on that one. The next play I made was easy, but I don't think I could have made another."

Series Statistics

By The Associated Press

	W.	L.	P.C.
NEW YORK (AL)	4	1	.800
BROOKLYN (NL)	1	4	.200

First game (at Yankee Stadium):

	R.	H.	E.
BROOKLYN	2	6	0
NEW YORK	3	6	1

Davis, Casey (6), Allen (7) and Owen, Franks (7); Ruffing and Dickey.

Second game (at Yankee Stadium):

	R.	H.	E.
BROOKLYN	3	6	2
NEW YORK	2	9	1

Wyatt and Owen; Chandler, Murphy (6) and Dickey, Rosar (9).

Third game (at Ebbets Field):

	R.	H.	E.
NEW YORK	2	8	0
BROOKLYN	1	4	0

Russo and Dickey; Fitzsimmons, Casey (8), French (8), Allen (9) and Owen.

Fourth game (at Ebbets Field):

	R.	H.	E.
NEW YORK	7	12	0
BROOKLYN	4	9	1

Donald, Breuer (5), Murphy (8) and Dickey; Higbe, French (4), Allen (5), Casey (5) and Owen.

Fifth game (at Ebbets Field):

	R.	H.	E.
NEW YORK	3	6	0
BROOKLYN	1	4	1

Bonham and Dickey; Wyatt and Owen.

Figures for fifth game:

Attendance (paid)	34,072
Total receipts	$ 161,921
Advisory Council's share	24,288.15
Each club's share	34,408.21
Each league's share	34,408.21

Figures for five games:

Attendance (paid)	235,733
Total receipts	$1,007,762
Advisory Council's share	151,165.60
Players' share	431,378.91
Each club's share	106,305.94
Each league's share	106,305.94
Winning players' share	181,179.14
Losing players' share	120,786.10
Amount divided among second, third and fourth place clubs in each league	129,413.67

Note—Figures do not include radio rights.

BROOKLYN FANS SAY—WAIT 'TILL WE MEET AGAIN

Sports Scribe Exposes High Lights And Low Lights Of Series

By WHITNEY MARTIN

Ebbets Field, Brooklyn — (The Special News Service)—The plaintive bleat of "Wait 'till next year" again echoed along the banks of the Gowanus Monday night as the Dodger fans finally were convinced that everything not only happens in Brooklyn, but to Brooklyn.

For what happened to their Bums shouldn't happen to a dog and if the breaks had just bent a little their way it would be over the river to the Yankee Stadium this Tuesday, instead of just over.

And before sticking the 1941 Dodger nightmare in mothballs to be unwrapped piece by piece on cold winter nights, a few high lights, and low-lights, might be exposed while they're still fresh. These might include:

Best all-around player—Joe Gordon.

Goat—name your own. We won't name Mickey Owen. He was simply the most unfortunate. He played great ball except for one lapse.

Sentimental hero—Fat Freddy Fitzsimmons, the pitching antique who had the Yanks tamed when he was kneed by a line drive.

Biggest bust—Dolph Camilli.

Most timely hit—Charley Keller's two-bagger in the "borrowed time" victory in the fourth game.

Least timely hit—Phil Rizzuto's single in the sixth inning of the last game with two out, and Ernie Bonham up next.

Best catch—Joe Medwick's spear of Joe DiMaggio's drive in the first game. Runner-up: Any one of half a dozen by Gordon.

Loudest noise—Leo Durocher squawking over DiMaggio's hit down the third base line in the fourth game. Runner-up: The loud speaker system.

Loudest silence—The center field bleachers when Pete Reiser fanned in the eighth inning of the final game. The Dodgers died right there.

Most unfair—The booing of DiMaggio when he fanned, and after his run-in with Whit Wyatt.

Maddest—Wyatt when the umpire made it ball four on what Wyatt thought was a perfect strike.

Biggest mistake—Hugh Casey giving Charley Keller a hitable ball after the count was nothing and two in the ninth inning of the fourth game.

Fastest play—Durocher getting

More of BROOKLYN on Page 11

LANCASTER NEW ERA
Sports

95 Out of 115 Scribes Rank Minnesota Tops

Sports Revue

Is Bell New Pilot? Scholastic Stars. Shame on Emmanuel.

by GEORGE W. KIRCHNER

PUTTING ONE WORD AFTER THE OTHER . . . And don't be too surprised if Les Bell, who managed Harrisburg to the Inter-State League championship last fall, turns up as the manager for our Red Roses . . . The owners are more than just merely interested in Bell now that he's not with Harrisburg . . . The story behind all of this was that Pittsburgh, which has taken over for the Capitol City association, was going to ship Bell to its "A" farm at Albany . . . But to date this has not been done and there's a possibility that Les may be scouting around . . . In which case, the Roses were interested . . . but definitely . . . Bell's one big selling point, other than his championship team, is that he discovered and tutored Billy Cox, who looks like he might make the grade with the Pirates next season . . . But he'd have to be a better than average magician to duplicate the trick with the ball players we had in our infield last year . . .

Columbia High had too much power for Catholic last week and as a result the Crusaders couldn't come up with anything resembling a dangerous aerial attack . . . Nevertheless, Pitchin' Phil Fittipaldi gave all the earmarks of being a right nice guy to have around when you want to cover some ground by air . . . He throws a long, soft ball that floats along accurately and is easy to catch . . . He'll be through this year, so the college scouts might just as well get busy here and now . . .

Out McCaskey High way they were saying that "everything is cut and dried" for Don Schneider to enter Penn State next fall . . . In fact, Bob Higgins, the State coach, paid a visit here to talk with him . . . But several other schools are also interested, so the chances are he won't make up his mind until later . . . For which you can't blame him . . . The kid has plenty on the ball right now and is in a position to listen to all bids . . .

Bobby Braner, who played in the outfield for the Roses last year, is looking for business manager Bill Cowdrick . . . And not just to shake his hand, either . . . Speaking of Braner, Bob's younger brother, Larry, seems to be doing alright with the Pitt Freshman football team and you're likely to see him at one of the tackle positions with the Panthers next fall . . .

The report today is that Gordy Peters, Columbia High's hard plunging back for all of his 136 pounds, will follow in the footsteps of his brother, Hubie and enter Millersville . . . Hubie, who used to star for Columbia a couple of years ago, is carrying on in fine style for Poss Stehman's Teachers and right now the Columbia boys have Gordy all set to join his big brother . . .

For a guy who has been around as long as "Snaps" Emmanuel, the York High coach, he certainly surprised everybody by his unnecessary actions during Saturday's game with McCaskey . . . Snaps has been in this business long enough to know better, and the sooner he realizes this the better off he and his team are going to be . . . The demonstration that he put on here certainly did not reflect favorably on either the coach or York High . . . It's tough to lose, everybody admits, but there's nothing so unpopular as a hard loser, who wants to put the blame on everybody but the right person, which, in most cases, is himself . . . Emmanuel, who used to be popular when he played with the old All-Lancaster team and who was respected when he was performing for Gettysburg, lost a lot of prestige by his actions on Saturday . . .

Teachers Point for Albright

Countians Resume Drills for Thursday's Tiff at Reading

Coaches Ivan "Poss" Stehman and Bernie Santaniello put the Millersville State Teachers College football team through a week of hard practices and will taper off with several light signal drills this week in preparation for their Turkey Day game, at Reading, with Albright College. This is the first time that these schools have arranged to play each other.

The Millersville coaches are hoping for a good clear day so that their squad will be able to use their much improved running attack. Two of the Black and Gold players who occupied starting positions will not be available for this contest. Kenny Herr, who started at fullback but had to retire at mid-season because of a shoulder injury is still on the injured list. The other player who is out because of a head injury which was obtained in the Kutztown game is Don Hoover, a guard.

The Millersville team clinched a tie for first place with West Chester Teachers, in the Mythical State Teachers College Conference, when they defeated the Golden Avalanches of Kutztown.

The DiMaggios and Little Joe

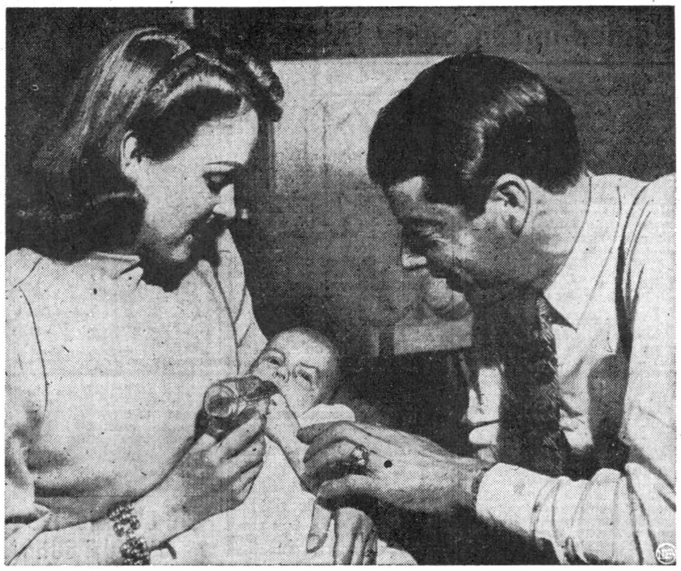

Little Joe DiMaggio, Jr., goes before the camera for the first time with his proud parents in their New York City home. Joe Jr. was born shortly after the World Series and just before his famous father was voted the most valuable American League player.

Texas Aggies Placed Second With Duke 3d

Gophers, With 17 Straight Wins, Seen Likely to Retain Title; Notre Dame 4th With Duquesne Moving to 5th Spot

By BILL BONI

NEW YORK, Nov. 25—(AP)—Minnesota's Golden Gophers, unbeaten and untied—and unbeatable, since their season is over—ride high again today in first place in the Associated Press football ranking poll.

Winners of 17 straight games and their second successive Western Conference championship, Bernie Bierman's boys were made first choice by 95 out of 115 sports experts throughout the country. Sixteen writers ranked the Gophers second, three listed them in third place and one rated them fifth, for a total of 1,124 points out of a possible 1,150.

Likely To Keep Title

With one more poll to go, Minnesota appears a good bet to retain its 1940 No. 1 ranking when the final votes are counted next week.

The Gophers' only serious rivals are two more of the country's four major all-winning teams—Texas A. and M., which still must protect that record against Texas in Thursday's climactic Southwest Conference engagement and against Washington State December 6, and Duke, the Southern Conference powerhouse which, like Minnesota, has completed its regular schedule.

The Aggies, given only two first-place votes to Duke's 15, got 41 votes for second and 40 for third in accumulating 922 points. Duke was only 10 points behind in third place. Notre Dame, unbeaten but tied by Army, also retained the fourth position it was voted a week ago the Irish got two votes for first and 778 points, on a basis of 10 for first, nine for second, eight for third, etc.

Duquesne Is Fifth

Unbeaten and untied Duquesne moved up a notch to fifth, changing places with Michigan. The Wolverines, though tied with Ohio State in their game last Saturday and also in the final Western Conference standings, considerably outdistanced the Buckeyes in the poll, which gave Ohio State only 71 points and 15th place.

The rest of the first 10 consisted of Missouri, the Big Six champion, moved up from eighth; Fordham, back in the charmed circle on its walloping of St. Mary's; Northwestern, probably the best 1941 football team that lost three games, and Texas. Outside of Texas, all of

(See FOOTBALL—Page 15)

Peckinpaugh Given New Post by Indians

Stoe in Last Fight Before Joining Marines

Andrew "Hutz" Stoe, the St. Joe youngster, will be making his last appearance in the squared circle before a local crowd on December 4 at the "Hill" arena.

"Hutz" has joined the U. S. Marines and this will be his last fight here. The younger brother of "Pinkie" has had only a few fights, but has shown much promise. He has made a tremendous hit with the fans by his aggressive style of boxing, and is one of the most promising boys in Coach Johnny Hauck's stable. Young Stoe will probably meet a soldier or sailor.

It appears as though the fans will be in for another thrilling show, such as was staged by the Hill Club a few weeks ago. Things can be expected to happen when Army meets Navy in some of the bouts.

In the heavyweight division husky Todd Cole of the Army will swap punches with Horrace Tompson of the Navy.

Sergeant Leo Connors of the Army team will bring some new boys here for the coming show. They are Irish Micky Hogan, Corporal Mike Mostasko, Steven Dziadik, Chuck Connors, and Dave Karess.

Chief Petty Officer T. L. Crocker of U. S. N. will bring his best boy, Jessie Harris, who meets Joe Smith of the West Lancaster A. A. Coach Hauck has seen the sailor in action and feels certain that Harris and Smith will give the fans something to talk about after they swing into action.

SEVENTH WARD WINS, 35-29

Seventh Ward A. C.	G	F	Tl.	Coatesville	G	F	Tl.
Meshey F	7	0	14	Victor F	3	0	6
Edwards F	1	2	4	De Pendo F	1	0	2
Myers C	3	0	6	Wasko C	0	1	1
Sheckard G	1	0	2	Tammey G	2	1	5
Austin G	2	0	4	Francisson G	3	1	7
Frank F	1	0	2	Forte F	4	0	8
Arnold G	0	0	0				
Schaeffer G	1	1	3	Totals	13	3	29
Totals	16	3	35				

SEVENTH WARD	7	10	6	12—35
COATESVILLE	10	4	4	11—29

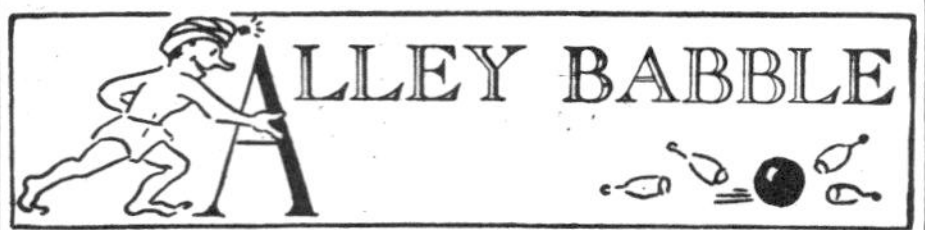

THE boys turned up with quite a few nifty triple totals last night and when it comes right down to stepping up to the front of the list, you can pass that pleasure on to Francis Richer of the Moose "C" League and Hen Erisman of the Machine League . .

Both scored very well with Richer getting 243-177-211 for a 631, while Erisman came through with 244-207-169 for a 630..

Leon Miller had a 222 and George Graham a 216 for other high Machine League scores..

The boys in the Hotel League also did right well with Paul Severin getting 212-198-205 for 615; George Sherman landing 171-224-206—601; Dick Graef 224; Wack Foulk 221; Walt Coble 243; Cleon Fisher 229; Jerry Bitzer 224, and Jake Shinsky 212-193-201—606..

R. Kendig and G. Schanberger paced the P. & L. League with 193, while Jim Kline's 209 and Les Nelson's 206 and 208 were the leading figures in the I-J League.

Harry Martin's 221 was the top number in the Y. M. C. A. "A" League, while Newswanger of Emmanuel, paced the Church League with his 224 and 575..

Gus Hertz's 213 and Screenie Welsh's 594 took top honors in the St. Joe League, while Edgar Wagner's 208 and Charley Koehler's 207 featured the W. and S. circuit..

The Hollinger girls were in prominence with one leading the Watch Girls League with 187, while the other—(or is it the same one?) took honors in Girls Distributors League with 166.. Lena McConnell's 464 was high triple for the Watch gals.

Here are a few more match game scores:

Rohrerstown	894-922-904—2673
S-L	780-925-801—2506
Quarryville	708-789-700—2297
Moose Specials	893-839-833—2475
Lebanon	894 863 862—2619
Moose Travelers	880-927-931—2738
Reading	824-873-890—2587
Ephrata Buds	849-869-874—2592
Reinholds	834 907-881—2622
Fleetwood	911-774-856—2541
Ephrata Owls	979-900-1021—2900
Hbg. Bakers	916-910-911—2737
Eph. Owls Girls	790-754-752—2296
Hbg. Dairy	645-725-754—2124
Roxboro Girls	696-623-709—2028
Eph. Owls Girls	792-757-749—2298

In the Lebanon Valley League, Myerstown won three points from Manheim.

The boys up in the other Moose Leagues also fared well . . . For instance, Jake Shinsky hit 247 and Harry Stoe 232 in the ABC League, while Bob Huss got 212 in the "B" League . .

Webber got himself a nifty 221-191-200 for 612 to pace the boys in the First Baptist League, while John Snyder's 185 and 467 led the Elks Duck Pin League . .

Kathryn Huss' 149 and 425 were high in the St. Paul's M. E. circuit with Williams' 135 leading the Linoleum Ladies . .

Tribe Moves Manager to Front Office

CLEVELAND, Nov. 25.—(AP)—The Cleveland Indians' manager Roger T. Peckinpaugh was promoted today to the top front office job of general manager.

President Alva Bradley, who made the announcement, said he hoped to announce soon a successor to Peckinpaugh as the Tribe's field chieftain.

The 50-year-old "Peck" succeeds Cyril C. Slapnicka, who surprised Bradley by resigning this fall after the Indians slumped into a tie for fourth place in the American League. Peckinpaugh, the Indians' 1928-33 manager, came back to them in the same position last season to replace Oscar Vitt.

KUCZYNSKI NAMED CAPTAIN

Philadelphia—(AP)—Bernie Kuczynski, star end, was elected captain of the 1942 University of Pennsylvania football team at a meeting of lettermen. He is a Philadelphian.

Minnesota Loses 15 of 1941 Team

MINNEAPOLIS, Nov. 25—(AP)—It was farewell to arms today for that great Minnesota football team.

Just before the annual athletic convocation this afternoon, the lettermen pick a 1942 captain and at the ceremony to follow Captain Bruce Smith will pass on the torch of leadership.

Certainly the new leader will have his job cut out for him, for he will be pledged to hustle for the alma mater as no other Golden Gopher ever hustled before. His responsibility will be to get that 1942 outfit tuned up to pick up that 17 game winning streak.

A lot of guns behind the blasting 1941 drive to the pigskin heights will be missing, for 14 men besides Captain Smith have played their last college football.

Heading the holdovers are such stars as tackle Dick Wildung and fullback Bill Daley and the guessing was that one will be the captain unless it is made a co-captaincy.

Wilt Wins Race

East Lansing, Mich.—(AP)—Frederick L. Wilt, slim Indiana University runner, Monday capped his first "big time" harrier season by slipping away from a picked field for an easy individual triumph in the fourth annual National Collegiate Cross Country championships.

Wilt's victory, however, failed to help Indiana's team title defense in the four-mile event, and Rhode Island State College, compiling 83 points, added the National crown to the I. C. 4-A title it won last week for the second straight year.

Wilt was clocked in 20 minutes, 32.3 seconds, a trifle slower than the record-breaking 20:30.2 set by Gilbert Dodds of Ashland College last year. But since the 1941 course was altered, Wilt's time established another course and meet record.

WOODWARD FIVE WINS, 27-25

No-Nodds	G	F	Tl.	Woodward Five	G	F	Tl.
Denlinger F	7	1	15	Keller F	4	0	8
Grau F	1	0	2	Greenawalt F	0	0	0
Waltef C	2	0	4	Grau C	2	2	6
Greiter G	0	1	1	Roher G	2	3	7
Arnold G	1	1	3	Tracy G	0	0	0
				Greenawalt G	3	0	6
Totals	11	3	25				
				Totals	11	5	27

WOODWARD FIVE	8	10	5	4—27
NO-NODDS	4	6	12	3—25

WEATHER

Eastern Pennsylvania—(Early Forecast)—Fair Thursday.

Intelligencer Journal Stormograph Reading—Fair With Fresh Winds Thursday.

Intelligencer Journal.

The Leading Newspaper in the Garden Spot of America, Home Owned for Home Folks Since 1794

Football
Franklin and Marshall College closes season with Ursinus here today.
Details Page 8.

VOLUME LXXVIII.—NO. 66. FINAL EDITION The Intelligencer Founded 1799 The Journal Founded 1794 LANCASTER, PA., THURSDAY MORNING, NOVEMBER 27, 1941. Entered at Post Office at Lancaster, Pa as second class mail matter 14 PAGES, 112 COLUMNS.—THREE CENTS.

PACIFIC PEACE PROPOSAL GIVEN JAPS

VALUE TOBACCO CROP AT OVER $7,000,000

Early Stripping Reveals Some 'Ton To The Acre' Crops

1941 Crop Is Largest And Most Valuable Since Depression Crippled Farm Prices; Growers Expected To Get Average Of $205.30 Per Acre; Approximately 35,000 Acres Harvested

Lancaster county tobacco growers this year produced the largest and most valuable crop of Pennsylvania cigar leaf tobacco since the depression crippled farm prices.

From a low point of only 17,220 acres and a crop worth $1,918,640 in 1934, according to official figures of the Pennsylvania Department of Agriculture, representing the start of AAA crop control operations in this county, Lancaster growers now are beginning to strip the 1941 crop, which is worth more than seven million dollars. Year by year the acreage and value of the local tobacco crop have moved gradually upward.

The 1941 tobacco acreage in Lancaster is put at approximately 35,000 acres, an increase of around 3,000 over last year, according to estimates made by County Agent F. S. Bucher and Dr. O. E. Street, director of the Lancaster Tobacco Experiment station.

51,100,000 POUNDS IN CROP

With the Federal-State Crop Reporting Service forecasting an average acre yield of 1,460 pounds for the 1941 crop of Pennsylvania cigar leaf, the present crop in the sheds of Lancaster county farmers amounts to a total of 51,100,000 pounds and, at last year's prices, is worth $7,185,500.

With a per acre yield of 1,460 pounds—1,260 pounds of wrappers and 200 pounds of filler leaf—the gross return per acre averages $205.30 for the county crop.

This is based on a conservative average price for last year's to-

More of TOBACCO on Page 5

JOSEPH C. FEAGLEY ELECTED DIRECTOR OF ARMSTRONG CO.

Succeeds John J. Evans, Sr., Who Resigns; W. D. Martz Named Assistant Treasurer

The resignation of John J. Evans, Sr., as a member of the Board of Directors of the Armstrong Cork Company and the election of Joseph C. Feagley to succeed him was announced Wednesday by H. W. Prentis, Jr., president of the company.

JOSEPH C. FEAGLEY

Mr. Prentis' announcement followed a meeting of the board held Wednesday. He said that Mr. Evans' resignation was accepted by the board "with keen regret."

At the same time Mr. Prentis said that W. D. Martz has been appoint-

More of FEAGLEY on Page 12

"We Lead All The Rest"
FARM CORNER
By
The Farm Editor

FARM WAGES SHOW PROGRESSIVE RISE

State Report Traces Increase Since January 1, 1940, Also Shows Growing Labor Shortage

Harrisburg—The extent to which farm labor and farm wages have been affected since January 1, 1940, when the defense program began being more fully felt is shown by records of the Department of Agriculture in which a progressive rise in wages is recorded while the supply of labor has been steadily downward.

According to the reports the monthly wage with board on farms in this State averaged $25.50. On October 1, this year, that figure had climbed to an average of $34.75. The average monthly wage rate without board on the former date was $40.50, but on the latter date this average had gone to $51.25. The daily wage rate with board increased from $1.60 to $2.25 and the average rate of pay per day without board changed from $2.15 to $2.85.

As the wage rate advanced the supply decreased progressively. On January 1, 1940 the supply of farm labor stood at 89 per cent of normal, but this figure on October 1, this year, was reduced to 56 per cent. As the available labor diminished the demand naturally increased and on the former date the demand was 82 per cent of normal but this figure has advanced to 99 per cent on last October 1. On the former date the supply was 109 per cent of the demand but on October 1 this condition had changed to 57 per cent.

Industry engaged in defense work is said to be the greatest contributing factor in the farm labor situation.

HAMP TO BROADCAST FROM ELKS LODGE

WGAL To Carry Program By Orchestra Playing At Lodge's Thanksgiving Dance

Johnny Hamp and his orchestra will broadcast through radio station WGAL for network listeners at 10:30 p. m. Thursday. The local boy making good will present his Rainbow Room Orchestra from the B. P. O. Elks Lodge No. 134. Earl Stauffer, exalted ruler of the Lancaster lodge, will give a brief Thanksgiving message during the dance.

YULE DECORATIONS SHORT CIRCUITED

Firemen Summoned To Benesch's Store, 4 W. King St., But Services Are Not Required

A short circuit in electric wiring used in the Christmas decorations at Benesch's Store, 4 W. King St., was responsible for a fire alarm at 5:50 p. m. Wednesday, according to Chief Harry Miller. Engine Company No. 1 and Truck Company B responded but their services were not required.

Intelligencer Journal Weather Calendar

COMPARATIVE TEMPERATURES

Station	High	Low
Intell Journal	53	32
Water Works	55	21
Ephrata	55	27
Last Year (Ephrata)	35	21
Official High for Year, July 28		102
Official Low for Year, January 14		11
Character of Day		Clear

HOURLY TEMPERATURES

Wednesday			
		Noon	48
3 a. m.	33	1 p. m.	51
4 a. m.	33	2 p. m.	52
5 a. m.	33	3 p. m.	53
6 a. m.	34	4 p. m.	52
7 a. m.	34	5 p. m.	49
8 a. m.	34	6 p. m.	46
9 a. m.	35	7 p. m.	45
10 a. m.	38	8 p. m.	45
11 a. m.	46	9 p. m.	44

SUN

Rises—7:01 a. m. Sets—4:41 p. m.

More of WEATHER on Page 12

Lone Lancastrian Opens War On Starlings

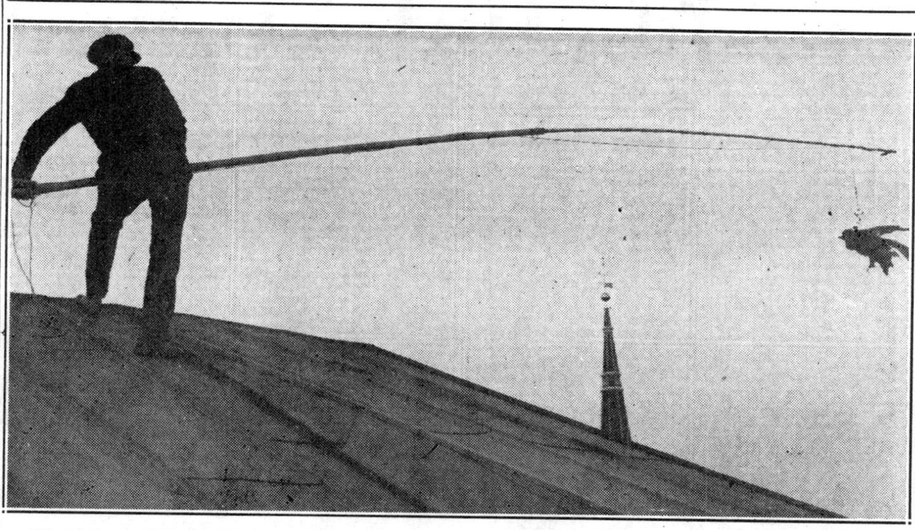

Elias W. Parmer, 131 Juniata St., who has declared a one-man blitz against the starlings roosting on the court house roof, dangles his newest invention, a "dipping hawk," at the birds. In the distance is the tower of the First Presbyterian Church. (Intell Photo)

SINGLE PHYSICAL EXAMINATION PLAN DROPPED IN PENNA.

Army Says Change Proposed January 1 Would Overtax Medical Corps

The single physical examination system for draftees throughout the nation, scheduled to go into effect January 1, had been abandoned as far as Pennsylvania is concerned, it was learned Wednesday.

COUNTY BOARD NO. 1 MEN ARE IN 61 CAMPS

Selectees and enlisted men from County Draft Board No. 1 are stationed at 61 camps in 26 states it was revealed Wednesday in a survey made by the board. Nine are serving outside the country. Camp Lee has the largest number of men, 21; Camp Croft, 18, and Fort Belvoir, 16.

The plan, which would give prospective selectees but one examination, at the hands of a traveling board of Army physicians, and thus eliminate preliminary physical examinations by private physicians connected with draft boards, has been under discussion for several months.

"The proposed change," an informed source said, "would entail additional responsibilities upon the Medical Corps which it cannot take at this time."

The present set-up of a draft board examination and a pre-induction examination at Harrisburg will be continued, it was learned. The pre-induction system of examination by Army physicians at Harrisburg was placed into effect last May and has been found to be "very satisfactory."

MODIFICATIONS POSSIBLE

Some modifications may be made, after January 1, in the procedure of local examinations, it was learned,

More of DRAFT on Page 12

'Porky's' Voice Too Shrill, So Opera Does Without Him

Chicago—(AP)—A high soprano voice was missing from Wednesday night's performance of "Martha" at the Civic Opera House.

Helen Jepson was there to sing the title role, but "Porky," her pet pig, stayed home. The snow-white baby pig had been presented to Miss Jepson by a friend. Then some one thought his presence might lend reality to the setting of Baron Von Flotow's bucolic romance.

"Porky" was given a chance at rehearsal. His high-pitched squeals drowned out the rest of the cast, however, and Stage Director William Wymetal ordered him banished.

Parmer Gets Early Start This Year With New Device

Amateur Naturalist Uses "Dipping Hawk" At End Of 22-Foot Pole To Chase Birds From Court House Roof; Crowd Watches Initial Round

The 1942 model of the starling exterminator—a "Dipping Hawk"—the brain child of Elias W. Parmer, 131 Juniata St., was given its initial test Wednesday by its inventor.

The simulated "hawk," feathers bristling and claws drawn, was dangled from a 22-foot pole by Parmer from the court roof while hundreds of pedestrians gasped—at the inventor's nimbleness and the weirdness of the "hawk."

SECOND ROUND

This is Parmer's second blitz on the thousands of starlings which hibernate on the court house roof.

This year's one-man crusade, however, was begun months earlier than last year.

The 1941 model of the amateur naturalist which made its bow, February 27, was a spider-like contraption composed of tail feathers of a golden pheasant and gourds fashoned and painted to resemble a hawk and a snake combined.

"This year," Parmer, "I've decided to get rid of these starlings and I'm starting early.

DETERMINED TO GET 'EM

"I've been a naturalist since I have been a kid, he continued as he walked over the roof dangling his invention, "and I have learned that the hawk is the natural enemy of the starling."

Parmer vowed he'd be "after these starlings until the last one disappears. I think this thing will do the trick," he added.

Parmer's 1942 model threw consternation among the ranks of the starlings. They darted in all directions but after the inventor had packed up his brain child they were observed cannily coming back to roost—on the court house roof.

UNIDENTIFIED MAN KILLED BY TRAIN AT DOWNINGTOWN

Body Still In Wreckage An Hour After Crash; Woman Taken To Chester Co. Hospital

Downingtown, Pa.—(AP)—An unidentified man was killed and a woman injured Wednesday night in an automobile-freight train crash at a crossing at East Downingtown.

Pennsylvania Railroad officials said the man's body still was pinned in the wreckage under the train an hour after the collision. The woman whose identity also was not learned immediately, was taken to a hospital in West Chester, the railroad said.

The train, consisting of a locomotive and two cars, was traveling

More of WRECK on Page 12

LIVESTOCK SHED BURNS NEAR EASTLAND

Cattle Freed From Building On Farm Of James Wood In Little Britain Township

A livestock shed on the farm of James Wood, near Eastland, Little Britain Twp., was razed by fire of unknown origin shortly after 2 p. m. Wednesday.

Wood, with a hired man, was working in a corn field near the shed when they noticed flames coming from the building. The Rising Sun Fire Company was called and kept the blazes, which burned the roof off the silo, from spreading to other buildings.

The farm was formerly owned by John Sprout, and about eight years ago a barn burned. This shed was erected over the barn's foundation. Three cows in the shed at the time of the fire were released by Wood. The damage amounted to several hundred dollars.

F & M TO PLAY NYU IN '42; MAYBE 1943

Contract Is Signed For Game To Be Played In New York City Next Season

A football game between Franklin and Marshall College and New York University has been arranged for 1942. It is understood that a contract was signed at F. & M. Wednesday afternoon, scheduling the game to be played in New York.

Reliable sources report that a return game will be played on the local field in 1943.

OVER-ALL PRICE CEILING PROPOSAL DROPPED BY HOUSE

Plan Embodying Baruch's Ideas Rejected By Decisive Vote Of 218 To 63

Washington—(AP)—By the decisive vote of 218 to 63, the House Wednesday rejected the proposal that a rigid limit be imposed upon all wages and prices.

With that done, it pushed on to issues presented by the administration bill to establish ceilings for the prices of selected commodities amid an increasing demand that the legislation be sent back to the banking committee for additional study.

Ahead lay decisions on several prickly questions, on all of which most of the political or regional blocs customary to the House were widely split. The issues awaiting settlement included:

Regulating the prices of farm commodities.

Establishing a licensing system for dealers selling commodities to be regulated.

Granting the government authority to stabilize prices by large-scale buying or selling of commodities.

Giving broad powers of administration to the present price control office headed by Leon Henderson.

If the licensing provision is included, Rep. Martin, Rep., Mass., the Republican leader, said there would be virtually solid Republican sentiment for recommitting the bill. A party conference on the subject was held during the day.

Rep. Dies, Dem., Texas, chairman of the committee on unAmerican activities, said on the floor that he would vote to recommit the measure if it contains its

More of HOUSE on Page 12

Church Services Will Usher In Observance Of Thanksgiving Day

Union Services To Be Held By Many Congregations, Record Crowd Expected At F & M-Ursinus Grid Game

Services in nearly all the churches of the city and county will usher in Lancaster's observance of Thanksgiving Day and the remainder of the day will be devoted to turkey, touchdowns and terpsichore.

Traffic was heavy Thanksgiving Eve, with many people coming home for the holiday—and others sallying forth to find entertainment in other cities.

The Franklin and Marshall-Ursinus football clash is expected to draw a record crowd in the afternoon, and many dances are planned for the evening.

UNION SERVICES

Many of the churches in Lancaster will hold union services uniting in thanksgiving for the spiritual and material blessings provided in America.

The Moravian church, St. John's Lutheran, Bethany Evangelical, Covenant U. B., Church of God and St. John's Evangelical will hold a joint service at 10 a. m. in the latter church.

The First and St. Paul's Evangelical and Reformed Churches will unite for a service at 10 a. m., in First church; and the three Presbyterian churches, Bethany, Memorial and First, and the First Baptist, will hold a service in the First Presbyterian Church at 10 a. m.

Union services will be held at 10 a. m. in Temple Shaarai Shomayim, with St. Peter's Evangelical and Reformed Church and the

More of THANKSGIVING on Page 12

FAIR AND COOL WEATHER FORECAST FOR HOLIDAY

Fair and continued cool weather were promised for Thursday, Thanksgiving Day. The mercury dipped to 21 degrees Wednesday morning at the Water Works and under a warm, clear sky rose to 55 degrees.

Early Edition

This edition of The Intelligencer Journal was printed at 9 p. m. Wednesday to allow employes to celebrate the Thanksgiving holiday.

Document Based On "Non-Aggression" Doctrine Of Hull

Secretary Of State Presents Paper To Tokyo's Envoys; Reception Considered Highly Uncertain; Acceptance Of Offer Seen As Achieving At Least Temporary Truce

Washington—(AP)—The United States Wednesday night handed Japan what was believed to be a blue-print for peace in the Pacific, but it was based on the "non-aggression" doctrine preached for years by Secretary of State Hull and hence its reception was considered highly uncertain.

Japan's two envoys, Ambassador Kichisaburo Nomura and Special Emissary Saburo Kurusu, were given what was officially described as a "document" when they called on Hull about 5 p. m. for a crucial conference.

After an hour and 15 minute talk with the Secretary of State, they emerged smiling but silent. Hull, who escorted them to the door, also smiled.

Then the waiting press corps was informed by a State Department official that the Japanese were handed, for their consideration, a paper that was the culmination of several conferences in recent weeks.

It is unnecessary to repeat, the official said, what has been said so often in the past that it (the document) rests on certain principles with which the correspondents should be entirely familiar in the light of many repetitions.

Hull has repeatedly emphasized the necessity of absinence from the use of force, non-interference by one nation in the affairs of another, settlement of all problems by peaceful negotiation, and observance of the sanctity of treaties.

However, he also has emphasized the need for equality of commercial

More of PEACE PLAN on Page 12

HITCH SUGGESTED IN NEGOTIATIONS OF NAZIS, FRENCH

Petain Reported Holding Out Against Outright Membership In Axis

New York—(AP)—Reliable reports received in New York Wednesday night suggested the possibility of a hitch in German-French negotiations, with Marshal Petain of France holding out against outright membership in the Axis.

These reports, coming from well-informed neutral sources, seemed to be supported by the failure of leaders of the two countries to meet the middle of this week, as had been expected.

Petain's reported resistance to German bids was said to be based largely on recent war developments from the various fronts. His chief reasons were listed as these:

1. The Italians again have pressed their aspirations for French territory in recent talks with the Germans.

2. The French have received reports that German losses in Russia are extremely heavy, although not as great as the Russians claim. The Russians have said the Germans have suffered more than 6,000,000 casualties.

3. Uncertainty of the fighting in North Africa. This was coupled with reports that the Germans now have no large troop concentrations in Bulgaria, leading the French to believe that the Axis will be unable to develop a pincers move-

More of FRENCH on Page 12

MAN HELD ON ZIG-ZAG CHARGE AFTER CRASH

Four-Year-Old Boy Suffers Laceration Of Lip In Collision In Rohrerstown

A charge of operating a motor vehicle while intoxicated was preferred against William W. Duffy, 48, of 30 N. Mulberry St., following a collision between two automobiles in Rohrerstown at 5:30 p. m. Wednesday.

Donald Hartman, four-year-old son of Mr. and Mrs. Sylvester Hartman, of Lancaster R1, was cut on the lip when he was thrown against the gear shift lever of the car in which he was sitting with his parents. The car was parked in front of a store on the south side of the Marietta Pike.

State Policeman W. F. Petrie, who brought the charge against Duffy, before Justice of the Peace Charles Sheeler, of Rohrerstown, said that Duffy was driving east on the highway when his car collided head-on with Hartman's car.

TWO BRITISH ARMY LINES IN LIBYA UNITE FORCES

Move Against Apparently Inferior Axis Grouping As Big Battle Looms

(By the Associated Press)

Two arms of the British offensive in north Libya, which had fought forward to a junction in the Rezegh area about Tobruk, moved Wednesday night as one powerful striking force against an apparently inferior Axis army in the preliminaries of a great new battle upon which hinged the whole of the North African campaign.

This merger was effected by the arrival in the Rezegh theater of a New Zealand column beating westward along the Mediterranean coast to its rendezvous with the main British armored infantry and south African concentrations.

The German commander, General Erwin Rommel, thus was confronted at a time when he was somewhat weakened by his dispatch of a German column eastward across the Egyptian frontier in a counter-offensive which the British command termed an unsuccessful diversion. This cost him a third of the tank strength of the column and imperiled the remainder.

Moreover, it appeared for the first time that not even in the earlier full-scale clash of mechanized weapons had the British command thrown its whole strength into action, for previously unused tank formations were reported moving up into the sprawling and ill-defined British lines in support of the imperial infantry—many of them American machines which informed persons stated had shown the low-

More of WAR on Page 12

AUTO RUNS DOWN MAN AT SILVER SPRINGS

John Stively, 68, Seriously Hurt In Accident While Returning Home From Work

John Stively, 68, Silver Springs, was seriously injured at 5:30 p. m. Wednesday when he was struck by an automobile driven by Paul B. Sauder, 214 E. Orange St., as he was crossing the Marietta pike in front of his home.

Stively was admitted to the St. Joseph's Hospital suffering a possible fracture of the skull, a deep laceration of the scalp and cuts about the face.

State Policeman A. E. Discavage said Stively, who is employed at the United States Army Depot project at Marietta, was returning home from work when the accident happened. He had alighted from an automobile driven by Louis Marion, 455 Rockland St. Walking from the right side of the car Stively rounded the front and stepped into the path of Sauder's eastbound car, Discavage said. He was conveyed to the hospital in the institution's ambulance.

WEATHER
Eastern Pennsylvania: Mostly Cloudy And Warmer Monday, Light Rain Or Snow In North Portion At Night.
Intell Journal Stormograph Reading: Unsettled Weather, Increasing Winds And Warmer.

Intelligencer Journal

The Leading Newspaper in the Garden Spot of America, Home Owned for Home Folks Since 1794

Football
Chicago Bears ... 34
Chicago Cardinals 24
Details Page 12.

VOLUME LXXVIII.—NO. 75. CITY The Intelligencer Founded 1799 The Journal Founded 1794 LANCASTER, PA., MONDAY MORNING, DECEMBER 8, 1941. Entered at Post Office at Lancaster, Pa as second class mail matter 18 PAGES, 144 COLUMNS.—THREE CENTS.

U. S., BRITISH NAVIES BATTLE JAPS AS TOKYO DECLARES WAR ON AMERICA; ROOSEVELT BEFORE CONGRESS TODAY

'Heavy' Naval And 'Large' Army Loss

Washington—(AP)—Bombs from Japan made war on the United States Sunday and as death tolls mounted President Roosevelt announced he would deliver in person Monday a special message to Congress.

In the background as the Commander-in-Chief went before the joint session of the House and Senate was a government report of "heavy" naval and "large" losses to the Army.

Whether Mr. Roosevelt will ask for a formal declaration of war by this country, to match the action taken in Tokyo, was left uncertain after a hurriedly summoned meeting of his cabinet and congressional leaders of both parties Sunday night at the White House. Also uncertain was whether that declaration might extend to Japan's Axis allies, Germany and Italy.

RESOLUTION TO BE PRESENTED

It was clear from a statement made by the participants, however, that Congress would be requested to adopt a resolution of some nature, and equally clear that it would quickly give its approval. A request for governmental power equivalent to that under a war declaration was expected as a minimum.

War came suddenly to the United States early Sunday afternoon. Without warning, and while Japanese diplomats were still conducting negotiations for peace, the Japanese air force struck at Honolulu, Pearl Harbor, and Hickam Field, all in the Hawaiian Islands. Soon afterward, Japanese bombs were raining upon Guam and, later, portions of the Philippines were attacked.

As quickly as word of the first bursting bomb was received, the President as Commander-in-Chief called upon the Army and Navy to repel the attack. Far in advance of any action which Congress may take Monday, the United States was fighting an attack.

Tokyo later announced its declaration of war on this

More of WASHINGTON on Page 4

Jap Planes Attack Pearl Harbor

This is a scene in Pearl Harbor, Hawaii, where it was announced in Washington that Japanese planes had made an attack.

U. S. Battleship Is Reported Sunk

New York—(AP)—The Berlin radio Sunday night broadcast a Tokyo announcement that the U. S. Battleship West Virginia had been sunk and the Battleship Oklahoma set afire in an engagement between the Japanese and the U. S. and British navies. The broadcast was heard in New York.

The Berlin broadcast said that the battle was "still going on" and that altogether three U. S. ships were hit. The third was not named.

The broadcast was heard shortly after 11 p. m., E. S. T.

The broadcast said, in part:

"From British reports just received it can be learned that the Japanese forces already have bombed with great success the Hawaiian Islands, the Philippines and the Island of Wake. Great material damage was caused.

"Near Honolulu oil tankers were set afire. One transport of unknown nationality was sunk at the Philippines. According to a report from Manila which was received in New York Japanese forces have attacked Singapore.

"The Imperial headquarters at Tokyo reports just now that a naval battle between Japanese, British and North American naval forces is going on in the Western Pacific.

"During this naval battle, which is still going on, between the Japanese navy and the British and American naval forces three American ships have been hit, according to a U. S. A. report. The U. S. A. Battleship West Virginia has been sunk and the U. S. A. Battleship Oklahoma has been set afire by shelling."

Meanwhile, roundabout, unconfirmed reports from Panama and London said that a Japanese aircraft carrier from which planes operated to attack Pearl Harbor had been sunk by United States navy ships.

These circulated in Panama and were broadcast from London by CBS Commentator Bob Trout as having been heard there. Trout also said unofficial news bulletins in London announced the sinking of two British cruisers at Singapore.

Bulletins

JAP CRAFT FLEE MALAYA

Singapore—(Monday)—(AP)—An official report from the northern Malaya front said today that all Japanese surface craft fled at high speed under British fire after leaving a few troops on the beaches. The troops were heavily machine-gunned, the report said.

SAY ATTACK "GREAT SUCCESS"

New York—(AP)—The German radio said Sunday night that a Japanese communique described the attack on Oahu, largest of the Hawaiian Islands, as a "great success." The broadcast was heard by NBC.

All Private Airplanes Grounded; Amateur Radio Operation Banned

Washington—(AP)—The Federal Communications Commission Sunday night prohibited all amateur radio operation in the United States and its possessions except for stations specifically authorized by federal, state and municipal authorities in connection with emergency matters.

Chairman James Lawrence Fly said he had been in touch with all major communication companies "with relation to the execution of pre-existing plans of the government and the companies for cooperation in the emergency."

Washington—(AP)—The Civil Aeronautics Authority issued orders Sunday night grounding all private airplanes in the United States and its possessions, except commercial airliners.

The CAA suspended temporarily all pilot licenses except those held by pilots on regular air lines.

Robert Hinckley, chairman of the CAA Air Safety Board, sent telegrams to the governors of the 48 states, Alaska and the Canal Zone asking them to assign police immediately to all known landing fields to protect facilities and to hold aircraft on the fields unless they were engaged in scheduled air transportation, were publicly owned or were operated under contract with the Federal government.

This action was to remain effective, Hinckley said, until accredited representatives of the CAA or commanding officers of Army or Navy air fields issued instructions permitting specific planes to fly.

It was to remain effective also, Hinckley said, until the Office of Civilian Defense issued further instructions for the formation of a Civil Air Patrol.

The order suspending pilots' licenses was signed by D. H. Connolly, CAA administrator, and made provisions for reinstatement of private licenses.

Pilots at schools engaged in training operations for the Government may regain their licenses when supervising Army, Navy or CAA officials are satisfied the holder "is an American citizen of unquestionable loyalty."

Pilots at aircraft manufacturing plants and at other defense manu-

More of PLANES on Page 8

Intelligencer Journal Weather Calendar

COMPARATIVE TEMPERATURES

Station	High	Low
Intell Journal	37	27
Water Works	46	25
Ephrata	39	26
Last Year (Ephrata)	48	26
Official High for Year, July 28		102
Official Low for Year, January 14		11
Character of Day		Partly Cloudy

HOURLY TEMPERATURES (Sunday)

3 a. m.	31	4 p. m.	37
4 a. m.	29	5 p. m.	35
5 a. m.	29	6 p. m.	34
6 a. m.	28	7 p. m.	33
7 a. m.	28	8 p. m.	33
8 a. m.	27	9 p. m.	32
9 a. m.	28	10 p.m.	32
10 a. m.	29	11 p. m.	32
11 a. m.	31	Midnight	31
Noon	33	(Monday)	
1 p. m.	34	1 a. m.	31
2 p. m.	35	2 a. m.	31
3 p. m.	36	3 a. m.	31

SUN
Rises—7:08 a. m. Sets—4:35 p. m.

LANCASTER BOY IS AT HICKAM FIELD, MANY IN WAR ZONE

At least one Lancaster man is stationed at Hickam Field, Hawaii, scene of a savage bombing raid by Japanese fliers Sunday which resulted in a number of American casualities.

L. Z. WISE

He is Leroy Z. Wise, who resides with his aunt, Mrs. H. C. Woodrig, at 132 S. Prince St. Wise, a first class private, is attached to the 22nd Materiel Squad of the Air Corps.

Wise enlisted in the Air Corps at Lancaster in November, 1939. He has been stationed at Hickam Field since May, 1940.

Two former Lancaster Newspapers carriers are serving with the armed forces in Hawaii. Thomas R. Toner, Jr., 17, 451 S. Duke St., is a sound operator aboard a submarine of the Pacific fleet based at Pearl Harbor.

He enlisted in Lancaster in 1941 and served at New London, Conn., and on the west coast before being assigned to Hawaii.

The other former carrier is Private John W. Odenwalt, 18, son of Mrs. Naomi Cramer, 425 Church St. He is a member of the Headquarters Battalion of the 25th Division, stationed at Schoefield Barracks, Honolulu. He was graduated from the Edward Hand Junior High School in 1940, and enlisted in June of this year. On August 20 he was

More of BOYS on Page 8

ELWOOD RAUM

RUSSEL SUMPMAN

Among Local Boys In War Zone

ROBERT L. FRIMD

JOHN W. ODENWALT

THOMAS R. TONER, JR.

OSCAR A. SMITH, JR.

ORDER ALERT IN EAST

New York—(AP)—Civilian defense authorities in the second region—New York, New Jersey and Delaware—were instructed Sunday night to be on the alert by Maj. Edward G. Riekert, executive director of the Second Region of the Office of Civilian Defense.

GAP WORKER DIES

Jonestown—(AP)—John O'Hare, 40, Indiana county painter employed at the Indiantown Gap military reservation, died suddenly early Sunday of what Coroner W. H. Brubaker said was a heart attack.

CITY SPEEDS PLAN FOR STRENGTHENING DEFENSE PROGRAM

The Japanese declaration of war burst like a bombshell here Sunday but before the night was over Lancaster had moved on a score of fronts to strengthen defense activities.

The Lancaster County Defense Council is awaiting the recommendations of the State Council of Defense which will convene at Harrisburg at 2 p. m. Monday. Governor James emphasized that the special concern now was sabotage.

Lancaster's company of Home Guards was in a state of readiness, vacations and furloughs for both city and state police were cancelled and defense industries prepared to increase their precautions against sabotage.

ANGRY RESENTMENT

News of the attacks by the Japanese upon Hawaii and the Philippine Islands left the citizenry speechless but as the shock wore off an angry resentment was evident. Crowds of people were on the downtown streets, united in one thought—defense of country.

They crowded around the bulletin board in front of the Lancaster Newspapers Office eagerly scanning the news flashes. Faces were grim. The crowd increased several times in size waiting for the special war

More of DEFENSE on Page 8

24-HR. PRODUCTION SCHEDULE IS URGED

Washington —(AP)— Undersecretary of War Patterson called Sunday night for production of all war munitions on a 24-hour basis.

Patterson issued instructions to chiefs of the War Department procurement agency that "all steps must be taken to increase the speed with which contracts are let and to speed up maximum production."

Patterson also directed that all officers and civilian employes of the War Department agencies under his control "be required to work as many additional hours each day as is necessary to get the day's work done."

LINDBERGH ISOLATED

West Tisbury, Mass. — (AP) — Charles A. Lindbergh, visiting at Seven Gates farm in this Martha's Vineyard Island village, refused Sunday night to see newspapermen or accept any messages.

Surprise Attacks On U. S. Possessions In Pacific

(By The Associated Press)

Japanese warplanes made a deadly assault on Honolulu and Pearl Harbor Sunday in the foremost of a series of surprise attacks against American possessions throughout the Pacific.

Three hours later the Japanese government declared war on the United States and Great Britain.

Soon a second wave of Japanese bombers roared over shocked Honolulu.

The Japanese also bombed Singapore, and the British announced that the Japanese had landed in North Malaya and were being engaged. The Tokyo radio said the British colony of Hongkong also was attacked and that 63 American soldiers had been disarmed at Tientsin, China.

The Japanese aggression, which the United States officially and unequivocally described as treacherous and utterly unprovoked, bore these first fruits for the Empire, as summed up from official and unofficial sources:

Up to 350 U. S. soldiers killed and more than 300 wounded at Hickam Field, Hawaii Islands;

The U. S. battleship Oklahoma set afire and two other U. S. ships at Pearl Harbor attacked;

More of BATTLES on Page 4

Plan Vigilantes As Police Probe Barn Fire, And 2 Arson Attempts

Vigilante patrols were proposed by county firemen Sunday as State Police listed another barn fire and two unsuccessful attempts to fire barns Saturday night, to a growing list of crimes attributed to vandals.

The latest fire brings to four the suspicious blazes being investigated by State Police who believe they may be the work of the same person or group who have been desecrating cmeteries and churches and burning corn shocks in the northern end of the county.

State Police Sunday night listed the following fires as being of suspicious circumstances:

A $25,000 fire which destroyed a barn and equipment on the farm of Noah E. Denlinger, a mile and a half northeast of Leaman Place Saturday night.

An $18,000 fire which destroyed a barn and tobacco shed on the farm of John S. Miller, Lancaster Junction on October 18.

An $18,000 fire which destroyed a barn, implement shed, tobacco shed and chicken house on the farm of John W. Martin, midway between New Hol-

More of VIGILANTES on Page 8

WAR EXTRA

Intelligencer Journal

WAR EXTRA

The Leading Newspaper in the Garden Spot of America, Home Owned for Home Folks Since 1794

VOLUME LXXVIII.—NO. 76. | The Intelligencer Founded 1799 The Journal Founded 1794 | LANCASTER, PA., TUESDAY MORNING, DECEMBER 9, 1941 | Entered at Post Office at Lancaster, Pa as second class mail matter | 22 PAGES, 176 COLUMNS.—THREE CENTS.

ENEMY AIRPLANES OVER CALIF.; NOT RESISTED; HUNT CARRIER

San Francisco—(AP)—The all clear was sounded at 3:27 a. m. (Tuesday), ending the third air raid alarm of the night.

Headquarters of the Fourth Interceptor Command said that unidentified planes again had been sighted off the coast and that it had ordered the police and fire departments to sound the alert.

The Command did not say at what distance the planes had been seen, nor did it indicate whether pursuit ships had been sent aloft to meet the strangers.

The alarm was the third of the night. It was preceded by a shutdown of radio stations which normally broadcast through the night. They said orders to cease operations came from the Federal Communications Commission.

Vallejo, site of the great Mare Island Navy Yard, was completely blacked out at 2:30 a. m. by the pulling of master switches controlling the entire electric system.

The Army said the blackout covered the entire San Francisco area, including East Bay Oakland and Berkeley.

"The planes are heading toward shore, and so far as we know, they are still coming," a spokesman said.

At Sacramento, 90 miles inland, McClellan air depot blacked out for the second time at 2:15 a. m. and instructions to douse lights were transmitted to all airports in the Sacramento vicinity. The blackout was ordered on the basis of the report that unidentified planes were approaching the coast.

San Francisco—(AP)—Army information sources confirmed early Tuesday (today) that two squadrons of enemy planes—numbering about 15 planes to the squadron—crossed the coast line west of San Jose last night and reconnoitered the San Francisco Bay area and other sections of California.

The two squadrons flew inland to the southern tip of San Francisco Bay, a short distance north of San Jose; then one squadron split off and disappeared in the south while the other headed due north up San Francisco Bay to the huge naval construction base at Mare Island.

This squadron flew over the Mare Island and Vallejo section, then turned out to sea in the vicinity of the Golden Gate and flew away to the southwest.

No attempt was made to bomb any of the strategic defense areas around San Francisco Bay, so far as information sources could learn.

The Army said that the presence of these two squadrons of planes indicated in all probability that an enemy aircraft carrier was lurking off the coast, possibly as far out as 500 or 600 miles.

The aircraft warning network lost track of the squadron which branched south from the San Jose area and, the Army say, no further report has been received on the course of this squadron.

While the air raid warning was in effect, a blackout lasting two and a half hours was put into effect in the San Francisco areas but, because of the hasty procedure, it succeeded in putting out only a fraction of the city's countless lights. Neon signs and other illuminated installations gleamed brightly. The sky was clear.

Army sources said that Brigadier General William Ord Ryan, commander of the Fourth Interceptor command, had reported the aforementioned information to Major General John L. DeWitt, commander of the Fourth Army, and that General DeWitt had forwarded it to the War Department in Washington.

The Army said their information was substantiated by Navy reports, which also estimated the number of unidentified planes at two squadrons.

Some United States planes were reported unofficially to have followed the enemy squadron out to sea after it headed southwest from the Golden Gate after reconnoitering the bay area.

So far as the Army reports indicated no anti-aircraft fire was directed at the enemy squadrons and the planes themselves did not fire a shot.

Practically every major city along the west coast from Canada south to San Diego was blacked out at one time or another Monday night and the precautions were being continued on into the night, it obviously being feared that the reconnoitering flights might be followed by actual raids on military or naval bases or defense plants.

San Diego, headquarters of the 11th Naval District, was blacked out at midnight in what the Navy termed a precautionary measure.

Mayor Angelo J. Rossi of San Francisco, said that high Army and Navy officials, including Major General John L. DeWitt, commander of the Fourth Army, had confirmed personally to him that unidentified planes, supposedly of enemy forces, tried to approach San Francisco.

More of PLANES on Page 6

Japanese Are Off Aleutian Islands

Victoria, B. C. — (Canadian Press) — A warning the "Japanese are off the Aleutian Islands" came from Mayor Andrew McGavin Monday night shortly after Air Commander A. F. Godfrey said "there is every reason to believe there will be an attack in the Pacific northwest."

"The Japanese are off the Aleutian Islands; we expect them here any time. The situation is very serious," Mayor McGavin said.

Commodore Godfrey said the Canadian Air Force was "standing by," and that instructions were issued to all cities for a complete blackout.

He said air patrols were intensified.

In Victoria a complete blackout of coastal British Columbia and the lower mainland was ordered because "the war situation is such that an attack by Japanese forces on the Pacific northwest coast is imminent."

All motor traffic on Victoria

More of ALEUTIANS on Page 6

U. S. Declares War On Japs; President To Speak Tonight

White House Says Jap Attack Instigated By Tokyo, But Lend-Lease Aid To Britain Will Continue Undiminished; President Forecasts "Inevitable Triumph" For America; War Vote All But Unanimous

Washington—(AP)—America declared war on Japan Monday after that nation's air bombers had dealt the Navy the severest blow in its history and inflicted losses which raised the harsh possibility that the Japanese fleet may now enjoy a temporary superiority in the Pacific.

Some details of the savage Japanese attack—which admittedly cost the Navy a battleship, a destroyer, a number of smaller craft, and killed or wounded 3,000—will be given to the nation by President Roosevelt Tuesday night in a ten o'clock radio address.

His speech will supplement the brief message with which he asked Congress for a declaration of war Monday—a request which both Houses followed up with action that was breathtakingly swift and, save for one vote, unanimous.

GERMANY IS ASSAILED

These developments came at the close of a day which saw this country not only declare war on Japan but also accuse Germany of doing its utmost to push the Japanese into the conflict, with the purpose of impeding the program of American assistance to Great Britain.

But, a White House statement said, the program of American help to the British "will continue in full operation." The announcement

More of WASHINGTON on Page 20

GERMANY ADMITS WINTER STALLED DRIVE ON MOSCOW

(By The Associated Press)

Berlin—Winter has stopped the Germans short of Moscow and the capture of the Soviet capital is not expected this year, a military spokesman declared Monday night.

It seemed likely from the spokesman's statement that until Spring there could be no further major German offensive except along the extreme southern front.

This word reduced the Russian campaign to secondary interest for the Germans for the first time, and attention focused instead on Japan's war with the United States in the Pacific.

DNB asserted that nearly 10,000,000 Russian troops had "been put out of action" since Germany invaded Russia last June.

Explaining a statement by the high command that the conduct of the war in Russia "now is dictated by the setting in of winter," the spokesman said:

"The cold is so terrific that even the oil freezes in motorized vehicles. Soldiers and officers trying to take cover simply freeze to the ground.

"Fighting under these conditions is practically impossible. This does not mean, however, that the front will become stagnant or fixed. There will be local operations, local air attacks and local straightening out of our front in such a manner as either to shorten it advantageeously or, as in the space between

More of GERMANY on Page 4

Intelligencer Journal Weather Calendar

COMPARATIVE TEMPERATURES

Station	High	Low
Intell Journal	44	29
Water Works	46	22
Ephrata	47	25
Last Year (Ephrata)	47	32
Official High for Year, July 28		102
Official Low for Year, January 14		11
Character of Day		Clear

HOURLY TEMPERATURES (Monday)

3 a. m.	31	4 p. m.	43
4 a. m.	31	5 p. m.	42
5 a. m.	30	6 p. m.	40
6 a. m.	29	7 p. m.	38
7 a. m.	29	8 p. m.	38
8 a. m.	30	9 p. m.	38
9 a. m.	30	10 p. m.	38
10 a. m.	31	11 p. m.	38
11 a. m.	36	Midnight	38
Noon	40	(Tuesday)	
1 p. m.	42	1 a. m.	38
2 p. m.	44	2 a. m.	37
3 p. m.	44	3 a. m.	37

SUN

Rises—7:13 a. m. Sets—4:39 p. m.

More of WEATHER on Page 20

JAPAN CLAIMS 2 U. S. BATTLESHIPS SUNK IN PACIFIC

Severe Damage To 8 Other War Vessels, Destruction Of 300 Planes Reported

By The Associated Press

Tokyo (Tuesday)—(Official Radio Pickup)—Japanese Imperial headquarters announced the sinking of two U. S. battleships and a mine-sweeper, severe damage to four other American capital ships and four cruisers and the destruction of about 100 American planes in Japan's surprise blows at Hawaii, the Philippines, and Guam.

The official news agency Domei quickly interpreted "these magnificent early gains" as giving Japan naval mastery over the United States in the Pacific, and said that any force which the U. S. could muster now "would be regarded as utterly inadequate to accomplish any successful outcome in an encounter with the thus-far-intact Japanese fleet."

CLAIM 300 PLANES

Domei said it was "understood Japanese forces have destroyed more than 300 American planes, including 200 in dogfights and on the ground in Hawaiii.

The remainder, it said, were "believed" destroyed in the Philippines.

Of the total the news agency

More of TOKYO on Page 20

20th CASE OF POLIO REPORTED IN COUNTY

The twentieth case of infantile paralysis in Lancaster county since early in the summer was reported this week to County Medical Director, Dr. A. J. Greenleaf.

The patient is Mary C. Lawrence, two daughter of Maxwell R. Lawrence, 548 N. Third St., Columbia, she has the disease in a very mild form, Dr. Greenleaf said. She contracted it on December 3, and the mild involvement of one arm and one leg is clearing up, he added. She is being cared for by Dr. J. H. Pickle, Columbia.

Dr. Greenleaf's weekly health report also includes 17 cases of chicken pox; three of mumps, three of whooping cough, and one each of German measles, measles and pneumonia.

The City Board of Health report includes three cases of pulmonary tuberculosis, two of chicken pox and one each of measles and German measles.

Bulletin

DNB REPORTS AMERICAN AIRPLANE MOTHER SHIP SUNK OFF HONOLULU

Berlin, Tuesday—(AP)—A DNB dispatch from Tokyo today said Japanese Imperial Navy headquarters announced an American airplane mother ship had been sunk off Honolulu.

Some Local Men With Navy Units Japs Say They Sank

Others At Army Posts In Hawaii, Philippines Which Were Bombed

A number of Lancaster men are serving on several units of the U. S. fleet which unconfirmed reports said were sunk and at several posts in Hawaii and the Philippines which were bombed within the past two days. Approximately 100 local boys have been reported in the war zone by relatives.

Two brothers, Paul C. and Melvin Girard, formerly of 1222 Clark St., are on the U. S. Battleship Pennsylvania, flagship of the Pacific fleet which was reported destroyed.

Commander Jesse L. Kenworthy, Jr., of Coatesville, was reported on the Battleship Oklahoma, which unofficial sources said was set afire and capsized at Pearl Harbor. Kenworthy was executive officer.

Lancaster countians are also stationed at Fort Stotsenberg, Wheeler Field and Hickam Field which were subjected to bombings.

Richard Trissler, 320 N. Mary St., 27th Bombardment Squadron; Clarence Rutt, 220 Green St., Quarter-

More of MEN on Page 20

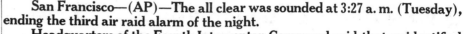

PAUL C. GIRARD

MELVIN E. GIRARD

Paul C. Girard and Melvin E. Girard, sons of Mrs. Jennie Girard, formerly of 1222 Clark St., who are stationed on the U. S. Pennsylvania, flagship of the Pacific Fleet, which was stationed at Pearl Harbor. Both are completing four years of service in the Navy. Both are mechanics.

JAPANESE TROOPS LAND ON LUBANG, THREATEN MANILA

REPORT BANGKOK TAKEN

London—(AP)—Japanese troops entered Bangkok, capital of Thailand, shortly after 9 p. m., Monday, Reuters reported from Tokyo.

Manila, P. I., (Tuesday)—Japanese troops were reported today to have landed with the probable help of "fishermen" Fifth-Columnists on Lubang island near the entrance to Manila Bay as Japanese planes carried out widespread raids on military objectives throughout the Philippines, including moonlit assaults on Manila itself.

The report of the landing on Lubang, some 60 miles southwest of the big American Naval Base of Cavite was not confirmed officially, but enough credence was placed in it that defense officers were trying urgently to contact the provincial governor.

Japanese Fifth-Column activity also was reported unofficially from Davao, on the big southern island of Mindanao where 25,000 Japanese present a vital threat to Philippine security. One report said 3,000 armed Japanese already were resisting.

MILITARY AIRDROME HIT

The U. S. Aircraft Carrier Langley was reported attacked in Malalag Bay near Davao in a series of daylight raids culminating in the raids early this morning on

More of MANILA on Page 6

Nicaragua Rounds Up All Japanese--- Both Of Them

Managua — (AP) — Nicaragua followed up her declaration of war on Japan Monday by immediately jailing the country's entire Japanese population: Gusudi Yakata and Juan Hissi.

PANAMA DECLARES WAR

Panama,—(AP)—Panama Monday declared war on Japan.

Home Guards Mobilized As City Places Itself On War Footing

Assigned To Guard Two Bridges Spanning Susquehanna River At Columbia; Recruiting Stations Rushed

Moving swiftly to the demands placed upon her by the declaration of war upon the Japanese, Lancaster placed itself upon a full wartime footing Monday.

These rapid - fire developments took place:

Company H of the Pennsylvania Home Guard was mobilized for active duty.

Home Defense organizations put into motion plans made months ago.

Crowds of men, boiling over with anger at the Japanese attacks, surged on Army, Navy and Marine recruiting stations.

City Council at a closed session pledged the city's support to both the State and National Governments.

The mobilization of the Home Guards by Governor James came unexpectedly Monday night. Word of the order was broadcast over WGAL and motion picture theatres flashed the call on their screens. Within a short time the State Arm-

More of GUARDS on Page 6

LANCASTER NEW ERA

WEATHER

Partly cloudy and somewhat colder tonight; Wednesday, cloudy followed by light snow in southwest portion by night. (Details on Page 3).

Examiner Founded 1830.
New Era Founded 1877.

Published Every Evening Except Sunday by New Era Company.
Entered as Second Class Matter at Post Office, Lancaster, Pa.

LANCASTER, PA., TUESDAY, DECEMBER 9, 1941 — CITY EDITION — 22 PAGES—176 COLUMNS—THREE CENTS

N.Y. HAS TWO AIR RAID ALARMS

30 Jap Planes Scout 'Frisco Region

SMITH'S TRIAL IS OFF UNTIL SHIRK'S WAR SERVICE ENDS

Night Club Operator's Case Will Be Postponed Unless District Attorney Is Relieved of Duty.

HOSTERMAN IS NAMED TO SERVE IN COURT

The second trial of Buford D. Smith, night club operator, charged with conspiracy, may have to be postponed until the March term of Criminal Court.

District Attorney K. L. Shirk made this announcement shortly before leaving the Court House this morning to take command of a detail of Pennsylvania Home Guards assigned to guard the Columbia-Wrightsville bridge. Shirk is a 2nd Lieutenant in Company H, which was mobilized last night for active duty.

"All I know we have been ordered to guard the bridge until relieved," Lieut. Shirk said. "That may mean only several days or it may mean weeks or months.

"During my absence in court, S. V. Hosterman, Esq., will take my place before the Grand Jury while my assistant, John Hamaker, will try the cases I was scheduled to try in court.

"In regards to the Smith case, however, I certainly would not ask either Hamaker nor Hosterman to undertake to go through with the trial. If I am not relieved of wartime duty, this case will have to be postponed."

Shirk, wearing his Home Guard uniform, did not appear in the court room but conferred with President Judge Oliver S. Schaeffer in chamber on the appointment of Hosterman as Special Assistant District Attorney.

Smith and William D. Sahm, Jr., confessed bank embezzler, are accused to conspiring to defraud the Northern Bank and Trust Company of $70,000. Sahm, who pleaded guilty previously to five charges involving the embezzling of $307,000 from the bank, entered a plea of nolo contendere to the conspiracy charge but will appear as a Commonwealth witness against Smith.

Shirk has announced that he would not call Sahm for sentence until the Smith case has been disposed of. Sahm has been in prison here since his return from Chicago, where he was arrested last July 16.

Smith's first trial resulted in a

(See COURT—Page 19)

CHRISTMAS BONUS BY 2 COMPANIES

A Christmas bonus to employes of two local companies was announced today.

Some 1,500 employes of the U. S. Asbestos Co., Manheim division, will share in a 5 per cent bonus on earnings; a total of $100,000.

Hager and Bro. announced this plan: "All employes regularly employed before January 1, 1941, will receive one week's pay; those regularly employed after January but before July 1, will receive one-half week's pay."

ROOSEVELT ADDRESS OVER WGAL TONIGHT

President Roosevelt's address to the nation will be broadcast over WGAL at ten o'clock tonight.

The Chief Executive will discuss what has happened in the U. S.-Japanese conflict thus far.

Home Guards on Duty At 2 Columbia Spans

Theodore L. Brubaker, local attorney, a member of Co. H., Lancaster Home Defense Unit, shown at his post guarding the Pennsylvania Railroad bridge at Columbia today.

55 Local Officers and Men Mobilized in 2 Hrs.; Called from Bathtubs, Movies, Beds and Motorbuses

From bathtubs, movies, beds and motorbuses they rallied last night, and within two hours after the mobilization was issued Company H of the Pennsylvania Home Guard was in uniform at the Lancaster Armory and ready for duty.

The first task assigned the 55 officers and men was the guarding of the Columbia-Wrightsville bridge, and the P. R. R. bridge over the Susquehanna, and it began immediately. Permanent company headquarters have been established at the armory here on a 24-hour basis, and a platoon headquarters has been set u pat Columbia.

Captain Appel Gets Call

Captain James Z. Appel received the mobilization order at 7:45 p. m. and summoned the company by telephone, radio and movies.

Members who were listening to the radio responded at once. Movie announcements notified several.

District Attorney K. L. Shirk, second lieutenant of the company, was one of the hardest to find. He was scheduled to make a speech last night, speak on the radio, and attend a meeting.

When found, the prosecutor confessed the call couldn't have come at a worse time from his standpoint. It is Quarter Sessions week. He appeared at the court house in the blue-back uniform of the guards this morning to furnish his assistants with papers necessary to carry on court work, and then went to Columbia to take charge of the platoon there.

Sergeant Mercer E. Gibson had just seated himself comfortably in a local theatre for a double-feature,

(See HOME DEFENSE—Last Page)

DISCUSS GUARDING LANCASTER PLANTS

Sheriff William D. Leed entered into negotiations with local industrial plants today relative to strengthening the guards on duty inside and outside the plants.

The Sheriff, who conferred with Judge O. S. Schaeffer during a recess in court, said he has been in contact with Washington and that as chief of the forces of law and order in the county he was taking the lead in the program.

Big manufacturing establishments handling defense orders here have their own guards but Federal authorities are encouraging a redoubled force responsible to local government officials.

CHARGE HAWAII DEFENSE ASLEEP

Court-Martialing of Army and Navy Leaders Will Be Demanded.

WASHINGTON, Dec. 9—(AP)—Rep. Dingell (D-Mich) told the House today he proposed to demand that court martial proceedings be instituted against four high-ranking Army officers and the commander of the Pacific fleet for "what happened in Hawaii."

Dingell named specifically Lt. Gen. Walter C. Short, commanding the Hawaiian department; Major Gen. H. H. Arnold, deputy chief of staff for air; Maj. Gen. Geo. H. Brett, chief of the Army Air Corps, and Admiral Husband Kimmel, commander of the Pacific Fleet.

Then, Rep. Bulwinkle (D-NC) immediately arose to say "it behooves members to keep their feet on the ground" and not act without knowing the full facts.

Bursts of applause greeted his remarks, as well as a statement by Rep. Van Zandt (R-Pa.) that he resented criticism of Kimmel. Van Zandt said that the House members did not appreciate the advancement of aircraft and when all reports were in there would be no criticism of any of the Admiral's staff or personnel.

Vinson Denounces Dingell

Dingell's action was denounced by Chairman Vinson (D-Ga) of the House Naval Committee as "nothing but a cheap effort to get newspaper publicity."

Vinson said he resented the insinuation that the naval and military men in the Pacific, who, he said were "offering their lives on

(See CRITICISM—Page 6)

MANILA ARMY BASE BOMBED IN 4-HR. RAID

5th Column Aids Invasion Party on Isle Near Philippine Capital.

HANGAR DAMAGED, BARRACKS BURNED

MANILA, Dec. 9—(AP)—The Army announced today that one United States soldier was killed and 12 were injured in this morning's pre-dawn raid on Nichols field, near Manila. Two other soldiers were hurt when a bomb landed near Fort William McKinley, also in the Manila area.

The Army spokesman said 10 Japanese bombers raided Nichols Field, damaging one hangar and burning an officers' quarters.

The two soldiers wounded near Fort William McKinley were injured by a stray bomb, he declared.

Because Nichols Field is near crowded Paranque, that district will be evacuated, probably today, marking the first Army-sponsored exodus from Manila.

Manila's populace began its second day of war busily, meanwhile, with heavy traffic rolling through sunny streets and the markets jammed with food buyers.

Citizens Hurry To Country

Many, leaving on their own initiative, were hurrying to the country with suitcases piled high on taxis, buses and even horsedrawn carriages.

There was an evident air of nervousness but, for the most part, Manilians still were complacent, gathering idly to watch anti-aircraft guns and flocking to the bay front in hopes of seeing an air battle.

Alarm Lasts 4 Hours

The Nichols Field air alarm lasted more than four hours—from 3.09 A. M. to 7.20 A. M. Because of the lapse of time, many Manilians, including some soldiers, thought the all-clear was a new alarm and there was a moment's flurry as crews manned their guns.

One anti-aircraft gun fired a single shot although no planes were visible.

Langley Declared Safe

U. S. Naval sources here denied reports that the seaplane tender Langley was bombed during a Japanese attack on Davao yesterday. They said the carrier was safe and carrying out routine duties.

The Philippine islands, target of repeated and widespread Japanese air raids, faced a new threat today as reports reached here that Japanese troops had seized Lubang Is-

(See MANILA—Page 13)

LOCAL GERMAN ALIEN IS ARRESTED AND TAKEN TO PHILA.

HARRISBURG, Dec. 9.—(AP)—FBI agents and the Pennsylvania State Police arrested eight men, listed as aliens, in this section of the state last night and took them to Philadelphia for questioning, it was learned today. Two agents of the Federal Bureau of Investigation asked the state force for help in taking the men into custody.

Five men were picked up in Harrisburg, one in nearby Lemoyne, one in York and one in Lancaster. Their names were withheld. Authorities said all were German aliens.

* * *

Sergeant Sheaffer, of the local sub-station, confirmed the arrest of an alien here but declined to disclose the identity of the man. He said the individual submitted to arrest without vigorous objection.

Air Raid Observers At 27 Local Stations

Coincident with the reports of possible enemy airplanes along the Atlantic seaboard, the observers of the 27 Aircraft Warning stations in Lancaster county went on duty today.

Chief observers of the 27 stations have been called to a meeting tomorrow evening so that a plan for continuous service can be established, by Captain John M. Groff. Some of the warning stations were manned last night and have been observing without interruption ever since.

Signs War Measure

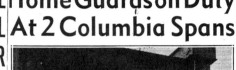

The President is shown signing the act which puts us officially at war with Japan, soon after Congress passed the resolution with but one dissenting vote.

'PUBLIC HAS ALL,' EARLY INSISTS

Secretary Tells Press F. D. Has No News; Speaks Tonight.

WASHINGTON, Dec. 9—(AP)—A bold Japanese foray that threatened to carry the horrors of the Pacific war to the continental United States put the nation on notice today that "it can happen here."

The detection of enemy aircraft over the strategically vital San Francisco area and the threat of an enemy carrier lurking off shore served as a realistic introduction for the report President Roosevelt has promised the country on the progress of hostilities with Japan.

The White House said Mr. Roosevelt had no information on these planes beyond that available to the press.

Most of his day was reserved for preparation of a radio address tonight which his secretary, Stephen Early, said would have to do to a large extent, "with what might be called the Nazi pattern of the whole situation."

No News To Issue

Early said Mr. Roosevelt had concluded a careful reading of all dispatches and a comparison of them

(See WASHINGTON—Page 6)

3 ALARMS BUT NO BOMBS FALL ON CALIF. CITY

Planes Fly Over Plants, Navy Yard, Then Disappear at Sea.

NAVY AND AIR FORCE ARE SEEKING CARRIERS

(By the Associated Press)

The Army and Navy were on the prowl today for an enemy aircraft carrier which sent at least two squadrons of planes in reconnaisance flights over industrial plants ringing San Francisco Bay — without dropping a bomb.

The 30-odd planes ranged from San Jose at the south tip of the Bay to the huge Naval Yard at Mare Island, the fourth army interceptor command reported.

The flight caused the first blackout in San Francisco's history. Two other blackouts followed in the darkness of early morning, but army authorities did not disclose whether enemy planes again approached.

Interceptors Lose Enemy Planes

Army interceptor planes followed the first of the enemy squadrons, but were unable to determine where they finally went. The Navy then took up a search for a plane carrier, presumably lurking off California's coast, and possibly 500 to 600 miles at sea.

"I don't think there's any doubt the planes came from a carrier," said Lieut. General John L. DeWitt, commander of the Fourth Army and the Western Defense Command.

Japanese Reported Off Alaska

Reports that other Japanese forces were off the Aleutian Islands, in the narrow Bering Strait between Alaska and Siberia, stirred new alarms today in the three-day-old battle of the Pacific.

Planes at Portland (Ore.) air base hopped off at 8:15 A. M., today, the 2nd interceptor command announced, to hunt 600 miles to sea for two or three Japanese aircraft carriers and some submarines reported operating off the coast.

Simultaneously, Brig. Gen Carlyle H. Wash, head of the interceptor command, reported planes warming motors here and at other Western Washington fields, ready to take the air as soon as "perfect attack weather" moderated.

Order Blackout Tonight

General Wash, in charge of last night's Pacific Coast blackout, ordered radio broadcasting stations

(See WEST COAST—Page 13)

Late War Bulletins

BERLIN TO CLARIFY STAND TOWARD U. S.

Berlin, Dec. 9—(AP)—An authorized spokesman said today he was unable to state whether German-American relations would change within the next 24 hours, but well-informed sources said a "clarifying statement" on the American-Japanese war was expected soon.

"The situation has not changed," the spokesman said.

There were unconfirmable reports that the Reichstag would meet tomorrow to receive a statement on Germany's official stand.

Washington, Dec. 9—(AP)—Secretary of State Hull indicated today that this country should be on guard against a sudden German move supporting Japan in fulfilment of the Axis Tripartite Pact.

Any preliminary military move of the character of the Pearl Harbor attack, he said, would only arouse the American people to resist with all the speed and all the might this nation can exert.

ARMY TO GRANT CHRISTMAS FURLOUGHS

Washington, Dec. 9—(AP)—The Army went ahead with preparations today to give Christmas holiday leaves to large numbers of troops.

The war likewise has failed to halt thus far the discharge from active service of many men who have reached the new top draft age limit of 28, or who have dependents.

MANILA HAS 2 MORE ALARMS

Manila, Dec. 9—(AP)—Manila had two air alarms tonight, the second coming at 9:50 P. M. (8:50 A. M.,) (This apparently meant at least one return of Japanese raiders whose presence over Manila was learned from radio reports in Ne·· York this morning.)

REPORT HOSTILE PLANES OFF BOSTON

Portland, Me., Dec. 9—(AP)—Authoritative sources here, which did not wish to be named, said it was reliably reported that "hostile forces" were an hour outside of Boston at 2:00 P. M., Eastern Standard Time.

"Enemy Airplanes" Reported Off Coast North to Portland

Million School Children Sent Home as Sirens Sound; Source of Reports Indefinite But Army Sends Hundreds of Planes into Air to Balk Any Attack

BULLETIN

New York, Dec. 9—(AP)—Public safety officials revealed today that a series of air raid alerts and alarms which electrified the eastern seaboard this afternoon were merely a dress rehearsal and that reports of approaching enemy planes were false.

(By the Associated Press)

New York's seven millions experienced a touch of wartime reality today as hostile airplanes were reported two hours away from the giant metropolis and two air-raid alarms sounded.

The first, at 1:25 P. M., lasted 20 minutes. The second began at 2:05 P. M., EST.

The second all clear sounded at 2:40 P. M. It later developed that the second alarm was the result of a small fire which broke out at Mitchel Field and in the confusion of a fire alarm, a second alert had been sounded.

The first alarm followed a reported "official warning from Washington" that enemy warplanes were sweeping in from the Atlantic—as they had been reported on the Pacific coast where three air-raid alarms sounded in San Francisco during the night.

U. S. Army and Naval forces were reported still scouring the waters off San Francisco in search of an enemy aircraft carrier.

In New York, untold numbers of interceptor planes swarmed into the skies to meet the supposed invaders.

A few minutes later, a Panama Radio broadcast said Japanese planes were reported flying over the Panama coast this morning—but no bombs were dropped.

It was not clear from whence the reports originated and in Washington the White House said it had been unable to confirm through the air force the presence of any hostile planes.

Nevertheless, New Yorkers were directed by frequent commercial radio announcements to keep calm and stay off the streets. There was little excitement and, generally, citizens appeared to be taking the warnings calmly, many going ahead with their usual business as if nothing was happening.

Rear Admiral Adolphus Andrews, commander of the north Atlantic naval frontier, said the Navy and Army were patroling.

Capt. Lynn Farnol, public relations officer at Mitchel Field, said the field was on the alert and that every necessary precaution had been taken. He said the reported presence of planes did not originate with the Air Corps, but that the Air Corps was acting on the theory that the reports might be substantiated.

U. S. Army planes from Mitchel Field, Long Island, which received the warning from Washington, immediately swept into the skies.

All families were evacuated from the field and "every plane was off the ground," it was stated.

Shortly after the warning of planes off New York, Secretary of State Cordell Hull indicated in Washington that the United States should be on guard against a sudden German move supporting Japan in fulfillment of the Axis tripartite pact.

The State Department made it clear, however, that there was no connection between Hull's warning of a surprise N··· thrust and the report of planes off New York, of which he was then unaware.

Subsequently, the White House announced it had been advised by Lieut. Gen. Delos Emmons, chief of the Air Corps

(See EAST COAST—Page 13)

WASHINGTON

(Continued From Page One)

with press reports and that there was no news to issue.

"You have it," Early told reporters. "You have as much as we have. Most of the dispatches this morning had to do with the west coast condition of last evening. You know as much about it as he does."

To a question how the Japanese could get within striking distance of San Francisco, where three air raid alarms have been sounded, Early replied:

"There's no answer to that. It is certain that the Army and Navy, under the President's instructions, are on the alert for the defense. That doesn't apply only to San Francisco or the West Coast. The picture is much broader."

Will Report On Ships

To a question whether reports would be issued on the facts relative to rumors of the sinking of several battleships in Pearl Harbor, Early said that certainly would be done. The President insists that the rumors and reports be given the press as received and then sifted to obtain the truth, he asserted. The sifting process now is underway, Early added.

Replying to an inquiry as to whether the Chief Executive in his radio address tonight would tell the people as much as possible, Early said this would not be done on any one operation.

To a question on whether reports of American naval damage from Rome, Berlin and Tokyo were designed primarily to shake the country's faith in the Navy, Early said he would not answer. But he added:

"You can take the same reports they have been putting out ever since the war. Until yesterday they applied mostly to the British. You know them for what they are."

Speaks At 10 P. M.

Mr. Roosevelt's address—his first since the nation declared war on Japan—will be broadcast at 10 P. M., E. S. T. The speech, which the White House said would contain a "more complete documentation" of the war than has yet been possible, will be carried by all networks.

The presence of hostile aircraft off the Golden Gate—5,200 miles from Japan—stirred the Capital, and was taken as notice that the front lines of the struggle may be in the main streets of Pacific coast cities as well as in the bomb-battered gun pits of Hawaii.

The interception and repulse of the raiders was a general source of gratification, but this was tempered by the fact the planes were identified as a reconnaisance mission and by the realization of the extremely audacious strategy the Japanese would risk in their all-or-nothing bid for supremacy in the Pacific and Asia.

Naval Bases May Be Targets

The California area with its vast aircraft plants and shipyards offered a tempting cluster of targets for air raiders, informed sources agreed, but their shrewdest guess was that the Japanese hoped to strike a surprise blow at one of the major Navy bases with the idea of inflicting further damage on the fleet's operating facilities ashore.

Capitol Hill studied last night's reports from California against the background of a statement by Senator Gillette (D-Iowa) who said he had information that Hitler had promised Tokyo active assistance by February.

Gillette said his information came from a source so reliable in the past that it had predicted two months in advance that Japan planned to attack the United States in December. The Hitler pledge, he explained, was predicated on Nazi expectations to gain full control of the French fleet at the start of 1942.

The possibility of the French fleet falling into Axis hands, now as always, aroused unfeigned concern in Congressional circles, which had already heard reports of former French submarines serving in Japan's Pacific offensive and of Axis pilots manning Japanese dive bombers in the blasting of Pearl Harbor.

These latter reports, which still lacked confirmation, were among the reasons that prompted Senator Pepper (D-Fla), fiery foe of the Axis, to predict that it was "just a matter of time" before Congress voted to extend the war declaration of yesterday to include Germany and Italy.

Long War Expected

Members of Congress, like the man in the street here, were talking in terms of a long war—just as long as it took to bring the conflict to the "successful termination" which the declaration of war stipulates.

Estimates ran from three to six years, with Senator Taft (R-Ohio) talking in terms of a six-year war and American casualties as high as 2,000,000 dead.

Such discussion, however, was directed toward the achievement of victory, and not toward quibbling about its cost.

Everything bespoke a nation girding for a mighty effort, mustering all its resources, treasure and manpower for the campaigns ahead.

Budget Director Harold D. Smith went to work on a war budget, calling in ranking Army and Navy officers for consultation. Informed estimates were that the budget, which will go to Congress early next month, would be between $35,000,000,000 and $50,000,000,000.

150 Billion Victory Program

But this represented only a beginning. The Supply Priorities and Allocations Board already was mapping an all-out "victory program" which defense officials said called for an outlay of $150,000,000,000, over and above the $70,000,000,000 appropriated or authorized for military and lend-lease purposes.

SPAB told Americans yesterday that "every activity of our national life and our civilian economy" must be enlisted in the victory drive.

Chairman Vinson (D-Ga) of the House Naval Committee announced that all naval construction had been ordered on a 24-hour basis in a tremendously intensified drive to build warships at a rate unequalled in history. He promised that all methods for a further speed-up would be examined.

Rush Of Volunteers

Although no special call for Army and Navy recruits has yet been issued, there was a rush of volunteers to the colors from coast to coast. In New York, enlistments doubled the record of the first recruiting day in 1917's World War. In all branches of the service the enlistments ran from 10 to 100 times the daily total of recent months.

There was a corresponding rush of men and women to sign up for the various civilian defense services, and the Pacific Coast's experience last night with wailing air raid sirens and blackouts was expected to swell the tide.

Agents of the Federal Bureau of Investigation rounded up German and Italian aliens throughout the country during the night, just as they yesterday took Japanese aliens into custody. It was another evidence of protective measures being taken on a national scale, which extended also to cities on both coasts and inland as well.

More Evidence of Unity

Manifestations of national unity continued unabated. Former President Herbert Hoover asserted last night that "we must fight with all we have....We must have and will have support for the President of the United States in this war to defend America. We will have victory."

Labor leaders, great and small, added their voices to the chorus, pledging the all-out efforts of the army of union members in overalls to win the battle of production. Strikes—long the bane of the defense program — virtually disappeared.

SAN FRANCISCO CAUGHT NAPPING

Still Incompleted Warning System Adds to Confusion.

SAN FRANCISCO, Dec. 9.—(AP)—San Francisco learned of the early evening air raid alarm—yesterday—first on the mainland—and blackout lasting two and a half hours.

Afterward, while searchers still sought whereabouts of one group of 15 planes that flew southward from San Jose, 50 miles south of San Francisco, blackouts were placed in effect in almost every major west coast city.

Army sources said the enemy planes flew inland over the coast line west of San Jose about 6 P. M. (PST), then the formation split into two squadrons of 15 planes.

One squadron flew southward and vanished.

The second squadron flew northward past the San Francisco Bay cities and up the bay to the vital Mare Island Navy Base, 25 miles from San Francisco.

Scout U. S. Navy Yard

After scouting the Navy yard from a great elevation, this squadron flew westward and through the Golden Gate out to sea.

Reports from the Army did not indicate any anti-aircraft fire. The enemy planes themselves did not fire a shot.

General Dewitt, talking with newsmen, said finding the carrier at sea might prove difficult.

"The carrier would have moved after they (the planes) were launched, and they would rendezvous in another spot," the General said.

Women Evacuate District

At Los Angeles, principal concern was felt for the San Pedro Harbor district, with highly important oil resources and defense works. An area of 15 miles around the harbor was blacked out. Simultaneously, 200 women and children, families of army officers, were evacuated from the Fort MacArthur military reservation at San Pedro.

Coming with startling suddenness to a city that had never even practiced a blackout, the first air raid alarm caught San Francisco with a still incompleted warning system.

Police ordered motorists to drive with only parking lights. Street cars turned off most of their lights, and motor buses preceeded without lights.

Radio Stations Go Off Air

From district firehouses all over the city came the wail of fire sirens, as engines were driven into the streets and their emergency noise-makers turned on. All local broadcasting stations were off the air.

Along the city's Western Beach, and at the blacked-out Presidio of San Francisco, 15 huge searchlights were placed in operation a half-hour after the air raid alarm.

Their rays plunged miles into the cloudless skies, but found nothing.

In an area a mile or two removed from the searchlight batteries, observers heard the roar of airplane engines but was unable to see any planes. The sound faded gradually in the west.

They said it was a tense and confused time for the 630,000 people in San Francisco, and that many more other persons in Oakland and other San Francisco Bay cities.

Oakland Turns Off Lights

The lights went off in Oakland and most of her sister cities, too, and there were strange reports of planes being heard overhead but no confirmation.

Before there was a full explanation from various authorities as to whether the alarm was merely a practice measure, or a genuine alarm, the police in San Francisco relayed "all-clear" signal. Then before the lights were all back on again, a second alarm and blackout request came from the army.

Local Boys in the Pacific War Zone

SAMUEL P. ZANGARI

PAUL C. GIRARD

BENJAMIN G. WALTZ

Well-known local softball player, who is now stationed with the 64th Field Artillery at Schofield Barracks, Hawaii.

Waltz enlisted in September, 1940, and was sent from Fort Slocum, N. Y., on November 13, 1940 to Hawaii, where he has been stationed ever since.

His parents, Mr. and Mrs. James Waltz, 32 Laurel street, heard from him last week at which time he wrote of his plans for coming home on a 90-day furlough. No word has been heard from him since.

Waltz played softball with the old Ritchey-Wise team and often played against his brother, Bill, another popular Eighth Ward player.

KENNETH R. ROTHFUS

Private first class, who has been stationed at Schofield barracks and was expected to return here for Christmas after his discharge. He served 26 months and was last heard from November 10. He is a son of William H. Rothfus, 65 Locust street, city.

ANTHONY A. ZANGARI

MELVIN E. GIRARD

Paul C. Girard and Melvin E. Girard, sons of Mrs. Jennie Girard, formerly of 1222 Clark street, who are stationed on the U. S. Pennsylvania, flagship of the Pacific Fleet, which was stationed at Pearl Harbor. Both are completing four years of service in the Navy. Both are mechanics.

PAUL B. MARTIN

CORPORAL WILLIAM L. BURD

22, now of Schofield barracks, Hawaii, who recently re-enlisted for three years. A son of Mrs. Marie Lyle, 337 South Ann street, he recently urged his mother to come to Hawaii for a visit. She was thinking it over Sunday when the radio flashed news of the bombing of Honolulu.

FRANCIS L. ZANGARI

Two brothers who are stationed in the war zone are Private First Class Samuel P. Zangari and Private Anthony A. Zangari, sons of Mr. and Mrs. Joseph Zangari, Lancaster R3. Samuel is a member of the Third Engineers at Schofield Barracks, and Anthony is attached to the 45th Pursuit Squadron of the Air Corps.

Private First Class Francis L. Zangari, son of Mrs. Domonic Zangari, 212 Manheim Pike, and cousin of Samuel and Anthony Zangari, who is stationed at the Schofield Barracks, Hawaii, as a member of the Third Engineers.

RICHARD SHENK

Richard Shenk, 19, son of Mr. and Mrs. J. P. Shenk, 17 E. Walnut St., a member of Company C, 21st Infantry, stationed at Schofield Barracks, Hawaii. He was last heard from on November 20.

HAROLD E. MARTIN

Paul B. Martin and Harold E. Martin, sons of Mr. and Mrs. Clayton R. Martin, 530 Ross St., who are on duty in the war zone. Paul is attached to the Gun Boat Tulsa on patrol duty in the Philippines. Harold is attached to the 61st Bombardment Squadron, which was stationed at Spokane, Wash., but has been ordered to the Pacific.

ROBERT B. RANDALL

Robert B. Randall, 538 East Ross street, son of Mr. and Mrs. Frank Randall, who is a third class yoeman on the Battleship California, stationed at Pearl Harbor, Hawaii.

ROBERT M. MISHKIN

Robert M. Mishkin, son of Mr. and Mrs. Hyman Mishkin, 935 West Walnut street, attached to the Signal Corps at Fort Shafter, Hawaii. He was graduated from the McCaskey High School, class of 1938, and joined the Army July 10, 1940.

DONALD A. ZIEGLER

Private First Class Donald A. Ziegler, 21, son of Mr. and Mrs. Lawrence C. Ziegler, 118 Crystal street, stationed with the 24th Battalion of the 13th Field Artillery at Schofield Barracks, Hawaii. He was graduated from the Lancaster Catholic High School in 1939 and enlisted in April, 1940.

HENRY SUMMY

Henry Summy, 20, son of Mr. and Mrs. Ira Summy, of Manheim, a member of the crew of the Battleship Tennessee, which is stationed at Pearl Harbor, Hawaii.

ROBERT H. MARTIN

Sergeant Robert H. Martin, son of Mr. and Mrs. Harry A. Martin, 621 Fourth St., weather station supervisor of Hickam Field, Hawaii, and instructor of mathematics and meteorology at the field. He was graduated from the Lancaster High School, class of 1934, and the Pennsylvania State College in 1939. He enlisted in the Air Corps in New York City, in August 1939.

Pvt. Stoltzfus, son of Mr. and Mrs. J. William Stoltzfus, 140 East Chestnut street, city, has been stationed at Fort McKinley near Manila, with the 91st Bombardment squadron, U. S. Air Corps, since December 1, according to word received here.

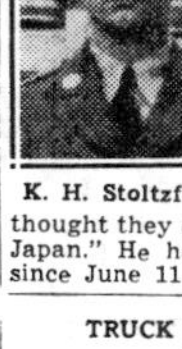

K. H. Stoltzfus

In a letter received only yesterday by his family he said the men "were on a 24-hour schedule and thought they expected trouble from Japan." He has been in the Army since June 11.

Private Frederick R. Usner, son of Mr. and Mrs. William Usner, 738 Lafayette St., is stationed with the 59th Coast Artillery at Fort Mills, Philippine Islands. He is serving his third enlistment with the Army, having served two years in Panama and three years at Fort Howard, Md.

F. R. Usner

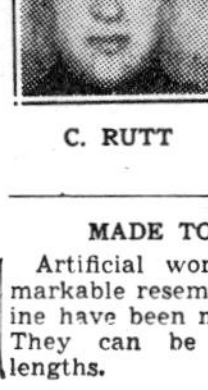

C. RUTT

Clarence Rutt, 23, son of Mr. and Mrs. John Rutt, 220 Green street, a private in the 13th Quartermaster Corps at Hickam Field, Hawaii. Members of his family received a letter from him last Thursday. He joined the Army in July, 1939.

TRUCK DRIVER FINED

COATESVILLE, Dec. 9—Charles Bailey, Coatesville, was fined $10 on Monday night when arraigned before Mayor A. G. Luebert in Coatesville police court on a charge of disorderly conduct. Police said Bailey was driving a truck in an improper manner and barely missed colliding with the police radio car on Saturday night at Seventh avenue and Lincoln Highway.

MADE TO FOOL FISH

Artificial worms bearing a remarkable resemblance to the genuine have been made for fishermen. They can be cut into desired lengths.

Many Await News Of Kin in War Zone

Additional List of Local Men and Women Who Are in Pacific Area; Some at Places Reported Bombed

Relatives and friends of men at sea in the war of the Pacific continued to wait anxiously for specific word of results in those quarters today, and additional local men in the war zone were reported.

Commander W. W. Behrens, son of Mr. and Mrs. Henry Behrens, 108 Race avenue, was scheduled to arrive in the United States recently, but no word has been received. His wife and 16-year-old daughter are in Honolulu.

Veteran in Manila

J. Clay Shay, 43, a veteran of the World War who is still in the service in Manila, sent a birthday postcard to his sister, Mrs. Riley Steffy, 565 North Shippn street, last month, the first word she had from him in 11 years. He said he was busy and would "write later." She also received a radiogram recently from a half-brother, Charles K. Engroff, Jr., 26, of the 64th Field Artillery, Schofield barracks, who said "everything is o. k."

Two brothers, Paul C. and Melvin Girard, formerly of 1222 Clark St., are on the U. S. Battleship Pennsylvania, flagship of the Pacific fleet which was reported destroyed.

Commander Jesse L. Kenworthy, Jr., of Coatesville, was reported on the Battleship Oklahoma, which unofficial sources said was set afire and capsized at Pearl Harbor. Kenworthy was executive officer.

At Places Bombed

Lancaster countians are also stationed at Fort Stotsenberg, Wheeler Field and Hickam Field which were subjected to bombings.

Richard Trissler, 320 N. Mary St., 27th Bombardment Squadron; Clarence Rutt, 220 Green St., Quartermaster Corps; Joseph Elliott, Jr., Manheim, Fifth Bombardment Squadron; Donald Angstadt, Manheim, 482nd Ordnance Company, and Sergeant Robert H. Martin, 621 Fourth St., weather station supervisor, are all stationed at Hickam Field.

Edward Witmer, Strasburg R1, of the Engineer Corps is at Stotsenburg. Private Anthony A. Zangari, Lancaster R3, of the 45th Pursuit Squadron, and Miller Garnett, Parkesburg, of the Air Corps are at Wheeler Field.

In War Zone

Additional men from this vicinity stationed in the war zone are:

Richard Shenk, 17 E. Walnut St., 21st Infantry, Schofield Barracks, Hawaii.

Corporal William L. Burd, 337 S. Ann St., Infantry, Schofield Barracks, Hawaii.

Donald A. Ziegler, 118 Crystal St., 13th Field Artillery, Schofield Barracks, Hawaii.

Ralph E. Thomas, 516 E. Chestnut St., Air Corps, Pearl Harbor, Hawaii.

Blair McClune, Parkesburg, U. S. Navy, Pearl Harbor.

Harry B. Conway, Jr., Parkesburg, radioman, U. S. S. Idaho.

Lieutenant Charles B. Frank Mount Joy, Veterinary Corps, Manila.

Miss Emily Frailey, 329 E. New St., who was reported to have been on nursing duty with the U. S. Army at Hawaii, is stationed in the United States, it was announced Monday. Miss Frailey is a graduate of the Lancaster General Hospital School of Nursing.

Henry Summy, Manheim, Battleship Tennessee, stationed for a time at Pearl Harbor.

Clarence Rutt, 220 Green street, city, 13th Quartermaster corps, Hickam field, Hawaii.

Harold E. Martin, 530 Ross street, 61st bombardment squadron, stationed at Spokane, Wash., ordered to the Pacific.

Frederick R. Usner, 738 Lafayette street 59th coast artillery, Fort Mills, Philippines, serving his third enlistment with the Army. He formerly served in Panama and Fort Howard, Md.

Samuel P. and Anthony A. Zangari, sons of Mr. and Mrs. Joseph Zangari, Lancaster R3, are attached to the Third engineers at Schofield barracks and the 45th Pursuit squadron, Air Corps, both in the war zone. Their cousin Francis L. Zangari, son of Mrs. Domonic Zangari, 212 Manheim pike, is a member of the Third Engineers at Schofield barracks, Hawaii.

In a recent letter from Sergeant Robert H. Martin, weather station supervisor at Hickam field, Hawaii, to his parents, Mr. and Mrs. Harry A. Martin, 621 Fourth street, he foresaw trouble with Japan and said that "according to experts, our Navy could blow them out of the sea in a pitched naval battle." Martin, honor student when he was graduated from Lancaster High in 1934, worked at Hamilton Watch company a year before enrolling at Penn State. He enlisted in the Air Corps and is Weather School supervisor and instructor of math and meteorology.

William, Frank O'Connor, son of Mr. and Mrs. Thomas O'Connor, 724 E. Fulton st., is on the U. S. S. Louisville, and a letter was received from him yesterday, mailed November 24.

Norman Almoney, son of Mr. and Mrs. Ross Almoney, Lititz, is at Schofield barracks, Hawaii.

Dean Stahr, son of Mr. and Mrs. Vance D. Stahr, is at Fort Kamchameha, Hawaii, according to his parents.

CRITICISM

(Continued From Page One)

the altar of service to their country," had not been true to their trust.

"This is no time to rock the boat," Vinson said. "If the Navy has suffered casualties at Pearl Harbor, there's just one simple thing to do—buckle up our belts and make a determined effort that will win the war that much sooner."

Vinson commented that "Congress can't fight this war," adding that that job must be left to the men trained for the task.

Charges Hawaii "Was Asleep"

Dingell's outburst came a short time after the House Naval committee heard Rep. Vincent (D-Ky) assert that someone responsible for Hawaii's defense "was asleep."

In the Senate, Chairman Walh (D-Mass) of the Naval committee announced that President Roosevelt, as Commander in Chief, would reveal more details on American losses in the Pacific. He said the Navy Department declined to give him information until after the President speaks tonight.

Senator Tobey (R-NH) interrupted Walsh to say that it was "imperative that the American people be fully informed" especially after rumors that a "lareg part of our naval and military forces in the Pacific have been wiped out."

Tobey said that 24 hours before the Japanese atack Secretary Knox had issued a statement the gist of which was "the Navy is ready."

He asked Walsh if he did not agree that the American pride in its Navy and confidence in some of its officials had not been "seriously hurt and impaired."

Walsh Asks Work, Less Talk

"All I can say is," Walsh replied, "is that talk ought to cease now and work, energy and enthusiasm ought to be manifested by all the officials of the government. I hope this talk will cease.

"Whatever injury may have happened to our Navy, the job ahead of us is to rehabiltate and go ahead with more enthusiasm than ever before."

Senator Vandenberg (R-Mich) asked Walsh if the discussion had not emphasized the need for some kind of "liasion committee, representing the united Congress' to maintain contact with the President and receive such information as it might be essential or desirable for Congress to have."

"Personally," Walsh replied, "I think that may be desirable, but I prefer no suggestion and no comment now."

Naval Enlistments Frozen

Rep. Vincent made his statement just before the House Naval committee approved a bill, already passed in the Senate, to "freeze" all Navy enlistments for the war's duration.

His criticism developed when he sought to learn whether high ranking naval officers were physically fit for their jobs. In that connection, Vincent asked specifically about Rear Admiral Hart, naval commander at Manila.

"We must assume," interposed Chairman Vinson (D-Ga). "That all these officers have complied with the physical requirements."

"I assumed," retorted Vincent, "that the boys would be awake at Hawaii. I assumed that the boys would patrol every inch of the waters around Hawaii."

U. S., GERMANY, ITALY AT WAR!

LANCASTER NEW ERA

WEATHER

Fair and slightly colder tonight; Friday cloudy and cold. (Details on Page 3).

Examiner Founded 1830.
New Era Founded 1877.

Published Every Evening Except Sunday by New Era Company. Entered as Second Class Matter at Post Office, Lancaster, Pa.

LANCASTER, PA., THURSDAY, DECEMBER 11, 1941 — CITY EDITION — 32 PAGES—256 COLUMNS—THREE CENTS

CONGRESS SOLIDLY VOTES WAR UPON AXIS

U.S. Warplanes Sink Jap Battleship

Army Fights 'Chutists Who Capture Airport To North of Manila

BULLETIN

TWO JAP WARSHIPS SUNK

Washington, Dec. 11. — (A. P.) — The Navy announced today that four separate attacks on Wake Island had been repulsed by defending United States forces in the last 48 hours and that one light cruiser and one destroyer of Japanese forces had been sunk.

WASHINGTON, Dec. 11 — (AP) — The sinking of the 29,000-ton Japanese battleship Haruna by Army bombers off the northern coast of Luzon in the Philippines was announced today by Secretary of War Stimson.

At his press conference, Stimson said the Navy Department had confirmed the sinking, previously reported by the Army as a battleship of the Haruna class.

Determined resistance by American forces, Stimson reported, have confined Japanese landings on Luzon to the vicinity of Aparri at the extreme northern tip of the Island.

(From Manila, however, came reports that Japanese parachutists had seized an airport six miles from Iligan in Eastern Luzon. Ippara is on the northern coast.)

The War Secretary said there were continued attacks by Japanese aircraft in the vicinity of Manila yesterday, particularly on the air fields at Cavite and Nichols Field.

Stimson said that losses of planes in the attack on Hawaii Sunday, although heavy, already were being replaced.

These losses can be made good, and they are being made good now, the Secretary said. He reported that a flight of four motored army bombers arrived in Hawaii during the Japanese attack.

The first of the planes was shot down, but the crews of the remaining ships, with a few moments warning, brought their ships in at various air fields in the Islands, and only two of the planes suffered any damage.

"The American people have been put through a very heavy test in the last four days," Stimson said. "When we survey the situation in cold blood and in perspective, we must realize that initial reverses are almost inevitably to be expected in a contest between a Democracy and an autocratic government.

"This is particularly true when the autocratic government has been preparing and fighting for several years and its men are veterans. We must be very careful not to underestimate the ability of the Japanese seamen.

"On the other hand, all students of history know that every war has three periods. They have been designated as the period of onset, the period of drag, when the war begins to weigh on the nations involved, and the finish."

Stimson said of the attack on Hawaii that the War Department itself as yet does not have a complete report, but said that this was no time for recriminations or accusations of blame.

"Anything like that, it seems to me, is a sign of an immature government and people," Stimson said. "The present is not the moment for investigation. That will come later. The present moment is one for action and preparation."

The Army, the Secretary said, was now engaged in strengthening its defenses everywhere—"in Hawaii and everywhere else."

Stimson handed correspondents the Department's third war communique, explaining that since its preparation the Navy had confirmed that the Japanese battleship sunk was the Haruna. It follows:

"Philippine theater: The Commanding General, Far Eastern command, confirms the sinking of a 29,000-ton Japanese battleship yesterday by the American army air forces, North of Luzon. This battleship is believed to be the 29,000-ton Haruna, or a vessel of the Haruna class.

"Continued attempts by strong Japanese forces to establish themselves along the northern coast of Luzon were reported. Determined resistance has confined this action to the attack in the vicinity of Aparri, at the extreme northern tip of Luzon, where the Japanese attempted to establish a beach head yesterday. Air activity continued

(See PHILIPPINES—Page 20)

First Local Casualty

SERGEANT ROBERT H. MARTIN

CITY MAN HURT IN JAP ATTACK

Weather Expert at Hickam Field, Hawaii, Wounded in Sunday Bombing.

Sergeant Robert H. Martin, of Lancaster, was wounded Sunday in the Japanese bombing of Hickam Field, Hawaii, where he is weather station supervisor, his family was notified today by the War Department. The extent of his wounds was not disclosed by the telegram.

(Chairman Walsh (D-Mass) of the Senate Naval Committee said today in Washington that the Navy's Pearl Harbor casualty list had arrived this morning by clipper and that telegrams would be sent immediately to the next of kin. The list will not be given to the public for two or three days.)

Martin was Lancaster's first casualty of the war, as far as was known here. Sixteen Pennsylvania men have been reported killed to date by the War Department.

The telegram, addressed to Mrs. Harry A. Martin, 621 Fourth street, Lancaster, the officer's mother, said:

"The Secretary of War desires me to express to you his deep regret that your son, Sergeant Robert H. Martin, was wounded in action in defense of his country at Hickam Field, Territory of Hawaii, December 7, 1941.

"Adams, Adjutant-General."

Enlisted In 1939

Martin, who is twenty-five, was also instructor of mathematics and meteorology at Hickam Field. He enlisted in the Air Corps in New York in August, 1939. He is a graduate of Lancaster High school, class of 1934, and Penn State College, class of 1939.

According to letters received by the parents here, Sergeant Martin found his work interesting and was delighted with the Hawaiian climate. He attended evening school at the University of Hawaii for a time. Recently he was on a cruise, setting up new weather stations.

He has four brothers, Earl, Paul and Lester, all of Lancaster, and Melvin, Akron; and two sisters,

(See LOCAL BOYS—Page 30)

24-HOUR SCHEDULE AT MARIETTA DEPOT

The regulating station at the Marietta Army depot announced at 2:50 p. m. today that it wanted "all men who have been laid off" to come back to work at once.

Construction work on the project will return to a 24-hour-day basis tomorrow," Captain William T. Hartman, adjutant, said.

The Scribbler

THE day following the bombing of Pearl Harbor, a local travel agency received a letter from a Japanese tourist company inviting travelers to visit the Philippines.

MRS. GEORGE HOUCK, Columbia, stepped out of her house yesterday to show John Lockard, Mountville, where to plant several trees.

She locked the door behind her John drove to Lancaster and got a key to the house from Mr. Houck.

THE PRESIDENT'S WAR MESSAGE

"On the morning of December 11, the government of Germany, pursuing its course of world conquest, declared war against the United States.

"The long-known and the long-expected has thus taken place. The forces endeavoring to enslave the entire world now are moving toward this hemisphere.

"Never before has there been a greater challenge to life, liberty and civilization.

"Delay invites great danger. Rapid and united effort by all of the peoples of the world who are determined to remain free will insure a world victory of the forces of justice and of righteousness over the forces of savagery and of barbarism.

"Italy also has declared war against the United States.

"I therefore request the Congress to recognize a state of war between the United States and Germany, and between the United States and Italy."

Complete "Blackout" Air Raid Test In City Area December 22

All Lights to Be Out for 15 Minutes, Starting at 10 P. M.; Appeals for Volunteer Fire Wardens and Airplane Spotters

Lancaster's first complete "blackout" and air raid drill will be held in the metropolitan area at 10 P. M. Monday, December 22, for 15 minutes, the Defense Council announced today.

The area embraced will be all of Lancaster city, and most of the adjoining townships—Manheim, Lancaster, West and East Lampeter.

Both the air raid warden system and the fire warden system will be in complete operation by that time, it was said, and the darkening will be carried out in form similar of that done experimentally in other eastern cities.

Blackuto in Areas Near City

City and township officials met this noon with Col. Charles P. Stahr, chief of the air raid warden system, Col. J. Hale Steinman, chairman of the Defense Council, Mayor Cary, Richard A. Mehring, of the State Council of Defense, and other appropriate officials to discuss the plans. Details will be announced as they are perfected.

Roughly, the area to be blacked out includes suburbs and countryside south to Lyndon, east to Bridgeport, west beyond West Lancaster, and north to Neffsville and Eden.

Following the meeting, Amos Keen, chief fire warden, issued an urgent appeal for more volunteers for fire warden service in both city and county.

City volunteers are asked to enroll at the Defense Council headquarters in Old City Hall. County volunteers are asked to volunteer directly to the fire chief in their respective districts.

More men also are needed for the air raid warden service, and they also are asked

(See HOME DEFENSE—Last Page)

ADMITS FIRES AND VANDALISM

Bareville Man Confesses Sending Threats; Damaged Tombstones.

Melvin Buchen, twenty-seven, Bareville, a concrete worker and neighborhood handyman, today confessed, according to State Motor Police, that he battered and broke tombstones in three county cemeteries, last month, and started a $26,000 barn fire and attempted to fire two other structures over the last week-end.

Buchen, police said, also confessed writing a series of threatening notes to farmers throughout northern Lancaster county threatening to burn their barns, to school officials and others in recent weeks. He confessed also to entering and damaging the Leola school building last June.

Insists He Worked Alone

Police said that Buchen insisted that he was alone in his one-man crime wave and battered the tomb-

(See CONFESS—Page 20)

Call Defense Meeting For Tuesday Evening

There will be a meeting Tuesday at 8 P. M. of the Defense Groups of all County towns with the Defense Committee of Lancaster County. **Notices are being sent giving the time and place of meeting. It is an important meeting at which instructions will be issued to Air Raid Wardens and Emergency Fire Wardens.**

14 ARMY FLIERS DIE IN CRASH OF BOMBER IN WEST

SAN RAFAEL, Cal., June 5—(AP)—Fourteen Army fliers died in the crash of a heavy bomber near here last night, the Army said today. Flames consumed the wreckage when the plane hit a hilltop as the pilot circled for an emergency landing.

The plane developed trouble soon after a takeoff and radioed nearby Hamilton Field to clear a runway. The pilot circled toward the field.

The big ship lost altitude and then dived into a hillside on the Herzog ranch, three miles northwest of Hamilton Field.

As it crashed great flames swept through the wreckage. Not a man escaped.

"JERRY HAS GOT THE "JITTERS," SAYS COMMANDO LEADER

LONDON, June 5.—(AP)—Germans fired upon Germans during the British Commando raid early yesterday against Boulogne-le Touquet defenses. One Nazi patrol boat was sunk and another was grounded in flames and smoke columns marked areas of destruction, eyewitnesses said today.

"Jerry has got the jitters," commented a 23-year-old officer of the British special service troops.

Dropped from Naval craft into the surf of the Channel coast of occupied France where an Allied expeditionary force may land one day, the raiders were heavily armed and lightly clad. Many wore only shorts, stockings and soft woolen headgear.

Late War Bulletins

TOBEY CHARGES "DERELICTION" AT PEARL HARBOR

Washington, Dec. 11—(AP)—Senator Tobey (R-NH) declared in the Senate today that "dereliction and inefficiency" in the Navy had been responsible for "disaster that's almost unspeakable" in the Japanese attack on the United States fleet at Pearl Harbor.

Tobey asaserted that the fleet's listening devices "weren't working" that the ships "lay at anchor and no steam up" and that more ships were sunk than had been disclosed by the President.

ARMY CALLS FOR 10,000 MORE NURSES

Washington, Dec. 11—(AP)—The Army called for 10,000 recruits for its corps of nurses today to fill existing vacancies and those anticipated in the immediate future. Major General James C. Magee, Surgeon General of the Army, said that both regular army nurses and reserve nurses were needed.

PHILIPPINE ARMY ROUTS INVADERS

Manila, Dec. 11—(AP)—The Philippine army was reported unofficially but reliably tonight to have recaptured the region around Aparri, on the north coast of Luzon, and to be driving the Japanese back to the seashore.

U. S. Acts Few Hours After Being Notified Of Break by Hitler

Axis Dictators Invoke Warfare Against This Nation at Same Time; Berlin Note Blames Sinking of Ships

(By The Associated Press)

The Congress of the United States without dissent voted war against both Germany and Italy today, swiftly countering Axis declarations of war against this country.

Not a single "no" vote was registered in either Senate or House.

The Senate voted 88-0 for war against Germany, 90-0 for war against Italy.

The House vote for war with Germany was 393, with one member voting merely "present." Against Italy, the House voted 399-0 with one "present."

Montana's Republican woman Representative Jeanette Rankin, who cast the lone vote against war with Japan and who voted against the war with Germany in 1917, was recorded as "present."

Congress' lightning speed in passing both resolutions — even more rapidly than in voting war against Japan — came after a message from President Roosevelt urging a "rapid and united effort" for victory "over the forces of savagery and barbarism."

"The long-known and long-expected has taken place," Mr. Roosevelt said, in a noon message to Congress.

"The forces endeavoring to enslave the entire world now are moving toward this hemisphere. Never before has there been a greater challenge to life, liberty and civilization.

"I therefore request the Congress to recognize a state of war between the United States and Germany, and between the United States and Italy."

Only a few hours earlier, the Axis dictators had invoked war against the United States, with Premier Mussolini exhorting crowds in Rome that "it is an honor to fight together with the Japanese."

Reichsfuehrer Adolf Hitler, lengthily addressing a wildly cheering Reichstag, reiterated his theme that the war would determine the history of the entire world for the next 500 to 1,000 years.

To cheering throngs in Berlin and Rome, Adolf Hitler and Premier Mussolini made the fateful declarations at approximately 8 A. M., Lancaster time.

In a brief, six-paragraph message to Congress, which followed declarations of war on this country by the two Axis partners, Mr. Roosevelt asserted that "the forces endeavoring to enslave the entire world now are moving towards this hemisphere."

Never before, he said, has there been "a greater challenge to life, liberty and civilization."

Declaring that delay invites greater danger, Mr. Roosevelt added that "rapid and united effort by all of the peoples of the world who are determined to remain

(See WAR DECLARED—Last Page)

WRECKAGE LEFT BY JAPANESE BOMBS IN HAWAII

Blazing from the Japanese bombing attack on Hickam field, Hawaii, are B-17 Army bombers, seen behind two motors of one of the bombers which escaped damage during the Dec. 7 raid.

Furniture and other household goods in Honolulu were moved to a safer place as Jap planes touched off the war with a raid on Pearl Harbor.

A view of wreckage in Honolulu after Jap bombing attack on Dec. 7.

Firemen and civilians rushed fire hoses to the scene to save homes and stores in the Jap and Chinese section of Honolulu during the Japanese attack.

Bystanders gaze at still smoking ruins of homes in Honolulu's residential district, blasted by Jap bombs which rained on Ouahu Island in "sneak" raid by Japs. In background, fire fighters work on smoldering ruins.

Two-man Jap submarine beached on the Hawaiian Island of Oahu during the surprise attack on Pearl Harbor. Released by Navy Dept.

BRITAIN SPEEDS COORDINATION

Commons Told All Steps Have Been Taken to Unified War Plans.

LONDON, Dec. 17—(AP)—Government spokesmen told the House of Commons today that all steps had been taken to coordinate British, American and Allied war plans in accord with President Roosevelt's call for "world scale strategy" but that Britain had not asked Russia to declare war on Japan.

These statements were made by Richard Law, Undersecretary for Foreign Affairs, and Lord Privy Seal Clement R. Attlee, in a session largely devoted to the question of cooperation among anti-Axis allies.

Law said that China had full legal status as a British ally.

Members of the House, foreshadowing a querulous tone for forthcoming secret debate on the war situation, bombarded the government with questions about the creation of a unified Allied War Council, adequacy of the Empire defense, strategy in the Far East and joint British-American efforts to obtain naval bases in Eire.

The government, despite statements that Allied war plans were being coordinated, gave no sharp indication on the idea of an overall war council. President Roosevelt's concept was brought into the debate by Edgar Louis Granville.

Duncan Sandys, Financial Secretary of the War Office, rejected what he called the "implications" of a question by Russell Thomas as to a "gross underestimate" by the High Command of the British position in Burma but said that information was being received on the subject.

Replying to alarm expressed by Reginald Purbrick over loss of airfields in Malaya, Sandys gave assurances that all officers were fully acquainted with instructions for defending airfields. This has been a subject of particular parliamentary concern since the British lost the Greek Island of Crete to the Nazis "vertical envelopment."

Laborite Hubert Beaumont proposed an increase of £100,000,000 ($400,000,000) annually in the allowance for dependents of service men in an effort to correct what he called discrimination in favor of men earning large wages in reserved occupations.

One member, supporting the measure, declared, "we are laying up an awful legacy of social unrest for the end of the war.."

Lady Astor, Conservative, said, "I blame the cabinet as a whole for pay discrimination which is creating bitterness and affecting troop morale. The unfairness of it is simply appalling. The cabinet is entirely out of date and far behind the country."

Capt. Frederick J. Bellenger, Laborite, commented that "we are now selecting our commissioned ranks in the RAF very largely or to a certain extent on the size of their bank balances."

AWNING IS BURNED

COATESVILLE, Dec. 17 — Fire broke out at 11:15 o'clock last night at the St. Regis restaurant, Second avenue and Lincoln Highway, Coatesville. Firemen said an awning in front of the building had caught fire and was destroyed. Men in the restaurant eating at the time formed a "bucket brigade" and succeeded in putting out the fire just as firemen arrived on the scene.

Ban on Tire Sales Extended 2 Weeks

WASHINGTON, Dec. 17—(AP)—OPM officials said today that the prohibition on manufacture and sale of automobile tires and tubes, except to fill top defense orders, would be extended until the first week in January. The original order, effective December 11, was to have expired December 22.

Designed to halt a consumer's buying wave which developed after the Japanese attack on American island possessions in the Pacific, the prohibition bars tire stores, both wholesale and retail, filling stations, automobile dealers or other persons from selling any type of new automobile, truck, bus, motorcycle or farm implement tire or tube except on high defense preference ratings.

Young Reserve Ensigns Show Nerve During Hawaii Attack

Take U. S. Destroyer to Sea After Regular Officers Were Killed; Knox Praises Other Acts of Bravery

WASHINGTON, Dec. 17—(AP)—Secretary Knox revealed yesterday that during the sudden Japanese attack on Pearl Harbor December 7 four naval reserve ensigns were the only surviving officers on board one destroyer, yet they took the ship to sea in pursuit of the enemy and, said Knox met all emergencies, operating the vessel like veterans. The young reserves had never had such responsibility before, Knox said in reporting their action under enemy fire.

He related the incident in giving further details of the battle of Pearl Harbor which he first reported on Monday, when he disclosed that the principal loss to the fleet was destruction of the battleship Arizona.

Knox said that had the attack taken place a short time later it would have found hundreds of Navy men at divine services. Actually it came a short time before "church call" and one chaplain was killed while preparing his compartment for services.

The Navy secretary did not name the ensigns nor the chaplain. He reported these other incidents:

"One enlisted man who went to sea after the attack on his own ship said on leaving the harbor, 'After that stab in the back I hope I live to show them what an American can do.' Another said, 'I know what the big shots meant when they spoke of the treachery of the Axis'."

"Several men under treatment on the hospital ship tried to rejoin their regular vessels and get into the fight. They were held back by officers and nurses with difficulty, and a few did manage to escape the vessel and join fleet units.

"A number of women, many being wives of officers and men and even in some cases women widowed by the attack, volunteered their services in the hospitals.

"Ship handling was excellent throughout the action, and among destroyers working at high speed and in close quarters, there were no collisions.

"A gun captain noticed a powder case had jammed in his gun. He quickly obtained a hacksaw and cut off a section so the breach could be closed. The gun continued in service throughout the action.

"On a destroyer tender some spare machine guns were broken out. These guns were speedily placed on top of deckhouses and welded into place by welders who carried on their work at the height of the attack and amid a storm of bullets and bombs. All of these guns were in the final action.

"Communications functioned perfectly throughout the action. Although many lines were cut by shrapnel communication with the mainland was maintained throughout. Men remained at their posts in radio rooms of some ships until the last."

6-MOS.-OLD GIRL HURT IN AIR RAID

MANILA, Dec. 17—(AP) — The youngest person injured in Japanese air raids on Luzon Island——an unidentified six-months-old girl—was given an even chance to survive by doctors at Manila hospital today.

The child was found on a Cavite street. Authorities believe her parents were killed in the attack.

ITALIAN GENERAL IS REPORTED LOST IN SUBMARINE

LONDON, Dec. 17.—(AP)—An Italian submarine carrying an Italian General and 19 other military officers from Libya to Italy has been sunk in the Central Mediterranean, the Admiralty said today. The Admiralty said the general was not among 53 survivors who were made prisoners.

The general was identified as Guido Lami.

The submarine was reported by the British to be the Ammiraglio Caracciolo, one of Italy's newest ocean-going submersibles, displacing 1,461 tons. The British said the submarine was sunk by the destroyer Farndale.

General Lami was said authoritatively to be the chief executive engineer of Italian Army headquarters in Rome.

REPORTER KILLED IN ACTION AT SEA

ALEXANDRIA, Egypt, Dec. 17.—(AP)—A. Massey Anderson, Naval correspondent of Reuters, British News Agency, has been killed in action at sea.

Anderson, who previously had been manager of Reuters in Alexandria, had witnessed many naval actions and had been praised for his coolness in attending some wounded men during the aerial bombardment of the aircraft carrier Illustrious last January.

(It is possible that Anderson was killed in the same action, not yet announced by the British, in which Larry Allen, Associated Press correspondent with the British Mediterranean fleet, was injured. Allen is now in an Alexandria hospital suffering from face and body bruises. Both Allen and Anderson were veterans of the Illustrious bombing.)

BOYS IN RUSSIA CRIPPLE NAZI MOTOR TRANSPORTS

MOSCOW, Dec. 17.—(AP) — The Germans were caught without crank handles to start their motors because all had been stolen by Russian boys, a writer in Izvestia reported from a village beyond recaptured Klin today.

Terming it "an incident as heroic as it is funny," the writer, Evgenii Petrov, said the Germans then "had to run in a most natural manner, using their own feet."

"The boys were the first to scent that the Germans were about to flee," said his account. "They pilfered all the handles. As soon as our troops appeared in the village the boys solemnly presented them with the handles."

NAME UNIT AFTER FIRST WAR HERO

DETROIT, Dec. 17 —(AP)— Capt. Richard Gillespie, acting army recruiting officer for Michigan, said today that a Colin P. Kelly, Jr., Aviation Cadet Unit No. 1 would be formed in honor of "the first real hero of the war."

"Priority over everything else will be given to the recruiting of the 20 men who will make up the unit," Capt. Gillespie said.

Capt. Kelly, a former aviation cadet, scored direct hits on a Japanese battleship off the north coast of Luzon on Dec. 9 and died in action in the Philipippne battle area.

Permission to form the Kelly unit was given, Capt. Gillespie said, by Maj-Gen. Emory S. Adams, adjutant-general of the U. S. Army at Washington.

BRITAIN ADOPTS 18-50 DRAFT BILL, WOMEN INCLUDED

LONDON, Dec. 17—(AP)—The government conscription bill which will make British women subject to compulsory national service and extend conscription of men for military services to the ages of 18 1-2 to 50 years was enacted today by the House of Lords. It will take effect upon the King's assent.

The measure already had been passed in the House of Commons.

Previous conscription ages for men were 19 to 41.

MISSIONARY TO SPEAK

Ida Shumaker, a returned missionary from India, will be at the Akron Church of the Brethren on Sunday. Services will be held morning, afternoon and evening.

URGES FARMERS TO PROVIDE OWN FOOD

WASHINGTON, Dec. 17— (AP) — Secretary of Agriculture Wickard told farmers today they could help the war effort greatly by providing their own food and feed supplies.

"The farm family that grows its own vegetable and egg and milk supply increases the nation's productive capacity in several ways," said Wickard. "First of all, such a family is better fed, stronger and able to work harder. Second, such a family does not call for the use of scarce tin and other containers to put up its food in city factories; it does not require the use of rail or highway transport to get part of its food supply, and it releases part of the commercial supply of these greatly needed foods for use by our own people, and the people of the nations allied with us."

NAZI FIGHTER PLANES DOWNED IN MALAYA

LONDON, Dec. 17.—(AP)—The Air Ministry News Service declared today that the Japanese are using both Messerschmitt 109's and 110's—German fighter planes—in the air battle of Malaya.

ME-109 is a single-engined plane and the ME-110 is the twin-engined. Both can be used as bombers.

The Japanese previously had been reported manufacturing fighter planes based on Messerschmitt models but there had been no indication before that they possessed planes made in Germany.

CHINESE ARE URGED TO JOIN U. S. FORCES

MANILA, Dec. 17—(AP)—The Chinese Consul General, acting on orders from Chungking, today advised thousands of Chinese living in the Philippines to offer their services to the government.

The census bureau estimated meanwhile that there are 3,443,500 men between 18 and 50 years of age in the island upon whom the army can draw in event an all-out defense is needed.

MANILA IS BUILDING PUBLIC RAID SHELTER

MANILA, Dec. 17—(AP)—Construction of Manila's first public air-raid shelter now is under way in one of the areas bombed recently by Japanese warplanes.

The shelter, of reinforced concrete, is designed to accommodate 100 persons. Many individual shelters also are being built.

ABOUT RAINDROPS

The ordinary raindrop is made up of 8,000,000 water particles. The drops vary from one-sixteenth to one-fifth of an inch in diameter, according to weather conditions.

LADIES ARE GUESTS AT LIONS' MEETING

The Lions Club held a party for ladies yesterday noon in the Hotel Brunswick, with approximately seventy-five present.

Ralph Taylor, dressed as "Uncle Sam", distributed defense stamp books, partially filled, to the ladies.

A program of entertainment was presented by Robert Stetler, accordionist; Dorothy Morrow and Doris Stoll, tap dancers. Group singing was led by John W. Eckenrode, Jr.

SONS, DAUGHTERS AT ROTARY MEETING

A magician entertained 60 sons and daughters of Rotarians yesterday at the club's annual party at the Brunswick Hotel.

The youngest child at the party was John M. Ranck, Jr., two-year-old son of Mr. and Mrs. John M. Ranck, of Strasburg.

Herman A. Wohlsen, president, announced that the president of Rotary International will give a radio address on a nation wide hook-up at 4 p. m. tomorrow. It will be carried by WGAL. The local station also will carry the weekly Rotary program "America Speaks."

BROWNSTOWN YOUTH IS HELD IN FORGERY

John Rice, nineteen, Brownstown, charged with forgery, was arrested yesterday by Motor Policeman Farra and jailed for court following a hearing before Justice of the Peace Yeager, Ephrata.

He is alleged to have forged the names of his mother, Mrs. Emma K. Rice, and his brother, Rupert K. Rice, on a $14.85 CCC check which he presented to H. F. Weit, Ephrata, for payment of cigarettes and received the balance in change.

Al Capone's Son Weds

Albert (Sonny) Capone, 22, son of the former Chicago gang chief, is shown with his bride, the former Diana Ruth Casey, 21, of Chattanooga, Tenn., after their marriage in St. Patrick's Church, Miami Beach, Fla. Al Capone attended the wedding.

INCREASED FUNDS FOR PUBLIC LIBRARY

The Lancaster Free Public library's income for 1942 from the city and county governments will be $8,000, as compared with $4,800 which it received from the two units in the past year, officials said today.

The city budget provided $4,000 instead of $2,400 which was set aside a year ago, and county commissioners indicated they would match the sum. A representative of the library trustees called upon the commissioners recently to request the larger sum.

NEFFSVILLE FIRE CO. AUXILIARY PARTIES

The Ladies' Auxiliary of the Neffsville Fire company will hold a card party Saturday evening, January 10, in the Fire Hall.

The annual Christmas party meeting was held Tuesday evening, and a donation of $5 was given to the Red Cross.

The next meeting will be held Tuesday evening, January 27, and the feature will be Chandler R. Heagey, of Eden, showing motion pictures of local interest.

2 YOUTHS, GIRL HURT AT LITITZ

Auto Hits Tree When Driver Falls Asleep; 4 Injured in Truck Crash.

Seven persons were injured in two auto accidents reported early today.

Richard Froeck, seventeen, Lititz, R. 4, suffered lacerations of the temple and ear; Harvey Nissley, eighteen, Neffsville, a laceration of the head, and Ruth F. Wenger, seventeen, Bareville, R. 1, an injured right ankle and shock when their auto struck a tree at Broad and Orange streets, Lititz, at 12:30 A. M. They were conveyed to the General hospital, where Nissley told attendants he fell asleep at the wheel.

Miss Wenger was jammed in the wreckage and as she was being extricated, crossed wires threatened to set fire to the auto. Nissley, an auto mechanic, secured a wrench and disconnected the battery. The Lititz fire company was called but was not needed.

Robert Reese, sixteen, New Providence, R. 1, face laceration; Jay Finefrock, sixteen, New Providence, injured wrist; Charles A. Kauffman, seventeen, New Providence, R. 1, injured ankle and shoulder, and Alfred Longer, New Providence, R. 1, laceration of face, were treated at St. Joseph's hospital after their auto and a truck operated by Ted Crawford, 244 West Orange street, collided at Columbia and President avenues at 1:50 A. M. Longer told police he was headed east when he crashed into the side of the truck, attempting to make a left turn into President avenue.

OBJECTORS' TRIAL SLATED FOR MONDAY

Six "Wenger Mennonite" men from eastern Lancaster county are scheduled to go on trial next week in Federal court, Philadelphia, on charges of violating the Selective Service law by refusing to go to a conscientious objectors' camp. The case is listed to start Monday.

The youths, members of the Wenger Mennonite Church, were indicted last month. They are: Elam Sauder Shirk, East Earl R1; Isaac Martin Rissler, Bareville R1; George Martin Zimmerman, Ephrata R2; Daniel Weaver Hoover, New Holland R1; David Weber Shirk, Ephrata R3, and Isaac Shirk Eby, New Holland R1.

Officials of County Draft Board No. 4, where the youths are registered, received subpoenas yesterday to appear as government witnesses.

FRENCH NORMANDIE CALLED LAFAYETTE

WASHINGTON, Jan. 1—(AP)—The former French luxury liner Normandie, now being converted into a naval auxiliary, today was given the name U. S. S. Lafayette.

The huge passenger liner, seized by the Coast Guard on December 12, is the first American naval vessel to be named in honor of the Marquis De Lafayette, French hero of America's Revolutionary War.

A Navy announcement said that Secretary Frank Knox assigned the name Lafayette "by direction of the President."

The Navy declined to say more than that the 83,433 ton ship would be an "auxiliary," but previous speculation about the use of the big liner had given primary attention to her value as a troop transport. Extensive conversion would be needed to fit the liner as an aircraft carrier.

Thursday, January 1, 1942

TODAY'S HIGHLIGHTS

6:00 P. M. WGAL	DUQUESNE BREW CO. NEWS: Ken Kreider
7:00 P. M. NBC	FRED WARING IN Pleasure Time
7:30 P. M. WGAL	RED CROSS PROGRAM Mrs. John F. Horting
8:00 P. M. NBC	MARCH OF TIME News Dramatization
8:30 P. M. WGAL	BAFFLE BOARD Pensupreme Milk
9:00 P. M. NBC	AMERICA'S TOWN MEETING: "Outlook On The Atlantic"

2:00— NBC—Sugar Bowl Game: Fordham vs. Missouri: Gillette Safety Razor
5:00—WGAL—Holiday Special
6:00—WGAL—Duquesne Brew. Co., News
6:15—WGAL—Lawrence Welk's Orch.
6:30—WGAL—Sports: Robert Harnish
6:45—WGAL—A to Z in Novelty
7:00— NBC—Fred Waring Orch.
7:15—WGAL—Novatime
7:30—WGAL—Red Cross Program: Mrs. John F. Horting
7:45—WGAL—Melodic Contrast
8:00— NBC—March of Time
8:30—WGAL—Pensupreme Baffle Board
9:00— NBC—America's Town Meeting: "Outlook on the Atlantic"
10:00— MBS—Raymond Gram Swing
10:15—WGAL—New Music For The New Year
10:30— NBC—News Here and Abroad
10:45— NBC—Joe Sudy Orchestra
11:00—WGAL—United Press News
11:15— NBC—Bob Allen's Orch.
11:30— MBS—Britain Speaks
11:45— MBS—Dick Stabile's Orch.
12:00— NBC—War News
12:05— NBC—Boyd Raeburn's Orch.
12:30— MBS—Del Courtney's Orch.
12:55—WGAL—War News
1:00—WGAL—Sign Off

Friday, January 2, 1942

6:00—WGAL—War News
6:15—WGAL—Red, White and Blue
6:30—WGAL—Home Folk's Frolic
6:45—WGAL—United Press News
7:00—WGAL—Musical Clock & News
7:45— NBC—Reveille Roundup
8:00— NBC—European News
8:15— NBC—Ross Sisters
8:30— NBC—Jim Robertson
8:45—WGAL—Styles in Swing
8:55—WGAL—United Press News
9:00— NBC—Happy Jack
9:15— NBC—Breakfast Club
9:30— NBC—Breakfast Club, Swift & Co.
9:45—WGAL—Blauner's Music Box
10:00— QSN—Golden Bars of Melody
10:15—WGAL—Devotions. Rev. Butt
10:30—WGAL—United Press News
10:35—WGAL—Listen to Liebert
10:45— NBC—Stringtime
11:00—WGAL—Madero Money Man
11:15—WGAL—Bargain Bandwagon
11:30— NBC—Prescott Presents
11:45—WGAL—Luncheon Club
12:15—WGAL—Dolly Madison News
12:30— NBC—Farm and Home Hour
1:15— NBC—Ted Malone
1:30—WGAL—Year and the Farmer
1:45— NBC—News Summary
2:00— NBC—Concert Orchestra
2:30— MBS—Philadelphia Orchestra
—Adv.

RADIO PROGRAM

THURSDAY, JAN 1, AFTERNOON

2:00—WOR—Football: Alabama vs. Texas A. and M., Dallas; WJZ—Football: Fordham vs. Missouri, New Orleans; WABC—Football: Georgia vs. Texas Christian, Miami
4:30—WEAF—Lorenzo Jones; WOR—Happy Jim Parsons; WABC—Landt Trio
4:45—WEAF—Young Widder Brown; WABC—News; Mary Marlin
4:55—WJZ—News; Adventure Stories
5:00—WEAF—When a Girl Marries; WOR—Little Orphan Annie
5:15—WEAF—Portia Faces Life; WOR—Shafter Parker Circus; WJZ—Secret City; WABC—The Goldbergs
5:30—WEAF—We, the Abbotts; WOR—Jack Armstrong; WJZ—Flying Patrol; WABC—The O'Neills
5:45—WEAF—Civilian Defense; WOR—Captain Midnight; WJZ—Tom Mix; WABC—Scattergood Baines
5:50—WEAF—Vagabonds

EVENING

6:00—WEAF—Music; WOR—Uncle Don; WJZ—News; Talk; WABC—News Reports
6:15—WEAF—News; WJZ—Bill Stern; WABC—William L. Shirer
6:30—WEAF—Heirs of Liberty—Play; WOR—News; Here's Morgan; WJZ—Lum and Abner; WABC—Bob Hannon
6:45—WEAF—Three Suns; WJZ—Lowell Thomas; WABC—The World Today
7:00—WEAF—Fred Waring; WOR—Sports—Stan Lomax; WJZ—East Aces; WABC—Amos 'n' Andy
7:15—WEAF—European News; WOR—Music and Talks; WJZ—Mr. Keen; WABC—Lanny Ross
7:30—WEAF—Cugat Orch.; WOR—News; Sports; WJZ—Roth Orch.; WABC—Maudie's Diary
8:00—WEAF—Frank Morgan; WOR—Morton Gould Orch.; WJZ—March of Time; WABC—Death Valley Days
8:30—WEAF—Aldrich Family; WOR—Boake Carter; WJZ—Army Camp Program; WABC—Duffy's Tavern
8:45—WOR—Goodman Orch.
9:00—WEAF—Music Hall; WOR—Gabriel Heatter; WJZ—George V. Denny Jr., Moderator; Outlook in the Atlantic—Rear Admiral Clark H. Woodward; Jay Allen, Col. W. Steward-Roddie; WABC—Major Bowes
9:15—WOR—War at Sea
9:30—WOR—America Preferred
10:00—WEAF—Vallee Varieties; WOR—Raymond Gram Swing; WJZ—Opera Guild; WABC—Miller Orch.
10:15—WOR—Spotlight Band; WJZ—First Piano; WABC—Navy Program
10:30—WEAF—Frank Fay; WOR—Kaye Brinker; WJZ—News; Music
10:45—WOR—Tune Twisters; WABC—News; Music
11:00—WEAF, WJZ—News; Music; WOR—News; Music
12:00—WEAF, WJZ—News; Music; WABC—News; Music
12:55—WEAF, WJZ—News; Music; WABC—News; Music
2:00—WOR—News; Music (To 5:30 A. M.)

FRIDAY, JAN. 2, MORNING

5:30—WOR—Music; Digest
6:15—WABC—News; Music
6:30—WEAF, WJZ—News; WOR—News; WABC—Arthur Godfrey
6:55—WABC—News; Arthur Godfrey
7:00—WOR—News; Musical Clock
7:30—WEAF—News; Music
7:45—WABC—News
7:55—WJZ—News
8:00—WEAF, WJZ—News; WOR—News
8:15—WEAF—Studio X; WOR—The Goldbergs; WJZ—Music; WABC—Music; Talk
8:30—WOR—Happy Jim Parsons; WABC—Missus Goes A-Shopping
8:45—WEAF—News; Talk; Music; WOR—News; WJZ—Kitchen Quiz; WABC—Adelaide Hawley
9:00—WOR—Dear Imogene; WJZ—Woman of Tomorrow; WABC—News; Music
9:15—WOR—Victor Lindlahr
9:30—WEAF—Isabel Hewson; WOR—News; Going Places; WJZ—Breakfast Club
9:45—WEAF—Edward MacHugh; WABC—Stories America Loves
10:00—WEAF—Bess Johnson; WOR—Food Talk; WJZ—Clark Dennis; WABC—Talk
10:15—WEAF—Bachelor's Children; WJZ—Today's News; WABC—Myrt and Marge
10:30—WEAF—Help Mate; WOR—Consumers' Quiz; Music; WJZ—House in the Country; WABC—Stepmother
10:45—WEAF—Road of Life; WJZ—String Ensemble; WABC—Woman of Courage.
11:00—WEAF—Mary Marlin; WOR—News; Talk; WJZ—Richard Kent; WABC—Buddy Clark
11:15—WEAF—Right to Happiness; WJZ—Andrini String Trio; WABC—Man I Married
11:30—WEAF—The Bartons; WJZ—Variety; WABC—Bright Horizon
11:45—WEAF—David Harum; WABC—Aunt Jenny's Stories

AFTERNOON

12:00—WEAF—Don Goddard; WOR—John B. Hughes; WJZ—Nancy Boothe Craig; WABC—Kate Smith
12:15—WEAF—Words and Music; WOR—This is Life; WJZ—Civilian Defense; WABC—Big Sister
12:25—WJZ—News; Farm and Home Hour
12:30—WEAF—Vladimir Padwa, Piano; WOR—News; Judy and Jane; WABC—Helen Trent
12:45—WEAF—Music; Markets Report; WABC—Our Gal Sunday
1:00-WEAF—Mary Margaret McBride; WOR—I'll Find My Way; WABC—Life Can Be Beautiful
1:15—WOR—Government Girl; WJZ—Ted Malone; WABC—Woman in White
1:30—WOR—Front Page Farrell; WJZ—Dr. Daniel A. Poling; WABC—Vic and Sade
1:45—WEAF—Betty and Bob; WOR—Dance Orchestra; WJZ—News; Lopez Orch.; WABC—Road of Life
2:00-WEAF—Biblical Drama; WOR—Martha Deane; WABC—Young Dr. Malone
2:15—WEAF—Mystery Man; WABC—Joyce Jordan
2:30—WEAF—Valiant Lady; WOR—Philadelphia Symphony; WJZ—Variety Show; WABC—Fletcher Wiley
2:45—WEAF—Arnold Grimm; WABC—Kate Hopkins
3:00—WEAF—Against the Storm; WJZ—Orphans of Divorce; WABC—The Helping Hand
3:15—WEAF—Ma Perkins; WJZ—Honeymoon Hill; WABC—News
3:30—WEAF—Pepper Young; WJZ—John's Other Wife; WABC—Renfro Valley Folks
3:45—WEAF—Vic and Sade; WJZ—Just Plain Bill; WABC—Americans Map the Skies
3:55—WABC—News; Concert Orch.

Holiday Puzzle

HORIZONTAL
1 Pictured Roman god.
5 He is —— of this month.
8 Twelfth part of a year.
13 God of war.
14 Considerable in degree.
16 Mud.
17 Anger.
18 Made shirrs in
20 Sesame.
21 Music note.
22 Horse's gait.
23 Close to.
25 Afternoon (abbr.).
26 Sixty sixties (astron.).
28 Minute skin opening.
31 Electrical engineer (abbr.)
32 Symbol for tantalum.
34 Sweet secretion (pl.).
35 Nautical.
36 Indian Army (abbr.).
38 Symbol for tellurium.
39 Repairs.
41 Fountain.
43 Sun god.
44 European food fish.
46 One who apes.
48 I am (contr.).
50 Emmet.
52 Tuned again.
54 Eucharistic wine vessel.
55 Thailand.
57 Carries.
58 To irritate.
59,60,61 Greeting common today (pl.).

Answer to Previous Puzzle

VERTICAL
1 Imprison
2 Tapestry.
3 Born.
4 Pronoun.
5 Gravel.
6 Over (poet.).
7 Mend.
9 Mystic syllable.
10 Louse egg.
11 Part of ruminant's stomach, used as food.
12 Ship's steering apparatus.
14 Specter.
15 Golf mound.
18 Standing room only (abbr.).
19 To dibble.
22 Surgical perforations of the skull.
24 One who rotates.
27 Eagle's nest.
29 Black corvine bird.
30 Entirely.
33 Crafty.
37 Small island.
39 Craze.
40 Drone bee.
41 Supplied with nourishment.
42 Timekeeper
43 Headstrong.
45 English school.
46 Afresh.
47 Footlike part.
49 Entangles.
51 Light knock.
53 American Indian.
54 Constellation.
56 Military police (abbr.).
58 Symbol for iron.

NEW ERA PATTERNS

QUICK-TO-SEW PINAFORE APRON
MARIAN MARTIN
PATTERN 9931

If you like to sew, yet like to finish quickly, make a Marian Martin Apron! You have your choice of two styles in Pattern 9931—apron A is like a child's pinafore with contrasting ruffles at the shoulders and hem. Don't you like the ric-rac "border" on the center panel? In apron B, which is made all of one fabric, the ruffles are omitted and the pockets and center panel outlined with ric-rac. A third version, apron C, may use narrow ruffle trim on the bodice and pockets. Make this apron up in perky cotton . . . it's so practical for work because the back bodice buttons together!

Pattern 9931 may be ordered only in sizes small (32-34), medium (36-38) and large (40-42). Small size, view A, requires 1⅞ yards 35 inch fabric and 5-8 yard contrast; view B, 2⅜ yards 35 inch fabric and 2⅞ yards ric-rac.

Here's exciting news! The Marian Martin Spring Pattern Book is ready — ready and waiting to give your wardrobe a gay Spring Fling! It's the smartest collection of simple-to-use patterns we've ever presented, with stunning Ensembles . . . vivacious Sportswear . . . the new softer tailoreds . . . gay Cottons and Prints . . . Evening and Wedding fashions . . . clothes for the Junior Miss and the Pigtail Set . . and slimming Matron modes. Order a copy TODAY!

Send fifteen cents in coin for this pattern. Write plainly your name, address and style number. Be sure to state size. This New Fashion Pattern Book is fifteen cents extra.

Address all orders for Pattern and Fashion Books to Pattern Department, Lancaster New Era, 232 West Eighteenth street, New York, N. Y.

SEES NO FEAR OF DEPRESSION

E. J. Flynn Says Nations Will Need U. S. Supplies.

NEW ORLEANS, Jan. 1.—(AP)—The United States has little cause to fear a post-war depression in the opinion of Edward J. Flynn, chairman of the Democratic National committee, here today to see his alma mater, Fordham University, in its Sugar Bowl tilt with Missouri.

The fact that the United States experienced a business depression following the last world war, he declared in an interview, does not mean that the same result should follow this war.

"It's not the same kind of war," he said. "In the last war nearly all the destruction was in France. Now it's all over Europe and a large part of Asia. Who can supply all the materials for reconstruction? Only the United States."

He asserted he thought the United States' economic position was strong enough to make it unnecessary to worry about how war-stricken countries could pay for the things they needed.

"There have always been people saying we're going to hell in a hand basket," he said.

Flynn declared that political parties were the logical organizations for promoting the sale of defense bonds and stamps and the organization of civilian defense.

"We'll never get way from our two-party system in America and wouldn't want to see it happen," he continued. "It's the basis of our governmental system."

LANCASTER NEW ERA

WEATHER
Snow flurries in mountains; colder tonight. (Details on Page 3).

Examiner Founded 1830. New Era Founded 1877.
Published Every Evening Except Sunday by New Era Company. Entered as Second Class Matter at Post Office, Lancaster, Pa.
LANCASTER, PA., FRIDAY, JANUARY 2, 1942 — CITY EDITION — 20 PAGES—160 COLUMNS—THREE CENTS

MANILA AND NEARBY CAVITE NAVY BASE TAKEN BY JAPS

Sale of Autos Halted, 1,000 Are Held Here

Rationing System for New Cars Will Start Jan. 15; 300 to 400 Local Salesmen Laid Off; All Production Will Be Stopped and Plants Used for War Materials

Sale of new passenger cars and trucks was prohibited throughout the United States today under government orders mobilizing the entire American automobile industry for war production only.

The new cars and trucks now in stock with dealers will be sold only to government, lend-lease and the most essential civilian users, the order said, and plans are being speeded to establish a rationing system to handle distribution of these cars.

The rationing system is expected to be in operation by Janary 15 and if set up under present plans it would be administered in Lancaster by the Commodity Allocation committee, Paul A. Mueller, chairman; Dr. Arthur P. Mylin and Clyde E. Gerberich.

Mueller said this morning that his committee has received no official word that his group will ration the automobiles but that he "had a feeling" it will be assigned the task. The committee earlier this week appointed members of the eight tire rationing boards.

1,000 New Cars Here

A survey of the leading dealers revealed that the city and county has on hand approximately 1,000 new automobiles, fully equipped. Some distributors called their salesmen into conference, gave them two weeks pay and told them to go out and find jobs in defense industries.

It is estimated that between 300 and 400 salesmen in the Lancaster area were laid off this morning. In most cases distributors retained one salesman. In addition, the sales staffs of the wholesale dealers serving the local area out of Philadelphia were dismissed.

To Close Salesrooms At 6 P. M.

Members of the Lancaster Automobile Trade Association in session this afternoon agreed to close all sales rooms at 6 P. M. daily. This will not include the service departments.

Service departments of the garages will continue to function as usual and in most cases the dwindling supply of second hand cars will be handled by the heads of distributing firms themselves and a skeleton crew. Some dealers in dismissing their sales staffs told them to "get into defense and then come back as soon as the war has been won."

Action Seen Shortening War

Sidney Hillman, associate OPM director, predicted today at Washington, that complete utilization of the automobile industry's machines and men "might shorten

(See AUTOS—Page 15)

No Rationing Jobs

The Commodity Allocation committee this afternoon issued a plea to the public to refrain from appealing to members of the various boards for jobs and for detailed information.

There are no paying jobs avilable and no detailed information, the committee said. The public will be kept informed through the newspapers as rapidly as instructions are received.

TIRE RATIONING PLANS SPEEDED

Application Blanks Arrive For 8 Local Boards; Start System Monday.

Application blanks for prospective purchasers of automobile and truck tires and tubes have been received by Lancaster County's Commodity Allocation committee, it was announced today.

Paul A. Mueller, chairman, said the blanks are being distributed to the eight tire rationing boards as quickly as possible. The rationing system starts on Monday.

Mueller said his office is being deluged with calls for information and that the organization is being pushed to completion so that the eight boards named earlier this week, will be ready to start functioning Monday.

Questions to be answered by the

(See TIRES—Page 15)

JAIL ESTES 3 MOS. IN AUTO DEATH HERE

David M. Estes, 60-year-old Belair, Md., lumber dealer, convicted of involuntary manslaughter by a jury that recommended mercy at the September term of Criminal Court, and who subsequently was denied a new trial, was fined $300 and costs and sentenced to three months in the county prison by Judge C. V. Henry this afternoon.

The charge, brought by Policeman Howard Snyder, grew out of a truck-auto collision June 17 at Prince and Orange streets in which Frank A. Wills, seventy, of Germantown, chairman of the board of the Supplee-Wills-Jones Milk Company, Philadelphia, was injured fatally.

W. Hensel Brown, attorney for Estes, made a plea for leniency on the grounds that his client was of good repute and was now engaged in defense work.

F. D. HITS FIRING OF ALIEN WORKERS

WASHINGTON, Jan. 2—(AP)—President Roosevelt urged all private employers today to adopt a "sane policy" regarding employment of aliens and foreign-born citizens.

He said in a formal statement he was "deeply concerned" over reports, in increasing number, of employers discharging workers who happened to be aliens and in some instances foreign-born citizens.

"This is a very serious matter," he declared. "It is one thing to safeguard American industry, and particularly defense industry, against sabotage; but it is very much another to throw out of work honest and loyal people who, except for the accident of birth, are sincerely patriotic."

The Scribbler

LANDIS KOFROTH, of Chester St., went to Marietta the other day to install some plumbing at the army supply depot. After several hours hard work he remarked that he wished he knew where to find a drink of water.

"That's the water boy over there—the fellow with the pressure pump on his back," somebody explained.

"Oh I saw him, but I thought he was the fire warden," Landis replied.

MANILA, CAPITAL OF PHILIPPINES, OCCUPIED BY JAPANESE FORCES

Manila, which the U. S. War Department announced today was occupied by Japanese invasion forces, is shown above. The river front and business district, depicted in the picture, were repeatedly bombed by the Japanese after the capital had been declared an "open city" in an effort to save the population from attack. However, the American and Filipino forces continued to battle the Japanese on several fronts on Luzon Island of which Manila is the largest city.

BROKE PROMISE TO WED, JAILED

Man Who Showed Court License 7 Weeks Ago Is Held in Contempt.

Joseph Cummings, twenty-nine, Paradise R. 1, who appeared in court seven weeks ago and displayed a license to wed Edith Brown, twenty-three, Kirkwood R. 1, the mother of his three children, today was jailed for contempt. He had failed to use the license.

Cummings had been brought into court several times for failure to pay an $8 support order. He had promised to marry the mother of his children but failed to do so and on November 14 he was directed to appear in court with evidence of the marriage.

On that day, Cummings produced the marriage license and informed the Court that they planned to be married in Gap on Friday, November 21. "I hope you get along fine," Judgel Appel told the couple as he extended the hearing indefinitely. Assistant District Attorney John L. Hamaker suggested the ceremony be performed in court then and there.

Again Promises To Marry

This morning, Cummings and his promised bride, who held the youngest of the children in her arms, appeared in court.

"I understand you have not married, neither have you paid anything toward the support of the children since you were here last. Is that true?" Judge Appel asked Cummings.

"Yes sir. But I'll marry her this

(See COURT—Page 17)

COUNTY COUPLE GETS FIRST '42 LICENSE

The first marriage license of 1942 was issued to Everett P. Frey, Millersville R1, and Esther W. Smtih, 129 North Fifth street, Columbia, who were married New Year's Day at Stehman's U. B. church, Manor township.

William Wagner, assistant clerk of the Orphans' Court, granted the license a day in advance when he learned the marriage plans. He dated it January 1.

British Take Bardia, Free 1,000 Prisoners

Libyan Port's Axis Garrison Falls to Tank Troops and RAF; Russians Speed on Despite Hitler's Arrival at Smolensk

(By the Associated Press)

British and South African troops have captured Bardia and released 1,000 British prisoners who were held there by the Libyan port's Axis garrison, it was announced from Cairo today.

The announcement came in a special GHQ communique, which said the Britons were released when Bardia's citadel was taken.

Capture of the port, near the Libyan-Egyptian frontier and some 300 miles east of the main British spearhead now engaging the bulk of Axis African forces at Agedabia, came after an intensive attack lasting several days in which the South Africans were supported by British tanks and artillery and the RAF.

In addition to releasing the British prisoners, the capture of Bardia also resulted in the seizure of more than 1,000 German and Italian troops.

"The number of enemy prisoners taken is not yet known," said the special communique, "but our casualties are reported to be light."

(Apparently the Allies yet have the task of reducing pocketed Axis resistance in the Salum area on the Libyan-Egyptian border. Today's Italian communique said Italian troops were still holding out at Salum, south of Bardia, and in the Halfaya area, between Salum and Bardia, "as a threat to British supply lines westward from Egypt.)

Hitler At Russian Front

Russia's Red armies were reported smashing today at German-held Mozhaisk, the last of the great

(See BARDIA—Page 18)

SNOW AND COLD IN MIDWEST

Mercury in High 40's Here, But Colder Weather Is Forecast.

Temperatures were in the high 40's here today as the midwest dug out of a traffic-blocking snowfall, with temperatures below or near zero.

Snow flurries yesterday turned to rain last night, but today a bright sun was shining. A strong northwest wind started blowing during the night and continued throughout the forenoon.

Colder weather is forecast for the local area tonight.

Generally the snow which swept over the mid-continent New Year's day had ended. Movement of the storm was a wartime, military secret guarded by the Weather Bureau.

Road crews in Iowa, one of the states hardest hit, attacked snow which reached 18 inches on the level and much deeper in wind-whipped drifts. Sioux City had the

(See WEATHER—Page 17)

FIRE AT HOME NEAR SMHTHVILLE

Fire of undetermined origin destroyed a small wash house at the home of George Snyder, on the Smithville-New Providence road, shortly before noon today. The main dwelling is of stone construction and was saved.

The wash house was destroyed and heat cracked several windows in the dwelling.

The Quarryville and Willow Street Fire companies responded.

JAIL NAZI SPIES FOR LONG TERMS

Alien Who Stole Bombsight Secret Gets 20 Yrs.; 3 Women Sentenced.

NEW YORK, Jan. 2.—(AP)—Prison sentences ranging up to 20 years were imposed today on 33 members of a fantastically-operated spy ring which networked the world in gathering and delivering all kinds of military, commercial and industrial intelligence to Germany.

Judge Mortimer W. Byers, sitting in Brooklyn Federal Court where 14 members of the ring were convicted of espionage December 12 after a 14-weeks trial, sentenced them and 19 others including three women who previously had pleaded guilty.

They were charged specifically with failure to register as agents of the German Reich and with conspiracy to deliver vital American defense secrets to Germany. Maximum possible sentence on the two counts was 22 years.

3 Women Jailed

Judge Byers sentenced the women defendants as follows:

Lilly Barbara Carola Stein, 38,

(See SPIES—Page 15)

$500 PICNIC FUND GIVEN TO RED CROSS

Employes of the United States Asbestos Division plant, Manheim, will not hold a picnic this summer.

The $500 from the canteen fund, usually used for the picnic, was turned over today to the Lancaster Chapter of the American Red Cross for the War Relief Fund. The contribution was credited to the Manheim chapter.

CITY DEFENDED FOR 25 DAYS

Manila Was Hit Hard By Bombing Since First Attack Dec. 10.

(By The Associated Press)

Manila, prime prize of the Philippines, came to its darkest hour clamped hard in the vice of a Japanese military machine pledged to wrest from the United States her most distant outpost in the Pacific.

Already the Philippine capital which rose from poverty to a flourishing position as a trade center since the Spaniards handed it over to the United States in 1898 had been hit hard from the air.

Its ancient buildings of the old Spanish days lie in blackened ruins and many of its citizens are dead or wounded from the rain of bombs loosed by the Japanese after the city was declared undefended and stripped of its guns.

The Japanese, at first timing their drive against Manila to celebrate its capture on the New Year's holiday, were thrown off schedule by the valiant Filipino and American resistance which wiped out one landing party in the Lingayen gulf during the first week of the war, repulsed others and confined three to the areas around Vigan, 200 miles north of Manila; Aparri, 250 miles north of the Capital, and Legaspi, 250 miles southeast of the city.

Bombing Started Dec. 10

The Japanese were slow — in comparison with the terrifying suddenness of the raids on Dec. 7 against Hawaii—in opening up on Manila. They bombed military bases up and down the Philippines on the day after hostilities opened, but it was not until two days afterward—Dec. 9—that the air raid sirens sounded and it was not

(See MANILA DEFENSE—Page 6)

NO ALIEN'S FIREARMS TURNED IN HERE

The Federal order to aliens to turn all firearms, cameras, radio transmitters and short wave receivers to police has brought no response here so far, officials said. They have until 11 P. M. to comply with the order.

Some radio dealers said that a few aliens have brought their radio receivers to the repair shops and ordered the short wave receiving circuits removed so that only the normal broadcast can be picked up.

It is estimated that there are about 1,500 unnaturalized persons who were born in Axis countries. There are no Japanese here.

FORMER LOCAL MAN ON PRUSA IS SAFE

John A. Long, 754 Poplar street, has learned that his grandson, Joseph Cannon, who was aboard the S. S. Prusa when the ship was torpedoed at sea, has been saved. Cannon, a former resident of Lancaster, was adrift in a lifeboat for nine days.

Cannon was taken to Honolulu where he is now in a hospital. Previously he was reported as lost.

The Cannon family left Lancaster about seven years ago and went to New York.

U. S. Forces Continue Last Ditch War Along Bay and in Jungles

MacArthur Consolidates Defense Army on Luzon Island; Fall of Capital Will Not Lessen Resistance, War Department Declares

WASHINGTON, Jan. 2. — (AP) — Manila and the nearby Naval Base of Cavite fell to the Japanese today.

Both places, the War and Navy departments said, had been evacuated of military and naval supplies and equipment before advance units of the enemy arrived.

"The loss of Manila, while serious, has not lessened the resistance to the Japanese attacks," the War Department said.

At Manila all military installations were removed or destroyed when the capital of the Philippines was declared an open city, and all troops, both Filipino and United States, were removed, the War Department said.

The Navy said all equipment, records and stores not destroyed by Japanese bombers had been removed from Cavite, but that the Naval Hospital personnel remained to care for the wounded.

All industrial and supply facilities, including fuel, were destroyed.

The advanced units of the Japanese entered Manila at 3 P. M. (1 A. M., E. S. T., the War Department said.

The Navy had more than $25,000,000 worth of property and supplies on hand in the Philippines in June this year, most of it centered around Cavite.

This total does not consider how much material had been sent there from June 30 to the opening of hostilities December 7. Neither did it include the value of planes and ships and other fighting equipment.

(In Tokyo, the Japanese declared officially that General Douglas MacArthur's defense forces had fallen back to the Fortress Island of Corregidor and the mountainous Batan peninsula for a "last stand after giving up Manila.

(Domei reported that the general, himself, had moved to the heavily-armed fortress island of Corregidor at the entrace to Manila Bay.

(Tokyo declared the American forces were kept under repeated air attack as they crossed to the island,

(See MANILA—Page 6)

Series of Forts Along Manila Bay Are Prepared for Long Siege

WASHINGTON, Jan. 2—(AP)—The loss of Manila today left General Douglas MacArthur's unified remaining forces within a great arc north and northwest of the city with Manila Bay, the South China Sea and the fixed fortifications at the entrance of the bay to their rear.

The abandonment of the $9,500,000 Cavite Naval Base to the southwest of the Philippine capital indicated that all major resistance to the Japanese would now be centered to the north, on terrain presumably chosen by General MacArthur as lending itself to defensive warfare.

Prepared for a long siege, the fixed fortifications on the bay are Fort Mills, on Corregidor Island, and outlying Forts Hughes, Drum and Frank, on smaller islands.

Manila's fall came just 18 days, after the Japanese, in overwhelming numbers, landed their first mass invasion force on the shores of Lingayen Gulf, some 120 air miles north of the capital.

The morning of December 22 a flotilla of 80 enemy transports was sighted there, the gateway to the valley avenue of approach of the capital.

Almost simultaneously another heavy force landed at Atimonan on the Pacific coast some 75 miles southeast of Manila, and the defenders were forced to divide their forces to deal with the separate jaws of a great pincer.

Since the first Japanese attacks on December 7, General MacArthur's air fields had been

(See FORTS—Page 6)

War Bulletins

26 NATIONS OPPOSING AXIS PLEDGE FULL RESOURCES, NO SEPARATE PEACE

Washington, Jan. 2.—(AP)—Twenty-six nations of the new and old worlds have formally pledged themselves, the White House announced today, to employ their full resources against the Axis powers, and to enter into no separate armistice or peace. President Roosevelt signed for the United States and Prime Minister Winston Churchill for Great Britain.

WAVELL SLATED FOR PACIFIC COMMAND

Canberra, Jan. 2.—(AP)—The Australian Associated Press said today it was learned authoritatively that General Sir Archibald Wavell, British Commander for India and Burma, would be placed in command of land, sea and air forces in the Pacific.

Youth Will Serve

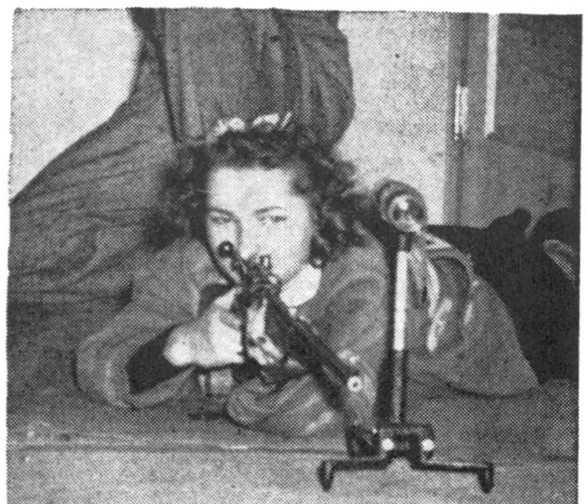

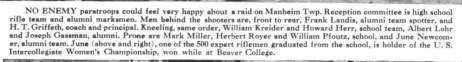

NO ENEMY paratroops could feel very happy about a raid on Manheim Twp. Reception committee is high school rifle team and alumni marksmen. Men behind the shooters are, front to rear, Frank Landis, alumni team spotter, and H. T. Griffeth, coach and principal. Kneeling, same order, William Kreider and Howard Herr, school team, Albert Lohr and Joseph Gassman, alumni. Prone are Mark Miller, Herbert Royer and William Pfoutz, school, and June Newcomer, alumni team. June (above and right), one of the 500 expert riflemen graduated from the school, is holder of the U. S. Intercollegiate Women's Championship, won while at Beaver College.

YESTERDAY'S NEWS isn't dead. It's important in the role of waste paper for war industry. Here Troop 5 Scouts, including Bill Snyder, John Stehman and Paul Shotzberger, show how troop collected, weighed, baled and sold 40 tons in four years.

AMERICA FIGHTS BEST with its back to the wall. That's the way city school pupils are learning to take air raids in drills which are run through much more seriously than fire drills these days. Here's how students at Reynolds Junior H. S. will line up in case the sirens blow in earnest—against the walls, and away from doors and open spaces where flying glass would be a peril. Younger pupils march into the auditorium where they sing to keep occupied. Similar drills are being held in all city schools.

TEEING OFF at the Lancaster Municipal Airport is Helen Jones, who won't get far off the ground in this new "plane" recently installed. It's a "wind tee," bright yellow indicator of wind direction for days when the regulation "sock" is hard to see. All local flying is confined to within 10 miles of the airport unless special permission is granted by the CAA.

KINDERGARTEN STUFF is the chart of airplanes shown at the window through which James Lamey watches. Scoutmaster Clyde Kauffman says his boys, who have made airplanes a troop hobby, "have forgotten more about planes than most observers ever knew."

OUTPOST for defense of Lancaster is New Holland aircraft observation station, where Boy Scouts who would know a B-19 or a Messerschmitt on sight work under supervision of adults. Here James Wenger marks down details while Ralph Grubb and Richard Strong call off number and type of planes and direction of flight. Models made themselves aid their observation.

LANCASTER NEW ERA

WEATHER
Fair and much colder tonight. (Details on Page 3).

Examiner Founded 1830. New Era Founded 1877.
Published Every Evening Except Sunday by New Era Company. Entered as Second Class Matter at Post Office, Lancaster, Pa.
LANCASTER, PA., SATURDAY, JANUARY 10, 1942 — CITY EDITION — 14 PAGES—112 COLUMNS—THREE CENTS

JAPS ARE 240 MILES FROM SINGAPORE

SEEK 2 MORE WITNESSES TO FATAL CRASH

Speed of Truck and Exact Position of Bus Still Being Investigated.

1ST OF 3 FUNERALS HELD THIS AFTERNOON

Two additional persons, believed to have been eye-witnesses to the bus-truck crash which caused the deaths of three persons at the entrance to Maple Grove park Thursday night are being sought by Motor Police.

The three young people who escaped being run down by the burning truck which killed their two campanions while waiting to board the bus after ice skating, told police that a man and woman were standing nearby just before the crash. In the excitement they disappeared.

The bus driver, lone occupant of the Maple Grove "ice special" died at the wheel from injuries and burns.

"Accidental Death" Certificate

Dr. A. V. Walter, county coroner, said that he has issued death certificates for Betty Landis, fifteen, 152 East James street; Jack Kuhn, sixteen, 438 South Shippen street, the two skaters run down by the flaming truck, and for Robert Schulmeister, thirty-five, 632 East Fulton street, driver of the bus. Each certificate is marked "accidental death."

The coroner said his investigation has not been completed and his future action will depend largely upon the finding of the two additional eye-witnesses to the actual crash.

No Inquest Planned

Dr. Walter said he will not hold any inquest into the fatal crash.

Dr. Walter said yesterday that "If the bus driver was making a left turn from the pike as indicated by several stories obtained by police, then he was to blame for the crash" The coroner pointed out that with the bus driver dead authorities are handicapped in piecing together the story.

The funeral of the bus driver was held today. Miss Landis will be buried tomorrow and Kuhn will be buried Monday.

Sergeant W. E. Price, of the State Motor Police, in charge of the investigation quizzed Claude Warner, 224 South Queen street, York, driver of the truck which overturned and burned after crashing with the bus. Price said he learned that Warner, who escaped injury, had 16 hours sleep during the 24 hours preceding the crash. Warner only recently received a ci-

(See CRASH—Page 11)

LEBANON POLICEMAN, EX-PATROLMAN HELD IN ROBBERY CASE

WASHINGTON, Jan. 10 — (AP) — Henry Charles Nestor, 33, a former policeman who was arrested at Lebanon, Pa., has been charged with being a "principal in a robbery by pre-arrangement."

He was taken into custody Thursday night and charged along with Policeman Charles A. Scott, 37; An-Anthony P. Passero, 36-year-old cab driver, and Harry E. Thomas, 39.

The warrants alleged that the others took $900 from Nestor last summer when he was a collection agent for a laundry. Records showed that Nestor had reported that a man jumped on the running board of his car August 30, produced a pistol and took the money from him. Nestor also is under indictment on a charge of breaking into two laundry branches. Patrolman Scott holds a bravery medal.

2 POLICE CRUISERS IN MINOR CRASHES

The two city police radio cruisers figured in minor accidents caused by slippery condition of streets early today.

A cruiser manned by Policemen Resh and Sandoe skidded into a Yellow taxi cab operated by John Henry Dieter, 134 Broad street, on Chester street, between Rockland and Duke streets at 1:25 A. M.

A car driven by Russel M. Hamilton, York, skidded into the rear of a cruiser manned by Policemen Reading and Baltasser at Duke and Chestnut streets at 1:45 A. M.

MOUNTVILLE YOUTH MAY HAVE TETANUS

Kenneth Hendricks, twelve, son of Mr. and Mrs. Raymond Hendricks of Froelich avenue, Mountville, was admitted to the General hospital at 10:30 A. M. today to be placed under observation for tetanus.

Hendricks, while skiing last Sunday, fell and cut his left knee. He was treated by a physician and remained home all week, although the injury was not considered serious, Dr. A. J. Greenleaf, Mountville, was summoned last night and he ordered his removal to the hospital. He was taken to the institution by Elmer S. Hartman, a neighbor.

Lone Survivor

William H. Chesteen, of Waterford, Conn., master of the U. S. Army minesweeper Arnold, who was the sole survivor of the 98-foot craft's crew of 11 when it foundered about 20 miles off the Isles of Shoals while being towed to port. Chesteen was picked up by another minesweeper and brought to Camp Langdon Post Hospital, Portsmouth, N. H. The 10 casualties were believed to be all civilian employes of the Quartermaster Corps.

CANCEL ALL '42 GOLF TOURNEYS

U. S. Association Calls Off Open, Amateur and Women's Events.

NEW YORK, Jan. 10—(AP) — The United States Golf association today cancelled all of its 1942 national championships, including the Open, the Amateur, the Women's Title event and the Poblic Links' tournament.

While cancelling all of its national championships, the USGA said it would not take any action on sectional tournaments, leaving that to sectional officials to determine.

Joe Dey, secretary of the USGA, pointed out that the action would have no effect on the winter tournaments, since they are controlled largely by the Proffessional Golfers' association. Both organizations, however, are working together on exhibitions for the benefit of various War Relief funds, he said.

The USGA amended its by laws to permit amateur golfers to receive up to $100 in defense bonds as prize money in any tournament. Heretofore, amateurs won only trophies. Approval also was given for three nation-wide one-day tournaments to be played May 30, July 4 and Sept. 7 as part of the "Hail America" physical program.

The three tournaments will be held on a medal play handicap basis at the associations member clubs. The USGA suggested a nominal entry fee be charged to take care of prize monies and expenses with all the surplus being turned over to the American Red Cross.

NO CHANGE AT HERSHEY

HARRISBURG, Jan. 10—(AP)—Officials of the Hershey Open Golf Tournament said today that the decision of the U. S. Golf Association to cancel its tournaments this year would not affect the annual links event here since it is held in cooperation with the Professional Golfers association.

HUMOROUS GAG USED ON BRITISH

CHUNGKING, Jan. 10.—(AP) — There was one humorous twist to the Japanese propaganda tactics in the siege of Hongkong, which fell Christmas Day.

Loudspeakers blaring from somewhere across the harbor frequently played such tunes as "Home Sweet Home" and "Swanee River," presumably to try to make the garrison — of Britons, Canadians and Indians—homesick.

INCOME TAX EXEMPTIONS MAY BE CUT

10 P. C. Increase in Farm Parity Price-Fixing Levels Is Sought.

CIVIL DEFENSE MAY COST HALF-BILLION

Developments in Washington are:

Still lower income tax exemptions likely in hunt for new war funds.

Government outlay of half-billion dollars seen for basic civilian defense needs; directorship dispute before conference group.

Farm Senators propose raising parity levels by 10 P. C. after winning an initial decision on farm products price fixing.

WASHINGTON, Jan. 10.—(AP) — The Treasury was reported today to have proposed substantially smaller individual income tax exemptions as one of many methods of bringing in $9,000,000,000 additional revenue proposed by President Roosevelt in the new budget.

Lowering of the present $1,500 exemption for married persons to $1,000, and reduction of the present $750 exemption for a single person to $500 was said to have been discussed in a preliminary conference of Democratic and Republican legislators with Secretary of the Treasury Morgenthau and his advisors yesterday.

Some members of the Senate Finance committee said, however, that these suggested changes would provide only relatively small portions of the $7,000,000,000 the President has requested in general taxes. About $2,000,000,000 in additional social security taxes is expected to be asked in separate legislation later.

Some members of Congress began discussing the practicability of payroll or sales taxes. Others advocated increased excise levies on such commodities as liquor, tobacco and gasoline.

Senator Taft (R-Ohio), a member of the Senate Finance committee, said it was becoming evident that either a withholding tax—

(See WASHINGTON—Page 9)

NEW FRIGID WAVE IS FORECAST AFTER OVERNIGHT RESPITE

A new cold wave was reported moving this way today after an overnight respite in which temperatures failed to hit zero or below for the first time in four days. Much colder weather is forecast for tonight.

The City Water Works reported a low of 11 degrees above zero—21 degrees higher than the low reading in the previous 24 hours when the temperature dropped to an official 10 degrees below zero. Ephrata reported a low of 14.

A light snow fell during the night. Towards noon the temperature rose above the 20-degree mark, but then started dropping.

2 DAYLIGHT BILLS MUST BE ADJUSTED

WASHINGTON, Jan. 10. — (AP)— The House and Senate were at odds today on a daylight saving time bill to conserve electricity for war production.

The Senate last Wednesday passed a measure permitting President Roosevelt to advance clocks as much as two hours whenever and wherever he saw fit. Yesterday the House adopted a bill to set clocks ahead one hour, all over America, until six months after the war, leaving the President no discretion.

The differences are expected to be settled in a conference committee.

Plane Watchers Battle Bitter Cold

Typical of the ingenuity displayed by spotters of the Air Raid Precaution Service here is Post 34-A, on the Amos Witmer farm between Safe Harbor and Letort, sponsored by the Society of the 28th Division. The post is an old truck body, with a glass-enclosed observation tower built on it. A coal stove serves to keep the spotters warm these bitter nights. However, frost on the glass often makes it necessary to open the windows. Manning the tower, left to right: Peter Simone, R. J. Munster, and Albert Blank.

MORE SPOTTERS ARE NEEDED

Precaution Service Members Called "Unsung Heroes of This War."

Tales of ingenuity, dogged determination and sacrifice are being told as several hundred men and women keep watch at the county's 27 Air Raid Precaution Service posts 24 hours per day as a safeguard against enemy planes.

Many and ingenious are the ways the men and women devised to protect themselves from the winter's most severe cold wave this week as the mercury dropped as low as 10 below zero. The task of keeping guard at night has been assigned to men thus far while women and Boy Scouts contribute their bit during the daylight hours.

Each air raid spotter pays his own expenses, carries his own bucket of coal to the lookout shack, wears out his own tires which can't be replaced and pays for his own gasoline.

"They are the first unsung heroes of this war," according to Captain John M. Groff, chief liason officer. "Serving without credit or praise they are sticking to their posts with a patriotic loyalty that will be told many times when this war is over."

It is the hope of the Air Raid Precaution Service to eventually have not less than 42 persons to each post. That will permit each person to serve a four hour stretch per week. If more can be enrolled, then the watchers will have companions for the night vigils.

More spotters are needed at once to man several of the posts more adequately. One post near Colum-

(See SPOTTERS—Page 11)

Reports of Revolt in Germany Force Official Nazi Denial

Correspondents Called from Bed by Foreign Office to Deny Revolution Stories; Berlin Admits, However, Russian Situation Is Critical as Reds Sweep On

SOMEWHERE on the German Frontier, Jan. 10—(AP)—Advices reaching this border point state that persistent reports of incipient revolution in Germany following increasing reverses on the Eastern front have impelled the Nazi Foreign Office to make a middle of the night denial.

Foreign correspondents one night this week were called from bed to be told individually by telephone of the reports, which the Foreign Office attributed to British and American sources, and to hear the official denial.

While correspondents themselves could confirm that no open or organized revolutionary movement existed in Berlin, some expressed surprise that the stories created so much concern in Wilhelmstrasse that an immediate denial was considered necessary.

The German press, now acknowledging the seriousness of the situation on the Eastern front, has denied, however, reports that the Germans are building a defense line along the Oder river in Eastern Germany.

Claim All Is Quiet

In a back-handed way, the Berlin Radio broadcast a dispatch from Bucharest to show that all was quiet in Berlin itself.

"Rumors of growing dissatisfaction in Germany, spread by Anglo-American propaganda, were launched in the hope of influencing the forthcoming (Pan-American) conference at Rio De Janeiro, according to the Berlin correspondent of the Rumanian news-

(See GERMANY—Page 9)

GRAIN ELEVATOR LOSS $2,250,000

G-men to Probe 2 Blasts at Superior, Wis.; 1,500,000 Bus. of Wheat Burn.

SUPERIOR, Wis., Jan. 10—(AP)— Two explosions, followed by fire, destroyed the Great Northern Railroad's elevator X, giant grain storage plant, today with loss estimated at $2,250,000. Seven persons, including two firemen, were injured fighting the blaze in subzero temperatures.

Firemen were trying to prevent the blaze from speading to other elevators and oil storage and coal docks in the heart of the city's vital lakefront defense production section.

The fire was fanned by a high wind and all buildings in the area were threatened.

The first explosion rocked the building, injuring five employes.

(See ELEVATOR—Page 11)

Giant Tanks Force British Back 50 Mi.

CRUDE RUBBER CAPITAL FALL IS CLAIMED

Kuala Lumpur Reported Occupied By Do-or-Die Jungle Fighters.

SINGAPORE PERIL IS DECLARED GREAT

(By The Associated Press)

Japanese field dispatches indicated late today that British troops had abandoned Kuala Lumpur, the world's crude rubber capital, 240 miles north of Singapore, as Japanese troops advancing 50 miles in 24 hours through the Malayan "green hell" jungles reached the outskirts of the city.

There was, however, no confirmation from the British that they had yielded Kuala Lumpur.

Earlier, an official Tokyo radio broadcast declared that Japanese forces, led by monster tanks, had opened a general assault on the southern part of the city this morning.

An official German broadcast recorded by the Associated Press quoted a Domei report saying that Kuala Lumpur had been abandoned by the British but no such report came directly from the Japanese.

Another Berlin broadcast of a Tokyo dispatch said fighting was going on in the state of Negri Sembilan. It is south of Selangor on the road to Singapore, but one arm of the state juts up between Selangor and Pehang, little more than 20 miles east of Kuala Lumpur.

British Far East headquarters tersely acknowledged that battle-wearied British Imperial troops had withdrawn "farther to the south" from the latest of a series of defense lines 50 miles north of Kuala Lumpur. No details were given.

Domei, Japanese News Agency, said the Mikado's invasion forces were closing in on the city from two directions—one moving down from the northwest, the other from the north.

Domei said the north column had swept within 10 miles of Kuala Lumpur by 5 P. M. yesterday after smashing through British lines at Tanjong Malim 50 miles to the north. The northwest column was reported 15 miles from the city.

Front line dispatches said the Japanese advance was marked by the bloodiest fighting of the month-old campaign, with the invaders hurling themselves recklessly into death-trap British defense positions.

Heaviest-type Japanese tanks

(See PACIFIC WAR—Page 9)

JAPS REINFORCE ARMY IN LUZON

Artillery Duels Indicate New Offensive; U. S. Liner Is Sunk.

WASHINGTON, Jan. 10—(AP)—The War Department reported today intensive patrolling and artillery duels between the Philippine defenders and the Japanese and said heavy enemy reinforcements were being brought up.

New Jap Offensive Seen

These developments were apparently ordered in preparation for a renewed Japanese offensive drive on Luzon.

Also the department said, a considerable number of enemy vessels had appeared off the coast of the southernmost Philippine island of Mindanao, indicating the probability of additional Japanese landings there.

United States and Dutch navy announcements told of Japanese submarine and air raids in Netherlands Indies waters. Authoritative quarters in Batavia believed a ma-

(See PHILIPPINES—Page 9)

30 JAP AIR BOMBS MISS DUTCH SHIP

BATAVIA, Netherlands East Indies, Jan. 10.—(AP)—Japanese raiders striking at the oil center of Tarakan, off North Borneo, for the second straight day hurled 30 bombs at a Dutch warship in the harbor but scored no hit, the Netherlands command reported today.

Five members of the crew of a merchant ship anchored nearby were wounded slightly by one of the few bombs which came near the ship, the Dutch command added.

Witness Tells How Cruiser Sank in 3 Min.

Larry Allen, Recovered, Writes First Eye-Witness Account

Editor's note: On Dec. 16 the Associated Press received word that Larry Allen, its correspondent with the British Mediterranean fleet, was in an Alexandria hospital after having swallowed much oily water and suffered cuts and bruises in a 45-minute plunge into the sea.

Today, recovered from his injuries and permitted by British censorship to explain how he came by them, Allen tops a long list of dramatic eye-witness accounts of sea war in the Mediterranean with the following first-person account of the destruction of the British cruiser Galatea and his own narrow escape from death.

By LARRY ALLEN

ALEXANDRIA, Egypt, Jan. 10—(AP)—The British light cruiser Galatea, struck by three torpedoes from an Axis submarine, flopped over like a stabbed turtle and went down within three minutes off the Egyptian Mediterranean coast in the inky darkness just after midnight the morning of Dec. 16.

The torpedoes, launched from close range, smashed in swift succession against the Galatea's after port side, amidships and forward, tearing into her interior with loud blasts and spurting flame.

On the dying cruiser's quarterdeck I clung tenaciously to the starboard rail until the list of the ship flung me into the cold, choppy sea.

Then I battled through thick, oily scum for 45 minutes before being rescued.

(The British Admiralty announced yesterday that a submarine had sunk the 5,220-ton Galatea, but did not specify the date, place or number of casualties. The Germans claimed on Dec. 16 that they had sunk a cruiser of this class in the Mediterranean.)

Dive-Bombed For 7 Hours

We had been dive-bombed for more than seven hours on Dec. 14 while patrolling with a squadron of cruisers and destroyers off the Libyan coast, but the Galatea successfully beat off those attacks and headed eastward.

At midnight on Dec. 15 the cruiser's announcer system warned: "First-degree readiness heavy armament."

Gunners thus were ordered to stand by for expected action.

(See WITNESS—Page 9)

War Bulletins

LEVINE HELD FOR SMUGGLING ALIEN TO U. S.

New York, Jan. 10.—(A. P.) — Charles A. Levine, who flew the Atlantic as an airplane passenger in 1927, was arrested today on a Federal indictment for smuggling into the country an alien whose name was given as Edgar Scinek, alias Edward Siegel. Levine waived removal proceedings and was held in $1,000 bail.

ITALY CONFISCATES TEXAS OIL PROPERTY

Berlin, Jan. 10.—(Official Broadcast Recorded By A. P.)—The German radio broadcast a dispatch from Rome today that all property of the Texaco Oil Company in Italy had been confiscated by the state. This was said to include an extensive network of gasoline filling stations.

LANCASTER NEW ERA
Sports

All in a Nutshell

THIS must be the "open" season for rumors . . . Anyway, the latest reports have E. E. (Hooks) Mylin leaving his grid coaching post at Lafayette to take over the chief tutor's position at Yale . . . Spike Nelson quit there to take a U. S. defense job and now Mylin's name is creeping into the picture . . . But Hooks, like the late Will Rogers says he knows "only what he reads in the papers" . . . Which could mean almost anything . . .

Hooks Mylin

And another "rumor" of especial interest locally has Muhlenberg shopping around trying to find a replacement for "Doggie" Julian, its chief basketball and football coach . . . But the last time we talked with Muhlenberg authorities they were pretty well satisfied with "Doggie" . . . That, however, was before F. & M. beat his football team . . . But also before his team upset Gettysburg . . . But, anyway, there are the rumors . . . You take them for what they're worth . . .

F. & M.'s athletic teams fared well on Saturday with Shober Barr's basketeers getting off to a good start in the Eastern Pennsy League by jolting Lebanon Valley, 49 to 39 at Lebanon, while the Diplomat swimmers took Temple into camp by a 45 to 30 score at home . . . And in the Church Basketball League, the First M. E. five ran into its second straight snag when Trinity handed it a 41 to 38 setback . . . This put both teams in a tie for first place and made the League race tighter than ever.

Norm Butz

Norm Butz, former Catholic High star, scored nine points as St. Joseph's College of Philadelphia downed C. C. N. Y., 44 to 33 Saturday night in New York . . . Matches in the World's Three Cushion Billiard championship were resumed today after a layoff on Sunday . . . Babe Ruth spent the week-end in the hospital although earlier plans were to release him last Friday . . . His wife, however, says he is "getting along nicely" . . .

Jack Kramer topped Wayne Sabin, 6-0, 6-0, 6-3 to win the men's singles title in the Dixie Tennis tournament . . . Francisco Segura teamed with Kramer to win the doubles from Sabin and Gardnar Mulloy, 6-3, 14-12, 6-4 . . . Now Fat Freddie Fitzsimmons, the pitcher, has joined the list of baseball players who are bowling alley owners during the off-season . . . No doubt, all their places feature strikes . . .

St. Bede Academy of Peru, Ill., wound up the 1941 sports season with 34 consecutive victories in major sports . . . Starting last Feb. 28 when they lost in a State basketball tourney, St. Bede won three court games, 17 in baseball, eight straight in football and six more in the current cage campaign . . . Would you say "Hard to Bede?" . . . Ouch . . . GWK . . .

ALLEY BABBLE

IT'S been a long time since we heard anything from the boys out in the St. Anthony League, but now they turn up . . . and with some mighty good scores, too . . .

Heading the parade was Jim Rittenhouse who had a 159-225-241 for 625, while Bernie Fulmer had 232; Sam Madonna had 224 and Ralph Ochs 222. . . .

The boys in the Moose ABC and "B" Leagues were going right to town. . . . In the "B" League, Earl Brown hit 137 and then jumped to 257 and finished off with 239 for a 633. . . .

In the ABC circuit, the scoring was high with Dick Pfyer getting 192-236-213 for 641, while Charley Bauers had 151-211-258 for 620; and Jake Shinsky put together 212-211-196 for 619. . . . Nifty singles included Bud Deen's 224 and 218; Whitey Baumler's 224; Harry Stoe's 224 and Johhny Hale's 232. . . .

George Snyder's 233 and Pisani's 604 were the feature numbers in the L-C League while Ben Kuntz hit 225 to pace the Newpennebay circuit and Johnny Styer's 235 paced the Ladies' and Men's League. . . .

Let Hershock's 227; Les Flawd's 225 and Roy Knaisch's 225 were the big numbers in the Home League, while Kittinger's 170 topped the Keystone loop and Pete Herman's 215 featured the Lino Inspection League. . . . Morrison's 178 was high for the Lino Shop League, while Sullenberger went all the way to 255 to pace the Lino Rotary circuit. . . .

Helen Snyder's 184 took top honors for the St. Joe Ladies with Lesher's 154 leading the Hydro Ladies' duck pin circuit and Seber's 149 featuring the Odds and Ends League . . . . Kittinger's 194 was high in the Cigar League. . . .

Charley Greener hit 230, Ray Goodwin 225 and Roy Brown 223 to be the leaders in the Broad Street Men's League, while Emma Shreiner's 159 was high for the ladies. . . .

An even 200 by Hen Kern paced the Elks Duck Pin circuit with Lichty getting 217-197-226 for 640 and high honors in the Paradise Defense League where Ammon also came through with a 268 and Miller added 223. . . .

In match games, the Helm Club beat the Phalanx; the Moose Travelettes downed the Arc-Over Ladies; the Moose Travelers "A" team beat the Reading Orioles "A" outfit and the Moose "B" boys nipped the Reading "B" boys . . . . Bill Schmidt hit 646 as St. Joe beat the News. . . .

Mary Smith's 184 and 533 topped the Ephrata Owls girls, while Bair's 226 was high for the Ephrata Owls in the Lebanon Valley League. . . .

Defending Champs Running Into Trouble

Defending champions in the Big Ten basketball conference, the University of Wisconsin cagers are now running into considerable trouble after having swept through their warm-up games to run their winning streak to 20. Coached by Harold (Bud) Foster, the Wisconsin first team lines up with Kotz and Charlie Epperson at the forwards; Harold Scott at center, and Bob Alwin and Fred Rehm at the guards. Last season Wisconsin won the N. C. A. A. title.

Barons Draw Near to Bears In Hockey Race

(By The Associated Press)

A bit of drama was injected into the Cleveland conquest of New Haven in the American Hockey League last night when it became known during the game that defenseman Wilf Simon of the Eagles had been recalled by his Canadian regiment.

Even Simon's presence couldn't help New Haven win as the Barons, 1941 playoffs kings moved closer to the leading Hershey Bears in the western half standings. Simon leaves today for Army duties.

Takes Crack At Fan

Cleveland triumphed handily, 4 to 1, in a rough contest that saw 12 penalties dealt out, one of 10 minutes going to Dizzy Desilets for taking a poke at a spectator with his stick.

The Indianapolis Caps won, 5 to 1, over the Philadelphia Rockets and clung to the third rung in the western ladder with 37 points—one more than Springfield needs to hold first in the eastern sector.

Eddie Shore's Indians were the 5 to 1 victims of an aroused Buffalo six as 7,120 Bison fans watched. It was the first loss in six starts for Springfield which has an eight point drag on the second place Providence Reds.

The Rhode Island aggregatiion got two of those points Sunday night by administering the fifth defeat in six games to Ching Johnson's free skating Washington Lions, 3 to 2.

Saturday night Springfield crushed the Lions, 8 to 0, while Hershey, the western boss, was trouncing New Haven 8 to 3. Cleveland measured Philadelphia, 2 to 1, that night and Pittsburgh trimmed Providence, 4 to 3.

The standings:

CLUBS	W	L	T	Pts	goals for	goals agst
WESTERN DIVISION						
Hershey	20	6	4	44	121	74
Cleveland	20	7	2	42	94	70
Indianapolis	17	12	3	37	100	75
Buffalo	12	12	2	26	69	62
Pittsburgh	8	20	3	19	74	123
EASTERN DIVISION						
Springfield	16	10	4	36	99	75
Providence	12	15	4	28	115	111
New Haven	12	16	1	25	84	105
Washington	10	18	3	23	82	105
Philadelphia	8	19	2	18	80	118

Bowlers Halted

CHICAGO, Jan. 12—(AP)—Bowling in hundreds of Chicago's 2.500 alleys was stopped at 1 A. M. today by police, acting on orders of Police Commissioner James P. Allman who announced a decision to enforce an old ordinance closing the alleys at that hour.

In many of the city's alleys where the biggest business normally is from midnight to 3 A. M., thousands of customers were surprised to learn of the closing order.

Leaders of bowling organizations said that the ban on early morning bowling came as a complete surprise. Many alleys had been operating 24 hours a day while hundreds of others remained open from 2 to 7 A. M.

COLLEGE BASKETBALL

Season a Success at Carnegie, But Leaders Finding It a Big Headache

NEW YORK, Jan. 12—(AP)—The infant basketball season, hardly out of its rompers, already is a howling success at Carnegie Tech—but a full grown headache at Wisconsin, Dartmouth, George Washington and the University of California at Los Angeles.

The Pittsburgh Scots, who hadn't tasted victory in two solid years, finally halted their losing streak at 27 games Saturday night by defeating Case of Cleveland, 42 to 37.

However, Wisconsin, whose coach labelled his present aggregation as good as his 1941 National Collegiate champions, is resting at the bottom of the Big Ten circuit with three straight losses and for the thirty-seventh consecutive time the UCLAns have been repulsed by Southern California.

Dartmouth Upset

Dartmouth, who has held the Eastern League title almost since its present athletes were in the kindergarten, was spilled in its 1942 opener by Harvard and highly regarded George Washington bowed to Duke, the Southern League's defending champion, although Matt Zunic hammered in five baskets.

Although this week's program is spotted with vacant dates because of impending mid-year examinations, virtually every contest is of a top-flight character.

In the southwest circuit, Rice and Arkansas will determine which of the two title favorites is the better in a twin bill at Houston this week-end. Oklahoma A. and M. and Tulsa, who played second fiddle to Creighton's champions in the Missouri Valley circuit a year ago, collide at Stillwater Thursday.

The Big Ten, where four teams have subdued all their league foes, tries to remedy the situation tonight with Minnesota likely to spill unscathed Iowa; unbeaten Purdue mixing with Indiana in the Hoosier civil war; all-winning Illinois at Ohio State and Northwestern protecting its unblemished record with Michigan the guest.

2 Southern Leaders

Tennessee and Auburn are the leaders in the southern circuit and right now the Vols are sweeping out the gym for the coming of Coach Adolph Rupp and his Kentuckians. Rupp enjoys road games best when he draws at least one boo from each spectator.

Collapse of the highly regarded George Washington Colonials has lifted an unheralded William and Mary five to the top in the southern circuit, one victory ahead of Duke. The Blue Devils meet V. M. I. at Lynchburg tonight while William and Mary's big test is Tuesday against Richmond in the latter's new arena.

Wyoming and Colorado, the Big Seven favorites, each has a double task this week, the former at Brigham Young Friday and at Utah Saturday. The Buffaloes' foes are Utah State at Boulder Friday and a joust with Colorado State at Fort Collins the next night.

Kansas, along with Iowa State one of the Big Six title seekers, takes high scoring Charles Black to Missouri for the annual Tiger-Jayhawk feud on Wednesday.

Penn Plays Big Green

Only four games are billed in the eastern circuit with Columbia at Yale Wednesday and Penn attempting to give Dartmouth its second licking at Hanover the same night. Yale is at Penn and Cornell at Dartmouth on Saturday as examinations slow up the dribblers.

Southern California continued its monotonous domination over UCLA in the only league game in the southern half of the Pacific coast loop and this week tangles twice with California.

Washington's speedsters lead in the northern half and travels to Oregon State for a week-end twin bill while Oregon State entertains Washington State tonight and tomorrow.

Among the nation's independents and schools from smaller conferences, West Texas State's immense five gained further stature by downing Depaul, 60 to 43, last week.

SPORTSMEN MEET TUESDAY

Prizes for the largest spread of deer horns, heaviest pheasant, rabbit and squirrel will be awarded at the monthly meeting of the Mill Creek Sportsmen's Club to be held Tuesday evening, at 7:30 o'clock, in the Mechanicsburg Fire Company hall of Leacock. Special music will be presented. The president, Harry E. Harsh, Bareville, will preside.

Linoleum Cage League Starts Here Tonight

The Inter-Departmental basketball league of the Armstrong A. A., will get underway tonight with four games being scheduled for Biesecker gym of F. and M. College. Nine teams are entered.

The League this year decided to stage a Shaughnessy playoff among the first 4 teams at the conclusion of the regular schedule on March 9. It also decided to play halves instead of quarters. Games will be played every Monday night starting at 7 o'clock.

The teams and their managers are:

Warehouse, Herb Grau.
Yard, Milton Weidel.
Factory Clerks, David Wireback.
Asphalt-Tile, Al Spinner.
Mechanical-Cement Preparing, George Flick.
Rotary, Gordon Remley.
General Office, George Pugh.
Inspection, Pete Herman.
Central Technical Lab., Norm Johnson.

The schedule tonight follows:

7 P. M. . . . Warehouse vs. Rotary.
8 P. M. . . . Inspection vs. Mechanical-Cement.
9 P. M. . . . General Office vs. Factory-Clarks.
10 P. M. . . . Asphalt-Tile vs. Central Tech. Lab.

Hogan Best Golfer Of '41, Records Show

LOS ANGELES, Jan. 12 —(AP) — Benny Hogan was America's best professional golfer in 1941 according to the average strokes per round statistics. He was also the country's money winner.

Hogan according to figures released by the Professional Golfers Association of America today, had an average of 70.28 shots per round in tournament play. It represented 101 rounds.

In order behind the little Hershey, Pa., Texas-born pro were Sam Snead, 86 rounds, 70.70; Byron Nelson, 82 rounds, 70.92, Jimmy Demaret, 50 rounds, 71.22; Henry Picard, 35 rounds, 71.22; National Open king Crag Wood, 79 rounds, 71.26; Clayton Heafner, 85 rounds, 71.58, to list the leaders.

WANT BASKETBALL GAMES

The Burger Reserves desire games for Sundays with Class "C" teams. Get in touch with Manager Jack Licht, Jr., 511 Ruby Street, city.

Cooper's 210 Tops Pro Stars

But Many Fear Harry Will Crack in Los Angeles Finals Today

LOS ANGELES, Jan. 12—(AP)—It was Harry Cooper against the field today in the final round of the Los Angeles open and the last crack at the biggest purse on California's winter tournament trail.

The hurry-up veteran of 39 went into the finale with a two stroke lead over his brother pros, who were inclined to believe that he wouldn't have it when the curtain came down tonight.

Billed out of Minneapolis, Cooper had rounds of 69-71-70—210 for the par 72 of Hillcrest Country Club's tree lined, well trapped course. He bolstered his position yesterday after starting out on even terms with the tournament favorite, Benny Hogan, America's top money winning pro and low scorer in 1941.

Hogan Is Second

Hogan shot a creditable 72 to go with his previous 70-70 for a 54 hole score of 212.

Cooper's fellow professionals were definitely not pulling against him. But off the record, as far as their names were concerned, they feared the pressure and last round jitters would get him.

The pressure undoubtedly was on "Lighthorse Harry" but he captured this tournament in 1926 and repeated his triumph in 1937. He might hang on to the finish.

Hogan, who had an official average of 70.28 strokes in 1941, showed no trace of cracking up under the strain despite his 72.

2 Challengers

Lurking behind, and a threat to both Cooper and Hogan, were two men just three blows out of first place. They were Slammin' Sam Snead, who shared the pre-tournament honor spot with Hogan, and long hitting Jimmy Thomson, of Del Monte, who won the tournment five years ago.

Snead, of Hot Springs, Va., looked like the biggest threat. He hadn't had a hot round, but coasted into a 213 total behind rounds of 70-71-72. And still very much in contention was Horton Smith, the first round leader, with a 72 yesterday for 214.

Dudley Shoots 68

P. G. A. President Ed Dudley of Augusta, Ga., and Colorado Springs, turned in the low score for the third round—a 68—but young Chick Harbert of Battle Creek, Mich., provided the dizzy thrill. He quit the course with the puzzling score of 39-30-69 for the par 36-36-72 route. He had eight birdies and five bogies. The bogies were all on the front nine and at the seventh hole he told his caddy he was going to withdraw. Instead he stayed in, scored his eight birds and sliced six strokes off par on the back nine. It put him in the money with 215, tied with Willie Goggin of White Plains, N. Y.

Ex-National Open Champion Byron Nelson handed in a 70 for 216, and popular Denny Shute and Jimmy Demaret went into today's play at 217. Many picked Shute to get in closer to the top. Two other former National Open champs, Lawson Little and Ralph Guldahl, lagged behind, Little with 222 and Guldahl with 226. The 1941 L. A. winner, Johnny Bulla, had 225.

Local Swimmers Lose

Newark, N. J.—It's getting to be a habit with the Lancaster Swimming Club women's team—this tying point totals, but losing meets by the count of first and second places.

It happened last year against the Newark Athletic club women's squad and again Friday night at the Orange YMCA with the Watchung swimming club.

The latest occurrence was Saturday night. The Lancaster team and the Newark A. C. Nacettes met again and tied at 33-all, but that old bugaboo of tabbing first and second places once more sank the Pennsylvanians.

150 yard medley relay—First, NAC (Florence Reilly, Dorothy McElroy and Evelyn Sofield); second, LSA. Time 1:40.20.
200 yard free style—First, Charlotte Book, LSA; second, Florence Schmitt, NAC; third, Ellen Gantz, LSA. Time 2:35.30.
100 yard breast stroke—First, Pauline Globisch, LSA; second, Dorothy McElroy, NAC; third, Dorothy Grieve, NAC. Time 1:28.
50 yard free style—First, Evelyn Sofield, NAC; second, Mary C. Heckel, LSA; third, Mary Colon, LSA. Time :30.7.
100 yard back stroke—First, Florence Reilly, NAC; second, Mary Catherine Heckel, LSA; third, Charlotte Book, LSA. Time 1:15.1.
100 yard free style—First, Charlotte Book, LSA; second, Florence Schmitt, NAC; third, Irene Ashmead, LSA. Time 1:10.4.
Diving—First Dorothy Grieve, NAC; second, Imogene Mellon, NAC; third, Betty Owens, LSA. Points 39.5.
200 yard free style relay—First, LSA (Mary Colon, Pauline Globisch, Charlotte Book and Mary Catherine Heckel); second, NAC. Time 2:01.

Sportsmen To Meet

Election of officers for the ensuing year will be the principal business to be transacted at a meeting of the Federated Sportsmen of Lancaster County in the Hotel Brunswick, Friday night, at 8 o'clock.

Champ Passes Army Exam

World's heavyweight boxing champion Joe Louis, who did his bit for the Navy when he flattened Buddy Baer in a bout which benefited the Navy Relief Fund, is shown in a soldier's cap at the New York draft board number 20, where he made arrangements to have his induction papers transferred from Chicago. Joe was given his final physical examination today and passed. He will be inducted in the service Wednesday at Camp Upton.

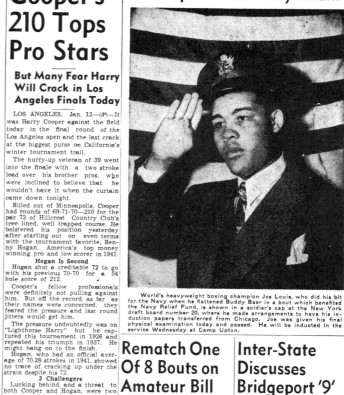

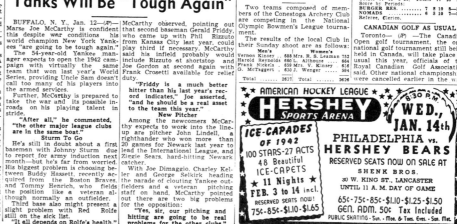

Rematch One Of 8 Bouts on Amateur Bill

As time is getting closer, the big amateur boxing show to be held for the benefit of the Red Cross on Thursday is creating more interest as the fans know what to expect when these young simon pures swing into action for this charity event.

Johnny Hauck paid a visit to Baltimore where he completed all arrangements to bring two of the leading clubs of that city here for Thursday's show.

Brother Benedict's St. Mary's boys', who always make a tremendous hit here, will have Gordon Neal, the Southern A. A. U. featherweight champ here to battle Nick Tazzi, Judd Eby's new champion who hails from New Jersey. Eby claims Tazzi is one of the best boy's he has. Tazzi and Harry Kurl put up some terrific training bouts. Eby claims it would not be surprising if Tazzi steals the show.

A club that will be making its first appearance in this city, "The Poodles A. C." of Baltimore, will be brought here by Heinie Welsh.

A bout that has created a tremendous amount of interest is the one between Kurl and Chuck Connors of the U. S. A. These two boys met at the last St. Joe show with the Army boy gaining an unpopular decision.

Coach Hauck scored a bull's eye when he secured Connors to come here for a return match with Kurl as this is one bout the fans want to see.

Another contest that is creating plenty of interest is the one between Louie Scheuchenzuber of St. Joe and Mike Stichak of the U. S. A. Stichak is a two-fisted battler who holds a decision over Kurl. The soldier is certain to give Scheuchenzuber the battle of his life. There will be 8 or more contests on the program, the first scheduled to start 8:30 P. M.

Inter-State Discusses Bridgeport '9'

WILMINGTON, Del., Jan. 12.—(AP)—Club owners and managers of the Interstate Baseball League came here today for their annual meeting, faced with the possibility that the Bridgeport (Conn) franchise will be dropped by the National League Boston Braves.

"There is some doubt about the Braves operating in Bridgeport," League President Arthur H. Ehlers of Baltimore said. Quinn (John Quinn, vice president of the Boston club) was to interview some people in Bridgeport about turning the franchise over to them but I don't know what has transpired.

"Quinn did tell me that the Boston club was not ready to place its $1,200 franchise guarantee up at the meeting."

Schedule Drawn

The 140-game schedule for the eight-team, Class B circuit's 1942 campaign has already been prepared but Ehlers said it would not be adopted until the league's membership is definitely settled.

Teams now holding franchises are Bridgeport, Wilmington, Del., a Philadelphia Athletics farm; Harrisburg, Pa., operated by the Pittsburgh Pirates; Trenton, N. J., which will work with the Phillies; Hagerstown, Md.; Allentown, Pa.; Lancaster, Pa., and Reading, Pa., owned by the Brooklyn Dodgers.

Ehlers said he believes th[illegible] will have little effect on th[illegible] unless night games are ba[illegible] conserve power.

If that should happen, h[illegible] "I don't think we could surviv[illegible]

Favor New Player Plan

The league is expected to vote for the new player setup of 12 veterans and four limited class men. Heretofore, the rules called for 10 veterans and six limited class players. It was changed at the recent minor league convention in Jacksonville, Fla.

The $2.400 a month salary limit remains the same.

Lancaster Big Five Downs Coatesville

The newly organized Lancaster Big Five, strictly an amateur quintet, ran rough shod over the Lukens team, of Coatesville, on the State Armory court, by a score of 52 to 35, Sunday afternoon.

A mere handful of fans turned out to see the amateur club make its debut but they were rewarded with some brilliant basketball on the part of the local favorites, Ehemann, Von Nedia and Emich who scored fifteen, fourteen and twelve points respectively.

Keehn, Coatesville guard, was the high scorer for the losing quintet with eleven points to his credit.

Lancaster Big Five		G	F	Tl
Emich	F	5	2	12
VonNedia	F	5	4	14
Ehemann	C	7	1	15
Bishop	G	1	1	3
Wuen'll	G	2	0	4
Graeff	G	2	0	4
Best	F	0	0	0
Totals ..		22	8	52

Lukens, Coatesville		G	F	Tl
Eagle	F	4	0	8
Jatkinson	F	0	0	0
Palmer	C	1	0	2
Markwood	C	4	0	8
Bown	G	0	0	0
Keehn	G	4	3	11
J.Entriken	F	1	0	2
A.Entriken	F	2	0	4
Totals ..		16	3	35

LANC. BIG FIVE ..... 15 17 7 13—52
LUKENS, COATESVILLE 6 6 17 6—35
Referee, Harry Hess.

Burger Five Drops First Game of Year

The L. G. M. quintet, of Coatesville, handed the Burger Catholic Club team its first setback of the season by a score of 38 to 36 on the Nevin Street court, Sunday afternoon.

Mulenek, Coatesville guard, was outstanding with five field goals and five foul goals for a total of 15 points. Kirchner, Stengle and Carpenter shared the honors for the home-town club.

In a well played preliminary tilt, the Burger Juniors won over the Nomads by a score of 33 to 26.

Burger C. C.		G	F	Tl
Flosser	F	0	0	0
Kirchner	F	4	4	12
Carpenter	C	4	1	9
Stengel	G	4	1	9
Doman	G	2	0	4
Maher	G	0	0	0
Fralich	F	1	0	2
Totals ..		15	6	36

L. G. M. Coatesville		G	F	Tl
Cosgrove	F	2	1	5
Pitcherella	F	4	0	8
Matuson	C	3	2	8
Lommey	G	1	0	2
Mulenek	G	5	5	15
Totals ..		15	8	38

Score by Periods:
L. G. M. COATESVILLE 11 14 10 3—38
BURGER C. C. ...... 0 11 14 11—36
Referee, Gavan.

Nomads		G	F	Tl
Fralich	F	2	5	9
Kuntz	F	1	0	2
Bagnolio	C	2	0	4
Segro	G	5	1	11
Totals ..		10	6	26

Burger Res.		G	F	Tl
Lytle	F	4	1	9
Licht	F	6	2	14
Trapnell	C	1	0	2
Fischer	G	4	0	8
Totals ..		15	3	33

Score by Periods:
BURGER RES. .... 7 8 10 8—33
NOMADS .... 6 3 10 7—26
Referee, Clerico.

Competes In Tourney

Two teams composed of members of the Conestoga Archery Club are competing in the National Olympic Bowmen's League tournament.

The results of the local Club in their Sunday shoot are as follows:

Men's		Women's	
Vernon Kinsey ..	688	Mrs. R. S. Leaman	752
Harold Reynolds	660	L. Althouse	664
Frank Nickels .	659	Mrs. V. Kinsey .	616
G. McTaggert .	630	J. Wenger	594
Total	2637	Total	2626

CANADIAN GOLF AS USUAL

Toronto— (AP) —The Canadian Open golf tournament, the only national golf tournament still being held in Canada, will take place as usual this year, officials of the Royal Canadian Golf Association said. Other national championships were cancelled earlier in the war.

Yanks Will Be "Tough Again"

BUFFALO, N. Y., Jan. 12—(AP)—Marse Joe McCarthy is confident this despite war conditions his world champion New York Yankees "are going to be tough again."

The 54-year-old Yankee manager expects to open the 1942 campaign with virtually the same team that won last year's World Series, providing Uncle Sam doesn't call too many of his players into the armed services.

Further, McCarthy is prepared to take the war and its possible inroads on his playing talent in stride.

"After all," he commented, "the other major league clubs are in the same boat."

Sturm To Go

He's still in doubt about a first baseman with Johnny Sturm due to report for army induction next month—but he's far from worried. His biggest problem is choosing between Buddy Hassett, recently acquired from the Boston Braves, and Tommy Henrich, who fields the position like a veteran although normally an outfielder.

Third base also might present a slight problem with Red Rolfe still on the sick list.

"It all depends on Rolfe's health," McCarthy observed, pointing out that second baseman Gerald Priddy, who came up with Phil Rizzuto from Kansas City last year, could play third if necessary. McCarthy said his infield probably would include Rizzuto at shortstop and Joe Gordon at second again with Frank Crosetti available for relief duty.

"Friddy is a much better hitter than his last year's record indicates," Joe asserted, "and he should be a real asset to the team this year."

New Pitcher

Among the newcomers McCarthy expects to work into the line-up are pitcher John Lindell, a righthander who won more than 20 games for Newark last year to lead the International League, and Ziggie Sears, hard-hitting Newark catcher.

With Joe Dimaggio, Charley Keller and George Selkirk heading the parade of clouting Yankee outfielders and a veteran pitching staff on hand, McCarthy pointed out there are two big problems for the opposition:

"Yes, sir, our pitching and hitting are going to be real problems for the other clubs."

SPORTS AT A GLANCE

MONDAY'S SPORTS EVENTS
Basketball

City-County League—
Broad Street at St. Joseph C. C.
Coral A. C. at Reamstown.
Western County League—
Columbia Union A. C. at Mt. Joy.
Mt. Joy at Elizabethtown.
Southern End Church League—
Kirkwood vs. Wrightsdale.
Mechanic Grove vs. Union.
Bi-County League—
Rossmere at New Holland.

SUNDAY'S SPORTS RESULTS
Basketball

Western County League—
Columbia North Ends 40, Mount Joy 29.
Penn State League—
Lebanon 79, York 36.
Harrisburg 45, Shamokin 37.
Other Basketball Results
Lancaster Big Five 52, Lukens of Coatesville 35.
L. G. M., of Coatesville 38, Burger C. C. 36.
Burger Reserves 33, Nomads 26.
Columbia Merchants 52, Lititz Big Five 32.
COLLEGE BASKETBALL RESULTS
St. Bonaventure 33, Ithaca 31.
ICE HOCKEY RESULTS
National League—
Montreal 2, Brooklyn 0.
Chicago 6, Detroit 5.
American League—
Cleveland 4, New Haven 1.
Indianapolis 5, Philadelphia 1.
Buffalo 5, Springfield 1.
Providence 3, Washington 2.

CHURCH LEAGUE STANDING

Teams	W.	L.	P.C.
First Methodist	7	2	.778
Trinity	7	2	.778
Broad St.	6	3	.667
St. John's	6	3	.667
Bethany	5	3	.625
St. Luke's	5	4	.556
Emmanuel	4	5	.444
St. Andrew's	4	5	.444
Memorial	4	6	.400
Church of Christ	1	8	.111
Pearl St.	0	9	.000

American Association—
Minneapolis 7, St. Louis 2.
Kansas City 4, Fort Worth 3.
Eastern Amateur League—
Boston 8, Johnstown 1.
Washington 4, New York 3.
River Vale 4, Baltimore 3.
Professional Basketball
Rochester N. Y. 40, New York Renaissance 39.

SATURDAY'S SPORTS RESULTS
Basketball

Central Pennsy H. S. League:
William Penn 41, York 35.
Eastern Collegiate League:
Franklin and Marshall 49; Lebanon Valley 39.
Albright 80, Ursinus 33.
Muhlenberg 64, Bucknell 62.
Church League:
Trinity 41, First Methodist 38.
St. Andrew's 38, Emmanuel 37.
Broad Street 48, Memorial 46.
St. John's 66, Church of Christ 36.
St. Luke's 52, Pearl Street 22.
Central Pennsy Jr. H. S. League:
Hannah Penn 34, John Reynolds 26.
Hannah Penn J-V 33, John Reynolds J-V 13.
Other Basketball Results
Lebanon Valley Frosh 34, Franklin and Marshall Frosh 29.
Professional Basketball
American League:
Wilmington 31, Philadelphia Sphas 27.
National League:
Akron 54, Indianapolis 44.
Swimming
Franklin and Marshall College 45, Temple University 30.
Penn 44, Allegheny (Meadville, Pa.) 22.
Columbia 32, Cornell 36.
Pennsylvania 56, Penn State 19.
Penn Frosh 47, Bucknell J. C. 27.
Brooklyn College 38, Swarthmore 37.

PARRY NAMED PRESIDENT

Philadelphia—(AP)—John C. Parry, Jr., of Philadelphia, is new president of the Middle States Lawn Tennis association. Other officers elected at the association's 19th annual meeting here were:

BURGERS WANT GAMES

The Burger Catholic Club basketball team would like to schedule games away from home with Class "A" and "B" teams. Write to Manager John Ganse, 245 Elm Street, city.

WEATHER
Eastern Pennsylvania: Light Rain South Portion Tuesday Afternoon, Somewhat Warmer South Portion.

Intelligencer Journal

The Leading Newspaper in the Garden Spot of America, Home Owned for Home Folks Since 1794

Help To Fill RED CROSS War Relief Chest

VOLUME LXXVIII.—NO. 118. CITY The Intelligencer Founded 1799 The Journal Founded 1794 LANCASTER, PA., TUESDAY MORNING, JANUARY 27, 1942 Entered at Post Office at Lancaster, Pa. as second class mail matter 14 PAGES, 112 COLUMNS.—THREE CENTS.

YANKS TORPEDO JAP PLANE CARRIER

A. E. F. LANDS IN NORTHERN IRELAND

Thousands Of U. S. Troops Pour Ashore After Secret Crossing Of Atlantic Ocean

Only Small Crowd Of Curious Persons On Hand For Welcome; "When Do We Eat," Soldiers Ask On Arrival

(By RICE YAHNER)

With The AEF In Northern Ireland, Jan. 26—(AP)—Several thousands of steel-helmeted Yanks—"all pepped up and rarin' to go"—landed here safely Monday as the vanguard of United States troops dispatched to Europe in the second World War.

Escorted safely by the U. S. and British navies, their commander, Maj.-Gen. Russell P. Hartle, 52, stepped ashore to the strains of "The Star Spangled Banner," and waves of cheers from those lining the dock.

After the General came First Class Private Milburn Henke, 22, of Hutchinson, Minn., whose German-born father's parting words were: "Give 'em hell."

Most of the huskies were from the Mid-west, seasoned regulars and drafted men. Women nurses also were in the convoy, and the Navy described the crossing as "a routine operation."

BRITISH, IRISH, AMERICAN OFFICIALS ON HAND

The American troops marched down the gangplank, formed ranks under the stock-taking gaze of British, Irish, and American officials.

"Your safe arrival marks a new stage in the World War, and a gloomy portent for Hitler," said Sir Archibald Sinclair, British air minister, who welcomed them.

"Your welcome arrival here today reveals part of one great plan to smash the dictator powers wherever they may be found.

"Its significance will not be lost on General Tojo."

General Hartle said: "It's a pleasure to be here."

There was no flamboyant welcome. The secret apparently was well-kept, and the curious who had gathered on the docks appeared to sense the evident grimness of the stiff-lipped doughboys who came down the gangplank.

CROSSING UNEVENTFUL

The Atlantic crossing I made with troops on a 20-year-old ship was uneventful, broken only by well-disciplined deck drills in case of submarine attacks.

With me was Harrison (Bob) Roberts, Associated Press photographer from New York, who also was assigned to this AEF.

"The Navy never lost a troopship, you know," the old tars reassured soldiers making their first sea trip. No uneasiness was apparent among the men throughout the voyage.

The Irish port suddenly loomed out of the mist, and the soldiers leaped to the rails. Few ragged cheers could be heard from ashore, and also the identical strains of "God Save The King" and "America" played by the Royal Ulster Rifles' Band.

As our ship drew alongside the dock this band switched to the "Star Spangled Banner." The men silently awaited their turn to land. There were few waves of the hands, orders were snapped and the men landed in the gray chill without much fanfare. That came later when the town generally got word of the arrival.

Besides Sir Archibald Sinclair, the welcoming party included Lieut.-Gen. H. E. Franklyn, general officer commanding the British troops in northern Ireland, Maj.-Gen. V. H. B. Majendie, general officer com-

More Of AEF On Page 4

"We Lead All The Rest"
FARM CORNER
By
The Farm Editor

DRAFT BOARDS MEET WITH FARM WAR BODY

Map Out Plan Of Cooperation In Vital Farm-Labor Problem In Lancaster County

The Lancaster County Agricultural War Board and representatives of four Selective Service Boards embracing most of the farming area in Lancaster County mapped out a plan of cooperation on the vital farm-labor problem at a meeting Monday at the Hotel Weber.

Under the plan, the board will act as a clearing house, supplying information to the draft boards on the cases of registrants who apply for deferment on the claim they are needed in agricultural pursuits.

This information, spokesmen for several of the draft boards said, would enable them to more accurately evaluate claims for deferment.

Paul Leaman, Bird-in-Hand R1, chairman of the Agricultural board, presided at the meeting. James Walker, of the state board, attended the meeting as did representatives of County Draft Boards 2, 3, 4 and 5.

SEVERAL TOBACCO SALES

There was little activity in the tobacco market while the Harrisburg Farm Show was in progress, Jan. 19-23, but several crops have been picked up by independent

More Of FARM CORNER On Page 9

Intelligencer Journal
Weather Calendar

COMPARATIVE TEMPERATURES

Station	High	Low
Intell Journal	37	31
Water Works	41	32
Ephrata	37	32
Last Year (Ephrata)	32	21
Official High for Year, January 2		53
Official Low for Year, January 11		—10
Character of Day		Cloudy

HOURLY TEMPERATURES (Monday)

3 a. m.	35	4 p. m.	32
4 a. m.	35	5 p. m.	32
5 a. m.	34	6 p. m.	32
6 a. m.	34	7 p. m.	32
7 a. m.	33	8 p. m.	31
8 a. m.	32	9 p. m.	31
9 a. m.	32	10 p. m.	31
10 a. m.	31	11 p. m.	31
11 a. m.	31	Midnight	31
Noon	31	(Tuesday)	
1 p. m.	32	1 a. m.	31
2 p. m.	32	2 a. m.	32
3 p. m.	32	3 a. m.	32

SUN
Rises—7:18 a. m. Sets—5:16 p. m.

More Of WEATHER On Page 9

MAJOR GENERAL R. P. HARTLE

SAM ROSEN CALLED BY DRAFT BOARD; WAS 1ST ON LIST

Man Holding No. 158 Was Deferred Twice Previously; Will Leave Next Month

Samuel Rosen, 220 N. Prince St., who had No. 158, the first to be pulled in the Selective Service lottery to determine order numbers in 1940, is among a list of local men who have been notified to appear for induction early in February, it was revealed Monday.

Rosen's name is among those announced by City Draft Board No. 3, with whom he registered on October 16, 1940.

He was classified as available for general military service in 1940 and appealed the board's decision on the grounds that his mother was dependent upon him. His appeal won for him a deferred status.

MOTHER DIED LAST YEAR

In the Spring of 1941 his mother died and the board reclassified him as a 1-A man, fit for service and scheduled him for induction in July. Before he could be sent, Congress passed the 28-year law, which placed men over that age in Class 1-H, which gave Rosen another deferment.

The war declaration abolished Class 1-H and City Board 3 reclassified him again as available for service. He passed the local board physical examination and Army physicians passed him several weeks ago at a final examination at Harrisburg.

City Board No. 3 announced this list: Vernon H. Elsen, 309 Pearl St.; Arthur P. Bechtold, 721 High St.; Harry C. Pfeffer, 561 E. Strawberry

More Of ROSEN On Page 4

BOMBERS OVER GERMANY

Berlin (From German Broadcasts), Tuesday — (AP) — British bombers penetrated Germany as far as the outer districts of Berlin during the night, it was announced officially today. Bombs were dropped on several towns in northern Germany.

WARTIME PRICE CONTROL BILL WINS APPROVAL

House Votes 286 To 112 For Measure After Blocking Opponents

NOW GOES TO SENATE

Washington—(AP)—After a three-hour attack by Republicans and a few Democrats the wartime Price Control bill was approved finally by the House Monday and sent to the Senate, where speedy action was forecast.

A powerful coalition led by Rep. Wolcott, Rep., Mich., came within 20 votes of sending the controversial measure—compromised between original Senate and House bills—back to conference with instructions to revise it. The coalition wanted to knockout a system of business licenses designed to enforce price control and also believed a board of review should be set up to pass on price ceilings that might be fixed.

ATTEMPT DEFEATED

But, after Democratic Leader McCormack, of Massachusetts, had asserted that those and other Republican-sponsored objections were unnecessary or meaningless, the House defeated Wolcott's attempts on a rollcall vote, 209 to 189. Then members went on to pass the legislation on another rollcall, 286 to 112.

McCormack took occasion during the animated debate to say that reports that the President might veto the bill were unfounded, but he did say he believed that additional legislation might have to be passed "to correct some of the defects in the present bill."

The legislation, first requested by President Roosevelt last July, would give a price administrator, who presumably will be Leon Henderson, authority to fix ceilings on prices in his discretion, as well as rents in defense areas. Licenses could be required for the conduct of almost any business. If provisions of a license were violated, the offending party would be warned, then the government could petition a state court to suspend it. That court might, after a hearing, suspend the license for not longer than 12 months and the aggrieved

More Of PRICES On Page 4

SUGAR RATIONS OF ¾ POUND A WEEK OR LESS INDICATED

Henderson Says Sales May Be Held Down To Assure Equitable Distribution

Washington—(AP)—Price Administrator Leon Henderson said Monday night that initial sugar rations may be restricted to no more than three-quarters of a pound a person a week.

Announcement was made last Saturday that rationing of sugar would begin some time in February. At that time, officials said each person's allowance would be about 50 pounds a year, or approximately a pound a week.

Henderson explained Monday, however, that part of the per capita average of 50 pounds a year would be consumed by persons who eat in hotels, restaurants and institutions.

Sales for home use, he said, will have to be curtailed to the extent necessary to allow for use in such establishments.

MAY HOLD BACK SUPPLIES

Henderson noted also that some sugar would have to be held back early in the year to meet seasonal demands for home canning during the summer months and for the winter holidays.

"It may also be necessary at the outset of the plan to hold sales

More Of SUGAR On Page 4

SEES SUBMARINE RAID ON FRISCO PROBABLE

Admiral Greenslade Points Out Possibility Of Craft Firing Deck Guns On City

San Francisco—(AP)—A submarine raid on San Francisco is "very probable," Admiral J. W. Greenslade, commandant of the 12th Naval District, said.

Such a raid, with a submarine coming to the surface and firing on the city with its deck guns, would have only a nuisance value for its effect on civilian morale and use in Japanese propaganda broadcasts, he said.

SMALL LIBRARY TAX SUGGESTED BY COMMITTEE

Report Plan Almost Universally Used Where Good Work Is Being Done

OPPOSITE GRUBB SITE

A recommendation that a "small, special tax" be levied for the maintenance of a Free Public library, is contained in a report completed Monday by the special library committee, and submitted to the Trustees of the Milton H. Garvin Library Fund. The report was examined late Monday by the trustees, and returned to the committee without comment, according to F. Lyman Windolph, one of the three trustees.

The report explained that a special library tax could only be levied and collected after it had been approved by the voters in a referendum.

"We have found that this is the plan almost universally used in libraries that are doing good and effective work in their communities," the report said. "This important question should be given careful consideration, and in order to equalize the assessment may require a city and county library tax. We suggest therefore the appointment of a special committee to study the question of library maintenance and support."

NO SITE SUGGESTED

The report quoted the opinions of a number of prominent librarians, who unanimously favored a central site for the library, and disapproved the Grubb estate. The committee recommended that these opinions be given consideration, and that a committee be appointed to examine available sites with a view to securing as soon as possible a definite location for the library.

The report "strongly urged" that every effort be made to increase the number of books in the library, and approved the "Buy a Book" campaign now being planned by the library authorities.

The committee recommended that $25,000 given under the will of Milton T. Garvin to the "Lancaster County Museum of History, Science and Art," should be used to establish a Fine Arts section in the new library. (The Garvin Li-

More Of LIBRARY On Page 4

CANADA PROPOSES CONSCRIPTING MEN FOR FARMS, PLANTS

Will Be Included In Plan To Draft Soldiers, King Tells Commons

Ottawa—(AP)—Prime Minister W. L. MacKenzie King told the House of Commons Monday night the government's plans for conscription include providing manpower for war industries and agriculture as well as the armed forces.

The government has announced that a plebiscite would be called soon on conscription. The Dominion people will be asked to release the government from its pledge of non-conscription for overseas service.

King declared Monday night the government's plans "will compre-

More Of CANADA On Page 4

MacArthur Spends Birthday Planning For Future Victory

With the U. S. Army in Luzon— (AP) —Gen. Douglas MacArthur, as always a figure of supreme confidence, spent his 62nd birthday anniversary Monday working on immediate battle problems and future plans for an eventual democratic victory.

He declined any special observance beyond accepting the congratulations of officers and men.

The General always looks as if he has received the best possible news, and his calm assurance sets an example for his men.

3 JAP SHIPS BOMBED

Melbourne, Australia, Tuseday—(AP)—Three Japanese ships in Rabaul harbor, New Britain, were damaged in a bombing attack last night, a Royal Australian Air Force communique reported today.

Flying Fortresses Helping To Hammer Enemy Convoy, Score--11 Sunk, 23 Battered

Toll May Be Still Greater In Big Naval Battle Being Fought In Indies Waters, No U. S. Ships, Planes Reported Lost

ADMIRAL THOMAS C. HART

Washington—(AP)—An American submarine torpedoed and probably sank a Japanese aircraft carrier in the battle of Macassar Strait Monday while surface warships and big flying fortresses took further terrific toll of an invading enemy convoy.

At least 11 ships have been positively sunk and 23 others heavily battered by American and Dutch forces since the great engagement began last Friday between Borneo and Celebes islands.

Northward in the Philippines, a tiny torpedo boat zipped again into Subic Bay, past net and boom defenses and heavy shore batteries, and sank another 5,000-ton enemy vessel, duplicating a similar daring attack of last week.

So fierce was the action and so brilliant the success of American arms, supported by Dutch forces, against the Japanese invasion convoy in the Macassar Strait approach to Java that a Navy communique late in the day said it was "still impossible to estimate total damage inflicted by our combat vessels" but that "the known results are substantial."

PLANE CARRIER "BELIEVED TO HAVE SUNK"

It also was not ascertained whether the torpedoed aircraft carrier went to the bottom but it was "believed to have sunk," the communique announced. Authorities here credited the Nipponese last October with eight aircraft carriers built and two under construction, ranging from 7,100 to 26,900 tons. The largest ones can carry 50 to 60 planes but have a normal complement of 30.

The sinking of the second 5,000-ton enemy ship in Subic Bay brought the count of Japanese vessels definitely sunk by American action since the Pearl Harbor attack to 51—or 52 if the aircraft carrier be counted.

A torpedo boat commanded by Ensign George R. Cox of Watertown, N. Y., scored on this latest raid. The communique also mentioned two lieutenants participating in the attack as squadron commander and squadron engineer, possibly indicating that other boats beside Cox's were involved.

At home, too, there was action. The sinking of the American ore carrier Venore off the Carolina coast with the loss of 22 of her crew was disclosed, bringing to eight the number of vessels attacked in the current wave of submarine warfare off the Atlantic coast of the United States, and to 97 the toll of the dead. (Picture on Page 7.)

But these desultory Axis stabs at American shipping paled to nothing in the face of the terrific destruction wrought by cruisers and destroyers of Admiral Thomas C. Hart's Asiatic fleet and by seven flying fortresses of the Army on a Japanese convoy seeking since Friday to thread the 90 miles of the

More Of BATTLE On Page 4

ROLL OF LINOLEUM KILLS WORKER AT ARMSTRONG PLANT

Lenard C. Kilburn, 31, New Danville, Loses Life As Crane Jumps Track At Intersection

Lenard C. Kilburn, thirty-one, New Danville, was killed instantly at 4:30 p. m. Monday when a roll of linoleum fell on him at the Armstrong Cork Company plant

Dr. Henry B. Davis, Manheim township coroner, said Kilburn suffered a fractured skull and issued a certificate of accidental death.

A preliminary investigation, company officials said, disclosed that Kilburn was pinned under a large roll of linoleum after a crane he was operating apparently jumped the track at an intersection. He was engaged in moving the roll of linoleum in the inlaid stoves department at the time, officials said. He had been employed in the inlaid department since March, 1941.

The victim was born in Russelville, Ala., a son of Mr. and Mrs. Robert V. Kilburn, Steele, Mo.

Mr. Kilburn served in the United States Navy for ten years and was honorably discharged in 1939. He was a member of the Marticville Methodist Church.

His wife, who was Hazel Mae Smith, Marticville, before marriage, four sisters, three brothers and his parents survive.

RAIN AND WARMER FORECAST

A light sleet and snow storm swept over this area early Monday but above freezing temperatures quickly melted the downfall. Little interference with traffic was reported. Temperatures ranged from 32 to 37 degrees. Light rain and somewhat warmer weather was forecast for Tuesday (today).

LARGE SALES DAY CROWDS EXPECTED IN CITY TOMORROW

Merchants Planning To Give All Customers Prompt And Courteous Service

Preparations for Lancaster's 44th semi-annual Sales Day, scheduled for Wednesday, are being completed by participating stores, according to Frank W. Tracy, member of the retailers special committee on arrangements.

"Merchants expect Wednesday's shopping crowd to exceed that of any previous mid-winter sale", said Mr. Tracy, "and are planning accordingly in order to give all customers prompt and courteous service. Extra sales personnel will be on duty in many stores. Merchant cooperation has been excellent as is evidenced by the 18 pages of special bargains advertised in yesterday's Sales Day Newspaper Supplement by the 97 participating stores. These stores may be identified by the large Sales Day streamers printed in red and black being displayed on windows. The Police

More of SALES DAY on Page 4

Four County Sections Top Goals In Red Cross War Relief Drive

County To Date Has Turned In $38,566.76 Toward Goal Of $75,000; Total Fund Now At $123,537.05

Four sections in the county have now passed their goals in the Red Cross War Relief Fund drive. They are Safe Harbor, Churchtown, Northern (Denver), and Rothsville. The county to date has turned in a total of $38,566.76 in its drive to raise a goal of $75,000. A number of sections have reported on their drive but have not yet turned in the funds to the headquarters.

The drive to date has netted a total of $123,537.05, of which $84,970.29 has been contributed from the city.

Actual funds turned in to date from the county include the following:

District 1, Roy B. Sheetz, chairman: Mount Joy, $4,284.82; Landisville, $75; Millersville, $2,691.91; Rohrerstown, $602.70; total, $7,654.43.

District 2, Rev. George Shea, chairman: Christiana, $1,042.88; Quarryville, $2,469.41; Safe Harbor, $1,428.85; Strasburg, $1,143.50; Willow Street, $1,417.08; total, $7,501.72.

District 3, Rev. John R. McClellan,

More Of RED CROSS On Page 9

Groundhog Lodge Tapers Program; Emphasize Patriotism, Sacrifice

Members To Meet Only To Observe Patron Saint; Members Urged To Aid Red Cross, Buy Defense Bonds

Since war his cast its grim shadow over the entire world, members of the Slumbering Groundhog Lodge of Quarryville, in observing whether or not their patron saint sees his shadow on February 2, will eliminate much of the colorful ceremony of the past, emphasizing patriotism and self sacrifice.

During the first World War the lodge refrained from celebrating in parade and feast, and simply observed the Groundhog's movements in order to make their prognostications of whether there would be six more weeks of Winter and similar procedure will be followed during the second World War.

In the first official notice to all esteemed and worthy brothers, William Uhler Hensel, 2nd, secretary and bondless treasurer of the lodge, points out that "from the homes of our members sons have gone forth to battle and numbers await the call to arms . . . Under all these circumstances we think the times are not propitious for

More Of GROUNDHOG On Page 9

Today's New Era

LANCASTER NEW ERA

WEATHER
Light to moderate snow in north portion; rain or snow over south portion; slightly colder tonight. (Details on Page 3).

Examiner Founded 1830. New Era Founded 1877. Published Every Evening Except Sunday by New Era Company. Entered as Second Class Matter at Post Office, Lancaster, Pa.
LANCASTER, PA., WEDNESDAY, JANUARY 28, 1942 CITY EDITION 14 PAGES—112 COLUMNS—THREE CENTS

U.S. Fliers Hit 3 More Jap Ships, Smash Air Attack; Atlantic Sub Toll Now 14

COUNTY WILL PAY $430,000 BRIDGE BONDS

Payment Major Item of '42 Budget; $300,000 Will Remain to Be Paid.

TAX RATE FOR YEAR IS NOT YET FIXED

The County of Lancaster is prepared to pay off holders of $430,000 worth of bridge bonds on Monday, the maturing date on which the remaining debt on the span is callable and payable.

There will then remain only $300,000 to be paid out of $1,400,000 which the county borrowed in 1930.

The payment is the major amount of expenditure in the 1942 budget framed by County Controller E. M. Miller's office and turned over to the County Commissioners today. Chairman G. Graybill Diehm said the commissioners had not decided on the '42 tax rate and that no conclusions could be drawn from the budget alone.

Some indication that the 1.9 mill tax would be retained, or at least not increased, was seen in the fact that the County is still paying all bills on the institutions (which consume 1.5 mills) and the amount set aside for other expenses is unchanged from last year.

New Problems

Framing of the 1942 budget presented several new problems—

Bridge guards will be a new item of expense this year.

Gasoline tax returns will fall and reduced income from the State is expected.

Abolition of the Home for Friendless Children will reduce that expenditure.

The Defense Council represents a new cost.

Income from personal property is believed likely to fall because more persons are buying non-taxable securities.

The budget disclosed that the county estimated its needs in 1941 at $1,062,950, and they amounted to only $756,168. This year the Controller estimated the needs for 1942 at $1,187,472.

The Commissioners' failure to appropriate any funds to the General, St. Joseph's or Columbia hospitals in 1941 was disclosed by the budget. They set aside $15,000 for possible payments to the institutions, but used none of it. The same amount is set aside in the budget this year.

Some payments were made to the hospitals in other forms, Diehm said. In cases in which the County hospital was not equipped to handle the patients, they were taken to the other institutions and paid for by the county.

Heavy Road Damage Expected

Highway construction damages may also constitute a major item of expense this year, particularly the straightening of rout 222 at Pugh's Mill. The commissioners set aside $119,000, the same as a year ago, although only $48,141 was used in 1941.

The County has already assumed more than $70,000 worth of damage obligations this year because

(See COUNTY—Page 11)

ONE-STORY BUILDING AT 36-38 N. QUEEN

A permit for the erection of a one-story building on the site of the old Lancaster Trust company building, 36-38 North Queen street, has been granted to Max A. Gluck, according to Henry Huth, city building inspector.

The contractor will utilize a portion of the old structure which was not razed. It is understood that the building will be occupied by a jewelry store and a shoe store.

Lash Faces Draft

Joseph P. Lash, 32, youth leader who has been trying to get a commission in the naval reserve, is being put into class 1-A by New York selective service officials along with others over 28 transferred from class 1-H.

BLASTS DAMAGE CLOISTERS

Saal Rafter Jarred Loose; Road Contractor to Modify Charges.

Blasting for the cloverleaf intersection adjacent to the Ephrata Cloisters has damaged one of the ancient buildings slightly, and the State Historical Commission has called upon the State Highway Department and the contractor to use lighter explosive charges.

A rafter in the Saal was jarred loose by one of the detonations, and much of the heavy plaster fell.

"We were alarmed about the possibility of greater damage, as the blasting has only started," Dr. Donald A. Cadzow, secretary of the State Historical Commission, said today. "The contractor has promised to pull his punches henceforward and I think it will be safe."

Instead of charges at 20-foot depths, the cloverleaf-builder plans to use only 5 and 10-foot charges.

Discovered Yesterday

The damages were discovered yesterday by Historical Commission and Highway Department representatives who met at the property to discuss the location of

(See CLOISTER—Page 2)

RCA TO BUILD PLANT HERE; TO HIRE 1,800

Company Buys 98-Acre Tract From Frank McGrann For $160,000.

WILL MANUFACTURE RADIO TUBES FOR NAVY

The RCA Manufacturing Company, of Camden, N. J., has purchased 98 acres in southeastern Manheim township for the erection of a radio and electronic tube factory which may cost an estimated $400,000, the firm announced last night.

The company paid Frank McGrann, of the New Holland pike, $160,000 for the land, according to a deed filed at the court house.

A one and two-story main building will be erected between March 1 and September 1, according to the company, and the plant should be in operation a few weeks after it is completed. It will produce defense materials for the duration of the war, but will turn to peacetime products afterward, the company said.

The U. S. Navy is cooperating with the RCA firm in building the plant.

Expects To Employ 1,800

Ultimately, the company said, it expects to employ 1,800 persons, most of whom will be women. Many will get opportunities to develop new skills. Because of the need for cleanliness, the building will be constructed of brick and be air-conditioned. It will contain about 326,000 square feet.

The tract involved is bounded by the New Holland Pike, Pleasure Road, and the Pennsylvania Railroad mainline. It has been in the McGrann family's possession for 50 years, and includes two farm houses and the coachman's residence, and the carriage house of the former Hardwick mansion.

One official privy to the negotiations said he understood that only one of the houses would have to be razed immediately and that the erection of the plant would not disturb the city police pistol range,

(See RCA—Page 11)

MOTORIST KILLED IN TRUCK CRASH

Tom Craig Injured Fatally, Passenger Hurt on Harrisburg Pike.

Thomas Craig, thirty-eight, 304 Pearl street, was injured fatally when the auto he was driving and a loaded cattle truck collided on a curve on the Harrisburg pike in front of the Oreville hotel at 2 A. M. today. He died in St. Joseph's hospital an hour and a half later.

Dr. A. V. Walter, county coroner, said death resultde from internal hemorrhages, due to a punctured lung and crushed chest. After conferring with State Policemen Baxter and Kweder, the coroner issued a certificate of accidental death, exonerating the truck driver.

Richard Albright, twenty-one, 326 Chester street, who was riding with Craig, suffered abrasions and contusions of the face and hand and was admitted to the hospital.

Police said the truck, which contained a load of cattle and belonged

(See ACCIDENT—Page 2)

B. F. GOOD DIES SUDDENLY

Tobacco Dealer Was Former Football Player and Coach.

Benjamin Franklin Good, Jr., forty-three, of the Lititz Pike, died suddenly this morning, at 10:25 o'clock at his home of coronary occlusion, after an illness of three weeks.

He was in the leaf tobacco business and was widely known as a former football player and coach.

Born in this city, the son of Elizabeth Bellemere Good and the late Benjamin F. Good Sr., he was a resident of Lancaster all his life.

He belonged to the Elks club and the Tobacco Board of Trade. He was a member of St. John's Lutheran church.

Good was graduated from Mercersburg Academy and attended Franklin and Marshall Academy and was a player and coach of the All Lancaster Football team for many years. He also coached St. Joseph's Catholic football team.

Besides his mother, he is survived by his wife, the former Florence Trissler, and two sons: Benjamin Franklin Good, III and Donald E., both at home; also one sister, Dorothy, wife of Guy L. Diffenbaugh, of Tallahassee, Fla.

HEAVY BUYING MARKS 44TH SALES DAY

Heavy buying of household necessities was one of the features of Lancaster's 44th Sales Day today.

Reports gathered from cooperating stores indicated that the early morning crowds were the largest in years and buying was heavy. Merchants said there was a tendency on the part of many housewives to buy in quantity. Merchants were ready for the rush with an ample store of merchandise.

Light snow flurries shortly before noon failed to halt the crowd.

TWO QUAKES NEAR MACASSAR STRAIT

NEW YORK, Jan. 28—(AP)—Two earthuake shocks recorded on the Fordham University seismograph were estimated by the Rev. Joseph J. Lynch, seismologist, to have been in the vicinity of the Banda sea, American and utch naval forces east of Macassar Strait where have been battling the Japanese.

SYDNEY, Australia, Jan. 28—(AP)—Strong earth shocks believed centering in the Arafura sea between New Guinea and Australia were recorded here at 12:36 P. M. today.

Once Over

by H. I. Phillips

Private Purkey on the Pearl Harbor Verdict

Dear Ma.—Well I serpose you read the report on Pearl Harbor and it bares out what I always sed. It's the men at the bottom witch have all the brains. The most important thing in the report of what happened was that part witch told how a non com was about the only fellow around Pearl Harbor who was wide awake to the danger of a sneak punch.

H. I. Phillips

* * *

He was the only man there who thought it wood be a good idea to keep a lookout for enemy planes. In fact when the post was shut down at 7 a. m. by the general's orders he asked could he stick around by himself and keep watching overtime. A few minutes later he spots the big fleet of Jap planes 130 miles off and right away he flashes the tip to the central station. So what happens? He gets a lieutenant witch is the same as finding nobody there.

* * *

He tells the lieutenant all about the planes and the lieutenant asks is he sure and when he says sure he is sure the lieutenant says he guesses they is all skywriters or something and not to worry no more.

And while all this is going on there has already been a fight between a Jap sub and a couple of U. S. ships. This is reported to the naval base but no alarm is sounded. I guess everybody was so jumpy they didn't want no noise or something.

Anyhow if this non com could of been boss he wood have stirred up the whole works and had everybody out on the run in time to get the planes off the ground. He wood of saved the U. S. planes, got 'em up in the air in time to give the Japs a battle and probably have saved hundreds of lives. When our

(See PHILLIPS—Page 8)

LINER IS SUNK OFF BERMUDA, 347 MISSING

U. S. Plane Sees U-Boats in Gulf of Mexico Near Oil Ports.

MOTHER SHIP BASES SUBS OFF U. S. COAST

(By the Associated Press)

Axis submarines, ranging the eastern American coast from the Gulf of Mexico to northern Canadian waters, have sunk at least 14 American and Allied ships since the undersea raiders appeared off Nova Scotia Jan. 12.

Survivors of a Norwegian tanker and Greek freighter who reached a Canadian port expressed belief that a German mother ship had released a pack of U-boats off the North Atlantic coast, declaring that one of the attackers was not a long-range submarine.

374 Missing From Liner

Latest announced blow was the torpedoing of a large Allied passenger liner carrying 450 passengers and crew from Bermuda to an eastern port. Only 71 have been saved, five bodies recovered, and 374 persons are missing from the liner.

As this blow was announced the navy at Corpus Christi, Tex., said that a submarine "doubtlessly German" had been sighted 15 miles from nearby Port Aransas and that probably another U-boat was in the vicinity.

This announcement followed upon last night's report of a U-boat's sinking the 7,096-ton American tanker Francis E. Powell off Lewes, Del., with an indicated loss of three lives.

The fate of another American tanker, the Pan-Maine, 7,237 tons, remained in doubt following a radio report yesterday afternoon that she was being attacked. The Pan-Maine carried 38 men.

Thirty-three survivors from a Greek freighter and a Norwegian tanker arrived at an eastern Canadian port last night and reported that 51 men were missing or dead in successful attacks on their vessels.

99 Lives Lost In 14 Days

Official Navy statements list eight ships sunk off the eastern American coast in 14 days. These

(See U-BOATS—Page 5)

NOTARY AND AUTO DEALER PROSECUTED

J. Emerson Young, a notary public of Salunga, and Mervin R. Murry, Harrisburg used car dealer, charged with conspiracy to commit and unlawful act, waived a hearing and posted bail for court before Justice of the Peace Weidman, Mount Joy township.

Prosecution was brought by W. H. Metzger, of South Enola, who alleges the seal of the notary public was stamped on the certificate of title of a motor vehicle so it would appear that he had signed and sworn to the assignment when in truth, Metzger claims, he had not done so.

Part of Wages in Bonds Seen Likely

WASHINGTON, Jan. 28—(AP)—Compulsory part payment of salaries and wages in defense bonds, and even higher taxes, were foreseen today by the National Resources Planning Board in an analysis of the trends of war needs and post war policy.

The board, a Federal agency, scouted any theory that a post-war depression was inevitable.

With respect to the war period, the agency, in a special pamphlet prepared by Alvin H. Hansen, Harvard economics professor and special adviser to the Federal Reserve Board, said the following policies were indicated:

1. High corporate-income and excess-profits taxes; 2. Sharply progressive estate taxes; 3. Broadening of individual income-tax base together with steeply graduated surtax rates; 4. Sharp increase in excise taxes on commodities competing with the war program; 5. Part payment of wages and salaries in defense bonds; and 6. "Qualitative shift in the components of consumption."

Tanker Goes Down Off N. J. Coast

The Norwegian tanker Varanger goes down 35 miles off the New Jersey coast, torpedo victim of an enemy submarine. The vessel sank during the early morning darkness of Jan. 25 and the stern was resting on the bottom when this picture was taken by the Bomber Command of the First Air Force.

Winant Sees 7-million U.S. Army With Women in Active Roles

U. S. and Britain Forming Quick-Hitting Invasion Units of Field Army Size to Cross Any Ocean in the World

LONDON, Jan. 28—(AP)—United States Ambassador John G. Winant told a national defense luncheon today that the United States plans to recruit an army of 7,000,000 men.

"If it is necessary for the women of America to scrub, drive or transport or man anti-aircraft batteries or pilot planes or whatever else, they will do it gladly," he said.

"Idleness has been no part of our national life . . . that is not America," the Ambassador added.

He said "we know the story of the battle of the Atlantic and if it is necessary that our Navy take time to re-establish its supremacy in the Pacific with whatever auxiliary airforce that is required, it will be done and its complete supremacy re-established."

Land-Sea Surprise Expeditions Planned

WASHINGTON, Jan. 28.—(AP)—Official statements indicated today that the United States and Britain have worked out a long term land-sea victory plan for surprise expeditions of field army size to strike suddenly across any ocean.

Disclosures of President Roosevelt, Prime Minister Churchill and Congressional leaders gave broad outlines of the plan and Congress rushed legislation to carry it out. The House passed 388 to 0 and sent to the Senate last night the $17,722,565,474 Naval appropriations bill, including a special emergency provision for the developing amphibious strategy.

The bill provides $3,900,000,000 for emergency construction of 1,799 special vessels. The House Naval committee disclosed in a report that this provision would give "the necessary ships with which to conduct the amphibious operations which it is contemplated may be necessary to prosecute the present war to a successful conclusion."

Mr. Churchill, meanwhile, had

(See ARMY—Page 5)

NAZI WAR LOOT DUMPED HERE

Agents Are Charged With Flooding U. S. Markets With Seized Diamonds.

NEW YORK, Jan. 28.—(AP) — The German High Command and their agents in New York City were accused in a Federal indictment today of dumping plundered loot and spoils of war in United States markets, the proceeds to be used to finance propaganda work in North and South America.

A New York corporation, its president, and three other individuals were named in the conspiracy indictment.

Those indicted were the Pioneer Import Corporation; Werner Von Clemm, its president, said by Federal agents to be a cousin of the wife of German Foreign Minister Von Ribbentrop; Carl Von Clemm, Werner's twin brother, said by authorities to be a German emissary in Italy; Ernest Cremer, manager of the Diamond Control Office, a regulative body established by the Nazis in the low countries fol-

(See INDICTMENTS—Page 11)

BOY SLAYER MUST SERVE LIFE TERM

BOSTON, Jan. 28.—(AP)—Life imprisonment, instead of death by electrocution, was decreed by Governor Leverett Saltonstall today for Raymond L. Woodward, Jr., 16, who pleaded guilty to the mutilation murder of Constance Shipp, 15-year-old Reading schoolmate, last summer.

The commutation, subject to the approval of the Executive Council, was granted by the Governor on condition that Woodward "be permanently confined to the state prison and never transferred to any institution from which there is a substantial risk of escape."

BOY RUNNING TO BUS IS INJURED BY AUTO

Henaga Maisells, eight, Lancaster R. 1, suffered lacerations and brush burns of the right cheek and upper lip when struck by an auto driven by Harry R. Kulp, Lancaster R. 3, at the intersection of the Oregon and Lititz pikes this afternoon. He was admitted to the General hospital.

The boy was accompanied by his mother, Mrs. Rosa Maisells, and ran across the Lititz pike to board a bus when struck, according to hospital attendants.

SAYS BRITAIN IS MISLED

Critics of Pacific War Handling, However, Assure Vote of Confidence.

LONDON, Jan. 28—(AP)—The government was accused today of misleading the country with "childish inconsistency" and unfulfilled promises of security in the Pacific War area but, in almost the same breath, Prime Minister Churchill's critics in the House of Commons assured him the vote of confidence that he demands.

Starting the second day of debate over the government's war leadership, launched yesterday with the Prime Minister's accounting to Parliament and the nation, Clement Attlee, his lieutenant in the House, formally proposed the vote of confidence.

Labor members decided by a large majority to support it, but there were signs that some might abstain and that a few might even vote against the government. Liberals were reported also to have decided to support him.

Any shred of doubt over the out-

(See CHURCHILL—Page 5)

LOCAL GARAGE MEN DISCUSS WAR WORK

Local automobile dealers met this afternoon to discuss taking small war contracts by mobilizing the machinery in their garages and shops.

The discussion followed a meeting at Harrisburg yesterday, when Mark S. James, State Secretary of Commerce, outlined a general plan for mobilizing garage equipment to do war work.

Automobile dealers here said they are willing to give every possible cooperation with the government. However, they pointed out, that Lancaster garages have little if any equipment that could be used in the production of war materials.

Everything That Americans Buy In Stores Liable to Rationing

Only F. D.'s Signature Needed to Make Price Fixing Legal; Expect Henderson to Retain Post of Administrator

WASHINGTON, Jan. 28.—(AP)—Everything that Americans buy at the stores became liable to rationing today, and legal price fixing was only one short step away.

The War Production Board delegated to Acting Price Administrator Leon Henderson full power to ration retail commodities, only a short time before the Senate completed Congressional action yesterday on a much-amended price control bill and sent it on to President Roosevelt.

Democratic leaders said they expected the Chief Executive to sign the measure, although some of its farm price sections were known to be distasteful to him. He had asked for the legislation more than six months ago, as a check against inflation. Living costs have risen more than 11 per cent since September, 1939, government economists say, and parallel price rises have added several billion dollars to the cost of the nation's armament program.

Henderson To Keep Post

The Capital generally conceded that Henderson would be retained in the price administration post he now holds by virtue of an executive order. The added ration-

(See RATIONING—Page 5)

TOKYO LOSSES PUT AT 30,000 IN MACASSAR

Giant Yankee Bombers Sink Another Transport, Set Second Afire.

SINGAPORE DEFENDERS FALL BACK AT 3 POINTS

(By the Associated Press)

American fliers were officially credited today with striking furious new blows at a Japanese invasion armada trapped in Macassar Strait, where 25,000 to 30,000 Japanese were said to have drowned already, while U. S. "Flying Tiger" volunteer pilots wiped out one-third of a 37-plane Japanese formation over Rangoon, Burma.

A Dutch East Indies communique said giant four-motor U. S. bombers sank a big Japanese transport, left another in flames and straddled a cruiser with sticks of bombs in the 400-mile Macassar Strait north of Java.

The Yankee volunteers achieved another air-fighting miracle east of Rangoon when in a daylight dogfight they destroyed six Japanese fighter planes by unofficial count, probably destroyed six more and damaged nine others.

The American fighters returned to their base without suffering any casualties.

Unofficial reports said that a formation of RAF bombers inflicted heavy damage in a raid last night on Bangkok, capital of Japanese-occupied Thailand.

A U. S. War Department bulletin in describing the action in Macassar Strait, said a formation of eight U. S. Army bombers engaged in the attack. One of the bombers was lost in the raid which centered about Balik Papan, the oil port the Dutch abandoned last week.

A direct hit was scored on the cruiser.

The transport was sunk in the river at Balik Papan but the cruiser was outside the harbor.

In a previous attack by U. S. planes at Balik Papan one enemy transport was sunk and another set afire.

Jap Ship Toll Now 36

Pounding home Japan's greatest naval disaster of the war, United States fliers thus boosted to at least 36 the number of Japanese ships sunk or damaged in a five-day battle.

Macassar Strait, the roadway to Java, headquarters of Gen. Sir Archibald P. Wavell's United Nations command, lies between Dutch East Borneo and Celebes Island.

An N. E. I. communique acknowledged that the Japanese had apparently occupied the burned-out oil center of Balik Papan, in East Borneo on Macassar Strait.

It was apparent, however, that

(See PACIFIC—Page 12)

Bulletin

BRITISH ARE FALLING BACK TO SINGAPORE

SINGAPORE, Jan. 28.—(AP)—The British military authorities late today ordered the evacuation by noon Friday of all civilians from a mile-deep strip on northern Singapore island and it appeared that the defenders were preparing to fall back upon that great base itself.

This action followed upon reports that the present British line still was being bent back in areas less than 50 miles above Singapore where Japanese pressure was enormous and still rising.

WEATHER
Eastern Pennsylvania: Rather Cold Tuesday, Snow By Night.

Intelligencer Journal

The Leading Newspaper in the Garden Spot of America, Home Owned for Home Folks Since 1794

VOLUME LXXVIII.—NO. 142. CITY The Intelligencer Founded 1799 The Journal Founded 1794 LANCASTER, PA., TUESDAY MORNING, FEBRUARY 24, 1942 Entered at Post Office at Lancaster, Pa. as second class mail matter 18 PAGES, 144 COLUMNS.—THREE CENTS.

JAP SHELLS DROP ON CALIFORNIA

Sub Hits Oil Pump As President Speaks

Large Submersible Fires Between Dozen And Two Dozen Shells At Plant Near Santa Barbara While Lying Mile Off Shore; Eye-Witnesses Say Aim Was Poor And That Most Shells Landed In Fields; No Casualties Reported; No Evidence That Craft Was Attacked

Santa Barbara, Calif.—(AP)—A submarine appeared Monday night near Goleta, some seven miles north of here, and fired between a dozen and two dozen shells at an oil refinery near the shore.

This was the first attack on the United States mainland in this war. An authoritative source said there were no casualties.

However, G. O. Brown, an oil field worker who witnessed the shelling, said one shot struck an oil well derrick and blew it and the pumping plant to bits.

He said the sub appeared to be aiming at an oil refinery on the beach but missed it with all the shells and that a score or more of men at work in the field were uninjured.

Witnesses pointed out that the shelling started about the time the President began to give his fire-side chat.

Police were informed the submarine appeared at about 7 o'clock (10 o'clock Lancaster time) and that the shelling continued for several minutes.

Asked by police about damage, the manager of the refinery, who reported the incident, replied:

"I don't know. I'm too busy dodging shells."

Location of the refinery was given as between Goleta and Elwood.

At Los Angeles President L. L. Aubert of the Bankline Oil Co., which owns the refinery in the field, said there was practically no damage and only one piece of equipment was hit. He declined to say what the equipment was.

Eye-witnesses said most of the shells exploded in a field and one went over highway 101, bursting in the foothills.

The Barnsdall and Rio Grande Oil Companies own wells in the area.

The attack was accompanied by word that a blackout had been ordered in this city.

The reception of the President's speech at many points along the coast was blacked out as radio stations went off the air.

Lawrence Wheeler, proprietor of an inn 11 miles north on Coast Highway 101, said he heard the first explosion at 7:15 p. m., while listening to the President's talk.

"The first explosion sounded distant," he said. "They grew nearer and nearer. Beginning with the third, they shook our building. I rushed out of the house and saw a shell explode against the cliff about three-fourths of a mile from our place. A geyser of dirt was shot into the air at what seemed like a great height.

"Another shell whined over my head and landed in the canyon on the Staniff place, which is across the road from us."

Mrs. Wheeler didn't hesitate in saying that when the shelling started she was "scared to death."

"I saw several shells explode on the beach," she said. "Great fountains of dirt were shot into the air, just like pictures in news reels. The shelling was so heavy it shook our house, just like an earthquake."

G. O. Brown, an oil worker in the Elwood Field, who lives on the Staniff place, was one of the first to report seeing the submarine.

"It was about a mile offshore," he said. "I could see it very clearly. It was so big I thought it might be a destroyer or cruiser. I have seen many submarines and this was larger than any of those in the U. S. Navy that I have seen. It was lying idly on the surface.

Between 8:30 and 9 o'clock observers here reported sighting three flares above Santa Barbara Channel 25 to 30 miles south of Elwood. At about the same time, Rev. Arthur Basham, of Pomona, who was visiting here, said he observed a boat flashing signal lights at the south end of Santa Barbara Channel.

The Ventura County sheriff's office was informed that flares had been sighted at several points along the coast near Hueneme, south of here.

Brown said the submarine appeared to be aiming at the Barnsdall Oil Company's main absorption plant, located almost on the beach.

"They missed with all their shots at this plant, though some of the shells landed awfully close, throwing up geysers of dirt and sand near the building," he added. "One shell hit a well and blew the pumping plant and derrick to bits. That was the only real damage they did.

"There must have been 20 or 25 men working in the field at the time and nobody was injured. It seemed to me as if the enemy vessel was firing a 5 or 6 inch gun. Their shooting wasn't very good, because the absorption plant was a beautiful target and they didn't hit it."

"Then it began shelling, shot after shot, with great regularity. I counted 12 shells that burst, most of them on the Staniff Place and the Barnsdall Oil Co. The first shot was fired at 7:15 and the firing continued for 20 minutes. I spotted the last shell at 7:35 p. m."

"The submarine still lay on the surface," Brown continued.

"It started to get twilight. I watched it as long as I could distinguish its form and then it grew dark. It didn't submerge and there were no airplanes heard.

"There were a couple of horses in the pasture near where I watched the shelling. They went mad. Shells were exploding in the pasture and the horses screamed and raced about."

Persons at the oil field at the time of the attack said no fires were started and no one was injured. A fire truck was stationed one mile north of Wheeler's but no glow in the sky indicated that any fire had been started.

All traffic on the highway was stopped by the Highway Patrol and the U. S. Army guards in that area blocked all movement, either by car or on foot.

Although this was the first attack on U. S. soil, the first in the hemisphere occurred a week ago yesterday (Monday) when a submarine fired shells into the oil refinery tank farm on the Dutch West Indies isle of Aruba as part of an offensive in which several shallow draft oil tankers were sunk in that area off the Venezuelan coast. The shell-fire caused only a dent in

More of SHELLS on Page 4

President Declares Allies Will Take The Offensive Soon

Says We Have Been Forced To Yield Ground But Points To Growing Production

WARNS AGAINST RUMOR

(Text of address on Page 6)

Washington — (AP) — President Roosevelt said Monday night that America had been "compelled to yield ground" to its enemies, but he added that with constantly increasing war production, the Allies would take the offensive soon and drive on to victory.

"We and the other United Nations are committed to the destruction of the militarism of Japan and Germany," he said. "We are daily increasing our strength. Soon, we and not our enemies, will have the offensive; we, not they, will win the final battles; and we, not they, will make the final peace."

Despite cruelly long distances involved, the President disclosed, "a large number of planes" manned by American pilots, "are now in daily contact with the enemy in the southwest Pacific." and, he said, "thousands of American troops" are also in the area.

PRODUCTION MEETING GOALS

The Chief Executive also said recent surveys had disclosed that the prodigiously high production goals established two months ago would be attained, and this, he repeatedly emphasized, was the key to victory.

Mr. Roosevelt spoke by radio from

More of PRESIDENT on Page 6

OUTLINES 3 PURPOSES "FOR EVERY AMERICAN"

Washington — (AP) — President Roosevelt outlined "three high purposes for every American" in his address Monday night. They are:

"1. We shall not stop working for a single day. If any dispute arises we shall keep on working while the dispute is solved by mediation, conciliation or arbitration—until the war is won.

"2. We shall not demand special gains or special privileges or advantages for any one group or occupation.

"3. We shall give up conveniences and modify the routine of our lives if the country asks us to do so. We will do it cheerfully, remembering that the common enemy seeks to destroy every home and every freedom in every part of our land."

BRITISH BEING SLOWLY PUSHED BACK IN BURMA

Yank Airmen Hammer Japanese-Held Airport On Bali Island

SHIP LOSS RECOUNTED

(By The Associated Press)

The struggle for Burma was turning sharply against the British Monday night, while the position in the invaded Bali Island approach to Dutch Java was at a delicate balance in which thus far no one had wholly won and no one had wholly lost.

As to the Burmese theater the outnumbered British Imperial forces, their line along the Bilin River having fallen, were slowly being driven back upon the Sittang, which is within 20 miles of the Rangoon-Mandalay-Lashio railway leg of the Burma supply road to China, and British informants conceded the probability of the fall of Rangoon itself.

After this, it was feared, would come the deluge: A Japanese invasion of the whole of the colony pushing the active front back toward India proper.

The Japanese apparently had been reinforced by troops released from the Malayan campaign after the fall of Singapore. There was indication that the Rangoon cable had been cut.

In his spring upon Bali the enemy had gained an apparently strong lodgment and had seized the airport at Denpasar within 200 air miles of the great United Nations naval base of Soerabaja on Java, but those of his troops that got ashore had been left isolated by strong American-Dutch air and sea action that had smashed crippled

More of WAR on Page 4

Coast Guard Cutter Lost

The U. S. Coast Guard cutter Alexander Hamilton (above) was torpedoed by an enemy submarine off Iceland, and had to be sunk by gunfire when it capsized while being towed to port. The Navy said there was "moderate loss of life" in the mishap.

SUB TORPEDOES U. S. COAST GUARD CUTTER IN ATLANTIC

Sinking Off Iceland Is First In That Area Since Dec. 7

Washington—(AP)—The first reported sinking of a United States warship in the Atlantic since this country entered the war December 7 was disclosed Monday with announcement by the Navy Department that the Coast Guard cutter Alexander Hamilton had been lost through enemy submarine action.

The 2,141-ton patrol vessel, one of seven known as "The Pride of the Coast Guard," was torpedoed and crippled in the waters off Iceland. Efforts were made to tow her into port, but en route she capsized and had to be sunk by gunfire.

There were no deaths reported as a result of the capsizing of the ship, but there was a "moderate" loss of personnel when the torpedo struck and exploded, the Navy said.

More of CUTTER on Page 4

SAILOR, KNOWN IN COUNTY, KILLED ON DUTY IN ATLANTIC

Alfred W. Steller, Jr., Grandson Of Witmer Man, Had Served Two Years

Alfred W. Steller, Jr., twenty-three, of Welsh, W. Va., grandson of Jacob Steller, Witmer, has been killed in action with the United States Navy somewhere in the Atlantic. He was a fireman, second class, and had served for two years and eight months.

ALFRED W. STELLER, JR.

Steller, a former football star at

More of SAILOR on Page 4

D. W. SHAUB HEADS AIRCRAFT WARNING SYSTEM IN COUNTY

Deputy Air Raid Warden Will Be In Charge Of 27 Local Stations

The appointment of Daniel W. Shaub, as Civilian director of the Aircraft Warning System in Lancaster County was announced officially Monday by Brigadier General John C. McDonnell, commanding the First Interceptor Com-

DANIEL W. SHAUB

More of SHAUB on Page 4

3,500 WALK OUT AT SHIPYARD, WANT EIGHT-HOUR DAY

CIO Spokesman Says It Is No Strike, But Protest Against 10-Hour Day

San Pedro, Calif.—(AP)—Nearly 3,500 CIO workers at the Bethlehem Shipbuilding Corp. yards walked out Monday in what spokesmen said was a protest against the ten-hour day, initiated Feb. 12.

"This definitely is no strike," said a spokesman. "We merely called the men off the job at the end of eight hours to bring the company to terms."

The spokesman said the night shift, which began work at 5:30 p. m., would quit work at the end of eight hours.

Approximately 5,000 construction men are employed at the shipyards and work in two shifts.

Bethlehem officials declined to comment, other than to say they were conferring with navy officers.

ARMOR FOUNDRY CLOSED

Granite City, Ill.—(AP)—The Granite City plant of American Steel foundries, which produces cast armor for army tanks and gun mounts for the navy, was closed Monday after the CIO Steel Workers' Organizing Committee threw a picket line around the entrance to collect delinquent dues from its members.

In telegrams to government defense officials, company executives

More of LABOR on Page 6

WAR RELIEF FUND REACHES $163,156.09

City Has Subscribed $101,538.56, County $61,617.53; More Contributions Listed

The Red Cross War Relief Fund now stands at $163,156.09, it was announced at chapter headquarters Monday. Of the total, $101,538.56 was contributed by the city, and $61,617.53 by the county.

The contributions include $92 as proceeds from a benefit dance held at the Elks club Saturday night, Miss Geraldine Haman, chairman; $72.19 as proceeds of the recent stamp auction; $43 from a special patriotic service held at St. John's Episcopal church Sunday, and $16.50 as the proceeds from a dance held Sunday night by the Italian American Club Ladies Auxiliary, Mrs. Elizabeth Fulginitie, president, and Mrs. Mary Rose, dance chairman.

ARMY ENLISTMENTS ARE GROWING HERE

February Quota Will Probably Set New High For A Single Month

Army enlistments for February will probably set a new record high for a single month Sergeant William Byrd, in charge of the local office, announced Monday.

Among the men enlisted recently were: Robert S. Burns, 16 Caroline St.; Samuel Newlin, 518 Howard Ave.; Carl A. Schoff, Pequea; Walter J. Null, Holtwood R2; Joseph R. Rineer, Jr., 528 S. Lime St.; Robert E. Adams, Manheim; William A. Flood, Jr., Manheim.

Leon M. Sheaffer, 214 S. School Lane; Robert E. Parmer, Jr., 166 W. Strawberry St.; Donald A. Beecher, 334 E. New St.; Howard R. Riegert, Lebanon; Henry W. Bisalski, 591 N. Plum St.; Claude A. Hartsol, Quarryville R2; Melvin C. Flowers, Mount Joy; William H. Strawser, 615 E. Walnut St.; John P. Schnitzer, 544 W. Lemon St.

Robert F. Keppel, Jr., 436 N. Lime St.; Harry G. Miller, 547 Spruce St.; John D. Zook, 113 Ruby St.; Robert F. Wenditz, 366 Ice Ave.; Clyde E. Bowser, 218 N. Mulberry St.; William G. Conrad, 17 N. Plum St.; George K. Hartman, 217 Nevin St., and Milton B. Hess, Jr., Millersville.

Red Army Within 50 Miles Of Smolensk In Big Drive

Moscow—(Tuesday)—(AP)—Soviet forces have driven to within 50 miles of the German Winter headquarters at Smolensk in a full-scale central front attack which started yesterday morning, the Russians announced today.

The Soviet Information Bureau said the spearhead of this drive had reached Dorogobuzh, northeast of Smolensk on the Dnieper river. This town lies about 15 miles south of the main Smolensk-Moscow railroad and is the terminus of a connecting branch line.

Dorogobuzh also is beyond Vyazma, one of the key Nazi Winter defense pivots.

The midnight communique which told of stubborn battles in this area said that in addition to Dorogobuzh, a number of other populated centers were liberated.

HEAVY AERIAL FIGHTING

Heavy aerial fighting accompanied the Russian advance and the official announcement said that yesterday 28 German planes were destroyed, eight of them on the ground. Twelve Soviet planes were acknowledged lost.

Elaborating on the information bureau's communique, a radio an-

More of RED ARMY on Page 4

WARNS DEMOCRATS AGAINST BATTLE FOR GOVERNORSHIP

Philadelphian Urges Harmony, Party Speculates On Guy K. Bard As Candidate

Harrisburg—(AP)—James P. Clark, Philadelphia Democratic City Chairman, warned in a speech at a Washington Birthday Dinner in Philadelphia Monday that the Pennsylvania Democrats "face a grave responsibility" in the coming elections.

"There is a terrible danger that if the Democrats let themselves be drawn from their duty to President Roosevelt by engaging in a ruinous war over the governorship, we may lose the Democratic members of Congress. Our war-time Congress must remain Democratic as it is today," he asserted.

"We in Philadelphia are for harmony; we are not for any single candidate. We plead with the leaders of the Democratic party in Pennsylvania to reach a speedy accord."

DIFFERENCES DEVELOPED

Sharp differences have developed in Democratic ranks, with U. S. Senator Joseph F. Guffey backing Common Pleas Judge Ralph H. Smith, of Pittsburgh, for governor, and State Chairman Meredith Meyers throwing his personal support to Dr. Luther A. Harr, former Philadelphia city treasurer.

David L. Lawrence, National Committeeman, was understood to favor Auditor General F. Clair Ross but he has not definitely committed himself.

Other speculation centered on

More of DEMOCRATS on Page 4

"We Lead All the Rest"

FARM CORNER

By *The Farm Editor*

LIST FOUR MEETINGS FOR COUNTY FARMERS

Will Show How To Check Condition Of Implements In Use, Ordering Of Repair Parts

Leo Bull, farm machinery department of State College, will have charge of four meetings arranged by the local Agricultural Extension Service for the benefit of county farmers this week. A number of cultivating and harvesting machines will be used in the demonstrations. The purpose is to show how to check the condition of implements in common use on farms and the ordering of repair parts, where needed.

The sessions are scheduled to be held at the following business places:

Thursday: New McCormick Deering store, one-half mile south of Ephrata, at 9:30 a. m.; and Arthur Young Co., Kinzer, at 1:45 p. m.

Friday, H. S. Newcomer and Son store, Mount Joy, at 9:30 a. m.; and C. E. Wiley and Son Co., Wakefield, at 1:45 p. m.

It is an annual practice on some farms to check over machinery and implements and to repair and dress harness at this time of the year, but the number of farmers who do this is "woefully small," County Agent F. S. Bucher said. The average farmer waits for the tear or the break and then wants the repairs immediately. He warned that those who fail to look after their

More of FARM CORNER on Page 4

DR. CLAYTON GABEL DIES IN 78TH YEAR

Practiced As Dentist In This City For Fifty Years; Ill A Short Time

Dr. Clayton G. Gabel, seventy-seven, 150 E. Walnut St., a practicing dentist in Lancaster for the past fifty years, died at 8:07 p. m. Monday at St. Joseph's hospital after a short illness.

He was born in Intercourse, a son of the late Dr. Isaac and Susan Ranck Gabel, and attended Millersville State Normal School and later the Philadelphia Dental College, from which he graduated in 1886. Dr. Gabel started practicing in Lancaster in 1892. He was a member of the Harris Dental Society, the American Dental Association and the First Presbyterian Church, this city.

Survivors include his wife, Annie A. Hoffer Gabel; these children: Dr. Arthur B. Gabel, of the University of Pennsylvania Dental School, Philadelphia; Percy H., this city; Mildred A., wife of George H. Irvin, Beverly Hills, Cal.; Anne G., wife of Milton A. Hildenbrand, Philadelphia; and a brother, Dr. T. W. Gabel, this city.

Intelligencer Journal Weather Calendar

COMPARATIVE TEMPERATURES

Station	High	Low
Intel. Journal	38	22
Water Works	41	20
Ephrata	42	23
Last Year (Ephrata)	41	25
Official High for Year, January 2		53
Official Low for Year, January 11		—10
Character of Day		Clear

HOURLY TEMPERATURES

(Monday)			
3 a. m.	23	4 p. m.	38
4 a. m.	22	5 p. m.	36
5 a. m.	22	6 p. h.	35
6 a. m.	23	7 p. m.	33
7 a. m.	23	8 p. m.	31
8 a. m.	23	9 p. m.	29
9 a. m.	24	10 p. m.	28
10 a. m.	26	11 p. m.	27
11 a. m.	28	Midnight	27
Noon	32	(Tuesday)	
1 p. m.	34	1 a. m.	26
2 p. m.	35	2 a. m.	26
3 p. m.	38	3 a. m.	25

SUN

Rises—7:46 a. m. Sets—6:49 p. m.

More of WEATHER on Page 6

MAN HELD FOR COURT

Edwin E. Getz, Ephrata, charged with assault and battery by Edwin Stief, Ephrata, posted bail for court following a hearing before Justice of the Peace Burkholder, Ephrata, yesterday. Stief previously posted bail for court on similar charges brought by Getz.

Hardy Family Coming to Colonial Theatre Tomorrow in "The Courtship of Andy Hardy"

Andy Hardy finds a new romance and successfully gets out of it to become a free man again in "The Courtship of Andy Hardy," which begins tomorrow at the Colonial theatre. Not only does Andy meet a new girl, but he also rescues his sister from a dramatic "scrape," gets into trouble with the police, and barely escapes the clutches of Polly Benedict, who returns to further complicate his young life. The picture introduces an attractive newcomer to the famous Hardy family series in Donna Reed. Playing her fourth film role, she is a personality certain to climb to stellar heights in Hollywood. The story centers around Andy's efforts to show Miss Reed, as Melodie Nesbit, a good time, on request of his father. Judge Hardy has taken pity on the girl, after trying the case of her separated parents in his court. Realizing that she has led a hopelessly sheltered life, with no opportunity for fun, the Judge calls on Andy for help. When Andy takes her to her first dance, she proves to be the "wall-flower" he had anticipated, but he bears up boldly under it. Experiencing a severe crush on him and realizing her own shortcomings, she learns how to make herself attractive before asking Andy to the next dance, and then becomes the sensation of the evening. Lewis Stone again gives a masterful performance as the wise, small-town judge, with Fay Holden at her best as "Ma" Hardy. Cecilia Parker, as Andy's sister, has her finest role in the series, while Ann Rutherford and Sara Haden add their charm to the family picture.

WILL AID MISSIONS

Blue Ball—The sum of $206 was lifted in an offering Sunday morning at the Weaverland Mennonite Church for the support of the Mennonite missions in Tanganyika Territory, Africa.

HERE'S A LAUGH — "The Man Who Came To Dinner" with Bette Davis, opens today at the Fulton.

BEST SELLER—Harry Pulham brings Bill King, his school chum, home to meet his mother in "H. M. Pulham, Esq.," M-G-M's filmization of the best-seller novel of Boston life by John P. Marquand. Opening Wednesday on the Joy screen, the picture stars Hedy Lamarr as Marvin Myles, Robert Young as Harry Pulham and Ruth Hussey as Kay Motford. Van Heflin plays Bill King, with Fay Holden cast as Mrs. Pulham.

LORETTA YOUNG

STIRRING — The romantic drama, "The Men In Her Life," opens at the Grand theatre today. It stars Loretta Young. Dean Jagger, John Shepperd, Conrad Veidt and Otto Kruger head the supporting cast. Starting Friday, "Kings Row," with Ann Sheridan, Claude Rains, Ronald Reagan and hundreds of others.

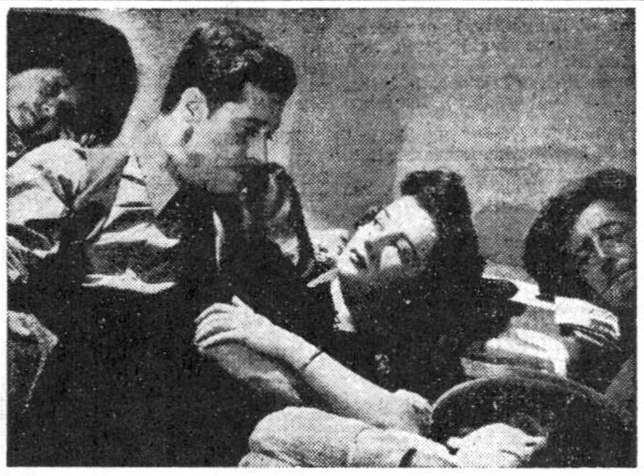

ROMANCE—They meet in a bomb-shelter . . . and it's the most peaceful moment in their romance. Don Ameche and Joan Bennett in a scene from "Confirm or Deny," opening Wednesday at Lititz and Moose theatres. Don is cast as "Yank" Mitchell, tin-hatted and tough war correspondent, while Joan is a fighting English girl with a heart full of courage and love!

BLACK BEADS BACK

Jet beads like grandma wore are good again. The next time you wear the white evening dress, change the accessories to black lace gloves, black evening, slippers and a long strand of jet beads, looped at different lengths.

COME HITHER is plainly written in the eyes of seductive Veronica Lake, as Joel McCrea obeys the command. They're the romantic comedy team of "Sullivan's Travels," new Paramount comedy due Wednesday at the Main Theatre Ephrata. Preston Sturges wrote and directed the new film.

UNCLE EF SAYS:—
With spring here, all the world except its human inhabitants is given over to providing new life. But we must sow plenty of death among the Japs and Germans, if we expect to survive.

LANCASTER NEW ERA

WEATHER
Snow probably turning to rain in north portion, and rain in south portion tonight; slowly rising temperature. (Details on Page 3).

Examiner Founded 1830. New Era Founded 1877. | Published Every Evening Except Sunday by New Era Company. Entered as Second Class Matter at Post Office, Lancaster, Pa. | LANCASTER, PA., THURSDAY, APRIL 9, 1942 | CITY EDITION | 22 PAGES—176 COLUMNS | 20c PER WEEK—4c Per Copy

BELIEVE BATAAN HAS FALLEN

Jap Planes Sink 2 British Cruisers

CHARGE FRAUD IN AGREEMENT ON MAGNESIUM

Defense Plant Agency's Dealings With Ohio Firm Seen Sinister.

PROBE IS DEMANDED BY NEVADA SENATOR

WASHINGTON, April 9—(AP)—Senator Bunker (D-Nev) charged in a Senate address today that an agreement between the Defense Plant Corporation and Basic Magnesium, Inc., of Cleveland, O., for construction of a $63,000,000 magnesite refinery at Las Vegas, Nev., "is so sinister as to indicate that some officials of our government are guilty of malfeasance."

He demanded a thorough investigation of the Defense Plant Corporation, a subsidiary of the Recdnstruction Finance Corporation, and added:

"If the agreement between the Defense Plant Corporation and Basic Magnesium, Inc., represents a cross section of conduct on the part of the Defense Plant Corporation, I can come to only one conclusion: We are tolerating the existence of an agency of the government that is s corrupt that it would make profiteering in the last war look like petit larceny by comparison.

"The fraud that is being perpetrated on the Defense Plant Corporation is a betrayal of the President and the American people."

4,280 P. C. Profit Seen

Last week Bunker told the Senate that Basic Magnesium, Inc., stood a chance of making a profit of 4,280 per cent in one year on an admitted investment of less than $50,000.

Previously, the special Senate committee that is investigating national war projects reported that hearings it conducted at Las Vegas at Bunker"s request indicated that Basic Magnesium, Inc., was guilty of "one of the most flagrant attempts at war profiteering."

Bunker, youngest member of the Senate, declared today that the ramifications of the transaction were so far reaching as to "project Basic Magnesium, Inc., into the picture of international intrigue, involving English and German interests."

Forty-five per cent of the stock in Basic Magnesium, Inc., he said,

(See MAGNESIUM—Page 19)

TWIN GIRL AND BOY BORN 12 MI. APART

Twins, a boy and a girl, were born to Mr. and Mrs. Robert Buchter, Brunnerville, today.

The boy was born at home at 11:30 A. M., with Dr. D. C. Martin, Lititz, in attendance. The mother and baby were placed in the General hospital ambulance and taken to the hospital, 12 miles from the home, where the girl was born at 12:30 P. M.

The twins and the mother were all reported "doing nicely" by hospital attendants this afternoon.

The Scribbler

H. S. MELLINGER, Akron coal and lumber dealer, went to the General Hospital recently to visit a friend. Entering the automatic elevator he closed the door and waited ten minutes for the operator to come. Finally he decided to push one of the buttons and ring for help. He pushed the button and by chance the elevator delivered him exactly to the floor he wanted to visit.

DETECTIVE John Kauffman, after a couple of night's work on his victory garden, became confused as to where he had planted things and what he had planted. To avoid future mistakes, he went to a seed store on South Queen street where he purchased wooden paddles which will now mark both the planted area and furnish information on the produce he may expect.

EVEN a draft board clerk can run afoul of the stringent censorship.

D. J. Keener, of County Board No. 3, walked up to a soldier directing the Army through Lancaster and asked, by way of friendliness:

"Where are you from?"

"I'm sorry, I can't tell you" was all he got, he admits.

High Schools to Aid In Training Pilots

Refresher Courses in Mathematics and Physics Planned in All Schools Where 15 or More Prospective Cadets Enroll

WASHINGTON, April 9—(AP)—The nation's high schools soon will be geared to the elementary training of pilots to fly America's great air armada.

J. W. Studebaker, U. S. Commissioner of Education, disclosed today that the plan contemplates the teaching of aeronautics in all high schools where 15 or more prospective air cadets can be enrolled.

"It is expected," Studebaker said, "that recommendations for pre-pilot refresher courses in physics and mathematics soon will be sent to all school systems of the country—these recommendations to be followed soon thereafter by the publication of detailed suggestions emanating from the Army and Navy as to the court outlines and instructional materials."

The Office of Education and representatives of the Army, Navy and Civil Aeronautics Administration now are conferring to determine what the high schools can do immediately to speed the pilot training program, in view of the President's goal to produce 60,000 planes this year and 125,000 in 1943.

Plan For Present Semester

Studebaker outlined tentative plans agreed upon as follows:

1. For the present semester, mathematics and physics applicable to the work of pilots might be handled as extra subjects in the boys' schedules, or taught before and after regular school hours.

2. Intensive refresher and pre-pilot training courses might be given in the summer schools of the larger communities and boys from nearby communities permitted to attend, tuition-free.

3. Next Septemebr a full semester's work in aeronautics should be offered in every high school in which as many as 15 prospective physically qualified air cadets can be enrolled. Boys who have taken such courses will be enabled, upon their induction into air cadet training, to devote more time to flying. Fewer boys will be "washed out" in the ground school phases of their first three months' training period.

A Voluntary Proposition

Definite plans for the administration of such courses will be issued soon. The outline of the plans made no mention of compulsion, it being assumed that eligible youths would make up their own minds whether to take the courses.

Studebaker said the high schools also could acquaint older boys in and out of school of the need for men to serve in the air forces, of the standards for selection of men to undergo training as air cadets; the schools could have physicians examine prospective air cadets to advise them and their parents whether they may hope to meet the physical standards required; and the schools could help these boys to obtain remedial physical

(See PILOTS—Page 12)

Cross Saves His Life

Second Lieutenant Clarence Sanford (above) of Auburn, N. Y., reported from "somewhere in Australia" that his life had been saved by a silver crucifix from natives of a small Pacific island after he had bailed out of his fighter plane while chasing Japanese warplanes.

"GAS" SUPPLIES CUT ONE-THIRD

Card Rationing Plan May Be Dropped, If Public Aids, Ickes Says.

WASHINGTON, April 9—(AP)—The War Production Board today ordered gasoline deliveries to service stations in 17 Eastern States, Oregon, Washington and the District of Columbia cut one-third compared with average deliveries last December, January and February. The curtailment compares with a 20 per cent cut already in effect, resulting from tanker sinkings and transportation shortages.

The new reduction, effective April 16, will require proportionate reductions in gasoline deliveries during the latter half of April.

Meanwhile, Secretary Ickes, the petroleum coordinator, told his weekly press conference that rationing by use of cards might be avoided if the public cooperated in the filling station supply limitation program.

"If this works satisfactorily," he said, "we may go to Mr. Henderson (the price administrator) and say there is no need for card rationing."

The coordinator reported that oil stocks of the seaboard dropped another 1,049,000 barrels last week, and that the overall stocks of then seaboard area now are 13,275,000 barrels under April of 1941.

Ickes announced he would support a proposal of the Petroleum Industry War Council for the industry to produce a minimum of 300,000 tons of synthetic rubber for civilian use, over and above the 700,000 tons already planned by government agencies.

MAN HIT BY BULLET WHILE ON TRACTOR

Corporal Harry Fitzgerald of the State Police is investigating the shooting of Ross Albright, fifty-five, Bareville, R. 1, who was treated by Dr. Ralph J. Goldin, Brownstown, for a superficial scalp wound Tuesday afternoon.

Albright told police he was operating a tractor while plowing a lot for Fary Herr at Talmage, when wounded by a stray .22 caliber bullet. He said the noise from the tractor engine drowned out any report of a shot and he was unable to give police any information as to the identity of the owner of the firearms.

7 ARMY NURSES, 2 SOLDIERS HURT IN INDIANTOWN CRASH

INDIANTOWN GAP, April 9—(AP)—Seven nurses and two soldiers were injured last night in a collision of their automobiles on the Indiantown Gap Military Reservation.

The nurses injured were Marie Shillen, 35, of Clearfield, condition critical; Dorothy Whitsill, 28, Mount Vernon, Ill.; Phyllis Pentz, 26, Grampian, Pa.; Leona E. Horan, 27, Brentwood; Anna Singleton, 26, Chester; Meredith Miller, 31, Bellefonte; and Mary Lally, 34, dietician at the post hospital, Olyphant, Pa. All except Miss Lally have the rank of second lieutenant.

The soldiers injured were Private Herman Wilson, 25, of Independence, La., and Private George Kimbrough, of Allensville, Ky.

NAVAL BATTLE REPORTED IN BENGAL BAY

New Jap Landing 30 Miles From India's Frontier Is Rumored.

BRITISH NAVAL BASE ON CEYLON BOMBED

(By the Associated Press)

Two British 8-inch-gun cruisers, the 10,000-ton Cornwall and the 9,975-ton Dorsetshire whose torpedoes finished off the German battleship Bismarck little less than a year ago, have been sunk by Japanese bombers ranging the Bay of Bengal and battering at thin-stretched British naval communications to India, the Admiralty in London announced today.

The sinkings constituted a blow to the British naval strength immediately available to cope with Japanese aircraft carriers and warships reported increasing their activities astride the sea lanes to Calcutta in the bay between the bombed coast of India and invaded Burma.

London naval reporters said the "biggest naval battle in all history seems about to blaze up in the Bay of Bengal between the Japanese and British fleets."

Axis reports last week declared powerful British naval forces had been sighted speeding around the Cope of Good Hope en route to the Indian Ocean and the Bay of Bengal.

Other Ships Apparently Near

There was no intimation what other warships were operating with the Cornwall and Dorsetshire. But 1,100 crew members out of 1,330 were saved, London announced, indicating that other ships were on hand. The commander of the cruisers were among the rescued.

The Rome radio reported that the remaining units of the British squadron were engaged in a running sea fight with stronger Japanese naval forces. London did not disclose when the cruisers went down.

Japanese broadcasts quoted Im-

(See PACIFIC—Page 12)

RUBBER COVERS FOR FOOD PACKAGES ARE PROHIBITED BY WPB

WASHINGTON, April 9.—(AP)—Use of rubber covers or rubber sealing rings in containers for packaging more than 40 groups of products, including coffee, tea, tobacco, candy, spices and various sauces, was prohibited today by the War Production Board, effective May 9.

Beginning ten days from today, the order further provides, no rubber product or compound may be purchased or used for manufacture of glass jar covers for these products.

WPB said the action was necessary to prevent a sharp increase in the use of rubber for jar covers by manufacturers of foods which can no longer be packed in tin cans.

The effect of the order, it was understood, would be to prevent use of glass containers for animal food, macaroni, spaghetti, and whole fruits and vegetables on the tin-can prohibited list unless further research discloses some method of packing them in glass without using the rubber tops or ceiling rings.

The Heroic Chapter Ends . . . .

Driven back successively from line 1, to line 2, to line 3, the heroic American defenders of Bataan today apparently had been driven to the tip of the narrow peninsula they had defended so amazingly for three months. How many of General Wainwright's 36,853 effective troops were able to reach Corregidor and other forts in Manila Bay which still are held by the Americans was not known.

CRUISER IS SUNK BY BRITISH SUB

10,000-Ton Italian Vessel Lost in Mediterranean; Rommel Is Held.

(By The Associated Press)

Britain's desert armies, swiftly countering the threat of a new drive by 125,000 troops under Field Marshal Erwin Rommel, were reported seizing the initiative with attacks on advanced Axis positions in North Africa today, while at sea, the British reported the sinking of a 10,000-ton Italian cruiser in the Central Mediterranean.

A London Admiralty communique said that a British submarine torpedoed the cruiser, which was escorted by destroyers and aircraft, and that eight minutes later the warship "was heard to break up and sink."

Premier Mussolini's high command acknowledged that the British were counter-attacking on the Libyan front, but asserted they had been beaten off.

British headquarters at Cairo said that British troops were engaging Axis forces at Sidi Bregisch, about

(See BRITISH—Page 2)

DAVIS HERE TONIGHT TO OPEN CAMPAIGN

U. S. Senator James J. Davis will launch his campaign for the Republican nomination for Governor at a meeting of G. O. P. county leaders from eastern Pennsylvania at the Stevens House here tonight. Kenneth Kressler, Northampton county, Davis' campaign manager, is making arrangements.

Thirty-seven county leaders and numerous Philadelphia ward leaders have been invited and County Commissioner G. Graybill Diehm, of Lancaster, said he would attend the event. Diehm has made no public commitment of a candidate since his withdrawal from the gubernatorial race last Saturday, but has been a long-time friend of Davis.

Major General Edward Martin, the other aspirant for the nomination, speaks at a rally at Oil City tonight. Northwestern leaders are expected to attend.

EPHRATA RE-OPENS MISSING $363 CASE

Motor Police at the Ephrata substation renewed their investigation of the theft of $363 of Ephrata borough funds, missing for three years, but said today the sole lead in the case was a dud.

According to Councilman William B. Carter, H. Wilson Hertzog, of Ephrata, had made a statement that he knew what happened to the money. Borough authorities asked the police to investigate the matter.

Corporal Simpson, of the Ephrata sub-station, said he interrogated Hertzog, but that the latter said he made the statement in anger and had no basis for it.

UNDERSTANDING IN INDIA AT HAND

Agreement on Setting Up National Government Is Reported.

NEW DELHI, India, April 9—(AP)—A general understanding on the main points at issue between the British and politically articulate Hindus appeared to be at hand today, with reported assent by leaders of the All-India Congress Party and the Hindu Mahasabha to establishment of a National Government for India.

Such a government would serve India pending the post-war dominion status offered by Britain.

Britain's chief negotiator, Sir Stafford Cripps, was understood to have telegraphed Vinayak Damodar Savarkar, president of the Hindu Mahasabha, asking if that organization of political moderates had any objections to joining a national government.

Savarkar was understood to have replied through the Governor of Bombay, Sir Roger Lumley, that his organization had no objections, even though it still opposed a clause in the British plan allowing provinces to remain outside the proposed Indian Union.

It was reported that the Mahasabha would get two seats in the national government.

Reports on the status of the negotiations with the Congress Party, the dominant political group, var-

(See INDIA—Page 2)

FIND BABY DIED AFTER CARRYING HER ACROSS ICY LAKE

STURGEON FALLS, Ont., April 9.—(AP)—The story of a dramatic race against death across the treacherous, thaw-weakened ice of Tomiko Lake was disclosed here today. Seeking medical aid for their nine-months-old daughter, Mona, who was suffering from bronchial pneumonia, Mr. and Mrs. Joseph Lavalee started across a seven-mile strip of honey-combed ice separating their cabin from Crystal Falls.

Four or five times the ice broke beneath them and they narrowly escaped going through. Heavy snow further impeded their progress as they carried the sick child across the ice. It required a full day to make the trip that usually took only a few hours. They arrived at Crystal Falls at dusk, only to find the child was already dead.

FATHER WEARS HIS CHILD'S ANKLETS

MARYVILLE, Mo., April 9—(AP)—Ellis Meek wore a snazzy pair of blue socks to work. Returning home at night, Meek's 7-year-old daughter greeted him frigidly.

The socks, he learned, were his daughter's anklets.

36,853 DEFENDERS FACE DEATH OR SURRENDER; BAY FORTS STILL STAND

Roosevelt Gives Wainwright Free Hand; Stimson Reveals Attempt to Reinforce Besieged Army; Some Supplies Got Through

WASHINGTON, April 9.—(AP)—The Defense of Bataan, America's heroic modern chapter in the book of history, appeared ended today.

Capture or death at the hands of invading Japanese hordes faced the bulk of the 36,853 gallant American-Filipino defenders, closing an heroic three-months battle against numerically overwhelming forces.

Exhausted by day and night fighting, short rations and disease, and virtually cut off from supplies despite costly efforts which provided them some ammunition but did not relieve the food shortage, the doughty defenders gave way before the Japanese who already had overrun the rich Dutch Indies and Britain's Singapore and Malaya.

Secretary of War Stimson related the first details concerning the defenders today, after a special communique had announced that the defense of Bataan had probably been overcome, and said President Roosevelt had authorized the Philippine commander to make any decision he deemed necessary in the light of events.

A round-about radio report from Berlin, quoting a Shanghai newspaper report, said that Lieut. Gen. Jonathan M. Wainwright, commander on Bataan, had sought an armistice, but this was not confirmed in any other quarter.

U. S. Still Holds Forts In Bay

Latest reports, Stimson said, indicated that Corregidor and other fortresses guarding Manila bay were still in United States hands, as was about half of the area of the Philippines, but he declined to make predictions how long the forts could be held. He said he saw no reason why resistance by small, isolated forces would not continue.

"This is only a temporary loss," Stimson said. "We shall not stop until we drive out the invaders from the islands."

Among Our Worst Military Reverses

The Secretary's disclosure of the number of American and Filipino troops involved made it evident that the Bataan disaster was among the most severe reversals suffered by American arms in any foreign war.

Officials believed the manpower loss might be the heaviest sustained by an American force in any single engagement with a foreign foe. Losses were heavier in the Meuse-Argonne offensive of 1918, but were spread over a campaign of weeks.

Stimson said the figure of 36,853 effectives was in the report received yesterday from General Wainwright. He stressed that this figure included only the men fighting on Bataan at that time.

Excluded were American and Filipino troops guarding the defenses of Corregidor and the other islands, the wounded, nearly 20,000 civilian refugees, and some 6,000 Filipino laborers who were non-combatant.

Hurley Headed Reinforcement Task

Stimson disclosed that under the direction of Brigadier General Patrick J. Hurley, former Secretary of War who is now Minister to New Zealand, urgent efforts were made beginning last January 11 to reinforce the besieged Philippine forces.

From a base in Australia several ship loads of supplies were sent to the Philippines, and part of these supplies reached Corregidor and Bataan.

"But for every ship that arrived, we lost nearly two ships," Stimson said.

Because of these supplies, the defenders were never short of ammunition, the Secretary said, but had been on short rations.

Stimson said he saw no reason why resistance by isolated, relatively small forces should not continue in northern Luzon, on the island of Mindanao and elsewhere where blows have been struck, aside from further defense of Corregidor.

The War Department's sober early-morning communique stating "the probability that the defenses on Bataan have been overcome" was the latest news the War Department had received up to 10:30 A. M., Eastern War Time, today, Stimson said.

"Our troops, outnumbered and worn down by successive attacks by fresh troops, exhausted by insufficient rations and the disease prevalent in that peninsula, finally had their lines broken and enveloped by the enemy," the Secretary said.

"We do not know the details

(See PHILIPPINES—Page 12)

Wenger Mennonites "Strike" at Camp

Unwilling to work for "other churches" but obedient to the government, six Wenger Mennonites at the conscientious objectors' camp near Wells Tannery, Pa., are now doing their share of the soil conservation work there.

The Wengerites, who were sent to the camp by Federal court after they refused to go willingly, are understood to have staged the equivalent of a sit-down strike when they arrived there in January. Not only did they refuse to work, but they refused to do any of the camp maintenance chores.

Managers From Mennonite Church

The camp managers are supplied by the Mennonite church from which the Wengerites broke away several generations ago, and with whom they have had no denominational affiliation since that time. The attitude of the smaller group was that they could not, in good

(See OBJECTORS—Page 12)

THE AMERICAN WAY: Today's Mother Finds Time for Home, Baby and War Job

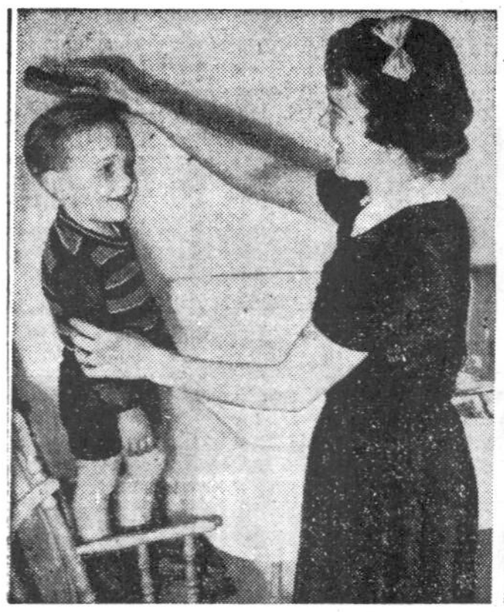

5 A. M.: Mrs. Max Sell, of Yonkers, N. Y., rises before dawn, gets breakfast, dresses healthy 2-year-old son, Clemens.

6:30 A. M.: Off to 25-cents-a-day nursery school where Clements gets trained care.

7 A. M.: Mother mans her loom to turn out duck for Army and Navy in world's biggest carpet mill. She earns $32 weekly.

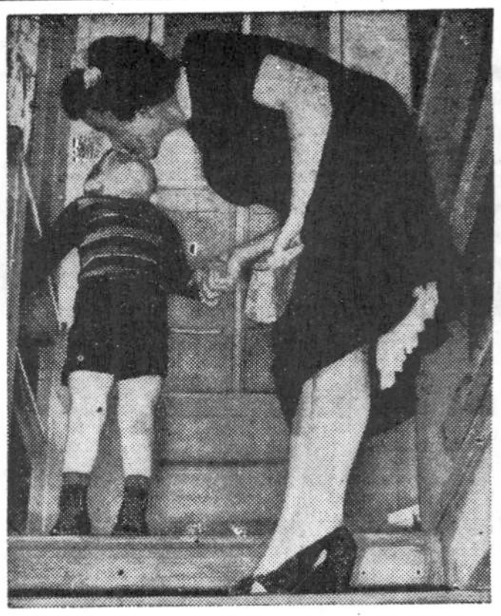

2 P. M.: Factory work done, home work begins. Father, a baker soon to be drafted, brings baby home from nursery.

3 P. M.: After walking baby, Mrs. Sell washes, irons, cleans, cooks big supper.

7 P. M.: She crochets to relax, plans budget. Sells together earn $70 weekly, spend most on food, clothes for baby.

BOOK CLUB ELECTS

Mrs. Paul Landis, of Millersville, was hostess Monday to members of the Village Book Club at her home. During the business meeting officers were elected as follows: President, Mrs. Gilbert Sharff; secretary-treasurer, Mrs. Allen Geist. The club also decided to dispense with the annual banquet this year and give a contribution to the Red Cross. After the business meeting a paper on the "Life and Poetry of Paul Lawrence Dunbar was read by Mrs. Raymond Hovis.

Stop Abusing Your Two Feet, Start Wearing Sensible Shoes

By HELEN JAMESON

March, march, march, the girls are marching! And some of them—especially those who hopped into the family car when they had to go only a few blocks—are having a pretty bad time of it. It never has occurred to them that their feet needed special care. They have petted their complexions, fondled their tresses, embellished their finger nails, kept their bodies neat and slender, but the poor little trotters got along as best they could. That's not playing fair. Feet are the faithful horses that drag the body around. Why be mean to them?

Before the age of seventeen a girl is seldom conscious of her feet. Her mother has provided her with suitable shoes. Then she develops a yen for spiked heels and her troubles begin. Her poor little dogs have tendons distorted, the musculature undergoes a change for the worse, toes go into a huddle. Chiropodists will tell you that the majority of foot ills are caused by shoes that are not properly fitted. Their customers are mainly women, victims of vanity. Men are vain too, some of them, but not to the extent of making themselves miserable and uncomfortable.

Between the age of thirty and fifty, feet get the meanest break. By the time a woman is fifty she is likely to encase her feet in suitable shoes. She has found that there's no more reason for clumping around on high heels than there is a reason for wearing a ring in one's nose.

Runover heels are a hazard. When the heels wear off on the outer side the legs will be slightly bowed. If the slant is on the inner side, look out for knock-knees. When the rear of the shoe wears more quickly than the forward portion it is because the foot comes down heels first, keeping the toes lifted more than they should be. This practice jars the spinal column.

The big toe should point straight ahead with no inward bend. If it curves toward the second toe there is a chance of developing a bunion, and the afflicted one had better provide herself with shoes that are wide, with firm soles, heels that are fairly low. The big toe will have a chance for readjustment.

The feet should be bathed daily if comfort is to be enjoyed. They are jailed in airtight coverings that prevent evaporation of skin moisture. The chemical deposits left by perspiration are irritating to the skin, causing smarting and burning, especially in the summer season.

Tired feet make for clumsy, awkward movements. They have a deplorable effect upon posture and they'll curdle the sweetest disposition. They make one unfit for the job, no matter what the job may be. When feet hurt one hurts all over; even the spirit is sick.

RUMMAGE SALE

The Junior Red Cross will hold a rummage sale Friday evening and all day Saturday at the corner of Caroline and Manor Sts. Anyone having rummage is asked to contact Jane DeBolt, 108 Jackson St., and the articles will be called for.

Saving Oils And Fats Is a Wartime 'Must'

By MRS. GAYNOR MADDOX

It is a wartime "must" to take good care of kitchen fats and oils. Mothers should enlist their younger daughters in a domestic campaign against waste. Dr. Louise Stanley, chief of the U. S. Bureau of Home Economics, supplies the following instructions:

There are a lot of ways to waste fat—by using too big pats of butter, by pouring bacon grease or drippings down the sink, and by storing leftover fat improperly.

Don't serve too frequently foods that need a lot of fat, such as pastries, doughnuts and croquettes.

There are a number of foods that supply us with fat. They include fat meats, fat poultry, fat fish, nuts, chocolate, coconut cream, egg yolk, nut butters, olives and avocadoes.

Many fats can be saved and re-used. Keep bacon fat and drippings for seasoning vegetables. Fat used for deep-fat frying may be used a number of times, if it is strained through several thicknesses of cheesecloth or other clean white cloth before you put it away each time.

Any surplus fat trimmed off at home—suet, pork, lamb, and chicken fat—may be ground or cut into very small pieces and rendered down: Heat it in a double boiler. Cover and stir occasionally. When the fat is all melted, strain and store it.

Clarifying fat will free it from objectionable odors, tastes, or colors in most cases: Melt the fat with an equal amount of water. Heat for a short time at a moderate temperature with occasional stirring. Cool, remove the layer of fat, and scrape off any bits of meat and other material which may cling to the underside.

Store all fats in a closely covered container, in a dark, cool place and away from strong flavored foods.

Young cooks will like this Girl Scout recipe using carefully saved fat:

NOODLES AND APPLES

Four cups boiled noodles, 8 apples, 4 tablespoons sugar, salt, 4 tablespoons bacon fat, 4 tablespoons butter.

Cook noodles. Wash, pare and cut apples in eighths. Melt butter and fat in a frying pan, put in half the noodles, then apples. Sprinkle with sugar, a speck of salt and cinnamon, cover with remaining noodles. Let bake until apples are soft and noodles are browned. Keep covered the first 10 minutes.

HOROSCOPE

Today's birthday child is a positive individual, very aggressive, but will listen wisely to offered counsel. He or she should foster the talent for music that they possess, and be guided by their first impressions. Business and domestic affairs will progress satisfactorily during the next year provided heavy expenditures and attempted fraud or deception are avoided. The heart should not be allowed to rule the head. A loving, kind, grenerous disposition will be possessed by the child who is born on this date. He or she will be ever ready to help others, but must be taught early to guard against imposition and excessive generosity.

BOOK REVIEW GIVEN

Dr. Richard D. Altick, of the English Department of Franklin and Marshall College, reviewed the book, "Hollywood," by Leo C. Rosten, at the monthly book review of the YWCA last evening. These reviews are sponsored by the General Education Department of the 'Y'. Mrs. M. Ray Adams was in charge of this session and introduced Dr. Altick.

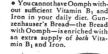

Matched In Crochet

by Laura Wheeler

When you've crocheted this pretty chair set in string you'll want to make the pillow too, for matching accessories are smart today! Pattern 322 contains charts and directions for making the articles shown; illustrations of them and stitches; material required.

Write plainly pattern number, your name and address.

Send ten cents in coin (plus one cent to cover cost of mailing) to Needlecraft Dept., Lancaster New Era, 82 Eighth avenue, New York, N. Y.

UNCLE EF SAYS:—
Donald Nelson says he may need a law to draft business executives because the politicians have them scared so badly they won't volunteer. It wouldn't require drafting if the hecklers would lay off.

LANCASTER NEW ERA

WEATHER
Mild temperatures tonight. (Details on Page 3).

Examiner Founded 1830. New Era Founded 1877.

Published Every Evening Except Sunday by New Era Company. Entered as Second Class Matter at Post Office, Lancaster, Pa.

LANCASTER, PA., MONDAY, APRIL 27, 1942 | CITY EDITION | 16 PAGES—128 COLUMNS | 20c PER WEEK—4c Per Copy

F.D. ASKS FREEZING OF ALL WAGES

33 Autos Destroyed, 36 Damaged As Fire Razes Old Convention Hall

Ruins of about 33 automobiles and trucks stored in an annex of the Whiting Motor company, destroyed by fire which razed Convention Hall. In this wreckage are about 22 new automobiles and trucks, the sale of which was restricted by federal automobile rationing. Thirty-six other cars were damaged.

(Other fire pictures on last page)

The War Today

by DeWitt Mackenzie

Hitler Within Six Weeks May Be Fighting a New Army—the Invisible Legions of the Conquered Nations

As the time draws near for the joining of the crucial battle of the Hitlerian conflict, there emerges the possibility that this Armageddon may see uprisings in many places by the invisible army of the subjugated peoples.

Should this happen on an extended scale — and it might—it likely would produce bloody chaos in the affected areas. The fury of a revolting populace, even though lacking proper arms, can be very terrible.

MacKenzie

Word long ago was spread throughout the conquered countries by Allied radio and by underground telegraph that the hour of deliverance would come, and the V-For-Victory symbol became a flaming torch of hope. Indeed, the campaign inspired so much premature violence that the British began urging these Hitler-ridden folk to hold their peace until the signal came for an uprising. It has been hard to keep them in haid, for the yoke of bondage has been cruel.

But now suddenly Britain's "Colonel Britton" — the radio voice which has been fostering and guiding the V-for-Victory army on the continent —has electrified his hearers by calling on them to prepare for united action. Probably within six weeks, says the spectral "Colonel," the sign will be given for the civilian uprising. Meanwhile the people are to lay plans to do the greatest possible damage to the Nazis by sabotage and other means.

* * *

Already France, Belgium, Norway, Holland and the countries of Eastern Europe have given us many grisly examples of what the invisible army can accomplish. Almost ever day adds to the list. Mysterious hands have been reaching out of the darkness of the night to snatch the lives of German soldiers. Even broad daylight has brought its swiftly moving assassinations. Troop trains have been wrecked, and bombs have been thrown. In short, there have been constant sabotage and killings despite the warnings from "Colonel Britton" to go slowly and not arouse Nazi ire until the time is ripe.

That the Nazis see the danger is shown by their wholesale executions of hostages in an effort to terrify the populations into submission. Poland and other countries have charged the Germans with great massacres. But slayings have only made the fire of hatred burn hotter.

Fear that unrest might even boil up in his own country was indicated in Hitler's Reichstag speech yesterday. His demand for obedience from the people carried a note of grave concern to the ears of expert radio observers in London.

* * *

Just when the all-out Allied-Axis clash will come is still a matter of conjecture. Probably "Colonel Britton's guess that the volcano will erupt in six weeks or less is a fair one. Of course, whatever else hap-

(See WAR TODAY—Page 13)

AUTOIST NABBED 3 TIMES IN YEAR

Table Tennis Champ Faces Loss of License as Habitual Violator.

Alfred G. DiCola, twenty-one, 146 East New street, Lancaster's table tennis champion, faces the loss of his driving privileges from one to three months as an habitual violator following a hearing this morning before Inspector Charles H. Stormfeltz in speeders' court.

Commissioner of Police Carlson, who had DiCola cited, forwarded to the State his record of three arrests within a year. DiCola was arrested March 16, 1941, for driving too fast for conditions, on October 29, 1941, for speeding over intersections, and again on February 27 this year for driving too fast for conditions.

"What reason can you give for your apparent disregard for the city speed laws?" Stormfeltz asked the youth. DiCola did not answer.

"Don't you realize you may kill or injure someone if you keep this up?" the inspector continued.

"Yes sir, but frankly there was only one time that I thought I was speeding," DiCola replied. "That was the second time I was arrested and that time I was late for work." DiCola said he was employed by the U. S. Ordnance Department at Philadelphia.

Policeman Paul Way testified DiCola was speeding at 40 miles an hour on October 29, 1941, and failed to reduce his speed while crossing three intersections.

70 MPH Speeder Going Into Army

Edwin P. Miller, Gap, R. 2, clocked at 70 miles an hour on March 14, said his speedometer was found to be 28 miles slow but adedd, "it doesn't matter if I lose my license or not for tomorrow I'm going into the Army." He explained he was drafted and is scheduled to leave tomorrow to be inducted.

Eight motorists failed to appear for hearings. One of them, Howard E. Whitney, Conestoga, R. 2, was represented by his attorney, W. Hensel Brown, who submitted a written application for a restricted

(See SPEEDERS—Page 4)

3 DIE, 40 INJURED IN CRASH OF BUSES

HALETHORPE, Md., April 27—Two inter-State buses collided with terrific impact Sunday afternoon, killing three persons and injuring more than 40 others. The roof of one bus was torn off. While neither overturned, both vericles were turned completely around by the force of the crash.

The dead were listed by police as Mr. and Mrs. Daniel S. Murphy, of Jersey City, N. J., and Gladys Lewis, of Washington. The Murphys' 8-year-old son was uninjured.

Ten persons were treated at the scene while 25 others were taken in 10 ambulancs to hospitals in Baltimore.

Traffic was backed up in both directions for 10 miles before it could be rerouted.

TRANSPORT GROUPS MEET TOMORROW

Members of the four groups of the Lancaster Transport Conservation Committee will meet tomorrow evening at 7:30 o'clock in the Council Chambers of the Municipal building.

A tentative program has been mailed to the members of the committees on conservation of transportation facilities for industries, deliveries, schools and farms. Members will discuss this program and make definite plans at tomorrow's meeting.

David R. Baker is chairman of the committee and E. G. Seidle is co-chairman.

19 Nearby Homes Damaged, 60 Routed

Flames Sweep Old Western Markethouse, Causing $350,000 Damage; Owner Carried from Building; 2 Ill Women Moved

Thirty-three automobiles, twenty-two of them new models frozen by federal rationing, were destroyed and 36 others were damaged when fire razed Convention Hall formerly the Western Market House, southeast corner of Orange and Pine streets early today. Approximately 19 nearby homes were damaged and about 60 adults and children routed from their homes.

Officials said 24 of the damaged automobiles were water soaked and charred and 12 others are badly drenched. Some of the 24 are damaged beyond repair, firemen said. All the automobiles were in the show rooms, repair shop and annex of the Whiting Motor company which occupied the first floor of the building. J. H. C. Whiting, owner of the company, is president and treasurer. The company is distributor for the Plymouth and Dodge automobiles.

The second floor was occupied by the Olympic Skating Rink operated by Jack Dalton.

Damage is estimated at $350,000 and upwards. Stores of oil and gasoline in the garage helped feed the fire.

A. Leaman Futer, who resided on the second floor, was carried to safety by a city fireman. He had been overcome and was lying in bed with flames only a few feet away when Clair Lefever, member of Company No. 1 battered down a door and reached him. Futer holds a life interest in the building which is owned by the B. Franklin Futer estate.

City firemen said the fire was

(See FIRE—Last Page)

2 DIE IN CRASH; 2 BADLY HURT

Auto Crashes Into Tree Near York; Probe Is Continued.

Two men, one a resident of Lancaster and the other a former resident, were killed and their two companions were seriously injured when the auto in which they were riding crashed through a fence into a tree near Stony Brook on the Lincoln highway, three miles east of York, late Saturday night.

Raymond Winters, twenty-six, 1049 Langley avenue, Philadelphia, formerly of 453 West Vine street, identified as the driver of the car, was killed instantly.

Carl Anthony Wendel, twenty-four, 647 St. Joseph street, died a few hours later.

2 Are In Serious Condition

James Binkle, twenty-seven, 706 Manor street, was reported in a serious condition at the York hospital, while Francis Harmes, twenty-eight, 706 Poplar street, the fourth occupant of the car, was reported "questionably fair." Hospital attendants said both suffered fractured legs, arms and head injuries.

Dr. L. U. Zech, York county coroner, who described the accident as "one of the worst I've ever seen," said the auto, traveling west on the highway toward York, crashed against the tree on the north side of the road with such force that it was demolished. The engine was torn from the chassis and hurled a distance of ten feet where it partially buried itself in the soft ground.

Coroner Zech added that the car apparently traveling at a high rate of speed and that Winters lost control. He said he was continu-

(See ACCIDENTS—Page 14)

1776 CANNON GOES INTO SCRAP SUPPLY

CAMDEN, N. J., April 27—(AP)—Camden County is throwing a Revolutionary War cannon into the fight against the Axis.

The gun, displayed on a lawn since the 18th century, was given to the Industrial Salvage committee. Its metal will go into war production.

TRADE SUGAR REGISTRATION

All Units Must Give Data Tomorrow, Wednesday; Halt Sales Tonight.

Machinery was in readiness today for the registration of "trade units" which require sugar in large quantities, to take place tomorrow and Wednesday at three city high schools and at 35 borough and township high schools over the county.

At the same time, retail sugar sales will be stopped at midnight today until May 5.

Rationing officials pointed out that the individual consumers do not register until next week, May 4-7 having been set aside for this task. This means the issuance of rationing books to Lancaster county's 212,000 residents, and a larger organization than the trade registration.

Early Registration Urged

It was expected that between 2,000 and 2,500 stores, bakeries, industries and institutions would register tomorrow and Wednesday in Lancaster county. One official said he hoped that all would apply tomorrow so that if the data was not complete it would be obtained the next day and finished up then.

Each of the five county rationing

(See SUGAR—Page 14)

RETAIL FOOD COSTS ARE UP 22 P. C.

STATE COLLEGE, Pa., April 27—(AP)—Retail food costs rose 20 to 22 per cent in Pennsylvania in March over 1940 figures while the State's industrial activity climbed to a new peak, with the index rising to 181.4 in March, a gain of 25 per cent, the Pennsylvania State College reported today.

The college's monthly business survey said retail food costs in leading cities were up 24 to 28 per cent since the start of the war. The gain in industrial activity for March over February, 1942, was one per cent.

Al l time records were made in factory employment and payrolls, industrial power sales, telephone service and sales of electricity.

'OLDSTERS' RUSH TO REGISTER

Draft Enrollment Ends at 9 P. M.; Many Wait in Line.

Registration of the "oldsters," between 45 and 65 years old, proceeded in Lancaster county today at the rate of about 1,000 an hour.

An expected 20,000 will have been added to the Selective Service records by the 9 P. M. deadline for registration tonight, it was estimated, bringing the total manpower registered in Lancaster county to about 60,000 thus far in the war.

By mid-afternoon there was a decided lull in the registration, and the boards looked forward to a rush this evening.

It was a good-humored, willing, group of men who went to the 36 registration places today. Many had served in World War 1, and not a few commented: "Give me a gun, and I'll go again."

13,000,000 Register In U. S.

The story was the same throughout the nation, and President Roosevelt was among the 13,000,000 who put their names on the books. The fourth registration of its kind, it brought to about 40,000,000 the number of men on record.

To cut the rush today, City Board No. 1 and County Board No. 4 kept their Breneman building basement room open from noon yesterday until 6 P. M., and for the first few hours had a line of men waiting which extended to Grant street at one end and to the Hamilton club at the other.

Today, the same boards reserved their system and had the men enter by the back and come out the front door, with the result that the line was inside the building instead.

Chinamen Register

Eng Poy, local Chinese restaurant proprietor, of 107 W. King St., was among the registrants this morning at City No. 1. "I hope we beat

(See DRAFT—Page 13)

TRONDHEIM SEETHES, RUSSIANS REPORT

SAN FRANCISCO, April 27—(AP)—The Khabarovsk radio, in eastern Siberia, today reported widespread sabotage and revolt among the people of Trondheim and strong measures by the German Gestapo to cope with the situation.

Trondheim is the port city of occupied Norway where important units of the Nazi war fleet are believed to have been based recently.

"The city and suburbs have been transformed into military camps by the Germans," said the broadcast, quoting Stockholm sources. "Thousands of Norwegians are forced out of their homes. Schools are changed into barracks. Hitlerites have forced thousands of Norwegian workers into building fortifications along the shoreline and harbor of the city.

The report was picked up here by the CBS shortwave listening station.

CONVICTS PURCHASE $43,000 IN BONDS

LEAVENWORTH, Kas., April 27—(AP)—Warden Robert Hudspeth modestly points out that his boys at the Federal penitentiary are co-operating in the war effort.

Inmates have purchased $43,000 worth of war bonds, donated $807.24 to Red Cross war relief. $167 to the Salvation Army war fund, $146.75 to the Navy relief and $124.05 to the U. S. O.

"And they've given I don't know how much blood for the blood bank," Hudspeth said.

RUSSIA AIMS KNOCK-OUT AT FINLAND

Seeks to Turn German Flank as RAF Pushes Greatest Offensive.

HITLER SPEECH BARES FEAR OF LONGER WAR

(By the Associated Press)

While the RAF hurled its greatest offensive of the war through the skies of western Europe, there were signs today that Russia had launched upon an offensive to knock Finland out of the war and outflank the Germans on their main northern anchors about Leningrad and southward.

Nearly 2,000 Finnish soldiers were reported killed last week in this apparent offensive, likened in hitting power to the knock-out blow dealt the Finns by the Red Army two years ago to end their short winter war.

Russia and Finland fought that earlier war, with Germany on the sidelines, over the Russian demand for Finnish territorial leaseholds to shield Leningrad. The battle lines now are drawn up well inside the Finnish frontier of 1939, said dispatches through London.

The present Russian drive might have the additional effect of protecting the lease-lend ports of Murmansk and Archangel while Adolf Hitler's main forces still mark time in the slush and mud from Leningrad south to the Crimea.

The Finnish High Command said the Russians were attacking on the Karelian Isthmus and in the vicinity of the Stalin Canal north of Lake Onega but asserted that the attack had been repulsed.

RAF Threatens Nazi Power

The unprecedented ferocity of the RAF offensive in Western Europe constituted a strategical factor upon which the whole course of the conflict may depend.

It threatened devastation of the centers of German power, one by one, in the deliberate manner of the last four nights of consecutive

(See EUROPE—Page 13)

TORTURES, SLAYS HIGH SCHOOL GIRL; SAVED FROM MOB

PUEBLO, Colo., April 27—(AP)—A 26-year-old father, was spirited through an angry crowd to the State prison today after police Chief J. Arthur said the man admitted torturing and slaying Alice Porter, 16-year-old high school girl. Grady termed it "the most amazing, most gruesome confession in my 38 years on the force."

Missing since Wednesday night, Miss Porter's nude body was found yesterday, badly mutilated ,in a cistern at an abandoned ranch house. A few hours later police arrested Donald H. Fearn, father of a 10-day-old daughter and a small son.

Chief Grady said that after questioning, Fearn related in a signed statement that he beat the girl, heated wires and applied them to her back and abdomen, raped her, struck her in the head with a hammer, and then shot her twice with a .32 caliber pistol.

U. S. AID TO INDIA DISTURBS GHANDI

AHMEDABAD, India, April 27—(AP)—American military assistance to India "amounts in the end to American influence if not American rule, added to the British," Mohandas K. Ghandi wrote today in his newspaper Harijan.

"We have foreign soldiers enough," the Indian leader declared. "Now we have the promise of a never-ending stream of soldiers from America, and possibly from China. I must confess I do not look upon this event with equanimity.

"Cannot a limitless number of soldiers be trained out of India's millions? Would not they make as good fighting material as any in the world? Then why foreigners?"

U. S. LOSES DESTROYER OFF FLORIDA

Sturtevant Sunk By "Underwater Explosion"; Loss of Life Small.

WASHINGTON, April 27—(AP)—The Navy announced today the destroyer Sturtevant had been sunk off the coast of Florida "by an underwater explosion within the past 24 hours."

Loss of life was small, the Navy communique reported, and most of the crew of the 22-year-old vessel reached port safely, indicating that the ship may have gone down quite slowly.

The Sturtevant, a 1,190-ton, flush deck, four-stacker, normally had a wartime complement of around 145 to 150 men.

Whether the explosion was a torpedo fired by a German U-boat raider, such as blew up the Jacob Jones off the Jersey coast earlier this year, or whether it might have been a floating mine, possibly even one which had broken loose from America's own mine fields was not stated, and some authorities suggested it would be extremely difficult to determine just what had happened.

7th Lost in Atlantic

The Sturtevant became the seventh naval vessel announced as lost in the Atlantic area since last fall. Four have been destroyed by enemy action. They were the destroyers Reuben James and Jacob Jones, the Coast Guard Cutter Alexander Hamilton and the Coast Guard Tender Acacia. Two vessels were lost in heavy seas off Newfoundland—the destroyer Truxtun and the store ship Pollux.

One naval vessel lost in the Caribbean area, in addition to the above, was the submarine S-26, sunk by collision with a surface ship.

The announced total of U. S. naval vessels lost to date in the war now stands at 31.

Among those the heaviest sufferers have been the thinly armored but valiantly fought old destroyers such as the Sturtevant. The first naval ship of the war to be lost in action with the enemy was the destroyer Reuben James of that type and all the United States war vessels of the destroyer class lost in the western Pacific were old four stackers.

The Sturtevant was commissioned in 1920.

Army to Control Entire East; 52,000,000 People in Area

All of Penna. to Be Subject to Military Rule at "Early Date"

NEW YORK, April 27—(AP)—The conduct of 52,000,000 civilians soon will be subject to Army regulation and control through designation of the entire Atlantic seaboard as the Eastern Military Area. All of Pennsylvania is in the Area.

This sweeping wartime measure covering a 400,000-square-mile sector bigger than Germany and Italy combined was announced yesterday by Lieut. General Hugh A. Drum, commanding general of the Eastern Defense Command and First Army, as effective at "an early date."

Chief object in establishment of the military area, the announcement said, is to control the conduct of "enemy aliens as well as of all other persons" as a safeguard against subversive activities.

The first step in enforcement of restrictions already has been taken, the commanders of the four Corps Areas involved having been directed to assume control over all lighting on the coast to prevent silhouetting of ships and their consequent destruction by enemy submarines.

N. England Coast Darkened

Swift action by Major General Sherman Miles, commanding general of the First Corps Area, with

(See ARMY—Page 4)

Shaded states show the Eastern Military Area. All the residents — 52,000,000 — soon will will come under control of the Army.

WOULD LIMIT NET INCOMES TO $25,000

Opposes Suspension of 40-Hour Work Week and Overtime Pay.

TO ADDRESS NATION ON RADIO TOMORROW

WASHINGTON, April 27.—(AP)—President Roosevelt said today that during the war "no American citizen ought to have a net income, after he has paid his taxes, of more than $25,000 a year" in proposing to Congress a seven-point program designed to combat the upward spiral in living costs.

The President proposed stabilization of wages and salaries of individuals, saying "I believe that stabilizing the cost of living will mean that wages in general can and should be kept at existing levels" and asked repeal of the provisions of the price-fixing law which allow farm commodities to rise to 110 per cent of parity (Parity is the price designed to give the farmer a return, based on industrial purchases, enjoyed in a 1909-14 base period).

Mr. Roosevelt also declared it was "indefensible that those who enjoy large incomes from state and local securities should be immune from taxation while we are at war" and urged that state, municipal and similar bonds "be subject at least to surtaxes."

"We must fix ceilings on the prices which consumers. retailers, wholesalers and manufacturers pay for the things they buy," the President said as he outlined his plans to keep the cost of living down, and added "ceilings on rents for dwellings in all areas affected by war industries" to the steps that must be taken.

Wants 40-Hour Week

Flatly opposing suspension of the 40-hour work week law, the President said:

"Most workers in munition industries are working far more than 40 hours a week, and should continue to be paid at time and a half for overtime. Otherwise, their weekly pay envelopes would be reduced."

Mr. Roosevelt reported that "all strikes are at a minimum."

Radio Address on Tuesday

The President will discuss the program for the nation in a radio address tomorrow night, Senate Democratic Leader Barkley said after a White House conference. The hour was not announced immediately.

TEXT ON PAGE 4
The text of President Roosevelt's message on living costs is on Page 4.

The program, outlined in a message to Congress, was the administration's plan for gearing the economy of the nation and its people to emergency war conditions.

The Chief Executive also proposed heavy taxes, holding personal and corporate profits to reasonable levels, stabilization of prices received by farmers, discouraging credit and installment buying, rationing of all essential scarce commodities, and stimulation of the purchase of war bonds.

Only taxes and stabilization of farm prices, Mr. Roosevelt said, require legislative action.

But he added in his message, read to the Senate and House by clerks:

"I assure the Congress that if the

(See ROOSEVELT—Page 4)

Charter Day Ceremonies, Buchanan Program Open City's Anniversary Celebration

Delegates, bearing the standards of their organizations filed into the auditorium of McCaskey High School at the beginning of the 200th anniversary program, according to the date of their organization's founding. About 150 clubs, churches, and societies sent a total of more than 450 delegates.

The newly restored West Bedroom at Wheatland was presented to the Wheatland Foundation by local and state Sons of the American Revolution Societies at a program yesterday afternoon. Miss Henrietta Reist, right, is arranging flowers in preparation for the inspection of the mansion by guests at the program, while Mrs. Montgomery Lampe, is seated at the left. Authentic French wallpaper was secured for the walls of the room, and a footbath of this period is seen in the left foreground. The rug on the floor is also an example of the finest workmanship of Buchanan's time.

In the finale of the tableau, "Men of Lancaster" local soldiers, sailors and marines presented the city, state and national flags, while the entire assemblage sang the national anthem. In the picture, left to right: Staff Sergeant Charles D. McGonigle, of the Marines; Sergeant O. L. Lewis, of the Army; Chief Water Tender Alvin C. Rementer, Navy; Sergeant Donald Sweigart, of the U. S. Army Air Corps; Third Class Seaman Herbert Dohner, Navy; Sergeant William T. Byrd, Army; and Staff Sergeant Roy E. Heineke, Marines.

CITY CELEBRATION

(Continued From Page One)

symbol of the value of the human spirit in the sight of God and of man....And we will stay free if we unite all our resources; but a house divided against itself will fall. If we lose, nothing will be of value any more."

"Out of this united determined, sacrificial response," Dr. Klein concluded, "will come a victory for all based on justice, freedom, and the dictates of humanity."

Representatives From 150 Groups

Headed by representatives of Trinity Lutheran Church and the First Reformed Church, who were founded even before Lancaster's incorporation, delegates of 150 religious, fraternal, civic and social organizations marched to their places at the beginning of the program.

Each group of three carried a placard bearing the name and date of the founding of its organization, and the procession was described by the stirring voice of the narrator, E. Cameron Hawley, who emphasized that the delegations represented a cross section of our social fabric, and that all were united in their citizenship in this community.

Then, in the completely dark auditorium, a spotlight was thrown on either side of the stage, where appeared alternately men in the uniforms of the eight wars in which Lancaster men have taken part. As a finale to this part of the program, the curtains were opened and a color guard and color bearers composed of men now in the armed forces came forward. The marines presented arms, and the entire audience rose to sing the national anthem.

Prentis Presides

H. W. Prentis, Jr., presided at the program, and in his address he pointed out that honesty, thrift and a capacity for hard work exist in Lancaster today, as they did 200 years ago. Referring to the delegates seated in the front of the auditorium, he pointed out that their organizations had only survived because the members believed in them.

"A government is like everything else," he said, "to preserve it, we must love it."

He urged that the "ancient altar fires of freedom that burned so fiercely in the Lancastrians of an early day should now be rekindled in the hearts and minds of all our people. Vital as they are, physical armaments in themselves are never adequate alone. Intellectual and spiritual ramparts such as have been built so firmly here in Lancaster are equally essential."

Civic Chorus Sings

The civic chorus, under the direction of Harold Shaar, Samuel B. Smith, Helge Pearson and Dr. Harry A. Sykes, sang four selections, during various parts of the program, two of them compositions of Dr. Sykes.

During the last number, "Onward Ye People," by Sibelius. Earle Thompson was baritone soloist. Accompanists were Frank Thompson, Dr. Sykes and Leslie Harnley.

Seated on the stage were members of the committee in charge of the bicentennial celebration, and officials of county towns.

Beck Presents Tablet

Dr. Herbert H. Beck, president of the Lancaster County Historical Society, presented a commemorative tablet of the bicentennial of Charter Day, to the city, represented by Mayor Cary. He traced the history of Lancaster's importance in the development of our national government and the principals for which it stands, and concluded—

"In presenting this tablet to the City of Lancaster, I am solemnly conscious of the fact that this thin marble plate, like liberty, independence and democracy, which its noble inscription features, is fragile. It could be demolished with the butt of a rifle. American precious national heritage, which our local forefathers lived for, fought for, and died for, is symbolized by this fragile tablet.

He then expressed confidence that "this symbol of liberty, independence and democracy will gloriously survive its present day supreme challenge for existence.

The tablet was unveiled by Miss Hildegarde Pilgram, of Philadelphia, the daughter of the Rev. and Mrs. Robert J. Pilgram and the great- great- great- great- granddaughter of Sebastian Graff, one of Lancaster's first two burgesses.

In accepting the tablet for the city, Mayor Cary said in part, "The citizens of Lancaster accept this marble tablet in the spirit in which it is presented. It will be installed within the wall wherein is established our municipal government. It should afford inspiration and encouragement to all our citizens, and to the future generations that come and go, to hold fast to the spirit of liberty, independence and democracy which is the symbol of our glorious republic.

Participants in the pageant were: French and Indian War, Harold Keller and Arthur Rudy; Revolutionary War, James Drumm and Robert Ross; Mexican War, J. Richard Gaintner and C. W. Dudley; Civil War, Robert Peters and Gloid Long; Spanish American War, Norman Adams and Paris Hinkle; World War, Ralph Schreck and John Sullivan.

The Very Rev. George W. Brown, pastor of St. Mary's Catholic Church, read Washington's prayer.

The invocation was given by the Rev. William H. Bollman, pastor of the First Evangelical and Reformed Church, and the 122nd Psalm was read by Rabbi Daniel L. Davis, of Congregation Shaarai Shomayim.

ARNOLD SEES WAR AS ECONOMIC PURGE

PITTSBURGH, May 2—(AP)—U. S. Assistant Attorney General Thurman Arnold declared last night that the full production demands of war will "operate like a purge" on the American economic system. Addressing the final meeting in a series of legal institutes sponsored by the Allegheny County Bar Association, Arnold told 700 lawyers:

"War is going to operate like a purge. War is going to revive our competitive capitalist system. We must not permit private grounps once again to seize control of production, either by patents or other restrictions, in order to regain domination over the necessities of life.

"Where patent privileges are used as instruments of business policy rather than for the purpose of increasing royalties it should be considered a criminal offense."

F.&M. TO HONOR 4 AT INAUGURAL

Honorary Degrees Will Be Conferred at Distler Ceremonies May 16.

Franklin and Marshall College will confer four honorary degrees at the inauguration of President Theodore A. Distler on May 16. Dr. Dixon Ryan Fox, president of Union College, Schenectady, New York, will deliver the address.

Men Getting Degrees

The honorary degrees and their recipients follow:

Doctor of Laws, Robert Livingston Johnson, president of Temple University, Philadelphia.

Doctor of Science, Clarence Erwin McClung, of Swarthmore, managing editor of the Journal of Morphology published by the Wistar Institute of Anatomy and Biology, Philadelphia, and one of the distinguished biologists of the world.

Doctor of Science, William Henry Welker, professor of physiological chemistry at the University of Illinois.

Doctor of Letters, Charles Sanford Tippetts, headmaster of Mercersburg Academy, Mercersburg.

Alumni Luncheon

The inaugural exercises will be held in Hensel Hall at 11 o'clock and the alumni luncheon is scheduled for 1 o'clock on the same day in the Biesecker gymnasium. Dr. Harry Woodburn Chase, president of New York University, and Dr. William Mackey Smith, professor of mathematics and registrar of Lafayette College, will be principal luncheon speakers.

Dr. Chase will represent the alma mater of Distler and Dr. Smith will speak for Lafayette College where the president of F. and M. served as Dean for eight years.

Dr. Adrian Jacob Barnouw, Queen Wilhemina Professor of Dutch Language and Literature at Columbia University, will deliver the Phi Beta Kappa oration in the Little Theatre on May 15.

Commencement May 18

Lowell Thomas, radio and movie news commentator, will speak at the 155th annual commencement exercises on Monday, May 18, at 10:30 a. m., in Hensel Hall.

Class Day exercies for the graduating class will be held at 9 o'clock Tuesday morning in Hensel Hall. The event is usually held during commencement but because of the accelerated program at the college it has been advanced this year.

Class Day Program

The program, in charge of the class president, Frank Graham, will include several glee club selections, the class history by A. Leroy Lightner; the class will by Richard Bromer and the class poem by Coby Swank. Franklin Schaffner will deliver the class oration and William Cox, vice president of the class, will deliver the mantle oration. The capping of Blue Key men, another event usually held in conjunction with commencement week-end, will also occur on the program. Nevin Kirk, Blue Key president, will make the presentations.

The committee arranging the exercises consists of John Keelen, A. Leroy Lightner, Floyd Worley, Charles Frey, Robert Dell and Jesse Schulman. Officers of the class are Frank Graham, president, William Cox, vice president; Phillip Geib, secretary and John Badorf, treasurer.

3 BICYCLE RIDERS GROUNDED 15 DAYS, ONE IN ACCIDENT

Three boys, including one who had been involved in an accident, had their riding privileges suspended for 15 days by Policeman David Strayer, acting for Commissioner of Police Carlson, in Bicycle Court this morning.

James Stauffer, 52 Green street, admitted that he had turned his head to talk to a companion who was following on another 'cycle when his bicycle struck and knocked down S. Edward Gable, president of the Lancaster Auto Club, at Prince and Mifflin streets, last Saturday night. Mr. Gable is still confined to the General hospital.

James Adamire, 238 East Walnut street, and Charles Haines, 657 Fremont street, were suspended for riding without lights.

151st Anniversary of Buchanan's Birth Is Observed at Wheatland

Prentis Presides at Meeting, Reading Historian Speaks; State Sons of Revolution Present Restored Bedroom to Foundation

The first program in Lancaster's bicentennial celebration was held yesterday afternoon at Wheatland, where the 151st anniversary of President James Buchanan's birth was commemorated with the presentation of a restored room in the mansion by the State society of Sons of the American Revolution.

Buchanan was described as one of the leaders in the preservation of democracy, and H. W. Prentis, Jr., who presided, recalled that Buchanan was a great leader in one of the most perplexing periods in the history of the nation.

Speaks of Buchanan

"Now when the nation is involved in a great struggle, it is helpful to turn our minds to the things of the past, and to gain inspiration from the experiences of our forefathers," Prentis said. He also recalled that Buchanan was Minister to Russia in 1832-33, and to England in 1853-56, pointing out the fact is significant when we think of the vital importance of the roles the two nations are playing today."

Prentis introduced J. Bennett Nolan, Reading attorney and historian, who played a distinguished part in the World War, and has written numerous books on historical personages.

Nolan spoke on the bond which ties Berks and Lancaster counties together, and of the prominent personages whose fame both counties have shared. His own great-great-grandfather, Frederick Smith, visited Buchanan at Wheatland, when both were district attorneys of their respective counties, he said. The speaker spoke more particularly of the connection of Daniel Boone, native of Berks county, with Lancaster county, saying that during the first 16 years of his life when he lived in Berks county, Boone came into contact with many of the prominent citizens of Lancaster, particularly on his hunting expeditions.

"The long rifle which he took with him to Virginia and Kentucky, was made in Lancaster county, and he passed through the county on his last pilgrimage to Virginia," Noland said.

Dr. Beck Accepts Room

Presentation of the room in Wheatland was made by Daniel Rhoads, regent of the Lancaster Chapter of the Sons of the American Revolution, and the room was accepted for the Buchanan Foundation by Dr. Herbert H. Beck, one of the trustees.

Rhoads described the furnishings which went into the bedroom, including a set of French Royal Dalton china, which Buchanan used when he lived in the mansion. The State SAR contributed a large sum toward the restoration, and the balance was made up by individual subscriptions, he said. The work was started a year and a half ago by Major W. Sanderson Detwiler, then regent of the local chapter, continued by Col. Daniel B. Strickler, and completed by Rhoads.

SAR Official Speaks

Thomas Ridgeway, secretary of the State SAR, in a brief speech, declared that "Lancaster is lucky in having the one spot where lived the only Pennsylvanian to be in the White House."

Dr. Beck, in his acceptance speech, declared that "Wheatland is the shrine of the spirit of liberty, independence and Democracy of which the great proprietor, James Buchanan, was a champion."

"The contribution to Wheatland is similar to other contributions which have been not only encouraging but stimulating to the group which started this project," he said.

The invocation was given by the Rev. Robert C. Batchelder, rector of St. James Episcopal Church.

Patriotic selections were rendered by the band of the McCaskey High school, under the direction of Leigh E. Wittell.

NIP SMUGGLING OF GOLD TO U. S.

N. Y. Refiner Faces 18 Years in Jail and $30,000 in Fines.

BUFFALO, N. Y., May 2—(AP)—Convicted of gold smuggling and conspiracy, in a plot which the government contends resulted in more than $1,000,000 worth of bullion being smuggled from Canada to the United States, a New York City gold refiner faces a possible 18 years in prison and $30,000 in fines.

Bernard M. Kushner was found guilty by a Federal Court jury yesterday on five counts of gold smuggling and one of conspiracy. U. S. District Court Judge John Knight fixed May 11 for sentencing and continued the 48-year-old defendant's $7,500 bail.

As the trial opened April 21, four other defendants, Jack N. Rubin, David Roth and Harry Julius, all of New York City, and Charles Abrahams, Buffalo, pleaded guilty to conspiracy charges. All but Abrahams testified as government witnesses.

Defense counsel Samuel M. Ostroff said last night an appeal would be taken. Terming the verdict a miscarriage of justice, he maintained that the three defendants who testified "hoodwinked the jury into believing Kushner guilty."

Judge Knight granted Ostroff's request for permission to reserve all motions to set aside the verdict until the scheduled sentencing date.

Assistant U. S. District Attorney Robert M. Hitchcock held that Kushner made more than $16,000 annually as the result of smuggling activities over a four-year period starting in 1938.

The indictment against the five men was returned in January. Julius and Abrahams were arrested at the International Peace Bridge in Buffalo Oct. 4, 1941, and $10,000 worth of gold bullion was seized. The others were apprehended in New York City.

CLAIM $200,000 IDLE PAY FRAUD

State Charges Stevedores Received Illegal Payments For 3 Years.

HARRISBURG, May 2—(AP)—Fraudulent collection of $200,000 in jobless benefits was charged to Philadelphia stevedores today as the State Unemployment Compensation Bureau pushed its drive against illegal payments.

Lewis G. Hines, Secretary of Labor and Industry, said investigation of payroll records of 8,000 stevedores showed that 2,200 filed false claims during 1938, 1939, 1940 and the early part of last year.

The findings will be turned over to the Bureau's legal division and those accused given a chance to "pay up or be prosecuted," declared the official.

He disclosed plans for similar inquiries in the garment industry at Easton, Pittsburgh, Scranton and Wilkes-Barre.

Hines said the bureau during the week ending April 24 obtained restitution of $3,974 which was collected from 409 individuals who obtained compensations through misrepresentation. He reported 5,839 similar cases now under investigation.

Hines said that when the Bureau was first established in 1938 there was "a lot of lost motion which made it easy for a stevedore to say he was working or was not working." This, explained the secretary, made it hard to trace the claimant due to the method of hiring such workers.

Hines went into office in 1939 and asked help of the International Longshoremens Association to handle claims. He said the union started to "discourage cheating on the bureau and has been cooperating fully with us."

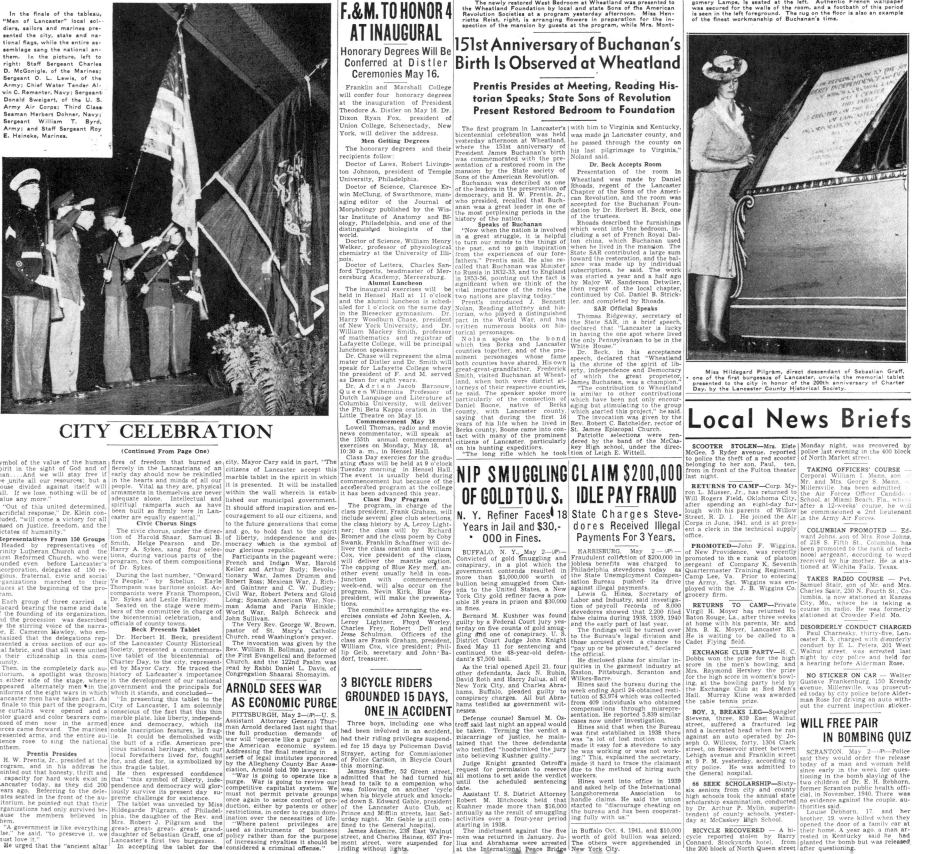

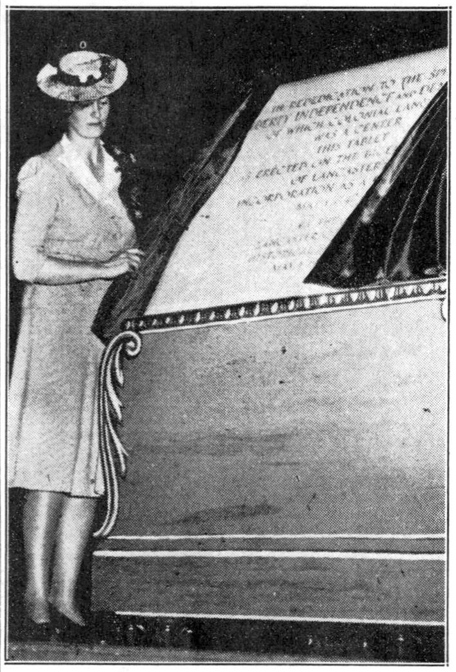

Miss Hildegard Pilgram, direct descendant of Sebastian Graff, one of the first burgesses of Lancaster, unveils the memorial tablet presented to the city in honor of the 200th anniversary of Charter Day, by the Lancaster County Historical Society.

Local News Briefs

SCOOTER STOLEN—Mrs. Elsie McGee, 5 Ryder avenue, reported to police the theft of a red scooter belonging to her son, Paul, ten, from in front of the Fulton theater last night.

RETURNS TO CAMP—Corp. Myron L. Musser, Jr., has returned to Will Rogers Field, Oklahoma City, after spending an eight-day furlough with his parents of Willow Street, R. D. 1. He joined the Air Corps in June, 1941, and is at present a clerk in the technical supply office.

PROMOTED—John F. Wiggins, of New Providence, was recently promoted to the rank of platoon sergeant of Company K, Seventh Quartermaster Training Regiment, Camp Lee, Va. Prior to entering the Army, Sgt. Wiggins was employed with the J. B. Wiggins Co. grocery firm.

RETURNS TO CAMP—Private Virgil H. Moyer has returned to Baton Rouge, La., after three weeks at home with his parents, Mr. and Mrs. B. K. Moyer, Lancaster R5. He is waiting to be called to a Cadet Flying field.

EXCHANGE CLUB PARTY—H. C. Dobbs won the prize for the high score in the men's bowling, and Mrs. Raymond Hershey the prize for the high score in women's bowling, at the bowling party held by the Exchange Club at Red Men's Hall. Murray Kline was awarded the table tennis prize.

BOY, 3, BREAKS LEG—Spangler Stevens, three, 839 East Walnut street, suffered a fractured leg and a lacerated head when he ran against an auto operated by Joseph O. Willcox, forty, 1304 Clark street, on Reservoir street between Lehigh avenue and Franklin street at 9 P. M. yesterday, according to city police. He was admitted to the General hospital.

66 SEEK SCHOLARSHIP—Sixty-six seniors from city and county high schools took the annual state scholarship examination, conducted by Dr. Arthur P. Mylin, superintendent of county schools, yesterday at McCaskey High School.

BICYCLE RECOVERED — A bicycle reported stolen by Harry Connard, Stockyards hotel, from the 200 block of North Queen street Monday night, was recovered by police last evening in the 400 block of North Market street.

TAKING OFFICERS' COURSE — Corporal William I. Mann, son of Mr. and Mrs. George S. Mann, of Millersville, has been admitted to the Air Forces Officer Candidate School, at Miami Beach, Fla., where after a 12-weeks' course, he will be commissioned a 2nd lieutenant in the Army Air Forces.

COLUMBIAN PROMOTED — Edward Johns, son of Mrs. Rose Johns, of 218 S. Fifth St., Columbia, has been promoted to the rank of technocal sergeant, according to word received by his mother. He is stationed at Wichita Falls, Texas.

TAKES RADIO COURSE — Pvt. Samuel Stair, son of Mr. and Mrs. Charles Stair, 230 N. Fourth St., Columbia, is now stationed at Kansas City, Mo., where he is taking a course in radio. He was formerly stationed at Crowder Field, Mo.

DISORDERLY CONDUCT CHARGED

Paul Charnesky, thirty-five, Lancaster R. 3, charged with disorderly conduct by E. L. Peters, 201 West Walnut street, was arrested last night by city police and held for a hearing before Alderman Rose.

NO STICKER ON CAR — Walter Gustave Frankenburg, 150 Kready avenue, Millersville, was prosecuted today by city police before Alderman Rose for driving an auto without the current inspection sticker.

WILL FREE PAIR IN BOMBING QUIZ

SCRANTON, May 2—(AP)—Police said they would order the release today of a man and woman held since early in the week for questioning in the bomb slaying of the two children of Dr. E. H. Rebhorn, former Scranton public health official, in November, 1940. There was no evidence against the couple, authorities said.

Louise Debhorn, 17, and her brother, 19, were killed when they opened the door of a family car at their home. A year ago, a man arrested in Kentucky said he had planted the bomb but was released after questioning.

WEATHER
Eastern Pennsylvania: Rising Temperature Wednesday.

Intelligencer Journal

The Leading Newspaper in the Garden Spot of America, Home Owned for Home Folks Since 1794

VOLUME LXXVIII.—NO. 203. The Intelligencer Founded 1799—The Journal Founded 1794. Entered at Post Office at Lancaster, Pa., as second class mail matter. LANCASTER, PA., WEDNESDAY MORNING, MAY 6, 1942. CITY 16 PAGES, 128 COLUMNS. 20c PER WEEK—4c Per Copy

CORREGIDOR FALLS TO THE JAPANESE

CONFUSION AS SUGAR SALES ARE RESUMED

Officials Explain Each Coupon Entitles Holder To One Pound Of Commodity

66,765 MORE REGISTER

Resumption of sugar sales under the rationing program started Tuesday—but immediately there was confusion over the value of each coupon. Rationing officials said they had received complaints that a number of grocers would sell only one-half pound of sugar for each coupon, whereas each coupon entitles the holder to a pound.

NEW JERSEY MAN REPORTS HOLDING 15,000 LBS. SUGAR

North Bergen, N. J.—(AP)—A North Bergen man reported Tuesday as he signed up for sugar rationing that he had 15,000 pounds of the sweetener.

Ralph Mazzei, local rationing administrator, said the man, whose name was withheld, declared he bought the sugar two years ago in anticipation of the present shortage.

Mazzei said he would ask state officials what should be done.

Rationing officials explained that while the ration is one-half pound per person per week, each stamp covers a two-week period. Thus, the first stamp is good for the period from May 5 to 16 and is to be used for the purchase of one pound of sugar. The second stamp cannot be used until the following period—May 17 to 30—and will permit the purchase of one pound of sugar for that period.

STAMPS WILL EXPIRE

In connection with the explanation, officials pointed out that a stamp not used in the period specified for it becomes void. It cannot be used to purchase additional sugar in the succeeding period.

Meanwhile, Franklin Ferrier, custodian of rationing supplies, reported an increase Tuesday in applications for rationing books. He said that 66,765 applications were received Tuesday, compared to 56,439 on Monday. There were 63,287

More of SUGAR on Page 9

"We Lead All The Rest"

FARM CORNER

By *The Farm Editor*

BETTER BREEDING PRACTICES URGED

State College Specialists Cite Need For Better Dairy Herds To Meet Production Demands

With officials calling for an increase of dairy products, more attention must be given to "better breeding" practices by herd owners, according to State College specialists. Given good care and adequate feed, any cow is limited in her production by her inherited ability. Although a dairyman cannot change the capacity of cows already in production, he can improve the future members of his herd by breeding—better breeding.

The experts cite 1940 production records which were obtained on 61,139 cows in dairy herd improvement associations. The average production of these cows was 345.4 pounds of butterfat, with an average return of $118 above feed cost.

On the other hand, the average production of all cows in the state for the same year was 200 pounds of butterfat. Such cows gave a return of only $47 above feed cost. Thus, there was a difference of $71 in favor of the dairy herd improvement association cow over the average cow of the state.

When the 400-pound butterfat producers are considered, it is found that after they paid for their feed $144 remained to pay for labor, housing, interest, depreciation, and other items of cost.

"Faced with these facts and

More of FARM CORNER on Page 9

Intelligencer Journal
Weather Calendar

COMPARATIVE TEMPERATURES

Station	High	Low
Intell Journal	71	53
Water Works	85	47
Ephrata	79	48
Last Year (Ephrata)	87	53
Official High for Year, May 1		95
Official Low for Year, January 11		-10
Character of Day		Clear

HOURLY TEMPERATURES

Tuesday			
3 a. m.	62	4 p. m.	69
4 a. m.	59	5 p. m.	70
5 a. m.	56	6 p. m.	71
6 a. m.	54	7 p. m.	70
7 a. m.	53	8 p. m.	69
8 a. m.	53	9 p. m.	67
9 a. m.	54	10 p. m.	65
10 a. m.	55	11 p. m.	60
11 a. m.	58	Midnight	59
Noon	60	Wednesday	
1 p. m.	62	1 a. m.	58
2 p. m.	65	2 a. m.	57
3 p. m.	67	3 a. m.	56

SUN

Rises—5:59 a. m. Sets—8:02 p. m.

More of WEATHER on Page 14

Government Places Stiff Controls On Installment Buying

Federal Reserve Board Also Decrees Charge Accounts Covering Many Articles Used In American Homes Must Be Paid Up By 10th Day Of Second Month Following Purchase

Washington—(AP)—Stiff regulations controlling the installment purchases of nearly every article in common use in the American home were promulgated Tuesday night by the Federal Reserve Board which, in addition, decreed that ordinary charge accounts involving such articles must be paid up relatively quickly.

The charge account rules, first ever issued governing this type of buying, provided that an article must be paid for by the 10th day of the second month following the purchase.

46 ARTICLES COVERED

Effective at midnight Tuesday, the regulations were issued in compliance with President Roosevelt's recent request that people pay off their bills and stay out of debt as much as possible. Hitherto, the purchase on credit of a score of articles had been regulated, but Tuesday night's rules lengthened the list to 46 classifications, and stiffened the requirements.

The new list of restricted articles included all civilian clothing, kitchen articles and dishes, linens, jewelry, auto accessories, all electrical appliances, luggage, umbrellas, sports equipment, used furniture and yard goods, in addition to the score of previously limited items such as furniture, radio, vacuum cleaners, bicycles and clocks.

The rules apply only to the 46 listed types of articles and no other

More of CREDIT on Page 14

SEALED VERDICT IS RETURNED IN MRS. SHERTS' SUIT

Case Goes To Jury After Two-Day Trial; Terre Hill Man Awarded $12,707

After deliberating two hours and 15 minutes, a jury returned a sealed verdict Tuesday in the damage suit brought against the Fulton National Bank by Mrs. Anna G. Sherts, widow and executrix of the estate of H. Edgar Sherts. The verdict will be opened before Judge Joseph B. Wissler at 9:30 a. m. Wednesday.

Mrs. Sherts is asking damages from the bank, charging that the bank appropriated two special accounts of Sherts and applied them to his personal indebtedness. The suit has been pending since June, 1939, and it took two days for the testimony to be offered. Mrs. Sherts claims that as a result of this action on the part of the bank, her husband suffered a complete nervous and physical breakdown.

ASKING 2 KINDS OF DAMAGES

"This suit was not brought merely for vindication," the jury was told by F. Lyman Windolph, who with William B. Arnold represent Mrs. Sherts, but added it was brought also for monetary compensation. "We are asking two kinds of damages," Windolph explained, "compensatory damages and exemplary damages."

George T. Hambright, counsel

More of COURT on Page 14

MAN BURNED WHEN TRUCK CATCHES FIRE

James Dougherty Tries To Push Blazing Vehicle From Barn Near Media Heights

James Dougherty, twenty-seven, Lancaster R6, suffered second degree burns of the right leg and left hand about 10:45 p. m. Tuesday when he attempted to push a burning truck out of a corn barn on the farm where he lives, near the Media Heights Country Club. He was treated at St. Joseph's Hospital.

According to Chief Earl Barley, of the Willow Street Fire Company, Dougherty was burned when some gasoline which was being drained from the tank of a truck was ignited and set the vehicle on fire. Dougherty said he attempted to push the truck from the shed and his clothes caught fire.

Robert Shank, Willow Street, a passing motorist, went to Dougherty's aid and towed the truck out of the shed with his machine. Chief Barley said the truck was badly damaged and the tires were burned. The shed was damaged slightly. The loss was estimated by Chief Barley between $400 and $500. The West Lampeter Fire Company also responded to the call. The farm is owned by U. Grant Barr.

$100 STOLEN FROM WOMAN AT MARKET

Shopping Bag Containing Two Purses Stolen From Stand At Arcade Market

Mrs. Ella Miller, Landisville, reported to city police Tuesday evening the theft of a shopping bag, in which there were two purses containing over $100 in cash, from a stand in the Arcade market.

Mrs. Miller told police she placed the bag in a paste board carton on the floor in the rear of a stand operated by her son, Arthur, and went across the aisle to talk to another woman. When she returned the bag was gone.

WPB ANNOUNCES 50 P. C. SLASH IN GASOLINE USE

Say Many Autoists Will Have To Get Along On 5-6 Gallons A Week

STARTING ON MAY 16

Washington—(AP)— Gasoline consumption in the east will be slashed 50 per cent below normal starting May 16, the War Production Board announced Tuesday night. This means that many of the area's 10,000,000 motorists probably will have to get along with as little as five or six gallons a week.

The reduction becomes effective the day the seaboard area begins using ration cards.

While the overall curtailment will be one-half, informed sources explained that it would amount to about a 60 percent cut for non-essential users of automobiles, since necessary vehicles will continue to receive their full requirements of fuel.

The WPB action, taken on recommendation of petroleum coordinator Harold Ickes, came shortly after Joseph B. Eastman, defense transportation director, declared "every owner of a motor vehicle in public or private service should realize that he holds this vehicle in trust for the national war effort and that it should be used only for purposes of necessity."

This statement of Eastman's applied to the whole country, not merely to the east.

Simultaneously with the gasoline order, WPB directed that deliveries of light fuel oil be reduced also by 50 per cent below last year, beginning May 16 in the 17 eastern states and the District of Columbia.

This was the first cut on fuel oil, used for house heating, and the order applied to deliveries to suppliers.

Gasoline consumption in the east and Oregon and Washington already is cut by one-third below normal, by a limitation on supplies to filling stations. Tuesday's new order made no mention of the northwestern states, where improved supply conditions have

More of GASOLINE on Page 9

MAN HANGS SELF WEEK AFTER HE GETS DRAFT CALL

Russell Geiman, Elizabethtown, Found Dead In Woods Near Borough

Apparently brooding over a draft call received last week, Russell Geiman, thirty-six, 439 E. High St., Elizabethtown, Tuesday hung himself in a wooded section along a little-traveled road about three miles northwest of the borough, according to Frank Miller, deputy coroner of Elizabethtown. He was due to report at Harrisburg May 13 for his physical examination and possible induction.

The body was discovered by a Boy Scout, James Roland Daggett, seventeen, Elizabethtown R1, who was walking along the road. Miller said the victim had been dead ten or twelve hours.

WORKED MONDAY NIGHT

Geiman, an employe of the Klein Chocolate Co., Elizabethtown, had worked Monday night. Apparently he went to the woods shortly after leaving the factory when the midnight shift changed, Miller said. The victim's automobile was parked at the side of the road and his body was hanging by a rope from a tree limb only a short distance away, the deputy coroner said. The section is known as Furnace Hill and is located along a road leading from the Harrisburg pike to the abandoned Conewago railroad station.

Daggett ran two miles to the nearest telephone to notify the deputy coroner. Miller and Dr. Troy

More of MAN on Page 9

Ask Older Firemen To Answer Alarms, Youngsters In Army

Walter Shaffer, president of the Elizabethtown Fire Company, has made an appeal to older men of the organization to respond to all fire calls—because so many of the younger members who ordinarily turned out are in the Army.

In urging the older group to become more active, Shaffer pointed out that 22 company members already have been inducted. Many of those now in the Army were active fire fighters, he said, adding that quite a number more are awaiting calls.

SEES WAR CHEST AN EXPERIMENT IN AMERICAN UNITY

Dr. Stephen S. Wise Addresses 600 Campaign Workers; Lauds Work Of Russians

"This United War Chest is an experimental station in the new American unity," Dr. Stephen S. Wise, noted Jewish leader, told more than 600 campaign workers for the United War Chest, at a meeting in the Hotel Brunswick Tuesday night officially opening the campaign to start May 11. The local war chest is one of the first in the country to be organized and underway, officials said.

"The war can only be won by unity," Dr. Wise declared, adding that every right of every group is trivial compared with the principal right of all—"freedom for us and all the United Nations. 'Let ALL peoples go' that they may serve God in freedom—that is the great ideal we are fighting for."

APPLAUD FOR PRESIDENT

The speaker drew forth thunderous applause when he referred to President Roosevelt as "today's greatest leader of the Democratic way of life."

Speaking of the appeals which go to make up the local drive, Dr. Wise declared that "we are under the deepest obligation to the Chinese people, for actually this war started in China ten years ago. We must feed them, clothe them, give them medical supplies, for they have proved themselves

More of WISE on Page 14

Control Center Staff Works Out Problems Likely During Air Raids

First Test Of Vital Defense Unit "Very Satisfactory" Says Col. J. Hale Steinman, Commander

Flames from the blazing dome of the Court House licked the sky—homes in the west end of Lancaster were demolished, entrapping occupants while falling walls killed and injured others—a big department store in the heart of the city was gutted by fire—

All this happened between 8 and 9 o'clock Tuesday night when Axis airmen attacked this city for 60 minutes and Lancaster suffered its first bombing raid in history—

Police and firemen sped to the scenes of devastation; rescue squads, ambulances, physicians, Red Cross workers and demolition squads responded immediately—

The above were "problems" worked out in practice of a simulated air raid at the first test given the entire staff of the Lancaster Control Center on Tuesday evening.

Reports of bomb hits, extent of damage, probable casualties and general situation were phoned into the control center by fire and air wardens from numerous points in the city during the practice test.

More of TEST on Page 14

Surrender Of Other Fortified Islands In Manila Harbor Also Announced

A picture of the barracks at Fort Mills on the Philippine island of Corregidor. In the background is the Bataan Peninsula from which the Japs launched the landing attack on Corregidor.

SEN. BULOW TRAILS IN SOUTH DAKOTA SENATE PRIMARY

All-Out Roosevelt Supporter Leads Incumbent; House Veterans Behind In Indiana, Ala.

(By The Associated Press)

An all-out Roosevelt supporter, former Governor Tom Berry, took a lead of more than 2 to 1 over Senator William J. Bulow in South Dakota's Democratic senatorial primary Tuesday night, headline contest of primaries held in four states.

The voting, on nominees for two Senatorial and 23 House seats, also found Rep. William T. Schulte of Indiana, a veteran of five terms, and Rep. Luther Patrick of Alabama, serving his third term, behind on early returns from their Democratic races.

Returns from 804 of South Dakota's 1,944 precincts gave Berry 12,285 and Bulow 5,619. Edward Prchal ran third.

Berry, a former cowboy, charged Bulow with "isolationism" while the Senator, campaigning from Washington by means of recorded broadcasts, pledged support to the war effort but reserved the right to criticize domestic administration policies he might deem unwise. Party leaders indicated that patronage matters also were a factor in the campaign.

In the Republican Senatorial contest there, Gov. Harlan J. Bushfield, candidate for the vice presidential nomination in 1940, took a 3 to 2 lead over Olive A. Ringsrud, Secretary of State. Bushfield led 25,088 to 15,787 in 764 precincts. Rep. Karl Mundt held a commanding lead for renomination.

The State's Republican gubernatorial fight was a nip-and-tuck affair among three of the four candidates.

ALABAMA RESULTS

In Alabama, the only other State

More of PRIMARIES on Page 9

Girl, 10, Survives Long, Wild Ride In Runaway Team

A runaway horse left a trail of excitement along a two and one-half mile course between Goodville and Blue Ball Tuesday afternoon and imperiled the life of a ten-year-old girl who rode most of the distance in the wildly swaying buggy.

It started as Daniel Esh, of Churchtown, accompanied by his daughter, Barbara, was driving westward down a steep hill.

The bridle broke and the horse, frightened, bolted. Esh leaped out and attempted to stop the animal—without success.

With Barbara screaming with each lurch of the wagon as the horse gained speed, farmers left their fields to make vain efforts to halt the animal's flight. Old Dobbin promptly crossed them up. He went into the fields.

That only lasted a short time, however, and the horse came back to the road—to find one farmer in an automobile taking up the chase.

Near Blue Ball Barbara managed to leap from the wagon to a soft bank along the road—and escaped without injury.

A short distance farther the horse smashed the wagon against a pole in front of the A. J. Rodgers, general store in Blue Ball, dashed across the road into the sales barn of Eby Brothers and Martin—and docilely "surrendered."

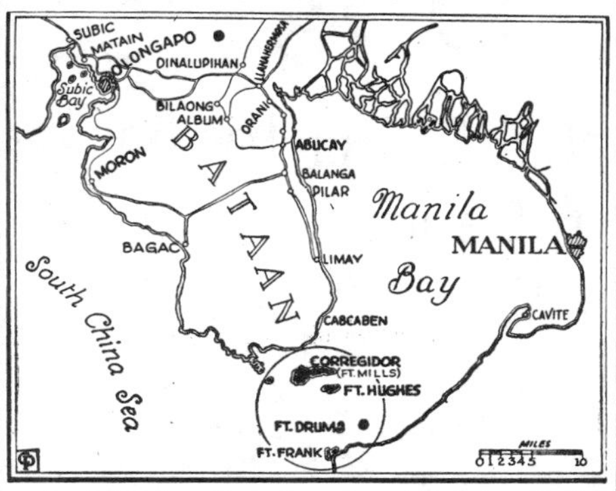

Location of Corregidor is shown above. This fortress, together with other island strongholds had prevented Japanese use of Manila Bay.

Allies Evacuating Troops And Civilians From Burma

Japanese Push Across Border Into China; British Press On In Madagascar; Vichy Rejects U. S. Warning Against Resistance

(By The Associated Press)

As the Japanese began landing on the shell-pocked Philippine fortress-island of Corregidor Tuesday night, Allied transport planes evacuated exhausted troops and civilians from collapsed Burma into India.

The Japanese horde in Burma pressed on into southern China, too. This was the dismal Allied picture in Asia.

In India the Allied airmen pressed every transport type of aircraft into service to salvage what they could of the Burmese equipment and personnel.

Some Pan-American craft designed to haul 21 persons actually took aboard 70 in the shuttle service across Burmese jungles into India. It appeared likely a considerable number of both British and Chinese troops would be captured by the Japanese.

BRITISH MOVE AHEAD

Punishing though the blow, Corregidor's prospective collapse had long been discounted militarily and was far more than counter-balanced by one of the most far-reaching Allied coups of the war.

A powerful British landing force was moving in on the Diego Suarez naval base on Vichy's Madagascar island, beating the Axis to a vital position and greatly improving the Allied situation from the Indian ocean to the South Atlantic.

This action, which late in the night still was in progress against spirited French resistance, appeared to have caught the Japanese flat-footed; to have the Nazis

More of WAR on Page 9

SNOWSTORM HITS NORTHWEST NEBRASKA

Snowplows Unable to Keep Roads Clear; Rains Overflow River in Southeast Part of State

Omaha—(AP)—A snowstorm which reached blinding proportions swept over northwestern Nebraska Tuesday night, while in the southeast corner of the state heavy rains overflowed at least one river.

Stalled cars dotted roads near Chadron, where 12 inches of snow had fallen and snow plows were unable to keep the roads clear. Traffic also was blocked near Crawford.

No serious flooding was reported from the affected Falls City area. At Omaha the Missouri River was rising but the crest was not expected until Thursday and then at considerably less than flood stage.

REVEAL REPULSE OF FIVE ATTACKS ON MIDWAY ISLAND

Admiral Nimitz Says Pacific Outpost Assaulted Every Month Excepting April

Pearl Harbor —(AP)— The repulse of five Japanese attacks on Midway Island, the last on March 10, was revealed officially Tuesday. Midway is 1,149 miles northwest of Hawaii.

The announcement followed the return of Admiral Chester W. Nimitz, commander-in-chief of the Pacific fleet, from inspections and the awarding of honors to Marine corps aviators and Naval personnel for their heroic defense of the Hawaiian outpost.

NO ATTACKS IN APRIL

Nimitz revealed Midway had been attacked each month since Dec. 7 except April. He personally decorated the Marines for shooting down a four-engined Japanese patrol seaplane making the last attack March 10.

The bomber was destroyed before it reached its objective.

Capt. James L. Neefus, leader of the intercepting fliers, was given the Navy cross. Distinguished flying crosses were awarded First Lieut. Charles W. Somers, Second Lieut. Francis P. McCarthy and Marine Gunner Robert L. Dickey. Dickey is recuperating at the Mare Island, Calif., Navy hospital and the medal is being forwarded to the mainland for presentation.

AWARDS MADE

In making the awards to the

More of MIDWAY on Page 9

THIEF SWAPS TIRES

Someone swapped an old tire for a better one on Miss Emma Sands' car while it was parked in a downtown parking lot last week. She reported to city police Tuesday. Miss Sands, who lives at Bird-in-Hand, said it was a Goodyear retread, 550 by 17.

Philippine Fortress Bombed 13 Times, Shelled Five Hours In One Day

DEFENDERS PRAISED

Allied Headquarters, Australia, (Wednesday)—(AP)—Corregidor and the other fortified islands in Manila harbor surrendered today, it was officially announced.

Besides the fortified rock that is Corregidor, the United States forts which had held out in the entrance to Manila Bay are Fort Mills, Fort Hughes, Fort Drum and Fort Frank.

The end came in the second day of the final Japanese assault, launched at midnight Tuesday, Manila time, with landings from Bataan peninsula after Corregidor, particularly the American forts, had been pounded again and again by Japanese big guns and aerial bombs.

Corregidor alone had 300 air raids since Dec. 29 when 35 Japanese bombers attacked for three hours.

Washington—(Wednesday)—(AP)—The Japanese have assaulted Corregidor in a landing attack, the War Department announced last night, and the capital feared that resistance of American troops was near an end.

The attack on the exhausted, hungry defenders of the crowded fortress began at midnight Tuesday, Manila Time (10 a. m., Lancaster time, Tuesday) and early today there was no official word of its trend or outcome. It was disclosed earlier, that the garrison was short of ammunition.

A total of 7,000 men or more were believed to be on Corregidor and other island forts in Manila Bay, although there was no official word of the number. The defenders included both Americans and Filipinos.

The attack followed a day which saw the rocky, island fortress bombed 13 times, and shelled continuously for a period of five hours. Presumably the landing attempt was made from nearby Bataan Peninsula, the scene of an epic resistance but inevitable defeat several weeks ago.

Informed opinion in Army quarters was that Lieutenant General Jonathan Wainwright and his men on Corregidor could not hold out much longer. Not only has the fort been bombed from the air, but it has been pounded unceasingly by big guns emplaced both on Bataan and on the Cavite shore.

It was generally considered that this battering had destroyed the fort's shore or beach defenses including barbed wire entanglements, pill boxes and the like, thus facilitating the Japanese landing.

ROOSEVELT'S MESSAGE

Word that the soldiers on Cor-

More of CORREGIDOR on Page 9

AIR RAID ALERT IN WEST

San Francisco—(AP)—Radios in the San Francisco Bay area went off the air at 9:18 p. m., Pacific War Time, under an alert flashed by the Fourth Interceptor Command. The "all clear" was given at 9:48 p. m. The alert extended as far east as Sacramento, the state capital 95 miles away.

New Pitcher Looks Good; Roses Snap Back to Win First Twin Bill

Cuccurullo Holds Rocks to Four Hits as Locals Take First, 4-0; Harig's Triple Wins 2nd; Kell, Kardash Show Power at the Plate

By GEORGE W. KIRCHNER

THE Red Roses are still a good way off from becoming a real honest-to-goodness contender in this hotly-contested Interstate League race, but several encouraging factors were brought out yesterday as the locals captured a twin bill from Wilmington, 4 to 0 and 10 to 9.

In their order they appeared something like this:

First:—Art Cuccurullo, the southpaw pitcher bought from Harrisburg last Friday night looks like he might prov[illegible] some help with a few wins. [illegible] held the Blue Rocks [illegible] hits, one of them qu[illegible] and the other a freak ground[illegible] that hit the third base sack. He didn't allow a run, walked only three men and fanned four.

Kell Hitting Well

Second:—George Kell, the shortstop who was shifted to first base to replace Tom Davis, who was hurt on Saturday, turned out to be a pretty good first sacker on the field, and a potent man at the plate, getting six hits in the eight times he went to the plate in the two games.

Third:—Mike Kardash, w[illegible] has been fieldi[illegible] we[illegible] since [illegible] joined the Ro[illegible] [illegible] turned on the heat w[illegible] his getting three for four in [illegible] first game and driving in [illegible] runs, and then finishing off w[illegible] two for four for a total of f[illegible] for eight for the day.

Fourth:—Chuck Harig [illegible] went hitless in the fir[illegible] [illegible] has been weak at the plate all year, showed old form in the second fray, getting three for five, including a triple in the eighth that drove Kell home with the winning run. And if you want a couple of other signs, Basil Elliston got one for two in the first and three for four in the second, while the Roses, as a whole, showed a fighting spirit by overcoming a four-run lead to tie the score in the second and then go on to win out in the extra eighth.

Beaten By Allentown

These were the encouraging signs and while there is still a lot to be desired, the picture today was, at least, brighter than it was on Saturday when the Roses were humiliated, 11 to 3 and 8 to 3 by Allentown, a team which has won seven straight from the home-boys this year without a single loss.

What most of the 1,800 customers liked yesterday was the way the locals polished off the Rocks in the first game. On the offensive, they collected nine hits for their four runs, taking the lead with a tally in the third and then clinching it when they put together two hits, together with a Wilmington error, for three runs in the seventh.

Cuccurullo Looks Good

Meanwhile Cuccurullo, making his first start, hurled a beautiful game. He gave two of his three free tickets in the first inning, but after that settled down and had the Rocks eating out of his hand. All told he gave up four hits, but one of these was regarded by some as an error on the part of rightfielder Red Mincy, who had a bad day, while the other was one of those rare grounders that hit the third base sack squarely and could not be fielded in time for a play.

The other two hits were solid blows, but were well scattered.

[illegible] those who like plenty of hits [illegible], that second game was a [illegible] the Roses collected 14 hits [illegible] 10 runs, while Wilmington [illegible] 13 for its nine.

[illegible]oses used three pitchers, [illegible] Lefty Verderame and fol[illegible] with right-hander Ed Boris before Glenn Young came in to finish and get credit for his third win of the year. Wilmington called on four, but this quartet of Heft, Feeney, Burrowes and Coleman was not enough to stop the locals.

A seven-inning game by agreement, the boys ended the seventh with the score tied at 9 all, the R[illegible]s leaving three men on the [illegible]n the last half of the inning. [illegible]oung retired the Rocks in [illegible]hth, the Roses won out on [illegible]single and Harig's triple.

Break Rocks' Streak

[illegible] virtue of this double triumph, [illegible]Roses snapped an eight-game [illegible]ning streak for the Rocks and, [illegible] the same time, won their first [illegible]uble-header of the year.

Harrisburg stopped Hagerstown's six-game win streak by grabbing [illegible]e second game, 3 to 1, after the Owls won the opener, 6 to 5, in 11 innings.

Trenton and Allentown split even with George Hennessy beating the Wings, 7 to 1, on his four-hit pitching in the opener, while the Wings rallied to win the nightcap, 3 to 1.

Two on the Hook

(First Game)

Wilmington	ab	r	h	o	a	Lancaster	ab	r	h	o	a
Rullo 2b	4	0	0	3	5	Long 3b	4	0	0	2	3
Scheldt 1b	4	0	0	10	0	Kar'sh ss	4	0	3	2	2
Mack'cz cf	3	0	2	1	1	Whea'n cf	4	0	0	3	0
Duke rf	3	0	1	2	0	Gleason c	3	0	1	5	0
Rutner 3b	4	0	0	3	1	Mincy rf	4	0	0	1	0
Pelton lf	4	0	1	2	0	Kell 1b	4	1	3	11	0
Adkins ss	3	0	0	2	5	Harig lf	3	2	0	2	0
Devlin c	2	0	0	1	0	Elliston 2b	2	0	1	1	2
Frye p	2	0	0	0	1	Cucc'lo p	3	1	1	0	2
Coleman p	1	0	0	0	0						
						Totals	31	4	9	27	9
Totals	30	0	4	24	13						

WILMINGTON .... 000 000 000—0
LANCASTER .... 001 000 30x—4

Error—Frye. Runs batted in—Kardash 2, Cuccurrullo. Two base hit—Pelton. Sacrifices—Elliston, Kardash. Double plays—Adkins to Rullo to Scheldt; Rullo to Adkins to Scheldt; Long to Kell. Left on bases—Wilmington 6; Lancaster 6. Base on balls—off Frye 2; Cuccurrullo 3. Struck out—by Cuccurrullo 3. Hits—off Frye 7 in 6 1-3 innings; Coleman 2 in 1 2-3. Wild pitch—Frye. Losing pitcher—Frye.

Umpires—Tatler and Ingram. Time—1:35.

(Second Game)

Wilmington	ab	r	h	o	a	Lancaster	ab	r	h	o	a
Rullo 2b	5	1	2	3	3	Long 3b	0	1	0	0	2
Scheldt 1b	4	0	3	8	0	Kar'sh ss	4	1	2	2	6
Mack'cz cf	5	0	2	2	1	Whea'on cf	4	0	0	0	0
Duke rf	4	0	0	1	1	Thack'n c	5	1	2	2	0
Rutner 3b	2	1	0	3	1	Mincy rf	4	2	0	0	1
Pelton lf	5	2	1	1	0	Kell 1b	4	2	3	12	0
Adkins ss	4	2	3	2	2	Harig lf	5	2	3	4	0
Yarmul c	2	3	2	2	3	Elliston 2b	4	1	3	3	2
Heft p	0	0	0	0	2	Verd'me p	0	0	0	0	0
Feeney p	0	0	0	0	1	Boris p	1	0	0	0	1
Bur'ws p	1	0	0	0	1	Young p	2	0	1	1	6
xDevlin	1	0	0	0	0						
Coleman p	0	0	0	0	0	Totals	33	10	14	24	18
Totals	33	9	13	z22	15						

x-Batted for Burrows in 7th.
z-One out when winning run scored.

WILMINGTON .... 124 110 00— 9
LANCASTER .... 214 200 01—10

Errors—Scheldt, Yarmul, Verderame. Runs batted in—Long, Kardash, Thackston 2, Mincy, Harig, Elliston 2, Boris, Rullo 2, Scheldt, Mackiewicz, Duke, Pelton, Adkins, Yarmul 2. Home run—Pelton. Three base hits—Harig, Yarmul. Two base hits—Thackston, Adkins 3, Mackiewicz, Kardash. Sacrifices—Heft, Rutner, Scheldt. Stolen bases—Kardash, Adkins. Double plays—Feeney to Yarmul to Scheldt. Left on bases—Wilmington 12; Lancaster 11. Base on balls—off Heft 2; Feeney 2; Burrows 4; Verderame 3; Boris 1; Young 4. Struck out—by Burrows 1; Young 1. Hits—off Heft 4 in 1 1-3 innings; Feeney 2 in 1 1-3; Burrows 6 in 4 1-3; Coleman 2 in 1-3; Verderame 3 in 3 1-3; Boris 4 in 1 2-3; Young 6 in 5. Wild pitch—Young. Passed ball—Yarmul. Winning pitcher—Young. Losing pitcher—Coleman.

Umpires—Ingram and Tatler. Time—2:20.

Archer Is Released

When Freddy Archer, the southpaw, was blasted all over the lot as the Roses dropped a 11 to 3 decision to Allentown here on Saturday, the crowd sensed that he had sealed his doom.

They were right, too, and yesterday Manager Tom Oliver announced that the veteran had been given his release.

LANCASTER NEW ERA Sports

PAGE 12 MONDAY, JUNE 1, 1942

CHAMPIONS IN SPORTS

CONGRATULATIONS, BARNEY—YOU, TOO, MR. SNEAD

Penn State captured the IC-4A championship, thanks to the amazing performance of Lancaster's triple-threat, Barney Ewell, who won the 100 and 220-yard dashes and the broad jump. Ewell, right, above, is pictured being congratulated by Asa S. Bushnell, Secretary of the IC-4A.

"Slamming Sammy" Snead, left, and Corp. Jimmy Turnesa, U. S. A., are shown holding the famous P.G.A. championship cup, which Snead won yesterday by 2 and 1 in Atlantic City. Turnesa came from behind, defeating Byron Nelson, for his crack at the title.

"I Just Run," Ewell Says After Becoming First to Win 9 Titles

Local Boy Climaxes Brilliant College Career With Triple Win; Set Marks in 100, 220, But Officials Ruled Against Both Because of Wind

BARNEY Ewell accomplished what no other track and field athlete in the sixty-six year history of the Intercollegiate Amateur Athletic Association championships ever achieved, and his only explanation was that "I just run."

First To Win 9 Titles

By virtue of his magnificent triple scored in the Triborough Stadium at Randall's Island, New York, last Saturday afternoon, he became the first athlete in these famous games to capture nine titles in three consecutive outdoor campaigns.

At the turn of the century, Alvin Kraenzlein, a hurdler for the University of Pennsylvania, annexed eight titles. His achievements stood the wear and tear of competition until Barney popped his kinky head into the competitive market in 1940 and began his grand slams that culminated in his obliterating from the books the skilled athletic labor manifested by the former wearer of the Red and Blue.

Like a Movie Plot

And it all worked out like a Hollywood plot that Barney should produce his finest performance in his exit from IC4-A competition. The sleek Negro boy from Lancaster's Seventh ward, who started his career at East Junior under Abe Herr, continued at Lancaster High under Dick Madison, and then to Penn State under Chick Werner, had to win three events and he did.

The 23-year-old athlete who started to "just run"—and win—credits luck, too, with lifting him to cinderpath glory.

"Most sprinters usually are thrown out of competition awhile with leg injuries, he said. "I've never been laid up even for one meet and that's luck."

It was Ewell's triumphs in the 100, 220 and broad jump which paced Penn State to its first outdoor IC4-A championship Saturday at New York.

State Wins Both Meets

The Lions thus became the first team to win both the indoor and outdoor titles in the same year. In March, Ewell led them to their first indoor championship when he shattered the broad jump mark.

The Negro star now has 12 association records—indoors and out—to his credit, and that's tops in IC4A history.

He turned ice-veined under fire Saturday and became in temperament like Joe Louis, the sober, dead panned young man who completes a task no matter how great the odds.

The first job he pulled successfully was to get the 100-yard title into the bag. He lined-up against a good field, was away from his marks fast, and boomed into the yarn a good five yards in the van of his competition in the remarkable figures of 9.5. But the officials turned their backs on his record-breaking performance because, as they put it, there was a favorable wind behind him. The opponents strewn along the way in his record breaking, but disallowed, performance were Hal Stickel, Pitt; Charlie Shaw, Cornell; Billy Carter, Pitt; Dave Lawyer, New York University; and Don Dolbin, a teammate from Penn State.

Tied 100-yard Mark

So in annexing the century, Barney, who actually broke the record, had to be content with the 9.6 mark he created in Friday's winning heat at which time he tied the figure held by Frank Wykoff, former Southern California star, and himself. In his semi-final heat, he buzzed down the stretch in 9.7. So in his three appearances in this event he did quite well with 9.6, 9.7, and 9.5 times.

He sewed up the broad jump on Friday afternoon when he leaped 24 feet 6 1-4 inches to beat Peter Guernsey of Yale in the trials. So he didn't bother jumping on Saturday.

Denied Second Record

To create his grand slam for the third year in a row it would take a first place medal in the 220-yard dash. It was on this race that Barney concentrated. He uncorked a 21.7 in winning his Friday heat. Then he romped home the winner over Willis Clark of Yale in the clocking of 20.8 in the semi-finals. In the finals, he was away fast, flying at the 100 mark, and then when he barged into the tape there was at least a streak of five yards of light between himself and second placer, Charlie Shaw of Cornell. The clockers all huddled around in a group. The official time as announced was 20.5. But again the record was disallowed because a favorable wind was behind the Penn State star. Barney however, holds the accepted IC-4A mark of 20.7 which he established last year.

It was strictly a one man show. Try as they might to push the New York favorite, Leslie MacMitchell, into the spotlight, they couldn't overshadow the brilliance of Barney, because the Lancaster boy was capable of duplicating his feats for the third consecutive year, while MacMitchell, who appears to be burned from too many high powered indoor miles this winter, couldn't keep up with the pack in the half mile race after he had won the mile, and finished last in a field of six in which the spotlight was dominated by Lynn Radcliffe, brilliant 880 star from Syracuse University.

The only other athlete on the card, who came through with a duplication was Al Blozis, the Georgetown giant, who copped firsts in the shot and discus for the third straight year to give him six titles, three less than the grand total collected by Barney.

Expects To Enter Army

Ewell expects to enter the army this month, but before he goes he hopes to compete in the NCAA and the National AAU championships. Last year he won both NCAA dash crowns and took the AAU 100.

Zink Wins Title

Bob Zink, of Mount Joy, won the singles championship of the Inter-County High School Tennis League Saturday when he defeated a teammate, Harold Fellenbaum, in the final round. Fellenbaum took the first set but Zink was too steady in the final two and won out.

Preliminary Round—Moseman, Manheim, defeated Fred Copeland, Columbia, 6-4, 7-5.

Semi-final Round—Harold Fellenbaum, Mount Joy, defeated Harold Smoker, Columbia, 6-1, 6-1. Bob Zink, Mt. Joy, defeated Moseman, Manheim, 6-1, 6-2.

Final Round—Bob Zink, Mount Joy, defeated Harold Fellenbaum, Mount Joy, 5-7, 7-5, 6-4.

392,280 See Holiday Games in Majors

N.Y. Gains In League

Split Even With A's, But Still Gain as Indians Fall

By AUSTIN BEALMEAR
Associated Press Sports Writer

Major League baseball enjoyed a rest today after the busiest weekend of the season, which brought disaster in double doses to many of the pennant contenders and success in the same quantities to those who could withstand the pressure of four games in two days.

A total of 392,280 fans swarmed to the ball parks, 197,820 of them on Decoration day and 194,460 of them yesterday. And that didn't include the hundreds of service men who were admitted free.

Here are some of the more important happenings witnessed:

The New York Yankees stretched their American League lead to eight games, although their eight-game winning streak was snapped by the Philadelphia Athletics in yesterday's second game.

The Brooklyn Dodgers boosted their lead in the National League to six games by stopping the Boston Braves twice yesterday after dividing a pair with the New York Giants the day before.

Indians Drop To Fourth

The Cleveland Indians skidded into fourth place in the American League while the Detroit Tigers took over second place and the Boston Red Sox moved up a notch to third.

The St. Louis Cardinals replaced the Boston Braves in second place in the National League by winning two out of three over the week-end

(See BASEBALL—Page 13)

The Baseball Standings

AMERICAN LEAGUE

	W	L	PC	GB
New York	31	11	.738	—
Detroit	26	22	.542	8
Boston	23	20	.535	8½
Cleveland	24	21	.533	8½
St. Louis	23	24	.489	10½
Chicago	18	26	.409	14
Philadelphia	19	30	.388	15½
Washington	17	27	.386	15

YESTERDAY'S RESULTS

New York 11, Philadelphia 7 (1st).
Philadelphia 4, New York 2 (2nd).
Chicago 9, Detroit 4 (1st).
Chicago at Detroit (2nd, postponed).
Boston 11, Washington 1 (1st).
Boston 4, Washington 3 (2nd).
St. Louis 5, Cleveland 4 (1st).
St. Louis 8, Cleveland 3 (2nd).

TOMORROW'S GAMES

Detroit at Philadelphia (night)
Chicago at New York
Cleveland at Boston
St. Louis at Washington (night)

NATIONAL LEAGUE

	W	L	PC	GB
Brooklyn	32	13	.711	—
St. Louis	25	18	.581	6
Boston	25	22	.532	8
New York	23	23	.500	10
Cincinnati	22	22	.500	9½
Chicago	21	24	.467	11
Pittsburgh	19	27	.413	13½
Philadelphia	14	32	.304	18½

YESTERDAY'S RESULTS

New York 3, Philadelphia 2 (1st).
New York 7, Philadelphia 1 (2nd).
Cincinnati 8, Pittsburgh 2 (1st).
Cincinnati 3, Pittsburgh 0 (2nd).
St. Louis 3, Chicago 0 (1st).
St. Louis at Chicago, (2nd, postponed).
Brooklyn 10, Boston 2 (1st).
Brooklyn 3, Boston 1 (2nd).

TOMORROW'S GAMES

Philadelphia at Cincinnati
New York at Chicago
Brooklyn at Pittsburgh
Boston at St. Louis (night)

INTERSTATE LEAGUE

	W	L	PC	GB
Hagerstown	20	11	.645	—
Wilmington	21	14	.600	1
Allentown	17	15	.531	3½
Harrisburg	15	15	.500	4½
Lancaster	12	18	.400	7½
Trenton	10	22	.313	10½

YESTERDAY'S RESULTS

Lancaster 4, Wilmington 0 (1st).
Lancaster 10, Wilmington 9 (2nd).
Trenton 7, Allentown 1 (1st).
Allentown 3, Trenton 1 (2nd).
Hagerstown 6, Harrisburg 5 (1st, 11 innings).
Harrisburg 3, Hagerstown 1 (2nd).

TOMORROW'S GAMES

Lancaster at Trenton
Hagerstown at Wilmington
Harrisburg at Allentown

Wagner Moves Up, Athletics Trade Hayes

PHILADELPHIA, June 1.—(AP)—The trading of Frankie Hayes to the St. Louis Browns climaxes the success story of Hal Wagner, who now becomes the No. 1 catcher for Connie Mack's Athletics.

Hayes, veteran A's backstop, went to the Browns last night in exchange for pitcher Bob Harris and catcher Bob Swift. No cash was involved.

Developed By Mack

The story of Wagner is the tale of a rookie taken in hand and developed gradually by Connie Mack, whom many consider the smartest manager in the game.

During the last two years Wagner, a 6-footer who lives at nearby Riverton, N. J., has spent much of his working hours sitting beside Connie on the bench. As different situations developed on the diamond, Connie explained fine points of the game.

"He's got it up here," Connie said early this season, tapping his forehead with a long forefinger.

Wagner, now 27, was discovered at Duke University in 1934 by Russell Blackburne, coach of the Athletics. He joined the A's in 1937 and was optioned to Portsmouth. In 1938 he played with Spartansburg and caught 33 games for the Mackmen toward the end of the season.

He caught 62 games for Newark in the International League in 1939, then returned to the A's and has been under the Mack's eye ever since.

SUNDAY'S SPORTS RESULTS

Baseball

Western County League—
Eden 5, East Petersburg 1 (1st).
Eden 3, East Petersburg 0 (2nd).
Ronks 3, Columbia 2 (1st).
Ronks 4, Columbia 1 (2nd).
Mountville A. A. 5, Mountville S. C. 1 (1st).
Mountville A. A. 11, Mountville S. C. 6 (2nd).

Lancaster-Lebanon League—
Manheim 5, Schaefferstown 4.
Hopeland 3, Bowmansville 2 (10 innings).
Schoeneck 1, Hinkletown 0 (1st).
Schoeneck 7, Hinkletown 5 (2nd).

Lebanon Valley League—
Wernersville 7, Adamstown 5.

MONDAY'S SPORTS EVENTS

Baseball

Inter-State League—
Hagerstown at Wilmington.
Trenton at Allentown.
Other clubs not scheduled.

Legion Junior League—
Fulton vs. St. Anthony at PRR Field.
Rangers vs. Stock Yards at Geo. Washington Field.

Softball

City Church League—
Redeemer at Pearl Street.
Emmanuel at Church of Christ.
Broad Street at St. Paul's.

Sixth Ward Jr. League—
Army vs. Marines.

Other Softball

Eighth Ward Girls vs. Hen Peck Ten at Chestnut and Plum Streets, 6:45 o'clock.

Seventh Ward Girls at New Providence, 6:30 o'clock.

Seventh and Eighth Ward Teams Triumph

The Seventh and Eighth Ward nines came through with victories in the American Legion Senior Baseball League games yesterday afternoon.

The Seventh Ward made their seven hits count and turned in a 7 to 1 victory over the Legion outfit on the George Washington diamond.

Likewise the Eighth Ward came through with ten hits to defeat the Sixth Ward by a score of 10 to 7 on the P. R. R. Field.

Seventh Ward	ab	r	h	o	a	Legion	ab	r	h	o	a
Under'r 2b	3	0	1	1	2	Duss'er p	3	0	0	0	2
Geist c	4	1	1	2	1	Hicks 2b	3	0	1	1	2
J.Keays 3b	3	1	0	1	2	Cush'an ss	3	0	0	2	1
Asplin p	3	2	1	1	3	Todd cf	3	1	2	1	0
Reese ss	2	2	2	1	1	Rhen 3b	2	0	0	1	0
W.Keays cf	2	0	0	1	0	S.Hurst 1b	3	0	1	5	0
Kramer lf	3	1	1	4	0	R.Hurst lf	3	0	0	1	0
Smith rf	2	0	0	0	0	Smeltz lf	3	0	0	2	0
Taylor 1b	4	0	1	9	0	McLain c	2	0	0	8	0
Quade rf	1	0	0	0	0						
LeFevre ss	1	0	0	1	0	Totals	25	1	4	21	5
Totals	28	7	7	21	9						

SEVENTH WARD .... 032 020 0—7
LEGION .... 000 100 0—1

Eighth Ward	ab	r	h	o	a	Sixth Ward	ab	r	h	o	a
Smeltz 2b	4	2	2	3	4	Moyer cf	5	1	1	1	0
N.Stro'r ss	3	1	1	0	0	Mon're rf	2	1	0	0	0
Wise 3b	4	3	2	0	3	Leaman 1b	4	2	1	12	2
E.Stro'r lf	4	2	0	3	2	T.Ma'na lf	4	1	1	2	3
Poole c	4	0	2	11	1	Kendig 3b	5	0	2	0	2
Kline cf	5	0	0	4	0	S.Ma'na p	4	0	1	2	2
Houck 1b	3	0	1	8	0	McClure c	4	0	0	5	1
Kohler rf	3	1	0	0	0	Warner ss	3	0	1	2	3
Souders p	4	1	2	0	3	Fragari lf	1	0	0	0	0
						Shoe'er 2b	3	2	1	2	2
Totals	34	10	10	27	13	Gibble rf	3	0	0	1	0
						Davis p	1	0	0	0	0
						Totals	39	7	8	27	15

EIGHTH WARD ...... 000 103 303—10
SIXTH WARD .... 200 110 003— 7

MOYLAN DEFEATS BELLIS

Philadelphia—(AP)—Ed. Moylan, of Trenton, ended the four-year reign of Izzy Bellis as Philadelphia and District Men's Tennis champion by beating Bellis, 7-5, 6-2, 6-2, in the finals of the annual tournament at the Cynwyd Club.

D. L. Armstrong Wins Country Club Play

Dwight Armstrong, veteran of many a tournament, returned to top form at the Lancaster Country Club by winning the Decoration Day 18-hole medal handicap play with a 74 card. Playing in the first division, Dwight shot a 38-39—77 with a handicap of three.

H. E. Seaman and Ben Shaub split honors in the second division with 70 cards. Both had gross cards of 95 and each had handicaps of 25.

Neal Begerow won the weekly Syeepstakes tournament yesterday with E. M. Hoffecker as runnerup.

The winners are as follows:

First Division

	Gross	Hdp.	Net
Neal Begerow	80	7	73
E. M. Hoffecker	78	4	74

Second Division

	Gross	Hdp.	Net
S. C. Martin	86	13	73
Robert Davis	89	14	75

Clarkson and Wolf Win Meadia Play

Dr. P. V. Clarkson and C. E. Wolf carried off the prizes in the Blind Bogey golf tournaments held Saturday and Sunday at the Meadia Heights Country Club.

The results are as follows:

SATURDAY'S RESULTS

	Gross	Hdcp	Net
Dr. P. V. Clarkson	81	7	74
F. R. Patterson	85	12	73
M. F. Manby	93	20	73
S. M. Ireys	91	18	73
G. Miller	94	17	77
Richard Oblender	92	15	77
Samuel Small	92	15	77

Other scores: Jack Peek 79, F. Groff, 79; H. E. Frailey 85, R. Eicholtz 85, H. Hassler 85, W. F. Coble 85.

SUNDAY'S RESULTS

C. E. Wolf	99	18	81
F. Travis	96	15	81
Dr. P. V. Clarkson	81	7	74
J. M. Eshelman	90	20	70
William Boothman	95	25	70
G. Miller	91	12	85
W. S. Taggart	91	6	85

Other scores: Russell Shelley 76, William Birrell 76, Fred Ritz 84.

PGA Title To Snead

Sammy Chips Out to Climax Rally in Win Over Turnesa

By GAYLE TALBOT

ATLANTIC CITY, June 1.—(AP)—Sammy Snead, they said, never would win a national golf championship, because something always seemed to happen to him in the closing stages of a tournament when the galleries were running wild and the players' hearts were in their throats.

They were wrong. Sammy held the Professional Golfers Association championship today and had $2,000 worth of war bonds in his pocket as he left for Washington to be inducted into the Navy's physical training program.

Finally Came Through

The 30-year-old star from the hill country, after having suffered probably more major disappointments than any top flight golfer, finally came through with a 2 and 1 victory over Corp. Jim Turnesa in yesterday's 36-hole title match at the Seaview Club here.

It was a fighting victory, too. Sam stood three down at the halfway point. The crowd of 3,000 was vociferously pulling against his every shot and rooting for the swarthy little soldier from Fort Dix. And under those circumstances Snead went out to shoot some of the greatest home-stretch golf ever seen.

Crowd Cheers Turnesa

A triumph for Turnesa undoubtedly would have been more popular. The little guy with the nerves of steel and no business whatsoever in the finals of a P. G. A. championship, had captured the fancy of everybody. The crowd had been cheering his every shot for two days as he scored upset victories over Ben Hogan and Byron Nelson, two of golfdom's greatest players. Yet Snead richly deserved his victory.

Three down through the 23rd hole and with Turnesa refusing to crack, Sammy turned on the heat and blazed home. Starting on the 24th hole, he shot 433 444 344 442. On the 27th hole he squared it with Turnesa, on the 28th he passed him, and from there on the scrapping corporal could only hang on.

Terrific Finish

Snead's finish would have dazed any opponent. The 35th hole, where the match ended, was typical. Sam overdrove the 213-yarder by some 60 feet and then chipped into the hole for a birdie two.

Turnesa, 29-year-old member of the numerous Turnesa golfing clan, also earned all of the superlatives lavished on him. He "made" the tournament. Completely unheralded, the stocky, dark little fellow dropped over from his army camp to play the finest golf of his life and completely upset the professionals' "routine." Odds of 50 to 1 could have been had against him at the start and there were no takers.

$750 Prize Goes To U. S.

Unfortunately for Turnesa, army regulations forbid his pocketing the $750 prize he won and, besides, he promised to donate anything he might win to the Army emergency relief fund.

So pleased were officials with the tournament they decided to hold their next championship on the same course. They don't know when that will be—probably after the war has ended—but it will be in Atlantic City.

LITITZ MERCHANTS TRIUMPH

The Lititz Merchants defeated the Seventh Ward Girls' softball team by a score of 23 to 12 on the Edward Hand diamond.

The Seventh Ward Girls will play at New Providence this Monday evening, at 6:30 o'clock.

Sox Sell Foxx to Cubs

BOSTON, June 1.—(AP)—The Boston Red Sox today announced the outright cash sale of first baseman Jimmy Foxx to the Chicago Cubs of the National League. No other players were involved, the club announced.

It was necessary for owner Tom Yawkey to get waivers from other American League clubs in order to make the sale of Foxx, who long had been regarded as one of the game's modern stars.

5 Years With Sox

Team captain of the Red Sox, Foxx has played five full seasons in Red Sox regalia. He was purchased from Connie Mack's Athletics, with whom he broke into the big time as a catcher in 1926.

"The beast" as he is affectionately called by his mates, has led the league in batting twice, in 1933 and 1938.

He has been incapacitated lately by sinus and by several cracked ribs he suffered when hit by a line drive while pitching batting practice. Ironically, the batter at the time was Harvard's Tony Lupien, who was brought up as his successor at first base.

Foxx, a member of several all-star American league teams, began his professional career with Easton in the eastern shore league in 1924 as a catcher.

GRAYSON'S SCOREBOARD

by HARRY GRAYSON

HAWAII shows you what happens to an American university in the actual theater of war.

There were 2300 students before Dec. 7. Only 700, mostly women, enrolled for the second semester.

The campus was transformed into shelters, dugouts, blackout rooms. The Union Building housed evacuees. Courses emphasizing war activities were added—surgical and first aid, home nursing. Plans for feeding the population were prepared by the Home Economics Department. Housewives are instructed in planning meals giving the utmost in nutritive value with the available food supply. Instructions on home gardens are given by the Agriculture Department.

Many faculty members are employed in full-time war work.

The University ROTC, a majority of the male students, volunteered en masse.

There is no varsity or intramural sports program.

COACH Tommy Kaulukukui closes by telling us what happened to the best Hawaii football squad in years, which the day before the attack won its ninth of 10 games by smothering Willamette University, 20-6, in a Shrine Hospital benefit before 25,000.

Fullback Bob Henderson and Linemen Harold Kometani, Tom Pedro, Ray Asmar, Sadao Watasaki and Kai Bong Chung rushed to the office of Chief of Police Gabrielson of Honolulu determined on apprehending so-called Americans who so ably scouted our military and naval weaknesses.

Unkei Uchima, giant tackle; Joe Yasuda, tackle; Wallace Doi, guard; and Jim Nishimura, halfback, all of whom Tojo would like to have leading interference, joined the Varsity Victory Volunteers, a group of Japanese boys out to prove their loyalty.

These boys set up barb-wire fences, build portable houses, do general construction work. Coach Kaulukukui is with them at Schofield.

CO-CAPTAIN NOLLE SMITH, Little All-America fullback, and Halfback Johnny Naumu no longer throw passes to one another. Instead they throw commands. Smith as a first lieutenant in the Territorial Guard and Naumu as the company commander of machine gunners.

End Bob Coulter and Halfback Dick Hart are second lieutenants in the Guard. Linemen Jere Smith, Jack Beaumont, Dan Hipa, Bill Amona, Ben Kaohi, Lloyd Skog, Emory Ornellas, Frank Catanha, Bill Paris and Albert Choy and Backs Mun King Wong and Moonie Kong are in the ranks.

Axel Silen, 220-pound tackle, was inducted into the Navy.

LINEMAN Judo Shibuya, Bob Fountain and Johnny Bellinger, Backs Larry Thim and Shiro Maehara and Student Managers Seichi Toda and Edwin Liu are with defense project constructors. Center Aaron Neff and Fullback Louis Collins are in the construction department at Red Hill. Co-captain and guard Chin Do Kim, End Lloyd Conkling and Quarterback Mel Abreu joined the fire department. Guard Spencer Kamakana and Tackle Charley Dawson hooked up with the telephone company.

May Day ordinarily is Lei Day in Hawaii.

This year it was War Bond Day.

Walter Mentzer Wins At Country Club Hgts.

Walter Mentzer captured the Hale America Blind Bogey golf tournament which was staged at Johnny Hiemenz' Country Club Heights course over the holiday week-end. The proceeds were turned over to the Lancaster Chapter of the American Red Cross.

Other winners included: W. C. Bohney, Henry L. Frantz, Richard Tomilson, Robert Strantz, Richard Hoffer, Dick Harnish, Thomas McNelis, Leroy Overly and M. J. Hess.

The tournament was handled by Ralph Bruce, pro at the club.

Members of the Motor Corps of the local Red Cross also helped in the promotion of the tournament. They include: Mrs. William Brown, Mrs. Zecher, Bette Frailey, Betty Gilbert, Claye Bump, Stella Marie Haefner, Ethel Marrow, Edith Marrow, Mrs. T. G. Newton, Mrs. Elizabeth Cromwell and Mrs. Charles Gaige.

Three Golfers Tied In Overlook Tourney

Three golfers were deadlocked for top honors in the Hale America 18 hole medal handicap tournament played at the Overlook Country Club course over the week-end.

Allen Goberman, Charles Moffett and William Binkley were all tied with net cards of 69 strokes each.

Allen Goberman	75	6	69
Bill Binkley	76	7	69
Charlie Moffett	81	12	69
Tom Newswanger	76	4	72
Mickey Draude	74	1	73
Clair Alexander	78	5	73
Charlie Deyer	84	11	73
Gener Hayes	79	6	73
Dr. Poole	77	4	73
Russell Morrison	81	8	73
George Anderson	86	12	74
Pete Leaman	80	6	74
John Hottel	79	5	74
Charlie Mower	86	12	74
George Scheffer	78	4	74
Frank Poose	93	18	75
Pete Powers	90	15	75
Charlie Wenger	86	10	76
Charlie Pott	84	8	76
Lester Mumma	102	25	77
George Schenck	85	8	77
Dr. Keiser	93	15	78
Charlie Raezor	90	12	78
G. Elvin Simmons	79	0	79
Elwood Lineaweaver	97	14	83

No Cards—J. R. Coder, E. K. Forney, J. Griffeth.

UNCLE EF SAYS:—
50,000 people go to a horse race and bet more than $2,000,000. That must be real cheering to the boys on the war fronts.

LANCASTER NEW ERA

WEATHER
Somewhat cooler tonight. (Details on Page 3).

Examiner Founded 1830. New Era Founded 1877.
Published Every Evening Except Sunday by New Era Company. Entered as Second Class Matter at Post Office, Lancaster, Pa.
LANCASTER, PA., FRIDAY, JUNE 5, 1942 — CITY EDITION — 22 PAGES—176 COLUMNS — 20c PER WEEK—4c Per Copy

HUGE SEA BATTLE OFF MIDWAY

Japs Pursued After Attack On U.S. Island is Smashed

Outcome May Decide If Foe Is to Strike At Hawaii and Calif.

Jap Battleship and Aircraft Carrier Damaged, Many Attacking Planes Shot Down; Island Suffers Minor Damage

(By the Associated Press)

American defenders, spurred by initial successes, closed battle today with a strong Japanese sea-air task force in what may be a finish fight for possession of Midway island.

Washington sources said American and Japanese fleet units apparently were engaged in one of the greatest battles of the Pacific.

Flaming Sea Battle Continues

The flaming sea battle was believed to be progressing long after the original attack on Midway was beaten off, with both sides maneuvering for advantage in what may be a crucial fight to determine Japan's ability to strike at such vital points as Hawaii, the Panama Canal and the American Pacific coast.

Already the island garrison had scored hits on an enemy battleship, an aircraft carrier and possibly other war vessels. Raiding planes were brought down in great number during the dawn attack yesterday which touched off the battle.

"Our attacks on the enemy are continuing," said a bulletin from the headquarters of Admiral Chester W. Nimitz, commander-in-chief of the Pacific fleet.

Only minor damage and no casualties were inflicted on defenders of the tiny U. S. outpost, 1,149 miles northwest of Hawaii and 2,600 miles southeast of Tokyo, a communique said.

Turning the surprise attack into a staggering defeat, American fighters including marines, sea and air forces were officially credited with damaging a Japanese battleship, an aircraft carrier and possibly other warships, as well as taking a heavy toll of planes.

This latest assault on the tiny island outpost, last line of defense before Hawaii itself, began shortly after dawn yesterday.

It found the American forces keyed to fighting pitch by long preparation and patently strengthened in the months since they first repulsed such an attack December 7.

Forewarned By Dutch Harbor

It found them alert and forewarned by the preceding day's raid upon Dutch Harbor, 2,000 miles to the north. It seemed the enemy may have stepped unwittingly into a spot too hot to handle.

But it also appeared strongly possible the Japanese did not intend this as a hit-and-run affair, like their five preceding forays against Midway.

Presence of capital ships in the attacking force and the heavy toll the defenders were able to exact in the first few hours of the operation suggested the enemy was at hand with the sole purpose of taking over the island, completely and finally.

And Midway, with the tradition of Wake island as its guide, was obviously in no mind to let the issue go by default.

As great as the Japanese force appeared to be, however, there remained a possibility that it was engaged in a diversionary operation and that a main force was developing an attack elsewhere.

Battle For Pacific Grows

Thousands of miles to the west, other naval actions marked the growing struggle for control of the seas:

AUSTRALIA—Gen. Douglas MacArthur's headquarters announced that Allied planes guarding the vital lanes in which U. S. war supplies are flowing to Australia have sunk two more Japanese submarines and probably a third off the east coast of the "Down Under" continent.

The new successes made a total

(See PACIFIC—Page 6)

MAY DECIDE ON $46 ARMY PAY

Senate Group Proposes Compromise; Soldiers' Wives Voted $50.

WASHINGTON, June 5.—(AP)—Senate conferees on the military pay increase bill proposed a compromise to the House committeemen today calling for $46 a month for buck privates and $52 for first-class privates.

The House group took the proposal under advisement and another conference may be held later in the day.

The compromise offer compares with Senate-approved figures of $42 for buck privates and $48 for first class privates and House-approved figures of $50 and $54, respectively.

Neither conference group had all of its members present, but a majority was on hand for each five-man side seeking to adjust House and Senate differences.

Retroactive To June 1

The two groups reached one agreement today—to make the pay increase retroactive to June 1. Privates now get $21 a month for four months, when they are raised to $30.

There appeared a likelihood that soldiers, sailors and marines having dependents would be required

(See SOLDIERS' PAY—Page 19)

LESS QUARANTINE FOR SCARLET FEVER

HARRISBURG, June 5.—(AP)—The Pennsylvania Department of Health has decided to shorten from 30 to 21 days the quarantine period for scarlet fever.

Dr. A. H. Stewart, acting secretary, said the new regulation would become effective after all agencies had been properly notified. He explained mild cases of the disease are not considered contagious after the third week.

Report Store Bought For Montgomery Ward

The Court today confirmed sale by the Farmers' Trust Mortgage Pool of the building at the southwest corner of Penn Square and King street to Arthur W. Binns, Philadelphia real estate man, for $62,800.

It is reported that Binns made the purchase for the Montgomery Ward and Company. Representatives of the company said that any announcement about the building will come from the Real Estate department of the chain concern in Chicago.

The corner has been without a permanent tenant since it was vacated by the Sears Roebuck and company. Years ago it was occupied as Antes cafe.

PAYS FOR EMPLOYE'S GLASS EYE

Luther B. Jenkins, Negro, 522 Concord street, Columbia, who pleaded guilty to a charge of vio-

(See COURT—Page 19)

The Scribbler

MRS. Ruth Schwebel, West King street miliner, is still puzzled over a birthday gift. She received a letter telling her to call at a local department store for a pair of stockings. Now she's wondering wheher they have been added to her bill.

State Rationing Head

Raymond F. Ashenfelter, Pittsburgh department store executive, the newly appointed director of the Office of Price Administration in Pennsylvania, is 44, and a registered Republican. He will supervise all rationing in Pennsylvania and direct the Federal government's price control and rent structures.

F D OPENS STUDY OF GAS, RUBBER

Statement Is Expected Soon; Local Boards Can Rescind X-Cards.

WASHINGTON, June 5—(AP)—President Roosevelt and 11 government officials who are searching for a solution to the rubber and gasoline problems conferred at the White House today but apparently reached no definite conclusions.

One of the participants said flatly no decisions were made and he did not know when any might be expected.

But, Archibald MacLeish, director of the Office of Facts and Figures, asserted a statement would be issued "in the nearish future." He interpreted that to mean a "matter of days," and said the statement would come from the White House.

The meeting today, he said, constituted a "routine discussion of general matters."

Congressmen Seek Probe

In the meantime nearly 100 Congressmen met and adopted a resolution proposing a Congressional investigation of the gasoline-rubber situation, opposing nationwide ra-

(See GAS—Page 6)

ARMY TRAINING MEN TO TAKE CONTROL IN RECONQUERED AREAS

PHILADELPHIA, June 5.—(AP)—The United States Army is training a corps of officers "to restore and operate civil governments in the countries of Europe as they are reconquered," Clarence E. Pickett, executive secretary of the American Friends Service Committee, said today.

Sixty officers are studying such administration at a southern university, Pickett told the graduating class of Friends' Central School.

21 ARE KILLED IN BLAST AT U.S. ARSENAL

Mammoth Plant at Joliet, Ill., Is Shaken By Explosion in Shipping Room.

GEN. DOOLITTLE'S BOMBS MADE THERE

JOLIET, Ill., June 5—(AP)—An explosion rocked the mammoth Elwood Arsenal, one of the largest in the nation, early today, leaving at least "21 known dead," Capt. David P. Tunstall, Army press relations officer, announced.

Twenty-four men were injured, and 28 others working in the shipping building escaped unhurt.

Three of the dead were identified, but Tunstall did not announce the names of any of the 40 casualties.

The blast, heard for a radius of 50 miles at 3:45 A. M., destroyed the shipping building of group two of the Elwood Ordnance Shell Loading plant, which had been described by its director as the largest in the world.

Captain Tunstall said there was no hint of sabotage, but that its possibility would be investigated by a board of inquiry.

Lt. Col. Don M. Hoffman, commanding officer, probably will convene the board of inquiry, but Tunstall said the time and place had not been set.

Dr. H. L. Shultz, medical director, was in charge of rescue operations.

Tunstall emphasized that operations in the one group would be interrupted only a short time. The plant was designed with the view of preventing and minimizing explosions and was scattered over a large area of southern Will County south of Joliet.

The bombs that Gen. James Doolittle dropped on Tokyo possibly came from the Elwood Loading plant and its companion plant, the Kankakee Ordnance TNT Works, a government spokesman recently said.

The two plants were in production some time before Pearl Harbor.

Tunstall said the wrecked build-

(See BLAST—Page 6)

14 ARMY FLIERS DIE IN CRASH OF BOMBER IN WEST

SAN RAFAEL, Cal., June 5—(AP)—Fourteen Army fliers died in the crash of a heavy bomber near here last night, the Army said today. Flames consumed the wreckage when the plane hit a hilltop as the pilot circled for an emergency landing.

The plane developed trouble soon after a takeoff and radioed nearby Hamilton Field to clear a runway. The pilot circled toward the field.

The big ship lost altitude and then dived into a hillside on the Herzog ranch, three miles northwest of Hamilton Field.

As it crashed great flames swept through the wreckage. Not a man escaped.

"JERRY HAS GOT THE "JITTERS," SAYS COMMANDO LEADER

LONDON, June 5.—(AP)—Germans fired upon Germans during the British Commando raid early yesterday against Boulogne-le Touquet defenses. One Nazi patrol boat was sunk and another was grounded in flames and smoke columns marked areas of destruction, eyewitnesses said today.

"Jerry has got the jitters," commented a 23-year-old officer of the British special service troops.

Dropped from Naval craft into the surf of the Channel coast of occupied France where an Allied expeditionary force may land one day, the raiders were heavily armed and lightly clad. Many wore only shorts, stockings and soft woolen headgear.

F.D. SAYS JAPS ARE USING GAS AGAINST CHINA

Declares U. S. Will Retaliate If Tokyo Persists in Inhumanity.

STATE DEPARTMENT CONFIRMS PRACTICE

WASHINGTON, June 5—(AP)—President Roosevelt told today of official information that Japan was using poison gas against China and grimly declared that if the Japanese persisted in this form of warfare, the United States would mete out "retaliation in kind and in full measure."

The reports that Japan on several occasions had resorted to gas warfare were described by the Chief Executive to his press conference as authoritative. He read a brief formal statement, which he said the State Department had prepared, making it unequivocally clear that the United States would consider the use of gas against China or any other United Nation as an action against the United States.

The text of the statemen follows:

"Authoritative reports are reaching this government of the use by Japanese armed forces in various localities of China of poisonous or noxious gases. I desire to make it unmistakably clear that, if Japan persists in this inhuman form of warfare against China or against any other of the United Nations, such action will be regarded by this government as though taken against the United States, and retaliation in kind and in full measure will be meted out. We shall be prepared to enforce complete retribution. Upon Japan will rest the responsibility."

Just where or in what manner

(See POISON GAS—Page 6)

Patrol Finds Everything Okay

A trio of U. S. Navy Kingfishers, while searching for enemy submarines, swings past an ocean-going freighter to make sure it is not a disguised enemy raider and then roars away to complete its patrol.

Largest Arms Convoy Reaches India Safely

American and British Troops and Many U. S.-Built Planes and Tanks Sent to Defense of Far East

By PRESTON GROVER

NEW DELHI, India, June 5—(AP)—As Japanese forces pressed to a point 45 miles east of India's Burma frontier, the British announced today that the largest convoy of reinforcements ever to come to the defense of India had been unloaded at Eastern India ports.

The reinforcements included light and heavy anti-aircraft guns, British and American light and heavy tanks and a large number of both fighting and technical personnel.

The convoy put into Indian ports early in May and was so big it could not be handled at any one port. It came through without loss.

U. S. Crews Arrive

Among the troops were some Indian soldiers trained in Britain and other troops with battle experience in France and Libya.

Crews of Hurricane fighters and American-built Kittyhawks now operating in India arrived on the convoy.

The number of troops and materiel was described as possibly the largest ever to leave the United Kingdom.

Japanese troops have reached Homalin, 45 miles east of the Indian-Burmese border, and are continuing to rus h troops up the Chindwin river in Burma, a British spokesman said today.

The spokesman declared the Japanese evidently planned at least

(See CONVOY—Page 6)

WENGERITE GOES TO WORK CAMP

1st of Sect to Leave Voluntarily; Another Indicted in U. S. Court.

Leroy Martin Martin, New Holland R1, left for a conscientious objectors' work camp this morning, the first member of the local Wenger Mennonites to go to camp voluntarily.

Nine other members of the sect were arrested when they refused go to comp. One was given a prison term, six were taken to a work camp and two others are under indictment in the U. S. Court.

Martin was assigned to the Hagerstown camp after he had been classified by County Board 4 as a conscientious objector. He originally was assigned to the Sideling Hill camp, Fulton county, but the order was changed by the Federal government.

Martin was accompanied to the bus depot by his employer and a group of church friends. The group stood some distance from the bus as Martin said an abrupt farewell and started on his journey.

It was learned that the youth had made his own decision to go to camp rather than wait to be prose-

(See DRAFT—Page 6)

LOCAL GERMAN ALIEN STILL HELD BY FBI

FBI agents in Philadelphia today were still holding a German alien picked up here yesterday morning and taken to that city for questioning. His name was not revealed by agents, who said no charges had been brought against the man, a German soldier during World War I.

Such cases in this area, it was learned, usually are transferred to the U. S. Immigration Detention station at Gloucester, N. J., for a hearing before the Enemy Alien Board.

MAY DECIDE ON $46 ARMY PAY

Senate Group Proposes Compromise; Soldiers' Wives Voted $50.

WASHINGTON, June 5.—(AP)—Senate conferees on the military pay increase bill proposed a compromise to the House committeemen today calling for $46 a month for buck privates and $52 for first-class privates.

The House group took the proposal under advisement and another conference may be held later in the day.

The compromise offer compares with Senate-approved figures of $42 for buck privates and $48 for first class privates and House-approved figures of $50 and $54, respectively.

Neither conference group had all of its members present, but a majority was on hand for each five-man side seeking to adjust House and Senate differences.

Retroactive To June 1

The two groups reached one agreement today—to make the pay increase retroactive to June 1. Privates now get $21 a month for four months, when they are raised to $30.

There appeared a likelihood that soldiers, sailors and marines having dependents would be required

(See SOLDIERS' PAY—Page 19)

LESS QUARANTINE FOR SCARLET FEVER

HARRISBURG, June 5.—(AP)—The Pennsylvania Department of Health has decided to shorten from 30 to 21 days the quarantine period for scarlet fever.

Dr. A. H. Stewart, acting secretary, said the new regulation would become effective after all agencies had been properly notified. He explained mild cases of the disease are not considered contagious after the third week.

"ZIG-ZAGGER" GOT GAS WITHOUT CARD

Mearl L. Mellott, forty-three, Ephrata, R. 3, charged with drunken driving, was arrested by city police after he collided with an auto driven by Edward T. Lander, 158 East Walnut street, on Prince street between Lemon and James streets at 9:30 P. M. yesterday.

Police said Mellott was driving with a 1941 operator's license and did not have a gas rationing card. He claimed he got gas without a card, and an investigation was ordered.

LOSES 38 LBS. TO JOIN COAST GUARDS

CHICAGO, June 5—(AP)—Joseph Schmid, a Chicago salesman, wanted so much to join the Coast Guard that he lost 38 pounds in 51 days to bring himself within the weight limit.

He was rejected on April 14 because he weighed 198 pounds—38 pounds too much for his five feet, ten and onehalf inch height. He was approved on his second examination.

FRESH PANZERS ATTACK IN LIBYA

Thrown Into Battle After British Base Smashes Two Assaults.

(By The Associated Press)

Marshal Erwin Rommel was reported moving strong Axis reinforcements into the bloody 11-day-old battle of North Africa today as the British announced they had smashed an Axis tank assault on Bir El Hacheim for the second time in two days.

Bir El Hacheim, a desert water hole, is the southern anchor of a 50-mile British defense line stretched across the hot sands to the Mediterranean sea.

British Strike From Rear

British headquarters said British and Indian troops struck from the rear to relieve the Free French and Indian garrison at Bir El Hacheim after the defenders had twice rejected German demands that they surrender the key stronghold.

Front-line dispatches said Rommel was speeding fresh troops and tanks into the battle sector around Tobruk in an attempt to relieve pressure on a 9-mile corridor which Axis forces had driven into the British main defense line.

British mechanized forces were reported slashing at Axis tanks holding the breach, while German dive bombers pounded furiously at British positions blocking Rommel's advance toward Egypt.

A Rome communique said Ger-

(See EUROPE—Page 6)

BODY OF MISSING BOY FOUND IN BAY

CAMBRIDGE, Md., June 5—(AP)—The body of Benjamin Lewis, 2 1-2 year old Baltimore boy, missing since last Saturday was found in Chesapeake Bay early today, State's Attorney W. Calvin Harrington, Jr., announced. Harrington said the body was washed ashore on the bay side of Hooper's Island, where the boy had gone for the Memorial Day holiday with his parents, Mr. and Mrs. Benjamin Lewis.

An intensive search of the entire Island area and Bay channel started Saturday had been given up Wednesday by Dorchester County authorities. The child was last seen playing with a ball in the yard of his grandparents, Mr. and Mrs. Richard Lewis, early Saturday evening.

Washington *by Peter Edson*

Proposed Synthetic Rubber from Alcohol from Existing Whisky Distilleries Provokes Battle of the Giants

ANNOUNCEMENT of the War Production Board's program to obtain 475 million gallons of industrial alcohol from grain, including 200 million gallons for the manufacture of butadiene, ingredient of synthetic rubber, has spurred on efforts of the Senate Subcommittee on Agriculture to win for the agricultural chemistry industry a more important place in war production.

Edson

When the new WPB alcohol schedule was first announced, it was thought the investigation being conducted under the chairmanship of Senator Guy M. Gillette of Iowa might be killed. But the sop thrown the committee has made this group of tough farm bloc senators, including McNary, Wheeler, Norris, Smith and Thomas of Oklahoma, all the more determined to find outlets for surplus farm crops.

Behind the scenes, this is a battle of giants. These senators, and other congressmen as well, are beginning to get mad. As a preliminary to one of the subcommittee's recent hearings, they voiced their ire over what they felt was a run-around being given them by WPB. Their constituents have difficulty in getting contracts or attention. The industrial areas are getting rich off war production, while the farmers can't. And so on.

This should be the chance for agricultural chemistry to win a permanent place in the industrial scheme, to work off these huge crop surpluses, to get away from doling out all these millions of dollars for farm subsidies and farm benefits. Agricultural chemistry should compete equally with the mineral chemicals industries like petroleum products and coal by-products.

The farm bloc senators would like, ideally, to see a lot of smaller alcohol distilleries right in the farm belt. The alcohol in turn would be made into butadiene, which would be made into synthetic rubber.

The WPB argument is that this would take too much critical material, 1300 tons of steel and 70 tons of copper, for instance, to

(See EDSON—Page 6)

Last Chance to Order Anniversary Edition

Extra copies of Lancaster's 200th anniversary edition must be ordered before 9 o'clock tonight.

Orders can be placed at the Newspaper Office or by calling 5252 and asking for Circulation Department. Mail orders, postmarked tonight, will be accepted. A special order blank will be found on Page 19 of today's New Era.

Newsprint restrictions make it necessary to print just enough papers to supply regular subscribers and extra orders on file.

The Anniversary edition will tell the story of Lancaster past and present in pictures and featured articles.

The price is 4 cents per copy or 15 cents per copy mailed.

Lancaster's 200th Anniversary

THAT WAS PENN SQUARE!

PRE-WAR STUFF—Three-quarters of Penn Square were caught in the sweep of the camera, including the "Welcome" on City Hall, Hirsh's clothing store, Hendren's Cigars, and quite a few people. (Entered by Katherine Houck, Lancaster R5.)

REMEMBER when Christmas trees were still sold in Penn Square? Photo above may help. (Entered by Charles H. Tucker, 132 College Ave.)

ZOOOOOM!—No, that's not Superman passing through the Square (at left). It's a Garfield campaign parade in 1880, which didn't wait for the time exposure. (Entered by H. M. Dorwart, Lancaster R1.)

CITY IN MOURNING—This great crowd gathered in the square on Sept. 19, 1901, (at right) the day President McKinley was buried. (Entered by John Sachs, 228 W. James St.)

34-STAR FLAG gives a clue to the age of this rainy-day stereopticon view of an Odd Fellows parade passing through the square, dating it around 1870. (Entered by R. K. Rittenhouse, Lancaster R1.)

ALL DRESSED UP—The old Citizens Bank, on the southeast corner of the square, was togged out fit to kill to greet the Jr. Order of United American Mechanics convention when this was taken. It was Locher's Bank before that. (Entered by G. K. Biemesderfer, 322 S. Queen St.)

OLD DRAY MARE—The dray wagon that waited around the square for hauling jobs was about all the traffic in sight, and it wasn't moving, when this photo was taken. (Entered by Mrs. Edna K. Hammel, 502 W. James St.)

MISHLER'S BITTERS, the Anglo-Arabian Horse Powder Depot, the U. S. Assessor's office, and Myers & Rathvon, the tailors, competed for Penn Square signboard space back in the 1870's. None of these buildings remain. (Entered by Paul Peel, 45 W. Chestnut St.)

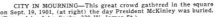

CIRCUS PARADE—The stagecoach and six-horse team attracted much attention among a highly horse-conscious crowd in the 1880's. The photo was taken from the second floor above Harnish & Leaman's paint store at 5 S. Queen St. (Entered by C. H. Tucker, 132 College Ave.)

The Weather
Eastern Pennsylvania: Moderately warm Sunday.

SUNDAY NEWS

3 A. M. Edition
The Sunday News carries the full report of two world wide news services—
LATEST NEWS by Associated Press, International News Service and Complete Local News

VOL. 19—NO. 42 | Entered at Post Office at Lancaster, Pa., as second class mail matter | LANCASTER, PA., SUNDAY, JUNE 21, 1942 | 50 PAGES, 272 COLUMNS.—SIX CENTS.

REPORT AXIS FORCES IN BARDIA

Navy Says Axis Mines Sown Along Virginia Coast Blasted 2 Ships

First Report of Enemy Mine Laying Here of War

Washington, June 20—(AP)—The first official report of enemy minelaying operations along the United States coast in this war came today in a Navy announcement that mines had caused the recent sinking of one merchant ship and damage to another off the Virginia shore.

The Navy said careful investigation had convinced it that the two ship casualties were not "as previously believed," the results of submarine attacks but were caused by the "vessels striking enemy mines."

"Undoubtedly, these mines were laid by an enemy submarine under the cover of darkness, when detection is extremely difficult," the Navy said.

Not Unexpected

That was the only official Navy comment regarding the minelaying, but the development had not been unexpected in naval circles. Germany is known to have a number of long-range submarines equipped for mine laying. Available records show several ocean-going U-boats of more than 1,000 tons displacement are fitted for minelaying and naval experts believe Germany has been busy building more. These are in addition to many coastal type U-boats used for laying mines in the waters around England and in shipping lanes leading from that country.

Moreover, the Germans recently announced what they called an intensive submarine campaign against all shipping along the coast of North America and extending east to the shores of Europe.

While the announcement set June 26 as the deadline for action in that area, it was possible the enemy had started off his campaign early with minelayers supplementing the already extensive operations of the torpedo-firing submarines.

After the United States entered the First World War, German mines were laid along the American coast.

Berlin Says U. S. Defense Stronger

New York, June 20—(AP)—The Germans acknowledged tonight that the Allies have "strongly increased" their defenses against Axis submarine attack, particularly along the Gulf and Atlantic coasts of the United States.

"The fight against enemy supply shipping and patrol and escort vessels of the enemy assumed particular fierceness in the past week," said the Berlin radio in a German-language broadcast for European consumption, recorded here by CBS. It continued:

"The enemy has strongly increased his submarine defense and convoy protection, and is using for the battle against the ever-greater submarine danger all available craft.

"It could be observed that along the east coast of the United States small and very small coastal ves-

MINES—Page 15

"Gasless Sundays" Of 1918 Recalled As Pumps Go Dry

The "gasless Sundays" of World War I seemed ready for a comeback here as approximately 20 percent of Lancaster county's service stations went dry for the weekend and thousands of "no gas" signs appeared along the Atlantic seaboard.

Two of the largest distributors in the local area reported that about one out of every five stations they supply has exhausted its quota until Monday. Other stations reported sufficient gasoline on hand to meet needs while still others were sharply restricting sales so as to spread the dwindling supply among more drivers.

Most stations that were open began curtailing sales to transient drivers. In most cases, sales were restricted to a single unit of a ration card—six gallons. Some few stations had adopted a similar policy with regular customers and allowed only one unit of gasoline per car.

Bulletin

Adamstown Man, 65, Killed on New Hwy.

William Fritz, about 65, Adamstown, was instantly killed this morning while walking along the new Reading highway near Adamstown. Dr. Luke Youndt, of Adamstown, pronounced the man dead. The name of the driver of the car could not be learned.

Rubber Salvage In Home Stretch

A THOUSAND RUBBER HEELS—AND HITLER, is today's war thought. J. Russell Graul, Duke and Vine, examines the contribution of an unidentified boy who turned them in for salvage.

1,000 Rubber Heels Get Into Scrap To Kick Axis

Tire Cache In Conestoga Creek, 'Mine' At Akron Boost Salvage Campaign

A thousand rubber heels, a ton of tires from the Conestoga Creek, and a "rubber mine" in an abandoned quarry at Akron have added to Lancaster county's growing pile of scrap rubber.

A boy turned in the rubber heels at Russel Graul's S. Duke and Vine Sts. service station Saturday. Graul said he had no idea where they came from. "He just asked me if I wanted 1000 rubber heels, then brought them in an hour or so later," Graul said.

Two boys, searching in the Conestoga creek, salvaged almost a ton of old tires in the vicinity of Slackwater. They are Lloyd Funk, 16, and his brother, Frank, 14, sons of Mr. and Mrs. Elvin Funk, who live at Slackwater.

Representatives of the Pennsylvania Salvage Company announced they will start excavations in the quarry of J. R. Withers, Akron, to investigate reports that many tons of old rubber from the Miller Hess Shoe Company plant are buried in the quarry.

Bits of rubber taken from near the surface of the ground-level of the quarry have been tested and found fit for salvage.

Much of the rubber in the quarry is in bales and represents trimmings from rubber soles and heels from shoes manufactured in the Akron

RUBBER—Page 15

Mother Gives Up Baby Boots For Rubber Salvage

Waltham, Mass., June 20—(INS)—A twelve-year-old boy walked into Ted Mills' filling station today carrying two bags of rubber articles.

He handed one of them to Mills, watched him weigh it and took his payment. Then he gave him the second container with a note, turned and walked quickly away.

The note read:

"The President's friend:

"These little rubber boots and beach sandals belonged to my little brother, who died ten year ago. He was only three then. I don't remember him very well, as I was only a year old at the time.

"My mother has often said that all the money in the world could not buy these things, but now she is giving them for the scrap rubber drive. Because they were so highly thought of by my mother, I don't want you to throw them in with the other old rubber. Sort of keep them in a special place of their own.

"Very truly yours,

"Peter Norton".

SALES TAX KILLED BY COMMITTEE

Plan to Collect Part of Individual's Income Taxes From Paycheck Is Approved

Washington, June 20—(AP)—The House Ways and Means Committee quickly killed sales tax proposals today, and then adopted a formula for collecting a part of each employed individual's income taxes from his regular paychecks beginning in January.

With the decisions, the committee virtually completed a tentative draft of new tax legislation intended to add at least $6,640,000,000 to Federal Revenue. Final action sending the bill to the House is expected to be taken next week.

The treasury had asked for $8,700,000,000, which Secretary Morgenthau said was the least that Congress should raise. Advocates of a sales tax had argued that a 5 per cent retail sales levy, with government and state purchases exempted, would produce $2,500,000,000.

Will Not Be Considered

At the end of a two-hour committee meeting today, Chairman Doughton, Dem., N. C., announced that a sales tax would not be considered in this bill, and members assumed that the subject would not come up again for many months, if at all. The vote against a sales tax was not announced but was reported to have been 13 to 8 with two proxies cast.

Representatives McKeough, Dem., Ill., and Healey, Dem., Mass., who led the fight against such a levy, contended that it would fall disproportionately heavy on those with low incomes.

By a 10 to 9 vote, the committee agreed tentatively to the pay-as-you-go system of collecting individual income taxes. It is designed to complete in two years a shift from the current system of paying one year's taxes the next year to a program of paying at least part of current taxes out of current income.

Generally speaking, the new plan would work like this:

An individual's annual personal exemptions would be determined and divided by 52 to ascertain the weekly exemptions. A 10 per cent "withholding tax" would be levied on that part of the weekly pay check not covered by the exemption.

Half of the pay deduction could be used as a credit against 1942 taxes due beginning next March 15, and the other half would accumulate as a credit against 1943 taxes due March 15, 1944. Beginning in 1944, the full 10 per cent deduction would be applied against 1944 taxes.

In order to reach those whose whose income is not in the form of regular checks, the treasury proposed a separate treatment for such persons as business men and recipients of rents.

The treasury proposed—and the committee approved—a stipulation that all persons pay a part of their 1942 tax liabilities next year in one lump sum in March, rather than in quarterly instalments. The lump sum would correspond to the amounts withheld at source from

SALES—Page 15

LEON HENDERSON OFFERS TO QUIT OPA JOB, IF—

Gives Reporters Two Reasons Why He Would Resign As Administrator

Washington, June 20—(AP)—Leon Henderson, embroiled in a patronage row with some members of Congress, offered today to resign his price administrator's job if:

Congress refused to enact price subsidy legislation so long as he remained in office, or

FINDS GAS RATIONING HAS BEEN 'INCONVENIENT'

Washington, June 20—(AP)—Price Administrator Leon Henderson, who bosses gasoline rationing in the East, some times is just another harassed motorist.

"Gas rationing has been damned inconvenient to me." he exploded, in the midst of a press conference today. "I think the government ought to look into some of these situations. I can't even go fishing any more."

Motorist Henderson has an "A" rationing card.

President Roosevelt wanted him to.

The price administrator's offer was made at a press conference at which he said he still believed that inflation could be prevented, but made clear that he thought little progress was being made currently toward that end.

Success or failure in the battle

HENDERSON—Page 15

War Workers May Be Allowed Tires

Washington, June 20—(AP)—The Office of Price Administration made war workers eligible to buy second grade tires today provided their need for them is certified by special rationing committees to be established in all war plants employing more than 100 workers.

Plants with fewer than 100 employes will not be eligible to participate in the new plan, nor will their workers be eligible to buy the tires.

OPA said the plant rationing committees would be made up of labor and management members and, in addition to determining a worker's need for tires, also would make certain that his automobile was being used in a transportation pool to carry other workers to and from their jobs.

F.-M. Airmen Hit Axis; One Shown On Army Poster

They're making a new kind of service flag out at F. & M. Instead of stars, it's to be covered with squadrons of little blue planes, each representing a graduate of the college pilot training program in active service.

There'll be three planes on the flag for men flying the long and perilous tangent of the African Air Ferries.

There'll be 25 to represent the young men in the Army Air Corps, and a dozen to salute those in Navy Air Corps service. One lone plane will signify that a graduate of the course is flying with the Royal Canadian Air Force.

As the new class of 40 men begin their studies on July 1, the winged flag will hang in their classroom to remind them of those who have gone before to the fronts of the world. They'll "live, eat, and sleep flying, ten hours a day for eight weeks," according to Prof. Frederic Klein, CPT Coordinator at the college.

Every one of the 40 will be already enrolled in the Navy or Army Air Reserves. Like a bigtime football team—or, a regular Air Cadet camp—they'll live together in a dormitory, with room, food and transportation provided them, up by 7 a. m. for calisthenics, ground school to noon, flight training at two airports all afternoon, back for boning on lessons at night.

In The Headlines

But their story is all in the future. It's the boys who have been handed their diplomas in the local course in the past two years who are up there in the clouds and the headlines.

Take Johnny Ryan, for instance. In flying togs, with goggles pushed up over his forehead and parachute strapped across his shoulders, he grins from the cover of one of the latest Army Air Corps recruiting leaflets. Johnny, whose family lives at 860 Helen Ave., is the embodiment of the kind of young pilot the

FLIERS—Page 15

"KEEP 'EM FLYING!"
AVIATION CADET

That big smile on the face of Flying Cadet John L. Ryan so pleased the Army Air Corps that they printed it like this on the front of a recruiting leaflet. Johnny, a graduate of the F. & M. flying course, is the son of Mr. and Mrs. Claude G. Ryan, 860 Helen Ave.

UNION FIRE CO. MEETS 182ND YR.

Judge Keller Calls For Elimination Of 'Blocs' During War

To win this war we must eliminate all blocs and become Americans, William H. Keller, president judge of the State Superior Court, said at the 182nd anniversary banquet of the Union Fire Co. No. 1 at the Arcadia Saturday.

He said the war would be won by those on the firing line and hoped those in authority would awaken to that fact and carry out the principal of "all for one and one for all." About 75 members and guests were present.

Mayor Dale E. Cary offered the toast, "To the Union Fire Co., may its existence be perpetual," first given by Mayor Sanderson in 1860. Other speakers were Earl F. Lefever, Quarryville, president of the Lancaster County Firemen's Association, Curtis B. Shaburg, York Director of Public Safety, L. Ellis Wagner, York fire chief, and James E. Chalfant, also of York.

C. H. Martin, historian of the company, traced the probable origin of the company from Ben Franklin's first company, in Philadelphia.

Dr. William A. Wolfe, vice-president, spoke in the absence of George H. Schenck, 88-year-old president of the organization. A prayer by the Rev. Will E. Glassmire opened the banquet. Assistant Fire Chief Frank Deen was toastmaster.

The committee on arrangements included George H. Schenck, chairman; Dr. William A. Wolfe, vice-chairman; secretary, George A. Arisman; treasurer, Alpheus M. Angstadt; publicity, Claude A. Villee.

UNION—Page 15

Summer's 1st Day, Sommer's Birthday

Today is the first day of Summer and the birthday of Sommer.

Everett Sommer, 714 S. Lime St., will be sixty-eight a few hours after Summer arrives at 9:22 p. m. A Spanish War veteran, he served 18 years in the Army and Marine Corps.

Mr. Sommer, who has three daughters, points out that today is also father's day. A coincidence all around, he thinks.

The mercury touched 90 degrees in the city Saturday and climbed to 94 at Ephrata, with moderate breezes and a shower bringing slight relief Saturday night. Moderately warm is forecast for today. The year's high thus far is 95, recorded May 1.

Man Is Injured When Hit By Auto

Harry McLaughlin, 230 North Prince St., was admitted to St. Joseph's Hospital after he was struck, city police said, on North Prince St. between Chestnut and Walnut Sts., by a car operated by Samuel J. Wickersham, 328 Chester St., Saturday night. He was slightly hurt.

Old Fort Gets Facial To Greet Army Women

Des Moines, Ia., June 20—(INS)—Venerable old Fort Des Moines, with its stately elm trees, shady walks and well-clipped grounds, is undergoing a facial.

Today construction work goes rapidly forward as carpenters renovate the old brick barracks to house—not army men—but the first contingent of women to enter the women's army auxiliary corps training school.

Will Arrive July 20

The WAAC's will be moving in July 20. When they arrive, they will find their quarters up to snuff in good old army style.

One faculty officer described the new barracks as "spacious."

"The women will have plenty of room. Their quarters will be strictly utilitarian, somewhat on the severe side, but comfortable, light and clean," he said.

"There'll be no great feminine marks of distinction in their rooms," he pointed out. "They'll have regular inspection. Yes, and they will make their own beds."

No K. P. Duty

In their routine at camp, the WAAC'S, at least the initial group attending the officer's candidate school, will be spared that one great headache of enlisted men—K. P. Duty.

"No doubt that will come later," our officer declared. "Right now, these women will have a plenty big job to do—learn the ropes in only eight weeks. K. P. duty would only hinder their more important training in what you might call this army "teachers college."

It was expected that later corps members will branch out in K. P. and a few other types of work left out of the initial curriculum.

Nazi Hordes Hammer Sevastopol Defenders

Strive To Take Base On Anniversary Of Russian Invasion

Moscow, June 21—(Sunday)—(INS)—Sevastopol's lion-hearted defenders clung grimly to the Crimean naval base today, inflicting fearful casualties on charging Nazi hordes that were apparently striving to gain a victory by midnight tonight when the first anniversary of the German invasion arrives.

Determined to foil Adolf Hitler's reported desire to proclaim a face-saving success before his war on Russia enters its second year, Soviet soldiers, sailors and airmen smashed new, record-breaking German onslaughts on Sevastopol through Saturday, killing more than 3,000 of the enemy.

The Russian high command said early today that thousands more of the enemy had perished and another 52 Nazi tanks were destroyed before the battlements of Sevastopol by Soviet troops and naval flyers in savage combat that raged without letup yesterday.

Batter on Three Sides

But the Germans in their desperate effort to beat the "anniversary deadline" kept pouring fresh hosts of reserves into the slaughter and more than 150,000 enemy troops were estimated battering at the northern, eastern and southern defenses of the ancient Crimean seaport.

A Soviet midnight communique, announcing continued failure of reckless day-and-night Nazi attacks on "Russia's Verdun," disclosed also that the Germans had launched what appeared to be a strong new push on the Kharkov front, some 400 miles north of the Crimean bastion.

The war bulletin said that "in one sector of the Kharkov front" the forces of Marshal Semyon

RUSSIA—Page 15

Gen. MacArthur 'Official Father'

Spokane, June 20—(AP)—Gen. Douglas MacArthur has been named "official father" for the 1942 observance of Father's Day.

Mrs. John Bruce Dodd, founder, said the International Father's Day Association had selected him in recognition of his inspirational leadership in the Philippines and Australia.

Actor Lionel Barrymore was given the designation last year.

Hope Allies Will Join Fight Soon

Moscow, June 20—(AP)—With the first year of the war in Russia drawing to a close the Red Army expressed the fervent hope today that United States and British forces soon would join it on the battlefields of Europe.

BRITAIN PLEDGES SECOND FRONT

Statement Made As Roosevelt And Churchill Confer In Washington

(By The Associated Press)

Britain pledged a second front in Western Europe Saturday and staked off a 36-square mile jumping off place pointed at the Dutch coast.

The pledge came from Sir Stafford Cripps, Parliamentary deputy for Winston Churchill while the Prime Minister and President Roosevelt—in the United States—were devising means to hit the Axis and hit it hard in Europe, Africa and Asia.

There were these other developments:

1. The disclosure that just before Cripps spoke, Churchill was in consultation by transatlantic telephone with at least one of his aides, Major Clement R. Attlee, Dominions Secretary.

2. An announcement by the German radio, which just gained notice Saturday, that German authorities, apparently in a defensive mood, had widened to the East and West the already extensive mine fields in the Skagerrak between Norway and Denmark.

Adding physical torment to the jangle of German nerves, the RAF returned to the attack with a

CRIPPS—Page 15

FOE WITHIN TEN MILES OF EGYPT

British Radio Says Enemy Probably Has Entered Town, After By-Passing Tobruk

New York, June 20—(AP)—The British radio quoted a dispatch tonight from its correspondent on the Libyan front as saying axis forces had "probably" entered the town of Bardia, 10 miles from the Egyptian frontier.

The BBC broadcast, heard by CBS, said:

"A dispatch that came in only a half hour ago from Richard Dimbleby, our observer in the desert, says that the enemy columns which withdrew from the frontier area last night, moved up again today and had by now probably entered the town of Bardia, some 10 miles from the frontier."

BRITISH STAND FIRM

Cairo, Egypt, June 20—(AP)—Britain's bloody but unbowed Eighth Army stood firm tonight 30 miles inside Libya from the Egyptian frontier after turning back two main columns of Axis forces which bypassed encircled Tobruk and drove to within 25 miles of Bardia.

The armored columns of the Axis Africa corps withdrew after a brief fight with the sun-blackened veterans of Lieut. Gen. Neil M. Ritchie and it appeared they were only testing the strength of the new British positions and consolidating their own stand.

Military experts said no Axis tank or man came nearer than 30 miles from the frontier—the approximate position of the new and stronger imperial defense line.

Patrols Still Operate

Although driven out of their main positions in the loose triangle bounded roughly by Tobruk, Ain El Gazala and Bir Hacheim, British armored patrols still were operating extensively in Cirenaica, especially in the inland desert stretches, and were harassing the enemy with repeated raids. Their attacks were exploiting the main problem confronting Marshal Erwin Rommel—his lengthened supply lines.

The Germans surround Tobruk but have not yet moved up to lay siege or assault that stronghold which hurled back every Axis attempt to take it last year in the eight months it was isolated. The strong defense works at the port continued to threaten the Axis rear.

The British also were consolidating their new positions, much nearer their supply bases, after withdrawing and getting into the strongest possible positions for both defensive and offensive action.

Military experts said the situation is similar to that of last year just before Gen. Sir Claude Auchinleck started his offensive which drove the Axis half way to Tripoli before stalling at El Agheila.

(The German high command said

LIBYA—Page 15

2 Dead, 6 Missing As Tornado Hits Indiana Town

Kokomo, Ind., June 20—(AP)—Two persons were dead, six missing, and at least 20 known injured in a tornado which struck the south half of Kokomo about six p. m. today.

More than 200 homes were unroofed by the storm which struck Kokomo after sweeping across the northern part of adjoining Clinton county. It cut a swath two city blocks wide and two miles long through the south part of the city.

FIRE BURNS BARN

Fire destroyed the barn and all the outbuildings on the farm of John Harnish, on Blue Rock Road, near Millersville, Saturday. About 70 chickens and the first cutting of hay were burned.

ANSWER TWO ALARMS

Four city fire companies responded to what city police said was a false fire alarm from the Bloch tobacco warehouse at Franklin St. and the Pennsylvania Railroad at 12:30 a. m. today. Companies 3, 4, 6 and Truck A went out. A fire that started in a pile of rags in a garage in the 100 block of East Marion street was extinguished by city firemen at 11:55 p. m. Saturday.

City Still Stands On Wilderness Site Squatters Chose In 1721

Lancaster, Muddy And Dusty, "Blacked-Out" For Half A Century; Was U. S. Capital For A Day

By GRACE SMITH HOFFMAN

The seeds of democracy, sprung from instincts for freedom in a new, untried world, already had thrust deep roots into rich soil two decades before a royal charter was granted Lancaster.

The struggle for existence in a hostile wilderness called for certain rules of settlement—sources of pure water, centers of slowly broadening travel, black loam to nurture life-sustaining crops.

That those who chose the site of what 220 years later was destined to be the thriving city of Lancaster, made their choice well and carefully is proven by the fact that the town mushroomed from the original squatter's location, and those who came after had no serious disposition to change it.

Rechristened

But if the site wasn't changed the name was, several times. First called Gibson's Pasture in 1721, honoring George Gibson, the inevitable tavernkeeper who was more than just that in early settlement days, the crossroads next was known in 1729 as Hickory Tree. This was because the 40 or 50 log houses were built around a giant tree of that name, an Indian council tree, where white men also held councils and decided weighty questions for the wellbeing of the community. There were in that year about 200 inhabitants, and the tiny village was located near what is now the second block of East King St. The little houses were clustered on the sunny slope, and bubbling springs dotted the area. Not too far away were several streams, one of which, the Conestoga, is synonymous with the forward march of Lancaster's development.

James Hamilton, inheriting from his father some 2,500 acres which included the site of Lancaster, feared the squatters might change the site of their town, so, to encourage them, he made a gift of land to the four county commissioners, Caleb Pierce, John Wright, Thomas Edwards and James Mitchell. This was with the understanding that buildings of administration be erected. Lots were to be purchased, for Hamilton was a good businessman and one of the richest in Pennsylvania.

First purchasers of lots in the heart of the village were Nicholas Bierly, Richard Marsden, Henry Hunt and Samuel Bethel. For some unknown reason few lots were sold during the next five years, but in 1740 they began to go rapidly and the town increased in size.

Keep Pigs In!

Although little data is preserved on the development of the town from 1730 to 1742, it is known that Commissioner John Wright named the infant city Lancaster after his former home in England. In the latter year when, by the wave of a pen, Lancaster became a borough, there were about 400 homes, almost all one-story and made of logs. To protect them from fire, the first burgesses enacted laws against allowing "chimneys to catch fire, spreading their fans of dangerous sparks." There is also a law, still unrepealed, forbidding residents to allow their pigs to run loose on East King street.

In 1742, James Hamilton instigated the incorporation and burgesses were elected. The town grew and thrived although its only sources of income were derived from markets, fairs and fines. By closest frugality money was accumulated by 1757 to erect a market house at the rear of City Hall. From those days henceforth, Lancaster has been famous for her markets, even after the picturesque curb markets were abolished because of growing vehicular travel.

Streets and roads, however, still left much to be desired. Streets were merely lanes, rivers of mud when it rained and inches deep in dust on clear days. In the "suburbs," cowpaths or slightly larger trails served as highways. Gradually these were improved and the outside world could travel to Lancaster once or maybe twice a week by stagecoach.

Town Went Elegant

But as the years rolled on—almost two decades of them before the initial fight for freedom—the town changed in appearance. It started to grow up as many of the original log houses were replaced by more substantial and "elegant" buildings, and others took on an outer garb of clapboard and new trim. A survey might show an amazing number of these log houses, still comfortable domiciles, their age concealed by the "face-lifting" process.

Much of the trading with the Indians died out and even eventually the colorful fairs which, in June and September, transformed main streets into gay festival scenes. One old Lancastrian, comparing the town of his venerable years with that of his childhood, wrote: "The most remarkable change (from the time of incorporation) is the Episcopal church that occupies the place of the time-worn edifice that I remember. It was built under a charter granted by George II and never had been entirely finished. So great was its age and infirmities, the congregation was obliged to have it taken down to prevent its tumbling about their ears."

The successor to this building was partly erected of stone in 1744. By lottery a steeple, galleries, bell and encircling stone wall were added. Trinity Lutheran, says Riddle's history, was built as early as 1736; rebuilt in 1785. Other early churches were those of the First Reformed and Moravian. These churches were well preserved. They were more than religious edifices; they were the symbol for braving new world terrors and the standard by which men counted the cost of a Revolution—the price they paid to worship God as they chose.

Lancaster in those trying days of the Revolution reflected the elation and depression of the young nation as the tide of battle ebbed and flowed. Much as in later wars, victories were celebrated, or fear took hold when rumors of the enemy's approach spread like wildfire. The war was very close and no hour of the day but saw the population varied by groups of prisoners and soldiers who came and went. But also like today there was some incedulity and sometimes a dangerous apathy.

Day In The Sun

The Declaration of Independence was read in the old log Court House, the one built in 1730, and which was destroyed by fire in 1781. The war was won and an example set for generations of all time to follow. But during and because of the struggle, Lancaster had its little hours in the sun when for 24 hours, September 27, 1777, it was the capital of the United States as the government retreated before the advancing Redcoats. On that day Continental Congress met in the old Court House.

Perhaps the taste of such glory went to the heads of the City Fathers, for some years later Chief Burgess Edward Hand offered the borough as the nation's capital. His letter of recommendation was a digest of the city of that day and furnishes concise data... "five public buildings, including an elegant Court House, fifty by forty-eight feet... possession of every advantage for water works... a larger number of wagons and good teams than can be found in the whole of the United States within a compass of ten miles. ....also 678 houses and 4,200 souls..." Then came a list of industries such as hatters, shoemakers, tanners, saddlers, tailors, butchers, weavers, blacksmiths, coopers, dyers, etc. This persuasion was, however, unavailing.

Construction of county buildings and a new market house marked the early 1790's, the corporation of the borough granting free a "spot of ground," but designating that the "public buildings shall be erected on solid ground of two storied height." The market house was built in 1798 and shortly thereafter Old City Hall, but for six years neither the burgesses nor the councils ever met there. It was used only by the county officers.

Pavement Was Ballast

The improvement in streets was conspicuous by its absence, especially when it rained. Water, which flowed on all four sides of the Court House, stagnated in the Square because of improper drainage. But after much to-do the roadway was filled and "piked" which made it compare favorably with the pavements around the Square, the bricks for which were brought over as ballast on the first English ships. These were probably the only sidewalks in town. Actually it was half a century later before Lancaster got proper paving. The citizenry continued to wallow in mud and dust, though they didn't like it.

In 1798 the State Assembly gen-

BORO DAYS — Page A-13

Lancaster's Royal Charter

George the Second by the Grace of God, of Great Britain, France and Ireland, King, Defender of the Faith, &c.

To all to whom these Presents shall come, Greeting. WHEREAS our loving Subject, JAMES HAMILTON of the City of Philadelphia, in the Province of Pennsylvania, Esq., owner of a Tract of Land whereon the Town of Lancaster, in the same Province, is erected, HATH on the behalf of the Inhabitants of the said Town, represented unto our trusty and well-beloved THOMAS PENN, Esq; one of the Proprietors of the said Province, and George Thomas, Esq; with our Royal Approbation Lieut. Gov. thereof, under JOHN PENN, the said THOMAS PENN, and RICHARD PENN, Esquires, true and absolute Proprietors of the said Province and the Counties of New-Castle, Kent and Sussex, upon Delaware, the great Improvements and Buildings made, and continuing to be made in the said Town by the great Increase of the Inhabitants thereof, and hath humbly besought them for our Letters Patent, under the Great Seal of the said Province, to erect the said Town of Lancaster into a Borough, according to certain Limits and Bounds hereinafter described and to incorporate the Freeholders and Inhabitants of the same with perpetual Succession, and to grant them such Immunities and Privileges as might be thought necessary for the well-ordering and governing thereof.

THEREFORE KNOW YE, That we favouring the Application of the said JAMES HAMILTON, on behalf of the said Freeholders and Inhabitants, and willing to promote Trade, Industry, Rule and good Order amongst all our Subjects, of our special Grace, certain Knowledge and mere Motion, have erected, and by these Presents do erect the said Town of Lancaster into a Borough for ever hereafter, to be called by the name LANCASTER, which said Borough shall extend, be limited and bounded in the Manner it is now laid out, pursuant to the Plan thereof hereunto annexed.

AND we further grant and ordain, That the Streets of the said Borough shall forever continue as they are now laid out and regulated.

AND we do nominate and appoint Thomas Cookson and Sebastian Grooffe to be the present burgesses; and the said Thomas Cookson shall be called the CHIEF Burgess within the said Borough, and Michael Byerly, Mathias Young, John Dehoffe, John Folkes, Abraham Johnson and Peter Worrall, assistants for advising, aiding and assisting the said Burgesses in the execution of the power and authorities herein given them: and Alexander Giblony to be High-constable; and George Sanderson to be Town-clerk: To continue Burgesses, Assistants, High-constable and Town-clerk until the fifteenth Day of September which will be in the Year of our Lord One Thousand Seven Hundred and Forty-four, and from thence until others shall be duly elected or appointed in their Places as is herein after directed.

AND we do by these Presents, for us, our Heirs and Successors, further give, grant and declare, That, the said Burgesses, Freeholders and inhabitants within the Borough aforesaid, and their Successors for ever hereafter, shall be one Body corporate and politick in Deed and in Name; and them by the Name of the Burgesses and Inhabitants of the Borough of Lancaster, in the County of Lancaster, one Body politick and corporate in Deed and Name, We do for us, our Heirs and Successors, fully create, constitute and confirm by these Presents; and by the same Name of the Burgesses and Inhabitants of the Borough of Lancaster, that they may have Perpetual Succession; and they they and their Successors, by the Name of the Burgesses and Inhabitants of the borough of Lancaster be, and at all times for ever hereafter shall be, persons able and capable in law, to have, get, receive and possess lands, tenements, rents, liberties, jurisdictions, franchizes and hereditaments, to them and their successors in fee-simple, or for term of life, lives, years of otherwise; and also goods, chattles, and other things of what nature or kind soever; and also give, grant, lett, sell and assign the same lands, tenements, hereditaments, goods and chattles, and to do and execute all other things about the same by the name aforesaid; and also, that they be, and shall be for ever hereafter, persons able and capable in law, to sue and be sued, plead and be impleaded, answer and be answered unto, defend and be defended, in all or any of our courts or other places, and before any Judges, Justices, and other persons whatsoever within the province aforesaid, in all manner of actions, suits, complaints, pleas, causes and matters whatsoever. And that it shall and may be lawful to and for the Burgesses and Inhabitants of Lancaster aforesaid, and their successors for ever hereafter, to have and use one common seal for the sealing of all business whatsoever touching the said corporation, and the same from time to time at their will to change and alter.

And we do for us, our heirs and successors, further by these presents, grant full power and authority for the Burgesses, Constables, assistants and freeholders, together with such inhabitants, housekeepers within the said borough, as shall have resided therein at least for the space of one whole year next preceding any such election as is herein after directed, and hired a house and ground within the said borough of the yearly value of five pounds or upwards, on the fifteenth day of September which will be in the year of our Lord one thousand seven hundred and forty-four, and on that day yearly forever thereafter, unless it happen to fall on Sunday, and then on the next day following, publickly to meet in some convenient place within the said borough, to be appointed by the chief Constable, and then and there to nominate, elect and choose by the ballot, two able men of the inhabitants of the said borough to be Burgesses, one to be high Constable, one to be town clerk, and six to be assistants within the same, for assisting the Burgesses in the managing the affairs of the said borough, and of keeping of peace and good order therein: which election shall be taken from time to time by the high Constable of the year preceding; and the names of the persons so elected shall be certified under his seal to the Governor for the time being within ten days next after such election; and the Burgess who shall have the majority of votes shall be called the chief Burgess of the said borough. But in case it shall so happen that the said freeholders and inhabitants, house-keepers aforesaid, shall neglect or refuse to elect or chuse Burgesses and other officers in manner aforesaid, that then it shall and may be lawful for the Governor for the time being to nominate, appoint and commissionate Burgesses, Constable, town clerk and assistants for that year; to hold and continue in their respective offices until the next time of annual election appointed as aforesaid, and so as often as occasion shall require.

And we further will and ordain, that the said Burgesses for the time being shall be, and are hereby impowered and authorized to be conservators of the peace within the said borough; and shall have power by themselves and upon their own view, or in other lawful manner, to remove all nuisances and incroachments on the said streets and highways within the borough aforesaid as they shall see occasion: with power also to arrest, imprison and punish rioters and other breakers of the peace or good behaviour, award process, bind to the peace or behaviour, commit to prison, and to make Kelendars of the prisoners by them committed; and the same to return, together with such recognizances and examinations as shall be by them taken, to the next court of Quarter-sessions of the County of Lancaster, there to be proceeded on as occasion may or shall require; and to do all and singular other matters and things within the said borough as fully and effectually, to all intents and purposes, as Justices of the peace in their respective counties can or may lawfully do.

But before any of the said Burgesses, Constable, Town clerk or other officers, shall take upon them the execution of their respective offices, they shall take and subscribe the oaths or affirmations of allegiance, and such other oaths and affirmations as are by the laws of our government in such cases provided, together with the oaths or affirmations for the due execution of their respective offices. And every chief Burgess so elected or appointed from year to year as aforesaid, shall within ten days immediately after his election, present himself to be qualified, by taking the oaths or affirmations aforesaid, before the Governor for the time being, or before such other persons as the Governor shall think fit to appoint for that purpose: and on failure of his so presenting himself, unless disabled by sickness or other reasonable cause, such as shall be allowed of by the Governor for the time being, another chief Burgess shall from time to time, and as often as occasion shall require be appointed in the stead of such person so failing to appear and qualify himself as before directed: which Burgess so to be appointed by the Governor for the time being, shall and may enjoy his office until the day of election next ensuing such his appointment. And the chief Burgess having qualified himself in a manner aforesaid, shall and may enter upon his office; and the other Burgesses, Constable, town clerk or other officers shall and may qualify themselves for their respective offices by taking and subscribing the oaths or affirmations aforesaid before the said chief Burgess, or before any of the Justices of the peace of the said County of Lancaster for the time being, who are hereby authorized and impowered to administer the same.

And we do further grant for us, our heirs and successors, to the Burgesses, freeholders and inhabitants, house-keepers aforesaid, and their successors, to have, hold and keep within the said borough two markets in each week, that is to say, one market on Wednesday, and one market on Saturday in every week of the year for ever in the lot of ground already agreed upon for that purpose and granted for that use by Andrew Hamilton, Esq., late of Philadelphia, deceased, as by the deeds thereof to John Wright, and other Trustees for the said County of Lancaster, may appear. And also two fairs therein every year, the first to begin on the first day of June next ensuing, and to continue that day and the next day following; and the other of the said fairs to begin on the twenty-fifth day of October following, and to continue that day and the next day after. And when either of those days shall happen to fall on Sunday, then the said fairs to be kept the next day or two days following together, with the free liberties, customs, profits and emolument, to the said markets and fairs belonging, and in any-wise appertaining, forever.

And we do hereby further grant and ordain, that there shall be a clerk of the market for the said borough, who shall have the assice of bread, wine, beer, wood, and all other provisions brought for the use of the said inhabitants, who shall and may perform all things belonging to the office of a clerk of the market within the said borough; and that John Morris shall be the present clerk of the market, who shall be removable for any Malfeasance in his office by the Burgesses and assistants aforesaid, and another from time to time appointed and removed as they shall find it necessary.

And we do further grant unto the said Burgess, high Constable and assistants, and their successors, as much as in us is, That if any of the inhabitants of the said borough shall be hereafter elected to the office of Burgesses, high Constable or assistants, and having notice of his or their election, shall refuse to undertake and execute that office to which he is chosen, it shall and may be lawful for the Burgesses, high Constable and assistants then acting to impose such moderate fines on the person or persons refusing as to them shall seem meet; so always that such fine imposed on a Burgess elect do not exceed ten pounds, and the Fine on the high Constable or an assistant elect do not exceed five pounds, each to be levied by distress and sale of the goods of the party refusing, by warrant under the hand and seal of one of the said Burgesses, or any other lawful way or means whatsoever, for the use of the said Corporation. And in any such case, it shall and may be lawful for the said inhabitants to proceed to the choice of some other fit person or persons in the stead of such who shall so refuse.

And it shall and may be lawful for the said burgesses, high constable and assistants for the time being to assemble town meetings as often as they shall find occasion: At which meetings they may make such ordinances and rules, not repugnant to, or inconsistent with the laws of the said province, as to the greatest part of the inhabitants shall seem necessary and convenient for the good government of the said Borough. And the same rules and orders to put in execution; and the same to revoke, and alter and make anew as occasion shall require. And also to impose such mulcts and amerciaments upon breakers of the said ordinances as to the makers thereof shall be thought reasonable; to be levied as above is directed in case of fines, for the use of the said borough, without rendering any account thereof to us, our successors, or to the proprietors aforesaid, their heirs or successors. Also at the said meetings to mitigate or release the said fines and mulcts, upon the submission of the parties.

And we do further will and grant, that where any doubts shall happen to arise touching this present charter, that the same shall in all courts of law and equity be construed and taken most favourably and beneficially for the said corporation.

In testimony whereof, we have caused these our letters to be made patent. Witness George Thomas, Esq.; with our royal approbation Lieutenant Governor of the province aforesaid under John Penn, Thomas Penn and Richard Penn, Esquires, true and abso-

CHARTER—Page 5A

MAY 1, 1742—That's the first-page date in the old Corporation Book which City Commissioner Daniel W. Coulter studies above. Among the city's most treasured possessions, it begins with a note of thanks for the new charter, and the boro's first ordinance—curbing violators of the Lord's Day peace.

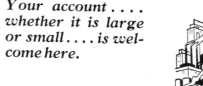

LANCASTER NEW ERA

WEATHER

Showers and scattered thunder showers and milder temperature tonight. (Details on Page 3).

Examiner Founded 1830. New Era Founded 1877.

Published Every Evening Except Sunday by New Era Company. Entered as Second Class Matter at Post Office, Lancaster, Pa.

LANCASTER, PA., MONDAY, JUNE 22, 1942 | CITY EDITION | 14 PAGES—112 COLUMNS | 20c PER WEEK—4c Per Copy

OREGON COAST SHELLED FROM SEA

Tobruk's Fall Shifts War's Strategy

ARMY OF 4,400 CIVILIANS WILL HAVE BIG PART IN 'BLACKOUT'

Mythical 'Disasters' Are to Be Reported By the Defense Workers Some Time During the Test.

AIR RAID WARDENS TO PATROL ALL NIGHT

An army of 4,400 civilian defense workers — air raid wardens, first ai workers, auxiliary policemen and firemen and others trained for special work—will take an active part in the all-night "blackout" here tomorrow night.

Some time during the night "disasters" — fire, sabotage, explosions, bombings — will be reported in various sections and the civilian defense army will swing into action immediately.

Homes and offices will be dimmed out for the entire night, from 8:30 P. M. to 5:30 A. M., and air raid wardens in most sections of the city and rural areas will maintain all-night patrols. But most of the civilian defense organizations will function only during the half-hour period of total darkness. when every light in the city, (with the exception of war production plants) will go out. The time of this complete blackout will not be known until the new air raid sirens spread the alarm.

Control Center Is Hub

All activities of the volunteer defense workers will be directed from the Control Center in the Greist building where all heads of the divisions will be stationed throughout the duration of the complete blackout. As soon as the "red" signal for the blackout, meaning the approach of enemy planes, is received at Control Center, telephone operators will begin calling air raid wardens. fire wardens, and emergency medical chiefs.

Disasters and "bombings" will be reported from the sector air raid headquarters in each ward, to the officials in the Control Center. Auxiliary services such as fire, police, and emergency medical divisions will be "dispatched" to the "scene" by the Control Center staff, but actually they will not leave headquarters. First aid workers have been assigned to each sector and air raid post headquarters.

In reality, the only volunteer civilian defense workers on the street will be the air raid wardens and auxiliary police, in some cases. Emergency traffic control officers will be stationed at suburban and county intersections.

The fire apparatus in the city will not leave the fire houses except in the case of an actual fire, Amos Keen, chief fire warden said today.

However, the fire apparatus in

(See BLACKOUT—Page 12)

First Coeds on F. & M. Campus

F. and M. took on a new appearance today as it turned coed for the summer course and girls invaded many of the campus spots sacred to male students. Above, Betty Long, left, and Marie Aierstock sitting on the library steps with Claire Simeral, left, and Louis Weisman whom they met on the campus. (Story on last page).

GAS STATIONS REOPEN WITH NEW SUPPLIES

Parcelling of 10-Day Quota to All Dealers Will Take Few Days.

LOCAL TRAFFIC RISES OVER THE WEEK-END

Many of the gasoline stations in the city and county, "dry" since last week, reopened this morning as bulk stations began delivering the new 10-days ration of "gas."

New deliveries brought some relief to local autoists who had trouble getting "gas" over the week-end, but the large distributing companies said the quota will not be "parceled out" until about Wednesday night. All stations are now eligible for the quota of gasoline which must meet their needs until July 1.

Despite the unprecedented gasoline shortage which closed many stations local automobile traffic increased over the week-end. Drivers apparently had conserved their supplies during the week for Sunday driving.

State Motor Police observed that "Traffic showed a surprising increase Sunday over the week days in the face of the gasoline shortage and rationing."

Distance Driving Declines

Long distance driving, however, was definitely on the decline. At the Columbia bridge, toll-takers said traffic yesterday was 60 per cent lower than on the corresponding Sunday of 1941.

Dry gasoline pumps stranded thousands of automobile drivers along the Atlantic seaboard yesterday as summer's first week-end brought an increase in travel and exhausting demands on filling stations.

As dealers hung up "No gas" signs, drivers with empty tanks either parked their cars by the side of the road or had them towed to garages.

In the eastern area, Philadelphia was hardest hit with all of its 3,500 stations closed by mid-afternoon

(See GAS—Page 5)

Axis Pushes Drive to Egypt, Pierces Sevastopol Defenses

Middle East Position of Allies Perilled; Axis Column Clashes With British 2 Miles from Border

By the Associated Press

The white flag that fluttered out Sunday morning over Tobruk's shattered barricades as a final, mute concession that a superior Axis force had reconquered Libya marks a major turn in the stratagems of war on two continents, if not in the whole world.

So extended and intertwined are causes and effects of this galling capitulation that military experts were hard-pressed to trace them all but it was obvious that the Axis triumph was forcing a drastic reshaping, if not postponement or abandonment, of some plans of the United Nations.

Watch Sevastopol

The bitter struggle for Sevastopol, in Russia, is being watched keenly by Allied observers for indications where the Axis will strike next.

Sevastopol defenders dropped back from the north and south fortresses guarding the Crimean naval base today before enormous German pressure, exerted ceaselessly despite the heavy casualties, estimated at 100,000, which Axis forces have suffered in less than three weeks.

A fresh Nazi wedge was forced in the fortifications to the north where the enemy massed a huge force of infantry, artillery and tanks, press accounts said.

Rome, first to claim the capture of Tobruk with six British generals reported among the prisoners proclaimed today:

"Occupation of Tobruk has been completed, and Axis troops are marching toward the Egyptian frontier."

Axis Pushes Toward Egypt

With Tobruk and virtually all Eastern Libya regained and with the British Eighth Army beaten, leaving thousands of its number in the Tobruk trap, the Axis African Corps rolled eastward today against Egypt, imperiling the en-

(See TOBRUK—Page 5)

Where 1st Shells Hit Canada

A Canadian government telegraph station at Estevan Point on Vancouver island, shown on the above map, was shelled by a submarine in the first attack of the war on Canadian soil. Several hundred miles to the south shells coming from the sea whistled over Seaside and Astoria, Ore.

SUB EARLIER SHOT AT FORT ON VANCOUVER

Army Says 6 to 9 Shells Landed Near Astoria in 15-Min. Attack.

NO CASUALTIES, LITTLE DAMAGE REPORTED

By the Associated Press

Gunfire today upon the Oregon coast from an unidentified craft lurking offshore on the heels of the submarine shelling of lonely Vancouver island in Canada's British Columbia brought war to the doorstep of an alert and expectant Pacific northwest.

The two attacks, at points separated by several hundred miles, came almost exactly 24 hours apart. Official reports indicated that no casualties and little damage were suffered at either spot.

First target was a Dominion government radio station at Estevan point, on the western coast of Vancouver island. The shelling there began at 10:35 P.M. (Pacific war time) Saturday and continued for a half-hour.

"The shells landed on the beach or on the rocks well beyond the building," said. Lieut.-Gen. Kenneth Stuart, commander-in-chief of Canadian west coast defenses. "A few windows in the radio office were broken by the concussion."

Shells Waken Oregonians

Then, at 11:30 o'clock last night, residents from Seaside on the ocean to Astoria on the Columbia river, at the northwest tip of Oregon, were awakened by the sound of gunfire and the whine of speding missiles.

"Six to nine shells landed in the area north of Seaside," the Army said in a communique from Western Defense headquarters at San Francisco, "apparently from an unidentified craft ofshore. Firing lasted 15 minutes. No damage or casualties reported."

Eyewitness Oregonians agreed with the Army that the firing had been of no effect, but many felt certain they had heard more than nine shots.

One was Robert Lucas, associate editor of the Astoria Budget.

Awakened by the sound, he said, "I hurried upstairs to have a look toward the sea, and heard from 12 to 16 shots. The shells seemed to be landing somewhere with a great thud, but I couldn't tell what the objective was."

Lucas and others also told of seeing flashes from a gun or guns, which the editor described as "bright orange and fan-shaped" and much like lightning playing on the horizon.

No shells landed in Astoria, Seaside or any other community, so far as could be determined from residents in the 30-mile area.

The Army's announcement that they fell "north of Seaside" suggested they might have plowed uselessly into some part of the 16 miles of sandy wastelands between the ocean city and the Columbia river.

This theory was held by at least one resident of the coast. "The Japs picked a swell place for harmless target practice," he remarked.

Seaside, primarily a resort city, is about 25 miles south of the mouth of the Columbia river.

A number of beach resorts and other small settlements lie between Seaside and Astoria, at the

(See SHELLING—Page 5)

SENTENCE SAHM IN U. S. COURT

Judge Bard Gives Him 10 Yrs. to Run Concurrently With Local Term.

William D. Sahm, Jr., 33-year-old former local bookkeeper serving 10 to 22 years in the Eastern State Penitentiary for embezzling $307,000 bank funds, was sentenced today to 10 years on Federal charges arising from the same case, the term to run concurrently.

Judge Guy K. Bard, presiding in the U. S. Court in Philadelphia disposed of the Federal charges against Sahm in this manner, explaining that he thought the penalty imposed in the local courts was sufficient.

When Sahm was called for arraignment, he immediately entered a plea of guilty on each of the 14 Federal counts of embezzlement. An FBI agent took the stand and had testified to finding a shortage of $179,000 when he was interrupted by Judge Bard, who remarked: "I know all about that." The FBI agent added that the entire shortage amounted to $307,000.

In calling Sahm for sentence, his attorney said his client started speculations in 1934, taking $100 to

(See SAHM—Page 5)

2 SPEEDERS ASK SPECIAL CARDS

Admit Going Over 50, But Deny Speeds Charged By Police.

Two out of six motorists appearing in Speeders' Court this morning admitted violating the 50-mile-an-hour law but denied the speeds charged by State Motor Policemen in the complaints.

Both of the drivers asked for restricted licenses. They are: C. J. Stroh, thirty-two, of 38 College ave., Elizabethtown, and Herbert N. Wolfe, thirty-seven, Coatesville R. 2. The hearings were held before Chief Inspector Robert E. Deal.

Stroh, a railroad fireman, said he received a call to report for work and was enroute to the Enola yards when clocked at the alleged speed of 66 miles an hour at Highspire on the night of April 3.

"I appeared at the office of Justice of the Peace Frank A. Stees, Steelton, three times before I paid my fine and costs and State Policeman H. C. Sheads was not present," Stroh said. "Stees told me: 'This fellow (Policeman Sheads) is having a joyride. He's making a plaything out of this thing.' He showed

(See SPEEDERS—Page 12)

CHILDREN IGNITE DOOR OF CHURCH

Children playing in front of St. Peter's Catholic church, Columbia, apparently ignited the basement door and caused a general fire alarm.

It was extinguished by Rev. Thomas Eovacious, the assistant priest, before the engines arrived, according to the priest, Rev. John Mahoney.

2,000 COUSINS LOSE $500,000 ESTATE

WASHINGTON, June 22.—(AP) — The 2,000 remoter cousins of the late Miss Mary Francis White today lost their fight in the United States Court of Appeals for a share of her $500,000 estate. Miss White, who died in April, 1939, at the age of 75, bequeathed $1,000 each to her cousins "irrespective of the remoteness of their relationship," with the residue after other bequests to go to five first cousins.

Claimants throughout the country and in Ireland were opposed by the first five cousins, whose lawyers contended that the whole human race could claim mutual descent from Adam and Eve and therefore kinship with Miss White. Their contention that the clause as to relationship was too vague was upheld.

ALL RETAILERS MUST FILE PRICES

All Lancaster retailers must file price lists of cost-of-living commodities with the State office of Price Administration in Philadelphia, Dr. James F. Bogardus, State Price executive of OPA, announced today. The deadline for filing is July 1 and national OPA officials warned that the deadline will not be extended.

National plans for filing the reports called for local War Price and Rationing Boards to handle the registration. The State office changed that order because local boards were not ready to handle it and because State officials want to study the reports.

Japs Only 585 Miles From Dutch Harbor

U. S. Army Fliers Hit Cruiser and Sink Transport at Kiska, Report Temporary Structures Erected by Invaders

WASHINGTON, June 22—(AP)—Under cover of fog and thick weather, Japanese landing forces have inched along the Aleutian island chain toward Alaska and now are establishing themselves at Kiska, which is only 585 miles from the United States Navy base at Dutch Harbor.

This was disclosed in a communique yesterday that told of the bombing of "a small force" of enemy ships in Kiska harbor. Army fliers reported hitting one cruiser and sinking a transport.

While the number of ships actually in Kiska harbor may have been small, observers pointed out that presence of a cruiser might indicate that a force of destroyers and auxiliaries was somewhere in the vicinity.

The communique said operations in the Aleutians "continued to be restricted by considerations of weather and great distances."

"Within the last few days, however," it added, "the weather was sufficiently clear at times to permit some restricted air operations aganist Kiska where tents and minor temporary structures were observed to have been set up on land."

The Navy reported on June 12 that a small enemy force had landed on Attu, a barren, rocky islet marking the westernmost tip of the Aleutian chain. At that time the presence of enemy ships at Kiska was noted, but they were reported shortly afterward to have been driven away.

Kiska, formerly used as a Navy coaling station, is about 275 miles east of Attu. About 20 miles long, it is sparsely inhabited by indians and a few white traders.

F. D. STRESSES SACRIFICES

Message to Governors Says Present War Is Struggle For Survival.

ASHEVILLE, N. C., June 22—(AP)—President Roosevelt said today that within the days and months to come the peoples of this world would determine "by their work, by their sacrifices, and through the instrumentalities of their armed forces whether generations to come shall live and work as free men or slave states."

He made the statement in a message to the National Conference of Governors, in session here.

The text of the President's message:

"My Dear Governors:

"The Governors' Conference meets this year at a most critical period in the history of our United States. Last year your conference dealt almost exclusively with problems of defense. A defense program which we all hoped would keep this country of ours out of the maelstrom of world-wide war, but at the same time prepare us for anything that might happen in a world torn loose from its moorings.

"Despite our efforts, however, we are in—all in—a war which

(See F. D. R.—Page 5)

The War Today by DeWitt MacKenzie

Fate of Egypt and Near East May Be Decided by Gigantic Air Battles Between American Warplanes and Hitler's Luftwaffe

MARSHAL ROMMEL'S capture of Tobruk, and the precarious position of Russia's great naval base of Sevastopol under furious German assault — operations vitally linked with Hitler's attempt to break in the Caucasus and Middle East—bring us appreciably nearer the moment when the Nazi chief will unleash his full pack and race for a kill.

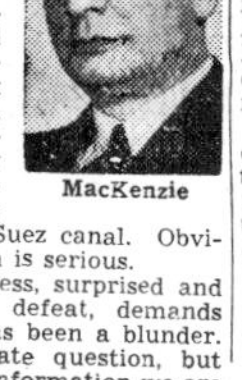

MacKenzie

Our immediate concern is with Tobruk, for Sevastopol still stands. The British now are back on Egyptian soil, preparing to defend their mighty base at Alexandria and block the road to the Suez canal. Obviously the position is serious.

The London press, surprised and angered at this defeat, demands whether there has been a blunder. That's a legitimate question, but pending further information we are entitled to say no more than that Rommel again has demonstrated that he is a master strategist and is perhaps even greater as a tactician on the actual battle field.

* * *

Still, while the British certainly must inquire into the circumstances of the defeat, the problem now is to defend Egypt and the Canal, for they must be held at all costs. We don't know how much the British have salvaged from their shattered eighth army which was operating in Libya, though a considerable force withdrew across the border. Apart from this, there are the Egyptian army of 40,000 well trained men and 100,000 Allied guardsmen.

So far as concerns land forces, it's doubtful whether Rommel could at this moment muster more men than the defense appears to have, although he is superior in tanks. However, it seems to me that the battle for Egypt is likely to turn on air power, in which case the British presumably will depend heavily on the United States for reinforce-

(See WAR TODAY—Page 12)

The Scribbler

MRS. William Mumma, Landisville, enroute home wearing a new hat was caught in a sudden downpour of rain. She removed the hat, wrapped it in paper and boarded a bus. Enroute home a blast of wind lifted the package from the seat and the new hat went out the window. An obliging bus driver turned around and helped recover the hat—undamaged.

IKE MOWERY, auto mechanic, has a solution for the tire shortage but— he still must perfect his dream of making one size tire fit all wheels.

MRS. Howard B. Warren, so we hear, went to the grocery store to buy what it takes to make potato salad. She returned home with everything except—the potatoes.

75 Mosquito Bites Per Person Common in Marietta Area

Situation Getting Worse, Burgess Rettew Complains; No Breeding on Army Property, Col. Douglas Declares

Some residents of Marietta and Maytown have as many as 75 mosquito bites and the insect situation is getting worse instead of better, Burgess George Rettew, Jr., of Marietta, said today.

"I have a little granddaughter in Maytown who is covered with bites from the knees to the ankles," he said. "Children are having a terrible time."

Not Breeding on Army Land

Col. L. B. Douglas, commanding officer of the Army depot at Marietta, said a careful examination of the 600 acres maintained by the War department showed that the mosquito breeding was not taking place on Army property.

"We have some barrels of water used in construction work," he said, "but we put some calcium chloride in this water to prevent any breeding."

Health department investigators went over the situation with Dr. Grover C. Kirk, depot medical director, and found swamps in the lowlands as Col. Douglas had indicated, he said. They said they would follow up the matter.

State Pushing Investigation

At Harrisburg, Dr. A. Hamilton Stewart, State Secretary of Health, said the investigation was going forward and results would be publicized as son as possible.

Burgess Rettew said a chemist told him a little puddle of water or merely a tin can filled with water might be a breeding place for hundreds of the insects. Although the mosquitoes might have come in lumber from the South, it is equally likely that they bred in stagnant water in the section, the burgess was told.

RAID TEST QUICKLY CLEARS BOSTON AREA

BOSTON, June 22 —(AP)— The crowded streets of Greater Boston were cleared as if by magic today when air raid sirens sounded at 11:36 A. M. (EWT) in a surprise daylight test described as the first and most comprehensive yet held in such a metropolitan area.

An etimated 3,000,000 people were held in places of safety or sent scurrying to shelter. Within three minutes after the first siren wailed downtown Boston took on the appearance of a deserted city.

The test was taken seriously. There was little levity among those sent hurrying indoors.

Bulletins

"I DESIRE GERMANY'S VICTORY," SAYS LAVAL

VICHY (From French Broadcasts, June 22.—(AP) — Pierre Laval told his compatriots flatly tonight: "I desire Germany's victory."

"We must either take part in the new Europe or be resigned to being cheated," the Chief of Government said in a broadcast.

"If I tell you this policy is the one to save France and guarantee a good future you must believe me," he said.

Germany, he declared, was making great sacrifices to create the "new Europe," and without fear "the Bolshevist menace would spread over Europe."

City Edition

LANCASTER NEW ERA

WEATHER
Rain, moderate to fresh winds and moderate temperature tonight.

VOL. 66—NO. 214 | Published Every Evening Except Sunday by New Era Company. Entered as Second Class Matter at Post Office, Lancaster, Pa. | LANCASTER, PA., SATURDAY, AUGUST 8, 1942 | 12 PAGES—96 COLUMNS | 20c PER WEEK—4c Per Copy

6 SABOTEURS ELECTROCUTED

Reds Set to Blast Oil Wells

NOW 30 MILES FROM MAIKOP, INVADERS SAY

"Situation Very Tense," Russians Admit; Nazis Nearer Stalingrad.

GERMANS ON ALERT FOR SECOND FRONT

By the Associated Press

Adolf Hitler's drive for the black gold of the Caucasus neared its first major goal today as the Germans smashed at the approaches of the Maikop oil fields, 170 miles south of Rostov, while in the north the invaders edged closer to the great steel city of Stalingrad.

"The situation is very tense," Soviet dispatches said referring to the Caucasus.

For the first time, the Russians acknowledged that the Germans had lunged far down the west side of the Caucasus land bridge to the Middle East after a major break through Red army defenses.

Dispatches to Red Star, the Russian army newspaper, said Marshal Semeon Timoshenko's armies had made a heroic but unsuccessful attempt to stem the Nazi onslaught in the loop of the Kuban river above Maikop, in the Armavir sector, 160 miles south of Rostov, and east of Krasnador.

Nazis 30 Miles From Maikop

German field headquarters asserted that Nazi troops had captured Kurgannaya, only 30 miles from Maikop, and the important rail junction of Armavir, 60 miles northwest of Maikop.

The Nazi high command said German columns also had broken through Russian tank and trench positions 20 miles north of Krasnador, 50 miles northeast of Maikop, and declared:

"Relentless pursuit of the enemy continues."

German planes striking ahead of the land forces were reported to have attacked Soviet columns on the march, transport and embarkations on the Black Sea coast. The German communique did not explain the Soviet "embarkations," but the implication seemed to be that the Russians were attempting to withdraw from a trap.

Nazi headquarters said German troops launched a fresh assault above Kalach, 50 miles northwest of Stalingrad, in the battle of the Don river bend.

But the gravest danger centered on the Maikop oil field, which produces seven per cent of Russia's oil.

Ready to Blow Up Field

With the invaders so near, Soviet demolition engineers presumably were ready to blow up the big field.

Masses of German tanks were reported thundering into action across the sun-parched steppes, while clouds of dive-bombers hammered the Soviet defenders.

British military sources said the Germans were throwing two panzer

(See—RUSSIA—Page 2)

Knudsen at Local War Plants

Lieut.-General William S. Knudsen, world-famous auto production expert and now Director of Production for the War Department, arriving at the Hamilton Watch company for an inspection tour of local conditions. G. P. Luckey, Hamilton vice-president in charge of manufacturing, is greeting the general.

NAZI SUBS CLAIM 17 MORE SHIPS

American Destroyer and an Escort Vessel Sunk, Berlin Asserts.

(Enemy announcements are printed for whatever news they may contain. Readers are cautioned to remember that they are enemy propaganda — that they may be misleading, or false).

BERLIN—(From German broadcasts)—Aug. 8—(AP)—The German High Command reported today in special and regular communiques that Nazi submarines had sunk 15 Allied merchantmen, an American destroyer and an escort vessel in attacks on North Atlantic convoys and in the Mid-Atlantic off the coasts of America and West Africa.

(There was no confirmation of this report from any source.)

Tonnage Put At 103,181

Tonnage on the merchantmen was listed at 103,181, including a 10,000-ton steamer bound for Alexandria with tanks and planes.

The North Atlantic attacks were described as especially difficult, with seven of the merchantmen totaling 49,000 tons and the escort vessel, not further identified, being sunk from "strongly escorted" convoys.

The destroyer and the eight other merchantman totaling 54,181

(See—U-BOATS—Page 2)

LONG WAY TO GO, SAYS GENERAL

Declares U. S. Only Half Way Into Production; Makes Suggestions

Lieut.-General William S. Knudsen arrived in Lancaster today for a quick inspection trip of three war industries, and smiled optimistically when asked whether production was progressing satisfactorily.

He commented favorably on the "outstanding work" being done in the Lancaster plants after visiting the Hamilton Watch company and the Closure and Floor Division of the Armstrong Cork company. He was scheduled to stop at the Merchant and Evans plant later this afternoon.

Only Half Way Into Production

As far as the national picture was concerned, he commented on the OWI announcement regarding production by saying "We are only half way into production, we have

(See—KNUDSEN—Page 9)

ARMS OUTPUT BELOW NEEDS OF U.S. FORCES

'We Could Lose This War' Warns OWI, If Volume Is Not Stepped Up.

SEES TOO MUCH DELAY IN SHIPMENTS ABROAD

The text of OWI statement is on page 4.

WASHINGTON, Aug. 8—(AP)—A gloomy picture of America's war effort to date was laid before the nation today in a warning by the Office of War Information that materials are failing to reach the fighting fronts in the time and the volume needed to win.

Reviewing the military and production situation, OWI asserted last night that output of fighting planes, tanks, most types of artillery and naval vessels fell behind schedule in June and expressed doubt that "all of us realize how hard we are going to have to work to win."

"To win a total war we must fight it totally," OWI said, "and we are not fighting it that hard."

A similar tone was expressed in Australia where war correspondent Norman Stockton of the Melbourne Herald asserted "our Allies have got to realize the grim fact that we are still fighting a losing war and that there is no possibility of an offensive from this country until real material aid is forthcoming."

Stockton described General Douglas MacArthur as an "offensive-minded" leader who apparently could not take the offensive because of a lack of material aid.

"Australia has been told too many rosy stories about United States military aid," he said. "The American press has fed the American public similar lines."

Predicts Attacks On U. S. Soon

Simultaneously, Premier Mitchell Hepburn of Ontario predicted in a speech at Fergue, Ont., that "we are going to have an attack on the Atlantic Coast very soon, and a

(See—O. W. I.—Page 4)

COURSES PROVIDED IN CAMOUFLAGE

HARRISBURG, Aug. 8—(AP)—A special course in industrial camouflage will be offered Pennsylvania architects, landscape architects, engineers and certain other professional men at Baltimore beginning August 31.

The State Council of Defense said today the four weeks' course will be sponsored by the Third Civilian Defense region each Monday, Tuesday, Thursday and Friday evenings.

The State Council, which said it would receive applications, disclosed a tuition fee will be charged to pay for text books and reference material.

Pay Penalty of Spies

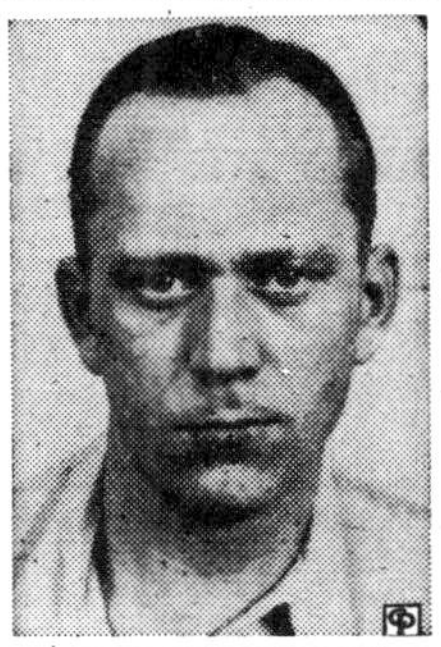

HENRY HARM HEINCK

WERNER THIEL

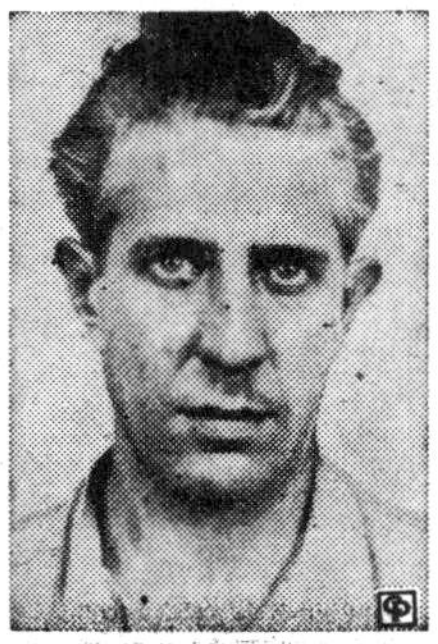

RICHARD QUIRIN

HERBERT HANS HAUPT

EDWARD J. KERLING

HERMAN OTTO NEUBAUER

2 Spared For Giving Evidence

White House Announces Electrocutions Began at Noon; Burger Gets Life Term, Dasch 30 Years at Hard Labor

WASHINGTON, Aug. 8.—(AP)—The White House announced today that six of eight Nazi saboteurs had been executed today, the first going to death by the electric chair at noon.

The two saboteurs spared were Ernest P. Burger, who was given a life prison sentence at hard labor, and George John Dasch, sentenced to 30 years at hard labor.

These, a White House statement said, had prison terms granted them rather than death sentences "because of their assistance to the government of the United States in the apprehension and conviction of the others."

The six who paid the death penalty for coming to the United States in Nazi U-Boats to burn and blast vital war installations were electrocuted in the District of Columbia Jail.

The executions were carried out a month to the day after a Military Commission began trying them on espionage and sabotage charges. The eight men came equipped with explosives and materials for incendiarism, four landing in Florida and four on Long Island.

The text of the White House announcement:

"The President completed his review of the findings and sentences of the Military Commission appointed by him on July 2, 1942 which tried the eight Nazi saboteurs.

"The President approved the judgment of the Military Commission that all of the prisoners were guilty and that they be given the death sentence by electrocution.

"However, there was a unanimous recommendation by the Commission, concurred in by the Attorney General and the Judge Advocate General of the Army, that the sentence of two of the prisoners be commuted to life imprisonment because of their assistance to the government of the United States in the apprehension and conviction of the others.

"The commutation directed by the President in the case of Burger was to confinement at hard labor for life. In the case of Dasch, the sentence was commuted by the President to confinement at hard labor for thirty years.

"The electrocutions began at noon today.

"Six of the prisoners were electrocuted; the other two confined to prison.

"The record in all eight cases will be sealed until the end of the war."

The six who were electrocuted were Edward John Kerling, Herbert Hans Haupt, Richard Quirin, Werner Thiel, Herman Otto Neubauer and Henry Harm Heinck.

The announcement of the executions was handed reporters by Stephen Early, Presidential secretary.

Several miles away, reporters outside the district jail watched ambulances drive into the prison yard at 1:24 P. M. EWT. No official word was given there that the six Nazis had been electrocuted, however.

The District of Columbia coroner, Dr. Magruder MacDonald, had come to the prison shortly before noon and army chaplains and three medical officers also were on hand. From 11 a. m. on, virtually all lights in the prison had been extinguished and helmeted soldiers guarded all the entrances.

(Unofficial reports from Washington yesterday said six of the eight Nazis had been ordered executed. One report said they were to have been executed before dawn today).

Since 8 a. m. (EWT), a curtain of strict military silence had hung over the prison. Correspondents on the inside were directed not to attempt any outside telephone calls.

Inside the jail when this ban was applied was Brig. Gen. Albert L. Cox, Provost Marshal of the Military District of Washington in whose custody the prisoners had been placed. With him were about a dozen high Army officers.

Outside the building, reporters and photographers gathered, waiting some official word from beyond the line of bayonets.

Major Thomas Rives, Assistant Provost Marshal, was seen by reporters to go to the telephone switchboard and check his watch against official time.

Chair Is Ready

Yesterday afternoon the execution chambers in the jail were prepared, although a high prison official, who declined use of his name, said this was done without suggestion from the military authorities who have custody of the prisoners.

As word of the enforced silence spread, the crowd increased outside the barred door of the District Jail, and additional Army officers arrived. They too declined to discuss the case in any way.

At 10:16 a man known to be a priest or minister arrived at the jail and hurried inside, refusing to identify himself.

U. S. PROBES USE OF BANNED NEWS

Biddle Claims 3 Dailies Violated Code on Battle of Midway.

WASHINGTON, Aug. 8—(AP)—Publication by three metropolitan newspapers of what Attorney General Francis Biddle termed "confidential information" concerning the Battle of Midway, became today a subject for Grand Jury investigation.

The investigation, recommended by the Navy Department and requested by Biddle after a preliminary inquiry, will concern possible violation of any criminal statutes, particularly the act of March 28, 1940, prohibiting unlawful communication of documents or information relating to national defense, the Attorney General announced last night.

The official announcement of the inquiry did not name the news-

(See—NEWSPAPERS—Page 2)

PLENTY OF COLOR FOR YULETIDE TOYS

WASHINGTON, Aug. 8.—(AP)—Little Johnny's Christmas toys will be as brightly colored as ever next Christmas, the war notwithstanding.

The War Production Board made this possible today by authorizing toy manufacturers to use pigments, oils and other materials required for paint and varnishes. Use of these materials had been prohibited but the Board explained that supplies of pigments now are ample, and that the restriction is no longer necessary.

Instead of metal, toys this year are being made from wood, cardboard and other less critical materials.

ASK DONATIONS OF GRAIN, HAY

Sisters of Gethsemane Need Aid to Replace $50,000 Fire Loss.

Old corn, wheat and hay are needed by the Sisters and Angels of Gethsemane, at Mountville, to keep their farm in operation until they have recovered from their recent $50,000 fire loss.

Anyone who can spare implements or feed or bedding for the livestock and poultry was asked to contact the institution. All of the equipment of the farm except a tractor and a side-delivery rake were lost in the blaze, and "all the wheat and hay to the last handful" Sister Philip said.

Tools ranged from rakes to cultivators, and included a threshing and binding machine. The loss, it was said, was covered by insurance to only about one-fourth of its value.

"Good farmers of the vicinity have showed their generosity in times past" Father A. J. Hoenninger, chaplain at the institution said. "This will be an opportunity to put the good-neighbor policy in action. Even a bushel of wheat or a bale of hay will be appreciated."

Trucks owned by the institution were burned, but volunteers are available to bring any goods offered to the farm.

FEWER POCKETS FOR WORK CLOTHES

WASHINGTON, Aug. 8—(AP)—From now on American workmen will wear clothes with fewer pockets and buttons and no unnecessary material.

The War Production Board issued an order yesterday setting the styles for workers to save needed materials. At the same time, WOB set a minimum yardage "to prevent skimping which would interfere with a worker's freedom of action."

The Scribbler

NOTES at random...Dr. Karl Compton, one of President Roosevelt's three appointees to the rubber investigation, was in Lancaster to accept a degree at F. and M. several years ago...The post-office can't understand why more people don't use the V-letters for overseas mail (the paper is free)...By Monday the job of Prothonotary in Lancaster county will have been vacant five months, with no appointment by Governor James...One of the gadgets the Wilmington pilot school will bring here is supposed to be a modern marvel. Pilot sits in it and operates it just as he would a real plane for a half an hour. Then he takes the hood off and can read a tracing of just what would have happened had it been a real plane—safe landing, off course, smash, or what. (Much safer than the real thing)...Hats off to 94-year-old Harvey Brush, Washingtonboro, the county's oldest school director. When his school board got in one of the most confusing mix-ups in local history, and had only two members left, the nonogenarian decided to take the situation in hand. He came to Dr. Mylin for advice, went back to the town and organized the board and got it functioning again...Happy reunions at the PRR station the other night. Some of Lancaster's boys in the navy got back in town for a few days.

SELECTEE POSTS BAIL FOR U. S. TRIAL

Weaver Weber Shirk, Ephrata, R. 3, charged with violating the Selective Service Act, was held for Federal Court following a preliminary hearing before U. S. Commissioner A. E. McCollough, Jr., this morning. His father, Joseph M. Shirk, posted $1,000 bail for his appearance in the U. S. District Court, Philadelphia.

Shirk, a conscientious objector, was charged with failing to report to the Sideling Hill camp for work of national importance on July 9. He was arrested Tuesday by U. S. Deputy Marshal Keeney.

Floyd Fraunfelter, clerk of County Draft Board No. 4, was the lone witness to testify at the hearing. He said Shirk had been sent his papers and failed to report and that the usual procedure had been duly carried out.

Late News Bulletin

U. S. HEAVILY ATTACKS JAPS IN ALEUTIANS

Washington, Aug. 8.—(AP)—Heavy attacks by United States naval forces on Japanese installations in the Solomon Islands in the Southwest Pacific and in the Aleutian Islands off Alaska were announced today by the Navy.

GERMAN PLANES BOMB LONDON AREA

London, Aug. 8.—(AP)—Enemy aircraft bombed the nearby home counties and drew gunfire from the London suburbs in daylight today while the city itself was under a half-hour air-raid alert.

G-MEN ARREST ALIEN WITH N. Y. HARBOR MAPS

New York, Aug. 8.—(AP)—The arrest of 33 enemy aliens, one a photo-engraver who possessed navigation maps of New York harbor and Long Island Sound waters, was announced today by the Federal Bureau of Investigation. Other contraband seized included two telescopes owned by a 23-year-old German who the FBI said took frequent bicycle trips up the Hudson river. P. E. Foxworth, assistant FBI director, said another German was a radio instructor for the National Youth Administration, a job he held at the time of his arrest.

DAVIS TURNS DOWN "WRITE-IN" OFFER

PITTSBURGH, Aug. 8—(AP)—Senator James J. Davis repudiated yesterday a Pittsburgh-inspired "write-in" campaign designed to boost him for Governor despite his defeat for the Republican nomination last May.

He said he has notified Joseph E. Harris, who organized the drive, that he has "no authority" from him to proceed with it. Harris is head of the "Independent Electors Committee of Pennsylvania," which has temporary headquarters here.

The committee has distributed circulars urging voters to write-in Davis' name for Governor in the November election.

WEATHER
Eastern Pennsylvania: Scattered Thundershowers In West Portion.

Intelligencer Journal

The Leading Newspaper in the Garden Spot of America, Home Owned for Home Folks Since 1794

VOLUME LXXVIII.—NO. 286. The Intelligencer Founded 1799—The Journal Founded 1794 Entered at Post Office at Lancaster, Pa. as second class mail matter LANCASTER, PA., TUESDAY MORNING, AUGUST 11, 1942. CITY 16 PAGES, 128 COLUMNS. 20c PER WEEK—4c Per Copy

U. S. MARINES LAND ON SOLOMONS, BATTLE FIERCE COUNTER-ATTACKS

ESTIMATES OF CORN, WHEAT CROPS BOOSTED

2,753,696,000 Bushels Of Corn, 955,172,000 Bushels Of Wheat Forecast

TOBACCO YIELD UP

Washington —(AP)— The Agriculture Department forecast Monday a 1942 corn crop of 2,753,696,000 bushels and a wheat crop of 955,172,000 bushels, based on Aug. 1 crop conditions.

Indications a month ago were for a corn crop of 2,627,823,000 bushels and a wheat crop of 904,288,000 bushels. Production of corn was 2,672,541,000 bushels last year and the 1930-39 ten year average was 2,307,452,000 bushels. The wheat crop was 945,937,000 bushels last year and the 10-year average 747,507,000.

The wheat crop includes 697,708,000 bushels of winter wheat, the preliminary estimate of production, compared with 675,482,000 bushels indicated a month ago, 671,293,000 bushels produced last year, and a ten-year average production of 569,417,000 bushels for 1930-39.

Spring wheat included is estimated at 257,464,000 bushels, compared with 228,806,000 bushels indicated a month ago, 274,644,000 bushels produced last year, and 18,090,000 bushels, the 10-year average.

Durum wheat included is estimated at 38,426,000 bushels, compared with 32,521,000 bushels a month ago, 41,800,000 produced last year, and 27,598,000 bushels, the 10-year average production.

OATS YIELD UP

Production of oats this year is indicated as 1,331,511,000 bushels, compared with 1,303,114,000 bushels a month ago, 1,176,107,000 last year, and 1,007,141,000 bushels the 10-year average.

Indicated production of potatoes is 378,175,000 bushels, compared with 369,825,000 bushels a month ago, 357,783,000 bushels last year

More of ESTIMATES OF on Page 6

"We Lead All the Rest"
FARM CORNER
By
The Farm Editor

POULTRY MANAGEMENT WILL BE DISCUSSED

A lecture on "Poultry Management," illustrated with lantern slides, by C. O. Dossin, Penn State poultry specialist, will feature a combination meeting of the Paradise and the Strasburg 4-H Community clubs to be held at the home of Lester Denlinger, near Paradise, Tuesday (today) at 8:30 p. m. Prior to the meeting, a ball game between teams of the two clubs will be staged at the Paradise High school grounds, starting at 6:30 p. m.

RAISE PENNA. APPLE GRADES

Harrisburg—Pennsylvania apple growers were authorized Monday to box their produce under three new grade labels to allow them to compete on a widened market, following a hearing by John H. Light, secretary of agriculture, at the request of growers who claimed they were handicapped by being forced to stay within previously-set grades.

Light explained that Army and Navy purchasers and chain store buyers have shown a preference for "fancy" fruits as graded under regulations set up several years ago by the State of Washington.

The new grades, similar to those used by Northwestern U. S. shippers, are "Extra Fancy," "Fancy," and "C." Previously the top grade allowed was U. S. No. 1.

"Pennsylvania growers contend they have improved their product to where it excels the Washington

More of FARM CORNER on Page 6

Intelligencer Journal Weather Calendar

COMPARATIVE TEMPERATURES

Station	High	Low
Intell Journal	85	64
Water Works	86	62
Ephrata	89	62
Last Year (Ephrata)	90	68
Official High for Year, July 19		98
Official Low for Year, January 11		—10
Character of Day		Clear

HOURLY TEMPERATURES (Monday)

3 a. m.	64	4 p. m.	84
4 a. m.	65	5 p. m.	86
5 a. m.	65	6 p. m.	74
6 a. m.	65	7 p. m.	75
7 a. m.	66	8 p. m.	74
8 a. m.	66	9 p. m.	72
9 a. m.	66	10 p. m.	70
10 a. m.	67	11 p. m.	70
11 a. m.	69	Midnight	69
Noon	73	(Tuesday)	
1 p. m.	78	1 a. m.	68
2 p. m.	81	2 a. m.	68
3 p. m.	82	3 a. m.	68

SUN
Rises—6:10 a. m. Sets—8:07 p. m.

More of WEATHER on Page 6

Germans Crack Russian Oil Field Defenses

Red army defenses before the oil fields of Maikop appeared to be cracking before the onslaught of the Nazi army, and dispatches told of explosions indicating the "scorched earth" policy was being applied. Black arrows show course of German drives, and white arrow direction in which Russians were counter-attacking.

BOARD REFUSES APPLICATION FOR SCHOOL BUILDING

Find Other Facilities Available; Approve Requests For Erection Of Farm Buildings

Applications for four rural building permits were approved, but the request for permission to erect a one-room brick schoolhouse at New Danville from the Mennonite Church was rejected by the Lancaster County Agricultural War Board.

The board announced Monday afternoon it has acted favorably on the following applications for building projects:

Phares K. Graybill, Lititz R2, to erect a reinforced concrete silo, costing $1,060.

Alvin W. Adam, Lititz R3, to erect a one-story, frame brooder house, costing $875. (Ordinarily, War Board approval is not needed for farm premises construction costing less than $1,000, but in this case there was earlier building on this place before April 9, when the new ruling became effective.)

Minnie and Ella Kendig, Millersville, to recondition a frame dwelling house, the work to cost $1,800.

Ira Hartz, Elverson R2, to erect a concrete slab silo, costing $1,600.

The board rejected the following application:

Lancaster Mennonite Schools, through Elmer B. Thomas, trustee, New Danville, permission to erect a one-story, one-room brick schoolhouse with basement at a cost of $4,200. The board noted on the application "other facilities available and we have the public schools."

All five applications were forwarded late Monday afternoon to Harrisburg for review by the Pennsylvania State Agricultural War Board.

GROUP OF LOCAL MEN ENLIST IN U. S. NAVY

A group of Lancaster County men were forwarded Monday for enlistment in the Navy, Chief Charles E. Heller, in charge of recruiting here, announced.

Richard C. Gaus, Columbia; Wilbur R. Hughes, Elizabethtown; and Harold E. Todd, Quarryville R1, enlisted in the regular Navy and were immediately assigned to training stations.

These reservists were called to active duty: Abraham C. Brubaker, Manheim; Albert Drachbar, 321 Laurel St.; and Raymond K. Herr, Lititz.

Five men were enlisted in the construction battalion of the Navy Reserves and returned to their homes to await a call to active duty. They are: William Bluh, Birdsboro; George T. Butzer, Conestoga R2; Paul E. Roschel, 631 George St.; Raymond S. Shenberger, 435 N. Queen St.; and John I. Strunk, Columbia.

FIRE DAMAGES MOTOR

Smoke from an overheated electric motor was responsible for an alarm of fire from the Freedman's Confectionery store, Lime and Ross Sts., at 7:26 a. m. Monday, according to Chief Harry Miller, who said there was no damage.

U. S. Air Force Will Join RAF Raids In "Immediate Future"

Major General Spaatz Pledges Yanks Will Help Blast Nazi Industries; New Contingents Of U. S. Troops Reach British Isles

London — (AP) — American fighter and bomber forces "within the immediate future" will join the RAF in blasting Hitler's great industrial cities and driving his planes from the English Channel.

This pledge came Monday from the commander of the U. S. Air Forces in the European theater, Major Gen. Carl "Toughy" Spaatz.

He declared further that U. S. Air Forces eventually would rise to 400,000 fliers and ground crew men and that there was complete cooperation and understanding with the RAF, which now has nearly three full years of active experience with Hitler's planes.

MORE TROOPS ARRIVE

Giving point to his assertions, made shortly after a flying inspection of U. S. airdromes in these islands, was the announced arrival of additional contingents of American troops. Air force men as well as units of all other combat forces were in the fresh convoy which arrived on an unspecified date.

Thousands upon thousands of American airmen and soldiers have been working day and night adapting British fields to their use, enlarging others and carving out additional bases. Every effort has been made to complete a vast amount of ground work necessary within a record time despite the

More of U. S. AIR FORCE on Page 6

SET ASIDE IRON, STEEL TO CONVERT OIL BURNING UNITS

WPB Says No Papers Required To Change Furnaces For Coal Burning

Washington—(AP)—The War Production Board set aside Monday iron and steel necessary for the conversion of oil-burning furnaces to coal.

"This action helps clear the way for conversion," the WPB commented. "All a home owner or a plant operator needs to do is place his order for the necessary equipment with his local plumbing or heating contractor." No papers are required.

The WPB set aside 11,009 tons of iron and steel for grate manufacturers during the last half of 1942.

Beause of the transportation situation, government officials for some time have been urging conversion of oil burners to coal in the east.

MEETING OF LANCASTER TWP. GROUP TONIGHT

Taxpayers of Lancaster Township will meet at 8 p. m. Tuesday in the James Buchanan School building for the seond general session relative to the protests they entered last week against the sewage charges imposed by the township supervisors.

WAR REDUCES NUMBER, SIZE OF NEWS PICTURES

Washington—War Production Board officials said Monday that newspapers, like other users, will have to cut in half the use of zinc to conform with recently issued orders on civilian uses of this critical metal.

This provision, it was said, would in effect reduce the number and size of zinc half-tones and other photographic reproductions.

Local VFW Post To Aid Forming Of Army Aviation Cadet Corps

Recruiting Office To Open At Penn Square Today; Committee In Charge Of Program Announced

Another Army Aviation Cadet Corps will be organized here through the efforts of the local Veterans of Foreign Wars Post, David Smith, commander, announced Monday.

The local post is participating in a national VFW Aviation Cadet recruiting program, authorized by Lieut. General Henry Arnold, Chief of the Army Air Force. Young men between the ages of eighteen and twenty-six may enlist through the local post at the Cadet Aviation office at Penn Square and West King Street, which will open Tuesday (today).

LIST COMMITTEE

Local VFW committeemen in charge of the program are: Col. John H. Wickersham, K. L. Shirk, Walter Gebhart, James Huebner, James Shand, Dr. J. R. Coder, Stephen J. Aument, Victor Ault and Frank A. Bonesky, chairman. Prof. Frederic S. Klein, of Franklin and Marshall college, is screening test director, and Dr. Harvey A. Smith,

More of LOCAL VFW POST Page 6

NAZI ARMIES REACH MAIKOP; REDS ADMIT

Russians Fighting Fierce Defensive Battles Along Broad Front

BACKS TO BLACK SEA

Moscow (Tuesday) — (AP) — Powerful German armies have swept to the vicinity of Maikop in the Caucasus and the Russians along a broad front are fighting a fierce defensive battle with their backs to the Black Sea, it was revealed by the Russian midnight communique today.

The Russians were engaged in what appeared to be the opening phase of a defense of the vital naval base of Novorossisk, 60 miles west of Krasnodar, where fighting was reported.

The Germans already had a firm foothold in the Maikop region, which produces 7 per cent of Russia's oil, and now appeared to be menacing the naval base—one of Russia's most important and one of the last refuges of the Soviet fleet in the Black Sea.

CLAIMED BY GERMANS

It was the first official indication by the Russians that their retreat in the face of smashes by German mechanized and air units had reached the Maikop region. The Germans claimed the capture of the city, important as a petroleum distributing center, Sunday.

The Russian communique said also the heavy fighting in this region extends to Krasnodar and Armavir, indicating a part of the German drive was veering toward the seacoast. Another German thrust appeared to be heading into the heart of the Caucasus, to the east.

This depressing news from the Caucasus was relieved somewhat by Russian reports of the vigor with which industrial Stalingrad was being defended. There were fierce battles near Kotelnikovski, 95 miles southwest of the industrial metropolis, and in the region of

More of NAZI ARMIES on Page 6

PRICE REGULATIONS ARE DISCUSSED BY LOCAL MERCHANTS

OPA Agents Report Government Beginning To "Crack Down" On Violators

The government is beginning to "crack down" on violators of the ceiling price regulations in its efforts to prevent inflation, two OPA representatives told local merchants at a mass meeting in Martin auditorium of the YMCA Monday night.

They urged that merchants not only have their own price ceilings listed, but to see that their neighbors also are complying with the regulations.

MANY DELINQUENT

Thirty-five per cent of the stores in Lancaster which they have inspected were found to be delinquent in price posting or in record keeping, they said, adding that most of the trouble seemed to be failure to maintain base period records.

The two agents, William Orr and Charles Wood of the Philadelphia OPA office, explained the basic purposes of price regulation, and, how, if carried out correctly, it will prevent inflation. They stated that now customers have recourse if they are charged above the ceiling price, and must be reimbursed either triple the amount of the overcharge, or $50, whichever is higher.

STRESSES IMPORTANCE

A. C. Darmstaetter, chairman of the Retailers' committee of the Chamber of Commerce, who introduced the OPA men, stressed the importance of the price ceiling reg-

More of PRICE on Page 6

TO TRAIN WOMEN AT OLD NYA CAMP HERE

The abandoned National Youth Administration camp at Kiwanis Park will be converted into a woman's technical training center, officials announced Monday.

While details of the training program remain to be worked out, officials said emphasis would be placed upon radio work.

The conversion is part of a nation-wide plan to train women in special skills which will free men in industry for combat duty.

Women from Lancaster County, it was revealed, will be given the first opportunity to enroll for the training courses.

Cruiser Lost, 5 Other Ships Damaged In Furious Assault; Foe's Losses Heavy, Navy Says

BOMB BASES

Yanks Attack Defensive Positions In Solomons, Hit Big Destroyer

RAID RABAUL AGAIN

General MacArthur's Headquarters, Australia, (Tuesday) — (AP) — Allied bombers again roared out over the waters off northeastern Australia Monday to attack Japanese positions on the island fringes of the Solomon battle theater, Allied headquarters announced in its daily communique today.

Off Northwestern Australia off the south coast of Timor Allied medium bombers scored at least three hits on a large enemy destroyer and left it badly damaged, The Allied command said. Two merchant ships were heavily attacked here, one left afire and heavily damaged and the other hit twice and probably sunk.

JAPS WITHDRAW

In addition Allied patrols fighting in the inland heights of New Guinea forced small but strong Japanese forces in the Kokoda area to withdraw to prepared positions, the Allied command announced.

Kokoda, west of the Gona-Buna area of New Guinea's Papuan Peninsula, is where the enemy has established a base threatening Port Moresmy, 60 miles away.

The Allied air operation apparently having most bearing on the Solo-

More of BOMB BASES on Page 6

L. B. HERR, JR., IS NAMFD INSPECTOR OF RESERVE CORPS

Will Check Set-Up Of All Branches Of County Citizens' Group

Lieutenant Colonel L. B. Herr, Jr., 1287 Wheatland Ave., has been appointed chief of the inspection service of the Lancaster County Citizens' Reserve Corps.

LT. COL. L. B. HERR, JR.

The appointment of Colonel Herr, who retired about six weeks ago from active Army service as commander of the Second Bat-

More of L. B. HERR, JR., on Page 6

WHAT, NO RAISIN PIE!

Washington—(AP) — The government Monday froze the entire 1942 production of dried apples, apricots, peaches, pears, prunes and grapes (raisins) in the hands of packers, to make them available for the Army, Navy and Lend-Lease shipment.

The freeze order issued by the War Production Board applied also to the carryover from the 1941 crop. Supplies not purchased by the government will be made available for civilians, WPB said. In addition, the entire 1942 crop of muscat, sultana, and Thompson seedless grapes was ordered diverted into the production of raisins.

In Charge

VICE ADMIRAL GHORMLEY

POLICEMEN BATTLE GANDHI'S ZEALOTS IN INDIAN RIOTS

Numerous Casualties Counted In Second Day Of Civil Disobedience Campaign

Bombay —(AP)— Mohandas Gandhi's "do or die" zealots defied police bullets time after time in Bombay and elsewhere Monday, rioting and striking in prolonged response to the All-India Congress campaign of mass civil disobedience designed to drive the British from this sub-continent.

In Bombay alone in two days of disorder police and troops fired on crowds "about ten times," a provincial government communique said Monday night. There were numerous casualties Monday, in addition to the eleven dead and scores injured on Sunday. Of Sunday's casualties, eight were slain and 158 injured in the Bombay area alone.

SITUATION WORSE

Late Monday the situation was growing progressively worse in northern sections of this city, with crowds stoning trains, cutting wires and smashing police lamps. A post office was attacked; several buses were damaged badly and

More of POLICEMEN BATTLE on Page 6

GERMANS EXECUTE 93 PERSONS IN PARIS

Vichy —(AP)— German authorities in Paris announced Monday night the execution of 93 "terrorists" as the result of a series of recent anti-German attacks.

The announcement was signed by Brig. Gen. Oberg, chief of the SS and police in occupied territories.

It warned the population it must "exercise the greatest vigilance to enable the detection of terrorist machinations, otherwise I will be obliged to take measures under which the entire population will suffer."

Gen. Oberg said the "terrorist attacks" were perpetuated by those in the pay of Britain.

COMMENT ON EXECUTIONS

New York — (AP) — The German radio, in its first comment on the execution of six Nazi saboteurs in Washington Saturday, said Monday the executions were "a serious event whose consequences enemy countries could not ignore." This quotation was attributed to a German foreign office spokesman.

By its action, the radio said, the United States "forfeited the right of protesting against the condemnation of saboteurs in the territory occupied by the German army."

2 SCHOOL DISTRICTS POSTPONE OPENINGS

The school directors of West Earl and Martic Townships have announced that they have delayed the opening of the schools until September 14 so that the children will be available to aid in harvesting crops.

Miss Evelyn V. Leaman, Bird-in-Hand R1, was elected as a teacher of the Sunnyside School in West Earl Township. She is a graduate of Millersville State Teachers' College.

ATTACK TULAGI

Admiral King Says Enemy Counter-Attacked "With Rapidity And Vigor"

WARNS OF LOSSES

Washington—(AP)—A force of hard-bitten American Marines, spearhead of America's first offensive in the Pacific, has landed on the strategic Solomon Islands flanking Australia and is now engaged in a terrific struggle with counter-attacking Japanese.

Disclosing this Monday, the Navy revealed that the furious assault, in which the Marines were strongly backed by warships and planes, had already cost the United States forces at least one cruiser sunk and two damaged, and two destroyers and one transport also damaged.

The Japanese, whose counter-attack was launched "with rapidity and vigor," have suffered a "large number" of planes destroyed and surface units put out of action, the Navy statement said.

How many lives have been lost in the grim amphibious struggle was not known, but such a landing attack is one of the most difficult operations in warfare, and the Navy statement warned that "considerable losses" must be expected.

The statement was issued by Admiral Ernest J. King, Commander in Chief of all American forces. He described the operation as "our first assumption of the initiative and of the offensive" in this war and declared the purpose is to drive the Japs out of the southeasterly Solomon Islands, their southernmost point of advance in the Pacific.

In a special statement on the progress of the three-day-old battle, the Admiral described the section directly contested as the Tulagi area. Tulagi, the capital of the Solomons, is situated on a small island of the same name, close to the nearby and larger Florida Island. The broad wording possibly meant that landings had been accomplished not only on Florida but also on the nearby large islands of Guadalcanal and Malaita.

Vice Admiral Robert L. Ghormley, 58, Naval commander in the South Pacific, is in direct charge of the assault actions under the general control of 57-year-old Admiral Chester W. Nimitz. Command-

More of ATTACK TULAGI on Page 6

Roses Take 4 From Rocks, Now 4½ Games From Playoffs

Big Leagues Hit Half-million in War Relief

American Loop "9s" Top $250,000 Goal

69,136 Paid to See Yanks, Show, While 50,758 Saw Tigers in Twin Bill; A's-Boston Tiff Netted Approximately $30,000

By AUSTIN BEALMEAR
Associated Press Sports Writer

"RELIEF," a word reserved for substitute pitchers in baseball language of the past, had a new meaning in the major leagues today after the last of the 16 teams chalked up their most important "assist" of the season—designed to help the families of the nation's fighting men.

The program, in which the receipts of eight regularly scheduled games in each circuit were earmarked for Army-Navy relief, was completed yesterday when the American League staged a fast finish with a trio of doubleheaders that boosted the contributions past the half million dollar mark.

69,136 See Yankees

A New York crowd of 69,136 paid an estimated $80,000 to see the Yankees and the Washington Senators. In Detroit, the Tigers and the St. Louis Browns drew 50,758 and a gate of $68,172. And approximately $30,000 came in at Philadelphia, where the Athletics met the Boston Red Sox.

These doubleheaders, redesignated as relef games after the first five American league Army-Navy contests brought in less than $75,000, enabled the junior circuit to surpass its quota of $250,000, although it fell short of the $270,000 produced by the National League.

Babe Gets 2 Homers

Babe Ruth and Walter Johnson were added attractions at Yankee stadium. The ex-slugger of the Yankees and the former pitching ace of the Senators faced each other in an exhibition between games and the Babe obliged by driving two balls into the stands.

As for the pennant races, the Yankees watched their American League lead shrink to nine full games while the Brooklyn Dodgers hiked their margin in the National League to seven and a half.

The Dodgers, who open an important four-game series with the second-place Cardinals in St. Louis tonight, turned back the New York Giants in both ends of a double bill that drew 32,886 although Babe Ruth was performing only a subway ride away.

Camilli Hits Homer

The first game went ten innings before Dolph Camilli came up with the bases loaded and blasted the only ball pitched by reliever Harry Feldman for a grand slam homer to trip the Giants, 6-4. Camilli also drove in both the other Dodger runs, but Mel Ott nullified these with a two-run homer and Johnny Mize gave the Giants a short-lived lead with a four-bagger that netted two runs in the top half of the tenth.

Darkness held the second game to five frames and again it was a last ditch rally that gave the Brooks the nod, 7-5. Ott hit his 24th home run of the year, but the Giants had to come from behind with four runs in the fifth to tie the score. Then Billy Herman decided the issue with a two-run single in the fifth.

Bucs Stop Cards

The Pittsburgh Pirates ended a St. Louis winning streak at eight games when a home run by Elbie Fletcher downed the Cards, 5-3, but Murry Dickson pitched the Red Birds to a 5-2 verdict in the afterpiece.

Claude Passeau and Lon Warneke hurled a pair of shutouts as the Chicago Cubs blanked the Cincinnati Reds twice by identical scores of 3-0. Passeau gained his 17th win, although he yielded nine hits, while Warneke tossed a two-hitter for his best effort of the year.

Braves, Phils Split

Boston and Philadelphia split, the Braves taking the first game, 3-1, and the Phils grabbing the nightcap, 2-0, on Rube Melton's four-hit pitching.

In the American League, the Senators handed Johnny Murphy his eighth straight setback when they rallied for three runs in the ninth inning to beat the Yanks, 7-6, but Ernie Bonham blanked Washington, 3-0, in the nightcap, which was halted by darkness after five and a half innings.

Red Sox Blank A's

The Boston Red Sox picked up a game on the leaders by shutting out the Athletics, 2-0 and 7-0. Tex Hughson pitched four-hit ball in the first for his 17th win and his 11th straight and Joe Dobson matched his performance in the second.

Three-hit pitching by Ted Lyons and a three-run rally in the ninth inning gave the Chicago White Sox a 3-1 decision over the Cleveland Indians, but Jim Bagby hurled the Tribe to a 1-0 triumph in the ten-inning nightcap with a five-hit job. Ken Keltner's third two-bagger brought in the winning run.

The St. Louis Browns pulled to within half a game of third-place Cleveland by stopping the Detroit Tigers, 2-1 and 4-2, the second game going ten innings. All four starting pitchers went the distance, with John Niggeling shading Hal Newhouser in the opener when the Brownies scored two unearned runs and Bob Muncrief edging out Dizzy Trout in the afterpiece when they pushed over two tallies in the top half of the tenth.

SUNDAY'S RESULTS

Baseball

Western County League:
Columbia 6, Eden 5.
East Petersburg 5, Mountville S. C. 1 (1st).
Mountville S. C. 2, East Petersburg 0 (2nd).
Ronks 3, Mountville A. A. 0 (1st).
Mountville A. A. 2, Ronks 0 (2nd).

Lancaster-Lebanon League:
Hopeland 8, Hinkletown 6 (12 innings).
Schaefferstown 7, Hinkletown 6.
Schoeneck 21, Bowmansville 1.

American Legion Playoff:
Lancaster Legion All-Stars 6, Coplay 5 (11 innings).

When George Herman Ruth Misses, He Misses

Here is one of the healthiest misses in baseball. George Herman Ruth, fondly called The Babe by Yankee fans, took one of his usual exuberant whacks at the ball tossed him by Walter Johnson. He missed. Benny Bengough, former Yank, has the ball right in his mitt with the Babe still fanning air. It was at the service benefit game in the Yankee Stadium. But Babe came back later and parked two into the right field bleachers.

Legion 9 Evens Series With Coplay

Locals Score 6 to 5 Win In Eleven Innings

The Lancaster Legion All-Stars and the Coplay Legion Post of Lehigh County will meet at Allentown Wednesday night at 8:30 p. m. on the Allentown Inter-State League diamond, in the third and deciding game of the American Legion's eastern sectional play-offs.

This third game was made necessary as a result of Lancaster's 6 to 5 victory over Coplay here yesterday afternoon at Stumpf Field in the second game of the series.

Conditions caused postponement of the third game yesterday which was to be played as part of a double-bill.

Coplay Wins First

Coplay won the first game at Coplay Saturday afternoon 17 to 2.

If conditions force further postponement of the game this Wednesday night, the contest will be played here Thursday night on Stumpf Field under the lights.

The eastern play-offs with Lewistown must be started Friday at Lewistown.

Arrangements for this week's games were made here Sunday by Leon Duckworth, eastern sectional director, State Chairman George Bellis of Philadelphia, and officials of the Lancaster and Coplay teams.

Errors Costly

Lancaster's rousing comeback here yesterday was even more decisive than the score indicates. Only some bad errors on the part of Lancaster enabled the visitors to stay in the game, and at least three of their runs were unearned.

Dick Rhen pitched his heart out for nine innings, but his mates tossed run after run away behind him. Bob Dommel finished out for Lancaster and was very effective. He was credited with the victory.

On the other hand the highly-touted Johnny Tomasic became the "goat" of the game when he relieved Hluschak on the slab in the ninth and walked in the winning tally in the eleventh.

Dommel Replaces Rhen

Dommel replaced Rhen for Lancaster and set the visitors down through the tenth and eleventh without trouble.

In the Lancaster half of the eleventh Bill Cushman singled and Simmons reached first on Tomasic's' error. Dommel sacrificed both runners around, and Strosser walked to load the bases. Jimmy Geist then outguessed Jimmy Tomasic and took four balls to force in Cushman with the winning run.

Bill Cushman played sensationally at shortstop for the Roses, while Dussinger was the hitting star with four for five, getting half of Lancaster's hits.

Coplay	ab	r	h	o	a	Legion All Stars	ab	r	h	o	a
Matika c	5	0	1	5	2	Stros'r lf	3	1	0	2	0
Hlus'k p	4	1	1	0	7	Geist rf	4	0	0	1	0
Tanz'h 2b	5	0	0	4	5	Hoff'an 3b	5	1	1	0	3
M. Ha'l 3b	5	1	1	3	5	Kratzer c	4	0	0	3	0
Lup'h lf	5	0	1	0	0	Todd cf	3	2	1	2	0
Abern'y 1b	4	1	0	12	0	Duss'r 1b	5	0	4	17	0
Fahr'r cf	3	0	0	1	0	Cush'n ss	3	1	1	5	6
A. Ha'l rf	4	1	1	2	0	Keays 2b	1	0	0	1	0
Erk'er ss	3	0	1	1	1	Rhen p	3	0	0	0	4
Kinoch 1b	1	1	0	3	1	Sim'ns 2b	3	1	1	2	3
Tomasic cf	1	0	1	0	0	Hicks xx	1	0	0	0	0
						Dommel p	0	0	0	0	0
Totals	40	5	7	x31	19	Totals	35	6	8	33	16

x—One out when winning run scored.
xx—Batted for Rhen in 9th.

COPLAY .... 012 000 002 00—5
LEGION ALL STARS 010 101 101 01—6

Errors—Hoffman, Kratzer, Keays 2, Simmons, Matika, Tanzosh, M. Harakal 2, Fahringer, Kimoch, Tomasic. Two base hits—Lupersheck. Sacrifices—Kratzer, Cushman 2, Dommel. Stolen bases—Lupersheck. Double plays—Cuskey (unassisted); Simmons to Cushman to Dussinger. Left on bases—Coplay 7, Legion All Stars 9. Bases on balls—Off Rhen 1, Dommel 1, Tomasic 2, Hluschak 5. Struck out—By Rhen 3, Hluschek 2, Tomasic 2. Hits—Off Rhen 7 in 9; Dommel 0 in 2; Hluschek 7 in 8; Tomasic 1 in 2 1-3. Hit by pitcher—By Hluschek (Geist). Wild pitch—Hluschek. Winning pitcher—Dommel; losing pitcher—Tomasic.
Umpires—Geiter and Keen. Time—2:40.

LIGHTNER NAMED COACH

Altoona, Pa. — (AP) — Robert Lightner, former Altoona High and West Chester State Teachers College football player, will report Tuesday as head coach of Roaring Spring High School.

GRAYSON'S SCOREBOARD

by HARRY GRAYSON

NEW YORK, Aug. 24. — Stop lionizing athletes in service, Comdr. James Joseph Tunney warns the boys in the press box.

Cut on sports ballyhoo, proposes the former heavyweight champion.

Forget athletic "extravaganza," like all-star football and baseball games.

Professional athleticism (he means sports) is "wonderful nonsense," to Comdr. Gene Tunney, who modestly remembers that he made $1,000,000 in 30 minutes by virtue of such silliness.

We hold no brief for the boys in the press box, who are simply trying to raise a few million dollars for Army and Navy relief through professional athleticism. After all, what is a few million dollars in times like these?

THESE criticisms by a high-ranking Naval official show a surprising lack of unanimity by the Navy.

Was the press responsible for these?

The Navy pre-flight program with its emphasis on big-time football, important coaches, big games and all the shortening that smacks of sports emphasis.

All-star Army football teams which play exhibitions against professional clubs.

Mickey Cochrane's touring baseball club.

The Great Lakes basketball team.

Professional fights between soldiers and sailors.

Commissions for sports writers to ballyhoo the Navy.

NO, the press hasn't asked for a thing. Unstintingly and at a goodly sacrifice, sports editors in almost every city have sweated—and are sweating—their hearts out to make some sense out of Commander Tunney's "wonderful nonsense" and get additional money for war funds.

A lot of us didn't know Commander Tunney felt this way about it, although we might have surmised as much when, at the meeting of the Service and American League All-Stars in Cleveland, he refused to co-operate to the extent of being seen with Lieut. Jack Dempsey of the Coast Guard.

Commander Tunney charged this to "Navy decorum."

Isn't there something in "Navy decorum" having to do with the boys in blue getting signals straight?

JUST tell us what you want us to do, fellows, and we'll do it whether it's filling pages with stories about the services or limiting ourselves to those quaint characters who frequent Jacobs Beach.

But, as they say in the Marine Corps, give one order and make it so easy that anyone can understand it.

Even the boys in the press box.

Major League Standings

AMERICAN LEAGUE

	W.	L.	P.C.	*G.B.
New York	81	42	.569	—
Boston	72	51	.585	9
Cleveland	64	58	.525	16½
St. Louis	64	59	.520	17
Detroit	61	64	.488	21
Chicago	53	64	.453	25
Washington	48	71	.403	31
Philadelphia	48	82	.369	36½

YESTERDAY'S RESULTS

Boston 2, Philadelphia 0 (1st).
Boston 7, Philadelphia 0 (2nd).
Chicago 3, Cleveland 1 (1st).
Cleveland 1, Chicago 0 (2nd, 10 innings).
Washington 7, New York 6 (1st).
New York 3, Washington 0 (2nd, called 6th, darkness).
St. Louis 2, Detroit 1 (1st).
St. Louis 4, Detroit 2 (2nd, 10 innings).

TOMORROW'S GAMES

Cleveland at Boston (2)
St. Louis at Washington
Chicago at New York

INTER-STATE LEAGUE

	W.	L.	P.C.	*G.B.
Wilmington	68	50	.576	—
Hagerstown	64	52	.552	3
Harrisburg	60	59	.504	8½
Allentown	58	60	.492	10
Lancaster	54	65	.454	14½
Trenton	49	67	.422	18

YESTERDAY'S RESULTS

Lancaster 4, Wilmington 1 (1st).
Lancaster 5, Wilmington 4 (2nd).
Hagerstown 4, Harrisburg 0 (1st).
Hagerstown at Harrisburg, (2nd, postponed).
Allentown 5, Trenton 3 (1st).
Trenton 4, Allentown 3 (2nd).

TONIGHT'S GAMES

Wilmington at Harrisburg.
Other clubs not scheduled.

Exhibition Games

Boston Braves (NL) vs. Lancaster Red Roses at Stumpf Field, 8:15 o'clock.
Detroit Tigers (AL) at Allentown 8 o'clock.

NATIONAL LEAGUE

	W.	L.	P.C.	*G.B.
Brooklyn	84	35	.706	—
St. Louis	77	43	.642	7½
New York	65	57	.533	20½
Cincinnati	59	61	.492	25½
Pittsburgh	55	63	.466	28½
Chicago	58	68	.460	29½
Boston	50	74	.403	36½
Philadelphia	34	81	.296	48

YESTERDAY'S RESULTS

Boston 3, Philadelphia 1 (1st).
Philadelphia 2, Boston 0 (2nd).
Chicago 3, Cincinnati 0 (1st).
Chicago 3, Cincinnati 0 (2nd).
Brooklyn 6, New York 4 (1st, 10 innings).
Brooklyn 7, New York 5 (2nd, 5 innings).
Pittsburgh 5, St. Louis 3 (1st).
St. Louis 5, Pittsburgh 2 (2nd).

TOMORROW'S GAMES

Philadelphia at Chicago
Boston at Pittsburgh (Night)
New York at Cincinnati (Night)
Brooklyn at St. Louis (Night)

WEEK-END SPORTS IN BRIEF
By The Associated Press

BROOKLINE, Mass.—Francisco Segura of Ecuador, defeated Lieut. Gardnar Mulloy, U. S. N., 6-3, 6-4, 7-9, 3-6, 6-1, in final 48th Longwood Bowl tennis tourney. Before Mulloy entered Navy he was Segura's amateur coach at Miami University.

OESTERSUN, Sweden—Gunder Haegg, Swedish fireman, ran 2,000 meters in record breaking time of 5:11.8, five full seconds faster than Archie San Romani's accepted world standard.

JASONVILLE, Ind.—James Counselman, of St. Louis, lowered own American record for 100-meter breast stroke from 1:15.3 to 1:13.1.

CAMP GRANT, Ill.—Chicago's football Bears used passes to defeat Camp Grant Eleven, 32 to 6, in prelude to game with College All-Stars Friday night.

SARATOGA SPRINGS, N. Y.—W. E. Boeing's Devil Thumb won Grand Union Hotel stakes for two-year-olds by going six furlongs in 1:12 2-5. Myron Selznick's Can't Wait took Saratoga handicap at odds of $37 to $2.

CAMDEN, N. J.—Ella K. Bryson's Mercury annexed Walt Whitman handicap by half a length from Ogma. Time for the six panels was 1:12 1-5.

CHICAGO—Blueberry Pie, owned by Mrs. Max Factor, Jr., clipped one-fifth second from track record in winning mile and quarter Meadowland handicap on Washington Park's turf course in 2:04 1-5.

P. I. A. A. Urges Its Schools To Keep Playing

HARRISBURG, Aug. 24.—(AP)—The Pennsylvania Interscholastic Athletic Association today called on its nearly 1,000 member schools to continue athletic programs "as far as possible along normal lines" during the war emergency.

"It appears that there is no alternative," declared executive Secretary Edmund Wicht, "except to face the situation as it exists and to meet the challenge by making use of available transportation facilities other than those to which we have been accustomed in order to continue our interscholastic programs and keep our athletes playing.

"It is hoped that the interscholastic athletic program will be continued and that where curtailment is necessary, such curtailment will be of a nature so as not to entirely deprive the boys and girls of our high schools of the opportunity to develop themselves physically and enjoy the pleasures of interscholastic competition."

Situation Critical

He advised PIAA members that school authorities had failed "to secure the consideration which was felt necessary to transportation, in buses, of our interschool athletes," and that the rubber situation "is so very critical that regulations are becoming more strict."

"Many inquiries have been received from all parts of the state relative to the present problem of carrying on our athletic program during the coming year," said the secretary. "There is no question but that this will be difficult for many schools and that most of the problems will have to be solved individually by the schools concerned."

Use Trains First

The opinion of the majority of school administrators and coaches, Wicht added, is that public transportation facilities such as trains, buses and trolleys should be utilized first even though this might necessitate overnight trips. Where public conveyances are not available, he said it may be possible to obtain voluntary help by transporting in private cars if the distances are not too great.

"In cases where some curtailment is necessary," declared the secretary, "old contracts could be voided by mutual consent and co-operation of schools concerned and new contracts made with nearer-at-home schools. Two games per school in football might also be the order of the day. Without question, it will be necessary to cut down the number of players taken on trips away from home."

Wicht said various leagues and conferences over the state are meeting the situation in different ways and are determined to carry on their athletic programs, adding "while the easy way would be to quit and discontinue such programs, such a course would not be meeting the needs of the boys and girls whom the army, navy and physical fitness groups requested us to 'make tough' so that they can meet the trying situations brought on by the war."

MONDAY'S SPORTS EVENTS

Baseball

Inter-State League:
Wilmington at Harrisburg.
Other clubs not scheduled.

Legion Jr. League Playoffs:
Stock Yards vs. Rangers at George Washington field.
Jr. Chamber of Commerce vs. St. Joseph C. C. at Ritchey-Wise field.

Exhibition Game
Boston Braves (NL) vs. Lancaster Red Roses at Stumpf Field, 8:15 o'clock.
Detroit Tigers (AL) at Allentown, 8 o'clock.

Softball

City Church League Playoffs:
Emmanuel vs. St. Lukes at College diamond.

Farnum Industrial League:
Farnum Barons vs. Lincoln A. C.

Other Softball
U. S. Army Signal Corps vs. Seventh Ward Girls at Stevens Trade diamond.

Columbia "9" Upsets Eden In Loop Game

WESTERN COUNTY LEAGUE

Teams	W.	L.	P.C.
Eden	21	6	.778
Mountville A. A.	17	9	.654
Ronks	17	12	.586
Columbia	11	15	.423
East Petersburg	9	15	.375
Mountville S. C.	6	23	.207

Scoring six runs in the seventh inning, the Columbia nine defeated the Western County Baseball League leading Eden batsmen, 6 to 5 on the Eden diamond Sunday afternoon. The second game was postponed.

In losing their sixth game of the season Eden pushed over two runs in the second and three in the ninth.

Playing at East Petersburg, the home team split its doubleheader with the Mountville Sports Clubs. East Petersburg won the first 5 to 1 while the Sportsmen took the second 2 to 0.

Ronks and Mountville A. A. divided a double-header. Ronks won the opener 3 to 0 and Mountville took the second contest, 2 to 0.

Eden	ab	r	h	o	a	Columbia	ab	r	h	o	a
Wiley ss	4	1	0	1	1	Kisca'n cf	5	1	2	3	0
Rylee lf	5	0	1	0	0	Rineer lf	5	1	1	1	0
H. Sl'h 1b	5	0	1	12	0	R. Ko'r rf	5	1	3	3	0
W. Sl'h cf	4	1	0	0	0	Young c	5	0	1	6	3
Fraser rf	4	1	2	1	0	Denlin'r 1b	5	0	1	8	0
Heinz'n 2b	3	1	2	0	3	Smoker 2b	3	1	1	4	1
Nye c	4	0	1	11	0	Lock'd 3b	2	1	0	2	1
Neff 3b	4	0	2	2	1	C. Ko'r ss	4	0	0	0	3
Falk p	4	1	3	0	5	Craig p	4	1	2	0	1
Totals	37	5	12	27	10	Totals	38	6	11	27	9

COLUMBIA .... 000 000 600—6
EDEN .... 020 000 003—5

(First Game)

Mountville S. C.	ab	r	h	o	a	East Petersburg	ab	r	h	o	a
R.Mow'r ss	3	0	1	3	2	Krein'r 3b	3	0	0	1	6
Zercher rf	2	0	0	1	0	Emich cf	4	1	2	2	1
Miller 3b	4	1	1	2	3	Neal lf	3	1	3	0	0
O'Brien 1b	4	0	0	11	1	Gavan 2b	4	1	0	1	1
Albright cf	4	0	1	1	0	Charles 1b	2	0	0	13	0
Youtz lf	2	0	0	0	0	Mowrer rf	2	0	0	0	0
Kauf'n 2b	3	0	0	3	2	Ellin'r ss	3	0	1	3	2
McCune c	3	0	0	1	1	Groff c	3	1	1	7	0
Shutt p	3	0	0	2	1	Jenkins p	3	1	0	0	4
H.Mourer	1	0	0	0	0						
Clair	1	0	0	0	0	Totals	27	5	7	27	14
Totals	30	1	3	24	10						

x-H. Mourer for Zercher.
xx-Clair for Youtz.

MOUNTVILLE S. C. .. 000 100 000—1
EAST PETERSBURG .. 002 000 12x—5

(Second Game)

Mountville S. C.	ab	r	h	o	a	East Petersburg	ab	r	h	o	a
R.Mou'r ss	3	1	1	0	2	Kreiner 3b	3	0	1	0	0
McCune lf	3	0	0	0	0	Emich cf	3	0	0	1	0
Miller 3b	3	1	0	1	0	Neal c	2	0	0	5	3
O'Brien 1b	3	0	1	10	1	Gavan 2b	1	0	0	1	0
H.Mow'r c	3	0	0	4	0	Charles 1b	3	0	0	12	0
Clair rf	2	0	0	2	0	Mow'r rf 2b	2	0	0	1	2
Albright cf	3	0	1	3	0	Ellin'r ss	2	0	0	1	1
Kauf'n 2b	3	0	0	0	2	Groff lf	2	0	0	0	0
Resh p	1	0	0	0	1	Landis p	2	0	0	0	1
						Miller rf	2	0	1	0	0
Totals	24	2	3	21	6	Totals	22	0	2	21	7

MOUNTVILLE S. C. ...... 001 001 0—2
EAST PETERSBURG .... 000 000 0—0

(First Game)

Mountville A. A.	ab	r	h	o	a	Ronks	ab	r	h	o	a
Shena'b'k	3	0	1	1	2	Cum'ings cf	4	1	1	4	0
Bell	3	0	0	7	0	Weaver 1b	4	1	1	7	1
Dambach	1	0	0	0	0	Hess c	4	0	0	8	0
Kittinger	2	0	0	2	0	Donley lf	4	0	1	1	0
R. Brooks	2	0	0	1	0	Wh'side 2b	3	0	0	4	4
Mummaw	3	0	0	1	1	Smeltz ss	4	1	1	1	2
Beck	4	0	2	1	1	Winter rf	4	0	1	1	0
V. Wallick	4	0	3	12	1	Trout 3b	3	0	1	1	1
Wile	4	0	0	0	0	Miller p	3	0	0	0	2
M. Brooks	3	0	0	1	0						
Pretzman	2	0	0	1	4	Totals	33	3	6	27	10
Totals	31	0	6	27	9						

RONKS .... 200 100 000—3
MOUNTVILLE A. A. .. 000 000 000—0

(Second Game)

Mountville A. A.	ab	r	h	o	a	Ronks	ab	r	h	o	a
Shen'b'k 2b	3	0	0	1	4	Cum'ings cf	2	0	0	1	0
Bell 1b	2	1	2	8	0	Weaver 1b	3	0	0	7	1
Kittin'r cf	3	1	1	0	0	Hess c	3	0	0	6	0
Mum'aw 3b	2	0	1	0	1	Donley lf	2	0	0	2	1
Beck ss	3	0	2	2	2	Wh'side 2b	3	0	0	0	1
Wile lf	2	0	1	0	0	Smeltz ss	2	0	0	1	1
Copel'd rf	3	0	1	1	0	Miller rf	2	0	0	0	0
R.Wal'k c	2	0	0	9	0	Trout 3b	2	0	0	1	2
R.Br'ks p	2	0	0	0	1	Winters p	2	0	0	0	4
Totals	22	2	8	21	8	Totals	21	0	0	18	10

RONKS .... 000 000 0—0
MOUNTVILLE A. A. .... 000 002 x—2

STEELTON NAMES TORETTI

Steelton, Pa.,—(AP)—The Steelton High School Board has selected Sever Toretti, former Penn State lineman, as assistant to football coach Charles Hoyt. He succeeds Nels Hoffman who resigned. John Keller, Stroudsburg, was to have taken the job but reconsidered, saying he would take over the business of his late father.

Locals Sweep Series In Wilmington; Play Braves Here Tonight

Gain Game on Allentown by Taking Four Straight from League-Leaders; Tulacz May Pitch Exhibition Game for Roses

AFTER climbing out of the Interstate League's cellar and pushing to within 4½ games of a fourth-place playoff spot by sweeping four games from Wilmington, Tom Oliver's red-hot Red Roses interrupt their League schedule tonight and tomorrow to tackle a pair of Major League teams at Stumpf field.

The first of these will be met tonight when Casey Stengel's Boston Braves come to town, while tomorrow night Del Baker will bring his Detroit Tigers here for an exhibition.

In order to give the pitching staff the rest it needs for its fight down the League's home-stretch, Business Manager Bill Cowdrick sent in a hurried call for Johnny Tulacz and Norm Hibbs, stars of last year's hurling staff, and Tulacz, at least, is expected to see action against the Big-Leaguers. Hibbs, now in the Army, was uncertain whether be would pitch.

Fans Are Excited

While this announcement, in itself, caused a stir in local sports circles, the Roses' four-game sweep of their Wilmington series had the boys and girls in ecstacy. This quartet of victories, completed yesterday when the locals won by 4 to 1 and 5 to 4, after they had taken Saturday's twin bill by 5 to 1 and 2 to 0, raised the hopes of local fans considerably, and today many were confident that the team would still reach the championship class.

No doubt about it, Manager Oliver's boys are red-hot right now. They still face a tough struggle to climb higher for both Allentown and Harrisburg were on the winning side of the ledger over the week-end and the schedule is nearing a close.

But there's still a chance and if the Roses continue to play the brand of ball they exhibited all of last week, they must be given consideration. It's questionable whether even the most rabid supporter expected the Roses to sweep four-straight from the Rocks in Wilmington this past week-end. Frankly, even the wishful-thinkers were muttering something about three out of four.

Won 13 Out of Last 14

But the Roses, who opened the series with a five-game winning streak, refused to be halted, running their streak to nine straight and showing a string of 13 out of their last 14 games.

Ben Eckert and Artie Cuccurullo took care of the Blue Rocks on Saturday night and yesterday Hickey Shufro turned in another masterful job to win the opening game by a 4 to 1 count. Gordon Mueller started the last game, but when he ran into trouble in the fourth inning Eckert came back to save the day.

The Roses had to do it the hard way, too, for the Blue Rocks, fighting to protect their League lead, threw their best pitchers at our boys. However, they simply refused to be impressed and kept pounding in runs. They collected 14 hits off Johnny Burrows and Dick McCahan in yesterday's opener, while Shufro was holding the Rocks to five, and they got nine off Freddie Caligiuri to win the nightcap which saw Wilmington collect six off Mueller and two off Eckert.

Homer By McCarthy

Behind Shufro's tight pitching, the Roses, backing him up with 14 hits, including a home-run over the left field fence by Bill McCarthy, had a comparatively easy time winning the first game by 4 to 1. Coupled with the two wins on Saturday, this gave the Roses the series, but Manager Oliver and his boys were not content to stop at that.

They went all-out and when Mueller showed signs of weakening in the second game, Oliver rushed Eckert to the mound to save the day. And Ben delivered.

Wheaton Comes Through

However, it was Woody Wheaton's bat that decided the issue here. Woody, whose sensational catches have saved many a game for the home-side, decided it was time to do a bit of punching with his willow and with the bases loaded in the second, he came through with a double that cleaned the sacks and sent our boys off to a four-run start.

The Rocks provided trouble later on, but that quartet of runs, coupled with another marker in the fourth, which, incidentally, Wheaton also batted in, proved enough to provide the one-run victory.

Tulacz May Pitch

Now tonight the Roses tackle the National League's Boston Braves and indications this morning were that Tulacz, once regarded as one of the Interstate's top pitchers, may get the starting assignment. Although out of organized ball this year because of his defense job, Johnny has been pitching regularly in semi-pro ball near his home in Poughkeepsie. He hurled a game up there on Saturday night and it may be that Manager Oliver will hold him over until tomorrow night. Oliver said he wouldn't decide on this until later today.

The Braves are bringing their full team here from Boston where they split even yesterday with the Phils. It is the first time that the Bostonians have ever played in Lancaster, and indications are that they will be greeted by a large crowd.

Hibbs in Town

As for Hibbs, Norm was in town over the week-end and Business Manager Cowdrick asked him to pitch. However, he was undecided, saying that he had not been in a baseball uniform since he was inducted into the Army early this year. There is a possibility, however, that he may don a suit and fill in at some other position.

While the Roses were sweeping that four-game series, Allentown took three out of four from Trenton, the one defeat giving our boys a chance to reduce the Wings' lead. The series' result enabled the Roses to stretch their lead over the last-place Senators. The latter team lost two straight on Saturday, but managed to gain an even split yesterday, losing the opener, 5 to 3, but winning the night-cap, 4 to 3.

Hagerstown blanked Harrisburg, 4 to 0, yesterday with the second game being postponed and the defeat left Harrisburg only five games ahead of our side.

JOHNNY TULACZ

(First Game)

Lancaster	ab	r	h	o	a	Wilmington	ab	r	h	o	a
Kell 3b	4	1	2	2	1	Sloboda ss	3	0	0	4	3
Oliver lf	4	0	2	7	0	Scheldt lf	4	0	1	3	0
Wh'ton cf	5	0	1	2	0	Mac'w'z cf	4	1	2	1	0
Kardash ss	4	0	3	1	3	K'opka 1b	4	0	1	7	3
Gleason c	4	0	0	6	0	Riley rf	2	0	0	1	0
Booker rf	5	1	1	0	0	Adkins 3b	3	0	1	1	3
McCar'y 1b	3	1	1	7	0	Broskie c	4	0	0	2	0
Elliston 2b	4	0	3	2	3	Rullo 2b	3	0	0	8	4
Shufro p	4	1	1	0	2	Burrows p	2	0	0	0	1
						a-Devlin	1	0	0	0	0
Totals	37	4	14	27	9	McCahan p	0	0	0	0	1
						Totals	30	1	5	27	15

a-Batted for Burrows in 8th.

LANCASTER .... 100 201 000—4
WILMINGTON .... 000 100 000—1

Errors—Sloboda. Runs batted in—Konopka, McCarthy 2, Wheaton. Three base hit—Mackiewicz. Home run—McCarthy. Sacrifices—Adkins, Kell, Gleason. Double plays—Adkins, Rullo and Konopka; Sloboda and Rullo. Left on bases—Lancaster 11; Wilmington 6. Base on balls—Off Shufro 2, off Burrows 3. Struck out—By Shufro 5, by Burrows 2. Hits—Off Burrows 13 in 8 innings; off McCahan 1 in 1. Hit by pitcher—By Shufro (Riley). Wild pitches—Burrows 2. Losing pitcher—Burrows.
Umpires—Brominski and Tatler. Time of game—1:39.

(Second Game)

Lancaster	ab	r	h	o	a	Wilmington	ab	r	h	o	a
Kell 3b	3	1	1	1	2	Sloboda ss	4	0	1	2	3
Harig lf	2	1	0	1	0	Scheldt lf	2	0	0	0	0
Wh'ton cf	4	0	2	2	0	Mac'w'z cf	4	1	1	3	0
Kardash ss	4	0	0	1	3	K'opka 1b	4	1	3	10	0
Gleason c	3	0	1	3	0	Riley rf	2	0	1	0	0
Booker rf	3	0	0	2	0	Daugh'rs rf	0	0	0	0	0
McCar'y 1b	3	0	0	7	0	Adkins 3b	3	0	0	1	2
Elliston 2b	3	1	2	4	2	Devlin c	2	1	0	2	0
Mueller p	2	2	2	0	0	Rullo 2b	2	1	0	2	4
Eckert p	1	0	0	0	3	Caligiuri p	2	0	2	0	4
Totals	28	5	9	21	10	Totals	25	4	8	21	13

LANCASTER .... 040 100 0—5
WILMINGTON .... 100 210 0—4

Errors—Sloboda. Runs batted in—Konopka 2, Caligiuri, Sloboda, Wheaton 4, Kell. Two base hits—Elliston, Wheaton. Three base hits—Mackiewicz, Wheaton. Home run—Konopka. Stolen bases—Harig, Daughters. Sacrifices—Booker, Kell, Adkins, Scheldt. Double plays—Kardash, Elliston and McCarthy; Kell, Elliston and McCarthy; Rullo, Sloboda and Konopka. Left on bases—Lancaster 7; Wilmington 9. Base on balls—Off Mueller 5, off Caligiuri 3, off Eckert 2. Struck out—By Mueller 2, by Caligiuri 2, by Eckert 1. Hits—Off Mueller 6 in 3 1-3 innings, off Eckert 2 in 3 2-3. Winning pitcher—Mueller.
Umpires—Tatler and Brominski. Time of game—1:[illegible]

Golf Pairings

Pairings for the annual Lancaster Country Club golf championship were announced today by A. B. Thorn, club pro.

S. R. Zimmerman Jr., won the Malone Bowl, it also was announced.

Dr. T. Harris Francis won the weekly Sweepstakes tournament.

The club championship pairings are as follows:

Jack Martin vs. H. C. Seaman.
John Ranck vs. Roger Hetzel.
Dr. T. Harris Francis vs. H. R. Peck.
D. W. Franck vs. R. K. Dodge.
J. M. Brenneman vs. B. M. Zimmerman.
J. H. Morrison vs. I. R Herr.
A. E. Pearce vs. E. M. Hoffecker.
S. C. Martin vs. Victor Despard.

MALONE BOWL WINNERS

	Gross	H'cap	Net
S. R. Zimmerman, Jr.	158	12	146
John Ranck	157	10	147
B. M. Zimmerman	165	14	151

WEEKLY SWEEPSTAKES WINNERS
(First Division)

	Gross	H'cap	Net
Dr. T. Harris Francis	80	7	73
D. L. Armstrong	78	3	75

(Second Division)

	Gross	H'cap	Net
Dr. Charles Gaige	90	13	77
G. W. Davis, Jr.	95	16	79

SZWEDKO ANNEXES CUP

Pittsburgh,—(AP)—Andy Szwedko, Etna millwright, won the Pittsburgh Municipal Golf Championship today at the Schenley Park Course, his 264 two-day aggregate edging out Carl Kaufmann by one stroke.

With Our Service Men

Corporal Harold R. Beam, who has arrived safely in Northern Ireland with a unit of the AEF, according to word received by his wife, Mrs. S. Mae Thomas Beam, of the Lincoln Highway East. Corporal Beam has been a member of the Army Air Force since April 30, 1941.

Staff Sergeant William M. Ginder, who was recently promoted from sergeant, is stationed somewhere overseas with a coast artillery division. He is the son of Mr. and Mrs. Herbert Ginder, of Manheim, and enlisted in the Army in May, 1940.

Corporal Technician Alfred B. Carpenter, who is serving overseas with the Army, according to word received by his parents, Mr. and Mrs. Norman S. Carpenter, of Rothsville. He has been in the service for two years.

Sergeant H. G. Beattie, son of Mrs. Hiram G. Beattie, of Boston, formerly of Lancaster, who enlisted in the Army in January, and is stationed overseas.

Pvt. Charles Miller, Jr., who has returned to Camp Shelby, Miss., where he is serving with an infantry unit, after spending a 14-day furlough with his parents at 426 Reynolds Ave. He has been in the Army since June and was formerly employed by the Bearings Company of America.

Marshall Webb, apprentice seaman in the Coast Guard, who is now stationed at Berkley, Va. Son of Mr. and Mrs. Charles Webb, of Mount Joy, he was graduated from the Mount Joy High school in 1939.

Pvt. George Tangert, son of Mr. and Mrs. Albert Tangert, 113 Reservoir St., who is stationed with an Army Engineer unit somewhere in Australia. He has been in service since November, 1941, and was previously employed as a bus driver for the Conestoga Transportation Company.

William Maynard Miller, 18, son of Mr. and Mrs. Harold Miller, 713 E. Chestnut St., who recently enlisted in the Navy and is stationed at Newport, R. I. He is a graduate of McCaskey High School, class of 1942, and was employed by the Pennsylvania Railroad.

2nd Lt. Richard M. Scott, of Lancaster, who recently reported for further flight training to the Greenville Army Flying school, Greenville, Miss., as a student officer. Upon completion of requirement there, he will be sent to another field to take supplementary training prior to receiving the "wings" of an officer pilot. Scott is the son of Mr. and Mrs. Roy V. Scott and is a graduate of the U. S. Military Academy, West Point, N. Y.

Pvt. William N. Hogarth, of 319½ Coral St., who is a recent enlistee in the Army, temporarily stationed at New Cumberland. He is the son of Mrs. Joseph Severin, of Harrisburg. His wife and daughter have remained in Lancaster.

Private John E. Zaring, of Brownstown, son of Mr. and Mrs. John Zaring, of Brownstown, who has been transferred from Fort Monmouth, N. J., to Fort Sam Houston, Tex.

Amelia and Paul Nicklaus, sister and brother, of Lancaster, are both enlistees in the U. S. armed forces.

Lieutenant Amelia Nicklaus, formerly of 135 N. Marshall St., enlisted in the Army Medical Corps and is serving as a nurse overseas, according to word received by her sister, Mrs. Albert Shaub. She is a graduate of Catholic High School and St. Joseph's Hospital School of Nursing. Before her enlistment she served for two years at the Mt. Alto State Tuberculosis sanatorium and one year at the Veteran's Hospital in Coatesville.

Apprentice Seaman Paul Nicklaus, formerly of 534 Lancaster Ave., enlisted in the Navy and was called to active duty in February. He is attending a metalsmith school at the U. S. Naval Training Station in Jacksonville, Fla. He is a graduate of Catholic High School and was formerly employed by the Armstrong Cork Company.

Robert H. Adams, son of Mrs. Laura L. Adams, 808 Fremont St., and nephew of Mr. and Mrs. H. Freelen Groff, Quarryville, who has been promoted to warrant officer and assigned to Camp Davis, N. C. He is a graduate of Franklin and Marshall College, class of 1939, and entered the Army with the local National Guard unit called in September, 1940.

Staff Sergeant Charles M. Baile, grandson of Mr. and Mrs. David N. Trapnell, Old Philadelphia Pike, who was recently graduated from the Officers Training School at Carlisle and commissioned a second lieutenant in the Medical Administrative Corps of the Army. He enlisted January 25, 1940, and served two years in Hawaii, including the time of the Jap raid on December 7, 1941.

Pvt. Earl W. Walters, who is stationed at South Hingham, Mass., with an Army infantry unit, is spending an eight-day furlough with his parents, Mr. and Mrs. Elmer Walters, Lancaster R5. He entered the service in February.

2nd Lt. John P. Schnitzer, 544 W. Lemon st., Lancaster, who was promoted from the rank of Corp. upon his graduation from the Anti-aircraft Artillery school of the Officer Candidate Division, Camp Davis, N.C. Schnitzer was formerly a sales engineer at the Armstrong Cork Co.

Carlton Moyer, stationed with the Army Air Forces at Key Field, Miss., has been promoted from private first class to corporal, technician 5th grade. He is the son of Mr. and Mrs. Perc Moyer, 216 E. Orange St., and was formerly employed by the Lancaster Newspapers.

Lester E. Gentzler, 21, formerly of 449 N. Market St., who has been promoted from private to private first class, according to word received by his friends here. He is stationed in Hawaii with an infantry unit, and has been in the Army for 13 months. Pfc. Gentzler is a former employe of the Hubley Manufacturing Company.

Fifth class Technician Clarence H. McKelvey, who has returned to his post at Fort Bragg, N. C., after spending a five-day furlough with his mother, Mrs. Roy E. Duke, 51 W. Farnum St., and his aunt, Mrs. Ben Miller. He has been in service for nine months.

Pvt. Edward S. Harrison, son of Mr. and Mrs. Jack Harrison, 141 E. King St., who is stationed at Camp Pickett, Va. He was inducted June 13.

UNIVERSITY CLUB OFFICERS

New Vice Presidents and Director Named; Committee Heads.

Lewis H. Wessinger was elected first vice president of the University Club of Lancaster by members of the board of directors last night. He succeeds Howard E. Campbell, employe of the Armstrong Cork Company, who resigned because of his transfer to Beaver Falls, it was announced by William G. Johnstone Jr., president of the club.

Robert B. Thompson was elected as second vice president to succeed Wessinger, while M. Norman Bair was elected to fill Campbell's vacancy on the board of directors.

Johnstone announced the appointment of Wessinger as chairman of the program committee; Bair as chairman of the membership committee, and Christian R. Herr as chairman of the entertainment committee.

TOTS FIND MONEY; REWARDED BY BONDS

PITTSBURGH, Aug. 28. — (AP) — Two Pittsburgh tots who found $440, then tried to exchange it with their grandmother for six cents to purchase ice cream cones, have war bonds today—along with enough money for quite a few cones.

"Grandma, Grandma," shouted five-year-old Donnie Hetricks, waving the money, "This is for you if you'll give us each three cents for an ice cream cone."

Terry Harkins, 3, stood by, nodding gleefully.

Mrs. Louise Tallent learned the children had picked it up out of an envelope on the street and then discarded the envelope. She found the envelope, bearing the name of Barney McGinley, prominent Pittsburgh sports promoter.

McGinley would only take $400. He gave each boy $20 and Mrs. Tallent said they both would buy $25 war bonds and still have money left for ice cream—all they want.

SIXTEEN PAGES OF PRINT

By ANNE DIAMOND

This is to Mr. Average Citizen. This is to the Common Man. Not only to you, but about you. You see, Sir, it's the little people that make the wheels go round. So it's important that they understand something as vital as the newspaper, especially during a war when the daily newspaper counts for so much.

I bought my paper last night just as I always do. I tossed out three pennies for sixteen pages of print. It's a matter of habit; we Americans are brought up on newspapers. And on the bus newspapers were everywhere. But did these people realize what a newspaper does, what it accomplishes?

A newspaper, I began confidently to myself, achieves...uh...it achieves...Well, there's the news, and the advertising. We get all kinds of information and news, and merchandising...

Then I realized I couldn't answer! What **does** a daily newspaper achieve?

To get a fuller picture of a commonplace American habit, I read back into newspaper history. I read of autocratic governments and ignorance plodding wearisomely along the road of humanity while news reporting was by mouth or by letter. When I looked for newspapers comparable to our present-day press, there were none! How could people live in this world for many centuries without a newspaper? I had to span the centuries to the **Acta Diurna** of Rome to find remarkable news reporting.

4th of the Kalends of April, 585

It thundered and an oak was struck with lightning on that part of the Mount Palatine called Summa Belia, early in the afternoon ...A fray happened in a tavern at the lower end of the Banker's Street, in which the keeper of the Hog-In-Armour Tavern was dangerously wounded....Tertinius, the Edile, fined the butchers for selling meat which had not been inspected by the overseers of the markets. The fine is to be employed in building a chapel to the Temple of the Goddess Tellus.

* * * * *

Rome's **Acta Diurna**, candidly brief, published the daily events of Rome. The Romans, regarding it as a public institution, placed their paper in the Hall of Liberty. At the death of Julius Caesar, the privilege of publishing news was withdrawn. For the following two thousand years the world was without a press system. For two thousand years absolute governments deliberately banned news dissemination. For two thousand years the people struggled hopelessly for power to assert themselves.

A newspaper could have given them strength and hope, but news instruments were suppressed. What was the magical quality in lines of print? What ethereal power did authority fear?

That the Hall of Liberty housed the **Acta Diurna** was strangely symbolical of the answer to this question. Tyranny deliberately suppressed news institutions because of the power they implied. The power to bring information and education to the masses. Power to become the voice of the people, to strike out for them in pursuit of—freedom!

The voice of the people, however, was checked. Human progress was cruelly, agonizingly slow. But there were a few who would know, a few who would fight to know. Their force settled ultimately in a strange new world. The men and women who landed on the shores of the New World were big men and little men—most of them just ordinary.

In 1671, Sir William Berkeley, governor of Virginia, wrote his English king: "But, I thank God, we have not free schools nor printing; and I hope we shall not these hundred years. For learning has brought disobedience and heresy and sects into the world; and printing has divulged them and libels against the government. God keep us from both."

Sir William's prayer beat against deaf ears. During the years of clearing land and working it, the little people grew away from England. They became hardy men with new, radical ideas, and they resented being pushed around. At first they were too busy to read. As a matter of fact, most of them didn't know how to read; but a literature slowly evolved. The pot of the Revolution was simmering. As the issues of rights came forward, the people demanded news. More important, they demanded a spokesman for their eager ideas. Newspapers sprang from heated discussions and contested views. The Revolution made the first American literature one of pamphlets and newspapers.

* * * * *

Printers and editors advanced timidly into the untested field of journalism. They were awed by its possibilities. It was as boundless, as tremendous as the strange country they were exploring. Benjamin Franklin reported quizzically: "That hence arises the peculiar Unhappiness of That Business, which other Callings are no way liable to; that they who follow printing being scarce able to do any thing in their way of getting a Living, which shall not probably give Offense to some and perhaps to many: Whereas the Smith, the Shoemaker ... may work indifferently for People of all Persuasions, without offending any of them..."

He almost disclosed the secret of the press. The press **is** the people. It is run for people about people by people. That is why the achievements of the people are the achievements of the press. That is why the will of the people expressed in print is invincible.

This was proved in 1776. To help the Colonists achieve their goals, the Colonial press grew and gained weight, literally and figuratively. In 1775 there were forty-eight papers, and in 1776 a letter to England complained of their influence: "Among other Engines, which have raised the present commotion next to the indecent Harangues of the Preachers, none has had a more extensive or stronger Influence than the Newspapers of the respective Colonies. One is astonished to see with what avidity they are sought after, and how implicitly they are believed, by the great Bulk of the people."

The Revolutionary War proved the new journalism a respectable enterprise. It helped the people voice their grievances. It made them, at last, articulate. It helped them defeat centuries-old tyranny and heartbreak. Thus the bonds were broken. Americans found voice; they found a machine for making their voice strong and vibrant. That they would not relinquish this was evidenced in 1791 when into the first amendment of the Constitution was written: "Congress shall make no law...abridging the freedom...of the press."

* * * * *

A free press! The world was aghast at the temerity of these Colonists. Not even the noble culture of Rome had dared a free press.

In 1800 a foreign visitor commented that "the influence and circulation of newspapers is great beyond anything ever known in Europe. In truth, nine-tenths of the population read nothing else... Every village, nay, almost every hamlet, has its press...Newspapers penetrate to every crevice of the nation."

In 1814 a Boston paper observed: "The insatiable appetite for news ...has given rise to a general form of salutation on the meeting of friends and strangers: What's the news?"

In truth, the news story is the greatest story we know because it is the story of humanity. All the multiple facets of the human mind and of human actions are portrayed by the paper. Once that printed story is quelled, the people are bound and progress marches haltingly. With a free press as a part of their basic thought, the American Colonists began an exhilarating advance.

After the Revolution, the people added to the task of building homes the task of building a country. The horizons were limitless and the people dauntless. The land bustled with industry. The hum of the presses became a growing crescendo. Under the eyes of Bennett, Greeley, Nelson, Dana, Godkin, Bowles, Raymond, newspapers doubled and tripled, newspaper functions expanded, newspaper influence became an incredible factor in the life of America.

In addition to news, the paper began to offer interpretation, entertainment, and information. It became a market place. It established itself as a forum where the public could meet in print to discuss, to argue, to buy and sell. It was a social and political leader because it became a natural well of information and power.

When a handful of papers and a little band of pioneers successfully asserted their rights to knowledge and government, they cut a new notch in man's progress. But they didn't declare a holiday, because they were busy showing the world they were right. The result is an American standard of living which leads the world. And when the little people shook off the chain of bondage and founded a new fellowship of freedom, they proved that the dangerous implication in a free press was freedom itself. A free press is a free people.

That's what I want to tell you, Sir. You may be just a little man working in a garage, or in a store, or at a desk; but you have more strength than the world has known. Because when you speak, you and your wife and all your relatives, there's a voice in this country that will reflect your wishes and make you powerful. But you must be jealous of this right, and you must treasure it. For the power of the press can be debased. In this decade, what we hold to be the straightforward, the honest in living was changed because of a so-called "new order" that thrived on brutality and trickery. We learned that freedom was suddenly old-fashioned and that a free press was outmoded. After watching the press grow to a constructive force, we saw it break men—the little men like you and me.

"The press is an instrument for the education of the people, which the state has to secure for itself with reckless energy, in order to place the same at the service of the state and nation."

These words were ominous. A controlled press is a horrible force; but Adolf Hitler was not speculating. In the first eighteen months of Nazi Socialist government in Germany, more than a thousand German newspapers died. Slowly, the voices of the German people were stilled.

"The freedom of the press which includes the right to work against the national interests to make itself an arena for intellectual acrobats has no place in the National Government."

* * * * *

Dr. Paul Joseph Goebbels frowned on a free press. In 1933, when he uttered these words, the first of many decrees was issued, and the German press began to "develop into a piano" on which the Ministry for Public Enlightenment and Propaganda might "play." Now there was only one voice in Germany.

Intent on goals which the world realized too late, Hitler would tolerate no obstructions. He isolated his people from the outside and from their own government. The press was the first to fall. From the past, the living voice of Thomas Jefferson: "No government ought to be without censors; and where the press is free, no one ever will." There could be no censors of the Nazi party; so there was no press.

The papers published were merely branches of Dr. Goebbels' propaganda ministry. They stopped fulfilling their rightful heritage which had taken so painfully long to achieve. The papers became appendages of the Nazi party. The press was a news-disseminating instrument—for the Party. The German press had been efficiently throttled. Now it no longer existed. Was it in vain that men had died for the right of humanity to speak?

Darkness mantled Germany. On all sides there was only the Nazi party. From all sides the hammer fell—Nazi, Nazi, Nazi. The news, too, was Nazi and, contrary to Nazi statistics, the ratio of readers to newspapers began to drop.

This artificial nursing of an entire country on half-truths, slanted stories, and bare lies was the first of its kind in the history of journalism. The results were tragic, at first, for the German people. In 1934 Edmond Taylor struck a dismal note: "It is hard to think of any place where the people live in such medieval ignorance as do the Germans." The results were tragic, at last, for the world. Since 1934 we have witnessed a parade of death, humiliation, sorrow, and subjugation that has brought us sharply to the retelling of values.

Liberty is dear today because we have seen others lose it. The press, as one instrument that will keep our liberty, has become suddenly precious. For it was with an enslaved press that the Nazis successfully isolated the German state, nursed the people on their miseries, and restored them to a new life of brutal mysticism.

America was on its way. Modern progress promised the unfolding of a better life. But we must stop again to fight for what we fought for two hundred years ago. The little man must suffer again and fight again. In the eighteenth century the press freed one people. In the twentieth, it destroyed another.

* * * * *

The present reveals two contrasting situations. In one, the party speaks; the people are dumb, their culture toppled, tragically undermined by the Nazi's use of modern weapons.

In this country, however, the people are free and the printed word is free. Liberty and life are synonymous. Our standard of living is the most advanced that history has recorded. This standard is based, not on one freedom but on three—social freedom, economic freedom, and political freedom.

We have a society built on the individual, not on class.

We have a society built on the highest standard of living attained by mankind.

We have a society in which every man is part of the government.

Who can boast better?

In two hundred years the press has helped establish in the United States people who are free socially, politically, and economically. These freedoms are combined into indistinguishable customs; but the results are clear. The American is mobile. His acts are not limited to a small area, his mind to a prejudiced view. You, Mr. Average Citizen, are a literate individual with an interest in an above-average life and a voice in your government.

The tradition of education and learning sprang from the remarkable newspaper-reading public which astounded outsiders in the nineteenth century. The press aided the schools in making the United States the most literate country in the world. In 1941, nineteen million high school students were graduated from high school courses. In one year, nineteen million educated boys and girls became dynamic factors in this country. And they'll stay that way. Their education was stimulated a century ago by newspapers, and the newspapers will add to their knowledge, will keep them not dumb, not silent, but a vital part of the United States of America.

* * * * *

As important as the newspapers' ability to stimulate interest in learning is their tremendous influence on individual freedom. In the eighteenth century, infant papers argued the freedom of man and his right to self-government. Newspapers have always defended this right and supported it. Nowhere today are men as personally free as in the United States.

This is due to newspaper reporting of American political life. The paper prints political news, discusses it, argues it, acts as a forum for it. The paper keeps alive the tradition of the New England town hall where every man's voice affected his government.

These social and political freedoms are themselves based on economic freedom.

Advertising, as we know it, is only a little less new to the world than our system of journalism. The new theory of advertising has been attacked and defended until the main issue has been forgotten. We realize, when we see others deprived of what we consider carelessly as necessities, that advertising has brought us benefits which will far outshine its faults. Because of advertising we use luxuries as a matter of habit.

Bathtubs were once a luxury in the United States. Advertising has made them a household necessity. The old $1,500 automobile is now the better-made $800 car. The twelve-cent can of soup once sold for twenty cents. But such statistics illustrating the driving power of advertising are endless.

Advertising created demands for better living. It created improved products at lower costs. It saved money for the consumer and repaid the manufacturer for his extra diligence.

There they are. The three most radical doctrines of human progress—social, political, and economic freedom. And the press was their publicity agent.

The newspaper doesn't just print news. Its jobs are vital, pertaining to these three parts of our lives. It offers the knowledge of men who interpret the news and give the story behind the story. Many times it puts the light of print on hidden plots and vicious desires. It offers its support when other institutions fail in responsible citizenship.

* * * * *

The newspaper is also a forum for controversy, for the crystallization of issues, all for the voice of every man—the average man whose voice is ultimately the government.

The newspaper spreads from the Atlantic to the Pacific a culture based on the benefits of industrial advertising. We wear better clothes, we eat better foods, we live all-round better lives because of our newspapers.

This is in my sixteen-page paper, and in the millions coming before it, and in the millions coming after. It's important for you and me to know that, Sir. Because, in this country, you and I have the last word.

Now you see what the press achieves. It's not all the glorious, munificent goals of which orators are inclined to spout. It's more than news, or interpretation, or entertainment. It's your freedom and mine. When a press points the way to a three-fold freedom, and holds the people to a three-fold freedom, that press has attained the simple and tremendous goal for which it was born.

Anne Diamond, senior in the School of Journalism at Syracuse university, is the 1942 winner of the gold medal and $1,000 cash prize offered by the American Newspapers Publishers' association to the student in a school or department of journalism who produced the best monograph on the achievement of the daily newspaper in public service.

Contestants, both men and women, from all parts of the United States competed for the prize which was awarded this year for the first time at the meeting of the American Newspaper Publishers' association just held in New York city. Valued at more than $1,000, the medal received by Miss Diamond, whose home is in Cedar Falls, Iowa, contains $600 worth of gold.

MEETING TONIGHT

The Women's Auxiliary of the Seventh Ward Republican Club will meet this Thursday evening in the club rooms, 134 Locust St.

BENEFIT CARD PARTY

A new deal card party will be held Thursday evening at 8:30 o'clock in St. Mary's hall for the benefit of St. Catherine's Catholic church, Quarryville.

BLACKOUT VIOLATOR FINED

Charles F. Stark, Mount Joy, pleaded guilty to charges of violating the blackout laws before Justice of the Peace George Schenck, Landisville, and was fined $10 and costs.

Prosecution was brought by County Detective Weller on the complaint of Jay T. Dombach, air raid warden of Sector 28, Landisville, who said Stark refused to stop his auto when whistled down by a warden during the surprise blackout test of Aug. 18.

OUT OUR WAY By WILLIAMS

WHY, THIS IS A BARGAIN AT THREE DOLLARS A MONTH! IT'S ONLY FOUR BLOCKS FROM HOME AN' THE ONLY OTHER ONE FOR RENT IS SEVEN BLOCKS--WITH A HORSE AN' CHICKENS IN IT!
YOU NEVER GET A BARGAIN--THEY GAVE YOU THE SIDE WITH NO SHINGLES ON THE ROOF! IF YOU'RE GOING TO KEEP THIS PLACE, PUT THE SIDE CURTAINS ON!
COPR. 1942 BY NEA SERVICE, INC. T. M. REG. U. S. PAT. OFF.
J.R.WILLIAMS 9-3

BORN THIRTY YEARS TOO SOON

Matinee				Evening			
ADULTS	68c	CHILDREN	22c	ADULTS	$1.00	CHILDREN	36c
U. S. Tax	7c	U. S. Tax	3c	U. S. Tax	.10	U. S. Tax	4c
Total	75c	Total	25c	Total	$1.10	Total	40c

Radio Program

THURSDAY, SEPT. 3, MORNING

5:30—WOR—Music; Digest; WABC — Reveille Sweetheart
6:30—WEAF—Charles Wooster; WOR — News; Digest; WABC—Arthur Godfrey
6:55—WABC—News; Arthur Godfrey
7:00—WEAF—News; Pat Barnes; WOR — News; Music; WJZ—Variety
7:30—WEAF—News; Let's Fight
7:45—WJZ, WABC—News
8:00—WEAF, WJZ—News; WOR — News; Aunt Jenny; WABC — News; Music; Talk
8:05—WEAF—Studio X
8:15—WJZ—Music
8:30—WEAF—News; Music; WOR—Happy Jim Parsons; WABC—Missus Goes A-Shopping
8:45—WOR—News; Music; WJZ—News; Songs; WABC—Adelaide Hawley
9:00—WEAF—Garry Moore; WOR—Dear Imogene; WJZ—Nancy Boothe Craig; WABC—News; Radio Reader
9:30—WEAF—String Orch.; WOR—News; Music; WJZ—Breakfast Club; WABC—Burl Ives
9:45—WEAF—Jack Turner; WABC—Thus We Live
10:00—WEAF—Bess Johnson; WOR—BBC News; WJZ—Music; WABC—Valiant Lady
10:15—WEAF—Bachelor's Children; WOR—The Johnson Family; WJZ — Helen Hiett; WABC—Stories America Loves
10:30—WEAF—Help Mate; WOR—Happy Jim Parsons; WJZ — Hank Lawson Knights; WABC—Honeymoon Hill
10:45—WEAF—Young Dr. Malone; WOR—Beauty—Richard Willis; WJZ—Chaplain Jim, U. S. A. WABC—Fletcher Wiley
11:00—WEAF—Road of Life; WOR—News; Bessie Beatty; WJZ—Music and Interviews; WABC—Mary Lee Taylor
11:15—WEAF—Vic and Sade; WABC — Second Husband
11:30—WEAF—Against the Storm; WJZ—House in the Country; WABC—Bright Horizon
11:45—WEAF—David Harum; WJZ—Jack Little Orch.; WABC—Aunt Jenny

AFTERNOON

12:00—WEAF—News; Music; WOR—Boake Carter; WJZ—Texas Rangers; WABC—News; Kate Smith
12:15—WOR—Variety; WJZ—Nancy Boothe Craig; WABC—Big Sister
12:25—WJZ—News; Farm and Home Hour
12:30—WEAF—President Roosevelt (Also WOR, WJZ, WABC, WQXR)
12:45—WEAF—Carey Longmire; WOR—Bill Hay; WABC—Our Gal Sunday
1:00—WEAF—Mary Margaret McBride; WOR—Legion of Friends; WJZ—Baukhage; WABC—Life Can Be Beautiful
1:15—WJZ—Edward MacHugh; WABC—Woman in White
1:30—WOR—News; String Ensemble; WJZ—Dr. Francis C. Stifler; WABC—Vic and Sade
1:45—WEAF—J. W. Vandercook; WOR—Karl Zomar; WJZ—Lopez Orch.; WABC—The Goldbergs
2:00—WEAF—Biblical Drama; WOR — Martha Deane; WABC—Young Dr. Malone; WABC—Joyce Jordan
2:15—WEAF—Lonely Women; WJZ—Ted Malone;
2:30—WEAF—The Guiding Light; WOR—News; Baseball Preview; WJZ—J. G. McDonald; WABC—We Love and Learn
2:45—WEAF—Hymns of All Churches; WABC—Pepper Young
2:55—WOR—Baseball: Giants-St. Louis
3:00—WEAF—Mary Marlin; WJZ—Variety; WABC—David Harum
3:15—WEAF—Ma Perkins; WABC—Brush Creek Music
3:30—WEAF—Pepper Young; WJZ—Interviews; Music; WABC—U. S. Navy Band
3:45—WEAF—Right to Happiness
4:00—WEAF—Backstage Wife; WJZ—War Bond Campaign Show; WABC—News; Listen Neighbor
4:15—WEAF—Stella Dallas; WJZ—Club Matinee
4:30—WEAF—Lorenzo Jones; WABC—Health Talk
4:45—WEAF—Young Widder Brown; WJZ—Swing Records
5:00—WEAF—When a Girl Marries; WJZ—The Sea Hound; WABC—Are You a Genius?
5:15—WEAF—Portia Faces Life; WJZ—Hop Harrigan; WABC—Mother and Dad
5:30—WEAF—Music; Tennis Summary; WOR—Superman; WJZ—Jack Armstrong; WABC—Landt Trio and Curley
5:45—WEAF—The Bartons; WOR—News; Music; Talks; WJZ—Secret City; WABC—Bernie Orch.

EVENING

6:00—WEAF—Funny Money Man; WOR—Uncle Don; WJZ—News; Music; WABC—Frazier Hunt
6:15—WEAF—George Putnam; WJZ—Joe Hasel; WABC—To Be Announced
6:30—WEAF—Petroleum Production; WOR—News; Here's Morgan; WJZ—Milt Herth Trio; WABC—Vera Barton
6:45—WEAF—Bill Stern; WJZ—Lowell

More of RADIO on Page 14

Thursday, Sept. 3, 1942

TODAY'S HIGHLIGHTS

9:30 A. M. BLU	BREAKFAST CLUB Swift & Co.
12:30 P. M. NBC	PRESIDENT ROOSEVELT International Student Assembly
6:00 P. M. WGAL	UNITED PRESS NEWS Sunshine Beer
8:00 P. M. NBC	MAXWELL HOUSE Coffee Time
8:30 P. M. NBC	ALDRICH FAMILY Comedy Serial

7:00—WGAL—War News
7:15—WGAL—Musical Clock
7:45—WGAL—Let's Fight
8:00— NBC—World News Roundup
8:15— NBC—Do You Remember
8:45—WGAL—Song Styles
8:55—WGAL—Pensupreme Dairy Dollars
9:00— NBC—Show Without A Name
9:30— BLU—Breakfast Club, Swift & Co.
9:45— NBC—Happy Jack
10:00— MUT—BBC News
10:15—WGAL—Devotions, Rev. Trumpeter
10:30— BLU—Hank Lawson's Knights
10:45—WGAL—Listen to Liebert
10:55—WGAL—United Press News
11:00—WGAL—Money Club
11:30— BLU—House in the Country
11:45— BLU—Little Jack Little
11:58—WGAL—Luncheon Club
12:15—WGAL—Dolly Madison News
12:30— NBC—President Roosevelt
12:45— BLU—Farm and Home Hour
1:00— BLU—Baukhage Talking
1:15— BLU—Gospel Singer
1:30— BLU—Everyman's Book
1:45— NBC—John W. Vandercook, News
2:00—WGAL—Safety Talk: Officer Strayer
2:15— BLU—Ted Malone
2:30— BLU—News Summary
2:45— BLU—Jack Baker, Songs
3:00— BLU—Prescott Presents
3:30— BLU—Men of the Sea
3:45— BLU—15 Minutes from Broadway
4:00— BLU—Club Matinee
4:55— BLU—Associated Press News
5:00— MUT—Willard Trio
5:15—WGAL—Bargain Bandwagon
6:00—WGAL—Sunshine Beer Presents United Press News
6:15—WGAL—Dinner Melodies
6:30—WGAL—Sports Parade: General Tire Co.
6:45—WGAL—Dick Jurgens Orch.
7:00— NBC—Fred Waring Orchestra
7:15—WGAL—U. S. Recruiting
7:30—WGAL—What Do You Know
8:00— NBC—Maxwell House Coffee Time
8:30— NBC—Aldrich Family
9:00— BLU—America's Town Meeting
9:55— BLU—Molasses 'N' January
10:00— MUT—Raymond Gram Swing
10:15—WGAL—Arms For Victory
10:30— BLU—Tommy Dorsey Treasure Show
10:45— MUT—To Be Announced
11:00—WGAL—United Press News
11:15— NBC—Dinning Sisters
11:30— NBC—Nocturne
12:00—WGAL—War News—Sign Off—Adv.

St. Louis Cardinals New World Baseball Champions

National Leaguers Top Yanks 4-2 In 5th Game On Kurowski's Homer

Johnny Beazley, 23-Year-Old-Rookie Pitcher, Wins Second Of Four Straight Games For Cards; Rizzuto And Slaughter Also Homer

OFFICIAL BOX SCORE

ST. LOUIS (National League)

	AB	R	H	O	A	E
Brown, 2b	3	0	2	3	4	2
T. Moore, cf	3	1	1	3	0	0
Slaughter, rf	4	1	2	2	0	0
Musial, lf	4	0	0	2	0	0
W. Cooper, c	4	1	2	2	1	0
Hopp, 1b	3	0	0	9	2	1
Kurowski, 3b	4	1	1	1	1	0
Marion, ss	4	0	0	3	5	0
Beazley, p	4	0	1	2	0	1
Totals	33	4	9	27	13	4

NEW YORK (American League)

	AB	R	H	O	A	E
Rizzuto, ss	4	1	2	7	1	0
Rolfe, 3b	4	1	1	1	0	0
Cullenbine, rf	4	0	0	3	0	0
DiMaggio, cf	4	0	1	3	0	0
Keller, lf	4	0	1	1	0	0
Gordon, 2b	4	0	1	3	3	0
Dickey, c	4	0	0	4	0	0
Stainback, z	0	0	0	0	0	0
Priddy, 1b	3	0	0	5	1	1
Ruffing, p	3	0	1	0	1	0
Selkirk, zz	1	0	0	0	0	0
Totals	35	2	7	27	6	1

z—Ran for Dickey in 9th.
zz—Batted for Ruffing in 9th.

ST. LOUIS (N. L.) ...... 000 101 002—4
NEW YORK (A. L.) .... 100 100 000—2

Runs batted in—Rizzuto, Slaughter, DiMaggio, W. Cooper, Kurowski 2. Home runs—Rizzuto, Slaughter, Kurowski. Sacrifices—T. Moore, Hopp. Double plays—Gordon, Rizzuto and Priddy; Hopp, Marion and Brown. Left on bases—New York (A. L.) 7; St. Louis (N. L.) 5. Earned runs—New York (A. L.) 2; St. Louis (N. L.) 4. Base on balls—Ruffing 1 (Brown); Beazley 1 (Priddy). Strikeouts—Ruffing 3 (T. Moore, Beazley 2); Beazley 2 (Gordon, Ruffing). Umpires—Magerkurth (N. L.) plate; Summers (A. L.) 1b; Barr (N. L.) 2b; Hubbard (A. L.) 3b. Time 1:58. Attendance—69,052 (paid).

Yankee Stadium, New York—(AP)—The unconquerable St. Louis Cardinals swept over the New York Yankees, 4 to 2, Monday and into the World's Championship of baseball as George (Whitey) Kurowski capitalized their indomitable spirit with a two-run ninth inning homer for their fourth straight victory in the five-game 1942 World Series.

It took a mighty battle to make the renowned Yankees drop their first World Series since another Cardinal club turned the trick in 1926, but the ripping, roaring Redbirds convinced a great crowd of 69,052 fans that they were made of the stuff of champions.

After winning three consecutive games with a show of dazzling speed, the Cardinals crushed the Bronx Bombers Monday at their own game — homer hitting — although they also continued their reckless running and received a wonderfully pitched seven-hit game from lean and confident Johnny Beazley, the 23-year-old rookie who also won the second game of the Series at St. Louis.

The climax came in the lowering dusk with visibility so poor that many of the fans in the huge concrete arena were unable to see where Kurowski's tremendous fly landed, but they could see leftfielder Charley Keller of the Yanks go tumbling head first over the low wall and into the front seats in an unavailing effort to reach the ball and they could see Walker Cooper and Kurowski trotting around the bases with the runs that ended New York's long domination of World Series play.

Cooper, whose hitting and catching throughout the Series had been nothing less than superb, opened the ninth with a sharp single to right-center and was sacrificed to second.

Charley (Red) Ruffing, the old Yankee wheelhorse who pitched hitless ball for 7 2-3 innings in the opener at St. Louis, striking out Kurowski three straight times and getting credit for New York's only triumph of the Series, then went to work carefully on the tow-headed rookie third baseman from Reading, Pa.

Kurowski Does It

He got the count to one and one and served up a half-speed pitch that must have hung exactly where Kurowski wanted it, because he took a lusty swing and the ball made one big arc into the lower stands.

It was a knockout and everyone knew it, although the Yanks got two men on base with none out in their final chance. The Cardinals responded to this threat with typical stamina. Joe Gordon opened with a single and second baseman Jimmy Brown fumbled an easy roller by Bill Dickey. However, Gordon was picked off second on a beautiful throw by Cooper. Brown redeemed himself by running onto the grass to scoop up a blooper by Gerry Priddy and then Brown threw out pinch-hitter George Selkirk for the final out as the crowd rose into a demonstration that hardly could have been louder or more appreciative if it had been at Sportsman's Park in St. Louis.

The defeat was the Yanks' first in nine World Series since 1926 and also the first time that any one pitcher had beaten them twice in a Series since Jess Haines and old Grover Cleveland Alexander each accomplished that assignment in '26.

Beazley, cool and calm as an iceberg, was tagged for a home run by little Phil Rizzuto the first time he took his bat off his shoulder in leading off for New York in the first inning. But it didn't faze the sensational right-hander, who won 21 games in the National League this season, and he did not get rattled either when the Yanks made explosive gestures in the fourth and fifth frames.

Slaughter Ties Score

Enos (Country) Slaughter, playing his first and last World Series before entering the army, had tied the score with a homer into the right-field stands to open the fourth and the Yanks battled back for a run in their half of the same inning.

Red Rolfe led off with a drag bunt down the first baseline, beat it out for a single and raced on to second as Beazley made a wild throw after fielding the ball. Rolfe advanced to third on a long fly by Roy Cullenbine and came home as Joe DiMaggio banged the first pitch for a single to left.

Keller also hit the first pitch for a single to right, putting DiMaggio on third, and for the moment it looked like Beazley might be tottering. Manager Billy Southworth came out of the dugout to soothe the youngster and he fanned Gordon on four pitches, then made Dickey hit into an easy force play.

The Yanks had their one other chance in the fifth when with one out Ruffing topped the ball between third and the pitcher's mound and beat it out for a hit. Rizzuto rapped an easy grounder to first baseman Johnny Hopp, who tried to catch Ruffing at second and instead made a wild throw

More WORLD SERIES on Page 11

FACTS—FIGURES

By The Associated Press

Final standings:

	W.	L.	P.C.
ST. LOUIS (N. L.)	4	1	.800
NEW YORK (A. L.)	1	4	.200

First game (at Sportsman's Park):

	R.	H.	E.
NEW YORK (A. L.)	7	11	0
ST. LOUIS (N. L.)	4	7	4

Ruffing, Chandler (9), and Dickey; M. Cooper, Gumbert (8), Lanier (9), and W. Cooper.

Second game (at Sportsman's Park):

	R.	H.	E.
NEW YORK (A. L.)	3	10	2
ST. LOUIS (N. L.)	4	6	0

Bonham and Dickey; Beazley and W. Cooper.

Third game (at Yankee Stadium):

	R.	H.	E.
ST. LOUIS (N. L.)	2	5	1
NEW YORK (A. L.)	0	6	1

White and W. Cooper; Chandler, Breuer (9), Turner (9), and Dickey.

Fourth game (At Yankee Stadium):

	R.	H.	E.
ST. LOUIS (N. L.)	9	12	1
NEW YORK (A. L.)	6	10	1

M. Cooper, Gumbert (6), Pollet (6), Lanier (7), and W. Cooper; Borowy, Donald (4), Bonham (7), and Dickey.

Fifth game (At Yankee Stadium):

	R.	H.	E.
ST. LOUIS (N. L.)	4	9	4
NEW YORK (A. L.)	2	7	1

Beazley and W. Cooper; Ruffing and Dickey.

Financial figures:
Fifth game:

Paid attendance	69,052
Gross receipts	$ 266,858.00
Commissioner's share	$ 40,028.70
Each club's share	$ 56,707.325
Each league's share	$ 56,707.325

Financial figures: (Five games)

Paid attendance	276,717
Gross receipts	$1,105,249.00
Players' share	$ 427,579.41
Commissioner's share	$ 85,299.60
Each club's share	$ 82,360.835
Each league's share	$ 82,360.835
U. S. O. share (x)	$ 362,926.65

(x)-United Service Organizations received entire $100,000 from sale of radio rights (not included in gross receipts) and 49 per cent of receipts from third and fourth games. U. S. O. also would have received all receipts from sixth and seventh games if they had been necessary.

Players shared only in first four games. Commissioner, leagues and clubs shared in first and second games and received all receipts of fifth game.

Yankees Pull Double Play On Cardinals

Jimmy Brown (sliding) of the St. Louis Cardinals was forced at second base on Enos Slaughter's grounder to Yankee Second Baseman Joe Gordon in the first inning of the fifth World Series game Monday, and this shows Shortstop Phil Rizzuto firing the ball to first to complete the double play. Umpire is George Barr.

Kurowski, Reading Youth, Clouts Homer To Windup Interesting Series

Yankee Stadium, New York—(AP)—Well, it's all over, chum—and if you don't believe it either, just think how Joe McCarthy feels.

A guy named Kurowski, out of Reading, Pa., busted it up with a homer. Wanna know why? It seems Whitey can't sleep on trains, and he didn't want to have to take that long ride back to St. Loo tonight in case the Yanks carried the Series into the sixth game. So, to give his railroad insomnia a break, he hit the jackpot off Red Ruffing.

Old Rufus the Red blew the decision, but he was certainly in there trying all the way. Reminds you of the time old Mike McTigue dropped a close "duke" to Paul Berlenbach and some back-slappers told him, "tough luck, Mike, you wus robbed."

"Ah, now," came back Mike, who'd been fighting about 20 years at that time, "look at the experience I'm gettin'."

Getting back to Kurowski, he's the same socker who hit the homer to beat the Dodgers, 2-1 on Sept. 12 and put the Cards in a tie for first place in the National League race. That's a nasty habit the kid has.

The Card's dressing room after the game was a nice quiet place for a guy with a nervous breakdown. They were running around and hollering so much you'd think they just won the World Series. Come to think of it, that's just what they did.

The Yanks' club-room was like the upstairs office in the First National Bank, with the president wondering whether he ought to loan Luke Glutz a fast fifty.

Before the game, Beazley was about as nervous as the inside of your icebox. He sat on the dugout steps whistling accompaniments to the band in center field. Needless to say, his whistle repertoire included neither "The Yanks Are Coming" or "Who's Afraid of the Big Bad Wolf?"

There was so much haze and overcast hanging over the outfield that Moore and DiMaggio in center were practically out of sight of the stands.

The fur-lined medal of honor for umpires goes to Cal (call me Tiny) Hubbard. He's the only ump who didn't have a row with a player throughout the Series. After all, when you're six-four and pack 240 pounds, nobody's gonna pick on you unless he's carrying brass knucks.

The first two times the Cards took their bats off their shoulder in the first inning, the net result was a strikeout and double play. This is how it was: Brown walked on four pitches. Moore had two strikes called on him, then fanned. Slaughter's first swing ended up in the twin killing. You can't say that was getting "the mostest of the bestest."

With casualties the way they were among Yankee infielders, it's no wonder Coach Art Fletcher thought twice before letting Frank Crosetti pitch batting practice. "And if you get hit out there," Fletch told him, "I'm taking the next boat to the Solomons before McCarthy catches up with me."

GEORGE KUROWSKI
(St. Louis Cardinals)

On the other hand, the first swing Rizzuto took for the Yanks, he belted a homer. This represented one fourth of the Scooter's four-bagger production for the entire regular season.

Brown took Keller's grounder in the second kneeling on the base line. It looked for a minute like he was going to meet it head on and rassle it three falls to a finish.

With Priddy on first in the third, Ruffing laid down a sacrifice that went for a double play. If that's sacrificing, what would you call hari kari?

Slaughter hit the first pitch of the fourth inning into the lower right field stands, right under the air-raid sign that reads "alert." Which is just what Country was on that one. After the inning was over and Slaughter went out to his right field spot, the bleacherites in the neighborhood gave him the biggest hand any ball player has received out that way since a guy named Ruth patrolled the same beat.

The American flag and World Series banners were so limp on the center field flagpole it looked like there wasn't a mouthful of air in the house.

Southworth pulled his infield in on DiMaggio in the fourth with a runner on third. This was like parting your hair with a meat cleaver, because Joe dumped a single over third for a run.

It was error, single, single in the fourth, and the Yanks began to look like—well, like the Yanks. Then the slow-moving Dickey tried to bunt with two away. Who's looney now?

The biggest surprise of the Series wasn't the Cards winning. It came in the fifth inning, when Beazley, who has no more use for a bat than an extra leg, poked a clean bingle into right. The only bigger rabbit that could have popped out of the hat would have been if McCarthy sent Lefty Gomez in to pinch hit—and Lefty clouted a homer.

The Yanks loaded the bags in the fifth and Southworth came out for a chat with Beazley. It's a safe bet it wasn't to ask how the folks are back in Nashville. When DiMaggio came up with the bags still loaded, Southworth popped out to the mound again. About the only thing you can tell a flinger in that kind of a spot is "it's every man for theirself, pal." But DiMag grounded into a force play and Beazley just got out of the hot water before he was parboiled.

In the sixth, Moore and Slaughter each whacked the first pitch for successive singles, and the Yankee pullpen came to life like a guy with bunions getting a hot foot. The next three batters went down, but a run came in on a fly, and for the second time the Cards had knotted it up all pretty like a wet shoelace.

Gordon went down weakly for the third time in a row in the sixth, and a fellow named Durocher, who had Gordonitis all during the 1941 Series, swore it wasn't true.

Ruffing teased Marion with so many dipsy-doo pitches in the seventh it was like a man trying to palm a rubber bone off on a hungry dog.

Brown led off the Cards in the eighth with a single and once more the fire alarm went off in the Yank bullpen. It was only a one-alarmer, though, and Ruffing put it out by himself.

Came the ninth—and you know what happened. Kurowski plastered one into the left field corner and school was out. Whitey got his master's degree on that one, and the Yanks went back to kindergarten.

Joins U. S. Navy

TOM OLIVER

Word was received in this city Monday, that Tom Oliver, who managed the Lancaster Red Roses, of the Inter-State Baseball League, this past season, joined the United States Navy, at a recruiting station in Birmingham, Alabama.

Quite A Bird, Ex-Pelican, Pitcher Mr. Johnny Beazley

By WHITNEY MARTIN
Wide World Sports Columnist

New York—A wonderful bird is the ex-pelican, Johnny Beazley. The test of a man is the way he stands up under trouble and what this New Orleans graduate stood up under as he pitched the St. Louis Cardinals to a world championship Monday wasn't exactly a canopy of roses.

Particularly in the fifth inning, when it seemed the best players on the Yankee team were Jimmy Brown and Johnny Hopp. The kid just stood out there, with the bases full, through no fault of his own, and only one down. He just stood there and pawed the dirt with his hoof like a milkman's nag smelling his oats near the end of the route. Then he forced Roy Cullenbine to pop out and the great Joe DiMaggio to hit into a force out.

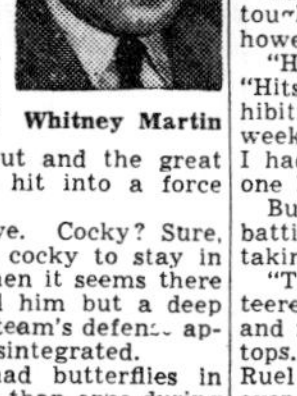

Whitney Martin

That took nerve. Cocky? Sure, a guy has to be cocky to stay in there pitching when it seems there is nothing behind him but a deep chasm; when his team's defense appears to have disintegrated.

He probably had butterflies in his stomach more than once during the long afternoon. Even while waiting, outwardly calm, for the teams to finish their batting and fielding practices, he was tied in a knot. A World Series game does that to a pitcher. We asked Bump Hadley about that just before Monday's game. In his 15 years in the majors the swart, stocky Bump pitched his share of World Series games.

"Sure, there's a difference," he said vehemently. "You're all tied up and think the game will never start. With me, and I think with most pitchers, though, the tension makes you pitch better. I know I surprised Bill Dickey by my control in one game, and I was plenty nervous to start with.

"I was a fast, wild pitcher," he grinned. "Later I developed some control but I lost plenty of games on walks."

Hadley, who was released by the Athletics last year and decided he'd better quit, as that was really going out through the trap-door in the basement, pitched against the Ruth-Gehrig powerhouses of the Yankee golden era. Gehrig was the toughest, he says.

"I never had much trouble with the Babe," he explains. "He was a wild swinger and I was a wild, fast pitcher, although I was known as a curve ball thrower. I'd just rear back and throw it past Ruth. I guess he always was expecting my curve.

Bump thinks Ted Williams is the toughest batter he has ever faced, however.

"He's really great," he explained. "Hits anything. I pitched an exhibition game against him about a week ago. I threw him the best I had, and he must have knocked one ball 475 feet."

Bump was standing behind the batting cage and Bill Dickey was taking his cuts.

"There's a catcher," he volunteered. "For giving you a target, and for all-around play, he's about tops. I think, though, that Muddy Ruel was the smartest catcher I ever worked with. The Yankees think a lot of this Walker Cooper of the Cardinals."

They should, for his single in the ninth put him on to score the winning run ahead of Kurowski in the ninth inning Monday, and his handling of pitchers has been superb. Particularly the way he handled the ex-pelican, Johnny Beazley, the kid from New Orleans.

We're a little worried about Beazley, though. The last we saw of him a bunch of frenzied Cardinal infielders were pounding and choking him to death over by first base.

COMPOSITE BOX SCORE

New York—(AP)—Following is the final composite box score of the five games of the 1942 World Series:

St. Louis (N. L.)	G	AB	R	H	2B	3B	HR	RBI	BB	SO	PCT	PO	A	E	PCT
Brown 2b	5	20	2	6	0	0	0	1	3	0	.300	6	16	3	.880
T. Moore cf	5	17	2	5	1	0	0	2	2	3	.294	15	0	0	1.000
Slaughter rf	5	19	3	5	1	0	1	2	3	2	.263	9	1	1	.909
Musial lf	5	18	2	4	0	0	0	2	4	0	.222	13	0	0	1.000
W. Cooper c	5	21	3	6	1	0	0	4	0	1	.286	24	2	1	.963
Hopp 1b	5	17	3	3	0	0	0	0	1	1	.176	46	3	1	.980
Kurowski 3b	5	15	3	4	0	1	1	5	2	3	.267	7	4	1	.917
Marion ss	5	18	2	2	0	1	0	3	1	2	.111	13	16	0	1.000
M. Cooper p	2	5	1	1	0	0	0	2	0	1	.200	0	1	0	1.000
Beazley p	2	7	0	1	0	0	0	0	0	5	.143	2	0	1	.667
White p	1	2	0	0	0	0	0	0	0	0	.000	0	0	0	.000
Gumbert p	2	0	0	0	0	0	0	0	0	0	.000	0	1	0	1.000
Lanier p	2	1	0	1	0	0	0	1	0	0	1.000	0	1	2	.333
Pollet p	0	0	0	0	0	0	0	0	0	0	.000	0	0	0	.000
Walker z	1	1	0	0	0	0	0	0	0	1	.000	0	0	0	.000
Sanders zz	2	1	1	0	0	0	0	0	1	0	.000	0	0	0	.000
O'Dea zzz	1	1	0	1	0	0	0	1	0	0	1.000	0	0	0	.000
Crespi zzzz	1	0	1	0	0	0	0	0	0	0	.000	0	0	0	.000
Totals	5	163	23	39	3	2	2	23	17	19	.239	135	45	10	.947

z—Batted for Gumbert, 8th inning, 1st game.
zz—Batted for Kurowski, 9th inning, 1st game; for Pollet 7th inning, 4th game.
zzz—Batted for Lanier, 9th inning, 1st game.
zzzz—Ran for O'Dea, 9th inning, 1st game.

New York (A. L.)	G	AB	R	H	2B	3B	HR	RBI	BB	SO	PCT	PO	A	E	PCT
Rizzuto ss	5	21	2	8	0	0	1	1	2	1	.381	15	14	1	.967
Rolfe 3b	4	17	5	6	2	0	0	0	1	2	.353	3	5	0	1.000
Crosetti 3b	1	3	0	0	0	0	0	0	0	1	.000	1	1	0	1.000
Cullenbine rf	5	19	3	5	1	0	0	2	1	2	.263	6	0	0	1.000
DiMaggio cf	5	21	3	7	0	0	0	3	0	1	.333	20	0	0	1.000
Keller lf	5	20	2	4	0	0	2	5	1	3	.200	12	1	0	1.000
Gordon 2b	5	21	1	2	1	0	0	0	0	7	.095	11	12	0	1.000
Dickey c	5	19	1	5	0	0	0	0	1	0	.263	25	1	1	.963
Hassett 1b	3	9	1	3	1	0	0	2	0	1	.333	15	1	1	.941
Priddy 3b-1b	3	10	0	1	1	0	0	1	1	0	.100	22	4	1	.963
Ruffing p-x	4	9	0	2	0	0	0	0	0	2	.222	0	1	0	1.000
Bonham p	2	2	0	0	0	0	0	0	1	0	.000	0	2	0	.000
Chandler p	2	2	0	0	0	0	0	0	0	1	.000	2	2	0	1.000
Breuer p	1	0	0	0	0	0	0	0	0	0	.000	0	0	1	.000
Turner p	1	0	0	0	0	0	0	0	0	0	.000	0	0	0	.000
Borowy p	1	1	0	0	0	0	0	0	0	1	.000	0	1	0	.000
Donald p	1	2	0	0	0	0	0	0	0	0	.000	0	0	0	.000
Stainback xx	2	0	0	0	0	0	0	0	0	0	.000	0	0	0	.000
Rosar xxx	1	1	0	1	0	0	0	0	0	0	1.000	0	0	0	.000
Selkirk xxxx	1	1	0	0	0	0	0	0	0	0	.000	0	0	0	.000
Totals	5	178	18	44	6	0	3	14	8	22	.247	132	45	5	.973

x—Batted for Bonham, 9th inning, 2nd game; for Chandler, 8th inning, 3rd game.
xx—Ran for Dickey, 9th inning, 2nd game; for Dickey, 9th inning, 5th game.
xxx—Batted for Bonham 9th inning 4th game.
xxxx—Batted for Ruffing, 9th inning, 5th game.

PITCHING

St. Louis (N. L.)	G	CG	IP	H	R	ER	BB	SO	WP	HB	W	L	PCT	ER AVG
Beazley	2	2	18	17	5	5	3	6	0	0	2	0	1.000	2.50
White	1	1	9	6	0	0	0	6	0	0	1	0	1.000	0.00
M. Cooper	2	0	13	17	10	8	4	9	0	0	0	1	.000	5.54
Gumbert	2	0	⅔	1	1	0	0	0	0	0	0	0	.000	0.00
Lanier	2	0	4	3	2	0	1	1	0	0	1	0	1.000	0.00
Pollet	1	0	⅓	0	0	0	0	0	0	0	0	0	.000	0.00

New York (A. L.)	G	CG	IP	H	R	ER	BB	SO	WP	HB	W	L	PCT	ER AVG
Ruffing	2	1	17⅔	14	8	8	7	11	0	0	1	1	.500	4.00
Bonham	2	1	11	9	4	5	3	3	0	0	0	1	.000	3.27
Chandler	2	0	8⅓	5	1	1	1	3	0	0	0	1	.000	1.13
Borowy	1	0	3	6	6	6	3	1	0	0	0	1	.000	18.00
Breuer	1	0	0	2	1	0	0	0	0	0	0	0	.000	0.00
Turner	1	0	1	0	0	0	1	0	0	0	0	0	.000	0.00
Donald	1	0	3	3	2	2	2	1	0	0	0	0	.000	6.00

COMPOSITE SCORE BY INNINGS

ST. LOUIS (N. L.) .... 201 701 318—23
NEW YORK (A. L.) .... 200 215 062—18

Earned runs—St. Louis (N. L.) 22; New York (A. L.) 13. Stolen bases—Rizzuto 2, Cullenbine. Sacrifices—Cullenbine, T. Moore 3, White, Hopp 2, Kurowski. Double plays—St. Louis 3 (Brown, Marion and Hopp), (Marion and Brown), (Hopp, Marion and Brown); New York 2 (Keller and Dickey), (Gordon, Rizzuto and Prddy). Left on bases—St. Louis 32; New York 34. Umpires—Summers and Hubbard (A. L.), Barr and Magerkurth (N. L.). Times of games—First, 2:35; second, 1:57; third, 2:30; fourth, 2:28; fifth, 1:58. Attendance by games—First, 34,385; second, 34,255; third, 69,123; fourth, 69,902; fifth, 69,052.

- - - Bowling Scores - - -

OVERLOOK "12" LEAGUE				
Spoons				
Longender'r	167	...	151	318
Fry	136	153	...	289
Aurand	...	167	137	304
Hall	152	186	151	489
Coder	133	147	135	415
Draude	184	182	190	556
	772	835	764	2371
Mashies				
Gibble	178	175	189	542
Hoffman	126	167	146	439
Leaman	...	...	147	147
Hurst	153	165	...	318
Forney	133	166	170	469
Slaugh	168	211	179	558
	758	884	831	2473
Jiggers				
McLane	160	187	164	511
Webster	149	189	165	503
Miller	167	176	155	498
Bitzer	151	167	148	466
Dowart	139	171	151	461
	766	890	783	2439
Putters				
Gorman	189	209	181	579
Eshleman	...	157	157	314
Martin	161	156	...	317
Morgan	164	171	181	516
Wingert	141	...	141	282
Deyer	188	176	181	545
	843	869	841	2553
Spades				
Mumma	162	163	183	508
Gammache	160	168	201	529
Getz	152	...	144	296
Dill	...	183	181	364
Collins	168	140	...	308
Hartley	179	198	149	517
	812	852	858	2522
Brassies				
Frey	152	208	...	360
Moffett	200	...	142	342
Donohue	...	156	144	300
Martin	153	151	160	464
Slaugh	234	161	197	592
Greiner	215	222	213	650
	954	898	856	2708
Sandwedges				
Sullenber'r	180	160	163	503
Dommel	184	154	167	505
McFalls	...	188	156	344
Witmyer	145	...	...	145
Dickinson	150	182	170	502
Pott	191	171	182	544
	850	855	838	2543
Niblics				
Morrison	174	118	183	475
Wade	153	184	153	490
Leinaweaver	111	153	112	376
Shertz	181	192	183	556
McElligott	180	192	152	524
	799	839	783	2421
Drivers				
Smithgall	197	160	183	540
Harnish	155	117	...	272
Aznavorian	...	...	114	114
Hiemenz	156	128	193	477
Herr	207	176	172	555
Daugherty	168	192	213	573
	883	773	875	2531
Baffies				
Flemming	183	147	191	521
Chandler	149	...	...	149
Musser	188	161	160	492
Gregg	179	146	167	492
Lerbscher	193	183	151	527
Simone	...	157	222	379
	892	794	891	2577
Mid-Irons				
Rineer	144	187	196	530
Slaugh	153	163	144	460
Radcliffe	94	163	150	407
Snader	143	202	195	540
Binkle	177	183	195	555
	714	898	880	2492
Cleeks				
Shelley	165	145	151	461
Scheffer	171	144	142	457
Farley	148	101	126	375
Hayes	185	209	166	560
Dombach	158	190	181	529
	827	789	766	2382
BURGER MEN'S LEAGUE				
Brooklyn				
Seber	184	176	128	488
Smith	131	125	166	422
Coyle	104	125	132	361
Yeager	172	97	157	426
Weber	144	157	178	479
	735	680	761	2176
Athletics				
Ranck	127	122	148	397
Shoenber'r	183	152	143	478
Koch	134	164	150	448
Bartch	199	125	139	463
Doe	104	97	128	325
	747	660	698	2111
Phillies				
Clerico	154	143	118	415
Dinkle	149	104	193	446
Peterman	143	103	144	390
Trimmer	161	170	142	473
Doe	96	89	101	286
	703	609	698	2010
Yankees				
Yeager	177	147	176	500
Fralich	135	163	146	444
Gottschalk	96	112	101	309
Fouchet	125	89	111	325
D'Annunzio	129	116	112	357
	662	627	646	1935
Red Sox				
Fr. Kane	124	144	148	416
Campbell	121	124	167	412
Licht	150	178	175	503
Flick	126	138	161	425
Freiler	138	158	188	484
	659	742	839	2240
Giants				
Fisher	199	163	150	512
Voci	124	...	...	124
Dinges	...	149	158	307
Baxter	160	139	138	437
Licht	177	162	167	506
Wiegand	149	148	189	486
	809	761	802	2372
P. AND L. LEAGUE				
Transformers				
Stetter	134	147	155	436
Kendig	139	133	151	423
Mummaw	139	124	139	402
Blank	150	...	143	293
Glouner	...	125	...	125
Shoff	204	168	157	529
	766	697	745	2208
Relays	...	...	...	...
Bair	136	89	135	360
Zahn	113	149	136	398
Scott	159	142	148	449
Burns	201	121	168	490
Doe	134	124	...	258
Scheid	...	...	158	158
	743	625	745	2113
Relays won roll-off last game.				
Meters				
Hershey	199	145	139	483
Martin	116	125	161	402
Seiple	129	117	139	385
Trapnell	171	158	154	483
Dougherty	196	144	173	513
	811	689	766	2266
Gas Ranges				
Shaub	169	185	210	564
Schadt	133	170	134	437
Harnish	110	105	99	314
DeLong	99	..	116	215
Groh	...	98	..	98
Schanerber'r	159	168	169	496
	670	726	728	2124
Watts				
Ziegler	133	170	152	455
Henny	131	113	138	382
Krentz	...	98	...	98
Waters	119	...	132	251
Colon	134	107	143	384
Troop	137	152	128	417
	654	640	693	1987
Water Heaters				
Haun	107	146	156	409
Leh	133	145	133	411
DeVerter	85	108	135	328
Herzog	141	131	146	418
Sullivan	159	139	124	422
	625	669	694	1988
Disconnects				
Spicer	...	184	177	361
Kieffer	145	150	197	492
Spangler	169	160	187	516
Eckert	199	166	139	504
Diffender'r	138	146	...	284
Buckwalter	124	...	140	264
	775	806	840	2421
Fuses				
Sharley	147	147	127	421
Campbell	137	149	133	419
Young	89	87	101	277
Morrison	112	79	108	299
Woodworth	201	165	146	512
	686	627	615	1928
W. AND S. LEAGUE				
Shoes				
Hagel	156	149	107	412
Shissler	162	162	133	457
Schoenber'r	160	170	154	484
Zangari	139	172	192	503
Clark	109	109	109	327
	726	762	695	2183
Rugs				
Watt	149	148	129	426
Reckard	152	162	141	455
Dennis	121	90	87	298
Mable	140	112	135	387
Duke	158	148	140	446
	720	660	632	2012
Suits				
Travis	170	163	174	507
Wagner	131	160	172	463
King	165	208	186	559
Wiley	124	146	122	392
Sullivan	168	163	161	492
	758	840	815	2413
Furniture				
Miller	144	128	156	428
Smith	134	142	179	455
Siple	119	163	125	407
Kempf	138	114	139	391
McCloskey	146	153	162	461
	681	700	761	2142
CHRISTIANA LEAGUE				
Drugs				
Diller	194	185	190	569
Graham	163	191	181	535
Kellenber'er	165	150	...	315
Jackson	161	179	169	509
Rittenhouse	186	193	202	581
Longeneck'r	...	...	151	151
	869	898	899	2666
Machine				
E.Ammon	145	182	201	528
Mervine	121	134	143	398
R.Ammon	141	159	180	480
Miller	126	130	143	399
Sillers	184	166	163	513
	717	771	830	2318
Christiana Fire Co.				
Ammon	144	191	112	437
Lechler	141	169	146	456
Pickel	135	180	147	462
Rowe	124	167	147	438
Simmons	202	157	194	503
	746	854	746	2346
Roses				
Brown	190	148	198	536
C.Hershey	156	157	141	454
May	253	170	144	567
Reinhart	142	133	..	275
Althouse	136	191	169	496
	877	799	817	2493
C. and B.				
Palmer	172	133	146	451
Ross	143	152	170	465
Reinhart	139	193	130	462
Trego	164	151	140	455
Albright	151	154	172	483
	775	783	746	2346
Gap				
Rank	199	154	...	353
Graham	168	154	170	492
Thompson	127	...	138	265
Wright	157	163	168	488
Hawk	188	159	129	476
Wettig	...	189	212	401
	839	819	817	2475
Pomeroy Fire Co.				
W.Bachman	136	163	153	452
Thorne	203	212	186	601
McLucas	161	212	167	540
H.Bachman	165	149	125	439
D.Bachman	126	...	128	254
McKinn	...	104	...	104
	791	840	759	2390
Parkesburg Lions				
Gillespie	162	172	132	476
Orr	136	140	147	423
Salage	121	138	164	423
Cardwell	127	138	152	417
Goldman	175	142	160	477
	721	730	755	2206
Paradise				
Troop	141	153	190	484
Lichty	154	146	225	525
Lechler	136	126	168	430
Miller	145	185	129	459
Grube	175	164	176	575
	751	774	888	2413
Paradise Lions				
Ranck	134	176	156	466
Harnish	131	136	148	415
Reed	144	167	122	433
Hershey	167	122	136	430
Lichty	138	186	148	472
	714	792	710	2216
Christiana Fire Co.				
Rowe	170	189	183	542
T.Hurst	156	159	151	466
Simmons	168	...	...	168
Large	150	144	167	461
L.Hurst	146	174	148	468
Low	..	..	185	185
Doe	...	115	...	115
	790	781	834	2305
Quarryville				
D.Miller	191	185	148	524
Wilson	195	195	195	579
Hassler	187	115	140	442
Fritz	150	...	...	150
B.Miller	138	...	...	138
Garvin	...	179	209	388
Rineer	...	163	135	298
	861	837	821	2519

N. Y. YANKEES CLIP RECORDS DURING SERIES

Charley Ruffing Creates Three New Marks And Ties Another

New York—(AP)—Although the New York Yankees lost the World Series, they carried off the lion's share of the records that were set or equalled during the five-game tussle with the St. Louis Cardinals.

Charley Ruffing, the Yanks' veteran pitcher, established three new records and tied another; little Phil Rizzuto equalled a few more; Joe DiMaggio picked up a couple and the Yanks as a club figured in still more record-breaking.

Both teams, of course, shared in the financial record-breaking as the largest crowds in World Series history turned out for the three games at Yankee Stadium.

For the Cards, Stan Musial, Max Lanier and Johnny Beazley turned in record performances of sorts but they didn't break any important ones.

When Ruffing pitched no-hit ball for seven and two-thirds innings of the opening game, he not only broke the mark of 7 1-3 hitless innings set by Herb Pennock in 1927, but by appearing in his seventh World Series, he tied a record set by Waite Hoyt for the Yanks and Athletics from 1921 to 1931. At the same time he won his seventh Series victory, going one ahead of Hoyt, Chief Bender of the Athletics and Lefty Gomez of the Yanks. Monday Rufus the Red broke the total-strikeout mark by whiffing his 61st World Series victim. Bender's old mark was 59.

Three of Rizzuto's record-equalling feats were in the field as he made 15 putouts in a five-game Series and seven of them in one game and had three assists in the second inning of the third game. His feat of hitting a home run to start Monday's game also equalled a record, made in 1917 by George Weaver of the Chicago White Sox.

DiMaggio had 20 putouts in the five games. That gave him a new record for putouts, one above his 1941 total, and equalled the record for outfielders' chances in a five-game series, set by Mike Donlin of the Giants in 1905 and equalled by DiMag last year.

Other Yankee records included Bill Dickey's having caught 33 World Series games since 1932, Charley Keller's two-home runs—equalling the highest mark for a five-game series although Babe Ruth once hit four in four games; the club's total of 178 at bats in five games their 18 runs (the most made by a loser in five games); their failure to hit even one triple and their using 20 players in five games.

Musial's feat of coming to bat twice in one inning on two different occasions gave him a record and he equalled another by making two hits in the fourth inning of the fourth game. Lanier's two errors in the ninth inning of the opening tied the mark for pitchers. Beazley's records were of the against-the-Yankees variety. He was the first rookie to beat them in a World Series since Paul Dean did it in 1934 and the first pitcher to beat them twice in a series since 1926.

The old attendance record of 68,540 and the single game gate receipts mark of $265,396, set by the Yanks and Dodgers last year, were broken in all three gan.. at the Stadium. The high marks of 69,902 fans and $269,408 were hit Sunday.

Total attendance of 276,717 also set a five-game mark, far above the Yanks-Giants 1937 total of 238,142, and the total gate receipts of $1,105,249 set a mark for a series in which the $100,000 radio receipts were not included.

St. Louis Gets Hep For Big Celebration

St. Louis—(AP)—A rousing reception, with band and confetti, was planned Monday night for the conquering St. Louis Cardinals, world baseball champions, when they return home at 7:00 P. M. E.W.T. this Tuesday.

Mayor William D. Becker, on a war plant tour with Britsih Ambassador Lord Halifax when he received the good news of the Redbirds' triumph, danced a jig and then immediately plunged into plans for the reception.

The mayor, happy civic leaders and expected thousands of loyal Cardinal fans will meet the players at Union station. Mayor Becker will welcome the players home in a brief address and then each one will be introduced to the spectators.

Sam Breadon, president of the club, was contacted tonight in New York and invited one and all to attend the reception. However, he requested that no plans made for a victory dinner for the players because of the war.

"8 West King St. Salutes Its 45 Fighting Comrades"

Warren L. Swartz
Ensign—U. S. Navy

Edward Drybred
Corporal—U. S. Army

William Thompson
Private—U. S. Army

Leighton C. Hacker, Jr.
Private—U. S. Army

A. Richard Kilgore
A.S.R.—U. S. Coast Guard

Herman L. Walzl
Private—U. S. Army

James Flick
Corporal—U. S. Army

Marshall M. Detwiler
Stf. Sgt.—U. S. Army

Raymond W. Smith
F. 1/c—U. S. Navy

Harold Godshall
Corporal—U. S. Marines

Leslie A. Peek
2nd Lieutenant—U. S. Army

These men, all of whom were employed in the Lancaster Newspapers building, are now fighting with Uncle Sam's forces to protect — FREEDOM OF SPEECH, FREEDOM OF RELIGION, FREEDOM OF ASSEMBLY and FREEDOM OF THE PRESS — thus preserving the American way of life.

We Salute Them

William T. Lightner
Ensign—U. S. Navy

Ross G. Miller
Candidate—U. S. Army

James E. Patton
Private—U. S. Army

James M. Ruble
Corporal—U. S. Army

Charles A. Corbett
Pfc.—U. S. Army

Alvin A. Hess
Apprentice Seaman—U. S. Navy

Harry P. Forry
2nd Lieutenant—U. S. Army
Reported Missing in Action

Woodrow W. Bierly
2nd Lieutenant—U. S. Army

Edward J. K. McLorie
Corporal—U. S. Army

E. Eugene Eshleman, Jr.
Pfc.—U. S. Army

David Brandt
Corporal—U. S. Army

Robert Beitzel
Seaman 2/c—U. S. Navy

Raymond K. Pierce
Private—U. S. Marines

John H. Zartman
Private—U. S. Army

Lester L. Nelson
Private—U. S. Army

Henry G. Pyzanowski
Tech. Sgt.—U. S. Army

Robert K. Shaub
Private—U. S. Army

Thomas Bradley
Pfc.—U. S. Army

Alvin B. Bealler
Private—U. S. Army

Franklin E. Wolpert
Corporal—U. S. Army

Paul W. Brunner
Stf. Sgt.—U. S. Army

Robert C. Harnish
Air Cadet—U. S. Navy

Clayton S. Frey
Private—U. S. Army

Paul F. Wiley
Private—U. S. Army

Russell Labrasca
Pfc.—U. S. Army

Franklin Schaffner
Midshipman—U. S. Navy

Clay H. Myers
Tech. Sgt.—U. S. Army

Paul E. Graeter, Jr.
Hosp. Ap. 2/c—U. S. Navy

Carlton Moyer
Corporal—U. S. Army

Howard Worner
Corporal—U. S. Army

(Picture Not Obtainable)

George Hersh
Private—U. S. Army

(Picture Not Obtainable)

Martin W. Weidman
Private—U. S. Army

(Picture Not Obtainable)

Richard Reinhold
Private—U. S. Army

Harold J. Eager
2nd. Lieutenant—U. S. Army

The Leading Newspaper in the Garden Spot of America—Home Owned for Home Folks Since 1794

Intelligencer Journal

Bible Thought for Today—
His commandments are not grievous. I John 5:3.

VOLUME LXXIX.—NO. 30. LANCASTER, PA., FRIDAY MORNING, OCTOBER 16, 1942 34 PAGES, 272 COLUMNS. 20c PER WEEK—4c Per Copy

Lancaster Women Doing Their Part On Industrial Production Lines

"Pied Piper" Pipes And Women Fall Into Line

From Homes, Shops, Schools, Lancastrians Are Answering Country's Call; Many Jobs Require Light Touch Of Feminine Hands

The "Pied Piper" of war industry is sounding his siren tune to women, and leitmotif of his song—

"Women, we need you—to win the war."

And with variations on the theme, pneumatic drills are chattering the tune, motors hum it, the clangor of steel on steel thunders it out.

The women are hearing it—heeding it. They're hearing the siren call in beauty shops, at jewelry counters, and at coffee urns; in comfortable homes, quiet libraries and schools, in hospitals, in restaurants, in bake-shops.

They're leaving these jobs to fall in line behind the Pied Piper, an earnest, clear-eyed band of pioneers. Though diversified their backgrounds, they've all a single thought in mind— to further the war effort, to fight on the assembly line as their sons, brothers, husbands, fathers, sweethearts, are fighting on America's far-flung battle fronts.

RESTRICTIONS GONE

Gone are many of the pre-war restrictions that once limited the opportunities of women in industry. Age, marital status, previous experience and education are pushed into the background. The all-important requirement is aptitude and ability to learn some one skill of the many that are needed. And the capable hand that rocked the cradle, or wrapped packages, or applied cosmetics, or mastered today's many labor-saving household implements, is found to be more than deft and facile at the machines on the production lines of Lancaster's war industries.

More

Many of the hundreds of Lancaster women now in war industry are getting their first taste of really hard manual labor, of the feel of their fingers on cold steel instead of on shining hair or bridge cards. But what price broken fingernails, or sacrifice of glamour bobs? They'd rather be "angels with dirty faces," each releasing a fighting man to the front.

However, many of the jobs in industry are exactly the opposite of heavy physical labor. Instead, they require the delicate sensitive touch of light feminine fingers, where masculine fingers would be too large and too strong. In fact, this recent influx of women into factory production in Lancaster is blasting a heretofore popular misconception among the ladies that operating a factory machine requires the physique and stamina of an Amazon. The need for all sorts of precision instruments and smaller products essential to the war has developed all kinds of power-run. machines, many of which, because of ingenious automatic controls, are simpler and easier to run than a sewing machine or automatic mixing machine. Modern war production plants are light, airy, spick and span and neat as a pin—a sharp contrast to the grimy industrial plants of pre-war days.

CROSS SECTION OF LIFE

The roster of women in industry reads like a cross section of life.

At Hamilton Watch women with greatly diversified backgrounds have forsaken other jobs or are working for the first time—all in the interests of the war industry.

Mrs. Pearl Mentzler, Lancaster RD, who is now a plate-tapping machine operator, is the mother of eight children and has a brother who is a bombardier in the Air Corps. Betty Burns, 16 Caroline St., who works along side of her, has a brother who is a corporal in the Army. Another wife behind the war effort at Hamilton is Mrs. Norman Wintermyer, Columbia, whose husband is a lieutenant in the Army Air Corps. She now assembles primers at Hamilton. Mrs. Arlyne Niesen, 435 W. Orange St., formerly a cashier, now operates a centerless grinder, while her husband, a technical sergeant in the U. S. Ordnance, is on active duty.

A mother and daughter working in the same department at Hamilton—Mrs. Carl Draude, and her daughter, Rose Marie Forberger, 476 Fremont St. Mrs. Draude has five other dependent children and now laminates plates at Hamilton. Rose Marie, a former sales girl, now shellacs closing screws across the aisle from her mother.

FORSAKES SCHOOL ROOM

Formerly employed in the office of the Quarryville High School, Mrs. Willis Stroble has forsaken school rooms for the assembly line at Hamilton, while her husband is away in the army. Mary E. Frey, a former cashier, now expertly handles a lathe at Hamilton.

Machines that spin escape wheels and pinions are skillfully operated by four girls who never before operated machines. Frances Elizabeth Troop, Bird-in-Hand R1, is a former office worker; Beatrice E. Markle, 607 N. Lime St., formerly worked in an insurance office; Kathryn E. Myer, Leola, is a former beautician, and Mrs. Anna C. Boyd, Mountville, is a former dressmaker and milliner, and has a brother in the Air Corps.

In other local war production plants are to be found women with equally diversified backgrounds.

For instance, among the girls selected by the personnel department of the new Lancaster plant of RCA Victor to be sent to the company's Harrison, N. J. plant for training in preparation for the opening of the plant here are four girls working side by side and sharing an apartment together.

MET BEFORE DEPARTURE

A Junior Leaguer, a jewelry salesgirl, a coffee dispenser and a book store clerk, none of them ever saw each other until two days before they left for Harrison. Now firm friends, they will be aiding the war effort when the RCA Victor plant opens here.

The four are Kitty Scully, 1064 Wheatland Ave.; Miriam Book, 1196 Elm Ave.; Verna Rineer, 426 W. Chestnut St.; and Betty Hildebrand, 445 E. King St. Miss Scully, who has given many hours of volunteer service to the community as a Junior League member, formerly assisted at a nursery school, worked as a temporary salesgirl, and her interest in aviation led her to take up flying which included the ground school course at Franklin and Marshall College. She is in training for instructress work on mounting of tube parts.

Miss Book clerked in a large department store here, handling such pretty things as handbags and costume jewelry, a job she held in two other stores previously. She also is in training as an instructress in mounting, which means making parts inside tubes. Miss Hildebrand, who is in training as an instructress in stem making, worked back of the coffee counter at a large cafeteria since 1936, and Miss Rineer was a clerk in a large office equipment and book store here before she began her training as instructress in mounting.

Other girls taking the course at RCA Victor have just as diversified backgrounds. Mary Louise Heckman, 316 E. Orange St., a graduate of Dickinson College with a B. A. degree, was an investigator with the Department of Public Assistance since 1933. She will be in training as an instructress in tube testing.

Beatrice Bennett, 756 Marietta Ave., was a candy packer, and now is training on a machine. Madeline Russell, 1113 E. King St., formerly was a dental assistant, and now is training on a machine which seals tubes. Vilet Leaman 916 N. Duke St., was a buyer in a large department store for several years—now also is in training as an instructress.

MUST STUDY

Training for instructesses at RCA Victor doesn't stop at machine and assembly work These girls are given courses to equip them to get along amicably with the other girls with whom they will work when the Lancaster plant is opened. Their program includes courses in human relations, public speaking, public relations, first aid and related subject.

Working for Uncle Sam, these girls have become the new glamour girls of 1942. And Uncle Sam's boys, whom they meet at parties and USO dances, are mighty proud of them.

At the Armstrong Cork Company, the cross section covers even a wider area, due to the large number of women now employed in the war production department, making airplane wing tips, shells and munitions and devising camouflage.

For instance, there's the wife of the dean of Franklin and Marshall College, Mrs. Richard W. Bomberger, 440 College Ave., who is just completing the aircraft training course, after which she will go to work rivetting and welding in the manufacture of wing tips. Then there's Mrs. Themma Eyde, 443 Lancaster Ave., formerly a teacher in the city schools, who is now inspecting shells. Mrs. Dorothy Marie Emmerick, 239 Fairview Ave., the mother of three children, formerly was a pretzel roller, and is now in the aircraft department. Mrs. Mary Irene Fox, 306 Coral St., mother of four children, used to be a telephone operator for the Lancaster Newspapers, Inc., and is now in munitions assembly. Miss Alice Foust, daughter of Warden and Mrs. Walter N. Foust, graduated from West Chester State Teachers College last spring, and turned down half a dozen teaching jobs to join the war production line.

Mildred Edythe Wolfe, 38 E. New St., has exchanged the position of a psychiatrist's assistant for a job in the camouflage department, and Mrs. Dorothy Rush Weaver, Strasburg R1, is a student in the aircraft school, keeping in mind her hero brother, Col. Hugo Rush, whose outfit sank several Italian ships recently.

Mrs. Dorothea Dick Thomas, Lancaster R6, forsook the classrooms of the Warwick Township schools, and is now in the aircraft training course. Her first day at work, instructors nearly introduced her to her own husband, Frank Thomas, an inspector in the department. Frankie Adeline Strickler, 507 W. James St., also gave up expounding the three "R"s to children in the Freysville schools, and now is an operator in the aircraft department.

Mrytle Irene Cunningham, Lancaster R3, formerly was a beauty shop operator, and is now in munitions assembly. Previously a WPA recreation supervisor, Bernardine Clara Ruhl, 9 S. Prince St., is now in the aircraft department, where also is employed Mrs. Catharine May Cunningham, mother of four children and formerly a nurse.

ESPECIALLY INTERESTED

Mrs. Sarah Elizabeth Dommell, 616 S. Lime St., who formerly was a cigar machine operator, and is now working in aircraft, is especially interested in the war effort, for she has a son, Elvin R. Loller, and a brother, William Becker, in the Army. Mrs. Rose Marie Schilling, Ronks R1, is reliving her experience of World War I. Now an inspector in the shell production department, during World War I, as a young girl, she helped in the shell shop. Later she worked in the inlaid department at the plant.

Among those planning to take the aircraft training course in the future are Mrs. Bernard M. Zimmerman, 547 N. President Ave., wife of the city solicitor, who is now in the U. S. Ordnance Department, and her sister, Miss Mary Luetta Eshelman, Lititz Pike. Neither have been employed before, but both have given volunteer service to the community as members of the Junior League and other service organizations. Their sister, Clara Mae, will leave shortly for officer training with the WAVES.

These women, selected at random from the long lists of the "weaker sex" now hard at work in the heart of the war effort, illustrate vividly the changes wrought in a democracy at war.

They are just a few of the many pioneers who already are at work on machines for the first time, and it is certain that even greater advances by women in the industrial field will be underway within a few months.

Trained personnel department employes in the local industries, courteous; pleasant and easy to meet, are intensely alive to the importance of painlessly probing the possibilities of every last applicant.

Of course, some women, like some men, are not adapted for industrial employment. But recent experience in our local plants has proven that the number is surprisingly few. Sometimes the first assignment doesn't prove out, but there are plenty of other assignments to try, and the personnel workers see to it that every possibility is exhausted in finding for each curvacious Peg the proper well-rounded niche in the war production picture.

A little anecdote reveals a sidelight on some of the changes in economic situations. Mrs. A., formerly employed Mrs. B. to help her at home, and after some months, called Mrs. B. again to do more work for her.

"Oh, I can't possibly come," Mrs. B. replied. "I'm working in war industry now, and I have some one come in to help me."

A quartet of women war workers, who never before operated machines, assemble parts for wing tips at the Armstrong Cork Company. Left to right, they are Mrs. Richard W. Bomberger, wife of the dean of Franklin and Marshall College; Mrs. Sarah Elizabeth Dommell, who has a son and brother in the Army; Mrs. Dorothy Rush Weaver, sister of Col. Hugo Rush, U. S. Air Corps hero, and Mrs. Dorothy Marie Emmerick, mother of three children.

Mrs. Norman Wintermyer, Columbia, has a special reason for actively helping the war effort, for her husband is a lieutenant in the U. S. Army Air Corps. She is shown assembling primers at the Hamilton Watch Company.

Mrs. Arlyne Niesen, formerly a cashier, is now busy operating a centerless grinder at the Hamilton Watch Company. Her husband is a technical sergeant in the U. S. Army Ordnance Department.

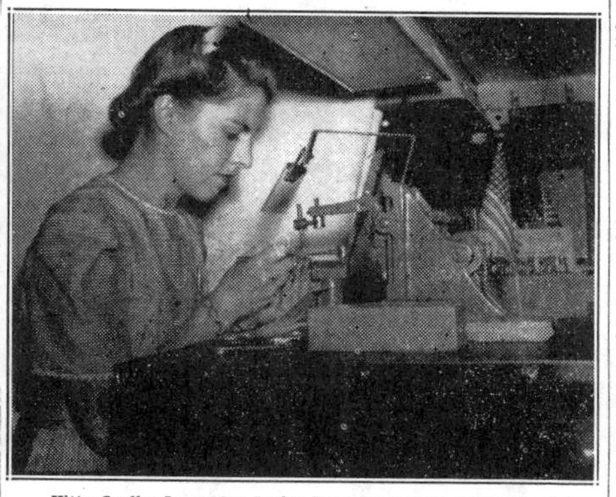

Kitty Scully, Lancaster Junior League member, is shown at her work in the Harrison, N. J., plant of RCA, where she is in training for instructress work on mounting of tube parts.

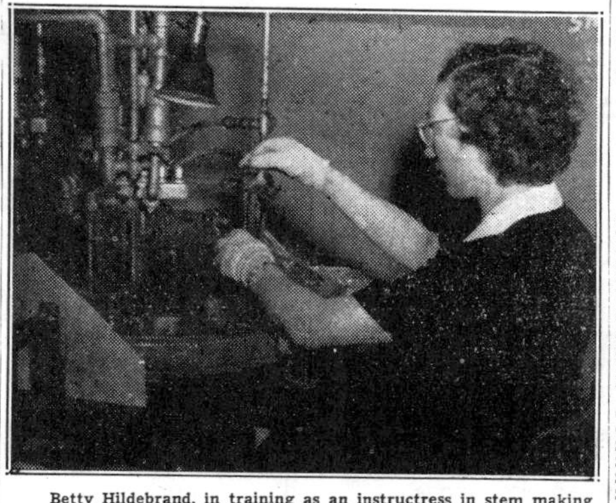

Betty Hildebrand, in training as an instructress in stem making at the Harrison, N. J., plant of RCA, formerly was employed at a local cafeteria.

We, The Women

By Ruth Millett

One way in which housewives might help relieve the labor shortage with little effect on their homes and familes is for those whose children are of school age to take on part-time jobs.

Ruth Millett

Thousands of women could work half a day, and still not neglect their primary job of home-making if they reorganized their lives.

They would have to give up their bridge and child - study clubs. They would have to simply their housekeeping and reduce their entertaining to having good friends in for evenings that break up early. They would have to give their children a little more responsibility, and count on them for more help around the house.

But they could—if they are strong and in good health—simplify their lives enough to take on paid jobs.

It is time more housewives started thinking along these lines, as the "Help wanted—evperience not necessary" ads in the newspapers grow longer and longer.

Not only would taking on part-time jobs help relieve the labor shortage—but wives would be helping their husbands out financially.

FAMILY FINANCES WILL NEED HELP

And many a husband is going to need help, as taxes eat up a larger and larger hunk out of every dollar.

The biggest hurdle most housewives will have to take is becoming part-time workers is getting used to the idea of combining paid jobs with housework.

It is hard for the woman who hasn't worked, or even toyed with the idea since she has been married, to see that if she hasn't any children under school age dependent on her she is one of the women needed in business and industry.

But once she has accepted that idea, the rest isn't so hard. From there on it is a matter of reorganizing her life—a job every mother has had to do each time she added a new member to the family. Making room for a job shouldn't be any more difficult than making room for a baby.

Name Additional Workers For Salvage Drive

Additional canvassers who are assisting the Women's Salvage Committee of Lancaster and the immediate vicinity, in the salvage drives being held here were announced on Thursday night by Miss Florence C. Bowers, general chairman.

They included: Lancaster Township, (Section 3), Mrs. Wallace Bork, Miss Barbara Charles, Mrs. Lewis Spencer, Mrs. Amos Shenk, Mrs. Marion Yost, Mrs. Mabel Schnelli and Mrs. Catherine Gochenauer.

Additional workers for the Ninth Ward are Miss Ethel Mohr, Mrs. Harold Shader, Miss Esther Kroeger, Mrs. Wallace Robinson, Mrs. H. R. Ritz, Miss Mary Krieder, Mrs. George Acker, Mrs. Samuel Swarr, Miss Helen Bitzer, Mrs. Margaret Walmer, Mrs. Richard Adams, and Mrs. Helen Ambler.

Third Ward, Mrs. Byron Burdic, Miss Dorothy Martin and Miss Matilda Fulmer.

Democratic Card Party Is Tonight

The Women's Democratic Club of Lancaster City and County, will hold its weekly card party at 8:30 o'clock this Friday evening in the club rooms, 124 E. King St. The committee in charge consists of Mrs. Katherine NcNiss, Mrs. Mary Daugherty, Miss Mary Bolbach and Miss Julia Bolbach, chairman.

The party next week will be held Thursday night, October 22, and it was announced that all parties in the future will be held at 8:30 instead of 8:45.

Need Volunteers For Stamp Booths

Miss Betty Martelli, chairman of the sales of war stamps at the theatre booths, has announced that volunteer workers are needed for the booths in all theatres.

Volunteers are needed for both afternoon and evening work, and those interested should contact Miss Martelli at her home on N. Mulberry St.

Social - Personal

Sergeant Lloyd Landgraf, of Lebanon, arrived Thursday morning for a brief visit with his brother-in-law and sister, Mayor and Mrs. D. E. Cary, E. King St. Sergeant Landgraf is stationed with the Coast Artillery at Quincy, Mass., and this is his first furlough since he entered the service last March.

The following instructors of Millersville State Teachers College will spend this Friday at Shippensburg State Teachers College where they will attend an educational meeting: Dr. Mark E. Stine, who is president of the higher education section of the Southern Convention District, Dr. Lee Boyer, Harold Bailey, Miss Ethel Powell and Miss Margaret Swift. They will be accompanied by Sanders P. McComsey and Dr. Maxwell Myers.

Mr. and Mrs. Eli S. Martin, of Bareville, and Mr. and Mrs. Ben Herr, of Farmersville, have returned to their homes from a trip to the Skyline Drive, and the Civilian Public Service Camps in Virginia.

Mr. and Mrs. Paul Sollenberger and daughter, Lottie Anna, of near Dallas, Tex., and Mr. and Mrs. Harry Sollenberger, of Oreville, Ohio, have returned to their homes from Leola, where they spent several days as guests of Mr. and Mrs. Ralph Miller.

Mr. and Mrs. J. H. Gentry and son, Sergeant Herbert Gentry, of Lancing, N. C. were recent guests of the former's son-in-law and daughter, Mr. and Mrs. Frank Hudler, of near Kirkwood.

Arthur P. Mylin, Jr., son of Dr. and Mrs. Arthur P. Mylin, of N. West End Ave., has been appointed a member of the Glee club of Mercersburg Academy, it was announced Thursday.

Mr. and Mrs. Thomas Pennypacker, of Mountville, have returned to their home from Fort McClellan, Ala., where they visited the former's brother, Corporal Frank Pennypacker.

Will Mark Anniversary October 23

The Normal Literary Society of Millersville State Teachers College will hold a meeting at 8 o'clock Friday evening, October 23, in the college chapel, in celebration of the 86th anniversary of the organization.

Allan D. Cruickshank, lecturer for the National Audubon Society, will be guest speaker, using as his subject, "Bird Life".

The meeting will open with a call to order by the president, Guy Eaby, class of 1911, and the college glee club under the direction of Melzer Porter will sing, "The Star Spangled Banner," Francis Scott Key; and "Forever Free," an ancient Dutch melody by Channing Lefebre.

Following a few remarks by the presidents, the Secretary, Miss Clara A. Withers, class of 1933, will read the minutes of the 85th meeting, and Miss Jane Gray, class of 1933, violinist, will play "Second Violin Concerto," from Wieniawski' "Romance," and "Poem," by Fibith. Mrs. Marion Perry Torchia, class of 1935, will accompany Miss Gray. Mrs. Torchia will also play several piano solos including Waltzes, opus 39, numbers 8 and 15, (Brahms) and from "Holberg's Time," Allegro Vivace, (Grieg).

The program will close with the glee club singing, "Evening on the Sava," (A. Arkkangelsky) and "Autumn," (A. Gretchinoff).

Following the program, a reception will be held in the college reception room.

Music Conference Will Be Held Here

Dr. Gomer C. Rees, retired pastor, residing in Allentown, will conduct a music conference at Christ Lutheran church, on Saturday. For 25 years Dr. Rees has served as a leader on the ULCA Committee on Church Music. The conference has been planned by the choir of Christ church, under the direction of Miss A. Margaret Lantz, and organist J. Edwards Smith, 3rd.

From 4 to 5:30 o'clock Dr. Rees will meet with organists, choir-directors and pastors to discuss the Spirit of Lutheran music. A supper meeting will be held at 6 o'clock, when he will discuss the Hymn tunes of the Common Service Book and their congregational use. The final period, at 8 o'clock, will feature an interpretation of the Common Service Liturgy. The public is invited to attend the last two periods.

The conference will be attended by representatives from the 11 ULCA Lutheran churches of Lancaster city and from several out-of-the-city churches.

Name Hostesses For Card Party

Hostesses for the St. Anthony's Parish card party, to be held next Tuesday evening at 8:30 o'clock, will be: The Misses Carolyn Ransing, Theresa Reichert, Mary Reichert, Hildegarde Reinche, Bernadette Reiner, Pauline Roehm, Grace Rohrer, Caroline Rohrer, Anna Roth, Catherine Rottmund, Rachael Rowan, Martha Rudy, Joan Ruof, Rose Russo, Anna Sabatine, Rebecca Sales.

Magdalene Sabinash, Agnes Sauer, Cecelia Schmoll, Margaret Schmoll, Carrie Seber, Mary Sekinger, Louise Sekinger, Emma Sekinger, Stella Sekinger, Mary Serbak, Catherine Serbak, Catherine Shenk, Elizabeth Shenk, Magdalene Simon, Elizabeth Smith, Grace Snavely, Florence Snyder, Helena Steinwandel, Anna Stephan and Dorothy Stork.

ELKS CLUB OPEN HOUSE

The bowlers of the Elks Club will hold their annual open house program for Elks and their ladies on Saturday night at the Elks Club. A program of entertainment has been planned, including a floor show, and dancing.

MALTA CARD PARTY

The Knights of Malta will open a series of card parties for the fall and winter season on Saturday evening. The parties will be held at the Malta Temple, 235 E. King St.

TOONERVILLE FOLKS By Fontaine Fox

HEY! YOU! ENNY SCRAP METAL FOUND ALONG THAT RIGHT O' WAY WILL BE SOMPIN' THAT BELONGS ON THIS CAR!
McNaught Syndicate, Inc.

(Follow Fontaine Fox's Family Folks In The Sunday News)

WEATHER
Eastern Pennsylvania—Occasional Rain Ending Saturday Afternoon, Moderate Temperature.

Intelligencer Journal.

CITY & COUNTY SCHOOLS Are Building SCRAP MOUNTAINS *Are You Helping?*

The Leading Newspaper in the Garden Spot of America, Home Owned for Home Folks Since 1794

VOLUME LXXIX.—NO. 31. Entered as second class matter June 23 1928 at the Post Office at Lancaster, Pa., under the Act of March 3, 1879 LANCASTER, PA., SATURDAY MORNING, OCTOBER 17, 1942 CITY 14 PAGES, 112 COLUMNS. 20c PER WEEK—4c Per Copy

GREAT BATTLE RAGES ON GUADALCANAL

Farm Wages May Be Regulated And All Salaries Controlled

Wickard Given Broad Authority To Deal With Problem In Agriculture

SUBSIDIES RUMORED

Washington — (AP) — Economic Stabilization Director James F. Brynes granted Secretary of Agriculture Wickard broad authority Friday night to regulate wages of agricultural workers, and there were reports that subsidies might be used to keep farm hands on the land.

Byrnes directed that machinery be established immediately to deal with the wage problem. His action was taken shortly after a House Agriculture committee had warned that the nation faced a food shortage because workers were leaving farms for higher pay in war industries.

Officials who asked that they not be quoted by name said they believed the authority gave Wickard power to fix agricultural wages at levels designed to help keep remaining workers on farms and to attract such workers into lines of agricultural production deemed most essential for war purposes.

MAY REQUIRE SUBSIDIES

The wage problem in agriculture, they said, was not one of excessive pay. Consequently, regulations would be one designed, they said, to bring farm wages more nearly in line with industrial pay. They said such control may require payments of subsidies to farm operators which would enable them to pay higher wagese.

Control of farm wages would not be a new field for the Agriculture Department. It now sets minimum rates for workers in sugar beet and sugar cane production. Employers must pay the minimum rates in order to become eligible for government sugar benefit payments.

The department has in recent months set up state wage boards to determine minimum rates which farm operators must pay in order to obtain transient farm workers being moved to areas of farm labor shortage by the Agriculture Department.

The department's first action under the Byrnes order probably would deal with labor shortages in the dairy industry. Because of the

More of WICKARD on Page 9

Byrnes Extends Stabilization Control To Salaries Under $3,000

BANS LONG DISPUTES

Washington—(AP)—In blunt language, James F. Byrnes Friday informed cabinet officers and other high-ranking officials that there must be no long-drawn-out disputes about economic stabilization and that he himself would resolve all disagreements swiftly.

At the first meeting of the officials, assigned to advise him as director of economic stabilization, Byrnes declared:

"In most cases common counsel should result in common agreement. But we are at war and we cannot wait upon the counsel of perfection. We will make mistakes. But in war, inaction is the greatest of mistakes. If, after an adequate exchange of views differences still persist, I shall resolve those differences and promptly communicate to you my decisions."

ANNOUNCES STEPS

Byrnes then announced that to implement President Roosevelt's recent stabilization order he had:

Arranged with the War Labor Board and the Treasury Department to "bring all salaries under control."

Started work, in conjunction

More of BYRNES on Page 9

SEARCH RIVER FOR MISSING COLUMBIA BOY

Jacob Henry, Jr., 16, Preparing To Hunt For Ducks When Last Seen

SUSQUEHANNA ROUGH

Jacob Henny, Jr., sixteen, 321 Perry St., Columbia, who is believed to have gone out on the Susquehanna River in a small rowboat to hunt ducks Friday, was still missing at an early hour Saturday morning.

Chief of Police Harold Shortlidge, of Columbia, and State Policeman Frank Leventhal and Albert Kendig, of Columbia, circled the section in a motorboat owned by C. A. Etzweiler, of Columbia, for more than three hours Friday night in an unsuccessful attempt to locate the missing youth. The search was finally abandoned for the night when the wind and strong current made it nearly impossible to keep the motor on their boat from stalling.

SEARCH ISLANDS

Shortlidge and Leventhal said that they searched every small island in the section and also scoured the shores of the river, but could find no trace of the youth or boat. Shortlidge said as far as he could learn the youth was alone when he started out on his duck hunting trip.

His parents, Mr. and Mrs. Jacob Henny said their son left home about 1 p. m. Friday with his older brother, Daniel. They said the boys then met Jack Reese who said Jacob could use his boat. The youth then left the two other boys and that was the last he was seen, the parents said.

His father said that this was

More of SEARCH on Page 9

For Democrats

MRS. PINCHOT

MRS. PINCHOT WILL BACK DEMOCRATS, R. S. BLACK SAYS

Wife Of Former Republican Governor To Take Stump Next Thursday

Harrisburg — (AP) — Ramsey S. Black, third assistant postmaster general and chairman of the State Democratic Campaign Committee, said Friday that Mrs. Cornelia Bryce Pinchot, wife of former Governor Gifford Pinchot, would take the stump to support Democratic candidates.

Black said Mrs. Pinchot will make her first platform appearance at a Bristol (Bucks County) rally next Thursday evening and that she will speak later in Allegheny County and Williamsport. Auditor General F. Clair Ross, Democratic candidate for governor, has made repeated bids for the support of what he called "Pinchot Republicans."

HITS PAY INCREASES

Meanwhile, at Butler, Ross charged that recent pay raises for state employes, announced by Governor James, was a "last minute righting of a prolonged wrong."

Asserting "the Republican policy is that starvation wages are all right for state employes until two weeks before election," Ross said:

"The fact that Arthur James, stubborn and selfish, finally has recognized that you cannot live in Pennsylvania and raise a family on $23.08 a week, shows that the pressure was on from the Republican high command."

The Democratic candidate said the raises came "as a result of the stand of the liquor store clerks' union; they got it because of the Democratic campaign; they got it because even James and (Adjutant General Edward) Martin (Republican gubernatorial candidate) fear the decency and sense of fair play of Pennsylvania voters in this election year."

FERRY IS SUNK OFF CANADIAN COAST, 137 DIE

Victims Include Women And Children; Navy Craft Rescue 101 Persons

SUBMARINE SURFACES

Sydney, N. S.—(AP)—Torpedoed in darkness, the Newfoundland-Nova Scotia ferry steamship Caribou was sunk in Cabot Strait Oct. 14 with the loss of 137 lives in the greatest announced marine disaster of this war in the coastal waters fringing on Canada.

Some Americans were reported among the casualties.

Canadian naval craft saved 101 passengers and crewmen after the 2,200-ton ship, owned by the Newfoundland government, had been sent to the bottom of the sea near the enr of her overnight run from North Sydney, N. S., to Port Aux Basques, Newfoundland.

The submarine that sank her surfaced and watched her go down within a few minutes while her victims struggled in the water.

The victims included eight U. S. service men and five American civilians. The others who lost their lives included women and children, Canadian service men, the Caribou's skipper, Capt Benjomin Taverner of Channel, Newfoundland, and his two sons, both officers of the ship.

(The sinking raised to 494 the Associated Press count of announced Allied ship losses in the western Atlantic since Dec. 7, 1941.)

HEADED FOR SUB

The survivors, landed here the day of the sinking, told how the captain steered his settling craft at the surfaced submarine in an apparent effort to ram the attacker. But the Caribou slid under before she could get her icebreaker's prow against the U-boats hull.

In surfacing the submarine was believed to have contributed to the loss of life by capsizing one

More of FERRY on Page 9

F & M Trustee

JUDGE WALTER I. ANDERSON

JUDGE ANDERSON, OF YORK, ELECTED TRUSTEE OF F & M

Alumnus To Serve Unexpired Term of Late S. Forry Laucks; Named At Fall Meeting

Judge Walter I. Anderson, of York, Pa., was elected to the Board of Trustees of Franklin and Marshall college at the Fall meeting of the Board Friday. He will fill the unexpired term of the late S. Forry Laucks, also of York, Pa.

Judge William H. Keller, first vice-president of the Board of Trustees, presided at the meeting in the absence of Dr. Paul Kieffer, of New York City. Aside from the election of a trustee, only routine business was transacted, Dr. Horace R. Barnes, secretary, said Friday night.

GRADUATE OF F & M

Judge Anderson is a graduate of F & M in the class of 1922. He began his term as judge of the Court of Common Pleas of York county on January 1, 1942, having previously served as district attorney. He is one of the youngest jurists in the state and in no case which he tried has the verdict been set aside by a higher court.

While he was a student at Franklin & Marshall, the new trustee was a member of the Green Room Club, Student Senate and Lambda Chi

More of JUDGE on Page 9

Jap Forces Bring Up Artillery, Shell American Positions

Climactic Engagements Being Fought In Air And On Sea, But Little Is Known Of Progress; Germans Advance In Stalingrad; French Flier Killed In "Fight" Over Dakar; Disorders Break Out In France

(By the Associated Press)

U. S. Marines and troops were under shellfire on Guadalcanal Island from artillery hauled ashore by large enemy landing forces, Friday night, and the first great battle between the Japanese and American armies since Bataan was raging without quarter.

At sea and in the air climatic engagements were being fought, although very little was known about their course. But it was evident that America's hold on the South Solomon Islands was truly in the balance.

"There's a real fight on out there; it's a stiff fight," Secretary of the Navy Knox told newspapermen. Asked if he thought our forces would hold, he replied :"I certainly hope so. I expect so."

Evidently it was the enemy's intention to envelop and smother the American positions ashore after endeavoring to soften fire points and crush airport facilities with a cross-fire of cannonade from shore and sea.

There were yawning time gaps in the news from the Solomon Islands; there was much that was missing, but this was the situation as told by the Navy's communique No. 156:

Determined and fully-equipped Japanese troops—"a large number" of them, got ashore on Guadalcanal with artillery and other equipment, possibly tanks, and have turned their mobile guns on the beach-head and airport positions held by the Marines and their Army reinforcements.

A new Japanese fleet, in addition to various enemy units up to capital strength now around the Solomons, has been located about 260 miles from Guadalcanal, near Shortland Island.

U. S. torpedo boats, the first to be reported in the battle, have attacked the enemy heavy and light warships which shelled the American positions on Guadalcanal. One Jap cruiser probably was hit with a torpedo.

American search planes, dive bombers and fighters were attacking transports and grounded planes at sea and on the enemy-held beach at Rekata Bay on Santa Isabel Island. Nine of these planes were dam-

More of GUADALCANAL on Page 9

5 PC VICTORY TAX WINS APPROVAL OF JOINT COMMITTEE

Levy On All Income Above $624 Is Biggest Tax Increase Ever Voted

Washington — (AP) — The biggest tax increase ever voted on individuals—the 5 per cent victory levy on all income above $624 yearly—won approval Friday of a joint conference committee rapidly adjusting Senate and House differences over the new revenue bill.

With only minor changes, the committee agreed to accept the new tax written into the bill by the Senate in place of a House-approved provision for a 5 per cent withholding levy on wages, interest and dividends. The latter would have served merely to advance the collection of the regular income tax.

BUSINESS TAXES

Turning to business taxes, the conferees agreed to a combined rate of 40 per cent on the normal and surtax earnings of larger corporations instead of the 45 per cent previously voted by the House. The present rate is 31 per cent.

Retention of the present $5,000 flat exemption from the excess profits tax was agreed upon, despite the House vote to raise this to $10,000. The committee delayed action until Saturday, however, on post-war rebate features inserted by the Senate in approving the 90 per cent excess profits rate previously voted by the House.

The victory levy, softened some-

More of TAX on Page 9

Gravest Flood In Capital's History Menaces Washington

President Roosevelt Inspects Critical Areas Along Swollen Rivers; 2,000 Persons Homeless, Four Dead In Four-State Section

Washington—(AP)—Swirling flood waters of the Potomac and other rivers Friday menaced sections of the national capital, caused four deaths and wide destruction and left at least 2,000 people homeless in a large area of Maryland, Virginia and West Virginia.

Acting upon reports that the flood here might be the gravest in Washington history, President Roosevelt toured the critical areas in and around this city and appealed to authorities to take every precaution to protect the capital.

With the Rappahanock and other streams on the rampage as well as the Potomac, many persons have been evacuated from lowland homes, some in rowboats, and the Weather Bureau warned others to be ready to leave.

RED CROSS ACTIVE

The American Red Cross said it was provided for 2,000 persons in the Virginia-West Virginia-Maryland-District of Columbia area. Front Royal, Va., was completely marooned and both Winchester and Culpepper, Va., were isolated.

Red Cross headquarters here said its field offices were checking several reports regarding other deaths or missing persons. Representatives at Fredericksburg, Va., were informed that two men died when tneir car went into a landslide south of that city. At Front Royal, field workers were investigating a report that a man and wife who failed to leave a threatened area

More of FLOOD on Page 12

ERROL FLYNN HELD ON ATTACK CHARGE INVOLVING GIRL, 17

Movie Star Surrenders After Being Charged With Raping Girl At Party

Los Angeles—(AP)—Errol Flynn, swashbuckling film star, surrendered Friday on a charge of raping a 17-year-old girl at a party and was released under $1,000 bail.

"I'm bewildered," he told reporters. "I can't understand it. I hardly touched the girl."

The complaint, issued by District Attorney John F. Dockweiler, after the county Grand Jury had failed to indict Flynn Thursday, charged him with raping Betty Hansen, 17, at the Bel Air mansion of Fred McEvoy, wealthy British sportsman and former Olympic bobsled champion, the night of Sept. 27.

LIVED WITH SISTER

She had come here recently from Lincoln, Neb., to live with a sister, Mrs. Jack Marsden.

"It is obvious," said Dockweiler, "that the grand jurors have not considered the evidence, for, from

More of ERROL FLYNN on Page 9

FOUR PERSONS HURT IN WEST END CRASH

Four persons were slightly injured in an automobile accident at Chestnut and Pine Streets at 10:30 p. m. Friday.

Kenneth Painton, eighteen, 33 E. Ross St., one of the drivers, was admitted to St. Joseph's Hospital under observation after being treated for two lacerations of the head. The other injured were: Donald Painton, twenty, Lancaster R3, laceration of the right hand; Norman Darrenkamp, sixteen, 56 Campbell Alley, laceration behind the right ear and Miss Jacqueline Keemer, eighteen, 62 Campbell Alley, brush burns of the left forearm, who were riding with him.

City police who investigated the accident learned that Painton was driving north on Pine Street when his automobile collided with a car being driven west on Chestnut Street, by Joseph P. Coonan, 522 W. Chestnut St. The Painton car was thrown onto the curb on the northwest corner by the impact, according to the police report.

Objector Wants To Fight After Reading His Bible

Local Man Cites Writings Of St. Peter In Asking Transfer From Work Camp To Army Air Corps; Draft Officials Refuse To Identify Him

A conscientious objector, now at a Civilian Work Camp, petitioned his local draft board Friday for a change of classification which will enable him to join the Air Forces—for combat duty. The wish will be granted.

The identity of the youth, registered with County Draft Board No. 4, which embraces eastern Lancaster county, was not made public immediately on the advice of Selective Service headquarters.

FIRST CASE HERE

It is the first case on record locally where a conscientious objector asked to be reclassified for actual combat duty. One other youth sought and was accepted for non-combatant service.

"I would like to have my 4-E (conscientious objector) class changed to 1-A (general service)" wrote the youth, who has been at the work camp for six weeks. "I was thinking on the matter and considering the wrong the Axis powers have done and how they murdered numberless innocent p[illegible] ple, the Bible says in Peter, [illegible] chapter, verses 13 to 17, that nations are ordained of God to punish

More of OBJECTOR on Page 9

HALLOWE'EN MASKS BANNED FOR ADULTS

Wearing of masks by anyone over 12 years old on Hallowe'en will be banned, as an emergency war-time measure, Mayor D. E. Cary announced Frida. The ban will affect only those who parade the streets and other public places during the celebration.

Because enemy agents might disguise themselves in Hallowe'en costumes in order to gain entrance to strategic places, the action was taken with the approval of Civilian Defense authorities.

EXPLOSION AT PITTSBURGH

Pittsburgh (Saturday) — (AP) — A terrific explosion at the Duquesne works of the Continental Roll and Steel Foundry Company shook the Ohio river communities of Sewickley and Coraopolis late last night. Patrolman William Walker reported that at least 45 persons were injured, many seriously.

MAN LOSES LIFE IN TRUCK CRASH; TWO ARE INJURED

Paul J. Dunlap, Lampeter, Fatally Hurt At Clay As Vehicle Hits Bridge

A man was fatally injured and two others slightly hurt when a light delivery truck in which they [illegible]re riding was demolished after twice striking a concrete bridge on Route 222 in Clay at 2:15 p. m. Friday.

P. J. DUNLAP

Paul J. Dunlap, thirty-one, Lampeter, the driver of the truck, died at 6:40 p. m. in the Lancaster General Hospital of internal hemorrhages caused by a ruptured spleen and fractured ribs, according

More of MAN on Page 9

LANCASTER COUNTY HIGHWAY DEATHS

38

Since January 1, 1942
Same Date—1941—46

PROPERTY PURCHASED BY STATE TO COVER ASSISTANCE GRANTS

For the first time in Lancaster county, the Commonwealth of Pennsylvania purchased the property of a deceased relief recipient at public sale Friday to reimburse itself for assistance grants distributed to the owner, Benjamin Mease.

Approximately $1,900 had been extended to the owner through the Department of Public Assistance, it was reported and the premises in Manheim township near Neffsville, was bid in at $810 for the State by Maxwell S. Michael, claim settlement agent for the DPA. The property was appraised at $1,200 for inheritance tax transfer purpose but a right of way dispute invloving the premises is believed responsible for the lower sales price.

Harold E. Martin, special deputy attorney general, will prepare a new deed, clearing the dispute, and the State will then offer the property at public sale again.

While State purchase of such property is a novelty in Lancaster county, Martin, representing the Commonwealth, has bid on various premises in the county but in all cases heretofore, public bidding exceeded the set figure to reimburse the DPA for its relief advances and outsiders were permitted to buy the premises.

Four cords of hard wood, in three separate piles, sold to the highest bidders at $6.75, $6.25 and $4.25, rsepectively. The sale was in charge of Lester H. Mease, executor of Benjamin Mease, deceased. Elmer V. Spahr, was the auctioneer and A. W. Reese, the attorney.

OBJECTOR ARRESTED AS HE BUYS HORSE

Harry Hoover Martin, Bareville R1, a conscientious objector who failed to report for a civilian work camp September 25, was arrested Friday by U. S. Deputy Marshall Clayton Keeney just as he was purchasing a horse at a sale in New Holland.

Given an immediate hearing before U. S. Commissioner A. E. McCollough, Jr., Martin was held for the U. S. Federal court at Philadelphia. His father, Menno M. Martin, New Holland R1, posted $2,500 bail.

Martin is a registrant of County Board No. 4. He is listed as a member of the Wenger Mennonite Church.

Nelson Says Newspapers Drive For Scrap Was Magnificent Job

WPB Chairman Tells Publishers Results Surpassed "The Fondest Hopes That I Entertained"

Washington—(AP)—Donald M. Nelson told the nation's newspapers Friday that they had done a magnificent and unprecedented job in carrying on the nation-wide household scrap salvage campaign during the past several weeks.

Addressing a group of publishers and executives who have served as members of the Newspapers' United Scrap Metal Drive Committee, the War Production Board chairman said:

"The job that the newspapers have done is absolutely unprecedented in this country. It has been magnificent. The results surpassed the fondest hopes that I entertaind when I asked the publishers to come in a few weeks ago and discuss the problem of our materials shortage and how the newspapers could help."

URGES INDUSTRIAL SALVAGE

With that statement Nelson urged the newspapers to turn increasing attention to the problems of industrial scrap salvage.

Richard W. Slocum, General Manager of the Philadelphia Evening Bulletin and committee chairman, and other publishers and executives, told Nelson they felt certain that newspapers throughout the country would accept the new challenge and gladly work to stimulate

More of NELSON on Page 9

BRIDGE COMMISSION DISCUSSES GUARDS AT SECRET SESSION

Toll collections on the Lancaster-York inter-county bridge for the first fifteen days of October was $15,680.45 and expenses, $4,380.11, Superintenent Monroe Bentz reported to the bridge commission at a meeting Friday.

The expenses included $1,859.90 for administrative salaries; $253.35 for maintenance, and $2,267.86 for bridge guards.

The commission held an hour's executive session but G. Graybill Doehm, president, said nothing was accomplished. During the closed meeting conduct of several of the guards and a proposal to boost the pay of guards was discussed, it was learned.

George S. Love, York County solicitor, was asked to investigate a request of the First National Bank of Wrightsville for a reduction in the amount of collateral bonds it must post to secure toll collections.

A complaint from R. E. Moore, Wrightsville, that a motorcycle operated by a bridge guard struck and damaged his parked automobile on September 20, was read. Major Benjamin Charles, in charge of guards, promised an immediate investigation.

"We Lead All the Rest"
FARM CORNER
By
The Farm Editor

DEMAND FOR MILKING MACHINES REFLECT SHORTAGE OF LABOR

Six of the ten applications for new equipment approved by the Lancaster County Farm Machinery Rationing board at a session Friday afternoon were requests to purchase milking machines, a reflection of farm labor shortage.

At the same time the board rejected the applications of ten other farmers to purchase equipment, mainly on the ground that "not sufficient need" for the machinery had been established. One plea was disallowed with the notation that the applicant's "present machinery can be repaired." Requests rejected were applications to purchase four hammer mills, two farm tractors, two pickup balers, one disc harrow and one manure spreader.

The fact that six of the ten requests approved on application Friday were to purchase milking machines is an indication of the serious labor shortage here, especially on dairy farms, members of the board pointed out.

Applications approved included: Karl L. Knosp and Brother,

More of FARM CORNER on Page 9

Intelligencer Journal Weather Calendar

COMPARATIVE TEMPERATURES

Station	High	Low
Intell Journal	50	49
Water Works	68	63
Ephrata	64	61
Last Year (Ephrata)	67	48
Official High for Year, July 19		98
Official Low for Year, Jan. 11		-10
Character of Day		Raining

HOURLY TEMPERATURES (Friday)

3 a. m.	56	4 p. m.	58
4 a. m.	56	5 p. m.	57
5 a. m.	57	6 p. m.	56
6 a. m.	57	7 p. m.	55
7 a. m.	56	8 p. m.	53
8 a. m.	55	9 p. m.	52
9 a. m.	54	10 p. m.	50
10 a. m.	54	11 p. m.	50
11 a. m.	55	Midnight	49
Noon	55	(Saturday)	
1 p. m.	56	1 a. m.	49
2 p. m.	57	2 a. m.	49
3 p. m.	58	3 a. m.	48

SUN

Rises—7:15 a. m. Sets—6:23 p. m.

More of WEATHER on Page 12

The Weather

Eastern Pennsylvania—Showers In East Portion Sunday. Colder West And East Sunday Afternoon.

SUNDAY NEWS

3 A. M. Edition

The Sunday News carries the full report of world wide news services—LATEST NEWS by Associated Press, International News Service, Wide World, and Complete Local News.

VOL. 20—NO. 9 | Entered as second class matter September 21, 1923 at the Post Office at Lancaster, Pa., under the Act of March 3, 1879. | LANCASTER, PA., SUNDAY, NOVEMBER 1, 1942. | 52 PAGES, 288 COLUMNS—SIX CENTS

4TH U. S. PLANE CARRIER LOST

BOMBS HIT SHOPPERS IN DOVER

Biggest Raid Since 1940 Leaves 10 Dead; Big Battle Over Straits

London, Oct. 31—(AP) — Fifty German bombers smashed with bombs and machine-guns at Southeastern England today in the biggest Nazi attack since the 1940 battle of Britain, concentrating their assault on shopper-crowded streets at Canterbury where Mrs. Franklin D. Roosevelt was a visitor only yesterday.

Roaring in at dusk, the raiders dropped bombs in haphazard fashion and machine-gunned a working class area and then a shopping street.

"They chose a time when the streets would be full of shoppers," said the Air Ministry, which also announced that nine of the planes participating in this attack and other raids on East Anglia today were shot down.

Informed of the Canterbury raid, Mrs. Roosevelt expressed deep concern and inquired whether several places she visited had been hit.

During the activity an air raid alarm was sounded in the London area tonight.

Operating with their old-time efficiency despite the long lull in large-scale battles over Britain, RAF fighters shot down six of the attackers with a loss of two of their own planes, while ground artillery accounted for the other three.

10 Persons Killed

Ten persons were known to have been killed at Canterbury, and some were injured. Six persons were killed in a crowded bus near which a bomb exploded. Another bus was machine-gunned, the driver being killed. The Air Ministry said the daylight attacks in East Anglia caused little damage and few casualties.

In one of the East Anglia attacks 13 raiders participated. Another group of 20 roared across the countryside at zero altitude and machine-gunned a coastal-bound express train hitting the engineer.

Meanwhile, American pursuit pilots shot up a freight train near Berck-Sur-Mer, France. They said steam was spouting from cannon holes in the boiler of the engine when they left.

Factories and industrial objectives in northwest Germany and Belgium were raided during the morning and afternoon, the Air Ministry announced. Seven planes were lost, three of them bombers. Many hits were observed.

Other RAF bombers and fighters blasted industrial objectives and

BOMBS—Page 17

Death Of O'Brien As She Went To Aid Wasp

This photo, one of the most remarkable pictures of the war, was taken just as an enemy torpedo struck the side of the U. S. destroyer O'Brien as she went to the rescue of the burning carrier Wasp in the background. The wake of the torpedo that sent the destroyer to the bottom is clearly visible. The Wasp, flaming furiously after being hit by three torpedoes, was finished off by a U. S. destroyer. This is U. S. Navy photo.

Ship Not Identified Sunk In Solomons; Jap Cruiser Bagged

Will Withhold Name Until Kin Of Men Are Told—Sunk By Navy After Battle In Which Porter Was Lost Last Sunday

Washington, Oct. 31—(AP)—Sinking of another U. S. aircraft carrier—the fourth—in the furious air and sea battle for control of the South Pacific, was announced by the Navy tonight, leaving only three American carriers known to be still in action.

The latest victim of two Japanese aerial attacks was not identified by the Navy.

She went down near the Santa Cruz Islands, a tiny spot in the Pacific about 250 miles northeast of Guadalcanal in the same battle which cost the U. S. fleet the destroyer Porter last Sunday night (Washington Time).

The first assault on the carrier, which came before noon, caused heavy damage. She was put in tow in an effort to salvage the big vessel, but the Japanese returned in the afternoon. Bombing and torpedo planes roared in to attack. This time the attackers inflicted damage below the water line of the helpless carrier.

She began to list. Orders were given for removal of the personnel and most of them were saved. Then came the final orders—instructions to complete destruction of the crippled ship.

The Navy said the name of the lost ship would not be disclosed until after next of kin of all injured or missing had been notified.

The vessel presumably came from among four vessels listed in Janes registry of fighting ships—the Saratoga, a converted carrier, commissioned in 1925, with a tonnage of 33,000; the Hornet, commissioned 1940, tonnage 19,900; the Ranger, commissioned 1933, tonnage 14,500 and the Enterprise, commissioned 1936, tonnage 19,900.

Each of these carriers has a normal complement of between 1,800 and 2,100 officers and men. Each, too, carried a striking force of about 85 airplanes—bombers, torpedo planes and fighters.

3 Previously Lost

Previously the Navy had announced the loss of three of the seven carriers which the United States had at the start of the war.

Among them was the Wasp, newest of the carriers, which went down in the battle of the Solomons on September 15. The Lexington was lost in the Coral Sea battle May 8 and the Yorktown in the battle of Midway June 7.

Loss of the Porter brought to 21 the number of destroyers lost so far in the Pacific. Other American vessels suffered lesser damage.

But on the other side of the ledger, the enemy also suffered heavy losses. One Japanese carrier was badly damaged, another damaged, an enemy cruiser badly damaged and a battleship hit.

That battle was the last major sea and air engagement reported in the vicinity of the Solomons before Navy Secretary Knox announced Friday that the Japanese fighting ships had disappeared from the Guadalcanal zone.

Official Report

The loss was reported in Navy communique No. 175, (about 175):

"South Pacific: (All dates are East longitude)

"1. The U. S. aircraft carrier

CARRIER—Page 17

Second Cruiser Badly Damaged

Gen. MacArthur's headquarters, Australia, Sunday, Nov. 1 —(AP)—Allied bombers striking for the third successive day at Japanese shipping in the northern Solomons and New Britain sank a heavy cruiser, severely damanged a light cruiser and scored direct hits on at least three merchant vessels, a communique said today.

Most of the damage in the latest raids was done at Buin, in the Solomons, but 21 tons of explosives were dropped on the harbor area of Rabaul, New Britain, where the results could not be fully observed because of low clouds. The Allies did not lose a plane in either raid.

New Intuition?

MARSHAL ROMMEL

Bern, Switzerland, Oct. 31—(AP)—Field Marshal Erwin Rommel may be slated to become Hitler's personal military adviser, the Neue Zuricher Zeitung said today.

The newspaper added there has been no official clarification of many rumors coming from Germany, but that evidence grows that Gen. Franz Halder has been ousted as chief of the German general staff, and has been replaced by Gen. Zeitler.

The Neue Zuricher Zeitung said that Rommel presumably is directing the Axis defense in Africa, but that there has been no official statement that he is still in command in that area.

RUSSIANS TAKE THE OFFENSIVE IN STALINGRAD

Main Battleground Shifted To Caucasus As Nazis Make New Gains

Moscow, Sunday, Nov. 1—(AP)—The Germans made new gains yesterday in their offensive across the Nalchik plains at the foot of the Caucasus mountains, the Soviet midnight communique said today, but the Red Army seized the initiative inside Stalingrad and won new successes northwest of the Volga city and on the Black Sea front.

The fact that the Russians had gone over to the offensive in Stalingrad was indicated by a statement in the communique that they had fought "battles to improve their positions" after beating off a number of German attacks.

(A Moscow broadcast said "the Russians in Stalingrad have gone over to the attack and that they have already dislodged the enemy at one point," the London radio reported in a broadcast heard Saturday night by CBS. Northwest of Stalingrad, the broadcast said, the Russians are "slowly but surely pushing the Germans back." The Rome radio broadcast that the Russians have launched a new mass counter-attack in the last 24 hours against the Germans at Stalingrad.)

The midnight communique said that about a battalion of German infantry had been wiped out in Stalingrad and that ten tanks and five blockhouses had been destroyed. Northwest of Stalingrad the Russians were said to have strengthened their positions and

RUSSIAN—Page 17

"Hidden" Taxes Start Biting The Pocketbook

If That Nickel Cigar Now Costs 6 Cents You Can Blame The War; Whiskey Will Cost More By Bottle Or Drink

Washington, Oct. 31—(AP)—If that nickel cigar costs six cents tomorrow, "blame the war and pass the contribution" because Uncle Sam's collecting higher excise taxes.

A lot of taxes the experts used to classify as "hidden" are coming out of their foxholes to bite the purchaser in the pocketbook. Cigar taxes are one of these, the levy on the nickel brands being increased from the present $2 per 1,000 to $4. Manufacturers and sellers may absorb this in some instances, but the fellow who smokes one will do most of the chipping in.

It's all in a good cause, however, for Uncle Sam expects increases effective Sunday in a miscellaneous array of taxes to bring in an additional $495,900,000 during the course of a year. This will be about enough to build five battleships and a cruiser.

More On Dec. 1

He will up that take by $157,700,000 Dec. 1 when a new 3 per cent tax goes into effect on the transportation cost of freight and express shipments, except for coal, where the government's charge will be 4 cents a short ton.

Those who like to keep warm in another way will find it more expensive beginning tomorrow. Whisky taxes are going up from $4 to $6 a gallon on 100 proof stuff. That means bonded whisky will cost 50 cents more a quart, straight drinks about 5 cents more apiece.

Beer also may be more expensive by the bottle but probably not by the mug, the tax increasing from the present $6 a barrel to $7. The tax on wines goes up, too, ranging from the increase from 7 to 10 cents on a half pint of sparkling wine or champagne to an increase from 65 cents to $1 a gallon on wines containing between 21 and 24 per cent alcohol.

Christmas perfume, if imported and containing alcohol, is going to be higher also, the tax increasing from the preset $4 to $6 a gallon.

Keep Track Of 'Phone Tax

There is at least one tax you can put down in your notebook against the day when Uncle Sam

TAXES—Page 17

Lititz Hallowe'en Has Photo Finish

Lititz children thought up a new one Saturday night—but Chief of Police C. R. Kreider thought faster.

The kids had been taking pieces of photographic film, wrapping them in paper and setting them afire to throw on porches and in doorways.

This was great fun until the chief got hold of an unburned strip of film, had a rush job of developing done on it, identified the children shown in the picture, and obtained a promise from their parents that they would desist. The incendiary bombings stopped.

Mishaps To Two Army Bombers Cost Six Lives

St. Paul, Oct. 31 — (AP) — Three crewmen, one of them a pilot who survived a flaming plane crash a year ago almost to the day, were killed at the airport here today when a B-24 Consolidated four engined Army bombing plane plummeted to the ground on the takeoff.

The victims were Captain Clarence Bates, Minneapolis, pilot, Robert James Raley, Duluth, Minn., co-pilot, and Robert Delman Bunn, Minneapolis, radio engineer.

4-MOTOR PLANE FALLS

Newsport News, Va., Oct. 31—(AP)—An Army Air Corps four-motored bomber en route to Langley Field from Patterson Field, O., crashed in the woods about two miles from Hampton, Va., tonight, killing its crew of three. Victims were:

Capt. William J. Foley, father, N. K. Foley, of Taff, Texas; First Lieut. James H. Moore, next of kin, Mrs. E. J. Moore, Beverly Hills, Calif.; Private First Class Gilford Wright, mother, Mrs. Bessie Mae Wright of Sterlington, La.

ATTORNEY HELD IN CHESTER CO. GUNNER'S DEATH

9 Hunting Accidents Reported In This Area On First Day

(Special to Sunday News)

Coatesville, Oct. 31—Stephen Devereux, forty, of West Caln Twp., prominent Chester county attorney, is being held in the Chester county prison at West Chester for questioning in connection with the fatal shooting of a hunter on Devereux's farm, seven miles west of here, during an alleged trespassing argument.

The victim Willard Copeland, thirty-eight, of Sadsburyville, operator of the Spanish Cabins near here, was instantly killed when shot above the heart with a revolver, State Motor Police reported.

Corporal J. F. Updyke and Private E. F. Sharpe, of the local substation of the State Motor Police, said no charges had been filed against Devereux but he is being held without bail for further questioning.

Deputy Coroner Fred B. Manship, who also is conducting an investigation, said Devereux and Copeland's wife, Pansy, who had accompanied her husband on the hunting trip, "told entirely different stories of the shooting."

Mrs. Copeland told him, Manship

SHOOTING—Page 17

BRITISH SMASH RELENTLESSLY AT ROMMEL FORCES

Consolidate New Positions On Desert, Repel Counter Attacks

Cairo, Oct. 31—(AP)—The British Eighth Army methodically whittled down German strength today in the Western Egyptian desert, consolidated its newly won positions and repulsed counter-attacks while maintaining air supremacy with the help of American planes.

(The German radio said the British resumed the attack early Saturday wheeling up reinforcements especially of artillery and tanks. The assertion by DNB came only 12 hours after the Nazis had claimed the offensive had collapsed).

Still there was no major tank battle and the German counter-attacks were made only with infantry and light armor.

Aussies Repel Four Attacks

The Australians repulsed four waves of Axis infantry Friday, attacking new lines which enveloped hundreds of square yards of territory wrested from the enemy Thursday night.

Two attacks were supported lightly by tanks, but heavy casualties were inflicted on the Axis in each instance, delayed dispatches from the front said. Another 200 prisoners were taken, of them conscripted Poles, Dutch and Czechs. Others were formerly in the French Foreign Legion.

The battle, now in its second week, was one of attrition and the British were determined to "de-

BRITISH—Page 17

Army Thanks Navy For Transporting 800,000 Overseas

Washington, Oct. 31—(AP)—Armed forces of the United States overseas now total 800,000 men, it was diselosed today in an exchange of correspondence between General George C. Marshall, Army chief of staff, and Admiral Ernest J. King, commander in chief of the United States fleets.

The figure was included in a letter written by Marshall extending Navy Day congratulations to King.

Marshall said that the Army's men were "deeply grateful for the skillful seamanship that has escorted 800,000 of them safely across the submarine-infested waters of the Atlantic and Pacific."

In his reply, King referred to close cooperation between the Army and the Navy at Bataan, Midway and in the Solomons.

SPECIALIST CORPS IS ABOLISHED

Men Appointed From Civil Life Will Get Commissions In Regular Army

Washington, Oct. 31—(AP)—The Army Specialist Corps, set up early in the war to procure officers directly from civil life for special service with the Army, was abolished by Secretary Stimson today "in the interest of efficiency."

Acting on recommendations by Major General Dwight Davis, head of the organization, Stimson announced that any further officers appointed from civil life would be given commissions as specialists in the regular army itself. Men now in the corps will be offered commissions in the army if qualified and if they are needed.

In a statement announcing the decision, the War Department said it was found "not advisable to have two uniformed services."

"The purposes of the corps could not be accomplished to the best of advantage in the midst of the war because of the civilian status of those appointed in it to serve with the army," it was explained.

The summary action was coupled with an announcement of added restrictions to prevent abuse in granting commissions to civilians and a prediction that the need for such men would diminish as the output of officer training schools increased.

U. S. Ship Sinking Raises Toll to 510

Washington, Oct. 31—(AP)—The Navy announced today that a medium sized U. S. merchant vessel was torpedoed and sunk by an enemy submarine during the latter part of September in the Atlantic off the northern coast of South America. Survivors have landed at an East Coast port.

The Associated Press count of announced losses in the Western Atlantic since Pearl Harbor rose to 510 with this sinking.

State Stores Have Beat-Tax Hangover

Shelves at the state liquor stores were bare when the rush buying to "beat-the-tax" ended Saturday night. Effective Monday most liquors will carry a tax of $2 a gallon.

The employees of the stores said the buying was heavier than during the Christmas rush and many of the most popular brands were completely sold out. One store estimated that their stock at the close consisted of only about 15 brands. They said the stock of rye whiskies was completely exhausted and the supply of Scotch and Bourbon whiskies were deeply depleted.

Cigarets which also will carry an additional tax were being bought in large lots and some stores were sold out of the leading brands.

Uniforms, Costumes Blend For Hallowe'en In City

The uniforms of men in the armed service gave a military air to Lancaster's first wartime Hallowe'en celebration Saturday night. Groups of soldiers, sailors and marines joined in the funmaking on the city streets but they weren't dressed for a masquerade—they were home on furlough after months spent in training camps and in some cases, after service on the battlefront.

Large crowds of merrymakers jammed the downtown area, throwing confetti, torn paper and streamers. Children in costumes and masks tooting horns and noisemakers added to the carnival spirit. In accordance with orders issued by the city council, no adults were masked.

Several young couples circled the Square and N. Queen St., in salvaged Model A's but motor traffic was not abnormally heavy. Complaints of mischief were much fewer than in previous years, police said.

Women and youngsters predominated among the merrymakers and there was comparatively little noise and "roughhousing." Extra police had been stationed throughout the city as a precautionary measure to direct traffic and prevent any attempts at vandalism.

Some damage was reported from county districts, including the burning of corn shocks in fields. A cottage near Salunga had its foundations damaged by marauders. Some windows were broken elsewhere.

Celebrating was restrained in the residential areas and there were few private parties, in keeping with the pleas being made for wartime economy. Several of the college fraternities held masquerade dances.

Pair of City's New Policemen Drafted, Mayor Asks Why

Mayor Cary said Saturday that he asked City Draft Board 1 to explain the drafting of two recently appointed city policemen.

"Both of the men were married before Pearl Harbor and in view of the announcement that no men married before Dec. 7 will be called in the November draft, I would like an explanation," the Mayor said. "Since one of the men has already been sworn in, I would like to find out what to do."

Members of the board, which held a special meeting Saturday night, said they had received no request for a ruling and consequently had not reconsidered the cases.

Kenneth Witmer, 455 S. Shippen St., was sworn in and received a notice from his draft board when he arrived home. Brandt Hipple, 549 S. Christian St., was scheduled to take the oath Saturday but it was postponed pending a clarification of his draft status. He is the father of one child.

Three other men sworn in as city policemen were:

Edward Van Egri, 145 E. Vine St.; Paul E. Kauffman, 117 S. Duke St., and Paul Fierstein, 39 Hager St.

HUNTER KILLED BY LOCOMOTIVE

Harry Rigel, 58, Columbia, Was Lying On Track, Official Says

Harry Rigel, fifty-eight, 110 Cedar St., Columbia, a hunter, lost his life the first day of the 1942 small game season when struck by a freight train near Chickies at 11:40 a. m. Saturday.

The victim was apparently lying on the tracks when he was struck by the train operating on the Columbia-Harrisburg branch, Dr. G. P. Taylor, of Columbia, deputy coroner, reported.

Dr. Taylor said Rigel was instantly killed, death caused by a crushed chest. The coroner issued a certificate of accidental death. The body was badly mutilated, Dr. Taylor said, as Rigel was dragged for about a quarter of a mile before a member of the crew noticed blood on the tracks and brought the engine to a halt.

Hunting With Son

Rigel, accompanied by a son, left home to hunt in the vicinity of Chickies Rock and during the morning the two became separated, Dr. Taylor said he learned. The father apparently stumbled as he was crossing the tracks and fell on them as members of the train crew

HUNTER—Page 17

Soldier Hit By Car Is Seriously Hurt

Pvt. Henry C. Conrad, thirty-eight, Ft. Mead, was hit by a car driven by Richard P. Snyder, 320 W. King St., about 1:40 a. m. today, according to city police. He was reported to have been crossing Prince St. south of Conestoga when struck. Lancaster General Hospital attendants report that he had a broken right leg, broken right hand, and possible skull fracture.

Today Is Deadline For Overseas Gifts

Today is the deadline for mailing Christmas packages to men and women in the armed forces who are stationed overseas. Presents for those in camps in this country should be mailed no later than December 1.

Tiwce as many packages have been mailed at the local postoffice during the past month than during October of last year. Supt. of Mails Oliver Cochran attributed the increase to the number of men in camps here and abroad.

The volume of mail for foreign lands is much heavier than during World War 1, Cochran said.

Women Barricade Halls So Nazis Can't Take Men

Bern, Switzerland, Oct. 31—(AP)—French women, barricading tiny town halls against German doctors sent to examine their men for the Hitler labor draft, have won one of the first victories in the campaign in the unoccupied zone against forced work in the Reich.

A new series of strikes was reported to have broken out, in Haut-Savoie.

The strikes in every case followed orders to factory owners designating the number of workers they were expected to furnish in the deal made by Pierre Laval for exchange of workers for war prisoners.

The men, upon receiving the announcement, simply quit work and in most cases their fellows walked out with them, the reports said.

Women, young and old, mothers, wives and sweethearts of the men, refused to obey orders and disperse after they collected angrily in front of the city halls, Journal Geneve reported.

Police were said finally to have helped the German doctors into the buildings, but then the men did not show up for the physical examinations they were expected to take before entraining for Germany. There the matter stood, with heavy police guards placed about cities and factories involved.

The strikes begun on Thursday at Annecy, Marnaz, Scionzier and Annemasse in the watchmaking region of Haute-Savoie continued. These had been supplemented during the week by walkouts at Toulouse, Grenoble, Avignon and Marseille.

Usually well-informed foreign circles with Vichy connections said these demonstrations were responsible, in large degree, for the Germans giving Laval two more weeks in which to declare formal conscription.

While Laval already has been trying to force the workers to go, officially he has emphasized that labor enlistment was on a voluntary basis. The two-week extension to Nov. 15 was said not to affect the Nov. 30 deadline for actual delivery of his quota of 150,000 French workers, a quota still far from fulfilled.

There were indications that the Germans would be glad to withdraw from their demands for the full 150,000 if they could discover a way to save face.

The eagle has been universally regarded as the emblem of might and courage from ancient times.

50 MPH SPEEDER IN TRUCK NABBED; 3 OTHER AUTO CASES

James A. Searer, Lewistown, charged with speeding at 50 miles an hour in a truck on the Harrisburg pike in Mount Joy township, was prosecuted by State Police before Justice of the Peace Weidman yesterday.

Mrs. Ethyl Walker, Middletown, was charged with making an improper pass in Elizabethtown.

Russell St. Clair, 639 Lake St., charged with illegal parking by State Police, was fined $2 and costs before Justice of the Peace Martin, Manheim township. Harold B. Heiss, Lancaster R. 6, charged with driving without an operator's license, was prosecuted by city police last night before Alderman Rose.

Borneo apes build platforms in trees on which they often sleep for several nights.

ENSIGN NEY TO WED GREER GARSON

HOLLYWOOD, Nov. 5—(AP)—Ensign Richard Ney, who was Greer Garson's son in the movie "Mrs. Miniver," will become her husband. The wedding will be at the actress' Bel-Air home over the weekend.

In applying for a marriage license at Santa Monica yesterday, Miss Garson said she was 31 and Ney gave his age as 29.

Ney, a former New York stage actor, received his Navy commission Oct. 29 and is on a two weeks furlough, so their honeymoon will be brief. It will be the second marriage for each.

Local Soldier Marks 21st Birthday in Ireland

Lester G. Alexander, son of Mr. and Mrs. John W. Alexander, 501 Ruby St., who recently graduated from the Army Engineering School at Fort Belvoir, Va., has been promoted to Corporal Technician and is now stationed at Fort Belvoir.

Sergeant Melvin R. Mayer, stationed in the Army Air Force at Ellington Field, Tex., who has been promoted to the rank of staff sergeant, according to word received by his mother, Mrs. L. M. Mayer, 327 E. King St. Mayer has been in the service since July 16, 1941. He has two brothers serving in the Army Air Force, Private Donald K. Mayer, at Brooks Field, Tex., and Private James Mayer, at Keesler Field, Miss.

Pfc. Peter Lincoln Foster, who is with a detachment somewhere in England. Private Foster is a grandson of Peter Lincoln Frailey, who was formerly connected with the Hamilton Watch Company, and the son of Mr. and Mrs. Wilmer Strong Foster. He is well known here.

Private George E. Hubley, son of Mr. and Mrs. George H. Hubley, 542 N. Plum St., who has passed his examination for entrance into the Armored Force Officer Candidate School at Fort Knox, Ky.

Private Russel Webb, formerly stationed at Engel Island, Cal., who is now on his way to an overseas destination, according to a letter received by his mother, Mrs. Mary Webb, 240 W. Grant St. Private Webb, who enlisted June 15, is the nephew of George Singleton, formerly of Lancaster, who has been in the Army for 20 years.

Private Leon M. Warfel, 18, son of Mr. Leon C. Warfel, Pequea R1, who enlisted in the U. S. Marine Corps Oct. 18 and is now stationed at Parris Island, S. C.

Pfc. Robert P. Shertz, 23, son of Mr. and Mrs. Albert Shertz, 219 Coral St., who has returned to Camp Rucker, Ala., after spending a short furlough at his home here. Pfc. Shertz who entered the Army in April, is attached to the station hospital at Camp Rucker.

Private John S. Miller, Jr., son of Mr. John S. Miller, 605½ East Marion St., who is stationed at Lincoln, Neb., with the U. S. Army Air Corps. Private Miller, who was inducted July 27, was formerly employed by the Hamilton Watch Company.

Private Salvador Michael Nobile, Jr., who spent a five-day furlough recently with his parents, Mr. and Mrs. Michael Nobile, 540 N. Third St., Columbia. Private Noble, who enlisted August 26, is stationed at New River, N. C.

Private Clifford L. Fasnacht, who celebrated his twenty-first birthday somewhere in Ireland today. He is the son of Mr. and Mrs. Charles F. Fasnacht, 330 N. Lime St., and the brother of Mrs. Florence Hurst, 312 Pershing Ave. Private Fasnacht left Lancaster with one of the first groups of National Guards in September, 1941.

Private Charles L. Sterback, who recently visited his wife, Mrs. Susanna Sterback, 18 E. Farnum St. Private Sterback has been transferred from St. Petersburg, Fla., to Mitchel Field, N. Y. He entered the Army Sept. 1.

Sergeant Paul E. Rohrman, U. S. Army Air Corps, who recently spent a few days with his parents, Mr. and Mrs. E. G. Rohrman, 602 N. Lime St., while enroute to Miami Beach, Fla. He enlisted in August, 1941. He will enroll in the Officers Candidate School of Physical Education.

Galen R. Herr, son of Carl B. Herr, 212 E. Frederick St., who enlisted in the U. S. Navy Oct. 21, has been sent to the new Naval Training Station at Bainbridge, Md., for his basic training.

Private John W. Odenwalt, son of Mrs. Naomi L. Kramer, 425 Church St., who has been with the U. S. Army somewhere in the Hawaiian Islands for 17 months.

Luther E. Harnish, Jr., who is stationed at the Naval Base at Fresno, Cal., recently spent a furlough with his parents, Mr. and Mrs. L. E. Harnish, 518 South Queen St.

Second Lieutenant Paul E. Byer, formerly a school teacher at Gordonville, who is stationed somewhere in England, according to word received recently by his parents, the Rev. and Mrs. F. J. Myer, Hollidaysburg, Pa. Lt. Byer is a navigator on a Flying Fortress. He is a nephew of Mr. and Mrs. Charles Whiteman, Gap, R1. Byer, a graduate of Juniata College, Huntingdon, in the class of 1935, taught at Gordonville until his enlistment in February, 1941.

Corp. Richard A. Mowery, son of Mr. and Mrs. Arthur Mowery, Conestoga R2, who has arrived safely in Northern Ireland, according to word received here. He has been in the service for two years.

Corp. Victor E. Shoff, son of Mrs. Minnie Shoff, 634 E. Walnut St., who has been overseas for more than a year. He enlisted in the Air Corps in August, 1940, and has not been home since July 23, 1941. His mother recently received a letter, the first word from him in three months.

Clayton Trout, Jr., son of Mr. and Mrs. Clayton Trout, 523 N. Pine St., who enlisted in the U. S. Navy Oct. 12 and left Friday morning for Bainbridge, Md. Before enlisting, Trout was employed in the mailing room of the Lancaster Newspapers.

Russell C. Gruel, 20, who recently spent a furlough with his parents, Mr. and Mrs. Clayton Gruel, 522 S. Queen St., has been transferred from the Great Lakes Naval Training Station to Treasure Island, San Francisco, Cal. He enlisted in the Navy Sept. 9.

Corp. Technician Woodrow Wilson Stump, who is stationed somewhere in Africa, according to word received by his mother, Mrs. Elsie Long, Elizabethtown. Prior to being sent overseas he was stationed at Aberdeen, Md. Corporal Stump, who was inducted Dec. 5, 1940, was the first selectee to leave Elizabethtown.

Melvin Hohenwarter, son of Mr. and Mrs. Charles J. Hohenwarter, 634 West Orange St., who spent a recent furlough at his home here. He is stationed at the Fresno, Cal., Naval Base.

Aviation Cadet William Witmer, son of Mr. and Mrs. Edward C. Witmer, Strasburg, R1, who recently reported to the Greenville Army Flying School, Greenville, Miss., for further flight training. Upon completing his training he will receive his "wings" and a commission as Second Lieutenant.

Private Robert G. Zercher, who enlisted in the Air Corps Sept. 7, has been transferred from Miami Beach to Madison, Wisc. He is the son of Mr. and Mrs. John Zercher, 601 S. Lime St. Private R. Paul Weagley, who lived with Zercher family, enlisted in the Marine Corps Aug. 19 and is now stationed at Parris Island, S. C. Weagley formerly was employed in the office of the Armstrong Cork Company.

Private Walter Stephens, who is stationed with the coast artillery anti-aircraft unit at Fort Bliss, Tex. He is the husband of Mrs. Irma Stephens, Landisville. Private Stephens enlisted Sept. 22.

Private Charles Joseph Long, formerly of 911 E. Orange St., who has been transferred from Olmsted Field, Middletown Air Depot, to Selfridge Field, Mich. He enlisted in the U. S. Army Air Corps ground crew as sheet metal worker Aug. 28.

Staff Sergeant Howard Glenn Anderson, 23, who has arrived safely in Northern Ireland, according to word received by his wife, Mrs. Dorothy Anderson, Lancaster R. 1. Sergeant Anderson, the son of Mr. and Mrs. George P. Beard, Washington, Pa., left Lancaster Sept. 16, 1940, with one of the first contingents of National Guards.

Pfc. Robert J. Fritsch who has arrived safely in England, according to a "V" letter received by his mother, Mrs. E. M. Smith, 133 Coral St. Private Fritsch, who entered the Army in May, 1942, was formerly employed by the Pennsylvania Railroad Company.

Pfc. Karl L. Bernhardt, who has arrived safely somewhere in Ireland, according to word received by his parents, Mr. and Mrs. Harry B. Bernhardt, 1 Fairview Ave.

WILL HONOR HEAD OF SALVATION ARMY

Several members of the Lancaster Salvation Army will go to Philadelphia tomorrow to meet General George L. Carpenter, London, international head of the Salvation Army, and Mrs. Carpenter.

General Carpenter will speak on the present world crisis and postwar conditions at a luncheon given in his honor at the Bellevue-Stratford Hotel.

The Weather
Occasional Rains And Slightly Warmer Sunday.

SUNDAY NEWS

3 A. M. Edition
The Sunday News carries the full report of world wide news services—LATEST NEWS by Associated Press, International News Service, Wide World, and Complete Local News.

VOL. 20—NO. 10 | Entered as second class matter September 21, 1923 at the Post Office at Lancaster, Pa., under the Act of March 3, 1879. | LANCASTER, PA., SUNDAY, NOVEMBER 8, 1942 | 50 PAGES, 272 COLUMNS.—SIX CENTS.

U. S. INVADES FR. AFRICA

F. D. Declares Move Forestalls Seizure By Axis; Yanks Land In Morocco, Algeria, Tunis, Senegal

AFRICAN FRONT MAY BE KEY TO VICTORY

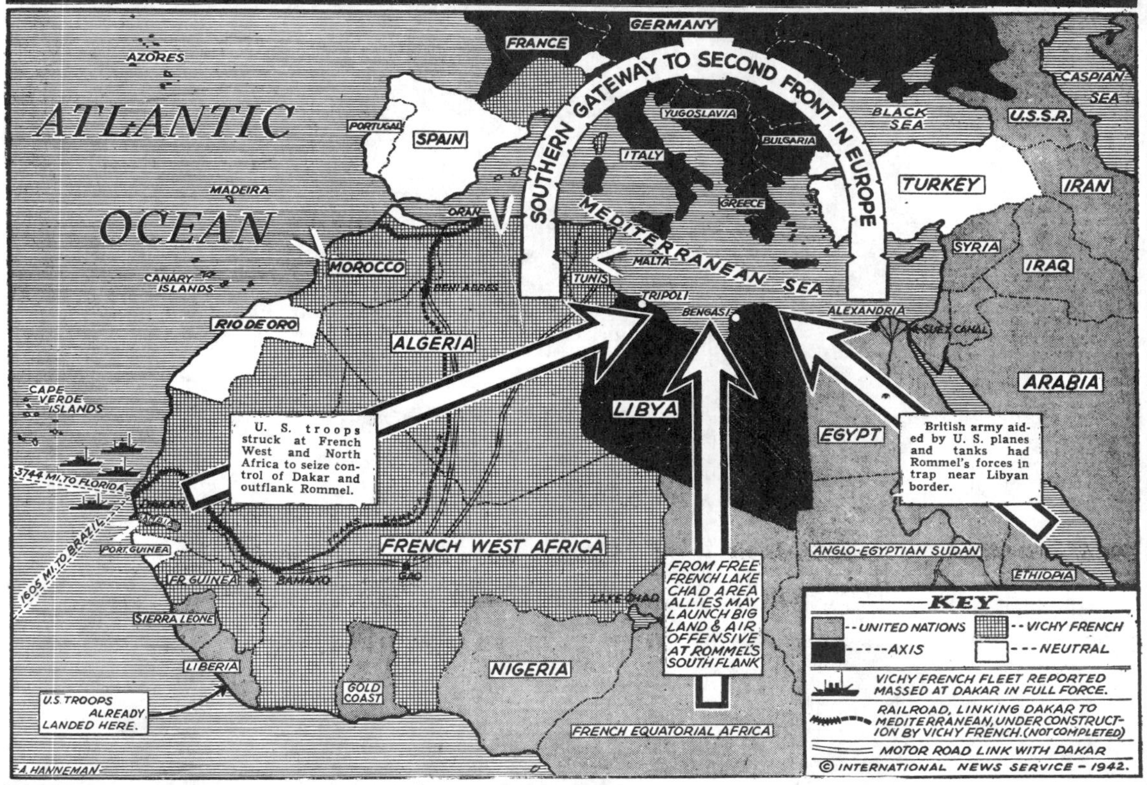

White "V's" in map above, pointing to Dakar, Morocco, Algeria and Tunis, show where American forces are landing in Africa.

First Big-Scale AEF Offensive Is Hailed As 2nd Front Move

Washington, Nov. 7—(AP)—Powerful American expeditionary forces are landing on the Atlantic and Mediterranean coasts of the French colonies in Africa in the first big-scale offensive of the war under the Star Spangled Banner.

An electrifying announcement of the action, obviously aimed at winning complete domination of the Dark Continent and reopening the Mediterranean sea for the United Nations in conjunction with the victorious British drive westward from Egypt, was made in a simultaneous announcement tonight by President Roosevelt and communique from the War Department.

The White House statement said the purpose of the move was two-fold:

1. To forestall an Axis invasion there which "would constitute a direct threat to America across the comparatively narrow sea from Western Africa."

2. To provide "an effective assistance to our heroic allies in Russia."

Thus the Axis had an emphatic answer to its attempts to "fish for information" by broadcasting accounts of heavy Allied troop convoys escorted by warships mustering at the Rock of Gibraltar in recent days.

Troops From British Isles

The troops apparently were some of those which have been concentrated in the British Isles for some time, itching for action as they went through the final stages of their battle training, for they were commanded by Lieutenant General Dwight D. Eisenhower, commander-in-chief in the European theater whose headquarters had been in Britain.

Eisenhower broadcast a message to the people of French North Africa on behalf of the President assuring them that "we come among you solely todestroy your enemies and not to harm you" and issued a proclamation instructing them how to cooperate.

To signify cooperation, the General directed that they fly the French tri-color and the American flag, one above the other, or two tri-colors by day and shine a searchlight vertically into the sky by night. He also directed French naval and aviation units to remain idle.

Pouring Ashore In Morocco

Eisenhower's message indicated that the troops were pouring ashore in Morocco, which has both Atlantic and Mediterranean shores, and the remainder of French North Africa which comprises Algeria and Tunis on the Mediterranean.

Landings also presumably were being made in the French West African colonies, including Senegal, whose capital of Dakar lies only 1,870 miles across the South Atlantic from the bulge of Brazil.

The announcement gave no details of the composition of the troops and their equipment, for obvious military reasons, but said that they were equipped with "adequate weapons of warfare" and that they would, "in the immediate future, be reinforced by a considerable number of divisions of the British Army."

Tanks and Artillery In Number

There was no doubt that the expeditions were made in heavy force with tanks, artillery and all the accoutrements of modern warfare for this new and pomising phase of the conflict. The offensive far surpassed in weight the American invasion of the Solomon Islands in the South Pacific undertaken just three months ago this day.

Announcement of the landings was timed to coincide with the actual debarkation of the troops on their destinations at 9 p. m., eastern war time (3 a.. Sunday, West African time), and was made only after a reassuring message from Mr. Roosevelt's own lips had been broadcast to the French people, asking for their aid to rout their own enemies.

The landing, the announcement said, was being assisted by the British Navy and Air Forces, and "it

INVASION -Page 15

BRITISH SMASH INTO FLEEING ROMMEL TROOPS

Axis Prison Toll Exceeds 100,000 Men As Allies Sweep Onward

Cairo, Egypt, Nov. 7—(AP)—Approximately 100,000 men of Marshal Rommel's Axis army of 140,000 were reported captured or pinned down in pockets far behind the swiftly moving African front today as the British Eighth Army swept on toward the Libyan border after smashing the German armor in its second attempted stand.

NO PRISONERS TODAY

Cairo, Nov. 7 — (AP) — The movement of events in the Egyptian battle are so rapid that some German and Italian soldiers are having difficulty finding anybody who has time to take them prisoner.

One large party of Germans overtaken at an advance airbase asked RAF men to take them prisoners, but were told they were too busy.

"Run off and get captured by somebody with more time to spare," an RAF officer said.

Disregarding the thousands of foot soldiers left in the dusty backwash of the battlefront, Lieut.-Gen. Bernard L. Montgomery's British and American tanks tore into the disorganized flanks of their main prize—the battered remnants of the German armored divisions—west of Matruh in an effort to eliminate them entirely. They already had caught up with this fleeing force once and sent it into headlong harassed retreat a second time.

Montgomery spurred his men on to swifter pursuit of the enemy with the admonition that the "Battle just won is only the beginning of our task." The British object apparently was to harry Rommel's men constantly so they could not rest or regroup their shattered forces.

"Only Beginning"

Montgomery's observation was contained in the following order of the day to the Eighth army:

"I feel sure that the battle we have just won is only the beginning of our task. There is much to be done yet, and it will call for supreme effort and great hardship

BRITISH—Page 15

LONDON CALLS IT '2ND FRONT'

Landing Of AEF In Africa Played Up Over Allied Victory In Egypt

London, Sunday, Nov. 8—(AP)—London acclaimed the United States landings in French North Africa today as the opening of the long-awaited Second Front and both the British government and Fighting French sources were quick to express gratification.

News of the landings electrified the British capital, which had been filled with rumors that something big was brewing. London morning newspapers made over their last editions to give the story precedence over the Allied victory in Egypt.

Typical of the press reaction were blazing eight-column headlines in the News of the World, which proclaimed:

"Second Front Is Opened—U. S. Forces Invade French African Colonies At Many Points."

The British Foreign Office issued a formal statement declaring that the government "subscribed in full to the policy and ideals" set forth in President Roosevelt's announcement of the landings.

"His Majesty's government have but one desire in relation to France, and that is to hasten the day when Frenchmen everywhere will join to restore the independence and greatness of France," the statement added. "The operation initiated by the United Nations in north Africa marks a step toward that day."

SMASH NAZI SUB BASE AT BREST

RAF Reported Active Over Northern Italy In Second Successive Raid

London, Nov. 7—(AP)—United States heavy bombers smashed at the big German submarine base at Brest in a daylight attack today and reports from France and Switzerland indicated the RAF had its big bombers out tonight for a new attack on Northern Italy.

The raid on Brest was made by Flying Fortresses and Liberators (Consolidated B-24) accompanied by RAF fighters. A communique said bombs were seen striking the target—the docks and submarine pens—but no details of the damage were given.

All the bombers returned safely, despite heavy anti-aircraft fire. One

RAIDS—Page 15

Paratroops Capture Vital Airdromes

By ROBERT G. NIXON

With Allied Headquarters In North Africa, Nov. 8—(Sunday)—(INS)—Combined United States armed forces spearheaded by hardy Commando-trained Rangers and Parachutists and covered by a heavy American-British naval and air screen, landed with tanks at numerous points on the French North African coast early today.

Simultaneous landings were successfully completed and beachheads won at many places along the French African coast by the Rangers, whose units participated with British Commandos in the memorable Dieppe assault last August, and by some U. S. Marine and Naval units.

At the same time, swift-striking paratroops of the United States Army were showered from planes farther inland where in short order they captured a number of important military airdromes.

HUGE INVASION ARMADA USED

Gibraltar Center Of Large Scale Fleet Activity, Axis Reports

London, Sunday, Nov. 8—(AP)—Possibly the greatest invasion armada assembled in Europe since the start of the war undertook the invasion of French North Africa today in the first large scale action in the European theater in which the United States has participated.

A force of 24 warships, transports and freighters, followed by the great battleship Rodney and a heavy air escort were reported by the German News agency DNB to have left Gibralter Thursday night.

Carriers In Armada

A possibility that as many as four aircraft carriers accompanied the attack fleet was seen in Axis reports. German broadcasts said the Furious the Argus and another unidentified "flattop" had been observed in the harbor at Gibraltar and a later Vichy report said four carriers were seen there.

100 At Gibraltar

In addition to the vessels which set out eastward into the Mediterranean, DNB said, at least 100 other ships waited at Gibraltar.

Among the 125 originally there, the German reports said, were six cruisers, one auxiliary cruiser, 26 to 28 destroyers, four submarines

ARMADA—Page 15

Reporter Sees Troops Start Big Invasion

By WES GALLAGHER

Allied Headquarters In North Africa, Sunday, Nov. 8—(AP)—American soldiers, Marines and sailors from one of the greatest naval armadas ever put into a single military operation swarmed ashore today on the Vichy-controlled North Africa shore before dawn, striking to break Hitler's hold on the Mediterranean.

Tall, decisive Lieut. Gen. Dwight D. (Ike) Eisenhower, supreme commander of the huge forces involved in the operation, worked throughout the night directing the first great American blow at the Axis.

Ranger Air Units Included

Included in the forces were crack combat troops Rangers (air borne units) and the cream of America's airmen.

British naval and air force units supported the American landing forces, who were preceded by a snowstorm of leaflets and a radio barrage promising the French that the United States had no intention of seizing French possessions and only sought to prevent Axis infiltration.

It undoubtedly was the longest overwater military operation ever attempted, with hundreds of ships in great convoys coming thousands of miles under the protection of British and American sea and air might.

I came on one of these big convoys.

Did Not Know Destination

Fighting-fit American soldiers and airmen, who did not know their destination until a few hours before scrambling into assault barges, crowded the ships to the very funnels and were guarded by aircraft carriers, racing cruisers and destroyers.

Split-Second Timing

Our big convoy arrived at its destination with the split-second timing of a subway train despite storms for many days at sea and danger from planes and submarines.

The entire operation was carried out with the delicate synchronization of an expensive watch, justifying the months of careful planning by Eisenhower and his British-American supreme command.

The vastness of the project, not only from the number of troops involved but from the distances cov-

GALLAGHER—Page 15

GENERAL EISENHOWER

Report Survey Here For Army Hospital

Agents from the New York office of the War Department were reported Saturday to be making a survey of the land between the Lititz and Oregon Pikes and south of the Roseville Road as a possible site for a 300-bed U. S. Army hospital. No confirmation was obtainable from the War Dept.

Parade Today Recalls AEF's Victory Of 1918

More than 2,000 persons representing military, civilian defense and other patriotic organizations will participate in the Armistice Day parade and community celebration at Williamson Field, Franklin and Marshall Campus, this afternoon.

The parade, which will form at Duke and Lemon Sts. at 1:30 p. m., will move South on Duke St. to Chestnut, and West on Chestnut to College Ave. From there the parade will go North on College Ave. to Williamson Field.

Daniel C. Hartbauer, commander of the Pennsylvania Department of the American Legion, will be the guest speaker and will review the parade from Williamson Field in celebration of the 25th Anniversary of the signing of the Armistice. Wednesday, Nov. 11, will be observed as a legal holiday.

Chief Marshal of the parade will be Col. Charles P. Stahr, who will be in the reviewing stand with Hartbauer. Daniel W. Shaub is chairman of the parade committee.

The program to be presented at the field will include: invocation, the Rev. Ernest J. Hoh, pastor of Emanuel Lutheran Church; music, Malta band, William Price, conductor; opening exercise, John C. Kiehl, chairman of the Armistice Day committee; address, John C. Weise, commander of Post 34, American Legion; address, Mr. Hartbauer; music, Malta band; benediction, the Rev. Mr. Hoh; taps, John Emig, Legion Post 30 drum and bugle corps, and echo,

PARADE—Page 15

'They Remember Last December'

POST HASTE—A year after Pearl Harbor, Lancaster's civilian defense shows its armor. On this page are photos of headquarters for City Sector 5, located in the basement of 615 W. Chestnut St. Typical of the efficiency sought in the entire set-up are city and sector maps, handy lights and report forms, and unique "on duty" board above the desk at which Sector Warden John H. Pfenninger presides. Billboard tells at a glance who is on call for all CD jobs at the moment. As in other sectors, supplies were purchased through neighborhood donations. Each of the other six posts in Sector 5 is as completely equipped as headquarters with fourth the quantity.

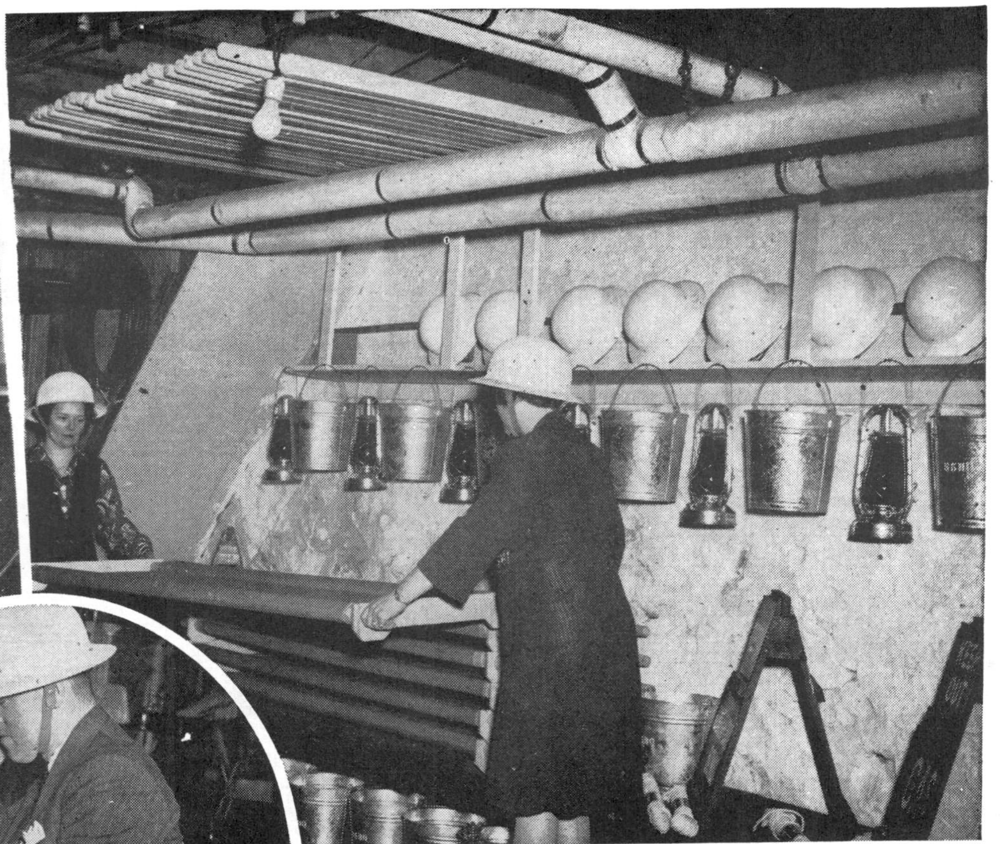

CARRY ON—Spirit of Pearl Harbor anniversary is symbolized by men and women of Civilian Defense in Lancaster who have given long hours to develop the techniques of mercy learned in the London blitz. Sector 5 headquarters equipment is lined up ready to grab. Air Raid Wardens Mrs. E. O. Voris and Mrs. George Brett here lift a stretcher.

THEY'RE DROPPING INCENDIARIES! Here Senior Post Warden E. O. Voris phones report to GHQ.

HIT THAT LINE—White traffic line from steps back to post door serves as guide to wardens in a blackout. All posts are marked with white signs. Many county posts still lack complete equipment—helmets, arm-bands, etc.—available in city.

IN THE BAG—Even first aid bags carried by wardens have post and sector numbers stenciled on. First Aid squads have more complete equipment.

CURTAINS FOR THE AXIS—Home front contribution to war is maximum security for civilians. Post 5 Sector 5 has blackout curtain around doorway. Wardens can work on reports at long table.

BELIEVE IN THESE SIGNS—Cards covering all possible contingencies of an air raid are ready with stands; also garden hose for fire emergencies, axes, first aid kits, ropes—in fact, the works.

PICK YOUR SHOVEL—To dig in rubble of bombed buildings or bury an incendiary, shovels are hanging ready.

STORM CELLAR—All set for service the wardens go out where things are happening. Wardens E. O. Voris (right), John L. Byerly (left), and M. A. Lazarus below), leave Sector 5 headquarters.

LANCASTER NEW ERA

WEATHER
Not so cold; light snow in west and north portions tonight.

VOL. 66—NO. 341 | Entered as second class matter January 21, 1924, at the Post Office at Lancaster, Pa., under the Act of March 3, 1879. Reg. U. S. Pat Off. | LANCASTER, PA., WEDNESDAY, JANUARY 6, 1943 | CITY EDITION | 12 PAGES—96 COLUMNS | 20c PER WEEK—4c Per Copy

ALL PLEASURE DRIVING OUTLAWED

POLICE ASKED TO STOP CARS; OFFENDERS TO LOSE RATION

All Holders of A, B, and C Cards in East Are Affected; Detailed Rules Due Tomorrow.

STILL MORE DRASTIC ORDER IS PREPARED

WASHINGTON, Jan. 6—(AP)—The Office of Price Administration today outlawed all pleasure driving by holders of "A," "B" and "C" gasoline ration cards on the Atlantic seaboard and prescribed the cancellation of gasoline rations as the penalty for failure to comply.

The order is effective at noon, Eastern War Time, tomorrow.

The aid of all state, county and municipal law enforcement agencies in the 17 eastern states and District of Columbia is being asked to help the Federal government in preventing pleasure driving, by reporting violations to local ration boards or local OPA offices.

"The presence of passenger cars at any gathering for purposes of sport or amusement will be taken as prima facie evidence that gasoline rations and tires are being dissipated needlessly and illegally," OPA said. "The ban on pleasure driving will also apply to driving to purely social engagements."

Simultaneously, OPA declared fuel oil heating rations of all buildings except those used for residential purposes in the east would be "cut substantially within the next 24 hours." No details were given.

The drastic prohibition on pleasure motoring was reinforced by an OPA warning that "even more serious measures" are being prepared to be ready for immediate use "if the current situation gets worse."

The action was taken at the instance of the Petroleum Administrator for war, OPA said, in a joint effort to plug every leak in the "dangerously scant supplies" of petroleum products on the Eastern Seaboard.

OPA said: "Pleasure driving will be interpreted broadly." Details will be contained in a regulation to be issued not later than tomorrow.

When a police officer encounters a motorist whom he believes to be driving for pleasure, the burden of proof as to the essential nature of the trip will "rest wholly on the motorist," OPA said.

The driver must satisfy his ration board that his use of gasoline was justified by his occupation or the essential character of his errand.

The Board may permanently cut off the ration or reduce it to the extent it considers necessary.

Obvious evidence of the misuse of gasoline—such as the presence of a parked car at a race track or movie theatre—may result in

(See GASOLINE—Page 4)

Held by Japanese

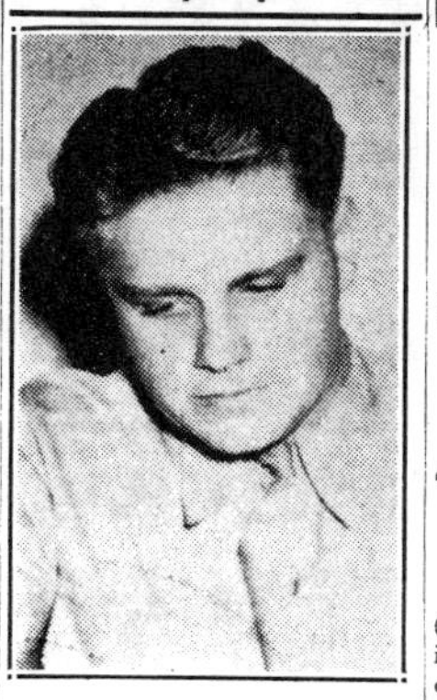

RICHARD P. LINDEMUTH

MAYTOWN MAN IS JAP CAPTIVE

Chief Warrant Officer Lindemuth Was on Bataan When It Fell.

Chief Warrant Officer Richard P. Lindemuth, 25, son of Mr. and Mrs. Willis Lindemuth, Maytown, who was reported missing in action in the Philippines in August, is alive and a prisoner of the Japanese, according to official dispatches received here.

A message from the War Department to Mr. and Mrs. Lindemuth on December 29 informed them that their son was a prisoner, and on Monday they received another message, giving an address to which they can write to him.

Lindemuth enlisted in the Army in 1935, after his graduation from the Maytown High school, and is serving his third enlistment. When he was reported missing he had the rating of technical sergeant in the Army Air Corps but later his family received a letter written several months previously, notifying them of his promotion to Chief Warrant Officer.

A veteran of the bitter fighting in the Philippines, Warrant Officer Lindemuth was on Bataan when it fell into enemy hands.

BRITISH SUBS SINK BIG AXIS TRANSPORT, SHELL PORT IN ITALY

LONDON, Jan. 6—(AP)—The Admiralty announced tonight that a large enemy troop transport and a supply ship had been destroyed and that two other ships had been hit and probably sunk by British submarines in the Mediterranean.

The big troop transport was encountered off Sicily while bound southward—toward Africa—with a heavy escort but she was hit by three torpedoes and sunk, the communique said.

The communique said a submarine also had scored "a large number of hits" in a bombardment of a brick railroad viaduct near Palinuro, Italy, 80 miles southeast of Naples, and had inflicted considerable damage. Another, it said, shelled harbor installations in the enemy occupied Greek port of Kyme. Kyme is in the Aegean Sea, on the east coast of Greece.

BOOK DRIVE OPENED; 'WAR AND PEACE' 1ST

WASHINGTON, Jan. 6—(AP)—Tolstoi's "War And Peace," contributed by Elmer Davis, Director of War Information, is the first book collected in the 1943 campaign to obtain millions of volumes for the armed forces.

OWI, in announcing Davis' contribution, called upon Americans for "good" books.

DEMOCRATS RULE HOUSE BY THIN EDGE

Rename Rayburn Speaker By 11 Votes as 78th Congress Opens.

"INDEPENDENT" NOTE AS SESSION STARTS

WASHINGTON, Jan. 6—(AP)—By the slimmest margin in a decade, Democrats kept control of the House and returned Sam Rayburn, of Texas, to the Speakership today in organizing the 78th Congress for President Roosevelt's report tomorrow on a year of war and the way to victory.

Rayburn defeated Rep. Joseph Martin (R-Mass), who, as a result of the outcome, automatically became the minority leader. Rep. McCormack, another Bay State lawmaker, was renamed Democratic floor leader at a party caucus yesterday.

The vote for Speaker was: Rayburn 217; Martin 206, on strict party lines.

After his re-election, Rayburn told a cheering House that when victory at war is won "this time there must be no stopping until the vandalism and paganism of Berlin, Rome and Tokyo are wiped from the face of the world."

The Senate's first session lasted exactly 30 minutes, with 89 members present. It was largely devoted to the swearing in of new and re-elected members. The first business was the presentation by Senator Connally (D-Texas) of the credentials of Senator O'Daniel (D-Texas). First Senators sworn in were Bailey (D-NC), Ball (R-Minn), Bankhead (D-Ala) and Bridges (R-NH).

With a larger membership, and more routine to be followed, the House could not complete its first-day doings so quickly.

Even before the election of the Speaker there was the ritual of a roll call by states, which in itself took about 30 minutes. This showed the presence of 216 Democrats, 206 Republicans and four minor party members.

Traditional Opening

It was the first Congress in a quarter of a century to convene with the nation at war. The opening followed the traditional pattern of initial sessions of new Congresses. Most members were in their seats before the stroke of twelve, and the galleries were well filled in advance.

Introduction of bills and resolutions started simultaneously with

(See CONGRESS—Page 4)

MARTIN NAMES 7 TO CABINET

Dr. Stewart, Miss O'Hara, Dr. Marts Are Retained From James' Regime.

HARRISBURG, Jan. 6. — (AP) — Governor-elect Edward Martin today named seven members of his cabinet, three of them retained from the outgoing administration of Governor Arthur H. James.

The appointments announced were:

Dr. A. H. Stewart, retained as Secretary of Health.

Brigadier General Robert M. Vail, Adjutant General, who served as Deputy Adjutant General under Martin.

David W. Harris, Republican city chairman of Philadelphia, Secretary of Revenue.

Charles M. Morrison, of Philadelphia, Secretary of the Commonwealth. Morrison was Martin's campaign publicity director.

Miss S. M. R. O'Hara, present Secretary of the Commonwealth, as Secretary of Welfare.

Miles Horst, Secretary of the Pennsylvania State Grange, as Secretary of Agriculture.

Dr. A. C. Marts retained as executive director of the State Defense Council.

Martin previously named George I. Bloom, of Washington, Pa., as secretary to the Governor.

The Governor-elect, who will be inaugurated on January 19, said remaining cabinet appointments would be announced next week.

"In selecting my cabinet," asserted Martin, "I have kept in mind ability to do the job, loyalty to me personally and that the members when selected could work together as a team. Many of the members are making sacrifices to take the places and these acceptances are deeply appreciated."

Martin said that the State Defense Council post was regarded as of cabinet rank.

Germans Reported in Flight, Blast Bridges in Caucasus; U.S. Fleet Shells Munda

BOMBERS AID WARSHIPS RIP KEY JAP BASE

Flying Forts Also Blast Enemy Ships at Buin and Shortland Isle.

10 TOKYO SHIPS SUNK OR HIT AT RABAUL

By the Associated Press

American warships boldly steaming into the heart of the Japanese defense zone in the Solomons have successfully bombarded the airfield at Munda, New Georgia island, 180 miles northwest of Guadalcanal, where the enemy has been developing an important base.

The foray, announced in a Navy Department bulletin, was the deepest northwest thrust by U. S. surface ships so far reported in the immediate waters of the Solomon archipelago.

The communique said Japanese bombers tried to intercept the warships but were driven off by four Grumman "Wildcat" Navy fighter planes which shot down four into the Pacific and probably destroyed two others. It said the action occurred in the pre-dawn darkness of yesterday.

Part of 2-Fisted Assault

The sea attack was part of a two-fisted assault by Allied forces on Japanese bases menacing the American hold on Guadalcanal. Heavy bombers were credited officially today with sinking or damaging 10 enemy ships in Rabaul harbor, New Britain.

In the background of these attacks was an Australian warning that Japan was massing a new war fleet in the Southwest Pacific.

The Navy communique said that B-26 "Marauder" medium bombers followed the warships in another attack on enemy installations at Munda and that Flying Fortresses, heavy B-17 bombers, attacked an enemy cruiser at Buin, on Bougainville island, but that the results of neither attack were observed.

The text of the Navy's commu-

(See PACIFIC—Page 2)

TIRE IS DAMAGED ON OPEN MANHOLE

The right rear tire, tube and wheel on an auto driven by John K. Brubaker, twenty-six, 32 N. George St., was damaged when he ran into an open manhole while driving northeast on Manor St., between Fairview Ave., and Ruby St., this morning, according to city police.

Brubaker said he did not see the open manhole until after the accident.

Axis Planes Left Behind by Fleeing Nazis

When General Montgomery's Eighth Army marched into Derna, in Libya, they found that the Axis forces under Rommel had fled. At the air field, just outside the town, the British found these wrecked Nazi planes. Most of the bombers and fighters had been damaged by R.A.F. bombings and strafings. Those that had escaped were hastily demolished by the retreating Germans.

ALLIES REGAIN TUNISIAN HILLS

Commandos, Paratroops Aid in Mateur Drive; U. S. Bombs Cruiser.

By WES GALLAGHER

ALLIED HEADQUARTERS IN NORTH AFRICA, Jan. 6.—(AP)—British troops, including Commandos, attacking 15 miles west of Mateur, have driven the enemy from strategic hills and are now mopping up in the first activity on the northern Tunisian front in some time, an official spokesman announced today.

Mateur is 20 miles southwest of the Tunisian naval base of Bizerte.

This success was stated to have been achieved against some of the best German forces in Tunisia. The Germans had been digging in there for weeks. A Nazi counterattack was reported to have failed.

Parachute troops took part in the British attack, it was added.

A month ago the British tried a similar assault but were beaten back, mainly because they lacked air support.

The attack was supported by RAF Hurricane bombers and fighters, and an RAF spokesman announced that during yesterday four Nazi Fooke-Wulf 190 fighters and one JU-87 dive-bomber were shot down for the loss of one British plane.

U. S. Planes Bomb Cruiser

Flying Fortresses—U. S. four-motored B-17 bombers—raiding the enemy port of Sfax were said to have scored hits on or near a cruiser leaving the harbor and to have left the power station in flames. American medium B-26

(See AFRICA—Page 9)

Davis Says Halsey Wrong In Seeing War End in '43

OWI Chief Warns U-Boat Menace Is Still Serious, Says Nazis Building Subs Faster Than Allies Sink Them

WASHINGTON, Jan. 6—(AP)—Elmer Davis, Director of War Information, spoke out today against over-optimism about an early end to the war and stressed particularly the "continuing serious submarine menace."

Davis, who in his New Year's message to the people last week advised them to expect casualties and losses inevitable in war, took specific exception to a prediction of Admiral William F. Halsey, South Pacific commander, that the war will end this year.

Has No Such Information

"I have no information to support such a prediction, although I have been trying to get some," Davis told a press conference.

The Information Director said that, to the best of his knowledge, the Germans were still building more submarines than the United Nations were sinking, while the toll that the German subs were taking of Allied shipping was creating "heavy losses in ships and in the cargoes that go with them, and sometimes trained men on them."

However, Davis said that the United Nations, particularly the United States, are now building ships faster than Axis submarines were sinking them.

Admiral Land of the Maritime Commission announced yesterday that this nation's shipyards alone

(See DAVIS—Page 9)

RATION BOARD TO MOVE JAN. 15

Central Headquarters Will Be Located in Odd Fellows' Hall.

Lancaster's central rationing headquarters will move to a new location about Jan. 15, it was announced today.

The new location will be in the Odd Fellows' Hall, West Chestnut street, just west of Water street. In the meantime the central rationing staff will continue to maintain the offices on the fourth floor of the Woolworth building where all business will be transacted until the new headquarters is established.

Moving of the rationing headquarters to a building where all departments will be on the ground floor has been considered for several months. The plan, rationing officials believe, will help end the congestion which occurred daily because offices were scattered in several rooms and because all per-

(See RATIONING—Page 9)

BOY BORN ON WAY TO LOCAL HOSPITAL

The stork overtook the Ephrata American Legion ambulance, enroute to the General hospital with Mrs. David Wenger, Ephrata R. 3, a maternity patient, and the baby, a boy, was born at 3 A. M. today, just as the ambulance reached the city limits.

Ralph Haines and Roy Weaver, who were in charge of the ambulance, after caring for the mother and baby, continued to the hospital, arriving at 3:15 A. M.

Mother and baby both were reported "doing fine" by hospital attendants.

9000 MINERS IDLE OVER UNION DUES

9 Penna. Hard Coal Mines Closed Or Curtailed By Dispute.

WILKES-BARRE, Jan. 6—(AP)—Nine thousand miners remained away from their jobs in nine of the largest collieries in the Pennsylvania anthracite fields today in a factional dispute centering around a 50-cents a month increase in union dues.

The movement, condemned by the United Mine Workers of America, developed while the UMW and mine operators worked on a plan to increase production for war needs, in accordance with a request from Solid Fuels Coordinator Ickes.

7 Collieries Are Closed

Seven collieries were closed and operations in two others, which were surrounded by pickets, were curtailed. Together the collieries produced 8,000,000 of the 30,000,000 tons of anthracite mined during 1941 in Luzerne county, a center of the industry.

A dues increase from $1 to $1.50 was voted at a UMW convention

(See COAL—Page 9)

SOVIETS PRESS WIDE ADVANCE IN DON AREA

500,000 of Hitler's Finest Troops Being Routed From Southern Zone.

COSSACKS WIELD SABERS ON ENEMY

MOSCOW, Jan. 6—(AP)—The German Army was reported in full retreat in the Caucasus today, blowing up bridges and mining roads in a desperate effort to check the surging advance of Russian forces driving hard at its heels.

Red Star, organ of the Soviet army, said Russian forces, which already had stormed and won the important towns of Mozdok, Nalchick, Prokhladnenski, Kotlyarevskaya and Maiskoye, continued their sweeping advance along a wide front, winning back a large number of additional towns.

The entire province of North Osetia, lying between Ordzhonikidze and Nalchik, had been won back under the Red banner by Soviet forces operating along the west bank of the Terek river, while other Russian troops rolled the Germans back to the north, Red Star asserted.

125 Miles From Rostov

To the north, along the Lower Don, the Russians were reported fighting forward after overrunning the important Nazi bridgehead town of Tsimlyansk and thus driving a second spearhead within 125 miles of Rostov, whose fall might doom the entire German force in the Caucasus.

The first spearhead was thrust earlier southwest of Kamensk to a point about 100 miles northwest of the great Don mouth port of Rostov.

(Reuters, British news agency, estimated in London that more than a half-million of Adolf Hitler's finest troops were in full retreat in the Caucasus and the Middle Don.)

Red Star said the main line of German fortifications at the eastern end of the Caucasus front was shattered Monday when the Russians stormed the approaches to Nalchik and occupied the city after a terrific street battle.

Soviet troops were said to have pursued the Germans northward from this sector across a western branch of the Terek river. In a 12-mile final thrust yesterday, Red Star said, the Russians drove into and captured the town of Prokhladnenski, 30 miles northeast of Nalchik.

Prokhladnenski is the juncture where the trunk line Caucasus railroad from Rostov to the Baku oil-

(See RUSSIA—Page 9)

So Your Husband's Gone to War?

by Ethel Gorham

Chapter Three

Holding The Home Front

If you have children it is not only wiser, it is infinitely more normal and sound to try and keep your physical home together. Taking the children back to Grandma, even if you find you have to work, is only a limited solution. One way, of course, is to try to get a good housekeeper who can help you manage your apartment and child while you go out to work. That presupposes a good salary and a well-planned economic existence. It also presupposes that you have the phenomenal luck to find a domestic worker with the brains and willingness needed to take over the household duties. They are few and far between and if you have one such, bless Allah.

If you do get a good maid she will be worth her good wages in the money and worry she can save you. Shopping economically, planning wisely, she can make the going much easier for you. She will give you peace of mind on your job all day because you will know that your house, your child, your budget are well cared for.

However, if you can't get a good maid for love or money, or you can't afford one no matter how much she can save you,

(See HUSBAND—Page 4)

Last Suspected Cases Of Smallpox Taken Off List

Several "Suspicious" Patients Do Not Have Ailment, Doctors Report; Vaccination Rush Continues; 59 Still Under Observation

No new cases of smallpox have been reported in Lancaster since noon yesterday and all "suspicious cases" have been removed from the observation list, health authorities said this morning. There are nine active cases of the disease in Lancaster.

Health authorities said mass vaccination in both city and county continued and physicians and health officials praised the people for their willingness to cooperate in the determined fight to prevent spread of the infection.

59 Under "Observation"

Fifteen homes, and two Catholic convents, housing about 59 persons, remained under "observation" quarantines as precautionary measures.

The ninth case was S. H. Suter, 65, 822 N. Duke St., reported at noon yesterday. Several hours later, Dr. A. J. Greenleaf, county medical director, said that a "suspicious case" at Columbia was removed from the observation list.

Re-vaccinate Teachers

School teachers in most of the borough and township schools have been asked to be re-vaccinated. The question of vaccinating teachers and re-vaccinating older pupils is being left entirely in the hands of local School Boards.

Dr. P. V. Clarkson late yesterday afternoon completed his inspection of local markets to determine whether all handlers of food had been vaccinated. Dr. Clarkson said only five persons in five markets had failed to comply with the order. All left the markets willingly, he said.

The order for broader vaccina-

(See SMALLPOX—Page 9)

Bulletin

ORDERS 50-CENT BOOST IN PRICE OF HARD COAL

WASHINGTON, Jan. 6.—(AP)—Price Administrator Leon Henderson today authorized an increase of approximately 50 cents a ton on Peennsylvania anthracite coal. He said the increase "reflected higher production costs involving the extension of the 35-hour week to six days" and other cost increases in the industry.

WEATHER
Eastern Pennsylvania: Wednesday Continued Cold.

Intelligencer Journal

6TH WARD
Fat Collection
Saturday, Jan. 30

The Leading Newspaper in the Garden Spot of America, Home Owned for Home Folks Since 1794

VOLUME LXXIX.—NO. 118. | Entered as second class matter June 23, 1928 at the Post Office at Lancaster, Pa., under the Act of March 3, 1879 Reg. U. S. Pat. Off | LANCASTER, PA., WEDNESDAY MORNING, JANUARY 27, 1943 | CITY | 16 PAGES, 128 COLUMNS. | 20c PER WEEK 4c Per Copy

ROOSEVELT AND CHURCHILL MEET IN AFRICA TO MAP 1943 OFFENSIVES

Agree Upon Plan To Force Unconditional Surrender Of Germany, Italy And Japan

President Flew 5,000 Miles To Attend Conference At Casablanca; Highest Military Figures Of U. S., Great Britain Also In Attendance As Were French Leaders De-Gaulle And Giraud; Stalin, Generalissimo Chiang Both In Touch With Decisions To Give Them Full Aid

Casablanca, French Morocco— (AP) —President Roosevelt and Prime Minister Churchill, in the most unprecedented and momentous meeting of the century, have reached "complete agreement" on war plans for 1943 designed to bring about the "unconditional surrender" of Germany, Italy, and Japan, it was disclosed Tuesday.

Defying every tradition, the President of the United States flew across 5,000 miles of the Atlantic ocean for a 10-day meeting with Winston Churchill which saw the leaders of the two nations bring General Charles de Gaulle and Gen. Henri Honore Giraud together for the first time in a little villa just outside this city.

WAR STAFFS PARTICIPATE

Virtually the entire war staffs of both nations participated in day and night discussions which ended Sunday afternoon with a press conference before a group of war correspondents flown secretly from Allied headquarters halfway across North Africa.

These are the high spots of the conference, which Roosevelt and Churchill agreed was unprecedented in history and may decide the fate of the world for generations to come:

1. The leaders of American and Brtiain, both military and civil, have agreed on a war plan for 1943 designed to maintain the initiative in every theater of the war;

2. Churchill and Roosevelt agreed that peace can come only through "unconditional surrender" of Germany, Italy, and Japan;

3. Generals Giraud and De Gaulle, meeting for the first time under sponsorship of the President and Prime Minister, are negotiating for a united French movement designed to put French armies, a navy and an air force again into the field against the Axis.

4. Premier Joseph Stalin of Russia was kept informed of the results of the conferences. In fact, Churchill and Roosevelt offered to meet Stalin "very much farther to the east," but the Russian chief was unable to leave the U.S.S.R., due to the need of his directing the present Red Army offensives.

The President and Prime Minister also have been in communication with Generalissimo Chiang Kai-Shek and "have apprised him of the measures which they are taking to assist him in China's magnificent and unrelaxing struggle for the common cause."

5. Maximum material aid to Russia and China will be one of the prime aims of the U. S. and Britain.

6. Roosevelt visited American troops in the field in North Africa, the first American president to visit an active war theater since Abraham Lincoln.

The meetings were held in a closely-guarded, barbed-wire-surrounded inclosure at a hotel in Casablanca under the greatest secrecy.

CHURCHILL ARRIVES FIRST

Prime Minister Churchill arrived for the meeting first. When President Roosevelt arrived by plane a few hours later, he dispatched Harry Hopkins to the Churchill villa, and the Prime Minister immediately came to start the meetings.

The first began at 7 o'clock in the evening of Jan. 14 and lasted until three o'clock the next morning.

President Roosevelt met correspondents in the garden of his villa Sunday afternoon.

Protecting American fighters and Spitfires roared overhead as the conference was held. The only woman present was WAAC Captain Louise Anderson of Denver, Colo., a stenographer from Lieut. Gen. Dwight D. Eisenhower's headquarters.

Hopkins was among the first to arrive, along with the President's flying son, Lieut. Col. Elliott Roosevelt, who was wearing the Distinguished Flying Cross recently awarded him.

While the President's envoy, Robert Murphy, flitted in the background, Generals Giraud and De Gaulle, clad in French army uniforms, appeared from the President's quarters. They were closely followed by Roosevelt himself, wearing a light grey suit with the usual cigarette holder held at a jaunty angle.

Churchill, in a dark grey suit and with the inevitable cigar, fol-

More Of ROOSEVELT On Page 11

Conferred At Casablanca

PRESIDENT ROOSEVELT

PRIME MINISTER CHURCHILL

COMMENT

Most Of Official Washington Encouraged And Stimulated By News

SOME DISAPPOINTED

Washington — (AP) — The words "inspiring," "stimulating" and "encouraging" were freely used Tuesday night as official Washington discussed the Roosevelt-Churchill conferences in Africa, but there also were some expressions of disappointment.

These centered largely around the fact that a union of all French factions was not announced as something accomplished, but something to be striven for. In addition, Senator Wheeler, Dem., Mont., frequent critic of Roosevelt foreign policy, declared that while the President's journey was "spectacular," the announcements contained nothing essentially new.

HULL GRATIFIED

On the other hand Secretary of State Hull expressed gratification over the conferences, which he described as "most wise and timely."

Hull said:

"The proceedings and the decisions of the conference, which were most wise and timely, are of the most far-reaching importance.

"They will prove of the greatest interest to all of the nations

More Of COMMENT On Page 11

REDS MOP UP TRAPPED NAZIS AT STALINGRAD

Report 50,000 Axis Troops About Liquidated; U. S. Troops Take Tunisian Pass

250 DIE IN MARSEILLE

(By the Associated Press)

The Russians announced Tuesday night the substantial liquidation of the 50,000 Axis troops that had survived in the Stalingrad trap, the bloodiest defeat ever suffered by one of Hitler's armies and one which had resulted in capture or death for more than 200,000 German and mercenary troops.

"The troops of the upper Don front, continuing their offensive against German Fascist troops encircled in the area of Stalingrad, have broken through numerous and powerful enemy fortifications after fierce battles and have in the main completed the liquidation of the German Fascist grouping," the Soviet command proclaimed in a special communique.

DAILY 12,000 IN ACTION

Only 12,000 of this lost Army remained in action, Moscow added, and that force was split in two and isolated. Moreover, the three big railroads fanning out from Stalingrad were declared wholly freed of the invader in a restoration of one of Russia's most vital communications centers.

The German High Command itself, which already has acknowledged in effect that the army before Stalingrad was done for, had admitted earlier Monday that its troops had been "concentrated in

More Of REDS On Page 11

Beauties To Entertain

DOROTHY LA FERN

BETTY BRUNKE

GERALDINE MAE POWELL

BEAUTY WINNERS WILL APPEAR HERE AT BIRTHDAY BALL

Miss Phila., Miss Chicago And Miss Eastern Pennsylvania To Entertain Friday Night

Three American beauties will entertain at the President's Birthday Ball Friday night in the Moose Home, it was announced Tuesday by Christian C. Rudy, general chairman of the committee in charge of the affair.

They are: Miss Chicago, first runner-up in the last beauty pageant to Miss America, who is Miss Betty Brunke, Chicago; Miss Philadelphia, who ranked high in the last beauty contest held in Atlantic City, who in private life is Miss Geraldine Mae Powell, Philadelphia and Miss Dorothy LaFern, who was chosen as Miss Eastern Pennsylvania, last year. She is from Philadelphia.

"We were lucky to obtain these girls because their presence is demanded all over the country," Rudy announced. The entertainment committee has worked hard and this is part of the result.

TO CROWN LOCAL QUEEN

Rudy also announced that Jay and Mary Meiskey, co-chairmen of the entertainment program, have arranged to have a local girl crowned as "Queen of the 1943 Birthday Ball."

There will be prizes galore, novelties, floor shows and music by three outstanding bands.

"We have left nothing undone to afford one of the best evening's entertainment," Rudy said. "And by attending, each one will help swell the fund for the Infantile Paralysis Chapter in Lancaster which has been doing such fine work in co-operation with the Crippled Children's Society of Lancaster. With this annual ball, our com-

More Of BEAUTIES On Page 11

"We Lead All the Rest"
FARM CORNER
By
The Farm Editor

42 FARM MACHINERY PERMITS ARE ISSUED

The 1942-43 tobacco crop which, in the closing days of buying, hit a top price, is moving rapidly to the warehouses, but according to verified reports, its packing is moving slowly because of a lack of manpower. Many of the oldtime tobacco case packers are in other jobs, mostly war industry, and many of the younger men, who have had experience, are sticking close to the farms on account of the deferment regulations.

It is generally understood that draft boards are taking a common sense viewpoint; that the valuable tobacco crop has to be processed and are not interfering with those in the farm deferment group who take jobs as tobacco packers in the different warehouses so long as they quickly return to the farms as soon as farm work opens up in the Spring.

THREE FARMS CHANGE HANDS

Thomas T. Graff sold his 48-acre farm in Hensel to Amos Moore, near Pleasant Grove, at private sale. Graff purchased a small property in Hensel from Roy J. Steele. Possession of both places will change April 1.

A. M. Keener, Lancaster real estate agent, announced sale of a 40-acre farm in Paradise township, near Iva, for John Dushl, Lancaster, to Daniel M. Buckius and wife, of Paradise, at private terms.

Also, sale of a 23-acre farm for Walter F. Lefever, at Hessdale, Strasburg township, to Tobias S.

More Of FARM CORNER On Page 11

Intelligencer Journal Weather Calendar

COMPARATIVE TEMPERATURES

Station	High	Low
Intell Journal	[illegible]	18
Water Works	51	30
Ephrata	47	27
Last Year (Ephrata)	[illegible]	32
Official High for Year, Jan. 24		58
Official Low for Year, Jan. 14		[illegible]
Character of Day		Cloudy

HOURLY TEMPERATURES
(Tuesday)

3 a. m.	36	4 p. m.	24
4 a. m.	34	5 p. m.	24
5 a. m.	33	6 p. m.	23
6 a. m.	32	7 p. m.	23
7 a. m.	31	8 p. m.	22
8 a. m.	31	9 p. m.	21
9 a. m.	30	10 p. m.	20
10 a. m.	29	11 p. m.	19
11 a. m.	28	Midnight	18
Noon	27	(Wednesday)	
1 p. m.	26	1 a. m.	17
2 p. m.	25	2 a. m.	16
3 p. m.	25	3 a. m.	15

SUN
Rises—8:17 a. m. Sets—6:17 p. m.

More Of WEATHER On Page 11

MILK BOTTLE DEPOSIT OF TWO CENTS FIXED FOR LANCASTER AREA

The Pennsylvania Milk Control Commission Tuesday fixed a two-cent deposit on milk bottles in the Lancaster Milk Marketing Area 14. Effective Feb. 1, Area 14 will include all of Lancaster County under a recent order of the commission which was approved by former Governor James. It now consists of Lancaster city, Columbia and all the area within five miles of the city lines.

The new order also provides a deposit of five cents on gallon jugs, 25 cents on cases and 50 cents on bulk can containers. The deposit charges only apply to multiple use containers.

The commission said its action was designed to bring about retrun of containers to their owners "so as to avoid waste of materials and reduce the cost of distribution of milk."

"One general result," it added, "has been more careful handling of bottles and prompt return to the dealers who own them. The over-all picture shows a saving of material as well as much less broken glass in streets where it may become a menace to children and to automobile tires."

The commission said it had been found that consumers in general approve of a bottle deposit as soon as they become accustomed to it. It said a hearing held in Lancaster on Dec. 16 produced testimony "for a bottle deposit of the kind and amount carried in the order."

The Office of Price Administration has ruled that a bottle deposit on mulitple use containers does not constitute a price increase so long as the deposit is not out of keeping with the original cost of the container.

Set Five-Can Limit On Holdings Of Canned Goods

OPA Announces Penalty Of 8-Point Stamp For Each Excess Can When New Ration Books Are Issued In Several Weeks

Washington—(AP)—Every person in the United States may possess without penalty a total of five cans of fruits and vegetables when rationing of those goods begins.

The Office of Price Administration announced this limit Tuesday. It apparently reflected a pessimistic view about the size of canned goods inventories throughout the country, since up until a few hours before the announcement high officials of the agency hoped that the allowable limit might be between eight or 10 cans a person.

The penalty for having more than five cans of vegetables or fruit (not counting home canned goods or cans containing less than eight ounces each) will be the loss of an 8-point stamp for each excess can when new rationing books are issued in three or four weeks.

NOT ALL ARE HOARDERS

An OPA spokesman said this penalty was designed to discourage hoarding. However, officials acknowledged that not everyone who

More Of SET LIMIT On Page 11

SLEET, SNOW HERE; THREE PERSONS HURT

A combination of freezing rain, sleet and snow Tuesday turned highways by nightfall into glazed pathways of danger for what little traffic ventured onto them. Three persons were injured in falls on sidewalks.

Heaviest snowfall was in the Elizabethtown area, where the depth was reported as three inches. Mount Joy and Landisville reported about an inch about midnight. Lebanon county reported moderate snowfall over ice, while Chester county had no snow.

State Highway Department officials employed 165 men and 47 trucks to cinder danger spots on highways and city streets. Much colder weather is forecast for Wednesday.

James Ritz, thirty-five, 24 Chester St., was admitted to the Lancaster General Hospital with a possible fracture of the right ankle suffered in a fall at 11 p. m. Tuesday in the 300 block of East King St. Violet Reeder, forty-one, 242 S. Queen St., was treated at the hospital for a fractured right wrist. She told attendants she slipped and fell on Water Street. Mrs. Cecelia Skiles, fifty-four, 29 W. Vine St., was treated at St. Joseph's Hospital for a fractured left wrist.

SPEAKER EXPLAINS PROGRAM TO SOLVE TEACHER SHORTAGE

Includes Speed Up Of Courses In Teachers' Colleges, State Official Says

A definite program to meet the problems of teacher supply and to forestall a still more serious acute teacher shortage has been formulated by the Department of Public Instruction, Prof. S. B. Stayer, director of teacher training at Millersville State Teachers' College, declared at an area conference sponsored by the State Department at MSTC Tuesday.

The program includes, he said,

More Of SPEAKER On Page 11

SWISS SIRENS HINT AIR RAID ON ITALY

London (Wednesday)— (AP) —Air raid warnings were sounded in Basel and Zurich, Switzerland, shortly after midnight this morning Reuters reported. This might indicate that Allied planes were headed for an attack on Italy.

Squadrons of American, British and Dominion fighter planes made sweeps over Axis targets on the Continent Tuesday, the Air Ministry announced, while Ventura medium bombers raided railway installations at Bruges, Belgium.

The Allied fighters in their forays over Northern France and Belgium were reported to have knocked down three enemy fighters in combat, while themselves losing four planes. The bomber attack on Bruges was carried out without loss, the Ministry said.

A small number of enemy aircraft were reported to have dropped bombs during the day on two towns on the southeast and southwest coasts, causing some damage and a few casualties. One of the raiders was shot down off the southwest coast.

REPORTER KILLED BY AA GUNFIRE ON WAY TO PARLEY

Canadian Correspondent Hit By Bullet In Plane Over Spanish Morocco

Casablanca, French Morocco, Jan. 24 (Delayed) — (AP) — Enroute to cover the biggest story of his career, war correspondent Edouard Baudry of the Canadian Broadcasting Corporation was killed by anti-aircraft fire over Spanish Morocco when the plane in which he was riding with other correspondents became lost in bad weather.

Baudry was one in the group of correspondents flown in three transport planes halfway across North Africa from Lieut. Gen. Dwight D. Eisenhower's headquarters to cover the historic meeting between President Roosevelt and Prime Minister Churchill.

FLEW OVER SPANISH MOROCCO

Baudry's plane encountered bad weather and flew over a city in Spanish Morocco.

Ground defenses opened fire and a machine-gun bullet hit him while the pilot was turning the plane out to sea.

An emergency landing was made at Port Lyautey, but Baudry died a few hours later in a hospital.

(His death was disclosed Monday in Montreal. Baudry is survived by his widow and one child.)

He was buried with full American military honors at Port Lyautey with correspondents and Brig. Gen. Robert McClure in attendance.

One crew member of the transport was injured, but the rest of the correspondents escaped injury.

The correspondents, all accredited to Allied headquarters in North Africa, were notified suddenly to

More Of REPORTER On Page 11

RATION BANKING GOES INTO EFFECT TODAY

Washington—(AP)—Ration banking—a new kind of checking account to keep track of ration coupons for merchants and wholesalers—will go into effect throughout the nation Wednesday.

The plan has been tested the last three months in several New York state communities. It was adopted by the Office of Price Administration both to simplify and safeguard the handling of the millions of coupons involved in wartime rationing.

Consumers are not involved, and small merchants need not use the system, which is designed mostly for business men handling large quantities of coupons which might otherwise get lost or stolen.

The ration account will operate almost exactly the same as an ordinary checking account except that coupons are deposited and checked out instead of money.

EXPLOSIONS HEARD IN NORWAY SECTOR

London, (Wednesday) — (AP) — A Reuters Stockholm dispatch early today reported that throughout the Swedish province of Jaemtland violent explosions were heard from the direction of Norway, suggesting a raid on the German-held port of Trondheim.

GIRAUD, DE GAULLE AGREEMENT MAY BE TEDIOUS PROCESS

Agree To Fight Germans; How, When And Who Is To Lead Remain Unanswered

Allied Headquarters In North Africa (Wednesday) —(AP)— Gen. Charles De Gaulle, fighting French leader, and Gen. Henri Giraud, North African high commissioner, have "met and talked" in Africa at the insistence of President Roosevelt and Prime Minister Churchill, but well-informed sources asserted last night that any definite settlement between the two is going to be a long, tedious process.

OFFICIAL COMMUNIQUE

Out of a two-day meeting between the two French leaders at the historic Roosevelt-Churchill conference at Casablanca, French Morocco, there has come little more than this official communique issued by the two generals:

"We have met. We have talked. We have registered entire agreement on the end to be achieved, which is the liberation of France and the triumph of human liberties by the total defeat of the enemy.

"This end will be attained by union in war of all free Frenchmen fighting side by side with all Allies."

They both agreed that French-

More Of GIRAUD On Page 11

RICKENBACKER WOULD HIT JAPS AT HOME THROUGH AIR POWER

Washington — (AP) — Foreseeing no final victory until 1944, Capt. Eddie Rickenbacker said Tuesday he agreed "100 percent" with General Douglas A. MacArthur that "we must hit the Japanese at home—through the air with tremendous striking power."

Rickenbacker said our victories at Guadalcanal, Buna and Gona were tremendous but "we can not defeat Japan by an island-to-island campaign—we must strike at the heart of Japan through air power." MacArthur had asserted Sunday that the successful Papuan campaign pointed to "offensive power in swift massive strokes rather than the dilatory and costly island-to-island advance that some have assumed to be necessary."

Rickenbacker said Japan might hold out for years if it had time to take back to its mainland the fruits of conquest.

The air line executive also asserted the United States should plan now "protection for post-war air transport" to assure the nation a ranking place in commercial aviation.

MILITARY FUNERAL FOR LAST VETERAN

Camp No. 19 Sons of Union Veterans, will conduct a full military funeral at 2 p. m. Wednesday for George Paules, of Marietta, last of the county's Civil War veterans who died Saturday. Services will be held at the Samuel Frey Memorial Funeral Home, 101 W. Market St., Marietta. Members of American Legion, Veterans of Foreign Wars and United Spanish War Veterans posts in the Marietta vicinity will assist.

FULL PAGE OF ROOSEVELT STORIES ON PAGE FOUR

Stories of various angles of the historic Roosevelt-Churchill conference as well as pictures of some of the stars of the big show in Africa will be found on Pages Four and Five.

AIRCRAFT: Mrs. Catherine Cunningham, 614 N. Duke St., mother of five grown children, took Armstrong's Aircraft Training Course last August. Now she's a full-fledged riveter. Owen Good, ex-bricklayer, New Holland R. D. 1, "bucks" the rivet.

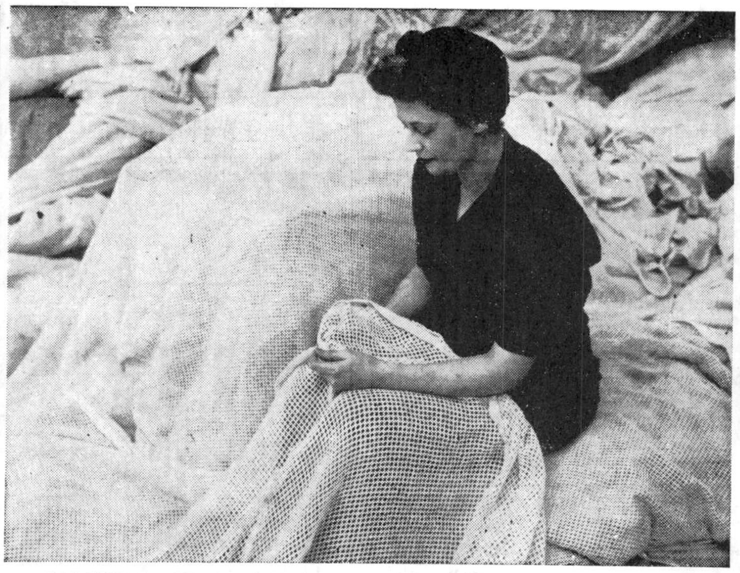

CAMOUFLAGE: Miss Margie Krall, 326 S. Queen St., sold dresses before she took her war job at Armstrong's. Now, without any previous experience, she's mending camouflage nets. "Anybody that's handy with a needle and thread can do this job," she says.

BOMB RACKS: Andros Kusuplos, 302 W. Vine St., used to be a shoemaker but now he's working at Armstrong's to back up his three sons in the service. He's proud of his job in the department that made the racks for bombs that were dropped on Tokio.

SHELLS: Mrs. Elsie Grill, of 7 S. Duke St., swapped her job in a local cafeteria for the job of banding shells. She's in this war "to the finish" and believes that "more production" should be America's motto.

COULD YOU DO ONE OF THESE WAR JOBS?

MAYBE you've been wondering whether you could do an essential war job—whether you have the training or experience such a job requires. If that has been in your mind, meet these twelve war workers who have signed up for good paying war jobs at Armstrong's. Most of them had never seen the inside of a factory before. But now they are successfully doing interesting and important work on aircraft, camouflage, shells, bomb racks, and other vitally needed war materials.

Here are just a few of the hundreds of patriotic men and women from every walk of life who are now doing war work at Armstrong's. Some of them are busy mothers and housewives who have taken these war jobs because they want to do their part. Some are business and professional men. Others are here because some relative is in the armed forces. Many have joined Armstrong's ranks because they recognized that their old jobs were not essential. All are here to back up our armed forces with plenty of the things our fighters need.

If you want to do vitally needed war work, Armstrong has interesting jobs that almost anyone can do. Age or inexperience is no drawback. Armstrong will train you to do the work —pay you while you are learning.

Any day, except Sunday, take a "Linoleum Plant" bus from Penn Square and come out to our Employment Office for a friendly interview. The office opens at 8 in the morning and stays open until 9 at night for the convenience of people who are busy in the daytime.

Persons now fully engaged in war work need not apply.

ARMSTRONG CORK COMPANY

West Liberty St. Lancaster, Pa.

FLOORING: Abner E. Snyder, Manheim, R. D. 1, inspects asphalt tile destined for a large aircraft plant. Other workers make special Armstrong floorings for camps, ships, powder plants and arsenals.

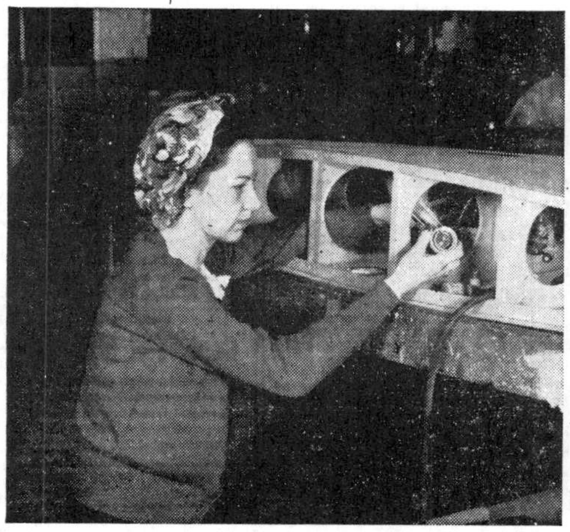

AIRCRAFT: Mrs. Harriet McGallicher, 715 Manor St., ran a restaurant. At Armstrong's she learned to be a skillful electrical worker in four weeks. Now she installs wiring in bomber wing tips.

BOMB CASTING: Anthony Tretter, Lancaster R. D. 3, a paperhanger for 20 years, learned how to make bomb castings in a few days after he came to work at Armstrong's. Now he's hard at work on bombs to blast Hitler and Hirohito.

BOMB RACKS: Miss Rose Tallarico, 321 E. Chestnut St., worked in a candy shop until she came out to Armstrong's over a year ago. Now she's an expert at her important job—inspecting and gauging bomb racks.

PROJECTILES: It took Mrs. Emma A. Yost, Lancaster R. D. 6, only one day to learn to run a drill press. A former office worker and mother of two children, she's helping to make projectiles at Armstrong's.

CAMOUFLAGE MATERIAL: Agnes N. Donaghy, 222 W. Vine St., former dental laboratory employee, applied for work at the Employment Office Tuesday evening. On her first day at work she started in a war job—making camouflage material at Armstrong's.

SHELLS: Verne Richards, 510 W. Lemon St., is one ball player the Boston Red Sox will have to do without this year. He's busy inspecting and packing shells to smash the Axis.

AIRCRAFT: William L. Miller, 208 Walnut St., Columbia, was an automobile salesman before the war and well known as the former chief of the Columbia Fire Department. Now, with two sons in the service, he helps to "keep 'em flying" by handforming aircraft parts.

Ruth Drew $80,000 A Year, And Was Grossly Underpaid

Sultan of Swat One of Game's Top Pitchers

Third of a series.
BY HARRY GRAYSON
NEA Sports Editor

GEORGE HERMAN RUTH is down in history as the Sultan of Swat, but he also was one of the greatest of left-hand pitchers. Of all his records, Babe Ruth is proudest of having pitched 25 scoreless innings in the World Series — for the Boston Red Sox against the Brooklyn Dodgers in 1916 and Chicago Cubs in '18.

Most other pitcher-outfield converts made the change only after their arms failed — Smoky Joe Wood, etc. — but with Ruth that, of course, was no consideration. The Bambino was still the best left-handed pitcher in the American League when Ed Barrow moved to the New York Yankees with him and made him an outfielder because of his thumping. The Bam played acceptably at first base, was a left-handed catcher in his youth.

Ruth never made a bad play, such as throwing to the wrong base. He wasn't a long thrower like Long Bob Meusel, but was remarkably accurate—a left-handed Joe DiMaggio in that respect. He never played the sun field, yet the only work of fiction suggested by his amazing career was written by the late Heywood Broun and called, The Sun Field.

In his younger days, Ruth was a crafty base-runner and an accomplished slider.

Still Most Popular Figure

Ruth was baseball's most glamorous figure. He was the game's highest-salaried performer — $30,000, $52,000, $70,000, $80,000 in '30 and '31, $75,000, $50,000, $35,000.

Even at $80,000 he was grossly underpaid, for he was the biggest bucks office magnet in the annals of the sport. Only last summer, at the age of 48, he packed Yankee Stadium with 80,000 admirers—and hit a home run off Walter Johnson! He remains the most popular man who ever played. He was also baseball's heaviest-fined bad boy and as time marched on, its forgotten man.

Ruth became a home run specialist while pitching and pinch-hitting for the Red Sox. In the days of choke hitters, he gripped the bat 'way down at the end. He was the first batter to concentrate on home runs. He shot for the works. He instituted something new and sensational when baseball was sadly in need of a tonic—following the Black Sox scandal.

Ruth had a double swing, looked good striking out. He had perfect rhythm. It was the power in his wrists at the end of his tremendous swing that enabled him to uppercut the ball and belt it for such remarkable distances.

Balloon On Toothpicks

The fabulous feats of Ruth fill a book. Ball players would be arguing about how far the ball was hit by him while it was still in flight. He was the only batter visiting players would watch in practice. I'll never forget the two little Waners watching Ruth and the late Lou Gehrig in batting practice before the World Series opened in Pittsburgh in '27. Their eyes popped out of their heads as the two giants, who seemed like men from another world, popped one ball after another into and over the right field stand.

There was the World Series game with the Cubs in Chicago in '32, when Ruth pointed to the left field stand, and hit the next pitch into it — smack dab. He was so good he could call his shots.

Ruth was a slender kid when he first came up, stood six feet two and weighed 215 pounds at his peak. In later years, he blew up until he looked like a balloon on toothpicks.

Ruth had a devouring appetite. Had he been sawed in two on any given playing day, half of Stevens' concessions would have been found inside him.

He is inherently bright, an excellent bridge player and golfer.

He remembered few names, called everybody Kid.

Here's the $64 question which keeps bums in saloons up half the night: Who played right field for the Yankees before Babe Ruth?

Sammy Vick is the answer, but nobody believes it.

NEXT: Walter Johnson.

Nobody ever hit the ball quite like Babe Ruth.

3-Day Benefit Card Arranged At Bay Meadow

NEW YORK, March 30—(AP)—Conferences, controversies, confusion and chaos have contributed to a hectic 24 hours for racing that left the average $2 bettor spinning as dizzily as a revolving door in a bargain basement.

But when the period was over the turf fraternity had a tentatively scheduled Navy relief program for the first three days of April at Bay Meadows, a mystery at Oriental Park in Havana and new owners for Agua Caliente in Mexico.

3-Day Charity Card

Jerry Giesler, chairman of the California racing board, said last night that he had tentatively arranged for the three-day charity meeting this week-end at Bay Meadows after first announcing that the abbreviated session would not be held.

Giesler made his two decisions at Washington where he had come for a conference with rubber director William M. Jeffers. Jeffers, Giesler said, "dumped" the Bay Meadows problem back into the laps of Giesler and two fellow Californians. A public meeting will be held in San Francisco Monday to determine if the track is to operate further.

Can't Agree On Bill

Oriental Park announced Sunday it would offer six programs a week to compensate for the blackout among United States tracks but yesterday horsemen there were reported not in accord with the track's plans and a decision is not expected until almost post time today.

Until Bay Meadows tentatively scheduled its three-day meeting all parks in continental United States were to be idle from March 27 to April 8.

John S. Alessio, manager of the Banco Del Pacifico in Ti Juana, Mex., said the newly formed Caliente Jockey Club, owned by Mexican capital, had purchased the Baja California Jockey Club, which controls Agua Caliente.

He indicated the group, of which Edward Nealis of Los Angeles is president, would conduct racing at the plant. Under the pari-mutuel betting system only. It has been closed since Oct. 18 because of a labor dispute.

Alley Babble

THE name of Hen Greiner is one that has been mentioned frequently around the bowling lanes for Hen is generally to be found among the scoring leaders . . . Last night he made certain that his name would be on top for he put together a 658 that paced the Overlook 12 League . . .

Greiner started off with 211, added 246 and finished with 201 for his fine triple. . . But, at that, he had stiff competition for Bud Sullenberger was right in there with 208-232-209 for 649, and Bill Binkle was right behind with 232-225-163—620, followed by Gene Daugherty with 220-177-215—612. . . Other nifty singles included Harry Miller's 226; Lew Morrison's 224; Bob Moore's 222 and a pair of 211s by Bill Donohue and Charley Deyer. . . Bob Leinaweaver made the 5-6-10 pin split and Heck Forrey turned in the 6-10-7 pin split. . .

Hen Frey and Bill Sidler shared top honors in the Fulton Major League, each getting 622. . . Sidler had 181-247-194, while Frey turned up with 209-256-157. . . Walt Coble was next with 169-238-210 for 617 and Clarence Smith posted 201-207-193—601. . . Bill McAdoo hit 231 with Harold Stumpf, J. Tompkins, Bill Lines and R. Fralich each getting 213. . .

Frank McLain was right in the groove for the Church League, knocking off 218 and 607, while Sam Smith had 217 and 563. . . John Rodman made the 4-7-10 pin split. .

Bill Shertz took top honors for the Armstrong Aircraft boys with his 232 and 606, while Walt Reinfried knocked off the 5-9-7 and 5-7 pin splits.

Roy Weit was the big gun in the Lititz League last week with his 213-202-207—622, while Amos Kraybill's 218 led the YMCA "A" League and R. Benner's 216 and 533 topped the Moose "C" circuit. . . Luke Buckwalter made the 6-9-7 pin split. . .

The gals in the Watch Girls League were right in stride with Kathryn Huss getting 216 and 525, while Reba Braner had 211 and 508 and Erla Witmer contributed 199 and 517 with Anna M. Shaeffer knocking off 505. . .

Alice Vermot hit 200 and 462, while Charley Regar grabbed 212 and 598 for high honors in the Monday Night Mixed circuit, with Ruth Echternacht getting 198 and Marian Connell 191 and 529 for the top places in the Retail Ladies League. . . Ginnie Mowrer stepped up with 188 and 529. . . Dolly Caccomo made the 2-5-10 pin split while Mildred Leisey contributed the 6-7; Nora Gilgore the 5-7-9 and Irene Grossman the 5-6-7. . .

Sally Aierstuck went all the way to 218 and 481 to lead the Acco League, her 218 setting a new high single mark. . . Bud Montgomery's 200 and 583 and Evelyn Bowman's 157 and 439, together with Ethel Nonnemacher's 157 paced the Ladies and Men's League. . . Catherine Wiebush made the 4-7-10 pin split. . .

Winners at Boothman's included: (ten pins): Hank Sharley's 225 and Bee Rinehart's 185; (duck pins) Dick Harral's 263; Bob Johnson's 222; Russ Blank's 218; Bill Goodwin's 214; Paul Shaffstall's 211; John Murphy's 187; Bill Baumler's 184; Walt Scott's 184; Alice Vermot's 180; Christy Groff's 175 and Lib Zahn's 151. . .

Church League Cage Title At Stake Tonight

After a full week's layoff Broad Street and St. Andrew's, the Church League finalists, will meet in the second of their three game series tonight at 7:45 o'clock on the YMCA court.

St. Andrews won the first tilt by piling up a lead in the first half and then going on to win out by a two-point margin, 40 to 38. They will therefore be out to turn in another win which will clinch the series and give them the first Church League pennant they have won. Broad Street, on the other hand, realize that in order to remain in the running they must come out on top tonight, and will throw everything they have into this tussle.

St. Andrew's will line up with Eshleman and Fuhrman at Forwards, Hershey at Center, and Gibble and Boettger at Guards; with Fisher in reserve to fill in at one of the forward spots. Opposing this team will be E. Shreiner and Hurst at Forward for Broad Street, with Pollack at Center and P. Shreiner and McCue at Guard.

Is His Face Red? Player Reports To Wrong Draft Board

ASBURY PARK, N. J., March 30.—(AP)—An embarrassed George Stirnweiss, whose speed helped him steal 73 bases in the International League last season, trudged slowly back to the New York Yankee training camp today to "explain everything" about his draft status.

Stirnweiss, a rookie shortstop, left here Sunday, telling his mates he had been ordered to appear for his physical examination at Hartford, Conn.

Instead he went to Norfolk, Conn., near his home at Kent. There he was told the board had no record of him and he was not examined. Previously Stirnweiss had said he was in 3A because he helped support his mother.

But from Norfolk, Va., came word that he was registered there, was due this morning for induction and that he had been in 1A all along.

The ball player explained that he had registered in Virginia but had requested a transfer when he obtained a job as a coach in Connecticut. When he received his orders he went north instead of south in beilef his papers would be there.

Denver Boy Among Hurlers Working Out Here With Toronto

Dick Knerr, Who Played With Teams in Virginia League, After Career on County Sandlots, Vies With Veterans for Team Berth

By GEORGE W. KIRCHNER

MAYBE he won't quite make the grade, but no one can ever say that husky Dick Knerr from out Denver way didn't give it the old college try.

The Lancaster county boy, who acquired pitching experience in Class "C" baseball, is now among the 20 or so men reporting daily as Burleigh Grimes sends his Toronto Maple Leafs of the International League, through their spring workouts at Stumpf field.

You won't find his name on the printed roster which the Leafs are circulating around the town, but you'll find husky Dick—(he must weigh over 200)—out there on the field going through the motions just like such veterans as Luke (Hot Potato) Hamlin, who was sent to Toronto in a deal involving Frankie Coleman and the Pittsburgh Pirates.

Strictly on His Own

Knerr, as Manager Grimes will tell you, is strictly on his own. He wrote to General Manager Peter Campbell and asked for a tryout and now he's crossing his fingers and hoping to make the grade.

Dick, who had experience with teams up around Denver and Reading, first broke into organized ball a few years back when he was on the hurling staff for Chief Bender's Newport News team of the Virginia League. That was during the 1941 season and he pitched a few innings against Billy Rogell's Lancaster Red Roses in an exhibition spring training game at Newport News.

From this team, Knerr finally landed with Petersburg, also in the Virginia League and his record of 17 wins against 13 losses was one of the factors that convinced Campbell he was worth a tryout.

Grimes Non-Committal

Grimes was non-committal on Knerr, just as he was on Tom Davis, who played first base for the Roses at the start of last season, and Major Bowles, the pitcher, who joined the Leafs in their workout yesterday. Bowles, it was pointed out, is still the property of the Roses, and is only working out, but it's a safe guess that if the Major shows something that interests the Leafs a deal may be arranged.

Davis, however, belongs to Toronto. After he was given his release by the Roses midway last season, Tom returned to North Carolina and finished with the Landis, N. C., club. When Toronto bought that franchise, Davis became the Leafs' property and was ordered to report here.

"We haven't had much chance to study any of the players individually," Grimes remarked after yesterday's double-session, "but we'll probably get around to that in a few days. Right now, veteran and rookie, alike, are strictly on their own."

The Leafs' pilot hoped to be able to split his squad into two teams for a few innings of practice this afternoon, planning to increase the number of innings and shift the lineup with each day. The visitors open their spring program on April 6 when they go to Wilmington to play the Athletics.

Of the advanced roster, only four players are still missing. Ralph (Red) Kress, the veteran infielder who was signed to act as lieutenant to Grimes, is driving here from the coast and is expected any day now. Al Smith, recently sold to the Leafs by Harrisburg, is also said to be enroute, as is George Motto, an infielder, and Harry Davis, another infielder, who is not expected to report until Friday.

Here's The List

All the others, however, are here and these include:

PITCHERS — Dick Conger, Sid Goldstein, Luke Hamlin, Jimmy Hopper, Ralph McCabe, Paul Mulach, Walt Smola, Nick Strincevitch, Joe Sullivan and Knerr.

CATCHERS—Herb Crompton and Dewey Williams.

INFIELDERS — Tom Davis, Charles Letchas, Al Rubeling with Harry Davis, Al Smith and George Motto due to report.

OUTFIELDERS—Ed Black, Pete (one-armed) Gray, Jim Gruzdiz, Kerm Kitman and the veteran Jimmy Ripple.

Lynn Myers, who used to play around here, is on the roster, but has not reported and Toronto officials say he is undecided whether he'll play or continue on his defense job.

Hockey Finals

New Haven, Conn.—(AP)—League President Maurice Podoloff Monday set Wednesday, March 31, as the date for the opener of a five game American Hockey League Championship series between Indianapolis and Buffalo.

Both the opener, and the second game, set for Saturday, April 3, will be played at Buffalo. The teams then move to Indianapolis for the third game, Sunday, April 4.

EAST END CLIPPERS WIN, 58-33

East Lampeter		G.	F.	Tl.	East End Clippers		G.	F.	Tl.
Shaeffer	F	5	1	11	Flory	F	6	0	12
Sheid	F	4	0	8	Reese	F	10	0	20
Kreider	C	0	0	0	Zook	C	10	2	22
Flory	G	4	0	8	May	G	0	0	0
Jenks	G	2	2	6	Duke	G	1	0	2
Barley	C	0	0	0	Grabill	G	1	0	2
					Bachman	F	0	0	0
Total		15	3	33					

LILIES EASILY WIN, 70-29

Lilies		G.	F.	Tl.	Wolves		G.	F.	Tl.
Finney	F	5	1	11	Palumbo	F	2	0	4
Wolfer	F	10	0	20	Sherbaun	F	1	0	2
Coolidge	C	6	5	17	Turton	C	0	0	0
Rineer	G	6	4	16	Shumaker	C	0	1	1
Martin	G	3	0	6	Hershey	G	3	0	6
					Hagy	G	8	0	16
Total		30	10	70	Total		14	1	29

Barker to Add Spring Football Drills to F. & M. Gym Classes

Three Hershey Bears Gain Places On All-Star Team. Kuhns Pays Bowling Bet. Other Bits Of Sports Notes.

by GEORGE W. KIRCHNER

PUTTING ONE WORD AFTER THE OTHER . . . And just in case you didn't know it, the Hershey Bears placed three men on the American Hockey League's All-Star team . . . They included Rodger Jenkins, defense, Wally Kilrea, center and Harry Frost, right wing . . . The team was picked by the 112 players of the seven clubs in the League and since these boys were in the thick of the action all year long they certainly are qualified to select the outstanding . . . Which, of course, gives the selection of the three Bears added significance . . . Just in case you're interested the entire team consisted of Bell, Buffalo, goalie, Beisler, Buffalo, defense, and Brown, Indianapolis, left wing . . . Hank Lauzon of the Bears, was picked for the second team which consisted of Karakas, Providence; MacKenzie, Cleveland; Cunningham, Cleveland, Summerhill, Cleveland and Locking, Cleveland . . . For the all-star coach, the players selected "Cooney" Weiland, coach of the Bears . . .

You'll be interested to know that "Bud" Allen, who played guard for Poss Miller at F. & M. some years back and later went to Shillington High as football coach, is now a Lieutenant in the Navy . . . He was in town last week to see his old pal, Carvel Malcolm, now recuperating at his home following an operation . . . Allen looks right snappy in his uniform . . .

About a year ago, Rufe Kuhns, well-known in local bowling circles, told a group of boys at Overlook that if "Pink" Wiley, a veteran maple-spiller, ever bowled over 650, he, Rufe Kuhns, would buy all present a steak dinner at the Stevens House . . . A week or so ago, Pink turned up with a sparkling 712 and as a result the boys enjoyed a steak (just imagine steak these days)—dinner with all the trimmings . . . Nick Motto, who first came to town as trainer when the Red Roses moved here from Hazleton, is now doing his training for Uncle Sammy . . . He's in the Navy and was in town the other night . . . Nick was with the Roses at the start of last season, but quit to take a job with the Scranton Miners in the Eastern League . . . Then after the baseball season he joined the Gobs . . . Likes it very much and looks to be in the proverbial pink . . .

Harry Westerby, trainer for the Toronto Maple Leafs, now working out here, came on this job a day or two after finishing his chores as trainer for the New York Rangers' hockey team . . . It's his first attempt at baseball training . . . You can just bet that Howard Gordon, general manager of the York club of the Inter-State League, will be over here to look over the Maple Leafs . . . The reason: Gordon sent a few of his Harrisburg players to Toronto and since both clubs have working agreements with the Pittsburgh Pirates, it appears that the Yorkers will land those boys whom Burleigh Grimes feels need additional experience . . .

When the pessimists talk of abolishing sports for the duration, they'll do well to consider what the National Professional Football League did for service charities last year . . . Elmer Layden, president of the League, announced today that his circuit raised $680,384.07 last fall, the largest amount raised by a single athletic organization . . . And certainly a figure worth consideration . . . Now if you'll stop and think over the amounts raised by baseball, horse racing, golf and other sports, you're apt to arrive at the conclusion that sports have their places in these hectic times . . . Of the money raised by the gridders, Army Emergency Relief received $463,206.90 and $51,464.56 was paid into the Navy Relief Fund . . . The balance, $161,712.61, was distributed among other war relief agencies, including the Red Cross, USO, United Seamen's Service and canteen funds . . . The boys seem to be in line for a few congratulations . . . So step up and give them a big pat on the back . . . The line forms to the right, but don't push . . .

OUT OF "DOGHOUSE" NOW

Everything's Just Fine With Medwick Now That He's Dodgers' Head Man Again

By SID FEDER

BEAR MOUNTAIN, N. Y., March 30—(AP)—Don't look now but Ducky (don't call me Muscles) Medwick is out of the Brooklyn Dodger doghouse, which just goes to show you even an elephant might forget.

The big temperament and left-field man is not only palsy-walsy with every one of the daffiness boys but no one even seems to remember that when the 1942 season ended he was about as popular as a combined case of batting slumpitis and charleyhorse.

Had Tiff With Mates

There was talk that he'd had more than just wistful words with several of the boys, and the hints were about as heavily veiled as a hula dancer that he benched himself the last few days of the season to save his .300 batting average—which is exactly what he wound up with. And there's no denying that over the winter, the Dodgers definitely put him on the trading block, but their price was too fancy.

But now, he's the little white-haired boy once more. Guys walk around patting him on the back. He smiles at everyone and actually wishes everyone a good morning and a good evening, rain or shine. Incidentally it's been mostly shine at this Dodger camp and the Bums are well along in their training.

He's Now No. 1

There's no doubt that Medwick has received word all is forgiven. One story is that the Brooklyn front office "suggested" that this type of treatment be given the muscle man, because with Pete Reiser and his big bat gone into the Army, Ducky is now No. 1 on the Dodger hit parade.

All hands realize that when Medwick knows he's the Mr. Big, he's a different guy altogether. With Reiser as the chairman of the Brooklyn "knock-their-brains-out" committee the last couple of years, Joe has been just a guy named Joe at the plate. Sure, he hit .318 for '41 and .300 for '42, but just compare that with his .329 average for his 11 years in the big time. This year, he's strictly the Dodger power, and that's a role he can play as if he wrote it himself.

All Set For Season

Right now, he knows he's one of the three fellows whose jobs are set for '43. The other two are Mickey Owen, heading the catching department, and Dolph Camilli, who's the watchman at the first-base gate. The rest of the lineup is still strictly a quiz program.

And Muscles also knows he's the guy who's supposed to hit. So this is fair warning to rival pitchers in the National League—Muscles is on the prowl again; you'd better keep the door to the bomb shelter a-swinging.

JOE MEDWICK

FIGHTS LAST NIGHT

DETROIT—Willie Pep, 129¾, Hartford, Conn., outpointed Bobby McIntyre, 135, Detroit, (10).

BALTIMORE—Lulu Constantino, 130, New York, outpointed Frankie Carto, 128½, Philadelphia (10).

CHICAGO—Tommy Bell, 147½, Detroit, outpointed Johnny Rozina, 149½, Milwaukee (8).

PROVIDENCE—Tony Costa, 131, Woonsocket, R. I., outpointed Patsy Brandino, 127¾, Hamilton, Ont. (10).

HOLYOKE, Mass.—Tommy Jessup, 137, Springfield, Mass., stopped Norman Rahn, 145, Philadelphia (2).

NEWARK, N. J.—Pvt. Clint Conway, 180, Cleveland, stopped Willie Thomas, 207, Philadelphia (7).

NEW YORK—Lee Oma, 177, Detroit, stopped Jimmy Gordon, 178, Tampa, Fla. (2).

Only 6 Players From Last Year Still Available

Spring football practice at Franklin and Marshall College will be more in the form of a different type of exercise for the gym classes rather than with any definite idea of moulding a team together for next fall, Dick Barker, Diplomat coach, announced today.

No date has been set for the opening of the spring drills, Barker added, but there is a possibility that the pigskin sport will again make its appearance within the next ten days.

Only 6 Players Here

As matters stand right now, F & M. has only six players remaining from last year's squad and of these five are in the Marine Reserves, subject to an early call, while the sixth plans to join the Navy.

The holdovers from last year include Joe Tomcho and Duane Doty, centers; Joe Hersh and Sammy Sardo, guards and Dave Jacobs and Eddie Trees, backs. All excepting Trees are in the Marines while Trees expects to take a test for the Navy soon.

"With such uncertain conditions," Barker commented, "it would be foolish to plan a spring practice with the purpose of making plans for next fall. Instead, we'll try a little football with the gym classes and in that way we'll be able to accomplish a two fold purpose. The boys will be getting their exercise and those who have football ambitions will be learning a few of the fundamentals of the game. Besides, there's always a chance that we might uncover some football talent."

Uncertain On Team

F. & M. is still uncertain about next season. Whether it will be represented on the gridiron is something that college authorities are unable to say today, and they announced that they are still going ahead on the day-to-day basis in sports.

Only 49 Out For Drills At Notre Dame

SOUTH BEND, Ind., March 30.—(AP)—The once mighty football legions of Notre Dame have dwindled to a corporal's guard.

The effect of war on collegiate athletics was felt with full force on the campus yesterday when Coach Frank Leahy called the Irish boys out for the opening of spring practice.

Only 49 Report

Whereas in past years the coaching staff has been overrun with 100 or more aspirants for places on the famed Irish gridiron teams, Leahy found himself yesterday with just 49 athletes—and 21 already have been summoned to report for active military duty at the end of the present semester May 1.

That left just 27 possibilities for next fall and almost to a man they said their military status was uncertain.

Approximately 40 of the 48 were freshmen and there were only five letter winners, not one of whom plays in the backfield.

Navy Holds Key

Leahy frankly admitted that the Navy holds the key to Notre Dame football hopes. If special trainees sent here by the Navy are permitted to play and if there are enough good football players, things might look better in the fall.

"I haven't any idea how many of these boys, if any, will be back to play next fall," he said. "Neither has anyone else. However, it looks like our only hope of having a representative team lies in what help the Navy may give us in special trainees it will send to Notre Dame in the future.

"Not knowing anything about that now, it may well be that all of us will have to start from scratch next fall and spring practice won't mean a thing. The only consolation, as far as I can see, is that all other coaches and schools are in the same boat."

Twelve of the 48 candidates who reported yesterday were backfield men—but 11 are freshmen. One experienced aspirant was Ed Krupa, of Flint, Mich., who has six minutes of varsity competition to his credit.

Big Boys Battle For The Right To Play St. John's

NEW YORK, March 30—(AP)—If height makes might, then two of the country's most powerful basketball teams clash in Madison Square Garden tonight for the national collegiate crown.

Wyoming, western finalist, is led by 6-foot 7-inch Milo Lomenich while Georgetown, standard bearer for the east, has John Mahnken, an inch taller than his rival.

And the personal duel between these scoring giants not only should settle the NCAA title, won a year ago by Stanford University, but also will determine which team opposes St. John's of Brooklyn Thursday night in a contest whose entire receipts go to the Red Cross.

St. John's, sparked by the 6-foot 9-inch Harry Boykoff, last night drubbed Toledo University, 48 to 27, for the national invitational championship. In a consolation game, Washington and Jefferson spilled Fordham, 39 to 34.

Boykoff won the award as the tourney's most valuable player by dropping in 13 points and proving outstanding on defense.

Gets Coaches' Award

New York — (AP) — The late George Keogan, Notre Dame mentor, was voted the annual award of the National Association of College Basketball Coaches for 1942-43. The award goes to the man who, in the opinion of the coaches, has contributed the most to basketball as a sport over a period of years.

Wins Berth, But Goes Down With Measles

By The Associated Press

RED SOX—After proving himself man enough to win the shortstop berth, Eddie Lake came down with the measles. His illness makes it impossble for the Sox to hold infield drill as Bobby Doerr has not yet reported and Manager Joe Cronin's excess poundage keeps him from playing.

CUBS—Now that Outfielder Bill Nicholson has signed his contract, Manager Jimmy Wilson has quit worrying about Lou Novikoff. But Wilson would like to see Catcher Clyde McCullough and Shortstop Eddie Stanky report soon. Both are the top candidates for their positions and both are good hitters.

INDIANS—Pitchers have reached the stage where each should be working at least five innings at every start, Manager Lou Boudreau said today, then added that "there aren't enough games to go around." The manager is concentrating on the seven freshman flingers and is permitting the older players to take care of their own conditioning.

ATHLETICS—The Athletics, in camp for only a week, open their spring exhibition schedule today with a contest against the University of Delaware nine. Orie Arnitzen, who won seven of eight for Williamsport last year, has changed his mind about quitting baseball for the duration and is expected to report today.

GIANTS—Manager Mel Ott took one look at Napoleon Reyes, Cuban baseball player, and decided to give him a chance of winning the first base job. Reyes, who has spent the past two seasons on the Giants' Jersey City farm, is 6 feet, 1 inch tall and weighs 205 pounds. He will be on the sidelines, however, until his size 12 shoes arrive from Havana.

PHILLIES — With only three infielders available, Catcher Mickey Livingston may play first base in the Sunday exhibition against the A's. Bucky Harris, however, says he is talking deals for three shortstops and a first baseman, all of whom have either played in the Majors or in the Double A Minors.

BRAVES—Casey Stengel says his outfield is all set with Charles Workman, who clubbed .327 for Nashville last year, in center; Tommy Holmes in right field; and Chet Ross in left. But Stengel feels that his ace batter, Catcher Ernie Lombardi, has given up baseball for the duration.

YANKEES—Manager Joe McCarthy has used Johnny Lindell, towering pitcher, on the mound, at first, at third and in the outfield but said today the lanky athlete would be in the outfield when the exhibition schedule starts Sunday.

WHITE SOX—Thornton Lee, a pitching liability last season, has rejoined his mates after a week-end siege of the flu but says none of the 1942 arm pain is present now and he hopes to return to the form of 1941 when he won 22 games.

PIRATES — Rookie Frank Colman, once a pitcher but now a .330 hitting outfielder up from Toronto, is the star rookie of the camp. In addition to his hitting, his fielding has been outstanding and Manager Frankie Frisch is using him regularly in right field.

BROWNS — The Browns have scheduled a doubleheader for Sunday against the Lambert Field Naval Air Station team which has Johnny Berardino, former Brown shortstop, and Bob Scheffing, Chicago Cub catcher, on its roster. Catcher Frankie Hayes arrived in camp late yesterday.

REDS—Manager Bill McKechnie won't predict a pennant but he is convinced "we have a better team than we had last year and I know we will win more games." McKechnie says the addition of Eddie Miller gives the Reds the best infield in the National League.

SENATORS — Joe Jacobs, 17-year-old Wichita, Kas., player, may give Manager Ossie Bluege some unlooked for trouble at shortstop. With Joe Sullivan and Ellis Clary slated to share the position the youngster was the star of yesterday's practice game with a pair of fielding plays that cut off apparent hits.

SEVENTH WARD WINS, 56-31

Wildcats		G.	F.	Tl.	Seventh Ward Aces		G.	F.	Tl.
Smith	F	0	0	0	Charles	F	9	0	18
Shelly	F	0	0	0	Yunginger	F	4	0	8
Stamm	C	4	1	9	Brenneman	C	7	0	14
Long	G	3	0	9	Stockbar	G	6	0	12
Brown	G	7	2	16	Jones	G	0	0	0
					Arnold		2	0	0
Total		14	3	31	Total		28	0	56

LANCASTER NEW ERA

WEATHER

Showers and a few scattered thunder storms ending early tonight; colder tonight and Friday morning.

VOL. 66—NO. 414 | Entered as second class matter January 31, 1924, at the Post Office at Lancaster, Pa., under the Act of March 3, 1879. Reg. U. S. Pat Off. | LANCASTER, PA., THURSDAY, APRIL 1, 1943 | CITY EDITION | 26 PAGES—208 COLUMNS | 20c PER WEEK—4c Per Copy

100 "FORTS" BLAST ESCAPE FLEET

HUNDREDS ASK MORE GAS TO GET TO WORK

Holders of "A" Books Apply; Farmers May Mail Applications.

Hundreds of holders of "A" ration books who use their automobiles to travel to and from work are running short of gasoline and have filed applications for supplemental supplies, it was reported today at ration headquarters.

When the OPA lifted the ban on pleasure driving it extended the valid period of stamps for Period 5 and thus reduced the holders of "A" books to an approximate 1 1-2 gallons of gasoline per week.

The OPA announced last week that "A" books need not be used for occupational driving. To get gasoline to drive to and from work, however, car owners must prove that they are sharing their ride with fellow employes or that such car sharing is impossible because of irregular hours. Persons who have some regular means of transportation to and from work may use their own automobiles but must limit their gasoline buying to "A" books.

Farmers May Apply By Mail

At the same time, ration officials announced that farmers may mail applications for farm gasoline and receive coupon books by mail. This service was introduced to save time for farmers during the spring planting season. Farmers may get a six-months' supply of gasoline instead of three as in the past.

The OPA also made tires for rear wheels of tractors available and announced that persons who hold certificates for the purchase of tires for passenger vehicles may do the buying at their convenience. Previously, certificates to buy tires had to be used within 30 days.

Local Ration Boards will issue no more temporary gasoline rations to operators of commercial vehicles.

In the past, local ration boards made gasoline available while operators of commercial vehicles appealed to the ODT for operating certificates or appealed their ratings. In the future, requests for temporary supplies of gasoline must be made to Harrisburg.

RULE ON SAFETY SHOES

Workmen who need special shoes for safety in their work must use Stamp No. 17 in their Ration Books before they may ask for supplemental shoe rations, it was announced today.

If the workers No. 17 stamp has already been used, the individual may apply to his ration board for a special shoe certificate even though a member of his family has an unused stamp.

In no case the OPA said, may safety shoes be acquired without surrendering a stamp or a certificate.

BAKERIES TO POST PRICES

Bakeries producing pastries, doughnuts, pies, cakes and sweet yeast raised goods and selling directly to ultimate consumers must print the retail ceiling price on the wrappings or packing materials.

The OPA said the order is now in effect.

SEED POTATOES RESTRICTED

Seed potatoes must be tagged as such and must not be sold in quantities of less than 50 pounds, the OPA announced today.

Seed potatoes originally were exempt from all control but abuse of the right to buy at will diverted some stock into the black markets for consumption, the OPA said.

Importing of Farm Boys For City Jobs Banned

Police Threaten Prosecution on Juvenile Delinquency Charge After 3 Lads Are Picked Up Here

City police took action today to stop the practice of using county children for work in the city in jobs other than specified in the special permits allowing them to be absent from school to help on farms.

Found $13,901

Meet Honest Frank Kominski, 13, who found $13,901.28 in two paper bags in a New York junk yard and promptly turned it all over to police.

After conferring with Arthur P. Mylin, county school superintendent, police announced that in the future persons importing county school children into the city for work will be prosecuted on charges of contributing to juvenile delinquency.

Police Pick Up 3 Boys

The question was raised this morning when Policeman Jason Nonnemacher picked up three boys at King and Water Sts. At police headquarters, they gave their names as Jacob Trostle, Jr., fourteen, Willow St.; Walter Werner, fifteen, New Providence R1, and Samuel Homsher, fourteen, Grofftown Rd.

Police said Werner, a pupil at the Mt. Airy school, produced a permit issued by his county school board to work on a farm. Trostle said his father was going to lift his permit on Saturday, while Homsher admitted being a truant from the Burrowes School.

Shortly afterward, F. William Scheller, New Providence R1, came to the police station in behalf of Trostle and Werner. He said the two boys had worked on his farms at various intervals and each Thursday he brought them into the city to distribute circulars.

"They only make a few pennies on the farm, so I give them this opportunity to pick up a few dollars," Scheller told police. He explained that although he had two farms, he also took charge of distributing the circulars each week.

Mylin Issues Warning

County School Superintendent Mylin and police both impressed upon Scheller the fact that the special working permits granted to school children under 16 years were for farm work only to relieve the labor shortage caused by the war and that the labor could not be used elsewhere.

Police later released Trostle and Werner to Scheller with the instructions that they should be returned to their homes and not be brought back to work in the city.

Homsher was returned to the Burrows School after police learned that his father had already been prosecuted by Miss Elizabeth R. Martin, supervising principal of Lancaster township schools, before Alderman Doebler for violation of the compulsory school attendance act.

NEW ARMSTRONG CONTROLLER

Keith Powlison Succeeds Geo. Arisman; Warnock Named Treasurer.

H. W. Prentis, Jr., president of the Armstrong Cork Co., announced today the election of Keith Powlison, treasurer of the company, to the position of vice president and controller.

Powlison succeeds George M. Arisman, former controller, whose resignation from the company has been accepted by the Board of Directors.

Warnock Is Treasurer

Announced at the same time was the election of M. J. Warnock to succeed Powlison as treasurer and the appointment of Cameron Hawley to succeed Warnock as a director of advertising and promotion.

Gray Playter and John P. Waters were named assistant directors of advertising and promotion.

Powlison Joined Firm In 1922

Powlison joined the Armstrong Cork Co. in 1922 as a member of the sales organization of the floor division. He left the company to return to academic work receiving the degree of doctor of philosophy in economics at Johns Hopkins University in 1928. After a period of association with the Security-First National bank of Los Angeles he returned to the Armstrong Cork Company as assistant treasurer in 1932. In 1938 he was elected treasurer.

Warnock, a graduate of the University of Oregon, joined the company as a salesman in 1926. He served for a number of years as manager of the company's branch office in Seattle and came to Lancaster as assistant manager of the floor division in 1930. He was named director of advertising and promotion in 1941.

Hawley joined the Armstrong Cork Company in 1927, and has served in a number of sales advertising and sales promotion capacities. Since 1941 he has been assistant director of advertising and promotion.

ASK TO MOVE 5 BUS LINES FROM SQUARE

CTC Files PUC Petition on City Orders; Washington Line Hearing.

The Board of Directors of the Conestoga Transportation company met at noon today and announced that acting on orders from the city they have filed with the Public Utility Commission a petition asking for permission to change the terminals of five suburban bus lines from Penn Square to the Conestoga Building, E. Orange Street.

The petition to make the change is being presented in the face of numerous protests against the proposed plan, it was announced.

The lines are:

Elizabethtown, Lititz, Manheim, Leaman Place, also serving Mellingers and Strasburg. Routes of these lines in and out of the city could be changed slightly to avoid passing through Penn Square.

The plan was announced several weeks ago following a conference of representatives of the Transportation company, city officials and police.

Cite Needs For Bus Line To Baltimore, Washington

A bus line between Lancaster and Conowingo, Md., is needed to transport war workers to their jobs in Baltimore and Washington and to provide better communications between the Sheriff's office and FBI headquarters in the capital, according to witnesses who appeared at the ICC hearing in the Post ffice today.

The Safe Way Trails, Inc., already has a permit to operate buses between Conowingo and Baltimore. It then filed application for permission to operate buses between Lancaster and Conowingo to connect with its Maryland line and to operate a spur from Conowingo to Perryville.

Drop Perryville Route

Today, the company withdrew its application for permission to operate the spur to Perryville and as a

(See BUS—Page 23)

Some British Casualties at Mareth Line

In conquering the Mareth Line, the British Eighth Army was not without casualties. In the picture above, first aid is being administered to British Tommies at the side of the Wadi Zigzau In the Mareth battle area, after their successful flanking maneuver. (Radiophoto from Cairo.)

RECORD RAIDS WRECK SHIPS INTENDED TO SAVE ROMMEL

26 Vessels Hit, 57 Axis Planes Ruined in Sardinian Harbor; Allies Press on in Tunisia.

By the Associated Press

Allied headquarters in Africa disclosed today that an armada of nearly 100 U. S. Flying Fortresses, the largest single force of its type ever massed, has begun smashing at Axis ships off Southern Sardinia in what appeared to be an attempt to wreck an enemy "Dunkerque Fleet" for escape from Tunisia.

Dispatches said the great striking force of Fortresses, strongly escorted by fighters, attacked the Sardinian port of Cagliari yesterday, hitting five merchant ships and 21 smaller craft.

In addition, the Allied raiders destroyed or damaged 57 aircraft on the ground and shot down 14 Axis fighter planes in attacks on three Sardinian airdromes, it was announced.

All Allied planes returned from the mission, the communique said.

American Mitchell bombers, escorted by fighters, also blasted enemy ships in the Sicilian Narrows, attacking a six-vessel convoy with these results: A large merchant ship sunk, another left burning and sinking, two others in flames, a large transport hit twice.

Six German fighters which attempted to intercept the Mitchells were shot down into the sea.

Meanwhile, Allied military quarters said British Eighth Army troops had advanced 12 miles beyond newly-recaptured Oudref in Southern Tunisia, on the coastal highway to Sfax, and were skirmishing with Axis rearguards dug-in well above the Gabes bottleneck.

The wording of a United Nations communique suggested that Field Marshal Erwin Rommel might be attempting a new stand after four days of retreat from the Mareth Line.

To Montgomery's left, United States armored units from the command of Lieut. Gen. George S. Patton, Jr., pushing eastward in the El Guetaria Pass area encountered deep mine fields which made progress difficult, but the junction with the Eighth Army appeared near.

First Army Presses On

In the north, the British First Army was reported making "good progress" in its four-day-old offensive toward the big Naval base at Bizerte, with vanguards less than 34 miles away.

An Italian communique listed 60 killed and 62 injured in the attack on Cagliari, which lies 140 miles north of Bizerte, and dispatches from Allied headquarters said the Sardinian port had been crippled as a major base for sending both planes and ships to the Axis armies in Tunisia.

All Types of Boats Blasted

Schooners, coastal craft and motorboats—the same variety used by

(See AFRICA-EUROPE—Page 8)

5 TO 10 PTS. DUE ON HAMBURGER

Butchers Puzzled as OPA Charts Fail to Recognize "Dutch" Cuts.

Rationing officials made no provision for Lancaster county hamburger when the meat rationing program was outlined and as a result butchers in the so-called Pennsylvania Dutch areas today had a mathematical headache.

The meat ration chart says that a butcher must ask five ration points for a pound of hamburger made of beef ground from necks, flanks, shanks, briskets, plates and miscellaneous beef trimmings and beef fat.

Not Made That Way

But in Lancaster county and nearby territory, butchers don't make hamburger that way. Usually, they will buy a young bull and grind most of the carcass into hamburger. The Pennsylvania Dutch sections demanded it that way for generations.

Butchers and county slaughterers have deluged the OPA for an answer to the problem and as a result—Lancaster county hamburger now appears under the more dignified name of "ground beef" and it may cost up to 10 or more points per pound depending upon the point value of the meat that went into the grinder.

Meat Cuts Also Different

Coupled with that came a new complication today when inspectors discovered that Lancaster county meat cuts are just a little different than in any other part of the country. "Tricks of the trade" handed down from generation to generation have enabled butchers to carve choice servings out of a carcass that have been just a bit different.

Butchers say the present meat ration chart is based largely upon the method used to make meat cuts in the south. As a result the cuts described on the point ration chart do not cover local methods of operations.

But that's not all the butchers faced. The new registration law requires each butcher to put his registration number on every cut of meat or parcel of meat product he sells. The government provided the formula for the marking, but the base is grain alcohol and the druggists wouldn't sell the alcohol without a prescription.

"Tell me," said one butcher today, "how I am going to write a number on a pound of unstuffed pudding meat or good old scrapple. The "big boys" just don't know how we folks eat here in Lancaster county."

OPA TO ANNOUNCE NEW MEAT PRICES

WASHINGTON, April 1.—(AP)—The Office of Price Administration today polished up new standardized retail prices for beef, veal, lamb and mutton, which along with rationing, are expected by officials to iron out many of the kinks in the meat distribution machinery.

These price rules, which probably will be released Monday, will be similar to the standardized retail pork prices that go into effect today, although they probably will not be effective until about April 15.

As in the case of today's pork prices, the new rules on beef, veal, lamb and mutton will set up two prices, one for small independent stores and the other for large independents and chains, in each of 11 zones into which the country has been divided. The two prices probably will be a cent to a few cents apart, with the small stores permitted to charge the higher prices because of higher relative operating costs.

TWO PROSECUTED BY STATE POLICE

State Police from the local substation prosecuted two motorists today.

David Graybill, Paradise R1, was charged with driving on the left side of the highway, while Frank Henne, Lancaster R1, was prosecuted for failure to carry owner's cards.

Invasion Jitters Hit Axis In All Areas of Europe

Allied Paratroopers Reported to Have Norwegian Base; Italy and the Balkans Agog as Nazis Strengthen Defenses

LONDON, April 1.—(AP)—Signs of increasing Axis invasion jitters from the Balkan frontier to the Scandinavian peninsula were highlighted today by a roundabout report that Allied parachute troops had established a base in the Norwegian mountains and had sallied out in raids on Nazi-controlled factories.

The Norwegian government-in-exile here, commenting upon the report, declared that "Quisling and the Germans appear to be genuinely alarmed," but said it could not give any confirmation.

The story came to London in Stockholm dispatches which said the Allied parachute base was somewhere in the Hardanger Vidda mountain lakes area, an ideal district for an airdrome and that it was equipped with a meteorological station.

The London Daily Press quoted the German radio as announcing that Nazi troops are hunting the parachutists, said to be British and Norwegians.

On the southern border of the Allied invasion arc, meanwhile, Italian propaganda Minister Alessandro Pavolini announced that Sicily, off the toe of the Italian boot, had become "a fortified outpost of the European continent itself against any and all attacks coming from the Mediterranean." Only yesterday Italy announced a new mobilization law to be applied in event of invasion.

The Daily Mail said in a dispatch from Madrid that 350,000 tons of French shipping immobilized in Mediterranean ports since the German occupation of Southern France had been ordered sent to Genoa, Spezia and ports in Sardinia and Sicily.

"The obvious inference is that a Dunkerque fleet is being collected

(See INVASION—Page 8)

Italy Reported Preparing Hospitals For 90,000 Men

MOSCOW, April 1— (AP) —A Tass dispatch from Lausanne, Switzerland, broadcast today by the Moscow radio, said that concentrations of transport and hospital ships and railway trains had been observed in ports of Southern Italy.

"There is every indication that Italian authorities are preparing for mass evacuation of Axis troops from Tunisia," the dispatch said.

It said also that hospitals which would accommodate at least 90,000 patients had been set up in Naples, according to Italian reports.

LEADERS IN COUNTY URGED TO ATTEND WAR BOND MEETING

Every county township and borough should be represented tomorrow evening at the meeting of War Bond drive chairmen, Milton H. Ranck, county war bond chairman, said today. The meeting will be held at 8 o'clock in the Court House, Court Room No. 2.

This will be the only meeting of county drive leaders to be held before the drive begins April 12, Ranck said today. Instructions will be given leaders to pass along to workers in their own communities, the chairman declared.

"We know everyone is busy and that the drive means work and sacrifice from us all," Ranck said, "but our fighting men are giving their lives, and the least we can do is lend the money to give them the equipment they must have."

SYNTHETIC RUBBER AS GOOD AS CRUDE

WASHINGTON, April 1 — (AP) — Rubber Director William M. Jeffers told Senate investigators today synthetic rubber has been perfected to the point where its quality answers virtually all requirements without the need of mixture with crude, then proudly displayed what he called the nation's first all-synthetic heavy duty truck tire.

Conceding that the outlook in terms of quantity has not passed the critical stage, he nevertheless defended curtailment of guayule planting on the ground that the projected acreage was more sorely needed now for good crops than for this natural rubber.

Presentation of the tire—built by Goodyear with butadiene produced from alcohol manufactured at an Institute, West Va., plant which utilizes grains, — created excitement at the hearing, called to study an order drastically curtailing the guayule program.

ROMMEL ARMY IS STILL INTACT

Stimson Sees Possible Union With Von Arnim, and Heavy Fighting.

WASHINGTON, April 1.—(AP) — Secretary of War Stimson said today that German Marshal Erwin Rommel apparently still has the bulk of his Tunisian force intact and that a strong chance remains he can effect a union with Axis forces under Colonel General Von Arnim in the north.

In such an event, the Secretary told a press conference, the enemy in Tunisia could offer strong resistance and before the final phases of the North African campaign, "there will in all probability be a good deal of heavy fighting."

Rommel suffered an important defeat at the Mareth Line, the War Secretary said, due principally to the skill and leadership of General Bernard L. Montgomery and the courage of his British 8th Army.

Axis Loses Seen Heavy

Estimates of Axis losses are incomplete, Stimson continued in a review of the war, but large numbers of German and Italian soldiers have been killed, several thousands wounded and taken prisoner, and the Allies have captured and destroyed large amounts of Axis equipment.

On other fronts, Stimson reported:

The bomber commands of both the U. S. Army Air Forces and

(See STIMSON—Page 8)

POLICE LODGER FACES DRAFT QUIZ

Gordon Boyer, Royalton, who applied for lodging at police headquarters last night and was unable to produce his Selective Service card, was jailed for 30 days on vagrancy charges by Alderman Rose in police court this afternoon. The alderman said he would be released when his draft status was clarified.

Agnes Maley Dempsey, fifty, this city, arrested in the 100 block of E. King St., last night, was fined $10 and costs.

DUKE ST. TROLLEY AND TRUCK CRASH

The front end of a Duke St. trolley car was damaged when struck by a truck, operated by Henry Tennis, Lititz R1, on the northeast corner of Queen St. and Penn Square at 12:45 P. M. today. No one was injured.

J. F. Rineer, 731 S. Lime St., was operating the trolley car. The truck was owned by Charles Zook, Lititz R4.

1ST H. S. PUPILS ASK FARM JOBS

96 at West Lampeter Volunteer For Work Away From Home.

Ninety-six West Lampeter Township High school pupils, 51 boys and 45 girls, have volunteered to do farm work away from home this summer, it was announced today by Wayne B. Rentschler, supervisor of vocational agriculture at the school.

West Lampeter is the first school in the county to announce results of a survey of In-School Youth for Emergency Work in Agriculture in the program of the U. S. Office of Education and U. S. Employment Service seeking to recruit a Volunteer Farm Corps to help alleviate the shortage of farm labor. Six other school districts in the county also have begun enrolling pupils in the Farm Corps.

39 P. C. of Student Body

The farm volunteers at West Lampeter represent 39.5 per cent of the total student body. Of the 243 pupils in the survey, 152 of the group said they would prefer employment other than farm work.

Rentschler announced that a community organization in West Lampeter township will be developed by the school in the near future, to register the farmers in that vicinity who need help this summer and to supervise the work of placing the boys and girls on the farms there as they are needed.

Plan Special Training

The supervisor explained that the volunteers will be given special training in the school to give them background for useful har-

(See PUPILS—Page 23)

MERCURY AT 84; SHOWERS PROBABLE

Temperatures were slightly lower in the Lancaster area today after soaring to 84 degrees yesterday—the highest point reached in March since 1938.

A stiff northeast wind drove the mercury down to 39 degrees last night but the temperature rallied to the high 50's by noon today.

Warmer weather with some thunder showers are a probability. The highest temperature ever recorded in March in Lancaster was 86 degrees on March 22, 1938.

SEES 4,000 MORE MOTHERS IN JOBS

State Official Says 2,000 Additional Children Will Need Care Here By 1944

At least 4,000 additional women will be taken into local war industries before January, 1944, and these women will have 2,000 children who must be cared for, Mrs. Benjamin Ludlow, State director of Child Care for the Office of Civilian Defense said here today.

Mrs. Ludlow spoke at a meeting of the Child Care committee this morning in the Community Building, when further plans for opening Lancaster's First Child Care Center were made. The Center is expected to be opened in May.

Cites Need For Nurseries

Mrs. Ludlow emphasized the need for nurseries and the fast-increasing rate at which mothers of small children are being employed. "Many women's husbands are making a great deal of money, and they don't want to go to work, but I don't think it will be a matter of choice much longer," Mrs. Ludlow declared.

Pointing out that mothers of 50,000 children under 14 will go into war work in Pennsylvania alone this year, Mrs. Ludlow said that the Child Care committee must prepare for the future, as

(See CHILD CENTER—Page 23)

The Scribbler

At least one April Fool's day joke kicked back on the jokester today.

Mrs. Mary Brady, 138 N. Mulberry St., told Edna Snead to look at the red bird outside her window. Miss Snead looked and Mrs. Brady yelled "April fool" but Edna laughed last because there was a red bird sitting on the tree.

WILBUR KENDIG, a boss in the aWrehouse Tabulating office at Armstrong's, was the victim of an April Fool's joke .... While playing pinochle during his lunch period, Kendig received a telephone cal to come to a building two blocks away to identify another employe. He walked there only to learn it was just a gag.

All Fools' Day Fun Is Fun —When It Isn't Sabotage

War's Restrictions Put New Complexion on Tricks Such as Salt in Sugar Bowl or Letting Air Out of Tires

This is April Fool's Day—sometimes known as All Fools' Day, which doesn't leave any doubt as to what the ancients thought about most folks.

But in view of the war's restrictions on what some fools consider fun, the Society for the Prevention of Practical Jokers today warned its members to proceed with caution in the matter of pranks—otherwise, there may be casualties.

For instance:

Don't put any bricks under old hats on the sidewalk, for passing pedestrians to kick. It's sabotage—shoes are rationed.

Don't use that old wallet-on-a-string trick. If the sucker bends over to pick it up, he may bust his suspenders. Rubber elastic is scarce.

Don't put salt in the sugar bowl. One cup of coffee ruined by a spoonful of salt is considered grounds for justifiable homicide.

Don't let the air out of your neighbor's tires — unless you've made your will.

Don't drain his gasoline out on the ground. Not a lawyer in the country would dare touch your case.

Don't sneak into an army camp with a bugle and blow reveille an hour early. Tearing you limb from limb would expend valuable military energy.

Above all, don't jump up and surprise your acquaintances by shouting: "Heil Hitler!"

They may not know what day it is—and there's enough absenteeism without taking time out to attend fools' funerals.

P. S.—April Fool! There's no such thing as a Society for the Preservation of Practical Jokers.

NEED FURNISHINGS AT INDIANTOWN GAP

An appeal for articles to furnish a day room for soldiers at Indiantown Gap was issued today by Lancaster Chapter, Red Cross. The chapter is asked to furnish the room through its Indiantown Gap Camp Council.

Articles needed include library tables, lamps, chairs, sofa, radio, phonograph, records, ping pong table, pictures, piano, and curtains. The Indiantown Military Reservation hospital also is appealing for book cases, electric fans, floor and table model radios, and a punch bowl.

Further details may be obtained from Mrs. O. J. Schneebeli, local Red Cross chairman of the Camp Council, phone 2-1295, or Mrs. Charles D. Addams, phone 2-1423.

STAR ROLES—Two sisters, one loving, the other hating—each other, are the roles played by Ida Lupino and Joan Leslie in "The Hard Way," playing at the Grand theatre. Dennis Morgan, Jack Carson and Gladys George head the cast opposite the stars.

BURIED ALIVE—Beth Ainsley (Jane Wyatt) holds the light while Lieut. Harvey (Kent Taylor) and Capt. Mason (James Ellison) struggle against the tons of earth that has blocked the entrance to the improvised front line hospital in a tense situation from RKO Radio's thrilling war drama "Army Surgeon", at the Fulton, in which they are starred.

MUSIC GALORE—Four of the nation's most famous swing bands are heard in "Reveille With Beverly," novel new musical comedy opening tomorrow at the Capitol theatre, with lovely Ann Miller featured. Shown above in scenes from the film are, Duke Ellington, Bob Crosby, Freddie Slack, Count Basie and their bands. "Silver Skates," starring Kenny Baker, Patricia Morison and Ted Fio Rita and his orchestra is showing today for the last times at the Capitol.

FREED ON PAYING COSTS

Stewart Dixon, Negro, 329 Locust St., charged with assault and battery and disorderly conduct by Martha McPhail, 310 North St., pleaded guilty before Alderman Rose yesterday and paid the costs.

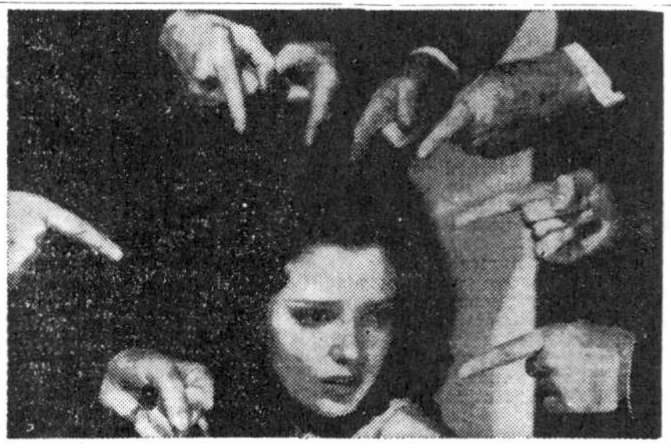

DRAMA—"City Without Men," sensational film production, comes to the Hamilton theatre Thursday and Friday. Starring the lovely and talented Linda Darnell, shown above, with a supporting cast including Glenda Farrell, Edgar Buchanan, Leslie Brooks, Doris Dudley and many others.

PLANS RAPID-FIRE DRAWINGS AT USO LOUNGE PROGRAM

Caricatures, comic drawings and more serious sketches will be drawn for service men at the USO Lounge at 7:30 P. M. Saturday by Jimmy Landreth, local entertainer. The "chalk talk" will include rapid-fire evolution stunts, comic trick formation, and caricatures of prominent personalities.

The Veterans of Foreign Wars Auxiliary will serve the weekly supper from 5:30 to 6:30 P. M. Sunday and Miss Dorothy Erisman will be guest pianist. Miss Louise Roy, a member of the entertainment committee is in charge of entertainment for the week-end.

HELD OVER SECOND WEEK—The above scenes are from Paramount's great musicomedy, "Star Spangled Rhythm," which begins its second week tomorrow at the Colonial Theatre. Top: "If Men Played Cards As Women Do" is portrayed by Fred MacMurray, Franchot Tone, Ray Milland and Lynne Overman. Center: Three Paramount glamour girls, Paulette Goddard, Dorothy Lamour and Veronica Lake do a little number entitled, "A Sweater, A Sarong and A Peek-a-boo Bang." Bottom: An embarrassing moment for Bob Hope. The gentleman who seems unable to take a joke is William Bendix.

ROMANCE with a capital "R" is provided in "Hello, Frisco, Hello" by Alice Faye and John Payne. The gay, new Technicolor musical due Wednesday at the Ephrata Main Theatre boasts a host of attractions, not the least of which is its cast which also stars Jack Oakie and Lynn Bari. Bruce Humberstone directed the picture, which was produced by Milton Sperling, 1st Lieutenant, U.S.M.C.R.

LANCASTER NEW ERA

WEATHER
Colder with frost and diminishing winds tonight and rising temperature Sunday morning.

VOL. 66—NO. 440 | Entered as second class matter January 31, 1924, at the Post Office at Lancaster, Pa., under the Act of March 3, 1879. Reg. U. S. Pat Off. | LANCASTER, PA., SATURDAY, MAY 1, 1943 | CITY EDITION | 14 PAGES—112 COLUMNS | 20c PER WEEK—4c Per Copy

F. D. ORDERS GOVERNMENT SEIZE CLOSED MINES, ARMY GUARD THEM

Yanks Start Shelling Mateur

BLOODY HILL CAPTURED BY PATTON UNITS

Nazi Planes Fail to Silence U. S. Guns at Gateway to Bizerte.

By the Associated Press

American troops have captured three more "important localities" and seized 200 prisoners on the Northern Tunisian battlefront, Allied headquarters said today, while the British First Army fell back slightly for the second time in 24 hours along the center of the 100-mile western barrier.

Frontline dispatches said United States troops captured the bloody Djebel Tahent—Hill 609—in savage fighting yesterday 16 miles southwest of Mateur, gateway to Bizerte, and shelled Mateur itself for the first time in the campaign.

The bombardment of Mateur, an important road junction 18 miles from Bizerte, brought an immediate counter battery fire and the heaviest artillery dueling since the American attack began April 23.

The Germans dispatched 15 or 20 Focke-Wulf 190's in a vain attempt to locate and silence the U. S. guns.

In the skies, Allied warplanes unleashed "full effort" attacks against Axis shipping, and at sunset yesterday the sea off Cap Bon was dotted with five burning hulks.

Direct hits were scored on at least eight ships, including a cruiser and two destroyers. The cruiser was left engulfed in flames and apparently sinking; both destroyers were believed sunk.

In addition, the Admiralty in London announced that British submarines had sunk 10 more Axis ships in the Mediterranean.

Allied communique No. 176 said exceptionally heavy fighting raged throughout yesterday, with the Germans lashing out in repeated counter-assaults in the critical Medjez-El-Bab zone which guards the open plain before Tunis.

"In one area, our forward troops were forced to make a slight withdrawal, but elsewhere all our positions were firmly held," Gen. Dwight D. Eisenhower's headquarters announced.

The Allied command stressed bloody losses inflicted on the Germans as the enemy battled with desperation-born fury to maintain his mountain defenses protecting Tunis and Bizerte.

"On the Eighth Army front, slight local gains were made."

Axis reports said Gen. Sir Bernard L. Montgomery's big guns were laying down a tremendous barrage along the Enfidaville line in the south—the usual prelude to a new offensive — and simultaneously

(See AFRICA—Page 4)

"Whistle Dress"

One of the premier "pin-up" girls of the Armed Forces, Jinx Falkenburg models a creation called a "whistle dress" by servicemen. Boy sees girl. Boy whistles. He can't be blamed, at that.

MAN, 30, KILLED UNDER TRACTOR

Driver Crushed as Machine Upsets on Him Near Mount Joy.

William Eckman, 30, Mount Joy, R2, was instantly killed this morning when a tractor he was operating ran up an embankment, overturned, and pinned him beneath it.

Eckman, a laborer employed on the farm of Herman Ginder, Mount Joy, R2, was hauling manure to a field at 9:45 a. m., when he lost control of the tractor.

The only witness to the accident was Charles Morton, Mount Joy, a rural mail carrier, who was passing at the time. He called Ginder, and the two men, with help from a nearby farm, moved the tractor and pulled Eckman from beneath it.

The man was dead when Dr. H. C. Kendig, Mount Joy, who was called, arrived on the scene.

Dr. William Workman, deputy coroner, issued a certificate of accidental death. He said Eckman died instantly from a crushed chest.

Eckman is survived by his widow, the former Christine Heisey, and two children, Joseph, 7, and Eli, 2.

EPHRATA CHIMNEY FIRE

The Ephrata Fire Company extinguished a slight chimney fire at the home of Raymond Martin, Ephrata R3, about 10:30 A. M. today. There was slight damage.

$15,216,595 BONDS SOLD; GOAL TOPPED

2d War Loan Total Here Is Expected to Reach $17,000,000.

Lancaster's Second War Loan campaign topped its $15,000,000 goal today, with returns still coming in.

With late sales still unreported, the total amount subscribed in the drive is $15,216,595.

"We are tremendously pleased to reach our assigned goal on the last day of the drive," Milton H. Ranck, county chairman, W. Hensel Brown, city chairman, and J. F. Aierstock, chairman of banking and finance, said this morning. "But this doesn't mean that the people can stop buying bonds, we want to get all the bonds we possibly can."

The committee added that when final reports are in, they feel confident that Lancaster's total subscriptions will reach at least $17,000,000.

"While the work of the solicitors is not entirely completed," the committee added, "we desire to express our thanks to all the workers in the city and county, with the added thought that all solicitation not completed should receive renewed impetus from these encouraging returns, and that the workers should now try harder than ever to boost Lancaster's total Second War Loan."

It is impossible at this time to compute the final figures on purchases by individuals and by banks, the committee said, but they added that "we feel confident that if the workers continue to do their canvassing, we will have the $10,000,000 from individual subscriptions, which is an important part of Lancaster's goal."

"The second war loan in this district has been successful beyond expectations," Alfred H. Williams, president of the Federal Reserve Bank, Philadelphia, and chairman for the campaign in the Third Fed-

(See BONDS—Page 11)

MAY DAY IS WINDY, MERCURY IN 40'S

High winds battered Lancaster county throughout last night and today as snow flurries and near-freezing temperatures were reported in many sections of Western Pennsylvania.

The mercury dropped to 40 degrees at the City Water Works last night and remained around that point during the morning. It was May Day on the calendar but Lancastrians held firmly to their winter garments.

1943 MERCANTILE PAYMENT IS DUE

Payment for 1943 mercantile licenses is due today, Mercantile Appraiser A. A. Krimmel, Jr., announced today. The 1942 mercantile licenses expired yesterday.

The present number of licenses issued exceeds last year by 500, Krimmel said, as he urged all merchants to pay promptly so that tires and gasoline will not be wasted in collecting the returns.

SENATOR JOHNSON IS SERIOUSLY ILL

WASHINGTON, May 1.—(AP)—Ailing Senator Hiram Johnson of California did not have "so good a night," it was reported today from the Naval Hospital at Bethesda, Md., but "he is holding his own."

Capt. Robert E. Duncan, hospital official, said the 76-year-old Senator is suffering from an acute upper respiratory infection and a "certain amount of pleurisy." He entered the hospital Wednesday.

FISH EXPERT QUITS TO GO ANGLING

CHICAGO, May 1. — (AP)—Alfred C. Weed, 61, who as curator of fishes for the Field Museum of Natural History has worked for 22 years among fish, announced he was retiring to get some rest. One of the things he said he would do while resting would be to do a little fishing.

MELLINGER LEAVES JAIL; SHIRK IGNORED

District Attorney Calls New Parole Board's Action "Absurd."

Edward P. Mellinger, described by police as the "kingpin" of Lancaster bookmakers, was released from the county prison today by the new Pennsylvania Parole Board after he had served slightly more than 19 months of a three-year jail term.

The action of the new board, while an application for commutation of sentence by Mellinger was pending before the old State Pardon Board, aroused District Attorney K. L. Shirk.

"It's ridiculous, absolutely absurd," Shirk said, when notified that Mellinger had been released from the county prison shortly after 6 a. m. "I had no knowledge that the new Parole Board was considering the matter. I wasn't even consulted.

"Such procedure is very unusual to say the least and I question the advisability of the new Parole Board taking jurisdiction when an application is pending before the State Pardon Board."

According to C. B. McDivitt, district superintendent of the new Parole Board, members of the board heard an application in behalf of Mellinger on April 22, the day after his application for commutation was heard before the State Pardon Board at Harrisburg. After considering the case from every angle, McDivitt said, the new board agreed that Mellinger should be given a parole as of May 1.

"This sentence against Mr. Mellinger still stands," McDivitt said.

(See MELLINGER—Page 11)

NAVY CADET WEEK PROCLAIMED HERE, BEGINNING MAY 3

Lancaster city and county will unite next week to promote the enlistment of recent high school graduates for the Naval Aviation Cadet company at Franklin and Marshall College.

Mayor Cary, on behalf of the city, and County Commissioners on behalf of the county, issued a proclamation today fixing the week of May 3 as "Fly With the Navy Week."

The Junior Chamber of Commerce and Lancaster Lodge of Elks are cooperating in the enlistment campaign. Candidates will be interviewed in the building on the southwestern corner of Penn Square next week from 3 P. M. to 9 P. M. Those accepted will be sent to college July 1 to start basic training.

Coal No Longer Goes To War

One of the empty coal cars at Montour Mine No. 10 at Library, Pa., bears the sign: "Coal Goes to War" on its side.

200,000 Pa. Miners Desert Collieries to Obey Lewis

Operators, Hoping Men Would Heed F. D. R.'s Plea Not to Strike, Watch in Vain for Sign to Prevent Shutdown

PITTSBURGH, May 1.—(AP)—Collieries whose spiral-like tipples dot the slopes of Pennsylvania's coal producing hills and mountains were virtually deserted today as the state's 200,000 miners obeyed the "no trespass" edict of their union leader, John L. Lewis and joined the nation's greatest strike since it went to war.

Throughout the night operators in the soft coal regions, hoping the miners might heed the plea of President Roosevelt not to strike against their government, had watched in vain for a sign that might reverse the trend towards a complete shutdown which set in a week ago.

40,000 Await Order

Hours before the midnight deadline—when the extended United Mine Workers contract with the operators expired—more than 40,000 coal diggers already had checked in their lamps and gone home to await word from Lewis.

Some mines change to "early" day shifts at 9:30 P. M., others at 10:30 and 11. But, by large, the heavy "regular" day shift is the one going into the pits around 7 A. M. Reports from all parts of the vast soft coal region now employing 117,000 men were the same —none but maintenance men, necessary to keep the mines in condition, entered the mines.

The ranks of the idle were swelled by 83,000 who produce the nation's entire anthracite supply from mines in nine counties in Eastern Pennsylvania. The hard coal miners had only brief notice that their representatives in New York had failed either to agree on a new contract or an extension of the old which expired at midnight Friday.

Thus for the first time since 1922 both hard and soft coal miners were idle.

Few Pickets Posted

The standstill came virtually without incident. Long accustomed to stoppages and strikes in the union's never-ending fight to

(See MINERS—Page 4)

3 CAFES ROBBED, $150 STOLEN

Burglars Routed From 4th Taproom By Woman's Threat to Shoot.

Three hotels were broken into by a gang of burglars who stole approximately $150 in cash last night, city police reported today. The thieves also attempted to break into a fourth cafe but were routed by a woman.

The places robbed: Buckius' Cafe, 201 W. Orange St., the Little Dutch Cafe, 201 W. Walnut St., and the Shamrock Cafe, 312 W. Walnut St.

An attempt was made to enter Benedict's Cafe, 209 N. Prince St., but the proprietress, Mrs. Margaret Benidict, who had been kept awake by a cold, heard the thieves tampering with a side window. She saw a man standing in the shadows and he fled when she threatened to shoot him with a rifle, according to Detective David Kauffman, who investigated. Mrs. Benedict told police the attempted burglary occurred at 2:15 a. m.

Harry Buckius, proprietor of Buckius' Cafe, serves meals to the "graveyard" shift of employes at the Commercial Crystal Co., engaged in war work, and he said

(See ROBBERIES—Page 11)

CITY ORDER CLOSES ROOMING HOUSE

The rooming house at 105 S. Queen St., long a landmark for itinerants in the central section of the city, closed today under an order from the Bureau of Health, according to B. F. Charles, city health officer.

The place was ordered closed after a roomer was overcome by coal gas and died. Charles C. Lebo, operator of the rooming house, also was overcome by the fumes but recovered.

Officials of the Bureau of Health said that caretakers will remain in the property. It was explained that the place can be reopened providing orders to clean up and make necessary repairs are obeyed.

Late News Bulletin

5 JAP BASES HIT BY U. S. FLIERS

Washington, May 1—(AP)—The Navy announced today that American bombers and fighters had attacked five Japanese bases in the Solomon Islands Thursday and Friday, starting large fires among installations at Kieta and Kahili.

ICKES INSTRUCTS MINE FIRMS TO OPERATE

Washington, May 1—(AP)—Solid Fuel Administrator Ickes today sent telegrams to 3,400 bituminous coal mining companies instructing them to operate their mines in the name of the United States government and to apply for troop protection if they need it.

CLAIMS ORDER WILL ANTAGONIZE MINERS

Bellaire, O., May 1 — (AP) — Adolph Pacifico, vice president of District 6, United Mine Workers, asserted today President Roosevelt's order taking over closed coal mines would "in my opinion do more to antagonize the miners of America than any other one thing."

U-Boats in North Atlantic Being Kept on Defensive

Air Patrol Extended Over Convoy Lanes; Japs Adopt Nazi "Wolf Pack" Tactics East of Australia

BY JOHN M. HIGHTOWER

WASHINGTON, May 1. — (AP) — Signs that the German U-boats soon may be the hunted instead of the hunters in North Atlantic sea lanes coincided today with hints that Japanese subs have shifted their undersea strategy and started raiding South Pacific supply lines in Nazi wolf pack style.

Reversal of the German role was seen in a Canadian announcement disclosing realignment of commands and greatly expanded protection for vital convoys moving between Canada and England.

M'Arthur Discloses Switch

The switch in Japanese undersea tactics — hitherto limited largely to battle action in conjunction with warships — was indicated in a communique from General Douglas MacArthur's Allied headquarters in Australia. It said the Japanese have opened a submarine attack "in some force in the waters east of Australia."

East of Australia means the Coral Sea and beyond there the ocean lanes used by the Allies for reenforcement and supply. Thus, it would seem the enemy attack is definitely directed against the supply lines from America and between Australia, New Guinea, New Zealand and New Caledonia, despite the communique's dearth of details — details which MacArthur said would be supplied as soon as they will not assist the enemy.

Such a supply line stab would mark the first Japanese try at wolf pack hunting style and Nippon's

(See U-BOATS—Page 4)

Will "Deal Bluntly" With Crisis In Talk To U. S. Sunday Night

Pleads Again With Miners to Return; Directs Ickes to Operate Collieries in Which 503,000 Are Idle; Stimson to Send Troops If Protection Is Needed

By The Associated Press

President Roosevelt today ordered government operation of the nation's struck coal mines — with troops ready to provide any needed protection — and at the same time called upon miners to "return immediately to the mines and work for their government."

Moving quickly to remedy the war production crisis threatened by the walkout of 503,700 men, Mr. Roosevelt sent orders to Fuels Administrator Ickes and War Secretary Stimson and promised to talk to the miners themselves in a nationwide radio address at 10 P. M. tomorrow.

The White House action came less than two hours after John L. Lewis and the rank and file of his United Mine Workers allowed to expire a 10 A. M. back-to-work ultimatum.

The President ordered Secretary of the Interior Ickes to take possession and operate the mines with such workers as he can provide, and told Ickes he could call on the Army for protection for the mines if necessary.

"Except in a few mines the production of coal has virtually ceased," the President said. "The national interest is in grave peril."

Only Month's Supply

Meanwhile, coal-eating war plants reported their supplies of fuel were down to only a few weeks supply and the nation as a whole was estimated to have about one month's supply above ground.

More than 165,000 of the 409,000 soft coal miners stayed away from work with the expiration last midnight of their wage contract, obeying the dictum of President John L. Lewis of the United Mine Workers "not to trespass" on company property.

There was no noticeable disorder. All anthracite mines likewise quietly closed, with some 80,000 workers idle.

The White House let pass the ten A. M. hour, beyond which Mr. Roosevelt had said he would exercise his powers as President and Commander-in-Chief, with only this statement from Early:

"At ten P. M. tomorrow night the President will make a brief but very important statement on the radio. It will be carried by all networks.

"It would be safe to surmise that it will deal bluntly with the question of the need of coal to win the war."

Lewis was silent.

Lewis At Hard Coal Parley

At 10 A. M., Lewis was closeted with several mine union representatives in the United Mine Workers office on the 11th floor of the Hotel Roosevelt, New York City. When he entered the offices a half hour earlier, he had refused all comment, but his office said he intended to attend negotiations between hard coal miners and operators scheduled today.

Secretary Early had no comment on a published report that an order had been prepared directing the Army to move into the coal fields.

(See COAL STRIKE—Page 4)

HEAVY BUYING OF MEAT HERE

Supply Cut as Expiring Stamps Were Used Yesterday.

Lancaster's meat supply was reduced sharply today as the result of a rush by housewives to use their A, B, C and D ration stamps which expired at midnight last night.

Some butchers in Central Market reported that yesterday's market was the largest in four years. Today's early morning markets, however, fell off sharply.

Housewives who had saved their ration stamps apparently decided to "plunge" as the deadline neared for the four stamps and butchers reported that cuts of meat requiring a large number of stamps were in best demand. Buying of other commodities also was reported heavy on the local markets.

A revision of the point system announced yesterday gave round steak a higher point value by one point, and reduced the points on spareribs, brains and tongue.

OPA Admits Shortage Of Table Potatoes Here

The Office of Price Administration today admitted that a definite shortage of table stock potatoes exists in the Lancaster area and sounded a warning that seed potatoes must not be used for food.

The OPA said it has authority to permit the use of seed potatoes for

(See RATION—Page 4)

PROHIBIT HAULING OF CANS TO DUMP

KANSAS CITY, May 1. — (AP) — City Councilmen heard a WPB plea to save metal, and tentatively approved an ordinance prohibiting hauling of tin cans over city streets to a dump. Penalties: $5 to $25 fine and 30 days in jail.

The Scribbler

"POP" GREINER, Lititz, retired farmer and one of the town's best known citizens, is busy explaining an error in his spring planting. "Pop" offered to plant pasture land for Elmer Beck with blue grass but somehow got hold of the wrong bag and planted 10 pounds of rolled oats.

NORMAN WARFEL and Richard Groff, auto mechanics, had better stick to their "gas" buggies, according to friends. They hired a horse to do the plowing on their Victory garden but couldn't make the horse move. Dick even tried holding a bundle of feed in front of the horse to coax it to move. A farmer friend was summoned and gave a snappy "giddap"—and away went the horse.

"Woody" Wheaton Named Manager Of Lancaster Roses

'Vet' Centerfielder Sends Local Outfit Through Initial Drill

Manager William Cowdrick Announces Exhibition Games With York Club Next Week-End; Locals Open Season Here May 11

By JACK MARTIN

"Woody" Wheaton, of Drexel, Pa., has been named playing manager of the Lancaster Red Roses of the Inter-State Baseball League, it was announced Sunday by Business Manager William Cowdrick.

Manager Cowdrick also announced that the Lancaster Red Roses will play two exhibition games with York, of the same circuit, next week-end. The Lancaster Roses are scheduled to open their league season with Wilmington Blue Rocks on the Stumpf Field, Tuesday, May 11.

Wheaton's name is not new to Lancaster sports fans as he made his debut here when the club was transferred from Hazleton to this city to complete its season and annex its first and only championship since it has been playing at Stumpf Field.

Centerfielder Wheaton started his baseball career at Upper Darby High School where he was a pitcher on that team. Upon his graduation he became the property of the Philadelphia Athletics and Connie Mack farmed him out to Williamsport. Wheaton played with the Eastern League club 1937-38 and '39 and joined Hazleton, of the Inter-State League, in 1940.

"WOODY" WHEATON

Wheaton can wield the hickory in fine style and rates as a good consistant hitter with a .300 average. Last season the Red Rose swatter was well up around .400 until July and then he struck a slump and finished the season with .259.

Wheaton has been nominated to the All-Star team of the Inter-State Baseball League each season and rates as one of the finest defensive players in his position in the circuit.

Sunday found the new manager sending the squad of about fifteen players through their real first workout which consisted of infield running and batting high ones to the outfielders in a sort of limbering up manner.

Practice sessions will be held daily with this Monday's scheduled for 12:30 o'clock.

Sports Trail

By ORLO ROBERTSON
(Pinch-hitting for Whitney Martin)

New York —(AP)— We think that baseball is getting a little the shaggy end of it when the crowds attending the games are compared with the crowds at other sports events, particularly horse racing. The inference is that baseball is trying to plam off two-bit entertainment as the real thing and thus is losing its grip on the public.

Before proceeding further it might be mentioned that if baseball isn't up to standard this year, which is admitted by all concerned, the game should be darned proud, as it means a great many of its star performers have more important things to do right now.

The comparison with horse racing is particularly unfair, as the two sports have entirely different foundations. One is based on gambling, the other on its attraction purely as a spectator event.

We sometimes wonder a little what would happen if they took the mutuel machines away from the race tracks and installed them at the ball parks so the fans could bet on hits and errors and strike-outs and the like, and if the good stake horses were drafted instead of the good ball players. Those really would be draft horses, wouldn't they?

Anyway, under those circumstances we imagine they could fill Yankee Stadium every day for games between the Yankees and Athletics, while you could fire cannon all afternoon at the horse parks and not hit anyone but maybe a stable boy.

When comparisons between the two sports are made fairly they would have to be made on the same basis. That is, both with or without gambling. We think baseball would stack up pretty well under those conditions.

People will gamble. They always have so they might as well let them do it legally. Our resentment is against the intimation that the sport owes it's popularity purely to its spectacle as a sport. A good horse race is a thrilling sight, but not thrilling enough to make the fans pack special and "relief" trains to get out there and watch it purely for the thrill of watching it.

We have an idea that if roulette wheels were the lure at the tracks instead of the horses the crowds still would out-draw baseball, the betting fever is so wild among sports fans.

Our other cause for resentment is that the fans often use devious methods frowned upon by the government to reach the tracks, which often are so situated as to make ordinary public utility means of transportation impracticable.

If the major league ball parks were so situated and the fans used their cars or taxis or forced the railroads to put on special trains to get them there we would say the same thing about baseball. Maybe we're wrong, but when the government says it is necessary to conserve gas and rubber and curb unnecessary railroad travel we think it advisable to cooperate.

You can't compare baseball to once-a-week or so fights, either. If the fights were held daily in the afternoon they wouldn't be bragging about the attendance.

All of which means that, everything considered, baseball isn't doing so badly, although not as good as normally. We think it still is tops among those who like sports purely for sports sake.

The Standings

National League

Teams	W.	L.	P.C.
Brooklyn	8	2	.800
Pittsburgh	6	4	.600
St. Louis	6	4	.600
Boston	4	3	.571
Cincinnati	5	5	.500
Chicago	3	7	.300
New York	3	7	.300
Philadelphia	2	5	.286

American League

Teams	W.	L.	P.C.
New York	7	3	.700
Cleveland	6	3	.667
Washington	7	5	.583
Detroit	5	4	.555
St. Louis	4	4	.500
Boston	4	6	.400
Philadelphia	4	8	.333
Chicago	2	6	.250

SUNDAY'S RESULTS

National League

Boston 3, Philadelphia 1 (1st).
Philadelphia 6, Boston 5 (2nd, 12 innings).
Pittsburgh 3, Chicago 0 (1st).
Pittsburgh 1, Chicago 0 (2nd).
Brooklyn 3, New York 2 (1st).
New York 2, Brooklyn 1 (2nd).
St. Louis 7, Cincinnati 6 (1st).
St. Louis 6, Cincinnati 3 (2nd).

American League

Boston 7, Philadelphia 6 (1st).
Philadelphia 8, Boston 1 (2nd).
New York 11, Washington 3 (1st).
Washington 4, New York 1 (2nd).
Cleveland 5, Detroit 2 (1st).
Cleveland at Detroit (2nd, game postponed.)
St. Louis 3, Chicago 2 (1st 11 innings).
St. Louis 5, Chicago 1 (2nd).

International League

(First games)
Syracuse 4 Rochester 1
Newark 3 Montreal 1
Jersey City 7 Toronto 6 (10 innings)
Baltimore 7 Buffalo 5
(Second games)
Rochester 7 Syracuse 1
Newark 2 Montreal 1
Jersey City 2 Toronto 0
Baltimore 7 Buffalo 0

American Association

(First games)
Toledo 5 Louisville 1
Minneapolis 6 Kansas City 5
St. Paul 7 Milwaukee 4
Indianapolis at Columbus, both games postponed.
(Second games)
Minneapolis 5 Kansas City 0
Milwaukee 24 St. Paul 3

Southern Association

(First games)
Atlanta 11 Knoxville 9
Nashville 8 Chattanooga 7
New Orelans 2 Little Rock 1 (16 innings)
Birmingham 18 Memphis 5
(Second Games)
Knoxville 11, Atlanta 10.
Memphis 9, Birmingham 8.
Nashville 3, Chattanooga 2.
New Orleans 4, Little Rock 2.

Pacific Coast League

(First games)
Seattle 2 Sacramento 1
Los Angeles 7 Hollywood 6
Portland 8 San Diego 3
San Francisco 2 Oakland 1
(Second games):
Seattle 1, Sacramento 0.
Los Angeles 1, Hollywood 1 (tie, called end five innings).
Oakland 2, San Francisco 0.
San Diego 5, Portland 4.

MONDAY'S GAMES

New York—(AP)—Probable pitchers in the major leagues this Monday (won-lost records in parentheses):

National League

Philadelphia at Brooklyn—Gerheauser (0-1) vs. Higbe (0-0).
Pittsburgh at Cincinnati (morning)—Butcher (0-0) vs. Vander Meer (2-1).
(Only games scheduled).

American League

Boston at New York—Dobson (0-2) vs. Chandler (1-0).
Chicago at Cleveland—Dietrich (0-2) vs. Bagby (2-0).
(Only games scheduled).

Cleveland Defeats Detroit Clan, 5-2

Detroit —(AP)— The Cleveland Indains regained sole possession of second place in the American League Sunday by hammering three pitchers for 11 hits to defeat the Detroit Tigers, 5 to 2, in the opener of a doubleheader before 22,040 spectators.

The second game was postponed because of weather.

Ray Mack's very first 1943 hit, a homer off Johnny Gorsica in the fifth inning, provided the wining margin. Bespectacled Mel Harder, leaving 11 Tigers stranded in a fancy exhibition of clutch pitching, gained his second victory against one defeat but needed help from Giant Mike Naymick.

Singles by Ken Keltner and Jeff Heath plus a wild pitch and an error gave Cleveland two first inning runs. Dick Wakefield and Pinky Higgins each drove in a run to tie it up in the third, and then Mack homered. The Indians got single runs later off Hal Newhouser and Roy Henshaw.

Cleveland	ab	r	h	o	a
Hockett rf	4	0	2	1	0
B'dreau ss	4	1	0	4	3
Keltner 3b	4	1	2	0	1
Heath lf	4	1	2	1	0
Edwards cf	3	0	1	3	0
Denning 1b	4	0	0	9	0
Rosar c	4	0	2	6	1
Mack 2b	4	2	2	3	2
Harder p	3	0	0	0	3
Naymick p	0	0	0	0	2
Totals	34	5	11	27	12

Detroit	ab	r	h	o	a
Hoover ss	4	0	0	3	4
Harris cf	4	1	1	2	0
W'field lf	5	0	2	1	1
York 1b	5	0	0	11	1
Higgins 3b	4	0	3	3	1
B'lworth 2b	4	0	0	6	4
Radcliff rf	3	0	2	0	0
Parsons c	2	0	0	0	2
Gorsica p	1	1	0	0	0
Ross z	1	0	0	0	0
Newh'er p	0	0	0	0	1
Wood zz	1	0	0	0	0
Henshaw p	0	0	0	1	0
Totals	34	2	8	27	15

z-Batted for Gorsica in 6th.
zz-Batted for Newhouser in 8th.
CLEVELAND .... 200 010 011—5
DETROIT .... 002 000 000—2

Errors—Bloodworth, Denning, Mack. Runs batted in—Wakefield, Higgins, Mack, Heath, Hockett. Two base hit—Wakefield. Home run—Mack. Stolen base—Harris. Sacrifices—Parsons 2, Naymick. Double plays—Keltner, Mack and Denning; Hoover, Bloodworth and York. Left on bases—Cleveland 6, Detroit 11. Bases on balls—Off Harder 4, Gorsica 2, Newhouser 1. Strikeouts—By Harder 4, Naymick 2. Hits—Off Harder 8 in 6 1-3 innings; Naymick none in 2 2-3; Gorsica 6 in 6; Newhouser 3 in 2; Henshaw 2 in 1. Wild pitch—Gorsica. Winning pitcher—Harder. Losing pitcher—Gorsica.
Umpires—Rue, Pipgras and Weafer. Time—2:07.

Miss Frances Mathai Annexes Tennis Title

Bryn Mawr, Pa. —(AP)— Miss Frances Mathai of Garrison, Md., and Bryn Mawr College, won the Middle States Intercollegiate girls tennis championship Sunday by defeating Miss Isabel Grant, of Los Angeles and Swartmore College, 4-6, 6-3, 6-3 on the Bryn Mawr clay courts.

Miss Mathai, seeded second, eliminated Carolyn Clothier, University of Pennsylvania, 6-0, 6-4, in the semi-finals while Miss Grant, a niece of Edward Everett Horton, the actor, upset top-sseded Joan Wheeler, also of Swarthmore, 2-6, 6-3, 6-4.

BASEBALL'S BIG SIX
By The Associated Press
BATTING (Three leaders in each league)
(Based on 15 or more times at bat)

Player, Club	G	AB	R	H	Pct.
Gustine, Pirates	7	15	2	7	.467
Stephens, Browns	8	30	4	13	.433
Litwhiler, Phillies	7	18	5	8	.444
Frey, Reds	10	40	7	17	.425
Higgins, Tigers	9	29	3	12	.414
Stirnweiss, Yankees	9	35	5	14	.400

RUNS BATTED IN

American League		National League	
Spence, Senators	12	Vaughan, Dodgers	9
Stephens, Browns	10	Owen, Dodgers	8
Gordon, Yankees	10	D'Maggio, Pirates	6
		Litwhiler, Phillies	6
		Rowe, Phillies	6

HOME RUNS

American League		National League	
Gordon, Yankees	1	Litwhiler, Phillies	3
Keller, Yankees	1	Twelve tied with	1
Mack, Indians	1		
McQuinn, Browns	1		
Laabs, Browns	1		

Count Fleet Wins 69th Running Of Kentucky Derby

Count Fleet crosses the finish line in this overhead view of the Kentucky Derby at Louisville, to win the 69th running of the classic by three lengths from Blue Swords. Third is Slide Rule, and that's Eddie (Rochester) Anderson's Burnt Cork bringing up the rear.

Washington Wins Nightcap, 4 To 1

New York Yankees Clinch Opener Before 32,000 Fans, 11 To 3

Washington —(AP)— The Washington Senators gained an even break with the New York Yankees in a doubleheader Sunday before 32,000 fans, taking the nightcap 4-1 behind rookie Ewald Pyle's six hit hurling after dropping the opener, 11-3.

Pyle steadied after a shaky start and never was in serious trouble after the first, when the Yanks pushed across their lone tally on an error, a fielder's choice and Joe Gordon's double.

The Senators got to Charley Wensloff for seven blows. Washington scored twice in the first on hits by Ellis Clary, Stan Spence and Jimmy Vernon. Another run came in the third on a walk, a stolen base and an outfield fly. A walk and hits by Spence and Gerry Priddy produced Washington's fourth run in the eighth.

In the opener, Ernie Bonham scattered Washington's nine blows effectively. He was never in trouble after Charley Keller blasted a home run over the right field wall with two mates on base in the fourth.

The Yankees belted the offerings of Early Wynn, Lewis Carpenter and Rae Scarborough for 10 hits, garnering five runs in the eighth. Wynn was the losing hurler.

(First Game)

New York	ab	r	h	o	a
Stirnw's ss	5	1	2	2	4
Weath'y cf	5	2	1	3	0
Keller lf	3	2	1	5	0
Gordon 2b	2	1	0	2	1
Etten 1b	5	1	2	12	0
W.J'son 3b	5	1	2	3	3
Sears c	5	0	1	0	0
Lindell rf	5	2	1	0	0
Bonham p	3	1	0	0	4
Totals	38	11	10	27	12

Washington	ab	r	h	o	a
Clary 3b	3	1	2	1	2
Case rf	5	0	1	2	0
Spence cf	5	0	1	3	0
R.J'son lf	4	1	2	3	0
Vernon 1b	4	1	1	8	0
Priddy 2b	4	0	0	4	3
Early c	4	0	1	4	2
Sullivan ss	3	0	0	2	4
Wynn p	2	0	0	0	0
Carp'er p	0	0	0	0	0
Moore z	1	0	1	0	0
Scarb'gh p	0	0	0	0	0
Myatt zz	1	0	0	0	0
Totals	36	3	9	27	11

z-Batted for Carpenter in 7th.
zz-Batted for Scarborough in 9th.
NEW YORK .... 000 302 150—11
WASHINGTON .... 001 000 020— 3

Errors—Stirnweiss, Clary, Scarborough 2, Sullivan. Runs batted in—Spence, Keller 3, W. Johnson 2, Gordon 2, Stirnweiss, Etten 2, Vernon, Early. Two base hits—Clary, Etten, R. Johnson, Vernon, Sears. Home run—Keller. Sacrifices—Bonham 2. Double play—Stirnweiss and Etten. Left on bases—New York 9; Washington 9. Bases on balls—Bonham 3, Wynn 1, Carpenter 2, Scarborough 4. Strikeouts—Wynn 3, Carpenter 1. Hits—Off Wynn 7 in 6 1-3 innings; Carpenter 0 in 2-3; Scarborough 3 in 2. Winning pitcher—Bonham. Losing pitcher—Wynn.
Umpires—Rommel, Berry and Hubbard. Time—2:23. Attendance—31,000 (estimated).

(Second Game)

New York	ab	r	h	o	a
Stirnw's ss	5	0	2	1	2
Stainb'k cf	4	0	1	2	0
Keller lf	3	1	0	1	1
Gordon 2b	3	0	1	2	1
Etten 1b	4	0	0	11	0
W.J'son 3b	4	0	1	2	1
Hemsley c	4	0	1	5	0
Lindell rf	4	0	0	0	0
Wensloff p	3	0	0	0	5
Grimes x	0	0	0	0	0
Totals	34	1	6	24	10

Washington	ab	r	h	o	a
Clary 3b	4	1	1	3	1
Case rf	2	2	0	4	0
Spence cf	4	1	2	3	0
R.J'son lf	4	0	0	4	0
Vernon 1b	4	0	2	9	0
Priddy 2b	4	0	1	0	4
Early c	2	0	1	3	0
Sullivan ss	2	0	0	1	3
Pyle p	2	0	0	0	1
Totals	28	4	7	27	9

x-Batted for Wensloff in 9th.
NEW YORK .... 100 000 000—1
WASHINGTON .... 201 000 01x—4

Errors—Early, Sullivan. Runs batted in—Gordon, Spence, Vernon 2, R. Johnson. Two base hits—Gordon, Clary. Stolen bases—Spence, Case. Sacrifices—Pyle, Sullivan. Left on bases—New York 9, Washington 5. Bases on balls—Pyle 3, Wensloff 3. Strikeouts—Wensloff 2, Pyle 3.
Umpires—Berry, Hubbard and Rommel. Time—1:55. Attendance—32,000.

Montgomery-Armstrong Head Boxing Program

New York—(AP)—Bob Montgomery and Henry Armstrong continue their preparations for bouts with Beau Jack, New York recognized lightweight champion, by taking on lightly regarded opponents in the feature bouts on this week's boxing program.

Montgomery, who has a title engagement with Jack at Madison Square Garden May 21, takes on Henry Vasquez of Spain in a 10-rounder at Holyoke, Mass., this Monday night. Armstrong, who like Montgomery came through last week, tunes up for a June match with Jack by meeting Tommy Jessup in Boston Friday. It also is scheduled for 10 rounds.

Johnny Greco, Canadian army private, returns home after building up a reputation in the U. S. and meets Terry Young of New York in a 10-rounder at Montreal Saturday.

PRO PINMEN WIN

Toy				
White	167	160	153	480
Flosser	[illegible]	...	218	[illegible]
Fasnacht	183	180	177	[illegible]
Kauffman	176	[illegible]	210	[illegible]
Benner	187	177	179	[illegible]
Long	...	143	...	143
	803	814	937	2554

Leaman's Pros				
Leaman	173	225	200	598
Hess	140	...	196	336
Kline	151	169	187	507
Peters	170	164	152	486
Rebman	...	161	...	161
Gibble	198	181	189	568
	833	900	924	2657

Count Fleet To Prep For Famous Preakness

Louisville, Ky—(AP)—Count Fleet packed his bags Sunday and hopped a train for Baltimore and what looked like a sure-shot $50,000 in the Preakness, while behind him Derbyville still argued long and loud over the question—"is the Count Fleet?"

Certainly, there's no reason to believe the Hertz hurricane won't blow through the Preakness next Saturday with just as much fun as he swept through the Kentucky Derby for a $60,275 payday at Churchill Downs Saturday. There's nothing making the trip up from here that figures to do more than spend the afternoon chasing him. And from all reports, the gee-gees waiting for him in the East would need 12-cylinder motors and high-octane gas to take the big pot away from him.

Meantime, however, the "experts" were having a hot old time debating whether The Count is "the greatest since Man O' War" or just a young fellow lucky enough to come along when there isn't any competition to make him prove it.

On only a couple of points could the boys and girls get together. One was that if Ocean Wave hadn't been forced to withdraw from the Derby because of a wrenched leg, The Count would have really had to work for his payroll, instead of practically loafing through the last eighth of a mile to finish three lengths in front of Blue Swords and nine ahead of Slide Rule. The other was that in taking this "street car" Derby in the horse-car time of 2:04, the Count could hardly be put down as a P-38 on the prowl.

The Wave has demonstrated to one and all that he really can roll up that stretch at high tide, and when he was scratched Saturday, and possibility of a horce-race was scratched with him. Although he won't be ready to start in the Preakness, it is the general opinion that when the Wave comes back to the wars, probably early next month, he's going to make The Fleet pitch and toss a bit.

"We're going to let him rest a while and get completely sound again", trainer Ben Jones said Sunday." "We're sorry we couldn't run him Saturday. I'm not sure we could have beaten Count Fleet, but the Wave would have made a real horse race out of it."

Some of the boys pointed to Count Fleet's last quarter mile time of 26 2-5 seconds and insisted that such a milk-wagon performance makes any resemblance between him and Man O' War purely coincidental. Certainly Big Red won't feel very flattered.

At the same time, there was no reason for the Count to go any faster. By that time the others were all out of it and Mrs. John D. Hertz' whiz-bang and jockey Johnny Longden could almost have stopped for lunch and still finished in front.

Whirlaway ran that last quarter mile at the Downs two years ago in 24 seconds flat. The first half mile Saturday may have been the direct cause of the last quarter crawn. With Gold Showers and Burnt Cork trying for a few yards to match their zip with the Count's get-up-and-go, they sizzled through the half in 46 3-5—exactly the time when Whirly came from behind to his all time low.

Of the Derby horses, only Blue Swords and Slide Rule are going to be stubborn about it and take another crack at the Count in the Preakness.

Picks 'Em Right

DONALD M. McCOLLOUGH

Count Fleet, Blue Swords, Slide Rule, that is the way they ran in the Kentucky Derby and that is just the way Donald M. McCollough, of the Intelligencer Journal staff, filed his selections April 5 with the authorities at Churchill Downs, Ky., as his choices for the 69th running over the Derby.

Of the 443 'selectors' there were 319 who picked Count Fleet to win.

The winning time Saturday was 2:04 whereby McCollough posted 2:03 1-5.

Sam Molen, of radio station WCHS, Charleston, West Virginia, had the first three horses and the time correct.

Prize winners will receive War Savings stamps for their effort.

FOURTH TIME

Norman, Okla.—Selection of Center Gerald Tucker of the Helms Foundation All-American basketball team of 1943 marked the fourth time in history that a University of Oklahoma player had been thus honored.

Previous selectees were Vic Holt, 1928; Bruce Drake, present Sooner coach, 1929, and Omar ("Bud") Browning in 1935.

FUNNY BUSINESS

"I think Private Wiggins is carrying things a bit too far by tying nuts on his foliage!"

St. Louis Browns Win Pair, 3-2; 5-1

Chet Laabs Eleventh Inning Homer, Sundra's Pitching Features

Chicago —(AP)— An eleventh inning homer by outfielder Chet Laabs in the opener and Steve Sundra's steady seven-hit pitching in the nightcap gave the St. Louis Browns a double-header over the White Sox, 3 to 2, and 5 to 1, before 4,525 fans Sunday and enabled the St. Louisians to return home Sunday night at the .500 mark.

Rookie Gordon Maltzberger, who had pitched shutout ball after replacing Thornton Lee at the start of the seventh, was the victim of Laabs' homer. In a second effort to make a normal salary clause replace the $1 a year contract he's now operating under, Lee allowed two runs and four hits in six frames before his convalsecent arm tightened. Bob Muncrief, who pitched the last two innings for the Bronws, was the winner. Johnny Niggeling was excused after a strong nine frames, in which he allowed five hits.

The Browns sewed up the nightcap by scoring four runs, all of them unearned, off Johnny Humphries in the first two innings.

(First Game)

St. Louis	ab	r	h	o	a
G'ridge 2b	4	1	1	3	1
Clift 3b	4	1	1	3	2
Laabs lf	4	1	1	7	1
Chartak rf	4	0	0	0	0
Stephens ss	5	0	1	2	8
McQuinn 1b	5	0	1	13	0
Kr'vich cf	4	0	1	1	0
Ferrell c	4	0	1	4	1
Nig'ling p	1	0	0	0	1
Criscola x	1	0	0	0	0
Muncrief p	0	0	0	0	1
Totals	36	3	7	33	16

Chicago	ab	r	h	o	a
Tucker cf	5	1	2	2	0
Appling ss	2	0	0	1	4
Kuhel 1b	3	0	0	16	0
Solters lf	4	0	0	2	0
Kol'way 2b	5	1	1	4	6
Moses rf	5	0	2	4	0
Culler 3b	5	0	1	0	3
Tresh c	4	0	0	4	1
Lee p	2	0	0	0	1
Hodgin z	1	0	0	0	0
Maltb'r p	1	0	0	0	1
Totals	37	2	6	33	16

x-Batted for Niggeling in 10th.
z-Batted for Lee in 6th.
ST. LOUIS .... 000 101 000 01—3
CHICAGO .... 100 001 000 00—2

Error—Lee. Runs batted in—Laabs, Stephens 2, Solters, Culler. Two base hits—Gutteridge, Stephens, Tucker. Home run—Laabs. Stolen bases—Clift, Appling, Kolloway, Culler. Sacrifices — Niggeling 2. Double plays—Niggeling, Gutteridge and McQuinn; Kolloway and Kuhel; Kolloway, Appling and Kuhel. Left on bases—St Louis 6; Chicago 8. Bases on balls—Niggeling 5; Lee 3; Maltzberger 1. Strikeouts—Niggeling 3; Muncrief 1, Lee 2, Maltzberger 1. Hits—Off Niggeling 5 in 9; Muncrief 1 in 2; Lee 4 in 6; Maltzenberger 3 in 5. Hit by pitcher—By Niggeling (Kuhel). Wild pitch—Niggeling. Passed ball—Ferrell. Winning pitcher—Muncrief. Losing pitcher—Maltzberger.
Umpires—Summers and Stewart. Time—2:12. Attendance—(Estimated) 6,000.

(Second Game)

St. Louis	ab	r	h	o	a
Gut'dge 2b	4	1	1	1	4
Clift 3b	5	1	3	1	2
Laabs lf	5	1	0	1	0
Chartak rf	3	0	0	3	0
Step'ens ss	5	0	1	2	7
M'Qui'n 1b	4	0	0	14	2
Byrnes cf	4	1	2	1	0
Hayes c	4	1	1	2	0
Sundra p	4	0	0	2	4
Total	37	5	8	27	19

Chicago	ab	r	h	o	a
Tucker cf	4	0	0	2	0
Appling ss	4	0	0	0	2
Kuhel 1b	4	0	0	10	0
Solters lf	4	0	2	1	0
Kol'way 2b	4	1	3	3	3
Moses rf	4	0	1	3	1
Culler 3b	3	0	0	1	4
C'right xx	1	0	0	0	0
Turner c	4	0	0	7	2
Humph's p	2	0	1	0	1
Kalin x	1	0	0	0	0
Grove p	0	0	0	0	0
Total	35	1	7	27	13

x--Batted for Humphries in eighth.
xx-Batted for Culler in ninth.
ST. LOUIS .... 220 100 000—5
CHICAGO .... 000 100 000—1

Errors—Stehens 2, Appling, Culler, Turner. Runs batted in—Stephens 2, Hayes, Moses. Two base hits—Kolloway, Humphries. Three base hit—Byrnes. Stolen bases—Clift, Laabs. Left on bases—St. Louis 7; Chicago 7. Bases on balls—Humphries 1; Grove 1. Strikeouts—Sundra 1; Humphries 5; Grove 2. Hits—Off Humphries 8 in 8; Grove 0 in 1. Losing pitcher—Hymphries.
Umpires—Stewart and Summers. Time—1:38. Attendance 4,525.

Lino Aircraft Bowlers Enjoy Turkey Dinner

Twenty-six persons attended the first annual banquet of the Lino Aircraft Bowling League held Sunday afternoon at the Ephrata American Legion Home. A turkey dinner was served.

The principal speaker for the occasion was Henry James Marshall an official of the company.

The same officers were re-named for next year as follows: Walter Reinfried, chairman; Vic Butz, secretary; treasurer, George Jacob Flick.

Prizes were awarded to the following winners: high average, Vic Butz, 188; high triple, Bill Shertz, 606; high single, Rodney Hawthorne, 253; each member of the Spot Welders, first-half champions and winners of the roll-off were presented with a shirt. Hand Formers won the second-half laurels.

Entertainment was offered by "Jiggy" Dommel. Movies also were shown.

MURTAUGH HURT

Philadelphia — (AP) — Danny Murtaugh, second baseman for the Philadelphia Phillies, was accidentally kicked in the head and forced to leave the game in the seventh inning of the first game of Sunday's doubleheader. Murtaugh was injured by Clyde Kluttz, Boston catcher, when the latter slid into second.

Bosox Split Double Card With Macks

Red Sox Win First Tilt, 7 To 6 And Drop Second Contest, 8-1

Boston —(AP)— The Boston Red Sox split a twin bill Sunday with the Philadelphia Athletics, coming from behind to win the opener, 7-6, and then collapsing in the nightcap as the A's racked up an 8-1 verdict.

Cecil "Tex" Hughson, Boston pitching ace, sought his third straight victory in the opener but was roughly treated during the five innings he worked. He gave up six runs on six hits and three errors, two oof the miscues being committed by himself. Anton Karl relieved him and got credit for the victory when the Sox pushed over the tying and winning runs in the einghth on singles by Roy Partee and pinch hitter "Dee" Milles, a base on balls to Bobby Doerr and an infield roller by pinch hitter Johnny Peacock.

The A's landed on Ken Chase in the nightcap and piled up a lead which the Sox were unable to challenge with knuckle-baller Roger Wolff holding them to six scattered hits.

(First Game)

Philadelphia	ab	r	h	o	a
Welaj cf	5	1	1	6	0
White lf	5	2	2	0	0
Mayo 3b	4	1	2	1	3
Tyack rf	4	0	1	0	0
Siebert 1b	3	1	2	9	1
Suder 2b	4	0	1	1	3
Hall ss	3	0	0	4	3
Valo x	1	0	0	0	0
Wagner c	3	0	0	3	1
Mac'w'z zz	0	0	0	0	0
Arntzen p	2	1	0	0	2
Christo'r p	1	0	0	0	1
Estal'a xxx	1	0	1	0	0
Totals	36	6	10	24	16

Boston	ab	r	h	o	a
N'some ss	3	0	0	4	2
d-Miles	1	1	1	0	0
Conroy c	0	0	0	1	0
McBride cf	5	1	1	4	0
Doerr 2b	5	0	2	1	3
Simmons lf	4	0	2	2	0
Lake ss	0	0	0	0	0
Lupien 1b	3	0	0	8	1
Tabor 3b	4	0	0	3	2
Lazor rf	3	1	1	0	0
Partee c	4	2	3	4	2
Fox rf	0	1	0	0	0
Hughson p	1	0	0	0	1
a-Cronin	1	1	1	0	0
Karl p	1	0	0	0	0
b-Peacock	0	0	0	0	0
c-Garrison	0	0	0	0	0
Ryba p	0	0	0	0	0
Totals	35	7	12	27	11

x-Batted for Hall in 9th.
xx-Ran for Wagner in 9th.
xxx-Batted for Christopher in 9th.
a-Batted for Hughson in 5th.
b-Batted for Karl in 8th.
c-Ran for Peacock in 8th.
d-Batted for Newsome in 8th.
PHILADELPHIA .... 200 130 000—6
BOSTON .... 003 020 02x—7

Errors—White, Tyack, Hall, Hughson 2, Tabor. Runs batted in—White 3, Tyack, Hall, Newsome 2, Miles, Doerr, Simmons, Hughson, McBride. Two base hits—Mayo, Doerr, Simmons. Three base hit—White. Stolen bases—Welaj, McBride. Sacrifice—Newsome. Double play—Lupien to Newsome. Left on bases—Philadelphia 5, Boston 9. Bases on balls—Off Arntzen 1, Christopher 3, Karl 1, Ryba 1. Strikeouts—By Hughson 2, Ryba 1. Hits—Off Arntzen 6 in 4 1-3 innings; Christopher, 6 in 3 2-3 innings; Hughson, 6 in 5 innings; Karl 3 in 3 innings; Ryba, 1 in 1 inning. Winning pitcher—Karl. Losing pitcher—Christopher.
Umpires—Grieve, McGowan. Time—2:11. Attendance—15,000 (estimated).

(Second Game)

Philadelphia	ab	r	h	o	a
Welaj rf	4	2	2	3	0
White cf	5	0	2	1	0
Mayo 3b	5	1	2	0	3
Estal'la lf	5	0	2	1	0
Siebert 1b	5	1	2	10	1
Suder 2b	5	1	1	2	1
Hall ss	5	0	1	7	4
Swift c	4	2	3	3	0
Wolff p	3	1	0	0	0
Total	41	8	15	27	9

Boston	ab	r	h	o	a
L.New'e ss	1	0	1	0	0
Lake ss	3	0	0	1	4
McBride cf	4	1	1	4	0
Doerr 2b	4	0	2	1	4
Simmons lf	4	0	0	0	0
Lupien 1b	3	0	0	10	0
Tabor 3b	3	0	1	1	0
Lazor rf	4	0	0	3	1
Conroy c	4	0	2	7	0
Chase p	2	0	0	0	4
Peacock z	1	0	0	0	0
H.New'e p	0	0	0	0	1
Miles zz	1	0	0	0	0
Total	34	1	7	27	14

z--Batted for Chase in 6th.
zz-Batted for H. Newsome in 9th.
PHILADELPHIA .... 110 201 003—8
BOSTON .... 001 000 000—1

Error—Lake. Runs batted in—Mayo 2, Estalella 2, White, Suder, Hall, Swift, Simmons. Two base hits—Siebert 2, Welaj, Mayo, Doerr. Sacrifce—Wolff. Left on bases—Philadelphia 10; Boston 9. Bases on balls—Off Wolff 3, Chase 3. Strikeouts—By Wolff 3, Chase 2, H. Newsome 2. Hits—Off Chase 11 in 6 innings; H. Newsome 4 in 3 innings. Losing pitcher—Chase.
Umpires—McgGowan and Grieve. Time—2:01. Attendance—17,050.

Two Pirate Players On Ineligible List

Pittsburgh—(AP)—Two Pittsburgh Pirates were placed on the ineligible list of organized baseball Saturday but the club president, William E. Benswanger, explained there was nothing discreditable in the listing.

The players are catcher Babe Phelps and pitcher Russell Bauers who decided to remain on defense jobs.

Benswanger said because of uncertainty about whether the men would be drafted ro stay in their present jobs it was impossible for him to put them on the national defense list or to have them apply for places on the voluntarily retired list.

Regulations require official disposition of players who fail to sign contracts or report 10 days after the season opens.

Pimlico Entries

Post Time—12:00 Noon

FIRST: Purse $1,300, maiden, 2-year-olds, colts and geldings, 4½ furlongs. Director J. E. 118, Plane Shadow 118, Col. Hockwald 118, x-Jons 113, True American 118, Mouse Hole 118, Victory Blue 118, Tarfun 118, Powdered Milk 113, Quarter Moon 118, Ataman 118, x-Silent Hero 113.

SECOND: Purse $1,200, claiming, 2-year-olds, 4½ furlongs. Marquest 113, Free Dutch 113, Little Bunny 110, Honest George 113, Meadow Clover 106, Sir Winks 113, Patsy T. 106, a-Which Ace 118, Light Sandwich 106, a-Tumble bBoy 116, x-Supreme Jean 108, Felt Hat 109.
a-Massey and Rogers entry.

THIRD: Purse $1,100, climing, 3-year-olds, 6 furlongs. x-Marron 109, a-Daring 114, His Banker 114, a-Gold Tint 10?, Hi-Kerry 114, Aiken 114, Sun Valley 114, Fireglas 109, Big Sneeze 114, Chance Oak 114, On The Line 114, Stella's Sun 114, Pilate's Heart 114, Chief Mate 114, Maecase 112, x-Hokum 104.
a-Straus and Winkleman entry.

FOURTH: Purse $1,500, claiming, 3-year-old, 6 furlongs. a-Hadawin 112, Maeames 108, Dr. R. Young 112, Nellie Mowlee 115, Partido 112, a-Granding 108, Brass King 112.
a-Lafaivre-Lindley entry.

FIFTH: The Jervis Spencer handicap steeplechase, $2,500 added, 4-year-olds and up, 2 miles. Knight's Quest 147, Ossabaw 138, Cottesmore 155, a-Stiegel II 132, c-The Beak 141, d-Mandingham 159, Caddie 139, d-Frederick II 141, d-Good Chance 139, e-Lechlade 138, e-Bladen 142, c-Royal Archer 138, Nayr 136, a-Iron Shot 147.
a-Kline and Widener entry.
c-Mrs. F. A. Clark entry.
d-Rokeby Stable and Bieber entry.
e-H. Lamontagne entry.

SIXTH: Purse $1,500, 3-year-olds, 6 furlong. x-Mercury 117, Vincentive 119, Little Wizard 116, Dimout 105, Sollure 113, Black Grip 116, Monday Sun 119, a-New Moon 113, a-Cream 111.
a-Straus and McHenry entry.

SEVENTH: Purse $1,500, 4-year-olds and up, 1 1-16 miles. x-Sweeping Lee 117, Nell Mowlee 104, x-Bunny Baby 107, Galley Boy 114, x-a-Alhalon 119, John's Star 109, Hornblende 114, Harebell 117, Spoon Bread 114, a-Pompeco 109, Wise Timmie 124.
a-J. H. Louchheim entry.

EIGHTH: Purse $1,000, claiming, 3-year-olds, 1 mile and 70 yards. Lalage 104, Battle Flame 107, First Girl 107, Miss Kalola 104, x-Gloryland 104, Winning Smile 104, Miss Addie 107, Tippy 104, Watch Flag 104, Alfred Stuart 109, Flying John 109, Briarlass 104, x-Hand Me Down 104, Pious Display 109, Cheater 104, Attache 109.
x-Apprentice allowance claimed
Track fast.

"Newspapers are essential to the war effort."
War Manpower Commission

LANCASTER NEW ERA

WEATHER
Scattered showers and thunder storms and continued warm to night and Sunday morning.

VOL. 66—NO. 456 | Entered as second class matter January 31, 1924, at the Post Office at Lancaster, Pa., under the Act of March 3, 1879. Reg. U. S. Pat Off. | LANCASTER, PA., SATURDAY, MAY 8, 1943 | CITY EDITION | 14 PAGES—112 COLUMNS | 20c PER WEEK—4c Per Copy

ALLIES MOPPING UP AXIS FORCES FLEEING FALLEN BIZERTE, TUNIS

1,400 LOCAL CANDIDATES TO BE CHOSEN

3 County, 2 City Commissioners, Judge to Be Elected.

Over 1400 local candidates to fill the slates of the two major parties will be selected at the fall primary on September 21. Approximately 700 of this number will be elected November 2 to fill city, county, borough and township offices.

Control of the Court House is at stake this year and all but two of the "Row" offices will be filled. Three County Commissioners, two City Commissioners and a judge of the Lancaster County Court will be elected.

G. Graybill Diehm, chairman of the board of County Commissioners, will complete sixteen years as a Commissioner this year. The other County Commissioners are Harry R. Metzler, Rep., and Fred W. Wagner, Democrat. Commissioners serve four-year terms.

Others whose terms expire include Prothonotary Mahlon S. Delp, Clerk of Quarter Sessions Lawrence Aument, Register of Wills Adam Z. Moore, County Treasurer B. Scott Fritz, Sheriff William D. Leed and District Attorney Kenelm L. Shirk. Delp was named Prothonotary by Gov. James last December to fill the unexpired term of Elmer E. Kling who died last March. The other officers have served their four-year elective terms.

Schaeffer's Term Expires

The term of Judge Oliver S. Schaeffer expires this year.

Judge Joseph B. Wissler and T. Roberts Appel, the other two County judges, still have several years of their terms to serve. Judges are elected for ten-year terms.

The terms of City Commissioners Donald M. Mylin and Daniel W. Coulter expire this year as well as the terms of School Directors Byrt W. Fisher, Clay M. Ryan, vice-president of the board Dr. Charles V. Snyder and Ira M. Honaman.

Republicans will retain control of City Hall and the city School Board regardless of the outcome of the election. Mayor Cary and City Commissioners Kreisle and Bowman are Republicans as are the five school directors whose terms do not expire. Honaman and Snyder were appointed last year to fill vacancies caused by the resignation of Kendig C. Bare, who entered the Army, and Harry A. Schnitzer.

Other county officers whose terms expire are County Surveyor Henry H. Koser, Coroner Dr. A. V. Walter, Prison Keeper Walter N. Foust and the board of prison inspectors.

County-Wide Vacancies

Virtually every elective office in Lancaster County's 41 townships and 18 boroughs also will be filled in the November election.

An auditor, constable, township supervisor, judge and inspector of elections and school directors will be elected in each of the townships for four-year terms. Justices of the peace will be chosen for six-year terms.

In the boroughs, justices of the peace, auditors, high constables, constables, assessors, judges and inspectors of elections and members of borough councils and school directors will be selected.

Tax assessors will be elected in each of the city's nine wards and an alderman will be elected in the ninth ward to replace Warren E. Broome who resigned to accept a defense job.

On Active Service

Former Governor of Minnesota, Lt. Commander Harold E. Stassen, is now billeted at the U. S. Naval Training Station, Great Lakes, Ill., and will later be transferred to the Indoctrination School at Ft. Schuyler, N. Y.

ROBBER AT CAFE FLEES IN CHASE

2d Attempt to Enter Hotel; Man Robbed By Companion in Uniform.

A thief who attempted to break into Benedict's Cafe, 209 N. Prince St., was routed and chased for four blocks by John Kendig, son of the proprietress, before making his escape at 12:45 a. m. today.

It was the second time within a week that robbers were frustrated at the cafe. Early last Saturday, Mrs. Margaret Benedict, who operates the cafe, was awakened by prowlers who fled when she threatened to open fire with a rifle. That same night, three other cafes were broken into and $150 in loot stolen.

Mrs. Benedict told police they had just closed the cafe and turned out the lights last night, when they heard a prowler tampering with the rear door. Her son opened the door and saw a youth running through a back alley. Kendig gave chase to Market St., then ran south on Market to the parking lot in the rear of Hotel Pennsylvania.

The prowler suspect ran through the parking lot to Queen St., continued north on Queen to Chestnut and then west on Chestnut where he lost his pursuer.

Man in 2d Lieut's Uniform Robs S. C. Visitor of $115

Howard M. Elkridge, fifty, Columbia, S. C., reported to city police today he was robbed of $115 by a man wearing a Second Lieutenant's uniform whom he befriended at the Corine hotel last night.

Elkridge, who came to Lancaster in search of work, picked up a sailor hitch-hiker enroute and then took the sailor to a cafe near the hotel. They had several drinks, Elkridge said, and then the sailor left. While standing at the bar, Elkridge was joined by the Army officer and they had more drinks, he told police.

The Second Lieutenant told him he had no place to stay here, so Elkridge invited him to the hotel to share his room. They drank from a bottle furnished by the Army officer and then Elkridge fell asleep. When he awoke at 11 p. m., he found the Army man gone and $115 missing from his wallet, concealed on his person. Elkridge told

(See ROBBERIES—Page 5)

TWO-BILLION LIVING COST SUBSIDY SEEN

May Extend 10 P. C. Cut in Meat, Coffee, Butter Prices to Many Foods.

WASHINGTON, May 8—(AP) — A two-billion-dollar-a-year Federal program for subsidizing the American cost of living was reported authoritatively today to be under consideration in high administration quarters.

The report followed yesterday's official announcement that meat, coffee and butter subsidies will be swung in to support price ceilings in the nation's stabilization fight on June 1.

Those subsidies will cost approximately $400,000,000 a year, according to unofficial estimates. The $2,000,000,000 program reported under study was said to include plans for subsidizing canned fruits and vegetables, and a long list of other foods—but nothing except foods.

The first program, announced by Price Administrator Prentiss M. Brown, is aimed to force a 10 per cent cut June 1 in the retail cost of beef, veal, pork, lamb, mutton, coffee and butter. It will be financed by the Reconstruction Finance Corporation, through one of its subsidiaries, under what officials said was a specific authorization contained in last October's price control act. Flat payments of a cent or more per pound will be made to meat packers, butter manufacturers, and coffee companies for their products, on condition that they cut their prices according to the program. In adopting this plan, the government rejected a proposal to buy direct from producers and resell at a loss to processors.

Despite the "conditional" implication that the program might operate on an optional basis, the unofficial consensus was that it would be compulsory throughout, with the penalties provided under the price control act. Officials, however, declined to discuss this phase of the plan immediately.

With few details of the program yet available, Brown predicted reduction would trim 3 cents a pound off present prices of beef and veal, 4 cents a pound off pork, 4 to 5

(See SUBSIDIES—Page 11)

SELECTEES' QUOTAS FOR MAY START FINAL ARMY TESTS

Movement of local draft boards' May quotas to Harrisburg for their physical examinations and induction into all branches of the service began today. Men from County Board No. 1, at Mount Joy, and County Board No. 2, Columbia, were the first to go to Harrisburg.

The other six boards will send their quotas next week. The majority of the boards are sending large numbers of married men without children, while several of the boards have a few teen-age youths and men with collateral dependents only.

Also in the groups this month are a number of men who originally were scheduled for induction in April but received a month's respite when the April quotas were cut.

HAPPY FRENCH BEDECK YANKS IN BIZERTE

Strew Flowers on U. S. Tanks as Port Falls; Tunis Is Wild With Joy.

By HAROLD V. BOYLE

BIZERTE, Tunisia, May 7—(Delayed)—(AP)—American tanks were strewn with flowers by the deliriously happy French populace as they rolled in their power through the streets of this seaport stronghold of the Axis today.

Axis "suicide squads" of combat engineers blew up docks and fled across the canal to the Bizerte marshes.

One company of tanks and two companies of tank destroyers swept in this great Mediteranean seaport at 4:15 p. m., five minutes before the British Army took Tunis and six months less one day from the time the Americans first landed in Morocco and Algeria.

(Today's Allied headquarters communique said the British First Army entered Tunis at 2:50 p. m. and the Americans entered Bizerte at 4:15 p. m. There was no immediate explanation of the conflict.)

Yankee tankmen up from the south, wheeling through artillery shells and past long lines of prisoners, won the race for Bizerte by a narrow margin from French infantry pushing in from the western hills.

The cheering French followed them into the battered and ruined city in which the few remaining residents wept with joy and waved fingers high in the sign of victory.

Ten minutes after they took Bizerte, tankmen took the flowers off their vehicles to reply to a bombardment from the few German guns still manned in the marshes across the canal.

British Tanks Reach Tunis, Civilians Are Overjoyed

By DANIEL DE LUCE

TUNIS, May 7—(Delayed)—(AP)—British tanks rolled down through the hilly vineyards into Tunis today and battled from street to street against a few batteries of enemy 88-millimeter guns which fought to the end, but the majority of Nazi troops already were withdrawing toward Cap Bon.

French civilians—men, women, the young and the old—wept tears of joy and brought out jugs of wine for the khaki legion which had advanced 15 miles across the Tunis Plain today to exploit their decisive

(See BIZERTE-TUNIS—Page 5)

$50 REWARD PAID IN STOLEN CAR CASE

Payment of $50 reward to Ellsworth Cox, 735 Fourth St., for furnishing information leading to the arrest and conviction of a man who stole the car of S. Edward Gable was authorized by directors of the Lancaster Automobile Club at their monthly meeting last night. The reward is in line with a standing offer of the auto club on cars reported stolen by club members.

The directors voted to omit regular meetings of the club in May and June because of motoring restrictions.

Where Axis African Doom Was Sealed

With the fall of Bizerte and Tunis, Allied armies are pursuing the remnants of the defeated Axis forces into the hills of Cape Bon Peninsula where the final chapter in the African war is expected to be written. The routes over which the Allies reached the key cities, paced by an unprecedented aerial onslaught, are indicated on the upper map by arrows.

The course of the war now seems destined to spill over into the Mediterranean. Lower map shows distances to possible insular and continental invasion points from Africa.

ONE FUND DRIVE HERE IN OCT.

Plan Joint Campaign to Finance Welfare and U. S. War Fund.

A joint fund-raising campaign, for the support of the Welfare Federation and to raise Lancaster county's share of the National War Fund, will be conducted here in October, it was announced today at the Federation office.

The campaign will be held at the time usually selected by the Federation for its annual drive and will replace the United War Chest drive heretofore held in the spring of the year.

The goal will be set to cover the needs of the Welfare Federation's seventeen agencies during 1944 and the amount assigned to Lancaster as its share of the National War Fund. A joint committee composed of representatives of the Federation and the present War Chest organization will be in charge of the drive.

Included in the National War Fund are three types of agencies, covering services to the men and women of our armed forces, Allied War Relief groups, and aid to the people of the United Nations.

In the services to the Armed Forces are the USO, Aid to War Prisoners, United Seamen's Service and American Social Hygiene Association. The Allied War Relief group includes U. S. Committee for Care of European Children World Emergency and War Victims Fund, National CIO War Relief Committee, Refugee Relief Trustees and United Nations Relief of the A. F. of L. In aid to the People of the United Nations will be assistance to the Belgians,

(See WELFARE—Page 5)

YANKS WERE LED BY GEN. BRADLEY

Commanded 2nd Corps Since April 17, Replacing Gen. Patton.

ALLIED HEADQUARTERS IN NORTH AFRICA, May 8—(AP)—General Dwight D. Eisenhower disclosed today that Maj. Gen. Omar N. Bradley commanded the victorious drive of the U. S. Second Corps into Bizerte, having taken over from Lieut. Gen. George S. Patton, Jr., when the Americans were shifted to the north on April 17.

Gen. Eisenhower at the same time expressed his "delight" over the fall of Tunis and Bizerte but asserted that the fight would go on "as long as there was a single armed German on African soil."

Bradley, regarded as one of the Army's best infantry commanders, took over command from Patton when the Americans were transferred from the Maknassy area to the rugged mountain region of the north.

The reason for the change in command, it was explained, was

(See BRADLEY—Page 5)

COLUMBIA GIRL IS HONORED AT COLLEGE

Nancy Roye, daughter of Mr. and Mrs. Walter Roye, of 820 Walnut St., has been elected treasurer of the Class of 1945 at the New Jersey College For Women, New Brunswick, N. J.

She is a graduate of the Columbia High School, class of 1941 where she was a member of the High School Glee Club. She is a commercial art student at the College and a Junior Hostess at the New Brunswick USO. Elected a member of the College Glee Club she is also a Junior Guide of the school.

Many Are Captured, Rest Are In Flight Toward Cap Bon

Eisenhower Says Battle Will Continue Until All Armed Germans and Italians Are Wiped Out; French Take Pont Du Fahs; British Narrow Salient in South

ALLIED HEADQUARTERS IN NORTH AFRICA, May 8—(AP)—Allied troops hammered scattered pockets of resistance and pursued enemy detachments fleeing from conquered Tunis and Bizerte today in a battle which Gen. Dwight D. Eisenhower said would continue "as long as a single armed German is on African soil."

Six months to the day after Allied landing barges grounded on French North African beaches, the Allied communique said significantly: "The advance continues."

French troops captured Pont Du Fams and high ground to the east to roll up the right wing of Axis lines still holding on the southern front to contribute to the offensive in which Americans seized Bizerte and the British First Army took Tunis yesterday.

Reports from the battle front indicated the disorganized enemy, seeking haven from the merciless air and ground bombardments, was heading for the mountainous Cap Bon Peninsula in an effort to delay for a few days the final defeat expected to be a prelude to the Allied invasion of Europe.

British armor, hurling aside a force of 35 enemy tanks, captured Bir M'Cherga, on the Tunis road 12 miles north of Pont Du Fahs, and also War Ksar Tyr, midway between Bir M'Cherga and Medjez-El-Bab to narrow the Axis' southern salient.

U. S. Troops Quell Resistance

Troops of the U. S. Second Corps—operating under a new commander—quelled intermittent resistance overnight in the streets of Bizerte and British forces likewise mopped up Tunis.

Fighting continued beyond both cities. Hundreds of prisoners, their numbers still uncounted, streamed to the rear.

One of the drives through to Tunis cut the roads of retreat of German and Italian forces in the Bizerte region and pockets were being wiped out in this and other areas by the speedy pushes of both Americans and British.

Disclosing that Maj. Gen. Omar N. Bradley, 50-year-old infantry officer, had succeeded Lieut. Gen. George S. Patton, Jr., the tank specialist, in command of the Second U. S. Corps for the campaign across mountainous North Tunisia, General Eisenhower praised both.

Eisenhower Is Elated

"Naturally I am highly delighted with the developments which brought us into Bizerte and Tunis," the Allied Commander-in-Chief said, "but so far as I am concerned as long as a single armed German is on African soil there is still a battle and I want to destroy the rest of his resistance."

He said the result of the unification of the British, French and Americans under Deputy Commander Gen. Sir Harold Alexander "speaks well for the tremendously difficult tasks lying ahead of the United Nations."

Civilians Were Unaware

Advanced elements reaching Tunis said civilians and Nazi soldiers alike appeared unaware of the proximity of Allied forces on the outskirts. Confusion resulted, with some fighting in the streets and sniping from buildings, but this was quickly cleared up.

Midnight reports said the American forces faced a similar situation in Bizerte, but the important naval base—first entered by the 894th Tank Destroyer Battalion of the American Ninth Division—was soon completely under control.

French troops found extremely heavy mine fields when they drove into Pont Du Fahs, indicating the Germans had planned a prolonged defense, and Eighth Army patrols probing the Axis line along the coast above Enfidaville said mine fields there were the most exten-

(See AFRICA—Page 5)

CAPITAL HAILS SPEEDY TRIUMPH

Defeat of Axis in Africa Was Not Expected Before June.

By WILLIAM FRYE

WASHINGTON, May 8.—(AP)—The speed with which Allied troops shattered the Axis bastion of Northern Tunisia brought surprise as well as obvious delight in Washington today.

Since the North African invasion last November, officials—particularly in military circles—have carefully avoided any predictions on the length of the campaign, but observers got the definite impression that the defeat of the Axis armies was not expected before June.

As described here, the final phase of the fight which resulted in the fall of Tunis and Bizerte appeared to have begun a week ago when the doughboys of the II U. S. Army Corps under Lt. Gen. George Patton stormed the precipitous slope of Djebel Tahent—also called Hill 609—just 13 miles southwest of Mateur.

On this steep, 2,000-foot eminence the Germans had pegged their defense of the approaches to Bizerte, and when it fell the Axis line collapsed. The advancing Americans seized it May 1, and two days later had swept into Mateur, vital rail and highway junction of Northern Tunisia.

From Mateur, American artillery, including the huge self-propelled 155 millimeter gun mounted

(See WASHINGTON—Page 11)

LONDON DRIVES OFF 3 NAZI BOMBERS

LONDON, May 8.—(AP)—A German raid on London in which only three planes were believed to have participated was turned back from the outskirts of the city today after Londoners had undergone a breakfast alarm.

The capital's anti-aircraft defenses brought down an enemy craft in flames at Benfleet, Essex, 25 miles from London at the mouth of the Thames, and two other Nazi machines were knocked down during night raids over Britain. Another was shot down over Northern France.

The three Nazi planes which made for the capital before being driven off by short, sharp anti-aircraft artillery bursts, unloaded their bombs on the home counties after veering off from London.

The German radio said targets in Western and Southern England were hit in night attacks.

Clapper In Sweden

Social Services Unaffected by War; New Low Priced Cottages, Owners Get 60 Yrs. to Pay

BY RAYMOND CLAPPER

STOCKHOLM, May 8.—(By Wireless)—When you consider that Sweden is surrounded by Nazis, that all communication is cut off except by air though she is dependent on the outside for coal, foodstuffs and materials, it is amazing how little life here is affected by the war.

Clothing is rationed, but people all seem well dressed. Only a third of a small bar of soap is allowed each person each week, yet everyone is spotlessly clean. I have seen numerous kitchens, all spotless.

Social services, for which Sweden is famous, continue unaffected by the war. Expansion has been checked, although an enormous hospital is just being finished. I saw rows of new low price cottages being built, with the aid of government subsidy—owners put up prefabricated houses, supplied by the government on long cheap credit. The owner's labor is accepted as down payment, with 60 years allowed to pay the balance.

* * *

I spent a whole day looking at apartments, homes, nurseries and hospitals with Mrs. Myrdal, wife of Professor Gunnar Myrdal, who is well-known in America because of extensive investigation of social conditions there. She says that Sweden has advanced well toward its goal in state medicine, still has much to do in housing, and is lagging badly in schools.

The school age is seven to 14, when 80 per cent go to work, 10 per cent go to college and 10 per cent go to trade schools—against an average 10 year compulsory schooling in America, with over half continuing into high school.

The trend in medicine is toward socialization. Public hospitals dominate, with 96 per cent of all

(See CLAPPER—Page 11)

War Bulletins

EISENHOWER SAYS REST OF FOE SOON WILL BE DEAD

New York, May 8. — (AP) — Lieut. Gen. Dwight Eisenhower declared today in a broadcast from Allied headquarters in North Africa that the only Axis soldiers remaining in North Africa "soon will be in their graves" and that "we have set our heads on complete victory."

U. S. PLANES STEP UP ATTACKS ON ATTU

Washington, May 8.—(AP)—American planes operating from new advanced positions in the Aleutian islands have stepped up their attacks on Japanese-held Attu island, the Navy disclosed today, raiding it seven times Thursday.

The same day Army fighters attacked the Japanese base on Kiska Island which so far has been the most heavily bombed of the two bases, five times.

TOULON AND NICE ORDERED PARTLY EVACUATED

London, May 8. — (AP) — Reuters reported from Zurich today that occupation authorities had ordered a partial evacuation of Toulon, where the French fleet was scuttled, and Nice, French city near the Italian frontier.

DR. STEELE GETS NAVY COMMISSION

Dr. John W. Steele, local dentist, son of Dr. and Mrs. M. K. Steele, Quarryville, has been commissioned a lieutenant (jg) in the Navy and will report Monday at the Sampson, N. Y., Naval Training Station to begin active duty.

He is a 1942 graduate of the dental college at the University of Pennsylvania, and has been in the office of Dr. C. V. Halpin, this city.

Buchanan Relics Given To Wheatland Foundation

Mrs. George W. Hensel, Jr., Presents Decanter, Sword and Signed Picture; Open House Planned on Saturday

Three gifts are being presented to Wheatland by Mrs. George W. Hensel, Jr., Quarryville, it was announced at the annual meeting of the Buchanan Foundation for the Preservation of Wheatland yesterday.

The gifts are a whiskey decanter brought back from England by President Buchanan, a signed picture of Buchanan and a sword given the late George W. Hensel, Jr., by B. Frank Kready.

Mirror Formerly at Mansion

Other acquisitions at Wheatland this year include a mirror which formerly was used in the mansion, a Pembroke table, a Sheraton breakfast table, and tie-backs given by Harriet Lane Johnson, Buchanan's niece, to Mrs. Mary Speer Denny, of Baltimore. These articles were bought at a sale of the Denny estate.

Four new trustees were elected by the Foundation. They are Mrs. Lawrence H. Dunlap, Mrs. Clifford J. Backstrand, Herbert B. Weaver and James M. Huebner.

Open House Saturday

Reports were given by Fred Heinitsh, treasurer, and Mrs. James C. Dunlap, on the open house celebration to be held Saturday from 2 to 6 p. m. Plans were made to distribute literature on the mansion to service men through the USO.

Dr. H. M. J. Klein, president, was in charge of the session. Martin M. Harnish was chairman of the nominating committee, assisted by Fred Heinitsh and Mrs. M. L. Lampe. Other directors attending were Mrs. Arthur B. Dodge, Mrs. John E. Malone, Mrs. H. Dorn Stewart, Mrs. James C. Dunlap, Mrs. William Shand, Frank C. Beckwith and H. W. Prentis, Jr.

JOE FOSS LAUDS LOCAL 'CHUTES

Firm Also Receives Praise From Sailor After Jump to Safety.

Two messages of congratulations for the vital equipment they are making for the war were received recently by the Eagle Parachute Corporation, 424 N. Queen St., from Naval airmen in active service.

Rear Admiral John S. McCain, U. S. Navy, chief of the bureau of aeronautics said in a telegram received Friday:

"You men and women of the Eagle Corporation who are helping to provide chutes for Navy fighter pilots will be proud to read the following combat report on your product by Captain Joe Foss, U. S. Marine Corps, America's greatest air ace: 'In all my time on Guadalcanal I never knew of a parachute failure.' In several months of furious air action in the Pacific area, Captain Foss knocked down 26 Japanese planes. His words of appreciation of the vital equipment you are furnishing to the Navy reflect the gratitude of all our fighting airmen who often against terrific odds have won imperishable victories in the South Pacific skies."

A letter from Aviation Machinist Mate First Class Roman E. Sompolski at Quonset Point, R. I., said that a 'chute manufactured by the Eagle Corporation saved his life when he was forced to jump from a plane March 31. The letter said, in part: "On the day of the flight the ceiling was low and the visibility was bad. Upon reaching our destination the weather closed in preventing us from landing. After trying to reach several other fields, our gas ran low and the pilot ordered us to jump."

The company has completed four Navy contracts and is working on a fifth.

3-DAY CONFERENCE FOR YOUNG PEOPLE AT CALVARY CHURCH

Ministers, missionaries and students from Eastern cities and colleges will be among the leaders at the Young People's Conference to be held from Friday through Sunday at the Calvary Independent Church, N. Duke and Frederick Sts., it was announced today.

Dr. T. Roland Phillips, pastor of the Arlington Presbyterian church, Baltimore, will speak at 7:45 p. m. Friday and at 6 a. m. and 3 p. m. Saturday. Robert Hall Glover, M. D., F. R. G. S., Philadelphia, home director for North America, of the China Inland Mission, will speak at 7:45 p. m. Saturday.

The speaker for Sunday afternoon and evening will be C. John Wyrtzen, New York City, director of The Word of Life Fellowship, Inc. Fred A. Fels, Jr., student at Faith Theological Seminary, Wilmington, Del., will be song leader, and Miss Doris Wynkop, student at King's College, New Castle, Del., will be the pianist. "The Four Easterners," a male quartet from the Eastern Baptist Theological Seminary, Philadelphia, will sing. The Rev. Frank C. Torrey, pastor, will speak on "The Rock, Christ Jesus" at the Sunday morning worship service, which will be broadcast over station WGAL.

Paddock In Shape

SAN FRANCISCO, May 20—(AP)—Captain Charles W. Paddock is proving that a former track athlete can regain his once streamlined proportions after long inactivity.

As Charley Paddock of the University of Southern California, he was the original "world's fastest human," holder of some 95 sprint records in his prime and competitor in three Olympic games.

Capt. Paddock, who served in World War I, is aide to Major General W. P. Upshur, commanding general of Marines in the department of the Pacific.

And the Marine Corps reports that after nine months' conditioning, Capt. Paddock's physical measurements are nearly identical to those when he was a sprint star twenty years ago. He was 22 years old in 1923 and is 42 today.

Observance Of Father's Day Is Now Widespread

Governor Martin Calls For Observance

Calls For Observance In Spirit of Love and Reverence

Harrisburg — Governor Martin in a statement Tuesday called for observance of next Sunday as Father's Day.

"The day should be observed throughout the Commonwealth of Pennsylvania in a spirit of love and reverence," he declared. "We should honor, in fullest measure, the patriotic courage and determination with which our fathers have always fought and are fighting today to preserve the sacred traditions of the American home.

"Let us join, in our churches, and in our homes, in this important wartime observance and put into action the Father's Day slogan: 'Honor a fighting American—your Dad'."

Last year thirty-two governors issued proclamations setting aside the third Sunday in June as official Father's Day. This year, forty sttaes have been asked to observe the day by their governors. Thus the observance has become a truly national American event.

GOVERNOR MARTIN

War Camps Plan Tribute

War Plants In United States Also to Honor Family Heads

Appropriate ceremonies in honor of the observance of Father's Day, June 20, will be held in Army camps throughout the country, according to the National Father's Day Committee.

The committee, composed of notables throughout the nation, united for the uniform promotion of a better understanding between father and child, has decreed that Father's Day this year be set aside for the honoring of the fathers on the battlezones. So, in a sense, fathers are honoring fathers.

However, the homefront fathers will not be overlooked on June 20. Plans are already underway to select the most prominent Father in many war plants.

Thirty-five per cent of all divorces in the United States occur within the first five years of married life.

The game of handball originated more than 1000 years ago in Ireland.

Sacrifices Called For On Part Of Men Who Are To Be Honored

Father's Day, 1943, falls on Sunday, June 20, and as was anticipated, it is geared to the war.

This year, however, Father's Day calls for a sacrifice on the part of the father. He is expected to buy a bond in his exuberance at being out for family honors.

The National Father's Day Committee believing that every father in America wants to contribute everything he can to the war's prosecution, is asking that the 33 million fathers buy 1 billion dollar's worth of war bonds during the month, beginning May 20 and continuing to June 20, Father's Day.

Father Hero Of The Day

This year, on the 33rd birthday of Father's Day, the nation has come to realize with sudden awakening that father is the hero of the day. As soldier, producer of vital tools, banker for the war, defender of the home, backbone and personnel of the arm—father is the No. 1 general on all fronts.

All over the globe, on hundreds of first lines, fathers are proving they can take it. Just read the proof in the desert stretches of North Africa, in the sandy pits of Wake Island, in the shell mangled jungles of New Guinea.

Making Fighting Tools

Fathers are not only fighting, they are making the fighting tools which daily leave our harbors for war centers. Mechanical skill and scientific training have never been at a higher premium, and these are products of long years and assiduous study, not usually in the possession of youths. Talented fingers to fashion machines of exquisite per fection are more precious than those of a Carnegie Hall pianist. Those hands are the hands of older men, family men, with a long background of experience.

There are many ways we can show our appreciation to father on his one day. Wear the patriotic new Father's Day war stamp boutonniere with a red rose heart traditional flower of the day. Remember father with some little token of esteem. Fathers themselves, ever happier giving than receiving, will celebrate the day by joining the U. S. Treasury approved billion dollar bond drive in honor of all fighting sons.

BUS STRIKES END IN 2 PENNA. CITIES

PITTSBURGH, June 16. —(AP) — A walkout of 325 AFL drivers and mechanics of the Greyhound bus lines ended at midnight last night after paralyzing East-West traffic of the company here and delaying hundreds of travelers for 12 hours.

Meanwhile, 50 drivers of the Penn Transit company at McKeesport remained idle in protest against a cut in work schedules necessitated by an ODT order to save gasoline.

At Johnstown, war workers and others travelled normally to and from their jobs today for the first time this week, with the ending of a bus and trolley operators' strike there.

FIGHTS LAST NIGHT

By The Associated Press

NEW YORK—Jackie Cooper, 149, Chicago, outpointed George Kochan, 160, U. S Coast Guard (8).

NEW YORK—Joe Mulli, 150, Brooklyn, outpointed Ernest (Cat) Robinson, 148¾, New York (8).

PORTLAND, Me.—Maurice (Lefty) Lachance, 128, Lisbon, Me., knocked out Ted Christie, 128, New York (4).

SCRANTON, Pa.—Charley Sabatella, 142, Dunmore, Pa., stopped Tony Grey, 145, Brooklyn (8).

NEW BEDFORD, Mass.—Jimmy McLarnin, 133, New Bedford, outpointed Russell Sawyer, 133, New York (8).

BUFFALO—Johnny Green, 145½, Lackawanna, N. Y., knocked out Joe Spangler, 147, Richmond, Va. (5).

LOS ANGELES—Luther (Slugger) White, 134½, Baltimore, outpointed Juan Zurita, 133, Mexico, (10).

Fathers and Sons In Service

General Eisenhower

Son John Eisenhower

Maj.-Gen. James Doolittle and son James, Jr.

Gen. Henry H. Arnold and son William.

Ship's cook Romie V. Burgess and son.

Adml. Chester W. Nimitz and son Chester, Jr.

Son Joseph, Jr., and Lieut.-Gen. Joseph Stilwell

Fathers of America in 1943 are justly proud of their sons and daughters who are working and fighting for victory, and perhaps the proudest of all are the fathers whose sons are serving beside them in the armed forces. As No. 1 father of 1943, Gen. Dwight Eisenhower has a son at West Point. Major-General Doolittle looks with pride on his son in the Air Force. General Arnold's son has just graduated from West Point, Admiral Nimitz's son is a sub commander, and General Stilwell's son is in the army.

Hero Father And His Son

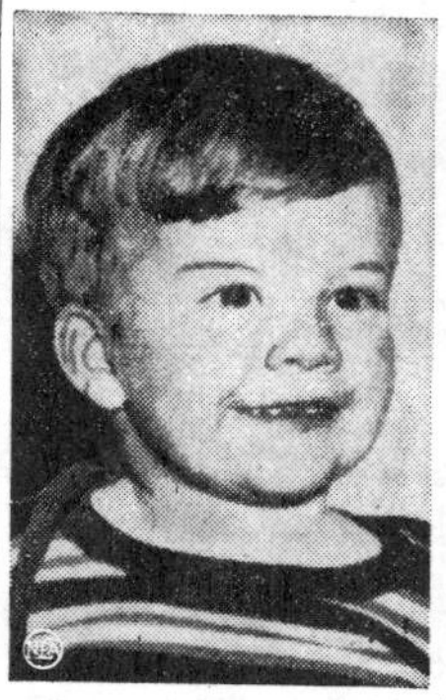

Among the first American heroes of the war was Captain Colin P. Kelly, Jr., (right) U. S. flier killed as he sank a Japanese battleship a few days after this nation entered the war. Above is his son, Colin, 3rd, who will become a cadet at West Point when he grows older. His name was proposed by the President of the United States as a measure of the esteem in which this nation holds his father.

JAP WAR WEAPONS WILL BE DISPLAYED

War weapons used by the Japanese will be displayed at a meeting of the Lancaster County Detachment of the Marine Corps League at 8 p. m. Friday at the home of Mr. and Mrs. Benjamin Tracey, 538 St. Joseph St. The implements of war were collected on Guadalcanal by their son, Private Jack F. Tracey, of the U. S. Marine Corps.

Parents of Marines and ex-Marines have been invited to attend the meeting.

MULLI WINS FIGHT

New York—(AP)—Joe Mulli, 150-pound Brooklyn battler, outpointed Ernest (Cat) Robinson, 148¾, New York, in a free-swinging eight rounder before 4,000 spectators at MacArthur stadium Tuesday night.

Red foxes eat grapes to round out their diet.

THE ATLANTIC SHRINKS

The ocean, which used to form a five- or six-day barrier between America and Europe by even the fastest ship, is today an aeronautical millpond. This map shows how its eastern and western boundaries have been pulled together since four Navy flyers made the first plane crossing in the NC-4. The time set by the modern bomber is not necessarily the speediest possible performance, because ferry command regulations prohibit deliberate efforts to set records. The crossings shown all occurred in May, when transocean flying conditions are gen-

Lititz Has 3 Nonagenarian 'Dads,' Oldest 97 On June 6

Martin Bollinger Likes to Reminisce About Olden Days; "Grandpa" Baum Interested In Victory Garden; "Pa" Buch Says He Still Has Much to Learn

Lititz has three nonagenarian fathers, the oldest is Martin Bollinger, who celebrated his ninety-seventh birthday anniversary on Sunday, June 6th. He was a farmer and drover in his youth and is fond of reminiscing and telling about the time he would drive for days buying cattle.

He has three sons, Elmer and Howard Bollinger of Lititz and Phares Bollinger, who lives on a farm near Downingtown.

The next oldest is "Grandpa" Baum (Wilson Baum) who was ninety five in February. He worked as a tailor until he was eighty six when he retired. He enjoys going to the fire house in the evening and playing cards with the "boys". Another interest is his victory garden which he spends much time cultivating. He lives with his daughter, Mrs. Esther Brunner and has two grandsons in the service, Major William Jaynes stationed at San Gabriel, Cal., and Joseph Jaynes, of San Diego who has been in the service twelve years as an instructor in the coast guard air corps.

Keen and Alert

"Pa" (Frank) Buch, keen, alert and versatile at ninety-one, was a cigar maker for many years and since early youth an enthusiastic hunter. He recalls when a youth of fifteen he was working on his father's farm at Kissel Hill when he heard a shooting match being conducted at Lititz, two miles away. He started to run and climbed to a high tree where he could watch the affair and when it was over he ran back to his work in the corn field and no one was the wiser.

Taxidermy was a hobby through the years and he had many specimens of pheasants, squirrels, owls, foxes, ground hogs, skunks and deer heads. He gave 75 of these to the Sportsmen's Association a few years ago and retains only a few of the finer ones.

Still Can Learn

Although ninety-one "Pa" remarked he has much to learn yet. When asked what fields were left for him to explore, he replied he had never learned to smoke but "Ma" Buch slyly remarked "but tell about the one time you tried it" then he said that many, many years ago ma had house plants that became covered with lice and he thought he would surprise her by killing them. He got a cigar, lit it and placed the end with the fire in his mouth and smoked them, adding that "it laid them flat, but it laid me flat too, I became so desperately sick I never tried to smoke anything again". Mr. and Mrs. Buch are married over sixty-one years and have two daughters, Mrs. Erla Stultz and Mrs. John Brubaker with whom they reside.

Star Graduates

Movie star Joan Leslie, 18, poses in the cap and gown she will wear when she receives her high school diploma at the University High School, Brentwood, Cal., along with 310 graduates.

NET PLAY ADVANCES

Philadelphia —(AP)— Three players, including Mrs. David W. Gray of Washington, District of Columbia champion, moved into the quarter finals of the Philadelphia District Grass Court Tennis Tournament Tuesday.

Mrs. Gary advanced by beating Jane Austin of Lower Merion, Pa., 6-2, 6-1. Virginia Redford defeated Anne Le Duc, Philadelphia girls' champion, 8-6 and 6-2, while top seeded Cecilia Riegel downed Jean Cook of Radnor, Pa., 6-4 and 7-5.

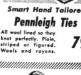

WEATHER
Eastern Pennsylvania: Continued Warm Saturday.

Intelligencer Journal

Treasury Award — Made to Lancaster Newspapers, Inc., its newspaper boys, and subscribers for their patriotic support of the War Savings Program.

The Leading Newspaper in the Garden Spot of America, Home Owned for Home Folks Since 1794

VOLUME LXXIX.—NO. 247. Entered as second class matter June 23, 1928 at the Post Office at Lancaster, Pa., under the Act of March 3, 1879. Reg. U. S. Pat. Off. LANCASTER, PA., SATURDAY MORNING, JUNE 26, 1943 CITY 14 PAGES, 112 COLUMNS. 20c PER WEEK—4c Per Copy

CONGRESS ENACTS ANTI-STRIKE BILL

Report 150,000 Nazi Troops Massed At Brenner Pass; U.S.-RAF Bombers Hit Ruhr

CLAIM 8th ARMY IN SYRIA

Suggest Germans Concerned Over Possibility Italy Might Collapse In Event Of Allied Landing; Virtually All Other Nazi Strength Reported Already Pulled Back From Sicily, Italian Boot And Sardinia

London—(AP)—The Germans were reported unofficially Friday night to be massing about 10 divisions of up to 150,000 men in northern Italy to guard the Brenner Pass, southern portal to Germany, against invasion, while the Berlin radio itself said the famous British Eighth Army had been sent to Syria to spearhead an Allied attack from there.

The German troop movement was reported by an unofficial source with close continental connections, and it was suggested that the Nazis were concerned over the possibility that Italy might collapse in event of an Allied landing.

This source, who cannot be identified, said about five divisions were taking up new positions, below the pass, and the remainder would form a mobile troop reservoir that could be sped to the Riviera or southeast into the Balkans in case of emergency.

Except for the German air force and special service forces, virtually all the other Nazi troop strength was reported already pulled back from the crisis zones—Sicily, the toe of Italy, and Sardinia.

SAY 8TH ARMY IN SYRIA

Transfer of the Eighth Army, flushed by its victories in Libya and Tunisia, to Syria was reported by a German military commentator in a broadcast recorded by Reuters. The report was wholly unconfirmed and it was recalled that King George VI visited the

More of CLAIM on Page 9

LIBERATORS RAID GERMAN AIRDROME NEAR SALONIKA

Find Defenses Weak At Major Base Of Nazis Grecian "Siegfried Line"

Cairo—(AP)—American Liberators bombers have violently raided the big German airdrome of Sedes near Salonika, a major air base in the Nazi's "Siegfried line" in Greece, and found surprisingly weak anti-aircraft defenses.

U. S. air headquarters here announced Friday that more than 50 Liberators dropped well over 125 tons of bombs at Sedes Thursday without a single loss. It was the first American blow at German-held Greece since September.

SCORE DIRECT HITS

"Direct hits were scored on three hangars and all are believed to have been destroyed," said a Ninth U. S. Air Force communique.

"Dispersal areas were covered by bursts and at least three enemy aircraft were seen to be destroyed. Administrative buildings northeast of the hangars received hits and several strings of bombs criss-crossed the field itself.

"Oil fires were observed west and south of the hangars and gray and black smoke covered the target area when the bombers departed.

"No enemy fighting opposition was encountered.

"All our aircraft returned safely."

Not bombs and fire alone, but

More of LIBERATORS on Page 5

SEVERE LOSSES

Say Reich Evacuating 4 To 5 Million Persons From Industrial Valley

WEEK-LONG RAIDS

London (Saturday)—(AP)—The Royal Air Force bombed Germany again last night, rounding out a week of Allied heavy air attacks on Germany, Italy and German-occupied Europe.

London—(AP)—Fleets of U. S. heavy bombers pounded northwestern Germany Friday on the heels of another RAF town-crusher attack Thursday night upon the Ruhr, the bomb-shattered industrial valley where 4,000,000 to 5,000,00 persons were reported evacuated to escape the mighty Allied air offensive.

The big American bombers hammered undisclosed targets in adverse weather against strong fighter opposition, and lost 18 ships for a total of 173 Allied bombers as the cost of more than six days and nights of tremendous attacks. Thirty-eight were American and 135 British.

Flying Fortresses made up at least part of the raiding force, and Fortresses from one station alone destroyed 24 enemy fighters and probably 14

More of SEVERE on Page 9

MERCURY RISES TO 99, NEW HIGH FOR THE SEASON

Friday Was The Hottest June Day Since June 17, 1939

NO RELIEF EXPECTED

The stifling 10-day heat wave which claimed two deaths thus far, intensified its grip on this area Friday, shooting the mercury to 99 degrees, a new high for the season.

The 99-degree reading at the Ephrata weather station, surpassed by two degrees, the previous high of 97, set Monday.

Friday was the hottest June day since June 17, 1939 when the temperature was 100 degrees. The low for the day was 69 degrees.

No relief is in sight, the Weather man said, and he forecast continued warm for Saturday.

GARDENS DAMAGED

The prolonged heat wave and lack of rain during the past two weeks are damaging hundreds of Victory Gardens. Some vegetation is beginning to turn brown under the the strong rays of the sun and the lack of moisture.

Jaded residents took to porches and yards to sleep again Friday night, while parks and swimming pools were jammed earlier in the day.

TO START STREET SHOWERS

The daily street showers, a part of the annual playground program, will start on Monday it was announced Friday by Grant D. Brandon, director of the Recreation association.

The schedule for the showers, which are given with the cooperation of the city Water Department and Parks department, is as follows: Lehigh Ave. and Reservoir St., 1:15 to 1:45 p. m.; Burrowes Ave., 1:30 to 2 p. m.; Ice Ave., 1:45 to 2:15 p. m.; Water St., 2 to 2:30 p. m.; Fremont St., 2:30 to 3 p. m.; Beaver St., 2:45 to 3:15 p. m.;

More of MERCURY on Page 5

Missing

Hope for the safety of Brig. Gen. Nathan Bedford Forrest, missing since the bomber on which he was an observer was shot down in the June 13 raid on Kiel, Germany, was advanced Friday night by the U. S. 8th Air Force which announced that at least eight persons of the 12 aboard were seen to parachute from the crippled plane.

FURTHER CUT IN GAS SUPPLIES OF EAST IS FORESEEN

Officials Disclose OPA Considering Suspension Of A-Card Coupons

Washington—(AP)—Suspension of A-card coupons in the East is one of the steps being considered by the Office of Price Administration (OPA) in view of increasingly tight supplies of gasoline for civilians, officials revealed Friday night.

They emphasized, however, that this would be done only as a last resort because they consider that many A-card holders use their gasoline for essential purposes.

SETS ALLOTMENT

Secretary of Interior Ickes, in his role of Petroleum Administrator, set aside for civilians a daily allotment of 328,000 barrels for July, August and September.

One OPA official, who declined use of his name, commented that "it looks as if new ration cuts will be necessary unless we can somehow get more gasoline."

The possibility of suspending A-card coupons was mentioned freueqntly last spring, but resisted by the OPA.

Friday indications came from OPA sources that the agency might appeal from the allotment figure set by Ickes for the next three months.

MAY SEEK OTHER WAYS

Conceding that "appeals don't create gasoline," OPA rationers were said to hope nevertheless that Ickes might be prevailed upon to seek some means of providing transportation for additional petroleum for the east.

In announcing the supply certification, Ickes declared he was "fully aware that the [illegible] civilian gasoline cons[illegible] must necessarily resu[illegible] con-

More of FURTHER on Page 5

LIMITED ACTIVITY IN SOUTH PACIFIC

Allied Headquarters In Australia (Saturday) — (AP) — A Beaufort bomber scored a near miss on a merchantman in a small Japanese convoy off Cape St. George yesterday, the high command announced.

Cape St. George is on the southeastern tip of New Ireland.

In a report of extremely limited activity, the communique told of a sweep by medium bombers southwest of Madang, New Guinea, where five Japanese-held villages were strafed from treetop height. Native structures were set afire and a machinegun post silenced.

PRESIDENT HITS DEADLINE SET BY MINE UNION

Chief Executive Says He Will Not Recognize Date Set By Lewis

MANY MINERS IDLE

Washington—(AP) — President Roosevelt, saying he would not recognize the United Mine Workers' Oct. 31 deadline for continued coal production, declared Friday that many people seem to forget we are at war and the life of the nation is at stake.

The President's grim reminder at a press conference that a prolonged stoppage of coal production could throttle the nation's war effort came against the background of these other developments:

OTHER DEVELOPMENTS

1. A spread of absenteeism in the Pennsylvania coal fields that had some 145,000 of the state's 200,000 miners idle. Pickets were attempting, too, to shut down other mines. A survey of all major coal mining states indicated about half of the 521,000 miners were still out of the pits. Union leaders said they had sent out organizers to try to get the men back to work on Monday, and it appeared the opening of the mines then would furnish the crucial test of whether the miners will accept the back-to-work order adopted Tuesday by the union's policy committee.

2. An apparent sharp controversy within the administration over whether disciplinary action should be attempted against the United Mine Workers. The War Labor Board (WLB) took to war mobilization director James F. Byrnes a request that the government compel the UMW to sign a contract, as ordered by WLB, or punish it for refusing. On the other hand, Secretary of Interior Ickes, the Federal boss of the mines, said he knew of no way to make any "private individual or group" sign an agreement.

3. A conference of Ickes with some 30 executives of major mines

More of PRESIDENT on Page 9

HOUSE ACTS TO END PROGRAM FOR FOOD SUBSIDIES IN U. S.

Labor Leaders Declare Rollback Must Be Effective Soon Or Higher Pay Will Be Asked

Washington — (AP) — The House voted to end the administration's food subsidy program Friday only a few hours after two labor leaders declared the rollback must be fully effective by July 15 or workers will insist on higher pay to meet increases in the cost of living.

The House action came while the Senate was debating a similar curb, and shortly after President Roosevelt commented that Congress will have to shoulder the responsibility if it takes the path toward inflation.

[illegible] AMENDMENT

Approving a bill extending the [illegible] the Commodity Credit Corp., the House adopted an amendment by Rep. Wolcott, Rep., Mich., providing in effect, that neither CCC nor any other government agency may make subsidy payments on production or distribution of farm-originated products, in order to reduce or maintain prices.

It was the second House vote against the price rollback, declared by Price Administrator Brown to be essential if living costs are to be driven back to the Sept. 15, 1942 level ordered by Congress. The rollback already has reduced the retail prices of butter and meat, and has been projected for coffee. Last week the House stripped OPA of $47,000,000 of the $177,000,000 recommended for it in the next fiscal year, and provided that none of the approved fund could be used to administer such subsidies.

SET "DEADLINE"

The July 15 "deadline" for effective rollbacks was set by both president Philip Murray of the CIO and Boris Shishkin, economist of the AFL. Appearing before a

More of HOUSE on Page 9

TOBACCO DUST BURNS; ENDANGERS LUMBER

Tobacco dust, ignited by a lighted cigaret stub Friday, threatened the Lancaster Iron Works' pile of lumber stored at their plant near Prince and Seymour streets, according to Fire Chief Harry Miller.

Chief Miller said the tobacco dust, at the W. H. Winstead Tobacco Plant at the same address, was ignited and the burning material started to ignite the lumber at the adjoining plant. He said the damage was slight. Engine No. 2 re-

Roosevelt's Veto Is Overridden With Surprising Speed

Senate Votes 56 To 25, House 244 To 108 To Put Law On Statute Books Providing Fines And Imprisonment For Persons Instigating Or Aiding Wartime Strikes In Government-Operated Industries

Washington—(AP)—Congress overrode President Roosevelt's veto Friday and slapped on to the statute books legislation providing fines and imprisonment for persons instigating or aiding wartime strikes in government-operated mines or war plants.

VETO FIRST A CONGRESS OVERRODE DURING WAR

Washington — (AP) — Legislative reference sources said Friday night that so far as they could recall Friday was the first time a Congress ever had overridden a presidential veto during war-time.

Six vetoes by Woodrow Wilson were overridden while he was President, but all were during a time when the nation was not at war, the sources said.

In the memory of those at the capitol, Friday's action was the fastest overriding of a veto by both branches of Congress.

The measure, hammered out by the legislators during the strikes by John L. Lewis' coal miners, was rejected by Mr. Roosevelt on the grounds that some of its provisions would foment rather than deter strikes. Some union leaders had protested it would "crucify" labor.

Mr. Roosevelt asked that Congress give him instead the authority to induct persons up to age 65 for non-combat military service—an authority which would allow strikers to be put into Army uniform and sent back to work.

The legislators bowled over the veto with breath-taking speed, completing action on the measure scarcely two hours after the Chief Executive's message reached the capitol. It becomes law immediately.

PASSES SENATE, 56-25

First, the Senate voted 56 to 25 to override, acting five minutes after it heard the message read. House action was delayed an hour and a half by the fact that the veto arrived when that body was in a parliamentary situation where immediate consideration could not be given to it.

TEXT ON PAGE 11

The text of President Roosevelt's veto message on the anti-strike bill will be found on Page 11.

Once the question was put, the House quickly backed up the Senate by a vote of 244 to 108. Two-thirds approval in each branch was necessary for Congress to over ride the veto.

The House division found 11 Democrats and 130 Republicans voting to override the veto, and 67 Democrats, 37 Republicans and four minor party members balloting to sustain it.

It was the first time since he has been in office that the President has suffered a major defeat in Congress on labor legislation.

Administration leaders sought to

More of ROOSEVELT on Page 9

DEMOCRATS SELECT BOK AS SUPERIOR COURT CANDIDATE

Philadelphia Jurist Endorsed By State Committee; Selection Urged By Guffey

Harrisburg—(AP)—The Democratic State Committee Friday selected Common Pleas Judge Curtis Bok as the organization's candidate for Superior Court and roundly assailed Republican Governor Edward Martin's administration along with the record of the legislature he controls.

The party's governing body in a one-hour convention unanimously endorsed the 46-year-old Philadelphia jurist after no other names were offered for the $18,000 judgeship now held by Claude T. Reno, former attorney general appointed to the court late last year to fill a vacancy.

EXPECT RENO TO RUN

Reno is expected to have Republican organization support for a full 10-year term. The judicial post is the only statewide office at stake in this year's elections. Both Democratic and Republican candidates probably will be nominated in the September 14 primaries without opposition.

State Chairman David L. Lawrence announced before the committee meeting that Judge Bok had agreed to make the race. Selection of a Philadelphia candidate had been urged in a letter to the gathering by U. S. Senator Joseph F. Guffey who was unable to attend.

In Philadelphia, Judge Bok said, "I confirm that I will be the Democratic candidate for the state Superior Court at the September 14

More of DEMOCRATS on Page 5

WPB ORDER CITES SCRAP DEALER FOR CODE VIOLATIONS

A War Production Board suspension order announced Friday charged Daniel Kauffman, Lancaster R6, scrap dealer, with "willful" violations of Supplementary Order N-9-b and Priorities Order No. 1, and forbids him to order, purchase, or receive any copper or copper base alloy in scrap form, or otherwise, until his total inventory has been reduced to 3,000 pounds.

The regional compliance division of the WPB at Philadelphia, explained that Order N-9-b forbids a dealer to accept delivery of copper or copper alloy scrap at any time when his existing inventory exceeds in weight the amount he has sold or otherwise disposed of during the preceding 60 days.

Kauffman was charged with having accepted deliveries in substantial amounts of copper scrap during the period of March 10, 1942 and February 11, 1943. He also was charged with failure to maintain proper records and make proper reports to the WPB.

Under the suspension order, which began Thursday, Kauffman must reduce his inventory to 3,000 pounds "by actual weight" before he may purchase or receive further deliveries.

"JUST BE PATIENT!"

Washington— (AP) —Navy Secretary Knox had these three words of comment Friday when asked at a press conference about the anticipated 1943 naval offensive in the Pacific:

"Just be patient!"

LIST DATES TO MAIL YULE GIFTS TO THOSE SERVING OVERSEAS

Washington—(AP)—In the air conditioned Postoffice Department building, even a June hot spell does not preclude thoughts of Christmas.

The Department announced Friday that Christmas gifts for Army personnel overseas must be mailed between September 15 and October 15 to assure delivery on time.

The dates for gifts to Navy personnel overseas were fixed at September 15 to November 1.

REPORTS THEFT OF AUTO

Elwood L. Kreider, Columbia R2, reported to city police Friday night the theft of his 1936 Ford coupe from in front of a gasoline filling station at Prince and James Sts. The car carried license No. 2RD47 and was painted gray.

"We Lead All the Rest" FARM CORNER By *The Farm Editor*

H. H. HAVERSTICK BUYS JOHN R. CASSEL FARM

H. H. Haverstick, of Lyndon, has purchased at private sale the John R. Cassel farm of approximately 105 acres in Penn township, between East Petersburg and Manheim, from the Cassel Estate. This is a noted tobacco and potato growing farm. The purchase price is said to have been $400 an acre.

$425 TOPS HOLSTEIN SALE

Forty-four head of cattle sold for $11,063, an average price of $251, at the eighth Garden Spot Holstein Consignment sale held Friday afternoon at the farm of C. M. Brubaker, near Willow Street.

Top price at the auction was $425, which was paid for a 2-year-old heifer, consigned by Naaman Stoltzfus, of Morgantown, by George S. Wolbert, of Baltimore. Wolbert was the heaviest buyer at the sale, purchasing 14 head in all. He paid over $400 for two animals, and over $300 apiece for nine other cattle.

Local consignors included:

Willis Glick, Elverson, 2-year-old heifer sold at $225 at Noah E. Denlinger, Paradise; her heifer calf sold at $32.50 to John B. Witmer, Lampeter; another 2-year-old heifer sold at $230 to Ivan S. Bowman, Ronks RD.

Henry A. Schell, Jr., Phoenixville, cow sold at $250 to Clarence Hershey, Ronks RD.

Jonas Gruver, Thomasville, cow sold at $350 to Ivan S. Bowman, Ronks; her bull calf sold at $20 to Henry R. Hess, Willow Street R1.

Other buyers included:

Henry E. Shenk, Manheim, heifer at $245; Lloyd Rosenberry, New Holland, heifer at $225; John C. Metzler, Christiana, cow at $315; Benamin L. Landis, Lancaster R4, heifer at $220; Elmer N. Hershey, Gordonville R1, cow at $340; John M. Esh, Gordonville, cow at $175;

More of FARM CORNER on Page 5

ARMY AND NAVY WILL ACCEPT VOLUNTEERS FOR AIR TRAINING

By agreement between the Army and Navy, changes in procedure of induction into the armed forces have been effected which make it possible for young men to volunteer for air crew training, the Army announced Friday.

Under the plan, the privilege of choice of service is offered again, limited, however, to men who are physically and otherwise qualified to meet the high standards required for Aviation Cadet training.

Young men between eighteen and twenty-six, may apply through voluntary induction for air crew training to become bombardiers, navigators and pilots. Those between seventeen and eighteen may apply for enlistment in the Air Corps Enlisted Reserve.

Details can be obtained at the Army recruiting station in the post office building.

FIRST DAY TODAY FOR PRIMARY PETITIONS

Saturday (today) the two major political parties in Lancaster county will start circulating petitions for the primary election.

Obtaining of signatures for these petitions is permitted Saturday (today) for the first time. A number of persons called at the court house Friday for the petitions, and G. Graybill Diehm, chairman of the County Election Board, said they are available "although not too many have asked for them."

REPORTS NAVY AIR CRASH

Green Cove Springs, Fla.—(AP)—Sheriff J. P. Hall of Clay County said he had received a report that a Navy plane crashed in the St. Johns River near here Friday with the apparent loss of 12 lives. The sheriff said additional details were not available and that the Navy was investigating the accident.

Intelligencer Journal Weather Calendar

COMPARATIVE TEMPERATURES

Station	High	Low
Water Works	96	67
Ephrata	99	69
Last Year (Ephrata)	80	53
Official High for Year, June 25		99
Official Low for Year, Feb 13		[illegible]
Character of Day		Clear

SUN

Rises—5:37 a. m. Sets—8:37 p. m.

STARS

Morning—Mars, Saturn
Evening—Jupiter, Venus.

More of WEATHER on Page 5

Navy Reveals Submarine R-12 Lost Off East Coast

Undersea Craft Carried Normal Complement Of 28 Men; Indicate Some Were Saved; Was Engaged In Training Exercises "Recently"

Washington—(AP)—Loss of the submarine R-12 while engaged in training exercises off the east coast was announced Friday night by the Navy.

The R-12 had a normal complement of 28 men but the Navy indicated some of these were saved after the sinking. The Navy said the loss was probably due to accident and not enemy action.

HAPPENED "RECENTLY"

The sinking, the time of which was placed only as "recently," raised to nine the number of United States submarines lost since Pearl Harbor either through enemy action or accident.

The Navy's communique said:

"A number of officers and men were unable to escape from the vessel before it sank. The depth of water makes it impossible to salvage the submarine and hope has been abandoned for recovery of the bodies of the missing personnel. The next of kin have been informed.

"Information obtained from survivors indicates that the loss was probably due to accident and not enemy action, and an investigation is now in progress to determine the available facts of the case.

ATTEMPTED RESCUE

"Announcement of this incident was withheld until attempts to locate and raise the R-12 were discontinued, in order that enemy submarines might not be given in-

More of NAVY on Page 9

SEEKING PERSONS HERE TO CARE FOR EVACUEE CHILDREN

City Homes Already Registered; Paradise, Leacock Twp. Residents Register Next Week

The Lancaster County Committee on the Care of Unaccompanied evacuee children announced Friday that it is continuing its efforts to obtain homes for several thousand children in case it becomes necessary for children to be evacuated from the seacoasts of our own country.

Registration of homes in the city where evacuee children might be cared for have already been taken, and at the present time it is planned to register homes in Paradise and Leacock Twp.

Therefore, in cooperation with the Red Cross Emergency committee of the two townships, arrangements have been made for people in these localities to register their homes and discuss the matter with persons at the sugar ration headquarters next Tuesday and Wednesday. They may register their preferences for boys or girls and the age

More of SEEKING on Page 5

LIST VALIDITY DATES OF NEXT RED STAMPS

Validity dates of four new series of red stamps, used in the purchase of rationed meats, fats, oils and cheese, were announced Friday by the Office of Price Administration. The stamps are good through July 31.

The dates the stamps will become valid: P., June 27; Q, July 4; R, July 11 and S, July 18. Dates for Stamp T will be announced soon, the OPA said. Each series of red stamps is worth 16 points.

The currently valid red stamps, J, K, L, M and N, expire June 30

Co. H, State Guard, To Participate In Field Training Camp Week Of Aug. 14

Encampment Part Of Program To Train Men For Any Possible Emergency Arising From Enemy Action

First Lieut. William D. Andes, commanding officer of Co. H, Pennsylvania State Guard, announced Friday that practically the entire company will participate in the first state field training camp at Indiantown Gap during the week of Aug. 14.

"The encampment," Lieut. Andes said, "will give the Lancaster soldiers a chance to use in the field the many details of military skill which they have practiced in the local armory and in week-end field work as part of their training in readiness for possible emergency arising from enemy action."

Lieut. Andes also announced that recruiting is being constantly continued for Co. H and that a steady flow of eligible men is needed to keep it at the strength now authorized for Lancaster.

Applicants should be between seventeen and a half and fifty

More of COMPANY H on Page 5

FACTORY BUILDINGS ON WATER ST. SOLD

The four-story brick factory building with a one-story cinder block building attached and a one and one-half story brick garage at 118-120-122 and 124 N. Water St. were sold for $20,000 yesterday to Morris Levy and Sons at public sale.

The property, now being used for storage by a tobacco company, was sold by the Farmers Bank and Trust Company, substituted fiduciary of the trust mortage pool of the Farmers Trust Company. Victor D. Kling was the auctioneer. It was not revealed what the new owners expect to do with the premises.

BREAKS IN WIRES DARKEN WEST END

Homes in a large portion of the west end were in darkness for two hours last night when three "feeder" lines carrying 4,000 volts of electricity each were broken at Mulberry and Strawberry Sts.

One of the wires broke between two poles along the west side of Strawberry St., between Vine and St. Joseph Sts., and the other two fell from a pole at Strawberry and Mulberry Sts.

Radio Comedienne

HORIZONTAL
1 Pictured comedienne, —— ——
11 Vegetable
12 One in debt
14 Sedan
15 Manuscript (abbr.)
16 Egypt (abbr.)
17 Urge on (Scot.)
19 Jewel
21 Size of shot
23 Oriental dwelling
24 Lawful
26 I am (contr.)
28 Greek letter
29 Quakingly
31 Portuguese title
32 Wine vessel
33 Copies
38 Compass point
41 Boat
42 Indian
44 Aggregate animals of a region
46 Group of three
47 Symbol for tin
48 Laughter sound
50 She is a radio ——
51 Oxford English dictionary (abbr.)
52 Sun god
53 Symbol for cerium
55 Footed vase
56 Revoke
59 Esteem
61 Echo

VERTICAL
1 Automobile storage place
2 Railroad (abbr.)
3 Limb
4 Price
5 That thing
6 Indian mulberry
7 Prevaricate
8 Lower limb
9 Half-em
10 Required
11 Antic
13 Muse of poetry
14 Young horse
18 English street car
20 Tropical timber tree
22 Sesame
25 Boundary
27 Mine
30 Diminutive of Daniel
33 Genus of barn owls
34 More uncommon
35 Device for applying acid
36 Weapon
37 Street (abbr.)
38 Act of sewing
39 Trap
40 Merit
43 Exclamation
45 Like
47 Sagacious
49 Genus of maples
52 Reverend (abbr.)
54 Girl's name
57 New England (abbr.)
58 Symbol for erbium
59 Of the thing
60 And (Fr.)

Answer to Previous Puzzle

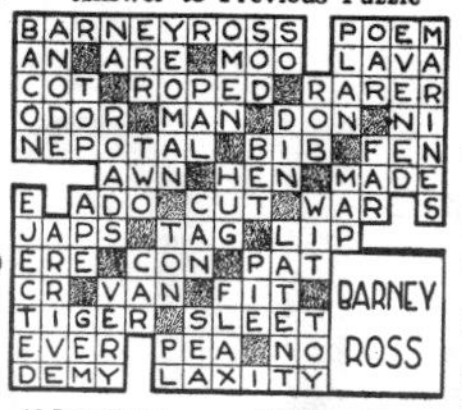

Physician Drops 7½ Miles On His First 'Chute Jump

WASHINGTON, July 1.—(AP)—The Colonel comes from Missouri and laboratory tests left him skeptical—he had to see it to believe it.

So. Lieut. Col. William Randolph Lovelace, 2nd, surgeon and Air Forces expert on high altitude equipment, made a parachute jump from 40,200 feet—the highest on record in this country—to convince himself and everybody else that the emergency oxygen equipment furnished to Army airmen is all that laboratory tests indicate.

It was his first jump, and he said yesterday at a press conference that it would be his last for a while, although his only injury was the freezing of his left hand. The jerk of his opening 'chute flipped off his heavy glove in a 50-below temperature.

Otherwise, Lovelace reported, he suffered no discomforts—the heavy regulation clothing, including oxygen mask, goggles and helmet, protected even his face from the cold.

Lovelace jumped from an Army bomber near Euphrata, Wash., last Thursday. The parachute opened automatically, and the shock "blacked out" the Colonel. He regained consciousness at about 30,000 feet, and by the time he got down to 8,000 feet was recovered.

It took him 23 minutes and 51 seconds to float down, he said, adding with a grin that this time "was almost exactly what laboratory calculations said it would be."

17-YR.-OLD YOUTHS LEAVE FOR NAVY

Four local youths left today to enlist in the Navy at Philadelphia from where they will be assigned to training camps. One left yesterday.

The group, all seventeen, include: Henri Pierre Berit, 422 N. Queen St., who left Wednesday; and Harold Metzger Detwiler, Third and Locust Sts., Columbia; Edward Myron Maharg, 51 E. Lincoln Ave., Lititz, and William Harry Thatcher, 340 Nevin St., and William Richard Coldren Jr., 50 S. Lime St., both of the city.

ORDERED TO PAY COSTS

Jacob H. Parke, twenty-two, 33 Filbert St., charged with disorderly conduct by Albert Newlin, Locust and Strawberry Sts., was ordered to pay the costs following a hearing last night before Alderman Wetzel. Similar charges against Jacob Moyer, sixty-four, 317 S. Duke St., were dismissed.

Scientists have been able to train fishes to accept and reject foods dyed different colors.

How's Your U. S. History I.Q. ???

MANY top-rank educators are growing uneasy over Americans' ignorance of American history. The Fourth of July should be a good time to check up on YOUR knowledge of great chapters in American history since that first Independence Day in 1776. You're unusually good if you can come up with 15 or more right answers; if you get less than 9 right you provide the educators with a good argument.

1782—This was most important surrender in American military history. Who were principals and where was it?

1803—What deal did we make with French and what was cost?

1813—Who sent what message following one of decisive battles of War of 1812?

1844—This trail indirectly led to the political slogan, "54-40 or fight!"

1848—Yankees storm Chapultepec. What war?

1848—Sensational news came from an obscure California mill. Whose mill?

1865—Two famous generals end Civil War. Where did they meet?

1869—What was the occasion of this famous meeting?

1876—America's worst defeat in its wars with the Indians. Where was the battle fought?

1889—Most exciting land rush in American history. Shot was fired as starting signal.

1898—Name Dewey's ship at Manila.

1914—Who was chief engineer in building "The Big Ditch"?

1920—Caption on ladder should be good clue.

GREAT INVENTORS

1793—His invention made agricultural crop "king" in South.

1831—Labor saving device which paved way for huge grain farms.

1844—"What hath God wrought?" was question he asked.

1876—He said to helper, "Come here Mr. Watson, I want you."

HERE ARE THE ANSWERS—TURN UPSIDE DOWN

1782—Cornwallis surrenders to Washington at Yorktown, Va., ending Revolutionary War.

1803—Louisiana Purchase, $15,000,000.

1813—Commodore Perry, after Battle of Lake Erie, said, "We have met the enemy and they are ours."

1844—The Oregon Trail. We almost fought Britain over territory boundary dispute.

1848—Mexican War.

1848—Sutter's Mill, where gold was discovered.

1865—Lee surrenders to Grant at Appamattox, Va.

1869—Last spike is driven in trans-continental Union Pacific Railroad.

1876—Custer's Last Stand, fought at Little Big Horn, Mont.

1889—Oklahoma Land Rush.

1898—The Olympia.

1914—Chief engineer in construction of Panama Canal was George W. Goethals.

1920—Women gained right to vote.

INVENTORS

1793—Eli Whitney and the Cotton gin.

1831—Cyrus McCormick and the reaper.

1844—Samuel F. B. Morse and the telegraph.

1876—Alexander Graham Bell and the telephone.

This Week's PICTURE SHOW—AP Features

"Newspapers are essential to the war effort."
War Manpower Commission

LANCASTER NEW ERA

WEATHER
Moderate temperature tonight and Sunday morning; scattered thundershowers early tonight.

VOL. 66—NO. 499 | Entered as second class matter January 31, 1924, at the Post Office at Lancaster, Pa., under the act of March 3, 1879, Reg. U. S. Pat Off. | LANCASTER, PA., SATURDAY, JULY 10, 1943 | CITY EDITION | 12 PAGES—96 COLUMNS | 20c PER WEEK—4c Per Copy

'BATTLE OF EUROPE' LAUNCHED BY ALLIED INVASION OF SICILY

Roosevelt Sees Blow "Beginning of End" For Axis Europe

WASHINGTON, July 10—(AP)—President Roosevelt considers the Allied invasion of Sicily as virtually "the beginning of the end" of Hitler's Europe, the White House disclosed today.

The Chief Executive expressed his reaction to the invasion at a formal dinner at the White House last night for General Henri Giraud. He predicted confidently the liberation of France, referring to it in a manner which suggested the possibility that military operations designed to drive the enemy from French soil will develop eventually from England as well as Sicily.

"General Giraud," the President said, "can rest assured that the ultimate objective—we will do it and in the best way—is to liberate the people of France, not merely those in the southern part of France but the people in Northern France—Paris."

Giraud is French Commander in North Africa.

President Roosevelt strongly indicated that the major moves had been well planned, for he continued:

"And in this whole operation, I should say rightly that in the enormous planning we have had the complete cooperation of French military and naval forces in North Africa — gradually the opposition has cooled and the older regime is breaking down.

"We have seen what has happened or is happening at the present moment in Martinique and Guadeloupe."

This was a reference to the Vichy-controlled islands in the Antilles, now in the process of coming under control of the French committee of liberation.

The State dinner, which started quietly about 8:15 p. m., (EWT), wound up with dramatic excitement after the President disclosed the attack on Sicily and General Giraud, responding with a toast to the President's toast to France, which climaxed his comments, proposed the health of the President and the glory of the United States. Giraud referred to this country as the great nation through which peace and freedom will be restored in the world.

White House Secretary Stephen Early today reported the Chief Executive's remarks at the dinner and told in general terms of General Giraud's reply.

Early related that the dinner ran quietly until about 9 o'clock when the President received word that the actual landings had been made on Sicily. All persons in the dining room were officials in some capacity or other. All but two of them were military or Naval officers.

General Giraud sat on the President's right and General George C. Marshall, Army Chief of Staff, sat on his left.

Across from Mr. Roosevelt were a lineup of notables including Secretary of State Hull, Admiral William D. Leahy, the President's Chief of Staff, and Admiral Ernest J. King, Commander In Chief of the U. S. fleet.

For almost an hour Mr. Roosevelt kept his exciting news to himself—at least he made no open announcement of it. Then at the conclusion of the meal, shortly before 10 o'clock, the President prepared to propose a toast and this gave him the opportunity to announce the invasion and discuss the present situation in Europe.

"I have just had word of the

(See ROOSEVELT—Page 4)

2 OFFICERS DIE IN AIR CRASHES

Lloyd Bergstresser Dies In Calif., F. & M. "Grad" In Ohio

LLOYD BERGSTRESSER

A Lancaster man and a graduate of F. and M. college, both lieutenants in the Army Air Corps, have ben killed in accidents in this country, according to word received by relatives yesterday and today.

Lieut. Lloyd Bergstresser, twenty-four, 819 N. Shippen St., was killed in an airplane accident at Merced Field, Calif., according to a telegram received here today by his sisters from the War Department. No details were given.

Lieutenant Bergstresser was married May 26 to the former Anita Broderick, Trenton, N. J.

Born in Waterfall, Pa., he attended and graduated from Juniata college and then came to Lancaster. He was employed as an investigator for the Retail Credit Corp. when he enlisted in June, 1941. He received his wings at Luke Field, Arizona in May, 1942.

His parents, Mr. and Mrs. Hayes W. Bergstresser are dead. In addition to his wife he is survived by three sisters, Mabel, Sara and Dorothy, all of this city, and two brothers, State Motor Policeman Ralph

(See OFFICERS—Page 2)

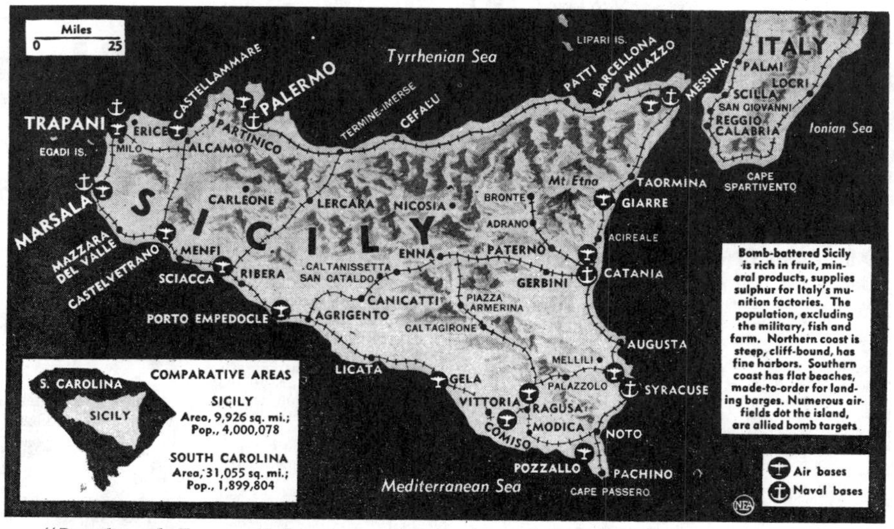

"Battle of Europe" Starts on Eastern and Southern Coasts of Sicily

Axis and Allied reports indicate today that Gen. Eisenhower's sea-borne invasion of Sicily, shown on the above map, struck before midnight at three areas on the eastern and southern coasts. Thus, the "Battle of Europe" is under way through one of Italy's strongholds.

The comparative size of Sicily with South Carolina is shown in the inset. The western and southern coastlines of Sicily, nearest Africa, are mostly flat, although there are few points where other than shallow-draft vessels can approach. Good harbors abound in the northern coast, but it is steep and cliff-bound, difficult to assault. Along the east, also fringed by bold cliffs, Mt. Etna towers into the sky.

The major portion of Sicily's transportation skirts the coast, making it subject to crippling attack.

(Detailed map of whole Mediterranean theatre is on Page 2.)

HURT ESCAPING FIRE IN HOME

Harry M. Huss, 58, West Lancaster, Trapped In Smoke-Filled Room

Trapped in a smoke-filled room of his burning home at 4:30 a. m. today, Harry M. Huss, fifty-eight, Cornell and Ridge Aves., West Lancaster, shattered a window with his hands to escape, receiving deep lacerations in his right hand and arm. He was treated at St. Joseph's hospital.

The West Lancaster and Bausman fire companies were called, the latter making its first run since the company was organized. Three sharp blasts on the Bausman fire siren, repeated after 30-second intervals, were heard in the city and were mistaken by many residents in the west end for an air raid warning.

Fire Chiefs Walter Landis, of West Lancaster, and Jacob Weber, of Bausman, estimated the fire loss at $500. They said the flames damaged an over-stuffed chair, radio, rug, a side wall and hard wood floors of the bungalow type dwelling.

Was Sleeping In Chair

Huss, whose wife died recently, was sleeping on a chair in a first floor room and narrowly escaped suffocation.

Firemen said that the over-stuffed chair in the living room near the radio caught fire and smoldered during the greater part of the night, creating intense heat and burning the floor and through some grill work in the side of the wall.

When Huss awoke, he told firemen, the room on the first floor in which he had been sleeping was filled with smoke. In some manner, the lock on the door leading from the room, he said, became jammed and in his dazen condition he was unable to open it. Going to the nearest window, he shattered the glass with his hands and escaped to the outside.

Neighbors Summon Firemen

Huss aroused neighbors who summoned firemen. Because of the small amount of water available in the neighborhood and due to their pumper being disabled, West Lancaster called upon Bausman for aid. Chief Weber and his firemen responded with the 178-gallon Bausman booster apparatus, which combined with chemicals, was used to quell the blaze after a half hour's battle.

Norman H. Hackenberger, a neighbor, conveyed Huss to the hospital for treatment.

CITY POLICE 'CYCLE DAMAGED BY AUTO

A city police 'cycle, operated by Policeman S. Kenneth Cliff, twenty-four, 321 N. Charlotte St., was slightly damaged when struck by an auto driven by Jacob S. Shirk, forty-nine, Paradise, on Queen St., between Orange and Chestnut Sts. at 11 A. M. today.

Police said Shirk was parked in front of 109 N. Queen St., and drove from a parking space, striking the police motorcycle, headed north on Queen St.

Most Sicilians May Prove Friendly to Yank Troops

Rome Used to Say Majority of 4,000,000 People on Island Were Anti-Fascist; Mountain Villages Are Picturesque

By RICHARD G. MASSOCK
Former Chief of (AP) Bureau in Rome

WASHINGTON, July 10 — (AP) — American troops on landing barges saw a great background of mountains before their boats scraped bottom on the shores of Sicily.

In those mountains live a people on whom they might count for eventual support, after the tough fighting of the initial invasion, for they used to say in Rome that most Sicilians were anti-Fascist and many of them, even, had never really accepted assimilation into Italy. It seemed as though Sicily was the unreconstruction south.

In Rome it formerly was said that there were only two real Fascists in Sicily, the provincial secretary of the Fascist Party and the Prefect, or Governor. And there was some doubt about the Prefect.

Exaggerated though that may be, there was another rumor current in Rome—that the far-famed Mafia had never been completely suppressed by Mussolini, but only driven underground. The criminal net work that had its own way in the island for almost a century, however, always had been invisible to strangers, leaving them alone. So the soldiers probably won't meet the boys who used to extort tribute, run elections and commit murders of blood vengeance.

Instead the troops are likely to encounter ordinary folk in modern cities, poor peasants in mountain villages and almost as poor sulphur miners—frugal and good-natured, but lively, hot-blooded and deeply religious.

Capital Is Modern

Palermo, the capital with a tenth of Sicily's 4,000,000 inhabitants, for instance, is much like any other Italian city. It has an opera, open air cafes, boulevards for promenades, the latest fashions in dress, naval shipyards and textile mills.

The mountain villages are more

(See SICILIANS—Page 4)

U. S. Getting Ready to Bomb Jap Mainland, Axis Claims

LONDON, July 10.—(AP)—The German radio, quoting Japanese dispatches, said today there were "various signs" that the American air force in China was planning a new attack on the Japanese mainland.

The Nazi broadcast, heard by the Ministry of Information here, said it was reported that American air bases at some points in China had been reinforced with planes, gasoline and supplies and that U. S. forces had abandoned "guerrilla warfare tactics."

BLOCKBUSTERS ROCK MUNDA

Naval Guns Also Blast Jap Base; Commandos Raid Burma

By The Associated Press

U. S. warships, planes and artillery were reported thundering destruction on the key Japanese stronghold at Munda today as American troops pressed a two-way "squeeze" within three miles of the fortified base on New Georgia island in the Central Solomons.

Dispatches from Gen. Douglas MacArthur's headquarters said U. S. naval gunners violently bombarded the enemy citadel while more than 100 bombers rocked the fortress with 2,000-pound blockbusters.

More than 70 tons of explosives were rained on Japanese bivouacs and supply dumps in the Munda defense area in the heaviest aerial attack yet to fall upon that much-bombed air base.

On the western flank of the 700-mile Allied offensive arc, U. S. Mitchell bombers renewed the assault on Japanese troops on Bobdubi ridge, only five miles below the big enemy base at Salamaua, New Guinea. There were no reports

(See PACIFIC—Page 4)

ALLEGED DESERTER NABBED IN CITY

Pvt. Bernard Highley, twenty-three, 17 W. Main St., Ephrata, sought since June 12 when he allegedly escaped from the post stockade at Gulfport Field, Gulfport, Miss., was apprehended this morning by City Detective John Kauffman and Deputy Sheriff Abe Lane. He was committed to the county prison, pending the arrival of military authorities.

Highley, according to police, had obtained employment as a truck driver and was arrested on an inter-state truck when he arrived here today.

"ODD-LOT" SHOES OFF RATION LIST

WASHINGTON, July 10 — (AP) — The OPA authorized today general sales of "odd-lot" shoes without ration stamps.

Officials said the sales will not be limited to special types of shoes as they have been in the past, but will be designed to clean out of dealers' stocks the normal accumulation of unusual sizes and slow-selling types. Merchants will be limited in designating non-rationed shoes by percentages of their stocks, however, so that the number of shoes released from rationing by the new order will not be large.

In the case of shoes already stocked by retailers, the non-rationed sale of odd-lot shoes will be limited to the two-week period of July 19-July 31. No time limit was set on odd-lot shoes hereafter sold by wholesalers or manufacturers to the retailers.

REDS CLAIM NAZI DRIVE CRUSHED

Put German Losses At 40,000 Men, 2,036 Tanks In 5 Days

By The Associated Press

Soviet dispatches declared today that the Red armies had crushed Field Marshal Guenther Von Kluge's tempestuous offensive on the Kursk salient as the Germans threw masses of tanks, planes and infantry into the assault with "crazy stubbornness."

Soviet troops were declared to have stopped the attack dead, although Von Kluge rushed up reinforcements of nine infantry divisions and a tank division in an attempt to breach the Russian lines on a 60-mile front between Kursk and Orel.

In the first five days of the six-day-old Nazi summer offensive, Russian headquarters said, the Germans lost 40,000 killed, 2,036 tanks knocked out of action, and 904 planes destroyed.

Countering Moscow's account of the Russians holding fast, Berlin asserted that German columns striking from the southern end of the 165-mile Orel-Belgorod front had lunged 36 miles northward toward Kursk.

The Germans admitted that Von Kluge's forces in the north "could gain ground only inch by inch" in the Orel area.

Soviet field reports said the Germans were battling frantically to expand the slim wedge driven into Red army lines two days ago on the southern flank, but declared there was little change in the situation yesterday.

Huge-scale tank and infantry battles were reported flaming all along the "bulge" some 200 miles

(See RUSSIA—Page 4)

DRAFT BOARDS GET QUOTAS FOR AUGUST; LARGER THAN JULY

The local draft boards received their August quotas today and the calls, in the majority of the cases, are considerably higher than the July figures, board members indicated.

Several of the boards said the new call "will exhaust practically all the available men under present regulations." One of the boards has just begun to call married men without children and the members said that "even under this condition we'll have difficulty filling the August quota."

Termination of occupational deferments for some registrants will help a few of the local boards, the officials said.

Eisenhower Strikes Isle in 3 Areas With 450,000 Troops

General Reported Using 2,000 Planes in Assault on Italy's "Fort"; Axis Rushes Reinforcements; Other Allied Moves Strongly Hinted

By the Associated Press

American, British and Canadian troops invaded Sicily today, striking with powerful air and sea-borne forces in the first major land blow aimed at Hitler's Europe.

Axis estimates indicated that a mighty host of at least 30 Allied divisions—perhaps 450,000 troops—had been thrown into the invasion, together with 2,000 planes.

London sources pictured the attack as being evenly divided between battle-hardened American and British troops, supported by Canadian forces moved into the Mediterranean since the Battle of Africa ended last June 10.

Sicily's importance, both to Italy and as the gateway to Europe, was emphasized long ago when Garibaldi issued his famous proclamation: "Here we make Italy or we die."

A bulletin from Italian headquarters said Allied parachutists spearheaded the assault and reported that fighting was in progress along the southern and eastern coasts, nearest to Italy.

First unofficial reports, according to the British news agency Reuters, said operations were going "according to plan."

American and British warships formed part of the invasion spearhead. The zero hour of invasion was 3 A. M. (9 P. M. Eastern War Time last night).

Land In Three Areas

Axis and Allied reports indicated today that Gen. Eisenhower's sea-borne invasion forces landed in at least three areas of Sicily.

A German broadcast said the Allies landed "in the southeastern part of Sicily," and declared it could not be stated whether landing attempts had been made at other points on the island.

An Algiers radio report said Allied forces also swept ashore on the rock-studded western tip of the island, near the bomb-ruined port of Trapani.

Axis Pours In Reinforcements

Heavy Axis reinforcements were reported streaming across the narrow Messina Strait from Southern Italy to combat the invasion.

London quarters hinted that the assault on Sicily might be accompanied at any moment by coordinated moves elsewhere along the Mediterranean front.

These quarters said the invasion now in progress should not be regarded as the only landing nor even as "the" landing planned by the Allies, thus implying that even greater events might be in the offing.

Dispatches from Ankara said there was a strong possibility of action in the Balkans this weekend, with the Germans feverishly reinforcing their defenses in the traditional "powder-keg" countries as well as key islands in the Aegean Sea.

British newspapers warned readers to expect heavy losses and possible setbacks before the conquest of Sicily, Italy's strongest island bastion, is completed.

A Fascist communique said:

"The enemy started last night, with support of strong air and sea formations and with dropping of parachutist units, the attacks against Italy. Axis armed forces are decisively counterattacking the enemy's action."

Dispatches from Allied headquarters said Gen. Dwight D. Eisenhower's combined forces swarmed ashore in bright moonlight, under cover of a terrific barrage by Allied warships.

Sicily lies 260 airline miles from Rome and its eastern tip is only two miles across Messina Strait from the "toe" of Italy.

"The battle of Africa is over; the Battle of Europe has begun!" an Algiers broadcast said, in a message to the conquered nations of Europe.

Hours after the great test began, the enemy made no claim of having beat off or defeated any part of the Allied sea-borne forces—nor was there any claim of the shore-bound Italian fleet having swung into action.

Tersely, the German high command said the Allies "immediately encountered strong defenses on the ground and in the air. Fighting is still progressing."

A Nazi propaganda broadcast asserted that Allied parachutists were "encircled and rendered harmless" and declared that Axis coastal batteries and bombers sank a number of landing craft filled with troops and supplies.

"The invasion forces were immediately engaged in heavy fighting which proved extraordinarily costly for them," the Berlin radio said.

Batter Way Inland

Dispatches from Gen. Eisenhower's headquarters said Allied troops, slipping ashore in snub-nosed, shallow-draft boats from convoys a mile or more off the coast, cut through wire barriers and hot machine-gun defenses and then, with hardly a moment's pause, began battering their way inland.

Swarms of Allied planes filled the skies, forming a vast aerial umbrella over the invasion forces and smashing at Axis fortifications.

American, British and Canadian forces of Eisenhower's command struck from landing barges by night, opening the big push they had awaited since they cleared North Africa of the Axis two months ago.

Swarms of Allied bombers, fighter-bombers and fight-

(See INVASION—Page 2)

War Bulletins

Roosevelt Assures Pope Allied Soldiers Will Respect Neutral Status of Vatican

WASHINGTON, July 10.—(AP)—President Roosevelt advised Pope Pius XII today that as American and British soldiers fight to rid Italy of Fascism "the neutral status of Vatican City as well as of the Papal domains throughout Italy will be respected."

The President's message to the Pope, given out at the White House, clearly held forth the prospect that the invasion of the Italian island of Sicily would be followed by similar operations against the Italian mainland.

U. S. WARSHIPS AGAIN BOMBARD KISKA

Washington, July 10—(AP)—Another bombardment of Japanese positions on Kiska island in the Aleutians by American Navy guns was reported by the Navy Department today. Shore batteries returned the fire but caused no damage, the Navy said. This was the second bombardment of Kiska in three days.

NAZI BASES IN FRANCE HEAVILY ATTACKED

London, July 10—(AP)—Strong formations of U. S. heavy bombers and flights of RAF light bombers attacked German fighter bases in France today.

WEATHER

Eastern Pennsylvania: Continued Rather Warm Monday. Scattered Thundershowers Monday Afternoon.

Intelligencer Journal

"Newspapers are essential to the war effort."

War Manpower Commission

The Leading Newspaper in the Garden Spot of America, Home Owned for Home Folks Since 1794

VOLUME LXXIX.—NO. 272. Entered as second class matter June 2¼ 1928 at the Post Office at Lancaster, Pa., under the Act of March 3, 1879. Reg. U. S. Pat. Off. LANCASTER, PA., MONDAY MORNING, JULY 26, 1943. CITY 12 PAGES, 96 COLUMNS. 20c PER WEEK—4c Per Copy

ITALIANS OUST MUSSOLINI

Badoglio Is New Premier; Americans Occupy Trapani

KING WILL LEAD ARMY

Il Duce's 21 Years Of Italian Dictatorship Ends Sensationally; Marshal Badoglio Heads Military Government "To Stand Against Those Who Have Wounded The Sacred Soil Of Italy"; Mussolini's Whereabouts Unknown

London (Monday) — (AP) — Benito Mussolini's 21 years of Italian dictatorship and international bullying ended sensationally last night when King Vittorio Emanuele deposed him and installed Marshal Pietro Badoglio as head of a military government "to stand against those who have wounded the sacred soil of Italy."

A royal proclamation announced Vittorio Emanuele had assumed supreme command of all Italian forces. It was preceded by an announcement that the King had accepted the "resignation" of the man whom Prime Minister Churchill termed Adolf Hitler's "tattered lackey."

However, crushing Axis defeats in Sicily and swiftly rising Allied threats to the Italian mainland supported the belief that Mussolini actually was dismissed by the King.

The 71-year-old Badoglio, called out of retirement to become the new premier, said:

"The war continues."

Mighty Allied war fleets roaring over Italy, increasing defections in the Fascist party ranks, rumored disagreements between Mussolini and Hitler, and reports of violence and sweeping arrests preceded the announcement.

FORESEE REPERCUSSIONS

World-wide repercussions, especially among the German and Japanese Allies, were expected.

There was no news concerning Mussolini's whereabouts, or what his status would be under the new government. Reports from Bern, Switzerland, that he and his cabinet members had been arrested found no confirmation here.

Badoglio signed a proclamation saying the King, who assumed supreme command of all Italian armies, had given him "full powers" to act at a time when onrushing Allied armies were sweeping across Sicily toward the Italian mainland.

Il Duce's fall, with the shadow of defeat and disaster hanging over his country, was widely regarded here as a crack in the solid front of the Axis.

A British authority said: "It's terrific news, but Italy still is in the war and it must be emphasized that the conditions remain the same—Italy can get out of the war only by unconditional surrender."

Mussolini's resignation — probably forced upon him—after more than a score of years of iron-handed rule probably means the death of the Fascist party he headed.

Significantly, the Rome radio which broadcast the proclamations by the King and Badoglio did not sign off with the usual Fascist party anthem, Giovinezza. It played only the Royalist hymn. The broadcasts were recorded by the Associated Press.

There was speculation that Adolf Hitler might march German troops into war-weary Italy where Badoglio warned all Italians that any attempt to interfere with his orders would be crushed.

ACCEPTS RESIGNATION

Rome's announcement began:

"The King-Emperor has accepted the resignation as head of the government, Prime Minister, and Secretary, submitted by his Excellency Caveliere Benito Mussolini, and has appointed as head of the government, Prime Minister, and Secretary of State, his Excellency Caveliere Pietro Badoligo, Marshal of Italy."

The majority view in London is that Italy won't be in the war much longer.

Badoglio, a close friend of the King, came out of retirement to take over the government. Mussolini had dismissed him as chief of staff Dec. 6, 1940, and during Il Duce's long term the old soldier had been known as a Fascist by compulsion and a Royalist by choice.

He told Italians to rally around the King and his proclamation added: "The war continues. Italy, grievously stricken in her invaded provinces and in her ruined towns, maintains her faith in her given word, jealous of her ancient traditions."

It was noted here that Badoglio's phrase "the war continues" was open to more than one interpretation. He did not necessarily say how long he or the King intends the war to continue.

The King's proclamation said Italy "by the valor of its armed forces and the determination of all its citizens will find again a way of recovery."

The ambiguity of this sentence suggested the possibility of an Italian capitulation after a period of what might be no more than token resistance—depending on how the Germans react meanwhile.

At a late hour Sunday night the only mention the Berlin radio had made of the affair was to quote the Italian Stefani News agency as saying that the change of government was believed to have been due to

More of KING on Page 7

KING VITTORIO EMANUELE

PIETRO BADOGLIO

BENITO MUSSOLINI

FINAL STAGE

Indicate Strong Stabilized Line On Northeastern Tip Of Sicily

PRISONERS MOUNT

Allied Headquarters In North Africa—(AP)—The campaign in Sicily reached its last and decisive stage Sunday as Gen. Dwight D. Eisenhower's headquarters announced the occupation of Trapani, last of the three major ports in the western part of the island, by the American Seventh Army.

While the American forces under Lieut. Gen. George S. Patton, Jr., rushed through the dust and heat to finish the mopping up of western Sicily, raising to more than 50,000 the total prisoners in their hands, there were strong indications that the enemy was establishing a strong stabilized line across the northeastern tip where he would make his last big stand in an attempt to block the door to Italy.

The Axis front now runs from the Dittaina River, about three miles south of Catania on the east coast, due west through Catenanuova, which is 12 miles west of Paterno and about 23 miles west and slightly north of Catania. From there it turns to Regalbuto, four miles to the northwest, and bends sharply northward to the sea.

(This would indicate that the Allies may be in possession of the north coast as far east as Acquedola, approximately 55 miles west of Messina Strait and 65 miles east of Palermo—or at least that the Axis may not be seriously opposing Allied advances into that area.

(Roundabout reports originating from the Algiers radio Saturday said the Allies had reached San Stefano Di Camastra, 50 miles east of Palermo.)

NAZIS HOLD SECTOR

German divisions are holding the sector from the river inland to Regalbuto, a winding line of 35 to 40 miles, and the Italians have been entrusted with the remaining 30 miles to the northern seacoast.

Dispatches indicated that the northern section of the line was still somewhat unsettled and it was known exactly here where it came up to the coast.

A small triangular section of Sicily is now left in Axis hands, with Messina at the tip. Both legs of the triangle are approximately 55 miles long and the base is about 60 miles across—an area approximately the size of Cap Bon where the remnants of Col. Gen. Jurgen Von Arnim's Tunisian army were destroyed less than three months ago.

Headquarters announced that Italian parachute troops had been dropped behind Allied positions at an unnamed place, but said they were captured and "effectively dealt with."

Sunday's communique said Cadaian troops under Maj. Gen. Guy Simonds "have been engaged in bitter fighting and have made good progress" ploughing through des-

More of FINAL on Page 2

WALLACE HITS ALL OPPONENTS OF ROOSEVELT

Says "Powerful Groups" Out To Destroy President's Domestic Program

WILL BE EXPOSED

Detroit— (AP) — Vice President Wallace asserted Sunday that "there are powerful groups who hope to take advantage of the President's concentration on the war effort to destroy everything he has accomplished on the domestic front over the last ten years."

Wallace spoke out in defense of President Roosevelt in an address before a crowd estimated at 14,000 at a meeting sponsored by Detroit labor and civic groups— an address in which he made no reference to the President's recent repreimand of himself and Secretary of Commerce Jones for a public quarrel over purchase of critical materials for the nation's war stock pile.

"Some people," Wallace said, "call these powerful groups 'isolationists,' others call them 'reactionaries' and still others, seeing them following in European footsteps, call them 'American fascists.'

"Sooner or later the machinations of these small but powerful groups which put money and power first and people last will inevitably be exposed to the public eye."

Referring to his recent visit to Latin America, Wallace said that "in South America I found that the lowliest peon looked on President Roosevelt as the symbol of his dearest aspirations in the peace to come."

The vice president called upon all Americans to begin now their "apprenticeship to world peace" by shouldering responsibilities for "enlightenment, abundant production and wolrd cooperation.

He asserted that "when we as victors lay down our arms in this struggle against the enslavement of the mind and soul of the human family, we take up arms immediately in the great war against starvation, unemploymnet and the rigging of the markets of the world."

Wallace declared that the nation was not confronted with a choice between an Americanized fascism and the restoration of pre-war scar-

More of WALLACE on Page 7

"We Lead All the Rest"

FARM CORNER

By *The Farm Editor*

SNAP BEANS, TOMATO VINES ARE ADDED TO CORN BORERS' VICTIMS

Harrisburg— (AP) —The dreaded European corn borer has added snap beans and tomato vines to its list of victims, the State Department of Agriculture reported Sunday.

Corn borers were seen in bean stalks in York county by Dr. Thomas L. Guyton, state entomologist, and on tomatoes in the southeastern corn borer infested area by Don M. James, Bureau of Markets.

Dr. Guyton reported he found empty pupa shells of the second generation corn borers in Cumberland, York and Dauphin counties, indicating second brood moths are flying and laying eggs that will hatch in four or five days.

The entomologist urged applications of rotenone dust beginning this week and continuing at not less than five-day intervals until mid-August since hatching of eggs and the emergence of young borers will be continuous over the three-week period. Borer moths are yellowish brown with a wing spread of about one inch. Borer eggs are laid in transparent masses on the underside of leaves.

ADDITIONAL MEETING

An additional meeting had been added to the schedule of eight tomato field meetings to be held Tuesday and Wednesday on var-

More of FARM CORNER on Page 2

Intelligencer Journal Weather Calendar

COMPARATIVE TEMPERATURES

Station	High	Low
Water Works	89	67
Ephrata	91	7:
Last Year (Ephrata)	86	64
Official High for Year, June 25		99
Official Low for Year, Feb 13		1
Character of Day		Partly Cloudy

SUN

Rises—5:56 a m Sets—8:24 p m

MOON

Rises—1:48. New Moon, July 31

More of WEATHER on Page 7

Roosevelt Denies Appeals Of 2 Local Draft Objectors

Decision Makes Men Again Eligible For Duty In Work Camps

LOCAL BOARD UPHELD

President Roosevelt denied the appeals of two Lancaster County conscientious objectors for farm deferment and affirmed the objector classification given them by County Draft Board No. 4, it was learned Sunday.

Affected by the decision are Amos Souder Shirk and Ivan W. Leid, both of New Holland R1, who recently were released from prison after serving several months of two and three-year sentences imposed for failure to report to work camps last year.

The decision of the presidential board, last resort in the appeal of registrants, automatically makes Shirk and Leid eligible for work camp duty.

The draft board now will send them to Harrisburg for Army physical examinations to determine if they are physically fit for service at a conscientious objector camp. If they pass, National Selective Service headquarters will set the date and the camp.

APPEALED BY HERSHEY

Their appeals as necessary men on the farm were carried to tht President by Major General Louis B. Hershey, National Selective Service director, after the Board of Appeals for Area 4 upheld the 4-E classification given them by County Board No. 4, and after Lt. Col. George H. Hafer, then acting Selective Service director in Pennsylvania, reviewed the cases and declined to appeal them.

The action of the presidential board apparently nullifies the contention of Federal Judge William H. Kirkpatrick, who sentenced the youths and then amended the sentences to the time served—four months.

In announcing the amended sentences Judge Kirkpatrick said: "I got in touch with draft authorities

More of ROOSEVELT on Page 2

Killed By Crane

SAMUEL L. SHEAFFER

SAMUEL SHEAFFER CRUSHED TO DEATH AT COATESVILLE

Well Known Farmer Of Near Quarryville Had Been Working At Steel Plant

Samuel L. Sheaffer, forty-seven, of near Quarryville, a well-known farmer, died at 7:55 p. m. Saturday in the Coatesville Hospital several hours after he was crushed by a crane at the Lukens Steel Plant according to hospital reports. Mr. Sheaffer, who had been employed by the McKee Construction Co., had been working at the plant for some time.

TO CONDUCT INQUEST

Fred Manship, deputy coroner, of Coatesville, announced he would conduct an inquest at the Wentz Funeral Home, Coatesville, at 7 p. m. Monday.

Hospital attendants said Mr. Sheaffer suffered a crushed pelvis, internal injuries and possible rib fractures.

Mr. Sheaffer, who was an independent Republican, at one time ran for the State Legislature. He also served as road supervisor in Eden Twp. and was one of the organizers of the Farmers' Creamery at Christiana. At one time he also

More of ACCIDENT on Page 2

HONEY BROOK WOMAN DIES IN AUTOMOBILE

Mrs. Ella E. Pim, seventy-five, widow of Samuel I. Pim, of Honey Brook, died suddenly from a heart attack about 12:15 p. m. Sunday in her automobile while returning home from the Honey Brook Presbyterian Church. Mrs. Pim, who was alone in the auto, apparently had been driving at a slow speed as the auto stopped when it struck a fence without any damage.

She was a member of the Honey Brook Presbyterian Church and was active in the organizations of the church.

Surviving is a sister, Mrs. Mary Trego, Downingtown.

AUDIBLE "ALL-CLEAR" FOR AIR-RAID DRILLS

A return to an audible "all-clear" to signal the termination of blackouts and air raid drills was ordered by the State Defense Council Saturday and local defense headquarters upon receiving notification of the change announced the new order will be compiled with immediately.

The new signal—a 15 second blast of sirens—has been approved by Major General Milton A. Reckord, of the Army's Third Service Command, and will replace the radio signal used in the State since February.

12 U. S. FLIERS DIE IN CUBAN COLLISION

Havana — (AP) — Two American B-25 bombers starting on a patrol Sunday collided in midair 2,000-feet above Cuban Army headquarters, killing 12 American airmen.

The planes were loaded with bombs, and some of the crewmen might have saved their lives by jettisoning the high explosives on the crowded beaches or Army headquarters, but they tried to make crash landings at sea and the planes blew up.

ALLIED AERIAL ARMADAS HIT AXIS TARGETS

RAF Pours Bombs On Hamburg; Flying Fortresses Stage Four Raids

31 BOMBERS LOST

(By The Associated Press)

Aerial armadas from Britain, North Africa and the Middle East, striking with greater weight and over longer distances than ever before, smashed at Axis targets from Norway to Sicily over the week-end, emphasizing repeated declarations of Allied spokesmen that heavier and heavier blows will be rained upon the enemy from the air.

Striking with pent-up fury after a period of poor flying weather, the RAF hit the great German shipping and submarine building center of Hamburg with 2,600 tons of bombs Saturday night—the heaviest raid in history.

DAYLIGHT ATTACKS

At daylight Sunday American Flying Fortresses took up the attack with their heaviest raids of the war. The American heavies pounded still smoking Hamburg, aircraft factories at Warnemunde near the Baltic port of Rostock, shipyards at Kiel and the seaplane base at Wustrow, all in Germany. RAF and American medium bombers escorted by American and British fighters pounded targets in Holland and Belgium. Among them the Fokker Aircraft Factory in Amsterdam.

The four big raids on Germany cost 19 of the big American bombers.

Hardly had they returned when the RAF roared off again to batter the continent Sunday night and early Monday.

More than 700 of Britain's four-engined bombers were estimated to have participated in the tremendous Saturday night blow, which in 50 fearsome minutes swamped Hamburg's ground defenses and sent clouds of black smoke billowing four miles into the air.

Only 12 of the bombers failed to return to England, a loss so insignificant by comparison to those incurred in previous mass raids over the Reich as to suggest that Germany's defense against the Al-

More of ALLIED on Page 7

Democrats List Candidates To File Petitions Today

Those Seeking Major City And County Offices Are Announced By Party Officials; More Petitions Filed

Democratic officials announced the following candidates will file their nominating petitions Monday (today):

District Attorney — James N. Lightner, local attorney and veteran of World War No. 1.

County Commissioner—Fred W. Wagner, Columbia, for re-election for a second term; H. Clifton Kuhns, Strasburg; salesman; Leo F. Houck, Lancaster, boxing instructor. Michael F. Donnelly, auditor, 317 Pearl St., filed his petition Saturday morning.

Sheriff—Roy S. Fritz, Quarryville.

Clerk of the Quarter Sessions Court—Lester R. McVey, Ephrata, veteran of World War No. 1.

Register of Wills, George H. Carpenter, Lancaster, insurance.

Prothonotary—Edward G. Wilson, Manheim Twp.

City Council—F. Melvin Martin, sports editor; Charles E. Weaver, coffee merchant.

School director—Mrs. Gertrude N. Ross, housewife, 43 N. Prince St.; Mrs. Mary Biemesderfer Frizzell, houseife, 840 Lake St.; Paul I. Gable, 527 N. Lime St. active lodge and church worker; Emanuel L. Bear, 132 E. Ross St.

County Treasurer—Mrs. Pearl F. Wagner, Denver, housewife, form-

More of DEMOCRATS on Page 2

RUSSIANS NEARING ENCIRCLEMENT OF NAZI BASE AT OREL

Reds Sweep Forward 2½ To 5½ Miles From Three Directions

London—(AP)—The great Russian counteroff[illegible]sive battering upon Orel from [illegible]hree directions engulfed 30 more p[illegible]ulated places and swept forward [illegible] to 5½ miles Sunday, Moscow announced in a special communique, and complete encirclement of the great Nazi base appeared only a matter of time.

Red Army columns driving down behind Orel have cut to within seven miles or so of the Bryansk railway feeding supplies and reinforcements into the stronghold.

The Russians are steadily nar-

More of RUSSIANS on Page 2

PROSECUTED AFTER CRASH

Harold G. Book, 310 W. James St., was prosecuted by city police for failure to yield the right of way as the result of a collision between two trucks at Lemon and Charlotte Streets at 9:15 a. m. Saturday. He will be summoned for a hearing before Alderman A. P. Newell. Book, who was treated for head injuries at St. Joseph's Hospital which he received in the crash entered the intersection at a fast rate of speed, police said, colliding with a truck driven by C. E. Yoder, 648 Ocean Ave.

WOMAN HURT IN FALL FROM TROLLEY CAR

Mrs. Helen Warfel, thirty-one, Millersville, who fell from a Rocky Springs trolley car at Duke and King Streets at 6:40 p. m. Sunday, was conveyed to the Lancaster General Hospital by city police for treatment for an injured spine. Mrs. Warfel told police she fell when her heel caught as she was leaving the car and a person in back of her pushed her.

Lancaster's Industrial Production For 1942 Valued At $202,299,000

Gain Of $23,000,000 Over 1941 Shown By Figures Compiled By State Department Of Internal Affairs

Lancaster county industry produced goods valued at $202,299,100 in 1942—the greatest in history—the State Department of Internal Affairs announced Saturday.

This is a gain of more than $23,000,000 over 1941 and $66,000,000 over 1940.

WAGES, SALARIES UP

Wages and salaries also showed a tremendous increase, from $36,000,000 in 1940 to $57,000,000 in 1942. In that period industries in the county added nearly 5,000 employes according to the figures released by Secretary of Internal Affairs William S. Livengood, Jr. Wage and salary earners increased from 34,493 to 39,116 in the two-year period.

Importance of Lancaster County factories is shown by the impressive figure under "value added by manufacture," Secretary Livengood pointed out. This total, which was almost 98 million dollars in 1942, means that this is the difference between the values of raw

More of LANCASTER'S on Page 7

BADOGLIO NOTED FOR HIS ATTITUDE AGAINST FASCISTS

Italy's New Prime Minister Long Personal Friend Of King Emanuele

(By Associated Press)

Tall and tough Field Marshal Pietro Badoglio, Italy's new Prime Minister, has long been noted for his anti-Fascist and anti-German attitude which made him a suspect by Mussolini's henchmen.

Long a close personal friend of King Victor Emanuele, the 72-year-old Marshal has for the most part held aloof from politics and on December 6, 1940 resigned as chief of staff of the Italian Army. Eleven days after his resignation, which was quickly accepted by Mussolini, German troops poured across the border into Italy proper.

MAN OF MYSTERY

Since that time he has been a man of mystery. Reports drifting to the outside world however had him under arrest by the Mussolini government and one of the leaders

More of BADOGLIO on Page 7

WOMAN FOUND WITH NECK LACERATED

Mrs. Elizabeth Brooks, sixty-three, 587 Pershing Ave., was admitted to the Lancaster General Hospital suffering from a razor wound of the neck, inflicted, city police said, in a suicide attempt at 1:30 p. m. Sunday. Her condition was reported as satisfactory by hospital attendants.

Mrs. Brooks was found in the bathroom at her home with a laceration along the right side of her neck by her nephew, Norman Smith, 585 Pershing Ave., according to the police report. Ill health was given by relatives as the reason for the act, police said.

JAPANESE BASES AT GASMATA AND MUNDA HAMMERED

Allied Bombers Rain Tons Of Bombs On Nipponese Holding Out At Munda

Allied Headquarters In The Southwest Pacific (Monday)—(AP)—Allied bombers, attacking Japanese positions in the southwest Pacific with ever increasing intensity, yesterday delivered the heaviest raids of the war against two of the enemy's most important bases.

More than 200 American planes swarmed over the key airbase at Munda, New Georgia, raining 186 tons of bombs upon the Japanese pinned within the airbase by American troops who control the surrounding jungle.

HAMMER AIRDROME

At the same time, medium bombers and long-range fighters, manned by Australians, swept up the coast of New Britain for a coordinated dawn attack on the Gasmata airdrome.

One plane was reported missing in the raid which also covered enemy gun positions on Bibolo Hill

More of JAPANESE on Page 7

REPORT FIFTH CASE OF TYPHOID FEVER

The fifth case of typhoid fever this year was reported Sunday by Dr. A. J. Greenleaf, Mountville, county medical director.

Evelyn Miller, fourteen, daughter of Mr. and Mrs. John Miller, New Holland R1, is confined to her home since she was stricken about July 5. Her condition is reported as improved by her physician Dr. A. B. Schnader, Terre Hill.

The source of the infection has not been traced the physicians said.

WEATHER
Eastern Pennsylvania: Slightly Cooler Friday And Friday Evening.

Intelligencer Journal

NEXT WEEK
Sept. 9th
TIN CAN
School Collection
"2 tin cans may save a life"

The Leading Newspaper in the Garden Spot of America, Home Owned for Home Folks Since 1794

VOLUME LXXIX.—NO. 306. Entered as second class matter June 23, 1928 at the Post Office at Lancaster, Pa., under the Act of March 3, 1879. Reg. U. S. Pat. Off. LANCASTER, PA., FRIDAY MORNING, SEPTEMBER 3, 1943 CITY 26 PAGES, 208 COLUMNS. 20c PER WEEK—4c Per Copy

ITALY INVADED

Allied Headquarters In North Africa (Friday) — (A P) — An announcement from Allied headquarters today said Allied troops had landed in southern Italy.

The British Eighth Army crossed from Sicily, the announcement said, and landed.

It was the first time Allied troops had set foot on European soil since the Dieppe raid in August, 1942, when Allied forces landed on the coast of France but later withdrew.

Canadian troops were included in the attacking forces, Allied headquarters disclosed.

BLOW STRUCK AT DAWN

The new blow was struck about dawn today.

Invasion of the continent came quickly on the heels of the cleanup of the Sicilian campaign, begun at dawn July 10 and brought to a victorious conclusion 38 days later with all Axis troops either killed, routed or prisoners.

A special communique, announcing the mainland landings, said the forces "of General Eisenhower continued their advance. British and Canadian troops of the Eighth Army, supported by Allied sea and air power attacked across the straits of Messina early today and landed on the mainland of Italy."

AIR AND SEA FLEETS PROTECT TROOPS

Thus, as in the Sicilian landings, powerful air and sea fleets gave protection to the landing troops.

By moving across the strait of Messina from the eastern shore of Sicily, the Allied forces had only a few miles of water to cross. The strait at its narrowest point at the extreme northeastern corner of Sicily is only a litle over two miles wide and can be crossed by fast boat in about 20 minutes.

The announcement of the landing was issued here shortly after 7 a. m. (1 a. m., Lancaster Time).

The complete text:

"Allied forces under the command of General Eisenhower have continued their advance. British and Canadian troops of the Eighth Army, supported by Allied sea and air power, attacked across the strait of Messina early today and landed on the mainland of Italy."

It was recalled that Canadian troops had been withdrawn from the Sicilian fighting some days before it ended. At that time, it was generally understood the Canadians were preparing to help spearhead some new attack.

(The American Seventh Army, which mopped up the greater part of the western half of Sicily, presumably was being held in reserve, for the time being at least.)

AMERICAN FLIERS TAKE PART IN ATTACK

Both American and British fliers took part in the air cover that accompanied the landing.

Significantly, the invasion came on the fourth anniversary of the day Great Britain declared herself at war with Germany.

It was possible this factor was taken into consideration at the recent Allied war conference at Quebec. Final plans undoubtedly were made during the historic meeting, for which Prime Minister Churchill crossed the Atlantic and President Roosevelt journeyed to the historic city of the United States' northern neighbor.

(A Mutual Broadcasting announcer in Algiers said the landing took place at 4:30 a. m. (or 10:30 p. m., Thursday, Lancaster Time.) This announcer said the landings were made opposite the town of Messina. Scilla and San Giovanni are the main towns directly opposite.)

COMMANDO RAIDS PRECEDED INVASION

(In a broadcast Friday morning from Algiers, John Daly, CBS correspondent, reported the invasion was preceded by a number of successful commando and reconnaissance missions in the past few nights.

(Daly said these missions were successful in helping to knock out enemy coastal defenses, and at the same time, he said, they reported valuable information back to attack headquarters.

(This report recalled that the Italians said several days ago a commando-type landing had been made in the region of Reggio Calabria. This was never confirmed.

(Daly said details were lacking as to exactly where the landings occurred, although in general they took place along the Calabrian peninsula. Daly said the Germans were believed to have done most of the initial fighting in the first phase against the invasion forces.)

LANDINGS PRECEDED BY HEAVY BOMBARDMENT

The landings were preceded by a heavy bombardment of the Italian coast by big Allied guns stationed on the Sicilian shore, which knocked out many enemy batteries and facili-

More of ITALY INVADED on Page 10

Where Allies Swept Into Europe

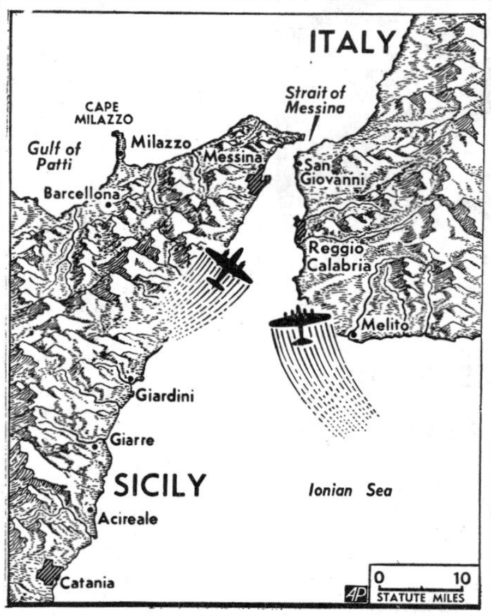

The long-awaited invasion of continental Europe by Allied forces began early Friday when an invasion force spearheaded by the crack British Eighth Army, stormed across the narrow Straits of Messina to land in Italy.

HOTEL STEWARD ARRESTED IN WAC SLAYING

Robert De Armond Is Held On Vagrancy Charge For Questioning

Indianapolis—(AP)—Saul A. Rabb, chief deputy Marion county prosecutor, announced Thursday night that Robert De Armond, 40-year-old Claypool Hotel steward who once served a five year prison term for rape, has been arrested for questioning in connection with the slaying of Corporal Mamoa L. Ridings of Camp Atterbury in the hotel Saturday night.

Charged with vagrancy, he was placed under $1,000 bond.

De Armond was employed days in the hotel and nights at Riverside Amusement Park. Rabb said he left the hotel job at 6 p. m. Saturday night and reported for work at Riverside an hour and thirty-four minutes later.

BODY PARTLY CLOTHED

The body of the WAC corporal, who checked into the hotel late Saturday afternoon, was found about 8:30 p. m., mutilated and only partly clothed, in her room.

Rabb said De Armond was convicted June 1, 1934, of raping a ten-year-old girl at Brookville, Ind., and was sentenced to two to twenty-one years. Nov. 13, 1939, he was transferred from the Indiana state prison at Michigan City to the Central Indiana (mental) hospital here. He was released from the hospital last April 28.

At the time of his conviction he

More of STEWARD on Page 10

"We Lead All the Rest"
FARM CORNER
By
The Farm Editor

JULY MILK YIELD IN STATE BELOW LAST YR.

Harrisburg—Through initial announcement of estimates to obtain a monthly total for milk production on Pennsylvania farms, it was learned Thursday that the total of 439 million pounds produced in July of this year was 10 million pounds below production for the same month in 1942.

Monthly production totals on milk will be compiled hereafter by the Federal-State Crop Reporting Service in the Pennsylvania Department of Agriculture according to Secretary Miles Horst. Previously this service had announced only the average milk production per cow in herds kept by crop correspondents.

"The necessity of converting average milk production per cow in herd figures as of the first of each month into some measure of total milk produced has long been recognized," the Secretary said. "It is believed that the new series of monthly milk production estimates for Pennsylvania will provide a more complete picture of the milk

More of FARM CORNER on Page 10

Intelligencer Journal
Weather Calendar

COMPARATIVE TEMPERATURES

Station	High	Low
Water Works	94	64
Ephrata	93	66
Last Year (Ephrata)	91	57
Official High for Year, June 24		99
Official Low for Year, Feb. 13		1
Character of Day		Clear

SUN
Rises—6:33 a. m. Sets—7:33 p. m.

MOON
Sets—9:50 p. m. First Quarter, Sept. 7

STARS
Morning—Mars, Jupiter, Saturn.
Evening—Venus

More of WEATHER on Page 10

Month Just Ended Was Driest August Since 1930's Drouth

The month just ended was the driest August since the great drouth of 1930, unofficial weather figures revealed Thursday, as the Federal-State Crop Reporting service reported additional damage to crops from the prolonged dry spell.

Available figures showed that about 1.3 inches of rain fell during the past month, compared with .92 of an inch in August 1930, when the greater portions of the farmland in the United States were turned into a barren desert.

In only two other years since 1930 did the August rainfall come anywhere near the low figure for the past month. In 1935, precipitation of 1.7 inches was measured and in 1938 1.82 inches was recorded. Normal rainfall for August is 4.26 inches.

Farmers watching their crops stand dormant for lack of moisture recalled that the rainfall in August, 1942 was 10.98 inches and back in 1933 total precipitation for that month was 12.70.

SHOWERS SPOTTY

Rainfall during August of this year consisted of showers which were spotty. The southern section of the county appeared to have received more rain than the northern.

Agriculturists emphasized again Thursday that only the surplus of moisture which was stored in the ground from last winter kept Lancaster county from facing a disastrous water shortage.

Continued excessive temperatures also continued Thursday. The mercury hit the 94-degree mark at the City Water Works. Cooler

More of MONTH on Page 10

TWO NEW CASES OF TYPHOID IN COUNTY

Two new cases of typhoid fever, the eighth and ninth this year, were reported Thursday by Dr. A. J. Greenleaf, Mountville, county medical director.

The victims are:

Mrs. Earl Wissler, Lititz R1, who is confined to her home and whose condition is regarded as fair by her attending physician, Dr. Paul H. Myerly, Lincoln.

Daniel Wenger, sixteen-year-old son of Mr. and Mrs. Harry M. Wenger, Ephrata R2, who is also confined to his home. Dr. John H. Reynolds, Akron, said his condition was fair.

Health authorities have taken samples of water from the water supply at the Wissler farm, where the Wenger boy was employed recently. Both victims became ill on the same day and both are believed to have been infected from the same source.

CREAMERY BUTTER TO BE 12 POINTS BEGINNING SUNDAY

Other Advances In Point Values Include Frozen, Canned Foods; Some Cuts In Meat

Washington—(AP)—A hike in the ration-stamp price of creamery butter, frozen foods and some canned fruits coincided Thursday with a reduction of a point or two in the value of 35 different cuts of meat.

All the changes—based on new surveys of what civilians want and what they can get—will go into effect Sunday.

The Office of Price Administration (OPA) boosted creamery butter from 10 to 12 points, blaming local shortages and reports that production is running five per cent behind original estimates. It cut

WHERE TO FIND THE CHARTS
The new chart for meat, fats, fish and dairy products will be found on Page Six and the new chart for processed foods will be found on Page Four.

the value of country farm-churned butter from ten points to six in an effort, it said, to get more of it to market to ease the demand for creamery butter.

STOCKS RUNNING LOW

Frozen foods and some canned fruits will go up in stamp value in

More of BUTTER on Page 4

MRS. F. D. R. IN AUSTRALIA

Canberra, Australia (Friday)—(AP)—Mrs. Franklin D. Roosevelt, wife of the President, arrived today by plane.

(The dispatch did not state from where the plane came but she previously had been in New Zealand.)

Police Reverse Role, Help Rush Ill Boy To Hospital

State Police, after chasing a fast traveling motorist on the Lincoln Highway at Soudersburg at 11 p. m. Thursday, reversed their role and led the motorist into the city when they learned the automobile contained a seriously ill child.

Samuel Garver, two, Paradise R1, the child, suffered a strangulated hernia and was taken to the office of Dr. George Beacher, Gap, where he was given ether to ease the pain and then referred to St. Joseph's Hospital.

Clarence Lefever, a neighbor of the Garver's, offered to bring the child to this city and was enroute when stopped by State Policemen D. J. Golden and R. G. Williams. The officers provided an escort to the hospital when they learned of the child's condition.

Attendants at the hospital said the condition of the boy was good early Friday morning.

Lancaster Girl Named Valedictorian Of Nurses At St. Joseph's Hospital

Major Charles H. Wilson, director of Medical Field Service, Carlisle Barracks, will be the principal speaker at the thirty-ninth annual commencement exercises of the St. Joseph's Hospital, School of Nursing, to be held at 4 p. m. Wednesday at the Catholic High School, Rossmere. A class of sixteen will be graduated.

Most Rev. George L. Leech, D.D., J.C.D., Bishop of the Harrisburg diocese, will address the students and award the diplomas. Rev. Harold E. Keller, A.M., Marietta, director of schools of the Harrisburg Diocese, will deliver the invocation.

Miss Barbara K. Spencer, daughter of Mr. and Mrs. John C. Spencer,

More of LANCASTER on Page 10

5 RED ARMIES HIT RETREATING NAZI SOLDIERS

Score Gains At Both Ends And Center Of 600-Mile Front

London (Friday)—(AP)—Russia announced early today that five Red armies plunging westward had cut the Bryansk-Kiev Railway 150 miles from Kiev, smashed German reinforcements in a six-mile gain on Smolensk, and rolled up Axis lines in a new 45-mile-wide spurt in the Donets basin.

Marshal Stalin's Thursday order of the day said that the Ukraine citadel of Sumy, 90 miles northwest of Kharkov, had fallen to Gen. Nikolai Vatutin's army, and a communique announced the capture of Krolevets and Yampol, two points on the vital Bryansk-Kiev Railway linking the enemy's Central and Southern Fronts.

MANY TOWNS CAPTURED

Lisichansk, Voroshilovsk, Slavyanoserbsk, and other cities were seized in the Donets Basin, while Budenovka, 20 miles from Mariupol, was taken in the push along the rim of the Sea of Azov, said the communique recorded by the Soviet Monitor.

The swiftness of the Russian advances and the tone of the communique indicated that the Germans were engaged in a large-scale retreat toward the Dnieper River, particularly in the huge Donets Basin. The bulletin, however, emphasized that the Germans were fighting stubbornly all along the 600-mile front.

More than 9,000 Germans were killed yesterday as the Red armies overran nearly 250 cities and villages, many of them strategic prizes, for a two-day bag of nearly 550 localities.

1941 LINES CRACKED

Germany's 1941 invasion lines now have been cracked by the Russians in a 1943 offensive that has carried the Red Army more than half-way along the come-back trail from historic Stalingrad to the Polish border.

The capture of Krolevets, 25 miles north of the rail junction of Konotop, put the Red Army 150 miles from Kiev after a 130-mile summer lunge from Kursk. Moreover, its fall further flanked Bryansk from the south and may force Germany's south-central armies to

More of RUSSIANS on Page 10

TROLLEY AND TRUCK DAMAGED IN MISHAP

A York Motor Express truck, operated by W. F. Wiest, East Petersburg, was slightly damaged when it was side-swiped by a Duke St. trolley operated by Jack Parke, 220 S. Christian St., on Duke St., between Ross and Clay Streets, at 9:50 a. m. Thursday, according to city police.

The trolley attempted to pass the tractor-trailer truck as it was passing a parked car when the collision occurred, police said. The left front fender and tire of the truck and the right front end of the trolley were damaged.

TWO COUNTY SOLDIERS LISTED AS WOUNDED

The War Department announced Thursday the names of two Lancaster county soldiers who were wounded in the North African area, presumably in Sicily.

They are: Pvt. Robert A. Esbenshade, son of Mr. and Mrs. Daniel Espenshade, Elizabethtown R3, and Pvt. Rodney D. Musser, son of Mrs. Daisy Musser, 253 S. Eighth St., Columbia.

The parents of the youths had previously been notified.

Lost & Found — Page 23

FATHER OF U. S. PARACHUTE TROOPS REACHES ENGLAND

Maj. Gen. Lee Turns Up In London With Gen. Arnold, U. S. Air Chief

London —(AP)—Gen. Henry H. Arnold, Chief of the U. S. Army Air Forces, and Maj. Gen. William C. Lee, Commander of an Airborne Division who is known as the father of American Parachute Troops, arrived in Britain Thursday from the United States.

Both these high-ranking representatives of American air power immediately plunged into a study of the military set-up and recent operations by the Eighth U.S.AAF.

CONFERENCES PLANNED

General Arnold is here for conferences with British Air Chief Marshal Sir Arthur Portal, Lt. Gen. Jacob L. Devers, Commanding U. S. Forces in the European theater; Maj. Gen Ira C. Eaker,

More of FATHER on Page 10

YOUR INCOME TAX DECLARATION EXPLAINED

The U. S. Treasury has found that a lot of people have a lot of questions about the September 15 declaration of estimated income and victory tax. It has issued a four-part explanation. Today's installment on Page 14 deals with the purpose of the declaration.

AMERICANS BOMB FRENCH TARGETS NEAR THE COAST

Largest Fighter Cover Used This Year Accompanies Planes On Missions

London (Friday)—(AP)—U. S. Flying Fortresses bombed air fields at Mardyck and Penain late yesterday and other battle planes made further attacks on French targets under the largest fighter cover used in air operations so far in 1943, it was announced today.

"Good bombing results were observed on all targets," said a communique issued jointly by U. S. Army headquarters and the Air Ministry.

THUNDERBOLTS ESCORT BOMBERS

Squadrons of P-47 Thunderbolts escorted and covered the Flying Fortresses.

"Marauders (B-26s) and RAF Bostons, Mitchells and Venturas bombed targets in Pas De Calais," the communique said. "Other Marauders attacked the power station at Mazingarbe and Bostons attacked the freight yards at Serqueux."

RAF, Dominion and Allied Spitfires escorted and supported the light and medium bombers.

Four enemy aircraft were reported destroyed, one by Fortress guns and three by Spitfires. One of the medium bombers, a light bomber and two fighters failed to return.

The raiders struck zones cluster-

More of AERIAL on Page 10

Heated Controversy May Prevent Writing Of New Tax Bill This Year

Washington—(AP)—A heated controversy between Treasury Secretary Morgenthau and the Congressional Tax staff broke open Thursday causing doubts in competent capitol hill quarters that a new general revenue act, with higher wartime levies, can be written in 1943.

The schism developed after the Congressional Tax staff sought to obtain information from the Bureau of Internal Revenue and other agencies, without channeling such requests through the treasury.

It is understood that Morgenthau resents the Tax staff engaging in such tactics to obtain information about the Treasury's efforts to draw up an administration revenue program. The cabinet member is

More of CONTROVERSY on Page 10

"Newspapers are essential to the war effort."
War Manpower Commission

LANCASTER NEW ERA

WEATHER
Cooler this afternoon; **somewhat** cooler tonight and Thursday **morning.**

VOL. 66—NO. 550 | Entered as second class matter January 31, 1924, at the Post Office at Lancaster, Pa., under the Act of March 3, 1879, Reg. U. S. Pat Off. | LANCASTER, PA., WEDNESDAY, SEPTEMBER 8, 1943 | CITY EDITION | 18 PAGES—144 COLUMNS | 20c PER WEEK—4c Per Copy

ITALY SURRENDERS AND IS GRANTED ARMISTICE

Steam Engine on Freight Train Overturns at Columbia

Six trainmen were injured when this steam locomotive drawing 120 empty oil cars was derailed and rolled over on its side at the Locust Street crossing of the Pennsylvania railroad in Columbia this morning. The injured were all riding in the caboose. A loose frog is believed to have caused the wreck.

SIX TRAINMEN ARE INJURED

Loose Frog Blamed at Columbia; Accidents at Dillerville, Parkesburg.

Six trainmen were injured at Columbia, shortly before 9 a. m. today when a large steam locomotive attached to a PRR freight train rolled over on its side in one of three train accidents in this section. No person was hurt in the other two accidents, one at Dillerville and the other at Parkesburg.

The six men injured at Columbia were riding in the caboose, about half a mile behind the derailed locomotive. All were hurled against the sides of the car when the air brakes were applied to the string of approximately 120 empty tank cars. The three members of the train crew in the cab of the locomotive escaped injury.

Injured In Columbia Hospital

The injured, all in the Columbia hospital, are: G. R. Mount, conductor, Harrisburg; J. V. Bowles, flagman, Summerdale; H. L. Craddock, brakeman, Newark; E. E. Kauffman, engineer, Enola; W. R. Lewis, brakeman, Burnham, N. Y., and Ralph L. Wise, flagman, Columbia. The injured men nad been relieved by an all Columbia crew and were riding to Enola.

In the cab with Engineer James Kunkle were M. J. Kimbal, fireman and William K. Gable, brakeman, all of Columbia. L. E. Ford, conductor of the train, riding in the caboose, was the only man in the car who escaped injury.

The locomotive rolled into a small ditch on the engineer's side and came within a few feet of striking a tall steel upright that supports one side of the wires which carry power to the electric trains that operate through Columbia.

So quickly was the train brought

(See WRECK—Page 14)

Price Panel Assistants Take Office, Learn Duties

Volunteers' Work Will Include Aid to Grocers; Will Make Periodic Check of Stores on Assignment Only

Volunteer assistants to the Price Panel of the War Price and Rationing Board were given final instructions and their oath of office, at a meeting last night at ration headquarters.

Three district officers of the OPA from the Harrisburg office attended the meeting, to explain to these men and women the part they will play in the OPA's program of price ceilings.

The work of these price panel assistants was outlined to include assistance to the grocer, in obeying the ceilings and posting requirements.

Checks On Stores

The assistants will make periodic check-ups in stores to which they will be assigned, as well as investigating specific complaints from consumers about ceiling price violations. However, they will not visit any store except on a specific assignment given them by the Price Panel, officials emphasized.

Consumers are strongly urged to report any price violations to the Price Panel, officials said. It is only by having reports of violations investigated and corrected that the OPA can be made effective, it was pointed out.

In making their investigations, the price panel assistants will carry identification cards which they will present to the manager or owner of the store. They will check on whether ceiling price lists and store classification is posted in a prominent place, on whether the meat ceiling prices are posted and being adherred to. They will also handle requests by store proprietors for additional information concerning regulations or lists, and will

(See PRICES—Page 14)

F. D. OPENS BOND DRIVE TONIGHT

Local Workers Ready to Start Solicitation Tomorrow.

President Roosevelt will open the $15,000,000,000 Third War Loan drive tonight with a 10-minute radio address as part of an hour-long program beginning at 9 o'clock and tomorrow hundreds of local volunteers will begin selling Lancaster's quota of $13,800,000 worth of bonds.

The radio broadcast tonight originating in Washington and Hollywood, will include an all-star cast of motion picture and radio headliners. Mr. Roosevelt will speak at about 9:45 p. m. **(The one-hour program will be carried over WGAL.)**

The Treasury's War Finance division meanwhile paid tribute today to the manner in which it said the nation's press is "forming a solid front-line for the record-breaking bond-selling" campaign.

Newspapers Help

Despite the handicap of a newsprint shortage and other wartime problems, the division reported that "a barrage of front-page news coverage, plus millions of lines of advertising is being laid down by the publishers and editors of the nation."

Hundreds of editorials have appeared, keynoting the drive's aim

(See BONDS—Page 14)

4 MEAT DEALERS REBUKED BY OPA

Four Lancaster meat dealers, cited for failing to post, tag and price their products according to regulations, drew sharp rebukes and were dismissed at hearings before an OPA officer in Harrisburg yesterday. The OPA did not make public the names of those who were heard. Representatives of the OPA said:

"These regulations are imperative in order to inform consumers of price charges so that they can protect themselves against violating the laws by paying more than over-ceiling prices.

Latest News

NAZIS REPORT TWO BIG CONVOYS OFF ITALY

London, Sept. 8.—(AP)—The German International Information Bureau reported today that two big convoys totalling 200 freighters and transports were moving off Italy and that their presence "suggests American troops are aboard to carry through yet another landing" on the mainland.

STALIN SAYS DONETS CLEARED OF GERMANS

New York, Sept. 8.—(AP)—Marshall Stalin triumphantly announced in a special order of the day today that "The Donets Basin is cleared of the Germans."

The announcement, broadcast by the Moscow radio and recorded by the federal communications, added, "our troops captured a number of cities, including the city of Stalino."

PLANS READY FOR INVASION OF N.W. EUROPE

But End "Is Not Yet in Sight" Gen. Marshall Says in Report.

WASHINGTON, Sept. 8—(AP)—Allied preparations for smashing Germany's European fortress—including an invasion of Northwestern Europe—are virtually complete, Gen. George C. Marshall disclosed today, and plans for decisive triumphs over Japan are well advanced.

"The end is not yet in sight," the Army Chief of Staff said of history's greatest war, "but victory is certain."

That the long-heralded "second front" was plotted as long ago as the Casablanca conference in January was made clear by his disclosure that "the plans for air and other operations in Northwestern Europe were reviewed and confirmed" at that meeting.

Marshall's conclusion as to the invincibility of Allied arms was set forth in an extraordinary report to Secretary of War Stimson in which he reviewed the early months of heartbreaking defeat suffered because of inadequate forces, revealed the swift measures taken to stem Axis aggression, told of historic decisions made in Casablanca and Washington, and showed how the enemy had at last been forced on the defensive road to defeat.

"Strategically the enemy in Europe has been reduced to the defensive and the blockade is complete," Marshall declared. "In the Pacific the Japanese are being steadily ejected or rather eliminated from their conquered territory.

"In the South and Southwest Pacific two facts are plainly evident to the Japanese command as well as to the world at large: Our progress may seem slow but it is steady and determined, and it has been accompanied by a terrific destruction of enemy planes and surface vessels. This attrition must present an appalling problem for the enemy high command."

Enemy Strength Declining

"In brief," he said, "the strength of the enemy is steadily declining while the combined power of the United Nations is rapidly increasing, more rapidly with each succeeding month.

"There can be but one result and every resource we possess is being

(See YANKS—Page 15)

TWO CO. MEN DIE IN WAR AREAS

Bowmansville and Christiana Soldiers Killed; City Man Wounded.

Reports of the deaths of two Lancaster county soldiers, killed in action, have been received by the men's families and the father of a city man was notified that his son was wounded, in telegrams from the War Department.

Pfc. Webster Gehman, of Bowmansville, died Aug. 10 in Sicily, and Pvt. Ross Benner, Christiana RD, died on July 15 in the Southwest Pacific area. Staff Sgt. Kenneth R. Rothfus has been wounded in the South Pacific.

Pfc. Gehman was killed in action with an Army infantry unit in Sicily, according to a War Department telegram received by his parents, Mr. and Mrs. Frank Gehman, last night.

The 23-year-old soldier was killed in action on August 10, the telegram stated, adding that he was in the "north African area." On August 18, Mr. and Mrs. Gehman received a letter from their son, written July 29, in which he said he was in Sicily.

He had been overseas since February, and had taken part in action in North Africa, as well as Sicily. Pfc. Gehman was inducted on June 12, 1942, and received his

(See 2 MEN—Page 14)

Fate of Italy Fleet, Nazis' Po River Line Unanswered

By The Associated Press

These questions arose from the Italian surrender today:

1. What becomes of the Italian fleet, which is built around seven battleships and is split between Pola on the Adriatic and Spezia on the Italian west coast?

2. Will the Germans retire from the Po valley in the north, where they have been reported to have as many as 15 or 20 divisions?

3. What happens to the 25 to 30 Italian garrison divisions in the Balkans and France? And to the 250,000 Italian workmen estimated in Germany?

4. What effect will the Italian surrender have on the wavering morale of Hitler's Balkan satellites of Hungary, Rumania, Bulgaria and Croatia? Hungarian policy has been linked more closely with Italy than with Germany and all the Balkan states have shown increasing signs of war weariness.

5. Does the surrender include the French island of Corsica, barely 30 miles from southern France, which the Italians occupied when the Allies landed in North Africa?

6. Will the scattered German units still in Southern and Central Italy be allowed to return to Germany?

STALINO FALLS TO RUSSIANS

Red Army Wins Back Last of Big Industrial Cities in Donets.

LONDON, Sept. 8.—(AP)—Capture of fiercely-defended Stalino by the Russians was acknowledged by the Germans today, restoring the last of the great industrial cities of the Donets basin to the Red army which already has won back two-thirds of the Ukraine's rich grain lands.

The Red Army advance also crossed the rail line to Mariupol, 65 miles southwest of Stalino on the Sea of Azov, making it almost certain that Nazi forces which have been fighting east of that town must withdraw to escape entrapment by the southward turning move.

Sever Main R. R. Line

The Red Army newspaper Red Star reported that other units had severed the main railroad from the Donets Basin to Dnieperopetrovsk, 115 miles west of Stalino.

The German communique, recorded by the Associated Press, said Stalino, Russia's 12th largest city, had been evacuated "to shorten the front" after all military installations had been destroyed.

Russian dispatches indicated Stalino fell in flanking moves rather than by direct assault.

This new victory followed upon Moscow's announcement that the Red armies had killed more than 420,000 Germans, wounded 1,080,000 and captured 38,600 in taking back at least 30,000 square miles of occupied territory since July 5.

Stalino, a city of about 500,000

(See RUSSIA—Page 14)

ALLIED CHIEFS WAITED WORD OF SURRENDER

Both F. D. and Churchill Obviously Knew Terms; Capital Jubilant.

WASHINGTON, Sept. 8—(AP)—President Roosevelt was seated at his momento-crowded desk in the White House offices and Prime Minister Churchill of Great Britain was busy elsewhere in the executive mansion when the world heard today that Italy had capitulated.

Both obviously had known the news for some time, since the terms were agreed upon last Friday. But from neither of the leaders was there immediate formal comment.

It was "big stuff" elsewhere. Suppressed excitement was evident among the White House staff when news dispatches gave the story to a jubilant American capital.

Secretary Stephen Early rushed into the Presidential offices with the dispatch and reported later that Mr. Roosevelt commented calmly:

"It is General Eisenhower's story. Let him tell it."

Churchill Stayed Over

The word was also conveyed to Churchill, whose reasons for tarrying in the American Capital so long after the Quebec conference now became apparent. Obviously awaiting the surrender announcement at any moment, Churchill and Mr. Roosevelt conferred into the late hours last night and were together again this morning.

Secretary of State Hull likewise withheld a statement when he held his press conference soon after the announcement.

Reports that "a break" were imminent spread through Washington last night and formal announcement of the Italian surrender brought enthusiastic expressions concerning a final victory for the United Nations from many leaders on Capitol Hill.

Comment included:

Seen "Cheerful News"

Rep. Bloom (D-NY) chairman of the House Foreign Affairs committee: "It is very very cheerful

(See CHIEFS—Page 14)

REBMAN ENDORSES BOND DRIVE PLAN

The Lancaster County War Activities program through which funds are raised to publicize local war drives in the Lancaster Newspapers and Sunday News, was endorsed yesterday by Earl F. Rebman, chairman of the Salvage Committee of Lancaster County.

"I think the program was a very good step," Rebman said. "It is good business and a sensible practice to have one method of collecting money and distributing the funds to publicize the various war activities."

Through the program manufactures, retailers, and professional men are given an opportunity to contribute on the basis of ten cents per employee per month to finance the local war drives, such as salvage collection, war bond drives, black markets, etc.

Italy's Value to Axis Was As A "Nuisance"

By RICHARD G. MASSOCK
(Chief of the former Home Bureau of the Associated Press)

WASHINGTON Sept. 8. —(AP)— An Italian people broken in morale by bombs and defeats on land sea and in the air capitulated to Allied might today to lop off the weakest Axis partner but leave for the moment unanswered:

How much Italian soil will the Nazi forces of Hitler attempt to hold? What of the future of the Balkans?

Italy's capitulation announced from North Africa by Gen. Dwight D. Eisenhower probably shortened the war some and undoubtedly will have an enormous phychological effect on Germany and her satellites.

Won Major Battle

Italy's surrender means the United Nations have won a major battle in the global war with the fighting that lies ahead likely to be long and bitter before the Germans and the Japanese in their turn surrender.

Italy for a long time especially since Benito Mussolini's downfall on July 25 has had little but nuisance value to her Axis partners in the war. That nuisance value is now lost.

Italy was unprepared for war when the Nazi attack on Poland brought it about in September 1939. After Italy was thrust into the fray on June 10 1940 when the mirage of a German victory dazzled Mussolini she lasted just three years two months and 29 days.

During nine months of non-bel-

(See VALUE—Page 10)

Lost & Found — Page 15

Italians Ordered To Quit Opposing Allies Everywhere

By EDWARD KENNEDY

ALLIED HEADQUARTERS IN NORTH AFRICA, Sept. 8--(AP)--Gen. Dwight D. Eisenhower today announced unconditional surrender of Italy in the greatest knock-out victory for Allied arms in four years of war.

Simultaneously, the Italian government ordered its troops to drop the fight against Allied forces, but to "oppose attacks from any other quarter."

Russia as well as the United States and Britain approved the granting of the armistice, Eisenhower announced.

It was signed in Sicily last Friday--on the very day that Italy was invaded--and Italy, accepting all the terms, agreed that it would become effective "at a moment most favorable for the Allies."

"That moment has now arrived," an official statement declared.

Italy will be obliged to "comply with political, economic and financial conditions" which the Allies will impose later.

Simultaneous announcement by the Allies and the Italian government was agreed upon in view of "the possibility of a German move to forestall publication of the armistice" by the Italians, headquarters said.

Hitler's "European fortress was cracked, the way was opened for new offensives, the course of World War II" immeasurably shortened.

Eisenhower called on the Italians to join the Allies in helping to eject the Germans from their country, and promised that all who do so will have the "assistance and support of the United Nations."

Marshal Pietro Badoglio's proclamation for the Italian armed forces to cease fighting but oppose attacks "from any other quarter" was closely related to this.

(In New York the FCC short wave listening post heard Badoglio broadcast his proclamation in person, in an address to the Italian people at 1:45 P. M., Eastern War Time. At that time the German and Japanese radios had made no announcement of the surrender.)

(CBS heard the Allied headquarters radio in Algiers broadcasting a message from Eisenhower to the Italian fleet. It admonished commanders of Italian ships to "take heed that you do not scuttle your ships or allow them to be captured." Those in the Mediterranean were advised to sail if possible to Gibraltar, Tripoli, Malta, Haifa, Alexandria or Sicily. Those in the Black Sea were told to sail to a Russian port.)

Surrender of Italian armed forces "unconditionally" was made by the government of Marshal Pietro Badoglio, successor of Benito Mussolini, the architect of Fascism.

Thus the Casablanca "unconditional surrender" ultimatum received its first application.

Announcing the brilliant news, Eisenhower, who led the Allied triumph in Tunisia and Sicily as well, declared:

"The Italian government has surrendered its armed forces unconditionally.

"As Allied commander-in-chief, I have granted a military armistice, the terms of which have been approved by the governments of the United Kingdom, the United

(See ITALY—Page 10)

Red Roses Hailed Among City's Greatest Baseball Teams

Sports

Blackout Helped To Save Our Red Roses; York Fan Lost $900 On Final Tiff. Crowd Sets New Record.

by GEORGE W. KIRCHNER

WINNING WITH THE ROSES . . . You've heard of boxers being saved by the bell, but it's ten, two and even that it's something new for a baseball team to be saved by—(of all things)—a blackout.

Yet, this is what happened with our Red Roses last night, and of the 7,267 fans who paid their way into Stumpf field, 7,266 agreed that the blackout played a big part in giving our boys a chance to comeback . . . The other guy was the fellow who stole the second-base bag and he, of course, couldn't be found . . .

The b. o. figured insofar as it cooled off Jim Walsh, the York pitcher who seemed to be just as fast as he was the first night here and all of us remember how he tamed our Roses then.

But after that hour's rest during which time Manager Woody Wheaton decided to relieve his starting pitcher, Jackie McClure, our side collected its power and decided then and there to use it at the earliest possible moment . . .

And that, of course, was just as soon as the lights came on . . . Then the boys really went to work and before the interrupted fourth inning could be completed, they had four runs across and were once again back on even terms . . .

Those two runs in the sixth put it on ice, but credit must be given the Yorkers for putting up such a stiff struggle, right up to the last man and last pitch in the ninth . . .

But then Bunny Griffiths and his boys were tough all the way through. They were supposed to be the weak-sisters of the four teams in the playoffs, but they changed that quickly by knocking off Hagerstown in three out of four . . .

Even then the fans wouldn't rate them with our side, and especially after our boys polished off Wilmington the way they did in that final game. But this opinion also changed with the first two games, and when the Yorkers took a 3 to 1 lead, why the thing became downright alarming . . .

However, that's when the Wheatonites really came back and that victory in York on Saturday night was just what the doctor ordered. They came back here to tie it up in a 14-inning struggle on Sunday and then went on to such a fitting and thrilling climax as that which they uncorked last night . . .

Speaking of doctors, the medicos were needed in the Roses' dressing room, too, for Johnny Greenwald, the first sacker, played the last game with a temperature of 101, suffering with the grippe, while Steve Sefick's middle finger was swollen three times its normal size . . .

But the way these guys got around, no one ever suspected but that they were anything but a couple of healthy young specimens . . . And that's just as well, too, for had the crowd known their condition, they would have had even more to worry about, and, as it was, York provided us with enough headaches . . .

That was a great series for us to win and a great way to finish it, but for one certain York fan it goes down as a costly one . . . This gentleman put up $900 against $300 that York would win, the bet being made when the White Roses were leading by 4 to 0.

Imagine how he felt when the Roses tied it up in the fourth, but don't try to think how he must have felt when it was all over . . . After all, a guy losing that kind of dough is entitled to exclusive rights to his moaning . . .

But if he moaned, the crowd cheered and so, for that matter, did the officials from Arthur Ehlers, the president, on down . . . It was the largest gathering ever to see an Inter-State League game and it is a figure which will long stand.

However, breaking records is nothing new for the Roses . . . At least five times this year they shattered the mark for Stumpf field attendance and every one thought that when they drew 5,987 paid customers on Sunday, that the peak was reached . . .

But you just couldn't stop that loyal mob of rooters, and last night they turned out in such numbers that their attendance there will go down on the record books not only as the greatest collection ever to see a playoff, but as a tribute to a team which they regard as one of the greatest assembled . . .

Manager Griffiths was not feeling too gay after it was all over, but Bunny's a No. 1 sportsman and he was among the first to congratulate Wheaton and his boys . . .

"It was a tough series to lose," he remarked, "but we lost it to a great team and that's something to remember."

And that's just one more statement which goes to show what a fine fellow Griffiths really is. York fans can well be proud of him, and the York management can well be satisfied with his piloting. He put a team that, on paper, at least, had no right to be there, right into the playoffs, and then inspired that club to put up one of the bitterest fights in the League's history. More than that no man can do.

But wasn't it great to win, and where were you during the blackout?

P. S.:—Woody Wheaton's glove, which was stolen during the dark period, was returned, but young Eddie Stumpf is still looking for that second base.

They Gave Lancaster The Inter-State League Championship

Presenting the Red Roses of 1943 who last night clinched the Governor's Cup in the Inter-State League playoff by nosing out York, 6 to 5. The Roses also won the League championship during the regular campaign.

In the picture, front row, left to right: Mark Hoskins, Brick Hoffner, Bill Rocap, trainer, Woodie Wheaton, playing manager, Vick Males and Irving Levy. Middle row: George Kell, Lou Flick, Tommy Peiffer, Billy DeMars, Steve Sefick, George Armstrong and Pat DeFelice. Back row: Edward Stumpf, owner of field, Charles Bowles, Lew Krausse, Paul Newell, Steve Gerkin, Johnny Greenwald, Jack McClure and William Cowdrick, business manager.

Say Three Local Players Brought $25,000

Kell, Wheaton, Flick Are Sold To Athletics

Although officials of both the Red Roses and Philadelphia Athletics refused to divulge the price paid for Manager Woody Wheaton, George Kell and Lou Flick, three local players who were sold to the A's, it was reported today that the amount was close to $25,000.

The only indication of the price which came out of authoritative quarters was that "it was considered to be the highest price ever paid for a Class "B" ball player," but the official statement refused to list which one of the three was the prize.

Kell Looks Like Prize

However, local fans have known for a long time that George Kell, the third baseman, who led the Inter-State League's batters with a terrific .396 average was the most sought-after player in the League, and it was assumed by nearly every one that Kell was the player referred to in the statement.

Business Manager Bill Cowdrick refused to talk price, as did owner Norman McClain, but both agreed that the A's parted with more money than did the Pittsburgh Pirates when they put up $20,000 for Billy Cox, the kid shortstop of two seasons ago.

This statement served to support the report that the price tag on the three reached nearly $25,000, although nothing was said about the amount paid to the Roses for pitcher Major Bowles, who joined the A's last week and pitched his first victory—(a 9 to 4 decision over the St. Louis Browns)—yesterday:

Kell Must Go Home

Kell will be with the A's for only today. He was ordered to report back to his Swiften, Ark., home last week in order to resume his school-teaching job, but asked for an extension of time to finish the playoffs here. He was granted only a short leave, so his stay with the Macks will be held to today's game with St. Louis. He's planning on returning to Lancaster tomorrow to pack his things and start for home.

Wheaton and Flick, however, are likely to finish the season although Flick seemed anxious to get back to his Tennessee home. Lou's sale came as a surprise, for while the fans felt all along that both Kell and Wheaton would go to the A's, there were few who included the ace-right fielder in the deal.

Mack Buys Six

The three Roses were three of six players acquired yesterday by Connie Mack, who parted with four. In the deals, Mack secured Jo-Jo Moore, veteran outfielder from Indianapolis in exchange for Roberto Estallella and cash; pitcher Luke Hamlin from Toronto in exchange for pitcher Orie Arntzen and cash; pitcher Norman Brown from Louisville for third-baseman Eddie Mayo and outfielder Johnny Welaj.

Last week, Mack bought second-baseman Joe Rullo, outfielder Bill Burgo and catcher Tony Parisse from Wilmington, and later, Major Bowles from the Roses.

BASEBALL'S BIG SIX

By The Associated Press

BATTING (Three leaders in each league)

Player and Club	G	AB	R	H	Pct.
Musial, Cardinals	150	600	106	215	358
Herman, Dodgers	146	558	72	184	300
Appling, White Sox	150	565	58	181	320
Witek Giants	146	594	64	188	317
Elliott, Pirates	151	565	80	179	317
W Cooper, Cardinals	119	435	51	138	317
Hodgin, White Sox	112	288	51	121	312
Wakefield, Tigers	149	611	87	188	308

RUNS BATTED IN

American League		National League	
York, Tigers	111	Nicholson, Cubs	122
Etten, Yankees	105	Elliott, Pirates	97
Johnson, Yankees	93	Herman, Dodgers	92

HOME RUNS

American League		National League	
York, Tigers	33	Nicholson, Cubs	28
Keller, Yankees	31	Ott, Giants	18
Stephens, Browns	20	Northey, Phillies	16

ALLEY BABBLE

LESTER FLEMING gave the boys in the Overlook "12" League something to shoot at last night when he came through with a 258 single and went on to a 594 triple . Ollie Morrison and Wilmer Gingrich grabbed 233 singles with Gingrich racking up 580 triple and Clem McElligott getting 220 and 586..

Bill Heist was the big gun in the Church League with his 234 single and 557 triple, while Newswanger's 211 and 542 ran next..Bill Shertz's 224 and Vic Butz' 215 featured the Armstrong Aircraft circuit..

Two 600 scores were posted at St. Joe with Polly Eckman getting 615 and Johnny Wendel 610...Single honors went to J. Eshbach, who had 232...Amos Shuman's 213 and 580 topped the Fulton Major League..

Maud Houghton joined the Ladies 200 club by grabbing a nifty 212 to pace the Hamilton girls...Maud went on to 524 triple with Hilda Baumler getting 512..Nice going, girls..

Bernie Kinderman's 234 and 576 featured the Y. M. C. A. "A" League where Doc Sam Appleyard made the 5-7-10 pin split...

Ed Mowrer, captain of the Elks team in the Elks duckpin league, set two high individual marks in a match last night. He rolled a 223 high single and a 566 triple as his team won three points from Charity.

Helen Artigiani hit 199 and 509, while Viola Harnish knocked off 516 and Irene Grossman 194 to feature the Retail Ladies League ...Hilda Baumler's 169 and Ann Sheaffer's 464, together with Edith Groft's upset of the 5-10 pin split, topped the Women's Sunday League..

Ruling Shows Baseball Is Not Essential

By JUDSON BAILEY
Associated Press Sports Writer

Major League baseball, fagged from a long, rough run, is wobbling toward the finish line and will just about make it before wilting completely.

The season this year, extending a week later than in the past because spring training was done in the North, has reached an anti-climax. With both pennants decided the fans apparently are thinking about the World Series, the players about their draft status and the managers about teams made up of 17-year-olds for next year.

The war manpower commission's ruling yesterday that baseball is not essential scarcely was a surprise. It had been said before in various versions, but this latest pronouncement on the specific case of Al Zarilla of the St. Louis Browns, a pre-Pearl Harbor father who had been classified 1A by his draft board, pointed up the problem anew.

Pilots Look For Players

Baseball's present player supply would dissolve soon, even if the season didn't. To meet this situation the managers of almost all clubs except the New York Yankees and St. Louis Cardinals, who are tuning up for the World Series next week, have turned the last week of the season into a wholesale tryout camp for new recruits.

Everybody expects baseball to continue next year, but the fans don't seem to care whether it continues this week or not.

At Cincinnati, where the Reds are striving to sew up second place in the National League, 767 customers paid to see Clyde Shoun pitch a five-hit 3-2 victory over the Phillies yesterday.

At Boston 714 fans, the smallest turnout since Tom Yawkey bought the ball club 11 years ago, was on hand as the Detroit Tigers routed the Red Sox 6-3.

Only 908 See Cards

Only 908 were present at St. Louis to see Lefty Ernie White test his lame pitching arm against the Boston Braves. As it turned out he was fast, but lacked control, and gave up ten hits while winning 6-3.

The Yankees beat the Cleveland Indians, 5 to 2, while the Chicago White Sox were outhit in both games of a twilight-night whipped the Washington Senators twice by identical scores of 2-1.

Bowles Beats Browns

The Athletics lost their 100th game of the year while dividing a doubleheader with the St. Louis Browns, winning the first game 9-4 and then dropping the second 7-6. Charles (Major) Bowles, up from Lancaster, was the winner in the opener, spacing out seven St. Louis hits.

Ace Adams broke the 1908 record of Ed Walsh by appearing in his 67th game of the season for the New York Giants, but the Chicago Cubs won 10-9.

CAUGHT 1914 SERIES

Boston —(AP)— Major Hank Gowdy, the first major leaguer to enlist in World War I, caught all four games as the Miracle Braves swept the 1914 Series against the Athletics. Gowdy batted .545, collecting six hits in 11 at bats.

Cards Re-sign Southworth To 1944 Contract

ST. LOUIS, Sept. 28—(AP)—Manager Billy Southworth's signature on the 1944 Cardinal contract comes under the heading of least unexpected news of the week.

For extension of Billy the Kid's contract yesterday—salary terms not disclosed—comes just a week before the world champion Red Birds try for their second crown.

Started In 1940

One of the last players to join the Cardinal's first championship team in 1926, Southworth came from the farm club to succeed manager Ray Blades in June, 1940. He lifted the team out of a slump into third place behind Cincinnati and Brooklyn, and trailed only the Dodgers at the close of the 1941 season.

Last year he demonstrated a memorable reliance in players by pushing them at a terrific pace sufficient to overcome a 10½ game lead in August. Carried over into the series, their spurt gave them four consecutive games to the Yankee's one. The Cards set a new record 10 days ago by annexing their league pennant again, after winning the World Series last year.

The only shutout in last year's series was pitched by Ernie White, who may be needed desperately next week in the Yankee stadium.

Great Finish, Boys

York	AB	R	H	O	A
Biros cf	4	0	0	3	1
Gracey 2b	5	1	2	1	2
Shoff 3b	3	0	1	1	1
Kinard lf	3	1	2	1	0
Griffiths ss	2	1	0	3	2
Schaedler 1b	4	1	1	5	1
Moran rf	4	0	1	1	0
Daniels c	4	1	2	9	0
Walsh p	3	0	2	0	0
xCampbell	1	0	0	0	0
Maricka p	0	0	0	0	0
Totals	33	5	11	24	7

Lancaster	AB	R	H	O	A
DeMars ss	5	1	3	2	2
Kell 3b	4	0	2	1	0
Flick rf	4	0	1	4	0
Wheaton cf	4	0	0	6	0
Levy lf	4	1	3	0	0
Greenwald 1b	4	0	0	6	0
Males 2b	2	0	0	1	1
Sefick c	2	2	1	6	2
McClure p	1	0	0	0	2
Hoffner 2b	3	2	2	1	1
McCrabb p	2	0	0	0	1
Totals	35	6	12	27	9

x—Batted for Walsh in 8th.

YORK	010 300 001—5
LANCASTER	000 402 00x—6

Errors—Greenwald, Walsh. R. B. I.—Moran, Daniels, Biros, DeMars 3, Kell 2, Kinard. Two base hits—Levy, Hoffner, DeMars, Kell, Gracey, Kinard. Sacrifices — Griffiths, Kinard. Stolen bases — Biros, Daniels. Double plays—Gracey to Griffiths to Schaedler. Left on bases—York 9, Lancaster 8. Base on balls—Off McClure 4, Walsh 3, McCrabb 1. Struck out—By Walsh 7, Maricka 2, McClure 3, McCrabb 2. Hits—Off McClure in 4 innings 6; off Walsh in 7 innings 11. Wild pitches—Walsh 3. Passed ball—Sefick. Winning pitcher—McCrabb. Losing pitcher—Walsh.

Umpires — King, Dzigan and Tatler.

Batting Leaders Appear Headed For 1943 Titles

NEW YORK, Sept. 28—(AP)—Threading through the final days of the Major League season, Stan Musial of the St. Louis Cardinals and Luke Appling, of the Chicago White Sox are about to move unmolested into the batting championships.

Musial, whose average has been rising from week to week down the stretch, brought it up to .358 yesterday, two points higher than a week ago and far out of reach of his closest pursuer, Billy Herman of the Brooklyn Dodgers, who has a .330 mark.

Appling Holds On

Appling, slipping from .324 to .320, is not so far in front of his teammate, Ralph Hodgin, but has a reasonable chance of maintaining his present eight point lead.

Hodgin, a late starter in the batting race, has been at bat 388 times and must go over 400 to be recognized by the American League.

The ten leaders in each league:

AMERICAN LEAGUE

Player and Club	G	AB	R	H	PCT.
Appling, Chicago	150	565	58	181	.320
Hodgin, Chicago	112	388	51	121	.312
Wakefield, Detroit	149	611	87	188	308
Cramer, Detroit	137	592	78	174	.294
Curtright, Chicago	133	468	64	136	.291
Case, Washington	139	606	101	176	.290
Fox, Boston	126	488	55	141	.289
Johnson, New York	148	562	69	161	.286
Cullenbine, Cleve.	131	464	60	132	.285
Higgins, Detroit	135	513	60	145	.283

NATIONAL LEAGUE

Player and Club	G	AB	R	H	PCT.
Musial, St. Louis	150	600	106	215	.358
Herman, Brooklyn	146	558	72	184	.330
Witek, New York	146	594	64	188	317
Elliott, Pittsburgh	151	565	80	179	317
W Cooper, St. Louis	119	435	51	138	317
Nicholson, Chicago	146	579	86	179	.309
McCormick, Cin	119	449	57	136	303
Vaughan, Brooklyn	142	584	112	176	301
Walker, Brooklyn	131	513	78	152	.296
Gustine, Pittsburgh	107	396	38	116	.293

FIGHTS LAST NIGHT

By The Associated Press

WASHINGTON—Holman Williams, 158, Chicago, outpointed John Garner, 165, Washington (10).

NEWARK—Joe Carter, 158, Rome, N. Y., outpointed Tommy Mollis, 150, Baltimore (10).

WEST SPRINGFIELD, Mass.—Ossie Harris, 159, Pittsburgh, Pa., outpointed Freddie Cabral, 154, Cambridge, Mass., (8).

BALTIMORE—Bobby Ruffin, 136, New York, outpointed Al Guido, 135, New York (10).

NEW HAVEN, Conn.—Bobby McIntyre, 136, Detroit, outpointed Julie Kogon, 133½, New Haven, Conn. (10).

PROVIDENCE, R. I.—Verne Patterson, 151½, Chicago, outpointed Jerry Fiorello, 146, New York, (10).

PHILADELPHIA—Terry Young, 137¾, New York, outpointed Cleo Shans, 134, Los Angeles (10)

CHICAGO—Corp. Lou Woods, 155, Detroit, stopped Eugene Simmons, 160, Indianapolis (8).

STANDINGS OF THE TEAMS

National League

Teams	W.	L.	P.C.
St. Louis	99	48	.673
Cincinnati	82	65	.558
Brooklyn	78	68	.534
Pittsburgh	78	71	.523
Chicago	69	77	.473
Boston	65	80	.448
Philadelphia	62	87	.416
New York	55	92	.374

American League

Teams	W.	L.	P.C.
New York	94	53	.639
Washington	82	67	.550
Cleveland	78	69	.531
Chicago	78	71	.523
Detroit	74	74	.500
St. Louis	71	76	.483
Boston	67	81	.453
Philadelphia	47	100	.320

YESTERDAY'S GAMES

National League

Cincinnati 3, Philadelphia 2.
St. Louis 6, Boston 3.
Chicago 10, New York 9 (13 innings).
Other clubs not scheduled.

American League

Philadelphia 9, St. Louis 4 (1st).
St. Louis 7, Philadelphia 6 (2nd).
Detroit 6, Boston 3.
New York 5, Cleveland 2.
Chicago 2, Washington 1 (1st).
Chicago 2, Washington 1 (2nd), (night).

International Playoff

Syracuse 2, Toronto 0 (Syracuse leads best of seven games series, 3 games to two).

Eastern Playoffs

Scranton 10, Elmira 2 (Elmira leads best of seven games series, 3 games to two).

Pacific Coast Playoff

San Francisco 5, Seattle 4 (San Francisco wins series, 4 games to two).

TOMORROW'S GAMES

National League

Philadelphia at Cincinnati (night)
Boston at St. Louis
Brooklyn at Pittsburgh
New York at Chicago

American League

Cleveland at Washington (twilight and night)
Detroit at Philadelphia (2)
Chicago at New York (2)
St. Louis at Boston (2)

7267 Fans See Locals Climax Uphill Battle By Nipping York, 6-5

By GEORGE W. KIRCHNER

WITH both the Inter-State League's pennant and Governor Cup in their possession, the Red Roses of 1943 were being hailed today as the greatest baseball team ever to represent Lancaster, even surpassing the 1940 combine that won the League's playoff championship, and with some going so far as to place them on a par with the Tri-Staters of old, whose diamond feats still hold a memorable spot in the annals of local baseball.

The Red Roses won the right to such high esteem by putting on one of the greatest uphill battles in the history of the Inter-State League, coming from behind by two games to tie up the final series with York and then going on to climax their fight by nosing out the White Roses, 6 to 5, here last night.

7,267 See Final

Exactly 7,267 fans, the largest number ever to see a League game in any city, cheered wildly as the Roses, trailing, 4 to 0 going into the last-half of the fourth, came out of the darkness of an hour's blackout to tie the score in their half of that inning and then go on to get two more runs for Lester McCrabb, who, as the relief pitcher, was officially credited with the deciding victory.

And with the cheers of the crowd still ringing in their ears, the Roses today broke up with three of them headed for tryouts with the Philadelphia Athletics, and six of them being recalled by their parent-clubs, leaving only nine players here to form the nucleus for another team next year. But with the war going on even these boys are in the doubtful class and owner Norman McClain was prepared to rebuild from the ground up.

3 Go To Athletics

Playing Manager Woody Wheaton, third baseman George Kell and right fielder Lou Flick were sold to the A's in a deal announced just before the start of last night's game, while pitcher Les McCrabb was recalled by Montreal; pitcher Jackie McClure, who started the final tiff, was called back by Kansas City and pitcher Lew Krausse, who was kept out of the playoffs by an operation, was recalled by Scranton.

The New York Yankees put in their bids by having Norfolk recall Johnny Greenwald, the first-sacker, and Binghamton recall Vic Males, the shortstop-second-baseman. Billy (The Kid) DeMars, the sensational shortstop who played such a big part in his short stay here, will have to go to Durham, owned by the Brooklyn Dodgers.

Nine Are Owned Here

This leaves the Roses with captain Brick Hoffner, who looked like the proverbial million in his comeback last night, Irv Levy, the left fielder whose contract was bought from Little Rock, together with Steve Sefick, the catcher, Steve Gerkin, the pitcher, Tex, Kardow, Paul Newell and young Tom Peiffer, three other pitchers, as well as Mark Hoskins, utility infielder and George Armstrong, second string catcher. But of these Gerkin has already been drafted and goes into the Army soon, while Sefick is due to return to his war job and the "kids" are expecting Uncle Sammy to nod any day now. Pat DeFelice, another pitcher, passed his physical two weeks ago, while Major Bowles, another pitcher, joined the A's last week.

Thus is the team scattering, but before they left, the Roses provided Lancaster's legion of baseball fans with so many thrilling diamond incidents that they'll be talking about them long after the snows cover the ground.

York Put Up Fight

Nosing out Wilmington, three games to two in the semi-final series, the Roses were heavily favored to take York, which had surprised everyone by knocking off hard-hitting Hagerstown in three out of four. But the White Roses soon changed this complexion by taking the first two games and even though our boys won the third contest, their position was not improved any when York came here and beat McCrabb, who had twice stopped the slugging Blue Rocks.

This put the White Roses ahead at three games to one as they carried the series back to York on Saturday night, but it was then that Manager Wheaton's boys rallied their forces and managed to win a thriller 9 to 8.

Then with 5,987 fans in Stumpf field, the Roses went 14 innings on Sunday to nip their rivals, 4 to 3 and get back on even terms. Last night they came from behind to win, but while they actually paid off on this one, every last member of the team agreed that it was Saturday's victory that really paved the way for the ultimate triumph.

"I knew that if we won that game on Saturday, we'd go on to win the pennant," Steve Sefick, the veteran catcher, remarked.

That's the way most of the other fellows felt and Manager Wheaton agreed.

"The boys had a tough struggle all year," the manager commented, "but they proved that they could come through when the chips were down. We had to fight to win the League championship; we had a tough time with Wilmington and then, finally, we had to come from behind to beat York. It was a terrific season and I'm glad we were able to pull it out of the fire. This was a great ball club and every man deserves a lot of credit."

Visitors Take Lead

York started out with Jim Walsh opposing Jackie McClure and when the visitors from across the river got to McClure for six hits and four runs in the first four innings, while Walsh's fast-ball kept our side in check, things looked mighty dark, indeed.

Then came the real blackout darkness out of which emerged a more determined Roses team . . . a team that had seemingly regained its full power in the dark and having regained it, unleashed it with a vengeance.

The score stood 4 to 0 favor York when Irv Levy who had three-for-four, stepped to the plate to lash out a double, starting the fourth inning. Johnny Greenwald and Vic Males fanned, but the Roses proved their rating of being "the best two-out club in the League" by rallying with two men down. Levy reached home on two wild pitches as Sefick was given a base on balls. Manager Wheaton put Captain Hoffner in to bat for McClure and the red-head lashed a double to centerfield. It was an easy triple, but it fell into the crowd out there and was held to a double by ground rules, keeping Sefick on third.

DeMars Comes Through

With two men on base, DeMars lashed one to right that was also held to a double and two more runs were scored. Kell then came through with his second hit—another double—and the score was tied.

You knew then that the Roses had regained their power, but it was not until the sixth that they finally pushed ahead. This time, Sefick started it by walking, Hoffner beat out a sacrifice to the pitcher and both runners advanced on Walsh's wild throw to first. Again DeMars came through and his single sent Steve across. Kell blasted one to deep center and while Biros made a great catch to rob him of a hit, the blow knocked in the sixth run.

Struggle In Ninth

Meanwhile, McCrabb, who had taken over after the blackout, had the Yorkers under control, but it was not without a struggle that he finally retired them in the ninth.

Sports Of All Sorts

By GEORGE W. KIRCHNER

PUTTING ONE WORD AFTER THE OTHER . . . And you'll be interested to know that the St. Joe C. C. is planning on coming back with amateur boxing . . . Right now the Hillians are trying to line up a card and hope to be able to present it before too many weeks slip by . . . Speaking of St. Joe, the club is likely to lose its president for Richard (Red) Danz is taking his local physical examination today and if he passes, it won't be long now . . . If you thought Steve Gerkin looked pretty good out there on the mound for the Red Roses, you ought to see him in his soldier's uniform . . . Looks the berries . . . Steve was inducted last Thursday and was back in town to pitch Sunday . . . Received a week-end pass from New Cumberland, so he came down here along with Lynn Myers, Chuck Harig and Ducky Detweiler, who also played for the Minor Stars . . .

Vic and Mrs. Males remained in town and both are now working at RCA. . . Irv Levy's doing his chores at Armstrong. . . Jerry Watts and Bertie Flick, who worked at Stumpf field all year, took time off to see two games of the World Sereis in New York last week. . . And both came back convinced that they had seen better baseball with the Red Roses. . . Maybe they have something there, at that. . . It's our conviction that Johnny Greenwald was a better first sacker than Nick Etten of the Yanks. . . And since Greenwald is owned by the Yankees, we can't understand why they don't move him up. . . It can't be because he's not a slugger, for Etten wasn't hitting the size of his hat-band on the days we saw him, and as for fielding, Johnny looks so much better. . .

Woody Wheaton, now the property of Connie Mack, is headed for the middle-aisle. . . He'll marry Helen Butler, of this city, Saturday. . . Add other Lancastrians to see the New York games of the series: Bill Cowdrick, business manager for the Red Roses, who, like the two girls, refused to be impressed by the type of baseball exhibited. . . And Freddy Jeffries also came back saying he'd just as soon see the Red Roses. . . Hook Mylin, who doesn't like this idea of loafing during the football season, is still in touch with Washington concerning some sort of war

job. . . Mike Santaniello, former Gettysburg guard—(and a great one, too)—is now a Lieutenant in the Army and headed upwards. . . He's Bernie's brother. . .

Nud Geraci, former well-known local ball player, is back from overseas, where he's in charge of a physical training class. . . He's a corporal and says he came up with unbeaten basketball, track and baseball teams. . . "They matched us against the English," Nud related, "and we beat the pants off them in everything." . . Expects to get back real soon, and hopes to stay in the Army after it's all over. . . Phil Stumpf, son of the owner of Stumpf field, is home from California on his first furlough. . . Looks better than ever. . . Vinnie Danz surprised his mother and brothers and sisters by accompanying his wife home from Florida. . . He's back in the south now after a pleasant visit with his young daughter. . .

Outside of football, Hugh McCullough's favorite sports are fishing and hunting, and the assistant grid coach at F. & M. takes advantage of every free moment to dip his line in county streams. . Hopes to do some hunting around here this fall . . . His wife, he says, is just as enthusiastic over the two sports and he's already telling his eight-months-old daughter all about the thrills of each . . . Walter Miller, the WGAL manager, took his father-in-law, a resident of Canada, to his first football game, and Walter's son Wayne reminded Grandpa to be sure to root for F. & M. as that was the surest way of being with a winner . . . As it resulted, the youngster was right for Grandpa saw the Dips beat Bucknell's Bisons last Saturday in Lewisburg . . . That our town has cooled off on baseball is proved by the fact that the Negro All Stars vs. Minor League Stars drew 1,200 paid in Trenton Sunday a week ago and less than 500 here last Sunday . . . Of course, the boys hit cool weather here and were also bucking the World Series, two factors which certainly helped reduce the crowd considerably . . . As it resulted, the promoters suffered at the gate . . . But it's time to dunk a doughnut.

La Motta Scores Quick TKO Over Walker

PHILADELPHIA, Oct. 12—(AP)—Jake LaMotta uncorked a terrific left hook that floored Johnny Walker in the first round of their scheduled 10-round bout at Convention Hall last night.

The bell saved Walker at the count of six, and he might as well have quit then, for LaMotta was given a technical knockout after 53 seconds of the second round.

It was LaMotta's first boxing appearance in his native city. Walker is a home town boy. LaMotta had a weight advantage of nine and a half pounds at 164. A crowd of 5,428 sat in.

Lee Oma, 185, Detroit, scored a technical knockout over Willie Thomas, 210, Philadelphia, at the end of the third round of the semi windup.

Dusty Wilkerson, 173, Philadelphia, technically knocked out Nat Paragine, 174, New York, in one minute and 42 seconds of the fourth round of the opening bout.

Tommy Bell, 145 1-4, Youngstown, O., won an eight round decision from Harold Smith, 148, Philadelphia, in the second bout.

Boss Congratulates Winning Pitcher

Boss Joe McCarthy gives Spud Chandler his blessing after Spud's pitching helped the Yankees win the World Series. All are happy players in the Yankees' dressing room, but standing next to Chandler, with a big grin, is Bill Dickey, hero of the final game.

Notre Dame Ranks First In Football

Irish Top Poll With Crisler Hailing Team as Best in History

NEW YORK, Oct. 12—(AP)—Ninety-nine of the nation's football writers agree with Coach Fritz Crisler of Michigan that Coach Frank Leahy of Notre Dame was enjoying a bit of under-statement when he termed his present team as only "fair."

BERTELLI

The scribes, voting in the Associated Press' second weekly poll of 1943, rated Notre Dame as the best team in the country with 86 of the writers unhesitatingly marking them as No. 1. None ranked them lower than third.

Crisler, who had a disheartening sideline study of the Irish Saturday, was quoted at Ann Arbor as saying "that it is by far the best Notre Dame team I have ever seen."

Notre Dame, triumphant by a 35 to 12 score over the Wolverines, collected only half of the first place votes in the inaugural poll last week but skyrocketed to 87 per cent this week after trouncing the tabulation's erstwhile second team.

Praises Bertelli

Crisler intimated that much of the Irish success this season should be credited to Angelo Bertelli, quarterback who reports to the Marines on Nov. 1.

"I've seen many quarterbacks who were fine ball carriers but none who could make the ball disappear and then turn up somewhere else like Bertelli," Crisler told newsmen after Saturday's game. "He's a magician and in my estimation he is better than Sid Luckman."

When Bertelli—who passed for two touchdowns, set up a third with passes, plunged for a fourth and converted all five of the Irish markers against Michigan—leaves for Parris Island at the end of this month he will be accompanied by Herb Coleman, center of the tough Rambler line.

Michigan, second last week, skidded to ninth place in the present voting with Army taking over the runner-up slot and Navy third.

Pennsylvania, Purdue, Duke, Iowa Pre-Flight and Southern California all ranked above the Wolverines and College of the Pacific grabbed the tenth rung. The far westerners, coached by Amos Alonzo Stagg, displaced idle Minnesota in the top ten.

The leading elevens with point totals (First place votes in parenthesis):

FIRST TEN

Notre Dame (86)	941	Duke	370
Army (1)	847	Iowa P.-F.	325
Navy (1)	669	South Cal.	309
Penn (1)	408	Michigan	273
Purdue	398	C of Pacific	125

Second Ten—Del Monte Pre-Flight (6) 124, March Field (4) 110, Minnesota 109, Great Lakes 70½, Memphis Naval Air Technicians 51, Dartmouth 48½, Southwestern 34, Texas A. and M 13, Washington 9, Georgia 8.

Also Rans—Tulsa 6, Colorado College 6, Missouri 6, Texas 5, Georgia Tech 4, Indiana 4, Texas Christian 2, Tulane 2, Ohio State 1, Randolph Field 1, North Carolina 1.

Duke Choice Over N. Carolina As Other Grid Powers Coast

By HARRY GRAYSON

NEW YORK, Oct. 12 — With the other haves picking on have nots or resting and marshalling their forces for big things ahead, national interest this week turns to the old neighborhood feud between North Carolina and Duke in Durham.

Wisconsin doesn't belong on the same lot with Angelo Bortolo Bertelli and his slingshot and Notre Dame. Penn State is just good enough to give Navy a workout. Red Blaik will have to put Oregon boots on young Ralph Davis and other backs to keep Army's score down against Columbia. Pennsylvania uses Lakehurst Naval as sparring partner.

Following the pasting by Notre Dame, Michigan requires a rest and the following week hopes to salve its feelings by beating Minnesota for the first time in 11 years. Dartmouth is also taking a day off.

So we travel to the Tobacco Triangle for the game of the afternoon and find the ancient backyard battle one of Navy V-12s, trainees supplementing Duke's holdovers coming from Georgia, Mississippi State and Wake Forest and new Tar Heels hailing from Alabama, Mississippi and North Carolina State.

Duke Is Long on Backs

After beating the Camp Lejeune Marines, 40-0; Richmond, 61-0; and North Carolina Pre-Flight, 42,0, Duke was made a slight favorite over vaunted Navy and lost little prestige in scoring with two minutes left to play and losing by the margin of the point after touchdown.

North Carolina righted itself after being pounced upon by Georgia Tech right at the start, proved itself by whacking Penn State, 19-0, and Jacksonville Navy, 23-0.

The teams are always up for a renewal of a series dating back to 1888, and the selection is Duke because its line matches that of North Carolina and the Blue Devils have more and better backs.

In other Dixie engagements, North Carolina Pre-Flight again takes it on the whiskers — from Camp Davis this trip, Wake Forest shades North Carolina State, Georgia Tech marches on against Fort Benning, Georgia figures to get over Daniel Field and Georgia Pre-Flight should not encounter too much trouble in Newberry. Memphis Navy's armament is too heavy for Louisiana State, Maryland gets a shaky vote over West Virginia and V. M. I. the call over Richmond.

Bucklings Overmatched

In the east, Cornell should successfully hurdle Holy Cross, but the Big Red will know it has been in a football game. Colgate shoved Rochester all over the field once and can do it again. Villanova should take the decision from Bucknell and Temple gets back into what is its own league these days and should dispose of Ursinus.

In the midwest, Ohio State's amazing Bucklings run into another team too big and experienced for them in Purdue in Cleveland, but will make their usual fine showing. Having found themselves against Wisconsin, Illinois' freshmen are likely to repel Pittsburgh. It's Northwestern over Great Lakes and Minnesota over Camp Grant in the Golden Gophers' final prep for Michigan. Clever Punchy Hoernschmeyer and Indiana have it on Iowa.

Iowa Pre-Flight with former professional Frank Maznicki in its backfield packs too many weapons for Missouri as Don Faurot directs against the school he rebuilt as a football power. This easily could be Iowa State's year against Nebraska and Kansas should win from Washburn.

In the southwest, Texas A. & M. is given a narrow margin over Texas Christian. The same goes for Tulsa against Oklahoma and Rice against Southern Methodist. Texas takes Arkansas in stride. Southwestern figures to shellack the North Texas Aggies. Oklahoma A. & M. should defeat Norman Naval.

California Disappoints

Disappointing California finally should get somewhere against U. C. L. A. Southern California remains boss of the Pacific coast in its match with San Francisco. Amos Alonzo Stagg's little College of the Pacific should keep up the good work against Del Monte Pre-Flight and Saint Mary's should win from the Alameda Coast Guard.

In the Rockies, Colorado College should smack Colorado Mines. Colorado should repulse Deming Air, but Denver may be attempting to unwrap too big a package in Fort Riley.

Now you're on your own.

Explains Early Closing of Duck Season in State

HARRISBURG, Oct. 12—(AP)—Director Seth Gordon of the State Game Commission said today the wild duck season in Pennsylvania was advanced 20 days this year to give sportsmen in the northwestern section a better break.

The season, fixed by the Federal government on recommendations from the commission, opened Sept. 25 and continues to Dec. 3, conforming with Ohio's season, but ending 20 days earlier than that in New Jersey.

Complaints Received

"There has been a bit of complaint from Delaware river hunters over the change," explained Gordon, who added the commission believed, however, the new season benefiitted the greatest number of Pennsylvania sportsmen.

He said hunters in northwest Pennsylvania and northeast Ohio in other years had to be careful they did not cross an imaginary line in Lake Erie and thus violate the law, while hunters in eastern Pennsylvania on the Delaware river did not face such difficulties because the boundary is well-defined.

Some Like Change

"Many of the Delaware river hunters like the change, though, since it gives them a longer season in which they can hunt. After Pennsylvania's season closes, they can go over into New Jersey and hunt there," Gordon added.

Hunters are allowed a daily bag of 10 ducks, but can shoot only three redheads, three buffleheads or three of those species combined and one wood duck a day.

Records Favored Cards, But Yanks Won

ST. LOUIS, Oct. 12.—(AP)—Well, it's all over . . . the New York Yankees are in as World Champions — and the 1943 series just goes to show there is no stable measure for comparing seasonal records before the classic starts.

The St. Louis Cardinals topped the Yankees during the season in just about every department—except home runs—which leads to pushing across those pay-off counters. They led by some 24 points in team batting, held a .976 to .974 advantage in team fielding.

And yet what happened in this series?

The blasting bombers backed up splendid hurling by both out-hitting and out-fielding the impotent Redbirds.

The National League Club just couldn't get the extra base blows when needed, but look what well-placed hits meant to the Bombers:

The deciding punch in the third game was a triple by Bill Johnson with the bases loaded. In the fourth contest, a double by Joe Gordon followed by Bill Dickey's single gave the Yanks a leading run. And later in the game Marius Russo's double placed him in position to score on a sacrifice and long fly.

Everyone knows the championship was won in the fifth meeting by Dickey's two-run circuit smash.

The Cardinals left 37 men stranded on base for lack of power at the

plate, only five short of the record set in five-game series by the Yankees in 1941.

The Cardinals were so helpless when scoring opportunities presented themselves in the first innings of the final contest that one Yankee follower volunteered the suggestion, "maybe somebody should try for a field goal.

You can't stop the Army department: When Murry Dickson relieved Max Lanier, it was the first time, so far as is known, that a soldier flashed his stuff in a World Series. Uncle Sam gave the slender hurler a special leave to be with the Cards during the World Series. If he had just brought along some heavy artillery . . .

Said Mort Cooper: "That home run pitch to Dickey was a fast inside ball across his chest. It was just what I meant to throw expect I intended it around his hips."

was perfect. Just where I wanted it."

Cardinal Centerfielder Harry Walker and Rookie Pitched Alpha (Bet) Brazle undoubtedly wish the series was still going on, but they would have been otherwise engaged today anyway. They reported for induction at Jefferson Barracks this morning.

The Redbird managament is letting a lot of dough slip through its fingers—but of necessity . . refunds to holders of tickets marked game No. 6 will be started Saturday morning.

And there is all that mazoola gone to waste on tickets already prepared for sale for the seventh game . . . optisism is a wonderful thing.

Bill Veeck, Milwaukee baseball team president, was nicked for $160 by the quick finger boys before he could bargain for their act to be booked in his Brewer Stadium.

Once there were two roommates, Billy Southworth, manager of the Cardinals, and Luke Sewell, St. Louis Browns manager. They shared the same apartment, one being on the road while the other stayed home . . . and do you know, Sewell didn't once tip off Southworth to the power of those Yankees? He had reasons to know of it . . . the Yanks trampeld the

Fellow Yankees congratulate Bill Dickey after he knocked out a homer in the sixth.

ALLEY BABBLE

THE boys in the Fulton Major League were in there bombing away like the Yankees last night with Dick Grossman getting high single of 233, while Bill Sidler put together 228-200-216 for 644 and high triple honors... Grossman added 188 and 179 to his high and finished with an even 600, tying Walt Coble, who had 204-215-181 for his 600.

Lloyd Eshelman hit 225; L. Webb 220 and Ernie Moser, F. Bennawit and Karl Ferrari each turned up with 215s..

Ed. Heltshe's 212 and 611 paced the St. Joe boys with Ed Schaller getting 225 and 592 and Frank Rottmund 214 and 586..

J. Kurtz and Lou Hogarth each grabbed 225s, but Charley Greener hit 612 for high honors in the Church League, finishing one pin ahead of Kurtz's 611... R. Newswanger's 570 also figured, while Ted Bixler of Grace, made the 7-9 pin split..

Bud Sullenberger was in top form in the Overlook 12 League with his 198-246-181 — 625, while Gene Daugherty had 221 and W. Gingrich 212... Charley Eshelman got his first big score of the year with a 212..

The boys in the YMCA "A" League came up with some nifty scores, paced by Bob Mowrer, who had 242 and 591, while Dick Hess had 215 and 585, Ferguson 224; Kraybill 222; Paul Schaffstall 213 and Doc Eby 210..

H. Shoff's 217 and 576 took top honors in the P. & L. League where Bob Groh made the 5-6 split twice in succession and Jerry Sullivan hit the 6-7-10 pin split..H. Shoff had 217 and 576 and G. Regar 214 and 560 with Schanerberger getting 550..John Eichelberger's 213 and Dan Dicely's 535 topped the Mac It League..

Polly Granger gave the gals in the Retail Ladies League something to shoot at last night when she hit a nifty 217, while Marie Leisey was right behind with 201 and Bea Sharpe came up with 197.. Janet Nolan's 515, Helen Ashmead's 513; Granger's 510 and Sharpe's 509 led in triples..

Erla Witmer's 186 and Kathryn Huss' 505 paced the Watch Girls with Erla getting the 5-7 pin split... Bea Rinehart's 177 and 478 topped the women, while Ed Lapham's 235 and 575 topped the men in the Monday Night Mixed League..

Schell Loft Wins

The Progressive Pigeon Club of Lancaster flew its first 200 mile young bird race of the 1943 series from Amherst, Virginia, on Sunday,

Loft	Entry	Arrival	Yds. per Minute
Schill	10	2:50-04	929.96
Stettler	4	2:51-30	929.02
Glick	8	2:50-47	928.47
Ursprung	8	2:50-58	928.20
Abel	7	2:56-12	925.26
Boxleitner	17	2:53-00	921.69
Dorwart	7	2:56-57	920.72
Meyer	9	3:40-26	836.84
Gilmartin	6	4:05-45	791.86
Dommell	6	No report	
Behmer	7	No report	
Scheid	7	No report	

The birds will be shipped for a second 200-mile race to Amherst, Virgania next week.

Win Tennis Match

Mexico City.—(AP)—Pancho Segura of Ecuador and William Talbert of Cincinnati, Ohio, top-seeded doubles team in the second Pan-American tennis tournament, won their first round match Monday against stubborn opposition.

The pair, winners of the first Pan-American tournament last year, subdued Octavio and Flavio Martinez, hard-hitting Mexican brothers, 6-3, 7-5, 4-6, 6-3.

FIGHTS LAST NIGHT

By The Associated Press

PHILADELPHIA—Jake Lamotta, 164, New York, stopped Johnny Walker, 154½, Philadelphia, (2).

SCRANTON, Pa.—Danny Devlin, 175, Allentown, Pa., knocked out Teddy Brown, 172½, New York (5).

NEW HAVEN, Conn.—Julie Kogon, 133, New Haven, stopped Sammy Rivers, 137 Mexico City (6)

BALTIMORE—Holman Williams, 156, Detroit, outpointed Joe Carter, 156, Rome, N. Y. (10).

NEWARK—Pvt. Clint Conway, 179½, Cleveland, outpointed Bobby Jacobs, 173, Philadelphia (10)

WASHINGTON—Georgie Parks, Washington, knocked out Nap Mitchell, Philadelphia (5) (heavyweights).

SAN FRANCISCO—Jack Chase, 157, Walsenburg, Colo., outpointed Paulie Peters, 161, San Francisco, (10).

CHICAGO—Al Gomez, 134½, Chicago outpointed Jimmy Joyce, 132, Gary, Ind (12), Lindy Elliott, 213, New York, knocked out Charley Roth, 195, Detroit

Facts and Figures

By The Associated Press

Final standing:

	W.	L.	P.C.
NEW YORK (A.L.)	4	1	.800
ST. LOUIS (N.L.)	1	4	.200

First game (At Yankee Stadium):

	R.	H.	E.
ST. LOUIS	2	7	2
NEW YORK	4	8	2

Lanier, Brecheen (8) and W. Cooper; Chandler and Dickey. Attendance—68,676

Second game (At Yankee Stadium):

	R.	H.	E.
ST. LOUIS	4	7	2
NEW YORK	3	6	0

M. Cooper and W. Cooper; Bonham, Murphy (9) and Dickey. Attendance—68,578.

Third game (At Yankee Stadium):

	R.	H.	E.
ST. LOUIS	2	6	4
NEW YORK	6	8	0

Brazle, Krist (8), Brecheen (8) and W. Cooper; Borowy, Murphy (9) and Dickey. Attendance—69,990 (record).

Fourth game (At St. Louis):

	R.	H.	E.
NEW YORK	2	6	2
ST. LOUIS	1	7	1

Russo and Dickey; Lanier, Brecheen (8) and W. Cooper. Attendance—36,196.

Fifth game (At St. Louis):

	R.	H.	E.
NEW YORK	2	7	1
ST. LOUIS	0	10	1

Chandler and Dickey; M. Cooper, Lanier (8), Dickson (9) and W. Cooper, O'Dea (5). Attendance—33,872.

FINANCIAL FIGURES

Fifth game:

Paid attendance	33,872
Gross receipts	$148,910.00
Commisioner's share	$22,336.50
Each club's share	$31,643.37
Each league's share	$31,643.37

Five-game totals:

Paid attendance	277,312
(Record for 5-game series)	
Gross receipts	$1,105,784.00
Players share	$488,005.74
Commissioner's share	$102,079.80
Each club's share	$76,831.24
Each league's share	$76,831.24
x-War Relief	$208,373.48

x-All receipts of the third and fourth games, after deduction of the players' share, go to the War Relief and Service Fund, Inc., which also received the $100,000 paid for radio broadcasting rights.

The players share in the receipts of the first four games only, while the Commissioner's office, the competing clubs and the two leagues share in the first and

Crosetti Is Hero In Yankees' Tenth World's Championship

By SID FEDER

ST. LOUIS, Oct. 12—(AP)—The scattered pieces of the busted St. Louis Cardinal bubble were being swept up for shipment to the nearest museum today as Frankie Crosetti was handed the bouquets and half a dozen Redbirds tried on sets of goat horns from the late lamented World Series.

One and all agreed no blockbuster ever went off any louder than the explosion of the Cardinal myth in this year's fall classic. When the New York Yankees wound it up on Bill Dickey's homer to win 4 games to 1 for the tenth World Championship in their history, the Cards were as well beaten as the parlor rug in spring house-cleaning—the same Cards, mind you, who had been built up as the runningest, fightingest, never-say-dyingest collection to come down the pike in quite a piece.

It was a nice fairy tale the St. Louis not-so-swifties had written by taking the 1942 series—about how they were the most sure-footed, sure-hitting, sure everything around; about how they never beat themselves. It was a nice fairy tale while it lasted, but the ending had a new twist. Instead of the old "they lived happily ever after" tag line, this one wound up with "we were only kidding."

Club Beat Itself

If ever a club beat itself, this year's Cardinals fit the picture. Mostly, they missed Terry Moore and Enos Slaughter in the outfield. After the second game, last Wednesday, which Mort Cooper won with a magnificent competitive performance, they folded up like a straw hat that's been sat on. As running specialists they were practically stationary. They appeared to be only going through the motions in the fourth game on Sunday. And in yesterday's convincer they had Spud Chandler on the ropes in six of nine innings, yet failed to throw a big punch and were put on ice for keeps by a 2-0 score on ancient Dickey's two-run sixth inning homer, which gave him a record of having been on eight series winning clubs since 1928.

And while the Cards were collapsing all over the place like pins in a bowling alley, the Yankees reminded the folks that when you're talking about teams that don't beat themselves, the bombers are better than green hands. They may have been over-confident last year, but they went at it like business men in this set. The result was while the not-so-swifties were making errors that cost them two games, and almost ruined a third, the Yanks got to the paying teller's window for the seventh time in eight series tries since 1932.

Dickey Among Heroes

Dickey was right up there in the voting for the series hero's spot, because in addition to catching five tough games, he got four of his five hits with men on bases and three of the four brought ducks home off the pond. So was Joe Gordon up there, for his first game homer and his all-around second-base magic; and Rookie Bill Johnson, whose bat was the loudest of them all, and Spud Chandler who chalked up two pitching victories.

But the majority of the boys and girls, while well divided on which Card was the No. 1 goat, pointed to the old guy at short, Frank Crosetti of the San Francisco Crosettis as the top hero. He's 33 and before the series one fellow said he was so banged up they had to tie him together with strips of tape and little pieces of wire. In fact, he wasn't supposed to be a Yankee regular at all this year, but Joe McCarthy finally had to send out the alarm for him to take over.

Supposed To Be Weak

So he did. And going into the series, the smart boys said shortstop was the weak link. Well, chums, it was weak like Joe Louis. Frankie's base running was the big factor in the first game win. He scored one of the runs in the losing second game. He was one of the key men in the big five-run eighth inning that won the third game—the batter the Cards had to walk with one away and runners on first

FRANK CROSETTI

and third so they'd have a play at any base.

His stop back of second on Walker Cooper's hit in the eighth inning of the fourth game, and the way he held Stan Musial at second on the play, was the big break of the tilt—the spot Manager McCarthy said was the turning point of the game. And yesterday he came up with three chances he had absolutely no right to get to haul Chandler out of the stew. He hit in four of the five games, scored in three, and was a defensive brick wall.

His Last Series

He told a couple of pals before the series that he expected this was going to be his last fall classic. Well, he bowed out with the bells ringing.

Generally, the series was a dull affair. It set a new attendance record for a five-game fuss by drawing 277,312 through the turnstiles, including the all-time one-game high of 69,990 who saw last Thursday's scramble in New York. And it paid off the players on a record pool of $488,005.74, from which each Yankee received $6,123.20 and each Cardinal $4,321.99. But for the customary series thrills and chills, it was strictly in waltz-time—no jumping jive.

NEW YORK (AL)	ab	r	h	o	a	ST. LOUIS (NL)	ab	r	h	o	a
Cros'ti ss	4	0	1	0	5	Klein 2b	5	0	1	3	1
Meth'y. rf	5	0	1	1	0	Garms lf	4	0	0	1	0
Lindell rf	0	0	0	0	0	Musial rf	3	0	0	1	0
John'n 3b	4	0	1	1	2	W C'per c	2	0	1	6	0
Keller, lf	3	1	1	1	1	O'Dea c	2	0	2	2	0
Dickey, c	4	1	1	7	0	Kur'ski 3b	4	0	2	3	3
Etten, 1b	3	0	1	11	1	Sanders 1b	3	0	1	7	2
Gord'n 2b	2	0	0	6	6	Hopp cf	4	0	0	1	0
Stain'k cf	3	0	1	0	0	Marion ss	3	0	1	2	3
Ch'dler p	3	0	0	0	2	M C'per p	2	0	0	0	1
						z-Walker	1	0	1	0	0
Totals	31	2	7	27	17	Lanier p	0	0	0	0	1
						Dickson p	0	0	0	1	0
						zz-Litw'ler	1	0	1	0	0
						Totals	34	0	10	27	11

z—Batted for M. Cooper in 7th.
zz—Batted for Dickson in 9th.

NEW YORK (AL)	000	002	000	—2
ST. LOUIS (NL)	000	000	000	—0

Runs bated in—Dickey 2. Home runs—Dickey. Sacrifices—Garms, Marion, Chandler, Stainback. Double plays—Crosetti, Gordon and Etten; Klein, Marion and Sanders. Earned runs—New York (AL) 2, St. Louis (NL) 0. Left on bases—New York (AL) 9; St Louis (NL) 11. Bases on balls—Off Chandler 2, (Musial, Sanders); Off M. Cooper 2, (Etten, Gordon), Off Lanier 2, (Keller, Gordon), Off Dickson 1 (Crosetti). Strikeouts—By M. Cooper 6 (Crosetti, Metheny, Johnson, Keller, Dickey, Chandler); By Chandler 7 (M Cooper, Musial 2, Hopp, Garms, Klein 2); By Lanier 1 (Metheny). Pitching summary: M Cooper 5 hits 2 runs in 7 innings; Lanier 2 hits no runs in 1 1-3 innings; Dickson, no hits, no runs in 2-3 innings; wild pitches—M Cooper. Losing pitcher—M. Cooper. Time—2:24. Attendance—33,872.

Composite Box Score

St. Louis—(AP)—Composite box score of the five games of the 1943 World Series:

NEW YORK YANKEES

Player	G	AB	R	H	2B	3B	HR	RBI	BB	SO	Pct.	PO	A	E	Pct.
Stainback rf-cf	5	17	0	3	0	0	0	0	0	2	.176	7	1	0	1.000
Crosetti ss	5	18	4	5	0	0	0	1	2	3	.278	9	16	3	.893
Metheny rf	2	8	0	1	0	0	0	0	0	2	.125	3	0	0	1.000
Johnson 3b	5	20	3	6	1	1	0	3	0	3	.300	2	9	1	.917
Keller lf	5	18	3	4	0	1	0	2	2	5	.222	10	1	0	1.000
Gordon 2b	5	17	2	4	1	0	1	2	3	3	.235	20	23	0	1.000
Dickey c	5	18	1	5	0	0	1	4	2	2	.278	28	3	0	1.000
Etten 1b	5	19	0	2	0	0	0	2	1	2	.105	46	2	1	.980
Lindell cf-rf	4	9	1	1	0	0	0	0	1	4	.111	8	0	0	1.000
Chandler p	2	6	0	1	0	0	0	0	0	2	.167	0	4	0	1.000
Bonham p	1	2	0	0	0	0	0	0	0	0	.000	0	0	0	.000
Borowy p	1	2	1	1	1	0	0	0	0	1	.500	2	0	0	1.000
Russo p	1	3	1	2	2	0	0	0	1	1	.667	0	2	0	1.000
xx-Stirnweiss	1	1	1	0	0	0	0	0	0	0	.000	0	0	0	.000
Murphy p	2	0	0	0	0	0	0	0	0	0	.000	0	1	0	1.000
x-Weatherly	1	1	0	0	0	0	0	0	0	0	.000	0	0	0	.000
Totals		159	17	35	5	2	2	14	12	30	.220	135	62	5	.975

x—Batted for Bonham in eighth inning of second game.
xx—Batted for Borowy in eighth inning of third game.

ST. LOUIS CARDINALS

Player	G	AB	R	H	2B	3B	HR	RBI	BB	SO	Pct.	PO	A	E	Pct.
Klein 2b	5	22	0	3	0	0	0	0	1	2	.136	10	13	2	.920
yyy-Walker cf	5	18	0	3	1	0	0	0	0	2	.167	10	0	2	.800
Musial rf	5	18	2	5	0	0	0	0	2	2	.278	7	2	0	1.000
W. Cooper c	5	17	1	5	0	0	0	0	0	1	.294	28	3	2	.939
Kurowski 3b	5	18	2	4	1	0	0	1	0	3	.222	8	8	2	.889
Sanders 1b	5	17	3	5	0	0	1	2	3	4	.294	42	5	0	1.000
Hopp cf	1	4	0	0	0	0	0	0	0	1	.000	1	0	0	1.000
yyyy-Litwhiler lf	5	15	0	4	1	0	0	2	2	4	.267	11	0	0	1.000
Marion ss	5	14	1	5	2	0	1	2	3	1	.357	7	14	1	.955
Lanier p	3	4	0	1	0	0	0	1	0	0	.250	0	3	1	.750
Brecheen p	3	0	0	0	0	0	0	0	0	0	.000	0	2	0	1.000
M. Cooper p	2	5	0	0	0	0	0	0	0	3	.000	0	1	0	1.000
Brazle p	1	3	0	0	0	0	0	0	0	1	.000	1	2	0	1.000
Krist p	1	0	0	0	0	0	0	0	0	0	.000	0	0	0	.000
Dickson p	1	0	0	0	0	0	0	0	0	0.	.000	1	0	0	1.000
z-Garms lf	2	5	0	0	0	0	0	0	0	2	.000	1	0	0	1.000
zz-O'Dea c	2	3	0	2	0	0	0	0	0	0	.667	2	0	0	1.000
zzz-Demaree	1	1	0	0	0	0	0	0	0	0	.000	0	0	0	.000
y-White	1	0	0	0	0	0	0	0	0	0	.000	0	0	0	.000
yy-Narron	1	1	0	0	0	0	0	0	0	0	.000	0	0	0	.000
Totals		165	9	37	5	0	2	8	11	26	.224	129	53	10	.948

z—Batted for Lanier eighth inning of first game.
zz—Batted for Kurowski ninth inning of second game.
zzz—Batted for Lanier seventh inning of fourth game.
y—Ran for Demaree 7th inning, fourth game.
yy—Batted for Brecheen 9th inning, fourth game.
yyy—Batted for M. Cooper 7th inning, fifth game.
yyyy—Batted for Dickson 9th inning, fifth game.

PITCHING SUMMARY

NEW YORK (A)

	G	CG	IP	H	R	ER	BB	SO	WP	HB	W	L	Pct.	ERA
Chandler	2	2	18	17	2	1	3	10	0	0	2	0	1.000	0.50
Borowy	1	0	8	6	2	2	3	4	0	0	1	0	1.000	2.25
Russo	1	1	9	7	1	0	1	2	0	0	1	0	1.000	0.00
Bonham	1	0	8	6	4	4	3	9	0	0	0	1	.000	4.50
Murphy	2	0	2	1	0	0	1	1	0	0	0	0	.000	0.00
ST. LOUIS (N)														
M. Cooper	2	1	16	11	5	5	3	10	1	0	1	1	.500	2.81
Lanier	3	0	15⅓	11	5	3	3	13	1	0	0	1	.000	1.80
Brazle	1	0	7⅓	5	6	3	2	4	0	0	0	1	.000	3.86
Brecheen	3	0	3⅔	5	1	1	3	3	0	0	0	1	.000	2.25
Krist	1	0	0	1	0	0	0	0	0	0	0	0	.000	0.00
Dickson	1	0	⅔	0	0	0	1	0	0	0	0	0	.000	0.00

COMPOSITE SCORE BY INNINGS

NEW YORK (AMERICAN)	000	405	062	—17
ST. LOUIS (NATIONAL)	011	510	100	—9

Earned runs—St. Louis, 7; New York, 12. Stolen bases—Crosetti, Marion, Keller. Sacrifices—Kurowski, W. Cooper, M. Cooper, Garms, Marion, Crosetti, Stainback 2, Chandler. Double plays—St. Louis, 4 (Klein, Marion and Sanders, 2; Marion, Klein and Sanders, 2); New York 3 (Gordon, Crosetti and Etten; Crosetti, Gordon and Etten, 2). Left on bases—St. Louis, 37; New York, 30. Interference—W. Cooper (Metheny 6th inning, second game). Times of games—first, 2:07; second, 2:08; third, 2:10; fourth 2:06; fifth 2:24. Attendance by games—first, 68,676;

Omission of 'Surrender' Terms In Pact Praised
—Editorial Page

LANCASTER NEW ERA

WEATHER
Light rain and warmer tonight; Tuesday cloudy and cooler.

VOL. 66—NO. 625 | Entered as second class matter January 31, 1924, at the Post Office at Lancaster, Pa., under the Act of March 3, 1879. Reg. U. S. Pat Off. | LANCASTER, PA., MONDAY, DECEMBER 6, 1943 | CITY EDITION | 18 PAGES | 20c PER WEEK—4c Per Copy

'BIG 3' ANNOUNCE PACT TO SMASH GERMAN ARMY FROM THREE SIDES

BRITISH REACH MORO RIVER, 5TH ADVANCES

Allies Push Nearer Rome; Soviet Advance Perils 3 Key Cities

By the Associated Press

The British Eighth Army drove to the banks of the Moro river less than 14 miles from the Adriatic port of Pescara while the American Fifth Army captured more Italian heights west of Mignano, commanding the road to Rome, Allied headquarters in Algiers announced today.

Russian armies pounding ahead in the worst snowstorms this year in White Russia threatened Mogilev, Zhlobin and Rogahev. The Germans were reported showing signs of lacking reserves. Several strongpoints in the Dnieper bend south of Kremenchug were taken and Nazi attacks in the Cherkasy area were thrown back. The Germans said the Russians were attacking violently in the by-passed Crimea, and had broken through south of Cherkasy.

Russia Warns Finland

As the Russian armies drove on, Moscow applied new pressure on Germany's satellites of Finland, Hungary and Rumania to quit the war. The magazine "War And The Working Classes" told the puppets that to "delay their withdrawal from the Hitlerite coalition will seriously worsen their fate."

The fighting in Italy was declared to resemble the bitter hand-to-hand combat at Verdun in the last war. The Germans reinforced their swaying line at the Moro, ten miles beyond the Sangro, with a regiment of 90th tank grenadiers, and launched a very strong counterattack which was repulsed in blood west of Venafro.

Supporting the Eighth Army advance, British destroyers bombarded the coastal supply route between Pescara and Giulianova and between Ancona and San Benedetto, sinking three German coastal craft.

In the Aegean, British submarines were credited with sinking 16 supply ships in recent forays.

Allies Bomb Salonika

Allied bombers strongly attacked the Greek harbor of Salonika and the Yugoslav harbor of Split. Bad weather curtailed most aerial operations.

The Fifth Army by-passed German strongpoints inland from the Mediterranean to carve out their new gains. Three commanding elevations were taken in the Maggiore and Camino mountain areas. The Germans were employing at least nine divisions in the Central Italian battle lines, with two others drawn back for rest.

Nazis Pushed To Balkans

Across the Adriatic, Marshal Josip Broz's Partisans said fresh German and Bulgarian reserves, including two divisions from Austria, had been thrown into the irregular Balkan fighting.

King Peter of Yugoslavia denounced the provisional government established by the Partisans and accused the Allies of stimulating its creation.

BOY, 13, IS JAILED 30 YRS. IN SLAYING

POUGHKEEPSIE, N. Y., Dec. 6.—(AP) — Thirteen-year-old Edwin Codarre, who pleaded guilty to second degree murder in the rape-slaying of a ten-year-old girl, was sentenced today to 30 years to life in Sing Sing Prison. Dutchess County Judge J. Gordon Flannery told the boy, attired in long pants for the first time since the beginning of the trial:

"I feel I must protect you and society from another such vicious attack. You will have to pay for what you have done."

Codarre, New York city schoolboy, changed his plea Nov. 23 from innocent to an indictment charging first degree murder in the slaying of Elizabeth Boigt.

JAPS SAY 100 U.S. PLANES HIT MARSHALLS

Tokyo Claims 20 "Carrier Based" Bombers Were Shot Down

By the Associated Press

American bombers struck at Japan's defense perimeter along an ever-widening line of aerial attack which the Tokyo radio reported included a raid yesterday by 100 carrier-based Allied planes on the Japanese-held Marshall Islands in the Central Pacific.

The Nipponese, in turn, carried out their first bombing mission against Tarawa and Makin islands since American capture of the Gilberts. They wounded three men and inflicted minor damage on Tarawa. There was no damage on Makin, the Navy's report said.

Japs Also Fail On Ground

On the ground, too, the Japanese failed in counterattacks seeking to throw back advancing Australians on the Huon peninsula in Northeastern New Guinea. In China, the Chinese High Command said Japanese forces in Northern Hunan province had been defeated.

Big American Liberators made their deepest recent strike at guardian bases of the Japanese empire in three raids on Hare island in the Kapinga-Marangi atoll 800 miles northwest of Guadalcanal and only 400 miles south by east of Truk, Japanese bastion in the Pacific. The latest attack, Dec. 2, smashed seaplane base installations of the little banana-shaped island.

Japs Claim 20 Raiders

Army Liberators bombed Mili in the Marshalls and Nauru, 500 miles west of the Gilberts, Saturday without encountering any enemy opposition. The Tokyo radio, in reporting new Allied raids on the Marshalls yesterday, asserted that 20 of the 100 raiders were shot down. It quoted the Japanese imperial headquarters as admitting some damage.

The broadcast claimed that Japanese naval fliers had pursued the Allied task force and had sunk one medium-sized aircraft carrier and a large cruiser. Two other ships were said to have been damaged. There was no Allied confirmation of the reported raid nor of the "sinkings."

Knox Sees Biggest Battles

In Washington, Secretary of the Navy Knox expressed the opinion that some of the heaviest naval fighting of the war probably will come next year.

"It is believed that 1944 will find the United States naval service

(See PACIFIC—Page 4)

4 OBJECTORS PLEAD INNOCENT IN COURT

PHILADELPHIA, Dec. 6—(AP)—Four Lancaster county men pleaded innocent in U. S. District Court today to charges of failure to report for induction. Their trials were set for next week before Judge George A. Welsh.

The defendants were sentenced to long prison terms last year on charges of failure to obey their draft board orders to report to conscientious objectors' camps. They were released shortly thereafter in the expectation they would be reclassified as "essential farm workers." Their classifications have not been changed.

They were boked as Ivan Weaver Leid, twenty-four; Mahlon Stauffer Martin, twenty-six; Amos Souder Shirk, twenty-five, all of New Holland, and Weaver Weber Shirk, twenty-seven, of East Earl.

WALLET WITH $40, PAY-CHECK STOLEN

Mrs. Dorothy K. Frey, 437 W. Chestnut St., reported to city police today the theft of a wallet containing $40 in cash and a $19.60 pay check from a muff-purse while she was at the American Legion Home, N. Duke St., Saturday night.

As Principals of the "Big 3" Powers Met in Iranian Capital

Joseph Stalin (left), Russian Premier, sits with President Franklin D. Roosevelt of the United States and Prime Minister Winston Churchill (right) of Great Britain, on the porch of the Russian Embassy at Teheran, Iran, during their four-day conference. This picture is released by the War Department in Washington. (12th Air Forces photo.)

DUCE EXECUTED CIANO, IS REPORT

Shot in Back as Traitor By Firing Squad, Swiss Hear

COUNT CIANO

LONDON, Dec. 6 — (AP) — Count Galeazzo Ciano, the 40-year-old son-in-law of Benito Mussolini, was executed this morning—shot in the back by a firing squad—according to unconfirmed reports reaching here from the Swiss border.

Executed As "Traitor"

This latest ironic twist to the Italian upheaval was reported both by Reuters and the Swiss Telegraph Agency which said the former Italian Foreign Minister, whose meteoric career was upset when he had a falling out with his father-in-law, had been sentenced to death by a special court of Mussolini's Republican Fascist government sitting in Northern Italy to try "traitors."

The life of the 40-year-old Count was a story-book tale of a rise to right-hand man to Mussolini in the hey-day of Fascism, of great popularity, prestige and wealth, and then, when the regime was tottering, a break with his father-in-law.

By last October, Mussolini's former affection for his esteemed son-in-law had changed until "his only feeling for him is sheer hate," Marshal Pietro Badoglio reported.

Voted Against Mussolini

For Ciano, at the last and fateful meeting of the Fascist grand council on the night of last July 24 was one of 19 members who voted in favor of Mussolini's resignation. Five voted for the Duce.

There was another reason for

(See CIANO—Page 4)

Christmas Ghost-Story To Make You Tingle

The Haunted Man, or The Ghost's Bargain, by Charles Dickens, starts today on Page 12 of The New Era.

Read the day-by-day account of a man who bargained with a ghost to forget his past! Written almost a century ago by the author of the well-loved Christmas Carol," this story answers a question still vital to human happiness.

Text Of Iran Declaration

LONDON, Dec. 6—(AP)—Following is the text of the declaration of President Roosevelt, Prime Minister Churchill and Premier Stalin at the conclusion of their Teheran conference:

We, the President of the United States of America, the Prime Minister of Great Britain and the Premier of the Soviet Union, have met these four days past in this capital of our ally Iran and have shaped and confirmed our common policy. We expressed our determination that our nations shall work together in the war and in the peace that will follow.

As to the war, our military staffs have joined in our roundtable discussions and we have concerted our plans for the destruction of the German forces. We have reached complete agreement as to the scope and timing of operations which will be undertaken from the East, West and South.

The common understanding which we have here reached guarantees that victory will be ours.

Sure of Enduring Peace

And as to the peace, we are sure that our concord will make it an enduring peace. We recognize fully the supreme responsibility resting upon us and all the United Nations to make a peace which will command the good will of the overwhelming masses of the peoples of the world and banish the scourge and terror of war for many generations.

With our diplomatic advisers we have surveyed the problems of the future. We shall seek the co-operation and active participation of all nations, large and small, whose peoples in heart and mind are dedicated, as are our own peoples, to the elimination of tyranny and slavery, oppression and intolerance. We will welcome them as they may choose to come into a world family of democratic nations.

Pledge Relentless Attacks

No power on earth can prevent our destroying the German armies by land, their U-boats by sea and their war plants from the air. Our attacks will be relentless and increasing.

From these friendly conferences we look with confidence to the day when all the peoples of the world may live free lives untouched by tyranny and according to their varying desires and their own consciences.

We came here with hope and determination. We leave here friends in fact, in spirit and in purpose.

200 PUPILS AID IN CITY STORES

Work Part-time to Relieve Labor Shortage During Yule Rush

Over 200 pupils of McCaskey High School started part-time work today in city retail stores, to help relieve the manpower shortage during the Christmas rush period. They have been granted leave of absence from classes in the afternoons, and more applications are coming in, according to Mrs. Mary B. Myers and Ernest S. Kilgore, deans at McCaskey.

This is the first year that the School Board has granted requests for early dismissal from school in order to ease the employe shortage. Part-time workers reported to jobs today, leaving school at 1 p. m. Half-day absence will be granted for those whose lessons will not be jeopardized from today through Dec. 17, and full-day absence may be taken from Dec. 20 through Dec. 22, when the regular Christmas vacation starts.

Of the pupils who have already started work, the majority are girls who will work in department stores and other retail stores. They include fifteen-year-olds and up.

(See PUPILS—Page 4)

3 MORE ADDED TO CASUALTY LIST

City Soldier Missing In Action; Lititz Man Reported Killed

Three more local soldiers have been reported casualties of war, and a fourth, previously listed as missing in action, is a Nazi prisoner, according to dispatches received here.

Hergenrother

Cpl. Richard P. Hergenrother, Lancaster, is the latest local man listed as missing in action.

Pvt. Oscar Weitzel, Lititz, R4, who had been missing in action, has been reported killed.

Pvt. Gordon Yingst, Lititz, has been wounded.

Pvt. Albert Emmerich, Lancaster, previously listed as missing, is a German prisoner.

Went Overseas Nov. 1

Mrs. Bertha Miller Hergenrother, wife of Cpl. Hergenrother, was informed by the War Department

(See DEAD—Page 4)

"BIG 3" MATCH PARTY TOASTS

Show Mutual Admiration At Birthday Dinner Given by Churchill

TEHERAN, Iran, Nov. 30.—(Delayed)— (AP) —President Roosevelt, Prime Minister Churchill and Premier Stalin matched eloquence tonight in a demonstration of mutual admiration as the British Prime Minister, at an enthusiastic birthday dinner he gave himself eased into his 70th year amid the exhilarating applause of his two fellow statesmen.

Stalin, who set the key to the evening's atmosphere, breezed into the British legation talking freely through an interpreter to the assembled guests, removed his great coat and lifted a glass to friend Churchill.

The dinner-jacketed Churchill, a ubiquitous, ebullient host, shepherded his guests into dinner in the victorian setting of the legation dining room. Thirty-four sat down around the long mahogany table under the stern gaze of Queen Victoria who looked down from one wall. From the other wall there looked down the sympathetic countenance of Edward VII. Roosevelt sat on Churchill's right and Stalin on Churchill's left.

Five-Star Guest List

Churchill's five-star gcest list, besides Roosevelt, who was the first to arrive, and Stalin, who was the last included Harry L. Hopkins, the President's official adviser; Foreign Secretary Anthony Eden; Admiral Sir Andrew B. Cunningham, chief of the British

(See BIG 3—Page 15)

$500,000 FIRE AT ATLANTIC CITY

ATLANTIC CITY, N. J., Dec. 6—(AP)—A beachfront block was in charred ruins and 150 persons were homeless today after a $500,000 fire which destroyed 16 boardwalk buildings, including two apartment houses. Fireman Harry Yard, 60, died at Atlantic City Hospital of a heart ailment aggravated by exertion in fighting the flames, Fire Chief Rex Farley said.

Coast guards from a training station here helped prevent further damage by dousing sparks on the roofs of other buildings in the area. City authorities had not determined the cause of the blaze.

STALIN SAYS U. S. PRODUCTION IS NECESSARY TO WIN WAR

TEHERAN — (Delayed)—(AP) —Premier Stalin solemnly got to his feet one night at a dinner attended by President Roosevelt and Prime Minister Churchill.

He looked soberly about him at the assembled military and diplomatic leaders of the United States, Great Britain and Russia and lifted his glass to American war production.

"Without American production the United Nations could never have won the war," the Soviet leader was reported to have declared.

The response to Stalin's unexpected gesture was terrific.

Allied Leaders Also Map Peace for All Nations of World

CAIRO, Egypt, Dec. 6—(AP)—President Roosevelt, Prime Minister Churchill and Premier Joseph Stalin have agreed completely on "the scope and timing of operations" to smash the German army from three sides, an announcement signed by the three statesmen in an epic four-day meeting in Teheran, Iran, and released here today disclosed.

The Allied leaders also charted a peace era in which all nations would be invited to join "a world family of democratic nations" based on the reaffirmed principles of the Atlantic Charter.

The history-making conference of the beads of the world's most powerful military and political combine was held in the Iranian capital from Nov. 28 to Dec. 1, attended also by scores of top-flight military chieftains and diplomats from the United States, Britain and Russia.

Staffs Meet In Cairo

Heavily underscoring the urgency of the military phase, the combined British and American general staffs subsequently returned to Cairo, scene of the Nov. 22-26 meeting of Chinese Generalissimo Chiang Kai-Shek with President Roosevelt and the Prime Minister, and staged concentrated planning sessions from last Friday through today.

Churchill joined in these and other sessions, leading to the probability that other disclosures of paramount international importance are still to come.

President Roosevelt's whereabouts since the Teheran conferences were not disclosed, however.

Two Declarations

Two Teheran declarations signed simply "Roosevelt, Stalin, Churchill," and dated Dec. 1 announced these results:

WAR—"Our military staffs have joined in our round table discussions and we have concerted our plans for the destruction of the German forces. We have reached complete agreement as to the scope and timing of operations which will be undertaken from the east, west and south.

"The common understanding which we have reached guarantees that victory will be ours.

"No power on earth can prevent our destroying the German armies by land, their U-boats by sea and their war plants from the air. Our attacks will be relentless and increasing."

PEACE—"We are sure that our concord will make it an enduring peace. We recognize fully the supreme responsibility resting upon us and all the United Nations to make a peace which will command the good will of the overwhelming masses of the peoples of the world and banish the scourge and terror of war for many generations.

"We shall seek the cooperation and active participation of all nations, large and small, whose peoples in heart and mind are dedicated, as are our own peoples, to the elimination of tyranny and slavery, oppression and intolerance. We will welcome them as they may choose to come into a world family of democratic nations."

The concluding paragraph of one declaration devoted to the status of Iran as an ally of the three nations apparently was the key to the envisaged "world family of democratic nations."

Aid Pledged to Iran

After expressing their respect for Iran's independence and territorial integrity, and promising economic aid to that country which has facilitated the flow of Allied supplies to Russia, the three leaders said:

"They (the United States, Britain and Russia) count upon the participation of Iran together with all other peace-loving nations in the establishment of international peace, security and prosperity after the war in accordance with the principles of the Atlantic Charter, to which all four governments have continued to subscribe."

The Atlantic Charter declaration by President Roosevelt and Prime Minister Churchill after their historic sea rendezvous in August, 1940, set out these general Allied principal and post-war aims:

1—They seek no territorial or other aggrandizement.

2—No territorial changes that do not accord with the "freely expressed wishes of the peoples concerned."

3—Respect for the right of

(See PARLEY—Page 15)

FD TALKS TO U. S. TROOPS IN IRAN

Praises Work Of Men In Persia, Wishes Them An Early Return Home

TEHERAN, Iran, Dec. 2—(Delayed)—(AP)—President Roosevelt made two informal speeches today to United States soldiers based at Camp Amirabad here, telling them of his meetings with Stalin and Churchill, praising their work here, and wishing them an early return home.

NO APPEAL MADE TO NAZI MASSES IN IRAN STATEMENT

WASHINGTON, Dec. 6—(AP) —Perhaps the most significant thing about the Churchill-Roosevelt-Stalin statement on Germany was what it didn't say.

There was no appeal to the German masses, over Hitler's head.

This throws Dr. Paul Joseph Goebbels' propaganda line completely out of joint. He had been warning the Germans for the past two weeks against just such an appeal.

The war of nerves goes on.

He said he and Stalin and Churchill had made progress in their effort "to plan for a world for us and our children when war would cease to be a necessity . . . But of course the first thing is to win the war . . And all of you who are here and farther south in Iran can always remember you have taken a very necessary and very useful part in winning the war."

Speaks At Inspection

Speaking first to a large body of men after an inspection, the President said:

"Officers and men:

"I seem at this moment to be thoroughly equipped with the weapons of war (two microphones).

"If you had said to me or I had said to you three years ago that we would meet in Iran today, we would have probably said that we were completely crazy.

"I got here four days ago to meet with the Marshal of Soviet Russia and the Prime Minister of England to try to do two things.

Progress On Two Things

"The first was to lay military plans for cooperation between the three nations looking toward the winning of the war just as fast as we possibly can, and I think we have made progress toward that

(See F. D.—Page 15)

PROBE THEFT OF 2 CHECKS FROM MAIL

City police are investigating the theft of two checks amounting to $150 from a mail box in the hallway of an apartment house at 341 E. Chestnut St.

Mrs. Sue Shultz reported a Christmas saving checks of $100 stolen last Wednesday, while a week prior to that a $50 check belonging to Mr. and Mrs. Harry Breniser was stolen.

Police said the Breniser check was drawn on an Elizabeth, N. J. bank and was a Christmas gift from Mrs. Breniser's father, Aaron Britt, of Elizabeth, N. J.

CHRISTMAS LIQUOR STOCK IS BURNED

PHILADELPHIA, Dec. 6.—(AP)—Not a bottle of the Christmas stock of liquor was saved when fire swept through a State Liquor store warehouse here today.

Firemen said they had to smash the front door and front and back windows to shoot hose streams inside. They could not enter until the one-story brick building was in ruins. Cause of the blaze was not determined. Damage was not estimated.

Lost & Found — Page 16

Latest News

U. S. PILOTS BAGGED 13,500 PLANES IN 2 YEARS

Washington, Dec. 6—(AP)—The Army air forces, now numbering more men than all U. S. branches were able to move into Europe in the First World War, have destroyed or damaged 13,500 enemy planes since the Pearl Harbor attack two years ago, Gen. H. H. Arnold disclosed today.

Swelled to 2,300,000 men, the air arm has flown more than 225,000 individual plane flights, fired 41,000,000 rounds of ammunition and chewed up 2,000,000,000 gallons of gasoline in that time.

WEATHER
Eastern Pennsylvania: Cloudy And Colder, Snow Flurries West And North Portion Tuesday; Light Snow Beginning Tuesday Night, Wednesday Snow And Continued Cold.

Intelligencer Journal

The Leading Newspaper in the Garden Spot of America, Home Owned for Home Folks Since 1794

VOLUME LXXX.—NO. 92. Entered as second class matter June 23, 1928 at the Post Office at Lancaster, Pa., under the Act of March 3, 1879 Reg. U. S. Pat. Off. LANCASTER, PA., TUESDAY MORNING, DECEMBER 28, 1943. CITY FOURTEEN PAGES. 20c PER WEEK—4c Per Copy

U. S. ARMY TAKES OVER RAILROADS; STEEL WALKOUT BELIEVED ENDED

Yanks Invade Cape Gloucester, Take Isle Off Huon Peninsula

Marines Push Inland After Sweeping Ashore In New Britain Without Losing A Man; Triple Landing Gives U. S. Navy Safe Passage Into Bismarck Sea

(By The Associated Press)

A three-pronged American drive on the southern shores of the Bismarck Sea, carried out by Marine veterans, opened up new reaches Monday for Allied air, sea and amphibious operations.

Marines swept ashore Sunday on either side of Cape Gloucester, most bombed spot in New Britain, without losing a man. Eighty-five miles to the west, other troops seized Long Island, off Huon Peninsula of New Guinea.

A communique Tuesday (today) from General MacArthur said the Marines were pushing inland, encountering principal opposition at Target Hill and already had brought the airstrip and Borgen Bay under artillery fire.

The triple landing, combined with the hold already established in the Arawe sector of New Britain, gives American naval forces a safe passage into the Bismarck Sea. It will open another segment of the long route back to the Philippines, sever Japanese barge communications between New Britain and New Guinea, add a new threat to enemy holdings on New Guinea, and increase Allied pressure on Rabaul, major fortress on New Britain and key to Japan's southern defense line.

TOJO WORRIED

The Allied "counteroffensive has become real and serious," Premier Hideki Tojo gravely told the Japanese Diet. The southwest Pacific war, Tokyo radio added, is in "the decisive stage in which the rise or fall of our nation will be decided."

In a futile attempt to beat back the New Britain invaders, the Japanese air force lost 61 planes. This brought their week-end losses to at least 132, and probably more than 150, counting battles over Rabaul.

A strong force of Marines, who learned about jungles and Japanese on Guadalcanal, landed on Cape Gloucester behind one of the heaviest naval and air bombardments ever seen in the southwest Pacific. This barrage, covering the beach with smoke and flame, came as the climax of almost daily air raids. The Americans had plunked down 3,784 tons of bombs on the area since Dec. 1.

The invading force, which embarked Christmas night, relied on sheer power for success.

More of YANKS on Page 4

Maj. Geu. William H. Rupertus (above) is commanding U. S. Marines who landed at Cape Gloucester, New Britain Island, to establish a second invasion front on the major Jap base.

REDS THREATEN MAJOR GERMAN RAIL NETWORK

Soviets Within 17 Miles Of Vital Line; Vitebsk 5 Miles Distant

London (Tuesday)—(AP)—Russia's First Ukraine Army plunged to within 17 miles of the vital Warsaw-Odessa rail network yesterday in a swift break-through toward the Rumanian frontier aimed at trapping hundreds of thousands of German troops in the Dnieper river elbow far to the east, Moscow disclosed early today.

Berlin said nearly 500,000 Russians were ripping at German lines, and all Axis broadcasts reflected anxiety over the spectacular development in the Kiev bulge.

SAY NAZIS RETREATING

Moscow officially declared that German troops were in retreat in some sectors on the approaches to Zhitomir, Berdichev, and Kazatin—all key rail cities in the area.

Far to the north in White Russia the Soviet first Baltic army cut the next-to-last German escape railway from Vitebsk, killed 2,000 enemy troops and smashed to within five miles of Vitebsk itself.

The capture of 100 towns and hamlets in the Ukraine and 30 on the Vitebsk front were announced in the communique broadcast by Moscow and recorded by the Soviet monitor.

In the push toward Rumania and southern Poland, Gen. Nikolai F. Vatutin's forces now were deeper in that German-held territory than ever before a total of 6,200 Germans were killed during the day, to boost Axis casualties to more than 26,000 in four days on all fronts, Moscow said.

Andrushevka and Vycherayshe, district centers of the Zhitomir region, were taken in the wheeling movement toward Rumania. Andru-

More of REDS on Page 12

Invasion Aide

AIR MARSHAL TEDDER

AIR CHIEF TEDDER IS NAMED DEPUTY TO EISENHOWER

Britain's Master Of Air Strategy To Lead Mightiest Assault In Invasion

London (Tuesday) —(AP)— The shaping of the team that will direct the main invasion of Europe took another step forward today with the announcement that Air Chief Marshal Sir Arthur Tedder has been appointed deputy to Gen. Dwight D. Eisenhower, supreme commander.

Thus, Tedder, Britain's master of air strategy, will lead the mightiest air assault the world has ever seen to pave the way for the opening of a new front from the west.

SURPRISE SELECTION

The selection—the first time an airman has been given such recognition—was greeted with surprise but pleasure in London, the London Express calling it "the most illuminating recognition of the importance of an air leader in the planning and execution of the greatest operation the Allies yet have undertaken."

Tedder, a pilot in the first World War, is referred to in London, as the originator of "carpet" or area bombing. The building of air strength, already under way, now is sure to gain new momentum.

Technically, Tedder would succeed Eisenhower if something happened to the commander in chief. Whether the air marshall actually would take over the No. 1 invasion post in such a case, however, is entirely speculative.

The selection of the man who swept the German Air Force from the skies of North Africa and then directed the air cover for the invasion of Sicily and Italy as Eisenhower's right hand in the west made it clear that a great share of the grand assault has been assigned to Allied air forces and that coordination of land and air troops is to be more tightly knit than ever before.

At the same time, it was announced that Gen. Sir Bernard

More of AIR CHIEF on Page 12

Roosevelt Acts In RR Case; Murray Ends Steel Walkout

WHEN WLB ACTS

CIO Leaders Issue Order After Board Reverses Itself On Retroactive Pay Clause

Pittsburgh (Tuesday)—(AP)—Back to work orders from union officials early today apparently signalled the sudden end of the big steel strike which threatened to imperil the nation's war-time production.

Quick on the heels of a War Labor Board directive which guaranteed pay retroactivity in their wage contracts. President Philip Murray of the United Steel Workers instructed the union to continue "uninterruptedly the production of steel."

BACK TO WORK MOVES

Work movements began immediately in some struck steel areas.

From Ohio, West Virginia and Pennsylvania, which felt most heavily the affects of the work stoppage, came reports from union officials that workers would resume work during the day.

Striking members of the union began reporting for work on the midnight shift at the South Chicago plant of the Republic Steel Company. Some workers in Ohio and Pennsylvania also were back on their early morning shifts for the first time since the interruption began Christmas Eve.

One Ohio union official said production would be well on the way back to normal by afternoon.

At Buffalo, Frank C. Farrell, Republic Steel district manager, said workers were returning to jobs on the midnight shift at the firm's Buffalo plant.

Commenting on Murray's statement, Joseph T. McNichols, union

More of MURRAY on Page 4

LT. GEN. SOMERVELL

M. W. CLEMENT

SURPRISE MOVE

President Issues Order Although 17 Non-Operating Unions Call Off Strike

Washington — (AP) — The Army Monday night took possession of the nation's vast railroad system, acting on orders from President Roosevelt who ordered the seizure so that transportation of war materials could continue in the face of a strike threat.

The seizure order was carried out by Lieut. Gen. Brehon B. Somervell, Chief of Army Services, acting for Secretary of War Stimson.

GROSS IN CHARGE

Major General C. P. Gross, Chief of the Army's Transportation System, was placed in charge of operating the lines.

Martin W. Clement, president of the Pennsylvania railroad, will serve as an adviser to the Army, Stimson said.

Mr. Roosevelt ordered the seizure as a move "essential to the prosecution of the war," even though 17 of the 20 railroad unions had abandoned their plans for a strike Dec. 30.

Directing the Army to seize the roads as of 7 p. m., Eastern War Time, tonight, he declared:

"Railroad strikes by three brotherhoods have been ordered for next Thursday. I cannot wait until the last moment to take action to see that the suplies to our fighting men are not interrupted. x x x

"The major military offensives now planned must not be delayed by the interruption of vital transportation facilities. If any employes of the railroads now strike they will be striking against the government of the United States."

Before the President acted, the unions representing 1,100,000 non-operating workers, and two operating unions numbering about 200,000, had decided to let Mr. Roosevelt arbitrate the case. Management also agreed to arbitration. Three unions of about 150,000 refused to do this.

Mr. Roosevelt decided forthwith the wage issues in the case of the two operating unions which agreed to abide by his decision—the Brotherhoods of Locomotive Engineers and Trainmen. Five cents an hour shall be paid starting immediately, he said, "as the equivalent of or in lieu of claims for time and a half pay over 40 hours (per week) and for expenses while away from home." He also awarded these workers a week's vacation a year with pay at the basic rates. In addition he affirmed the four cents an hour increase in basic wages previously awarded by an emergency board.

STIMSON STATEMENT

In a statement, Stimson said:

"In accordance with the Executive order of the President, issued

More of ARMY on Page 4

Sailor Decorated For Bravery When Cruiser Was Bombed

Warrant Officer Ralph H. Habecker, 445 W. King St., has been decorated with the Silver Star medal for "exceptional bravery" and "conspicuous gallantry" when the light cruiser Savannah was hit by a bomb at Salerno, Italy.

Habecker, a boatswain, was in charge of the damage control repair party, which took over when the bomb penetrated a turret and exploded below deck.

"Boatswain Habecker promptly and fearlessly went below through smoke and gas filled compartments" and restored the "firemain system for use in fighting the fires," said the citation accompanying the medal which was signed by Admiral H. K. Hewitt, commander of naval forces in North African waters.

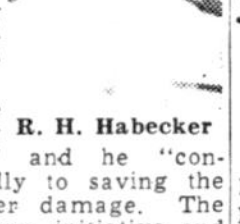

R. H. Habecker

"As a result he was overcome by smoke and gas" and he "contributed materially to saving the ship from further damage. The exceptional bravery, initiative and outstanding devotion to duty displayed by Boatswain Habecker were in keeping with the highest traditions of the Naval service."

"The Savannah means a lot to me," Habecker said Monday at his home where he is spending a 15-day leave with his wife and two children while his ship is being repaired.

'I helped commission her in

More of SAILOR on Page 12

EPHRATA MARINE KILLED IN ACTION IN PACIFIC AREA

Jay E. Sahm, Jr., Eighteen, Believed To Have Met Death At Tarawa

Marine Jay E. Sahm, Jr., eighteen, has been killed in action in the Pacific area—presumably at Tarawa—his parents, Mr. and Mrs. Jay E. Sahm, N. State St., Ephrata, have been notified by the Navy Department.

The telegram, signed by Lt. Gen. Thomas Holcomb, former Marine Corps commandant, announced the bare fact that the youth "was killed in action in performance of his duty and in the service of his country" and expressed "heartfelt sympathies."

The youth was known to have been in the Pacific area. He enlisted in the Marine Corps Reserves on August 12, 1942, when he was seventeen years old.

Besides his parent, he is survived by these brothers and sisters: Norman, Richard, Doris and Joyce, all at home.

POPE SAYS PLANE ATTACK ON VATICAN CITY WAS PLANNED

Implies He Knows Nationality Of Craft Which Bombed Holy City

New York—(AP)—Implying he knew the nationality of the plane which bombed Vatican City Nov. 5, Pope Pius XII said in a statement broadcast Monday night by the Vatican radio that the attack was "deliberately planned and dishonorably and unsuccessfully screened behind the anonymity of the pilot."

The Pope, whose remark was included in his response to Christmas greetings from the College of Cardinals, did not identify the attacker, however, according to the Federal Communications Commission, which recorded the broadcast.

"The air raid on Vatican City evoked the unanimous indignation of the entire world," the Pope was quoted as saying. "Such an attack, deliberately planned and dishonorably and unsuccessfully screened behind the anonymity of the pilot, on territory sacred to Christians.

More of POPE on Page 4

OPA PUTS CEILING ON PRICES CHARGED FOR NEW WHISKIES

Pennsylvania Stores Do Not Stock Brands Affected By New Order

Washington—(AP)—The OPA aimed a blow Monday at high prices on new brands of whisky which have appeared on the market within the past year or so.

Price ceilings were imposed at the processors level on all domestic distilled spirits. Since percentage markups for wholesalers and retailers are fixed, the action is calculated to roll back consumer prices of some brands. Effective Jan. 6, the flat maximum prices are applied to all new brands of domestic whisky introduced since March, 1942.

NONE IN LOCAL STORES

[Prices of few if any whiskys on sale at State Liquor Store will be affected by the OPA order placing flat ceiling prices on new brands of domestic distilled spirits, Donald A. Behney, stores director of the Pennsylvania Liquor Control Board, announced Monday night in Harrisburg.

["The brands we have listed are of origin before March, 1942," Behney stated. "We have taken on

More of OPA on Page 12

G. HAROLD WAGNER IS CANDIDATE FOR AUDITOR GENERAL

State Treasurer Will Seek Post On His "Efficient And Economical Administration"

Harrisburg —(AP)— State Treasurer G. Harold Wagner, of Luzerne County, announced his candidacy Monday for the Democratic nomination for Auditor General of Pennsylvania, starting the parade of candidates for next year's election.

Indicating he would make the race on the record of his four years as head of the state treasury, Wagner, 40-year-old veteran of World War 1 said in his statement of candidacy:

'I have tried to conscientiously render to the taxpayers of Pennsylvania an efficient and economical administration."

MEETING IN FEBRUARY

Wagner, himself, was unavailable to amplify his formal announcement, but a close associate said his name would be presented for endorsement to the Democratic State Committee when it meets here early in February to slate organization cnadidates for the April 25 primary. He was elected to the treasury post in 1940

More of WAGNER on Page 12

SOLDIER, HURT JUNE 18 WHILE ON WAY TO WED, SEEKS NEW LICENSE

Pvt. Anthony C. Geiger, 442 Pershing Ave., who was severely injured June 18 in an automobile accident at Somerville, N. J., while enroute to Lancaster to be married the next day, applied Monday at the court house with his fiancee, Dolores M. Shultz, 503 S. Lime St., for a new license.

For several months Geiger was confined to a hospital. When he and Miss Shultz applied for the license he still was using a cane.

Lost & Found — Page 12

"We Lead All The Rest"

FARM CORNER

By The Farm Editor

18 FARM GROUPS PLAN MEETINGS JAN. 18-20

Eighteen Pennsylvania farm groups and agricultural associations are planning to hold annual conventions in Harrisburg Jan. 18, 19, and 20, under the sposorship of the State Farm Products Show Commission.

Many Lancaster county farm residents plan to attend various meetings, which include livestock, dairy, poultry, potato, fruit, vegetable, beekeepers, and farm youth and farm women organizations.

NEW MACHINE RATION FORMS

All applications filed prior to Dec. 1 under the 1943 farm machinery rationing program automatically became void as of that date, the Lancaster AAA County Committee announced Monday. It therefore will be necessary, if such farmers still want to purchase the equipment, to file another application. The 1944 program for the rationing of farm machinery is now in effect and the new forms differ from the old. Applications are handled at the AAA office, 29 N. Duke St.

PLAN T.B. TEST HERE IN '44

The second triennial test of all dairy herds in Lancaster county for the detection of bovine tuberculosis will be made in 1944, officials of the Pennsylvania Bureau of Animal Industry announced. While no definite time was announced, County Agent F. S. Bucher said the testing

More of FARM CORNER Page 12

Arrested Six Hours After Being Freed As Christmas Gift

Six hours after Burt Henson, fifty-five, no home, was freed of drunkenness and disorderly conduct charges as a "Christmas present" by Alderman A. P. Newell, in police court, Monday, he was back in a police cell, booked on similar charges.

John W. Weaver, manager of The Village, the prosecutor, claims that Henson created a disturbance at the bus terminal at 7 p. m., annoying travelers with his demands for money. Henson had been arrested at the bus terminal by city police Sunday.

Leo Fluck, forty-two, 105 S. Queen St., was freed by Alderman A. P. Newell in police court Monday as a "Christmas present" when he appeared to answer charges of drunkenness and disorderly conduct. He was arrested Saturday after he fell and cut his head.

ALLIED AIRCRAFT HIT AXIS TARGETS

London, (Tuesday)—(AP)—Allied aircraft were heard crossing the channel early last night and shortly afterward heavy explosions rumbled from the invasion coast of Northern France.

The action broke the Christmas lull in heavy aerial activity which had persisted since last Friday's record raid of 1,300 American fighters and bombers on the same area, where German rocket emplacements may be the targets.

Report Diphtheria, Meningitis Cases In County, Both Victims Improved

A case of diphtheria and one of meningitis were reported Monday by Dr. A. J. Greenleaf, Mountville, county medical director.

Mrs. Arlene Feldser, twenty-three, Ephrata R2, West Earl Township, the victim of diphtheria, was reported as improved at her home where she has been a patient since she was stricken ill December 14.

Ward M. Kurtz, Leacock, state health officer, said he was unable to trace the source of the disease as Mrs. Feldser had not been away from her home for some time before she was taken ill.

The last cases of diphtheria in the county resulted in the deaths of Marian E. Huber, four, and her sister, Esther Mae, eight, daughters of Mr. and Mrs. Phares G. Huber, Lancaster R4. They died a week apart in St. Joseph's Hospital the latter part of November.

The victim of meningitis was a child who was stricken ill while visiting relatives in Manheim, according to Donald Brossman, Manheim Health Officer. Attendants at St. Joseph's Hospital where the child had been a patient said she was discharged a week ago after recovering from the disease.

Other cases of contagious diseases reported were, chicken pox, eighteen, scarlet fever, three and tuberculosis, two.

Two new cases of chicken pox and one of bronchial pneumonia were reported to the city board of health last week, according to the weekly health bulletin issued Monday.

SNOW FORECAST

There was no white Christmas but there may be a white New Year's Day. The Weather Bureau forecast a light snow Tuesday evening to continue Wednesday. Temperatures Monday ranged from 36 to 48 degrees.

ASK VOLUNTEERS TO AID RATION PANEL

Paul G. Murray, chairman of the Lancaster War Price and Rationing Board, issued an SOS Monday for hundreds of volunteers to assist in issuing truck gasoline rations which must be in the hands of truckers by January 1.

"We can use volunteers both day and night until January 1, beginning Tuesday," Murray said in urging high school students, clubs and civic organizations to lend a hand.

Murray said the board had a plan worked out which misfired. "Arrangements were made early in December to have students from the upper classes of the high schools assist with the work but local industries hired them for a week's work which upset all our plans."

NAZIS REPORT QUAKES

New York —(AP)— Three slight earthquakes were felt in the Wurttemberg region of southwestern Germany Monday night, but they caused "no damage worth mentioning," a DNB broadcast said. The dispatch was reported by the Federal Communications Commission.

SAVE THIS NEWSPAPER

After you have read this paper, please save it. Every bit of paper is vitally needed for war production.

Allied Bombers Hit Northern Italy As Weather Slows Ground Forces

Allied Headquarters, Algiers—(AP)—While pouring rains and snow turned the Italian front into a quagmire, restricting ground fighting and bogging all heavy bombers, the deadly diversity of the Allied aerial arm was demonstrated in a series of attacks by Marauder mediums on German communications in Northern Italy.

The Allied command announced Monday that the two-engined bombers splashed from runways in strong force to blast railway yards along an important lateral "feeder" line connecting the big inland junction of Florence with the West Coast ports of Pisa and Leghorn. The attacks further crippled enemy supply lines already badly damaged by Flying Fortress and Liberator assaults on the Brenner pass route.

Waves of the extremely fast Marauders hit railway yards at Prato and Pistoia, 10 and 15 miles northwest of Florence on the north branch of the line to Pisa and Leghorn, and at Empoli, 10 miles southwest of Florence on the south branch line. A communique said "good coverage" was obtained on the rail yards. The previous day Allied bombers had smashed the yards at Pisa.

While the air force was harassing the enemy rear, American troops scrambled forward in a driving rain to take two more high points of the Mt. Samucro Mass

More of ALLIED on Page 12

Weather Calendar

COMPARATIVE TEMPERATURES

Station	High	Low
Water Works	49	32
Ephrata	48	26
Last Year (Ephrata)	40	27
Official High for Year, July 25		99
Official Low for Year, Feb. 13		1
Character of Day		Partly Cloudy

SUN
Rises—8:25 a. m. Sets—5:46 p. m.

MOON
Sets—7:38 p. m. First Quarter, Jan. 2

STARS
Morning—Jupiter, Saturn, Venus
Evening—Mars

NEARBY FORECASTS
Maryland: Cloudy and not so warm Tuesday, rain and colder Tuesday night and Wednesday
Delaware: Cloudy and not so warm Tuesday rain and colder Tuesday night and Wednesday
New Jersey: Cloudy and colder Tuesday, Wednesday cloudy and continued cold with rain on the coast and snow in the interior.

INVASION BLUEPRINT: How Army Engineers Prepared to Blast Walls Of Hitler's Fortress

As American invading forces storm the beaches of Hitler's Europe, it was the Army's engineers who led the way. Their job is to wipe out enemy barriers and clear the way for the men and supplies that follow. These sketches show how they probably did it.

1. The engineers must know first the obstacles they will face. The invasion area probably is heavily mined, lined with barbed wire, tank blocks, pill boxes.

2. Before invasion, the beach is shelled from the sea to daze the enemy. As the shelling nears its end, the first wave of engineers goes ashore.

3. Working prone, engineers use mine detectors and bayonets to locate and remove mines, then mark the safe path with white tape. Next they blast wire with bangalore torpedoes—strips of sheet metal rolled around explosive.

4. Engineer in foreground blasts tank block. Others blind enemy in pill box with flame thrower. Paratroops landed in rear work toward beach.

5. Mat roads are laid for tanks and supply vehicles. Engineers lay burlap first, then steel matting. The beach is now clear, ready for a full force of invaders.

Comprehensive Chronology of the War, From Blitz of Poland to the Invasion

1939

Sept. 1: Germany invades Poland, annexes Danzig.

Sept. 2: France mobilizes. Italy proclaims neutrality.

Sept. 3: Britain and France declare war on Germany. Nazis bomb Warsaw.

Sept. 4: New Zealand and Australia declare war on Germany. United States proclaims neutrality. Fighting begins in front of Maginot line.

Sept. 10: Canada declares war on Germany.

Sept. 17: Russian troops strike into eastern Poland.

Sept. 27: Warsaw surrenders.

Sept. 28: Germans and Russians partition Poland.

Nov. 4: President Roosevelt signs neutrality law, repealing arms embargo.

Nov. 8: Bomb wrecks Munich beer hall just after Hitler leaves.

Nov. 30: Russia invades Finland.

Dec. 17: German pocket battleship Admiral Graf Spee scuttled outside Montevideo harbor after battle with three British cruisers.

1940

Jan. 16: President Roosevelt recommends further financial aid to Finland.

Jan. 20: Winston Churchill, first lord of the British admiralty, warns Europe's neutrals to join the Allies.

Feb. 2: Finland, still resisting fiercely, asks Russia for an "honorable peace."

March 11: Britain discloses she and France ready to aid Finland if requested.

March 12: Moscow announces treaty ending Russo-Finnish war.

March 20: Daladier resigns as French Premier and is succeeded by Paul Reynaud, his Finance Minister.

April 4: Churchill given general supervision over all units of Britain's military and naval strength.

April 9: Germany invades Norway and Denmark, Denmark giving in but Norway declaring war.

April 15: British land troops in Norway.

May 2: Prime Minister Chamberlain admits the Allies have given up fight for southern and central Norway.

British Flee Dunkerque

May 10: Hitler, announcing "The hour has come," sends his troops into Belgium, the Netherlands and Luxembourg while Nazi planes bomb northern France. Winston Churchill succeeds Chamberlain as British Prime Minister.

May 14: Dutch army capitulates. Allied troops battle Germans on Meuse front in Belgium.

May 19: General Maxine Weygand replaces Gamelin as Allied generalissimo.

May 28: King Leopold orders the surrender of his Belgian forces, exposing British flank.

May 29: Under heavy German attack, 400,000 British soldiers begin to escape from Dunkerque. Allies capture Narvik in Norway.

June 3: German planes bomb Paris.

June 4: Allies bomb Munich, Frankfort and the Ruhr.

June 10: Britain announces evacuation of Norway. Paris government leaves as Germans strike to within 35 miles of city. Italy declares war on Britain and France.

June 14: Germans march into Paris.

June 17: Marshal Henri Petain becomes premier and announces French surrender. Great Britain says she will fight alone.

June 20: French armistice with Germany signed at Compiegne.

June 24: French armistice with Italy signed.

June 28: Russia occupies Bessarabia in Romania.

July 5: Petain severs relations with Great Britain after British navy attacks French warships at Oran.

July 14: Estonia, Latvia and Lithuania annexed by Russia.

July 19: Hitler offers Britain "last chance" for peace. Britain says "no."

Aug. 4: German air force begins heavy attack on Britain.

Aug. 6: Italians invade British Somaliland.

Aug. 12: Five hundred German planes raid Britain.

Aug. 19: British withdraw from Somaliland.

Aug. 20: Britain disclosed agreement to lease naval and air bases in western hemisphere to the United States.

Aug. 30: Romania forced by Germany to yield half of Transylvania to Hungary.

Aug. 31: RAF bombers hit center of Berlin for first time.

Sept. 3: President Roosevelt announces trade of 50 over-age destroyers to Britain for naval and air base leases in western Atlantic.

Sept. 6: King Carol abdicates Romanian throne in favor of son.

Sept. 7: Heavy night raids on London begin.

Sept. 16: President Roosevelt signs Selective Service act.

Sept. 27: Japan joins the Axis, signing 10-year tri-partite pact in Berlin.

Oct. 3: Neville Chamberlain resigns from Churchill's cabinet, pleading poor health.

Oct. 4: Hitler and Mussolini meet at Brenner pass. Japanese Premier says U. S. must accept Axis order or face war.

Oct. 8: U. S. orders citizens to leave the Orient. German troops enter Romania.

Oct. 18: British disclose repulse of German invasion attempt on Sept. 16.

Oct. 27: Italy invades Greece.

Nov. 9: Chamberlain dies.

Nov. 14: British dig for 1,000 dead and wounded after raid on Coventry.

Nov. 17: Greeks rout Italians along 100-mile front.

Nov. 20: Hungary joins Axis.

Nov. 24: Slovakia follows Hungary and Romania into Axis alliance.

Dec. 12: Britain reports Italy's invasion armies in headlong retreat from Egypt; 20,000 prisoners taken.

1941

Jan. 3: Ireland raided by German bombers.

Jan. 10: Germany and Russia sign new friendship pact.

March 1: Bulgaria signs Axis pact; German troops march in.

March 10: British troops leave Alexandria for Greece.

March 11: President Roosevelt signs lend-lease bill.

March 25: Yugoslavia joins Rome-Berlin-Tokyo alliance.

March 27: Military coup ousts Yugoslav government which signed Axis pact; 17-year-old Peter enthroned as king.

March 30: U. S. seizes Axis ships in ports.

April 6: Germany attacks Yugoslavia and Greece.

April 17: Germany announces surrender of Yugoslav army.

April 18: Premier Korizis of Greece commits suicide.

April 27: Germans take Athens.

May 10: Rudolf Hess, Hitler aide, lands by parachute in Scotland.

May 20: Germans attack Crete in first air-borne action.

May 31: British withdraw from Crete.

June 14: President Roosevelt freezes Axis credits in U. S.

June 16: U. S. closes all German consulates.

June 22: Germany, Italy and Romania declare war on Russia.

Atlantic Charter Meeting

June 25: Finland enters war against Russia.

July 7: American naval forces land in Iceland.

July 13: Britain and Russia pledge joint action against Germany.

July 24: Japanese troops move into French Indo-China.

July 25: U. S. and Britain freeze Japanese credits.

July 26: Japan freezes U. S.-British credits. Roosevelt calls Philippine military forces into U. S. service.

Aug. 14: Rumored Roosevelt-Churchill sea conference confirmed by announcement of eight-point program later known as Atlantic Charter.

Aug. 25: British and Russian troops invade Iran.

Oct. 19: State of siege declared in Moscow.

Nov. 24: Russians begin counter-offensive west of Rostov.

Dec. 7: Japanese attack Pearl Harbor.

Dec. 8: U. S. declares war. Japs attack Midway.

U. S. Troops Reach Ireland

Dec. 10: Japanese land in Philippines. British lose Battleship Prince of Wales and Battle Cruiser Repulse off Malaya.

Dec. 11: U. S. declares war on Germany and Italy after earlier Axis declarations. Japanese Battleship Haruna sunk by U. S. Army airmen. Japanese landing forces attack Wake.

Dec. 12: Guam occupied. U. S. Navy takes over French ships in U. S., including Normandie.

Dec. 16: Germans retreating along entire eastern front.

Dec. 23: Wake falls after 14-day defense.

Dec. 25: Hongkong falls.

Dec. 27: Manila bombed despite declaration it open city.

1942

Jan. 1: United Nations pact signed pledging no separate peace with Axis.

Jan. 2: Japanese occupy Manila.

Jan. 14: First ship is torpedoed off Atlantic coast.

Jan. 17: Prime Minister Churchill returns to London after visit to U. S.

Jan. 21: Five-hundred mile British penetration into Libya checked by Rommel.

Jan. 23: Rio De Janeiro conference of 21 American republics recommends Axis break.

Jan. 27: First American troops arrive in Northern Ireland.

Feb. 1: U. S. Navy raids Gilbert and Marshall island.

Feb. 9: French liner Normandie ravaged by fire.

Feb. 11: American troops safeguard oil refineries on Dutch islands of Curacao and Aruba in the Caribbean.

Feb. 15: Singapore surrenders.

Feb. 27: Great naval battle begins off Java; U. S. loses Cruiser Houston and Destroyer Pope.

March 9: Japanese overrun Java. Rangoon, Burma's capital, falls.

March 16: War department announces "considerable numbers" of U. S. troops have arrived in Australia.

March 17: Gen. Douglas MacArthur reaches Australia from Philippines.

March 31: Japanese begin heavy attacks on Bataan.

April 3: Announcement says American "Flying Tigers" in China destroy more than 200 Japanese planes.

April 9: Fighting ends on Bataan.

April 18: U. S. Army bombers, under Lt. Col. James H. Doolittle, raid Tokyo.

May 6: Corregidor falls.

May 7: British occupy French island of Madagascar.

May 9: Gen. MacArthur announces five-day Coral sea battle in which 17 Japanese ships sunk or damaged.

May 12: Russians launch offensive against Kharkov.

May 26: Sixth Libyan campaign opens with Axis thrust toward Tobruk.

May 30: More than 1,000 RAF planes drop 6,000,000 pounds of bombs on Cologne in greatest air attack in history.

June 3: Japanese bomb Dutch Harbor, Alaska.

June 5: Japanese naval forces attacking Midway island smashed by American naval and air power in great battle.

June 11: U. S. and Russia sign mutual aid pact.

June 12: Japanese land in Aleutians.

June 18: Churchill comes to United States again.

June 21: British announce loss of Tobruk.

June 22: Japanese submarine shells Oregon coast.

June 23: Nazi armored forces roll toward Egypt.

July 1: Germans capture Sevastopol.

July 4: U. S. Army bombers stage first raid on western Europe.

July 5: Germans claim breakthrough to Don river in 100-mile advance.

July 17: Japs occupy three islands in Aleutians.

July 27: Russians evacuate Rostov.

Aug. 8: American forces land on Guadalcanal.

Aug. 19: Dieppe raid brings heavy losses to Allied forces; American Rangers take part.

Sept. 1: U. S. and Australian troops drive Japs from New Beachhead at Milne bay, in New Guinea.

Sept. 17: Nazis penetrate Stalingrad.

Sept. 23: Russians launch counter-offensive in Stalingrad area.

Oct. 23: Gen. Bernard L. Montgomery breaks Axis El Alamein line and starts the drive which was to hurl the Axis from North Africa.

Nov. 8: American and British forces land in French Northwest Africa.

Nazis Give Up In Tunisia

Nov. 11: Germans occupy all France. Americans capture Casablanca and Oran, ending French resistance.

Nov. 12: U. S. wins three-day naval battle in Solomons.

Nov. 13: Drafting of 18 and 19-year-olds ordered in U. S. British Eighth army takes Tobruk.

Nov. 19: Russians open winter offensive at Rzhev and Stalingrad.

Nov. 20: Bengasi taken.

Nov. 27: Most of French fleet scuttled at Toulon as Germans attempt to seize vessels.

Dec. 12: British reach their old highwater mark at El Agheila.

Dec. 24: Admiral Darlan assassinated.

1943

Jan. 18: Seventeen-month siege of Stalingrad broken.

Jan. 24: Tripoli, capital of Italy's last colony in Africa, falls.

Jan. 26: President Roosevelt and Prime Minister Churchill hold "Unconditional Surrender" conference at Casablanca.

Jan. 27: Heavy bombers make first All-American assault on Germany.

Feb. 10: Guadalcanal completely taken. Eighth Army crosses into Tunisia.

Feb. 21: Germans take Kasserine pass in Tunisia from Americans.

Feb. 25: Kasserine pass reoccupied by American troops.

March 3: Japanese convoy of 10 warships, 12 transports destroyed off New Guinea.

May 7: Tunis and Bizerte captured by Allies.

May 11: Churchill arrives in Washington.

May 12: All Axis resistance in Africa ends in the Cap Bon peninsula.

May 14: American troops land on Attu.

May 16: RAF blasts two Ruhr dams.

May 30: Japanese garrison on Attu wiped out.

June 11: Italy's island outpost of Pantelleria falls after heavy pounding from the air.

July 5: U. S. wins naval battle with Japanese in Kula Gulf.

July 5: German summer offensive in Russia is halted.

Reds Capture Kiev

July 7: American troops land on Munda.

July 9: Allied forces invade Sicily.

July 19: Rome bombed for first time.

July 22: Palermo, Sicilian capital, falls.

July 25: Mussolini resigns; Marshal Badoglio becomes Prime Minister.

Aug. 1: 175 U. S. Liberators from Middle East blast Ploesti refineries.

Aug. 2: RAF makes ninth attack on Hamburg in 10-day 8,000-ton record-breaking blitz.

Aug. 15: U. S. forces occupy Kiska in Aleutians.

Aug. 17: Conquest of Sicily completed.

Aug. 23: Russians take Kharkov for second time of summer.

Aug. 24: Roosevelt and Churchill meet at Quebec.

Aug. 25: Lord Mountbatten named Allied commander for attack on Burma.

Aug. 28: King Boris of Bulgaria dies after reported split with Hitler.

Aug. 29: Danes scuttle their fleet in revolt against Nazis. King is seized.

Aug. 30: Reds storm through Taganrog, southern pivot of German line.

Sept. 7: Amercian paratroops land behind Lae, New Guinea, encircle 20,000 Japs.

Sept. 8: Italy surrenders unconditionally, armistice was signed in Sicily Sept. 3.

Yanks Below Rome

Sept. 10: German troops shell and seize Rome.

Sept. 11: Most of Italian fleet escapes to the Allies.

Sept. 13: MacArthur takes Salamaua airfield in New Guinea.

Sept. 19: Italians seize Sardinia for the Allies.

Sept. 21: Churchill promises invasion of Europe from west.

Sept. 26: Smolensk falls to Russians.

Sept. 27: Americans breach Nazi line east of Naples. British capture Foggia.

Oct. 1: Fifth Army takes Naples.

Oct. 5: U. S. Navy and planes pound Wake island.

Oct. 12: Portugal grants Great Britain naval and air anti-submarine bases in Azores.

Oct. 13: Italy declares war on Germany.

Oct. 14: Biggest Pacific air fleet bombs Rabaul, smashes 177 planes.

Oct. 18: Hull and Eden in Moscow for conference with Molotov on unity in war and peace.

Oct. 26: Reds capture Dnepropetrovsk.

Nov. 1: Americans land on Bougainville.

Nov. 6: Kiev falls, Stalin calls second front near.

Nov. 21: U. S. forces have landed on Makin and Tarawa islands.

Dec. 4: Roosevelt-Churchill-Stalin meet at Teheran.

Dec. 12: Russians, Czechs sign 20-year pact.

Dec. 16: U. S. Sixth army makes surprise landing on New Britain.

Dec. 24: Eisenhower to direct invasion of Europe.

Dec. 30: U. S. Marines capture strategic airdrome at Cape Gloucester.

1944

Jan. 4: Reds smash across Polish line.

Jan. 17: Russia bars negotiations with Poland.

Jan. 22: Allies land behind Nazi lines about 20 miles south of Rome.

Jan. 31: U. S. amphibious troops invade Marshall islands at Kwajalein.

Feb. 17: Americans land on Eniwetok atoll in Marshalls.

March 1: American destroyer-borne troops land on Admiralty island. MacArthur on hand for surprise blow.

March 3: U. S. planes fly over Berlin for the first time.

March 10: Eire rejects U. S. call to oust Axis envoys.

March 20: German troops occupy Hungary.

March 24: German occupation of Romania is confirmed.

March 31: Russia ends Sakhalin oil concession to Japan.

April 3: Russians invade Romania.

LCT carries tanks, which go ashore over side ramp.

LCM carries tanks, motorized artillery, heavy vehicles.

Army Nurses Were Trained For Invasion Conditions

Photo shows U. S. Army nurses in training under canvas in Wales to run a field hospital during invasion.

WITH THE U.S. ARMY NURSES IN BRITAIN—(AP)—The first American women onto the Continent after the beachhead is gained will be the U. S. Army nurses. "That's what I'm waiting for," said 2nd Lts. Lilyan Emmons of Chicago and Marion L. Hemmesch of New Rockford, N. D.

Lilyan, a blue-eyed blonde, is attached to an evacuation hospital, intensively trained in tents to prepare for battle conditions. Marion, an attractive brunette in an Air Evacuation squadron, will fly in transport planes returning the wounded to U. S. Army hospitals in Britain.

Lessons learned in Bataan, in North Africa and in the Mediterranean have revised clothing and equipment for flying nurses and those on the ground for the Big Show.

Except for firearms Lilyan will get the same field equipment—gasmask, helmet, musette bag, mess kit, pistol belt to which is attached canteen, first aid kit, flashlight—issued G.I.Joe.

Marion's flying nurses equipment is about the same as heavy bomber pilots'. It includes jacket, trousers and helmet of leather; "Mae West" life preserver, oxygen mask, heavy fleece lined boots and parachute.

In the field both girls will sleep on cots minus sheets. They will wear slacks and leggings. Hospital duty will see them in brown and white seersucker, instead of the traditional white. Bataan taught that white was too easy a target to see from the air, and the laundry problem is a nightmare up front.

WACs, who will follow the nurses onto the continent, will have the same 50 pounds of equipment as the Army ground nurses.

WEAPONS FACING OUR INVADERS

BIG COAST GUNS, of which this is a typical example, add to the deafening roar of battle as they blast at targets many miles off shore. The type here shown is good for a 10 to 15 mile range.

IN an 8000 mile perimiter about his "Fortress Europe," Hitler has provided his huge defense forces with strategically located walls of concrete and steel. Our Allied leaders know well just what our invading forces face—and where! Whatever may or may not be the merits of the much-discussed giant rocket gun, any general check-up would include an assortment of ferro-concrete forts; gigantic guns; floating islands bristling with mines; barbed wire entanglements of ingenious construction—some electrically wired; and whatever may be left of the Luftwaffe, which many believe may show considerable strength in a crisis.

ALONG THE ENEMY'S strongly protected coasts are thousands of these squatty pill boxes from which anti-aircraft guns operate in revolving turrets. They are long since familiar to Allied fliers who made daily visits to key coastal areas.

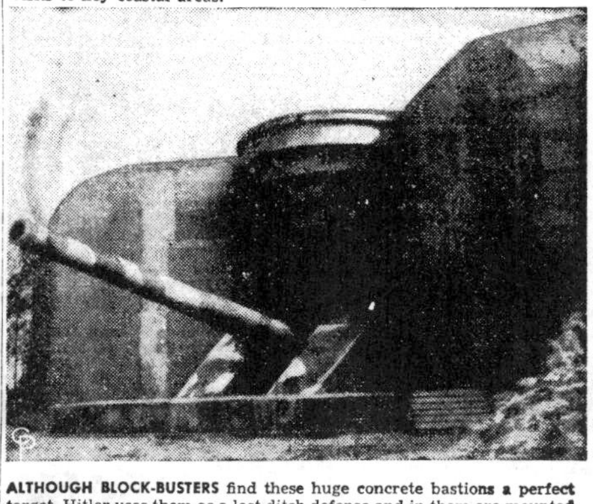

ALTHOUGH BLOCK-BUSTERS find these huge concrete bastions a perfect target, Hitler uses them as a last ditch defense and in them are mounted the naval-type rifles pictured here.

TURNED AGAINST Britain, these giant railway guns constantly threaten life and property across the Channel. They made their first appearance early in the war when French resistance was collapsing.

WEATHER

Eastern Pennsylvania: Occasional Light Rain Ending Late Friday, Continued Mild; Saturday Increasing Cloudiness, Moderate Temperature.

Intelligencer Journal.

Girl Scout
FAT COLLECTION
7TH WARD
"On the Door Step"
for Your Convenience
SATURDAY

The Leading Newspaper in the Garden Spot of America, Home Owned for Home Folks Since 1794

VOLUME LXXX.—NO. 119. Entered as second class matter June 23, 1928 at the Post Office at Lancaster, Pa., under the Act of March 3, 1879 Reg. U. S. Pat. Off. LANCASTER, PA., FRIDAY MORNING, JANUARY 28, 1944 CITY TWENTY-SIX PAGES. 20c PER WEEK—4c Per Copy

ALLIED ARTILLERY HEARD IN ROME

JAP SAVAGERY ON BATAAN REVEALED

HORROR STORY IS TOLD BY ARMY, NAVY

Escaped Officers Say Gallant Defenders Starved, Tortured, Murdered

Washington—(AP)—A horror story scarcely paralleled in the annals of modern war—how the Japanese starved, tortured and in some cases wantonly murdered the gallant defenders of Bataan—was told by the Army and Navy Thursday night.

Documented by sworn statements of officers who escaped from prison camps, the joint announcement described a cold-blooded campaign of savagery carried out after the 36,000 Americans and Filipinos on Bataan and Corregidor were overwhelmed by superior numbers.

THOUSANDS OF DEATHS

The 4,000-word account began by telling of thousands of deaths in Japanese camps (2,200 Americans died in two months in one camp) and then recited that:

When the Americans and Filipinos first were taken prisoner, those found with Japanese money or tokens were beheaded. Survivors were beaten along a "march of death" from the scene.

Twelve thousand men were kept penned in a 100-yard square area without food for a week. There was a 12-hour wait to fill canteens at the one water spigot.

A widely used torture was the "sun treatment." Captives were made to sit in the boiling sun all day without cover and with little water.

SIX BURIED ALIVE

Six men—three Americans and three Filipinos—ill from mistreatment were buried while still alive.

Men "literally were worked to death." It was not unusual for 20 per cent of a work detail to die and "in one instance, 75 per cent were killed that way."

Three officers who attempted

More of BATAAN on Page 23

"We Lead All The Rest"

FARM CORNER

By The Farm Editor

AYRSHIRE BREEDERS REELECT OFFICERS

Officers of the Lancaster County Ayrshire Breeders' Association were reelected Wednesday evening at the Farm Bureau building, 812 N. Queen St. Attendance at the dinner meeting totalled 160 breeders and their families.

The officers reelected are: Jacob Horst, Lititz R3, president; Enos Good, Lititz R3, vice-president; E. K. Buckwalter, Lancaster R4, secretary and treasurer. The officers together with John Ranck, Jr., New Holland, are Ralph Harnish, Christiana, R1, will serve as the executive committee.

The meeting was addressed by William Shaffer, of the Artificial Breeders' Association; and John Gable, of the Dunwoody Farm, and Ray Williams, manager of the Adrossian Farms, Chester county.

GOOD PRICES AT SALES

Farm equipment, animals and feed brought fancy prices at three sales Thursday.

At the Jacob G. Witmer sale, near Marticville, 5,000 tobacco lath sold for $1.51 per 100, the highest price received for this lath to date, it was reported. One horse brought $150, while another sold for $100. Acclimated bulls brought up to $108, while a 1940 tractor and harrow sold for $600. Mixed hay sold from $32 to $34 per ton, while corn brought $1.50 per bushel. Six shoats sold for $6 each, while locust posts brought $.50 each. Parke Shaub was the auctioneer.

A manure spreader at the sale of John B. Long, Warwick Twp., one and one-half miles east of Rothsville, brought $120, while Hampshire sheep brought from $12 to $18 each. White Rock laying hens sold for 21 1-2 cents per pound. An old dinner bell brought $5, and the same price was obtained for

More of FARM CORNER Page 22

Weather Calendar

COMPARATIVE TEMPERATURES

Station	High	Low
Water Works	64	29
Ephrata	62	32
Last Year (Ephrata)	27	22
Official High for Year, Jan. 26		62
Official Low for Year, Jan. 17		2
Character of Day		Cloudy

SUN
Rises—8:17 a. m. Sets—6:18 p. m.

MOON
Sets—10:05 p. m. First Quarter, Feb. 1

STARS
Morning—Jupiter, Venus.
Evening—Mars, Saturn.

NEARBY FORECASTS
Maryland, Delaware and New Jersey: Occasional light rain ending late Friday, continued mild; Saturday increasing cloudiness, moderate temperature

Lost & Found — Page 23

Lancaster County's Men Who Fought On Bataan

PVT. KARL H. STOLTZFUS (Dead)

S-S ROBERT E. BURCHFIELD (Dead)

CPL. WARREN E. MICKEN (Dead)

LT. COL. GUY H. STUBBS (Prisoner)

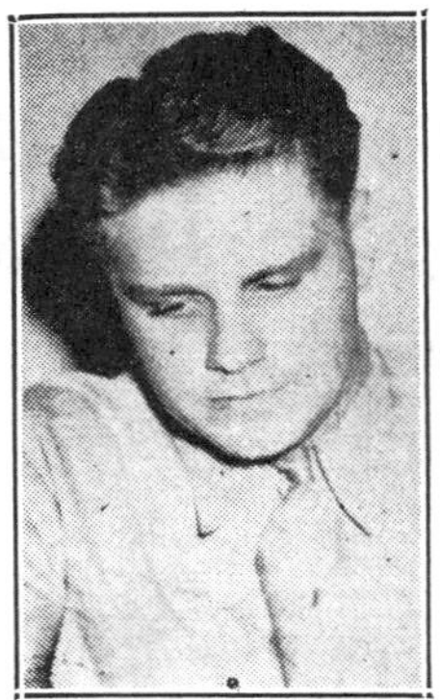
CWO. RICHARD P. LINDEMUTH (Prisoner)

SGT. LOUIS SACHWALD (Prisoner)

PFC. CHARLES M. FORRY (Prisoner)

PFC. FREDERICK R. USNER (Prisoner)

LT. CHARLES B. FRANK (Prisoner)

PVT. LEONARD E. YOHN (Prisoner)

SGT. EDWARD C. WITMER (Prisoner)

SC-2C HARRY G. KEATH (Prisoner)

HARRY M. BECKER (Missing)

SGT. CHARLES V. BEALLER (Missing)

S-2C PAUL B. MARTIN (Missing)

ELWOOD A. ROYER (Missing)

CONCERN FELT OVER ELEVEN FROM HERE HELD BY JAPANESE

Three Of Country's Valiant Defenders Of Philippines Dead In Prison Camps Already

With three Lancaster county soldiers already dead, great concern was expressed Thursday night over the welfare of 11 other known prisoners of the Japanese in the Philippines as the War and Navy Departments officially released a blood-curdling account of starvation and brutality in those camps.

SGT. RICHWINE (Prisoner)

Official casualty lists revealed that there were 19 Lancaster county service men among the valiant defenders of Bataan and Corregidor. Fourteen were taken prisoner by the Japanese, of which three died. Five more are still carried as missing in action.

MS. HUMPHREYS (Prisoner)

During the past few months sterotyped messages have been filtering to the relatives of the prisoners by means of the International Red Cross. All have been hand lettered, all recite the same fact, "am well and uninjured." No factual information was enclosed.

The first of the local prisoners to die was Pvt. Karl H. Stoltzfus, 140 E. Chestnut St. His name was contained in a list of more than 300 prisoner deaths announced in June, 1943.

NORMAN DAVIS (Missing)

The War Department at that time said Japan, through the Red Cross, claimed the deaths were caused by disease. Malaria, diphtheria, dysentery, pneumonia and beri-beri were among the diseases listed.

vived by two brothers and one sister, Charles, James and Gloria, all

More of CONCERN on Page 22

CONFEREES ADOPT LONG SERIES OF EXCISE TAX RAISES

25 Per Cent Levy On Cosmetics, Toilet Articles, Including Shaving Cream

Washington—(AP)—Congressional conferees on the new tax bill Thursday gave their final approval to a long series of excise tax increases designed to collect more than a billion dollars additional a year from wartime spenders.

Rouge, lipstick, face powder—all such cosmetics and toilet articles, including shaving cream — will carry a new 25 per cent tax rate in place of the present 10 per cent, or the 20 per cent approved by the Senate.

(The conferees approval virtually assures enactment of the excises.)

Patrons of cabarets, night clubs and juke joints must figure on handing Uncle Sam 30 cents for each dollar they spend. The present tax is 5 per cent and the Senate had voted to hold the increased rate to 20 per cent. The Senate also attempted to temper the tax by excluding service men from its application, but the conferees decided any celebrating soldiers should pay just like civilian playboys.

The tax on pool and billard tables becomes $20 per table annually;

More of CONFEREES on Page 22

U. S. Suspends Oil Shipments From Caribbean To Spain

Washington—(AP)—The United States has suspended all shipments from the Caribbean area to Spain for the month of February, it was learned on excellent authority Thursday night,

The step is understood to be part of a general reconsideration by this government of Spain's over-all position with regard to the war.

LIMITED AMOUNTS

Spain has been allowed an extremely limited amount of fuel oil and gasoline from the Caribbean area, practically her only source of supply. The agreed quotas supply most essential needs but make it virtually impossible for Spain to gather any reserves.

Matters involved in reconsideration of Spain's position regarding the war include that nation's failure to release Italian ships interned in her ports, to control adequately German agents operating on her territory, and reduce export of war materials to Germany.

The climactic step on Spain's part was the negotiation recently of an agreement with Germany providing 400,000,000 pesetas credit (about $40,000,000) to the Nazis.

The credit was accorded Germany as payment for debts incurred during the Spanish Civil War.

SEVERE BLOW TO ALLIES

This was a severe blow at Allied efforts to reduce strategic German imports, since during the past six months Germany has received very little from Spain because of the Nazis' lack of pesetas.

The most important material the Germans import from Spain is wolfram, ore from which tungsten is derived. The Allies have adequate supplies but have made vigorous efforts to prevent German acquisition of the vital metal, used

More of U.S. SUSPENDS Page 22

Bulletin

BAG 16 JAP PLANES IN MARSHALLS RAID

Pearl Harbor—(AP)—Seventh Army Air Force Mitchell medium bombers and fighters downed 16 and probably 22 planes Wednesday in the biggest aerial battle over the Marshall Islands since the Navy carrier-based raid of Dec. 4, Adm. Chester W. Nimitz announced Thursday night.

The air action over those invasion menaced mid-Pacific bases, carrying an air offensive there through the 21st day, occurred during an assault on Taroa airfield on Maloelap atoll.

All the American raiders returned.

POINT VALUES ARE LOWERED FOR MANY PROCESSED FOODS

Boost Ration Stamp Cost Of Most Cuts Of Beef, Lamb, Veal

Washington — (AP) — Most canned vegetables were assigned lower point values for February Thursday, but the ration stamp cost of most cuts of beef, lamb and veal was boosted slightly.

In announcing two-point reductions for such items as corn, beets, tomatoes and spinach, price administrator Chester Bowles heeded the request of commercial canners for lower values but at the same time, he dashed their hopes for outright removal of vegetables from rationing.

OPA SYMPATHETIC

Canners had reported "sympathetic reception" by OPA of their appeal which was based on estimates that supplies of home-canned vegetables are large.

"The rumors (of a point holiday) are without foundation," Bowles declared. "The truth is that our food needs are fully as great this year as last. The military demand is greater. Civilian purchasing power and demand are greater."

The new point tables, which go into effect Sunday, show increases in the canned fruit category for applesauce, fruit cocktail, peaches

More of POINTS on Page 17

GERMAN THRUST REPULSED BY ALLIED FORCES

Crack Hermann Goering Division Beaten Below Littoria In Pontine Marshes

Stockholm—(AP)—The roar of Allied artillery now is heard plainly in all parts of Rome and Allied aircraft swarm the skies about the city, the Rome correspondent of the Goeteborg Handels Sjoefarts Tidningen said in a dispatch Thursday.

The Swedish correspondent said naval officers in Rome estimated that at least 2,800 vessels of all descriptions participated in the Allied landings at Nettuno. He said the immense armada virtually covered the sea off the landing beaches.

CONFISCATE RADIOS

All radios in Rome have been confiscated, presumably in a German effort to keep the inhabitants in the dark concerning military operations, he said. Telephones, however, still are functioning.

German authorities were reported offering a reward of 200,000 lira ($2,000) for information about persons participating in "terroristic" activities. Armed guards patrol the city and Vatican guards have been strengthened considerably, the dispatch said.

Rome already has the appearance of a besieged town, with every inhabitant "a prisoner," the Rome correspondent of the newspaper Dagens Nyheter said.

PICTURE OF ROME

He gave this picture of Rome as the Allies and Germans prepared for the battle almost within sight of the ancient city:

Bicycling outside the city is forbidden. All roads are blocked. By 4 p. m., there is no sign of life on the streets. Curfew is at 5 p. m., but the shops close at 3 to permit employes to reach their homes. The trams halt at 3:30.

The curfew is imposed because of acts of sabotage, the correspondent said, but he added "an objective person must say the activity of the Partisans often is silly." He cited the throwing of small hand grenades at German army cars "which is of no military importance and the only consequence is that peaceful people must suffer."

Germans guard traffic junctions and sentries at all bridges have

More of GERMAN on Page 22

COUNTY SOLDIER KILLED IN ITALY; AIRMAN INJURED

Pvt. Harry F. Brendle, Adamstown, Reported Dead; Sgt. L. L. Wagner, Ephrata, In Hospital

A Lancaster county soldier was killed in Italy and a flier with the Eighth Army Air Force in England was injured in action, according to reports received here Thursday.

Pvt. Harry Franklin Brendle, nineteen, was killed in action in Italy according to word received by his parents, Lewis and Mary Stork Brendle, of Mohnton R. 2. Two days ago his parents received word that he was wounded Jan. 7 and later received the notice of his death, Jan. 9.

HAD SERVED AT SITKA

Brendle, who resided with his grandmother, Mrs. Sallie Brendle, of 155 W. Main St., Adamstown, attended the Adamstown schools, and was employed at the Adamstown Hat Co., before his enlistment Nov. 23, 1942. He had served with the First Special Service Force at Sitka, Alaska, for three months, returning to this country for a short time before being sent to Italy four months ago.

Besides the parents he is sur-

More of COUNTY on Page 22

Bulletin

RAF BOMBERS AGAIN HIT REICH CAPITAL

London (Friday)— (AP) —RAF bombers battered Berlin again last night, the British announced today, in a smashing renewal of the obliteration campaign against the German capital.

It was the first raid on Berlin since the night of Jan. 21, when a great force of British bombers struck at both the capital and Magdeburgh.

Last night's attack apparently was carried out in force. Observers on the English coast earlier had reported big formations of raiders sweeping out across the Channel following widespread daylight sweeps by British and Canadian aircraft over France and the Low countries in which 10 Nazi fighters were downed.

Marshall M. Cohen Appointed United States Commissioner

Marshall M. Cohen, 601 N. Duke st., Thursday was named to fill the vacancy caused when Commissioner A. E. McCollough, Jr., was inducted into the United States Army.

The commission, signed by all the judges of the United States court for the Eastern District of Pennsylvania, was delivered to Mr. Cohen Thursday.

Mr. Cohen attended the public schools in this city and served as attorney for the Home Owners Loan Corporation from 1936 to 1939 and was a special deputy attorney general of Pennsylvania from 1935 to 1939. He also served a term as a member of the House of Representatives from Lancaster city.

MARSHALL M. COHEN

SAVE THIS NEWSPAPER

Make this newspaper do double work—give it to your paper-salvage drive.

HONOR ROLL

★ WATT & SHAND

FOR STAMPS AND BONDS

Let's Back Up These And All Loyal Americans By Buying More War Bonds!

These former Watt & Shand employees are typical of millions of other loyal Americans offering their lives for their country! . . Let's back them up by buying more war stamps and bonds! . . During this 4th War Loan drive, this store has joined with all the Retailers of America to sell 5 billion dollars worth of war bonds. . . Come in and help one of our salespeople win one of the coveted "Merit Certificates" given for selling $200 worth of bonds.

P. M. FIRST CLASS LEROY ALGIERS is serving with the U. S. Navy somewhere in the Pacific. He was formerly employed in Watt & Shand's Furniture Department Warehouse.

SERGEANT ROY B. WEITZEL is serving with the U. S. Army at Fort Myer, Virginia. He was formerly employed in Watt & Shand's Rug Department.

PFC. HERBERT GISH is serving with the U. S. Army somewhere overseas. He was formerly employed in Watt & Shand's Rug Department.

MACHINIST MATE HENRY KOESTNER is serving with the U. S. Navy somewhere on the seas. He was formerly employed in Watt & Shand's Display Department.

MASTER SERGEANT MELVIN MAYER is serving with the U. S. Army at Ellington Field, Texas. He was formerly employed in Watt & Shand's Package Department.

PRIVATE FRANK B. HUTH, JR., is serving with the U. S. Army somewhere overseas. He was formerly employed in Watt & Shand's Display Department.

FIREMAN THIRD CLASS ROBERT MABEL is serving with the U. S. Navy at Sampson, New York. He was formerly employed in Watt & Shand's Display Department.

CORPORAL SAMUEL CACCAMO is serving with the U. S. Army in El Paso, Texas. He was formerly employed in Watt & Shand's Beauty Salon.

★

PFC. DONALD ULRICH is serving with the U. S. Army at Camp Campbell, Kentucky. He was formerly employed in Watt & Shand's Men's Furnishings Department.

SEAMAN SECOND CLASS WALTER TOMLINSON is training with the U. S. Navy at the University of Chicago, Illinois. He was formerly employed in Watt & Shand's Delivery Department.

PRIVATE HARVEY SHISSLER is serving with the U. S. Army somewhere overseas. He was formerly employed in Watt & Shand's Men's Clothing Department.

PRIVATE CHARLES R. GARRETT is serving with the U. S. Army somewhere overseas. He was formerly employed in Watt & Shand's Rug Department.

★

PFC. RICHARD KRUSCHINSKY is serving with the U. S. Army at Camp Campbell, Kentucky. He was formerly employed in Watt & Shand's Rug Department.

CORPORAL FRED BISHOP is in the 384th Field Artillery Bn., Headquarter's Battery at Camp Howze, Texas. He was formerly employed in Watt & Shand's Hoover Cleaner Department.

WEATHER

Eastern Pennsylvania: Considerable Cloudiness And Warmer, Thundershowers In The Mountains Monday; Tuesday Warmer, Thundershowers West Portion.

Intelligencer Journal

The Leading Newspaper in the Garden Spot of America, Home Owned for Home Folks Since 1794

Turn In Last Week's PAPERS For This Week's SCHOOL COLLECTION

VOLUME LXX X.—NO. 229. Entered as second class matter June 23, 1928 at the Post Office at Lancaster, Pa., under the Act of March 3, 1879 Reg. U. S. Pat. Off. LANCASTER, PA., MONDAY MORNING, JUNE 5, 1944 CITY TWELVE PAGES. 20c PER WEEK—4c Per Copy

ROME FALLS TO 5th ARMY

Allied Warplanes Saturate German Invasion Defenses

Batter Axis Targets Around Boulogne; Mediterranean Units Seek To Sever Two Main Rail Lines Between France And Italy; Suffer Light Losses

London—(AP)—Upward of 1,200 American heavy bombers struck Europe again Sunday — some 500 pounding German strongholds along the invasion coast while their comrades from the Mediterranean made a strong attempt to sever two main rail lines between France and Italy.

RAF bombers battered targets in enemy-occupied Europe again Sunday night, the British announced Monday (today), taking up the burden of the non-stop offensive. Specific objectives of the overnight assault were not immediately announced.

Swarms of medium bombers and fighter bombers from Britain kept the thunderous assaults going for the second straight day saturating defenses around Boulogne with 1,500 tons of bombs.

HIT NAZI RADIO CHAIN

Spitfire bombers and fighters hammered enemy radio installations along the northern coast of France Sunday evening and the air ministry announced that more links in the Nazi radio chain had been broken.

The U. S. army air forces announced early Monday that four heavy bombers and three fighters were missing from three raids Sunday against Nazi transport lines

More of ALLIED on Page 9

"We Lead All The Rest"

FARM CORNER

By The Farm Editor

AUTHORIZE WINTER COVER CROP PRACTICE

To encourage farmers to combat the ill effects of erosion in corn and other cultivated crops, the AAA has authorized a Winter cover crop practice as a part of the farm program, offering two dollars an acre as a "conservation" payment, State AAA headquarters, Harrisburg, announced Sunday.

Farmers who seed domestic rye grass in the last working of corn or any cultivated row crop, in buckwheat, soybeans, orchards and vineyards, will receive the $2.00 per acre as a conservation payment.

The AAA said Pennsylvania farmers are planting about 90,000 more acres of corn than in 1943 and "muddy rivers show cover crops are needed." W. Clayton Jester, chief of field operations for the AAA in Pennsylvania, pointed out "Corn is a valuable feed crop but likewise a soil depleting crop. Unless sound conservation practices are followed, we can destroy in one year a great deal of the progress we have made in soil conservation during the past ten years.

"Rye grass is one of the best cover crops. Its roots and blades form a protecting blanket against Fall and Winter rains. This blanket will hold soil on the hillsides and prevent the clogging of streams."

RURAL YOUTH SESSION TUES.

A business session followed by a "lengthy recreational period" will feature the June session of the Rural Youth of Lancaster County to be held at the Farm Bureau, this city, on Tuesday at 8:15 p. m., Richard Lefever, president, announced.

John Rothfus will conduct the devotions; Paul Huber will lead group singing; and Rhelda Eshleman will entertain with saxophone selections.

REFUSES $350 FOR MILKER

Cows sold from $80 to $199 per

More of FARM CORNER on Page 9

Weather Calendar

COMPARATIVE TEMPERATURES

Station	High	Low
Water Works	83	57
Official High for Year, May 13		90
Official Low for Year, Jan 17		2
Character of Day		Cloudy

SUN

Rises—5:36 a. m. Sets—8:29 p. m.

MOON

Sets—5:00 a. m. Full Moon, June 6

STARS

Morning—Venus.
Evening—Jupiter-Saturn.

NEARBY FORECASTS

Maryland, Virginia: Considerable cloudiness and warmer, thundershowers in the mountains Monday; Tuesday warmer, thundershowers west portion

New Jersey and Delaware: Considerable cloudiness, warmer Monday afternoon; Tuesday fair and warmer

SAVE THIS NEWSPAPER

Make this newspaper do double work—give it to your paper-salvage drive.

LEARN FATE OF TWO COUNTY SOLDIERS MISSING IN ACTION

Cpl. V. E. Meashey Dead; Sgt. F. A. Snavely Prisoner Of Germans

The fate of two Lancaster county soldiers previously reported missing in action was made known by the War Department over the week-end—one is listed as killed and the other a prisoner of the Germans.

Cpl. Vernon E. Meashey, twenty-five, formerly of Hershey, died Nov. 27, 1943, when a troop ship was sunk by the enemy in the European theatre, his wife, the former Caroline Cramer Meashey, of Lancaster R1, was informed.

CPL. MEASHEY T/S SNAVELY

Technical Sgt. Fred A. Snavely, radioman and gunner on a bomber in England, missing since April 22, is a prisoner of the German government his parents, Mr. and Mrs. Clayton B. Snavely, of Lititz, were informed.

Sgt. Snavely entered the Army Air Forces in January, 1941, and received his training at Scott Field. He had been in England since Oct. 10, 1942.

Cpl. Meashey, son of Mr. and Mrs. Chester Meashey, of Hershey, was the Army Air Forces and he had been reported missing in action Nov. 26, 1943.

Mrs. Meashey received a letter Saturday from the War Department saying that her husband "died as the result of the sinking of a troop ship by enemy action in the European theatre of war."

USE PENICILLIN TO TREAT SOLDIER ILL WITH INFECTION

Sgt. William U. Hensel, III, son of Mr. and Mrs. William U. Hensel, Jr., of Quarryville, is in serious condition at St. Joseph's hospital from a leg infection which developed as he was traveling to his home from Sheppard Field, Tex., to spend a furlough.

As physicians used the wonder drug penicillin to combat the infection, the sergeant's family said that he had suffered what was considered a minor leg injury two days before leaving the Texas army base.

The injury, physicians said, apparently became infected. He was taken to a physician Saturday afternoon immediately upon his arrival in Lancaster. The physician ordered his immediate removal to the hospital.

NEW COMIC STRIP

Beginning this morning, the Intelligencer Journal presents to its readers a new comic strip, Wash Tubbs. The strip replaces Flash Gordon, which has been concluded by its artist. Follow the adventures of Wash Tubbs and his pal, Captain Easy, daily in the Intelligencer Journal and in the Sunday News.

SOVIETS TOLD DIRECT FACTS BY JOHNSTON

U. S. C. Of C. Head Says Communists Wasting Their Time In This Country

Moscow— (AP) —Eric Johnston, president of the Chamber of Commerce of the United States, in an address to Soviet trade leaders Saturday and released Sunday, urged that Russians and Americans reconcile themselves to different economic systems and carry on a flourishing business.

The speech, probably the frankest and most provocative ever made in Moscow by a private individual, was at a luncheon given by Anastas I. Mikoyan, Soviet trade commissar, and issued by Johnston Sunday at a press conference.

Johnston prefaced his speech by warning the Russians, "I am going to tell you direct, harsh business facts."

"In economic ideology, the practice of my country is different from yours," he said. "You are state-minded, collective-minded. We are most private-minded, most individual-minded and gentlemen, make no mistake, we are determined to remain so or even to become more so."

He told the Russians to "realize how completely our American Communists have been wasting their time."

In a recent poll, he said, most organized workers answering a question as to their social class replied middle class.

2 HORSE-DRAWN VEHICLES STRUCK BY AUTOMOBILES

State Police Seek Hit And Run Driver In Crash Near Paradise

Two horse-drawn vehicles were struck by automobiles on county roads in two of a number of accidents reported over the week-end. In another accident, a cow was struck and killed.

State Police Sunday night were seeking a hit-and-run automobile driver which crashed into a horse-drawn wagon driven by Daniel I. Beiler, New Holland R1, near Paradise, at about 10:30 p. m. Sunday. State Policeman L. A. Mazakas, who is investigating, said a wheel was broken from the wagon Beiler was driving but that neither the horse nor the driver were injured.

At about 7:30 p. m. Sunday, a horse-drawn wagon driven by Harry N. Snyder, forty-three, Ephrata R3, was struck by an automobile near Hinkletown. Ephrata state police said the driver of the car was Richard Stauffer, sixteen, 42 E. Fulton St., Ephrata. They reported passengers in the wagon were shaken up but no one was seriously injured.

3 PERSONS INJURED

Three persons were injured when the automobile in which they were riding left the New Holland pike, a mile east of Lancaster, and overturned at 12:15 p. m. Sunday.

The auto was driven, State Police, said, by Fireman First Class Claude H. Hemperly, Jr., eighteen, 2 Ryder Ave. He was traveling east on the highway when the car left the highway, mounted a bank, ran over the trolley tracks and

More of ACCIDENTS on Page 9

Eternal City Falls To Allies

Allied troops captured ancient Rome Sunday and pushed beyond the Eternal City in pursuit of battered German forces. The above airview of Rome shows the Victor Emmanuel Monument at the upper left. Below its right corner is the Palazzo Venezia. The domed building in the center is the Pantheon. The River Tiber shows at the lower right.

ORDER SIX DRAFT OBJECTORS SENT TO WORK CAMPS

County Board No. 4 Told To Forward Recent Federal Parolees To Virginia Camp

National Selective Service headquarters has ordered County Draft Board No. 4 to forward to a civilian public service camp the six conscientious objectors who recently left the Sideling Hill camp after being discharged from Federal court probation.

The six, who were sentenced to the Pennsylvania camp in 1942, after they voluntarily refused to report, are scheduled to be at the Grottoes, Va., camp, June 15.

LIST REGISTRANTS

The registrants, who spent a little more than two years of the three-year sentence at Sideling Hill imposed by U. S. Judge Harry Kalodner, and who left the camp against the advice of the Federal Probation System, are:

Daniel Weaver Hoover, New Holland R1; Elam Souder Shirk, East Earl R1; George Martin Zimmerman, New Holland R1; Isaac Shirk Eby, New Holland R1; Isaac Martin Risser, Bareville R1; and David Weaver Shirk, New Holland R1.

The draft board, in announcing that it had been directed to forward the men to the Grottoes camp, said that five of the six recently passed pre-induction physical examinations. The sixth, who failed to report for his examination, has been ordered to report on a delinquent status.

The youths, who face their second call to camp, or possible prose-

More of ORDER on Page 9

MAN FOUND DEAD NEAR COATESVILLE

Coatesville—Abner Johnson, sixty-eight, was found shot to death behind a chicken coop at the rear of his home, Coatesville R1, Sunday morning. Police said a 16-gauge single-barrelled shotgun was found beside him.

State Policeman said Johnson's body was found by his son-in-law, James Smith, of the same address, at about 8:15 a. m., an hour after he was last seen. Pvt. G. F. Robinson, of the State Police, is continuing his investigation.

Soldier Returns From Service Abroad To Learn Best Friend Has Been Killed

Sgt. Albert L. McMullin, sent back to the United States for reassignment after two years in the Mediterranean area, arrived at the home of his parents, Mr. and Mrs. A. B. McMullin, 9 Rider Ave., to learn that while enroute his company had been transferred and his best friend killed.

The friend was Staff Sgt. David H. Meisky, twenty-one, son of Mr. and Mrs. Daniel L. Meisky, 217 Ice Ave.

BOTH IN 213TH CAAA

Both were attached to the former Battery E, 213th Coast Artillery, Anti-aircraft, a Pennsylvania National Guard unit, stationed in Lancaster.

When Sgt. McMullin said farewell to Meisky and his buddies the company was stationed near the Volturno River in Italy, protecting airfields.

When he arrived home he learned that the company, transferred

More of SOLDIER on Page 9

Near the Volturno River in Italy, Sgt. Albert L. McMullin reads the Intelligencer Journal, catching up on events in his home town.

U. S. Tanks Knock Out Scout Car In Front Of Bank Of Italy

(By Daniel De Luce)

Rome—(AP)—Rome, the Eternal City, was liberated Sunday night by tanks and infantry troops of the Allied Fifth Army which battled German rear-guards to the edge of the ancient forum.

A force from the old Anzio beachhead completed the mop-up of Nazi forces at 9:15 p. m. (3:15 p. m., Eastern War Time) by knocking out an enemy scout car in front of the Bank of Italy, almost within the shadow of the column erected to Emperor Trajan, who ruled the Romans from 98 to 117 A. D.

The Fifth Army force fought its way into the heart of the city after a four-hour battle against German armor in the suburbs of the ancient capital.

The city of seven hills was the first Axis capital to fall to Allied troops who were pursuing the Germans north of Rome with the aid of swarms of Allied planes battering at Nazi transport columns.

Shortly after 3:30 p. m. the Germans began a frenzied series of demolitions inside Rome. Huge clouds of smoke plumed above the city.

American and other armored troops flowed through the heart of Rome's governmental district, snuffing out the last bits of German resistance almost four years after Benito Mussolini plunged his countrymen into war against France on the side of Germany.

(Behind a doubled Swiss guard sealing off Vatican City, Pope Pius XII held urgent consultations Sunday with the Papal Secretary of State, Luigi Cardanaw Maglione, and prayed in his private chapel, the London Daily Mail's Madrid correspondent reported.

In a dawn dash from Borgata Finocchio, 13 miles distant on the Via Casilina, a spearhead of 24 Sherman tanks, eight armored cars and 150 U. S. and Canadian infantrymen pushed beyond suburban Torre Spaccata before they ran headlong into a German road block.

Old men and young girls and todding children were waving the Americans on when the fire of German 88-millimeter guns knocked out the leading tank and snipers starting pouring machinee-gun fire from hideouts next to a white church whose bells were ringing for early mass.

AMERICAN TROOPS OPEN DRIVE FOR 3 BIAK AIRDROMES

Allied Planes Bag 30 Jap Interceptors In Widespread Pacific Sweeps

(By The Associated Press)

Two columns of American troops began pushing slowly toward three airdromes on Biak island, within bombing range of the Philippines, after five days preparation for the offensive, Southwest Pacific headquarters announced Monday (today).

Japanese dug in along the hills, and supported by tanks, had stopped the original advance off the northwestern New Guinea coast. U. S. Sixth army troops moved along the beach and the commanding ridge in their renewed drive towards Mokmer, nearest of the three fields.

BAG 30 JAP PLANES

Topping widespread aerial sweeps over the Pacific, Allied planes shot down 30 Japanese interceptors in three air battles. Nine were brought down over Biak, 11 at Babo, also near the western end of New Guinea, and ten at Truk in the Caroline islands.

South Pacific American troops made a new landing back of Japanese lines near the mouth of the Jaba river, twelve miles from the Allied air base on Bougainville island in the Solomons.

American bombers swept almost unmolested over the extremities of Tokyo's eastern island defenses while Japanese ground forces pushed down central China in an effort to keep the Allies from establishing bases closer to the heart of her empire.

HULL AT HERSHEY FOR WEEK'S REST

Hershey, Pa. —(AP)— Secretary of State Hull came here Saturday for a week's rest but kept in constant touch with his office with a private telephone line.

The secretary said he has scheduled no conferences during his stay at the $31,000,000 Hotel Hershey and planned to spend his time on the putting greens and strolling over spacious hotel grounds, including scenic rose gardens.

Before leaving Washington, Hull brushed aside speculation that his Hershey visit might be the occasion for announced conferences with representatives of Britain, Russia and China on post-war peace plans.

"It's a marvelous place," declared the secretary after his first tour of the area. "I came here for a rest away from the tension of Washington."

He was accompanied by his wife and three aides who emphasized that the secretary is "taking it easy," recalling he has had hardly any vacation in several years.

EMMANUEL CHURCH TO ASK TRANSFER TO CENTRAL PA. SYNOD

Emmanuel Lutheran Church voted unanimously Sunday to amend its constitution and to apply for transfer to the Central Pennsylvania Synod to take effect at such time as is agreed upon by the two synods involved. This action is in harmony with the resolutions passed at the recent meeting of the Ministerium of Pennsylvania at which time this synod urged all of its congregations situated west of the eastern boundary of Lancaster County to apply for transfer to the Central Synod of Pennsylvania. The object is to overcome an overlapping of synods on the territory of eastern Pennsylvania.

At this same congregational meeting, the resignation of the assistant pastor, Rev. Ernest H. Flothmeier was accepted with sincere regrets, to take effect on July 1. Pastor Flothmeier has received and accepted a call from the Foreign Mission Board of the United Lutheran Church to serve in Liberia, West Africa. Pastor Flothmeier has served at Emmanuel Church since June 1, 1943. The pastor of the church is Rev. Ernest J. Hoh.

Yanks-Canadians Sweep North In Pursuit Of Nazis

Complete Mop-up Of Center Of Eternal City—First Axis European Capital To Fall To Allied Troops—After Bitter Fighting

Allied Headquarters, Naples—(AP)—Fifth Army troops captured ancient Rome Sunday night, smashing German resistance in the heart of the Eternal City and sweeping on northward in pursuit of battered German forces which had dynamited some installations.

The mop-up of the center of Rome—the first Axis European capital to fall to Allied troops—was completed at 9:15 p. m. (3:15 p. m., Eastern War Time) by Americans and Canadians under Lt. Gen. Mark W. Clark.

How much of the city was razed by the beaten German garrison was not immediately learned, but most of the bitter all-day fighting occurred in the suburban areas.

The last German rearguard unit was crushed by Allied gunners in front of the Bank of Italy, almost within the shadow of Trajan's column.

A smoke pall hung over parts of the city where the Germans began their demolitions shortly after 3:30 p. m. (The BBC in a broadcast recorded by NBC said this indicated the Germans had "probably destroyed the bridges over the Tiber" river, which runs southward through the city and then southwest to the Tyrrhenian Sea. Across the Tiber lies Vatican City).

ROOSEVELT TO DISCUSS FALL OF ROME TONIGHT

Washington—(AP)—President Roosevelt will discuss the fall of Rome, the first Axis capital captured by the Allies, in a 15-minute radio broadcast to the nation Monday night.

The White House announced Sunday night the President's talk will be carried over the four major networks between 8:30 p. m. and 8:45 p. m., Eastern War Time.

North of the city Allied warplanes shot up fleeing German transports, wrecking or damaging at least 600 motor vehicles along the clogged retreat roads. These "excellent targets" were encountered as far as Lake Bolsena, 50 miles above Rome, an indication that the next main German defense line may be in that area.

East of Rome the Germans had withdrawn into the Savine Mountains northeast of Valmontone in the area above Palestrina, about 25 miles east-southeast of Rome. The Allied Eighth Army was attacking in that sector.

CLARK APPEARS

Front dispatches from Edward Kennedy and Daniel De Luce, Associated Press correspondents who entered Rome with the Allied troops, said the final drive from the suburbs began after General Clark appeared in the fighting area, where bullets whizzed about his head.

The Germans had thrown up road blocks of wrecked vehicles and other material, and shelled important road intersections with 88-mm. self-propelled guns. This slowed the Allied drive by troops of the old Anzio beachhead, and the fighting continued to the edge of the ancient forum in the center of Rome.

The huge air-wreaked toll of Nazi transports on congested roads above Rome indicated the enemy intended no major stand in the ancient city—first European capital to be entered by Allied troops.

Opposition appeared to be taper-

More of YANKS on Page 9

Hitler Presents Plan For Making Rome 'Open City'

Reports Nazi Forces Withdrawn To Northwest, Says Fight To Continue

London—(AP)—Hitler announced Sunday night in two special communiques—broadcast after Allied troops had liberated Rome—the withdrawal of German troops to the northwest of the city and said the Allies had been offered a plan whereby Rome would be regarded as an "open city."

In the first word from the Fuehrer's headquarters in several days, it was asserted the fight in Italy would continue and that measures were being taken "to force final

More of HITLER on Page 9

Final Can Collection By Schools This Week; Special Efforts Urged

The last tin can collection for the present school year will be held Wednesday and Thursday, and Salvage officials urged Sunday that every can available be turned in at a school on those days.

"Unload all the tin cans possible so that there will be no backlog when the school collections are resumed in the fall," Earl F. Rebman, salvage chairman urged.

"Most important,'" he added, "continue to save and properly prepare cans over the summer months as tin is one of the most vitally needed metals at this time."

Members of families who have no school children are asked to "be personally responsible" that their prepared cans will be taken to the closest school building.

The Salvage committee also announced the names of school children who were presented with Merits of Award for collecting at least 900 tin cans during a month. Some children won the award twice.

MERIT AWARDS

The winners and the number of cans:

Poplar Street School, Columbia—Harold McKonley, 519 N. Second St.,

More of FINAL on Page 9

WEATHER
Eastern Pennsylvania: Warmer With Afternoon Thundershowers Tuesday; Wednesday Considerable Cloudiness And Much Cooler.

Intelligencer Journal.

SCHOOL TIN CAN COLLECTION WED. & THURS.

The Leading Newspaper in the Garden Spot of America, Home Owned for Home Folks Since 1794

VOLUME LXXX.—NO. 230. Entered as second class matter June 23, 1928 at the Post Office at Lancaster, Pa., under the Act of March 3, 1879 Reg. U. S. Pat. Off. LANCASTER, PA., TUESDAY MORNING, JUNE 6, 1944 CITY SIXTEEN PAGES. 20c PER WEEK—4c Per Copy

ALLIES INVADE FRANCE

Great Aerial And Sea Armadas Support Operations From LaHavre To Cherbourg

Supreme Headquarters, Allied Expeditionary Force (Tuesday) — (AP) —Gen. Dwight D. Eisenhower's Headquarters announced today that Allied troops began landing on the northern coast of France this morning strongly supported by naval and air forces.

Text of the communique:

Under the command of Gen. Eisenhower Allied Naval forces supported by strong air forces began landing Allied armies this morning on the northern coast of France.

The Germans said the landings extended between Le Havre and Cherbourg along the south side of the bay of the Seine and along the northern Normandy coast.

Parachute troops descended in Normandy, Berlin said.

Berlin first announced the landings in a series of flashes that began about 6:30 a. m. (12:30 a. m. Eastern War Time).

The Allied communique was read over a trans-Atlantic hookup direct from General Eisenhower's headquarters at 3:32 E.W.T., designated "Communique No. 1."

A second announcement by Shaef said that "it is announced that Gen. B. L. Montgomery is in command of the army group carrying out the assault. This army group includes British, Canadian, and U. S. forces."

The Allied bulletin did not say exactly where the invasion was taking place, but Berlin earlier gave these details:

SHELLING LE HAVRE

Allied naval forces, including heavy warships, are shelling Le Havre. "It is a terrific bombardment," Berlin said.

Allied parachute troops floating down along the Normandy coast were landing and being engaged by German shock troops.

Other Allied units were streaming ashore into Normandy from landing barges.

In a special order of the day issued to all soldiers, sailors and airmen under his command, Gen. Eisenhower said:

"We will accept nothing except full victory."

Eisenhower told his men they were "embarking on a great crusade toward which we have striven these many months," and warned them that they were facing a tough, well-prepared enemy.

Berlin said the "center of gravity" of the fierce fighting was at Caen, 30 miles southwest of Le Havre and 65 miles southeast of Cherbourg.

Caen is 10 miles inland from the sea, at the base of the 75-mile-wide Normandy peninsula.

Heavy fighting also was reported between Caen and Trouville.

One of Berlin's first claims was that the first British parachute division was badly mauled.

General Montgomery, hero of the African desert, was leading the assault of the Allied Liberation Army.

No other Allied commanders were announced, for the thousands of battle-trained Allied troops, although Gen. Omar Bradley has been in command of American ground forces in England for several months.

Bradley participated in the Tunisian victory.

Thousands of battle-trained American, British and Canadian troops hurled themselves at Hitler's western defenses after months of preparation.

Huge troopship armadas slipped out of English ports in the darkness and sped toward Europe where four years ago almost to the day Britain brought back the last battle-worn defenders of Dunkerque.

The Germans also declared that Calais and Dunkerque, immediately across the English channel from Britain, were under heavy air attack.

GERMAN RADIO FIRST

The German radio gave the first reports of the invasion while correspondents were hurriedly summoned from bed to supreme press headquarters and locked in a press conference room until the communique was released several hours after the landings were made.

It was made known at Shaef that the Supreme Command felt it necessary to yield the initiative in the war of words to the Germans in order to retain the initiative on land and keep the German High Command in the dark as long as possible.

The great Allied armadas dwarfed anything yet seen on the sea.

Huge transport planes filled with paratroopers and pulling airborne troops in gliders roared over the German westwall to drop their cargos in the rear.

Berlin said that masses of Allied parachute troops bailed out over Normandy, trying to seize airfields.

WISHED GODSPEED

Just before taking off in the darkness the paratroops were wished Godspeed by the lanky Kansas Supreme Commander, Gen. Eisenhower.

He was accompanied by several other of his commanders and his face was tense but confident as he strode down the long lines of fighting men.

All night long London and England resounded to the roar of thousands of airplanes, some carrying bombs, some carrying men. Returning RAF bombers met big fleets of Flying Fortresses on their way out.

The forces thrown into operation were by far the greatest ever used in an amphibious operation. They had to be. An estimated million German troops waited in their fortifications for the great onslaught under crack Nazi Field Marshals, Runstedt and Rommel.

It was reported earlier this week that Adolf Hitler himself had a special train ready to rush him to France to take over personal command as he did on the East front.

CHASERS FOR ROMMEL

Despite these reports Allied military men expected Rommel to be the main tactician on German defense but on the Allied side were the team of Eisenhower and Montgomery—the men who chased Rommel from Africa.

Although amphibious attacks are the most difficult in war, a quiet feeling of confidence characterized the Allied Generals.

Just what element of surprise, if any, the landing troops achieved was not immediately announced by Supreme Headquarters. There was no chance to hide the great convoys with only about five hours darkness on the channel.

SAILED OUT BEFORE

On several occasions thousands of troops, even with correspondents aboard, sailed out in great fleets to almost within shell range of German defenses in Europe as though they were going to attack while Nazi reconnaissance planes closely checked convoys.

These feints have been carried out on widely separated points.

The Supreme Command made no bones about its intention to attack but the surprise was that the Germans did not know where the main blow was coming.

In four previous big amphibious landings to date the Allies obtained tactical surprise three times—at Anzio, Sicily, and North Africa. At Salerno the Germans guessed the landing spot and were waiting.

Coast Of France Target Of Allied Troops

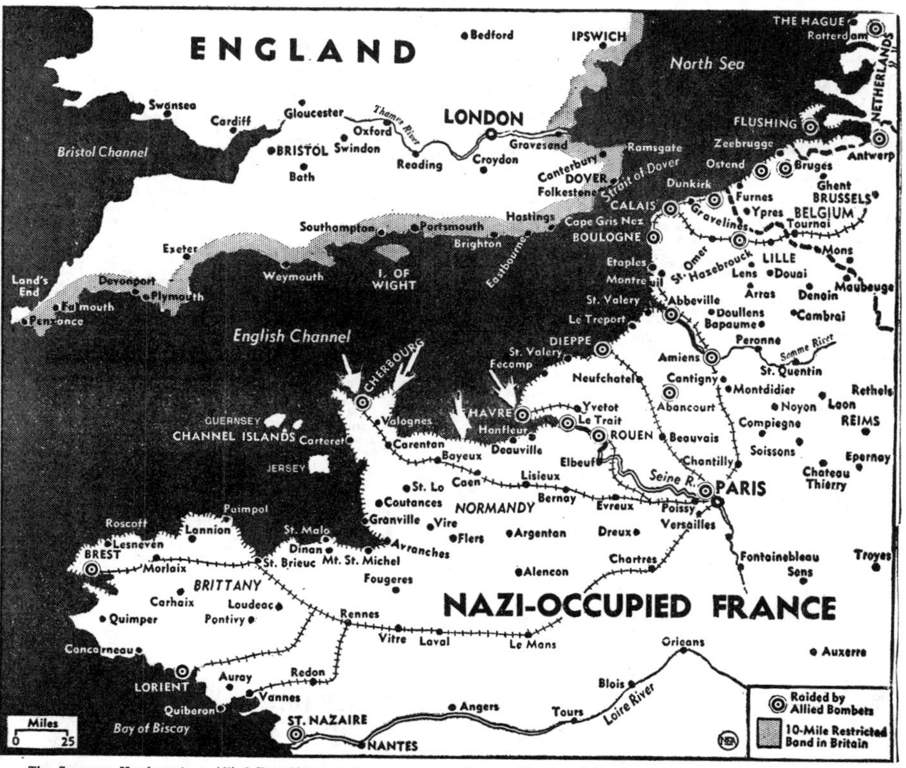

The Supreme Headquarters, Allied Expeditionary Force, announced early this morning that Allied troops are landing on the coast of France, spurred on by a special order of the day from Gen. Dwight B. Eisenhower which said "We will accept nothing except full victory." While the Allied communique did not say exactly where the Allied forces were landing, German broadcasts asserted that the coast between Le Havre and Cherbourg was the target of the soldiers. Berlin said the one center of fighting, probably by Allied paratroops, was about Caen, 30 miles southwest of LeHavre and 65 miles southeast of Cherbourg. The Germans also said that Calais and Dunkerque, immediately across the English Channel from Britain, were under heavy air attack, and reported that masses of Allied parachute troops bailed out over Normandy, trying to seize airfields.

Prayers Arranged for City's Observance Of D-Day

The invasion flash from General Eisenhower's Supreme Headquarters of the Allied Expeditionary Forces arrived in Lancaster at 3:33 a. m. Tuesday, and despite the earliness of the hour the news gradually spread over the sleeping city.

Workers at war plants, making the shells and equipment which the Allies were hurling at the Nazi legions at the very moment, were among the first to hear the news.

The news of the landing of Allied troops in France was broadcast to third shift workers at the RCA plant.

For the most part, however, Lancastrians slept through the initial stages of the invasion.

The Rev. Dr. James E. Wagner, pastor of St. Peter's Evangelical and Reformed Church, notified of the invasion, lighted the candles in his church at 4 a. m. Fifteen-minute prayer services will be held there at 7:30 a. m., 10:30 a. m., 1:30 p. m., 4:30 p. m., 7:30 p. m., and 10:30 p. m.

Practically every church in the city and county will be open for special "Liberation Day" prayers and services, asking divine aid and protection for the success of the forces of liberation in their battle with the Nazi hordes.

To hundreds of Lancaster families D-Day will have a special meaning—their sons, brothers and husbands are among the soldiers, sailors and airmen in England who are making the initial thrust against the German military might.

No demonstration or celebration of any kind has been planned for Lancaster as authorities felt that D-Day was a day to be spent in prayer.

DeGaulle, Free French Chief, Has Arrived In England

New York (Tuesday)—(AP)—Gen. Charles De Gaulle has arrived in England, it was announced today in a broadcast from Supreme headquarters, Allied Expeditionary Force. NBC monitored the broadcast.

Pershing Confident Allied Forces "Will Win Through To Victory"

Washington, (Tuesday) — (AP)— Gen. John J. Pershing, who commanded American armies in France in the World War, issued the following statement following the announcement that a new expeditionary force had landed in France:

"American troops have landed in Western Europe.

"As the overmastering military might of the Allies advances it will be joined by the men of the occupied countries, whose land has been overrun by the enemy but whose spirit remains unconquered.

"Twenty-six years ago American soldiers, in cooperation with their Allies, were locked in mortal combat with the German enemy. Their march of victory was never halted until the enemy laid down his arms in defeat. The American soldier of 1917-1918, fighting in a war of liberation, wrote by his deeds, one of the most glorious pages of military history.

"Today, the sons of American soldiers of 1917-1918 are engaged in a like war of liberation. It is their task to bring freedom to peoples who have been enslaved. I have every confidence that they, together with their gallant brothers-in-arms, will win through to victory."

KING HAAKON WARNS NORWEGIANS AGAINST PREMATURE UPRISINGS

New York, (Tuesday)—(AP)—King Haakon of Norway in an invasion broadcast today to his homeland warned his people against premature uprisings, said a broadcast from Supreme Headquarters, Allied Expeditionary Force, heard by NBC.

The King broadcast special orders to both organized and unorganized resistance groups in Norway.

NAZIS SAY ALLIED FORCES REINFORCED IN LEHAVRE AREA

London, (Tuesday) — (AP) — The German News Agency DNB said in a broadcast shortly before 10 a. m. (4 a. m. EWT) that Anglo-American troops had been reinforced at dawn at the mouth of the Seine River in the Le Havre area.

Sun Breaks Thru Heavy Clouds On First Day Of Allied Invasion

London (Tuesday)—(AP)—The sun broke through heavy clouds at times in the Dover strait area this first day of the Allied invasion of western Europe.

After a daybreak shower there was sunshine, but later banks of heavy clouds swept up from the northwest. There were further sunny periods, although the outlook was less settled.

The wind had blown fairly hard during the night, but lost some of its strength after dawn. A moderate sea was running.

Reveal Allies Conducted Series Of Feints In Advance Of Invasion

Supreme Headquarters, Allied Expeditionary Force (Tuesday)—(AP)—It can now be revealed that the Allies have been conducting a series of feints in advance of the invasion today.

These feints were predicted sometime ago by Prime Minister Churchill, and were designed to lull the Germans so they would never know when the blow was coming.

Japs Will Be Busy Alibiing For Tojo
—Editorial Page

LANCASTER NEW ERA

WEATHER
Thunder showers tonight; Friday clearing and cooler.

VOL. 66—NO. 817 | Entered as second class matter January 31, 1924, at the Post Office at Lancaster, Pa., under the Act of March 3, 1879. Reg. U. S. Pat Off. | LANCASTER, PA., THURSDAY, JULY 20, 1944 | CITY EDITION | 26 PAGES | 20c PER WEEK—4c Per Copy

HITLER ESCAPES BOMBING PLOT

British Tanks Advance Five Miles

Wallace Staging a Comeback; Gets 16 Votes From Kansas

Truman Gets Support of Frank Walker and His Backers Claim V-P Nomination on First or Second Ballot

CHICAGO STADIUM, July 20—(AP)—Henry A. Wallace, regarded by many as all but counted out only 24 hours ago, hit the comeback trail in his fight for renomination today while Senator Harry S. Truman, his leading rival, gained the open support of one of President Roosevelt's cabinet.

Postmaster General Frank Walker told reporters, "I'm for Truman."

Wallace's backers were cheered by addition of 16 Kansas votes to his column.

Two other cabinet members, however — Attorney General Francis Biddle and Interior Secretary Harold Ickes—stood firm for Wallace. Biddle is a Pennsylvania delegate, as is Walker, while Ickes is an Illinois delegate-at-large.

Wallace himself was absent from the convention today.

Kansas, its 16 convention votes previously unpledged, caucused and balloted to give them to the tousled Iowan—possibly indicating a new trend among some of the previously uncommitted delegations.

Backers of Senator Truman, however, conceded nothing—many predicting his nomination over Wallace on the first or second ballot.

Truman himself told reporters, however, "I'm not campaigning for anything."

Asked if he had talked to President Roosevelt, he replied "no."

Cities Support Truman

With 684½ votes still unpledged and unclaimed, Wallace had 154½ votes claimed and 165 pledged outright—total of 319½. Truman had only Missouri's 32 pledged outright, with 589 needed to nominate, but apparently had been promised support from big city organizations.

As the convention prepared to renominate President Roosevelt and hear his acceptance by radio tonight, the lines for the Wallace-Truman struggle were drawn by party leaders. These were headed by National Chairman Robert E. Hannegan, vigorously backing his 60-year-old fellow Missourian.

But Wallace, as today's first caucus vote and hotel corridor talk plainly indicated, made it tough for the strategists who wanted to eliminate him and name the chairman of the Senate's war-investigating committee on the first ballot.

Will Propose Byrd

Meantime, it was announced that the name of Senator Harry F. Byrd of Virginia would be placed in nomination for the Presi-

(See POLITICS—Page 24)

JACKSON WARNS OF "CHANGE"

Must Keep Commander-in-Chief, He Says

CHICAGO STADIUM, July 20.—(AP)—Senator Samuel D. Jackson of Indiana, declaring wartime is no time to change administrations, told the Democratic convention today that the ballot box must not become "Hitler's secret weapon." The Commander-in-Chief, he said, must not be taken from the fighting forces overseas.

Taking over as Permanent Chairman, Jackson told the convention he was confident of an election victory next November because "the American electorate will not vote for change, interruption and delay" in winning the war.

"America will win this war finally and completely, no matter who is elected President of the United States next November," he said.

"But how many battleshps would a Democratic defeat be worth to Tojo?

"How many Nazi legions would it be worth to Adolf Hitler?

"Frankly, could Goebbels himself do better to bolster Axis morale than the word that the American people have upset this administration — the administration that made it possible for the Russians to drive the Nazis back to the Russian border?"

Says G. O. P. Thwarted Peace

Jackson developed the theme also that the Republicans thwarted moves for a lasting peace after World War I, sought to hamstring defense preparations before the current conflict, and in three terms under Harding, Coolidge and Hoover "led us into the depths of depression."

He hit hard at 42-year-old Governor Thomas E. Dewey's references to "old, tired and quarrelsome men" in the Roosevelt administration, uttered when Dewey accepted the Republican Presidential nomination.

President Roosevelt, Jackson declared, "has more rugged vitality

(See JACKSON—Page 23)

INJURED WOMAN, 78, IS FOUND IN HOME

Mrs. Fannie A. Fiero, seventy-eight, widow of John C. Fiero, former city school truant officer, suffered a fractured hip and injured ribs when she fell down a stairway at her home, 435 S. Shippen St., sometime last night. She was admitted to the General Hospital.

A neighbor, Mrs. J. B. MacKenzie, 431 S. Shippen St., went to the house at 8:45 a. m. today and looking through the gass door, saw the woman lying at the foot of the stairway. Unable to gain entrance when she found the doors and windows locked, Mrs. MacKenzie called city police.

Sgt. Shank and Policeman L. Nonnemacher forced an entrance to the home. Due to the serious injuries, police summoned the hospital ambulance to remove the victim. A daughter, Miss Edna Fiero, of Merchantville, N. J., was notified.

MAIZE IS NAMED SECRETARY OF MINES

HARRISBURG, July 20—(AP)—Governor Martin has elevated Richard Maize to full Secretaryship in the Department of Mines following a long period as "acting" secretary under two administrations.

Maize was named acting Secretary by Governor James following the death of John Ira Thomas and retained his post when Governor Martin became the State's chief executive. His commission provided that he continue in office until a successor was named. In removing the "acting" part of his title Martin said "he has done a beautiful job." His salary of $10,000 per year remains the same.

DEWEY CONFERS WITH N. Y. CABINET

ALBANY, N. Y., July 20—(AP)—Gov. Thomas E. Dewey, Republican Presidential candidate, busied himself with a routine of State work today as the Democratic National convention at Chicago prepared to nominate President Roosevelt for a fourth term.

The Governor scheduled a meeting with his cabinet of State Department heads which might last through the afternoon balloting on the President's renomination. He did not listen to radio broadcasts of the Democratic convention's opening yesterday. Instead he chatted briefly with Rep. James W. Wadsworth (R-NY), co-author of the Selective Service Act, with whom he had conferred at length the previous night, then put in a full day at his gubernatorial duties during which he received a five-member delegation of the Women's Army Corps.

HARRY S. TRUMAN

5 IN PACIFIC 2 YRS ON WAY HOME

Local Marines Helped Start Offensive on Japs

Five Lancaster county men who served with the First Division of the U. S. Marines which started America's offensive operations against the Japs Aug. 7, 1942, are on their way home after 25 months' service in the Pacific.

The five men were part of a large contingent that landed at San Diego on July 7 and later started east aboard special trains. The Lancaster men are expected to leave the train at Wilkes-Barre or Jersey City and then resume the trip home over the Pennsylvania railroad. Their arrival in Lancaster is expected hourly.

The five men from Lancaster are:

Cpl. Alfonso Micciche, twenty-four, son of Mr. and Mrs. Vincenzo Micciche, Witmer.

Pfc. Edgar Lloyd McCoy, twenty-seven, son of Mr. and Mrs. Robers Myers, 115 High St., Manheim Formerly employed in the U. S Asbestos plant, Manheim.

Pfc. Donald L. Schramm, twenty, son of Mrs. Myrtle Schramm, 503 W. King St.

Pfc. Kenneth H. Yellets, twenty, son of Mr. and Mrs. Henry J. Yellets, 31 E. Frederick St. He was attending the Reynolds Junior High school when he enlisted.

Cpl. Charles L. Fisher, twenty-one, son of Harry M. Fisher, Lancaster R4. His wife, Mrs. Catherine L. Fisher and daughter, Kitty, re-

(See MARINES—Page 23)

PORT CHICAGO TOLL NOW STANDS AT 322

PORT CHICAGO, Calif., July 20—(AP)—The death toll of the explosion of two ammunition-laden ships here Monday night stood at 322 today with a Navy announcement of 213 names of men known to be dead or missing.

In addition to the Navy list issued last night known dead or missing included 69 merchant sailors, 31 members of armed guard crews aboard the vessels, five Coast Guardsmen and four civilians caught in the blast. A special court of inquiry will be convened by the Navy tomorrow to consider all phases of the catastrophe, the 12th Naval District has announced.

STORE IS BOMBED

PITTSBURGH, July 20—(AP)—Police today sought clues in the bombing of a suburban Brushton confectionery store after Richard Hall, the owner, could ascribe no motive for the early morning blast which caused damage of $1,500. No one was injured, but windows were shattered for a block around the scene by concussion of the bomb, which police said apparently was made of dynamite.

HEAVY ARMOR BATTLE RAGES NEAR TROARN

Nazis Unable to Stabilize Lines But Make Stand Inside Bourguebus

By Wes Gallagher

SUPREME HEADQUARTERS ALLIED EXPEDITIONARY FORCE, July 20—(AP)—British armor slashing forward in several directions has cut into good tank fighting country on a broad front five miles southeast of Caen and the Germans have been unable to stabilize their lines in the third day of the offensive despite their best efforts, Supreme Headquarters announced today.

Heavy fighting was raging however, around a German anti-tank screen in the Emieville-Frenouville area from two to three and a half miles southwest of Toarn, a railway center eight miles east of Caen.

The British were reported to have swept through the Troarn railway station just outside the town, and British tanks—led by a man once the prisoner of Marshal Erwin Rommel—were engaged in hot combat inside Bourguebus, five miles southeast of Caen.

Revolt In Belgium

Meanwhile, a special communique announced, French underground activity has been joined by an underground revolt in Belgium.

The French Maquis, it was said, have wrecked 26 bridges in 10 days and destroyed a full train load of flying bombs although forced temporarily to abandon three towns in the Ain department.

Just short of Vimont the armored drive led by Lt. Gen. Sir Richard Nugent O'Connor — who was captured in the African desert in 1941 but escaped from an Italian prison camp—jabbed into battered German positions after carving out a four-mile wide spreadhead south from the vicinity of Troarn, east of Caen.

The Germans have ordered French civilians to be evacuated from territory looping from Cabourg on the English Channel east of the Orne to Villers Bocage on the British right flank west of Caen.

9 More Towns Taken

At least nine more towns and villages fell in the last 24 hours to hard-fighting British and Canadian troops as they broadened and deepened their corridor east of the Orne river.

Two other German strongholds, Hottot and Vendes, were captured on the west flank. The newly fallen towns seized in the Eastern salient included Frenouville, Cagny, Ifs, Le Poirier, Four, Bras, Hubert-Folie, and Fleury-Sur-Orne.

Canadians striking down from the ruins of Faubourg De Vaucelles—Caen's major residential section south of the Orne—captured Fluery-Sur-Orne and stormed on southward and took Hill 67 whose crest dominated the bitterly-defended Nazi stronghold at Maltot across the Orne.

Fighting In Bourguebus

On the southeast, heavy fighting now is in progress in the streets of Bourguebus.

Marshal Erwin Rommel is commiting armor on an increasing scale with upwards of 30 Tiger tanks impeding the British advance in the thickly-wooded country between Cagny and Troarn.

(See INVASION—Page 23)

2 BOARDS GET AUG. INDUCTION QUOTAS

The first August induction quotas were received by two local draft boards from State Selective Service headquarters today, while all boards are preparing to send groups of selectees for pre-induction examinations in the middle of August.

City Board No. 3 and County Board No. 1, which today received the induction calls for early in August, announce that the quotas are slightly larger than the very small contingents sent for active duty with the Army and Navy this month.

SHOWERS FAIL TO END DROUGHT HERE

Intermittent showers which started last night continued today but the rainfall was not sufficient to break the drought.

Showers were heaviest in the northwestern section of the county shortly after midnight but some rain fell over most of the county. There was only a light shower in the southern section last night.

The mercury touched a high of 83 degrees yesterday and was around the 80-degree mark again

Latest News

FARLEY WILL VOTE FOR BYRD

Chicago, July 20—(AP)—James A. Farley, who fought a third term nomination for President Roosevelt, plans to protest against a fourth term by voting for Senator Harry F. Byrd of Virginia, it was learned today.

F. D. TO BE NAMED THIS AFTERNOON

Chicago Stadium, July 20—(AP)—Democratic National chairman Robert E. Hannegan said today, in a speed-up of plans, that President Roosevelt would be nominated for a fourth term at this afternoon's national convention session. The President will accept by radio tonight—probably late. The exact time has not been announced. Previously it had been planned to go through the certain business of nominating Mr. Roosevelt tonight.

CLAIM HITLER'S ATTACKERS "TRAILED"

New York, July 20—(AP)—The Berlin Home Radio said today "the would-be perpetrators of Hitler's assassination have escaped, but the police are on their trail," NBC reported.

No Change in Jap Militaristic Policy Indicated in Tojo's Fall

Losses in Pacific Forced Ouster of Premier and Selection of Two 64-Year-Old Militarists As His Successors

By The Associated Press

Premier General Hideki Tojo, who led Japan into war against America and Britain and had been virtual dictator for two and a half years, has fallen with his entire cabinet and Tokyo announced today that Emperor Hirohito had ordered another general and an admiral to form a new government "in cooperation."

Hirohito's mandate was given General Kuniaki Koiso, governor general of Korea, and Admiral Mitsumasa Yomai, Premier in 1940, two of the most powerful leaders of the fighting services. Tokyo broadcasts said completion of the new cabinet was expected tonight or early tomorrow (Tokyo time).

The choice indicates there will be no fundamental departure from the principle of military rule. Both Koiso and Yonai have been known as aggressive proponents of Japanese expansion.

The designation of two men is unprecedented and signifies a determination to combine all elements of the Army and Navy in a government to cope with the acknowledged peril of defeat by the United States and its Allies.

The announcements of Tojo's fall and the choice of two 64-year-old militarists as successors came in a series of broadcasts recorded by the Federal Communications Commission and the Associated Press.

Sequel to Series of Defeats

The ousting of Tojo was a sequel to the series of defeats climaxed by the loss of Saipan July 10, bringing American air and naval power within a few hours' bomber flight of the Japanese homeland and confronting the Empire with what Tojo himself called an "unprecedentedly great national crisis."

His fall constitutes one of the most drastic governmental upheavals of the second world war, since his position generally had been considered abroad similar to that of Hitler in Germany and Mussolini in Italy.

General Koiso and Admiral Yonai were commanded to pick a "new strong cabinet" to spare the Emperor further concern.

Domei, the official news agency, indicated that Tojo had fought a losing battle for the past week to maintain his power. One of the problems facing him, said Domei, was the necessity of "enlisting capable men in his cabinet and renovating the cabinet structure." He held a series of meetings with senior statesmen but failed and

(See JAPAN—Page 10)

TWO LOCAL MEN KILLED IN FRANCE

3 Others Listed Wounded in Invasion

Five local soldiers are included on the casualty lists today from the battlefields of France, including a paratrooper and an infantryman reported killed and three men who are reported wounded.

Sgt. Richard Eckman, 661 W. Orange St., and First Sgt. Robert Lee Ginder, Manheim, are reported killed in France. The wounded are S-Sgt. Milton Hoover, Groffdale; Pfc. Herman Koehler, 430 Reynolds Ave.; and Pvt. Richarr Paul Wolfe, Refton.

Another invasion casualty, Sgt. William V. Hess, Kirkwood, reported wounded yesterday, has been awarded the Purple Heart.

Paratrooper Killed In France on June 15

Sgt. Richard Eckman, twenty-nine, son of Mrs. Pearl Eckman, 661 W. Orange St., was killed in action in France, June 15, according to a telegram received by his wife, the former Catherine Wein, who resides with her parents, Mr. and Mrs. John Wein, 36 W. Liberty St.

Sgt. Eckman was serving with a paratrooper division and entered the service Oct. 12, 1942. He received his basic training at Ft. Benning, Ga., and was overseas since January.

A graduate of the Lancaster High School, he was formerly employed at the Middletown Air Depot. He was married last August.

Surviving him besides his wife and his parents are two sisters: Sara Jane Eckman and Colleen Eckman, both at home.

County Infantryman Killed in France

First Sgt. Robert Lee Ginder, thirty-two, a distant relative of General Dwight D. Eisenhower, supreme Allied commander in the European Theater of Operations, was killed in action in France, June 11, his parents, Mr. and Mrs. Aaron Ginder, Manheim, have been notified by the War Department.

Sgt. Ginder's mother and Gen. Eisenhower are second cousins. Mrs. Eisenhower visited at the Ginder home upon several occasions.

Sgt. R. L. Ginder

He entered the service on April 27, 1936, and received his basic training at Fort Howard, Md., and Camp Gordon, Ga. He was given advanced amphibious training at Camp Gordon Johnson, Fla., and arrived overseas in January of this year. He was attached to an infantry unit.

Besides his parents, he is survived by his widow, Mrs. Gladys Ginder, Augusta, Ga., and these brothers and sisters: Harry E., Miles E., and Mrs. Clarence Shonk, all of Manheim; Cpl. Earl R., in

(See MEN—Page 24)

26 CASES OF POLIO AT WELLSBORO

WELLSBORO, Pa., July 20—(AP)—An outbreak of 26 cases of infantile paralysis in rural Tioga County since May 15, with five fatalities, brought Dr. F. J. Dickey, of the State Health Department, to Wellsboro from Harrisburg today.

Dr. Dickey came here to aid local health officials after three new poli cases were reported yesterday. Printed warnings were distributed to local residents on preventive measures to be taken against infection. Wellsboro, has had 10 cases since May 15 with one fatality, local health officials said.

Earlier this week the State Health Department said 54 cases had been reported since January 1 throughout the State, an increase over the average number for the same period in previous years with most of them in Allegheny and

Underground Revolt In Belgium Reported

SUPREME HEADQUARTERS ALLIED EXPEDITIONARY FORCE, July 20—(AP)—An underground revolt in Belgium was reported tonight in a special communique from Gen. Eisenhower's headquarters.

The communique said the Belgian patriots had joined with the extensive French underground in harassing action against the Germans.

Extensive French activity was reported.

The French were said to have destroyed 26 bridges in ten days and made widespread attacks on the Germans.

REDS REACH EDGE OF LLOW, BREST

Germans Showing Signs of Breaking Before 7-front Offensive

By Daniel De Luce

MOSCOW, July 20.—(AP) — The German Army showed signs of breaking in the hotly contested battleground west of the Niemen River before East Prussia today as seven fronts flamed in battle.

(The German radio said Russian troops had reached Augustow, at the base of the Suwalki triangle which was annexed to East Prussia out of Polish territory in 1939. The town is eight miles from the pre-1939 frontier of East Prussia).

The string of German-held cities of Lwow, Brest Litovsk, Bialystok, Kaunas and Daugavpils was tottering, with the Russians fighting to the outskirts of Lwow in Southern Poland and possibly in the suburbs of Brest Litovsk in northern Poland.

Smash Bug River Defense

In the south the Russians for the first time had smashed through the Bug river defense which from 1939 to 1941 formed the dividing line between Russia and German-held Poland.

In the newest of their power-packed offensives near the Latvian Republic's northeast corner, Gen. Ivan Maslennikov's Third Baltic Army crossed the Velikaya river south of Ostrov and made swift progress toward Middle Latvia, the frontier only nine miles away.

The Soviet air force was out in a strength never before equalled, giving sure cover for masses of tanks, cavalry and infantry which swarmed upon the Germans from the western Bug river to the bogs of the north.

The scope of the 600-mile front made it difficult to set apart the

(See RUSSIA—Page 24)

JAPS REPORT YAP RAIDED BY YANKS

NEW YORK, July 20—(AP)—The Tokyo radio announced today that 27 U. S. Liberator bombers had attacked Yap island in the Carolines yesterday and said that three Liberators had raided Chichi Jima in the Bonins.

The broadcast, recorded by the Associated Press, asserted—without Allied confirmation—that 18 of the planes attacking Yap had been "heavily damaged," but did not claim any had actually been destroyed. It acknowledged the loss of one Japanese plane in air combat.

PLUNGES 14 STORIES

PITTSBURGH, July 20—(AP)—Police reported today that William Dickson, 65, of West View, plunged to his death from a fourteenth floor window of Allegheny Hospital.

NAZIS SAY PATTON UNITS IN FRANCE

LONDON, July 20.—(AP)—The Berlin radio, in an unconfirmed reference to Lt. Gen. George S. Patton Jr., said today:

"Further divisions of Patton's army, which consists of Canadians and Americans, are now being engaged on the invasion front. New Allied formations brought up to the front include a replenished Canadian second division which carried out the raid on Dieppe."

Supreme headquarters has not yet defined Patton's role in the invasion.

2 Who Met When Prisoners In Same British Hospital

Two local paratroopers, who landed in France with the D-Day forces, were wounded, captured by the Germans, met in a German prison hospital and were released three weeks later when the Yanks liberated the area, are now in the same hospital in England recuperating from their wounds.

The soldiers, Pfc. Ross E. Pearson and Pvt. Harry J. Sellers, in a letter to the New Era received today, write that their "wounds are very slight."

In the letter Pfc. Pearson states that: "I guess our boys made a bit of history on the night before D-Day, but I and a lot of others were among the unfortunates, whose planes got lost from their formations, when we hit a thick wall of flak and a heavy haze as we started over France.

"My plane had to give the 'go' signal quite a distance from our objective, and after 'hitting the silk' we found ourselves facing machine-gun

Pfc. Pearson

Pvt. Sellers

close, that it was cutting some of the boys' equipment from their bodies.

Only 4 Together

"When we hit the ground we were too far apart to get organized as a group, and only four of us were able to get together which was very little fire power to put up against the companies and regiments

REICH LEADER BURNED, FIVE AIDES INJURED

Scene of Attack Believed to Have Been at Rommel Headquarters

LONDON, July 20—(AP)—Berlin announced that Adolf Hitler was burned and bruised in an unsuccessful bombing attempt on his life today.

Three of Hitler's military leaders were seriously injured, while his chief military advisor Col. Gen. Alfred Jodl was less seriously hurt along with five other Generals and two Admirals.

(The FCC said one German broadcast said the attempt on Hitler's life was "by dynamite," another mentioned "explosives" and still a third said merely "an attempt was made on the life of the Fuehrer today, Thursday.")

The broadcast announcement did not give the scene of the attack, but it obviously took place while Hitler was surrounded by high members of the military staff—perhaps at Hitler's headquarters.

The announcement came 16 hours after Tokyo's announcement of the fall of Premier Hideki Tojo, and Berlin said Hitler after the attack received Benito Mussolini, third member of the ill-starred trio who led the Axis into war.

Hitler's Aide Badly Hurt

Among the seriously injured, Berlin said, was Lt. Gen. Schmundt, Chief of the German Army's Personnel Department and chief Military Aide De Camp to Hitler for several years.

Two lieutenant colonels named Brandt and Borgmann, and a "collaborator" named Berger also were listed as seriously injured.

Slightly injured were these:

Generals Jodl, Hitler's personal military aide; Karl Bodenschatz, aide to Hitler; Guenther Korten, Chief of Staff of the German Air Force, Buhle, Heusinger and Walter Scherff.

Admirals Voss and Von Putkammer.

Probably Occurred In Holland

A source in London with close European connections said the incident probably occurred at Breda, Holland, reported to be the headquarters of Field Marshal Erwin Rommel.

This same source, who cannot be identified by name, said the critical question of reserves for the German armies on three fronts had provoked a split between Rommel and Field Marshal Gen. Guenther Von Kluge, Commander of the forces in Normandy. He speculated that the incident might have resulted from a general division of the German staff, resulting in a brawl.

Follows General's Dismissal

The incident followed by a few days the dismissal of Field Marshal Gen. Karl Gerd Von Rundstedt from his command in the west in favor of Kluge, a shift which was interpreted abroad as a slap at the German military caste and a favor to the Nazi type of General such as Rommel.

Yesterday another old-line Junkers General, Col. Gen. Alexander Von Falkenhausen, was eased from his command in Belgium and Northern France.

Recently, dispatches from the German frontier said the death in an airplane crash of Col. Gen. Eduard Dietl, German commander in Finland who was closely attached to Hitler, might have been the result of sabotage by a rival military clique anxious to get possession of a secret document Dietl was carrying to Hitler.

When the German radio gave the story of today's attempt to the home audience—it still was being

(See HITLER—Page 24)

3,000 LWOW POLES SEIZED BY NAZIS

LONDON, July 20—(AP)—Acting to forestall an uprising as the Russians approach, the Germans have seized about 3,000 Poles in Lwow, including all the prominent persons, the Polish telegraph agency said today.

Quoting the Polish underground radio, the agency said Gen. Ledochowski, former commander of the Krakow military area a brother of the late Cardinal Ledochowski of the Jesuit order, was mong those arrested.

11 NAMES

(Continued From Page One)

Engle has four brothers and a sister in the Army. They are Pvt. Richard Engle, twin to Robert, who is now home on furlough enroute to his new base in Texas; Reed Engle, formerly with the Flying Tigers, now on his way overseas; Cpl. Andrew Engle, in France; Pvt. Isaac Engle, in Florida, and First Lt. Rachel Engle, a graduate of the Lancaster General Hospital School of Nursing, who is an Army nurse and is on her way overseas.

He was inducted Nov. 27, 1942, and received his training at Fort Meads, Md.; Camp Beale, Calif., and Camp Bowie, Tex. A graduate of the East Donegal Township High School, he went overseas about two months ago and had been in France three weeks.

Besides his parents and those in the service, are these brothers and sisters: George Engle, Marietta RD; Mildred, wife of John Fletcher, Richland, and Elizabeth, wife of Paul Raeder.

KILLED IN FRANCE

Pfc. Claude M. Stertzel, thirty-six, was reported killed in France, July 11, by the War Department in a telegram to his fiancee, Miss Edna M. Althouse, 103 Main St., Denver.

Attached to an infantry unit, Pfc. Stertzel entered the service June 3, 1942, and arrived overseas in March, 1943. He participated in the invasions of North Africa and Sicily.

Son of the late Mr. and Mrs. Martain Stertzel, he resided with Mr. and Mrs. Lester Aulthouse, Denver, and is survived by three sisters, Margaret, wife of Leroy Seidel, Annville; Mary Ellen, wife of William Christman, Bernville R3, and Mildred, wife of Stanley Williams, Rehrersburg.

Before entering the service he was employed at the Blue Line Hosiery Mills, Denver.

DIES IN ACTION

Pfc. Benjamin B. Firestone, twenty-four, was killed in action July 17 in France, his parents, Mr. and Mrs. Martin Firestone, Denver R1, were notified Friday by the War Department.

A member of the Engineers Corps, he was inducted Oct. 20, 1941, and arrived overseas in December, 1943. His last letter was written July 7.

Besides his parents he is survived by a twin, Cpl. Robert Firestone, stationed in England; a sister, Dorothy, wife of Pfc. Warren Leid, Denver R1, and two brothers, Richard and Roy, both at home.

KILLED IN EUROPE

Pfc. Robert M. Kleinhans, twenty-one, was killed in action in the European Theatre of War according to word received from the War Department by his parents, Mr. and Mrs. Harry Kleinhans, Conestoga R1.

Pfc. Kleinhans

He entered the armed forces in December, 1942 and was stationed at Camp McCoy, Wisc., until October 1943, when he was sent overseas.

Kleinhans was formerly employed at the Marietta Depot. He was a member of the Colemanville Methodist Church.

Surviving, besides his parents, are two sisters: Hazel, wife of Pvt. Frank Altland, and Violet, wife of John Gebhart, both of Conestoga R1.

KILLED IN FRANCE

Technician Fifth Grade Milo B. Helt, twenty-five, son of John K. Helt, of East Petersburg, formerly of Manheim, reported missing in France on June 8, was killed in action on June 9, according to a telegram from the War Department received by his sister, Mrs. Earl Diehm, of Manheim, with whom he resided for a year before entering the service.

Cpl. Helt

He entered the armed forces in May, 1941, and was trained at Camp Croft, S. C., Fort Devens, Mass., Fort Dix, N. J., Fort Benning, Ga., Fort Jackson, S. C., Camp Gordon, Ga., and at Camp Gordon Johnston, Fla. He went overseas in January, 1944.

He held the expert driver's medal and the good conduct award. Prior to his service with the armed forces, he was employed by the U. S. Asbestos Division in Manheim. He was a member of the Church of the Brethren.

Surviving are his father, John K. Helt, and step-mother, Lottie Landis Helt, East Petersburg; and these brothers and sisters: Mrs. Earl Diehm, Manheim; Ernest, Lancaster; Pvt. Earl Helt, Fort Sill, Okla.; Mrs. Norman Clinton, Columbia; Meda, Manheim; Dorothea and John, of East Petersburg.

HURT IN FRANCE

The War Department Friday notified Mrs. Mary S. Lichty, 46 S. Ann St., that her son, Pvt. Irvin A. Lichty, nineteen, was slightly wounded in France on July 16. He is serving with an Infantry unit.

Entering the service June 30, 1943, Pvt. Lichty was first in the paratroops until spraining his ankle while jumping. He then studied engineering under the RSTP at the University of Indiana and Texas A. and M., until he was transferred to the Infantry. Before going overseas in June of this year, he trained at Camp Butner, N. C.

A graduate of McCaskey High School class of 1943, Pvt. Lichty has a brother, Pfc. Leonard J. Lichty, in the Medical Corps at Valley Forge Hospital.

SLIGHTLY WOUNDED

Pfc. Richard F. Kiehl, nineteen, was slightly wounded on July 16 in France according to word received here by his parents, Mr. and Mrs. John Coldren, of 228 Lincoln St.

A V-mail letter was received from him the soldier telling of being wounded in the leg, and a War Department telegram also was received.

Kiehl, who is serving with an infantry unit, entered the service in March 1943 and has been overseas since May of this year. He is a graduate of Manheim Twp. High School, class of 1942, and was employed by the Calder Manufacturing Co.

IN ENGLISH HOSPITAL

The War Department has notified Mrs. Lester B. Fiester, 701 S. Prince St., that her son, Staff Sgt. Clyde M. Myles, twenty-one, was seriously wounded in France on July 15 and is now hospitalized in England.

A veteran of the African, Tunisian and Sicilian campaigns, the infantryman participated in the initial invasion of France and has been overseas for two years. He entered the service in October, 1940, and received his basic training at Fort Bragg, N. C. He has received several medals since going overseas.

S-S Myles

Sgt. Myles is a step-brother of Lt. Lester E. Fiester who was killed in action in an air raid over Romania on May 5.

A graduate of the Smithville High School, he was employed by the Pennsylvania Railroad before entering the service.

MISSING IN ACTION

Sgt. (T-5) Robert B. Riley, Jr., twenty-six, has been missing in action in France since July 13, according to a War Department telegram received Friday by his wife, the former Miss Dorothy Beecher, 634 S. Plum St. Letters from him dated July 16, have been received by several members of the family.

Sgt. Riley

The infantryman, a son of Mr. and Mrs. Robert B. Riley, 77 Locust St., was on the front lines, he had informed his wife previously. A veteran of six years in the service, he was stationed in Panama for two years, returning to this country in 1940.

Sgt. Riley trained at Camp Forest, Tenn.; Fort Jackson, S. C.; and Fort Leonard Wood, Mo., before going overseas eight months ago. Before entering the service he was employed by the Champion Blower and Forge Co.

The father of three children, one three months old whom he has never seen, Sgt. Riley has two brothers in the service, Staff Sgt. Warren N. Riley, with the Infantry in France, and Pvt. Roland Riley, who until recently was stationed on the Aleutian Islands.

MISSING IN FRANCE

Pfc. Walter H. Herman has been missing in action in France since July 1, according to word received by his mother, Mrs. Lena Herman, Bird-in-Hand R1, from the War Department.

Pfc. Herman, twenty-one, participated in the invasion of France with an infantry unit, having arrived overseas in May. He entered the service Feb. 19, 1943, and received his basic training at Camp McCain, Miss.

Pfc. Herman

Before entering the service, he attended public schools in Weavertown and Upper Leacock Twp. High School and was employed by the Spacht Furniture Store, Lititz.

WOUNDED IN HEEL

Mr. and Mrs. Edwin L. Hoover, Groffdale, have received word that their son, Staff Sgt. Milton Hoover, was wounded in the heel July 16 in France, and was hospitalized for five days.

The information was contained in a letter the soldier wrote to Miss Marion Kurtz, of Spring Garden. He said he was carried back to his lines by a buddy, Pfc. Harry C. Snader, son of Mr. and Mrs. Harry R. Snader, New Holland R2, a cousin of Miss Kurtz.

VATICAN URGES PEACE

Vatican City —(AP)— The Vatican City newspaper Osservatore Romano issued a strong appeal for peace Friday.

In a three column, page one, editorial, the newspaper asserted that the fundamental question was "put an end to the slaughter if results justifying it can no longer be expected x x x."

The editorial stated that all the belligerents claimed to be fighting for their rights but 'it has reached the point where it is necessary to preserve life "to existence again after this inferno is finished."

The paper said the war is increasing in its intensity and "under its crushing weight will emerge crushing treaties. Let us hasten peace. It is the only good on which one can still count."

TREATED AT HOSPITAL

Warren Pennell, thirty-three, 229 N. Christian St., who suffered an epileptic seizure while walking in the first block of West King Street Friday night, was conveyed to the Lancaster General Hospital by city police for treatment.

NOMINATE OFFICERS AT LEGION POST

Benjamin L. Schaeffer was nominated commander of American Legion Post, No. 34, at the regular meeting held Friday night in the Legion Home. C. Earl Welchans presided. The officers will be elected September 1.

Other nominations are: David David Graybill, first vice commander; Herman Ordell, second vice commander; Richard Smith, finance officer; Oliver Baublitz, chaplain; Jack McCartney, historian; George T. Hambright, legal aide; Leon Duckworth, employment officer.

Giles Andes was reelected for a three-year term as trustee.

The following were named representatives to the County Council: Henry Shank, Herbert Gansman, John Kiehl, Joseph Buch, David Graybill, Earl Welchans, Norris Donaldson, Leon Schaeffer, Guy Neel, Irvin Vandegrift, Charles Fry, Giles Andes, Walter E. Gebhart, George Macrides, Stephen Aument, Oliver Baublitz, Herman Ordell, Walter Marion, Francis Heidig.

It was announced that Post 34 subscribed $1200 to the Fifth War Loan drive, and won third prize for an increase in membership.

JAIL MAN FOR HEARING

Joseph A. Bell, 1652 Market St., Harrisburg, was committed to the Lebanon county jail Friday evening in default of bail, following a hearing before John A. Witmeyer, Justice of the Peace of Annville, on charges of issuing worthless checks. The charges were brought by Charles R. Ristenbatt, constable.

Bell, who has previously served time in York and Cumberland counties on similar charges, is also wanted in Lancaster, Berks, Schuylkill and Cumberland counties for the same offense, police said.

WITHDRAW PROPERTY

A property on the Oregon pike, offered for public sale Friday night in the auction rooms of J. G. Forney and Co., was withdrawn from sale, according to George T. Hambright, agent for the owner, Edward C. Hoover. The property contains one acre and thirty perches, on which is erected a two-story frame dwelling.

ALLIES

(Continued From Page One)

the south bank of the Arno) without damage to architecutral buildings of the city.

"He has thus enjoyed unlimited use of bridges over the Arno and has seen fit, when outfought south of the city, to destroy bridges of military value, to deny us use of bridges which up to now he has enjoyed."

The statement added that military bridges could be quickly thrown across the Arno inside Florence and that the destruction would not hold up the Allied advance for long or have any bearing on future operations.

The Allied statement threw but little light on the military situation inside Florence — not saying whether enemy troops had withdrawn entirely from the northern part of the city —but continued at length on German vandalism.

It called the "wanton destruction of bridges "just another example of Field Marshal Albert Kesselring's order to his troops to carry out demolitions with sadistic imagination."

"No doubt those responsible for allowing Rome's bridges to remain intact have been reprimanded by the Germans and even stronger measures were taken to ensure that the bridges in Florence should not fall into Allied hands and so be preserved for posterity," the statement said.

FIFTH ARMY QUIET

Florence's defenses collapsed only after weeks of bitter fighting in the hills to the south and southwest. It was announced that the Eighth Army had captured 5,000 prisoners in the past 24 days and that the enemy's losses in killed and wounded had been very high.

There was news only of patrol clashes and artillery exchanges from the American Fifth Army front, extending from the Tyrrhenian coast inland along the Arno river some 30 miles. German troops still clung to the northern half of Pisa.

WEATHER

(Continued From Page One)

general throughout Wisconsin. Minneapolis had a high of 84 degrees. Columbus reported a 95-degree maximum, two degrees under the city's all time record for Aug. 4. Indiana's temperatures averaged 9 degrees above normal.

In the south—Baltimore had its hottest day of the season as the mercury reached 99. Washington had clear skies and a 94-degree top temperature. Alabama, with heavy rains, had temperatures in the eighties. The past three months have been the driest in the 73-year history of the Knoxville, Tenn., weather bureau. Atlanta was sultry with thundershowers.

New Jersey baked. Friday in Philadelphia, was the hottest Aug. 4 since 1881. Boston's high for the day was 92 degrees.

But there were a few comfortable spots on the map:

Coalville, Utah, reported a minimum of 32 degrees in the morning. In the San Francisco Bay region the weather was "sunny and mild" with a maximum of 86 degrees. The Pacific Northwest reported simply that it was "comfortable." Nebraska's heat wave was broken with rains on Thursday night that pushed the mercury down to 61 in some sections. It also rained in Iowa and Friday's temperatures were a degree below normal. Colorado announced happily that it was enjoying a "slightly cooler summer than usual."

BABY'S THUMB LACERATED

Margo Ann Steffy, two and one-half, daughter of Mr. and Mrs. John M. Steffy, 435 High St., was treated in St. Joseph's Hospital Friday for a lacerated right thumb sustained when she fell on a bottle.

The University of Paris was the model for Oxford and Cambridge.

HOLD EVERYTHING

"At last we have Yankee navy outnumbered!"

FIRE EXTINGUISHED

A fire of undetermined origin caused a small loss at the home of Jacob Rogers, east of Leaman Place, on Lincoln Highway east, Friday morning at 6:45 o'clock.

The fire was discovered by Rogers in a clothes closet and some clothing was burned. Furniture and the carpet were damaged by smoke and water.

Intercourse and Kinzer fire companies were called but the fire was extinguished before they arrived. The loss is covered by insurance.

The Turks introduced coffee to Europe around 1683.

DUCK, BROTHER, DUCK!

London—(AP)—One anti-aircraft battery in southern England has a sign with this alliterative advice:

"If doodle dallies don't dawdle. Dive!"

There's only one voice like Crosby's!
There's only one picture like this!
Risë Stevens... hear her golden voice sing "Going My Way"
Bing and the Gang sing "The Mule"!
"Would you like to swing on a star, Carry moon-beams home in a jar, And be better off than you are, Or would you rather be a mule?"
"Going My Way"
Songs!
"The Day After Forever"
"Going My Way"
"Swinging On A Star"
plus "Ave Maria"
"Silent Night, Holy Night"
And 3 Other Old Favorites
"LIFE" Magazine says—
"Barry Fitzgerald's performance is one of the half-dozen finer things seen in 50 years of motion pictures!"
They may come bigger—but they don't come any tougher than STANLEY CLEMENTS!
A PARAMOUNT Picture with
BING CROSBY
BARRY FITZGERALD · FRANK McHUGH · JAMES BROWN · JEAN HEATHER
GENE LOCKHART · PORTER HALL · FORTUNIO BONANOVA
And RISË STEVENS Famous Contralto of Metropolitan Opera Ass'n. Produced and Directed by LEO McCAREY
B. G. DeSYLVA, Executive Producer · Screen Play by Frank Butler and Frank Cavett
Jim Brown and Jean Heather find going Bing's way is best!
STARTS TODAY
Colonial
FEATURE TIME:
12:00 - 2:10 - 4:25
6:50 - 9:10

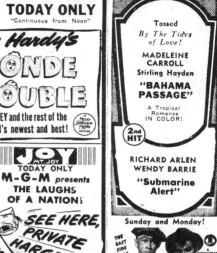

The equatorial circumference of the earth is 24,902 miles; the meridional circumference 24,860 miles.

The number of pound-miles of air express carried in the United States increased from 2,822,000,000 in 1936 to 8,300,000,000 in 1941.

Traffic accident deaths totaled 10,870 for the first six months of 1944.

A wikiup is an Indian hut.

B-29 GROUP HEAD—The War Department announced that Maj. Gen. Curtis E. Leway, 37, of Columbus, O., has been named to head the 20th Bomber Command, which operates the B-29 Superfortresses. The 20th Command is based in the China-Burma-India area, from which strategic attacks are being made on Japan.

SEEK TO RELAX BAN ON TELEGRAMS OF GREETINGS

Washington—(AP)—Two proposals to relax wartime bans against telegraphing of congratulatory and greeting messages were made before the Board of War Communications Thursday by representatives of the Western Union Telegraph Co., the American Communications Association (CIO) and the Commercial Telegraphers Union (AFL).

One of the proposals would permit telegraphing any type of congratulatory war greeting except in certain specified holiday periods, while the other would permit telegraphing such messages in those periods if the messages did not relate to the holidays.

TAX EXEMPTION FOR SERVICEMEN SPONSORED

Washington—(AP)—Rep. Lemke (R-N. D.), introduced a bill Thursday to grant an additional permanent income tax exemption of $2,000 to honorably discharged servicemen and women who have been wounded or disabled or have served more than 90 days.

STRONGER GUARANTEE

Vatican City—(AP)—The Vatican City newspaper Osservatore Romano contrasted United States and Japanese policies toward Philippine independence Thursday and concluded that "the reciprocal promises of independence and aid" between the Americans and Filipinos were a "certain guarantee" that their relations "will always became stronger."

The newspaper said the relations "draw their inspiration from the American administration which by treating Filipinos as equals gradually has led them toward independence."

SUCCUMBS TO HEAT

Warren, Pa. — (AP) — John Murray, 70, collapsed and died Thursday while digging potatoes in his garden in nearby Farmington Township. Coroner Ed Lowrey attributed death to a heart attack superinduced by the heat.

Pegler Defines
U. S. Communists
— Editorial Page

LANCASTER NEW ERA

WEATHER
Continued hot with warm nigh
scattered thunder showers in mour
tains tonight and again Wednesda

VOL. 66—NO. 839 Entered as second class matter January 31, 1924, at the Post Office at Lancaster, Pa., under the Act of March 3, 1879. Reg. U. S. Pat Off.
LANCASTER PA., TUESDAY, AUGUST 15, 1944 CITY EDITION 16 PAGES 20c PER WEEK—4c Per Co

SOUTH FRANCE INVADED

Paratroops Fight Way Far Inland; Nazi 7th Held In Normandy Trap

SECOND POLIO DEATH HERE, 2 NEW CASES

2 Others Under Observation; 5 Who Were at Camp Quarantined

A second death from infantile paralysis and two new cases of the disease were reported here today.

In addition, two additional patients, suspected of having the disease are under observation in the General Hospital and the State Department of Health ordered observation quarantines placed on five children here who were subjected to the disease at a summer camp.

Thus far, eight definite cases of the disease have been reported in the country this summer but several of the victims are well on their way to recovery. The first death was reported yesterday.

330 Cases in State

Health Secretary Dr. A. H. Stewart reported at Harrisburg that Pennsylvania's 330 cases of infantile paralysis have reached an "abnormally high" mark. Allegheny county continues to lead the state with 106 cases and nine deaths. Philadelphia has 65 and York reported four. Last year there were [illegible] cases in the state at this time.

In Philadelphia, city officials considered closing all swimming pools as a preventative measure. Dr. Yer Solis-Cohen, assistant director of public health in Philadelphia, said recommendations may be made to halt nose and throat operations on children and to ban children gathering in public places such as theatres. He said the greatest carrier of the disease is believed to be polluted waters.

Ross St. Child Dies

The second death from the disease in Lancaster was reported this morning when George Edward Leggett, Jr., five years old, son of George and Helen H. Eby Leggett, 232 E. Ross St., died at 3 A. M. in the General Hospital. He had been ill three days and was admitted to the hospital yesterday. The child's father is a patient in the General Hospital following an attack of heart disease.

The child was a member of the Otterbein United Brethren Sunday school. In addition to his parents, he is survived by two sisters, Beverly Ann and Yvonne E. Leggett, both at home; his paternal grandparents, Mr. and Mrs. S. W. Eby and his maternal grandmother Mrs. Ann Leggett.

Goldie Jones, seven-months-old daughter of Mr. and Mrs. David Jones, Washington Borough R1, died yesterday in Columbia. She was stricken with the paralysis several days ago.

2 New Cases

The two new cases reported here are John Bachman, fifteen, 1122 E. King St., and Joseph Cooper, seven,

(See POLIO—Page 14)

NEW HOLLAND GIRL IS "POTATO QUEEN"

HARRISBURG, Aug. 15 — (AP) — Governor Martin today crowned 18-year-old Sylvia Ann Hoober of New Holland, Lancaster County, "Miss Potato Blossom Queen of 1944."

Miss Hoober was selected by the Board of Directors of the Pennsylvania Potato Growers' Association to reign until blossom time comes again. She is a graduate of New Holland High School and plans to enter the University of Pennsylvania.

The crowning occurred in the Governor's office with the girl's parents, Mr. and Mrs. Roy K. Hoober, Secretary Miles Horst of Agriculture and President P. D. Frantz, Allentown, of the potato growers attending. Coronation exercises originally were scheduled for last week at Coudersport but were postponed due to infantile paralysis in Tioga County.

RAF BOMBS MEN IN CANADIAN LINES

WITH THE CANADIAN FIRST ARMY, Aug. 15—(AP)—British heavy bombers dropped a number of explosives behind Canadian lines yesterday while assaulting German positions, causing a number of casualties.

GEN. GEORGE S. PATTON, JR.

PATTON SPRUNG TRAP ON NAZIS

Leading 3rd U. S. Army in North France

By Howard S. Cowan

A SUPREME HEADQUARTERS ALLIED EXPEDITIONARY FORCE COMMAND POST IN NORMANDY, Aug. 15.—(AP)—Gen. Dwight D. Eisenhower announced today that Lt. Gen. George S. Patton, Jr., "Old Blood and Guts" of the Tunisian and Sicilian campaigns, is leading the American Third Army which has driven roughshod over the Germans in lower Normandy and Brittany.

Since Aug. 1 the Third Army had effected the cutoff of the Breton peninsula and helped close a trap on the German Seventh Army with a spectacular sweep northward from Le Mans.

Le Clerc With Patton

A French division of armor under Brig. Gen. Jacques Leclerc, who joined the Allies from Lake Chad in Africa, is fighting with Patton.

The announcement of Patton's command came after it was revealed that Lt. Gen. Omar N. Bradley is the overall commander of the newly-formed 12th U. S. Army group and Lt. Gen. Courtney H. Hodges has taken Bradley's former place as commander of the American First Army. The First and Third armies are included in the 12th U. S. Army group.

Patton roused a public storm in the United States when the

(See PATTON—Page 11)

COUNTY SIZZLES AGAIN TODAY

No Relief in Sight For At Least 48 Hours

Temperatures soared into the 90-degree bracket again today and the U. S. Weather Bureau said there is no relief in sight for at least another 48 hours.

Said the Weather Bureau — "Hot weather and high humidity this afternoon, tonight and tomorrow."

Yesterday, the mercury hit an even 90 degrees and dropped to 68 during the night as a light west breeze brought some relief.

It was the 34th day this summer that the mercury has hit 90 degrees or higher and Weather Bureau observers said it is now probably the longest, continuous heat wave on record.

CLAIM ROMMEL IS RECOVERING

LONDON, Aug. 15 — (AP) — Field Marshal Erwin Rommel is progressing well in his recovery after an accident, a German broadcast reporting a Berlin press conference said today.

Earlier accounts have said that Rommel, apparently the victim of an Allied air attack, sustained head injuries.

NEW U. S. WEAPON

LONDON, Aug. 15—(AP)—Toyko radio declared today that a new American weapon is a 14-pound anti-personnel bomb whose explosion is controlled from a plane by a steel cable wound around the missle.

ESCAPE ROUTE IN NORTH CUT TO 10 MILES

Wall of Bombs and Shells Halts Von Kluge's Army in Attempted Break

By Gladwin Hill

SUPREME HEADQUARTERS, Allied Expeditionary Force, Aug. 15.—(AP)—Allied armies clamped a giant nutcracker upon France today, hitting with massive invasion in the south even as the dying German Seventh Army struggled in an inexorably-tightening Normandy trap 450 miles to the north.

Four separate American, British and Canadian Armies, squeezing upon Field Marshal Von Kluge's forces of perhaps 100,000 to 200,000 men, pinched his escape gap below Falaise to only 10 miles, and sealed that off with a wall of bombs and shells.

The powerful new Mediterranean invasion, opening a fourth major front, is designed to chase the Germans from France, and link with Gen. Eisenhower's warriors in Normandy and Brittany. Americans who spanned the Loire below Brittany already are only 400 miles from these latest Allied liberators.

Nazis Try To Break Out

The trap upon Von Kluge meanwhile was nearly snapped shut. A front dispatch said that again this morning the Germans tried to break out eastward, but the route below Falaise was blocked by a wall of bombs and shells.

West of Falaise, the roof of his corridor "appeared to be collapsing today" under a British avalanche of tanks and men, a front report declared.

On all sides the Allies pressed in. Hundreds of captives were taken by Americans closing from the west. The pocket was slimmed to half its size. Thousands of Germans were still believed caught. A British staff officer said Von Kluge was throwing in reinforcement, but they were apparently 80 per cent "slave troops," tossed in as sacrifice rearguards while Von Kluge sought to save his armor and his best men.

By dawn today, the western invasion of Europe had been doubled

(See FRANCE—Page 11)

CO. MAN KILLED; 6 ARE WOUNDED

All Were in France; One Injured Second Time

A county man today was reported killed in France and six local men were listed as wounded in France, one for the second time.

The man killed was Pfc. John F. Horst, Brownstown.

The wounded are: Pvt. Charles Wenditz, 336 Ice Ave.; Pvt. Irvin A. Lichty, 46 S. Ann St.; Pvt. Robert Habalar, Terre Hill; Pfc. Paul H. Martin, 596 N. Plum St.; Pfc. Paul Graybill, 23 Chester St.

Brownstown Youth Killed In France on July 26

Pfc. John H. Horst, son of Marvin Horst, Brownstown, nineteen, was killed in action in France, July 26, according to a telegram received from the War Department by his father.

He was serving overseas with an Infantry unit since October 1943 and was previously stationed in Iceland and England. The last letter received from him was on July 26, the day he was killed.

He was inducted into the Army

(See MEN—Page 14)

Total War Casualties For City and County

Killed in Action	134
Killed in Accidents and Died in Camps	46
Missing	77
Wounded	292
Prisoners	64
Total	613

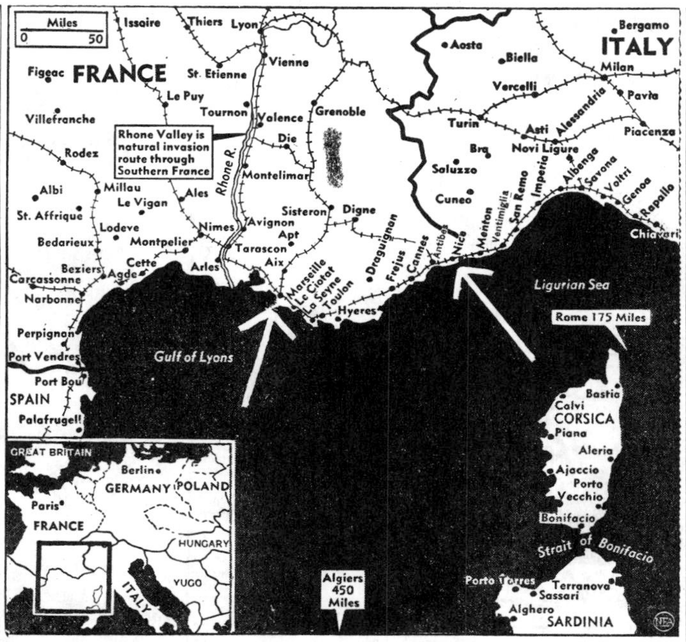

Where Allied Troops Land in Southern France

Map shows where Allied troops landed on the southern coast of France this morning between Marseille and Nice (white arrows).

No Major Opposition to Invasion Is Sighted in Flight of 20 Miles Inland

By Kenneth Dixon

ON A B-25 MITCHELL BOMBER OVER SOUTHERN FRANCE, Aug. 15 — (AP) — So far as I could see from a height of 1,000 feet above the beaches where the Allies smashed ashore less than an hour ago no major fighting had yet developed.

As far as 20 miles inland a complete lack of any sign of struggle marked the rugged landscape.

From this vantage point 1,000 feet up the new Allied blows at southern France this morning seemed to be meeting almost no resistance in the preliminary stages.

Gliders Landed Successfully

There was plenty of visual evidence, however, that the preliminary stages of the Allied operation —parachute and glider landings— were carried out successfully.

We came in with the first wave of glider troops to strike southern France. Some miles inland they cut loose from C-47 tow planes and glided down into little meadows between rugged crags just within the coastline.

With the exception of a few which crashed into ditches and fences or turned over on their backs the gliders seemed to make it safely.

Nowhere was there any sign of resistance to them. We sometimes got as low as 200 or 300 feet over the treetops and not a shot was fired at us.

The first sign of movement as scores of gliders skidded to a stop in clouds of dust came from near an overturned glider which apparently was badly wrecked. A small machine moved beetle-like from under the wing of a nearby glider and headed toward the one in trouble.

1st Jeep In Action

"There goes the first Airborne jeep into action in southern France," said Corp. Bill Luneback of Chicago, the bomber's 22-year-old radio operator.

"Everything must be going okay," he said with a grin.

Along the coast and out at sea there was a complete lack of gun

(See DIXON—Page 11)

HARD COAL SHORT SIX MILLION TONS

WASHINGTON, Aug. 15.— (AP) — Secretary Ickes said today the anthracite shortage this winter now is estimated at 6,000,000 tons—a million more than expected—and he ordered that maximum shipments to retail dealers be reduced from 90 per cent of their full requirements to 87 1-2 per cent.

Officials of the Solid Fuels Administration said an unauthorized strike in mines of the Philadelphia and Reading Coal and Iron company has contributed "substantially" to the change in regulations.

War Situation In France

By The Associated Press

Clamping a giant vise upon France, the Allies invaded the Toulon area in the Mediterranean today under tremendous naval and air support, quickly seizing initial objectives. To the north, 450 miles away, annihilation battles cut up the dying German Seventh Army in the tightening Normandy trap.

The greatest fleet ever to sail the Mediterranean carried American, British, and French troops rolling through the southern French wall. Thousands of parachutists leaped behind Nazi defenders. The full weight of Allied air power in the Mediterranean theatre backed the push.

Four separate American, British and Canadian armies to the north crushed in upon Field Marshal Guenther Von Kluge's wrecked Seventh Army. His Falaise escape neck was reduced to 10 miles. Hundreds upon hundreds of Germans were captured. Again Von Kluge tried a costly daylight rush in an effort to escape.

Overnight the western invasion had doubled in scope, exploding open a fourth front against Hitler after the German hold in Southern France had been weakened.

The Allied objective "is to drive out the Germans and join up with the Allied armies advancing from Normandy," asserted Gen. Sir Henry Maitland Wilson, commanding the southern invasion.

Gen. Dwight D. Eisenhower declared the Germans on the Normandy front "are taking a sound beating." But he warned that "we are still a long way from the Rhine," although this week has brought "a very definite climax" in one phase of the vast liberation campaign.

Latest News

SUPREME HOUR HAS STRUCK, NAZIS SAY

London, Aug. 15—(AP)—"The supreme hour has struck," the German radio said tonight. "It is the hour when we must throw into battle the last little ounce of strength."

LONDON HEARS GEN. DEVERS IN CHARGE

London, Aug. 15—(AP)—Reports were published in London that Lt. Gen. Jacob L. Devers, U. S. A., was commanding the forces which landed today in the south of France. Gen. Eisenhower's supreme headquarters declined comment. Devers is an expert in tank warfare and is deputy to the Mediterranean theater commander, Gen. Sir Henry Maitland Wilson.

YANKS CLINCH CONTROL OF ESCAPE ROADS

Supreme Headquarters Allied Expeditionary Force, Aug. 15.—(AP)—The Americans clinched control of the German escape roads to the south today by capturing La Ferte Mace between Domfront and Ranes.

REDS SEE VICTORY THIS YEAR

Moscow, Aug. 15—(AP)—"Victory this year," said many Russians today when they heard the first radio flashes that the Allies had landed in Southern France.

Army of France and Great Force of Americans and British Land on Wide Area About Toulon

By Edward Kennedy

ROME, Aug. 15.—(AP)—The army of France and a great force of battle-hardened Americans and British, struck Hitler on a fourth major front today, invading southern France and successfully completing all their landings along a broad section of Mediterranean beach around Toulon.

(A broadcast from one of the beachheads showed Allied troops had penetrated several miles inland. Only a few lives were lost in the landings, the broadcast added.

(London dispatches said 14,000 troops were landed in the first two hours. Allied bombing operations indicated the landings were centered in the 30-mile Raphael-Cap Camarat area between Toulon and Cannes.)

A special communique a few hours after the blow was struck said beaches along a considerable length of the Rivera had been seized by mid-morning according to schedule with scarcely any ground opposition and no air opposition.

Air-Borne Troops Pave Way

One of the greatest air-borne combat forces ever assembled paved the way for the assault and likewise carried out operations successfully far inland.

The great stab into the "underbelly of Europe," bringing the battle for France to full fury, was backed by more than 800 ships—one of the biggest fleets ever to churn the waters of the Mediterranean, which Mussolini once called his own, and by great air power.

The troops swarmed ashore with the avowed purpose of linking their Mediterranean theater with their front west of Paris where the Allies apparently were on the point of scoring a great victory which might speedily result in the liberation of most or all of France.

"The army of France is in being again, fighting on its own soil for the liberation of its country with all its traditions of victory behind it. Remember 1918," was the ringing declaration of the commander-in-chief of the invasion force, Gen. Sir Henry Maitland Wilson.

Hit On 125-Mile Beach Front

Striking after sunrise, seven waves of infantry splashed ashore in the first two hours and seized their initial objectives with great rapidity at many places along a 125-mile stretch of the Riviera between the great port of Marseille and Nice.

They encountered only the weakest opposition, for enemy defenses had been pulverized by five straight days of a powerful air offensive.

An Air Force spokesman said the landing area had been virtually isolated by the destruction of every rail bridge in the Rhone valley from Valence to Marseille—a distance of 120 miles—while the Riviera rail line into Italy had been blocked for several days.

This afternoon Liberators and Fortresses bombed five highway bridges crossing the Rhone between Valence and Avignon and the road leading from the beach to Frejus, near the mouth of the Argens river west of Cannes.

Enemy airfields in the Marseille area appeared to have been knocked out or abandoned.

The Germans apparently had pulled a large part of their effectives in southern France northward to meet the threat to Marshal Von Kluge's Seventh Army.

Shortly before dawn a large air-borne combat force descended into the rugged hills which rise from the coastline and went into a grapple with the German defenders for possession of key communication points and commanding vantage points.

The invasion was accompanied by the signal from the French National Committee and Allied commanders to all Frenchmen to rise up against their German oppressors and indications were that the well organized underground army of southern France had responded.

Scarcely Shot Fired At Big Planes

Scarcely a shot was fired at the big transport planes and gliders which put the air-borne troops down, and the

(See INVASION—Page 4)

Mighty Array of US Tanks Grips Nazis in Normandy

By Hal Boyle

WITH U. S. ARMORED FORCES AT ARGENTAN, Aug. 13—(11:46 p. m.)—(Delayed)—(AP)—Huge German army forces, trapped tonight by converging Allied armored spearheads, began immediate attempts to smash out of 300 square miles enclosed by the steel vise.

From a wheatfield overlooking Argentan at 7 p. m., I could see the vanguard of the great Nazi retreat try to stab its way through a bottleneck 12 miles wide between this town and the city of Falaise.

This narrow bottleneck is the greatest Allied armored roundup of the war and all roads are under heavy artillery fire from the Canadians on one side and the French and Americans on the other.

Chance To Shorten War

There is no way for the Nazis to escape unless they are able to fight their way out—and that is what these tank men who have already rolled 330 miles in two weeks, fighting most of the way—want them to try. They think such an attempt will shorten the war a matter of weeks.

Our artillery at this moment is beating to pieces a German convoy trying to escape through the Argentan road hub from the west. On a far away ridge, I can see our shells burst as they land among clouds of dust hiding individual vehicles in the convoy. Some have been hit directly and pillars of black smoke rise from the shroud of yellow dust.

Signals For Attack

In a ditch by the edge of a field, an air support officer, Capt. Albert G. Kelly, San Jose, Calif., is sig-

(See TANKS—Page 11)

LAND IN SWEDEN

Stockholm — (AP) — Two United States Liberator bombers made forced landings in southern Sweden Thursday. The 20 men making up the crews were uninjured.

"CHEWEY" ADOPTED AT FRENCH HOSPITAL—Lt. Alexe Bury (left) of Edmonton, Alberta, and Lt. Jean MacIntosh, Calgary, Alberta, pet "Chewey," a goat which wandered into the area of a Canadian general hospital in France and was adopted.

SAYS ALL ROADS TO SEINE JAMMED

By ROGER GREENE

With British Troops enroute to the Seine—(AP)—All roads to the Seine are jammed Thursday night. The great advance is on.

In columns stretching many miles across the countryside. Allied armies are rolling eastward in what we all believe is the final phase of the war. I have heard British officers wagering that the European war will be over within the next three weeks. There were few takers.

Across the Seine, Field Marshal Guenther Von Kluge is said to have massed every available soldier scraped from dregs of the German manpower reservoir to meet us.

"The enemy is leaving bits and pieces to try and delay us, but there is no major stand all the way back to the Seine," a field headquarters officer told the Associated Press.

On an 80-mile jeep ride to the front Thursday, I traveled through and sometimes over wreckage of Von Kluge's German Seventh Army. The scene was incredible.

Mile after mile, sometimes forced to drive over enemy corpses squashed in the mud, we bumped along deep-rutted roads where the Germans made their last frantic attempt to escape the Normandy trap. In ditches, in newly-harvested wheat fields, behind hedges lay hundreds upon hundreds of jack-booted enemy slain, dead horses, burned out tanks and charred skeletons of motor trucks.

Ancient Athens was once called "The City of the Violet Crown," because of the colors of the hills surrounding it.

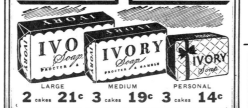

TRAVEL WHEN NECESSARY

Washington—(AP)—Col. J. Monroe Johnson, director of the Office of Defense Transportation Thursday asked civilians to abandon plans for Labor Day travel on trains or intercity buses unless their trips are directly connected with the war.

Help the Paper Pickup This Sunday

WEATHER

Eastern Pennsylvania: Occasional Rain And A Few Scattered Thundershowers, Not So Warm Friday; Clearing And Cool Saturday.

Intelligencer Journal

The Leading Newspaper in the Garden Spot of America, Home Owned for Home Folks Since 1794 — 150th Anniversary Year

SAVE PAPER AND TIN CANS For September SCHOOL COLLECTION

VOLUME LXXX.—NO. 305. Entered as second class matter August 9, 1944 at the Post Office at Lancaster, Pa., under the Act of March 3, 1879. Reg. U. S. Pat. Off. LANCASTER, PA., FRIDAY MORNING, SEPTEMBER 1, 1944 CITY TWENTY-EIGHT PAGES. 20c PER WEEK—4c Per Copy

AMERICANS ENTER OUTSKIRTS OF SEDAN

Reds Take Bucharest, Reach Bulgarian Border

PLAN TO REOPEN SCHOOLS HERE ON SCHEDULE

County Authorities Announce Decision; 21st Case Of Polio Reported

The county schools will open on schedule unless some unforseen development forces a postponement, it was announced by county health and school officials Thursday, as the twenty-first case of infantile paralysis was reported.

Dr. A. J. Greenleaf, Mountville, county medical director, and Dr. Arthur P. Mylin, county superintendent of schools, announced their decision after a meeting Thursday, during which time they were also in contact with State School officials.

The discussion was held to determine if the schools should not be opened in view of the number of cases of paralysis reported in the county to date.

The city schools will open as scheduled Wednesday morning, it was announced by Dr. Joseph Appleyard, city medical director.

NEWEST VICTIM

The newest victim of the disease is:

Wanda Myers, seventeen, daughter of Mr. and Mrs. Edward Myers, Lancaster R3, who is confined to her home, according to Dr. Greenleaf, with a slight attack of polio. She was stricken ill August 15th,

Dr. Appleyard, Thursday received a reply to a telegram he sent Wednesday to James P. Leake, National Institute of Health, U. S. Public Health Service, in reference to the opening of Lancaster schools. The text:

"Lancaster's present rate of ten cases of poliomyelitis per 100,000 population, which will probably be doubled before the season closes, would not ordinarily justify non-opening of schools by mid-September in our opinion.

"The State Department of Health

More of PLAN on Page 12

"We Lead All The Rest"

FARM CORNER

By The Farm Editor

BOOST IN FEDERAL FEED SUBSIDIES TO DAIRYMEN TODAY

Harrisburg—(AP)—Federal feed subsidies to more than 50,000 Pennsylvania milk producers will be increased Friday from 45 to 70 cents a hundredweight, and in 35 counties to 80 cents, in a production-supporting program that has cost $12,000,000 since last October.

Clyde A. Zehner, state chairman of the agriculture adjustment agency, said the increase was ordered last spring by the War Food Administration for the period when cows go on fall rations and will continue until March 31. The lower subsidy was paid while cows were on pasture.

The additional 10-cent subsidy will be paid in counties hard hit by the summer drought.

"Another survey of drought conditions will be made by the AAA in mid-September and if it is found insufficient rainfall has affected milk production in other counties the supplemental payments will be extended," Zehner said.

The milk subsidy was ordered by the Federal government last fall—after the OPA refused to approve a price increase to consumers ordered by the milk control commission—to pay for increased costs of feed without raising consumer prices.

Payments are now being calculated for the July and August period, Zehner said, and will be made in September. Subsidies under the new 70 and 80-cent rates will be paid in November on milk

More of FARM CORNER on Page 12

Weather Calendar

COMPARATIVE TEMPERATURES

Station	High	Low
Water Works	85	52
Ephrata	89	55
Last Year (Ephrata)	92	55
Official High for Year, Aug. 5		95
Official Low for Year, Jan. 17		2
Character of Day		Partly Cloudy

SUN

Rises—6:31 a. m. Sets—7:36 p. m.

MOON

Sets—4:44 a. m. Full Moon, Sept. 2

STARS

Morning—Saturn

Evening—Venus, Jupiter, Mars.

NEARBY FORECASTS

Maryland and Delaware: Cloudy, moderately warm and humid with occasional rain and a few thunderstorms Friday; clearing and a little cooler Saturday.

New Jersey: Occasional rain and a few scattered thunderstorms, not so warm Friday; clearing and cool Saturday.

SAVE THIS NEWSPAPER

Make this newspaper do double work—give it to your paper-salvage drive.

Truman Warns U.S. Against Choosing Inexperienced Man

SENATOR HARRY S. TRUMAN

Accepts Democratic Nomination For Vice-President; Praises Roosevelt

Lamar, Mo.—(AP)—Senator Harry S. Truman Wednesday accepted the Democratic nomination for vice-president in a colorful ceremony at his birthplace here in a speech warning the nation against choosing for president "a man who lacks experience."

Truman Text Page 25

The Missouri Senator, named last month at Chicago as President Roosevelt's running mate in the November elections, devoted almost his entire 18-minute speech to praise of the Chief Executive, declared that the nation in its efforts to make a permanent peace was "very definitely in mid-stream," and cautioned against entrusting "the negotiation of the peace of the world to those who are not familiar with world affairs."

HOME TOWN PARTY

Truman came back to his home town late in the afternoon to be greeted by several thousand townsmen who had decorated the old Barton County Courthouse Square with bright bunting, flags and pictures of President Roosevelt and Truman, while the streets leading into the square were blocked with sandwich stands to feed the big crowd attracted to the celebration, and listen to Truman's fulsome praise of the President, whom he called his "leader and comman-

More of TRUMAN on Page 12

U. S. SEIZES TEN MINES WHERE WORK HAS BEEN HALTED

Roosevelt Directs Seizure As Strike Of Supervisory Employes Continues

Washington—(AP)—The government reached into Western Pennsylvania Thursday and took possession of ten bituminous coal mines where a strike of supervisory employes newly-organized by the United Mine workers has caused 4,200 persons to stop work.

President Roosevelt, on request of the War Labor Board, ordered the interior department to seize the properties of:

Rochester and Pittsburgh Coal Company, Indiana, Pa., eight mines, 3,200 men.

Ford Collieries Company, Curtisville, Pa., two mines, 1,000 men.

The Solid Fuels Administration of the Interior Department announced that the mines will reopen for work Monday morning and said "every man is expected to be back on the job."

The presidents of the two com-

More of MINES on Page 12

NEW POLICE STATION FAVORED BY MAYOR IN POST-WAR YEARS

A new city police station will be erected in Lancaster city if the present administration is in office when the war ends, Mayor D. E. Cary asserted Thursday.

The mayor, remarking that a new city police station is advisable and has been talked about for a period of time, said he felt it should be situated at a convenient place, with easy access to the court house. He said he had no definite idea where it could be erected, although several sites have been discussed.

The mayor said that while he favored housing all branches of the city government in one building this was impossible because the present municpal building will continue to be used.

Asks Youth To Make Most Of Present Opportunities To Get An Education

"The three million high school boys and girls who have been working this summer must decide whether they are to become members of the clan of Jacob, the foresighted—or Esau—the weak and short-sighted." Dr. James E. Wagner, pastor of St. Peter's Evangelical and Reformed church, pointed out in urging boys and girls to return to school this fall.

"The first twins in history, according to the Bible, were Jacob and Esau, the sons of Isaac and Rebekah," Dr. Wagner reminds us. "Jacob's name is familiar because, among other things, he was far-sighted enough to look beyond the immediate moment and see what would get him most in the long run. His twin-brother Esau—perhaps also the first 'red-head' in history—is scarcely known at all, and when he is mentioned it is most frequently to speak of him as the boy who 'sold his birthright for a mess of pottage (vegetable-soup)

"The three million high school

More of ASKS on Page 12

DR. JAMES E. WAGNER

WIN RAIL-SEA BASE FOR PUSH INTO HUNGARY

Second Ukraine Units Enter "Little Paris Of Balkans" After 30-Mile March

London, (Friday) — (AP) — Red tanks and motorized infantry rumbled into the broad avenues of the capitulated Romanian capital of Bucharest yesterday, winning a great rail-air base for an overland sweep into Hungary and Southern Germany, and also reached the Bulgarian frontier in a 30-mile advance below the captured Black Sea port of Constanta.

The dusty Second Ukraine Army units under Gen. Rodion Y. Malinovsky, victor at Odessa, clattered into "the little Paris of the Balkans" after a 30-mile march southward from the burning Ploesti oil fields, wrested from the bitterly-resisting Germans Wednesday.

CHASE NAZIS TO NORTH

Other Soviet columns had turned northwest of Ploesti, chasing the retreating Germans nine miles beyond the great oil center along the roads leading across the Predeal pass into Transylvania.

A 20-salvo salute from 324 Moscow victory cannon marked the collapse of the Germans in Romania and the entry into Bucharest.

The parade of big Russians tanks and guns down the broad Calea Victorei, Bucharest's main thoroughfare, came three years and six weeks after Romania made the fatal mistake of joining the Germans in their June, 1941, attack Russia—a step that has cost the Romanianas more than 300,000 men, either captured of who perished on the vast Russian Steppes

More of WIN on Page 12

Hungarian Collapse Seen Near, Report Rail Strikes

London — (AP) — Hungary, new keystone of Adolf Hitler's southeastern defenses, seemed on the edge of a crack-up as neighboring Slovakia fell rapidly under the control of Czechoslovak armed forces and Bulgarian peace delegates waited in Moscow and Cairo, respectively, to sign terms of capitulation.

Moscow radio said information had reached Switzerland that railway strikes had broken out in Hungary and traffic on the three main lines into Budapest was completely paralyzed. The report said the whole country was "on the verge of a general strike."

The United Nations radio at Algiers said that German troops had occupied all strategic points in Budapest, and that all official buildings in the Hungarian capital were under guard of German machine-gunners.

Hungarian newspapers carried customary last-ditch appeals but also mentioned the growing peril from "military deserters, escaped prisoners-of-war, enemy mercenaries, criminals with no homeland who are capable of anything, partisans and saboteurs infesting the

More of BALKANS on Page 12

RAINFALL HERE NEARLY INCH ABOVE NORMAL FOR YEAR

Yet Some Sections Are Facing Near-Drouth And Water Shortages

Spotty rainfall this year has created a peculiar situation in Lancaster County — precipitation is nearly one inch above normal for the eight months yet some sections are facing near-drouth conditions and water shortages.

Total rainfall to Sept. 1, as recorded at the Lancaster Water Works, is 29.20 inches while normal for that period is 28.29 inches.

This situation is caused, weather observers explained, by the spotty rainfall, which sent a deluge in some sections

More of RAINFALL on Page 12

2-WEEK SUSPENSION FOR LOCAL GAS DEALER

Harrisburg —(AP)— A two weeks' suspension of gasoline sales was ordered Thursday for Earl W Wolfe, operator of a gasoline filling station at Queen and Liberty Sts., Lancaster, after an OPA hearing on a citation for an inventory excess of 520 gallons of gasoline.

Hearing Commission Ewald J. J Smith fixed the penalty on recommendation of enforcement Attorney Max Lichtenfeld and said the date of the suspension would be fixed in the order. Wolfe was represented by Attorney Lewis S. May.

In the case of H. D. Kuntzelman, of Elizabethtown, doing business as the Elizabethtown Creamery Company on a charge of selling butter without receiving ration points, Smith directed issuance of a warning notice and told Kuntzelman the current charge would be considered in event of future violations.

Foresee No Major Resistance Short Of Germans' Siegfried Line

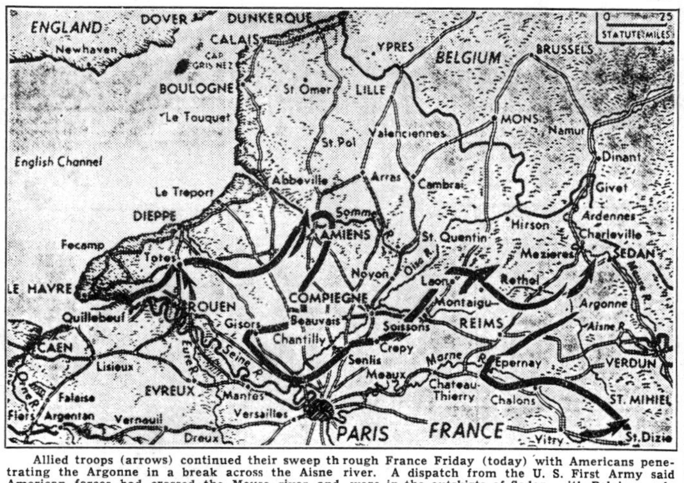

Allied troops (arrows) continued their sweep through France Friday (today) with Americans penetrating the Argonne in a break across the Aisne river. A dispatch from the U. S. First Army said American forces had crossed the Meuse river and were in the outskirts of Sedan, with Belgium only five miles away. Canadians entered Totes, within 17 miles of Dieppe.

Belgium 5 Miles Away; British Take Amiens; Patton's Men In Argonne

Supreme Headquarters Allied Expeditionary Force, (Friday)—(AP)—American troops have crossed the Meuse river near the Ardennes forest on the Belgian frontier in a tidal offensive stabbing into the outskirts of the historic battle city of Sedan, and field dispatches early today said the Yanks were unlikely to collide with any major German resistance short of the famous Siegfried Line, or West Wall, on the German frontier itself 55 miles east of Sedan.

The advance carried into the area of Maginot Line fortifications which failed France in 1940, an entrenched system of defenses which extended from the Belgian frontier northeast of Lille to the Rhine and thence along the Swiss and Italian frontiers to the Mediterranean.

5 MILES FROM BELGIUM

The Meuse apparently was crossed between Sedan—where the Germans broke into France in 1940 —and Charleville, and hard-riding Yank armored units then fanned out against both towns just five miles from the Belgian border.

A rabble of disorganized Germans was melting in the path of the Americans—fleeing in an effort to get into Germany, field dispatches said.

Leaping in a single day through the Argonne forest, where Gen. John J Pershing's doughboys battled for six weeks, freewheeling U.S. armored units may already have sprung the barrier of the Meuse, just south of Sedan.

Matching the speed of Lt. Gens. Courtney H. Hodges and George S. Patton, Jr., British tanks broke loose into the open plains of Piccardy, and advancing 60 miles in two days captured the cathedral and industrial city of Amiens, where the "black day" defeat of the German Army in 1918 induced Germans to make their first bid for peace.

From a strong bridgehead across the historic Somme at Amiens, Lt. Gen. Sir Richard Nugent O'Connor's armor plunged on 10 miles to Corbie, 55 miles from the Belgian border, and virtually sliced off half the Germans buzzbomb coast.

The Canadians, driving straight

More of SEE on Page 12

CITY MAN KILLED, 2 COUNTIANS ARE WOUNDED ABROAD

Pfc. Reneker Dies In France; Former Marine Officer Here Killed

Three additional casualties among Lancaster county service men fighting on the world's battlefields were reported Thursday. One was killed in action and two wounded.

The casualties:

Pfc. Kenneth Richard Reneker, twenty, 247 Elm St., killed in France.

Sgt. Richard W. Sweigart, Reamstown, wounded in France.

Pfc. David C. Huber, Columbia, wounded on Guam.

Word also was received of the death of a Marine officer formerly stationed here on recruiting duty, and the death of an airman with relatives in Lancaster county.

KILLED IN FRANCE

Pfc. Kenneth Richard Reneker, twenty, was killed in action in France on Aug. 8, according to a War Department telegram received by his parents, Mr. and Mrs. Raymond C. Reneker, of 247 Elm St.

He was serving with an infantry unit and has been overseas since

More of CITY on Page 12

DEMOCRATS TO OPEN HEADQUARTERS HERE

Democratic campaign headquarters will be opened at 49 N. Prince St., Friday, it was announced Thursday by Democratic County Chairman Albert H. Fritz.

"This campaign headquarters will be open to all voters, regardless of whether they are Democrats or Republicans," Chairman Fritz announced. "We are striving to get all qualified electors registered, and those who care to fill out their registration cards in the headquarters are free to do so."

Eisenhower Lashes German Land Greed In French Fight

Supreme Headquarters AlliedExpeditionaryForce—(AP)—Gen. Eisenhower, bronzed and smiling, voiced anew Thursday night his confidence that victory over Germany was possible in 1944, attributed the Nazis' utter defeat in France to their land-greedy defense strategy, and announced a change in his staff setup.

The Supreme Commander said that Lt. Gen. Omar N. Bradley, whose American armies are dashing head-long toward Belgium, had been made a full field commander of U. S. Forces in northern France, a command post equal to that of British Gen. Sir Bernard L. Montgomery, whose promotion to the rank of Field Marshal was announced later in London.

Eisenhower asserted the fight would be carried into Germany and he appeared convinced the Nazis were running out of manpower for their breached western defenses.

Underscoring Eisenhower's words was a huge battlemap behind him blazing with huge red arrows indicating the latest Allied advances toward Belgium and the German border in an invasion which he declared was already fully five days ahead of schedule.

Asked when he expected complete victory, the Supreme Commander said he would stand by his statement in Algiers just before he

More of EISENHOWER on Page 12

NEEDS FOR WAR MATERIEL STRESSED BY EISENHOWER

Urges "Maximum Rate" Delivery Across Atlantic Of Parts Modern Army Requires

Washington—(AP)—General Dwight D. Eisenhower urges "maximum rate" delivery across the Atlantic of "all those things, including spare parts, that a modern army and air force require in battle."

He cites 3,000 airplanes lost since D-day and 150,000 tons of ammunition expended a month as samples of the need.

The General's message to Lieut. Gen. Brehon B. Somervell, head of the army service forces, made public by the war

More of NEEDS on Page 12

FIRE ON POLE

A short-circuit, which burned off a "cut-off" and caused an alarm of fire at 10:35 p. m. Thursday, extinguished street lights in the southwestern portion of the city. Chief Harry Miller, who responded to an alarm turned in from Box 69, Water and Conestoga Streets, learned a pedestrian saw flames on a pole in the 200 block of South water Street and turned in the call. The services of firemen were not needed and the damage was repaired by employes of the Pennsylvania Power and Light Company.

JANE LOUISE GRILL IS REPORTED SOLD

Emanuel Frangos, proprietor, has sold the Jane Louise Grill, 101 W. King St., it was learned Thursday. The purchasers are Christ Moreos, 308 S. Beaver St., A. Frangakis, 326 S. Beaver St., and Helen Francos, 446 W. Lemon St., it was reported.

A certificate to conduct the business under the present name will be presented to the Common Pleas Court Tuesday, and a similar action will be filed with the Secretary of the Commonwealth on the same day.

Frangos, who operated the business for a number of years, was convicted recently, in the local court of operating a disorderly house. A motion for a new trial is pending.

Manheim Twp. GOP Kettle Boiling, Over New Constable This Time

Republicans of Manheim Township have started a new battle among themselves, it was discovered Thursday following the filing of a petition for constable of the township in the office of the Quarter Sessions Court in the Court House.

It appears that the organization Republicans filed a petition for the appointment of Alvin A. Leibley, 1117 Frances Ave., to fill the vacancy by the death of John L. Miller.

This petition, bearing the signatures of 14 Republicans, is scheduled to be presented formally to the court within two weeks. It was filed as of August 24, according to the date on the petition.

A second petition will be presented Friday, asking for the appointment of Elmer Lipp, Eden fire chief, it was reported Thursday.

Signers of Leibley's petition include D. H. Miller, 1023 Lititz Ave.; Edward J. Kessler, 962 Louise Ave.; Bruce A. Boggs, 1123 Louise Ave.; Viola M. Blumenstock, Lancaster R5; A. J. Kohler Lancaster R3; Janet R. Miller and C. Ralph Binkley, Neffsville; George H. Goll, Lancaster R3, David Mourer, 1251 Lititz Pike; Dr. C. Howard Witmer, Lancaster R3; Karl B. Kuhlman, 836 Janet Ave.; Jacob H. Esbenshade, Lancaster R3; Tom C. Shirk, 21 Fordney Road, and Hilda J. Markley, 824 State St.

BOY SERIOUSLY HURT IN 18-FOOT FALL

Melvin Gilbert, nine, 229 Green St., was seriously injured when he fell eighteen feet to a concrete pavement when he attempted to jump from a tree to a porch at his home at 5:30 p. m. Thursday. He was admitted to the Lancaster General Hospital suffering from a possible fracture of the skull, possible dislocation of the right shoulder and a laceration of the scalp

Attendants learned the boy was playing at his home and had climbed out on a tree limb and attempted to jump onto the front porch roof. The boy missed the roof and landed on the pavement below, attendants learned.

CHIMNEY SPARKS SET FARM HOUSE ON FIRE WITH $5,500 DAMAGE

Fire that started when sparks from a chimney ignited a shingle roof caused $5,500 damage to the two and one-half story frame farm house of Oscar Kaechel, midway on the road between Quarryville and Buck, in E. Drumore Twp., at 2:30 o'clock Thursday afternoon.

Flames burned through the second floor of the house, it was reported, but the occupants managed to save some furniture from the living room and kitchen on the ground floor. The Quarryville Fire Company, supervised by Robert Groff, engineer, responded to an alarm and brought the fire under control. The loss, it was said, is partly covered by insurance.

FOOD AND SUGAR STAMPS BECOME VALID

Five more blue stamps in War Ration Book 4, worth 10 points each, become valid for purchasing rationed processed foods beginning Friday (today). The stamps, G5, H5, J5, K5 and L5 remain valid indefinitely.

Sugar Stamp 33, also in War Ration Book 4, will become valid Friday (today) for an indefinite period, for the purchase of five pounds of sugar.

JAPANESE STUBBORNLY DEFENDING BURMA BASE

Southeast Asia Command Headquarters, Kandy, Ceylon—(AP)—Japanese troops are stubbornly defending Tiddim but Allied patrols have been operating within 400 yards of that western Burma base, Allied headquarters announced Tuesday.

Reverses were reported for enemy elements to the south.

Withdrawing from an unsuccessful attack near Goppe Bazaar, at the eastern end of one of the main passes across the Mayu range, Japanese reconnaissance troops left more than 60 dead, and British Fourteenth Army patrols harassed the withdrawal, killing more of the enemy around Taung Bazaar Monday, headquarters said.

The communique said road and rail communications were attacked successfully in central and northern Burma by Allied aircraft of the Eastern Air Command Monday and Sunday, despite adverse weather. Bridges were the main objectives.

12TH OFFENDER JAILED

James Henry Conway, forty-eight, no home, charged with vagrancy, was jailed for 90 days by Alderman Charles Uhland in police court Tuesday afternoon. He was a twelfth offender over a period of four years.

WEATHER HINDERS AIR OPERATIONS

London — (AP) — Formations of fast Allied bombers were over Western Germany Tuesday night, the Berlin radio reported, after a day of bad weather that kept most of the U. S. Eighth Air Force and RAF planes grounded on this side of the channel.

Extent of the Allied night operations was not disclosed. The American heavyweights were preparing to carry out orders to destroy the German city of Aachen if it does not surrender by Wednesday morning.

The pounding that Aachen will get if it rejects the American ultimatum may be a good example of what the future holds for other stubborn points on the way of the Allied march on Berlin.

"On our airfields bombers are awaiting the final order to take off," Aachen's resident's were warned in the ultimatum.

In the past month the Eighth Air Force alone has dumped 60,850 tons of bombs on German cities and has stayed at home only 11 days since Sept. 10 because of weather.

Berlin was reported without telephone service Tuesday, and Stockholm dispatches said the German capital had been without long-distance service since Friday, when about 1,000 American heavy bombers hit the city and wrecked telephone cables.

The German radio acknowledged that the steel works at Bochum was damaged considerably Monday night by an attack of 500 RAF Lancaster heavy bombers. Returning to their old tactics of saturation bombing, the RAF dumped thousands of incendiaries and many tons of explosives on the German industrial city and left fires which crewmen watched for many miles on the way home through cloud and fog.

Bochum was shattered by a big raid Sept. 29, 1943. In the intervening year the Todt Construction organization had been able to get some of the major industries going again, thus setting the stage for Monday night's blow.

FIGHTING AMONG SPANISH GROUPS IS REPORTED

New York — (AP) — Fighting has broken out between troops of Generalissimo Francisco Franco and Maquis forces of Spanish Republicans re-entering Spain from France, and is increasing in fury with Franco forced to bring up artillery and mechanized equipment against the Spanish Republicans, a Blue Network broadcast from London said Tuesday.

HEIFER BRINGS $20,000

Cheyenne, Wyo.—(AP)—A young heifer was sold for $20,000. The Wyoming Hereford ranch auctioned the animal, Lady Lill 15th, to John E. Owen of Riverside, Calif., and ranch officials said the price paid was a world's record. They said the previous high bid for a heifer was $13,850.

BLOOD DONORS: BE SURE TO KEEP APPOINTMENTS TODAY

WEATHER
Eastern Pennsylvania: Increasing Cloudiness And Colder Friday; Saturday Rain And Continued Rather Cold.

Intelligencer Journal.

The Leading Newspaper in the Garden Spot of America, Home Owned for Home Folks Since 1794 — 150th Anniversary Year

Girl Scout FAT COLLECTION
Northeast Suburbs (Grand View Heights Section, etc.)
SATURDAY MORNING

VOLUME LXXXI.—NO. 33. Entered as second class matter August 9, 1944 at the Post Office at Lancaster, Pa., under the Act of March 3, 1879. Reg. U. S. Pat. Off. LANCASTER, PA., FRIDAY MORNING, OCTOBER 20, 1944 CITY THIRTY-FOUR PAGES. 20c PER WEEK—4c Per Copy

M'ARTHUR IN PHILIPPINES

BLOOD DONOR CENTER SETS DAILY RECORD

205 Pints Blood Collected Here; Hope To Be Able To Exceed Week's Quota

An all-time record for the Lancaster Blood Donor Center was set Thursday when 205 pints of blood were collected—topping the daily quota by 45 pints, and the previous high daily record, set last January, by 27 pints.

However, serious deficits in daily quotas for last Monday and Tuesday left the Harrisburg Mobile Donor Unit still 16 pints short of the weekly quota of 800 pints. The unit will receive volunteers at the First Evangelical and Reformed Church today.

Red Cross officials expressed themselves as jubilant over the response, and said that if all the people who made appointments for Friday appear, the weekly quota of 800 pints will be reached.

HAD 231 DONORS

A total of 231 donors reported, including 100 men and 131 women, and of those reporting, 111 were new volunteers, a fact which was gratifying to the committee in charge, as new volunteers are constantly sought.

There were 59 who failed to keep their appointments, and 40 or 50 "drop-in" volunteers, who nearly made up for the absentees. The Center was unable to take care of all those who volunteered, but many of these will be taken Friday.

Of the donors, 120 gave for their second time or more, as follows: 46, second time; 25, third; 59, fourth time or more.

About 150 employes of Armstrong's were among the donors, and also a group from Stehli's Silk Mill.

Paul Taylor, whose home is in Gibraltar, was among the donors.

Seven donors became members of the Gallon club Thursday, as follows: Miriam Vollrath, 313 E. New St.; James F. Smith, 543 N. Duke St.; Gertrude Sprenkle, Lancaster R1; Mrs. William Troop, 733 E. End Ave.; Robert Greenawalt, 138 N. Duke St.; Samuel B. Smith, Jr., 716 First St.; Ira Styer, 639 First St.

"We Lead All The Rest"

FARM CORNER

By The Farm Editor

43-ACRE FARM SELLS FOR $9,240 AT SALE

A farm containing 43 acres and some odd perches, including a two and one-half story brick dwelling, large bank barn and attached tobacco shed, hog sty, garage and orchard was sold for $215 an acre, or a total of $9,240 Thursday during a public sale on the farm in West Hempfield Township to Isaac H. Seachrist, Mountville R2. The farm was sold by Levi B. Kneisley. The auctioneer was Edgar F. Funk.

A farm of 151 acres with 30 acres of timber, a meadow and stone buildings, situated in Brecknock Township, Berks county, along the road from Knauers to Adamstown, was withdrawn Thursday when offered at public sale, because of insufficient bids. The farm was offered by Jacob S. Newswanger and Esther S. Newswanger. The auctioneer was Benjamin F. Weaver.

A 74-acre farm in Manheim Township was sold Thursday to Noah W. Weaver, New Holland, for Mr. and Mrs. W. Raymond Bushong, Lancaster R3, through A. M. Keener, agent. The farm, formerly owned by the late Enos Hess and known as the Hess farm, contains a brick dwelling, large bank barn, tobacco shed and necessary farm buildings. The sale price was not revealed.

Weather Calendar

COMPARATIVE TEMPERATURES

Station	High	Low
Water Works	70	37
Ephrata	72	41
Last Year (Ephrata)	52	37
Official High for Year, Aug. 5		95
Official Low for Year, Jan. 17		2
Character of Day		Clear

SUN
Rises—7:19 a. m. Sets—6:18 p. m.

MOON
Sets—8:38 p. m. First Quarter, Oct. 24

STARS
Morning—Jupiter-Saturn.
Evening—Venus-Mars.

NEARBY FORECASTS
Maryland, Delaware and New Jersey: Cloudy, windy and colder Friday; Saturday rain and continued rather cold.

Dewey Voices Appeal For War Fund Drive Support

Albany, N. Y. — (AP) — Gov. Thomas E Dewey broadcast an appeal Thursday night for support of the National War Fund, which he described as "The American conscience in action."

Asserting the fund "unites the war work of 22 member agencies of scores of other participating services and of the agencies in your community," he said:

"It is inter-faith. It is non-governmental. It is wholly voluntary. It is the living, working proof of the vitality of the American idea of neighborly good will."

He paid special tribute to the USO, which he helped organize in 1941.

"The foreign relief and refugee agencies of the National War Fund follow, close up, in the wake of the war to salvage life and restore hope to the stricken people," he said.

"Our generosity will be a measure of the steadfastness with which our home front supports them (our fighting men) on the battle front. It will be an assurance to them of the tender affection in which they are held—and a promise of our will that they shall come home as soon as possible after victory to an America with freedom and opportunity for all."

United Drive Workers Told To Beware Of Complacency

With about 55 per cent of the United Drive goal of $484,000 already subscribed, campaign workers will resume their efforts today with the knowledge that complacency and overconfidence threaten their success.

The amount already contributed was revealed at the first report meeting at the Hotel Brunswick Thursday noon and totaled $267,877. Veterans of previous campaigns were quick to note that the total must be viewed in the light of the completeness of the reports made. It was explained that the first report was far more nearly complete than the first report last year, when $207,000 of a goal of $468,000 was subscribed.

This indicates that while subscribers are being signed up earlier this year than last, the total contributions from the same pledge cards is smaller. Thus, the task of raising the remaining $216,000 may be considerably more difficult than appears on the surface, unless each division concentrates on contacting every possible prospect and obtaining larger subscriptions than last year.

The advance divisions in Lancaster city area made the most complete reports and consequently their contributions at the two remaining report meetings may not be too impressive, although there are many potential subscribers still unreported. It devolves then upon the women's division in the Lancaster city area and the county division to make up much of the deficiency between the amount subscribed and the total goal.

NEXT REPORT MONDAY

The next report meeting will be held Monday noon and the final victory dinner is scheduled for Thursday, October 26, at 6:30 p. m., both at the Hotel Brunswick.

At the close of Thursday's report meeting Dr. James E. Wagner, general chairman of the United Drive, said:

"I am grateful for the work al ready done, but I am fearful that the Thursday noon report may be misleading. The simple fact is that many people, seeing that we reported more than 55 per cent of the goal, will be even more complacent with regard to the United Drive.

"That first report was as high as it was, not because people are giving more, but because more people had been solicited than in the corresponding period a year ago.

"Simple fact is that most of the work of the Industrial and Special Gifts division has been done and their contributions are below what they were a year ago.

POINTS OUT DANGER

"Our chief danger, right from the start, has been with people assuming that because the campaign went over the goal last year they can afford to let down on their giving

More UNITED DRIVE on Page 16

NAVIGATOR DIES IN CRASH; 6 WOUNDED, EPHRATAN MISSING

Mt. Joy Flier Killed In Accident; Two Pacific Casualties

First Lt. Robert F. Lindamuth, twenty-seven, of the Army Air Forces, reported by the War Department to have died in England Sept. 26, was fatally injured in the collision of two planes, according to additional information received by his mother, Mrs. Ellen Lindamuth, of S. Barbara St., Mount Joy.

The letter from the War Department said that Lt. Lindamuth, who had only arrived overseas in August was navigator on one of the planes which collided while on a practice mission.

Six additional casualties were reported Thursday, including a soldier missing in Germany and five wounded in action, two for the second time.

The casualties:

Sgt. Harry Turner, Ephrata, missing in Germany.

Pfc. Dallas Hirneisen, Reinholds, wounded in Germany.

Pvt. Gordon Yingst, Lititz, wounded in Italy.

Pfc. Richard C. Eshleman, 534 E. Chestnut St. wounded in Holland.

Cpl. Dean G. Pettis, Columbia, wounded in the South Pacific.

Pfc. William Studenroth, Columbia, wounded in the South Pacific.

Sgt. Harry Turner, twenty-three, who resides with his sister, Mrs. Anna Burkholder, 156 E. Walnut St., Ephrata, has been reported missing in action since Sept. 28, in

More of CASUALTIES on Page 16

HAND SERVICE GROUP TO HOLD SCRAP DRIVE

The ninth salvage drive will be conducted by the General Hand Service Plaque Association from 8 a. m. to 11 a. m. Sunday, it was announced by President John Dunlap Thursday.

The group is seeking to attain more scrap than in any of the previous drives, and President Dunlap stated that residents outside of the vicinity wishing to donate scrap are asked to dial 3-2109.

The association has mailed 129 Christmas boxes to service men and women. The group will also hold a rummage sale December 15 and 16 at at Rockland Street and Howard Avenue.

BELIEVE LANCASTER'S FALCON HAS RETURNED

The Peregrine falcon which roosted nightly for several months last winer on the highest ledge of the Griest building in Penn Square was reported by observers to have returned Thursday evening, just before dusk.

The bird, the observers reported, alighted on the same ledge on the northwest corner of the building, as it occupied nightly in its previous sojourn here.

The spectacle of one of nature's largest birds roosting in the center of the city brought out thousands of persons to observe its action during its last appearance.

The falcon disappeared this spring as mysteriously as it put in its original appearance.

U.S. Forces Seize Eastern Coast Of Leyte; "Pledge Redeemed"--FDR

SAYS NIPPONS TO BE TAUGHT NEEDED LESSON

President Sees Move Another "Way Station On The Road To Japan"

Washington (Friday)—(AP)—President Roosevelt said today that Gen. Douglas MacArthur's drive into the Philippines redeemed the pledge made when American troops surrendered on Corregidor two years ago and marked another "way station on the road to Japan."

"We promised to return, we have returned," Mr. Roosevelt said in a statement issued minutes after news of MacArthur's landings on the island of Leyte was flashed from the southwest Pacific.

PROMISES FREEDOM

Promising freedom to the Philippine Islands as soon as the Japanese invader has been driven out, the President said:

"We have learned our lesson about Japan. We trusted her and treated her with the decency due a civilized neighbor. We were foully betrayed. The price of the lesson was high.

"Now we are going to

More of ROOSEVELT on Page 16

Gen. Douglas MacArthur's Headquarters in the Philippines announced Thursday night that the eastern coast of Leyte Island had been seized in a major amphibious operation. Striking at Leyte MacArthur's forces at one blow split the Japanese forces in the Philippines. The carrier symbol and arrows show where U. S. Army task force has been striking.

M'Arthur Makes Good Vow, "I Shall Return," In Major Amphibious Operation In Central Philippines Splitting Jap Forces

General MacArthur's Headquarters in the Philippines (Friday) — (AP) — (By Army Radio Pool Broadcast)—Gen. Douglas MacArthur, making good his vow he would return to the Philippines, announced from those islands today his Navy and air-supported forces have invaded and secured expanding beachheads in the Central Philippines.

MacArthur, aboard a warship, went along with the huge convoy from New Guinea, and within four hours after his forces landed began making plans to go ashore.

"In a major amphibious operation, we have seized the eastern coast of Leyte Island in the Philippines, 600 miles north of Morotai and 2,500 miles from Milne Bay (New Guinea)," a special communique dramatically proclaimed from the invasion scene.

Striking at a point where he is in position to quickly cut off the island of Luzon, on which Manila is situated from Mindanao on the south, MacArthur poured supplies ashore in preparation for showdown battles with an estimated 225,000 Japanese under Field Marshal Juichi Terauchi.

Every able bodied man who escaped from Corregidor in Manila Bay before it surrendered May 6, 1942, went along on the invasion to liberate the Filipinos and their imprisoned fellow Americans from bondage.

On Leyte, a suitable air base island 300 miles southeast of Manila, the invaders secured Tacloban on the northeast end of the island "with small casualties," the communique reported.

Tokyo radio also reported landings at Cabalian on the southern tip and said earlier landings occurred at the entrance of Leyte Gulf on Suluan Island.

Eyewitness account from the scene reported the American Navy and Airforce were on hand in such mammoth strength that the Japanese navy was nowhere in sight and the Nipponese airforce, knocked out at all airfields in the Philippines, offered scarcely token resistance.

One correspondent said today "up to now no ship has been lost."

The preparation for the invasion included the destruction of more than 1,300 planes, the sinking of 86 ships, damaging of 127 ships and widespread devastation of airfields and reinforcement bases since Oct. 9 in task force blasts at the Ryukyus, Formosa and the Philippines.

HUGE INVASION CONVOY

Dean Schedler, Associated Press war correspondent, reporting from the scene said the invasion convoy stretched as far as the eye could see.

Tokyo radio accounts said Suluan Island, not mentioned by MacArthur, was invaded Tuesday (Manila Time) and the

More of PHILIPPINES on Page 16

Canadians Accelerate Drive Against Nazis In Holland

London (Friday)—(AP)—Canadian troops accelerated their drive against Germans pocketed in the Schelde estuary of Holland yesterday, one column bursting forward three miles, and last night the Berlin radio blurted out fresh speculation on the imminence of an all-out Allied assault across the Dutch-German frontier.

Late reports said the Canadians were fighting inside Breskens, just across the estuary from flooded Walcheren Island, while another Canadian column splashed through the marshes three miles to within one mile of Costburg, squarely in the center of the pocket.

DETERMINED EFFORT

This action was part of the determined effort to clear away German forces blocking the Schelde river leading to Antwerp and German military spokesmen have repeatedly maintained that a British-American "knockout blow" would be attempted somewhere between Aachen and Arnhem as soon as the Antwerp supply channel was opened to Gen. Eisenhower.

The Canadians were making steady progress, but in some cases meeting desperate opposition. German troops counterattacked fiercely against Lt. Gen. H. D. Crear's units on the three-mile wide spit of land stretching out to Walcheren and front dispatches said some of the enemy had won a foothold in the north edge of Woensdrecht.

CONVERGE ON TOWN

British troops advancing southward from captured Venray ploughed 3½ miles deeper into the German Maas river bridgehead in Holland Thursday and with a strong Amercian force converged upon the key town of Amerika, astride one of the main railroads leading eastward into Germany's industrial

More of CANADIANS on Page 16

STATE DEPT. HITS DEWEY'S REMARKS ABOUT ROMANIA

GOP Nominee's Blast Brings Administration Volley In Reply

Washington — (AP) — Governor Thomas E. Dewey's blast at what he termed President Roosevelt's "personal, secret diplomacy" brought an administration volley in reply Thursday including a formal State Department statement of "facts" it said the Republican Presidential candidate left out in discussing Romania.

Senator O'Mahoney of Wyoming, Chairman of the Democratic Senatorial Campaign Committee, declared in a statement that Dewey "recklessly demands what amounts to an open break with Russia while the war is still on." He called Dewey's address Wednesday night to the New York Herald-Tribune Forum "the most effective argument" yet advanced for re-election of President Roosevelt.

The State Department's statement was confined entirely to Ro-

More of STATE on Page 16

DEWEY ENDORSES STATE DEPARTMENT WARNING TO NAZIS

Republican Presidential Nominee Scheduled To Speak In Pittsburgh Tonight

Albany, N. Y.—(AP)—Gov. Thomas E. Dewey endorsed Thursday night a State Department warning to Nazi leaders that they would "pay the penalty for their heinous crimes" if they carried out reported plans to exterminate Poles, Jews and other non-German nationals held in concentration camps.

ISSUES STATEMENT

In a formal statement, issued a few hours before the Republican presidential nominee was due to leave for a labor speech in Pittsburgh Friday night, Dewey said:

"Information comes to this country from unquestionably reliable sources that the Nazis, trapped and knowing that they are faced with inevitable defeat, are now resorting to the known gangster terror device of threatening to exterminate their very victims—Poles, Jews and other non-German nationals—now imprisoned by them in their horrible concentration camps in parts of Poland and other counttries still occupied by the Nazis.

"The civilized world is now in a position in unmistakable terms to warn the Nazis — military commanders, members of the German government, their aiders, abettors,

More of DEWEY on Page 16

County Child Ill With Diphtheria; 8th Case Of Typhoid Fever Reported

A case of typhoid fever, the eighth this year, and a case of diptheria, the second this year, were reported by Dr. A. J. Greenleaf, Mountville, county medical director, Thursday.

The typhoid fever victim is Miss Minnie Nolt, thirty-seven, daughter of Mr. and Mrs. Isaac Nolt, New Holland R1, Earl Township.

The victim of diptheria is Emma Bannon, eight, daughter of Mr. and Mrs. T. K. Bannon, East Earl R1, Caernarvon Township.

Miss Nolt was stricken ill October 1 and is confined to her home. Her condition is regarded as fair by attending physicians.

She is the aunt of Titus Nolt, twenty, and Luke Nolt, twelve, New Holland R1, who were stricken with typhoid fever early in September. Another typhoid fever victim, David Brubaker, twenty-six, New Holland R1, who was taken ill shortly after the two Nolts, resides on a tenant house on the Isaac Nolt farm.

Ward M. Kurtz, Leola, State Health Officer, who is investigating the source of the four cases, said that samples of water have been taken from the Nolt farm for analysis.

More of COUNTY on Page 16

STATE-AID CHECKS FOR HOSPITALS HERE

A check for $9,250 has been mailed to the Lancaster General Hospital, and one for $7,300 to the Tuberculosis Society of Lancaster county for the Rossmere Sanatorium by State Treasurer G. Harold Wagner, it was announced in Harrisburg Thursday. These payments were among those made to state-aided institutions for the quarter ending August 31, it was announced.

American Army, Navy Losses Since Pearl Harbor Total 453,375

Washington—(AP)—Two months of fighting on the western front from the break-through on the Normandy peninsula to the time when German territory was invaded cost about 62,000 casualties among American troops.

This was disclosed Thursday in a War Department announcement that the total American Army casualties for that theater through October 3 were 174,780. An announcement last month by supreme headquarters of the Allied Expeditionary Force said that the total for western France through August 6 was 112,321.

Of the total casualties from the landing in Normandy on June 6 through October 3, the dead amounted to 29,842, wounded 130,227 and missing 14,711.

An exact comparison of the two casualty announcements, however, was impossible, since the August 6 total included Air Force casualties whereas that covering the period through October 3 did not.

American Army and Navy casualties in all theaters since Pearl Harbor now total 453,375. The War

More of AMERICAN on Page 16

ROAD TO BERLIN

(By The Associated Press)

1. Western Front: 302 miles (from west of Duren).
2. Russian Front: 310 miles (from Warsaw).
3. Italian Front: 558 miles (from south of Bologna).

STEVEDORE DROWNS

PHILADELPHIA, Oct. 27—(AP)—John Rinsley, 55-year-old stevedore from Haddon Heights, N. J., drowned last night when he fell into the Delaware River. Harbor police recovered the body.

ISSUE CITATION

A citation was issued in the estate of Jacob N. Townsend, late of Bart Twp., in Orphans Court yesterday to show cause why an account should not be filed. The petition stated that although letters of administration were granted to Edward K. Townsend, no account has been filed to date. The citation is returnable on Nov. 20.

PLAN SCAVENGER HUNT

The Intermediate Fellowship Society of St. Andrew's Evangelical and Reformed Church is planning a scavenger hunt to be held Nov. 2, immediately following the business meeting of the organization. The committee in charge includes: Nancy Peters, chairman; Joanne Sheer, Jean Piersol, Arlene Huber, Joan Tompkins, Joan Comfort and George Oswald.

MEN

(Continued from Page One)

Lime St., from the War Department.

Lt. Herr entered the service in April 1942 and received his commission as a second lieutenant at Ft. Sill, Okla. He has been serving overseas with a Field Artillery Unit since June.

Prior to entering the service, Lt. Herr was the Washington representative of the Legal Department of the Armstrong Cork Co.

He is a graduate of the West Lampeter High school and attended George Washington University, Washington, D. C. His brother, M-Sgt. Landis Herr, is in France.

Pfc. Strickler Killed In France on Sept. 15

Pfc. William C. Strickler was killed in action Sept. 15, in France, three days after his twenty-seventh birthday anniversary, the War Department notified his wife, Mrs. Anna Mary Strickler, who resides near Millway.

Son of Mrs. Harvey Strickler, of Sheridan, he entered the service in 1942 and trained at Fort Dix, N. J., and in Virginia. He went overseas in the spring of 1944 and was wounded in action Aug. 26. He returned to combat duty just a few weeks before he was killed.

Besides his wife and his mother, he is survived by a sister, Katherine, and these brothers: Robert, Harvey, Jay, George, Arthur, Paul, Ronald, James and Mark.

M-Sgt. Brimmer Dies In West Coast Hospital

Master Sgt. John Richard Brimmer, Jr., twenty-six, of the Army Air Forces, son of Mrs. Gertrude B. and the late John Richard Brimmer, 1014 Marietta Ave., died suddenly yesterday morning of a heart ailment at San Rafael, Calif.

M-Sgt. Brimmer

He attended Hebron Academy, Me., and was a senior at Franklin and Marshall College when he enlisted in the Air Corps in January, 1942.

In addition to his mother, he is survived by his widow, Thelma M. Brimmer; a son, John Richard Brimmer, III, and the following brothers and sisters: William Blair Brimmer, with the Army Air Forces at Hamilton Field, Calif.; Mrs. Robert M. Allard, Scarsdale, N. Y., and Mrs. L. Levan Cummings, New Haven, Conn.

S-Sgt. Fritsch Dies In Veterans Hospital

Staff Sgt. Joseph W. Fritsch, twenty-four, died at 5:30 p. m. yesterday at the Veterans Hospital, Washington, D. C., of aplastic anemia, following an illness of ten months.

S-Sgt. Fritsch

Sgt. Fritsch was striken ill while a member of a ground crew of a bomber group stationed in England and was confined to a hospital there for several weeks before he was brought to this country.

While confined to the hospital, he was visited by his brother, Pfc. Herman Fritsch, who was also stationed in England. The meeting was arranged by the Red Cross.

Sgt. Fritsch was born in this city, the son of William E. and Erla Vollerston Fritsch, 37 Rodney St., attended St. Joseph Schol and enlisted in the U. S. Army on August 12, 1942. He was sent overseas in October, 1943. He was a member of St. Joseph's Roman Catholic Church.

Besides his parents, he is survived by his wife, Mary Keller Fritsch, 426 Poplar St.; two brothers Cpl. William J., U. S. Army, South Pacific, and Pfc. Herman C., U. S. Army, Europe. Two sisters, Erla and Shirley, at home, also survive.

Pvt. Dusel Wounded In Germany on Oct. 6

Pvt. Adam J. Dusel, Jr., 20, son of Mr. and Mrs. Adam J. Dusel, 626 First St., was wounded Oct. 6 in Germany, according to a War Department telegram received by his parents.

Pvt. Dusel

He received his Basic training at Fort Knox, Ky., and left for overseas duty in November, 1943. In a letter to his parents, he said he is hospitalized in France.

Total War Casualties For City and County

Killed in Action	203
Killed in Accidents and Died in Camps	52
Missing	78
Prisoners	72
Wounded	485
Total	890

Pilot Is Missing Over Germany Since Oct. 7

Flight Officer Elvin Vernon Brooks, son of Mrs. Stella Brooks, Lancaster R3, and Elvin L. Brooks, 1013 N. Lime St., has been reported missing over Germany since Oct. 7 according to a War Department telegram received by his wife, who resides in Montgomery, Ala.

F. O. Brooks

F.-O. Brooks, twenty, was a pilot on a B-24 Liberator and holds the Air Medal with two oak leaf clusters and also has been cited for meritorious flying while in combat.

He enlisted in the aviation cadets in August 1942 and left for training in February, 1943. He received his pilot wings at the Army Air Field, Stuttgart, Ark., on Dec. 5, 1943 and left for England, April 1944.

His last letter written on Oct. 2, and received here on Wednesday, a few hours before the telegram from his wife arrived, said that he had completed 23 missions.

He is a graduate of the East Lampeter Twp. High School and his brother, William, has enlisted in the Aviation Cadet Reserves.

Pfc. Rineer Listed Missing in Holland

Pfc. David M. Rineer, twenty-three, son of Mr. and Mrs. Jesse Rineer, Quarryville, has been missing in the Holland area since Oct. 4, the War Department has notified his wife, the former Roberta Reese, of New Providence.

Pfc. Rineer

He entered the service Aug. 28, 1942 and received his training at Fort Knox, Ky., and Camp Chaffee, Ark. He left for overseas service July 2.

A graduate of the Quarryville High School, he was a prominent member of the Quarryville Fire Company and prior to entering the service was employed by the Armstrong Cork Co.

Pvt. Sheaffer Wounded, Receives Purple Heart

Pvt. Amos Landis Sheaffer, Jr., nineteen, has sent his Purple Heart award received for wounds in France, to his parents, Mr. and Mrs. Amos L. Sheaffer, Sr., of New Providence R1. His parents did not know he was wounded until they received the medal.

According to letters received from him, the infantryman was probably wounded in August, but no word of it has been received from the War Department. He wrote only that he was resting and they would be receiving a "surprise," but told nothing about the wounds.

Pvt. Sheaffer

Pvt. Sheaffer enlisted in the Army on Dec. 3, 1943, and after training at Camp Croft, S. C., and Camp Meade, Md., he went overseas in June of this year. He entered France after the invasion. He attended Quarryville schools and worked on his father's farm before entering the service.

His brother, Sgt. John L. Sheaffer, was formerly in a tank division but is now with the Army Air Forces at Sheppard Field, Tex.

Pfc. Dysinger Listed Missing in Holland

Pfc. John M. Dysinger, Jr., thirty-four, is missing in action in Holland since Oct. 5, according to a telegram from the War Department received Wednesday by his wife, who resides at 842 N. President Ave.

Pfc. Dysinger, Jr.

Pfc. Dysinger has been overseas since July 25, and was in England for a short while before going to France with an Armored Infantry Battalion. He entered the service July 1, 1943, and was stationed at Fort Knox, Ky., Camp Chaffee, Ark., Camp Phillips, Kansas, and Fort George R. Meade, Md., before going overseas.

T-Sgt. Lockard Missing, Awarded Air Medal

Technical Sgt. Victor V. Lockard, twenty, radio operator on a B-17 Flying Fortress, has been missing in action over Germany since Oct. 7, the War Department notified his parents, Mr. and Mrs. Eli Lockard, of Lancaster R1.

T/S Lockard

Shortly after the telegram arrived, his parents received a letter written October 4, three days before the mission from which he failed to return.

A graduate of the Columbia High School, class of 1942, he was inducted April 23, 1943, and received his basic training in Florida. He obtained his advance AAF training at Sioux Falls, S. D., and Yuma, Ariz., arriving overseas —in England—in July of this year.

According to a dispatch received here this morning from an Eighth Air Force Bomber Station, England, Sgt. Lockard has been awarded the Air Medal in recognition of "exceptionally meritorious achievement" while flying in a B-17 Flying Fortress in the air war in Europe as a radio operator and gunner. Sgt. Lockard has participated in long-range assaults on German industrial plants producing tanks, synthetic oil, guns, planes and other weapons.

Lt. Anderson Wounded In Germany on Oct. 8

First Lt. Robert C. Anderson was wounded in action Oct. 8 in Germany, the War Department notified his parents Mr. and Mrs Robert Anderson 35 Washington St.

Lt. Anderson

He entered the Army in May, 1942, and entered France on D-Day June 6, fighting through France and Belgium into Germany. He previously served with the 92nd Division.

A graduate of the McCaskey High School, class of 1941, he was employed by the Armstrong Cork Co., prior to entering the service.

His brother, Second Lt. Monroe Anderson was wounded in action in France Aug. 6, and has received the Purple Heart.

Pfc. Weitzel Awarded Purple Heart

Pfc. William K. Weitzel, twenty, son of Mr. and Mrs. Heber Weitzel, Denver R2, was wounded in New Guinea and awarded the Purple Heart, he informed his parents.

Pvt. Drake Wounded In France in Sept.

Pvt. Melvin Drake, twenty-five, son of Mr. and Mrs. Robert Drake, Drumore RD, was wounded in action in France in September, the War Department notified his wife, Mrs. Frances Drake, of Poplar St., Lancaster.

He arrived in North Africa in the spring and was stationed in Italy previous to participating in the invasion of France. In a letter to his wife, he said that he was wounded in the side, but that his injury was not serious.

Sgt. Bechard Wounded In Holland on Oct. 8

Sgt. Paul R. Bechard, son of Mrs. Mary Bechard, 506 S. Lime St., was seriously wounded Oct. 8 in the Holland area, the War Department announced in a telegram.

Sgt. Bechard

He entered the service Oct. 29, 1942, and trained at Camp Blanding, Fla. He went overseas on Jan. 15 of this year.

He is a graduate of the Lancaster High School and attended Millersville State Teachers College. Prior to entering the service, he was employed by the Hamilton Watch Co.

Pvt. Myers Wounded, Hospitalized in France

Pvt. Francis Myers has been wounded in Belgium, the War Department notified his parents, Mr. and Mrs. Ira Myers, of Quarryville. He is hospitalized in France suffering from a shrapnel wound in the leg.

S-Sgt. Constantine Receives Purple Heart

Staff Sgt. Milton Constantine, son of Chief Petty Officer and Norman R. Constantine, Ephrata, has recovered from wounds received in the European area, been decorated with the Purple Heart, and resumed his duties as a radio operator on a transport plane.

The information was contained in a letter he wrote his father, stationed at the Philadelphia Navy Yard.

TWO HOMES, FARM PROPERTY ARE SOLD

The brick building at 22, 24 and 26 East Main St., Lititz, was sold at public sale yesterday afternoon to Dr. M. H. Yoder, of Lititz, and others, for $12,650. The property was sold by Ethel R. and Alice Zook.

Paul G. Good sold his farm of 59 acres situated one mile north of Bowmansville at public sale to Amos Zimmerman of Blue Ball, at $149 an acre. Good has purchased a house at Bowmansville from Frank Gehman and will move there.

A two-and-a-half story frame house, the property of Emma R Graul, Penryn, was sold at public sale last night for $5,610 to Alvin Keath, Manheim R1.

MRS. PINCHOT TALKS TO LEBANON PAC

LEBANON, Oct. 27 — (AP) — Mrs. Cornelia Pinchot, wife of the former Republican Governor of Pennsylvania, spoke here last night at a Roosevelt rally sponsored by the Citizens Political Action Committee of Lebanon County.

Mrs. Pinchot told a large gathering that "all Republicans are not bad, and all Democrats are not good. Both make mistakes." The speaker then added "one of the greatest mistakes the Democrats made was in not renominating Henry Wallace, a truly great liberal, for Vice-President."

She confided to the gathering that she recently visited President Roosevelt at the White House and told him "there are not enough Democrats to re-elect you, but we Republicans will see that you are elected for another four-year term."

HENSELS HAVE GUEST FROM SOUTH AFRICA

Frank Boustred, head of a commission from South Africa now in the United States for post war planning of his country, has been visiting members of the Hensel family in Quarryville.

Boustred, is a brother-in-law of Mrs. George Forsythe, a native of Quarryville, who has lived in South Africa for the past 25 years. Mrs. Forsythe is a sister of W. U. Hensel, Quarryville.

NON-SUPPORT CHARGED

Frank Mimm, Jr., 106 Chester St., charged with non-support, posted bail for court before Alderman Wetzel today. Prosecution was brought by his wife, Mary E., 117 E. Vine St.

U. S. STUDENT WEDS CHINESE GIRL

SEATTLE, Oct. 27—(AP)—A Chinese girl in the United States on a student fellowship and a Caucasian youth six years her junior, both students at the University of California, were married here last night.

They are Ellsworth Charles Dougherty, 23, son of Ellsworth Y. Dougherty of Rapid City, S. D., and Miss Ching-Yi Hsu, 29, daughter of Dr. Kingman Hsu of Tientsin, China. They came to Seattle to be married because Washington is the only State on the Pacific coast without a law against mixed marriages, Dougherty said.

The average American family purchases 2,8 bed sheets a year.

WEATHER
Eastern Pennsylvania: Mostly sunny and warmer Wednesday; Thursday rain and becoming windy.

Intelligencer Journal

You Are ELECTED for Duration TO SAVE PAPER for War Needs

The Leading Newspaper in the Garden Spot of America, Home Owned for Home Folks Since 1794 — 150th Anniversary Year

VOLUME LXXXI.—NO. 49. Entered as second class matter August 9, 1944 at the Post Office at Lancaster, Pa., under the Act of March 3, 1879. Reg. U. S. Pat. Off. LANCASTER, PA., WEDNESDAY MORNING, NOVEMBER 8, 1944. CITY EIGHTEEN PAGES. 20c PER WEEK—4c Per Copy

ROOSEVELT WINS 4TH TERM

Yank Planes Score Heavily In Raid On Manila

BAG 2 WARSHIPS DESTROY 440 JAP PLANES

Third Warship Probably Sunk, Eight Others Are Damaged

U. S. Pacific Fleet Headquarters, Pearl Harbor—(AP) — Carrier-based Helldivers, Hellcats and Avengers destroyed 440 Japanese planes, sank two enemy warships, probably sank a third and damaged eight others in a two-day raid on the Manila area of the Philippines, the Navy disclosed Tuesday.

Additionally, three cargo vessels and an oil tanker were sunk, a trawler, and 14 cargo vessels were damaged and heavy destruction was spread among airfields, oil stores and installations.

The raids by planes of the U. S. Third Fleet were made Saturday and Sunday. An enemy sub chaser went down Saturday and a heavy cruiser probably sank. An enemy destroyer was sunk Sunday.

A light cruiser and three destroyers were damaged Saturday. Two destroyers and two destroyer escorts were hit Sunday.

At least 191 enemy planes were wiped out Saturday, the bulk of them on the ground. Another 249 were accounted for Sunday.

The enemy warship score increased to at least 72 the total sunk, probably sunk or damaged in actions related to Gen. Douglas MacArthur's invasion of Leyte Oct. 20.

Adm. Chester W. Nimitz announcing the continued neutralization of the Manila area in a communique Tuesday, reported additional "heavy damage" was inflicted on ground installations.

Three oil storage areas were set afire on the north strip at Clark Field and a tremendous explosion started another large fire in the northeast area of the same airdrome.

North of Malvar, a railway en-

More of BAG on Page 10

"We Lead All The Rest"

FARM CORNER

By The Farm Editor

LAST BEEKEEPERS' SESSION FRIDAY

A final bee meeting of the year, sponsored by the Lancaster County Beekeepers' association, is scheduled to be held at the farm of Roy Herr, a quarter-mile south of Lincoln Highway West, near Maple Grove, on Friday afternoon starting at 1:30 o'clock.

John Amos, extension bee specialist from State College, will discuss the market outlook for honey, fall feeding and winter management of colonies.

The session then will move to the home of Victor M. Swarr in East Petersburg where Roy Herr, of the Beekeepers' association, will discuss bottling and marketing of honey and its products. Honey products will be on display and served as refreshments.

HENSEL FARM SOLD

Hensel—Elmer Booth has sold his farm of 36 acres in Hensel at private sale to Richard Roland, of near Fairfield. Possession will be given next spring. The Booth's have resided on the farm 15 years.

Weather Calendar

COMPARATIVE TEMPERATURES

Station	High	Low
Water Works	56	35
Ephrata	54	36
Last Year (Ephrata)	69	43
Official High for Year, Aug. 5		95
Official Low for Year, Jan. 17		2
Character of Day		Clear

SUN
Rises—7:40 a. m. Sets—5:55 p. m.

MOON
Rises—7:43 p. m. First Quarter, Nov. 15

STARS
Morning—Jupiter-Saturn.
Evening—Venus-Mars.

NEARBY FORECASTS
Delaware and New Jersey: Mostly sunny and warmer Wednesday; Thursday rain and becoming windy.
Maryland: Mostly sunny and warmer Wednesday, rain beginning Wednesday night and ending Thursday morning, followed by clearing and windy.

EXTENDED WEATHER FORECAST
Extended weather forecast for period ending Sunday: Fair and rather cold Wednesday with hard freeze early morning, but sunny and mild in afternoon; cloudy and warmer Friday and Saturday with some chance of rain; clear and colder Sunday.

SAVE THIS NEWSPAPER
Make this newspaper do double work — give it to your paper-salvage drive.

Vote In City

(Complete)

(33 Districts)

PRESIDENT	
Roosevelt, D	11,504
Dewey, R	11,280
U. S. SENATOR	
Myers, D	11,309
Davis, R	11,102
CONGRESSMAN	
Burkholder, D	11,541
Kinzer, R	10,900
JUDGE, SUPREME COURT	
Jones, D	11,165
Hughes, R	11,133
JUDGE, SUPERIOR COURT	
Ross, D	11,327
Rhodes, D	11,290
James, R	11,069
Graff, F	11,115
AUDITOR GENERAL	
Wagner, D	11,289
Watkins, R	11,099
STATE TREASURER	
Black, D	11,270
Baird, R	11,116
STATE REPRESENTATIVE	
Cohen, D	11,164
Murray, R	11,220
STATE SENATOR (13th District)	
Newpher, D	11,265
Homsher, R	11,140

Vote In County

(Complete)

(145 Districts)

PRESIDENT	
Roosevelt, D	25,146
Dewey, R	42,480
U. S. SENATOR	
Myers, D	24,739
Davis, R	41,956
CONGRESSMAN	
Burkholder, D	25,619
Kinzer, R	41,265
JUDGE, SUPREME COURT	
Jones, D	24,325
Hughes, R	42,047
JUDGE, SUPERIOR COURT	
Ross, D	24,882
Rhodes, D	24,664
James, R	41,753
Graff, R	41.672
AUDITOR GENERAL	
Wagner, D	24,782
Watkins, R	41,879
STATE TREASURER	
Black, D	24,591
Baird, R	41,998
STATE REPRESENTATIVES	
Gross, D	13,351
Weaver, D	13,382
Nuss, D	13,296
Royer, R	30,924
Trout, R	30,810
Wood, R	30.763
STATE SENATOR—13TH DIST.	
Ivan Newpher, D	17,602
Homsher, R	27,394
STATE SENATOR—17TH DIST.	
Ziemer, D	7,058
Becker, R	14,672

CRITICAL FIGHT RAGES IN ORMOC VALLEY ON LEYTE

Reinforcements Rushed In By Japs To Oppose Yank 24th Division

General MacArthur's headquarters Philippines, (Wednesday) NO. 8—(AP)—The U. S. 24th division is locked in a critical fight in Ormoc valley on Leyte with elements of four Japanese divisions, including three rushed in as reinforcements, headquarters reported today.

This was the crucial battle presaged by Japanese convoy landings at Ormoc while the 24th was capturing Pinamopoan on Carigara Bay and swinging south.

Today's communique said elements of the First, 30th and 102nd Nipponese divisions had augmented the badly shattered 16th—the torturers of Bataan—in opposing the 24th. Three strong enemy counter-attacks were repulsed.

Heavy losses were inflicted on the enemy in these counter-attacks, made at night just south of coastal

More of CRITICAL on Page 6

Election Official Cuts Thumb On Poll Book Box

Jack E. Tangert, twenty-eight, 815 E. Madison St., an election official in the fifth precinct of the sixth ward cut his left thumb on a metal box Tuesday, and was treated at the Lancaster General Hospital. He said the injury occurred while sealing the election registration books in their container.

Dewey Concedes Defeat; Democrats Lead For Congress; President Ahead In City

Soldier Vote May Determine Cohen-Murray Contest

In an outpouring of voters which may break all recent presidential election figures, President Roosevelt, with the soldier vote still to be counted, carried Lancaster city for the fourth time, Tuesday by 224 votes, while the Republicans again built up large pluralities in the county.

Despite the large vote, estimated at 82 per cent in the city and 79 per cent of the eligible voters in the county, the final outcome in several contests will not be decided until the soldier vote is counted Nov. 22.

The votes of the men and women on the battlefronts will decide whether Marshall M. Cohen, Democratic candidate for State Representative from the city, or Paul G. Murray, his Republican opponent, has won.

Returns from the city's 33 voting districts show that Cohen, who served a term in 1940 as State Assemblyman, is trailing Murray by 56 votes. Murray polled 11,220 votes and Cohen, 11,164.

A total of 12,423 soldier ballots were mailed by the Lancaster County Election Board and by Tuesday night 4,487 ballots had been returned. Of this number 1.827 are from the city and 2,660 are from the county.

All soldier ballots postmarked Nov. 7 will be counted when the official tabulation of that type of

More of COUNTY on Page 6

WALLACE ASKS FOR "FULL STEAM AHEAD"

Washington—(AP)—Vice President Wallace, interpreting early returns as assuring the reelection of President Roosevelt, issued a statement Tuesday night calling for "full steam ahead."

The Vice President told the Associated Press:

"Roosevelt until 1948 means a country confident, moving with full steam ahead. The vote constitutes a mandate to Congress to prepare the way for 60,000,000 post-war jobs.

"Corner apple selling disappeared under Roosevelt. The people have determined to lick the dole. Full mployment postwar means prosperity to farm and city alike. Our plans will now go ahead for a permanent, enforceable peace."

FRANKLIN D. ROOSEVELT

HARRY S. TRUMAN

President And State-Wide Democratic Candidates Are Leading In Pennsylvania

STATE GOP CHAIRMAN WON'T CONCEDE YET

Harrisburg (Wednesday)—(AP)—Republican State Chairman M. Harvey Taylor said early today that Pennsylvania would be in the Dewey column when final returns come in from the rural counties.

"We have no thought of conceding defeat until the last vote is counted," said Taylor when informed more than 6,000 of the state's 8208 precincts gave President Roosevelt a lead of more than 40,000 votes.

WOMAN IN HOSPITAL, CRITICALLY BURNED

Mrs. Lizzie Earhart, sixty-six, wife of Jacob Earhart, E. High St., Elizabethtown, was admitted to St. Joseph's Hospital in a critical condition Tuesday evening suffering from first and second degree burns of her entire body. She was burned at her home when a spark from a stove ignited her apron. Neighbors said her husband attempted to put out the flames by putting water on them and then beat them out.

Philadelphia — (Wednesday) — (AP) — President Roosevelt rolled up a Pennsylvania majority of 59,777 early today and swept pivotal Philadelphia by a margin of 131,000.

With returns in from 7.374 of the state's 8.208 precincts, the unofficial count was 1,607,532 for Roosevelt and 1.547,755 for Dewey.

The President was well ahead in industrial Pittsburgh and the anthracite region, but Governor Dewey piled up majorities in upstate Republican rural counties.

U. S. Senator James J. Davis, Republican, and Rep. Francis J. Myers, Philadelphia Democrat, were running a close race for Davis' Senate seat.

Returns from 6,793 precincts gave Myers 1,441,694 and Davis 1,373.700.

Democrats were also leading for other state-wide offices.

Early returns indicated that Republicans would retain control of both houses of the Pennsylvania Legislature.

The vote for assemblyman in many districts, however, will remain in doubt until the soldier vote is counted Nov. 22.

The Democrats picked up three House seats in U. S. Congress in Philadelphia, and possibly several others elsewhere in the state.

Republicans hold a 20 to 13 majority in the state's congressional delegation. On the basis of early returns, it was considered possible that dominance will shift to the Democrats.

Neck-and-neck races were the rule in balloting for the state-wide offices at stake.

LIST RESULTS

The count at 4:20 a. m. today stood as follows:

State Treasurer, 6.303 of 8.208 precincts:
Ramsey S. Black (D), 1.288.167.
Edgar W. Baird, Jr. (R), 1,282,-172.

Auditor General, 6.303 precincts:
G. Harold Wagner (D), 1,313,-491.
G. Harold Watkins (R), 1,241,-710.

Supreme Court, 6,267 precincts:
Charles Alvin Jones (D), 1,-270,849.
Howard W. Hughes (R), 1,265,-230.

Superior Court, 6.250 precincts.
F. Clair Ross (D), 1.290,551.
Chester H. Rhodes (D), 1,272.-635.
Arthur H. James (R). 1,247.440.
J. Frank Graff (R), 1,235.749.

The latest vote from Allegheny county, embracing Pittsburgh and suburbs, with 753 of the 1,024 precincts reporting, gave President Roosevelt 255.929 and Governor Dewey 175,244.

Rep. Myers had 221,606 in the county and Senator Davis 153,697.

Roosevelt's Philadelphia majority was the lowest accorded him in

More of PRESIDENT on Page 6

GOVERNOR DEWEY CONCEDES DEFEAT IN RADIO SPEECH

Declares Republican Party "Emerges Revitalized From This Campaign"

New York—(Wednesday)—(AP)—Gov. Thomas E. Dewey told a press conference at 3:15 a. m. that "it's clear that Mr. Roosevelt has been reelected for a fourth term."

In a brief address carried by all radio networks the Republican presidential nominee said he was grateful for the support he had received and declared that the Republican party "emerges revitalized from this campaign."

"I am confident that all Americans will join me in the hope that Divine Providence will guide and protect the President of the United States."

Dewey smiled for a battery of cameramen as he pronounced his 1944 political swansong.

With more than 300 newsmen, photographers and employes of the Republican National committee clustered about him in the main ballroom of the hotel. Dewey sat down smilingly before a bat-

More of GOVERNOR on Page 6

Three County Nonagenarians Vote; 2 For FDR, One Dewey

Three Lancaster county nonegenarians cast their votes Tuesday—two for Roosevelt and one for Dewey.

Mrs. Mary J. Gochenauer, ninety-five, Milner Hotel, and Philip Shovitz, ninety-five, 204 Pearl St., both voted the straight Democratic ticket, as they have done all their lives—but once, when they both cast their ballots for the late Mayor Frank C. Musser running on the coalition ticket.

Mrs. Martha Annie Heim, ninety-three, 761 Walnut St., Columbia, believed to be Columbia's oldest voter, cast her vote for Dewey at 8 a. m. Tuesday in Columbia's sixth ward polling place. She has been voting ever since women were granted suffrage, and said she always voted the Republican ticket. She resides with her daughter, Mrs Annie Heim.

Mrs. Gochenauer, widow of a Civil War veteran, John C. Gochenauer, voted at 9 a. m. Tueday, and said she has always voted the straight Democratic ticket, like her father, Henry Smith, and her grandfather, Arnold Smith, before her. The only time she varied from this tradition was when she favored the coalition party, marching in the parade at the time, and casting her ballot for Mayor Musser, whom she said was a very fine man, and recalled, Tuesday, many of the improvements he had made in the city during his administration.

Mrs. Gochenauer, who listens daily to all the war news on the radio, and has followed the campaign closely, said that she voted for Roosevelt because she believes him to be one of the best presidents we ever had. She added that she did not believe Dewey was a big enough man to fill the office,

More of THREE on Page 10

Education For Peace Must Reach All Age Groups, Dr. Distler Says

"Education for an enduring peace must operate throughout all age groups," Dr. Theodore A. Distler, president of Franklin and Marshall college, said in a statement issued Wednesday in observance of American Education Week.

The text of Dr. Distler's statement follows:

"Education for an enduring peace is a continuous process. It must operate in childhood, youth, maturity and old age. It must operate not only in formal education, elementary school, high school, college, graduate school, but in all areas of our body politic. The educational program which would condition us for an enduring peace must of necessity stress the following elements:

"1. A knowledge and appreciation of the history, traditions and development of our own nation. Not only of our nation, but of our state and of our local community. Not only an understanding, but an appreci-

More of LOCAL on Page 10

Roosevelt Tide Also Felt In Gubernatorial Races In Nation

(By the Associated Press)

The vote-getting magic of Franklin Delano Roosevelt won him a fourth term in the White House today, and continued leadership in the vast unfinished business of war and peace.

Thomas Edmund Dewey, youthful New York Governor who declared in vain that "it's time for a change," conceded defeat at 3:15 a. m. (EWT).

Said Dewey at a news conference in New York:

"It's clear that Mr. Roosevelt has been reelected for a fourth term."

The Republican nominee had fallen farther and farther behind in tabulations pouring in during the early morning hours after a see-saw struggle in early counting. The ballots of nearly 27,000,000 Americans showed, at the time he gave up:

For Roosevelt, 14,411,965.
For Dewey, 12,165,763.

State after state had slipped away from Dewey. Roosevelt took command of 34, with an electoral count of 395. Dewey had only 14 with 136 votes at the time he announced it was all over.

The Roosevelt tide was felt also in Congressional and gubernatorial races. At the rate the President was going it looked as if he would carry a Democratic House with him. There never was much doubt about the Senate.

Even before Dewey conceded the trend had been unmistakable. At Hyde Park, the President told his neighbors late in the evening that it looked like another victory. Supporters carrying red flares flocked into the grounds of the world famous Squire of Dutchess County.

FDR GOES AHEAD

All over the country, except in the cornbelt, Roosevelt went out ahead when the election score sheets were halfway finished. The President got the Solid South and all five border states. He was far ahead in the mountain and western states, and he had a comfortable edge in the east and northeast.

There was an outside chance

More of NATIONAL on Page 6

GOV. DEWEY LEARNS PRESIDENT ROOSEVELT STILL WIDE AWAKE

Governor Thomas E. Dewey told reporters, in conceding defeat early Wednesday, that he had been informed by news reports that President Roosevelt had retired by midnight and as a consequence he had not sent the President any message of congratulation.

"I understand the President has gone to bed, so I have to do it this way," Dewey said, motioning to the battery of microphones.

Then he said: "I extend to President Roosevelt my hearty congratulations and my earnest hope that his next term will bring a speedy peace and we will establish tranquility among our people."

Shortly afterwards President Roosevelt sent the following telegram to Governor Thomas E. Dewey:

"I thank you for your statement which I have heard over the air a few minutes ago."

The telegram was dispatched from the President's Hyde Park home 15 minutes after Dewey had conceded his defeat.

WEATHER
Eastern Pennsylvania: Cloudy And Rather Cold, Light Snow Ending Friday Morning; Saturday Fair, Warmer In The Afternoon.

Intelligencer Journal.

Girl Scout
FAT COLLECTION
2nd & 7th Wards
SAT., NOV. 25th

The Leading Newspaper in the Garden Spot of America, Home Owned for Home Folks Since 1794 — 150th Anniversary Year

VOLUME LXXXI.—NO. 63. Entered as second class matter August 9, 1944 at the Post Office at Lancaster, Pa., under the Act of March 3, 1879. Reg. U. S. Pat. Off. LANCASTER, PA., FRIDAY MORNING, NOVEMBER 24, 1944 CITY TWENTY-EIGHT PAGES. 20c PER WEEK—4c Per Copy

B-29 ARMADA BOMBS TOKYO

French Armor Fights Into Heart Of Strasbourg

LAND ESCAPE PATH CUT FOR 70,000 NAZIS

Other French Units Closing In On Germans From the South

Supreme Headquarters Allied Expeditionary Force, Paris—(AP)—French armored forces fought their way toward the center of Strasbourg Thursday night after an 18-mile dash to the Rhine which sealed off the overland escape route for an estimated 70,000 troops of the German 19th Army, now pinned against the almost bridgeless river.

The second spectacular Rhine breakthrough in five days, imperiling nearly one-seventh of the forces the Germans are believed to have committed on the Western Front, came as the bitterest battle since the invasion thundered into its seventh day far to the north on the Cologne plain.

SEIZE BATTENHEIM

As the French Second Armored Division pressed into the outskirts of Strasbourg against light resistance, the First French Armored Division more than 50 miles to the south seized Battenheim, four miles north of Mulhouse, and pushed on north up the Rhine.

This was the southern jaw of a giant pincers reaching around the broken enemy Vosges Mountain Line, with the northern jaw formed by the French of the U. S. Seventh Army which had sped through Saverne Gap.

Although at Strasbourg they are farther from Berlin than their American and British Allies fighting inside the Reich in the Aachen

More of LAND on Page 24

French Reach Strasbourg

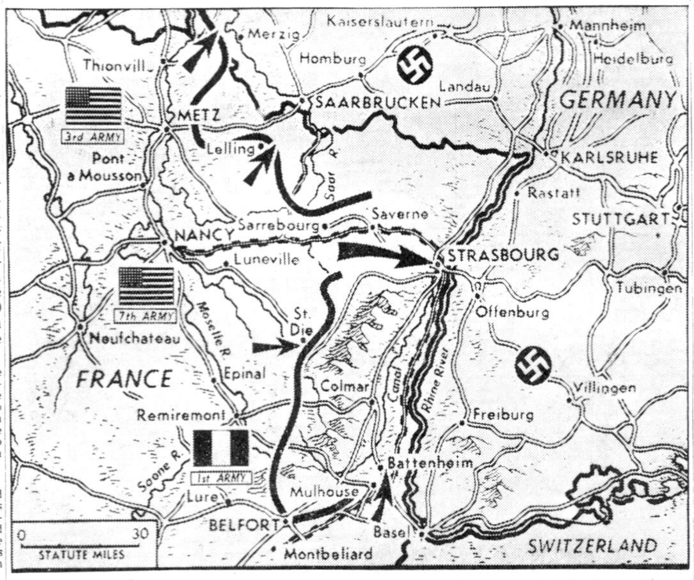

The French Second Armored Division of the American Second Army reached Strasbourg Thursday in a dash past Saverne. Farther south, French First Army units advanced from Mulhouse to Battenheim, pushing northward along the Rhine. The American Third Army threatened the Saar valley and Saarbrucken.

UNION LEADERS AGREE TO HALT PHONE STRIKE

Spreading Stoppage Collapses In Face of Intimated Gov't. Seizure

Washington—(AP)—The possibility of a nation-wide telephone strike in war time collapsed Thursday night in the face of intimated government seizure of the struck facilities.

Union leaders from Ohio and Washington, D. C., called off the strike and agreed to let the War Labor Board review the issue, whether normally non-resident switchboard operators are entitled to a cost of living bonus when brought into a city.

Company spokesmen expressed gratification that the strikers had agreed to go back to work and expressed belief service would soon return to normal.

Within a short time after the strike was called off, long distance calls again were being accepted for non-emergency purposes.

OTHERS HAD JOINED

The dispute, began in Dayton, Ohio, then spread to Washington and Detroit. Some 7,000 operators in Illinois and northern Indiana had voted to join walkout shortly before it was terminated and the strike seemed likely to involve metropolitan New York.

There were 2,700 workers involved in Washington, 2,000 in Detroit and approximately 5,000 in Ohio.

Spread of the work stoppage was checked when Robert G. Pollock, president of the Ohio Federation of Telephone Workers and Mrs. Mary E. Gannon, president of the Washington Telephone Traffic Union, told the War Labor Board they had asked their fellow workers to get back on the job.

The other sympathy walkouts, either already in effect, or proposed, thereupon ended.

No reports of violence had

More of UNION on Page 12

Nippon Heartland Blasted From New Bases On Saipan

U. S. 9TH FLEET HITS MATSUWA IN KURILES

U. S. Pacific Fleet Headquarters, Pearl Harbor—(AP)—U. S. Ninth Fleet warships shelled Matsuwa, Japanese Kurile Island base, in an unopposed strike Tuesday within 600 miles of the home island of Hokkaido, Adm. Chester W. Nimitz announced Thursday.

No American ship was damaged. Large fires and explosions were observed during the bombardment, while Japanese batteries on the fogbound coast were silent.

This was the third time Matsuwa has been bombarded by gunfire. The last task force striking against it, June 12-13, was a feint before the landing on Saipan June 14.

Nimitz's communique also reported land-based plane strikes on the northern Palaus, Yap and the Bonin Islands Monday, Wake Island Wednesday and the Marshells Tuesday and Wednesday.

Believe Force Of Brand-New 21st Bomber Command Of 20th AAF Greatest Ever To Hit Japan From Land Or Sea

Army Air Forces Headquarters, Pacific Ocean Areas — (Friday) — (AP) — A large force of B-29's, probably the greatest number yet to attack Japan, bombed industrial targets in Tokyo today, as the 20th's Thanksgiving Day message to the Japanese.

While Gen. H. H. Arnold's brief Washington statement, released simultaneously here by Lieut. Gen. Millard F. Harmon, deputy commander, 20th AAF, made only a general statement that "a sizeable force of B-29's," attacked industrial targets in Tokyo, it was believed here that:

The force was the greatest ever to hit Japan from either land or sea.

Yokohama and Kobe and the Tokvo area probably also were blasted.

Targets included vital hydroelectric plants and dams in the Tokyo area; Tokyo's inflammable industrial district; shipping, shipbuilding yards and repair docks in and around Yokohoma Bay; airfields in the entire target area.

DAYLIGHT MISSION

Washington (Friday)—(AP)—Tokyo was attacked today by Superfortresses in a daylight mission launched from bases in the Mariana Islands.

The War Department announced that "a sizeable task force of B-29 aircraft of the 20th Air Force today attacked industrial targets in Tokyo."

The mission was conducted by a newly-established 21st Bomber Command operating from bases in Saipan approximately 1500 miles to the south and east.

The text of the War Department statement:

"A sizeable task force of B-29 aircraft of the 20th Air Force today attacked industrial targets in Tokyo, General H. H. Arnold, in his capacity as Commanding General of the 20th Air Force, announced at the War Department.

"The mission was a daylight operation by the newly-established 21st Bomber Command, under command of Brigadier General H. S. Hansell, Jr., from bases on Saipan.

"A communique covering this operation will be issued when further details are available."

More than two years have elapsed between the first and second bombing of the enemy capital. The first attack was made by sixteen medium bombers launched from the deck of the Carrier Hornet on April 18, 1942.

That flight was commanded by the then Lt. Col.

More of NIPPON on Page 12

RAIN-POUNDED U. S. INFANTRYMEN TAKE LIMON ON LEYTE

Japan's First Division Practically Destroyed; Doughboys Push Past Bastion

General MacArthur's Headquarters, Philippines (Friday)—(AP)—Rain-pounded American infantrymen captured the Japanese bastion of Limon and have driven 1,000 yards south in a sudden upsurge of a battle which has practically destroyed the enemy's First division.

Headquarters reported today the 32nd Division plunged through shell-battered Limon Wednesday, in the biggest advance in more than two weeks.

The entire Yamashita Line, upon which the Japanese depend to hold Leyte Island, is in danger of being rolled up, the communique said.

As heavy rains continued to lash the battle front, the Yank infantrymen drove through the mountain village to the nearby Leyte River.

HEAVY LOSS FOR NIPS

Gen. Douglas MacArthur had identified Limon as apparently the Japanese-selected site for their major defensive battle to protect the vital Ormoc corridor. Capture of the town, said today's communique, means the Nipponese have lost a "critical defensive line."

The announcement said rolling terrain lies ahead of the Yanks in their drive down the main highway toward Ormoc, last Japanese

More of RAIN-POUNDED Page 12

Canada Acts To Send Drafted Men Overseas; Crisis Created

Ottawa—(AP)—The Canadian government, after fighting five years of war by sending only volunteers to fight abroad, abandoned the policy Thursday under a tidal wave of opposition which threatened to put the veteran Prime Minister W. L. MacKenzie King out of office.

Before a tense House of Commons called together expressly to debate a nation-shaking crisis arising from an immediate need for reinforcements on the Western Front, the Prime Minister announced that partial conscription for overseas service had been effected by an order-in-council and that 16,000 drafted men had been made available for service overseas.

King disclosed Wednesday that he had written earlier this month that he believed conscription for overseas duty would almost inevitably bring a general election and would risk national dissension and perhaps weaken Canadian unity and strength "for genera-

More of CANADA on Page 24

CHURCHILL ASSERTS U. S. IS WORLD'S STRONGEST POWER

Declares Allies Moving Irresistably Toward A Victorious Peace

London — (AP) — Prime Minister Churchill, in a surprise Thanksgiving speech to an Anglo-American audience, Thursday night hailed the United States as the world's greatest military power and declared that together the Allies were moving irresistibly "and, perhaps, with God's aid, swiftly towards victorious peace."

Nearly 8,000 people, including many hundreds of American servicemen, jammed huge Albert Hall to hear a gala concert dedicated to

More of CHURCHILL on Page 12

COLUMBIAN DIES OF INJURIES AFTER FALL FROM WINDOW

Charles Edward Blank, 69, Succumbs Without Regaining Consciousness

Injuries suffered in a 20-foot fall from the window of his bedroom to the sidewalk early Tuesday morning proved fatal to Charles Edward Blank, sixty-nine, 838 Walnut St., Columbia, Thursday. He died at 8:30 a. m. in the Columbia hospital, where he had been taken, without regaining consciousness. Dr. G. P. Taylor, deputy coroner, Columbia, is conducting an investigation.

Mr. Blank was found on the sidewalk of his home about 5 a. m. Tuesday by a neighbor, Christian Hamaker, who heard his groans. Hamaker aroused the injured man's son, Thomas E. Blank, who resides at the home, and they removed the injured man to the hospital.

C. E. BLANK

The son said he believed his father had gotten out of bed to raise a window and lost his balance, falling out of the window. He said there is a radiator in front of the window and that it making it necessary for anyone opening the window, to lean over.

Mr. Blank was born in Germany, a son of the late John L. and Matilda Greffin Blank, and came to America in 1914. For 26 years he was an agent for a national life insurance company, retiring from

More of COLUMBIA on Page 12

OPA OPENS DRIVE TO NIP RISE IN CLOTHING PRICES

Announce Ceiling Prices For Low Cost Infants' And Children's Garments

Washington—(AP)—The Office of Price Administration Thursday night launched a drive to nip a rise in clothing prices.

Price Administrator Chester Bowles announced that "simple, easy-to-understand" dollar - and-cent ceiling prices will be fixed on low-cost infants' and children's garments for which the War Production Board allocated 40,000,000 yards of cloth.

The second move was issuance of a regulation aimed at reduction of "over-finishing" and "fancying-up" of fabrics, a practice OPA said had "added greaty" to the cost of both cotton and rayon clothing.

Both programs, described as the first of a series of moves to hold clothing prices in line, follow closely Stablization Director Vinson's edict that a recent slight but "disturbing" rise in living costs "must

More of OPA on Page 24

"We Lead All The Rest"

FARM CORNER

By The Farm Editor

TO NAME COUNTY AAA COMMITTEE HERE ON MONDAY

Delegates To Convention Chosen At Series Of Community Meetings

Election of a Lancaster County Agricultural Conservation Committee to supervise administration of the AAA and special government programs involving agriculture during 1945 is scheduled for 2 p. m. Monday at a county convention of 39 AAA community delegates to be held in the Farm Bureau auditorium, this city.

Members of the 1944 county committee whose terms expire this year are: Chairman, Paul L. Leaman, Bird-in-Hand R1; vice-chairman, David J. Zartman, Ephrata R1; third member, Jacob M. Denlinger, Drumore R1; first alternate, John S. Shenk, Lancaster R6; and second alternate, C. C. Greider, Mount Joy R1.

A series of community meetings were held Tuesday night at which the delegates who are to attend the county convention on Monday were chosen by vote of the farmers. At the same time community committees to be in charge of local administration of the 1945 farm programs were elected for each district.

Due to the small number of farmers attending, it was impossible to elect delegates and a community committee in District No.

More of FARM CORNER on Page 4

Tokyo Radio Says American Marines Roughneck Bunch

(By The Associated Press)

The Japanese don't like the American Marines, the Tokyo radio said Thursday night, which seems to make it mutual.

The Marine Corps, the radio said in a broadcast recorded by the Federal Communications Commission, is composed of "a bunch of roughnecks" who "don't give a hang about their lives" in landing operations.

The radio went on that "it is said in America 'Tell it to the Marines.' This has the same meaning as 'don't be silly'. That is to say, the Marines are all so ignorant that they may believe you when the general public would not."

FINED FOR CARRYING LOADED GUN IN AUTO

Edward Albright, 616 S. Duke St., paid a fine of $25 Wednesday evening on a field receipt to Game Protector John M. Haverstick for possessing a loaded firearm in a vehicle in motion on a public highway.

Albright was apprehended about 6:25 p. m. in West Lampeter township by Fish Warden Robert Greener, while Greener was patrolling for game violators who were reported to be shooting pheasants from autos in that area.

PVT. A. S. BRANDT, 19, WOUNDED IN FRANCE

Pvt. Allen S. Brandt, nineteen, was seriously wounded in action in France, Nov. 9, the War Department notified his parents, Mr. and Mrs. Abram S. Brandt, Manheim R3, on Wednesday.

Pvt. Brandt

He entered the service Dec. 31, 1943 and received his training at Camp Blanding, Fla., and Fort Jackson, S. C. Attached to an infantry unit, he went overseas in September, 1943.

Prior to induction he was employed at the Manheim plant of the U. S. Asbestos Co. He has a brother in the service, Pvt. Ray S. Brandt, twenty-four, stationed at Fort Leonard Wood, Mo.

Weather Calendar

COMPARATIVE TEMPERATURES

Station	High	Low
Water Works	44	27
Ephrata	44	30
Last Year (Ephrata)	40	32
Official High for Year, Aug. 5		95
Official Low for Year, Jan. 17		2
Character of Day		Partly Cloudy

SUN
Rises—7:39 a. m. Sets—3:42 p. m.

MOON
Sets—1:22 a. m. Full Moon, Nov. 29

STARS
Morning—Jupiter, Saturn, Mars. Evening—Venus.

NEARBY FORECASTS
Maryland: Mostly cloudy and rather cold Friday; Saturday fair, warmer in the afternoon.
Delaware and New Jersey: Cloudy and rather cold, light snow ending Friday morning; Saturday fair, warmer in the afternoon.

SAVE THIS NEWSPAPER
Make this newspaper do double work — give it to your paper-salvage drive.

Indiantown Gap Army Show Will Aid War Bond Drive Wednesday

The War Bond Show from the Indiantown Gap Military Reservation, entitled "Thanks To You," will be presented at the Capital theatre, at 8 p. m. Wednesday, Nov. 29, in the interest of the local war bond drive to raise $12,000,000 in the city and county.

Admission will be by purchase of war bonds, and tickets will be available starting Friday noon at all the banks, on presentation of a War bond receipt and 25 cents for a service charge.

In two previous war loan drives, shows from Indiantown Gap netted more than $10,000,000 in war bond sales.

It was announced that the Theatrical Brotherhood association, 18 N. Water St., purchased $6000 worth of bonds on Wednesday, in connection with the Sixth War Loan Drive.

The new show, "Thanks to You," with WACs from the Harrisburg Recruiting headquarters appearing

More of INDIANTOWN on Page 24

Pa. Democrats Hold Margins In GI Vote; Count In 17th Senatorial District Listed

Philadelphia—(AP)—Challenged on technicalities, thousands of Pennsylvania G-I ballots were laid aside by election boards Thursday while meager returns showed servicemen voting along the same lines as the folks back home.

In Philadelphia alone, 5,000 of the 58,174 ballots returned by members of the armed forces were questioned on grounds the jurat, an avvidavit by the voter as to his qualification, was improperly filled out. Dauphin county tabulators held up 100 in Harrisburg districts for similar reasons with lesser figures in some other counties.

Validity of the ballots will be passed upon later by county arthori-

More of STATE on Page 24

SERVICE VOTE ELECTS JOHNSTOWN DEMOCRAT

Johnstown, Pa. — (AP) — Tabulation of the soldier vote Thursday night elected Frank J. Pentrack, Democrat, to the State Assembly by 70 votes, defeating Republican incumbent Walter E. Rose, who had previously led in the civilian vote.

Pentrack's 999 military votes wiped out a civilian majority of 113 held by Rose, who received only 816 military votes. Final totals, including the military ballots, were Pentrack 10,594 and Rose 10,524.

Figures were released Thursday on the tabulation of the military ballots in the Seventeenth Senatorial District of Lancaster County, completed early Thursday morning by a special tabulation board in the County court house.

One thousand, four hundred and forty votes were tabulated, according to the unofficial results. Of these, 430 were straight Democratic ballots and 667 straight Republican ballots. Of the split ballots, 190 votes were cast for President Franklin D. Roosevelt and 134 for his opponent, Thomas E. Dewey.

The board started the count at 10 a. m. Wednesday and concluded

More of LOCAL on Page 12

SENATE WILL PROBE RESIGNATION REQUEST

Washington—(AP)—Senator Kilgore (D-WVa) said Thursday the Senate War Investigating Committee expects to inquire into Attorney General Biddle's request for the resignation of his assistant, Norman M. Littell.

Informed sources said the resignation had been asked for on the basis of "incompatibility" between the two men.

GIFTS FOR EVERYBODY

A convenient Christmas shopping guide will be found under the above heading in the want-ad section of this paper and will appear daily. Suggestions and available items are listed by Lancaster stores under captions of For Him . . . For Her . . . For Boys & Girls . . . For Everyone. Save yourself a lot of "running around," turn to it now for helpful Christmas buying ideas.

1944 - SPORTS HIGHLIGHTS OF A WAR YEAR - 1944

by The Associated Press

PAYOFF PLAY AS CARDS WON SERIES—The Cardinals won the world baseball series in an all-St. Louis six-game struggle with the Browns. Here Ray Sanders, Card first baseman, comes home in fourth inning rally that won final game, 3-1.

SUCCUMBS — Death claimed Judge Kenesaw Mountain Landis (above), high commissioner of baseball for a generation. Pending naming of a successor, Ford Frick, Will Harridge and Leslie O'Connor were chosen to administer the office.

DIVE AT FOREST HILLS—Francisco Segura misses the ball and takes a dive in Forest Hills tennis match with Bill Talbert, who later lost in men's finals to Sgt. Frank Parker.

UTAH CAGERS WIN—Herb Wilinson and Arnold Ferrin of Utah, with competition from Bill Kostorfs (3) of St. John's, leap for a rebound in the Madison Square Garden basketball final which gave Utah the national title.

LIGHTWEIGHTS IN ACTION—With many fighters in the armed forces, boxing languished in the doldrums. One of the better title matches pitted Bob Montgomery (right) against Beau Jack in a 15-rounder won by Montgomery.

PENSIVE WINS KENTUCKY DERBY—Warren Wright's Pensive won the 70th running of the Kentucky Derby at Churchill Downs, with Broadcloth second and Stir Up third.

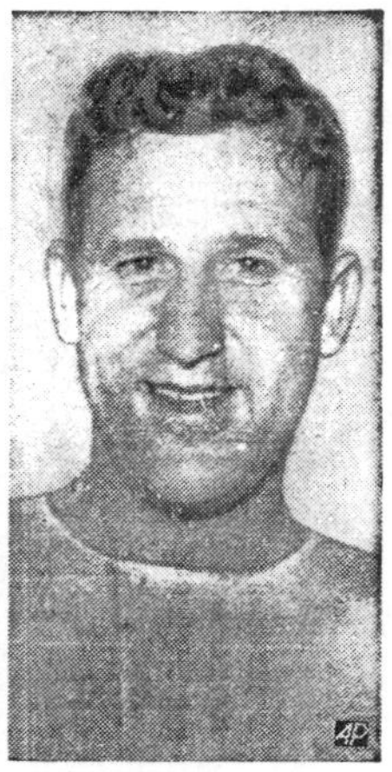

NO-HITTER— Jim Tobin (above), Boston Braves pitcher, won a place among baseball's elite with a no-hit game against Brooklyn April 27. Voted "most valuable" in their leagues were Tigers' Harold Newhouser and Cards' Marty Marion.

ARMY TOUCHDOWN ROMP— Standout football team of the year was Army, victor over all opposition, including Navy. Here John Minor runs to a score against Notre Dame, beaten 59-0.

MILER— Arne Andersson (above) of Sweden set a new world record of 4:01.6 for the mile at Stockholm July 18. Gil Dodds of Boston turned in a new indoor record, making a one-man race of the Bankers mile at the Chicago Relays in 4:06.4.

HORSE OF THE YEAR—Twilight Tear (above), three-year-old filly owned by Warren Wright, was named "horse of the year" for her string of 11 straight track victories and her triumphs in the Pimlico Special and Arlington Classic.

GRIDIRON STAR — Les Horvath of Ohio State University, shown with the Heisman trophy, was voted the outstanding college football player in a poll of 700 sports writers.

GI SPORTS IN FAR PLACES—Baseball, football and other typical American sports were seen in remote corners of the world. Here bronzed GI's play volleyball at a New Guinea camp.

THREE-TIME WINNER — Pauline Betz of Los Angeles won the women's tennis singles for the third year in succession. Above Miss Betz (left), holding the trophy emblematic of the title, talks with runner-up Margaret Osborne.

'CORN TASSEL' CLASSIC—Yankee Maid, with Henry Thomas driving, won the Hambletonian trotting classic, returned this year to its traditional site at Goshen, N. Y.

WEATHER
Eastern Pennsylvania: Light Snow And Becoming Colder Tuesday Followed By Clearing And A Cold Wave Tuesday Night. Wednesday Fair And Quite Cold.

Intelligencer Journal

SAVING PAPER
Is Not a Kid's Job
It's Everybody's Job
It's Your Job
Are you on the job giving paper to schools?

The Leading Newspaper in the Garden Spot of America, Home Owned for Home Folks Since 1794 — 150th Anniversary Year

VOLUME LXXXI.—NO. 102. Entered as second class matter August 9. 1944 at the Post Office at Lancaster, Pa., under the Act of March 3, 1879. Reg. U. S. Pat. Off. LANCASTER, PA., TUESDAY MORNING, JANUARY 9, 1945 CITY FOURTEEN PAGES. 20c PER WEEK—4c Per Copy

Ice Jam Causes Water Shortage At Columbia

JAPS SAY YANKS TRIED LUZON LANDING

Blizzard Shields Nazi Withdrawal In Bulge

ALLIED ARMIES DEAL GERMANS RENDING BLOWS

U. S. 1st, 3rd Units Only 10 Miles Apart; Strasbourg Threat Subsides

(By The Associated Press)

Shielded by the worst blizzard of the winter, German armor was pulling out of the tip of the Belgian salient Monday night under rending blows by four Allied armies.

American First and Third Army forces, hammering toward each other near the center of the salient, were only 10 miles apart and the entire enemy escape corridor was being swept by Allied artillery. A field dispatch said Marshal Von Rundstedt was sacrificing infantry to extricate three crack armored divisions which had opposed British forces at the western end of the salient.

More than 700 U. S. heavy bombers plastered the enemy's communications inside the bulge, bombing by instrument. It was conceded that Rundstedt probably would be able to withdraw his forces without serious loss. Only one main highway still was available to him, but there were innumerable dirt roads.

The Germans' secondary offensive in northeastern France appeared to have been stalled and at some points U. S. Seventh Army forces had seized the initiative. Counterattacks wrested back part of the enemy's bridgehead over the Rhine eight miles north of Strasbourg, and tension in that French city had subsided. The German radio claimed another bridgehead had been established south of Strasbourg, but this was not confirmed.

The Nazis' 15-mile deep salient below Bitche was rolled back as much as two miles, easing the threat to the vital Haguenau-Sarreguemines highway supplying American and French troops along the Rhine. Wingen and Lichtenberg were recaptured. An American of-

More of ALLIES on Page 9

Court Restrains Tobacco Deals By General Cigar

WFA Charges 'Freeze' Order Violated By Agreements To Deliver Crops

Philadelphia—(AP)—Federal Judge Harry E. Kalodner Monday signed a temporary injunction forbidding the General Cigar Company, Inc., of Lancaster, and its general manager, George Carmin, to "continue to violate" a War Food Administration order freezing the purchase, delivery, acceptance, use or processing of cigar fillers or binders until Jan. 31, 1945.

A final hearing of a petition for a permanent injunction sought by the WFA was set for next Monday.

The WFA charged that the company, a New York corporation with purchasing offices in Lancaster, violated the order in an agreement with a group of Lancaster County growers for delivery of an estimated 15 per cent of the county's 1944 production of cigar fillers.

United States Attorney Gerald A. Gleeson argued that "as a result of the action of the General Cigar Company Inc. x x x, other tobacco companies have begun to engage or are about to engage in the same practice, the result of which will be to demoralize the tobacco market in Lancaster county x x x."

Gleeson's petition also stated that unless the company "is immediately restrained from its activities" the tobacco market throughout Lancaster county and the WFA program for effecting a normal distribution and adequate supply of tobacco in the county "will suffer irreparable injury, damage and loss."

SAY REGULATIONS VIOLATED

Washington—(AP)—The Office of Price Administration cautioned

More of COURT on Page 9

Decorated

Staff Sgt. Paul H. Hossler, son of Mrs. Anna Hossler, Elizabethtown, is awarded the Bronze Star for meritorious achievement in performance of duty as crew chief of a Fighter Group of the Eighth Air Force in England. The award was bestowed by Brig. Gen. Jesse Auton.

TWO COUNTY MEN WIN AWARDS FOR WAR ACHIEVEMENT

Coxswain D. S. Rhoads, Sgt. Paul H. Hossler Given Bronze Stars

Two Lancaster county service men, one with the U. S. Navy and the other with the Army Air Forces, have been decorated with Bronze Star medals for meritorious achievement and performance of duty, it was announced Monday.

The recipients of the medals are Coxswain David S. Rhoads, son of Charles H. Rhoads, Quarryville, and Staff Sgt. Paul H. Hossler, son of Mrs. Anna Hossler, Elizabethtown.

SIGNED BY STARK

Rhoads was decorated for "meritorious performance of duty in action during the amphibious invasion of Normandy, France," on D-Day, June 6, 1944. He then held the grade of seaman first class.

The citation bestowing the

More of TWO COUNTY on Page 9

3 DAYS' SUPPLY IN RESERVOIR, COMPANY SAYS

All Plants Closed; Backwater Floods Pumping Station

Shifting ice packs that jammed in the Susquehanna River at various points from Turkey Hill to near Middletown sent flood waters cascading into the pumping station and filter plant of the Columbia Water Company Monday afternoon, effectively halting all industry—including several war plants—and precipitating a serious water shortage throughout the borough.

An immediate appeal from Theodore H. Kain, general manager of the Water Company, who warned that the sudden flood had cut Columbia's available pure water supply to a dangerously low reservoir of 3,800,000 gallons—"which might last three days"—brought full cooperation from local industry.

All plants, including the Columbia Malleable Castings Corporation, shut down operations at once. At Harrisburg, the division superintendent of the Pennsylvania Railroad ordered valves closed on all PRR water tank stations served by the Columbia Water Company, and said that steam-powered trains would bypass the area for the duration of the emergency.

Meanwhile, citizens of Columbia were reassured that the reservoir water was uncontaminated and could be used as usual—without boiling. However, all persons were cautioned that the situation was acute, and would continue to be so until it was possible to resume operations at the pumping station. This, Mr. Kain estimated, could not be done at least until Wednesday or Thursday, depending upon further developments of the river stage. He pointed out that it would be necessary to clean and repair the Diesel engines now cov-

More of ICE on Page 9

Flood Waters Enter Columbia Pumping Station

The ice-jammed Susquehanna brought grief to Columbia Monday afternoon as sudden flood waters spilled into the pump room of the Columbia Water Company, shown above. The semi-submerged Diesel engines in the picture will have to be dried and cleaned before Columbia's water supply can be returned to normal. Meanwhile, Water Company officials announced a reservoir water supply of 3,800,000 gallons, approximately enough for three days, and called upon consumers to draw "most sparingly" upon this reserve.

TOKYO RADIO REPORT SEEN RATHER VAGUE

U. S. Carrier Planes Scourge Island; Nimitz And M'Arthur Confer

(By The Associated Press)

An American attempt to land a division of troops on Luzon, main island of the Philippines, was reported Monday night by Tokyo radio in a vague broadcast which said the Yanks "are still unable to secure even a foothold."

The broadcast, lacking Allied confirmation, spoke in one breath of the Americans "attempting to land" and in the next boasted of "what awaits the anticipated landing operations."

SOME DIFFERENCE

Actually it did not say the Americans had left the transports which earlier Tokyo broadcasts have described as being in Lingayen Gulf, some 120 miles north of Manila, along with U. S. warships bombarding the coastline.

The broadcast, picked up by the Federal Communications Commission, said the Americans were employing some 70 to 80 landing barges, and that the defenders already have dealt a "staggering blow" to forces engaged in "an attempted landing."

A delayed dispatch of Rembert James, Associated Press war correspondent aboard the flagship of Vice Adm. John S. McCain disclosed that carrier planes scourged Luzon for the second straight day Saturday (U. S. date).

They found sizable enemy shipping had fled all the island's harbors, with big Manila and Subic Bays empty, and that the enemy airforce was amazingly small. For the two days, during which the attacks were continued around the clock night and day, 179 enemy planes were put out of action, the bulk of them on the ground.

Three ships and 11 small seagoing craft were sunk and 22 damaged.

Tokyo radio continued to fill the airways with invasion talk.

Earlier the Japanese radio reported an American armada of some 450 transports steaming toward Luzon, where the enemy for two days has reported a bitter battle between a fleet of 70 U. S. warships and shoreline fortresses.

At Pearl Harbor it was dis-

More of TOKYO on Page 9

"We Lead All The Rest" FARM CORNER

By The Farm Editor

TOBACCO GROWERS' CO-OP SEEKS CHARTER

Final plans for securing a charter for the proposed "Pennsylvania Tobacco Growers' Cooperative Association" were made at a meeting Monday night of the organization committee held at the Farm Bureau building. The application will be presented at Harrisbu[illegible] later in the week and a meeting of stockholders will be held for election of permanent officers and directors after the certificates of incorporation is issued.

It is planned to incorporate with an initial capitalization of $30,000 and with about 100 growers who have subscribed for capital stock to date. The Baltimore Bank for Cooperatives has pledged substantial financial backing to the co-op in plans to pack tobacco for Lancaster County farmers.

Voting rights and full membership require a grower to purchase one share of common stock at $10 and a share of preferred stock at

More of FARM CORNER on Page 9

Weather Calendar

COMPARATIVE TEMPERATURES

Station	High	Low
Water Works	36	23
Ephrata	36	22
Last Year (Ephrata)	30	20
Official High for Year, Jan. 2		46
Official Low for Year, Jan. 3		11
Character of Day		Clear

SUN
Rises—8:26 a. m. Sets—5:57 p. m.

MOON
Rises—9:14 p. m. New Moon, Jan. 14

STARS
Morning—Mars-Jupiter.
Evening—Venus-Saturn.

NEARBY FORECASTS
Maryland: Light snow; becoming colder west portion Tuesday, clearing and becoming much colder Tuesday night. Wednesday fair and quite cold.
Delaware and New Jersey: Rain or snow Tuesday followed by clearing and much colder Tuesday night. Wednesday fair and quite cold.

SAVE THIS NEWSPAPER
Make this newspaper do double work — give it to your paper-salvage drive.

SEES 100,000 YANK LOSSES IN EUROPE DURING DECEMBER

Chicago —(AP)— American casualties on the European war front for December probably will total 100,000 when the lists are completed, Lt. Col. K. D. Pulcipher, Washington, D. C., of National Selective Service Headquarters, said Monday.

"It is expected that 750,000 men will be needed for replacements in the next six months," he declared.

Addressing the National Auto Wreckers Association, Col. Pulcipher told the convention delegates that the casualty figures demonstrate the desperate man power situation now faced by the army and navy as well as on civilian fronts.

First Casualties Of German Drive Are Reported Here

First official War Department notifications of casualties sustained by Lancaster county soldiers in the German break-through in Belgium late in December began arriving here Monday.

Among the day's total of 10 casualties, five were reported missing. Of the five, four were reported missing in Belgium Dec. 17 and Dec. 19.

Three of the missing in Belgium were part of the force of 150 Americans, members of an artillery observation battalion, trapped by the Nazis. Eyewitness accounts told how German tank forces ruthlessly poured machine gun fire into their ranks. Two other Lancaster county soldiers in the battalion escaped by playing dead, it was revealed a few weeks ago.

Another of the missing is a Columbia Army Air Force officer, prominent Columbia athlete. The other casualties included a soldier killed in action in Germany and four wounded.

The casualties:

KILLED

Pvt. William F. Horn, 532 S. Lime St., in Germany.

More of FIRST on Page 9

"MEAT HOLIDAY" TO BEGIN HERE BY END OF THE WEEK

Butchers' Ass'n Asks Shops To Close As Present Supplies Are Sold

The "meat holiday" threatened by the Southeastern Pennsylvania Butchers' Association, allied organizations and individual retailers in Lancaster and Berks counties, in protest against OPA price control and regulations will begin at the end of this week, it was announced Monday.

Charles S. Winters, of Terre Hill, spokesman for the association, said that notices will be mailed Tuesday requesting its members and others who backed the plan at meetings held in Ephrata, to close their shops as soon as their present stocks are disposed of.

NO SPECIAL DAY

"No special day has been set for the closing," Winters said, "because various retailers, most of whom kill their livestock, have different stocks of fresh meats on hand. The shops will be closed as they use up present supplies."

Winters said that the closing of the shops generally, should occur about Saturday.

Meanwhile, in Philadelphia the "holiday" is scheduled to begin Wednesday when 315 Kosher butcher shops will close their doors.

Winters said that the grievances of the butchers and the slaughter-

More of MEAT on Page 9

Begin St. Joseph's Hospital Fund Drive Among Industrial Employes

About a hundred leaders in the St. Joseph's Hospital building fund campaign met Monday night at a dinner in the Hotel Brunswick that signaled the launching of solicitation in the county and among commercial and industrial employes.

The gathering heard Clifford J. Backstrand, vice president of the Armstrong Cork Company, hail the hospital's campaign as "a rare opportunity". He declared:

"The campaign is an emphatic reminder of how important we are in a nation and a town and a county such as ours. We are not told to join in this cause. We are

More of BEGIN on Page 9

WMC STARTS DRIVE TO OBTAIN MEN FOR WAR PLANT JOBS

Area Director Calls On Non-Essential Industries For Voluntary Cooperation

"It is high time that all tap rooms, night clubs, theatres, pool rooms, dance halls, amusement places and similar establishments release voluntarily all able-bodied employes for critical war work," emphatically declared Wilbur P. Gallatin, War Manpower Commission director for the Lancaster Area Monday as a new WMC program was inaugurated here.

The new five-point program for this area—Lancaster, Lebanon, York, Adams, Franklin, Perry, Cumberland and Dauphin counties—launched Monday, aims to bring into play every possible community force in each of the counties and every manpower resource "to man the 'must' plants for providing the combat materials desperately needed now . . . not when the war is over," declared Gallatin.

ASKS VOLUNTARY COOPERATION

The first step, Gallatin announced, will be the application of this program to "expand and intensify the call from less essential industries into critical war

More of WMC on Page 8

190 MORE VOLUNTEERS NEEDED TO GIVE BLOOD FOR PLASMA BANK

There are still 190 vacancies on the scehdule for the three-day visit of the Harrisburg Mobile Blood Donor unit to Lancaster Jan. 16, 17 and 18.

There are 66 vacancies for Tuesday, Jan. 16; 74 for Wednesday, Jan. 17, and fifty between 2 and 3 p. m. on Thursday, Jan. 18. The remainder of the appointments for Thursday are being filled by employes of the Armstrong Cork Co.

The quota for Lancaster remains at 200 pints a day, or 600 pints for the three-day visit. Red Cross officials pointed out that plasma is badly needed at the present time, on account of the many casualties of the battlefronts.

Donors will continue to have the privilege of signing their names on package labels in honor of whomever they desire. This custom will be permanent.

The unit will be stationed at St. James Parish house, and volunteers are asked to call the Red Cross chapter house, 3-3926, for appointments.

Navy Disagrees With Ingram View On Robots Hitting U.S.

Washington—(AP)—The Navy Monday night indicated it was not in complete accord with the view of Admiral Jonas Ingram, Commander in Chief of the Atlantic Fleet, that robot bomb attacks on the Atlantic coast are "probable."

In reply to questions about Ingram's news conference statement that it was "possible and probable" that buzz bombs might strike New York City and other Atlantic ports within the next 30 to 60 days, the Navy said:

"There is no more reason now to believe that Germany will attack with robot bombs than there was on Nov. 7, 1944," when a joint Army-Navy statement was issued.

That statement said that the War and Navy Departments considered such attacks "entirely possible" but it did not extend the idea to that

More of NAVY on Page 9

POLIO CASES' AID LISTED IN REPORT BY LOCAL SOCIETY

19 Of 42 Patients Have Recovered So Far, Crippled Children's Group Learns

Because of the epidemic of infantile paralysis in Lancaster county, it was necessary for the staff in charge to work "seven days a week from July to December, employ five extra full time graduate nurses, and travel during the year a total of 14,652 miles in visiting the cases," it was revealed Monday at noon during a meeting of the Lancaster County Society for Crippled Children, Inc., by Miss Edna F. Schreiber, orthopedic nurse for the Society.

"The funds for this extra work were made available through the Local Chapter of the National Foundation for Infantile Paralysis," Miss Schreiber stated in her annual report.

The continuance of this work and the need for support of the drive for the Infantile Paralysis Fund were stressed during the annual session, when directors and officers for 1945 were elected.

In her report of the activities of the year, Miss Schreiber revealed that of the 42 patients treated by the Kenny method, 33 are ambulant cases, of whom 19 have had a

More of POLIO on Page 8

Tokyo Reports Yankee Action

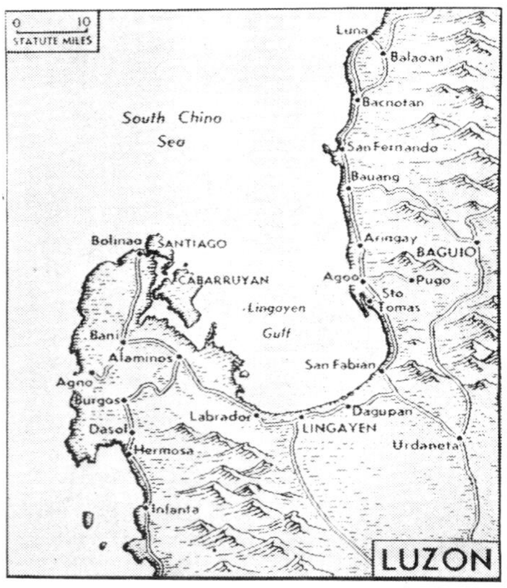

The Tokyo radio reported Monday night that American invasion forces have begun attempts to get ashore on the Lingayen coastal area of Luzon in the Philippines. The broadcast said the Yanks "are still unable to secure even a foothold," but was very vague as to whether MacArthur's units had really tried to land. The broadcast lacked confirmation from any Allied source.

WEATHER

Eastern Pennsylvania: Fair And Very Cold Wednesday. Thursday Considerable Cloudiness And Warmer With Light Snow In Mountains And Occasional Light Snow Southeast Portion.

Intelligencer Journal

The Leading Newspaper in the Garden Spot of America, Home Owned for Home Folks Since 1794 — 150th Anniversary Year

PAPER HOLIDAY Continued in Lancaster FOR DURATION *Carry Unwrapped Parcels—Save Paper*

VOLUME LXXXI.—NO. 103. Entered as second class matter August 9, 1944 at the Post Office at Lancaster, Pa., under the Act of March 3, 1879. Reg. U. S. Pat. Off. LANCASTER, PA., WEDNESDAY MORNING, JANUARY 10, 1945 CITY SIXTEEN PAGES. 20c PER WEEK—4c Per Copy

M'ARTHUR LEADS LANDING ON LUZON

Pipeline To York Sought To Aid Columbia

OPA Says Growers May Sell Tobacco At Packers' Ceiling

Spokesman Explains Growers, In Order To Qualify, "Must Perform All The Services, Assume All The Responsibilities" Of Packer

Washington—(AP)—Growers of cigar filler and binder tobacco may sell their crop at packers' ceiling prices when they meet certain conditions.

A spokesman for the OPA, explaining this Tuesday, said that to qualify for these higher ceilings growers "must perform all the services and assume all the responsibilities" of a packer.

"This means," he added, "that there can be no tie-in agreement with a manufacturer or another packer, especially with respect to leasing premises or equipment."

It is not necessary for a grower to have done his own packing in the past to qualify, as long as the operation is carried on independently, the spokesman said.

OPA ruled Monday that tie-in agreements between these growers and manufacturers and packers are in violation of regulations. The agency said that under such agreements some manufacturers and packers will pack the growers' tobacco "with the intention of buying it from the grower at ceiling prices for packed tobacco."

ASK GOVERNOR TO APPEAL FOR AID OF ARMY

More Strict Conservation Measures As Ice Holds In Susquehanna

Columbia's water shortage grew increasingly acute Tuesday night, when it was revealed that Governor Martin had been asked to appeal to the Third Service Command of the U. S. Army, at Baltimore, for immediate aid in the emergency.

Edward C. Shannon, president, and Theodore H. Kain, general manager, of the Columbia Water Company, called the Governor's Office by telephone at midnight Tuesday, it was said, to suggest an official petition for an Army pipeline to carry water from York for the duration of the emergency. The chief executive could not be reached at that time, they said, but George Bloom, the Governor's secretary, promised that the Governor would consider the proposal in the morning.

Nothing could be learned of the exact nature of the proposed pipeline, but it was assumed that such a line could be quickly established with the use of the new combat-area-type pipe sections, and it was estimated that Army engineers could link the stricken river town with the York Water system in a maximum of three days.

Meanwhile, all residents of Columbia were warned that every water-consuming public service in the borough must close Wednesday until further notice. All bars, barber shops, soda fountains and other establishments must shut down immediately, Mr. Kain said, as he pronounced the situation "extremely critical." Already, 30 industrial plants are closed, with a daily loss in manpower hours near the 12,000-mark. Residents were told that they must refrain from taking baths, shaving or otherwise using more water than is absolutely necessary.

These stringent restrictions were made necessary as ominous river conditions continued, and the dwindling reservoir supply of pure water was reduced by more than 200,000 gallons—or approximately one-third of its contents. The normal consumption is 1,200,000 gallons daily.

Experimental attempts to alleviate, in some measure, the acute shortage, will begin Wednesday, it

More Of ICE JAM On Page 11

Ice-Locked Plant Of Columbia Water Company

Shown here is the pumping station of the Columbia Water company, flooded by backwater from the Susquehanna River when an ice gorge dammed the normal flow of the stream Monday. An appeal was made to Governor Martin Tuesday night to petition Army officials to lay a portable pipe-line to York to carry water to the Columbia reservoir, in which an estimated two-days' supply of water remained Tuesday night. In the foreground is a section of the ice field which has choked the river.

LOSSES LIGHT AS YANKS HIT LINGAYEN GULF

Use 800-Ship Convoy, Push Into Flatlands 120 Miles From Manila

General MacArthur's Headquarters, Philippines (Wednesday)—(AP)—Tens of thousands of U. S. Sixth Army forces, accompanied ashore by Gen. Douglas MacArthur, landed Tuesday along 15 miles of Lingayen Gulf coast on Luzon Island from an 800-ship convoy and pushed deep into flatlands leading 120 miles south to Manila over ideal tank-war country.

Tanks were among the equipment put ashore in strength to make possible a powerhouse offensive.

Dispatches direct from the scene, said the gigantic landing operations were carried out with exceptionally light losses.

From the beaches, cleared of Japanese by fierce warship shellings and aerial bombings, the lightly opposed Yanks surged inland over the same crescent of sand dunes the Japanese employed three years ago. The invasion scene now is dry and suited for a war of movement.

SETS UP HEADQUARTERS

A field dispatch, disclosing that MacArthur already has set up headquarters on Luzon, said the landings were on the southern extremity of the gulf which includes the city of Lingayen.

At one point, only 11 enemy snipers could be found in an hour's hunt.

Just prior to the landings, fully 3,000 small amphibious craft, each with a full complement of troops, rotated near the transports while the last naval gunfire and blistering rocket barrage softened the four landing beaches.

When this curtain of fire lifted, troops crowded into armored amphibious tanks and tractors churned toward the landing points, extending roughly from San Fabian on the southeast west to Lingayen City.

Covered by salvos of bombarding battleships and exploding bombs of carrier and land planes which drove the enemy's main forces inland, they got ashore on the south and east sides of Lingayen at 9:30 a. m.

Within two hours after the first transports had disgorged the soldiers to landing boats, following a dawn shelling of the areas, MacArthur was back on the island where he fought the losing battles which opened the Pacific war.

WARSHIPS, AIR ATTACKS

The way for this showdown fight for all the Philippines was paved by a multiplicity of warships and aerial attacks. These included the destruction or damage of 262 enemy planes and the sinking or damaging of 73 ships in three days of carrier-based assaults on Luzon, Formosa and Okinawa, in the Ryukyu chain.

Spencer Davis, Associated Press War Correspondent aboard a flagship, said huge stores of equipment, guns and armor already have been put ashore for the drive toward Manila down territory suited for mechanized war.

Deep penetrations inland by some of the landing forces already have been made, Davis said.

(In a shortwave broadcast direct from Luzon, George Thomas Folster, of NBC, said the 70-mile-long convoy reached the gulf without the loss of a single soldier.

(He said 50 per cent more troops went ashore in the first wave than landed at Leyte. The waves of men sent in at Leyte were elements of four divisions.

("I visited the beaches with General MacArthur and we found no beach defenses worthy of the name," Folster reported.)

Covered by withering warship and aerial attacks, the troops suc-

More of LOSSES on Page 11

"We Lead All The Rest"

FARM CORNER

By The Farm Editor

GOVERNOR PRAISES FARMERS FOR HUGE FOOD PRODUCTION

Martin Lauds State Agriculturists; Groups Cite Need For Deferments

Harrisburg —(AP)— Governor Martin Tuesday night termed food "the greatest weapon of war" and praised Pennsylvania farmers for having "more than produced their share of the load."

Addressing a central meeting of more than a score of state farm organizations, the chief executive said that new production records have been set despite the lack of experienced help and farm machinery and other handicaps.

"On behalf of the state," he said in a prepared address, "i extend congratulations and thanks to all farmers, their wives and their children who have carried these extra burdens without complaint; and also to the thousands of men, women and high school pupils from towns and cities who have given such fine emergency aid."

With a possible manpower shortage a major problem facing farmers, the Pennsylvania State Council of Farm Organizations called for continued deferment from military service of young men holding full-time farm jobs. Selective Service recently called for their induction to the extent permitted by law.

A resolution adopted by the council declared present farm labor is inadequate and said thousands of farms are being operated by young men who are called up for physical examination.

WARN DRAFT OFFICIALS

"We express a word of caution of those in authority regarding the

More Of FARM CORNER On Page 11

8 NAMES ADDED TO COUNTY'S LIST OF WAR CASUALTIES

Eight names were added Tuesday to Lancaster county casualty lists, including one soldier reported missing in action, one a prisoner of the Germans, and six wounded, one for the second time.

The names of two men were removed from the casualty list. Previously reported missing, their relatives have now been informed that they are safe.

The men:

MISSING

Pfc. Carl Fry, Hopeland, in Belgium.

PRISONER

Pvt. Howard J. Scheetz, Elizabethtown, previously missing, prisoner of German government.

SAFE

Pfc. George A. Lorah, 32 S. Lime St., previously missing in Belgium.

Sgt. Robert Mearig, Lititz, previously missing in Belgium.

WOUNDED

Pfc. Charles Drescher, Jr., Columbia, in Belgium for second time.

Pvt. John P. Mundorff, Pequea R1, in European Theater of Operations.

Staff Sgt. Lester A. Sesseman, Lititz, in France.

Pfc. Alfred R. Grumelli, Bart, in Luxembourg.

Cpl. Samuel McFalls, Columbia R2, in Belgium.

Lt. Comdr. Lewis W. Dunton, 1028 Wheatland Ave., in Pacific area.

Pfc. Carl Fry, twenty-two, son of Enos Fry, Lancaster R1, has been missing in action in Belgium since Dec. 17, the War Department noti-

More Of 8 NAMES On Page 11

TRANSPORT VERSION OF B-29 SETS CROSS COUNTRY SPEED MARK

Washington— (AP) —A double-decked transport version of the B-29 Superfortress, known as the Army's C-97, apparently set a cross-continent speed record of approximately six hours Tuesday.

The time on this flight from Seattle to Washington, compares with the record of six hours, 31 minutes and 30 seconds set by a Mustang fighter plane flying from Los Angeles to New York last spring.

LOCOMOTIVE BOILER OF TROOP TRAIN EXPLODES

Rockville, Md.— (Wednesday)—(AP)—The locomotive boiler of a westbound Baltimore and Ohio Railroad passenger train carrying troops exploded near this suburban Washington community early today, derailing one car of the 13-car train. First reports said the engineer and fireman of the train were unaccounted for, but that none of the military personnel aboard was injured. Third Service Command officials said the troops were enroute from Fort Meade.

Weather Calendar

COMPARATIVE TEMPERATURES

Station	High	Low
Water Works	37	23
Ephrata	34	24
Last Year (Ephrata)	31	11
Official High for Year, Jan. 2		46
Official Low for Year, Jan. 3		11
Character of Day		Clear

SUN

Rises—8:26 a. m. Sets—5:38 p. m.

MOON

Rises—10:02 p. m. New Moon, Jan. 14

STARS

Morning—Mars-Jupiter-Mercury.
Evening—Venus and Saturn.

NEARBY FORECASTS

Maryland: Clear and quite cold Wednesday. Thursday warmer, partly cloudy east portion, considerable cloudiness with occasional light snow west portion.

Delaware: Clear and very cold Wednesday. Thursday partly cloudy and warmer.

New Jersey: Clear and very cold Wednesday. Thursday considerable cloudiness and warmer with occasional light snow.

EXTENDED WEATHER FORECAST

Extended weather forecast for the period ending Jan. 14: Light precipitation during end of period; temperature average below normal with rapid fluctuations; very cold at end of period.

WIEGAND'S OUSTER SOUGHT IN ACTION BEFORE GOP CLUB

Labor Leader Charged With Supporting Roosevelt In Last Fall's Campaign

Charges have been brought against Benjamin M. Wiegand because he openly supported President Franklin D. Roosevelt in last fall's political campaign and he may be ousted from the Young Republican Club, it was learned Tuesday. Weigand served two years as president of the club.

John W. Beyer, president of the club admitted Tuesday evening that the charges have been brought and said the membership will vote next Tuesday on the proposal to oust Weigand. Weigand has been notified of the charges, it was admitted by Beyer and Weigand, and of the date for the meeting when the action would

More Of WEIGAND'S On Page 11

NEW DRAFT ORDER WILL AFFECT 1,976 LOCAL FARM MEN

Officials Estimate 60 P.C. Of That Number Are Conscientious Objectors

The recent order of Selective Service directing local draft boards to reclassify for military service farmers and farm workers, eighteen through twenty-five, will affect 1,976 men in Lancaster county, a survey revealed Tuesday.

This is the number of men in that age group holding deferments as farmers. These men will be forwarded for pre-induction examinations, regardless of classification, on a staggered quota basis within the next few months.

By boards, the number of registrants varies greatly. For the five county boards the figure runs from 162 to over 800. For the three city boards, the number varies from none to two.

60 PER CENT C.O.'S

Of the 1,976 registrants, officials estimate that 60 per cent are conscientious objectors. Under existing regulations they would be made available for work of national importance at work camps, while their fellow workers who have no conscientious scruples against war, would don uniforms. The objectors, however, can volunteer for non-combatant service in the Medical Corps.

Meanwhile, Clyde A. Zehner, chairman of the Pennsylvania State War Board, said that he has appealed to National War Board

More Of NEW On Page 11

Allies Continue To Whittle Down Nazis' Belgian Bulge

Supreme Headquarters Allied Expeditionary Force, Paris—(AP)—American tanks clashed with German armor in a battle that raged all day Tuesday in a blinding blizzard as Field Marshal Sir Bernard L. Montgomery's two-army team whittled another mile off the northern side of the Belgian bulge and closed within three-fourths of a mile of the important communications hub of Laroche.

The U. S. Third Army, which had been forced to give ground late Monday under repeated counterattacks on the southern side of the salient, roared back Tuesday with gains up to a half-mile at several points despite the worst weather of the winter and continued fierce enemy resistance.

MAZIS INCREASE PRESSURE

As the Allied in Belgium pinched Marshal Karl Von Rundstedt's salient to a width of 9 miles between the areas of Laroche and Herbaimant, the Germans increased their pressure in Alsace and shelled Strasbourg with heavy artillery from the east bank of the Rhine.

American forces on the northern flank of the German bulge drove to within four miles of the last main escape and supply highway and Von Rundstedt was reported hurriedly shifting tanks from the Bastogne area northward to meet this threat to his lifeline.

Should the smashing Yank drive from the northern waist of the bulge sever the Houffalize-St. Vith highway, all German forces in the western half of the salient would be placed in a precarious position

More Of ALLIES On Page 11

SEES CHECKED NAZI PUSH POSSIBLE AID TO ALLIED CAUSE

Gen. Bradley Says Allies Took "Calculated Risk" On Ardennes Front

With the 12th Army Group—(AP)—Lt. Gen. Omar N. Bradley, breaking his silence regarding the German counteroffensive which was aimed at splitting the Allied line in his 12th Army group sector said Tuesday that the now-thwarted enemy move "may materially affect the Germans' ability to resist."

Gen. Bradley, who was awarded the Bronze Star by General Eisenhower Tuesday for his part in halting the Germans, stated at a press conference that Germany's ability to prolong the war may have been reduced, but added quickly that this did not mean the Allies could

More Of SEES On Page 11

83 BILLION DOLLAR 'TENTATIVE' BUDGET IS ASKED BY FDR

Drop From Last Year; Would Lift War Spending To 450 Billion

Washington—(AP)—President Roosevelt groped ahead Tuesday into a fiscal year that won't even begin until six months from now and pulled out a "tentative" budget of 83 billion dollars.

This would be a drop of 17 billion dollars from the present year, but woud increase the total war spending program (1941 through 1942) to the gigantic total of 450 billion dollars. This is nearly half a trillion.

You could read the President's annual budget message forty ways and you wouldn't find a prediction as to the length of the war.

Yet the estimates of government spending in fiscal 1946 evidently are based on a hope that Germany will give up some time within the next 18 months, because——

War spending was estimated at 70 billion dollars, about half way between the best and the worst that might happen. The President told Congress that war costs could be less than 60 billions or more than 80, depending on various assumptions as to the war.

Presumably they would be 80 billios if we had to keep fighting on

More Of 83 BILLION On Page 11

Yank Ingenuity Provides Christmas "Tree" On Ship Of Pacific Fleet

With the closest evergreen tree thousands of miles away, Harry B. Miller, electricians mate third class, and his buddies on a unit of the Pacific fleet, nevertheless, had a Christmas tree.

Its "growth," another example of American ingenuity, was described in a letter he wrote his parents, Mr. and Mrs. Harry W. Miller, 19 Howard Ave.

The base of the tree was a used five-inch powder case, the trunk was a brass tube and the branches copper wire. The "tree" was covered with friction tape and painted green.

To get the snowy-effect, the wet paint was sprinkled with epsom salts. To decorate the base, an old map of Japan was painted to resemble bricks. Swab sticks covered with cotton provided a fence.

The decorations were strings of lights one hidden within a star cut from tin, lathe turnings, and short pieces of bakelite tubing painted with brilliant hues.

"I think it was the best darn tree and the only evergreen in the Pacific," he wrote. The letter was written on Christmas Day.

NAME REEMPLOYMENT COMMITTEEMAN FOR CITY DRAFT BOARD 1

Selective Service announced Tuesday the appointment of Robert E. Groh, 611 W. Chestnut St., as re-employment committeeman for City Draft Board No. 1, and also named four associate committeemen.

Groh succeeds the Rev. Geo. W. Brown, pastor of St. Mary's Catholic Church, who recently resigned as re-employment committeeman.

The associate committeemen, who will assist Groh in obtaining for veterans their rights under the provisions of the Selective Service and Training Act, are:

Walter H. Doner, 108 E. Walnut St.; Dr. Charles V. Snyder, 219 E. Orange St.; C. J. Follmer, 347 E. Orange St., and William P. B. Brinton, 334 E. Orange St.

Reveal U-Boat Warfare "Flared Into Renewed Activity" In Dec.

Washington—(AP)—U-boat warfare "flared into renewed activity" during December.

President Roosevelt and Prime Minister Churchill so reported Tuesday night, describing the increased activity by German submarines as "but another index that the European war is far from over."

ALLIED LOSSES RISE

They said Allied losses of merchant shipping increased, but despite the losses "the United Nations are regularly continuing to supply their expanding armies over the world, enabling them to resist the attackers or drive back the foe."

"The Allies continue to sink the enemy undersea craft in widely-separated parts of the world," the monthly joint statement of the Anglo-American leaders said.

"The announcement of the recent landing of enemy agents from a U-boat on the Maine coast is yet another indication that the menace of Germany's undersea fleet is real and continuing.

Increased U-boat activity had been forecast by the President and Prime Minister in their joint statement on submarines and anti-sub-

More Of REVEAL On Page 13

Lancaster Mushes Through Deepest Snow In 17 Years

BIGGEST HILL around town, Seventh and President Aves., provides plenty of long thrills for sleds and a swell opportunity for the old toboggan.

SNOW ANTICS were part of the big blizzard's aftermath. George Pefley shows Roseanna how to do that face-washing stunt.

SNOW TRACERY transformed tree-lined streets into exotic patterns. This study by Clarence J. Thomas was taken at Duke and Orange eastward, showing First Presbyterian steeple in background.

DEEP IN THE HEART of Lancaster county the drifts pile up and the hills get round-shouldered from the snow. Although highway dept., plows opened 'em up in record time, there was still enough left in the lanes to preserve the wintry mood. This is the Gap-Smyrna road.

LANCASTER DUG out of its biggest snow in 17 years this week with a stride that nothing except a 1918 blizzard could stop. This week's was a big snow but only a drop in the bucket compared to four feet in 1918, 42 inches in 1888 and various depths before and between those dates. Story on page one, section two.

GET OUT IF YOU'RE UNDER is a switch on the old auto tune. Wierd and beautiful burials went on all over the place Tuesday and stayed that way until shovels got busy, days later. This is Buchanan Ave., west of College Ave.

SNOWS OF YESTERYEAR retain their freshness only in pictures. Here's one in Penn Square around Christmas time in the 'nineties. The Intelligencer was published in the building in the rear of the monument, now Conestoga Bank corner. The monument in the square has been measuring blizzards since 1873. Other photos in Section two.

ALL-TIME SNOW SCENE could be Lancaster in practically any period. These sleighs and the old farm blockies have surmounted blizzard problems around here for decades. A quick camera shutter caught this one at Marietta and Race the other day when going got too tough for autos.

ONCE-IN-A-LIFETIME in this area a kid gets a chance to really build a snow cave or an igloo. There are several around this week. This one was carved out by Johnny Long on College Ave., and is complete with everything but a dog sled.

CLEAR AS A BELL

New York—(AP)—A young man who likes to listen to police radio calls was under arrest here charged with grand larceny in the theft of a police automobile.

Found some time after the purported theft he said he really didn't steal the car, but took it just to listen to the calls over the short wave system.

"And did you hear the call for the car you took?" police said they asked him.

"Yes, came over clear as a bell," was the answer.

With The Service Men

Isaac W. Redcay recently was promoted to the rank of petty officer second class according to word received by his wife, who resides at Christiana R1. Petty Officer Redcay enlisted in the Navy Sept. 15, 1943 and has served six months in the Pacific theater of operations since completing his training in the U. S.

Isaac Redcay

Sgt. Frank C. Limon and Pfc. Mary Jane Limon returned to their stations after spending furloughs with the latter's parents, Mr. and Mrs. Harry F. Gieg, Mount Joy R2. Sgt. Limon is attending officer candidate school at Fort Benning, Ga., and Pfc. Limon is stationed at Camp Blanding, Fla., serving as a dental assistant in the WAC. Mr. and Mrs. Gieg also have three sons in the service. Pvt. James Gieg, with the AAF at Wendover Field, Utah; Pvt. John R., with the AAF in England, and Pvt. Harry, Jr., with the Third Army in Germany.

Pvt. Harry F. Ream, son of Mr. and Mrs. Charles F. Ream, Mount Zion, who is an aircraft mechanic serving as a crew chief on heavy bombers at the Davis Monthan Field, Tucson, Ariz., was awarded the Good Conduct ribbon by his commanding officer. He has been serving with the Second AAF since May 5, 1944.

Pvt. Ream

Pvt. Willis M. Houck, with an infantry unit, recently arrived in France according to word received by his wife, Mrs. Verna E. Houck, of Strasburg. Entering the service May 13, 1944, he trained at Fort Bragg, N. C., and Fort Jackson, S. C., before leaving for overseas duty. Prior to entering the Army he was employed by the New Holland Machine Company.

Lt. Joseph J. Carroll, son of Mr. and Mrs. Joseph Carroll, Marietta, pilot of a B-26 Marauder based in France, recently was awarded the Air Medal with two bronze oak leaf clusters for combat achievements in the European theater, according to word received by his family. Lt. Carroll arrived overseas in August of 1944.

William H. Williams, son of Mr. and Mrs. Hallet B. Williams, 30 Caroline St., recently has been promoted to the grade of chief petty officer while overseas, according to word received by his family. Chief Williams first trained at Richmond, Va., and later in the Solomon Islands.

Pvt. William X. Kane, Jr., 231 N. Mulberry St., recently received a certificate under the personal signature of his commanding general honoring him for combat duty with the 29th Infantry Division from D-day to St. Lo, according to a news release from his unit.

Technician Fifth Grade Jay L. Koser, Lancaster R1, is serving with a motor transport unit which moved more than 600,000 tons of war supplies to Russia through Iran according to a dispatch from his unit at Andimeshk, Iran.

In response to an appeal to soldiers assigned to Supreme Headquarters, European Theater of Operations, for blood needed at the front, one officer walked briskly into the clinic and took his place in line with the other volunteers.

He gave a pint of blood, drank a cup of coffee and started to leave. Then one soldier in line noticed that it was General Eisenhower and remarked, "Hey, that would be the blood to get!"

The General overhead the remark and replied:

"If you do, I hope you don't inherit my bad disposition."

Staff Sgt. Charles W. Reus, nineteen, son of Mr. and Mrs. William Reus, 48 Chester St., recently arrived at the AAF Redsitribution Station at Miami Beach, Fla., after completing a tour of duty outside the United States.

As a B-24 Liberator gunner, Sgt. Reus flew 35 missions while in the European Theatre of Operations and holds the Distinguished Flying Cross, and the Air Medal with three oak leaf clusters. He entered the service September, 1943.

Sgt. George J. Nicholaou, 329 W. Lemon St., is a member of a Bomber Group stationed in England which was recently cited for "distinguished and exceptionally outstanding performance of duty" on 200 missions.

Commanded by Col. Lorin L. Johnson, Payson, Utah, the group has been overseas for more than a year. The 200th mission was made on Armistice Day, the 100th on D-Day.

Targets attacked by the 392nd Liberators include Berlin, Gotha, Politz, Bremen, Hamburg and other objectives in Germany, France, Norway, Holland, Belgium and Poland.

Technician fourth grade James H. Flick, 676 Union St., has received a certificate personally signed by his commanding general honoring him for fighting with the Twenty-Ninth Infantry Division from D Day to St. Lo.

T-4 G Flick

The honor is a personal salute from Maj. Gen. Charles H. Gerhardt to the officers and men who battered their way through flooded areas and the Normandy hedgerows and stormed the key city of St. Lo in the campaign where the taking of every 500 yards was a major battle.

The Army reckons the Normandy fighting as one campaign, which entitles participants to one star on their theater ribbons, but General Gerhardt's certificate recognizes the unusual toughness of the fighting in the early days of the invasion.

Technician Flick entered the services Jan. 13, 1941 and has been overseas for 27 months. The thirty-one year old soldier is now in Germany. Before entering the service he was employed at the Lancaster New Era. He also attended Catholic High School.

Henry J. Westman, Ph.M. third class, USN, son of Mrs. Frank Westman, Bausman, is spending a leave with his mother and his wife, Mrs. June Westman, who resides at 310 W. King St.

Serving aboard an LST boat, he participated in the D-Day invasion of France. He entered the service March 6, 1943, and trained at Sampson, N. Y.

MAILING BILLS FOR THOSE 'UNFORGIVEN'

Washington—(AP)—The day of judgment is approaching for those who are unforgiven.

Yea, brethren, the Bureau of Internal Revenue announced Tuesday that separate bills are being mailed to about 4,000,000 citizens who postponed paying part of their "unforgiven" income taxes.

The collection will be taken up no later than March 15. The total amount due is $900,000,000.

In case you've forgotten about this forgiveness business: When the pay-as-you-go system started, Congress cancelled in most cases at least 75 per cent of the 1942 or 1943 tax, whichever was smaller. At least half of the unforgiven portion—if any—was due by March 15, 1944. The rest is coming due now.

The reason for sending separate bills in this: 50,000,000 people have to file 1944 income tax return by March 15, but only 4,000,000 of them have to pay any unforgiven taxes from 1943. The two transactions will be entirely separate because there's no use confusing the other 46,000,000 tax payers. Amen.

FINAL APPEAL DAY

Assessors from the Sixth, Seventh, Eighth and Ninth Wards of Lancaster city will sit in the offices of the county commissioners Wednesday to hear appeals from real estate and personal property assessments of 1945—the last appeal day this year.

Total county assessments for the current year are $143,100,000, according to the commissioners.

Gloria Jean and Mel Torme both in important roles, enliven Universal's newest comedy musical "Pardon My Rhythm," at the Fulton.

Bertrand Russell, English philosopher, mathematician and sociologist, belongs to one of the oldest families of England.

Ray Stannard Baker biographer and essayist, writes under his own name and also under the name of David Grayson.

WEATHER
Eastern Pennsylvania: Rain With mild temperature Tuesday; Wednesday Fair And Continued Mild.

Intelligencer Journal.

DAILY

The Leading Newspaper in the Garden Spot of America, Home Owned for Home Folks Since 1794 — 150th Anniversary Year

VOLUME LXXXI.—NO. 132. | Entered as second class matter August 9, 1944 at the Post Office at Lancaster, Pa., under the Act of March 3, 1879. Reg. U. S. Pat. Off. | LANCASTER, PA., TUESDAY MORNING, FEBRUARY 13, 1945 | CITY | FOURTEEN PAGES. | 20c PER WEEK—4c Per Copy

BIG 3 GIVE FORMULA FOR TRIUMPHAL WAR'S END IN EUROPE, START OF PEACE

TWO MORE HERE REPORTED ILL OF DIPHTHERIA

One Victim Is Woman Who Gave Birth To Child Friday

The mother of a four-day-old infant was one of two persons whose illness was diagnosed as diphtheria Monday. The other case was that of a eleven-year-old girl. These two cases raise the total for the county to three so far this year, one more than in all of 1944.

Mrs. Anna Magni, twenty-nine, 216 N. Water St., who gave birth to a daughter at 10:46 a. m. Friday after a caesarean operation, is a patient at the Lancaster General Hospital, where her condition is regarded as fair.

Grace Kirchner, eleven, daughter of Mr. and Mrs. Francis Kirchner, Kreider Avenue, Lancaster R3, the other victim, is confined to her home where her condition is regarded as good by physicians.

BABY "DOING NICELY"

Mrs. Magni, wife of Guido Magni, was ill when admitted to the hospital Friday, attendants said, and after the birth of the child was moved from the maternity section of the hospital. Her condition became worse and her illness was diagnosed as diphtheria and preventive measures taken.

The child, who is in the nursery at the hospital, was reported by attendants as "doing nicely."

The Kirchner girl, a student of the Brecht School, Manheim Township, was stricken ill February 8, according to health officers, who said the child had never been given an injection of toxoid for the prevention of diphtheria.

The other victim of the disease reported this year, Robert M. Yohn, nine-months-old son of Mr. and Mrs. Robert Yohn, Lancaster R6, was reported as improved Monday. He had been stricken ill January 9.

FARM CORNER
By The Farm Editor

LEBANON TOBACCO GROWERS TO MEET WEDNESDAY EVENING

A delegation of Lebanon county farmers, after conferring with officials of the Lancaster County Tobacco Growers' Cooperative association in this city Monday afternoon, arranged for a tobacco growers' meeting to be held at the Millbach school house in Mill Creek township, Lebanon county, on Wednesday evening, at 7:30 o'clock. Millbach is located Northeast of Schaefferstown. Growers of Northern Lancaster county also are invited to attend.

The acreage planted to tobacco in Lebanon county has increased sharply in recent years, with quite a number of Lancaster county families, principally Amish, buying farms there and continuing to raise cigar filler leaf north of the border. Only a small percentage of the 1944 crop in Lebanon county has been sold, the visitors said, and the purpose of the meeting is to explain the Lancaster Co-op plan and give interested growers an opportunity to sign up their crops.

Meanwhile, directors of the local Co-op announced Monday night an additional warehouse had been leased at Walnut and Plum streets in this city. This makes six different warehouses, four in the county and two in Lancaster city, that will be used by the Co-up for the receiving and packing of tobacco for its members in Lancaster and near-by counties.

PLAN ORCHARD MEETS AGAIN

Two orchard meetings, twice postponed because of the January blizzard and closed roads, now are scheduled by the local Agricultural Extension Service to be held in the

More Of FARM CORNER On Page 6

Weather Calendar

COMPARATIVE TEMPERATURES

Station	High	Low
Water Works	52	22
Ephrata	50	29
Last Year (Ephrata)	27	19
Official High for Year. Feb.	12	50
Official Low for Year. Jan.	25	-1
Character of Day		Clear

SUN
Rises—7:00 a. m. Sets—6:37 p. m

MOON
Rises—2:19 a. m. First Quarter, Feb. 19

STARS
Morning—Mars-Jupiter.
Evening—Venus-Saturn.

NEARBY FORECASTS
Maryland, Delaware and New Jersey: Rain with mild temperature Tuesday: Wednesday fair and continued mild.

Roosevelt, Churchill, Stalin Discuss Final Defeat Of Reich

Around the table at Yalta Crimea, Russia, sit President Roosevelt, Marshal Stalin and Prime Minister Churchill and their staffs as they decide military plans for final defeat of Germany. Around table are (clockwise from man at extreme left): Andrei Vyshinsky, Russian Vice Commisar of Foreign Affairs; Russian Foreign Minister Vyachenslav Molotov; Marshal Stalin; Ivan Maisky, Vice Commisar of Foreign Affairs; Andrei Gromyko, Russian ambassador to U. S.; Adm. William D. Leahy; U. S. Secretary of State Edward R. Stettinius, Jr.; President Roosevelt; Charles E. Bohlen, Chief of State Department Division of Eastern European Affairs; James F. Byrnes, OWM chief; unidentified; Anthony Eden, British foreign minister; Prime Minister Churchill; two unidentified men; and Sir Archibald Clark Kerr, British ambassador to Russia. (AP Wirephoto from Signal Corps.)

Yanks, British Take Kleve, Pruem; Reds Score Advances

(By The Associated Press)

Armies of the western and eastern Allies struck further spectacular blows against the reeling enemy Monday. Kleve and Pruem, strongholds of the Siegfried Line, fell to the Canadian First and U. S. Third armies, respectively, as the Nazis expressed fears that the Allies were massing tanks for a smash to the Rhine.

Russian forces swept to within 74 miles of Dresden, capital of Saxony, in a 15-mile advance that overran the Bober river fortress of Bunzlau. Sixty-two miles behind Bunzlau the German garrison of Breslau fought desperately to keep the Soviets from closing a 15-mile escape gap from the city.

REDS NEAR STETTIN

The Germans said Russian columns had spurted to within 15 miles of Stettin, Berlin's Baltic port, and had broken German defenses some 12 miles north of Sagan and 27 miles west of the farthest point Moscow had reported reached. The Red Army's month-old offensive had virtually completed the capture of Poland, seized most of East Prussia and driven within 32 miles of Berlin.

Canadian and British troops, grinding on beyond Kleve, original northern anchor of the Siegfried Line, were within 22 miles of Wesel and in position to drive along the Rhine and break into the Ruhr,

More Of YANKS On Page 6

FASTNACHTS SCARCE FOR FASTNACHT DAY

Today is Fastnacht Day and the old-time fastnacht "just ain't," according to veteran bakers.

Bakers in Lancaster city and county cut down considerably on fastnachts this year and many of the larger producers did not make a single one because of curtailment of supplies, shortening and sugar.

However, many of Lancaster's housewives scraped together a little shortening and went easy on are sugar to make a supply Monday. Markets Tuesday are expected to produce "few" in comparison to former years because of the shortage of needed materials.

BOY, 10, DISCOVERS MOTHER, 39, DEAD ON KITCHEN FLOOR

Coroner Says Mrs. Helen Croessant Ended Life With Illuminating Gas

Mrs. Helen A. Croessant, thirty-nine, wife of Carl F. Croessant, 526 New Dauphin St., was found dead on the floor of the kitchen in their home shortly before 4 p. m. Monday by her son, Ronald C., ten, who discovered the tragedy after school when he gained entrance to the dwelling by climbing through a cellar window. Dr. A. V. Walter, county coroner, announced death was attributed to suicide by inhaling illuminating gas.

Mrs. Croessant, who had been in ill health for some time, left a note to her husband asking "forgiveness for this act," according to Dr. Walter, who said the woman had locked the house and turned on the gas burners in the stove in her kitchen.

NOTIFIED FATHER

Upon finding his mother on the floor, the son turned off the gas burners and telephoned for his father, an instructor at the Thaddeus Stevens Industrial School. Superintendent John C. Stauffer informed Croessant of the tragedy, and both went to the residence.

Mrs. Croessant was a daughter of Mr. and Mrs. Edward Fox, Reading, and was a native of Tamaqua. She and her family resided in Lancaster for the past seven years. She

More Of BOY On Page 6

Dr. Distler Endorses Campaign To Raise $50,000 For Boy Scouts

Endorsement of the campaign to raise $50,000 for improvements to Camp Chiquetan being conducted by the Lancaster County Council, Boy Scouts of America, was made Monday by Dr. Theodore A. Distler, president of Franklin and Marshall college.

President Distler is a former Commissioner of Scouting in the Delaware Valley Area Council at Easton, and is now a member of the executive board of the Lancaster County Council. His son, Theodore A. Distler, Jr., is a second class Scout in Troop 22, of St. Peter's Evangelical and Reformed Church.

His statement follows:

"The Boy Scouts of America represents to me one of our outstanding democratic achievements. Its program is one of the finest we possess for the training of youth of our nation. Indeed, it is, in essence and operation, one of the outstanding youth movements of the entire world. It takes youngsters, and (by means of an intelligently conceived program) in a normally healthful environment, teaches them skills and aptitudes and lessons in personal and group living which make of them outstandingly fine citizens.

"One of the most important phases of Scouting is the year-round camping program which pro-

More Of DR. DISTLER On Page 6

EIGHT MORE NAMES ADDED TO LOCAL CASUALTY LIST

Soldier Killed In Action, One A Prisoner And Six Wounded

WAR CASUALTIES

Lancaster county war casualties announced Monday included:

KILLED

Pvt. John Ferguson, Jr., 442 New Holland Ave., in Belgium.

PRISONERS

Pfc. Ray R. Wolpert, 550 Pershing Ave., of Germany.

SAFE

Pfc. Irvin Garber, Lititz, previously missing.

WOUNDED

Pfc. J. Robert Charles, Washington Boro, in Belgium for second time.
Sgt. Charles DeVerter, 437 Beaver St., on Luzon.
Pfc. Benjamin B. Gainer, Pequea R1, in Luxembourg.
Pfc. John P. Bowers, Columbia, in France.
Pvt. Roy S. Bechtold, Jr., Refton, in France.
Pfc. Alvin Martzall, Ephrata, in France.

Eight additional names were added Monday to Lancaster county war casualty lists, including a soldier killed in action, one a prisoner, and six wounded. Another soldier, previously listed as missing, returned to his unit.

Pvt. John Ferguson, Jr., eighteen, son of Mr. and Mrs. John Ferguson, 442 New Holland Ave., was killed in action in Belgium, Jan. 13, according to a War Department telegram received by his parents.

Entering the service in June, 1944 after graduating from McCaskey High School, he trained at Ft. McCellan, Ala., and went overseas in December with an Infantry Unit.

At McCaskey High School he was a member of the Vidette staff for three years and was on the Vidette yearbook staff. He also was a member of the National Honor

More of CASUALTIES on Page 6

ELLIOTT ROOSEVELT PROMOTION OKAYED

Washington — (AP) — The Senate voted 53 to 11 Monday to confirm Elliott Roosevelt's promotion to brigadier general after the young Air Force colonel and his dog rode out a storm of Republican criticism.

The 34-year-old son of the President was called a military "amateur" by Senator Bushfield (R-SD) in a warm debate in which Blaze, young Roosevelt's bull mastiff, also was taken for a Senatorial ride.

When the skies cleared after two roll call votes—the other a motion to shelve the nomination by sending it back to the Military committee having been rejected, 49 to 14—the promotions of 77 other colonels to one-star generals were confirmed by voice vote.

Sen. Joseph F. Guffey (D-Pa) was listed as voting for confirmation of Col. Roosevelt. Pennsylvania's second Senator, Francis Myers (D), was not listed as voting.

Japs Discussed By President, Churchill At Malta Session

Valetta, Malta—(AP)—Plans for stepping up the war against Japan as well as finishing off the conflict in Europe were discussed on this war-torn Mediterranean island by President Roosevelt and Prime Minister Churchill.

They and members of their staffs then flew to their Crimea meeting with Premier Stalin.

This information came from a high-ranking U. S. officer and constituted the only mention of Japan in connection with the Big Three meetings.

Meeting here with Roosevelt and Churchill were many of the chief figures upon whom the final clean-up of Japan may rest.

The Prime Minister had with him Adm. Sir Andrew Browne Cunningham, First Sea Lord: Air Chief Marshal Sir Charles Portal, and Field Marshals Sir Henry Maitland Wilson, Sir Alan Brooke, and Sir Harold Alexander.

The President's party included chief of staff, Gen. George C. Marshall; Adm. Ernest King and many others. Adm. Chester W. Nimitz was reported to have been present, but this was not officially confirmed.

The Prime Minister arrived at this Mediterranean island base before Roosevelt and made his headquarters in a warship during his stay. There was a note of sadness connected with his visit, for 15 persons connected with his party were killed when their plane crashed in the Mediterranean. Bodies of the victims which were found were brought ashore and buried on the island and injured members were treated here.

The President landed on a Malta airdrome which swarmed with planes. He received a thundering

More Of JAPS On Page 12

DOUGHBOYS BACK NIPS INTO NARROW POCKET IN MANILA

Extinction Of Suicide Remnants Assured As Final Phase Approaches

(By The Associated Press)

American doughboys, fighting the final phase of the bloody battle for Manila, have backed Japanese suicide remnants into a narrowing pocket where extinction is assured.

Gen. Douglas MacArthur reported late Monday that battle-hardened American troops of three divisions have made juncture in war-torn south Manila and are going about the work of liquidating the fanatical Japanese who widely sabotaged the city with explosives and fire. The general termed the fighting "extraordinarily fierce."

BLAST PILLBOXES

In the Nichols Field area, on Manila's southeastern city line, the Yanks destroyed 111 pillboxes and captured much equipment including 75 pieces of artillery and 300 tons of ammunition.

Cleanup operations centered in the region of the Paco railroad station and Manila Polo Club where the Yanks were clearing vast land mine fields and enveloping and infiltrating the Japanese lines.

In one of the most furious aerial assaults of the Pacific war American bombers have unloaded 700 tons of explosives on southern Bataan and more than 200 tons on Corregidor gun positions. Patrol planes sank 35 Japanese barges off

More Of DOUGHBOYS On Page 6

STETTINIUS IN MOSCOW FOR A SHORT VISIT

Moscow—(AP)—U. S. Secretary of State Stettinius has arrived in Moscow for a short visit.

An official announcement said: "At the invitation of (Foreign Commissar) Molotov, Mr. Stettinius arrived in Moscow this afternoon by plane from the Crimea. He was accompanied by (W. Averell) Harriman, the American ambassador. His visit will be a brief one."

At Least 36 Die, Over 200 Hurt As Tornadoes Hit Alabama, Mississippi

(By The Associated Press)

At least 36 persons were killed and more than 200 injured, most of them on the outskirts of Montgomery, Ala., in a series of tornadoes which swept across Alabama and Mississippi Monday.

Twenty-two bodies, 15 of them Negroes, had been brought to Montgomery undertaking establishments four hours after a tornado cut a half moon path around the Alabama capital city's western and southern edge.

HIT ELSEWHERE

At least seven were killed and more than 45 injured in two small communities near Meridian, Miss., when the storm struck there an hour earlier.

One Negro was killed and between 15 and 20 other Negroes were injured at York, Ala., 125 miles west of Montgomery. Two trainmen were killed south of Livingston, Ala., when tornadic winds blew 39 cars of a southbound freight train off the tracks. Four other persons were fatally injured there.

At Montgomery, more than 50 cars of the Louisville & Nashville and Atlantic Coast Line railroads were wrecked by high winds and main line tracks were blocked by

More Of LEAST On Page 12

8-Day Conference At Yalta In The Crimea Concluded

Nine-Point Program, Announced Following Fateful Sessions, Seen Projecting U. S. Onto Center Stage In European Affairs

Washington — (AP) — The Big Three, winding up an eight-day conference around a white draped table in an old play spot of the Czars, announced Monday night their formula for the triumphal conclusion of a war and the beginning of organized peace.

Their nine-point program, announced at the end of the fateful day-and-night sessions, projected this nation fully onto center stage in European affairs.

That in outline is the record of the meeting concluded Sunday in the one-time summer palace of Czar Nicholas II on the Black Sea at Yalta in the Crimea, a conference that may shape tomorrow's world.

RELEASE JOINT COMMUNIQUE

The decisions were announced Monday in a joint communique from the participants, President Roosevelt, Prime Minister Churchill and Premier Stalin.

Here at home first reaction in Congress and elsewhere was overwhelmingly favorable for the report of the leaders of the Three Great Powers. That report covered these prime resolves:

Final extirpation of Naziisim and militarism; elimination or control of all German industry usable for war; no softening of unconditional surrender; and no break in the Allied front.

Collaboration in peace plans to be formally drafted at a United Nations conference at San Francisco April 25; and a settlement (its nature not yet disclosed) of the question of veto power for the great naions on peace council acions.

Joint action to effectuate the Atlantic Charter principle of self-government for liberated peoples, with U. S. paricipation on a far larger scale than heretofore.

On only one point that had figured strongly in preliminary speculation did the three leaders fail to report agreement or action. That was the question of possible Soviet participation in the war against Japan. Pointedly, Japan went unmentioned in the announcement.

Text on Page 4

However, by the time of the San Francisco conference, Russia's decision on whether it expects to abrogate or continue its non-aggression pact with Japan should be known. April 13 is the date on which the Soviets have agreed to give Japan the one-year's agreed upon notice if the pact is to be discontinued. Without such notice, it would be effective for another five years.

LIST NINE POINTS

The nine points of the Big Three communique are:

1. Detailed agreement among the United States, Britain and Russia on military plans against Germany which "will result in shortening the war." As if speaking to the German people over the head of Hitler, the communique warned them that "Nazi Germany is doomed. The German people will only make the cost of their defeat heavier to themselves by attempting to continue a hopeless resistance."

2. A final decision to split

More Of 8-DAY On Page 12

Solons Applaud Action Taken At Crimea Parley

Washington—(AP)—The Big Three statement won bipartisan applause Monday in Congress. Both Democrats and Republicans said it held out high hope for future peace.

Minority Leader White (Me) praised its "forthright terms" and told his colleagues "I feel a great work has been done." Majority Leader Barkley (Ky), who also addressed the chamber, said:

"It is a source of great gratification to me, and I am sure to all the peace-loving peoples of the world, that these heads of three great governments have been able to go so far in composing differences growing out of the war and the occupation of liberated territories."

The two, both members of the Foreign Relations Committee which will pass on treaties ending the war and determining the type of international peace organization to which this nation will become a party, spoke after the communique was read.

BLOOM COMMENTS

Chairman Bloom (D-N. Y.) of House Foreign Affairs Committee said "there is a reaffirmation (in the statement) of the Atlantic Charter and if we are falling back again on the Atlantic Charter we've got a pretty good basis to work from."

Referring twice to the "momentous document," Barkley said he was happy in the thought of its release on the anniversary of the birth of Abraham Lincoln, the Great Emancipator.

Hardly had the session recessed until Thursday before Senator Vandenberg (R-Mich), a foremost

More Of SOLONS On Page 6

WEATHER

Eastern Pennsylvania: Increasing Cloudiness And Colder, Followed By Snow Saturday And Saturday Night; Sunday Clearing, Windy And Cold.

Intelligencer Journal.

The Leading Newspaper in the Garden Spot of America, Home Owned for Home Folks Since 1794 — 150th Anniversary Year

VOLUME LXXXI.—NO. 136. Entered as second class matter August 9, 1944 at the Post Office at Lancaster, Pa., under the Act of March 3, 1879. Reg. U. S. Pat. Off. LANCASTER, PA., SATURDAY MORNING, FEBRUARY 17, 1945 CITY TWELVE PAGES. 20c PER WEEK—4c Per Copy

You Can Help BOMB TOKYO
By Giving Paper Used for Bomb Rings
Send Yours to Schools

YANKS RECAPTURE HISTORIC BATAAN; NAVY PLANES CONTINUE TOKYO RAIDS

Roaring Fight Now Raging On Ten-Mile Front In Kleve Area

Montgomery's Offensive Crunches Southeastward Yard By Yard Into Reinforced German Line Standing Between His Troops And Rich Ruhr, Rhineland

Paris—(AP)—A roaring battle raged Friday on a ten-mile front south and east of Kleve, where Field Marshal Montgomery's offensive crunched southeastward yard by yard into a strongly-reinforced German line standing between his forces and the rich Ruhr and Rhineland.

Over a battlefield where hundreds of big guns blazed, swarms of Allied warplanes attacked with bombs, bullets and rockets, trying to knock the Germans from rising ground before the three strategic road networks of Goch, Uedem and Calcar.

USING MORE TANKS

The Canadian First Army—now disclosed to be made up of 75 per cent British forces—was about two miles from Calcar, five miles from Uedem and two and a half miles from Goch. More Allied tanks were joining the bruising struggle as the ground firmed underneath.

German civilians, men, women and children, streamed from the battle zone, seeking safety behind the Allied lines.

Scottish infantry driving east and gaining nearly a mile were attacking bitterly-defended heights south of Moyland, possibly within two miles of Calcar and 17 from Wesel at the gateway to the industrial Ruhr valley.

The Germans had thrown in elements of eight divisions to block the path to the Ruhr—last great source of enemy munitions — and U. S. heavy bombers battered at those war factories as more than 3,500 warplanes of all kinds took to the skies of western Europe.

Massed German artillery and mortars earlier in the day pinned down the advance on pivotal Goch along the Niers river, but a late dispatch said that once more the British were advancing on Hassum,

More of WEST FRONT on Page 7

FARM CORNER
By The Farm Editor

BEEKEEPERS TO MEET WEDNESDAY EVENING

The annual meeting of the Lancaster County Beekeepers' association is scheduled to be held at the Manor township high school in Millersville on Wednesday evening at 8 o'clock, H. S. Sloat, assistant county agent, announced Friday.

John Amos, Penn State bee specialist, will give an illustrated lecture on spring management problems of colonies, including use of a pollen supplement for feeding purposes. The long period of cold weather has weakened many colonies, which will require careful attention and feeding, to survive, Mr. Sloat said.

Roy Herr, Lancaster, president of the Pennsylvania Beekeepers' association, will give a report of the national beekeepers' convention in Chicago several weeks ago. He will discuss plans adopted for improving the industry and better marketing of honey and allied products.

CO-OP TO GET TOBACCO DAILY

More than 200,000 pounds of tobacco were received from farmers at the Lancaster County Tobacco Growers' Cooperative association warehouse at Plum and Walnut Sts., Lancaster, on Friday.

The Co-Op will have at least

More of FARM CORNER on Page 7

Weather Calendar

COMPARATIVE TEMPERATURES

Station	High	Low
Water Works	50	29
Ephrata	49	33
Last Year (Ephrata)	39	24
Official High for Year, Feb. 12		50
Official Low for Year, Jan. 25		-1
Character of Day		Clear

SUN
Rises—7:56 a. m. Sets—6:42 p. m.

MOON
Sets—12:39 a. m. First Quarter, Feb. 19

STARS
Morning—Mars-Jupiter.
Evening—Venus-Saturn.

NEARBY FORECASTS

Maryland and Delaware: Snow or rain and colder Saturday, snow and much colder Saturday night; Sunday clearing, windy and cold.

New Jersey: Increasing cloudiness and colder, followed by snow Saturday and Saturday night; Sunday clearing, windy and cold.

EXTENDED WEATHER FORECAST

Extended weather forecast for the period through Feb. 21: Rather cold through Monday with temperatures near normal over Middle Atlantic states followed by warmer thereafter; rain over Virginia and rain or snow north of Virginia about Monday.

SAVE THIS NEWSPAPER
Make this newspaper do double work — give it to your paper-salvage drive.

Renominated

S. EDWARD GABLE

GUY E. ECKMAN, 50, DIES SUDDENLY OF HEART ATTACK

Builder And Contractor Was Active In Defense Council Work

Guy E. Eckman, fifty, 629 N. Pine St., was stricken suddenly at his home at 2 p. m. Friday and died before medical aid could reach him. Dr. George Gerlach, osteopathic surgeon, who was called, pronounced him dead, and Dr. A. V. Walter, county coroner, issued a certificate of death due to a heart attack.

GUY E. ECKMAN

The coroner said he learned Eckman had been to the bank Friday morning but had not complained of illness until stricken. He was active in the work of the Lancaster Defense Council serving as Warden of Sector Nine, comprising the

More of ECKMAN on Page 7

PUC ORDER BECOMES IN PP AND L CASE

Harrisburg — (AP) — The Public Utility Commission order dismissing the eleven-year-old rate complaints against the Pennsylvania Power and Light Co. became final Friday with the withdrawal of two petitions to intervene and file exceptions.

A commission member said that the company and the City of Bethlehem, the original complainant, still have 15 days in which to ask the commission for a rehearing and 30 days in which to appeal to the courts from the order.

The withdrawn petitions to intervene and file exceptions were those of the Lancaster Ice Manufacturing Co., Lancaster, and W. W. Heidelbaugh, Lancaster.

LOCAL AUTO CLUB NAMES S. E. GABLE TO SERVE AGAIN

Nominate Veteran President For 27th Consecutive Year After Members' Tribute

S. Edward Gable, president of the Lancaster Automobile Club, was nominated for re-election for the 27th consecutive year at a meeting of the club held at the headquarters, 10 and 12 South Prince St., Friday night. All other incumbent officers and directors also were nominated.

Dr. W. Giles Hess, Holtwood, paid tribute to Gable in placing his name in nomination. Under Gable's leadership, Dr. Hess pointed out, the Club has grown from a membership of less than 300 to over 16,500.

OTHERS NOMINATED

In addition to Gable the officers and directors nominated, all without opposition, are:

First vice-president, Dr. W. Giles Hess, Holtwood; second vice-president, D. Lyman Hamaker, Ephrata; third vice-president, Howard N. Homsher, Bartville; fourth vice-president, F. L. Spence, Columbia; secretary, H. C. Kreisle, Lancaster; treasurer, J. Wade Gayley, Strasburg.

Directors, District No. 1, Ira F. Honaman, George M. May and M. J. McNerney, all of Lancaster; District No. 2, Fred W. Wagner, Columbia; District No. 3, Dr. B. Scott Fritz, Marietta; John E. Schroll, Mt. Joy; Elwood S. Grimm, Elizabethtown, who is serving with the U. S. Army overseas; District No. 4, H. E. Trout, Manheim; Paul H. Bomberger, Lititz; District No. 5, E. L. Bertram, Manor Township; Tom C. Shirk, Manheim Township; J. H. Nissley, East Petersburg; District No. 6, Edgar G. Hess, Hollinger; District No. 7, Lloyd L. Winter, Quarryville; District No. 8, H. M. Rea, Christiana; District No. 9, Victor D. Kling, Intercourse; District No. 10, H. S. Shirk, Blue Ball; District No. 11, Samuel L. Snyder, Denver, Alger H. Shirk, Schoeneck.

The election will be held in connection with the annual meeting of the Club on Friday evening.

More of GABLE on Page 7

EISENHOWER LAUDS LOCAL SOLDIER

Master Sgt. Henry P. Bucher, one of five children of Mrs. C. R Bucher, 121 College Ave., in the armed forces, has been commended by General of the Army Dwight D. Eisenhower, commander of the Allied forces in the European Theater of Operations.

The commendation was for the help Sgt. Bucher gave the 101st and 82nd Airborne divisions during the German counteroffensive in Belgium.

Sgt. Bucher entered the service in 1942 and has been overseas nearly two years.

SOVIET SIEGE TROOPS CRASH INTO BRESLAU

Germans Report Red Capture Of Central Oder Stronghold Of Crossen

London (Saturday)—(AP)—Red Army siege troops crashed into the edge of Breslau yesterday, completely encircling that big Silesian capital on the Upper Oder river, while the Germans announced that other Soviet forces had captured the central Odor stronghold of Crossen, 63 miles southeast of Berlin.

An enemy broadcast late last night said that the "decisive battle" for Breslau had begun, with Soviet artillery slamming shells into the city from all sides.

DEATH GRAPPLE

Breslau is the biggest German city yet within the grasp of any Allied army. It had a 1942 population of 630,000, later swollen to 1,000,000 by the influx of refugees from Berlin and other bomb-shattered Nazi cities. Most of the civilians were believed to have been evacuated, and the stage was set for a death grapple in its ancient streets.

The Russians officially were declared to be only four miles from the heart of Breslau, a sprawling industrial city on the east and west banks of the Oder. They broke into the edge of the city with the seizure of Drachenbrunn, adjoining Bischofswalde, a forest on the southeastern side of the city next to the Zoological Gardens.

More than 100 miles northwest of Breslau a wild fluid battle had developed on the southeastern approaches to Berlin, and a late Moscow dispatch said the Germans were rushing reinforcements of veterans and unseasoned home

More of REDS on Page 7

11th Corps Lands Under Corregidor's Silenced Guns To Trap Jap Forces

Nips Admit Second Attack Over Capital Has Passed Third Hour

U. S. Pacific Fleet Headquarters, Guam (Saturday)—(AP)—Wave on wave of American rocket-firing and bombing planes from the world's largest assemblage of aircraft carriers are over Tokyo again today, with the enemy admitting the attack has passed its third hour.

Seven hundred fifty miles to the south, battleships and cruisers of Adm. Raymond A. Spruance's Fifth Fleet are keeping up the deadly accurate bombardment of Iwo Jima, begun yesterday.

The hundreds of tons of bursting steel already have knocked out the vital coastal batteries of that air base island, where Japan expects a Yank invasion at any moment.

Tokyo, in acknowledging Vice Adm. Marc A. Mitscher's carrier planes, 1,500 strong, returned to that metropolitan area today, reported three hours after first placing the planes over the city that air battles still were in progress. Tokyo said yesterday's attack lasted nine hours.

TERSE COMMUNIQUE

Adm. Chester W. Nimitz first announced the second day of attacks on Tokyo and Iwo Jima in a terse communique today.

Nimitz' announcement meant the Fifth Fleet, including some of the newest 45,000-ton battleships and the largest aircraft carriers, still remained within 300 miles of Japan, apparently unchallenged by Nippon's home defense fleet.

Al Dopking, Associated Press war

More of TOKYO on Page 7

While U. S. Naval airmen continued to operate in the Tokyo area Friday, Gen. MacArthur announced the capture of Bataan Peninsula, historic Philippine battleground of 1942. A combined army - navy - air operation put the 38th Infantry Division ashore at Mariveles on the southern tip of the peninsula, while troops of the Yank Sixth Division pushed down the east coast of Bataan to meet the 38th.

Doughboys Swing Around From Olongapo Naval Base In Subic Bay To Establish Beachhead At Mariveles; Protected By Naval Guns, Far East Airforce Planes

Manila (Saturday)—(AP)—Recapture of historic Bataan Peninsula was proclaimed today as 11th Corps Yanks, landed at the south tip Thursday under Corregidor's silenced guns, seized Mariveles Harbor and airdrome to clamp a trap on several thousand disoganized Japanese troops.

Protected by guns of the U. S. Seventh Fleet, which shelled Corregidor fortress, and by planes of the Far East Airforce, the Americans swung around from the Olongapo naval base in Subic Bay to establish a 500-yard beachhead at Mariveles. American losses were light.

A fourth division—the sixth—was thrown into the raging battle for Manila, meanwhile. The thus reinforced 14th corps drove through to the bay front on an 800-yard front to reduce Japanese holdings in the city's heart to a triangle of about 3,000 yards by 2,000. The enemy still was resisting bitterly.

On Bataan the Americans drove swiftly inland to close an 18-mile gap between them and a strong U. S. force moving down the Manila bay shore of the peninsula from the north.

"We have capturedBataan," Gen. Douglas MacArthur announced. Thus the five-star general hailed the capture of Bataan in a campaign of a little more than two weeks. It took Japan more than three months to do it in 1942.

The fight may not be over on Bataan, but with control of the single coastal road and command of the northern entrance to Manila Bay, the Americans have all they want or need for the moment that bears directly on the principal military objectives of the Luzon campaign.

Only Corregidor fortress, whose guns have been pounded into near helplessness, and the Cavite coast to the south now bar the way into Manila Bay.

DARING OPERATION

Maj. Gen. Charles P. Hall's 11th Corpsmen landed at Meriveles Thursday morning. Preceding the landing, the harbor was cleared of mines "in a daring and skillful operation," today's communique said.

The American battle for Bataan's recapture opened Jan. 29 with Yank landings on the Sambales province coast in a push toward Olongapo.

From Mariveles, big land guns can be set up to shell Corregidor.

Associated Press Correspondent Jim Hutcheson, aboard the attack force flagship, said the invasion fleet steamed unscathed past Corregidor, which fired only a half dozen shots.

The 38th Division units commanded by Brig. Gen. William C. Chase pushed quickly inland from a beachhead of 500 yards. Bombed and shelled Mariveles was occupied immediately. Two nearby airfields were seized.

The convoy had to sail through a gap a little more than four miles wide between the rock and Cochinos Point on Bataan.

Gunfire from Corregidor fortress was neutralized beforehand by cruiser and destroyer batteries, and by American warplanes.

The invasion started from the Olongapo Naval base in Subic Bay immediately north of Bataan on the Luzon wes coast. Colongapo was captured last month after a virtually unopposed amphibious landing on the Zambeles province coast.

MacArthur said the landing was made along the south coast of Bataan at a number of points centering about Mariveles Bay, which is immediately opposite Corregidor.

American losses were light.

(Tokyo radio announced earlier that a score or so of American minesweepers were clearing the channel in preparation for a likely invasion of warships and troopships.)

Sixth Division Yanks drove down the peninsula's Manila Bay coast

More of BATAAN on Page 7

YOUTH WHO FAILED TO REPORT TO WORK CAMP SENTENCED

Floyd Elam Fox, Nineteen, Ephrata R3, Given Four Year Term

Floyd Elam Fox, nineteen, Ephrata R3, was sentenced to four years in prison Friday by Judge George A. Welsh in U. S. Federal Court at Philadelphia, on charges of failing to report to a civilian work camp at Powellsville, Md., Nov. 21, 1944.

Fox, who was arraigned Wednesday, pleaded no defense to the charge.

ARRESTED DEC. 6

The youth, registered with County Draft Board No. 4, was arrested by the FBI Dec. 6 and was taken before U. S. Commissioner Marshall M. Cohen. He posted $500 bail for his court appearance.

Fox, the record of his case shows, wrote his draft board that if it needed men "put me in Class 1-A. I am listed as a conscientious objector but I am none."

The draft board reclassified him as 1-A, available for general military service. He then appealed that classification but the Area Board of Appeals upheld Lancaster County Board No. 4 and kept him in Class 1-A.

"The Pennsylvania Director of Selective Service, who reviewed the case, asked the appeal board to review its decision. The reviewd dcision put him in Class 4-E, a conscientious objector."

National Selective Service head-

More of YOUTH on Page 7

WOMAN FOUND DEAD IN KITCHEN AT HOME

A woman identified by police as Mrs. G. H. Smith, was found dead in the kitchen of her home, 33 N. Lime St. at 3 a. m. Saturday, apparently of natural causes, police said. Dr. A. V. Walter, county coroner, is investigating. Police were called by Mrs. Leman Hurst, 31 N. Lime St., who became suspicious after noticing a light burning in the kitchen since Friday night.

HOUSE SMOOTHES WAY FOR WALLACE TO CABINET POST

Pass Legislation Divorcing Commerce Department From The RFC

Washington —(AP)— Henry A. Wallace's rocky pathway into the Roosevelt cabinet was smoothed Friday when the House passed legislation divorcing the Commerce Department from the RFC

The bill, which opens the way for Wallace to become Secretary of Commerce without the vast lending powers wielded by ousted Secretary Jesse Jones, now goes to the White House.

SOME TROUBLE

Known as the George bill, the legislation was passed 399 to 2 on the final rollcall, but this was no measure of the struggle over it. Shortly before that, the Administration escaped defeat by a hair's breadth margin of eight votes when the House voted 204 to 196 not to recommit (shelve) the bill.

The Senate is due to vote March 1 on the Wallace nomination. Wallace backers predict he will be confirmed, whereas most legislators believed that if the George bill had not passed he would have been rejected.

Senator Barkley of Kentucky, majority leader, told a reporter late Friday:

"It is obvious that the action of the House in passing without

More of HOUSE on Page 7

THIEVES LOOT TRUCK OF LOCAL COMPANY

Philadelphia—(AP)—A 10-ton trailer truck was stolen Friday from a Philadelphia freight depot, looted of $20,000 worth of merchandise and abandoned two miles away.

Included in the loot were $13,000 worth of cotton and wool material consigned to army quartermaster depots, rationed shoes, cigars, sweaters and sportswear, and smoked meats, police said.

The theft occurred at Shirk's Motor Express Company depot. The company has headquarters in Lancaster.

BOYS, TEN, ADMIT THEFTS AT SCHOOL

Two ten-year-old boys admitted to State Police Friday that they broke into the two Temperance Home School buildings, near Rocky Springs Park, Thursday night and stole a quantity of school supplies. Sgt. S. H. Smith, of the State Police, who apprehended the boys, said they have been released in custodmy of their parents, pending completion of the case. Both have prior police records, police said.

BLOOD DONORS NEEDED FOR RED CROSS UNIT

Volunteers to act as blood donors next week are urgently needed, it was announced Friday by the local Red Cross Blood Donor committee.

The Harrisburg Unit will be stationed at St. James Parish house on Tuesday, Wednesday and Thursday.

There are 89 vacancies for Tuesday from 12:30 p. m. on, and 50 vacancies for Thursday, between the hours of 1:30 and 3 p. m.

The donor committee pointed out that odd fact that when our armies are forging ahead, attendance at the Blood banks drops off. They emphasized that when our forces are winning the need for blood plasma shoots up, because the casualties mount up. They added that the terrific casualties in January make the need for plasma especially urgent.

Survivor Tells Of Massacre Of Yank Prisoners By Nazis

The experiences which at least nine Lancaster county soldiers, members of an artillery observation battalion, went through at a little crossroads in Belgium, when they were cut off by advancing Nazis in their December counteroffensive, were graphically recounted Friday by a survivor.

The story was told by Pvt. James P. Mattera, son of Mrs. Rose Mattera, of Maytown, one of the few survivors of the group of 150, who were rounded up by the Germans and then mowed down by machine gun fire from tanks.

Pvt. Mattera

Of the nine known soldiers from Lancaster county in the group five were reported missing. Of the five, three have since been reported killed.

Besides Pvt. Mattera, the other local men and their status: Technician Fifth Grade Charles F. Haines, Columbia R1, killed; Technician Fourth Grade Sylvester V. Herchelroth, Marietta, killed; Pfc. Carl Frey, Hopeland, killed; Technician Fifth Grade Luke S. Swartz, Reinholds R1, missing; Sgt. Robert Mearig, Lititz, reported missing but now safe; Harold Hinkle, Marietta; Pvt. William F. Ream, Elizabethtown, and Technician Fifth Grade Harold W. Billow, Mount Joy, all safe.

Pvt. Mattera's story, as it ap-

More of MASSACRE on Page 7

FOUR NAMES ADDED TO COUNTY LIST OF WAR CASUALTIES

One Reported Killed, One Missing And Two Are Wounded

WAR CASUALTIES

Battle casualties from the Lancaster area reported Friday included:

KILLED

Pfc. Benjamin Harsh Oxford, formerly of Lancaster, in France.

MISSING

William F. Shepley, watertender third class, 148 E. Walnut St., in Pacific area.

PRISONER

Sgt. Harvey Turner, Jr., Ephrata, of Germans.

WOUNDED

Pfc. Willis Harvey, Jr., 35 W. Frederick St., in France.

Pvt. John H. Stoner, Quarryville R1, in France.

Four additional names were added Friday to Lancaster county casualty lists. One was reported killed, one is listed as missing and two were wounded. Also, an Ephrata soldier, previously listed as missing, is a prisoner of the Germans.

Pfc. Benjamin F. Harsh, twenty-seven, son of Mr. and Mrs. B. F. Harsh, of Hockessin Del., formerly of this city, was killed in action on Nov. 27, 1944, in France, according to word received by his family from the War Department in December.

He entered the service August, 1941 and was serving with an Infantry Division. Prior to his induction he attended local schools and was residing in Oxford where he was employed at the Cabinet factory.

He trained at Camp Croft, S. C.; Camp Roberts, Calif.; Ft. Meade, Md., and was stationed in the Canal Zone for more than a year. He was overseas approximately five months and his last letter was dated two days before his death.

His wife, Gladys, resides in Oxford. Besides his wife and his parents he is survived by three sis-

More of CASUALTIES on Page 7

Manufacturers' Association Adds Endorsement To Scout Campaign

Endorsement of the campaign to raise $50,000 for Camp Chiquetan being conducted by the Lancaster County Council of Boy Scouts was made Friday by the Manufacturer's association.

The campaign is now underway and will continue until the end of February.

In a letter addressed to J. Edward Mack, campaign chairman, Walter C. Miller, secretary of the Manufacturers' Association, says:

"The Manufacturers' Association of Lancaster, Pa., is glad to give its hearty endorsement to the Lancaster County Council Boy Scouts of American Campaign to raise $50,000.00 to equip the recently purchased Chiquetan Camp site.

"Manufacturers recognize the fine job of character building the Boy Scout movement has accomplished with the youth of Lancaster county, and you can rest assured that you will receive our hearty support and cooperation in your efforts to secure the funds to do an even better job among the youth of this county.

"Very truly yours,
"Manufacturers' Association of Lancaster Pa.
"Walter C. Miller, Secretary."

Miss Margaret K. Heinitsh, 85, Dies; Active Over 50 Yrs. At Trinity Church

Miss Margaret Keller Heinitsh, 229 W. Chestnut St., died at 12:35 p. m. Friday at the Lancaster General Hospital after a brief illness in her eighty-fifth year. Miss Heinitsh was born in Lancaster and lived here all her life.

Miss Heinitsh

"Miss Margie", as she was known, was a lifelong member of Trinity Lutheran Church and a teacher in it's varied activities from her youth on. So truly did she incorporate its spirit that she was chosen a few years ago, by common consent, to play the role of "Mother Trinity" in an aniversary pageant. A Sunday School teacher, Missionary Society member, and a King's Daughter, she was active in each of these organizations, but her special joy was in her service in the choir for well over 50 years. In 1910, she inspired the organization of the Trinity Guild and served as its treasurer continuously for 34 years.

Sh has sung for directors: Ambrose Schmidt, Carl Steinhouser, Benjamin Schreiner, Edwin Albright, alter Bausman, Carl Motts, Clarence McHose, William Westfall and Dr. Harry A. Sykes. She was a member of the Cecilian Musical society, which is no longer in existence. She was a member of the Musical Art society. As for hobbies she had two, singing was the main one, and crocheting came next. Several of her pieces of

More of HEINITSCH on Page 7

WEATHER

Eastern Pennsylvania: Partly Cloudy, Not So Warm East Portion Friday; Saturday Fair And Warmer.

Intelligencer Journal.

The Leading Newspaper in the Garden Spot of America, Home Owned for Home Folks Since 1794 — 150th Anniversary Year

Help Save PAPER
Carry Unwrapped Parcels
GIVE WASTE PAPER
To Nearest School

151st Year—No. 216 | Entered as second class matter August 9, 1944 at the Post Office at Lancaster, Pa., under the Act of March 3, 1879. Reg. U. S. Pat. Off. | LANCASTER, PA., FRIDAY MORNING, FEBRUARY 23, 1945 | CITY | THIRTY PAGES. | 20c PER WEEK—4c Per Copy

MARINES TAKE MT. SURIBACHI ON IWO

PATTON'S MEN SPAN SAAR AT 2 POINTS

Marines Of U. S. Fourth Division Hitting Beach On Iwo Jima Island

Fourth Marines dash from landing craft, dragging equipment, while others "go over the top of sand dune as they hit the beach of Iwo Jima, Volcano Islands, Feb. 19. Smoke of artillery or mortar fire in background. Photo by AP Photographer Joe Rosenthal on assignment with Wartime Still Picture Pool. (AP Wirephoto.)

American Marines, invading the Jap stronghold of Iwo Jima, Volcano Islands, dig in after taking what was an "impregnable" enemy pillbox (center background). Note Marine in center digging foxhole and bodies, some in open, some partly covered by sand, which caption did NOT identify. These are Fourth Division Marines in action Feb. 19. Photo by AP Photographer Joe Rosenthal on assignment with Wartime Still Picture Pool. (AP Wirephoto.)

7,000 ALLIED PLANES BLAST NAZI RR LINES

U. S. 3rd Completes Conquest Of Moselle-Saar Triangle, Takes Saarburg

London (Friday)—(AP)—The Swiss radio reported today that U. S. Third Army troops fought their way into Saarbruecken this morning. The report was not confirmed immediately by Allied sources.

Paris—(AP)—The rampaging U. S. Third Army broke across the Saar river at two points 65 miles from the Rhine Thursday and completed a whirlwind conquest of Germany's 80-square-mile Moselle-Saar triangle as 7,000 Allied warplanes struck simultaneously at enemy rail lifelines.

A field dispatch said Third Army officers and men were in high spirits as they ripped across western Germany's ramparts with a speed reminiscent of their historic dash in France, seizing the fortress city of Saarburg and 29 other Reich towns on a 55-mile front.

Saarburg, once a thriving city of 10,000, was deserted save for 100 aged civilians.

5 MILES FROM TRIER

This powerful thrust 18 miles deep into the Reich collapsed all enemy resistance in the triangle and rammed a steel spearhead to a point five miles from Trier, fortified city of 88,000 population on the mountainous route to the Rhine.

While Trier's battlements came under Lt. Gen. George S. Patton's guns, artillery to the south tore at the fortified hills into which the Germans had been chased east of the Saar river. The attackers were confident the enemy soon would be driven from these new positions.

To the fury of the Allied air attack—a new technique under

More of 7,000 on Page 12

FARM CORNER

By The Farm Editor

STATE'S POTATO CROP SIXTH IN U. S. IN 1944

Harrisburg—Pennsylvania farmers in 1944 regained for the State its prominence as a potato producing area when the crop of more than 19 million bushels was sufficient to rank the Commonwealth sixth among all the states in total production.

This was an advance from eighth place held in 1943, according to records of the State Department of Agriculture, compiled by the Federal-State Crop Reporting Service.

The best Pennsylvania ranking for potatoes held in recent years was fifth place in 1941, when the State also stood fifth in acreage and fourth in value of the crop. The next year the State still ranked fifth in acreage but dropped to seventh in production and fifth in value.

Drought, shortage of labor and machinery in 1943 brought the standing to its lowest wartime point, seventh in acreage, eighth in production and fifth in value. Return in 1944 to sixth in production was accompanied by sixth place in acreage and fifth in value.

Average yield per acre had much to do with the changes in Keystone State potato production ranking during these war years, the report shows. In 1941 Pennsylvania ranked 17th in the Nation with 130 bushels per acre. The next year it was 24th with an average of 112 bushels, but in 1943 advanced to 23rd with 106 bushels. Last year the average yield was 116 bushels per acre and the State advanced to 20th place. In each of the past two years a late, wet spring retarded planting, and summer

More of FARM CORNER on Page 12

Weather Calendar

COMPARATIVE TEMPERATURES

Station	High	Low
Water Works	44	32
Ephrata	44	32
Last Year (Ephrata)	39	25
Official High for Year, Feb.	12	50
Official Low for Year, Jan.	25	-1
Character of Day		Cloudy

SUN
Rises—7:47 a. m. Sets—6:49 p. m.

MOON
Rises—11:11 p. m. Full Moon, Feb. 26

STARS
Morning—Mars-Jupiter.
Evening—Venus-Saturn.

SUB FORECAST
Maryland and Delaware: Fair with moderate temperature Friday and Saturday.
New Jersey: Partly cloudy and not so warm Friday; Saturday fair and warmer.

SAVE THIS NEWSPAPER
Make this newspaper do double work — give it to your paper-salvage drive.

STALIN FORECASTS 'COMPLETE VICTORY' FOR ALLIES SHORTLY

Soviet Chief Says Drive Has Cost Germans Over 1,150.-000 Casualties

London —(AP)— Premier Marshal Joseph Stalin, in an order of the day commemorating the 27th anniversary of the Red Army, declared Thursday night the Soviet winter offensive had cost the Germans more than 1,150,000 killed or captured and predicted "complete victory" now is near.

In a breakdown of the German casualties as reported by the Moscow radio, the Soviet leader said the Russians killed 800,000 and captured 350,000 in driving the Nazis back on a 1200 kilometer front (about 745 miles) "within 40 days of January and February, 1945."

FIRST CONSEQUENCE

Stalin described the Russian blows as complementary to the Allied western front war and said the first consequence of the mighty Soviet offensive was to thwart the "German winter offensive in the west which was aimed at the seizure of Belgium and Alsace." This enabled, he said, the British and Americans, in turn, to launch attacks which linked their present offensive operations with those of the Russians.

The Soviet premier added that the Soviet armies "together with the armies of our allies are successfully completing the rout of the German Fascist army."

"Complete victory over the Germans now is near," he asserted. "But victory never comes of itself. It is won in battles and by persistent labor. As the doomed enemy hurls his last forces into action, hanging on desperately to escape stern retribution, he grasps and will grasp at the most extreme and

More of STALIN on Page 12

AMERICAN CASUALTIES CLIMB PAST 800,000

Washington — (AP) — Reported American casualties of World War II climbed past 800,000 Thursday.

The compilations by the Army and Navy came out along with hints of impending big-scale action which indicated little if any diminution in the rate of losses.

Representing a rise of approximately 100,000 in the past month, and up 18,982 for the week, the casualty figures were rising at a rate which would raise the total past 1,000,000 within two months.

The Army's total of dead, wounded, missing and prisoners since Pearl Harbor stood at 711,497, and the Navy's at 89,665, for an aggregate of 801,162.

Secretary of War Stimson said the Army's figures covered individual names compiled here up to Feb. 14.

HORSE KICKS, BADLY INJURES YOUTH, 18

Abner Stoltzfus, eighteen, son of Mr and Mrs. John Stoltzfus, Elverson R2, was seriously injured when kicked in the face by a horse while working on his father's farm Thursday, according to attendants at St. Joseph's Hospital. Stoltzfus underwent an emergency operaton Thursday night for a badly mangled nose, which attendants said was nearly torn from his face. His condition is reported as fair.

MISSING MAN NOW AMONG PRISONERS; ANOTHER MISSING

County Soldier Held By Germans; Bareville Man's Grandson Unaccounted For

The casualty status of a Lancaster county soldier was changed from missing to a prisoner of the Germans, Thursday, while the grandson of a Bareville man was reported missing in action.

Sgt. George William Hoshower, twenty-one, son of Mr. and Mrs. A. R. Hoshower, 1111 Washington St., Lebanon, and grandson of George Hoshower, Bareville, has been missing in action in France since Jan. 25, the War Department notified his parents.

Sgt. Hoshower

He entered the service Feb. 22, 1943, and had been overseas with an infantry unit since November, 1944. A graduate of the Lebanon High School, class of 1940, he trained at Fort Jackson, S. C. and Camp Gordon, Ga.

He was then selected for the Army Specialized Training Reserve Program and assigned to the Uni-

More of CASUALTIES on Page 12

Stettinius Says U. S. Seeks "Freedom From Fear, Want"

Mexico City—(AP)—Secretary of State Edward R. Stettinius, Jr., said Thursday night that American foreign policy aims at an Atlantic Charter peace of "freedom from fear and want" for all men.

That, he told the Inter-American conference here, is an essential fact in a five-point United States program which he asserted had been "greatly advanced" by the results of the Crimea conference.

In probably the most important speech he has yet made as Secretary of State, Stettinius reported that three days after the Crimea conference he had reviewed the work done there with President Roosevelt and "it is the President's firm conviction that the results of the Crimea conference have greatly advanced the basic objectives of United States foreign policy."

These are the basic objectives which Stettinius then set forth, evidently basing some of them directly on decisions made by the President, Prime Minister Churchill, and Premier Stalin at Yalta:

1. The "earliest possible final defeat of the aggressors.
2. Any steps necessary "to insure that neither Germany nor Japan will ever again have the military or industrial capacity to make war."
3. Participation in guaranteeing to the liberated peoples of Europe their own government and sovereign rights. In this "the United States will not shirk its responsibilities."
4. Creation before the end of the war "of an international organization to insure the peace of the world, by force if necessary." This is the aim of the April 25 meeting at San Francisco.
5. The development of an Atlan-

More of STETTINIUS on Page 12

Donated Salvage Materials Sold For Total Of $131,181

Salvage work in Lancaster county is a big business—not only in the fine collection record but in the money involved in the sale of donate salvage materials.

Earl F. Rebman, county salvage chief, in a report Thursday, announced that the sale of donated salvage up to Jan. 31 brought in $131,181.32.

This money was distributed among a number of organizations including Defense Councils, Red Cross, Boy Scouts, Girl Scouts, infantile paralysis fund, city and county schools, Blind Association,

More of SALVAGE on Page 27

729 PINTS BLOOD, 129 OVER QUOTA, DONATED HERE

Red Cross Officials Urge Volunteers To Make Appointment For Next Visit

A total of 729 pints of blood was obtained at the Lancaster Blood Donor center during the past three days, when the Harrisburg Mobile Blood Donor unit was stationed at St James Parish house. The total is 129 pints over the quota of 600.

Red Cross officials expressed themselves as exceedingly pleased at Lancaster's support of the project, on account of the heavy casualties being incurred at Iwo Jima. They pointed out that there will be a heavy drain on the blood plasma supply, and that Lancaster, by going over its quota, has done its bit toward helping to build up the reserve.

NEXT VISIT IN MARCH

Officials urged that people make their appointments now for the next visit of the Mobile Donor unit on March 20, 21, and 22, by calling the Red Cross Chapter House, 3-3926. The unit will be stationed at Holtwood on March 19.

On Thursday, final day of the visit here, 249 pints of blood were donated. A total of 279 donors reported, including 127 men and 152 women. There were 183 repeaters, of whom 43 gave for their second

More of 729 PINTS on Page 27

PUBLIC MEMBERS OF WLB ASK FDR HOLD WAGE LINES

See No Revision Until Victory Is In Sight; Labor Members Dissent

Washington —(AP)— Public members of the War Labor Board advised President Roosevelt to hold tight to the Little Steel wage formula so long as civilian goods and services must be restricted.

Inasmuch as the President has indicated he will rely heavily upon the four public members' findings in deciding whether to crack open the ceiling on base wage increases, the report indicated no revision until victory is fully in sight, especially not while hostilities continue in Europe. The whole recent trend has been to channel more and more of the nation's capacity into war.

The public members reported, at the President's request, on the status of wage earners in wartime.

The Little Steel formula, keystone of the administration's wartime wage stabilization policy, allows for 15 per cent higher pay than in January, 1941, to make up for cost of living increases up to May, 1942. The report accepted an earlier finding of the President's cost-of-living committee that living expenses rose 30 per cent by last December, but it made no recommendation that workers be given another 15 per cent wage hike to keep pace.

Industry members of the board announced their concurrence with the findings. Labor members, in separate statements, dissented.

The four public members are Chairman William H. Davis, Vice Chairman George W. Taylor, who wrote the "Little Steel Formula" two and one-half years ago; Frank P. Graham, president of North Carolina University, and Lloyd K. Garrison, dean of the Wisconsin University Law School.

The report, four months in the making, was submitted on the eve

More of PUBLIC on Page 27

U. S. CASUALTIES REACH 5,372 IN 58 HOURS

Deadly Jap Resistance; Yank Fleet Damaged; Navy Shells Paramushiro

U. S. Pacific Fleet Headquarters, Guam (Friday)—(AP)—Hard-fighting United States Marines, who have paid the Pacific's highest price for 58 hours of battle with 5,372 casualties at Iwo, wrested 546-foot Mt. Suribachi on the south tip of the island from the Japanese today.

The United States flag was raised on the crater's rim at 10:35 a. m. by the 28th Regiment, signalling the end of one phase of the five-day-old struggle.

DEADLY POSITIONS

From Suribachi, whose slopes had been blasted by battleships and divebombed by carrier planes, the Japanese had raked Marine positions throughout the southern sector with deadly mortar and artillery fire.

Adm. Chester W. Nimitz announced the victory in a brief communique soon after one which had reported only minor advances through Thursday against fierce opposition.

The earlier communique, covering Marine casualties only through 6 p. m. Wednesday, disclosed that 644 Marines had been killed, 4,168 wounded and 560 were missing. Since then severe battles have raged.

In the same 58-hour period, a total of 1,222 enemy dead were counted.

No invasion of the Pacific war for a comparative period has cost so many American casualties. At Tarawa, previously considered the bloodiest fight of the war, Marine casualties for its entire 72 hours slightly exceeded 3,000.

CASUALTIES MOUNT

Nimitz in his last previous communique covering the casualty count up to 5:45 p. m Wednesday

More of IWO JIMA on Page 12

YANKEES OCCUPY CAPUL ISLAND OFF SOUTHEAST LUZON

Move To Clear Japs From Main Shipping Route From U. S. To Manila

Manila, (Friday) —(AP)— Veteran Yanks of the Americal division invaded tiny Capul island in the San Bernardino Straits just off Luzon's long southern tip on Wednesday in a move to clear the Japanese from the main shipping route from the United States to Manila.

Opposition was light.

The small oval island, five miles long and two wide at the middle, commands the strait through which the Japanese sent a war fleet to Harass the American invasion of Leyte last October.

It lies directly between the extensive southeastern tip of Luzon and the northern end of Samar island, which is practically in American hands. It is 260 airline miles southeast of Manila and about 325 by sea.

In Manila, meanwhile, point-blank shelling of the thick East Wall of the Intramuros was intensified as First Cavalry Yanks made ready for a grand assault to clean up the Japanese garrison there. Howitzers and cannon were attemp-

More of YANKEES on Page 12

2 Democratic Congressmen Engage In Fist Fight On Floor Of House

Washington — (AP) — Shouts of "Communist" and "liar" exploded into a fist fight between two Democratic congressmen on the floor of the House of Representatives Thursday.

The contestants: Small, white-thatched John Rankin of Mississippi, who shouted "Communist," and strapping Frank E. Hook, New Dealer from Michigan, who retorted "liar."

The official reporter got Hook's remark as "—— —— liar" but in the press gallery above the fight most reporters heard it as "dirty liar." In any event, the ugly word was stricken from the record.)

GETS IN JABS

There wasn't one good, solid blow landed but Rankin managed to get in several short jabs at Hook's flushed face before other startled members separated them.

As soon as the fight was over talking about disciplinary action started. Although leaders hurried the House into adjournment to ward off a further flare-up, some Democrats spoke of introducing a resolution to expel Hook when the House meets Friday.

Thursday night, however, the project apparently simmered down

More of 2 DEMOCRATIC on Page 27

Old Man River Invades, Gives Home Front Troubled Week

RIVER ROLLS IN to engulf a town. At its height—over 10 feet, the flood at Washington Boro broke 1904 record for that spot covering railroad tracks, carrying off small shacks and boats, and forcing 19 families to leave their homes. Postoffice above was cut off by flood.

MIRROR LAKE merged houses and water along the Washington Boro river front climbing toward high porches. Gas pumps nearly submerged indicate high water mark at Sherick store which had 16 inches on floor.

TURKEY HILL 1904 indicates what that must have been like. So far, although the water is receding up river, the ice is still holding in the Turkey Hill narrows where flood started as water backed up.

IS YOUR TRIP NECESSARY? Flooded railroad tracks made it hard to decide where water ended and parts of the railroad began at Washington Boro. Are these lads rowing to Columbia? Could be.

PRIVATE LAKE with that setting in the background would be ideal under other circumstances, that is to say without river flood and ice. It's home of Frank B. Miller, Washington Boro.

WAR OF NERVES by the Old Susquehanna is still to be reckoned with after weeks of watchful waiting, and a week of actual flooding all along the Lancaster-York county river front. On the Lancaster side the waters recede after sweeping surges across the shoreline, and the menace passes slowly.

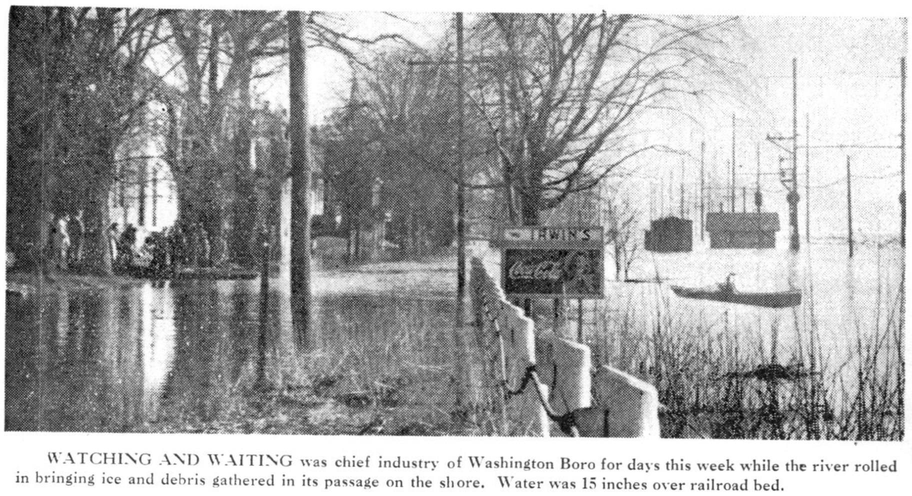

WATCHING AND WAITING was chief industry of Washington Boro for days this week while the river rolled in bringing ice and debris gathered in its passage on the shore. Water was 15 inches over railroad bed.

BUT THE ICE IS STILL THERE though the channels are carrying off some of the flood pressure. This is the York county side.

BACK COUNTRY FELT the pressure when flood waters pushed up the creeks. This is Chickies which flooded farm lands above Columbia earlier in the week. Course of stream is to left.

Never Too Old - - - - By Jack Sords

FRED FITZSIMMONS,
43-YEAR-OLD MANAGER OF THE PHILADELPHIA PHILLIES, PREPARING TO TAKE HIS TURN ON THE MOUND THIS YEAR IF NECESSARY
GOSH! THAT'S 184,000,000 FEET!
FITZ RECENTLY RETURNED FROM A 35,000-MILE U.S.O. TOUR OF THE PERSIAN GULF COMMAND AND AFRICA
PONCE DE LEON WAS WRONG — HE SHOULD HAVE GONE TO PERSIA
SORDS
HE CREDITS THE STRONG PERSIAN SUN FOR TAKING THE KINKS OUT OF HIS ARM AND GIVING HIM THE IDEA HE COULD PITCH AGAIN

JIM RAFFERTY WINS 4-A MILE

GUNDER HAGG IS DISMAL LAST IN FIELD OF FIVE

By PAT ROBINSON

NEW YORK, March 3—(INS) — Gunder Hagg, Sweden's greatest runner, came, ran and was soundly beaten in his debut in Madison Square Garden tonight.

Jim Rafferty, unbeaten in mile competition, won the special mile event, in a dawdling 4:16.4, which is usually only a warm-up jaunt for him.

Hagg finished last in the field of five, 80 yards behind Rafferty and was clocked in 4:31, which isn't even good time for schoolboys.

Forest Efaw ran a surprisingly fine race, and finished so close behind Rafferty it was almost a dead heat. Don Burnham was 20 yards back in third place and Rudy Simms 10 yards further to the rear but 50 ahead of Hagg.

Hagg quickly took the lead and at once had a fight on his hands as Simms kept toying to get in front.

Hagg fought him off time after time but on the seventh lap Simms took over as Hagg faded rapidly to the rear of the pack.

Two laps from home Rafferty took command and seemed to have the race in the bag until Efaw came surging up with a powerful spurt that just failed to nip Rafferty at the tape.

The time for the mile by quarters was :63.3, 2:10, 3:15.4 4:16.4.

Haakon Lidman of Sweden, Europe's champion hurdler, was given a chance to show his stuff in two special hurdle races at 50 and 60 yards.

He won the 60-yard race handily with Bill Mitchell of the Marines, the National Junior champion, second, and Owen Cassidy, of Columbia, the National champion, third. The time was 7.4 seconds.

Paul Robeson of Cornell, son of the famous singer, and Joe Conley of Dartmouth divided the high jump title each clearing the bar at 6 feet 3 inches.

Army swung back again when Jerry Morrow inched out George Hedrick of the Navy in the 60-yard high hurdles in 7.6 seconds.

In the 50-yard special hurdles, Mitchell and Cassidy finished in that order ahead of Lidman as the Swede clipped a couple of the timbers. The time was 6.4 seconds.

The pole vaulters were far off form, the event winding up in a five-way tie at a very mediocre 12 feet. Jim Halcomb, Ken Kochel, Phil Lansing and Augie Puchrik, all of Army and Charles Riehl of Navy were the point winners. Lansing usually clears at least 13½ feet in these things.

The Navy ran 1-2-5 in the 60-yard dash with Army taking third and fourth places. The winner was John Van Velzer with his Navy pal, John Pettit, only inches behind him and a foot ahead of Dick Newell of Army. The time was a snappy 6.3 seconds.

Stan Callender of N. Y. U. came in ahead in the 1,000-yard title. He jumped Dick Hall of Navy on the bell lap and beat him to the tape by six feet. Bernard Conor of Navy was three feet further back and a foot ahead of Floyd Cuff of Navy. The time was 2:17.

It was announced later that Callender had been disqualified for fouling which gave Hall the title and put Conor second.

Eleven started in the Intercollegiate Mile and it was merely a breeze for Vincent Barry of the Navy who led Henry Eckert, N. Y. U., to the tape by 50 yards in a slow 4:26.2. Jim Cavanaugh of Rhode Island was 10 yards further back in third place.

Armand Osterberg of N. Y. U. scored an easy 50-yard victory in the 2-mile run with Art Truxes of Army second and John Kandl of Cornell third. The time was a slow 9:44.7.

At this point Army had the team title clinched with 62½ points to Navy's 51½. N. Y. U. was in third place with 11 points.

Snead, McSpaden Golf Leaders

SUB-PAR SCORES FEATURE 3RD RD AT JACKSONVILLE

JACKSONVILLE, Fla., March 3 — (AP) — Turning on the power, slammin' Sammy Snead and Harold (Jug) McSpaden fired six-under-par 66's today to go into a first-place tie in the third round of the $5,000 Jacksonville Open Golf tournament.

Their 200 total for the 54 holes placed them two strokes ahead of Ky Laffoon, of Chicago, whose 66 today put him in second position with 202.

Big Bob Hamilton, of Chicago, national PGA champion, who lead during the first two rounds, carded a 71 for a 203 total and third place.

Next in line were Bruce Coltart, of Absecon, N. J., with 66 and a 205 total; Bryson Nelson, of Toledo, with a 72 and Sam Byrd, of Detroit, with a 66 were tied at 206. Craig Wood, of Mamaroneck, N. Y., duration open champion, had a 70 for a total of 207.

The final 18 holes will be played tomorrow with Snead ranking a slight favorite to beat out McSpaden for first money. The hot Springs, Va., slammer belted out prodigious drives today and his play around the greens was consistently accurate.

McSpaden, hailing from Sanford, Me., was bent on shaking off the jinx that has kept him from winning a single tournament this season. He played a flawless game despite the pressure and the 86-degree heat.

Hamilton took a 39 on the incoming nine after carding a 32 for the front side.

Nelson, the winter circuit's leading money winner, separated from the lead by only two strokes yesterday, also was beset by tournament gremlins. He took a seven on the 410-yard fifteenth.

Leading scorers:

Harold McSpaden, Sanford, Me.	134-66—200
Sam Snead, Hot Springs, Va.	134-66—200
Ky Laffoon, Chicago	136-66—202
Bob Hamilton, Chicago	132-71—203
Bruce Coltart, Absecon, N. J.	139-66—205
Sam Byrd, Detroit, Mich.	140-66—206
Byron Nelson, Toledo, Ohio	134-72—206
Craig Wood, Mamaroneck, N. Y.	137-70—207
xFred Haas, New Orleans, La.	138-70—208
Leonard Dodson, San Francisco, Calif.	143-67—210
Leonard Ott, Denver, Colo.	140-71—211
Willie Goggin, New York City	142-70—212
x-John Teal, Jacksonville	140-73—213
George Low, Clearwater, Fla.	142-71—213
x-Jim Lee, Jr., Tallahassee, Fla.	148-71—214
Frank Starra, Greenwich, Conn.	142-72—214
Johnny Revolta, Evanston, Ill.	148-67—215
Denny Shute, Akron, Ohio	140-75—215
Sam Schneider, Corpus Christi, Texas	144-71—215
Bob Stupple, Glencoe, Ill.	143-72—215

(x-Denotes amateur).

Story-Book Finish Gives New Holland Claim To County Hi Cage Championship

NEW HOLLAND, LANCASTER COUNTY CHAMPS OF 1944-45, reading from left to right: Front row, Melvin Ludwig, Edward Mersky, Clyde Bensinger, Capt. Harold Wright, Glenn Sweigart, John Sweigart, Coach Carl S. Driscoll.
Back row, Rodney Hoober, student manager; Robert Martin, George Musselman, Robert Collins, Glenn Smith, supervising principal, and J. Harvey Shue.

Capturing the Lancaster County Basketball Championship served as a glorious finale for the wonderful record of achievements established throughout the season by the New Holland High School team.

Their schedule was opened Nov. 28 with a game with East Hempfield, which the latter won 32-24, but the season was brought to a close with a championship playoff game between the same two teams and this time New Holland avenged its only defeat for the entire basketball campaign, winning a hard fought contest 24-23 in a story-book finish that will be long remembered.

After playing East Hempfield in the opener, the county champs followed through with several non-league tilts. Among its opponents was the high-ranking Downingtown High five, of Suburban League 3, which includes such teams as Coatesville, Pottstown, etc. Winning their first encounter 33-31, New Holland came through with a more impressive victory against the Mainliners later in the season, defeating them 50-16.

The official league schedule for New Holland opened Dec. 12 with E. Cocalico, whom they overpowered 64-18, and ended with a contest with Paradise in which the champs were victors 56-21. In their own league, New Holland encountered only light opposition, the closest game being with E. Lampeter, 27-25. All other league games, including a second contest with E. Lampeter, were won by margins of 14 points or better.

As for statistics, New Holland registered to date a total of 813 points to their opponents 423. Under the successful coaching of Carl Driscoll, New Holland has in the last two years won 35 out of 37 games played. Their record for this year is 18 victories out of 19 contests. This record gives them a percentage of .947, the highest of any high school team in the county. New Holland also was the only participant in the County League to emerge with a perfect record in the official league games played.

They became victors of their Section by winning all ten games. Only two rivals scored more than 30 points against them and no team scoring more than 32 points in any one clash with these lads of the Maroon and Gray.

As a result, the Driscoll-coached team was eligible to enter either Class A or B competition in the PIAA playoffs, but because of their comparative small enrollment, they chose to compete in Class B playoffs.

In the first round, New Holland bowed to Cornwall 39-32 in a game played on the Manheim Twp. High court Friday night.

Frisch Has Chance, Unless Draft Hits

Pittsburgh, March 3—(AP)—If enough key ball players from the Pittsburgh Pirates' present roster show up this season, Manager Frankie Frisch looks to have as good a chance as anybody of winning the 1945 National League pennant.

The club roster, released today, lists several promising recruits who, with a few important veterans, might easily show the way in the loop, especially considering that the champion St. Louis Cardinals lost such formidable stars as Stan Musial, Walker Cooper and others.

Among the youngsters looming big are outfielders Al Gionfriddi and Bill Rodgers, infielder Vic Barnhart and Pitcher Leonard Gilmore. Gionfriddi, Rodgers and Barnhart all batted better than .300 in class A baseball last season, while Gilmore, a righthander, won 21 games against six losses for Albany.

Another stranger to the Pittsburgh roster is catcher Bill Salkeld, up from San Diego of the Pacific Coast League.

Among the veterans slated to return, unless Selective Service or other elements interfere, are outfielders Frank Colman, James Russell, John Barrett and Tommy O'Brien. Vince DiMaggio's future with the club remains in doubt.

The roster lists, among others, these infielders: Pete Coscarart, Babe Dahlgren, Bob Elliott, Frankie Gustine, Lee Handley and Al Rubeling. Al Lopez and Virgil Davis are expected to be back as catchers, and a string of eleven pitchers includes Truett (Rip) Sewell, Max Butcher, Fred Ostermueller, Xavier Rescigno, Elwin (Preacher) Roe, Ray Starr and Nick Strincevich.

HERSHEY BEARS TOP FLYERS 3-2

Hershey, Pa., March 3—(AP)—The Hershey Bears moved closer to the playoffs in the American Hockey League by defeating the St. Louis Flyers, 3 to 2, here tonight, before 6,400 fans.

The Flyers, tail enders in the western half of the league, held two consecutive wins over the Bears on home ice.

Mike Shabaga and Hal Cooper annexed a pair of goals in the opener but with Art Strobel in the cooler, the Flyers moved up a point on George Blake's goal just before the bell. In the second period, the Bears widened the breach when Hy Buller rifled a 65-foot shot into the net from near the blue line.

The third period was scoreless until 18:30 when the Flyers scored as Jimmy Russell deflected a hard hit pass and the puck zipped into the net. In the last 30 seconds of play the Flyers unleashed a drive that threatened to tie the count. The bell saved the Bears.

Hershey	Pos.	St. Louis
Damore	E.	Highton
Johnson	R. D.	Lynn
Buller	L. D.	Holouka
Ritson	C.	Hergert
Cooper	R. W.	Kendall
Webster	L. W.	Evanshen

Referee—Rabbit McVeigh. Linesman—James Reynolds.

Hershey spares—Gooden, Shabaga, Strobel, Cooper, Scherza, Robertson, Drummond, Calladine, O'Neil, Maher.

St. Louis spares—Nakina, Smith, Blake, Carl Smith, Rimstad, MacIntosh, Russell, Giroux.

First period scoring: 1—Hershey, Shabaga (Drummond and Gooden) 5.26; 2—Hershey, Cooper (unassisted) 10.46; 3—St. Louis, Blake (Herbert and Giroux) 18.22. Penalties—O'Neill, Strobel, Blake.

Second period scoring: 4—Hershey, Buller (Ritson and Cooper) 9.23. Penalties—Hergert, Nakina, Smith, Buller, Scherza.

Third period scoring: 5—St. Louis, Russell (Nakina, Smith and Carl Smith) 18.30. Penalties—None.

Saves: Damore 28; Highton 25.

Little Gets New Post At Overlook

Bill Little, former manager of the I.O.O.F. alleys and Bowl-O-Drome, has been named manager of Sam Snader's bowling lanes at the Overlook Golf Club. He will start his new duties Monday.

BASKETBALL SCORES

Albright 61, Gettysburg 41.
W. Va. 66, Carnegie Tech 35.
Oklahoma U. 52, LaSalle 38.
St. John's 51, Ellis ICG 46.
American U. 70, Johns Hopkins 36.
Iowa 43, Illinois 37.
Minnesota 54, Wisconsin 50.
Temple 72, St. Joseph's 47.

NATIONAL HOCKEY

Toronto [illegible], Montreal 2.

AMERICAN HOCKEY

Buffalo 3, Pittsburgh 3 (tie).

Giants Sign Three Rookie Pitchers

New York, March 3 —(AP)— President Horace Stoneham of the New York Giants today announced receipt of signed contracts from three rookie righthanded pitchers. They were Ray Harrell, William Emmerich and Loren Bain.

Harrell won 20 and lost 18 for the San Francisco Seals of the Pacific Coast League last year and was purchased for cash, pitcher Ken Miller and the optioned contract of pitcher Ken Brondell.

Emmerich was selected from Rochester of the International League in the December draft. He won 12 and lost 13 for the Carjinal farm and was recommended by scout Hank De Berry who also advised purchase from Minneapolis of Bain. The latter compiled an 11-17 record for the American Association team.

BUCKEYES IN 3RD WIN

Columbus, O., March 3 — (AP) — Ohio States swimming team won its third victory today with a 60-24 job on Michigan State.

The Bucks won eight of the nine events, with the visitors registering only when Mueller won the 100-yard freestyle in 58.2.

Buch Scores 24 Pts. But E-Town College Bows To Wagner '5'

Guy Buch, Elizabethtown College's wonder man, racked up 24 more points to his total last night but his efforts were to no avail as the countians dropped a 74-47 decision to Wagner on the E-Town court last night. The visitors were leading 34-25 at halftime.

In a preliminary game, the E-Town girls defeated the Bridgewater girls, 21-17.

E-town		G	Fl	Tl	Wagner		G	Fl	Tl
Buch	F	8	8	24	Snee	F	9	4	22
Hershey	F	5	2	12	Brown	F	6	4	16
Myers	F	0	0	0	Franzen	C	2	0	4
Whitacre	C	4	3	11	Sackel	G	7	0	14
Bucher	G	0	0	0	Thomp'n	G	1	0	2
Lefever	G	0	0	0	Blonquist	G	6	2	14
					DeGroat	G	1	0	2
Totals		17	13	47	Totals		32	10	74

ILLINI HARRIERS SCORE

Champaign, Ill., March 3 — (AP) — Illinois' well balanced track team established itself as the team to beat in the Big Ten track meet at Chicago next Saturday when it defeated Michigan's defending championship squad, 58 to 46, in a dual meet here today.

E-Town Cager One of Year's Bright Stars

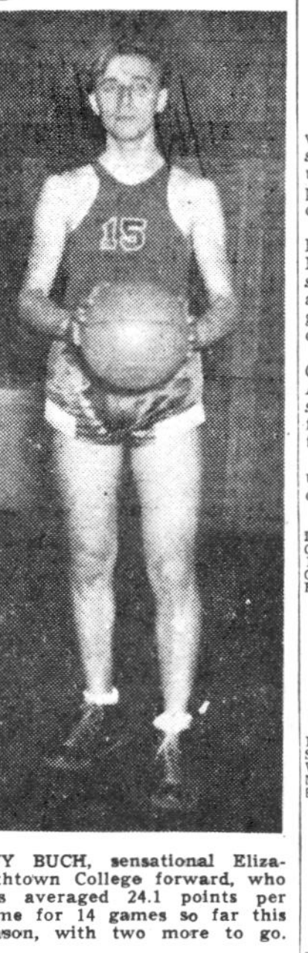

GUY BUCH, sensational Elizabethtown College forward, who has averaged 24.1 points per game for 14 games so far this season, with two more to go.

One of the unsung heroes of the rapidly closing basketball season, who has been pretty sensational in rolling up one of the finest individual records of the 1944-'45 campaign, is Guy Buch, forward on the Elizabethtown College team.

With the spotlight centered on most of the Metropolitan teams and players and the so-called contenders for national honors, the Elizabethtown star has been largely overlooked by the experts, and outside of Lancaster County is, in all likelihood, little known.

But the nineteen year old youngster, who stands 6 feet, and tips the beams at 160 pounds has compiled a record that will stand comparison with any other individual record in the nation this winter.

In fourteen games this year Buch has scored 338 points, with two games to go yet against Haverford and Wagner. His average score per game is 24.1 points.

Against Haverford earlier this season, he scored 38 points.

He had his biggest night against Susquehanna at Elizabethtown when he racked up a total 42 points, ringing 14 goals from the field, and 14 from the foul line. He was fouled 21 times in that game.

Against Albright, the team that licked both F & M and Muhlenberg, the rangy youngster scored 61 points, in two games, and it was reported that Albright had two men "on him" all the time.

Buch, who plans to enter the Bethany Bible School in Chicago next Fall, has preached at Elizabethtown and Pine Grove, his birthplace, during his college days at E-town College.

This his third and last year at Elizabethtown. His present home is at Fredericksburg, Pa.

He graduated from Pine Grove High School, and played two years of varsity basketball there.

According to his mentor Ira Herr, he is one of the finest all-around players he has ever seen.

He's a one-handed shooter, and equally accurate with either hand. He is very deceptive, and in addition to being a good dribbler, has an excellent change of pace. In addition to all of this he is a fine defensive player.

High scoring is not new to him, except that he has gotten better every year. Here's his three year record of total points scored:

1942-'43—16 games ...... 196 points
1943-'44—13 games ...... 218 points
1944-'45—14 games ...... 338 points
(2 games to go)

Unfortunately E-town College has not been able to cash in on Buch's great scoring power, and has won only 2 out of 14 games. But this makes Buch's individual performance all the more remarkable.

BROAD ST. AND CHRIST WINNERS

Playoff Standings

	W.	L.	P. C.
Broad St.	1	0	1.000
Church of Christ	1	0	1.000
Memorial	0	1	.000
St. Andrews	0	1	.000

Broad St. and Church of Christ, who finished first and second, respectively, in the regular schedule, opened the Church League playoffs with victories on the "Y" court last night.

Broad St., with Elwood Shreiner leading the way, turned back Memorial 56-36 in a game which saw a closely fought first period, after which the eventual winners gradually pulled away from their opponents.

Kenny Depoe led the Church of Christ boys as they defeated St. Andrews 45 to 27. He dropped six field goals and nine out of 11 foul tries to add 21 points to his teammates' total.

Next week, the same teams stack up against each other in the second of their three-game series.

Memorial		G	Fl	Tl	Broad St.		G	Fl	Tl
Leese	F	0	1	1	E.Shr'ner	F	9	4	22
Glossm'r	F	4	0	8	Hurst	F	5	3	13
Rineer	C	7	2	16	Brown	F	0	0	0
Coolidge	G	3	0	6	McCue	C	1	0	2
Bruba'r	G	2	1	5	Cameron	G	3	0	6
					Pollock	G	2	2	6
Totals		16	4	36	P.Shr'ner	G	2	3	7
					Totals		22	12	56

Score by periods:

BROAD ST.	12	13	13	18—56
MEMORIAL	11	3	9	13—36

Referee, Pew and Butz.

Church of Christ		G	Fl	Tl	St. Andrew's		G	Fl	Tl
Depoe	F	6	9	21	Kline	F	4	2	10
Snyder	F	4	2	10	R.Diller	F	4	0	8
Weber	C	4	2	10	Sheckard	C	4	0	8
Miller	G	0	0	0	Geist	G	0	0	0
Ruof	G	2	0	4	Gibble	G	0	0	0
					Rich'son	G	0	0	0
Totals		16	13	45	A.Diller	G	0	1	1
					Totals		12	3	27

CHURCH OF CHRIST	9	23	10	3—45
ST. ANDREW'S	5	12	6	4—27

Referees, Pew and Butz.

SET 2 NEW MARKS

Philadelphia, March 3—(AP)—Two National Intercollegiate swimming records were set as Temple University's girls team defeated Penn Hall 33-29 today in a dual meet.

Leola Thomas of Washington, D. C., covered the 50 yard backstroke distance in 32 6/10 seconds and Peggy Pate of Goldsborough, N. C., cut through the water in 35 5/10 seconds in the 50 yard breast stroke event, to establish the new marks. Both are from Penn Hall.

BOB FELLER AT CLINIC

Rochester, Minn., March 3—(INS)—Bob Feller, star pitcher of the Cleveland Indians, was in Rochester tonight undergoing a physical checkup at the Mayo Clinic.

Feller, now a Navy specialist, has been overseas for several months. He and his wife expect to remain in Rochester for the next five or six days.

Sees and Hears Same Fight

By CHIP ROYAL
(AP Newsfeatures Sports Editor)

New York, March 3—(AP)—There are fights that make us happy, and there are fights that make us sad. But the best way to be pleased by the ring battlers is to do what your agent did the other night.

I sat in a ringside seat and watched featherweight champion Willie Pep defend his crown against Phil Terranova and I listened to it the same time!

Besides being a lot of fun, the evening proved several points which have been bothering all of us.

After every main bout at Madison Square Garden, either the wife, or some friend will say:

"What did you think of the fight? I thought so and so won, the way it came over the radio."

OR

"I never hear the same fight I read about the next day. Why don't you reporters and radio announcers get together!"

Well, we got that way, and here's what happened.

The first preliminary started about 8:30 p. m. The radio men didn't start drifting in until 9:30. Besides Don Dunphy, the actual fight describer, there were Bill Corum, between-the-rounds color man, two engineers, a production man for the advertising agency, and another one for the network.

Besides those six, there were representatives of the sponsor, the network, and the men working on the program, in back of yours truly, and around the ringside.

That ain't all. There are two engineers and two announcers at the studio tied up by the broadcast.

As soon as the radio boys set-tled in their seats they started to worry. Four bouts had ended in early konckouts and the air time was set at 10 p. m.

A hurry call to promoter Mike Jacobs brought the information he would put on a four-round emergency. That helped a lot.

It was just about 10 p. m. when Corum went on the air with the introductions, etc.

Then, after the father of the boxing law, former Mayor Jimmy Walker, paid his fine tribute to Hype Igoe, the dean of the Broadway boxing writers who had died a week before, another hitch developed.

Pep came into the ring without **a mouthpiece. That left Corum** holding the mike—and how he held it.

Bill's really a master at the color business. Besides holding the interest of any listener with his word picture of what was going on, he gave the background of the two fighters and everything else leading up to the action.

Then came the gong and the first round.

The eyes watched and the ears

WELL, WOTTA YA KNOW- THIS IS THE SAME FIGHT I'M HEARING !!

listened. Back in our crop one of those little devils seemed to be saying: "Show me, Dunphy!"

Well, shout the words far and wide. Don dood it!

The kid (he seems like that although he's been broadcasting sports events for 15 years) gave a fight description worthy of a stenographic machine.

Sometimes the punches fly faster than Dunphy's voice and Corum's eyebrows. But Don gets them all in. Sure, he calls one or two wrong. Who wouldn't? The important part of the broadcast is that he makes the fight interesting.

Pep held, wrestled and jabbed when he wasn't dancing around the ring. Terranova missed a lot. Both boys cut each other up a bit.

Once they started a conversation. It could have been about anything. Dunphy told the radio audience about it. The moment the boys increased the tempo of their blows you could hear it in Don's voice.

Between rounds, Corum brought the listener up to date on any of the points Don missed. Sitting there, watching everything going on, this agent couldn't help but admire the excellent reporting.

The crowd mikes don't pick up the feelings of the mob as well as they do on football and baseball fields. The background was full of groans instead of words or cheers. But who cares about that.

There's only one complaint. The earphones, after 15 fast rounds, made the Royal head ache.

ANOTHER CHANCE?—Lou Novikoff, above, the famed "Mad Russian" of baseball whose contract troubles with the Chicago Cubs are almost legendary, has refused to sign with the Los Angeles Pacific Coast league club for the time being. Lou says he's pretty sure one or more major league clubs would like to have him on their rosters next season. Could be. (International)

Braves' New Boss Grew Up In Ballpark

Young John Quinn Followed Dad's Trail From St. Louis To Boston

BOSTON, Mar. 3— (AP) —If good wishes mean anything, John Quinn, the majors' youngest general manager, soon should have the pennant whipping atop the flagstaff at Braves Field.

Not a dissenting remark could be heard concerning the appointment of 36-year-old John to replace his father, genial Bob Quinn, as general manager of the Boston National League baseball club.

Bob stepped down as president and general manager on St. Valentine's day, his 75th birthday, to supervise and expand the Tribe's minor league holdings.

Son John cut his eye teeth on baseball and if ever an American kid lived and breathed the game, he did.

Born In Columbus

A quiet, self effacing young man, young Quinn was born in Columbus, Ohio, April 1, 1908, and his favorite team during his youngest years was his father's Columbus Red Birds.

The family moved to St. Louis in 1917 where Bob was an executive with the Browns. In addition to sitting in with his father learning the business end of baseball, John, with his brother, often sat on the players' bench.

John's particular pal then was Wally Gerber and he still can tell incidents of that master workman, George Sisler, or pitcher Urban Shocker and of the great outfield the Browns had in those days, Johnny Tobin, Baby Doll Jacobson and Dib Williams.

John and his brother, Robert, now a Dominican priest in charge of athletics at Providence College, were among the best umpire jockeys on the bench.

"They were pretty good at it, too," says their father.

John Quinn, 36, sits with his dad, Bob Quinn, 75, to get some inside baseball dope—and fatherly advice—on how to run the Boston Braves' front office.

The family came to Boston in 1923 when the elder Quinn headed the Red Sox. John, who was graduated in 1929 from Boston College, played freshman baseball and was a trackman in his freshman year.

He wanted to play pro ball but father said no, explaining that John "could run, field and throw but couldn't hit."

John, after working for an insurance firm, joined the Red Sox office force as a ticket seller and junior secretary in 1929, becoming secretary under Tom Yawkey in 1933 when father Bob moved to Brooklyn.

When the senior Quinn returned to Boston to head the Braves, John became secretary of the club.

Meantime John married a Newton girl in 1934 and now is father of five children, Joan, 10, Bob, 8, Jack, 7, Margaret, 4, and Susan 2. And if the boys want to be ball players it's OK with John.

Headed Farm System

Three years after his marriage, John was appointed president of the Braves' farm system which included Hartford, Evansville, Bridgeport, York, Erie, Beaver Falls, Zanesville and Bradford.

In 1943, when the present owners of the Braves took over, Bob remained as president and general manager and John became assistant treasurer.

Said John, "every advancement has been a thrill and this one is the biggest."

Few men in baseball are as well liked or as well trained as young Quinn.

He has done about every kind of job in a baseball office, including checking turnstiles and payrolls and counting tickets.

"LITTLE MEN" PACE DURHAM GOLF PLAY

Penna, Dodson Tied With 139's; Nelson Only A Stroke Away

DURHAM, N. C., March 31—(AP)—The "little men" of golf showed no inclination to give up today in the second round of the Durham Open, Toney Penna and Leonard Dodson deadlocking for the lead at the halfway mark of the 72-hole meet.

Penna, the smallest of the pros, added a 71 to his opening 68 and the slender Dodson pulled up even with the Dayton, O., wisecracker with 69-70—139.

NEW WELTER STAR—Presenting Jimmy Doyle, the California welterweight who has compiled a fancy record. Doyle, winner of nine bouts in the east after leaving his native Los Angeles, gets a hard test in his next bout when he meets the rising young Clevelander, Chuck Hunter, at the Cleveland Arena, Wednesday, April 4. Doyle has won 35 of 36 bouts.

Hard on the heels of the two little men, who haven't won a tournament in five years, came the hottest man in the game — Lord Byron Nelson.

Nelson scored a 69, the only subpar round of the day, for a 36-hole total of 140. Another shot back was Sammy Byrd of Detroit, the former ballplayer, with a 70-71—141.

Jim Gauntt, of Ardmore, Okla., had an even-par 70 to move into fifth place at 142, a stroke ahead of defending champion Craig Wood and Harold (Jug) McSpaden, one of the pre-tournament favorites. Wood had a 73 today, McSpaden a 72.

Sam Snead, winner of six Winter meets, practically blew himself out of consideration with a 74 for 145, needing 40 strokes on the out nine. PGA champion Bob Hamilton reversed the procedure by taking a 40 on the back nine for a 74 and a 147 total.

The field was reduced to the low 40 and ties for tomorrow's 36-hole windup for $6,666 in war bonds.

The leaders:
(x-Denotes amateur).

Toney Penna, Dayton, O.	68-71—139
Leonard Dodson, San Francisco	69-70—139
Byron Nelson, Toledo, O.	71-69—140
Sam Byrd, Detroit	70-71—141
Jim Gauntt, Ardmore, Okla.	72-70—142
Harold McSpaden, Sanford, Me.	71-72—143
Craig Wood, Mamaroneck, N. Y.	70-73—143
Gene Kunes, Hollywood, Fla.	70-74—144
Sam Snead, Hot Springs, Va.	71-74—145
Joe Zarhardt, Norristown, Pa.	71-74—145
Bobby Cruickshank, Richmond, Va.	70-75—145
x-Ed Furgol, Utica, N. Y.	71-74—145
Jimmy Hines, Chicago	73-73—146
Bob Hamilton, Chicago	73-74—147
Ky Laffoon, Chicago	72-75—147
Mike Turnesa, Elmsford, N. Y.	71-76—147
x-Wes Ferrell, Greensboro, N. C.	75-72—147
Purvis Feree, Winston-Salem, N. C.	72-75—147
George McCallister, Dayton, O.	76-73—149

M'Caskey High's Champion Wrestlers

An enviable record, including the District 3 PIAA championship, was compiled during the 1945 season by Coach H. Grant Hurst's McCaskey High School wrestling team. The boys were undefeated in team competition, winning ten meets. Pictured above they are: (back row), Frank Groff, George Glick, George Xakellis, Eugene Miller, Jack Charles, Arthur Husson, Herbert Schmid, Richard Miller, assistant manager; (middle row), Coach Hurst, Mervin Hemperly, James Case, Richard White, James Ferich, David Wiley, Harry Coyle, Charles Ambrose, Kent Bowron, Lloyd Webb, John Smucker, manager, and William Ambrose; (front row), Assistant Coach George Hershey, Wilbur Kraybill, Edward Wenger, Edward Clarke, Co-captains Henry Shaub and Walter O'Connor, Robert Miller, Stanley Shear, LeRoy Duke and Richard Clarke.

Horse Racing Ban Will Be Lifted V-E Day, Byrnes Says

WASHINGTON, March 31—Racing people tonight formally received from Jimmy Byrnes the word they have been awaiting for weeks—that the ban on their sport will be lifted V-E day.

While this announcement lacked an exact date, it nevertheless was accepted as being specific enough for racing to "get set" for the 1945 season.

In a report on war progress to the President and Congress, War Mobilizer Byrnes said, in part:

"Lagging production has made it necessary for various conservation measures to be placed into effect to include a reduction in travel, the suspension of racing, a reduction in the use of electricity in night lighting, and the closing of places of entertainment at midnight.

"These measures are of an emergency nature, and, with the exception of the travel measure, should be withdrawn on V-E Day."

In making this announcement, Byrnes praised racing people for their cooperation during the shutdown since January 3, 1945, and told reporters "they were just what you'd expect them to be . . Good sports."

In recent weeks, many a letter writer and many a caller at Byrnes' door or on his telephone has urged modification of the ban, but owners of tracks and horsemen were "with him," despite financial losses, and felt his decision was right, Byrnes said at a news conference.

Byrnes mentioned that thousands of miles (19,000) of telegraph wire, telephone facilities and manpower have been made available to the general public and war effort during the racing ban.

Harry Parr, 3rd, of Baltimore, president of the Thoroughbred Racing Association, and spokesman for most of the major tracks, said of Byrnes' announcement:

"That's swell. Now we can begin preparation. We'll still have a few problems, including transportation, but we can straighten most of those out and be ready to operate on about a 90 per cent basis 30 days after Germany falls."

Parr added that "chances are bright," with war progress so rapid, for running the Kentucky Derby, first Saturday in May, and the Preakness, following week, "Almost on schedule."

While racing may have to resume without being "tip-top," the sport will "not be seriously affected" by the shutdown since January, Parr said.

Lifting the ban apparently will come a little too late to accomodate some of the early eastern meets, such as Bowie, Md., which traditionally opens early in April.

Parr indicated that it will be up to racing officials to determne whether the season-long-program can be so rearranged as to make room for such meets.

Col. Winn Comments

In Chicago, Col. Matt Winn, president of the Churchill Downs, Ky., race track, said:

"I know racing enthusiasts will be happy and grateful for the good news. We at Churchill Downs believe that our track can be put in operation within six weeks after Mr. Byrnes gives the go-sign. Let's work together for speedy victory in Europe."

Benjamin F. Lindheimer, executive director of Washington Park and Arlington Park race tracks near Chicago, said his racing organizations "will be ready to go ahead with our plans to give the public the high class of racing which has become traditional at both tracks."

NOVA SUFFERS GASH

New York, March 31—(AP)—James J. Johnston, manager of Lou Nova, said today that seven stitches were required to close the gash the California heavyweight received above his right eye last night while losing a 10-round decision to Joe Baksi, Kulpmont, Pa., miner.

PHILS GET HIM — Whitlow Wyatt, former star pitcher of the Brooklyn Dodgers, has been traded to the Phils. Wyatt, bothered by a sore arm, won only two games against six losses last year.

ODDS FAVOR BOTH ST. LOUIS CLUBS

St. Louis, March 31—(AP)—Both St. Louis major league baseball clubs were named to repeat their championship showings in the 1945 American and National League pennant races in pre-season odds released today by James J. Carroll, betting commissioner.

The Browns were listed as 8 to 5 favorites (wager $5 to win $8) and the Cardinals odds-on at 4-5 (wager $5 to $4).

Some shifting of clubs compared with last season's final standings is indicated by the odds. The Philadelphia Athletics of the American League are advanced two notches from sixth to fourth place and the Boston Red Sox are dropped two positions.

In the National League the odds boost the New York Giants into fourth place and drop the Cubs into the second division.

The quotations:

American League — Browns 8-5, Detroit 2-1, New York 4-1, Philadelphia 5-1, Cleveland 10-1, Boston 15-1, Washington 25-1, Chicago 25-1.

National League—Cardinals 4-5, Pittsburgh 3-1, Cincinnati 4-1, New York 10-1, Chicago 10-1, Boston 25-1, Brooklyn 25-1, Philadelphia 25-1.

Jeff Heath Signs Cleveland Contract

Cleveland, O., March 31—(INS)—Jeff Heath, husky Cleveland Indian outfielder, has ended his perennial holdout and agreed to terms. Vice-President Roger Peckinpaugh of the Tribe announced tonight. Peckinpaugh said that Heath would report at the Indians' Lafayette, Indiana training camp next week.

Yankees Nose Out Red Sox, 15 To 14

Atlantic City, N. J., March 31—(INS)—The New York Yankees today staged a ninth inning, five-run uprising to take a raggedly played exhibition game with the Boston Red Sox, 15 to 14.

Joe Buzas, rookie shortstop, climaxed the rally with one out by slamming a triple to left center to drive home the tying and winning runs.

Buzas was charged with one of the nine errors contributed by the two teams, but offset this miscue by starting four double plays.

Each side received 10 bases on balls from an assortment of pitchers. The Yanks made 15 hits and five errors and the Sox 14 hits and four errors.

New York (A) 020 143 005—15 15 5
Boston (A) .. 023 231 201—14 14 4

Page, Turner (4), Moore (7); and Crompton; Johnson, Woods (4), Dreisewerd (7) and Walters.

PHILLIES BUSY

Wilmington, Del., March 31—(AP)—The Jays pounced on Dick Barrett for four runs in the third inning to defeat the Blues in a seven-inning intra-camp game today at the Philadelphia Phillies camp.

'Czar' Group Ready To Make Report

Chicago, March 31—(INS)—The four-man committee appointed by the major leagues to recommend a new high commissioner of baseball announced today that it is ready to report to club owners of the National and American Leagues.

A spokesman for the committee, meeting in Chicago, said "It is obvious that there can be no enlargement on this statement at this time."

Appointed by Will Harridge, president of the American League, and president Ford Frick of the National, the committee members are Don Barnes of the St. Louis Browns, Alva Bradley of the Cleveland Indians, P. K. Wrigley, Chicago Cubs, and Sam Breadon of the St. Louis Cardinals.

Numerous candidates, including Gen. Douglas MacArthur and Bobby Jones of golfing fame, have been suggested as a successor to the late Judge Kenesaw Mountain Landis.

The club owners will vote on the committee's recommendation either by telegraph or at a special meeting. The decision, apparently, will be made by Harridge and Frick.

DUROCHER WILL OPEN AT SECOND

Bear Mountain, N. Y., March 31—(INS)—"I'll definitely start the season at second base," Manager Leo Durocher of the Brooklyn Dodgers announced today.

Durocher said he planned to stay in the lineup until such time as Eddy Stanky is ready to take over. The latter only recently recovered from a serious illness and will not arrive in camp until the latter part of next week.

"It will take Stanky awhile to get in shape," Durocher said, "and I'll try to fill in until he is ready. However I won't stay in the lineup if I am hurting the club."

A Dodger-Army game scheduled at West Point was rained out today, but the Dodgers managed to get in a brisk batting and fielding drill.

Big Mort Cooper Getting Into Shape

St. Louis, March 31—(AP)—Pitcher Mort Cooper, winner of 65 games for the St. Louis Cardinals in the last three seasons, is rounding into form early and today pitched six innings of an intra-squad game which the regulars won 8 to 1.

The regulars played the infield manager Billy Southworth probably will use to open the season—Ray Sanders at first; Emil Verban, second; Whitey Kurowski, third, and Red Schoendienst, shortstop. Marty Marion still is a holdout. In the outfield were Augie Bergamo, right, Jim Mallory, center, and Dave Bartosch, left.

NAVY NINE AHEAD

Annapolis, Md., March 31—(AP)—The Naval Academy baseball team in its first game of the season won a 14-13 victory in 11 innings over North Carolina Pre-Flight today.

Pirates Swap Vince Di Maggio To Phils

Pittsburgh, March 31—(INS)—Outfielder Vince DiMaggio, in the Pittsburgh Pirate doghouse since the middle of last baseball season, has been traded to the Philadelphia Phillies for Pitcher Al Gerhauser.

Announcement of the transaction was made today by William E. Benswanger, Pirate president, who said the players were swapped yesterday by long distance phone.

Benswanger added that he had sent his "best regards" to the Californian—a brother of Joe and Dom DiMaggio—who had asked to be traded.

DiMaggio was used infrequently last season after a dispute with club officials over meal-tickets.

He reportedly had been disgruntled for some time, but had been regarded as a Pirate regular since he came to the club from Cincinnati in a trade for Johnny Rizzo in 1940. He led the National League in strikeouts during the last three seasons.

Gerhauser, a southpaw, had been with the Phillies for two seasons and last year won eight games 16 defeats.

PENNOCK HAILS TRADE

Wilmington, Del., March 31—(AP)—General Manager Herb Pennock of the Philadelphia Phillies, hailing the trade of hurler Al Gerheauser to the Pittsburgh Pirates for outfielder Vince Di Maggio, said today:

"I think Vince will hit a lot of home runs over that left field fence at Shibe Park."

Pennock—one of the busiest traders and purchasers during the spring training program—added Di Maggio to the Phils' weak outfield, yielding a pitcher from the Blue Jays' potentially powerful mound corps.

With Buster Adams and Coaker Triplett, veteran outfielders, still on the holdout list, Manager Fred Fitzsimmons said today he will use rookies Nick Goulish and Vance Dinges and Cuban Rene Monteagudo in the outfield when the Phils engage Bainbridge (Md.) Naval Training Station Monday.

VINCE DIMAGGIO

Nick Etten Signs With Yankee Nine

Atlantic City, N. J., March 31—(AP)—Nick Etten, New York Yankees' first baseman and leading home run hitter of the American League in 1944, signed his contract today, after a conference with president Larry MacPhail.

The salary, while undisclosed, was believed to be around $16,000. Etten, however, will be available for pinch hitting duties only, in the exhibition games tomorrow and Monday against the Giants, as he will need more conditioning. In the meanwhile, Oscar Grimes will be at first.

Etten's signing leaves shortstop Frank Crosetti and pitcher Ernie Bonham as the only important holdouts.

BRITISH RACING OPENS MONDAY

London, March 31—(AP)—England's horse racing season opens an eight-month stand at two historic tracks Monday and a record war time crowd of 100,000 followers in gala Easter holiday mood, stimulated by the apparent nearness of V-E Day, will bet an estimated $5,000,000.

Approximately 60,000 British bang-tail bettors will go to the Royal Ascot Park, 20 miles from London, even if they must stand in line four hours for the chance of buying a railroad ticket. Others will go by horse and buggy or on bicycle.

Ten races, twice as many as normal, are booked for the program that starts at noon.

Some 40,000 spectators, mostly war-workers, are expected at Pontefract in northern England for the inaugural that features the transplanted Lincolnshire Handicap.

The Jockey Club has arranged fixtures through June although the war economy still restricts programs to Saturdays with the exception of midweek meetings at Newmarket. But if the European war ends, racing is geared for an all-out schedule until November.

The Derby, England's premier event which in peace time always is run at Epsom Downs, will continue in its war time setting at Newmarket, even if V-E Day comes before the race's scheduled date of June 9.

See Boom Season

Track fans look for a boom season, noting there is a great demand for horses. Prices paid at the Blodstock sales last December were the second highest in British history and more thoroughbreds are expected to run this season than any year since the banner 1938 campaign when 5,143 were in training. Only 1,626 raced last year.

Prize money also is expected to soar after being cut from $2,927,304 in 1938 to $835,224 in 1944.

"People have more money to spend and less to spend it for—just like in the United States—so betting should set a record," said one track follower.

Admirals And Athletes

Halsey—Hard-Hitting Fullback

By FRANK ECK
(AP Newsfeatures Sports Writer)

Annapolis, Md.—"If he hits the Japs as hard as he used to hit in football—God help the Japs," said a former football coach of Adm. William Frederick Halsey. This terse sentence tells more than anything that Halsey knew his way around the gridiron.

'Pudge," as he was called during his days as a Midshipman at the U. S. Naval Academy, played fullback in the eighth and ninth Army-Navy games, 1902-03. He was one of 14 middies to win an "N" in his final season.

Brief Account

A brief account of the 1902 Army-Navy game can be found in the 1903 Lucky Bag, Navy classbook. It says:

"Halsey played well. He made a first down through left tackle. Later, with Army in possession, Halsey tackled H. B. Hackett, causing him to drop the ball which Halsey recovered."

A tackle and recovery by the tackler! a great play, even four decades later with streamlined and well-padded moleskins.

Halsey's play paved the way for a Navy touchdown, but the Middies bowed to Army, 22-8.

Halsey was active in founding Navy's athletic program and in 1904 he won the Robert M. Thompson trophy for promotion of athletics at the Naval Academy.

Liked Boxing

Had there been Navy boxing in those days, Halsey undoubtedly would have been out for the team, for he liked the sport. While wearing the three wide gold stripes of a captain he was Navy's officer representative for boxing from 1928 through 1930.

Halsey commander of the U. S. 3d Fleet, will be 63 on Oct. 30. Born in Elizabeth, N. J., he grew up in the Navy, attending Annapolis while his dad served as a lieutenant commander and later as full commander.

"Pudge" made his first Midshipmen's summer cruise in 1899 aboard the Monongahela. His father was executive officer and second in command. When his father was head of the Seamanship Department at Annapolis, young Bill was president of Navy's Auxiliary Athletic Association.

Adm. Halsey is shown as officer representative of the 1930 Navy boxing team, his third and last year in that capacity. First row, l to r: Bryan F. Swan, F. L. Wallace and Halsey, then captain. Second row: E. S. Cooke, A. E. Gates, Jr., and F. J Foley. Gates was killed at Pearl Harbor, Wallace lost his life in an air accident before the war, Foley is a commander and Swan has been retired from the Navy.

Commanded Destroyers

In World War I, Halsey commanded two destroyers—Shaw and Benham—winning the Navy cross for patrol and convoy duties. He once had command of the carrier Saratoga and later trained air squadrons for the carriers Yorktown and Enterprise. And he didn't learn to fly until he was 52.

Nine days before Pearl Harbor he sensed imminent danger. Taking a task force out of Honolulu he said:

"Shoot any Jap plane or ship on sight."

His victory in the Solomons, when you count ships sunk and casualties inflicted, is regarded as greater than Jutland.

At Guadalcanal he had the Japanese fleet crazy. Steaming through a Nipponese armada he so confused the enemy that the Japanese fired on each other, sinking several of their own ships. President Roosevelt made him a full admiral for his strategy.

"A real old salt," said Lucky Bag forty years earlier.

NEXT: Adm. Jonas H. Ingram.

Dodgers' Contest Is Washed Out

Bear Mountain, N. Y., March 31—(AP)—Brooklyn's scheduled exhibition game with the U. S. Military Academy was washed out today and so the Dodgers spent three hours in the Cadet fieldhouse polishing their hitting. Montreal will be met here tomorrow and the Dodgers will journey to West Point Monday for their postponed contest.

216 Kept Eligible For Reading Test

Reading, Pa., March 31—Two hundred and sixteen of the original 410 nominations of the foals of 1943 have been kept eligible in the Reading Fair Futurity as two-year-olds to be raced as a special feature of the Grand Circuit harness racing at Trenton, N. J., Sept. 10-13, secretary, Charles W. Swoyer, of the Reading Fair Futurities announced today.

These two-and-three-year-old classics will be raced over the Trenton mile track, due to the Reading Fair ground being occupied by the United States Army.

William E. Miller, Washington, D. C., tops the list with eight eligible colts, Cotave Blake, Newport Stock Farm, South Plainfield, N. J., and Fred Egan's Stable, Longwood, Florida, have seven.

American League Has Own Mad Russian

Metro, Athletics' New Slugger, Helped Browns When He Made Stephens A 4F

By FRANK ECK
(AP Newsfeatures Sports Writer)

Frederick, Md. — The Chicago Cubs of the National League or the Los Angeles Angels of the Pacific Coast League, or whatever club lays claim to Lou Novikoff's contract, can have the Mad Russian. The American League has its own Mad Russian.

He is Charlie Metro (Moreskonich) of Nanty-Glo, Pa., and Mayfield, Ky.

When you speak of the St. Louis Browns having won the 1944 American League pennant, give a little credit to Metro.

Break For The Browns

Without Shortstop Vernon Stephens there's no telling where the Browns would have finished. Stephens is 4F because of Metro.

Metro and Stephens were roommates when they played for Mayfield in the Kitty League in 1939. They got $75 a month and loved it. One day after a game at Hopkinsville, Ky., Metro and Stephens were in a playful mood. They agreed to an impromptu wrestling match.

Metro got a leg hold and when he let go Stephens' leg swelled up like a balloon. Stephens was rushed to the hospital. He was forced to wear a special brace. Metro had torn just about every cartilage in the knee.

That's why Vernon Stephens is 4F.

But today everything with Metro is on the serious side as he continues to make rapid strides to win over the left field post with the Philadelphia Athletics.

"This is the chance I've been waiting for," says Metro. "I'm going to make good because I feel like Al Simmons always felt: 'That I'm one of the best outfielders in baseball.' I've talked that angle into my head so that nothing can change my mind."

CHARLIE METRO
(Might Make Detroit Sorry)

That's exactly the way Charlie spoke a few hours before the opening exhibition game against the Curtis Bay Coast Guard. He promptly drove out a long hit to start a perfect five-for-five afternoon. He belted a triple, two doubles and two singles in accounting for six runs.

He is the A's left fielder after that exhibition of power hitting. Bobby Estalella, who hit .298 last year, will be in center, with eight-toed Hal Peck in right. Peck is the pull hitter who slugged so well for Milwaukee last season.

In 1936 Metro paid his own fare to New York and attended a Brooklyn tryout class. Failing to catch on, he says "I then chased Scout Paul Krichell of the Yankees all over town only to learn that no tryouts were being held."

After 125 games with Mayfield in 1939 he played at Palestine and Texarkana in the Cotton States League. In 1941 he hit .317 for the latter, received $125 a month and finished with Beaumont in the Texas League. He remained there through 1942.

His first major league trial came last spring with the Detroit Tigers. He batted only .200 in 44 games and General Manager Jack Zeller sought to ship him off to Indianapolis. Metro balked.

"What do you want then, your unconditional release?" asked Zeller.

Metro replied in the affirmative and the office girl handed Charlie the pink slip.

"Then I contacted several clubs and the Athletics signed me as a free agent. I got $8,000 for signing, and the Athletics have been treating me swell ever since," says Metro.

The 186-pounder, who lacks one-half inch of six feet, well remembers his first game with the A's.

"The Athletics were playing Detroit in Philadelphia and Doc Cramer was at bat," says Metro. "I played with Doc for almost two years with the Tigers and knew just where he'd be most likely to hit the ball.

"I moved over toward the left field foul line. Connie Mack, sitting on the bench, waved his scorecard at me. I followed instructions and moved a few steps toward center. Mr. Mack kept waving his scorecard. I thought he was all wrong, yet I moved to the exact spot.

"Well, Cramer hit a line drive right into my hands.

"You know, I think Mr. Mack is the best outfielder in both leagues."

THUMBNAIL PREVIEW

PHILADELPHIA ATHLETICS
Pitching—Good
Catching—Good
Infield—Fair
Outfield—Promising
Hitting—Lacking
Finish—1-2-3

Metro Follows Through

CLOSE RACES LOOM IN MAJORS

WONDER WHO'LL CATCH TODAY—Chicago, Ill.—Mrs. Grace Comiskey, "boss of the White Sox, looks over some new catching equipment for Jimmy Dykes' men. The "pale hose" owner is sure her 1945 team will do a lot better than the seventh place finish of 1944.

Ann Curtis Takes 440 To Strengthen Bid For "Triple"

Chicago, April 14—(AP)—Ann Curtis, who holds more swimming records than any other woman, tonight successfully defended her national AAU 440-yard free style swimming title, but failed by six seconds to equal the record for the event she set a year ago.

Miss Curtis, pacing the field all the way, came in 25 feet ahead of her nearest competitor, Marilyn Sahner, a teammate from the San Francisco crystal plunge, but was far off the pace she set in the preliminaries earlier today.

Her time for the event—one of her specialties—was 5:27.7.

The victory was her second of the evening. Earlier she had anchored the crystal plunge 400-yard free-style relay team to an easy victory over the Women's Swimming Association of New York in 4:17.3, aided by her sister Sue.

In both events, Ann, the only woman ever to win the Sullivan Award, easily was the class of the field.

In the 440-yard event, one of her pet races, Miss Curtis gained almost four feet on every length of the 75-foot Chicago Town Club pool. But at no time did she seem to really be exerting herself as she easily churned the water to continue to build up her lead over the rest of the field of five finalists. After the first two laps of the event, it seemed impossible any other competitor could catch her.

A teammate, Marion Pontac, of the Crystal Plunge, came up with another victory for the San Francisco Club when she won the 100-yard backstroke by inches from Barbara Wertin of the Town Club of Chicago. Leola Thomas of Penn Hall College, Chambersburg, Pa., was third.

The 220-yard breast stroke title went to Patricia Sinclair of the Women's Swimming Association, New York, in 3:13.1, with Clara Lamore, 16-year-old representing the Olneyville Boys' Club of Providence, R. I., a close second. Miss Lamore last night—probably the first girl ever to represent a boys club in a Women's National AAU swimming meet—won the 300-yard individual medley crown.

Miss Curtis will meet a stern test tomorrow when she faces Brenda Helser of Hollywood, Cal., in the 220-yard free-style event. Miss Curtis defeated Brenda Friday night by inches in the finals of the 100-yard free-style event. Miss Helser was defending her title in the race.

Hugh Devore, Irish Grid Coach, Is One Of Rock's Proteges

South Bend, Ind., Apr. 14—(AP)—If it hadn't been for a few words spoken 15 years ago by the late Knute Rockne, Notre Dame still might be seeking a football coach to replace Ed McKeever, who resigned to take the Cornell job.

Hugh Devore

Because of those few words, Hugh Devore, who is but 34, has the job.

It was in February, 1930, that Devore's coach at St. Benedict's High School in Newark, N. J.—where he had earned an all-state rating at end—told him somebody wanted to see him. It was Rockne.

"I didn't spend more than three minutes with him," Devore says in recalling the meeting. "He asked where I intended to go to college. I said I thought I might go to Pennsylvania . . . didn't think I was good enough for the Notre Dame varsity."

"Rock smiled and said: 'You never know until you try. We'd like to see you out to school next fall.' "

He went. Three days after he reached South Bend he was scrimmaging against such legendary men of the gridiron as Joe Savoldi, Marty Brill, Marchy Schwartz and Frank Carideo.

He was a starting end in his sophomore year and played three years for the Irish.

He stayed a year as assistant coach with Elmer Layden, spent three with Jim Crowley at Fordham, four at Providence, R. I., College, and returned to his Alma Mater last year.

He will be head football coach until the return of Frank Leahy, on military leave.

A's And Phils Clash In Exhibition Today

Philadelphia, April 14—(AP)—Philadelphia's two major league clubs, the Athletics and the Phillies, will play a pre-season exhibition game here tomorrow.

The teams had originally scheduled a two-game series, starting today, but the first game was cancelled because of the death and funeral services of President Roosevelt.

The A's are expected to call upon Don Black or Jess Flores for mound duty while the Phils will probably start Charlie Schanz, holding Dick Barrett in reserve.

Detroit Wings Trade 5 Players To Flyers

St. Louis, April 14—(AP)—The St. Louis Flyers of the American Hockey League acquired five players from the Detroit Red Wings of the National League in exchange for two players in a deal announced today by the Flyers.

The two St. Louis players transferred to the Detroit roster are Vic Lynn, wing and defenseman, and Carl (Winky) Smith, wingman.

Coming the Flyers are Dick Kowcinack, Frankcis (Red) Kane, William Thomson, Ted Garvin and George De Felice, all of whom were with Indianapolis part or all of the past season.

GROWING BOXER

State College, Pa. —(AP)— Leo Houck, Penn State's boxing coach, fought in every division from flyweight to heavyweight during his professional ring career.

Detroit Upsets Toronto 5-3 In Playoff

RED WINGS COME THROUGH AFTER LOSING 3 GAMES

TORONTO, April 14—(AP)—Coming from behind with three goals in the last period, the Detroit Red Wings beat the Toronto Maple Leafs tonight, 5 to 3, to keep alive their chance of winning the Stanley hockey cup. It was Detroit's first victory after losing the first three games of the final playoff series.

The Detroit third-period splurge nullified a brilliant individual scoring performance by 19-year-old Ted Kennedy of Toronto who tallied all three Toronto goals, two in the first period and one in the second.

Five players shared in the scoring for the Wings, who had been shut out three times in succession by Toronto goaltender Frank McCool. Defenseman Bill Hoilett scored in the first period and Center Murray Armstrong in the second. Then Eddie Bruneteau and Ted Lindsay tallied unassisted early in the third period to put the Wings ahead, and Joe Carveth made it more emphatic with a goal in the last three minutes on a breakaway play.

The result of the game was a disappointment to the 14,587 Toronto fans who had looked for the Leafs to finish off the series with four straight victories.

The game was the most wide-open of the series, neither team sticking for long at the tight-knit defensive play which characterized the first three games.

The Toronto team outshot the Wings by 24 to 20, holding an edge in each period except the second when the teams were even with seven shots apiece. Harry Lumley played a particularly brilliant game in the Detroit nets, overshadowing rookie-award winner McCool although the latter handled several difficult shots with ease.

The series now moves back to Detroit where the fifth game will be played next Thursday night. Should a sixth game be necessary it will be on Toronto ice next Saturday night.

FIRST PERIOD

A penalty to defenseman Babe Pratt of Toronto paved the way for the first goal Detroit has scored in the series. It came at 8:35 and was netted by Bill Hollett, who took a goal-mouth pass from Eddie Bruneteau. In less than four minutes, however, the Leafs took a 2-1 lead on a pair of goals scored by center Ted Kennedy with the help of rightwing Mel Hill. The first was tallied at 9:19, Hill passing to Kennedy after a neat bit of stick handling. The second was scored while defenseman Earl Seibert of Detroit was serving a hooking penalty.

SECOND PERIOD

Persistent Detroit rushes finally paid off with a goal by Murray Armstrong to tie the score. Armstrong tallied at the 9:20 mark, but a minute later Kennedy got his third goal to put Toronto ahead again 3 to 2.

THIRD PERIOD

Unassisted goals by Eddie Bruneteau and Ted Lindsay gave the Wings a 4-3 lead in less than four minutes of play. Bruneteau's goal came at 1:11 with the Wings a man short, Jackson having been penalized for charging. Bruneteau fired from just inside the blue line and Lindsay got his from the 30-foot range at 3:20. Carveth stretched the Detroit lead to two goals on a breakaway play during a Toronto attack. Final score Detroit 5, Toronto 3.

Summary:

Detroit		Toronto
Lumley	G.	McCool
Quackenbush	R. D.	Pratt
Hollett	L. D.	Morris
Carveth	C.	Kennedy
Liscombe	R. W.	Hill
E. Bruneteau	L. W.	Davidson

Referee—King Clancy. Linesman—Ken Mullins and Leo Gravel.

Detroit spares—Seibert, Jackson, McAtee, Couture, Lindsay, Armstrong, M. Bruneteau, Buckovitch.

Toronto spares: Hamilton, Stanowski, Bodnar, Carr, Schriner, Jackson, McCreedy, D. Metz.

First period—Scoring: 1—Detroit, Hollett (E. Bruneteau) 8:35; 2—Toronto, Kennedy (Hill) 9:19; 3—Toronto, Kennedy (Hill) 11:44. Penalties—Pratt, Seibert, Lindsay.

Second period—Scoring: 4—Detroit, Armstrong (M. Bruneteau) 9:20; 5—Toronto, Kennedy (Davidson) 10:20. Penalties—None.

Third period—Scoring: 6—Detroit, E. Bruneteau, 1:11; 7—Detroit, Lindsay, 3:20; 8—Detroit, Carveth (Hollett) 17:38. Penalties—Jackson.

NO CURVES NECESSARY

Brooklyn—(AP)—Whitey Johnson, young catching prospect on the National Defense List of the Brooklyn Dodgers, recently wrote Harold Parrott, the club secretary, from the European theater of operations:

"You don't have any trouble with curves over here. Everything comes at you straight."

Rip Sewell Doubts That His "Blooper" Pitch Can Be Blasted Out Of Ballpark

Muncie, Ind., Apr. 14 — (AP) — Gather 'round you town criers and take a message from this pennant conscious Spring training camp!

Rip (Blooper) Sewell of the Pittsburgh Pirates would like to see just how far the National League hitters can clout his famous arc pitch.

"Big Red," as his Corsair teammates call him, isn't kidding. He spent all winter demonstrating the specialty for servicemen. He's had letters from soldiers, sailors and marines all over the world.

They all want to know one thing:

"How far can the big leagers hit the ball?"

"Man, I wish I knew myself," insists Rip. "Then, maybe I'd forget it and work on my fast one!

One Triple Off Blooper

"All I know is that Musial hit a triple of the blooper, four other batters reached second, and the rest of the hitters, who touched it, wound up with singles.

"The whole thing gives me a laugh. I was out in the bullpen, near the close of the 1942 season, and got tired warming up. So I started to lope them over.

"Then I tried to put a spin on the ball and found that I could. When I got into a game, I tried it out, and it worked.

"So, in 1943, I mixed it up with my sidearm, overhand and underhand deliveries. It helped me win top honors in the league.

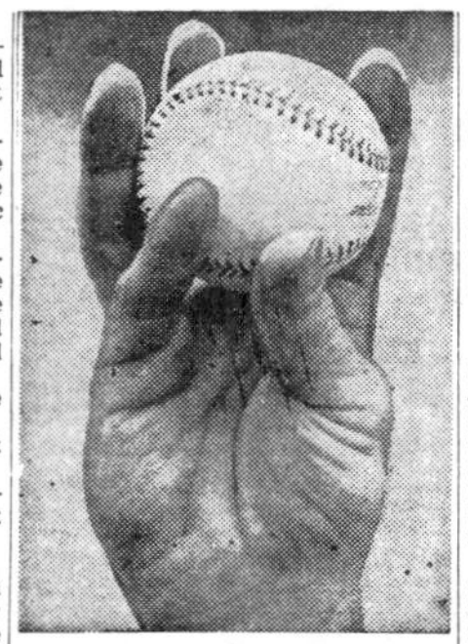

Here's how Rip Sewell grips his famed blooper pitch.

His Big Pitch

"Last year the blooper got me out of many a tough spot. I like to use it when I have two strikes on a batter. I can get it over the plate and they don't know what to do with it.

"I've had a million laughs out of the way some of the fellows go after it. I'd like to see someone hit a homer off that pitch. I don't think it can be done."

Well, there's the challenge, fellows, and the fans who sit in on all the games Rip pitches this year will be in for plenty of fun.

Meanwhile, the Pirates are talking about the first senior loop title at Forbes Field since 1927. Could be too, if Uncle Sam's draft boards behave.

Seven Holdover Hurlers

Manager Frankie Frisch will have nine pitchers to choose from, seven of them holdovers from last year. There are a couple of newcomers, Ken Gables, a reasonable facsimile of Freddy Fitzsimmons who has a world of stuff; and Leonard Gilmore, a 21-6 hurler from Class A Albany.

Al Lopez will take care of the catching while he breaks a record for the most games caught in the majors. The popular Pirate captain needs 49 contests to pass Gabby Hartnett. He will be ably assisted by Coach Spud Davis and rookie Bill Salkeld from San Diego.

Veteran infields and outfields are awaiting the first "Play Ball." There's a chance that Vic Barnhart, the son of an old Pirate favorite, Pooch Barnhart, may wind up at short.

The kid is an Army discharge, a snappy infielder and a fair hitter. He was with Albany last year and had a neat .328 average after being out of the game a couple of years. And, he had only one year of pro ball before he went into the service.

This is the way the Pirate pitcher lets it go.

Bill Rodgers and Al Gionfriddo, also from Albany, are the garden rookies who may make good. If either one of these two boys crash the lineup, outfielders Jim Russell, Johnny Barrett and Frank Colman may have a tough time getting back in there.

HOUCK SUGGESTS SERVICE SPORTS

State College, Pa., April 14—(AP)—A nation wide sport program for rehabilitation of servicemen was suggested today by Leo Houck, Pennsylvania State College boxing coach.

Houck made the proposal after his return from a three-months tour of Army bases in Greenland, Iceland and Bermuda. Accompanying him were Football Coach Harry Rockafeller of Rutgers University, Trainer Ed Zanfrini of Dartmouth College and Charles Berry, American League baseball umpire and former catcher for the Philadelphia Athletics.

The trip was a great success, said the veteran Penn State coach. It was the first outside of this country to be made under the Army Special Service Division's new athletic program. There was a great deal of interest in sports, Houck added, particularly among the wounded whom the party visited at an army hospital at Presque Isle, Me.

HAIL VICTORY ON SHELF

Miami —(AP)— Calumet Farm's hopes for Hail Victory for the 1945 Kentucky Derby—should it be run—have evidently been abandoned. The son of Blenheim II has been shipped to the farm at Lexington. Trainer Ben Jones still has formidable racers in Pot O' Luck, Good Blood and Battlefire.

PROBABLE OPENING DAY MAJOR LEAGUE PITCHERS

New York, April 14—(AP)—Probable opening day major league pitchers with their 1944 records in parentheses:

Monday

AMERICAN LEAGUE

New York at Washington—Donald (13-10) vs. Leonard (14-14).

Tuesday

AMERICAN LEAGUE

Detroit at St. Louis—Newhouser (29-9) vs. Jakucki (13-9).

Chicago at Cleveland—Lee (3-9) or Grove (14-15) vs. Reynolds (11-8).

Washington at Philadelphia—Haefner (12-15) vs. Christopher (14-14) or Newsom (13-15).

Boston at New York—Cecil (4-5) vs. Borowy (17-12).

NATIONAL LEAGUE

St. Louis at Chicago—M. Cooper (22-7) or Donnelly (2-1) vs. Derringer (7-13).

Pittsburgh at Cincinnati—Ostermueller (13-8) vs. Walters (23-8).

New York at Boston—Voiselle (21-16) vs. Javery (10-19).

Philadelphia at Brooklyn—Raffensberger (13-20) vs. Davis (10-11).

Lancaster's Dick Vaughan Equals National Mat Record

On the evening of March 24 in the Sportatorium at Dallas, Texas, when Dick Vaughan, former Franklin and Marshall college star representing the Hamilton R.A.C., pinned the shoulders of George Bollas, 340 pound colossus from Ohio State, to the mat in 2 minutes 50 seconds, it marked the third time in five years that Dick had won a National A.A.U. heavyweight wrestling title.

Only one other grappler in the long and colorful history of the Nationals duplicated that feat. His name was J. Gundersen, who did his wrestling for the Dover S. P. Gundersen won the heavyweight title in 1907, 1908 and 1913.

Dick won his first National crown at Baltimore in 1937. At the same Baltimore Y. M. C. A. he duplicated the feat in 1944.

Experience paid off for the local star in winning the crown this year. It wasn't the huge Bollas in the finals who gave Dick his stiffest argument. A fellow by the name of Bob Coffey, Southwestern A. A. U. heavy champ grappling for the Dallas Y. M. C. A., did that. Coffey and Vaughan tangled in a semi-final match.

With 20 seconds until the end of the match and Coffey out in front on points 4 to 1, Dick turned to his 19 years experience in the game. He reversed his position to take the offensive. This gave him two points. Then he went to work and scored a near fall just as the whistle sounded ending the affair to be given two more points and the match by a count of 5 to 4.

Dick said he didn't feel that Coffey was anything like a great wrestler. It was more that he, himself, just couldn't get going soon enough. Perhaps it was the fact that Dick hadn't encountered any actual match competition all season prior to this contest. Coffey, like Bollas was in the 300 pound class, actually tipping the beams at 310. Vaughan weighed 225.

The former Diplomat mauler actually started in the wrestling game in 1926 back in his home town of Newton, New Jersey. That first year as a 158 pounder, he failed to make Coach Henry Boresch's Newton High team. But the following season when he was 16, he took over a regular spot and that started him on his way.

DICK VAUGHAN

After he got out of high school he was employed in a bank in Newton but worked out every noon hour at the high school with some of Boresch's up and coming Newton grapplers. He did this for three or four years.

Four-Time State Champ

In 1933-34-35-36 he was the New Jersey State Heavyweight title-holder. Dick didn't feel he had sufficient experience to step into big time competition as yet, but ventured forth anyhow in 1937 when the National A. A. U.'s were held at the Baltimore Y. He got through the preliminary matches and into the finals on some very smart wrestling. In the finals he met a fellow by the name of Charley McKinney of the New York Athletic Club. He proceeded to give the 235 pound New Yorkers a going over, finally pinning him to win the title.

It was during this tourney that Dick met Uncle Charley Mayser for the first time. The Old Fox from College Hill convinced him that F & M would be as good a school as any to apply his grappling wares for the next four years. Dick thought the matter over and the following fall he matriculated to the Blue and White institution.

Vaughan figures the two biggest thrills he had out of the sport thus far happened in 1937 and 1940. In 1937 wrestling for the Newton Boys Club of New Jersey, he met Hal Scobey, the great Lehigh University Heavyweight who was operating in that same class for the Bath Fireman grapplers. Scobey had just returned with the United States Olympic team from the 1936 Olympic games which were held in Germany. He had been an alternate on the club.

Dick held no fear for reputations and went into battle with the Lehigh star and came out on top with a well earned point victory.

In 1940 with his match depending on a victory or a defeat for F & M. against a great Ohio State mat outfit, Dick met big Johnnie Downes in the final contest of the evening. After a nip and tuck tussle that went through two overtime periods, Dick came out on top with a close decision.

Dick's pet and most effective hold is a roll or wing with a body press. He used this one on Ohio State's Big Ten Champion, Bollas, to win the 1945 National crown.

About the future in wrestling, Dick just says he isn't being quoted as to whether or not he'll try for a fourth National A. A. U. Heavyweight title in 1946.

FANS AWAIT CRY OF "PLAY BALL!" SLATED MONDAY

By JACK HAND

NEW YORK, April 14—(AP)—Prospects of tight pennant races in both major leagues served to heighten interest in Monday's opening of a fourth wartime baseball season despite the shocking off-season deaths of President Franklin D. Roosevelt and Commissioner Kenesaw M. Landis.

Rookies figuring prominently in the hopes of major league outfits include such discharged veterans as infielder Jack Tobin of the Red Sox, outfielder Al "Red" Schoendienst of the Cards, infielder Al Cihocki of the Indians, outfielder Jack McHale of the Tigers, and pitcher Jim Wallace of the Braves.

The Cardinals again were a standout in the National League on their spring training lineup, but the imminent loss of both Johnny Hopp and Walker Cooper could draw them back to the pack. Manager Billy Southworth has his entire holdover world champion infield, but would have to rebuild his outfield. The pitching is Southworth's least worry.

Pittsburgh has been labeled the chief threat to a fourth straight Card flag but pitching is their problem. If Max Butcher, Preacher Roe, Nick Strincevich and Fred Ostermueller can back up Rip Sewell, they might make the grade. A strong infield packs punch in Bob Elliott and Babe Dahlgren and the outfield could be the best hitting trio in the league.

Pitching is Charley Grimm's headache in Chicago, too ,with Ace Claude Passeau and Ed Hanyzewski having arm trouble. Bill Nicholson, outfielder who clouted 33 home runs last season, is expected to join the club today and the Bruins now pack a real wallop with a holdover infield and capable outfield.

Cincinnati is threatened with a drop to the second division for the first time under Bill McKechnie with shortstop Eddie Miller sidelined by a knee injury. He must depend on old timers like Guy Bush and Hod Lisenbee to back up Bucky Walters..

Mel Ott's Giants have some punch in Phil Weintraub, Ernie Lombardi and Ott with Joe Medwick a doubtful factor due to a back injury. With an entire holdover team, Ottie counts on improved pitching to make the first division.

The Braves have more new players than any club in baseball with Manager Bob Coleman hoping for added speed and defense to make his good pitching look better. Brooklyn has infield problems galore, needs more catching and pitching, but boasts a strong outfield built around Dixie Walker. The Phillies have a green infield, added power in the garden with Vince DiMaggio, but they miss Ron Northey and Tony Lupien.

Detroit counts on Al Benton and Stubby Overmire to give Hal Newhouser and Dizzy Trout the help they didn't have last season. Loss of Dick Wakefield and Pinky Higgins has weakened the batting attack.

Browns Back Again

St. Louis has last year's pennant winners back with the exception of Al Zarilla and Denny Galehouse and has added one-armed Pete Gray and Boris Martin, a 350 hitter at Toledo.

New York's chances depend on how soon Johnny Lindell and Nick Etten are called for duty. Only pitcher Mel Queen is missing from the 1944 club leaving Joe McCarthy a well-rounded mound staff as its strongest asset.

Loss of Tex Hughson, Hal Wagner and Bobby Doerr probably cost the Red Sox last year's flag and they were socked again when Jim Tabor and Al Partee were taken.

FANS—Page 15

Tigers Still Moan About Loss

- - - O'Neill Now Using Mack Formula - - -

Evansville, Ind., April 14 —(AP)—Manager Steve O'Neill of the Detroit Tigers is going to steal a page out of Connie Mack's championship book this year—and he thinks it will bring the Bengals their first American league championship since 1940.

Even though he has lost two of his 1944 stars to the armed forces (slugger Dick Wakefield and third sacker Pinky Higgins, Steve is happier about his team's chances than he was a year ago.

"There isn't a day goes by but one of the regulars moans about a play, or a chance on the bases, where he faltered last year," reveals the Tigers' boss.

"That's a good sign! It shows the boys know how and where they lost the pennant through careless fielding and running!

'Connie Told Us'

"Don't think I'm not going to take advantage of their mistakes, too," smiles the confident O'Neill. "Away back in 1911, when I was playing with the Athletics, Connie Mack told us:

" 'Play every inning as if it were the last! If the other team gets a run, stop them from getting two; if they get two, don't let them score three.'

"I intend to make full use of Mr. Mack's theory this Spring," assures Steve. "It would have meant the difference between second and first place last year."

STEVE O'NEILL
Will Play 'Em Closer

Peeved Tigers

It seems that Hal Newhouser, Dizzy Trout, Stubby Overmire, Doc Cramer and Eddie Mayo, to mention a few, don't like the way the St. Louisans nosed them out last year.

"There were at least three games we should have won from the Browns," say these Tigers, "and anyone of them would have given us the pennant."

"And don't forget that flukey one the Athletics lost in St. Louis," pipes up Mayo, "when Bobby Estalella dropped a fly ball for the deciding run."

Looking over the American League figures, the Brownies were the only ones to win more games from Detroit during the 1944 season.

"But they were all early in the season," O'Neill is quick to point out. "We beat them six out of eight later on. We'll continue from there this year.

"Every championship team always had the strongest combination down through the middle," says Steve, "and that's where we'll have them.

"Our pitchers will be better than ever. We have the strongest catching staff in the league, the best short and second combination in Skeeter Webb and Eddie Mayo, and the top centerfielder in Doc Cramer.

"Any team that wins the pennant will have to beat us!"

Cooper Brothers In Pay Row, Each Demand $15,000 Of Cards

St. Louis, April 14—(AP)—Morton and Walker Cooper, baseball's outstanding brother battery, today told President Sam Breadon of the St. Louis Cardinals, he would have to increase their 1945 salaries to $15,000 each or they would not go to Chicago for the season's opener Tuesday.

Both players recently signed contracts for $12,000, the club's ceiling salary under the 1943 Wage Stabilization Act.

The Coopers said their grievance is based on an increase in salary over the club's ceiling given star shortstop Marty Marion.

"After Marion had been signed Mr. Breadon offered to increase our salary," Walker Cooper said. "He offered us $13,500, which he said was more than he had paid Marion.

"But we're holding out for $15,000. We've written to President Ford Frick (of the National League) telling him about our stand and asking for his advice.

"Unless we get what we are asking we won't go to Chicago with the club Monday night. If he can ask the board (WLB) to tilt to $13,500 he might as well ask it to tilt it to $15,000. You know you have to make your money over just a few years in baseball."

Breadon said he had told Walker no player on the club would receive more than he did.

"Marion felt he was entitled to an increase and I felt he was justified in his opinion and asked him to sign a contract increasing his salary above the 'ceiling,' condition upon the approval of the Internal Revenue Department," Breadon said in a statement.

"x x x I immediately called them (the Coopers) to my office and told them I had increased Marion's salary over the ceiling x x x and I offered them the same contract as Marion had received. Their reply was that they had signed for $12,000 and they would play for $12,000 but they would not sign a new contract unless I made it $15,000. I felt the club had been fair in offering an increase after they had signed their contracts."

A Healthier Borowy Goes For Lifetime Goal—20 Victories

Atlantic City, April 14—(AP)—Hank Borowy, the New York Yankees' top pitcher in victories and in earned runs permitted last season, is looking forward to his best year in the American League.

And it's not because he's fooling around with a knuckle ball, as some scribes would have you believe. True, Hank is working on the pitch, but he says he may not use it in a league game all season.

Won 23 In A Row

Hank went to college and is the sort of guy who won't attempt anything unless he can perfect it. He matriculated at Fordham where he compiled a record of 23 straight victories in two seasons before blowing a 5-4 decision.

But the reason that Hank thinks he'll surpass his 17 conquests of last season is his health. Borowy says he's in the best shape of his six-year career—three with Newark, three with the Yanks.

Now At Normal Weight

Just before last season, Hank made a trip to Alaska to entertain the soldiers. He didn't sleep any too well, ate odd meals at odd times and returned to the states a bit underweight. Today at 176 pounds, he is at his normal weight. Last spring he was down to 160.

"It didn't tell on me at first," says Hank, "because at one time last summer my record showed 13 wins and four losses.

"But then, I found it difficult to win. I finished with 17 and 12. It will be different this year."

HANK BOROWY
"Just Foolin' With Knuckler"

Someone ventured a guess that Hank might toss 25 wins into the Yankee pool. Hank says that's silly. He'll settle for 20. That's his lifetime ambition.

With Borowy, Jumbo Ernie Bonham, Atley Donald and Walter Dubiel as almost certain starters with plenty of help from Floyd Bevens, Allen Gettel and Karl Drews, the Yankees are in fine mound shape. Others on their very promising staff include Ken Holcombe, Lefty Joe Page, Emerson Roser, Elmer Singleton and Bill Zuber with 38-year-old Jim Turner on hand to put out fires.

"We're in better shape than we were this time last spring," smiles Manager Joe McCarthy. "I have more manpower and better balance."

But Buffalo Joe isn't doing any handsprings. It's a good wartime club but a far cry from any of his eight Yankee pennant winners.

WEATHER

Eastern Pennsylvania: Increasing Cloudiness And Continued Warm Friday. Showers And Scattered Thunderstorms Friday Night. Clearing And Becoming Cooler.

Intelligencer Journal.

The Leading Newspaper in the Garden Spot of America, Home Owned for Home Folks Since 1794 — 150th Anniversary Year

PAPER Is America's No. 1 Critical Item *Give Your Paper To Nearest School*

151st Year.—No. 258. Entered as second class matter August 9, 1944 at the Post Office at Lancaster, Pa., under the Act of March 3, 1879. Reg. U. S. Pat. Off. LANCASTER, PA., FRIDAY MORNING, APRIL 13, 1945 CITY THIRTY-FOUR PAGES. 20c PER WEEK—4c Per Copy

PRESIDENT ROOSEVELT DIES, TRUMAN SWORN INTO OFFICE

PLEDGES SELF TO POLICIES OF ROOSEVELT

32nd President Says 'Frisco Parley To Go On, Asks Cabinet To Stay

Washington—(AP)—Harry S. Truman, who 11 years ago was a Missouri County judge, became the 32nd President of the United States at 7:09 p. m. Thursday and solemnly pledged himself to the policies of Franklin Delano Roosevelt.

STALIN EXPRESSES HOPE FRIENDSHIP WILL CONTINUE

Premier Stalin sent a note to President Truman Thursday night.

"On behalf of the Soviet government and myself personally," the message said, "I express our profound condolence to the government of the United States of America on the occasion of the premature death of President Roosevelt.

"The American people and the United Nations have lost in Franklin Roosevelt a great politician of world significance and a pioneer in the organization of peace and security after the war.

"The government of the Soviet Union expresses sincere sympathy to the American people in their great loss and their conviction that the policy of friendship between the great powers who are shouldering the main burden of war against the common enemy will continue in the future."

Signed: Joseph Stalin.

Sworn in 2 hours and 34 minutes after Mr. Roosevelt's death in Warm Springs, Ga., as a shocked capital sought to weigh the import of the sudden change, Truman announced in quick succession:

1. He will try to carry on as he believes President Roosevelt would have done.

2. The San Francisco United Nations conference will go on as scheduled April 25.

3. He has asked the Roosevelt cabinet to stay on with him.

4. The war will be pressed to a "successful conclusion."

The new Chief Executive issued this statement:

"The world may be sure that we will prosecute the war on both fronts, east and west, with all the vigor we possess, to a successful conclusion."

Thus Mr. Truman acted immediately to steady a stunned nation and drive forward toward victory and a lasting peace.

About the White House crowds stood silently at the tall iron fence. Flags there, and on embassies and other public buildings, dipped to half staff.

BRIEF CEREMONY

After the brief and solemn induction ceremony, President and Mrs. Truman went from the cabinet room to the White House residential quarters to speak with Mrs. Roosevelt, who was leaving to fly to Warm Springs. Shortly after 7:30 p. m., they left by a rear entrance and motored to their apartment on Connecticut Avenue in northwest Washington.

Secret Service men and district police threw a cordon around the apartment building and visitors to the Truman suite were barred. All telephone calls, and they were myriad, were rejected except one from Mrs. Truman's brother, Frank Wallace.

Senator Green (D-RI) was among those who called in person to congratulate the new President, but he too was denied an audience.

Guards patrolled the third floor corridor all night. The neighborhood was quiet in contrast to the throngs which stood across from the White House for hours, far into the darkness.

SUMMONED TRUMAN

It was Mrs. Roosevelt, who summoned Mr. Truman from his capitol office to the White House and told him her husband was dead.

While waiting she sent messages to the four Roosevelt sons in the armed forces—James, Elliott, Franklin, Jr., and John—telling them of their father's passing.

He slept away this afternoon, she told them. He did his job to the end, as he would want to do. Bless you all and all

More of PLEDGES on Page 12

PRESIDENT TRUMAN

Suddeness Of Roosevelt's Death Shocks Community

The death of President Roosevelt burst upon this war-geared community with such stunning suddenness Thursday afternoon that for hours incredulous residents still sought confirmation of the shocking news.

Most Lancastrians were on their way home from war industries, stores and offices when the "flash" announcing the death of "The Chief" was received.

In minutes, however, hundreds of persons swamped the Lancaster Newspapers telephone switchboard seeking confirmation of news of the death of the President.

DAZED BY NEWS

Dazed by the news, crowds gathered on the downtown streets in the early evening waiting for the extra edition of the Intelligencer Journal, which appeared at 8:10 p. m.

Among the crowds that thronged West King Street were many sailors from the Bainbridge, Md., Naval Training Station, at Lancaster on liberty, who stared unbelieving at the bulletin telling them the President had died.

FLAGS AT HALF MAST

Mayor Cary upon hearing the news of the death of the President immediately ordered the flag on the Municipal building lowered to half-mast. He suggested that flags on both public and private buildings also be lowered, but spontaneously, the flags on many buildings had already been lowered.

The Lancaster School Board officially ordered flags on all school buildings be set at half-mast at a meeting Thursday night. School will remain in session as usual on Friday.

Leaders in industry, government, and politics and in the civic, educational and religious life of the county joined in paying tribute to President Roosevelt as a "humanitarian."

STOPPED HERE IN 1934

President Roosevelt, it was recalled Thursday, made a short stop in Lancaster on the evening of May 31, 1934. He was on his way to New York after delivering an address at the National cemetery at Gettysburg.

An estimated 20,000 persons gathered at the Pennsylvania Railroad Station to greet the chief executive, then in the midst of perfecting his great national reforms.

"I am glad to be here x x x and I want to return" x x x he said in a brief address from the observation platform of his special train.

More of DEATH on Page 12

7 NAMES ADDED TO CASUALTY LIST OF CITY, COUNTY

Missing Soldier Declared Dead; Two Are Prisoners, Four Are Wounded

WAR CASUALTIES

Casualties among Lancaster county service men, reported Thursday:

KILLED

Staff Sgt. Jacob S. Snavely, Manheim, over Austria.

PRISONER

Pfc. Raymond C. Haldeman, 314 Mill St., of Germany.

Pfc. George N. Buzzendore, Columbia, of Germany.

WOUNDED

Cpl. Harold Burns, 436 Chester St., on Iwo Jima.

Pfc. Clifford R. Graybill, 23 Chester St., in Germany.

Staff Sgt. Richard Kauffman, Ephrata, in Germany.

Pvt. Willis M. Houck, Strasburg, in Germany.

Seven names were added Thursday to Lancaster county's war casualty lists. One soldier, previously missing, was declared dead and two others were reported prisoners of war. Four servicemen were wounded, one for the third time.

GUNNER KILLED

Staff Sgt. Jacob S. Snavely, thirty-six, an aerial gunner with the Army Air Forces stationed in Italy, who was reported missing Feb. 25, 1944, was declared killed in action, according to a second War Department telegram received by his father, Abram B. Snavely, 226 S. Orchard St., Manheim.

S-S Snavely

Sgt. Snavely had been in the service since 1943 and went overseas only a few months before he participated in the mission in which he lost his life. Prior to entering the service he was employed by the U. S. Asbestos Co., Manheim.

Pfc. George N. Buzzendore,

More of CASUALTIES on Page 29

RULES FOR FLYING FLAG AT HALF-MAST

Washington —(AP)— The proper manner to display the flag in memory of President Roosevelt is at half-mast, from sunrise to sunset.

"Half masting of flags should only be done when a nation is in mourning," the Library of Congress said Thursday night. "Quite obviously that applies now."

Regulations adopted by Congress governing display and use of the American flag specify that it should be "first hoisted to the peak" of the staff for an instant and then lowered to the half-mast position. Similarly, the flag should be raised to the peak before it is lowered for the day. This applies to both public buildings and private homes.

Yanks Cross Elbe; Organized German Fight Seen Near End

Tanks Cross River On 6-Mile Front; Leipzig Threatened; News Blackout

Paris (Friday)—(AP)—U. S. Ninth Army tanks smashed across the Elbe river on a six-mile front just 57 miles from Berlin yesterday and U. S. First and Third armies in sweeps of nearly 50 miles thundered at the gates of the great city of Leipzig, 75 miles southwest of the capital.

A field dispatch said only orders from Lt. Gen. William H. Simpson were needed to send the Second Armored Division dashing on into Berlin, which could possibly be reached today. Wholly unconfirmed French reports said Allied parachute troops had been dropped at Brandenburg, barely 20 miles from greater Berlin.

The electrifying crossing of the Elbe—last big river barrier before the devastated capital—came with such speed that Supreme Headquarters was unable to confirm it, a spokesman saying that Sheaf was completely out of touch with Ninth Army spearheads.

The U. S. First and Third armies, after their long gains, were under a security blackout, but a field report said it was possible that one of them would reach Leipzig by today. They last were reported 23 to 24 miles from the city with nothing in front of them.

26-MILE GAIN

From out of the security blackout came the news that the First Army's Third Armored Division had reeled off a 26-mile gain on the First's north flank and had driven more than two miles beyond Sangerhausen, 84 miles southwest of Berlin.

The advances of these two powerful armies, bidding for a quick decision in the war in Europe by balking a die-hard stand in southern Germany, were expected to be western front sensations once the blackout is lifted.

(Paris radio said tank spearheads were 16 miles from Leipzig and 19 miles from the Czech border.)

Three tank columns of the U. S. Third Army ripped beyond the heart of Germany in dashes of more than 46 miles and were 129 miles from the Russian lines, 40 miles from the Czech border and 109 miles from Berlin. The Ninth Army was 115 miles from the Russian lines.

CAPTURE WEIMAR

The First Army, traveling east at a rate of 30 to 40 mies a day, had picked up a new batch of camp

More of TANKS on Page 12

Army Officials Tell Senators End May Come Within Few Days

Washington — (AP) — High Army officials told senators Thursday the end of organized fighting in Germany probably will come within a few days.

Describing the pell-mell dash of American Armies across Germany, general staff officers expressed the opinion to member of the Senate Military committee that a collapse of Nazi arms is imminent.

Those who attended the conference said the army chiefs said:

Only pockets of resistance will remain to be cleaned up after this collapse.

REDUCE SHIPMENTS

They feel so sure of results that orders have been drawn drastically reducing the shipments of durable equipment to Europe in preparation for reversing the flow toward the Pacific.

They hope that Hitler and his Nazi leaders will be captured, although they did not discount the possibility of escape by some.

A German broadcast heard in London today had Paul Joseph Goebbels, Nazi Propaganda Minister, saying that "the war cannot last much longer in my opinion."

In a review of problems developing with the imminent shift of major war activity to the fight against Japan, the Senators also were told by Gen. Brehon B. Somervell, chief of the Army's Service of Supplies, and other military leaders that the nation again is scraping the bottom of the barrel on steel.

This new crisis in steel production has developed, it was disclosed, because of the increased weight of bombs, plus needs for heavy equipment in the Pacific.

CIVILIAN PINCH

The civilian pinch in the Pacific war will be felt primarily in steel, cotton goods and shoes, the Senators heard. Steel lack may hamper the reconversion of the auto industry. Cotton is needed for lightweight uniforms. Shoes rot fast in the Pacific fighting areas. Civilians may be cut to one pair a year.

Plans have been worked out, the Senators were told, for a three-way trail of men and supplies from Europe to the Pacific. Some will go direct to the Orient. Some will come back to the United States and then go to the Pacific. Some will go direct from this country to the Japanese war zone.

POINT SYSTEM

The legislators were informed that the Army intends to adhere rigidly to a point system in deciding which of the fighting men in Europe shall come home, which shall stay there to help occupy Germany, which shall go on to fight

More of ARMY on Page 12

U. S. Leaders Mourn Loss Of FDR; Foreign Countries Receive News

(By The Associated Press)

Governor Thomas E. Dewey of New York Thursday night declared that President Roosevelt would be mourned "as a human being of warm human qualities and great capacities."

"It remains for all of us to preserve and strengthen our national unity in waging the war to total, uncompromising victory over all our enemies," the 1944 Republican presidential candidate said, adding:

COURAGE AND SPIRIT

"Coming to leadership of the nation at a critical period in our economic life he brought his courage and indomitable spirit to the task of meeting the most difficult of national problems, inspiring the people with fresh confidence and establishing basic liberal reforms."

Earlier, Dewey telegraphed Mrs. Roosevelt: "Please accept our deepest sympathy in your great loss which will be shared by every American and mourned by all the freedom-loving people of the entire world."

OTHER COMMENTS

Other comments included:

Mayor F. H. LaGuardia, of New York—"It is the greatest loss the peace-loving people of the world have suffered in the entire war.

More of COMMENT on Page 1

(By The Associated Press)

News of President Roosevelt's death, flashed to friend and foe, troops in the field and sailors at sea, reached into every corner of the world Thursday night, and expressions of sympathy, along with bitter enemy comment, poured into a bereaved American nation.

Cable dispatches and radio broadcasts carried the news to the capitals of the world and to Allied soldiers fighting toward a victorious end of the world's greatest war. The peoples of Europe were informed in a special broadcast by the American Broadcasting station in Europe, which declared that "the world has lost its greatest champion for peace."

EXPRESSIONS OF GRIEF

Expressions of grief came from London, Moscow, Paris, Rome, South America, Cuba, Canada and elsewhere, while the German radio, in a comment heard of FCC monitors, declared that the President "will go down in history as the man upon whose instigation the present war turned into the second World War." The Japanese carried a factual broadcast of the death, but was not heard to comment immediately.

Premier Stalin expressed his sorrow at the death of President Roosevelt in a message to Mrs.

More of FOREIGN on Page 12

THE LATE PRESIDENT ROOSEVELT

Reveal FDR Saw Expanding Role For U. S. In Pacific

Warm Springs, Ga.—(AP)—At his last news conference before his death President Roosevelt expressed the hope that he would be able to proclaim complete independence for the Philippines by autumn.

It was the 998th gathering, White House records showed, that the President had held with reporters.

SAW EXPANDING ROLE

He made his Philippines disclosure along with his view that the United States will play an ever-expanding role in the Western Pacific after the war to thwart further Japanese aggression.

He believed Japan, like Germany, should be policed internally when she is beaten, and that the United States and other United Nations must accept trusteeships over Japanese mandates and build new naval and air bases—in a combined move to stamp out Japanese militarism.

The Chief Executive expressed these views at a news conference April 5 at his pine mountain cottage near here.

VIEWS WITHHELD

For security reasons he asked that they be withheld from publication until he returned to Washington.

White House Secretary William D. Hassett authorized publication

More of REVEAL on Page 12

NIP SUICIDE CRAFT HIT YANKEE FLEET OFF OKINAWA ISLE

Sink Destroyer, Damage Other Ships; 4 More U. S. Divisions On Island

(By The Associated Press)

Another large force of Japanese suicide planes desperately attacked the American invasion fleet off Okinawa Thursday, sinking a U. S. destroyer and damaging other ships in a furious engagement in which 118 enemy aircraft were destroyed.

All the damaged American ships remained in operation.

Fighting ashore on Okinawa remained bitterly deadlocked as Fleet Adm. Chester W. Nimitz identified four more divisions as in the fight just 325 miles south of Japan itself.

These were the First and Sixth Marine Divisions, and the 27th and 96th Army Divisions. The Seventh and 77th Army Divisions already had been identified. All these forces are part of Lt. Gen. Simon Bolivar Buckner, Jr.'s new Tenth Army.

INVADE ISLAND

Americal Division troops of the U. S. Eighth Army charged ashore on Bohol Island Wednesday, Gen. Douglas MacArthur reported Friday (today), and with Filipino guerrilla aid started liberation of the last central Philippine island still in Japanese hands.

Covered by American naval and air bombardment, the Yanks landed at Tagbilaran on Bohol's southwestern shore and pushed inland against the surprised Japanese in "another thrust in the swift campaign to clear the bewildered enemy from the Visayas," MacArthur said.

On Cebu Island, west of Bohol, the Americans made gains in clearing northeastern hills, and on Luzon 14th Corps Yanks continued to close the trap on Japanese caught on Bicol peninsula in the southern part of the island.

Allied bombers out of the Philip-

More of NIP on Page 34

POSTPONE DINNERS

Washington —(AP)— Five hundred Jefferson Day dinners, planned by Democrats all over the country for Friday night, have been indefinitely postponed because of the death of President Roosevelt, who had planned to address them by radio.

Mrs. Roosevelt True Champion

Washington —(AP)— Mrs. Franklin D. Roosevelt, left the White House Thursday night for the sorrowful flight to her dead husband's side.

The Army supplied an airplane for the journey to Warm Springs but said that for reasons of personal safety the take-off time would not be announced.

"I am more sorry for the people of the country and the world than I am for us," the President's widow said of his death.

Going with Mrs. Roosevelt on the trip were Admiral Ross McIntyre, the late President's personal physcian, and his press secretary, Stephen Early.

She had received Vice President President Truman in her second floor sitting room in the White House. There she made the remark about being grieved first for the people.

She told Mr. Truman: "The President has passed away."

Truman asked: "What can I do."

"Tell us what we can do," Mrs. Roosevelt replied. "Is

More MRS. ROOSEVELT Page 12

STROKE FATAL TO PRESIDENT IN 64TH YEAR

Chief Executive Expires At His Cottage In Warm Springs, Georgia

Warm Springs, Ga.—(AP)—President Franklin D. Roosevelt, his strength sapped away as Commander-in-Chief in America's greatest war, died suddenly Thursday afternoon.

It was at 3:35 p. m. (4:35 p. m. Lancaster Time) that Mr. Roosevelt died of a cerebral hemorrhage.

LAST WORDS

Mr. Roosevelt's last words were:

"I have a terrific headache."

He spoke them to Comdr. Harold Bruenn, naval physician.

FUNERAL SATURDAY

The funeral will be in the White House East Room in Washington on Saturday. Burial will be at the Roosevelt ancestral home at Hyde Park, N. Y., Sunday.

The body will not lie in state.

Presidential Secretary William D. Hassett said Mr. Roosevelt's body would leave here around 9 a. m., Friday for the approximately 22-hour run to Washington.

Mr. Roosevelt, 63, was sitting in front of a fireplace in the little White House here atop Pine Mountain when the attack struck him.

MASSIVE STRIKE

Bruenn described it as a massive cerebral hemorrhage.

The President's negro valet, Arthur Prettyman, and a Fitipino messboy carried him to his bed room. He was unconscious at the end. It came without pain.

Mr. Roosevelt, in the third month of his fourth term as President, came here three weeks ago to rest.

The death removed from world councils one of the Big Three — Roosevelt, Stalin and Churchill — who worked together to win the war and laid joint plans for keeping the peace. Truman likewise has stressed the need for international cooperation.

Dr. Bruenn said, "at one o'clock he was sitting in a chair while sketches were being made of him by an architect. He suddenly complained of a very severe occipital headache (back of the head).

"Within a very few minutes he lost consciousness. He was seen by me at 1:30 p. m., fifteen minutes after the episode had started. He did not regain consciousness and he died at 3:35 p. m."

Only others present in the cottage were Comdr. George Fox, White House pharmacist and long an attendant on the President; Hasset, Miss Grace Tully, confidential secretary; and two cousins, Miss Laura Delano and Miss Margaret Suckley.

Bruenn said he called Vice Admiral Ross T. Mcntyre, Navy Surgeon General and White House physician in Washington and that McIntyre in turn called Dr. James E. Paullin, of Atlanta, an internal medicine practicioner and honorary consultant to the Navy Surgeon General.

Paullin was present when Bruenn gave the statement of the cause of death to reporters of three national news services.

GIVES ANNOUNCEMENT

Hassett gave newsmen the first announcement.

News of the President's death spread like wildfire around the Foundation and atop an adjoining mountain where guests were gathering for a barbecue.

The President's late arrival for the barbecue caused some anxiety. A telephone call was put through and a few minutes later representatives of the Associated Press, United Press and International News Service were told to rush immediately to the Carver cottage on the Foundation grounds for some news.

MANY A TEAR

News of the President's death spread quickly and caused many a tear among the 125 infantile paralysis patients at the foundation here.

Mayor Frank W. Allcorn of Warm Springs was giving a barbecue at his mountain cabin Thursday afternoon for the President and about 50 other guests. Allcorn was awaiting the President's arrival when reporters got word through the Army Signal Corps radio telephone and summer White House telephone communication to rush to the foundation.

Miss Louise Hackmeister, veter-

More of STROKE on Page 12

6 Who Planted Iwo Flag Symbolize U.S. Melting Pot

By TRUDI McCULLOUGH

New York, April 21 —(AP)—The six men who planted the flag atop Mount Suribachi on Iwo Jima are symbolic of the melting pot that is America and her fighting forces.

Among the six were a full blooded Pima Indian, the son of an immigrant Czech coal miner, a Kentucky farm boy. They ranged in age from 19 to 25; they had been in service from 18 months to six years. Their temperament varied from "one of the nicest, quietest boys in town", according to a local policeman, to "a daredevil who wanted action," according to his mother.

3 Died On Iwo Jima

All had been eager to enlist, and one out-slicked induction doctors to do it. Three of them died on Iwo Jima, and another was wounded: an index to the terrific cost of that bleak Pacific island.

But unknown to them, all were to become famous due to "a historic photograph in which." Admiral Nimitz wrote to AP Photographer Joe Rosenthal, "you caught a moment in the lives of six of our valorous Marines . . which will live forever in the minds of their countrymen."

Describing this moment, which as a painting will serve as the official poster for the Seventh War Loan Drive, Photographer Rosenthal said:

"There were a number of Marines on top of Mount Suribachi . . Probably 50 . . . Digging into rubble of Jap gun positions, some checking into caves to make sure no more live Japs were left. The men didn't talk much. The half dozen men who raised the big flag were working on the foundation for the pole . . . Finally the Marine in charge said, 'Okay, we're ready, let's go.' There was almost no conversation as the flag went up. Somebody said 'let's swing it fast.'

First man in the picture, reading left to right, is Pfc. Franklin R. Sousley. He was the Kentucky farm boy, whose name originally was withheld from the group identification until his mother, Mrs. J. H. Price, Ewing, Ky., had been notified of his death. He wrote home about the flag raising before he was killed in the mopping-up operations. The youngest of the group, Sousley, who still looked like a schoolboy, had been graduated from Flemingsburg high school in 1943 and worked a year in Dayton, Ohio, before he joined the Marines in January 1944.

Kin In Indian Village

The Marine with the slung rifle is one of the survivors, Pfc. Ira H. Hayes, 22. His parents Mr. and Mrs. Job Hayes live in a little village of 200 Indians at Bapchule, Arizona. Hayes attended the Pima Reservation School at Sacaton and the Indian School in Phoenix, where he starred in football and baseball. Sacaton superintendent A. E. Robinson remembers him as "always in the thick of things. He always stayed with anything he undertook."

Private Hayes, who also is a qualified paratroop jumper, has two Bronze Stars for gallantry at Vella Lavella and Bougainville. He has a brother, 19, in the service, and two other brothers, "just youngsters," whom he last saw on a 30-day furlough in Feb. 1944.

Barely visible beside Hayes in the photograph is Sg.t Michael Strank, 25, killed also in the mop up. Strank was the "quiet boy, one of the swellest in town". His pardnts came from Czechoslovakia to settle in Cambria county, a soft coal mining area in Pennsylvania. Michael was born there, went to high school at Franklin Borough where he was in the school orchestra and played basketball.

Has Brother In Navy

He worked for 18 months in a CCC camp and in 1939, offering as his reason, "I like the Marines," enlisted in the corps. A brother, 19, is in the Navy, another brother 21 and a sister 12 at home.

Pharmacist's Mate Second Class John H. Bradley, 21, now in San Diego with "stateside" leg wound, is the only non-Marine of the group. An undertaker's assistant before he joined the Navy 26 months ago, Bradley sought a pharmacists rating as an occupational aid. He was serving with "E" company, second battalion, 28th Marines, on Iwo as a medic. He was graduated in 1941 from high school in Appleton, Wis., where his father, a veteran of the last war, is a bar proprietor. In high school Bradley was a wrestler, came out of that sport with a trick knee, which he managed to get past the medical examiners in January, 1944.

Gagnon Is Engaged

Pfc. Rene A. Gagnon, whose helmet barely is visible beside Bradley in the photograph, the other unhurt survivor, identified the other men and said, "it makes you feel kind of strange to know that out of those six fellows, three of them are dead. They were my buddies." Gagnon, 20, is the son of Mrs. Irene Gagnon of Manchester, N. H. He is engaged to Miss Pauline Harnois, 19, whose picture he carried in his helmet throughout the Iwo fighting. They worked in the same room at Chicopee Mills before Gagnon enlisted.

He had tried to enlist in the Navy at 17 but was rejected becaused of high blood pressure. He carefully followed a physician's instructions and passed the Marine Corps physical a year later. Gagnon wants to be a policeman after the war. He told Gov. Charles M. Dale, of N. H., "The war is making some tough fighters. It will take some fellows with training to keep them in line."

Sgt. Henry O. Hansen, 25, the man at the base of the pole, is the "daredevil who wanted action," according to his mother Mrs. Madeline Evelley of Somerville, Mass. He joined the Marines in June, 1938 after serving a year in the Merchant Marine. He had an opportunity to remain in this country as a gunnery instructor when he re-enlisted last June but chose to go overseas. Three brothers are in the service and a sister is about to become a Navy nurse.

On 3,500,000 Posters

In the coming war bond drive, the picture of these six men will be reproduced on 3,500,000 posters, 15,000 outdoor panels, and 175,000 car cards. It also is expected to appear on a postage stamp and has been suggested for monuments.

Photographer Rosenthal, now vacationing on the West Coast, has been honored by the Catholic Institute of the Press, the Press Photographers Association of New York, by such letters as Navy Secretary Forrestal's — who was there and saw the incident—stating, "I think it is the outstanding photograph of the war." And there have been countless letters from parents of boys who fought on Iwo.

Rosenthal himself says, "I just hope the picture will help focus attention on the Marines for the terrific job they did at Iwo."

BIG INCH

(Continued From Page Nine)

develops. Looking like an engineer's blue print of the pumps and the lines in the next room, there are electrically lighted arrows and buttons which at a trained glance show how the fuel is flowing through the three pumps and how the mechanism of the pumps themselves is functioning.

"If, however," said Reich, "one of the pumps gets hot or something goes wrong with it, a red light indicates trouble in that pump. We press a button and automatically that pump is cut out and, without any stoppage in the flow, the pump is by-passed until repairs are made. The control goes even further than that. If the pressure along the line gets dangerously high, a pump will cut out automatically for the protection of the line. It will cut out, too, if the pressure gets extremely low. Pressure is followed carefully and recorded automatically on graphs which are circular discs and which show every pound of pressure on each disc over a 24 hour period."

1400 Miles At a Touch

"A man," Reich continued, "is on duty watching the control board and the graph all the time. So efficient is the control system, that within a minute and a half the whole line across the country can be shut down. For instance, if I get notification of a break from the dispatcher in Cincinnati, I merely push a button and all pumping stops at once. Through the two way radio system this can be done simultaneously over 1400 miles of pipeline."

Every two hours tests are made of crude for gravity and sediment and a report compiled. The gadget used looks like a milk separator. Because sediment normally gathers in the pipelines, once a month scrapers, called "pigs" are sent through the lines to keep them clean. But Engineer Reich, who has been in charge since last May, knows his oil so well that all he needs is his nose to tell from which field in Texas the oil is coming.

"Each has a distinctive odor," he says, "like different kinds of perfume."

LANCASTER CLEARINGS

Clearings for April 21, 1945 $327,954.27
Corresponding day last year $297,304.63

Dr. Jung Here Today, Will Talk On Aid For Victims Of War

With the approach of V. E. Day in Europe, the humilities, the suffering and hunger of the people in Europe comes vividly into focus. People are coming out of hiding—out of woods and forests, out of caves, out of sewers. They know that liberation has arrived. As they come out and into the open they bring their scantily clothed bodies, an endured hunger for food, and above all a spirit and desire to survive. They know there is but one direction to turn their outstretched arms for help—to America.

The United Jewish Appeal being conducted throughout the Communities of America is an answer to these peoples.

Louis J .Wainer, Chairman of the 1945 Campaign for the Lancaster United Jewish Appeal, whose program is to raise $45,000 toward a national drive of $82,000,000 to carry on the work of rescue, relief, and rehabilitation of the surviving Jewish populations in Europe and Palestine, will introduce Dr. Leo Jung who will tell this story this afternoon at the Mass Meeting, 3:30 p. m. at the Jewish Community Center, 219 E. King St.

Nationally Prominent

Dr. Jung has held the post of Rabbi at the Jewish Center in New York City since 1922 and is one of the outstanding speakers, scholars, and writers in the American Jewish Community. Rabbi Jung is a director of the National Conference of Christians and Jews, governor of the Jewish Academy of Arts and Sciences, Chairman of the Cultural Committee of the Joint Distribution Committee, a member of the Council of the Jewish Agency for Palestine, for the period 1928 to 1934, he was president of the Rabbinical Council of Union of Orthodox Jewish Congregations of America; he is the son of Rabbi Mayer Jung, formerly chief Rabbi of the Federated Synagogues of London, England.

Rabbi Jung has degrees from London and Cambridge Universities and has written in English, German, and Hebrew for the public in America, Europe and Asia. This is Dr. Jung's first appearance in Lancaster.

THE DANCE OF HOPE. Immigrants arriving in Palestine dance in rejoicing at the end of their long journey. The cost of their transportation from Europe to Palestine, their care and initial accommodation upon arrival, relief, vocational training, financial assistance and housing—all these are the responsibility of the Jewish Agency, whose source of support is the United Jewish Appeals in American communities.

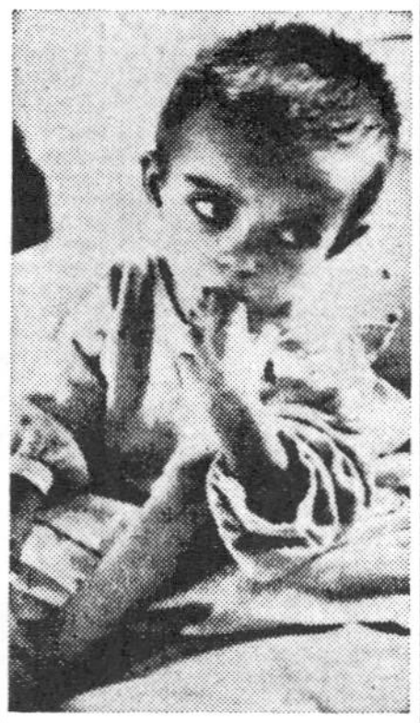

MOTHER IS DEAD, father deported to a foreign country. For two long years, fear and bitter hunger have been his companions, and undernourishment has left marks that will take years of tender care in the home for orphaned Jewish children supported by the Joint Distribution Committee, before he will be strong enough to run and play.

NEW HOMES IN THE HOMELAND. The rising influx of new immigrants has created a critical housing shortage. This housing development for workers near Tel Aviv was financed with the aid of the United Palestine Appeal. The Jewish Agency has set aside $2,400,000 in its budget for the current year for the construction of dwellings and the encouragement of private building activities.

NEW YORK CURB

Closing prices furnished by Reynolds and Co. Members N. Y. Stock Exchange and N. Y. Curb Exchange, 61 N. Duke St., Lancaster, Pa

APRIL 21	CLOSE		CLOSE
Aireon	5⅞	Natl City Line	20
Am Cyan B	42⅛	Pantepec	12⅞
Am G and El	34⅞	Niag Hud Pw	4⅞
Atlas Plywood	20⅝	Pennroad	6¾
Bliss E W	23⅞	Pgt S P and L	16½
Blumenthal	20¼	Radio Kth Wts	1¼
Bow-Bilt Pfd	35½	Raytheon	19½
Breeze Corp	17⅞	Repub Aviat	7⅜
Brewster	5⅜	Richmond Rad	4½
Cal Tungsten	6⅞	Root Petrol	7⅞
Cessna	4⅜	St Regis Paper	5⅞
Childs Pfd	110	Salt Dome Oil	9½
Cities Svc	20⅛	Segal	2¾
Creole Petr	28⅞	St Oil of Ky	19⅞
Cub Atl Sugar	23½	Technicolor	21¾
Detroit Mich	6½	Tilo Roofing	11¼
Divco Truck	15	Tr West Oil	54¼
Easy "B"	10¼	Un Cigar W	3⅜
El Bd and Shr	12¾	Un Gas	11⅝
El B-S 5 pc	96¾	Un Wall Paper	4¾
Glen A Coal	21	Venezuela Petr	11
Jacobs F L	12¾	Wright Hrg	3 13-16
Kingston Prod	4½		Asked
Lone Star Gas	12	Hm Wtch Com	19⅞
Natl Bell Hess	3	Hm Wtch Pfd	109
Molydenum	9⅞		

Penn State's golf teams have won 107 of 153 matches, in 23 seasons under Bob Rutherford, Sr.

George Harvey, Penn State's wartime track coach, has been an avid fisherman since boyhood.

N. Y. STOCK MARKET

By The Associated Press

Div. in $	Sales in Hds.	High	Low	Close	Net Chge.
Ad Exp (e.60)	11	15⅛	15	15⅛	+ ⅛
Air Redu (a1)	11	47½	47	47	− ½
Alaska June.	2	7	6⅞	7	..
AllegStl(g.40)	2	31½	31½	31½	− ½
Allied S (1)..	7	26	26	26	+ ⅜
All Chal(g.40)	13	47	46½	47	+ ⅜
Am Air(e1) ..	2	51¾	51⅝	51⅝	+ ⅜
Am Cable & R	13	12⅛	12	12⅛	+ ⅛
Am Can(3)..	2	95¾	95¾	95¾	−1¼
AmForPow2p	2	24	24	24	+ ¼
AmLoco(g.35)	4	34⅝	34½	34⅝	+ ½
Am P & L 5p	8	68⅜	68	68⅛	+ ⅜
Am Rad (.40)	30	14¼	13⅞	14¼	+ ¼
Am Roll(.80)	4	18¾	18⅝	18¾	+ ⅜
Am Roll p(4½)	*50	84½	84½	84½	− ½
Am Smelt(a2)	2	46½	46½	46½	+ ⅛
Am StlFdy(2)	3	31¾	31¾	31¾	− ⅛
Am Tel & T(9)	16	164⅝	164¼	164⅝	+ ¼
Am Tob B(a3)	5	74¾	74¼	74¾	+ ½
Am Type (g½)	6	14⅞	14⅞	14⅞	− ⅛
Am Visco (2)	3	49¼	49⅛	49¼	+ ⅛
Anac Cop (2½)	10	33¾	33⅝	33⅝	+ ⅛
Armour Co..	7	7¾	7¾	7¾	..
Arms'g (g½).	3	49¼	49	49⅛	+ ⅜
Asso Dry (1)	2	22¼	22⅛	22¼	− ⅛
Atch S F(6)	15	97	95¾	97	+ ⅞
AtlCoast(g1¾	5	70⅜	70⅛	70⅜	+ ⅜
Atl Refin (g½)	10	34	33¾	34	+ ¼
Atlas Cor (½)	4	16⅝	16⅜	16⅝	+ ¼
Baldwin (e1½)	3	29½	29½	29½	+ ⅜
Balt & Ohio..	32	17	16¾	16⅞	+ ¼
Balt & Ohio p	14	30½	30	30½	+ ¾
Barnsd(.80)..	70	24⅛	23½	24⅛	+ ⅝
Bath Iron(4)	9	20⅜	20¼	20¼	− ⅛
Bendix (3)....	5	52½	52¼	52¼	− ¼
Beth Steel(6)	4	76¾	76¼	76¼	+ ⅜
Blaw K(.60)..	4	15¼	15⅛	15¼	+ ⅛
BoeingA(g1).	5	18¼	18⅛	18¼	− ¼
Borden (g.40)	9	35⅞	35⅝	35⅝	− ⅜
BriggsM(2)..	10	41	40¾	41	+ ½
BuddMfg(g¼	12	11⅜	11¼	11⅜	..
Budd 5 p(5)..	*100	81	81	81	..
Budd W(g.15)	11	14	13⅞	13⅞	− ⅛
Burr Ad(g.10)	9	15	14⅞	15	..
Byron J (a1).	5	25	25	25	− ¼
Cal Hec (g.10)	5	6⅝	6⅝	6⅝	− ⅛
Can Pac (g½).	10	13⅛	13	13⅛	..
Case J I(g.40)	4	41	40½	41	+ ½
Caterpillar(2)	11	54¼	53½	54¼	+ ¼
Celanese(2)..	3	51⅜	50¾	51⅜	+ ¼
Cer de Pas(3)	5	34½	34¼	34½	+ ½
Ches & O (a3)	40	50¾	50⅛	50⅝	..
Ch G W p(g½)	4	26⅜	26¼	26⅜	+ ⅜
Chrysler(3)	6	104½	104	104½	+ ½
Climax(a1.20)	1	39¼	39¼	39¼	− ¼
ColgPalm(1).	3	35	34⅝	34⅝	− ⅜
Coll & Aik (1)	1	39½	39½	39½	..
Col GE(g.10)	132	5⅜	5⅛	5¼	− ⅛
Com InvTr(2)	7	49⅞	49⅛	49⅞	+ ⅜
Com Sol(e½)..	4	17¼	17⅛	17¼	+ ⅛
Com Ed (1.40)	7	31	30⅞	31	+ ¼
Comw'th & S	679	1⅛	1	1⅛	..
Con Edi(1.60)	20	28¾	28⅜	28½	− ⅛
C Film p(g½).	2	29¾	29½	29½	− ¼
ConVultee(2).	25	22⅜	22	22¼	− ¼
Contain (g½)	1	29⅝	29⅝	29⅝	..
Cont Bak (g½)	11	10	9⅞	10	..
Cont Can (1).	7	44⅝	44¼	44¼	− ¾
Cont M(g.20).	14	11	10⅞	10⅞	− ⅛
ContOD(g.40)	2	35	34¾	34¾	− ⅛
Corn P (2.60).	2	64¼	63¾	64¼	+1
Crane(1).....	4	31¼	31	31¼	..
Cruc St (e3).	1	45	45	45	+ ½
Cuba AS(e1).	9	16½	16¼	16¼	− ⅛
Curtis Pub ..	19	11¼	11	11¼	+ ⅛
Curtis W (e½)	17	5⅞	5¾	5¾	− ⅛
Deere(e2)....	2	44¾	44¾	44¾	+ ⅛
Del Hud (4)..	3	47	46⅞	46⅞	+ ⅛
Del Lack W..	17	9¼	9⅛	9¼	+ ¼
Dis S (h2.22).	7	50⅞	50⅜	50½	..
Dome (h1.20)	4	24½	24⅜	24½	+ ½
Douglas (e5).	1	69½	69½	69½	− ½
duPont(g1½).	3	171	170¼	171	+ ¼
EAirLines(1).	11	50¾	50⅛	50¼	− ¼
E Auto L(2).	1	50	50	50	..
El Boat(g½)..	10	16½	16¼	16½	+ ⅛
El Pow L 6 p	1	118	118	118	+1
Eng Pub Serv	25	21½	21⅛	21½	+ ¼
Erie R R(1)..	42	16	15¾	16	+ ¼
Erie p A (5)..	1	79½	79½	79½	+1⅞
Flintk't(g.15)	33	30½	29⅝	30½	+ ⅝
Food Fair (1)	4	19¼	18⅞	19¼	+ ⅛
Gen Cigar(a1)	1	29⅝	29⅝	29⅝	..
GenElec(1.60)	19	42⅝	42½	42½	..
Gen Fds(1.60)	11	42¼	42⅛	42¼	+ ⅛
Gen Motor (3)	15	68½	68⅜	68½	+ ½
Gen Mot p (5)	4	127½	127	127½	+ ⅝
Gillette (.80).	9	15	14⅞	15	+ ⅜
Gimbel(g½)..	14	26¾	26⅜	26⅝	+ ⅜
Goodrich (2).	5	61⅝	61	61⅝	− ⅛
Goodyear (2).	5	57½	57⅛	57½	+ ½
Gt N Ry p(e2)	11	53½	53	53⅜	+ ⅛
Greyh (a1.40)	6	24¾	24½	24¾	+ ½
Gulf M p(e5).	3	69¼	67¾	69¼	+2¼
Gulf Oil(a1)..	7	55⅜	55	55⅜	+ ⅛
Homestake M	2	46⅝	46⅝	46⅝	− ⅛
Houd H B(1).	3	22¼	21⅞	21⅞	− ⅛
Houston Oil .	20	18¼	18	18¼	+ ⅜
Illinois Cent.	41	30⅝	30	30⅝	+ ⅜
In'lake(e.35).	4	10	9⅞	10	+ ¼
In Har (a2.60)	4	84½	84¼	84½	− ¼
Int Nick(1.60)	16	33	32½	33	+ ¼
Int Paper....	25	25⅜	24¾	25⅜	+ ⅝
Int Pap p (5)	1	90¼	90¼	90¼	+ ¼
Int T & T....	43	27¾	27⅜	27⅝	+ ½
John M(g½)..	3	119	118¼	119	+1
Jones L (g1).	10	32	31¼	32	+ ½
Kans CitySou	45	21¼	20½	21⅛	+1¼
Kennecot(g½)	25	39¼	38¾	39¼	+ ¼
Kresge (a1)..	1	27⅞	27⅞	27⅞	− ⅛
Kroger (2)....	1	40⅞	40⅞	40⅞	+ ⅝
Lambert(a1½)	1	34⅛	34⅛	34⅛	− ¼
Leh Nav (e1).	5	13¾	13½	13¾	+ ¼
Leh'an (a1.20)	5	41⅝	41⅛	41⅛	− ¼
LOFGl(g½)..	5	62⅜	61½	62⅜	+ ⅜
LibMcN(g½).	21	8⅞	8¾	8¾	− ⅛
Lig My B (a3)	5	89	88¾	89	+ ½
Lockheed (2).	3	21	20⅞	20⅞	..
Loew's (a2)..	6	77⅞	77⅝	77⅝	− ⅜
Lorill'd(g½)..	1	22¾	22¾	22¾	..
Macy(1.60)...	3	34¾	34¾	34¾	+ ⅛
M Field (a.80)	2	20⅞	20⅞	20⅞	− ⅛
McKess (1.40)	1	25¾	25¾	25¾	− ¼
Mid Cont(g½)	38	30¾	30⅛	30¾	+ ¼
Mo Kan Tex p	18	26¼	25½	26¼	+ ⅝
MontgW(2)..	4	61	61	61	+ ¼
NashKel(½).	69	19⅝	19⅛	19⅝	+ ½
Nat Acme(2).	6	24¾	24½	24⅝	− ⅛
Nat Bis (1.20)	7	25⅜	25⅛	25⅜	..
NatCash(a1).	5	34½	34⅛	34½	+ ¼
N Dairy(1.40)	9	29⅞	29¾	29⅞	..
Nat Distil(2).	10	40¼	39⅞	40¼	+ ⅛
Nat Gyp (e½).	18	15¾	15⅝	15⅝	..
Nat Lead (a½)	9	28	27⅞	28	..
Nat Pow & Lt	192	9⅞	9½	9⅞	+ ½
Nat Steel (3).	2	71¼	71¼	71¼	+ ¼
NatSupply...	6	17	16¾	16¾	− ¼
New Ind (.80)	2	22⅞	22¾	22⅞	+ ⅜
N Y Cent (g1)	74	25	24⅝	25	+ ⅜
N Y C & StL p	4	134½	133	134½	+1½
N Y Ship(e3).	1	23⅛	23⅛	23⅛	+ ⅜
N Am Av(e1½)	5	10	9⅞	9⅞	− ⅛
No Am (f.70).	8	24	23⅞	24	..
NorthPac(g1)	59	25	24⅜	25	+ ¾
Ohio Oil (a½).	9	19	18⅞	19	..
Owens Ill (2).	1	68¼	68¼	68¼	+ ½
Pac G & El(2)	4	38	37⅞	38	+ ⅛
Pack M (g.15)	31	6¾	6⅝	6¾	+ ⅛
Pan Am Air..	22	17½	17¼	17⅜	− ⅛
Param't(2)...	19	31¼	30½	31¼	+ ⅝
ParkD(g.60).	4	30½	30¼	30⅜	..
Patino(g¾)..	13	20¾	20½	20½	− ⅜
Penney (a3)..	2	110¼	110	110¼	+ ¼
Pen Cent Air.	5	25⅝	25½	25⅝	+ ⅝
Pen R R (e2½)	19	37¾	37½	37¾	+ ⅛
Pepsi C (.70).	25	25⅛	24⅞	25	+ ¼
Phelps (1.60).	17	28⅜	28⅛	28⅛	− ½
Phila El(1.20)	3	25⅜	25¼	25⅜	..
Philco (g.20).	3	35⅝	35⅛	35⅛	− ½
Phillips P(2).	4	53⅛	52¾	52¾	− ¼
Press Stl(1)..	11	20⅛	19⅞	20	+ ⅛
Proc Gam(2).	7	57	57	57	− ½
Pub SNJ(1)..	7	21	20¾	21	+ ¼
Pub SNJ p(5)	*200	104⅜	104⅜	104⅜	..
Pullman(g½).	7	52¾	52¼	52¾	+ ¾
PureOil(e1)..	29	19⅞	19⅝	19⅝	− ⅛
Radio (g.20) .	24	11⅜	11¼	11⅜	+ ⅛
Radio p(3½)..	2	87¼	87¼	87¼	..
Radio Keith .	7	8¼	8⅛	8⅛	− ⅛
Reading (1)..	1	27¼	27¼	27¼	+ ½
Rem R (a1.20)	3	26⅜	26¼	26⅜	+ ¼
Repub Stl(1).	9	23	22⅞	23	+ ⅜
Revere Cop..	7	16¾	16¼	16¾	+ ½
ReyTB(a1.40)	13	34½	34⅜	34⅜	− ⅛
Safeway new.	8	22⅞	22¼	22⅜	− ¼
Sav Arms(g½)	100	9⅝	9½	9⅝	+ ⅛
Schenley(2)..	30	53¼	52¼	53¼	+1⅛
Sears Roe(a3)	5	106⅞	106⅝	106⅞	+ ⅛
Servel (1)....	13	21⅞	21⅝	21⅞	+ ¼
Shell Un(e1½)	6	27⅝	27⅜	27⅝	..
Simmons (g½)	13	41¼	41	41¼	+ ½
Sincl'r O (1)	27	17	16⅞	17	..
Socony(½)....	53	17¼	17⅛	17¼	..
So Pacific(3)	35	45⅝	45⅛	45½	+ ⅜
Sou Rwy(3)..	10	44¼	43⅛	44¼	+1
Sou Ry p(5)	5	75½	75¼	75⅜	−1¼
Sperry(e2)...	5	29¾	29⅝	29¾	..
Stan Br (1.20)	13	33⅛	32¾	33⅛	..
Stan O Cal (2)	7	43	42¾	43	+ ¼
S O Ind (a1)..	5	37⅜	37¼	37¼	− ⅛
S O N J(a1)..	16	61⅞	61¼	61⅞	+ ¾
Stone W (e½).	5	13¼	13	13	..
Studebak(g½)	25	27⅜	27	27⅛	+ ¼
Sunshin(.40).	8	13¾	13⅝	13⅝	+ ½
Swift (a1.60)	8	31⅜	31¼	31⅜	− ⅜
Texas Co (2).	7	54¼	54	54¼	+ ½
Tex G Sul (a2)	1	40⅛	40⅛	40⅛	+ ⅛
Tide W (a.80)	2	19⅜	19⅜	19⅜	..
Timk De(2)..	4	39½	39½	39½	+ ½
Timk R(2)...	3	54	54	54	−1¼
Transam (a½)	7	11¼	11	11¼	+ ¼
Trans W A.	*10	30½	30⅛	30½	+ ½
Twenth C(a2)	6	29	28⅞	29	+ [illegible]
Un Bag (g.15)	2	16⅝	16⅝	16⅝	+ [illegible]
Un Carb(3)	4	88¾	88½	88¾	− ½
UnPacific(6)	5	125	124¾	125	+ [illegible]
Un Pac p(4)	3	109	108⅝	108⅝	− ⅞
Unit A L(e½)	6	35	34¾	35	+ ⅜
UnitAir(e3)	8	29⅛	28⅞	29	+ ½
Unit Corp....	77	2	1⅞	2	..
Unit Drug ...	1	18¾	18¾	18¾	..
UnFruit(g2).	3	95½	95¼	95¼	−1
Un GasI(g.35)	3	16¾	16⅝	16¾	− ⅛
U S Gyps (2).	1	83½	83½	83½	..
U S Rub (2)..	13	59	58¾	58¾	+ ½
U S Steel (4).	37	66⅞	66¼	66¾	+ ⅜
U S Steel p(7)	1	146	146	146	− ½
Vanad'm(g¼)	4	25½	25¼	25½	+ ¼
Wal'th (e.60).	12	10⅝	10⅜	10⅝	..
Warner Pict	9	14⅝	14⅜	14⅝	..
West UA(2)	8	46⅜	46⅛	46⅜	+ ¼
WestAB(g½).	6	30½	30⅜	30½	− ¼
Westg E(4)	8	134⅞	134	134⅞	− ⅛
Whi Stl(g½)	2	38½	38½	38½	+ ½
White M (g½)	4	30½	30⅜	30½	+ ¼
Wilson Co	1	12¾	12¾	12¾	+ ¼
Woolwt (1.60)	8	46	45½	46	+ ⅛
Worth P (g½)	6	58	57½	57½	− ½
Y'ng Sh T(2).	11	49¼	48⅞	49¼	+ ⅝
Zenith(g1)...	1	39⅜	39⅜	39⅜	..

The 1946 season will mark Leo Houck's 24th year as Penn State boxing coach.

Bowling -- --Standings

FULTON MAJOR "A"
(Final Standings)

Teams	W.	L.	P.C.
Sergeants	72	48	.600
Majors	66	54	.550
Colonels	65	55	.542
Captains	63	57	.525
Generals	54	66	.450
Lieutenants	40	80	.333

Jake Shinsky—268
Generals—1091
Robert Liller—678
Captains—2965
Sec., Chas. Frey

FULTON MAJOR "B"
(Final Standings)

Teams	W.	L.	P.C.
Navy	70	50	.583
Coast Guard	68	52	.567
Air Corps	65	55	.542
Infantry	65	55	.542
Paratroops	58	62	.483
Marines	33	87	.275

Larry Sterling—245
Infantry—1011—2822
Norman Trimble—647
Sec., Chas. Frey

ST. PAUL'S METHODIST GIRLS

Teams	W.	L.	P.C.
Violets	36	20	.643
Pansies	34	22	.607
Roses	24	32	.429
Daisies	18	38	.321

J. Kurtz—212
Violets—803—2187
G. Long—509

CHRIST LUTHERAN

Teams	W.	L.	P.C.
Roses	38	18	.679
Daisies	34	22	.607
Lilies	27	29	.482
Poppies	26	30	.464
Pansies	22	34	.393
Violets	21	35	.375

Bob Buckwalter—243
Everett Wilson—651
Lilies—955
Daisies—2589
Sec., John Hoin

AUTOMOTIVE

Teams	W.	L.	P.C.
Hydra Matics	77	51	.602
Head Lights	74	54	.578
Plugs	73	55	.570
Bolts	70	58	.547
Mufflers	68	60	.531
Brakes	61	67	.477
Nuts	56	72	.438
Fire Balls	55	73	.430
Tail Lights	54	74	.422
Clippers	52	76	.406

W. J. Moorehouse—262
Plugs—982—2689
Wilbur Benedict—621
Sec., R. J. Schwalm

MIDDLETOWN AIRCRAFT
(Final Standings)

Teams	W.	L.	P.C.
Airacobras	36	12	.750
Mustangs	29	19	.604
Thunderbolts	27	21	.563
Lightnings	4	44	.083

J. Hohenwarter—256—650
Airacobras—871—2415
Sec., R. V. Shaeffer

CITY LADIES DUCKS

Teams	W.	L.	P.C.
Birchs	38	14	.731
Oaks	37	15	.712
Elms	29	23	.558
Spruces	29	23	.558
Willows	27	25	.519
Cedars	25	27	.481
Pines	14	38	.259
Maples	9	43	.173

A. Vermot—166—413
Cedars—599—1595
Sec., Alice Vermot

TUESDAY NITE MIXED

Teams	W.	L.	P.C.
Green	32	20	.615
Red	28	24	.538
Black	25	27	.481
Blue	19	33	.365

Ladies—Totty Wild—212
Men—Elvin Irwin and Ralph Licht—244
Blue—837
Ladies—Bea Rinehart—505
Men—Ed. Lapham—588
Red—2288
Sec., Freda Stretch

IOOF

Teams	W.	L.	P.C.
Eagles	40	20	.667
Crows	35	25	.583
Robins	26	34	.433
Owls	19	41	.317

Tiny Wiker—257
Robins—995—2754
Dick Weaver—658
Sec., Chris Kendig

MERCHANT LADIES

Teams	W.	L.	P.C.
Jewels	37	19	.661
Glassware	33	23	.589
Coal	29	27	.518
Bread	29	27	.518
Fashions	24	32	.429
Gas	16	40	.286

Eliz. Marabella—221
Catherine Judith—552
Jewels—869
Gas and Glassware—2289
Sec., Helen Davidson

CLOSURE

Teams	W.	L.	P.C.
Marines	46	14	.767
Commandos	43	17	.717
Air Corps	43	17	.717
Rangers	36	24	.600
Navy	32	28	.533
Marauders	26	34	.433
Army	23	37	.383
Flying Tigers	14	46	.233

John Timmins—271
Rangers—957
Willis Brenneman—647
Commandos—2588
Sec., Elmer C. Allwine

MERCHANTS BOWLING

Teams	W.	L.	P.C.
Brewmen	94	34	.735
Overlook	85	43	.645
Furniture	76	52	.555
Drugs	70	58	.495
S-R	70	58	.495
Ernies	62	66	.415
G. and W.	62	66	.415
Machines	58	70	.385
Hats	52	76	.325
Sportsmen	50	78	.305
Jewelers	46	82	.265
Cafe	43	85	.235

Bill Taggart—680
Machines—1081
Bob Smith—265
Overlook—3013
Sec., Bob Brill

MOUNT JOY TOWN

Teams	W.	L.	P.C.
Stuckeys	46	14	.767
Doughertys	38	22	.633
Alwines	31	29	.517
Schneiders	28	32	.467
Tronios	26	34	.433
Bennetts	24	36	.400
Barnharts	22	34	.393
Haas	21	35	.375

Ken Stuckey—276—687
Doughertys—1038—2802
Sec., J. S. Barnhart

OVERLOOK C. C.

Teams	W.	L.	P.C.
Mid-Irons	36	16	.692
Sandwedges	35	17	.673
Cleeks	31	21	.596
Brassies	30	22	.577
Spades	29	23	.558
Putters	28	24	.538
Spoons	25	27	.481
Niblics	24	28	.462
Baffies	23	29	.442
Jiggers	20	32	.385
Mashies	16	36	.308
Drivers	15	37	.288

Ollie Morrison—269
Red Webster—695
Baffies—1032
Mid-Irons—2751
Sec., Wm. S. Webster

ELKS—NATIONAL

Teams	W.	L.	P.C.
Badgers	42	14	.750
Deer	36	20	.643
Lions	35	21	.625
Comers	33	23	.589
Antlers	27	29	.482
Wolves	26	30	.464
Charity	12	44	.214
Wildcats	7	49	.125

DeCroce—225—496
Antlers—785
Badgers—2273
Sec., Netscher

ELKS—AMERICAN

Teams	W.	L.	P.C.
Leopards	42	14	.750
Cubs	37	19	.661
Fidelity	29	27	.518
Justice	29	27	.518
Tigers	28	28	.500
Bro. Love	26	30	.464
Bears	26	30	.464
Elks	13	43	.232

Keller—225
Mowrer—514
Bears—780—2188
Sec., Netscher

MANHEIM STOKOR

Teams	W.	L.	P.C.
Hoppers	40	20	.667
Worms	30	30	.500
Gravity	30	30	.500
Binfeed	28	32	.467
Controls	27	33	.450
Motors	25	35	.417

Diehl—209
Doerr—552
Controls—2382
Sec., Frank Thomas

ST. PAUL'S METHODIST

Teams	W.	L.	P.C.
Tigers	87	41	.680
Indians	70	58	.547
Cards	70	58	.547
Cubs	67	61	.523
Yanks	63	65	.492
Senators	62	66	.484
A's	50	78	.383
Browns	43	85	.336

Irwin Hixon—263—633
Indians—927
Tigers—2544
Sec., Geo. Brunner

QUARRYVILLE RECREATION
(Final Standings)

Teams	W.	L.	P.C.
Pins	43	13	.800
Misses	34	20	.601
Balls	30	26	.536
Strikes	23	33	.401
Splits	23	33	.401
Spares	15	41	.268

Frank Graver—244
Buzz Myers—637
Misses—942—2677
Sec., Bob Gabriel

POWER DUCKS

Teams	W.	L.	P.C.
Transformers	44	16	.733
Fuses	44	16	.733
Kilowatts	28	32	.467
Lights	28	32	.467
Plugs	19	41	.317
Amps	19	41	.317

"Tillie" Eitnier—184
Lillian Vollmer—429
Transformers—530
Fuses—1494
Sec., Lillian Vollmer

FIRST BAPTIST
(Final Standings)

Teams	W.	L.	P.C.
Seabees	41	15	.732
Marines	30	26	.536
Navy	30	26	.536
Army	25	31	.446
Coast Guard	21	35	.375
Air Corps	21	35	.375

Marines—931
Navy—2592
Neal Kalle—258—644
Sec., John Buchanan

RETAIL LADIES
(Final Standings)

Teams	W.	L.	P.C.
Jewelry	101	19	.842
Overlook	96	24	.800
H. Fashions	67	53	.558
K. Jewelry	65	55	.542
D. Coal	55	65	.458
R. Fashions	40	80	.333
A. Cafe	28	92	.233
H. Shoes	28	92	.233

"Ginnie" Mowrer—233
Overlook—926—2563
Lena McConnell—603
Sec., Jo Binkle

POWER AND LIGHT

Teams	W.	L.	P.C.
Relays	38	22	.633
Water Heaters	33	27	.550
Gas Ranges	33	27	.550
Transformers	16	44	.267

Ray Kendig—233
Relays—965—2648
Charles Burns—621
Sec., Robert E. Groh

TOY
(Final Standings)

Teams	W.	L.	P.C.
Texan	42	18	.700
Pirate	38	22	.633
Army	37	23	.617
Cowboy	23	37	.383
Dandy	22	38	.367
Winner	18	42	.300

Bill Jordan—236
Arlene Aukamp—235—555
Elwood White—622
Pirate—904
Texan—2553
Sec., J. H. Watson

BEARINGS
(Final Standings)

Teams	W.	L.	P.C.
Polishers	42	14	.750
Assemblers	34	22	.607
Beaders	31	25	.553
Collars	27	29	.482
Blanchers	26	30	.454
Grinders	8	48	.143

James Keenen—240
Elwood Rhen—620
Polishers—896—2546
Sec., Willis S. Mayer

YMCA "A"
(Final Standings)

Teams	W.	L.	P.C.
Reds	36	24	.600
Cards	34	26	.567
Giants	34	26	.567
Cubs	16	44	.267

Robert Rudisill—260—629
Reds—910
Giants—2676
Sec., Robert Rudisill

WATCH GIRLS

Teams	W.	L.	P.C.
Hands	41	15	.732
Barrels	40	16	.714
Stems	34	22	.607
Cases	19	37	.339
Pinions	19	37	.339
Clicks	13	43	.232

Verna Wile—231—573
Hands—813
Stems—2209
Sec., Helen N. Rinick

HOME

Teams	W.	L.	P.C.
Drapes	88	40	.696
Stools	84	44	.664
Pictures	69	59	.539
Shades	69	59	.539
Rugs	65	63	.507
Chairs	61	67	.476
Desks	61	67	.476
Lamps	57	69	.445
Radios	56	72	.437
Tables	55	73	.429
Curtains	53	75	.414
Beds	48	80	.375

Andy Doerstler—277
Geo. Nelson—672
Desks—1047
Rugs—2887
Sec., Chas. E. Burns

OVERLOOK LADIES
(Final Standings)

Teams	W.	L.	P.C.
Pars	73	47	.608
Flags	70	50	.583
Markers	62	58	.509
Birdies	54	66	.449
Eagles	54	66	.449
Cups	47	73	.391

Beulah Chandler—230
Birdies—818
Beulah Chandler—618
Pars—2253
Sec. Floss Leinaweaver

MEADIA HEIGHTS

Teams	W.	L.	P.C.
Bogeys	83	45	.649
Pars	69	59	.539
Birdies	63	65	.492
Aces	59	69	.460
Eagles	58	70	.453
Do Does	52	76	.406

Dick Owens—254
Bogeys—979
Do Does—979
C. Alexander—669
Bogeys—2848
Sec., R. J. Moyer

MAC IT
(Final Standing)

Teams	W.	L.	P.C.
Studs	40	20	.667
Keys	38	22	.633
Square Heads	31	29	.317
Headless	30	30	.500
Hollows	30	30	.500
Tool Posts	30	30	.500
Sockets	23	37	.383
Caps	18	42	.300

Daniel Dicely—244
Irwin Miller—595
Sockets—885
Keys—2426
Sec., Carl Neudorf

U. S. TREASURY BALANCE

WASHINGTON, April 21—(AP)—The position of the Treasury April 19:

Receipts	$ 82,731,699.56
Expenditures	$ 28,848,593.24
Net balance	$ 12,309,747,783.36
Working balance included	$ 11,546,816,188.85
Customs receipts for month	$ 20,626,391.70
Receipts fiscal year (July 1)	$ 36,450,659,707.70
Expenditures fiscal yr	$ 78,634,955,917.51
Excess of expenditures	$ 42,184,296,209.81
Total debt	$235,508,433,646.42
Increase over previous day	$ 22,938,880.92
Gold assets	$ 20,395,806,371.58

DOW JONES AVERAGES

Industrials	163.20	up	.37
Railroads	55.19	up	.25
Utilities	29.84	up	.04

2 Draft Boards Send Pre-Inductees

City Board 1 and County Board 5 forwarded groups for pre-induction examinations Saturday. Both boards sent smaller groups than were forwarded last month and many of the men sent formerly held occupational deferments.

Meanwhile, local boards are preparing to fill quotas received from State Selective Service headquarters for pre-inductees to be sent for examination in May. Several of the calls are larger than those received for April, but many are approximately the same size or slightly smaller, according to officials.

Extra

LANCASTER NEW ERA

Weather
Clear, cool, with light to heavy frost tonight; Wednesday fair with slowly rising temperature

Published Every Evening Except Sunday by New Era Company

Examiner Founded 1830
New Era Founded 1877

LANCASTER, PA., TUESDAY, MAY 1, 1945

Entered as second class matter January 31, 1924, at the Post Office at Lancaster, Pa., under the Act of March 3, 1879, Reg. U. S. Pat. Off.

HITLER KILLED IN BERLIN

Germans Report Fuehrer's Death; Admiral Doenitz Is In Command

LONDON, May 1 ---(A. P.)--- The Nazi radio at Hamburg announced tonight that Adolf Hitler had died this afternoon at his command post in Berlin.

The broadcast implied, but did not directly state, that Hitler was slain in battle with the Russians. (The British Broadcasting Company reported that Hitler actually died of a stroke.)

Admiral Karl Doenitz commandant of the German Navy, immediately announced over the Hamburg radio that he had succeeded Hitler, having been appointed by the Nazi dictator yesterday (April 30).

First Task To Save People

Doenitz said "my first task will be to save the German people from the advance of the Bolshevist enemy. For this aim only the struggle continues."

The Hamburg announcement said:

"From the Fuehrer's headquarters it is reported that our Fuehrer, Adolf Hitler, has fallen this afternoon in his command post at the Reichs Chancellery, fighting up to his last breath against Bolshevism."

Doenitz, following the announcer, said:

"German men and women, soldiers of the German army: Our Fuehrer, Adolf Hitler, has fallen.

"With deepest sorrow and reverence the German People bows. He had recognized the horrible danger of Bolshevism very early and consecrated his entire existence to the fight against it.

"At the end of this, his struggle, and of his straight and unerring road, he dies a hero's death in the capital of the German Reich."

No Mention Of Himmler

No mention was made of Heinrich Himmler, Gestapo chief who had been dickering in an attempt to surrender what remained of Germany to Britain and the United States but was turned down because he did not include Russia in his offer.

"At the Fuehrer's headquarters it is reported that our Fuehrer Adolf Hitler has fallen this afternoon in his command post at the Reichs chancellery, fighting up to his last breath against Bolshevism," said the announcement.

"Give me your confidence," Doenitz appealed to the German people. "Keep calm and be disciplined. Only in that way will we be able to stave off defeat."

The announcement said Hitler had appointed Doenitz April 30 (yesterday) as his successor.

Hinted Grave Announcement

The broadcast came approximately an hour after the Hamburg radio had told its listeners that it would shortly have a grave and important announcement.

"German men and women, soldiers of the German Army, our Fuehrer Adolf Hitler has fallen," Doenitz announced dramatically.

"With deepest sorrow and reverence the German people bows.

"He had recognized the horrible danger of Bolshevism very early and consecrated his existence to the fight against it. At the end of this his struggle and of his straight and unerring road he dies a hero's death in the capital of the German Reich.

Praised Hitler's Fight

"His life was entirely given to the service of Germany. His struggle against the Bolshevist storm floods was, furthermore, not only for Europe, but for the entire civilized world. The Fuehrer has appointed me to be his successor. Fully conscious of the responsibility, I take over the leadership of the German people in the fateful hour."

"My first task will be to save the German people from the advance of the Bolshevist enemy," Doenitz continued. "For this aim only the military struggle continues.

"For as long and as far as the reaching of this aim will be impeded by the Anglo-Americans, we shall continue to defend ourselves against them and fight them.

"The Anglo-Americans do not then continue the war for their own people but solely for the spreading of Bolshevism in Europe. What the German people has achieved fighting this war and what they have suffered at the home front is a historic unicum."

Order To The Army

Doenitz also addressed an order of the day to the German Army.

In addressing the people, Doenitz said, "in the coming times of distress I shall aim to give the brave German women, men and children bearable living conditions to the limit of my powers. For all tha I shall need your assistance.

"Give me your confidence, because your road is my road too. Maintain order and discipline in own and country. Let everyone do his duty at his post. Only thus shall we be able to mitigate the suffering which the coming times will bring to each one of us. Only thus will we be able to avoid the collapse.

"If we do what is in our power to do, the Almighty will not abandon us after so much suffering and after so many sacrifices."

Will Continue Figh

Doenitz, in a personal broadcast immediately after the reading of the proclamation, declared that Germany would continue to fight—but continued the Nazi propaganda line that this would be only to save the nation from Russia.

"My first task," said Doenitz, "will be to save Germany from the advancing Bolsheviks. Only for this do we continue to fight.

"Give me your confidence. Keep calm and be disciplined. Only in that way will be able to save off defeat."

Doenitz was introduced by the announcer, who said:

"Our new Fuehrer will speak to the German people."

In his order of the day to the Army, of which he now had become the supreme commander, Doenitz said:

"Adolf Hitler has striven all his life to save the peoples of Europe from Bolshevism. In this struggle he has sacrificed his life and found a hero's death."

Here a ghost voice broke into the broadcast, shouting:

"This is a lie."

Says Greatest Hero Gone

Doenitz continued, "with Hitler, one of the greatest heroes in German history has gone."

Then the ghost voice declared:

"The greatest of all Fascists."

When Doenitz said, "filled with proud respect and mourning we lower the banners before him," the ghost voice again interrupted with:

"His death calls upon us to act. Strike now."

Doenitz Takes Command

Doenitz continued, "The Fuehrer has appointed me his successor as head of the state and as supreme commander of the Wehrmacht. I take over the supreme command over all parts of the German Wehrmacht imbued with the determination to continue the struggle against the Bolsheviks until such

(See HITLER DEAD—Page 2)

Hitler's Many Roles On Way To Disaster

HITLER MAY HAVE DIED WEEKS AGO. OR REPORT MAY BE RUSE

By The Associated Press

Whether Adolf Hitler actually died at his command post in Berlin today as the German radio said, the world may not know with assurance for some time—perhaps never.

He may have been dead for days or weeks; he may still be living and this announcement only a ruse to help his escape plans.

However, the Hamburg radio announcement could mean that this is the official end of Adolf Hitler, as far as what authority remains in Germany is concerned.

Whether he is living or dead, it could mean that the Nazi heirarchy has decided that the myth of Hitler dead now suits its purposes better than the myth of Hitler living and leading the last forlorn hope in Berlin.

A legend of Hitler dying in a Goetterdaemmerung finale to the terrible tragedy he precipitated may also fit in with Nazi propaganda plans for the years or generations ahead.

The possibility remains that Adolf Hitler actually may have died as described.

MORE DRAFT BOARDS GET MAY QUOTAS

May induction calls received by several local draft boards are slightly smaller than those received in April, reflecting the diminishing calls being issued throughout the state, officials announced.

The state-wide quota for May is 11,880 men, approximately 2,000 less than the April call and substantially lower than the monthly calls of late in 1944 when military forces were being built to peak strength. According to State Selective Service officials the June quota will be further decreased, with calls for 10,236, a decrease of 1,644 from May.

LIONS WILL HEAR HEAD OF POW CAMP

Lt. Col. Samuel E. Tromley, commanding officer of the prisoner of war base camp at Indiantown Gap, will speak on handling of prisoners of war at the Lions' Club meeting at 12:15 P. M. tomorrow at Hotel Brunswick.

Col. Tromley formerly assisted in processing captured war prisoners in Europe.

A muskrat provides about one and a half pounds of edible meat.

FLAG ASSOCIATION WILL HOLD FESTIVAL

A meeting of the East End Flag Association was held last evening in St. Mark's Lutheran Church with Leon Metzger, vice president, presiding. Preliminary plans for a festival to be held the middle of June were made, and Richard Kipphorn and Phares Hostetter were named co-chairmen.

The next meeting of the association will be held Monday, May 28.

The earliest state income tax was instituted in Virginia in 1843.

Life History of Adolf Hitler

By LOUIS P. LOCHNER

Little did those of us who were assigned to duty as foreign correspondents in Germany during the days of the struggling Weimar Republic imagine that Adolf Hitler, the rabble rousing ex-corporal and one-time Austrian house painter, would one day play a role in history comparable to that of a Nero, a Caesar, a Genghis Khan, a Napoleon, or an Alexander the Great.

Yet in a measure he surpassed all these earlier devotees of carnage and conquest. For, it can be said of Adolf Hitler that no single man in the entire history of mankind brought misery to as many human beings as did Der Fuehrer of Greater Germany.

By that statement I do not desire to put Adolf Hitler down as a more cunning or brilliant or diabolically capable man than the dictators before him. The simple facts in the situation, however, are that Hitler was born in an era of mechanical inventions the like of which history has hitherto not known.

THE MODERN TOUCH

Through the radio he could reach more mortals than any world figure before him. With the airplane he could contact personally more groups of people than any campaigner preceding him. By the mechanization of warfare his troops could cover more ground than any army of World War I. Through the development of the science of explosives his mechanized forces could carry death and destruction over wider areas than had been possible to earlier exponents of "Schrecklichkeit."

Hence, when I award the palm for spreading human sorrow to Adolf Hitler, I do it to condemn a man who, had he used the instrumentalities provided by modern civilization to advance human progress rather than to attempt to throw it back into the Middle Ages, might have emerged as a benefactor of mankind.

I found myself unable during my long stay in Germany to explain to my own satisfaction how the strange phenomenon bearing the name of Adolf Hitler could acquire the hold upon the German people that he did. I thought then that once I had returned to America and would be able to contemplate the years spent under Nazism more dispassionately, I might find a satisfactory explanation.

But such is not the case. The other night I happened to stray into a movie in the course of which Adolf Hitler's voice suddenly is heard. I had not listened to a Hitler harangue since the days of my internment at Bad Nauheim, early in 1942, when a group of us had access to a tiny radio set which we managed to keep from the inquisitive eyes of our Gestapo guards.

I was bewildered. I understood Hitler's oratorical hold upon his people less than ever. That raucous voice — its hysteria — its jarring dissonance — its lack of beauty or even dignity of expression: how, I asked myself, could I, in the days of my reporting in Germany, sit there for several hours at a time and stand it? How could the German people stand it?

When I think of Adolf Hitler, I have a picture of the most unharmonious human being I ever met, of a man full of contradictions within his own self. Here are some of them:

A man who could hold audiences spell-bound for hours at a time, yet whose diction often was ungrammatical, his voice repulsive, his platitudes exasperatingly repetitious, his meaning frequently obscure;

A devotee of physical culture who took no exercise except occasional hiking, who could neither swim nor box nor run nor play tennis nor compete at football, who never hunted nor rode a mount, who never, as far as I knew, pulled an oar;

A fanatic for mechanization who knew not how to drive a car, never had the curiosity to sit in the cab of a moving railway engine, never piloted an airplane;

A political leader credited with hypnotic powers over those whom he could look firmly into the eyes, yet who squirmed and became visibly uneasy if anybody contemplated him deliberately and unflinchingly;

A MAN WITH 'FRONT'

A play-actor and stage poseur who seemed indubitably sure of himself and convinced of the infallibility of his decisions, but who was revealed again and again to be made up of inferiority complexes, who faltered and hesitated, and often made decision and action dependent upon the last man with whom he chanced to discuss a given question, provided he took a fancy to that man;

A politician who preached realism in government and military strategy but who personally relied on hunches and intuitions and was steeped in superstitions;

A lover of music who—an uncommon thing in Germany — never joined a Maennerchor or Gesangverein, played no instrument, hummed no tune, cared for almost no other music save that of Richard Wagner.

Yet it is undeniable that his own followers worshipped him and blindly carried out his instructions. Nobody, not even the ablest of German generals, dared stand up to him (except at the very end). His word was law.

BORN IN AUSTRIA

Adolf Hitler just missed by the breadth of the River Inn, a tributary of the Danube, being born in the Germany of which he later became the dictator. Braunauam-Inn, in Austria, can claim the notoriety of being the birth-place, on April 20, 1889, of Adolf, son of the illegitimate Alois Schickelgruber. Twelve years before his son's birth Alois had succeeded in obtaining permission to call himself by the family name of his presumptive father, a miller named Johann Georg Hitler, rather than continuing with the name of his mother, a domestic named Maria Anna Schickelgruber.

Braunau was pretty much of a counterpart of the average American Main Street town, except that it could look back upon an historic past with ruins of fortifications and of patrician residences dating back to the 15th century.

Possibly these romantic ruins, together with the medieval city gate, the ancient municipal fountain, and the venerable Church of St. Stephen, erected in 1439, had something to do with awakening in the future leader of Germany that romanticism which became that romanticism which became most obvious in his devotion to Richard Wagner's "Meistersinger."

STRAIN OF ILLEGITIMACY

However that may be, Adolf Hitler spent the earliest years of his life in Braunau as the son, by third marriage to a woman 20 years younger than himself, of an Austrian Imperial Customs Service functionary. According to one biographer. "Adolf Hitler's father had a rather extravagant marital existence for a customs officer. He had three wives, seven children, one divorce, one child before marriage, and two children born very soon after his marriages to their respective mothers."

One sees the family strain ran to illegitimacy! This parental proclivity probably explains in part why National Socialism, Hitler's creation, so consistently preaches that legitimacy of birth is of no account, whereas purity of race is paramount.

When father Alois reached the pension age, he bought himself a little farm near Linz and sent his son Adolf to the secondary school in the metropolis of the Upper Danube. Accounts of his contemporaries describe him as an "Eigenbroetler"—as a lad who sat off by himself and ruminated. He flunked in Linz and was transferred to a school at Steyr, in Upper Austria, where he managed to get through four classes.

After the death of his father, in 1903, the family moved on to Linz but only five years later his mother, of whom he always spoke with great veneration, also passed on, leaving young Adolf virtually uprooted. His ambition, to be accepted into the Linz Academy of Art, was not realized, for as he put it, "I was assured that, to judge by the drawings I had brought with me, I was obviously not fitted to be a painter, but that quite plainly my capacities lay in the sphere of architecture."

CHARITY FROM JEWS

From Linz young Hitler drifted to Vienna, where in his own words, recorded in Current Biography, he spent "five years of misery and desolation during which I had to earn my bread first as a workman on odd jobs and later as a decorator's man. And scanty bread it was, never enough to satisfy even an ordinary appetite."

What he does not mention is that, according to various trustworthy accounts which I have read, he often spent a night in a Jewish refugee home for shelterless tramps. It is claimed that his resentment at having to accept charity from

LOCHNER TELLS STORY OF REICH'S WAR MAKER

For almost two decades, Louis P. Lochner had a ringside seat at history, watching Adolf Hitler rise from obscurity to dictatorship—a dictatorship that in many respects has been unsurpassed in history.

Lochner, who chronicles that rise in the accompanying five articles, probably knows as much about Hitler as any living American. He joined the Associated Press in Berlin in 1924, and was chief of the Berlin bureau from 1928 until the bureau was closed when the United States entered the war. He now is a news commentator for Press Association, Inc., on the Pacific Coast network of the National Broadcasting Company.

When millions of people were inclined to dismiss Hitler as an unimportant, twopenny politician, Lochner was telling the world about the future Fuehrer's program as the result of exclusive interviews. He watched Hitler cleverly impose his program on the German nation, then ruthlessly drive to power and, finally, to the greatest war in history.

Jews furnished one of the reasons for his buning anti-Semitism.

The aloofness which characterized him even as a child and which became even more marked, the higher he rose, was obvious also to his fellow workmen and artisans in Vienna, with whom he was not at all popular.

SOLDIER OF BAVARIA

A year or two before World War I began, Adolf Hitler shuffled on to Munich. He had hardly had time to become acclimatized, when the war broke out. Such was Adolf Hitler's hatred of the House of Hapsburg, however, that he enlisted in the Bavarian army and was assigned to the List Regiment. The photograph extant of the future German Fuehrer as a Bavarian soldier shows a very average, unprepossessing steel-helmeted orderly with long, drooping mustache. One looks in vain for that hypnotic gaze of which people in Germany always spoke to me later when discussing his strange hold upon his co-nationals.

In 1916 Hitler was taken to a military hospital at Beelitz, near Berlin, suffering from a three weeks blindness which he claimed, resulted from his being exposed to English mustard gas. High medical authorities, including Dr. Victor A. Gonda of Loyola School of Medicine, Chicago, insist he suffered from hysterical amblyopia, or hysterical blindness.

Hitler wore as his only decoration the German Iron Cross of the First Class. His enemies asked two questions: first, why is there no record anywhere of the awarding of the Iron Cross of the Second Class which invariably precedes? Second, how come that a man who had been at the front, as Hitler claimed to have been, from the beginning of World War I, and who was awarded the Iron Cross, never rose higher than corporal?

NAZI PARTY IN POWER

When, during the first year after Hitler's assumption of power in 1933, we American correspondents met at each others' homes we would often, in mockery, give each other the Nazi salute and imitate Der Fuehrer's guttural voice with "Vierzehn Jahre der Schmach und der Schande" (Fourteen years of shame and disgrace).

For virtually every public speech of Hitler during that first year either opened with, or somewhere contained, his reference to the "Fourteen years of shame and disgrace" through which Germany had just passed and which, he insisted, came to an end with the triumph of National Socialism.

A POLITICIAN IS BORN

Having no job to which to turn immediately, Hitler upon return from the war continued to live in a Bavarian military camp and to receive his pay and his food from the army. Frequently he gave vent to his disappointment at the outcome of the war by hysterial tirades against the Jews and his version of the injustices of the treaty of Versailles.

He discovered himself in the process. "I decided to enter politics," he wrote later, apparently greatly pleased at noting that he possessed a certain "gift of gab."

A small group of unemployed and down-and-outers, who like himself blamed the "Marxists" and the Jews for all of Germany's woes, had formed a Deutsche Arbeiter-Partei (German Workers'

(See LIFE OF HITLER—Page 2)

SPORTS TRAIL

By WHITNEY MARTIN

New York—(AP)—He was as nice a looking young fellow as you might hope to see, and with his chest full of ribbons and stars and the captain's bars on his shoulders and the six overseas hash marks on his left sleeve he might have stepped right out of one of those "When He Comes" home ads.

His name is John F. Sullivan, Jr., and he's 27 years old. Despite the fact he was blown 40 feet out of a tank in the battle of Macknassy in Africa and took part in the landings at Sicily and Salerno and is one of the five living members of the group of 150 officers who went overseas with him, he is as chipper as they come.

His Dad is an instructor and golf coach at North High School in Worcester, Mass., and turned out the National Scholastic champions in 1942, but young John doesn't say much about his own golf game, as "everybody else in the family can beat me."

BOXING INTEREST

He played a little football at Boston University in 1938 before busting up a knee, and took part in intercollegiate boxing as a light-heavy. It was this interest in boxing that got him lined up in a coaching and managerial capacity overseas, first in England and later in Italy, where he was in charge of the Fifth Division team.

W saw him at a P.G.A. meeting, where he went to give that organization's rehabilitation program a boost. As a former hospital patient himself as a result of that flying trip out of a tank while with the Sixth Infantry Regiment of the First Armored Division, he knows what he is talking about when discussing what convalescent soldiers want, and he's sold on the P.G.A. plan.

"It's the best for the purpose I've heard of," he said, referring to the pros' project to provide golf facilities for all service hospitals.

"I'm sure that eight out of 10 service men would rather see a sports event than any other form of entertainment, and facilities for disabled vets to play golf themselves or watch exhibitions would be fine. I think baseball could lay out diamonds on hospital grounds and bring teams for exhibition games, too. About 75 per cent of the patients would be able to get out to the games some way."

The captain, home on leave, says schools are being conducted in Rome to develop instructors, coaches and officials for the extensive sports program which will follow V-E Day, and he hopes to take championship service teams on tours of the different European countries. He had much to do with the Italian tours of Joe Louis and Billy Conn, and took the Fifth Army team to the Oran tournament, where it lost only one bout.

He doesn't say much about all those rainbows across his chest, but with quite a little urging will admit he got nine citations, and the medals and stars include the British Military Cross and the French Croix De Guerre, as well as the Purple Heart. He's, well, he's a young fellow you feel quite proud to know.

Vanek Classified 1-A

Allentown, Pa. —(AP)— Ollie Vanek, playing manager of the Allentown Cardinals of the Interstate League, has been reclassified 1-A by his East St. Louis, Mo., draft board, club officials announced tuesday. He was formerly 2-B.

Vanek, a centerfielder, led the Cardinals to a pennant last year in his first season with the club. Before coming to Allentown, he had been playing manager of another St. Louis Cardinals farm at Lynchburg, Va.

The veteran, 33-year-old, player manager makes his home in St. Louis with his wife and two children, and during the winter works with the Railway Express Agency there.

HAYNES HURLS ONE HITTER AS CHISOX BLANK TIGERS 5-0

Detroit — (AP) — Righthander Joe Haynes, pitching one of the finest games in the major leagues this season, shut out the Detroit Tigers 5 to 0 on one hit Tuesday to keep the Chicago White Sox in first place in the American League.

Haynes faced only 28 batsmen in recording his near-perfect game, spoiled only by a clean single over second base in the third inning by ex-White Sox infielder Jimmy (Skeeter) Webb. No other Tiger reached first.

The Sox meanwhile knocked out rookie Walter Wilson, Detroit starting pitcher, in the sixth with their fourth extra base hit of the game. Wilson gave five hits and Leslie Mueller, his successor, allowed one in three innings.

Roy Schalk, Chicago second baseman, drove in three runs with a triple and single in three times at bat.

Chicago	ab	r	h	o	a	Detroit	ab	r	h	o	a
Moses rf	5	0	1	2	0	Borom 3b	4	0	0	0	2
Hock't cf	1	1	1	0	0	Mayo 2b	3	0	0	4	2
C'right cf	2	0	0	4	0	Cul'bine lf	3	0	0	2	0
D'shot lf	3	2	1	0	0	York 1b	3	0	0	8	1
Nagel 1b	4	0	0	14	1	Cramer cf	3	0	0	2	0
Cuc'lo 3b	2	1	1	2	4	Outlaw rf	3	0	0	4	1
Schalk 2b	3	1	2	0	2	Webb ss	3	0	1	3	2
Mich's ss	3	0	0	3	3	Swift c	2	0	0	3	0
Tresh c	4	0	0	1	0	Wilson p	1	0	0	1	2
Haynes p	4	0	0	1	3	Mueller p	1	0	0	0	2
						Hostet'r z	1	0	0	0	0
Totals	31	5	6	27	13	Totals	27	0	1	27	12

z-Batted for Mueller in 9th.

CHICAGO	000 400 010	5
DETROIT	000 000 000	0

Errors—None. Runs batted in—Dickshot, Schalk 3. Two base hits—Moses, Cuccinelloo. Three base hits—Dickshot, Schalk. Sacrifices — Schalk, Swift. Double plays—Outlaw and Swift. Left on base—Chicago 5; Detroit 1. Base on balls—Wilson 3; Mueller 2. Strikeouts—Haynes 1. Hits—Off Wilson 5 in 5 innings (none out in 6th); off Mueller 1 in 4. Balk—Wilson. Losing pitcher—Wilson. Umpires—Rue, Boyer and Summers. Time—1:40. Attendance—3,294.

Red Sox Win 4th In Row; Top Nats 5-4

Boston—(AP)—With Manager Joe Cronin and his crutches parked on their bench, the Boston Red Sox today won their fourth straight by breaking their Johnny Niggeling jinx while defeating the Washington Senators, 5-4.

It was the Sockers first triumph over kunckleballer Niggeling since 1942, when he was with the St. Louis Browns.

Emmett O'Neill, the rangy righthander, held the Senators to four hits, three of which were made by George Binks, who drove in all of the Washington runs.

Washington	ab	r	h	o	a	Boston	ab	r	h	o	a
Case cf	3	1	0	3	0	N'some ss	4	1	2	1	2
Myatt 2b	3	2	0	1	2	Steiner 2b	3	0	0	3	3
Kuhel 1b	3	0	0	9	1	M'vitch 1b	4	1	2	16	0
Binks rf	4	0	3	2	1	John'n lf	3	0	0	2	1
Clift 3b	3	0	0	1	3	Fox rf	4	0	2	0	0
Torres ss	4	0	1	0	3	Tobin 3b	3	0	0	2	5
Powell lf	4	0	0	1	0	Culb'n cf	4	1	3	0	0
Guerra c	4	0	0	7	2	Garb'k c	2	2	0	3	1
Nig'ling p	2	0	0	0	2	Holm c	1	0	0	0	0
Chipple x	0	1	0	0	0	O'Neill p	3	0	1	0	3
Pieretti p	0	0	0	0	0	Woods p	1	0	0	0	1
Totals	30	4	4	24	14	Totals	32	5	10	27	16

x-Batted for Niggeling in 8th.

WASHINGTON	100 001 020	4
BOSTON	120 002 00x	5

Error—Newsome. Runs batted in—Binks 4, Newsome 3, Fox, Metkovich. Two base hits—Binks, Culberson 3, Newsome. Stolen bases — Case, Myatt. Double play—Johnson and Steiner. Left on bases—Washington 4, Boston 7. Bases on balls—Off Niggeling 4, O'Neill 5. Strikeouts—By Niggeling 3, Pieretti 1, O'Neill 3. Hits—Off Niggeling 10 in 7 innings; Pieretti 0 in 1; O'Neill 4 in 7 1-3; Woods 0 in 1 2-3. Winning pitcher—O'Neil. Losing pitcher—Niggeling. Umpires—Steward, McGowan, Weafer. Time—1:52. Attendance—1,919.

Eastern Loop Opens 1945 Season Today

(By The Associated Press)

The Class A Eastern League opens its 23rd season this Wednesday amid predictions of a close race and a good brand of baseball, despite manpower depletions and wartime restrictions.

Most clubs are built around a nucleus of a few players with Class A experience or better, plus discharged servicemen and a raft of recruits, many without previous professional experience.

All are looking for quick reinforcements from parent major league aggregations.

The schedule, revised to cut 25 per cent mileage from last year's chart, calls for the 1944 first-place Hartford Laurels to open against the Senators at Albany, the Binghamton Triplets, playoff champions, to start against the Bluejays at Utica; the Wilkes-Barre Barons to face the Miners at Scranton and the Williamsport Grays to battle the Pioneers at Elmira.

Two days later the picture will be reversed as the opening day visitors stage their home unveilings.

GRIDDERS PLAY LACROSSE

State College, Pa.—Six Penn State football players are getting in shape by playing lacrosse this spring.

The six, four of whom are Navy V-12 trainees, will be serious contenders for gridiron berths next fall. Only one, Freshman Bronco Kosanovich of Aliquippa, played on the 1944 eleven.

COMMISSIONER'S SON KILLED

New York—(AP)—Maj. Gen. John J. Phelan (Ret.), former chairman of the New York Athletic Commission, was notified Tuesday that his son, Lt. Col. John J. Phelan, Jr., was killed in action on the Italian Front April 15.

Ten Named To Baseball's Hall Of Fame

Fred Clarke

Hugh Jennings

Roger Bresnahan

Wilbert Robinson

Jimmy Collins

Hugh Duffy

Here are six of the 10 diamond stars who glittered before 1900 and who have been named by a special old timers committee for inclusion in Baseball's Hall of Fame in Cooperstown, N. Y. Clarke and Duffy were outfielders, Robinson and Bresnahan were catchers, Collins and Jennings were infielders. Others named were Outfielder Ed Delehanty, First Baseman Dan Brouthers. Mike Kelly and James O'Rourke were the other two old-time stars selected for the Hall of Fame. Already included in the Hall of Fame are such historic diamond figures as Connie Mack,, Hoss Radbourne, Ty Cobb, Lou Gehrig, George Sisler, Babe Ruth, Hans Wagner, Christy Mathewson, Walter Johnson, Tris Speaker, Cy Young, Napoleon Lajoie, Buck Ewing, John J. McGraw, Ban Johnson, Rogers Hornsby, Eddie Collins.

ICE HOCKEY BILL UP TO FINAL VOTE

Harrisburg — (AP) — A Senate-approved bill to permit Sunday ice hockey games and exhibitions after local option votes barely escaped being sent back to committee and possible death Tuesday night.

The House voted down 80-76 a Democratic move to recommit the measure and placed it in position for final action Wednesday.

The House previously rejected amendments to broaden the proposal to permit Sunday basketball, bowling and to increase from two per cent to 20 per cent the number of voters who must sign petitions for local elections.

Debating the motion to recommit, Democratic Leader Hiram G. Andrews, said "this bill belongs back in the law and order committee because it has a trail of slime. This bill is worth $25,000 to some party's campaign fund and it isn't my party."

Andrews called the House's attention to the fact that the bill was introduced April 17, and referred to the Senate committee of forests and waters and game and fish.

"Such was the strange compulsion," said Andrews, "The fish committee gets a hockey bill on the 17th, the Senate gets a hockey bill on the 18th."

The Cambria lawmaker said ministers have written him protesting the speed with which the bill has gone through the legislature and declared the law and order committee should have a look at the proposal.

Rep. W. Henry Elder (R-Allegheny) objected to the motion and asked the House to vote it down but did not elaborate on his stand.

Bucs Invite Happy

Pittsburgh—(AP)—Sen. A. B. "Happy" Chandler, baseball's new commissioner, has been invited to be guest of honor at a War Relief-Red Cross game between the Pittsburgh Pirates and the Detroit Tigers at Forbes Field on the night of July 10, William E. Benswanger, president of the Pirates, announced.

BAKSI-LANE BOUT TONIGHT

Chicago—(AP)—Joe Baski, former coal miner of Kulpmont, Pa., will resume his campaign to regain top-ranking heavyweight honors Wednesday night by engaging Larry Lane, hard hitting 190 pounder of Trenton, N. J., in a ten-round bout at the Coliseum under the promotion of Jack Kearns.

Baski, favorite, will have a ten-pound weight advantage.

Baseball At A Glance

STANDINGS OF TEAMS

National League

Teams	W.	L.	Pct.
New York	8	4	.667
Chicago	7	4	.636
St. Louis	5	4	.556
Boston	6	5	.545
Brooklyn	5	5	.500
Cincinnati	5	6	.455
Pittsburgh	4	7	.364
Philadelphia	3	8	.273

American League

Teams	W.	L.	Pct.
Chicago	6	2	.750
New York	7	4	.636
Detroit	6	4	.600
Philadelphia	6	5	.545
Washington	6	6	.500
St. Louis	4	5	.444
Boston	4	8	.333
Cleveland	2	7	.222

Interstate League

Teams	W.	L.	P.C.
Lancaster	4	0	1.000
Wilmington	4	0	1.000
Allentown	2	1	.667
Hagerstown	1	3	.250
Trenton	0	3	.000
York	0	4	.000

TUESDAY'S RESULTS

National League

Chicago-Cincinnati not scheduled.

All other games postponed.

American League

Chicago 5, Detroit 0.

Boston 5, Washington 4.

Philadelphia-New York postponed (rain).

St. Louis-Cleveland night postponed (rain).

Interstate League

All games postponed (rain).

International League

Montreal at Newark, postponed (rain).

Buffalo at Jersey City, postponed (rain).

WEDNESDAY'S GAMES

National League

Cincinnati at Chicago—Heusser (2-0) vs. Derringer (3-0).

Boston at Brooklyn — Andrews (1-1) vs. Lombardi (1-0).

New York at Philadelphia—Feldman (2-0) vs. Lee (0-1).

St. Louis at Pittsburgh — (2) — Brecheen (1-0) and Donnelly (0-1) vs. Sewell (1-2) and Butcher (1-1).

American League

Cleveland at St. Louis (night)—Reynolds (0-1) vs. Potter (1-1).

Chicago at Detroit—Grove (1-0) vs. Benton (2-0).

Philadelphia at New York—Christopher (3-0) vs. Gettel (0-0).

Washington at Boston—Haefner (1-0) vs. Johnson (0-0).

Inter-State League

Lancaster vs. Wilmington at Stumpf Field. 8:15 p. m.

Allentown at York.

Hagerstown at Trenton.

COOPER TO JOIN FELLER AT G. L.

St. Louis — (AP) — Hey, Bobby Feller, here comes another good ballplayer.

Walker Cooper, great catcher and team captain of the World Champion St. Louis Cardinals, was inducted into the Navy Tuesday at Jefferson Barracks and is headed for Great Lakes (Ill.) Naval Training Station.

Walker, who thought he was through with baseball and headed for the Army for the duration, found he had a choice of services and he didn't hesitate in choosing the sea-going branch.

At Great Lakes, Feller, former Cleveland ace, has assembled one of the finest service teams in the country, loaded with former major league stars. Cooper's choice probably won't be bad news to the fire-ball king who pitched to Walker during one exhibition tour.

WAS MAINSTAY

The husky Cardinal star has been the mainstay of three championship teams in St. Louis. In all three years he has been overshadowed individually for "most valuable player" honors. First it was his big brother Morton, then outfielder Stan Musial and last year shortstop Marty Marion. But there has been little doubt among close observers of the club that Cooper was a major factor in guiding wartime pitchers past the 100-victory mark in all three years.

Walker said goodbye to the Cardinals last Thursday before they left on their current road trip. He enters the service with a contract argument still pending before baseball's high authorities. He and Mort wanted a $3,000 raise on their $12,000 contracts this season.

Trout To Arrive Here

One hundred cans of fingerling trout will arrive in this city Wednesday and be distributed among sportsmen's clubs here, Arthur H. Fox of the Federated Sportsmen announced.

The trout will arrive at 120 S. Prince St. and Fox said clubs desiring them are asked to furnish their own cans for distribution in county streams.

WILSON TAKES OVER BIG 10

Chicago—(AP)—Kenneth L. (Tug) Wilson Tuesday officially became athletic commissioner of the Western Conference, succeeding the late Maj. John L. Griffith, only previous commissioner.

The 48-year-old Wilson, who participated in the 1920 Olympic games as a javelin-thrower, predicted conference schools would broaden all branches of competitive sports to meet sharp acceleration in post-war enrollments.

West Coast Sportsmen Inspiration To Vets

LOUIS LEO JONES

AP Newsfeatures

Los Angeles—There are a couple of sportsmen out here who might be an inspiration to a lot of young fellows these days.

Louis Leo Jones, 51, father of five children, hasn't had any legs since he was 15. He lost them under a freight train in Illinois.

His golfing pal, Frank De Silver, 38, and also married, lost his left arm nearly up to the shoulder in an Oklahoma oil field accident in 1928.

OTHER SPORTS, TOO

Both play golf in the high 80's. Moreover, Jones is a crack swimmer, and De Silver plays badminton, tennis, billiards and boasts a 161 average in his bowling league.

They're businessmen who have never been on relief. Jones is a toolmaker by trade who now operates a thriving concession business. De Silver is an automobile salesman.

Jones wears wooden legs but uses a motor scooter to get around the golf course.

LEAD FULL LIVES

Both lead full lives despite their physical handicaps—they ask no favors and they except none. They admit it took them a while to reach that attitude.

"You have to get used to people feeling sorry for you—it's tough at first but wears off," Jones says. "After a while you get so you can do many things you never dreamed you'd be able to do when you first lost a limb."

That comes after you win the mental battle you have with yourself," De Silver adds. "The main thing's perseverance. Start off easy and little by little you find you're nearly 'normal' again."

On the normalcy note: De Silver with one hand ties his shoelaces as tight as anyone with two hands and lights his cigarettes from a book of safety matches with equal facility. Jones' gait is slightly stiff-legged but he walks almost as fast as the average pedestrian.

FRANK DE SILVER

Chandler Lays Plans For Post-War Sport; Discourages Betting

St. Louis—(AP)—Sen. A. B. "Happy" Chandler who has only to sign his contract to become the nation's new baseball commissioner disclosed Tuesday his plans for carrying baseball "back to the country" to capitalize on "the tremendous sports boom we will have after the war."

In his first press conference since his election to the commissioner's post a week ago he asserted baseball has two immediate responsibilities:

"We must provide some place for baseball's war veterans to play. We are obligated to find jobs for them."

"Thousands of players have been wounded and will need rehabilitating and they ought to be able to see baseball games."

Chandler's proposal is to locate leagues in the vicinity of government hospitals and in high schools and colleges.

NEW TALENT

"We'll have lots of opportunities to discover new baseball talent," he said.

Chandler was here to attend the American League pennant raising ceremonies of the St. Louis Browns.

As to baseball's present status, Chandler said he talked with President Truman a few days ago just before leaving Washington and "I came away with the impression the President thought baseball had justified its right to continue for the duration."

He said he had been told of instances in which baseball players classified 4-F had been inducted into the armed services just because they were ball players through abuse of authority by some draft board officials.

"I have informed President Truman of this," he declared.

NO GAMBLING

"Some of the finest men I know are in the racing industry," he said. "Cases involving ball players who overemphasize their racing interests will be judged on their individual merits. Gamblers must not and will not get into baseball and my advice to ball players and umpires is to stay away from race tracks."

He said serious discussion was being given to transferring the commissioner's office from Chicago to Cincinnati because the Ohio city was more centrally located, and added:

"Besides it's across the river rom Kentucky and I've been told I could get offices from where I could see into Kentucky all the time."

WANT OFFICE IN CHICAGO

Chicago — (AP) — Billy Niesen, president of the Old Timers' Baseball Association, Tuesday petitioned Mayor Kelly to induce Baseball Commissioner-elect A. B. (Happy) Chandler to retain the commissioner's office here. Chandler has indicated he favored moving it to Cincinati.

The association has a membership of 1,400 and listed the late Commissioner K. M. Landis as an honorary member. "Chicago is in the center of the United States and the commissioner rules over all of baseball," Niesen declared. "The baseball tradition of the city makes it worthy of the office."

ONE-LEGGED VET TO PLAY FOOTBALL

State College, Pa.—(AP)—A one-legged Army sergeant may be playing football for Pennsylvania State College this fall.

Sgt. Johnny Schroyer, who lost his right leg in a German prison camp but not his ambition to return to the gridiron, wants to get back into the game.

"There's one thing sure," Coach Bob Higgins said Tuesday, "he has the coach rooting for him."

Johnny recently wrote Higgins from Atlantic City's England General Hospital:

"What are my chances of playing football again? I love the game too much to give it up without a try."

PRAISES COURAGE

Commenting that he "hopes all my future players possess as much courage as Schroyer," Higgins said:

"I don't know too much about artificial limbs but if the Army does a good job in fitting him with one and Johnny can accommodate himself quickly, he may play football again.

"Johnny was a blocking back when he last played for me in 1942 but apparently he is willing to return to the line when he rejoins the squad. Our inside tackle doesn't run very much so that may be the spot for him to try."

The sergeant, a native of Connellsville (Pa.) and former high school running mate of Notre Dame's Johnny Lujack, says he is in condition now—all he needs is the new leg.

Speaks For Military Training Backed By National Health Law

Washington —(AP)— Tad Wieman, former Michigan and Princeton coach, spoke up emphatically Tuesday for not only universal military training but a nation-wide physical fitness program as well.

"One program without the other would be unsatisfactory in improving physical standards, found shockingly low in this war," he told a reporter.

Wieman, civilian consultant to the War Department on physical fitness, said that "physical fitness develops the man; military training develop the team . . the machine."

"It's like coaching a football team," he elaborated. "The coach needs good parts, good players. If he doesn't have good parts, he doesn't have a good team. The same thing is true of a nation."

When Germany folds up, the War Department will have a coordinated physical fitness-universal military training program ready for consideration by Congress.

F. And M. Nine Faces Ursinus Here Today

Franklin and Marshall's baseball team will entertain the Ursinus Bears on the home diamond at 3:30 p. m.

Coach Tom Floyd announced Tuesday night that the team will be without the services of its regular shortstop and second baseman. Tex Phillips, starting shortstop, will be out of the F. & M. lineup for the remainder of the season because of a fractured thumb suffered in a practice session.

The second baseman, Garner, is out of action this week as a result of falling down in his studies.

Floyd had to move his regular third sacker to shortstop, and the keystone sacker to the hot corner to plug the gaps. He is starting a new man at second.

The F. & M. lineup for Wednesday's game:

Urban, 3b; Keteltas, cf; Breneman, ss; Ramsey, lf; Fullerton, 1b; Wesp, 2b; Barnhart, rf; Schwerdfeger, c; Burns, p.

Hoppe Tops Cochran

Los Angeles— (AP) —Willie Hoppe defeated three-cushion titlist Welker Cochran, 60-35, Tuesday in another block of their travelling world's championship series.

It took Hoppe 41 innings to turn the tables on Cochran, who won both of Monday's blocks.

The win increased Hoppe's tournament lead to 48 points. Their totals at the end of this afternoon's block were: Hoppe, 3,029; Cochran, 2,981.

E-TOWN BOWS TO BUCKNELL

Bucknell	ab	r	h	o	a	Elizabethtown	ab	r	h	o	a
Murphy ss	3	1	1	1	0	Myers ss	3	0	1	4	4
Styron 2b	1	0	0	0	1	Bucher rf	2	1	0	0	0
Harris 2b	2	1	0	2	0	Buch 1b	4	1	3	9	0
Kil'n 1b	3	0	0	5	0	J.Lef'r cf	4	0	1	0	0
McG're rf	3	2	1	0	0	Eshel'n c	3	0	0	3	1
Trug'y cf	1	1	0	1	1	D.Lef'r p	1	0	0	0	2
Ath'ly cf	1	0	0	1	0	Hers'y 3b	3	0	0	2	1
Brocke 3b	2	1	0	0	2	Whit're 2b	2	0	0	1	0
McD'ls lf	3	2	2	0	0	Markey lf	2	0	0	1	0
Wag'r lf	0	0	0	0	0	Hald'n lf	0	0	0	1	0
Devore c	1	1	1	8	0	Wenger lf	0	0	0	0	0
Caldw'l c	1	0	0	3	0						
Ellis p	3	1	2	0	2	Totals	24	2	5	21	8
Totals	24	10	7	21	6						

BUCKNELL	050 500 0	10
ELIZABETHTOWN	200 000 0	2

Errors—Murphy, McGuire, Myers 2, Markey 2. Two base hits—McGuire, McDaniels 2. Stolen bases—Kileen, McGuire, Trugley, Ellis, Buch. Base on balls—Off Ellis 6; Lefever 4. Struck out—By Ellis 11; Lefever 3. Hit by pitcher—By Lefever 3; Ellis 1. Winning pitcher—Ellis. Losing pitcher—Lefever. Umpires—Seaman and Eppler.

BASEBALL'S BIG SIX
(By the Associated Press)
BATTING
(Three leaders in each league)

Player, Club	G.	AB.	R.	H.	Pct.
Stephens, Browns	7	23	8	10	.435
Ott, Giants	12	37	15	16	.432
Holmes, Braves	11	47	10	20	.426
Kreevich, Browns	7	23	3	9	.391
Ross, Tigers-Indians	8	29	3	11	.379
O'Brien, Pirates	10	38	3	14	.368

RUNS BATTED IN

American League		National League	
Derry, Yankees	13	Lombardi, Giants	16
Etten, Yankees	13	Nieman, Braves	15
Cramer, Tigers	8	Ott, Giants	11
Hayes, Athletics	8	Elliott, Pirates	11

HOME RUNS

American League		National League	
Derry, Yankees	4	Nieman, Braves	4
Hayes, Athletics	3	Ott, Giants	3
Stephens, Browns	2	Weintr'b, Giants	3
Johnson, R. Sox	2	Lombardi, Giants	3

All Games In County High Loop Postponed

Rain and cold weather caused postponement of all seven of the scheduled county high baseball games Tuesday afternoon.

Some of the washed out games will be played this Wednesday afternoon, but some of the teams moved their games to a later date.

The revised schedule follows:

Section A

Manheim Twp. at West Lampeter, Thursday, May 3rd; Manor at Strasburg this Wednesday.

Section B

East Donegal at Lititz this Wednesday; East Hempfield at Manheim Boro this Wednesday; Rothsville at Mt. Joy Thursday, May 17th.

Section C

Paradise at New Holland (pending); East Lampeter at Upper Leacock, Friday, May 11th.

Bowling Scores

OVERLOOK C. C. LEAGUE

Jiggers 1—Shelley 461, McNelis 475, Winger 529, Morgan 474. Spades 3—Dombach 585, Sprenkle 395, Leinaweaver 425, McEllicott 526, Kalle 535.

Brassies 1—Gingrich 593, Dorwart 463, Moffett 463, Getz 466, Hoffman 438. Spoons 3—L. Morrison 494, Fellows 504, Aznavorian 515, Deyer 564, Dougherty 518.

Putters 1—Morrison 481, Witmyer 461, Illeman 459, Gibble 545, Frey 509. Cleeks 3—Flemming 451, Schneider 456, Ashmead 500, Hiemenz 525.

Niblics 1—Rineer 458, Miller 499, Hartley 465. Baffies 3—Forney 475, Chandler 460, Musser 518, Smithgall 530, Slaugh 522.

Sandwedges 4—Dickey 505, Martin 480, Fry 539, Lerbscher 521, Greiner 550. Mashies 0—Bitzer 502, Dommel 470, Webster 524.

Mid-Irons 4—Simone 462, Yackly 566, Bates 448, Martin 440, Pott 600. Drivers 0—Bowers 489, McAdoo 558.

SLOAN SOLD BY GIANTS

New York—(AP)—Outfielder Bruce Sloan was sold Tuesday by the New York Giants to the Minneapolis Millers of the American Association.

Although the husky outfielder who batted .368 at Little Rock in 1943 but spent last year with the Giants as a utility man, had been accepted by the Army, it was understood he had been given a seven weeks' stay before induction.

RED ROSES TO MEET WILMINGTON TONIGHT

The first game of the series having been washed out, the Lancaster Red Roses and the Wilmington Blue Rocks clash this Wednesday night on Stumpf field at 8:15 p. m. The teams are tied for the league lead, both having won four and lost none.

Radio

WGAL

NBC • 1490 Kc. • Mutual

Wednesday, May 2, 1945

7:00—War News
7:05—Musical Clock
7:30—U. P. News, W. W. Moyer
7:35—Musical Clock
7:45—Reveille Roundup
8:00—World News, Penn Dairies
8:15—Do You Remember
8:30—Devotions
8:45—Listen to Leibert
8:55—Spotlight On Peace
9:00—Ed East & Polly
9:30—Good Morning Neighbor
9:45—Nations Rations
10:00—Henry Gladstone
10:15—Maxine Keith
10:30—Road of Life
10:45—Ei Capitan Money Man
10:55—U. P. News, Arrow Shoe Store
11:00—Happy Felton in Finders Keepers
11:30—Treasury Salute
11:45—Yes or No, Hershey Ice Cream
11:50—Interlude
11:55—Lanny & Ginger
12:00—Waltztime
12:10—Dick & Jeannie, Harolds
12:15—Dolly Madison News
12:30—Sons of the Pioneers
12:45—Band Box Revue
1:00—Sketches in Melody
1:30—This is Your OPA
1:45—Morgan Beatty: Crystal Rock
2:00—Guiding Light
2:15—Today's Children
2:30—Women in White
2:45—World at War
2:50—Rhapsody in Rhythm
3:00—Women of America
3:15—Ma Perkins
3:30—War Commentary
3:35—Song Styles
3:45—Right to Happiness
4:00—Backstage Wife
4:15—Stella Dallas
4:30—Lorenzo Jones
4:45—Young Widder Brown
5:00—U. P. News: W. W. Moyer
5:05—Matinee Dancetime
5:25—Baseball Scores
5:30—Superman: Kellogg's
5:45—Tom Mix
6:00—World News: Oblender & Co.
6:15—Musical Moments
6:25—Sports Parade: General Tire
6:30—Music of Manhattan: Hermans
6:45—Lowell Thomas
7:00—Chesterfield Supper Club
7:15—News of the World
7:30—Your Children at School
7:45—Tomorrow's World: Frick's Esso
7:50—Victory March
7:55—United Press Bulletins: Zook's
8:00—Mr. and Mrs. North
8:30—The Gay Mrs. Featherstone
9:00—Eddie Cantor
9:30—Mr. District Attorney
10:00—Kay Kyser
11:00—United Press News & Baseball Scores: Wise Jewelry Co.
11:15—Lazy River
11:30—Music for Tonight
12:00—War News—Sign Off—Adv.

8:00—WEAF, World News; WOR, P. Robinson, News; WJZ, The Fitzgeralds; WABC, News Roundup
8:15—WEAF, Listen to Lewis; WOR, Breakfast With Dorothy and Dick; WABC, Phil Cook Show; WJZ, Your Life Today
8:30—WEAF, News; WJZ, Nancy Craig; WABC, Missus Goes Shopping
8:45—WEAF, Rod Hendrickson; WABC, Margaret Arlen
8:55—WJZ, News
9:00—WEAF, Fun and Folly; WOR, Health Talk; WJZ, The Breakfast Club; WABC, News
9:15—WOR, Talks; Songs; WABC, Arthur Godfrey
9:30—WEAF, Adelaide Hawley; WOR, Alfred McCann
9:45—WABC, This Life is Mine; WEAF, Nations Rations
10:00—WEAF, Robert St. John; WOR, H. Gladstone, News; WJZ, My True Story; WABC, Valiant Lady
10:15—WEAF, Lora Lawton; WOR, Bessie Beatty; WABC, Light of the World
10:30—WEAF, Road of Life; WABC, Evelyn Winters; WJZ, Music With Melton
10:45—WJZ, The Listening Post; WABC, Bachelor's Children; WEAF, Joyce Jordan
11:00—WEAF, Happy Felton in Finders Keepers; WOR, P. Robinson; WJZ, Breneman's Breakfast in Hollywood; WABC, Amanda
11:15—WOR, Music; WABC, Second Husband
11:30—WEAF, Soldiers Came Home; WOR, Take It Easy; WJZ, G. Martyn, News; WABC, Bright Horizon
11:45—WEAF, David Harum; WOR, Your Idea?; Songs; WJZ, Jack Berch, Songs; WABC, Aunt Jenny's Stories
12:00—WEAF, News, Don Goddard; WOR, News, William Lang; WJZ, Glamour Manor; WABC, Kate Smith, News
12:15—WEAF, Maggi McNellis; WOR, Music at Mid-Day; WABC, Big Sister
12:30—WEAF, Music Room; WOR, H. Gladstone; WJZ, News; Drama; WABC, Helen Trent
12:45—WOR, The Answer Man; WABC, Our Gal Sunday
1:00—WEAF, Mary M. McBride; WOR, Jack Bundy's Album; WJZ, H. R. Baukhage; WABC, Life Can Be Beautiful
1:15—WJZ, Organ Music; WABC, Ma Perkins; WOR, Tello-Test Quiz
1:30—WABC, B. Flynn, News; WJZ, Galen Drake; WOR, Vincent Lopez Orch.
1:45—WEAF, Morgan Beatty; WJZ, Galen Drake; WABC, Young Dr. Malone; WOR, John J. Anthony
2:00—WEAF, The Guiding Light; WOR, News, Cedric Foster; WJZ, John B. Kennedy; WABC, Two on a Clue
2:15—WEAF, Today's Children; WJZ, Ethel and Albert; WOR, Jane Cowl; WABC, Rosemary, Sketch
2:30—WEAF, Women in White; WJZ, Sunny Side of Street; WABC, Perry Mason; WOR, Queen for Today
2:45—WEAF, Hymns of All Churches; WABC, Tena and Tim; WJZ, News
3:00—WEAF, Woman of America; WJZ, Appointment with Life; WABC, Time to Remember; WOR, Martha Deane
3:15—WEAF, Ma Perkins; WABC, Off the Record
3:30—WEAF, Pepper Young Family; WABC, Off the Record; WOR, Rambling with Gambling; WJZ, Beautiful Music
3:45—WEAF, Right to Happiness; WABC—Sing Along Club
4:00—WEAF, Backstage Wife; WJZ, News, W. Van Voorhis; WABC, House Party; WOR, News, J. Gambling
4:15—WEAF, Stella Dallas; WJZ, Musical; WOR, Jay Johnson, Songs
4:30—WEAF, Lorenzo Jones; WJZ, News From Europe; WABC, Feature Story; WOR, Food Forum
4:45—WEAF, Young Widder Brown; WJZ, Hop Harrigan; WABC, Danny O'Neil, Songs
5:00—WEAF, When a Girl Marries; WOR, Uncle Don; WJZ, Terry and the Pirates; WABC, Service Time
5:15—WEAF, Portia Faces Life; WOR, Superman, Drama; WJZ, Dick Tracy
5:30—WEAF, Just Plain Bill; WOR, House of Mystery; WABC, Cimaroon Tavern; WJZ, Jack Armstrong
5:45—WEAF, Front Page Farrell; WOR, Tom Mix; WJZ, Captain Midnight; WABC, Wilderness Roads
6:00—WEAF, D. Hollenbeck, News; WOR, Paul Schubert; WJZ, W. Kiernan, News; WABC, Harry Marble, News
6:15—WEAF, Serenade to America; WOR, Hal McIntyre Orch.; WJZ, What Are the Facts; WABC, Jimmy Carroll Sings
6:30—WOR, News, Van Deventer; WJZ, Whose War?; News; WABC, Eileen Farrell
6:45—WEAF, Lowell Thomas; WOR, Stan Lomax; WJZ, Peggy Mann, Songs; WABC, World Today; News
7:00—WEAF, Supper Club; WOR, Fulton Lewis, Jr.; WJZ, Headline Edition; WABC, Jack Kirkwood Show
7:15—WEAF, Morgan Beatty; WOR, The Answer Man; WABC, Music That Satisfies; WJZ, Raymond G. Swing
7:30—WEAF, Al Roth's Orch.; WOR, Can You Top This?; WJZ, The Lone Ranger; WABC, Ellery Queen
7:45—WEAF—H. V. Kaltenborn
8:00—WOR, Cecil Brown; WJZ, Ted Malone; WABC, Jack Carson Show; WEAF, Mr and Mrs. North
8:15—WOR, Curt Massey, Songs; WJZ, Lum and Abner
8:30—WEAF, Billie Burke Show; WOR, Barney Grant Show; WJZ, David Harding; WABC, Dr. Christian
9:00—WEAF, Eddie Cantor; WOR, Gabraiel Heatter; WJZ, San Francisco, Prog.; WABC, Frank Sinatra Show
9:15—WOR, San Francisco News
9:30—WEAF, Mr. District Attorney; WOR, Brownstone Theater; WABC, Which is Which?; WJZ, Spotlight Bands
10:00—WEAF, College of Musical Knowledge; WOR, Boston Blackie; WABC, Great Moments in Music; WJZ, Wendell Niles
10:30—WJZ, Adventures of Tom, Dick and Harry; WABC, Let Yourself Go; WOR, Symphonette
11:00—WEAF, News, Lyle Van; WJZ, News; Wm. Gailmore; WABC, News, Wm. L. Shirer; WOR, Van Deventer, News
11:15—WEAF, Richard Harkness; WJZ, San Francisco Report; WABC, Joan Brooks, Songs; WOR, News
11:30—WEAF, Music For Tonight; WJZ, Glen Gray's Orch.; WABC, Invitation to Music; WOR, Randy Brooks Orch.
11:45—WOR, Lionel Hampton Orch.

WYATT LEAVES TO JOIN PHILS

Buchanan, Ga. —(AP)— Whitlow Wyatt, veteran National League pitcher sold by Brooklyn to Philadelphia this spring, left here to join the Phillies.

Bothered with an army ailment the past two years, Wyatt has been working out at his home here for seven weeks and spent several days training with the Atlanta Crackers.

EXTRA! LANCASTER NEW ERA EXTRA!

69th Year—No. 21,088 | Entered as second class matter January 31, 1924, at the Post Office at Lancaster, Pa., under the Act of March 3, 1879, Reg. U. S. Pat. Off. | LANCASTER, PA., MONDAY, MAY 7, 1945 | HOME EDITION | 16 PAGES | 20c PER WEEK—4c Per Copy

VICTORY EUROPE

Germany Quits Unconditionally To U.S., Great Britain and Russia In Gen. Eisenhower's Headquarters

By Edward Kennedy

REIMS, France, May 7. — (AP) — Germany surrendered unconditionally to the Western Allies and Russia at 2:41 A. M. French time today.

(This was at 8:41 P. M., Eastern War Time Sunday).

The surrender took place at a little red school house which is the headquarters of Gen. Eisenhower.

The surrender which brought the war in Europe to a formal end after five years, eight months and six days of bloodshed and destruction was signed for Germany by Col. Gen. Gustav Jodl.

Jodl is the new chief of staff of the German army.

It was signed for the Supreme Allied Command by Lieutenant General Walter Bedell Smith, chief of staff for General Eisenhower.

It was also signed by General Ivan Susloparoff for Russia and by General Francois Sevez for France.

General Eisenhower was not present at the signing, but immediately afterward Jodl and his fellow delegate, General Admiral Hans Gorg Friedeburg, were received by the Supreme Commander.

They were asked sternly if they understood the surrender terms imposed upon Germany and if they would be carried out by Germany.

They answered yes.

Germany, which began the war with a ruthless attack upon Poland followed by successive aggressions and brutality in internment camps, surrendered with an appeal to the victors for mercy toward the German people and armed forces.

After signing the full surrender, Jodl said he wanted to speak and was given leave to do so.

"With this signature," he said in soft-spoken German, "the German people and armed forces are for better or worse delivered into the victors' hands."

"In this war which has lasted more than five years both have achieved and suffered more than perhaps any other people in the world."

Nazi Foreign Minister Says "Harsh Terms" Are Accepted

LONDON, May 7.—(AP)—German Foreign Minister Ludwig Schwerin Von Krosigk announced to the German people over the wavelenth of the Flensburg Station today that "after almost six years struggle we have succumbed."

"Nobody must deceive himself over the harshness of the conditions. We had to accept them," the broadcast said.

The Free Danish radio at about the same time reported without Allied confirmation that German forces in Norway had capitulated.

Just before, the Flensburg wavelength quoted Grand Admiral Karl Doenitz in an order of the day ordering all Nazi u-boats to cease hostilities.

The Paris Radio also broadcast a French Telegraph Agency report which said the "surrender of German forces in Norway has now been solved. They will all be transferred to Sweden and there disarmed. An o½cial announcement of the surrender is expected any time now."

The Flensburg Radio broadcast quoted a three-day-old order of the day by Doenitz to his submarine crews telling them "crushing superiority has compressed us into a very narrow area. Continuation of the struggle is impossible from bases that remain."

Events Which Led to Unconditional Surrender of All Germany to the Allies

German soldiers of the 21st Germany Army jam a road with their horse-drawn wagons as they pour towards the Allied lines May 3. The capitulation of this German Army group to Field Marshal Sir Bernard Montgomery's command ended the fighting in Northern Germany, Denmark and Holland previous to the complete capitulation of all Germany today. (Signal Corp Photo.)

Lt. Gen. Foertsch, commanding general of the German First Army (center), signs papers near Munich, Germany, May 5, for uunuconditional surrender of German Army Group "G" to American forces under command of Gen. Jacob L. Devers, commanding general Sixth Army group. Looking on at right is Brig. Gen. Pearson Menohher, chief of staff of U. S. 15th Corps. The two German officers (left) and the American officer (second from right) are unidentified. (Signal Corps Photo.)

Latest News

TRUMAN WILL MAKE OFFICIAL ANNOUNCEMENT

Washington, May 7—(AP)—President Truman was conferring with aides in the Executive offices today as news was flashed t othe world from Reims of the unconditional surrender of German arms.

Newsmen surged into the White House in anticipation of an expected V-E announcement.

OWI director Elmer Davis was among those at the White House. He told reporters:

"When there is any official announcement it will come from in there." (Indicating the President's office).

Mr. Truman arrived at his office at 8:27 A. M., EWT, accompanied by his Military and Naval aides, and went directly to his office.

Newsmen who have been staffing the White House around the clock for a week, jammed the big oval reception room. White House aides said they had nothing official to announce at once on a cessation of hostilities in Europe.

Signer of Nazi Surrender Once Hitler's Personal Aide

By The Associated Press

Col. Gen. Gustav Jodl who signed the unconditional surrender for Germany apparently is the same as Gen. Alfred Jodl who was wounded last July 20 in the attempted assassination of Adolf Hitler.

The surrender dispatch said Jodl was the new German Army Chief of Staff.

Precisely when he became Chief of Staff was not clear. Col. Gen. Heinz Guderian had occupied that position until the closing days of the siege of Berlin. His fate and whereabouts has not been reported since Berlin fell.

On March 17, Jodl inspected the Bavarian Redoubt where the Nazis had hoped to make their last stand. Back in 1942, Jodl was reported to have been Hitler's personal aide.

He attended many of the Hitler-Mussolini war conferences early in the conflict and was mentioned late in 1942 as a possible successor to Marshal Von Brauchitsch, commander of the German armies. He was chief of the German Armed Services Guidance staff early in 1943 and the following year assumed a command on the Russian front.

40,000,000 Lost In 2,319 Days of War

LONDON, May 7—(AP)—The greatest war in history ended today with the unconditional surrender of Germany.

The surrender of the Reich to the Western Allies and Russia was made at Gen. Eisenhower's headquarters at Reims, France by Col. Gen. Gustaf Jodl, chief of staff for the German Army.

This was announced officially after German broadcasts told the German people that Grand Admiral Karl Doenitz had ordered the capitulation of all fighting forces, and called off the U-boat war.

Joy at the news was tempered only by the realization that the war against Japan remains to be resolved, with many casualties still ahead.

The end of the Europea nwarfare, greatest, bloodiest and costliest war in huma nhistory—it has claimed at least 40,000,000 casualties on both sides in killed, wounded, and captured—came after five years, eight months, and six days of strife that overspread the globe.

Hitler's arrogant armies invaded Poland on Sept. 1, 1939, beginning the agony that convulsed the world for 2,319 days.

Germans Talked First

Unconditional surrender of the beaten remnants of his legions first was announced by the Germans.

The historic news began breaking with a Danish broadcast that Norway had been surrendered unconditionally by its conquerors.

Then the new German Foreign Minister, Ludwig Schwerin Von Krosigk, announced to the German people, shortly after 2 P. M. (8 A. M. Eastern War Time), that "after almost six years struggle we have succumbed."

Von Krosigk announced Grand Admiral Karl Doenitz had "ordered the unconditional surrender of all fighting German troops."

The world waited tensely. Then at 9:35 A. M., E. W. T., came the Associated Press flash from Reims, France, telling of the signing at Gen. Eisenhower's headquarters of the unconditional surrender at 2:41 A. M. French time (8:41 A. M., E. W. T.) Germany had given up to the Western Allies and to Russia.

London Goes Wild

London went wild at the news. Crowds jammed Piccadilly Circus. Smiling throngs poured out of subways and lined the streets.

(Cheers went up in New York, too, and papers showered down from skyscrapers.)

An announcement on the wavelength of the Flensburg radio, which has been carrying German communiques and orders for several days, said:

"German men and women! The high command of the armed forces has today, at the order of Grand Admiral Doenitz, declared the unconditional surrender of all fighting German troops."

The announcement was attributed to the new German Foreign Minister, Count Schwerin Von Krosigk.

Crowds In London

Crowds gathered in the flag-decked streets of Lodnon and crowded about microphones. Prime Minister Churchill had arranged to go on the BBC with the official Allied announcement whenever it was ready. It was announced last week that King George VI would broadcast to his empire at 9 P. M. (3 P. M. Eastern War Time) on V-E day.

Shortly after the broadcast attributed to Von Krosigk, the German communique was broadcast on the Flensburg wavelength.

This said "bitter fighting continues" in the area of Olmuetz" in Moravia where the Germans have been opposing the Russians. This communique usually has related the events of the previous day.

An order of the day attributed to Doenitz ordered German U-boats to cease fire.

Breslau Falls

The German-controlled radio in Prague announced the fall of besieged Breslau, capital of Silesia which had been encircled by the Russians since Feb. 17.

The free Danish radio said that Germans in Norway had capitulated.

"After almost six years struggle we have succumbed," the Krosigk broadcast said.

"Our sympathy firstly goes out to our soldiers. Nobody must deceive himself on the harshness of the terms which our enemies have imposed on the German people.

"Nobody must have any doubt that heavy sacrifices will be demanded from us in all spheres of life.

"We must take them upon us and stand loyally to our obligations."

HOOP, JR. CAPTURES DERBY BY SIX LENGTHS

Byerly Wins City-County Boys Net Title

PIAA CHAMPION TOPS J. STEHMAN IN FOUR SETS

Charles Byerly, PIAA singles tennis champion, defeated John Stehman, second man of the McCaskey squad, for the Lancaster City and County Junior Boys' tennis championship, sponsored by the Lancaster Tennis Club late Saturday afternoon on the Lancaster Club courts. The scores were 6-2, 5-7, 6-0, 6-1.

The doubles finals will be played this Monday.

The results of the singles follows:

Third Round

Byerly defeated Smith 6-1, 6-0.
Lebegern defeated Gould, default.
Piersol defeated Kessner, 7-5, 4-6, 6-2.
Stehman defeated D. Hoh, 6-2, 6-2.

Semi-Finals

Byerly defeated Lebegern 6-2, 6-0.
Stehman defeated Piersol 6-1, 6-1.

Finals

Byerly defeated Stehman 6-2, 5-7, 6-0, 6-1.

High Alumni Netmen Defeat McCaskey 4-2

A team of Lancaster High School Alumni defeated the McCaskey High varsity tennis team Saturday match.

In the feature match of the afternoon Charles Byerly, the present state singles champion, defeated Bob Smith, State champion in 1924, by the scores of 6-1 and 6-2.

In the feature doubles match Paul Shreiner and Clarence McCue, Alumni, defeated the McCaskey team of Byerly and John Stehman 6-2, 6-4.

The results:

Singles

Byerly, Varsity defeated Smith, 6-1, 6-2.
Shreiner, Alumni, defeated Stehman 6-2, 6-4.
McCue, Alumni, defeated Kessler, 6-2, 6-0.
Kennedy, Alumni, defeated Hoeel, 2-6, 6-1, 6-1.
Gerhart, Varsity, defeated Miller, 6-1, 8-6.

Doubles

Shreiner and McCue, Alumni, defeated Byerly and Stehman 6-2, 6-4.

Phils' Rally Falls Short, Drop 13th In Row To Brooks, 8-7

Brooklyn, June 9—(AP)—The Phillies hammered Ben Chapman off the mound in the ninth inning but their late attack which netted four runs and featured a homer by Jimmy Foxx, fell one short of tying the score and they lost to the Dodgers 8 to 7 tonight before 14,892.

It was the Phillies' 13th consecutive defeat and with it they moved to within one game of equalling the two longest losing streaks in the Philadelphia club's history. The Phillies of 1883 dropped fourteen in a row and the modern day skein of setbacks of that proportion was suffered in 1936 under the management of Jimmy Wilson.

The Dodgers scored what proved to be their winning runs off Oscar Judd in the seventh inning when they pounded the southpaw for five singles and three tallies.

Philadelphia	ab	r	h	o	a	Brooklyn	ab	r	h	o	a
Mont'o lf	4	0	0	1	0	Stanky 2b	4	0	1	3	4
Dinges cf	4	1	1	4	0	Rosen cf	5	3	3	2	0
Wasd'l rf	5	2	2	4	0	Galan lf	3	1	1	1	0
Foxx 1b	5	2	3	9	1	Walker rf	4	0	1	4	0
C'ford ss	5	1	2	0	4	Olmo 3b	4	2	1	0	0
Sem'k 3b	4	0	2	0	3	White ss	0	0	0	0	0
Peac'k c	3	0	1	0	0	Sch'ltz 1b	4	1	2	10	3
Manc'o c	1	0	0	1	1	Dant'o c	4	0	1	2	0
Pic'to 2b	3	0	0	5	1	Bas'ki ss	4	0	1	2	3
Karl p	2	0	0	0	0	Chap'n p	4	1	1	2	2
Trip't x	1	0	1	0	0	Lomb'i p	0	0	0	1	0
Judd p	0	0	0	0	0						
DiM'o xx	0	0	0	0	0	Totals	36	8	12	27	12
K'y xxx	0	1	0	0	0						
Totals	37	7	12	24	10						

x-Batted for Karl in 7th.
xx-Batted for Judd in 9th.
xxx-Ran for DiMaggio in 9th.

PHILADELPHIA	000 101 014—7	
BROOKLYN	104 000 30x—8	

Errors—Seminick 2, Picciuto. Runs batted in—Walker, Rosen 2, Olmo, Crawford, Seminick, Schultz 2, Dantonio, Wasdell, Foxx 3. Two base hits—Rosen, Crawford, Seminick, Tripiett, Wasdell. Three base hits—Olmo, Wasdell. Home runs—Rosen, Foxx. Stolen bases—Galan, Olmo. Sacrifices—Stanky. Double plays—Basinski, Stanky and Schultz; Stanky and Basinski. Left on bases—Philadelphia 7, Brooklyn 6. Bases on balls—Off Karl 1; Chapman 4. Strikeouts—Judd 1; Chapman 2. Hits—Off Karl 7 in 6 innings; Judd 5 in 2; Chapman 12 in 8 2-3; Lombardi 0 in 1-3. Winning pitcher—Chapman. Losing pitcher—Karl. Umpires—Goetz, Jordan and Henline. Time of game—2:06. Attendance—12,938.

First Three Horses In Derby To Race In The Preakness

Louisville, Ky., June 9—(AP)—The first three horses to finish in the Kentucky Derby today will be starters in next Saturday's Preakness at Pimlico.

Trainer Ivan Parke said he would ship Hoop Jr. tomorrow morning, along with Mrs. W. G. Lewis' Darby Dieppe. Warren Wright's Pot O' Luck also will head for Baltimore within the next day or two.

Ludell Ruff, trainer of Jeep, who finished fifth, will return the Col. C. V. Whitney colt to New York and then decide if he'll be a starter in the Preakness. He said, however, that if the track was like Churchill Downs' racing strip today that the Whitney colt would not go in the second half of the triple crown.

Alexis also is expected to be a starter in the Preakness.

ONE-HORSE STABLE

Mexico City, June 9—Gay Dalton, the Mexican Man o' War, is a one-horse stable.

Big Time Tennis Is Scheduled For Wimbledon Stadium

London, June 9—(AP)—Big time tennis will return to Wimbledon Stadium, the world's most famous lawn tennis ground, on June 30 with an exhibition between United States and British Empire service stars.

The roster includes a number of former Davis Cup players and internationally known stars like George Lott and Sgt. Charley Hare and others to whom a return to Wimbledon will be like a homecoming.

The war put an end to competitive tennis at Wimbledon in 1939. A German bomb took a large chunk out of the main grandstand in front of the center court, but otherwise the place was undamaged.

The one day series of contests—two singles matches and three doubles—will be held under the joint sponsorship of the Wimbledon association and the United States Army Special Services branch. The gate receipts will go toward renovating the stadium.

NAVY PLACES IN 11 NCAA FINALS

Milwaukee, June 9—(AP)—Navy used its all around power tonight to smother gallant bids by Illinois and Michigan and carry the National Collegiate Athletic Association track and field championship east for the first time in the 24-year history of the event. The Midshipmen scored in seven of the 14 events for a total of 62 points.

Milwaukee, June 9—(AP)—Navy's big, balanced squad operated as advertised today in the trials for tonight's finals of the 24th annual National Collegiate Athletic Association track and field championship meet, sending men into 11 title events.

The small, compact entries from Illinois and Missouri shaped up as the main opposition to the Midshipmen with six places each, with Purdue and Notre Dame landing four apiece.

Navy made its most impressive showing in numbers if not in performance, in the javelin in which Bill Patton, Frank Kelley and Peter Colot gained the finals. Patton came up with the best mark, an ordinary 181 feet, 11 3-4 inches. Joe Hall and Fred Boswan qualified in the broad jump, in which Fred Sheffield of Idaho leaped 23 feet, 7-8 inch for the top performance, and John Van Velzer landed second in his heat of the 100-yard test for another finalist place. Bob Crowson of Missouri and Bill Buster of Illinois, headed the sprinters, each winning a heat of the 100 and the 220-yard dash in the same time, 10.2 seconds in the century and :22.3.

Van Velzer, unbeaten this year in the furlong, was shut out in the first heat of the event which went to Dave Murphy of Notre Dame in 22.7 seconds.

Navy suffered a mild shock in the half-mile when Floyd Cutt failed to qualify, but got a man into the event when Francis Carlon ran second to Bill Maskill of Michigan State in the slow time of 2:00.7. Sylvester Stewart, stubby Negro from Miami, Ohio, University, won the other test in 1:59.9.

Navy's other qualifiers were Newbold Smith in the shotput and discus, and Frank Sorensen in the latter event, and Bill Kash who took his heat of the quarter-mile in 50.3 seconds. Best time in the quarter was turned in by Dick Forrestel of Michigan, at :50.1.

Missouri qualified Ed Quirk and Wilfred Bangert in the shot and discus, along with Crowson in the dashes. Buster headed the Illinois delegation with his places in the sprint, George Walker qualified in both hurdles and Henry Aihara and Marce Gonzalez earned positions in the broad jump and 440-yard dash, respectively.

Other schools qualified for places as follows: Drake, Michigan, Fresno, Calif., State, Western Michigan and Miami 3 each; Louisiana State, Marquette, Iowa State, Illinois Tech, Minnesota and Ohio State 2 each, and Iowa, Depauw, Utah, Wisconsin, Idaho, Michigan State, Texas and Oberlin, one each.

Boast 9th Straight Undefeated Season—

WINNERS of the District 3 championship for the eighth time in nine years, the McCaskey High track squad has just completed its ninth straight undefeated season in dual competition. Thirty-six straight dual meets have been won in the long span, this past season's victims being Coatesville, John Harris, Lebanon and York. A total of 291 1-2 points were scored against 129 1-2 points for the opponents.

This year's team produced two state champions, in Harry Coyle, high hurdler, and George Shoemaker, high jumper. Coyle will captain next year's squad.

The complete McCaskey squad, pictured above, includes:

First row, left to right: Theodore Schmidt, Fred Johnson, James Ault, George Betz, John Diffenderfer, Allen Eckert, Donald Harvey, William Snyder, Frank Bashore.

Second row: James Case, manager; Wilbur Kraybill, Robert High, Myron Jones, Richard Diller, Captain Robert Anderson, Donald Beck, James Jones, Henry Strock, Albert Spinner, John Smucker, Kenneth Mattern, assistant manager.

Third row: Coach S. W. Sponaugle, Jere Klivansky, Sumner Bohee, Kenneth Smeltz, George Shoemaker, David Wiley, John Kreider, Harry Coyle, George Stauffer, David Williams, Assistant Coach B. L. Sponaugle.

Fourth row: Joseph Giordano, Milton Gockley, Fred Johns, John Jarrett, Jay Miller, Robert Schmid, Charles Finefrock, Jay Vatter, Nowell Hoover.

Fifth row: Robert King, Richard Goodman, Morris Winer, James McCaskey, John Hartman, Bernard Levine, John Barton, Paul Schrenk, Donald White.

THE SCOREBOARD

STANDING OF TEAMS

National League

Teams	W.	L.	P.C.
New York	28	16	.636
St. Louis	25	19	.568
Brooklyn	24	20	.545
Pittsburgh	24	20	.545
Chicago	21	19	.525
Cincinnati	21	21	.500
Boston	20	21	.488
Philadelphia	10	37	.213

American League

Teams	W.	L.	P.C.
Detroit	24	16	.600
New York	26	18	.591
Boston	23	21	.523
St. Louis	21	20	.512
Cleveland	19	21	.475
Chicago	20	23	.465
Washington	20	23	.465
Philadelphia	16	27	.372

Interstate League

Teams	W.	L.	P.C.
Lancaster	27	12	.692
Wilmington	24	15	.615
Trenton	20	21	.488
Allentown	14	18	.438
Hagerstown	15	22	.405
York	12	24	.333

SATURDAY'S RESULTS

National League

Boston 4, New York 0.
Chicago 5, Cincinnati 1.
Brooklyn 8, Philadelphia 7 (night)
Pittsburgh 5, St. Louis 1 (night)

American League

New York 13, Boston 7.
Cleveland 2, St. Louis 1.
Detroit 7, Chicago 6.
Washington 3, Philadelphia 2.

Interstate League

Hagerstown 12, Wilmington 4.
Lancaster 10, York 4.
Allentown 15, Trenton 6.

American Association

St. Paul at Columbus (postponed, wet grounds).
Milwaukee at Indianapolis (postponed, rain).
Kansas City at Louisville (postponed, rain).
Toledo 6, Minneapolis 4 (night).

International League

Newark 8, Buffalo 2.
Syracuse 9, Rochester 1.
Jersey City 8, Toronto 4 (night).
Montreal 13, Baltimore 4 (night).

SUNDAY'S GAMES
(All doubleheaders)

National League

New York at Boston—Voiselle (8-3) and Hansen (4-2) vs. Cooper (4-0) and Tobin (4-2).

Cincinnati at Chicago—Heusser (5-3) and Dasso (3-3) vs. Passeau (3-2) and Prim (2-3).

Philadelphia at Brooklyn—Barrett (3-5) and Kennedy (0-3) or Wyatt (0-5) vs. Gregg (6-4) and Rudolph (0-0).

Pittsburgh at St. Louis—Roe (4-3) and Butcher (5-2) vs. Wilks (3-4) and Brecheen (3-1).

American League

Boston at New York—Ferriss (8-0) and Terry (0-1) vs. Borowy (7-1) and Dubiel (4-4).

Washington at Philadelphia—Haefner (2-6) and Pieretti (5-4) vs. Flores (1-2) and Knerr (1-3).

Chicago at Detroit—Grove (5-4) and Ross (0-0) vs. Overmire (4-1) and Trout (4-4).

St. Louis at Cleveland—Jakucki (3-4) and Muncrief (3-1) vs. Bagby (0-5) and Reynolds (4-5).

Interstate League

Lancaster at York.
Allentown at Trenton.
Wilmington at Hagerstown.

NOTRE DAME WINS, 55-17

Waterbury, Conn., June 9—(AP)—Notre Dame beat Kingsbury here yesterday 55 to 17, or at least that's what a little girl said when she called the Waterbury Republican sports department to report the result of a girls' baseball game between Notre Dame Academy and the Kingsbury grammar school.

Sports Are Asked To Cut Travel Down To A Minimum

Washington, June 9—(AP)—Sports were asked tonight by the Office of Defense Transportation to "reexamine their requirements and reduce travel to a minimum."

Col. J. Monroe Johnson, ODT director, announced a six-point voluntary program for the public which he said "may avert" the need of travel rationing.

Grouping sports with entertainment, commercial concerns and other enterprises as "large users of transportation," Johnson pointed out that "as yet no formal restrictions have been imposed but they will be if the need is indicated."

In answer to a query, an ODT official later said that baseball, bowling, high school and college athletics already have voluntarily adopted substantial travel reduction plans "but it may be necessary to go a step beyond that and formalize these programs."

Professional football, it was added, has not yet formally "come in with a curtailment program," although some reductions have been discussed. In some individual instances, however, reduced travel plans have been announced.

President Truman recently said that he will not hesitate to put travel under federal control if it becomes necessary.

Lower End Softball Champions—

THE Bart girls' softball team won the Lower End League title during the past season, winning nine games and tying one against five opponents. They defeated Little Britain, Drumore, East Drumore and Colerain twice during the season, and defeated and tied Fulton.

Seated in front is East Murphy, pitcher. In the first row, left to right, are: Mary Hershey, first base; Evelyn Rapp, second base; Marian Phenneger, short center; Geraldine Trout, shortstop; Martha Myers, center field.

The second row, left to right, includes: Hiram G. Troop, coach; Martham McMinn, catcher; Jean Troop, pitcher; Dorothy Murr, third base; Ada Rineer short center; Magdalene Reed, right field; Irene Stoltzfus, left field.

TIGER PITCHERS BAT OUT 7-6 WIN

Detroit, June 9—(AP)—A pair of Detroit pitchers proved far more effective at bat than on the mound today as the Tigers came from behind with four runs in the ninth to edge the Chicago White Sox, 7 to 6, and hold the American League lead.

Les Mueller, Tiger starter, gave six runs and 13 hits in seven innings but belted a two-run homer during a three-run Detroit rally in the fifth.

Zeb Eaton, who relieved Mueller in the eighth, allowed two hits and a pair of walks, but doubled off the left field wall, driving in two runs in the ninth and putting the tying marker on second.

Bob Maier and Bob Swift had singled ahead of Eaton in the surprise finish, both scoring on the relief pitcher's wallop. Skeeter Webb tried to sacrifice but was safe on fireman Earl Caldwell's error, putting Ed Borom, running for Eaton, on third.

Eddie Mayo provided the payoff blow, a mighty triple to center, scoring Borom and Webb and pinning the loss on Caldwell, who pitched to only two batsmen after relieving Joe Haynes in the ninth. Nobody was out when the winning run scored.

The White Sox pecked away at Mueller during his entire stay, getting one hit in the first and two in each of the next six innings.

A walk, a Tiger error and Mueller's balk helped Chicago to a 4-3 lead in the sixth after Detroit had bunched its first four hits off Haynes for three runs in the fifth.

Two more runs, on two hits and another Detroit error, made it 6-3, Chicago, in the seventh. Haynes, who had hurled a one-hitter in his last start against the Tigers, protected that margin until Detroit jumped on him with both feet in the ninth.

Chicago	ab	r	h	o	a	Detroit	ab	r	h	o	a
Moses rf	5	0	1	1	0	Webb ss	3	1	0	2	1
Far'll 1b	5	0	2	8	1	Mayo 2b	5	0	2	4	8
Hock't cf	5	1	3	4	0	C'nbine rf	4	0	1	0	1
D'shot lf	5	2	2	4	0	York 1b	3	0	1	10	1
Cuc'llo 3b	4	2	2	1	2	Cramer cf	4	0	0	3	0
Schalk 2b	4	0	0	2	2	Outlaw lf	3	1	1	1	0
Mich'ls ss	2	1	2	2	2	Maier 3b	4	1	1	4	1
Tresh c	4	0	1	2	0	Swift c	4	1	2	3	0
Haynes p	4	0	2	0	0	bHoover	0	1	0	0	0
Cald'l p	0	0	0	0	0	Mueller p	2	1	1	0	3
						aMcHale	1	0	0	0	0
Totals	38	6	15y	24	7	Eaton p	1	0	1	0	0
						cBorom	0	1	0	0	0
						Totals	34	7	10	27	15

y-None out when winning run scored.
a-Batted for Mueller in 7th.
b-Ran for Swift in 9th.
c-Ran for Eaton in 9th.

CHICAGO	010 003 200—6
DETROIT	000 030 004—7

Errors—Moses, Michaels 2, Caldwell, Webb, Mayo. Runs batted in—Michaels, Tresh 2, Swift, Mueller 2, Eaton 2, Mayo 2. Two base hits—Hockett, Cullenbine. Three base hit—Mayo. Home run—Mueller. Stolen bases—Cuccinello 2, Dickshot 2. Sacrifices—Schalk, Webb. Double plays—Farrell and Michaels; Mayo, Webb and York; Mayo, York and Webb; Mayo and York. Left on bases—Chicago 9, Detroit 7. Bases on balls—Haynes 3, Mueller 1, Easton 2. Strikeouts—Mueller 2. Hits—Off Haynes 9 in 8 innings; (none out in 9th); Caldwell 1 in 0; Mueller 13 in 7; Eaton 2 in 2. Balk—Mueller. Winning pitcher—Eaton. Losing pitcher—Caldwell. Umpires—Stewart, Weafer and Hubbard. Time—2:01. Attendance—6,484.

Meade And McCombs Denied Licenses

New York, June 9—(AP)—Jockeys Don Meade and Ken McCombs were denied licenses today by the (New York) Jockey Club, whose meeting was attended by Ashley T. Cole, chairman of the State Racing Commission.

The Jockey Club announced no reasons for the denials. Meade recently was suspended in Mexico City but that ban ended with the close of the meeting there.

LAFAYETTE WINS FIRST

Easton, Pa., June 9—(AP)—Lafayette won its first baseball game in 11 starts today when Dick Reed's triple with two out in the ninth drove in two runs to give the Maroons a 4 to 3 victory over Drew Seminary in the second game of a doubleheader. Drew won the opener, 8 to 7.

LOGAN OF BRAVES TOPS GIANTS, 5-0

Boston, June 9—(AP)—Bob Logan, veteran Boston southpaw, recently brought back to the majors, handed the New York Giants their second shutout of the season today, to give the Braves a 4-0 victory before 5,082 paid admissions.

In pitching the Braves to their fifth straight triumph, Logan held the league leaders hitless for five and two-thirds innings. George Hausmann got the first New York hit, a bunt single to third, followed by a solid single by Mel Ott.

Harry Feldman matched Logan's runless pitching for six frames, but singles by Carden Gillenwater, Phil Masi and Frank Drews produced the Braves first run in the seventh.

Boston added three more in the eighth off relief hurler Ace Adams, counting on two singles, a double, plus two Giant errors.

The victory was Logan's third of the season compared to one defeat while Feldman suffered his third loss against five victories.

New York	ab	r	h	o	a	Boston	ab	r	h	o	a
Ruc'r cf	4	0	1	3	0	Joost 3b	4	0	0	0	3
Hau'n 2b	4	0	2	2	2	Holm's rf	4	1	1	4	0
Ott rf	4	0	1	1	0	Mack 1b	4	1	1	8	0
Med'k lf	4	0	0	3	0	Work'n rf	4	1	0	4	0
Lom'di c	4	0	1	5	0	Gil'w'r cf	4	1	2	5	0
bTr'way	0	0	0	0	0	Masi c	4	0	3	2	0
Jurges 3b	4	0	1	1	1	Drews 2b	4	0	1	1	3
Kerr ss	4	0	1	2	2	Wiet'n ss	3	0	1	3	3
A.G'la 1b	3	0	0	7	0	Logan p	4	0	0	0	0
cFil'w'z c	1	0	0	0	0						
Feld'n p	2	0	0	0	1	Totals	35	4	9	27	9
aHudson	1	0	0	0	0						
Adams p	0	0	0	0	0						
dDeK'ng	1	0	0	0	0						
Totals	36	0	7	24	6						

a-Batted for Feldman in 8th.
b-Ran for Lombardi in 9th.
c-Batted for A. Gardella in 9th.
d-Batted for Adams in 9th.

NEW YORK	000 000 000—0
BOSTON	000 000 13x—4

Errors—Hausman, A. Gardella, Joost 2, Wietelmann. Runs batted in—Drews, Workman, Gillenwater, Masi. Stolen base—Kerr. Double play—Wietelmann, Drews and Mack. Left on bases—New York 9, Boston 8. Bases on balls—Adams 1. Strikeouts—Feldman 2, Adams 1, Logan 2. Hits—Off Feldman 6 in 7 innings; Adams, 3 in 1. Wild pitch—Logan. Losing pitcher—Feldman. Umpires—Barr, Dunn and Sears. Time—1:31. Attendance—5,082 paid.

Chipman's Draft Decision Delayed

Chicago, June 9—(AP)—Induction center officials today postponed until Monday a decision in the draft examination of Bob Chipman, southpaw pitcher for the Chicago Cubs. Chipman, previously classified 4-F, began his examination yesterday.

Outfielder Bill Nicholson of the Cubs was approved for military service here yesterday, but is expected to remain with the club for at least a month. A third Bruin regular, First Baseman Heinz Becker, was ordered to report for induction June 18.

Pot O'Luck Runs Second; 3rd Place To Darby Dieppe

LOUISVILLE, Ky., June 9—(AP)—Showing the way over practically the entire mile and one-quarter of muddy going, Hoop Jr. today won the 71st and richest of all Kentucky Derbies so easily it appeared his 15 rival three-year-olds were in another race.

With Eddie Arcaro in the saddle for this third triumph in America's premier race, the son of Sir Gallahad 3rd carried F. W. Hooper's blue and white silks across the line six lengths in advance of Pot O' Luck from Warren Wright's Calumet Farm.

Mrs. W. G. Lewis' Darby Dieppe, hoping to be the first grey horse to carry off honors in the classic run for the roses, was third, beaten a half length for runner-up honors. Lt. Com. T. D. Buhl's Air Sailor failed to land in the money picture by a neck as the other horses finished far back.

Track Was Soaked

Running over a track soaked by three days of rain and under overcast skies that threatened all day long to drench the crowd of 65,000, the Jacksonville, Fla. -owned Hoop Jr. stepped out in front of the pack inside of the first sixteenth of a mile and never was headed.

Arcaro, who won in 1938 with Lawrin and four years ago with Whirlaway, rated Hoop along in front of the pack until he hit the head of the home stretch—a quarter-mile from the finish line.

Then, acting as if he was up on another Whirlaway, the veteran Newport, Ky., Italian called on Hoop Jr. The race for the $64,850, winner's share of the gross purse of $86,875, was settled right there. When the Hooper bay crossed the finish line swinging on the bit, he enjoyed the biggest margin of victory since Whirlaway won by eight lengths.

Hoop Jr. ran all but the first quarter mile on the rail, where the going was heaviest, but he stepped the distance in 2:07—the slowest time since Gallant Fox needed 2:07 3-5 to win over a good track in 1930. The last time the Derby was run over a muddy track in 1929, Clyde Van Dusen was clocked in 2:10 2-5.

Arcaro's victory, scored with a colt that cost Hooper $10,200 as a yearling, tied him for jockey honors in the Derby with Earle Sande and Isaac Murphy each of whom rode three winners.

Pot O' Luck Was Choice

Hoop Jr. was the favorite parading to the post but by the time Reuben White gave them the word to go, the huge throng had established Pot O' Luck as its choice, apparently remembering the two previous triumphs of Wright's colors and one additional by Trainer Ben Jones.

As the result, the well built colt trained by Ivan Parke, who himself twice rode in the Derby but never tasted the fruits of victory, paid $9.40, $5.20 and $4.00 across the board. A $2 place ticket on Pot O' Luck returned $4.80 and a show ducat $3.60. Darby Dieppe paid $4.00 to show.

A total of $776,408 was wagered on the race, surpassing the previous high of $694,870 bet in 1926 when Bubbling Over won.

Breaking from near the outside on the large field, Hoop Jr. needed only two cracks of Arcaro's whip to send him bounding past J. K. Houssel's Bymeabond. He swung straight down the middle of the track, where the going was much better, opened a two-length lead as he passed the judges' stand and then went over to the rail.

Alexis An Early Threat

As Hoop Jr. rounded the first turn, with Bymeabond a length back, Alexis from Henry Lunger's Christiana Stable was running smoothly in third place. Pot O' Luck, Darby Dieppe and Col. C. V. Whitney's well backed Jeep were far back, with the latter out in the middle of the track.

Swinging into the back stretch, Arcaro still had a tight hold on the reins with Bymeabond holding to second place. Alexis found the pace too swift and dropped back as Air Sailor moved into third and Fighting Step, owned by the Murlogg Farm, entered the scene. Meantime, Doug Dodson on Pot O' Luck and Melvin Calvert on Darby Dieppe were gradually closing in but Hoop Jr. still was a long way up front.

There was little change in their positions as Hoop showed the way out of the backstretch, rounded the final turn and pointed his nose toward the finish line. Almost, as if he was shot out of a cannon, the Sir Gallahad offspring shook off his competitors. Bymeabond quickly called quits as Pot O' Luck and Darby Dieppe came charging up to get into the money. They were running strongly at the end but so was Hoop Jr.

Jeep also closed fast to finish fifth but he was beaten four lengths by the fourth place Air Sailor. Then came Bymeabond, Sea Swallow, Fighting Step, Burning Dream bidding for E. R. Bradley's fifth Derby, Alexis, Foreign Agent, Misweet, the only filly in the race, Tiger Rebel, Bert G., Jacobe and Kenilworth Lad.

4 New York Racing Groups Purchase Jamaica Holdings

New York, June 9—(AP)—Purchase of the stock holdings of the late Mrs. Matt Corbett in the Metropolitan Jockey Club, which holds its races at Jamaica, by the four other New York racing associations was announced late today by George P. Widener, president of the West Chester Association.

The purchase price was not announced. Earlier this week it was reported that William Helis, New Orleans sportsman, had bid $4,000,000 for the Corbett shares plus another block of 12 per cent.

Mrs. Corbett, widow of one of the four men who built the plant, owned an estimated 44 per cent of the stock when she died last year.

The four purchasing associations are the West Chester, which conducts its meetings at Belmont; Queens, with Aqueduct the site of its races, Saratoga and Empire City.

Mrs. Corbett left her race track holdings to various relatives. A bequest of $50,000 in cash went to her sister, Sister Miriam Bernard of the Society of the Sisters of St. Vincent De Paul.

Bucs Trip Cards, 5 To 1, Strincevich Allowing Six Hits

St. Louis, June 9—(AP)—Nick Strincevich allowed the St. Louis Cardinals six hits while Pittsburgh collected 10 blows to defeat the World Champions, 5 to 1, in the second game of their series at Sportsmans Park tonight.

The Pirates punched Red Barrett for four hits, scoring four runs, in the first inning, and the Cardinal hurler was relieved by George Dockins in the second.

In the ninth the Red Birds made their only run when Al Schoendienst scored after Buster Adams flied to left field.

Pittsburgh	ab	r	h	o	a	St. Louis	ab	r	h	o	a
Han'y 3b	4	0	0	2	3	Sch'd'st lf	4	1	2	3	0
J.Bar't cf	4	2	2	4	0	Hopp rf	3	0	1	3	0
Russ'l lf	4	1	1	1	0	Ber'mo rf	1	0	1	1	0
Elliott rf	4	1	0	0	0	Adams cf	4	0	0	2	0
Salk'd c	5	0	2	3	0	Sand's 1b	3	0	1	6	1
Dahl'n 1b	2	1	0	13	1	Kur'ki 3b	3	0	0	1	2
G'tine 2b	4	0	2	3	6	Garms 3b	1	0	0	2	0
Barn't ss	3	0	3	0	2	O'Dea c	4	0	0	2	3
St'vich p	3	0	0	1	1	Marion ss	3	0	0	1	1
						Verb'n 2b	3	0	1	5	0
Totals	33	5	10	27	13	C.Bar'tt p	0	0	0	0	1
						Dockins p	1	0	0	1	1
						Bart'h z	1	0	0	0	0
						Juris'h p	0	0	0	0	0
						Totals	31	1	6	27	9

z-Batted for Dockins in 8th.

PITTSBURGH	400 010 000—5
ST. LOUIS	000 000 001—1

Errors—Hopp. Runs batted in—Gustine 2, Barnhart, Elliott 2, Adams. Two base hits—J. Barrett, Barnhart, Schoendienst. Sacrifices—Strincevich, Russell, Barnhart. Double plays — Barnhart, Gustine and Dahlgren; Handley and Dahlgren. Left on bases—Pittsburgh 9, St. Louis 5. Bases on balls—Strincevich 2, C. Barrett 1, Dockins 2, Jurisich 2. Strikeouts—Strincevich 2, Dockins 1. Hits—Off C. Barrett 4 in 1 inning; Dockins 5 in 7; Jurisich 1 in 1. Losing pitcher—C. Barrett. Umpires—Conlan, Boggess and Pinelli. Time—1:46. Attendance—5195.

Owls Win Second From Rocks, 12 To 4

Hagerstown, Md., June 9—(AP)—Collecting 13 hits off the offerings of three Wilmington pitchers, the Hagerstown Owls made it two straight over the Blue Rocks tonight, 12-4.

Hagerstown scored seven runs in the eighth on three hits, two errors, a hit batman, two walks and a wild pitch.

Jake Kraft of the Owls gave up seven hits. Bob Martin stole home in the fourth. Valesquez led the Owls' attack with three hits.

Wilmington	ab	r	h	o	a	Hagerstown	ab	r	h	o	a
Col'bo 3b	5	1	2	2	1	Val'ez ss	5	1	3	2	3
Volan cf	4	0	1	1	0	Martin 2b	6	3	2	3	2
Gl'r 2b ss	2	1	1	5	4	King rf	1	2	1	2	0
Aug'n c	4	0	1	6	1	Mat'zo lf	3	1	1	3	0
Scal'e rf	4	1	1	1	0	Danek cf	5	2	1	1	1
Narl'y 2b	2	0	0	3	1	Dan'ls 3b	4	1	2	2	0
Neb'k 1b	4	0	0	5	1	Perc'k 1b	4	1	1	6	0
Sand's lf	4	0	1	1	0	Trench c	5	1	2	8	0
Chitw'd p	1	0	0	0	1	Kraft p	4	0	0	0	1
Holtc'p p	1	0	0	0	2						
Latchie x	1	0	0	0	0	Totals	37	12	13	27	7
Sch'tz xx	0	1	0	0	0						
Krsn'k ss	1	0	0	0	0						
Porter p	1	0	0	0	0						
Totals	34	4	7	24	10						

x-Batted for Holtcamp in 7th.
xx-Ran for Marlesky in 7th.

WILMINGTON	000 000 211— 4
HAGERSTOWN	210 100 17x—12

Errors—Narlesky, Glaser 2, Daniels 2, Porter, Augustyn, Volan. Runs batted in—Matarazzo 2, Valesquez 2, Sanders, Perchak, Krsnick, Daniels, Trench, Volan. Two base hits—Daniels, Danek, Perchak, Scalise, Columbo, Volan. Stolen bases—Martin. Sacrifices—Volan, Kraft. Double plays—Martin to Valesquez, Glaser to Nebarek. Left on bases—Wilmington 7, Hagerstown 11. Base on balls—Off Kraft 3, Holtcamp 3, Porter 1. Struck out—By Chitwood 2, Kraft 8, Holtcamp 3, Porter 3. Hits—Off Chitwood 6 in 2 innings; off Holtcamp 3 in 4 innings; off Porter 5 in 2 innings. Hit by pitcher—By Chitwood (Matarazzo), Porter (Daniels). Wild pitches—Porter. Passed balls—Trench. Winning pitcher—Kraft. Losing pitcher—Chitwood. Umpires—Schindler and Tatler. Time of game—2:05.

Lowly Senators Want To Match Pieretti Against The Sensational Dave Ferriss

Washington, June 9—(AP)—The lowly Washington Senators are getting high-falutin ideas — they want to knock off Dave Ferriss, pitching sensation of the Boston Red Sox.

And the rookie mound battle of the year is shaping up for next Friday night between Ferriss and the Senators' diminutive freshman, Marino Pieretti.

Owner Clark Griffith of the Senators has written his son-in-law, Joe Cronin, manager of the Red Sox, challenging him to pit Ferriss against Pieretti.

"Cronin is a pretty tough guy himself and likes a good scrap so I'm sure he'll accept this challenge," Griffith said, with one eye cocked on the box office.

Eight Straight Wins

Since Ferriss came out of service, he has hurled eight straight wins without a defeat and lifted the Red Sox up into the pennant race.

Pieretti's record reads 5-3 but the little hurler has established himself as a "clutch" performer.

He mowed down Big Al Benton, Detroit Tiger ace, in a 1-0 duel after Benton had won five in a row . . . he beat the Philadelphia Athletics, 4-3, in 12 innings, and the Yankees once went 13 innings to nose him, 2-1.

Pieretti came to the Senators from Portland of the Pacific Coast League with 26 wins and 13 losses last season, and a reputation as "a throw-back to the old school of rough-and-ready baseball."

The tiny—as big leaguers go—pitcher (about 5 feet, 6 inches tall) is a product of the rock roller gang of Telegraph Hill in San Francisco.

Learned At Golden Gate

He learned to play ball at Golden Gate park which sent Ping Bodie, Lefty O'Doul, Tony Lazzeri, the DiMaggio boys, Willie Kamm, Cronin and others to the big show.

Ferriss, in winning eight straight, already has tied the American League record for a first-year pitcher. Hooks Wiltse of the old New York Giants ran up 12 wins before he lost one in 1904, but Wiltse started his streak with three victories in relief roles.

The American League mark tied by Ferriss was set originally by Johnny Whitehead, freshman ace of the Chicago White Sox, in 1935.

"Pieretti is just naturally a giant killer, and he'll take Ferriss the same way he took Benton," Griffith enthused.

WEATHER

Eastern Pennsylvania: Considerable Cloudiness And A Little Warmer With Scattered Showers Friday; Saturday Partly Cloudy And Moderately Warm.

Intelligencer Journal.

The Leading Newspaper in the Garden Spot of America, Home Owned for Home Folks Since 1794

152nd Year.—No. 23. Entered as second class matter August 9, 1944 at the Post Office at Lancaster, Pa., under the Act of March 3, 1879. Reg. U. S. Pat. Off. LANCASTER, PA., FRIDAY MORNING, JULY 13, 1945 CITY TWENTY-SIX PAGES. 20c PER WEEK—4c Per Copy

500 B-29'S RESUME HONSHU POUNDING

Two-Alarm Blaze Damages 3 Sheds, 5 Buildings Here

Firemen, Assisted By Police, Civilians, Fight Fire At B. B. Martin Company, Lumber Dealers, Charlotte And James Sts.; Estimate Damage At $25,000

A two-alarm fire swept through a lumber storage shed at the B. B. Martin Company, lumber dealers, Charlotte and James Sts., at 2:59 p. m. Thursday, damaging two other sheds and five adjoining buildings before firemen, assisted by police and civilian volunteers brought the flames under control.

Damage to the buildings and the lost contents was estimated at $25,000 by officials of the company and Fire Chief Harry Miller. Among the lumber lost was irreplacable mahogany, white pine and poplar boards.

Chief Miller escaped injury and the coupe he was driving was slightly damaged when involved in a collision with another automobile when he was responding to another alarm as flames broke out anew in a pile of charred boards at 7:13 p. m. The accident occurred at Charlotte and Walnut Streets.

The first fire was discovered by Alvin Shenk, a yard employe, who noticed smoke pouring from the two story frame building located along Concord Street, in the rear of the yards. He ran to the office and notified other employes and then went back to the building with a fire extinguisher and attempted to fight the flames.

Office employes sounded the alarm from Box 49, James and Charlotte Sts., which brought Chief Miller, Assistant Chief Frank Deen, and Pumpers from Companies No 1, 4 and 6 and Truck B to the scene.

MASS OF FLAMES

When firemen arrived they found the building a mass of flames, with dense clouds of smoke pouring from the doors and a burned-through portion of the roof. Chief Miller sounded the second alarm and Truck A and the pumper from Company No. 3 responded.

The regular firemen were assisted in laying six plug streams by more than a score of civilians, including city policemen, who were preparing to report for the 4 p.

More of TWO-ALARM on Page 10

"We Lead All The Rest"

FARM CORNER

By The Farm Editor

TOBACCO ASSOCIATION STOCKHOLDERS TO MEET ON SATURDAY

A special meeting of stockholders of the Lancaster County Tobacco Growers' Cooperative Association has been called by the board of directors to be held in Martin auditorium, YMCA building, on Saturday, at 7:30 p. m. Certificates of stock, which will admit holders to the session, will be issued, starting at 6 p. m.

A proposal to increase the capitalization of the growers' marketing organization will be discussed since, the board announced, all the preferred stock has been taken and in order to admit new members it will be necessary to issue more stock. There are more than 40 members at present.

The Co-op has finished its present packing operations and a detailed report will be given on progress to date since the new marketing organization was formed by county tobacco growers last Winter. Other discussion will center on the "attempt of certain interests to institute an allotment plan for our 1945 crop."

Growers with a new address or who for other reasons do not receive notice by mail are urged to attend, coming early. It is a meeting for stockholders only, the board said Thursday.

Weather Calendar

COMPARATIVE TEMPERATURES

Station	High	Low
Water Works	78	46
Ephrata	80	47
Official High for Year, June 30	97	
Official Low for Year, Jan. 25	—1	
Character of Day		Clear

SUN
Rises—5:46 a. m. Sets—8:33 p. m.

MOON
Sets—11:32 p. m.
First Quarter—July 17

STARS
Morning—Mars-Venus-Saturn
Evening—Jupiter

NEARBY FORECASTS
Maryland: Considerable cloudiness and a little warmer with scattered showers Friday; Saturday partly cloudy and moderately warm.
Delaware and New Jersey: Considerable cloudiness and a little warmer Friday; Saturday partly cloudy with moderate temperatures.

GLENN L. MARTIN ACCUSED IN EXCESS RYE SPECULATIONS

Baltimore Aircraft Manufacturer Cited In Agriculture Department Complaint

Washington —(AP)— Glenn L. Martin, Baltimore airplane manufacturer, was accused by the Agriculture Department Thursday of buying rye futures in excess of limits set under the Commodity Exchange Act.

A complaint signed by Secretary Anderson stated that Martin and his agent, Henry L. T. Ullrich, of Wilmington, Del., bought 3,300,000 bushels of rye futures on the Chicago Board of Trade June 9. This was 1,300,000 bushels in excess of the daily trading limit established by the Commodity Exchange Commission in 1938.

This limit on trading is designed, the department said, to prevent "excessive speculation" in grain and grain futures contracts.

The penalty provided for such violation is loss of trading privileges on the nation's commodity contract markets for a period of time determined by the Secretary of Agriculture.

20 DAYS TO ANSWER

Martin and Ullrich were given 20 days in which to file an answer to the complaint. A hearing before an Agriculture Department referee was set for August 9.

Filing of the complaint came a few days after Rep. Keefe (R-Wis) urged Congress to investigate trading in rye and rye futures on the Chicago market. He declared that an inquiry would disclose a "national scandal" involving government officials and some members of Congress as well as some grain traders.

On May 28, a complaint was issued accusing General Foods Corporation, Charles W. Metcalf, its executive vice-president, Daniel F. Rice & Company, Daniel F. Rice,

More of MARTIN on Page 10

Longest Session Of Big Three Is Seen Coming Up

By ERNEST B. VACCARO

Aboard The Cruiser Augusta With President Truman— (AP) — President Truman neared Europe Thursday night for a conference which will cover so many problems that it may last longer than any previous "big three" session.

It was revealed aboard this warship that the conversations with Prime Minister Churchill and Premier-Generalissimo Stalin in conquered Potsdam will get under way Monday or Tuesday of next week.

The President was reported convinced that the meeting on Berlin's outskirts will outlast those of Quebec, Tehran and Yalta. The Yalta meeting lasted eight days.

Except for the date of the meeting itself, Mr. Truman's schedule

More of LONGEST on Page 10

Firemen Battle $25,000 Blaze In City

City firemen are pictured battling to control the $25,000 fire at the B. B. Martin company, Charlotte and James Sts., Thursday afternoon, which destroyed a large lumber shed stored with mahogany and white pine and damaged several adjoining buildings. The inset shows Pvt. Walter Snyder, 416 N. Charlotte St., of the U. S. Army Engineers, who volunteered to help fight the blaze, and who worked with the firemen until the fire was out. He is home on 30-day furlough after serving in the European Theater of Operations. He expects to be assigned to the Pacific.

DEATHS OF TWO CITY VETERANS IN EUROPE REPORTED

One Killed In Accident In Austria, Second Died In Prison Camp

WAR CASUALTIES

The deaths of two Lancaster soldiers in the European Theater of Operations were reported Thursday.

KILLED IN ACCIDENT
Staff Sgt. Melvin Miller, 644 Hebrank St., in Austria.

DIED IN PRISON CAMP
Pfc. Clarence F. Lahr, 734 E. Fulton St., in Germany.

The deaths of two Lancaster soldiers in Europe were reported Thursday. One was killed in an accident in Austria two days before he was scheduled to return to the United States, while the second died in a German prison camp.

Staff-Sgt. Melvin Miller, twenty-five, son of Mr. and Mrs. Ralph Miller, of 644 Hebrank St., died in an accident in Austria on June 21, two days prior to being sent home for discharge from service, according to a message received by his parents from the War Department. He would have observed his twenty-sixth birthday anniversary Thursday.

S-Sgt. Miller

The only details given about the accident were that a vehicle

More of DEATHS on Page 10

Senate Accepts Bill Change Allowing FEPC To Continue

Washington—(AP)—The Congressional fight over continuing the Fair Employment Practice Committee ended Thursday night with House and Senate agreement on a $250,000 appropriation to fund it in the 12 months beginning July 1.

The legislators got together when the Senate accepted by voice vote House language which nullified a previous stipulation that the agency must use the funds to liquidate.

The $250,000 is just half what FEPC had asked.

Senator Morse (R-Ore) made a futile effort to defer a decision until Monday. He said he hoped that if this were done the people at home would make their sentiments known and a larger appropriation would be given the agency.

He launched into what he termed "extended discussion" — sometimes another name for filibuster —in an effort to force delay but gave up the floor after an hour and a half.

"DEMOCRACY ON TRIAL"

During his speech Morse stressed the theme that democracy is on trial in the world and that it will be judged in part on the way it treats minorities.

By the time the FEPC fight was ended, the hour was so late that leaders delayed final action until Friday on a $750,000,000 war agencies appropriation bill which contains the FEPC item.

The House had been standing by, waiting for the Senate to act on FEPC, with expecation that the entire bill could be finally acted on. House leaders decided to let it go until Friday.

BILBO'S IN AGAIN

When Morse gave up the floor, Senator Bilbo (D-Miss), bitter foe of FEPC, threw a scare into Sen-

More of SENATE on Page 10

LAWYER TESTIFIES JUDGE JOHNSON ASKED "PAY-OFFS"

Surprise Witness Says Federal Judge Sought Two-Thirds Of Fee

Washington — (AP) — A Scranton, Pa., lawyer testified Thursday that former Federal Judge Albert W. Johnson asked for pay-offs on a receivership fee.

John Memolo, a surprise witness in the House Judiciary subcommittee's investigation of the conduct of the Middle Pennsylvania District Court judge, said Johnson made the request in 1938, asking two-thirds of a big fee Memolo expected.

"I was non-committal," Memolo added.

JOHNSON IS PRESENT

The judge, sitting 12 feet from the witness and watching him intently through a long account of alleged out-of-court dealings, had been expected to take the stand himself but was not reached Thursday.

Accompanied by three Luzerne county lawyers, Johnson was present for the first time since open hearings began Tuesday into his

More of LAWYER on Page 10

N. Y. NEWSPAPERS' DELIVERYMEN LOSE CONTRACT RIGHTS

WLB, In First Action Of Kind, Rescinds Order Extending Contract

Washington—(AP)—The War Labor Board by unanimous vote Thursday rescinded its order of June 14 extending the contract between the Newspaper Deliverymen's Union in New York and the New York newspaper publishers.

The board said this action was taken in view of the continuation of the strike by the independent union which has tied up delivery of 14 daily newspapers since June 30.

The June 14 order which was rescinded, extended the contract beyond the June 30 expiration date pending settlement of differences and with the understanding that any wage increases would be made retroactive to June 30.

Board officials said the order means that the publishers are relieved of any contractual obligations to the union and are now at liberty to hire any one they want.

The publishers, officials added, could even bargain with another

More of STRIKES on Page 10

RETURNS GIRL TO HOME

Judy Watson, four, 304 Ice Ave., who wandered away while accompanying her mother on a shopping trip to a grocery store Thursday night, was returned to her home after she was found by Ralph Graham, 736 E. Fulton St., in front of his home, according to city police.

Introduce Four New Jap Cities To Fire Saturation Raids

Sixth Superfort Strike In 13 Days Hits Industrial Centers; Navy Planes Range Nip Homeland, Turn Back Korea-Bound Convoys In Yellow Sea

Guam (Friday)—(AP)—More than 500 B-29s spilled 3,000 tons of fire and demolition bombs before dawn today on a Tokyo bay oil center and four Japanese cities after Marine and Navy planes had battered a big naval air station, factories and rail lines at the south end of the daily-pounded enemy homeland.

Shortly after the 21st Bomber Command disclosed the sixth Superfortress strike in 13 days at Nippon, fleet headquarters reported a "strong flight" of Marine Corsairs tore into the Kanoya naval air station on Kyushu the day before. On the same day, Navy search planes destroyed a factory, damaged another and wrecked rail traffic on Eastern Kyushu.

(A dispatch from the cruiser Augusta taking President Truman to the Big Three conference said the Chief Executive was in touch hourly with the powerful U. S. Third Fleet off Japan. This hinted at possible new blows, for the fleet has been under a security blackout since its big strike at Tokyo Tuesday.

(Building up toward "the air saturation of Japan", Gen. Douglas MacArthur announced at Manila that his veteran air leader, Gen. George C. Kenney had become top tactical air commander and had moved advanced headquarters of the Far Eastern Air Force to Okinawa.

(Kenney promptly said Japan would be bombed "from 10,000 feet and from ten feet, with fire and explosives, with bombers and fighters—and we will do it 24 hours a day.")

Along a 480-mile strip from the southern island of Shikoku northward to an industrial city 60 miles north of Tokyo, the sky giants dumped their cargoes of destruction, bringing to nearly 18,000 tons the weight of bombs they have unloaded on Japan since July 1.

SMASH OIL CENTER

The big Kawasaki oil center on a reclaimed island in Tokyo Bay, previously hit in an April raid, was the target of demolition bombs.

The four industrial cities, all raided for the first time, were showered with incendiary bombs in the same sort of saturation attack that has been erasing Japan's war industries one by one.

They were:

Utsonomiya, industrial city of 80,000 population 60 miles north of Tokyo.

Ichinomiya, west of Tokyo and nine miles northwest of the often-bombed munitions city of Nagoya.

Tsugurga, 55 miles northwest of Nagoya on the coast of the main home island of Honshu.

Uwajima, on the west-central coast of the southern home island of Shikoku.

The blows on the home islands coincided with new successes by U. S. air blockaders in the Yellow Sea and came close to the heels of heavy strokes at the empire climaxed by a 1,000 carrier plane raid on Tokyo's air fields.

CONVOYS DRIVEN BACK

Two heavily-gunned enemy convoys trying to run Nipponese troops from China to invasion-menaced Japan were driven back into port by the U. S. air blockade that is steadily throttling the island empire.

This operation, announced Thurs-

More of AIR WAR on Page 10

NEW SHOE STAMP IS VALID AUGUST 1

Washington — (AP) — The new shoe stamp which becomes valid Aug. 1, will be airplane stamp No. 4, in Ration Book No. 3, the OPA announced Thursday.

Airplane stamps Nos. 1, 2 and 3 remain valid indefinitely.

The new stamp is the first for shoes to become valid since Nov. 1, 1944, when rationing, because of limited stocks of shoes, went off a two-pair-a-year basis.

AUSSIES, DUTCH IN VIOLENT SLUGGING MATCH WITH JAPS

Allied Fighters Use Flame Throwers To Burn Nips From Positions

Manila (Friday —(AP) —A violent battle beyond Balikpapan was reported today with Australian and Dutch troops wielding flame-throwers in an attempt to encircle formidable Japanese ridge positions north of the captured Borneo oil port.

At the same time, a one-mile advance east of Balikapapn was scored by Australian troops fighting along Borneo's east coast toward the rich Sambodja oil fields.

Infantrymen of the Australian Seventh Division, supported by Dutch Colonial troops, were closing in on the core of enemy resistance north of Balikpapan, Gen. Douglas MacArthur's communique announced.

Paced by tanks and flame-throwers, they blasted their way through tough resistance in a two-mile advance and closed in on "smashed stone ridge," keystone of the enemy's positions.

Meanwhile Dutch forces farther east, pushing along Kariango peninsula, joined another Australian column and swung northeast, attempting to encircle the ridge.

RESISTANCE SLACKENS

The Australian forces driving along Borneo's east coast sent back word that Japanese resistance had begun to slacken as they advanced two and a half miles beyond Manggar airdrome, 13 miles east of Balikpapan.

The gain was ground out only after a week of heavy fighting, during which a number of enemy gains, mortars and light machine-guns were captured.

The advance placed the Australians about a dozen miles from Sambodja, pipeline control point and

More of AUSSIES on Page 10

Jap Statesmen In Dither Over Food Supply Of Nippon

San Francisco —(AP)— Premier Kantaro Suzuki—confronted with a tightening U. S. air blockade and a rising clamor of home front criticism — convened his cabinet and a phalanx of "elder statesmen" Thursday to consider the home islands' "worsening food situation."

Suzuki first called on Emperor Hirohito, then went into conference with his cabinet and such former premiers as Gen. Hideki Tojo architect of the Pearl Harbor attack, and Prince Fumimaro Konoye, who was sidetracked to private life when Japan took its fateful decision to war on the United States.

They listened to an explanation of the food situation — which has prompted recent cuts in rations — from Motoi Yukawa, agriculture and commerce vice-minister, said a Tokyo home front broadcast pick-

More of JAPS on Page 10

BOY BREAKS LEG

Russel Wolf, thirty months, 128 N. Pine St., was admitted to the St. Joseph's Hospital Thursday night suffering from a fractured right leg sustained in a fall. His condition is regarded as good.

Four Local School Youths Aiding In Taking Livestock To Greece

Four Manor Township High School youths have sailed from Baltimore as handlers on a ship loaded with cattle and horses for war-torn Greece.

The animals were gathered by the Brethren Service Committee as part of its "heifers for relief" program, mapped out by the Church of the Brethren to help war-ravaged Europe.

The youths who volunteered to make the trip, and sailed last week from Baltimore are Robert Herr and Elven Brown, both of Millersville; Joseph Owen, Mt. Nebo, and Jack Small, Lancaster R6.

Each of the youths will have charge of the handling of about 25 head of livestock. The boat is scheduled to dock at a port in Greece where the animals will be distributed.

The trip to Greece and back will take about two months.

CHILD IS INJURED WHEN CARS COLLIDE

Michael Mease, eighteen months, suffered a bruised forehead when an automobile operated by his mother, Mrs. Donald Mease, twenty-seven, Main St., East Petersburg, collided with another automobile at the intersection of a township road and the Fruitville Pike, seven miles north of this city, at 6: 20 p. m. Thursday.

State Policeman A. Novachek, who investigated, said Mrs. Mease was driving east on the township road when her automobile collided with an automobile being driven north on the Fruitville Pike by A. R. Kauffman, forty-five, Manheim R1.

If Anything Goes Wrong Today, Blame It On The Calendar

If things go haywire Friday (today), blame it on the calendar—Friday, July 13. Superstitious persons—everyone says they are not—will especially give a wide berth to black cats and other evil omens.

The weather man promises considerable cloudiness and a little warmer for the day. Thursday temperatures ranged from 46 to 80 degrees.

New Travel Curbs On Civilians "In All Categories" Planned

Washington—(AP)—The ODT disclosed Thursday that it contemplates new travel curbs on civilians, while the House heard a demand for a ban on the use of private railroad cars by wealthy families and railroad executives.

J. Monroe Johnson, director of the Office of Defense Transportation, told reporters that further travel restrictions are contemplated "in all categories, not aimed particularly at sports."

He made this remark after a conference with Harry A. Parr, III, president of the Thoroughbred Racing Association, and other racing officials. The conference dealt with ODT's order Wednesday prohibiting shipment of racing and show animals by rail or other public carriers.

Associates said Johnson, in mentioning further travel re-

More of NEW on Page 10

WEATHER
Eastern Pennsylvania: Partly Cloudy And Cooler Tuesday With Some Chance Of Showers Southeast Portion; Wednesday Fair With Moderate Temperatures.

Intelligencer Journal.

The Leading Newspaper in the Garden Spot of America, Home Owned for Home Folks Since 1794 — 150th Anniversary Year

SAVE WASTE PAPER
For City Play Ground Collection
Every Week

152nd Year.—No. 8. | Entered as second class matter August 9, 1944 at the Post Office at Lancaster, Pa., under the Act of March 3, 1879. Reg. U. S. Pat. Off. | LANCASTER, PA., TUESDAY MORNING, JUNE 26, 1945 | CITY | SIXTEEN PAGES. | 20c PER WEEK—4c Per Copy

CHARTER ADOPTED BY UNITED NATIONS

Huge Force Of B29s Hits 10 Jap Plants In Daylight Raid

Greatest Demolition, Pin-Point Mission Ever Flown Against Nip Targets

Guam (Tuesday) — (AP) — Between 450 and 500 B-29s struck 10 Japanese aircraft, ammunition and ordnance factories in daylight about noon today in the largest demolition, pin-point mission ever flown against Japanese war industry targets.

Five of the factories were in the Nagoya area; two in the Gifu area near Nagoya, and one was at Akeshi, 10 miles west of Kobe.

MEDIUM ALTITUDE

The Superforts were escorted by Iwo-based Mustangs of the Seventh Army Fighter Command. The strike was from medium altitude.

Good weather permitted visual bombing of several targets, but cloud cover required precision instrument bombing of some objectives.

The Superforts dropped more than 3,000 tons of high explosive bombs in the most powerful strike of the 21st Bomber Command's new phase in Superfort operations—complete blasting destruction of Japan's war industry, already seriously crippled by the fire-bombing campaign which burned out 112 square miles of Nippon's industrial areas.

Ten targets for one mission was the second largest number of objectives for a single day. On April 26, strikes were made against 11 Kyushu Island airbases in neutralizing raids in support of the Okinawa invasion.

ALL HIT PREVIOUSLY

All plants bombed today had been damaged previously. Six were engaged directly in aircraft

More of HUGE on Page 6

Hastening the clean-up campaign on northern Luzon, parachutists of the U. S. 11th Airborne Division, landing near Aparri (1), have put the squeeze on an estimated 20,000 Japs now sealed off from that major escape port. From the south (2) another American force was fast pushing toward a junction in Cagayan River Valley.

COMMUNISTS IN REICH REJECT SOVIET SYSTEM

German Party Asks Coalition Parliamentary Government And Free Enterprise

Moscow—(AP)—The German Communist party, in a manifesto issued in Berlin, Monday rejected a Soviet system for present-day Germany and instead asked for a coalition parliamentary government and the development of private enterprise and the profit system.

The appeal, signed by the Central Committee of the Communist party and reported by the Russian Tass news agency, was addressed to all German people everywhere.

ASK EQUAL RIGHTS

Calling for equal rights before the law and free elections, the manifesto demanded the confiscation of the big estates of the Nazis, Junkers and "imperialists" and their division among landless peasants.

It made clear that all Germans, except the Nazis and rich collaborators, should retain their property and that large-scale landowners and big peasants should keep their lands if they did not tie up with the Nazis.

In the document, the Communist party not only blamed the German people for their plight, but also blamed the German Communists themselves for being unable to weld together Democratic groups in defiance of the Nazis.

The Communist appeal also admitted that Germany should repay the Allies for the damage and harm done during the war.

The German Communist party, in the election of March, 1933, which swept Adolf Hitler into power, tallied nearly 5,000,000 votes and elected 81 delegates to the Reichstag. Only two parties were stronger —he Nazis and the Social-Democrats.

Leading signer of the document was 67-year-old Wilhelm Pieck, as-

More of COMMUNISTS on Page 6

Battle-Weary Yanks Sleep On Okinawa

Sprawled in a moment of precious sleep near the front lines are these weary Yanks of Company L, 383rd Infantry Regiment, 96th Division, of the victorious U. S. 10th Army.

Delegates Of Fifty Countries Complete 2 Months Of Work

President Truman To Deliver Message To Conference's Last Gathering Tonight; Signing Of Charter Itself Expected To Get Underway This Morning

San Francisco—(AP)—Delegates of 50 United Nations approved by standing vote Monday night a charter designed to maintain world peace.

The historic decision was made at 10:53 p. m. Pacific Wartime (1:53 a. m. Tuesday, Lancaster Time), in the crowded floodlit San Francisco opera house.

Delegates and spectators stood to their feet and applauded when the Earl of Halifax, presiding, announced the unanimous vote.

The delegates voted to approve both the United Nations charter and the statute of a new world court.

Also unanimously approved by leaders of 50-nation delegations was a suggestion by Cuba's Guillermo Belt to set up a preparatory commission which will hold its first meeting Wednesday morning in San Francisco.

Interim headquarters will be established in London.

After approval of the document for the new world organization which was hammered out here in nine weeks Halifax said.

"I think we all agree that we have taken part in a historic moment in world history."

In calling for a vote on the charter Halifax said that in view of the "world importance of this vote" it would be appropriate to depart from the practice of holding up hands.

TAKE RISING VOTE

"I would suggest," he said, "that leaders of delegations rise to vote on this charter. If I have your pleasure may I invite delegations to rise in their places and remain in their places while the votes are

More of DELEGATES on Page 6

COMPLETE CHARTER TEXT ON PAGE 11

The complete text of the United Nations charter will be found this morning on Page 11 of the Intelligencer Journal. The text runs more than 10,000 words.

Labor Picture Is Somewhat Brighter In Chicago, Detroit

(By The Associated Press)

Chicago's labor picture brightened Monday night as a union back to work order appeared to have broken the 10-day truck strike, but elsewhere in the nation more than 76,-000 workers remained idle.

End of the Chicago strike, in progress since June 16, was seen as officials of the Independent Chicago Truck Drivers' Union directed 6,-000 members to resume work Tuesday (today).

MANY RETURN

Officers of the AFL International Brotherhood of Teamsters reported Monday that 98 per cent of their 8,000 members had returned to their trucks. The strike, in protest against a War Labor Board wage award below the unions' demands, resulted in government seizure of 1,700 lines and use of soldiers as drivers and escorts.

A settlement appeared imminent in a Detroit AFL-CIO jurisdictional dispute which has left 30,000 auto workers idle and had threatened to spread to an additional 36,500.

Daniel W. Tracy, Assistant Secretary of Labor, disclosed at Washington that the AFL Building Trades Department already has approved the proposed agreement, details of which were not made public. CIO unionists accepted the proposal conditionally, pending a meeting with the rival union, thus averting immediate danger of a strike.

About 1,500 of these 30,000 idle were CIO maintenance workers and spread of the AFL-CIO dispute to embrace all the 38,000 CIO maintenance workers night force closing within a few days of 300 factories.

Included in the number idle in the Detroit AFL-CIO row were 22,000 at the Packard Motor Car Company, 7,500 at the Budd Wheel Company and 145 at Chrysler Corporation.

OTHERS IDLE

Other Detroit strikes kept additional thousands away from their posts over contract disputes including more than 6,000 in the Ford Motor Company's Rouge River plant, 650 at Hudson Motor Car Co., 975 at the Aeronautical Products Corp., 500 at the Stinson Aircraft plant and 700 in 12 yards of five retail lumber companies.

VOTE TO STAY OUT

In Akron, O., CIO United Rubber Workers voted for the third time in five days to continue their strike at the Goodyear Tire & Rubber Company. Eighteen thousand workers were idle and the union contended the strike was provoked by the company's failure to adhere to WLB directives for adjustment of grievances.

At Elkhart, Ind., Police Capt. William Sinon said two men were injured and that police fired two tear gas bombs to break up a skirmish that occurred when workers drove through a picket line at the northern Indiana Brass Company plant. The factory, making parts for B-29s and submarines, has been closed since June 5.

A union spokesman, Verne Griffith of the United Construction Workers, a United Mine Workers affiliate, said the stoppage would continue until the union was assured of a working contract.

SUSPEND PUBLICATION

The Pittsburgh Press suspended publication for the second day when truck drivers refused to pick up papers. The company said Local 211 of the AFL Newspaper Drivers was demanding immediate adoption

More of LABOR on Page 6

HOT AND SULTRY WEATHER HERE AS MERCURY HITS 93

Weatherman Promises "Partly Cloudy And Cooler" Weather Tuesday

Sultry, humid weather continued to keep Lancaster uncomfortable Monday night and at an early hour Tuesday morning there were few signs of any relief, although the weatherman promised "partly cloudy and cooler Tuesday, with some chances of showers in the southeast portion."

The fringe of a tropical storm, sweeping up the Atlantic coast, was not expected to bring any disturbance to this area.

SOLAR PHENOMENON

Resident here witnessed a solar phenomenon about noon Monday, when concentric colored rings formed a halo around the partially-hazed sun. At Philadelphia, Dr. I. M. Levitt, assistant director of Fels Planetarium, said that the solar halos were caused by—of all things!—the cold.

Said cold, however, was at an approximate altitude of 30,000 feet, and the halos were formed when rays of the sun filtered through ice crystals in the cold strata. Dr. Levitt also said the phenomenon is usually visible about the edges of storms and that, perhaps in a day or a day and a half, a storm may arrive.

Official temperature, recorded at Ephrata was 93 degrees Monday, three degrees short of the record reading of 96 on June 14. The Water Works reported a high reading of 92 degrees.

STOCK FOUND DEAD

Some 60 head of "small stock" among 60 cars enroute to New York were found dead when the stock was unloaded here for the usual feed, water and rest over the week-end. Most of the heat victims were swine.

Hogs have a tendency to crowd together and then smother, and it is not unusual for shipments from St. Louis to arrive at Lancaster with two or three dead per carlot in hot weather, according to George W. Adams, president, Un-

More of HOT on Page 6

CHEERING CROWDS WELCOME TRUMAN TO SAN FRANCISCO

President Arrives From Portland; To Close Parley With Address Today

San Francisco —(AP)— Cheering, applauding crowds running into many thousands gave President Truman a roaring welcome upon his arrival Monday to close the United Nations conference.

Standing in his open car, a trench raincoat about his shoulders, Mr. Truman waved his gray hat to the crowd and smiled his thanks for the biggest and noisiest acclaim since he assumed the Presidency.

BIG CROWD ON HAND

The city's police traffic bureau estimated the throng at 250,000 persons. It said there were 100,000 in seven long blocks on Market Street alone.

Mr. Truman traveled through 25 miles of suburban and city streets. In downtown San Francisco ticker tape floated from many windows and confetti poured down upon the parade, in which the chairmen of 50 delegations to the Security Conference participated.

The procession followed formal greetings at Hamilton Field and ended at the President's headquarters in the Fairmont Hotel where he held a reception for all the conference delegates.

His head bared to a stiff breeze which ruffled his hair, Mr. Truman obviously enjoyed the occasion.

He seemed, too, to have had a full measure of pleasure out of the playing of the "Missouri Waltz" at the airport.

While the band played the theme song of his campaign for the Vice Presidency last year, Mr. Truman kept pace to the music as he strolled briskly around troops drawn up for his review.

Earlier he had been given a military welcome by General H. H. Arnold, chief of the Army Air

More of CHEERING on Page 6

SEEK NEW TRIAL FOR JOHN MALONE IN MURDER CASE

Counsel Files Petition Listing 11 Alleged Errors In Verdict

A new trial for James John Malone, eighteen, was asked by his counsel, W. Hensel Brown, Monday afternoon.

Malone, on June 12, was found guilty of second degree murder in the "Russian Poker" killing of William L. Long, thirteen.

The jury's verdict carried a maximum penalty of 20 years imprisonment. Malone, now living with his mother in a bungalow near Pequea, is free on $5,000 bail pending the decision of the new trial petition.

Filing the petition, Mr. Brown asked Judge Joseph B. Wissler, who heard the case, for a rule "to show cause why a new trial should not be granted." This rule will be granted as a matter of course and the petition will be placed on the argument list during the week beginning Monday, Sept. 17.

LISTS 11 REASONS

Following the argument the Court will decide whether or not a new trial will be granted.

Eleven reasons for a new trial were listed by Mr. Brown in his petition, the first four being that

More of SEEK on Page 6

FIRE IN BIG ROCKY MOUNTAIN ARSENAL

Denver— (AP) —The Denver Fire Department reported Monday night a blaze which had broken out in a section of the big Rocky Mountain Arsenal, northeast of the city, was believed under control.

The fire department said the conflagration may have been caused by an explosion, but no details were available and it was not determined if there were any casualties.

Newsmen were turned away at the gate of the plant by civilian guards, who said arsenal officials would issue a statement on the "incident" Tuesday.

"We Lead All The Rest"

FARM CORNER

By The Farm Editor

PUBLIC HEARING ON PAY RATE FOR POW'S TO WORK IN COUNTY

A public hearing to establish wage rates to be paid for prisoner of war labor employed on Lancaster county farms this season is scheduled to be held in the Emergency Farm Labor Office, third floor of the YMCA building, Lancaster, on Saturday morning at 9:30 o'clock, R. S. Hovis, office director, announced Monday night.

County farmers who have applied to the office with requests for such labor are urged to attend the hearing. Hovis said, since they must pay the bill. A straight hourly wage rate for ordinary labor, and a piece rate for special crops or types of work are to be determined.

When the plan to set up a camp for war prisoners here in the county seemed likely, the office had requests for approximately 230 men, but the demand has been scaled down to about 100 war prisoners since military authorities vetoed the proposal. These will be transported daily from Indiantown Gap and camps in nearby counties during the summer months, Hovis said.

END FARM TRANSPORT GROUPS

Farm transportation committees set up in 3,022 agricultural counties in the United States by the AAA in late 1942 will be disbanded after June 30.

Beginning with July, farmers seeking certificates of war necessity or the purchase of new farm trucks should get in touch with their closest ODT office or local War Price and Rationing Board, E. J. Gardner, district manager, Office of Defense Transportation, Harrisburg, announced Monday night.

4-H PIG SHOW SEPT. 25, 26

Two hundred and forty-eight head

More of FARM CORNER on Page 6

Weather Calendar

COMPARATIVE TEMPERATURES

Station	High	Low
Water Works	92	63
Ephrata	93	67
Official High for Year, June 14		96
Official Low for Year, Jan. 25		-1
Character of Day		Clear

SUN
Rises—5:37 a. m. Sets—8:37 p. m.

MOON
Rises—9:45 p. m. Last Quarter, July 2

NEARBY FORECASTS

Maryland: Rains and windy near the coast, scattered showers in the interior Tuesday, followed by clearing and cooler late Tuesday; Wednesday fair with moderate temperature.

New Jersey and Delaware: Mostly cloudy in the interior, rain and windy near the coast and cooler Tuesday; clearing and cooler Tuesday night; Wednesday fair with moderate temperatures.

ROSS SAYS FEPC MAY CONTINUE ON VOLUNTEER BASIS

Member Of Agency Reports Plans For Demonstration As Fight Grows

Washington—(AP)—The fight over continuing the Fair Employment Practices Committee with new intensity Monday with the agency's head saying it may continue operating on a volunteer basis even if Congress gives it no money.

Chairman Malcolm Ross said the FEPC may go ahead regardless and another member, a Negro, reported plans for a demonstration "more dramatic than a march on Washington."

This member, Milton P. Webster, international president of the AFL Brotherhood of Sleeping Car Porters, told a news conference he couldn't disclose the nature of the demonstration now but "we are not going to take it lying down."

SLOW ACTION

He referred to slow action on legislation for a permanent FEPC. The House Appropriation Committee approved Monday a $125,000 fund earmarked for liquidation of the agency in the three months after July 1.

Southerners in Congress, meanwhile, girded for a filibuster to talk to death any attempt to give FEPC a congressional appropriation. Senator Bilbo (D-Miss) threatened to "talk 'till Christmas, if necessary, to stop funds for a lot of peckerwoods to go around and meddle into other people's

More of ROSS on Page 6

2 SALES PERSONS HERE WIN MYSTERY SHOPPER AWARDS

Reward For Challenging Woman Raised; Urge Greater War Bond Sales

Two local sales people "caught" the "Mystery Shopper" Monday, during her tour of local stores in the interests of the Seventh War Loan drive.

They are Miss Elizabeth F. Herr, of M. T. Garvin's store, and E. S. Little of Oblenders'. Each will be awarded a credit for a $1000 war bond purchase, and a pair of tickets to a local theatre.

AWARD TO BE RAISED

The award for challenging the Mystery Shopper will be raised to $2000 bond credit for the remainder of this week, Nathaniel E. Hager, chairman of the retailers division of the bond committee, announced Monday. The idea back of the Mystery Shopper is to stimulate the sale of war bonds, by encouraging sales people to ask customers to buy bonds.

Lancaster County has been asked to buy one million dollars worth of E-bonds this week to improve the local Seventh War Loan standing before the official end of the drive Saturday. War Finance Committees members reported Monday.

As the campaign entered its final week, the committee also called upon the 39 city and county banks to make a final drive on idle deposits and set each bank a six-day E-bond quota.

E-bond purchases up to Monday are $2,879,000, only 55 per cent of the county's $5,200,000 quota. Sales of all individual bonds stand at $8,-406,000, which is 88 per cent of the county's individual bond quota.

Brown Monday morning awarded

More of BOND DRIVE on Page 6

Youth "Burns" His Hands Testing Rope Fire Escape Here

An eighteen-year-old youth was "burned" while testing a rope fire escape at his home Monday night.

Richard Wagner, Jr., 1011 N. Duke St., who suffered severe rope burns of both hands, was discharged after receiving treatment at the Lancaster General Hospital.

Wagner told attendants he had rigged a rope line from a window of his third floor room to the ground as a "fire escape" and tried the arrangement Monday night, burning his hands as he slid to the ground.

FORMER F&M SPORTS STAR KILLED IN PLANE CRASH IN WALES

Word of the death of Technical Sergeant Kenneth W. Craumer, twenty-four, Hanover, an outstanding sports figure during his days at Franklin and Marshall Academy and college, in a plane crash, has been received here. Craumer, Central Pennsylvania Golf Association champion in 1941, was killed in Wales on June 8.

Sgt. Craumer

Sgt. Craumer, who was outstanding in sports during his Hanover High School days, entered F. & M. Academy in 1938 and F. & M. college in the fall of 1939. In 1941, he was a star forward on the college cage team which won the Eastern Collegiate league championship.

He also was a member of the 1942 undefeated F. & M. college golf team and retiring champion of the Hanover Country club when he was inducted into the Army, in July, 1942. At Tyndall Field, Fla., he became a gunnery instructor in the Air Force. He later volunteered for service overseas and was sent to England. He was cited for meritorious achievement while on a combat mission over Europe.

Besides his father, Walter J. Craumer, the youth is survived by a brother, Sgt. Jacob Craumer, USMC, in the Pacific; and three sisters, Mrs. Richard Zudrell, York; Mrs. C. L. Sheads, Fairfield; and Mrs. Pattie Rooney, Opa Locka, Fla.

SGT. W. F. ELSLAGER, COLUMBIA SOLDIER, KILLED ON LUZON

Sgt. William F. Elslager, thirty-seven, was killed on Luzon on June 8, according to a War Department telegram received by his parents, Mr. and Mrs. Frederick G. Elslager, Jr., of 845 Spruce St., Columbia.

Sgt. Elslager

Sgt. Elslager, who was serving with the 38th Infantry Division, entered the service in February, 1942 and trained at Camp Wheeler, Ga., and Camp Shelby, Miss. He was sent to the Hawaiian Islands 19 months ago and later served in New Guinea and the Philippine Islands.

His brother, Cpl. Frederick G. Elslager, III, recently visited him on New Guinea. Another brother, Pfc. George Elslager, is stationed at Fort Crockett, Tex.

He was a member of Holy Trinity Catholic Church, the Holy Name Society and the Columbia Beneficial and Fraternal Association No. 1, and was a graduate of the Holy Trinity parochial school.

Besides the parents and two brothers in service he is survived by three sisters, Emma, at home; Mary, wife of Albert Yeager, this city; and Elizabeth, wife of Staff-Sgt. Melvin Flosser, Columbia; and his paternal grandparents, Mr. and Mrs. Frederick Elslager, Columbia.

COUNCIL ACCEPTS 1945 TAX ABATEMENT ACT AT SPECIAL SESSION

At a special session, held just before 5 p. m. Monday, city council adopted a resolution accepting the provisions of the 1945 Tax Abatement Act passed by the General Assembly of Pennsylvania.

The special meeting was called, Mayor Cary said, when it was discovered that this was the last day on which action could be taken. Council considered the action earlier in the day, according to the mayor, and had decided to vote favorably on it Tuesday. However, a last-minute check revealed that the 30-day time limit expired Monday, and an immediate vote was necessary.

The Act provides that the city will abate certain tax penalties and interest on unpaid taxes, with certain exceptions, and prohibits the sale of real property for the non-payment of any such taxes for a certain period, preserving certain tax liens and providing for the extension thereof.

Victory Gardeners' Notebook— No. 22—Succession Cropping

At a time like now when all foods are needed, the patriotic gardener will make every available inch of soil produce "as much, and as many" crops as possible, says H. S. Sloat, assistant county agent. This mean what is known as "succession cropping"—the planting of a second crop on the same soil after an early crop has been harvested. However, the practice of rotation is recommended, wherever possible.

Succession cropping is most successful if those crops maturing about the same time are planted near each other. But it is wise not to follow crops with vegetables of the same family. For example, he says, do not follow early beets with late beets, but rather use some crop like late spinach, lettuce or kale. Likewise, members of the cabbage family, including cauliflower, broccoli, turnips and radishes, should not follow each other.

Cucumbers are one plant which can be started now; bush snap beans may be planted until mid-July. Celery for fall and winter may be set out for another three weeks, and late cabbage can still be started in the garden.

Beets and carrots for canning or storing may be seeded late this month after the earlier crops have been harvested. Late-planted beets and carrots will be tender and not overgrown, he says. Endive does best when sown in mid-July and

More of NOTEBOOK on Page 6

MANOR TWP. MAN ILL OF UNDULANT FEVER

John E. Keener, thirty-one, Manor Township, is confined to his home suffering from undulant fever, according to Dr. A. J. Greenleaf, Mountville, county medical director, who listed his case on a weekly health report issued Monday.

Keener was taken ill June 18 and the source of the infection was traced to a cow in the herd on the Keener farm, Dr. Greenleaf said.

Other cases listed on the report include, scarlet fever, fourteen; chicken pox, five; whooping cough, four and measles, two.

Two new cases of scarlet fever were reported to the city board of health last week, according to the weekly health bulletin issued Monday. There was one new case each of whooping cough and mumps.

Plan Final Drive For Building Of Recreation Center At Eden

Plans for a final drive for the construction of a community recreation center in Eden were formulated at a meeting of officers of the Eden Community Association Monday night at the Eden Fire company hall.

The need for such a center has been recognized and the matter has been talked about for two years or more but the officers of the association feel the time has arrived to do something definite, the Rev. L. M. Becker, pastor of Grace Evangelical and Reformed Church and chairman of the association, explained after the meeting.

MAJORITY WANT IT

"A large majority of the residents of this community want such a center," he said. "We do not want it for our young people alone. It should be open to any group from the city or elsewhere which desire to come for meetings or recreation. In fact, many of our residents work or have their offices or business properties in the city itself."

Mrs. A. B. Zarker, secretary of the association, emphasized the fact that there was no other place for the several hundred young people of the community to meet, adding, "but they will not be there all of the time. We do not plan a recreation center that will keep our boys and girls out of their homes and away from their parents every evening. Other groups always will be welcome".

The officers, including R. C. Heagy, treasurer, were unanimous in expressing the belief that the

More of PLANS on Page 6

54 Lancaster Men Listed as Dead and Missing

List 13 Officially Killed In Action

23 Others Described as Missing in Action; 18 Others Died or Were Killed in Accidents at Camps

At least 54 men from Lancaster city and county have been reported killed or missing in action, or have died at training camps since America entered World War 2.

Since December 7, 1941, thirteen local men have been officially listed as killed in action. Twenty-three others are listed as missing in action, and an additional 18 men died or were killed in accidents at training camps.

Four former local students, not included in the total of 54, have also been killed, one died in action, and two in air training accidents. A former Manheim man was also killed at Pearl Harbor.

These figures were gathered from reports of local casualties received in official War Department dispatches, and from information from the families of the men. However, since the War Department does not issue casualty lists until some time after the families of the men involved have been notified, there may be a number of local soldiers and seamen killed or missing, whose names are not known to the newspaper.

Ten Soldiers Killed

Of the men who have been reported killed in action eleven are soldiers, six of whom were in the Army Air Force; two were members of the Marine Corps and one was a sailor in the merchant marine.

Lieutenant Harry P. Forry, Army Air Force flier, has been reported killed in action for more than a year. He is the son of Mrs. Benjamin Hambright, of Florin. His personal possessions were recently returned to his mother.

Charles G. Palmer, the merchant sailor, of 669 W. Orange St., was killed in July, 1942 when a cargo ship sank in the Gulf of Mexico.

Sgt. Frank W. Kahl, twenty-three, an engineer and gunner on a bomber, was killed in action in northwest Africa on January 7, 1943. The 23-year-old flier was the son of Mr. and Mrs. Emory G. Kahl, 442 W. James St.

Sgt. Larry B. Hagan, twenty, was a gunner on a Flying Fortress. He was the son of Mrs. Jacob H. Hacker, Bausman, and was killed on November 20, 1942.

Staff Sergeant Robert Martin, of Goodville, was killed in action in Africa this winter. He was a bombardier, and the son of Mr. and Mrs. John R. Martin. His death was reported on March 1, 1943.

Technical Sergeant Elwood E. Miller, twenty-four, a gunner on a Flying Fortress was killed in action December 28, 1942. He was at first reported missing in action to his mother, Mrs. Mary E. Miller, Columbia R2.

Ephrata Man Was First

Pvt. Samuel W. Leiphart, eighteen, of Ephrata, was the first member of the Army ground forces to be reported killed—on November 23, 1942 he was listed among the casualties in the fighting on Guadalcanal. He is the son of Mrs. Kate Leiphart, Ephrata, and of Arthur M. Leiphart.

Cpl. Cyrus W. Connor, twenty-two, was killed in action last November, probably in Africa. He is the son of Harry D. Connor, 220 W. Vine St., and his death was reported on November 30, 1942. He received the Purple Heart decoration posthumously.

Pvt. Richard Lemmer, whose wife formerly lived at 460 S. Queen St., was reported killed in action on April 24, 1943. He had previously been reported missing in action.

Pfc. George W. Goodhart, Jr., twenty-six, was killed in action in North Africa on March 29, 1942. He was the son of Mr. and Mrs. G. W. Goodhart, 530 Third St.

Pvt. Norman E. Diehm, twenty-two, was killed in action on May 26 of this year in the "North American area." He was the son of Mr. and Mrs. Norman R. Diehm, Lancaster R1, and his death was reported on June 7.

Two Marine Casualties

The two Marine Corps casualties are:

Cpl. Robert E. Huber, twenty-nine, who was killed on Guadalcanal last November and Pvt. Charles Ludwig, twenty, who was also killed on Guadalcanal. Huber was the son of Mr. and Mrs. Jesse K. Huber, 1142 St. Joseph St., and Ludwig resided with Roy Ream of New Holland.

The 23 men missing in action include 13 sailors and eight soldiers, three of whom are members of the Army Air Forces. A Marine and a member of the Merchant Marine complete the list.

John Richard Kendig, a sailor, was reported missing in actionn June 17, 1942, following the battle of Coral Sea. He was aboard the destroyer "Sims" and had entered the Navy 17 years before. Kendig is the son of Mr. and Mrs. Frank Kendig, 633 N. Queen St.

Leon W. Weaver, also in the Navy, has been missing since the sinking of the "Langley", according to a report of May 26, 1942. He is the son of Mr. and Mrs. Raymond Weaver, Ephrata.

George W. Knapp, Jr., was reported missing in action with the Navy July 17, 1942. He is the son of Mr. and Mrs. G. W. Knapp, Richland, and was 23 at the time of the report.

Raymond St. Clair, son of John St. Clair, 639 Lake St., was reported missing in action Sept. 2, 1942. He had been serving on a destroyer.

William Ulmer, one of five sons of Mr. and Mrs. Robert Ulmer, 35 Church St., who are serving in the Navy, was reported missing in action Sept. 15, 1942.

Missing On Wasp

Walter D. Nye, also a sailor, was reported missing in action Oct. 28, 1942, following the sinking of the aircraft carrier "Wasp" in the Pacific. Nye's parents are not living, but he resided with Mr. and Mrs. Edwin L. Witmer, Kirkwood Rd.

Jack L. McBride, formerly of this city was reported Dec. 15, 1942, to be missing in action in the Solomons. He is the grandson of Mrs. Mary McBride, Lincoln Highway East.

Paul B. Martin was a fireman second class aboard the gunboat "Tulsa" which was reported missing in the Manila area June 23, 1942. He is the son of Mr. and Mrs. Clayton Martin, 530 E. Ross jstreet.

Fireman First Class J. William Helt was reported Jan. 14, 1942, to be missing in action in a Naval battle off the Solomon islands. He is the son of Mr. and Mrs. Francis W. Helt, 66 Hazel St.

Ensign Edward John Knudsen, of the USNR, has been missing in action aboard a merchant vessel since Nov. 22, 1942. He is the husband of Mrs. Kit Musser Knudsen, 147 E. Chestnut St., and a native of Matua, N. J.

Edward Francis Hampton, seaman first class, son of George Hampton, 120 Concord St., was reported missing Feb. 25, 1943. His wife, Mrs. Eva Mae Hampton, resides at 325 Coral St.

Petty Officer Third Class Martin E. Watson, son of Mr. and Mrs. Dwight W. Watson, 346 S. Queen St., was reported missing in action March 9, 1942.

Sub Commander Missing

Lieutenant Richard L. Helm, twenty-five, a native of Millersville and commander of a submarine, was reported missing in action June 7. He is the son of Mr. and Mrs. Hiram P. Helm, Harrisburg, formerly of Millersville, and the grandson of Mrs. C. E. Helm, Quarryville.

First of the nine Army men to be reported missing was Harry M. Becker, son of Mrs. Anna Becker, Lancaster R6, who has been missing since the fall of Corregidor, according to a report received May 26, 1942.

Elwood A. Royer also has been missing since Corregidor, according to reports received Aug. 27, 1942. He is the son of Harvey Royer, Manheim.

Technical Sergeant Charles V. Bealler was reported June 6, 1942, to be missing on Bataan. He formerly resided with his sister, Mrs. Merl Dommel, 557 S. Christian St.

Pfc. Norman C. Keller, Jr., formerly of 618 Penn Ave., is missing in action with the Army medical corps, it was reported Feb. 23, 1943.

Two From Ephrata

Private Carl Weinhold, son of Mr. and Mrs. Evan Weinhold, 28 N. Church St., Ephrata, was reported Feb. 23 to be missing in action in the "Western area."

A tail gunner in the Army Air Force, Staff Sergeant Herbert R. Fasnacht, nineteen, has been missing in action in New Guinea since Feb. 19. He is the son of Mr. and Mrs. Rueben Fasnacht, E. Locust St., Ephrata.

Lieutenant William S. Eichler, Jr., a bomber pilot with the AAF, has been missing in action in the Asiatic area since March 13, 1943. He is the grandson of Henry Eichler, Florin, and he lived here until three years ago.

First Lieutenant Edward A. Gast, 23, AAF bombardier, was reported missing in action in England June 30. He is the son of Mr. and Mrs. Earl M. Gast, 822 N. President Ave., and is believed to be the first member of the Elks

(Continued On Page 21)

LIEUT. HARRY P. FORRY (Killed in Action)

SGT. FRANK W. KAHL (Killed in Action)

2nd MATE LESTER W. LEAMAN (Missing)

PAUL B. MARTIN (Missing)

JOHN R. KENDIG (Missing)

HARRY M. BECKER (Missing)

N. E. Diehm R. W. Martin (Killed in Action)

G. W. Goodhart L. B. Hagen (Killed in Action)

R. E. Huber S. W. Leiphart (Killed in Action)

E. E. Miller C. H. Ludwig (Killed in Action)

LEON W. WEAVER (Missing)

JACK L. McBRIDE (Missing)

PFC. ELWOOD A. ROYER (Missing)

T|SGT. CHARLES V. BEALLER (Missing)

C. W. Connor (Killed in Action) C. Cook, Jr. (Killed in U. S.)

T|SGT. DONALD K. SWEIGART (Killed in U. S.)

H. R. Fasnacht (Missing) R. L. Helm (Missing)

RAYMOND ST. CLAIR (Missing)

M|SGT. KENNETH K. TREDWAY (Killed in U. S.)

A. B. Cavna (Plane Victim) R. A. Young (Plane Victim)

D. Shingler (Killed In U .S.) K. H. Stoltzfus (Died in Prison Camp)

William Ulmer (Missing) W. D. Nye (Missing)

M. E. Watson (Missing)

J. W. Helt (Missing) Carl Weinhold (Missing) E. F. Hampton (Missing) N. C. Keller (Missing)

Any excuse you can give for not upping your payroll savings will please Hitler, Hirohito and puppet Mussolini.

Out-doors for the Summer

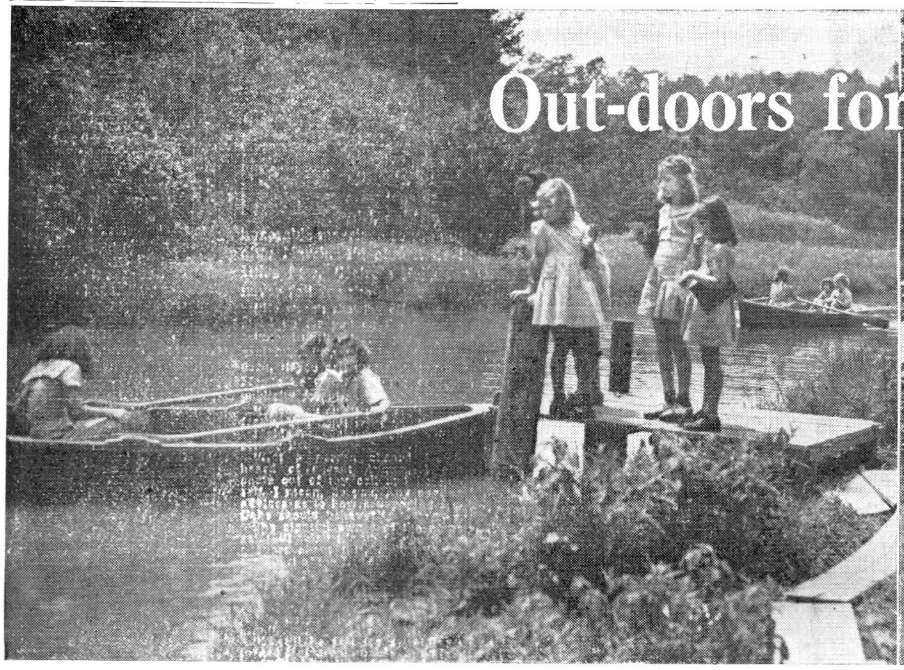

"JUNIOR WAVES" try their hand at the oars on the mill dam at Camp Andrews, summer camp of St. Paul's Reformed Church. Right, daily service on Vesper Hill conducted each evening by one of the children. Camp under direction of Harold W. Shaar and assistant, Milton E. Gockley, Jr., opened two weeks ago with the girls; boys were there last week.

***HOME CAMPS** are furthering the trend toward nearby Lancaster county sites as the camping season begins this year. Camp Chiquetan, new site for the Boy Scouts near Conestoga Center, and the St. Paul's Reformed Church camp now occupying the old Andrews Mill site below the Buck, are developing ample acreages which have the advantage of old buildings to be renovated for camp activities. Kepler Lodge at Martic Forge has developed that property over a long period of years into an ideal girls' camp as an example of what can be done with local sites, while day camps take up the slack for groups which as yet do not have permanent camps. But these too, have the use of suitable locations in the parks with which Lancaster is generously provided to complete a definitely local out-door recreation picture.*

YMCA DAY CAMP at Maple Grove is wartime substitute this year for annual Camp Shand program.

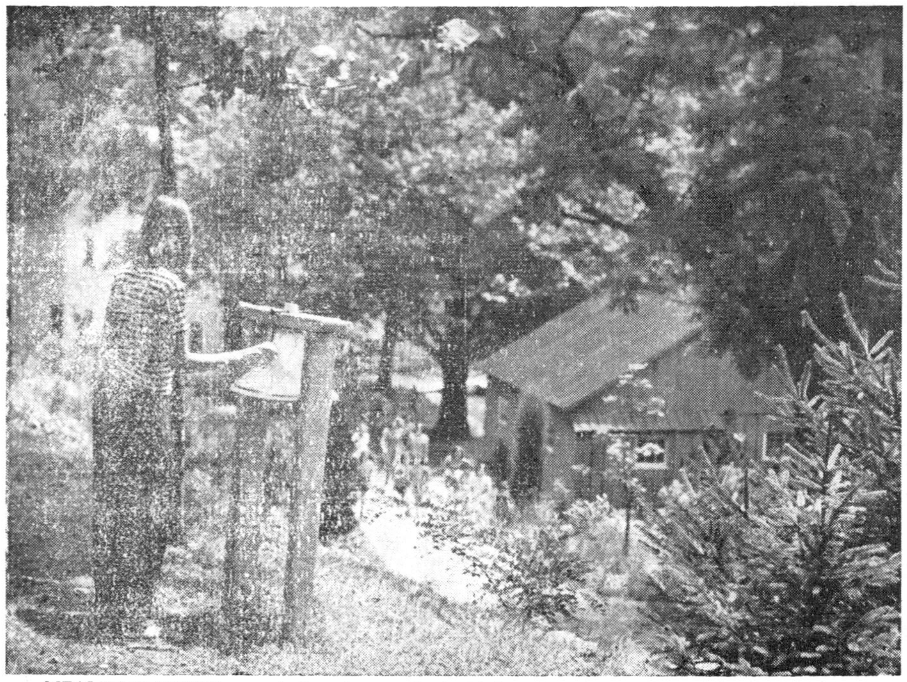

MEALTIME SIGNAL rsounds from just outside the kitchen door and campers wend their way from various activities at Camp Andrews to answer the call. The property consisting of the old mill, dwelling, and other buildings with some cabins added, provides a wide range of recreational development. Program now includes a craft shop, boating, games, etc.

COOL POOL invites Susan Foster's best dive at Kepler Lodge. Counsellor Nancy Weisser, Judy Troutman, Betty Mundorf and Louise Altdoeffer look on.

SALUTE TO FLAG is a morning rite every day at Kepler Lodge. The lodge, YWCA camp, divides the summer between girls by age groups and interests. The lodge near Martic Forge is one of Lancaster county's ancient dwellings preserved in antique style with swimming pool, craft shop and other recreational facilities. Chief counsellor is Mrs. Albert F. Kelso.

SEA-SCOUT SHIP won the award for Region III and was a feature of the camporee recently which was preliminary to the Camp Chiquetan season. The schedule for the new Boy Scout camp near Conestoga Center, opens today. Meanwhile the sea scouts, Robert Fulton Ship 201, Jacob S. Krupa, skipper, have switched to the real thing on a Chesapeake cruise.

OUTDOOR COOKING doesn't happen in Long Park where the Brownies attend day camp, but that little problem is solved with an open air fireplace behind the Brookside pool when the Brownies feel the pangs. Jackie Draude stirs up the embers at lunchtime which is an important interval in any day spent in Lancaster county's wide-open spaces.

Hitler's Scientists Curbed Just In Time
See Tucker — Editorial Page

LANCASTER NEW ERA

WEATHER
Partly cloudy, preceded by scattered showers in extreme east portion tonight; Tuesday generally fair; not much change in temperature.

69th Year—No. 21,152 | Entered as second class matter January 31, 1924, at the Post Office at Lancaster, Pa., under the Act of March 3, 1879, Reg. U. S. Pat. Off. | LANCASTER, PA., MONDAY, JULY 23, 1945 | CITY EDITION | 14 PAGES | 20c PER WEEK—4c Per Copy

Storm Damage Set At $300,000; U.S. Warships Strike In Tokyo Bay

6 FIRES SET BY LIGHTNING, 4 BARNS BURN

Northeastern Section Is Hardest Hit; 3 Bridges Are Swept Away

Lancaster county today dug itself from under mud, debris and damaged property left in the wake of a violent electrical storm and cloudburst which caused this area to shudder for nearly an hour yesterday afternoon.

Firemen, farmers and property owners estimate damage may reach in the neighborhood of $300,000.

It is estimated that between four and five inches of rain fell in the Mt. Joy section within an hour. The official rainfall recorded at the City Water Works was 1.04 inches.

The northeastern section of the county bore the brunt of the storm and in this irregularly shaped triangle floods and fire left most of the damage. A "flash" flood in the Conoy Creek swept away an Elizabethtown diner and imperiled the lives of four persons. Homes and business properties in the town were flooded and damaged. In the Mt. Joy section the Little Chickies creek overflowed and nine persons were saved from trapped automobiles.

Lightning Set 6 Fires

Lightning started six fires which destroyed four large barns, damaged a home and a Mt. Joy industrial plant. Damage from fires is estimated at $62,500. Chief Burgess J. N. Olewiler, Elizabethtown, estimated damages to public property in the borough at $50,000 exclusive of damage to private properties which includes homes and business places.

The storm hit the northwestern section of the county about 2:30 p. m., swerved to the south and then turned westward where it appeared to link up with a second storm from the northwest and brought torrential rains, high winds and a violent electrical disturbance. Roads were quickly flooded and traffic in the northeastern section of the county was either halted or marooned

Pikes Were Closed

At one time the Manheim, Marietta and Harrisburg pikes all were closed. Many automobiles were detoured while other drivers took refuge on high land and awaited the passing of the storm and the receding of the waters.

At the height of the storm the Lincoln highway was the only road between the Fruitville and Millersville pikes that could be used to move traffic.

The Harrisburg pike was closed at Oreville when the Little Conestoga Creek overflowed and the same creek closed the Marietta pike, just west of Lancaster. Roads crossing the creek southwest of Millersville also were closed.

3 Bridges Swept Away

H. L. Worst, superintendent of the Lancaster office of the State Highway Department, said three bridges were swept away by floods in the Elizabethtown-Mt. Joy section. He said the old covered bridge crossing the creek on the Mt. Joy-Milton Grove road was carried away and two spans on a township road northeast of Elizabethtown were destroyed.

The Lititz and Manheim sections also were hit hard by high water.

Lititz Park Flooded

The Lititz Springs park was flooded and water rose to the first floor of the band shell. About 4 p. m. yesterday a short circuit set fire to the band shell but the fire was extinguished before it caused any serious damage. Firemen

(See STORM—Page 7)

Where Elizabethtown Diner Landed After Being Washed 150 Feet Across Highway

This is where the large Elizabethtown diner (right) landed during the storm yesterday afternoon after being torn from its foundation (arrow, left) and washed 150 feet across the highway by the swollen Conoy Creek. Owner of the diner, Kenneth Baker, 715 N. Market Street, estimated the damage at $4,500. The damaged ice cream freezer can be seen (center) at the bank of the creek. The diner and kitchen moved as a single unit and was stopped as it hit the Forney's Service Station across the street. The owner's son, two boys, and a man were in the diner moving stock to higher shelves just as the building was ripped from its foundation. Three dived out as the structure moved across the highway and the fourth stayed inside until it reached the service station.

13 Are Rescued in County As Creeks Go on Rampage

4 Occupants of Diner Marooned When Building Was Swept Off Foundations; Nine Assisted from Cars

Thirteen persons were rescued when "flash" floods sent the Conoy and Little Chickies creeks swirling over their embankments in the Elizabethtown and Mt. Joy section in the wake of torrential rains yesterday afternoon.

Four persons were saved in a spectacular rescue when the Baker diner, N. Market St., just west of the Elizabethtown square, was swept from its foundation near the Conoy creek and carried across the street where it crushed an automobile and lodged against another building.

In the diner at the time were Kenneth Baker, Jr., fifteen, son of the owner; Robert Bishop, sixteen; Robert Bodman, fifteen, and John E. Copenhaver. All were trying to move diner supplies to high shelves because of the rising water.

Suddenly the flood swept down upon the diner and the building began drifting with the water. All but Bodman dived through the windows into the water and managed to reach a pole where they held on for 45 minutes before they were rescued. Bodman rode across the flooded street in the diner and finally was rescued.

Marooned 45 Minutes

"The flood came so quick we didn't know what happened," Bishop said this morning. "Somehow Copenhaver, Baker and I managed to get through the windows and hang on to that pole. We were there about about 45 minutes before we were saved finally.

The Elizabethtown Fire Co., was summoned but after trying with ropes to reach the three marooned on a pole they appealed to Charles Crow, Elizabethtown, who owns a rubber Navy boat which he recently purchased at Middletown. The boat was inflated and launched.

Use Life Raft

The current was too swift for the little craft but one of the rescuers finally tossed a rope to the boys on the pole. They caught it and helped guide the rescue craft. They were uninjured but Bishop said "I feel pretty stiff this morning."

Bodman who failed to escape from the diner with the other three said he had a short but thrilling ride.

"I couldn't get out with the others," he said, "so I just held on

(See RESCUE—Page 7)

WIDOW IS FOUND SUICIDE BY GAS

Policeman Entering House Made Ill by Fumes

Mrs. Elizabeth M. Brooks, sixty-four, widow of Charles Brooks, ended her life by inhaling illuminating gas in the kitchen of her home at 587 Pershing Ave. this morning.

Policeman Charles Resh, who responded to a call from the woman's nephew, Norman Smith, 585 Pershing Ave., was made ill by the fumes and taken to the General Hospital, where he was held several hours for observation.

Smith, a city fireman from No. 5 Engine House, told police his aunt suffered a nervous breakdown some time ago and had been a patient at the Marshall Square Sanitarium, West Chester. She had attempted suicide last July by slashing her throat. Dr. A. V. Walter, county coroner, issued a verdict of suicide.

According to Smith, his aunt had recovered and was in apparent good spirits over the week-end. She was last seen about the house last night.

Detects Odor Of Gas

At 6:45 o'clock, Smith's wife detected the odor of gas and she notified her husband when he returned from work at 8:10 A. M. Smith went next door to his aunt's home to investigate and found the windows and doors locked. He rang the door bell and when he failed to get a response, he telephoned, Jacob O. Hebble, 125 E. Vine St., a friend of the family.

When Hebble arrived and noticed the strong odor of gas coming through the mail slot on the front door he told Smith to call city police. Policemen Resh and Stammer responded and Stammer broke a dining room window to the rear of the house to gain entrance. They found Mrs. Brooks' body lying on the kitchen floor with five burners on the gas stove open.

Mrs. Brooks' husband died six years ago. Born in Lancaster, she was the daughter of the late Christian and Melinda Shay Vogt. She was a member of Faith Evangelical and Reformed Church. Surviving are one sister, Mary, wife of John Fasig, and four brothers: John, George Charles and Cyrus Vogt, all of this city.

LEOLA MAN, 60, SHOOTS HIMSELF

Craig Moorehouse, sixty, Leola, is in a critical condition at St. Joseph's Hospital after shooting himself in the right temple with a .32 calibre revolver at 8:30 a. m. today.

According to members of his family, Moorehouse had been in ill health. They heard a shot fired in a second-floor bedroom and rushed upstairs to find him lying across a bed with a bullet wound through his head and the revolver still in his hand. A Leola physician was summoned and ordered him removed in the hospital ambulance.

Connally Asks Senate For 'Courageous' Charter Vote

WASHINGTON, July 23 — (AP) — Senator Connally (D-Tex) called on the Senate today to ratify the United Nations Charter "by a vote that will be heard around the world."

Opening debate on the 50-nations agreement signed June 26 at San Francisco, the chairman of the Foreign Relations committee won applause from spectators banked in the galleries when he urged the Senate to show "the same courage toward the obligations of peace as we have in war."

Despite what he termed ample evidence that the Senate will ratify the Charter overwhelmingly, Connally said many representatives of other nations still are doubtful of the outcome.

"They know that the League of Nations was slaughtered here in this chamber," he shouted, pulling off his glasses and waving them in the air.

"Can't you see the blood—there it is on the wall," Connally continued, pointing at the rear wall of the chamber.

Would Provide "Impulse"

Declaring that Senate ratification would give other nations a "tremendous impulse," Connally said the Senate also ought to have the courage to offer its full cooperation in the proposed new league.

"There are some who say we can't send soldiers to back up the peace—that we mustn't have a vote on anything until it is checked back to Congress," he declared.

"Can't we show the same sort of courage toward the obligations of peace as we have those of war?"

With leaders pointing toward a ratification vote late this week, the chairman of the Senate Foreign Relations committee took the floor after the Senate had agreed to sweep aside such technicalities

(See CHARTER—Page 7)

MEAT POINTS TO DROP JULY 29

Beef, Lamb and Mutton Will Be Affected

WASHINGTON, July 23—(AP)—A slight but "fairly general" reduction in ration point values for beef, lamb and mutton will be ordered this week for the August ration period starting July 29.

This was learned today, although OPA withheld any official announce beyond acknowledging that "point reduction would appear logical" if meat supplies are showing improvement.

Pork points will not be reduced, because hog marketing has been slow.

The reductions will amount to only one or two points a pound on beef, it was learned, and will cover steaks, roasts and other preferred cuts as well as the less popular ones. For lamb and mutton the lowering of point values will be about the same, perhaps a trifle greater.

Reports from various parts of the country tell of increasing meat supplies in civilian distribution channels and prospects of further increases in the weeks ahead. In some areas consumers are said to be complaining of a shortage of red points in relation to the meat available.

Three Factor Involved

Three factors are reflected in the improved meat supply: (1) a slightly larger level of livestock marketings and slaughtering than had been anticipated by rationing officials.

(2) A reduction in military purchases due to the re-deployment program and a gradual release of some prisoners of war.

(3) Better distribution of civilian

(See MEAT—Page 11)

LOCAL DOCTOR'S CAR IN JERSEY MISHAP

WILDWOOD, N. J., July 23—(AP)—Three Camden children were slightly injured when an auto driven by Dr. Gerald B. McGarvey, 133 S. Queen St., Lancaster, Pa., swerved following a collision with another car and pinned two baby coaches in which they were riding against a fireplug here Saturday.

Raymond Lannon, three, 331 Bailey St., Camden, and his thirteen-months-old sister, Irene, were in one coach and Evelyn Janice, three, 320 Bailet St., Camden, in the other. The children are cousins.

BRETHREN PLAN WHEAT FOR HOLLAND

Local congregations of the Church of the Brethren which have been cooperating in the "heifers for relief of war-ravaged countries" project now are planning to donate wheat and flour for shipment to Holland, B. G. Bushong, Columbia R2, Brethren relief official, announced today.

"Preliminary plans call for one or several congregations to donate a carload," Bushong said. "Arrangements still are in their tentative stages."

EXPRESS DERAILED

LEWISTOWN, Pa., July 23—(AP)—Eastbound tracks of the Pennsylvania Railroad were tied up for several hours today by the derailment of the engine, baggage car and three coaches of the passenger train, The American, St. Louis-to-New York express, 25 miles west of Lewistown.

Railroad officials said no one was injured. They attributed the derailment to a broken driving axle on the engine.

Lawyers and Police Battle As Petain Goes on Trial

Aged Marshal Hustled from Court Room During 25-minute Disturbance; Reynaud Is First Witness Called by France

PARIS, July 23—(AP)—Disorder broke out today in a courtroom where Marshal Petain was making a plea before a special court trying him for his life. French police cleared the court and made arrests among the spectators.

The old Marshal, proudly wearing the medals France had given him, made what he said would be his lone statement of defense to capital charges of intelligence with the enemy and plotting against the security of France, both before and after he became Chief of State of the Vichy regime.

Prepared For Liberation

"While, Gen. De Gaulle continued the struggle abroad, I prepared the road to liberation," he argued.

The courtroom disturbance resulted from an altercation between prosecutor Andre Mornet and defense attorneys.

"There are too many Germans in this room," Mornet shouted.

Catcalls, protests and cries of "justice" rang from all sides of the crowded room especially from the benches where lawyers were seated.

Jacques Isorny, defense counsel, demanded a formal apology and Mornet retorted:

"I said there are too many people her serving the German cause. I didn't say they were Germans, but I consider them as the same thing."

Again the courtroom erupted with shouts and spectators rose.

Hearing Suspended

The court then ordered the hearing suspended and police started making arrests.

The public which had attended the opening of the trial on invitations of the Ministry of Justice was ordered to clear the gallery. The spectators protested furiously, waving invitation cards under noses of the gendarmes while newspapermen, witnesses and court attendants climbed on chairs and tables to watch the scuffling.

Lawyers ordered ejected battled with police to reenter the courtroom, contending they were immune to arrest under French law.

When the disturbances started, Petain himself was hustled from the courtroom by guards. His chair and table were overturned.

Just before the incident started, he had called upon those condemning him to ask themselves whether "they did as much" for France.

Heir To Catastrophe

"In the most tragic days of the history of France, she called on me," the Marshal said. "I was heir to an unprecented catastrophe."

He contended he had only carried out the advice of his military lead-

(See PETAIN—Page 7)

MARSHAL PETAIN

CEILING ON APPLES UP 25 CTS. BUSHEL

WASHINGTON, July 23—(AP)—The OPA today authorized an increase of 25 cents a bushel in grower prices for fresh apples produced in states along the Eastern Seaboard.

Beginning immediately and ending August 19, the FOB shipping poin ceiling will be $3.70 a bushel for apples grown in Maine, New Hampshire, Vermont, Massachusetts, Connecticut, Rhode Island, New York, Pennsylvania, New Jersey, Delaware, Virginia, Maryland, West Virginia, North Carolina, South Carolina, Georgia and Florida.

LOCAL MAN DIES IN GERMANY

Drowns in Wurm See; Marine Wounded

Two local men were reported on the casualty list today, according to word received here. A soldier died in a swimming accident in Germany and a Marine was wounded on Okinawa.

In all these cases the next of kin nave previously been notified and have been kept informed directly by the War Department of any change in status.

The list includes:

Sgt. Arthur Bell, formerly of this city, died in Germany.

Pvt. Lloyd Reickard, Jr., USMC, 1202 E. King St., wounded on Okinawa.

Sgt. Bell Drowned In Germany on June 21

Sgt. Arthur Bell, thirty, former soloist with Chet Lincoln's band, drowned in Germany, June 21, according to a War Department telegram received by his brother, George W. Bell, of Philadelphia.

The telegram said that he was boating in the Wurm See, Germany, and that the boat capsized. No other details were contained in the message.

Sgt. Bell, a graduate of the Stevens Trade School, class of 1934, was employed at the Armstrong Cork Co prior to the time he entered the service in March, 1941. While in Lancaster he resided at 519 E. Chestnut St. He was among the first group of local inductees to report for service.

He received his training at Fort Bragg, N. C., Camp Blanding, Fla., and Fort Sill, Okla., prior to going overseas in February, 1943.

His 30 months of overseas service were spent with the 939th Field Artillery in the ETO. He had five battle stars on his ETO service ribbon and escaped without

(See CASUALTIES—Page 11)

80,000 NAZIS TAKEN IN RAID BY U.S. TROOPS

Search Every House In Our Zone; Some Caught Wearing GI Uniforms

FRANKFURT ON THE MAIN, July 23—(AP)—Half a million American troops arrested upwards of 80,000 persons and searched every single house in the American occupation zone of Germany over the weekend, it was disclosed today.

It was perhaps the greatest mass raid in history.

The Americans were seeking weapons, ammunition and loot. Many of those taken in custody were members of the S. S., hunted as war criminals.

The 15,000,000 Germans in the American zone were caught completely by surprise and were bewildered and scared, but offered not the slightest opposition.

Brig. Gen. Edwin L. Sibert of Vineyard Haven, Mass., head of the G-2 division of U. S. forces in the European theater, lifted censorship on the raid today. He said that although orders for the raid were issued three weeks ago, perfect security was maintained and not a word leaked out.

German Shot To Death

Only two Germans tried to escape the search, he said, and at least one was shot to death.

Sibert said a considerable number of guns, ammunition and loot such as American uniforms, K-rations, gasoline and vehicles were uncovered, but that there was no sign of an organized German underground.

A lot of S. S. men—many posing as discharged Wehrmacht prisoners of war—were rounded up, he said. Details as to the exact number and identification of any leaders among them were not immediately revealed.

Some In U. S. Uniforms

The general said some of the persons arrested were in American uniforms. These declared that they had no other clothing. Most of those taken into custody, however, were booked for irregularities in identification papers, he said.

With "tallyho" as a code word, the American soldiers struck at daylight Saturday. They stopped every vehicle, including U. S. Army jeeps, checked the papers of civilians and soldiers and swept through every German house from cellar to attic.

Given Week of Grace

"It upset the civilian population quite a bit, which is good," Sibert said, explaining that the Germans

(See ARRESTS—Page 11)

TIE REDS IN WAR TO ULTIMATUM

Surrender Broadcast May Have Warned Japs

POTSDAM, July 23 — (AP) — A broadcast U. S. surrender ultimatum to Japan was viewed by many competent observers here today as a thinly veiled warning to the enemy that Soviet participation—at least to some extent—in the Pacific War is imminent.

It was known here that the Saturday night short-wave broadcast from Washington was authorized by President Truman and was cleared in Potsdam at the "Little White House." Significance was attached to the warning to Japanese leaders that they would not be able to deal with the United States alone unless they surrendered promptly.

President Truman's position now was squarely before the Pacific enemy as the "Big Three" conference entered its second week. Victory over Japan is the President's prime objective in this conference. Japan has been told that she must suffer the responsibility for any further hostilities when the time comes for post-war settlement.

Meanwhile, as the President met daily with Prime Minister Church-

(See PEACE—Page 11)

GEN. HANDLEY GETS BURMA-INDIA POST

CALCUTTA, Juy 23—(AP) — Maj. Gen. T. J. Handley, Jr., has assumed command of the U. S. Army Air Force in the India-Burma theater succeeding Lt. Gen. George S. Stratemeyer, it was announced today. Stratemeyer has become overall commander of U. S. Air Forces in China.

Gen. Handley, a graduate of West Point in the class of 1915, formerly commanded the India-Burma Air Service Command. His home is in Coshocton, Ohio.

HIT 4 SHIPS; 2 OTHER UNITS SHELL COAST

Top Blown Off Japanese Battleship, 791 Vessels Blasted in 14 Days

By Murlin Spencer

GUAM, July 23—(AP)—America's mighty Pacific fleet thrust boldly inside the mouth of Tokyo's outer bay today to wreck a four-ship convoy, and Adm. Nimitz said carrier planes sweeping over the same waters Wednesday blew the top off one of Japan's last two seaworthy battleships. In all, the carrier pilots sank or damaged 21 enemy vessels.

It was the 14th consecutive day the fleet prowled unopposed off Japan—14 historic days in which the fleet and far-ranging land-based air power of Admiral Nimitz and General MacArthur had sunk or damaged 791 vessels and small craft and destroyed or damaged 596 airplanes.

Bombard Chichi Jima

Significant of the total lack of opposition, the fleet today was operating in at least two widely separated units. While one light force ventured farther into Tokyo's outer bay than ever before in this war, another light force of warships bombarded Chichi Jima 550 miles southeast.

Japanese broadcasts reported a third American naval force shelled Paramushiro on the northern road to Japan yesterday.

Seventy-five to 100 Superforts added to the clouds of flying debris today with a 450-ton demolition strike on the Ube synthetic oil refinery on southwestern Honshu. Crewmen observed "excellent results," and all planes returned.

Typhoons Stall Okinawa

Movements of the combined fleet's heavy units remained hidden by radio silence. There was no indication that typhoons which stalled MacArthur's aerial thrusts from Okinawa for the second consecutive day had shifted into the fleet's zone of action—and Tokyo radio warned that new fleet attacks are expected momentarily.

The Japanese shipping toll ranged from the 32,720 ton battleship Nagato to junks and PT boats. The superstructure was knocked off the Nagato, one of the Emperor's two remaining battleships, last Wednesday when 500 carrier planes nosed down on Yokosuka naval base and camouflaged warships lying offshore in Tokyo Bay.

22 U. S. Airmen Lost

This was part of a combined 1,500 plane American and British carrier attack. The Allies swept over 90 miles of the Tokyo area, destroying or damaging 45 surface craft, 110 planes, six locomotives and all types of ground installations. Twenty-two American airmen, 12 U. S. and two British planes were lost.

The balance of the six day toll was taken from Tokyo Bay, down the China coast to Borneo.

In Washington, the Navy reported that pilots of Vice Admiral Marc A. Mitscher's Task Force 58 shot down 1,640 Japanese planes between March 14 and May 28, while opening and supporting Okinawa operations.

In addition, 619 enemy planes were destroyed on the ground and another 1,000 were listed as probably destroyed or damaged for a total of 3,259 destroyed or damaged during the 76 days.

Task Force 58 aircraft also sank 220 vessels, probably sank 150 and damaged 759 during the same period. In surface engagements ships

(See JAPAN—Page 7)

BUTCHER OF LIDICE TO BE TRIED SEPT. 1

MONDORF, LUXEMBOURG, July 23—(AP)—Karl Hermann Frank, the butcher of Lidice, will go on trial about Sept. 1 in Prague and whether convicted or not by the Czechoslovaks will be turned over to the United Nations War Crimes Commission for retrial at Nuernberg with other war criminals, Dr. Bohuslav Ecer, Czechoslovak representative on the commission, said today.

Ecer said Frank had admitted signing death warrants for at least 2,000 men, women and children. He estimated that Frank's trial would last about two weeks. The major war crime trials probably will begin any time after Sept. 15, he said.

WEATHER
Eastern Pennsylvania: Generally Fair And Moderately Warm But Less Humid Friday. Saturday Fair With Moderate Temperature.

Intelligencer Journal

The Leading Newspaper in the Garden Spot of America, Home Owned for Home Folks Since 1794

152nd Year.—No. 41. Entered as second class matter August 9, 1944 at the Post Office at Lancaster, Pa., under the Act of March 3, 1879. Reg. U. S. Pat. Off. LANCASTER, PA., FRIDAY MORNING, AUGUST 3, 1945 CITY TWENTY-SIX PAGES. 20c PER WEEK—4c Per Copy

BURN UP JAPAN
With Paper
Your Waste Paper
Helps Make Bombs
Turn Your Paper
In At Playgrounds

BIG 3 MAPS HARSH RULE OF REICH, CHARTS PLANS FOR EUROPEAN PEACE

Col. Strickler Lands In Boston With 28th Division Units

Lancaster Officer Says 28th Will Fight "Anywhere, At Anytime"

Boston—Col. Daniel B. "Dangerous Dan" Strickler, of Lancastr, Pa., landed in the States Thursday with his 110th Infantry Regiment of the 28th "Keystone" Division—the boys who earned the reputation of being able to "take it and dish it out."

"Dangerous Dan"—a nickname of admiration given by his troops which he led through a trail of combat across France, Belgium, Luxembourg and Germany—strode down the gangplank of the transport General Brooke with a selected group of his decorated men.

Asked the probable fate of the Japanese, which the 28th will take on after 30-day furloughs, Col. Strickler lost no time in repeating the Keystone Division's slogan:

"The 28th will fight anywhere at any time."

As the tooting whistles of harbor craft and music of army bands resounded through the pier, the Lancaster officer, veteran of the Ardennes breakthrough where his 110th with other elements of the 28th Division stood off nine German divisions, watched his regiment disembark.

COMMANDER DISEMBARKS

The General Brooke on which Col. Strickler returned, brought back 3,509 veterans of the 28th, including 343 from Pennsylvania. Docking a short while earlier was the James Parker, with 2,857 veterans of the division, including 305 Pennsylvanians, and Major Gen. Norman D. Cota, fifty-two, of Chelsa, Mass., division commander.

Col. Strickler wore service rib-

More of 28TH on Page 10

COL. DANIEL B. STRICKLER

MISSING SOLDIER KILLED IN ACTION; 2 ARE WOUNDED

Pfc. John M. Dysinger, Missing Since Oct. 1944, Killed In Holland

WAR CASUALTIES

Combat casualties reported Thursday, involving Lancaster county men in the armed forces:

KILLED

Pfc. John M. Dysinger, 842 N. President Ave., in Holland, previously reported missing.

WOUNDED

Robert F. Walther, pharmacist mate third class, Columbia, on Okinawa.

Cpl. Robert W. Long, USMC, 717 W. Vine St., on Okinawa.

A Lancsater soldier, previously listed as missing was reported killed in action, while two other service men were wounded, according to word received by their relatives Friday.

Pfc. Dysinger

Pfc. John M. Dysinger, thirty-five, was killed in action Oct. 5, 1944 in Holland, the War Department notified his wife, Mrs. Gladys Kutz Dysinger, 842 N. President Ave.

Mrs. Dysinger had been notified Oct. 20, 1944 that her husband was missing in action. The second telegram said that the delay in notification of her husband's death was due to "misinformation" and described it as a "most unusual circumstance."

Pfc. Dysinger, who entered the service July 1, 1943, was attached to the 48th Armored Infantry Battalion of the Seventh Division, and went overseas in July, 1944.

He received his training at Fort Knox, Ky.; Camp Chaffee, Ark.; Camp Phillips, Kan., and Fort Meade, Md.

Besides his widow, he is survived by his parents, Mr. and Mrs. John M. Dysinger, 610 N. Pine St.; one brother, Hulbert, West Lancaster, and two sisters, Katharine

More of CASUALTIES on Page 10

"We Lead All The Rest"
FARM CORNER
By The Farm Editor

LARGE WAREHOUSE HERE IS PURCHASED BY TOBACCO CO-OP

Buildings At 214-224 N. Water St. To Be Used By Association

A warehouse affording nearly 50,000 feet or over an acre of floor space was purchased by the Lancaster County Tobacco Growers Cooperative Association, 131 N. Duke St., Thursday, according to an announcement by officials of the association.

Located at 214-224 N. Water St., just north of Chestnut St., the property consists of a four story main building and basement 190 feet long by 50 feet wide, a smaller warehouse building, and two dwellings, most of which extends to N. Arch St., at the rear.

The main building was originally constructed by Charles F. Adams, for the manufacture of candy and is currently occupied by the Dodge Cork Company. Morris Levy and Sons, owners, sold the property to the association.

With a railroad siding giving access to both the PRR and the Reading Railroad, and four loading platforms at the rear of the building available from N. Arch St., of-

More of FARM CORNER Page 17

Weather Calendar

COMPARATIVE TEMPERATURES

Station	High	Low
Water Works	83	63
Ephrata	85	65
Official High for Year, June 30		97
Official Low for Year, Jan. 25		—1
Character of Day		Clear

SUN
Rises—6:03 a. m. Sets—8:16 p. m.

MOON
Rises—1:48 a. m. New Moon, July 7th

STARS
Morning—Mars, Venus, Saturn.
Evening—Jupiter, Mercury.

NEARBY FORECASTS
Maryland and Delaware: Fair and rather warm, but less humid Friday. Saturday fair and moderately warm.
New Jersey: Generally fair and moderately warm, but less humid in the interior Friday. Saturday fair with moderate temperature.

SAVE THIS NEWSPAPER
Make this newspaper do double work — give it to your paper-salvage drive.

116 JAP SHIPS, 278 PLANES ON REVISED SCORE

Nimitz Reveals New Details Of Great Fleet Raids Over Japan

(By The Associated Press)

American and British carrier raids knocked out a total of 116 Japanese vessels and 278 aircraft in Monday's Tokyo-Nagoya-Maizuru raids, Adm. Nimitz disclosed today (Friday).

Gen. MacArthur reported more than 250 far east Air Force planes heavily attacked Japan's big shipbuilding city of Nagasaki Wednesday and Gen. Spaatz said 151 Iwo-based Mustangs strafed and rocketed the Kobe-Nagoya region Thursday.

FEAF fliers left fires raging among shipyards and 10 vessels sunk.

Three other ships and a submarine were damaged in the strike. It was the second successive day of attacks on Kyushu coastal industrial centers and shipping. The Yank pilots in the two days destroyed or damaged 56 enemy vessels. In one of Tuesday's attacks near misses were scored on two carriers caught at the Sasebo naval base.

Japanese interceptor planes offered weak opposition to the raiders Wednesday losing six planes out of 20 which were surprised by only four American Mustang fighters off the south coast of the island.

Col. Frances Gideon, operations officer of the FAEF, said the appearance of the hitherto reluctant Japanese planes was a desperate attempt to halt air attacks which will soon complete the blockade of the enemy homeland.

SMASH FIVE SHIPS

Spanning the east China Sea to Shanghai, American Army and Navy bombers destroyed or damaged five more enemy cargo ships. Other Allied planes hit enemy ships

More of PACIFIC on Page 10

JAPAN BOASTS OF 100,000,000 NIPS READY FOR FIGHT

"Fight It Out" Theme Of Enemy's Propaganda As He Admits Blows

San Francisco—(AP)—Enemy broadcasts, conceding heavy blows by Superforts, boasted Thursday of an "iron defense" by 100,000,000 Japanese determined to scorn surrender and fight the war to a finish.

Some uneasiness was manifest, however, over repeated assaults by General MacArthur's air forces from Okinawa on the southern island of Kyushu, which the Japanese previously have declared was a "fortress."

Domei Agency said such attacks on transport targets were "systematic and thorough," were carried out by from 350 to 500 fighters and bombers daily and "will undoubtedly be intensified in the future."

The theme of most of the broadcasts, recorded by the Federal Communications Commission, was determination to fight it out.

As for Wednesday's record raid by 820 Superforts the Japanese named three cities as hit which were not listed in the 20th Air Force communique.

The Tokyo radio said that fires broke out in Toyama but "by

More of JAPAN on Page 10

More Than 166,000 Yanks Moved From France From June 15 July 31

The Paris, France, Assembly Area Command announced Thursday that more than 166,000 American soldiers moved through its 17 camps between June 15 and July 31. At the end of July more than 164,000 men were being processed in the camps.

The command also announced that the redeployment schedule of the 13th Airborne and 45th Infantry Divisions had been advanced. The former is now scheduled to move into the staging area at Le Havre from Camp Pittsburgh Aug. 8 instead of Aug. 12. The 45th Infantry is scheduled to leave Camp St. Louis for LeHarvre on

More of REDEPLOYMENT Page 17

REDEPLOYMENT BOX-SCORE

13th Armored, 20th Armored and Ninth Army headquarters—on the sea.

30th Infantry—Advance units sailed from Le Havre July 22. The main body less one regiment is en route to the United Kingdom for an August sailing on the Queen Mary. The 119th Regiment will sail from Le Havre at the same time.

35th Infantry, 45th Infantry and 13th Airborne—Advance units have sailed from Le Havre. The main bodies are at the Reims assembly area.

Tenth Mountain Division—Sailed from Naples, Italy.

Truman Shakes Hands With King

President Truman (right) shakes hands with King George VI as he is piped aboard the British battle-cruiser Renown, at Plymouth, England, where the two met after the President returned from Germany and Big Three conference, en route to the U. S. This photo was received via radio from London, Aug. 2.

TRUMAN STARTS ON VOYAGE HOME; SAW KING AT PLYMOUTH

President In Good Spirits As He Visits British Monarch

With President Truman Aboard Cruiser Augusta—(AP)—Obviously in high spirits, President Truman started home aboard this famous warship Thursday after concluiding the Big Three conference and holding a 20-minute luncheon conference with King George VI of England.

The talk with the British Monarch was held aboard H. M. S. Renown off the war-scarred port of Plymouth, England, as the world prepared to receive a communique on the historic Big Three sessions at Potsdam.

The President had flown to England from Potsdam aboard the famous C-54, "The Sacred Cow." He landed at Harrowber airport about eight miles north of Plymouth.

Accompanied by Secretary of State James F. Byrnes and Admiral William D. Leahy, his chief of staff, he drove to the Plymouth area to the cheers of English

More of TRUMAN on Page 10

City Police Play Nursemaid To Boy Found In Street

City police played nursemaid to a thirty-months-old boy Thursday night, after neighbors reported him wandering nude in the 200 block of West Orange Street at 9:13 p. m.

Cruiser men who responded to the call, found Lloyd Ulmer, Jr., 222 W. Orange St., playing near his home. From neighbors they learned that he left the apartment during the absence of his mother.

Taking the child to the apartment, police put him to bed, then went to the first floor to talk to other residents. A few minutes later Lloyd walked down the steps again and headed for the street.

He was stopped by police, dressed and taken to the police station where he stayed until his mother Mrs. Janet Ulmer called for him at 11 p. m. She had gone to a restaurant for lunch, police said.

PURSE, $143 STOLEN

Mrs. Emma Druschel, 800 Chestnut St., Columbia, reported the theft of her purse containing $143 in cash, ration books and other personal belongings Thursday morning while shopping in several downtown stores. Police said the purse was left lying on a counter after a purchase was made and had disappeared when the women returned.

Poland Gets Long Coastline, Danzig, But Denied Stettin

By RICHARD KASISCHKE

London—(AP)—The Big Three carved vast territories out of eastern Germany and awarded them to Poland in fixing the Poles' western frontier along the Oder-Neisse river lines—at some points less than 50 miles from the center of Berlin.

While leaving the final delimitation of this frontier to the peace conference, the three leaders handed over to Warsaw the immediate administration of practically all of agricultural Pomerania and industrial Silesia, about two-thirds of East Prussia and a big portion of Brandenburg.

But the Poles were denied the big German Baltic port and shipbuilding center of Stettin, which they had demanded. Stettin lies on the west bank of the Oder. It remains German.

The Poles also received less than they had expected of East Prussia, the northern third of which went to Russia.

"On the whole, however, I think our government is satisfied," said an authoritative source closely connected with the Warsaw government.

STETTIN DISAPPOINTMENT

"There was some expectation regarding Stettin, so we didn't get all we asked," he added.

Polish sources here said they still hoped for some concessions regarding Stettin—possibly a declaration that Stettin is a free city with commercial passage allowed to Poles and Czechoslovakians.

The Big Three decided that Poland's claims to reparations from Germany should not be paid separately, but instead from the share collected by Russia.

The new frontier as announced in the Big Three communique gave to Poland:

"The former German territories east of the line running from the Baltic Sea immediately west of Swindemuende, and thence along the Oder river to the confluence

More of POLAND on Page 10

COP'S ALERTNESS RECOVERS VEHICLE

An AWOL soldier was taken into custody and a missing station wagon recovered in this city Thursday afternoon through the alertness of a city police officer, who had just returned to his home after completing work.

George C. Wiley, twenty-two, formerly of this city and now listed as a resident of Wrightsville R1, is the soldier. He has been absent without leave from Camp Pickett, Va., and was turned over to the Shore Patrol.

Policeman Andy Kauffman, 679 Poplar St., had returned to his home from police headquarters when he saw a station wagon stop across the street and a soldier alight. He checked the license number and learned it corresponded with a license sent over the State Police teletype listing it as a missing automobile.

According to police, Wiley had loaned the automobile from Frank P. Hoffman, Wrightsville, several days ago, to make a trip to York. He was to have returned the car within a few hours but failed. Hoffman refused to prosecute, police said.

SEN. TAFT SCORES POTSDAM RESULTS; SEES NEW STRIFE

Deplores Agreement On Polish Boundary Expansion, Criticizes President Truman

Washington—(AP)—Democratic legislators generally applauded the Potsdam declaration Thursday night but Senator Taft (R-Ohio) charged that the agreement for a provisional westward shift of the Polish boundary "sows the seeds of future war."

Taft, chairman of the Senate Republican Steering committee, criticized President Truman for acting without consultation of the Senate.

Chairman Connally (D-Tex) of the Senate Foreign Relations committee told reporters that "as a whole" the Big Three understandings on the handling of European affairs met with his approval. Senator Thomas (D-Utah) commented that the Potsdam announcement showed the United States is stand-

More of TAFT on Page 10

LITITZ SETS DATE FOR FARM, POULTRY SHOW

Lititz will hold its annual Farm and Poultry Show this fall it was decided at a meeting of the Community Show Association held Thursday evening.

The Show will be held October 4, 5 and 6. There will be a parade.

Arthur Myers will have charge of the Poultry Show again.

Howard Regannas, president of the Association, announced that the Association will meet August 13, at which time committees will be appointed.

Sun Moves Back Into Weather Scene Here—Mercury Reaches 85

The sun moved back into the weather scene Thursday and immediately set about proving that it had lost none of its power while hidden behind heavy clouds for the better part of three weeks.

It succeeded quite well. The Ephrata Weather Station recorded a high temperature of 85 degrees. Generally fair and moderately warm but not so humid was forecast for Friday.

Prospects that a heat wave might be next on the season's wacky weather schedule appeared Thursday night. Cleveland, O., reported a high temperature of 90 and St. Louis a high of 97.

Meanwhile Lancastrians still struggled to open doors swollen by the extreme dampness and farmers hoped for more and more sunshine so that they could get back into fields badly damaged by the rains.

No Direct Reference Made To Russian Attitude Over Japan

Potsdam Communique Only Says Chiefs Of Staffs Conferred On "Military Matters Of Common Interest;" Reich To Pay Damages

Washington—(AP)—The Big Three Thursday night set up the mechanism for great powers to write the peace of stricken Europe and extract reparations from a guilty Germany forced to devote its energies to agriculture and peaceful industry.

But on the great question in the minds of people the world over—will Russia help smash Japan?—a 6,000-word communique on the Potsdam conference was silent.

It concluded, however, with a single, succinct sentence which may be expected to receive uneasy scrutiny from Japan's war-lords:

"During the conference there were meetings between the chiefs of staff of the three governments on military matters of common interest."

Issued simultaneously in London Moscow and Washington the communique was approved by Prime Minister Attlee, Premier Stalin and President Truman.

Appraising their work in the heart of a once powerful enemy state, they spoke of "important decisions and agreements," of strengthened ties, of a "renewed confidence that their governments and peoples, together with the other United Nations, will ensure the creation of a just and enduring peace."

Text Starts Page 19

Nearly half the Potsdam pronouncement dealt with Germany. Most of the rest covered European problems in detail. Perhaps significantly, the only point in the lengthy, historic document which was not amplified was the reference to consideration of military matters.

Now that the war in Europe is over, diplomatic analysts here were asking what other military matters remain to hold the attention of all the world's three most powerful nations.

The great powers set themselves up as severe rulers of whipped Germany. But they said it was not their intention to "destroy or enslave the German people." They said it might become possible for the Germans "in due course to take their place among the free and peaceful peoples of the world."

ERADICATE NAZIS

Germany, however, is to undergo "complete disarmament and demilitarization," with the elimination or control of all German industry that could be used for military production. The Nazi party is to be eradicated.

Germany's economy is to be decentralized, and in its organization, primary emphasis will be placed on development of agriculture and peaceful industries.

Payment of reparations, the Big Three determined, should leave enough resources to enable the German people to subsist without outside help. Their standard of living is not to exceed that of other European peoples.

Just how much reparations will be extracted, the communique did not say.

But Soviet reparation claims are to be met in large part from the Russian occupation zone in the east and from German external assets. Poland's share will come from what Russia gets.

The claims of the United States and Britain and other countries will be met from their western

More of BIG THREE on Page 10

11 SPECIFIC RESULTS OF POTSDAM MEETINGS

Washington—(AP)—Specific results of the Potsdam Big Three conference were 11 in number. Signatories to the declaration:

1. Established a permanent council of foreign ministers of the three powers and those of France and China. The council was assigned to "continue the necessary work for the peace settlements."

2. Promised that the writing of a peace treaty with Italy shall be the first task of the council; after the treaty is concluded the Big Three will seek to get Italy into the United Nations.

3. Blackballed Franco Spain from membership in the United Nations because its government was founded with Axis support and because of its "close association with the aggressor states."

4. Spelled out in detail their political and economic plans for Germany.

5 Agreed on how reparations are to be extracted from that shattered nation.

6. Assigned temporary western boundaries to Poland, with a final determination to await the writing of peace terms.

7. Reaffirmed their purpose of bringing war criminals to "swift and sure justice."

8. Decided that peace treaties with Rumania, Bulgaria, Hungary and Finland shall be concluded after the one with Italy.

9. Offered to all these, and to neutrals who qualify under the United Nations Charter, eventual support for memberships in the new World League.

10. Abolished the European Advisory Commission and agreed to revise procedures of Allied control commissions in Rumania, Bulgaria and Hungary.

11. Examined extension of the authority of Austria's provisional government but left the question open to detailed study later.

GIRL BICYCLIST FRACTURES ARM

A Girl Scout from Upper Darby, bicycling with a group of scouts on the Horseshoe Trail, fell from her bicycle and fractured her right arm Wednesday near Fivepointville.

Margaret Shook, sixteen, daughter of Mr. and Mrs. R. C. Shook, 162 Overhill Road, Upper Darby, was treated by Dr. Paul S. Schantz at his office at Ephrata, for a right arm fracture near the shoulder. Dr. Schantz X-rayed and reduced the fracture.

The group had stopped at the Bowmansville hostel overnight and were on their way back to Girl Scout Camp Elizabeth Borton, near Elverson, when the accident happened. The camp is for Delaware County Girl Scouts.

The girl was taken to her home by Dr. Schantz, who was on his way to Philadelphia.

Hal Boyle Describes
Visit to Pyle's Home
— See Editorial Page

LANCASTER NEW ERA

WEATHER
Showers and scattered thunder storms tonight followed by clearing with moderate temperatures Tuesday.

69th Year—No. 21,164 | Entered as second class matter January 31, 1924, at the Post Office at Lancaster, Pa., under the Act of March 3, 1879. Reg. U. S. Pat. Off. | LANCASTER, PA., MONDAY, AUGUST 6, 1945 | CITY EDITION | 14 PAGES | 20c PER WEEK—4c Per Copy

Atomic Bomb, Equal to 20,000 Tons of TNT, Dropped On Japan

SIZE OF ARMY DISPUTE HEADS TO PRESIDENT

Campaign For 3,000,000 Troops to Whip Japan Reported Gaining

WASHINGTON, Aug. 6—(AP) — **President Truman, as Commander-in-Chief, probably will have to step in to settle the mounting dispute over the size of the Army needed to whip Japan.**

This word came today from Capitol Hill, where a first class row has developed over the size of the fighting forces for a one-front war.

Senators Johnson (D-Colo) and Taft (R-Ohio) openly criticized the War Department over the week-end for its slowness in demobilization, and there were signs that their independent campaigns were picking up recruits among other lawmakers.

On the other hand, such Senators as Pepper (D-Fla) and Thomas (D-Utah) —the latter chairman of the Military Committee — were standing by Secretary of War Stimson in his decision to retain about 7,000,000 men in uniform as of next June 1.

Pepper said:

"The War and Navy Departments are charged with prosecution of the war and they know more about the size forces they need than the Senate does. With all due respect to the distinguished Senator from Colorado (Johnson), I think the size of the Army is a matter which should be left to the Commander-in-Chief and the Army General Staff."

Thomas already was on record with this statement: "It is time we stopped fooling around with the size of the Army x x x there is a general rush to collapse the armed services."

Taft Calls Plan Stupid

Taft called the War Department's big Army policy "stupid, stubborn," and Johnson challenged Stimson in a letter to disprove the Coloradoan's assertion that there can't be more than 3,000,000 effectives on the Pacific front by next year, due to transportation and supply difficulties.

Johnson said Gen. Douglas MacArthur ought to get all the men he can possibly use, but remarked that "discontented American soldiers marking time on this continent are not going to help MacArthur or hurt the Japs."

If Stimson's decision is carried out, Johnson said, it means—

"Millions of bitter, discontented men milling around the United States in uniform . . . a transporta-

(See ARMY SIZE—Page 7)

SEN. HIRAM W. JOHNSON

SEN. JOHNSON DIES, AGED 79

Californian Opposed League and New Charter

WASHINGTON, Aug. 6.— (AP) — Senator Hiram W. Johnson of California, militant opponent of the League of Nations and the San Francisco Charter for a United Nations Organization, died today at 79 years.

The veteran Republican Senator succumbed at Naval Hospital, where he had been confined for two and one-half weeks. His physician, Capt. Robert E. Duncan, USN, said he died from a thrombosis of a cerebral artery.

His political activities extended over a third of a century covering some of the most stirring events in the nation's history.

Defeated League Of Nations

A striking figure in the Senate since first elected to Congress in 1916, he played a leading part in defeating President Wilson's League of Nations covenant and later in opposing United States' adherence to the world court.

His wife, whom he referred to as "The Boss," was with him at the time of his death.

Senator Mc Kellar (D-Tenn), president of the Senate, today will appoint a committee to attend the funeral of the silver-haired veteran.

Oppose 'Teen Age Draft

One of his last great Senate fights was against passage of the 'teen age draft bill. He told his colleagues, with tears in his eyes, that he opposed "calling children to fight our battles."

He had been expected to take a lead in opposition to the recently approved World Charter, but illness prevented.

Another Senate battle, in which he lined up in opposition to Sen. Connally and others, was on the United States-Mexican Water Treaty. It finally was enacted, but not until Johnson had called upon all the arts of a long career to defeat it.

Johnson, who served as Governor

(See SEN. JOHNSON—Page 7)

BOMB SECRET NOT REVEALED TO WORKERS

125,000 Were Employed at Isolated Plants in 3 Areas of U. S.

WASHINGTON, Aug. 6—(AP)—The atomic bomb disclosed by President Truman today was developed at factories in Tennessee, Washington and New Mexico.

Mr. Truman in his announcement said that from 65,000 to 125,000 workers were employed on the project at Oak Ridge near Knoxville, Tenn., at Richland near Pasco, Wash., and at an unnamed installation near Santa Fe, N. M.

He said the work was so secret that most of the employes did not know the character of it.

Workers Were Recruited For "Bomb" Projects

RICHLAND, Wash., Aug. 6—(AP)—The secret which turned this sleepy little sagebrush hamlet into one of the major smaller cities of the Pacific northwest was revealed today after an atomic bomb—releasing the basic force of the universe—was dropped with disintegrating results upon a Japanese city.

For two years, the government has been recruiting workers all over the nation for the Hanford project, of which Richland became the residential center; Pasco the official headquarters and several smaller cities the mystery-shrouded nerve-center in the war's greatest secret.

Recruited All Over Nation

The Army employed Public Relation officers to tour newspaper offices reiterating pledges of secrecy. Mysterious directives issued from censorship authorities simultaneously with page advertisements all over the country calling for unskilled workers, electricians, millwrights and specialists by the hundred and the thousands for the Hanford project.

Just how the mystery-shrouded project would aid the war effort provided a major guessing contest throughout the Pacific northwest. It was known the DuPonts had something to do with it. It was known that armed guards turned

(See WORKERS—Page 7)

"Dust and Smoke" When Bomb Hit

Stimson, Awaiting Report, Says It Will Shorten War

WASHINGTON, Aug. 6.—(AP)—Secretary Stimson predicted today that the atomic bomb will "prove a tremendous aid" in shortening the war with Japan.

The War Secretary made his statement as the Army reported that an "impenetrable cloud of dust and smoke" cloaked Hiroshima after it was hit by the new weapon from the air.

An accurate assessment of the damage inflicted by the bomb is not yet available, however, the War Department said. As soon as details of its effectiveness are learned, the Department added, they will be released.

Staggers Imagination

Stimson said in his statement that the explosive power of the bomb is such as to "stagger the imagination." He added that scientists are confident of developing even more powerful atomic bombs.

Stimson said the security requirements do not permit disclosure of the exact methods of producing the bomb or the nature of its action. He did say, however, that urainium ore is essential to the production of the bomb.

Development of the bomb culminated three years of work by Allied scientists, industry, labor and military forces, Stimson said, adding that he was convinced Japan will not be in a position to use a similar weapon. While Germany worked "feverishly" to develop an atomic bomb, Stimson said, the Nazi defeat now has erased danger from that source.

Stimson promised that further statements will be released in the future to give additional details concerning scientific and production aspects.

Thousands Kept Secret

He disclosed that development of the bomb was carried out by thousands of persons "with the greatest secrecy." The work has been so divided, he said, that no one has been given more information concerning the bomb than was absolutely necessary to his particular job.

The possibility of using atomic energy in the manufacture of weapons, Stimson said, was brought to President Roosevelt's attention late in 1939. The Chief Executive named a committee to investigate and by June, 1942, Stimson said sufficient progress had

(See STIMSON—Page 7)

Where Atomic Bomb Hit Jap Base

President Truman disclosed today that an atomic bomb had been dropped on Hiroshima (bomb burst symbol), a Japanese army base. American B29s also rained incendiary and explosive bombs on six Japanese war centers (underlined) and fighters used rockets and machine guns on targets in Tokyo area (A). Air Force headquarters said that photos showed Toyama (B) raided Thursday was "totally destroyed." Mine symbols locate areas mined over weekend by B29s. (AP Wirephoto.)

U. S. Army Spends Two Billion Dollars on Most Terrible Weapon of All Times

WASHINGTON, Aug. 6 — (AP) — An atomic bomb, hailed as the most terrible destructive force in history and as the greatest achievement of organized science, has been loosed upon Japan.

President Truman disclosed in a White House statement at 11 A. M., (EWT), today that the first use of the bomb — containing more power than 20,000 tons of TNT and producing more than 2,000 times the blast of the most powerful bomb ever dropped before—was made 16 hours earlier on Hiroshima, Japanese army base.

The atomic bomb is the answer, President Truman said, to Japan's refusal to surrender. Secretary of War Stimson predicted the bomb will "prove a tremendous aid" in shortening the Japanese war.

Even More Powerful Bombs Coming

Mr. Truman grimly warned that "even more powerful forms (of the bomb) are in development." He said:

"If they do not now accept our terms, they may expect a rain of ruin from the air the like of which has never been seen on this earth."

The War Department reported that "an impenetrable cloud of dust and smoke" cloaked Hiroshima after the first atomic bomb crashed down. It was impossible to make an immediate assessment of the damage.

President Truman said he would recommend that Congress consider establishing a commission to control production of atomic power within the United States, adding:

"I shall make recommendations to Congress as to how atomic power can become a powerful and forceful influence towards the maintenance of world peace."

Both Mr. Truman and Secretary Stimson, while emphasizing the peacetime potentiality of the new force, made clear that much research must be undertaken to effect full peacetime application of its principles.

$2,000,000,000 Spent On Research

The product of $2,000,000,000 spent in research and production—"the greatest scientific gamble in history," Mr. Truman said—the atomic bomb has been one of the most closely guarded secrets of the war.

Franklin D. Roosevelt and Winston Churchill gave the signal to start work on harnessing the forces of the atom. Mr. Truman said the Germans worked feverishly, but failed to solve the problem.

The raid on Hiroshima, located on Honshu Island on the shores of the inland sea, had not been disclosed previously although the 20th Air Force on Guam announced that 580 Superforts raided four Japanese cities at about the same time.

The city of 318,000 also contains a principal port.

Harnesses Basic Power of Universe

Mr. Truman added:

"It is an atomic bomb. It is a harnessing of the basic power of the universe. The force from which the sun draws its power has been loosed against those who brought war to the far east."

The President disclosed that the Germans "worked feverishly" in search of a way to use atomic energy in their war effort but failed. Meantime American and British scientists studied the problem and developed two principal plants and some lesser factories for the production of atomic power.

The President disclosed that more than 65,000 persons now are working in great secrecy in these plants, adding:

"We have spent $2,000,000,000 on the greatest scientific gamble in history—and won.

"We are now prepared to obliterate more rapidly and completely every productive enterprise the Japanese have above ground in any city. We shall completely destroy Japan's power to make war."

The President noted that the Big Three ultimatum issued July 26 at Potsdam was intended "to spare the Japanese people from utter destruction" and the Japanese leaders rejected it. The atomic bomb now is the answer to that rejection and the president said "they may expect a rain of ruin from the air, the like of which has never been seen on this earth."

Will Intensify Offensive

Mr. Truman forecast that sea and land forces will follow up this air attack in such numbers and power

(See ATOMIC BOMB—Page 7)

Secret of Sun Harnessed To Make Atomic Bombs

By Howard W. Blakeslee

NEW YORK, Aug. 6.—(AP)—President Truman's statement that the atomic bomb is made of the force from which the sun draws its power explains the principle of this new explosive.

The sun's power is the sun's heat. For years scientists have known that this he could not come from ordinary fires like any known on the earth's face. The sun just wasn't big enough to have lasted the billions of years during which there is plenty of evidence it has been burning at the present rate.

In ordinary fire, molecules of wood, coal or whatever else is blazing, separate. As they come apart, the energy which held them together, is released in the form of heat, light and other rays, like X-rays. Even a hot fire gives off a bit of X-rays.

The sun burns not by separation of molecules but by two much more intensely hot methods. One is the atoms that form molecules separating from each other. This kind of separation releases incredibly greater amounts of heat and energy than molecule separations.

Made Up of Electrons

But an even greater source of sun power is the fact that the atoms themselves come apart to some extent. These atoms are made of electrons, protons and other electrical and non-electrical particles. Electrons and other particles fly off the atoms. This kind of separation releases even greater energies (including heat and all other sorts of rays) than the separation of atoms from each other.

Not all these inter-atomic forces are yet even known. Some are so powerful that they have only been guessed at. The popular phrase, smashing the atom, describes this

(See SUN'S SECRET—Page 7)

4 MORE CITIES LEFT IN ASHES

Fires Over Japan Visible 150 Miles at Sea

By The Associated Press

American airmen said they turned four more forewarned Japanese cities to ashes today as 750 Superforts and Mustang fighters reportedly swept the enemy's sacred islands with fire bombs, rockets and parachuted mines.

B-29 crewmen returning to their Marianas Island bases told of setting fires visible for 150 miles at sea. Some ran into intense anti-aircraft fire and strong interception including rocket planes as they raided cities Tokyo described as "defenseless."

3,850 Tons Of Bombs

Waves of B-29s dropped approximately 3,850 tons of incendiaries on the industrial cities of Nishinomiya, Maebashi, Imabari and Saga, and demolition bombs on the Coal Liquefaction Company at Ube.

Pilots reported Japanese opposition was light, although Capt. Lawrence Bird, Mapleton, Utah, reported seeing a Japanese jet fighter plane over Maebashi.

"At first I thought it was a flare or ball of fire. It came to within 500 feet of our B-29," he said.

Reporting on the results of the heavy raid on Saga, on Kyushu, 2nd Lt. Gordon P. Marchal, of Sacramento, Calif., said, "I could see lines of fire on the ground and believe me, the whole thing was definitely saturated."

Over Nishinomiya, however, one pilot reported seeing more flak, more fighters and more searchlights than in recent forays over

(See JAPAN—Page 7)

Speculate That Atom Secret Could Blow Up Planet

By The Associated Press

Cmdr Herbert Agar, aide to U S. Ambassador to Great Britain John G. Winant, said on June 29 that " if the war (European) had gone on for another six months it is quite possible that this planet would have ceased to exist because it was probable that someone would have learned to break the atom without controlling it."

Agar said "there was a danger that the Germans would learn how to split the atom first," and added: "I sincerely believe that in a very few years human beings will know how to destroy the human race."

Previously Lt. Col. John A. Keck of Greensburg, Pa., chief of the enemy equipment intelligence section of the U. S. Army Ordnance Division in the European Theater, had told of many highly advanced German secret weapons which had not yet reached the perfection stage when the war ended.

While revealing many German inventions Keck added that they were not all—that there were others which must remain secret because of the Pacific war.

Keck said the German scientists declared their belief that rockets within the next five to 10 years would speed a ton of mail across the Atlantic in 40 minutes and that within 15 to 25 years rockets would make regular passenger runs between Europe and the United States.

LIQUOR RATIONING ENDS IN CANADA

OTTAWA, Aug. 6—(AP)—The wartime alcoholic beverages order, under which the sale of liquor was rationed in Canada, was lifted today.

"In view of the termination of hostilities in Europe," said an announcement from the office of Prime Minister W. L. MacKenzie King, "the principal reasons for imposition of the restrictions on supply contained in the wartime alcoholic beverages order, 1942, no longer exist."

Only the provision barring liquor advertising remained in effect.

ERECT "STOP" SIGNS AT FIRST AND RUBY

Police today erected "Stop" signs at First and Ruby Sts.

The signs are erected to give traffic on Ruby St. the right-of-way. Residents of the area had petitioned city authorities for a safeguard at the intersection.

Hero of 108 Missions Is Lost on Eve of Discharge

GUAM, Aug. 6—(AP)—Tailgunner Kurt J. Hermann, who fought over two oceans and all three enemy capitals, is missing in action—just two trips short of his self-set 110-mission retirement goal.

The 26-year-old tech sergeant from Babylon, N. Y., passed up at least 100 chances to go home to stay. He wanted to complete 110 combat missions. On the 108th, over Kochi, Japan on July 4, his Superfort was lost.

The 20th Air Force yesterday disclosed his amazing record, topping even the 107-mission record of T-Sgt. Lewis L. Coburn, Niagara Falls, N. Y.

26 Days On Life Raft

Serving first in the Merchant Marine, Hermann survived a torpedoing, spent 26 days on a life raft, was rescued, and enlisted in the air forces in August, 1942.

He bagged his first German Messerschmitt as a waist gunner aboard a 12th Air Force Fortress based in North Africa. Transferring to a Marauder force, he knocked down three more enemy fighters. Parachuting from a badly damaged B-26 after a strike at Sardinia, he landed unhurt beside an American field hospital. And in July, 1943, he participated in the first bombing of Rome.

Furloughed, he hitch-hiked home by air, was called to Washington by Gen. Henry H. Arnold, the Air

T-SGT. KURT J. HERMANN

Forces chief, and got his requested transfer to the Eighth Air Force in England. He participated in

(See AIR HERO—Page 7)

RAIN FOLLOWS IDEAL WEEKEND

Shore Travel Up; More Crop Loss Feared

Rain returned here today to end a brief week-end rally by the sun that gave Lancaster its first pleasant "outdoor" weather in four week-ends.

Old Sol went back on a vacation that he kept during most of July to make room for more precipitation. Skies brightened slightly early this afternoon after heavy showers throughout the morning, but the weather bureau forecast more showers tonight with clearing weather tomorrow.

Reacting to the clear skies and moderate temperatures that prevailed here Saturday and yesterday, Lancastrians took advantage of the weather to make trips to nearby parks and shore vacation spots.

Rush To Resorts

Local travel authorities reported a 25 percent increase in train and bus travel over the previous three week-ends, mainly to the seashore. State police said there was a slight increase in highway traffic but the number of accidents and arrests remained "normal."

County farm officials said the clear week-end gave farmers a chance to salvage what wheat can be used and also to cut ruined wheat with reapers to prevent it from choking out clover crops. Farmers also took advantage of the dry weather to cultivate tobacco to alleviate moisture and control disease, it was pointed out.

Generally, officials said, the clear days gave impetus to other late

(See WEATHER—Page 7)

BOY, 2, HAS POLIO; 6TH CASE THIS YEAR

The sixth case of infantile paralysis here this year, a two-year-old county child, was listed over the week-end.

Health authorities reported that the illness of Albert S. Cumens, Jr., son of Mr. and Mrs. Albert S. Cumens, Manheim R3, was diagnosed as polio at General Hospital Saturday. The boy was stricken July 22.

The city board of health reported the following diseases in the city last week: Chicken pox, two cases; mumps, two; measles, one; and whooping cough, one.

MORE CLOTHES FOR CHILDREN

Larger Quantities Low-Cost Garments Promised

WASHINGTON, Aug. 6. —(AP)— The children's low-cost clothing situation is looking up.

An Associated Press survey showed today that a greater number of essential garments should begin appearing in stores next month despite a continuing general shortage of cotton clothing.

In fact, mothers from now on should be able to find a few necessary articles of clothing for their youngsters.

Will Supply Minimum Needs

But government and trade experts cautioned against any notion of stocking up on the garments because the program that is turning them out is aimed at meeting only minimum needs throughout the country.

More than 43,000,000 essential garments are scheduled for manufacture by the end of September under the War Production Board's infants' and children's clothing program.

Output is planned on a per child basis, with particularly large increases in garments for infants and small children to meet the war's larger birth rate.

Recognizing also some women shoppers' complaints about quality and cut of children's clothing, WPB said it has set up standards

(See APPAREL—Page 7)

MAJOR KIRK UNHURT IN CRASH WITH BUS

No one was injured but property damage estimated at $425 was reported in a bus-auto collision at Prince and Chestnut Sts. at 5:30 a. m. today.

Police said an auto driven by Major Norris J. Kirk, forty-one, 446 W. Chestnut St., who was enroute to the Pennsylvania Railroad station to board a train for Fort Dix, N. J., collided with a bus owned by Irvin H. Nolt, Willow Street and operated by Edgar M. Eckman, twenty-three, 239 W. Vine St. There were no passengers on the bus, police reported.

The bus was reported turned around by the car and the physician's car was crushed against the curb on the northeast corner of the intersection. The damage to the bus was estimated at $300 and the auto at $125.

4,000 Navy Yard Workers Are Idle Over Wage Tax

PHILADELPHIA, Aug. 6—(AP) — Nearly 4,000 Philadelphia Navy Yard workers living in New Jersey and in Delaware County, Pa., stayed away from work today in protest against the arrest of employes for non-payment of Philadelphia's one per cent city wage tax.

Leroy W. Owen, a member of the Wage Tax Protest League of South Jersey, said, "we believe we will have cooperation from the strongly organized CIO and AFL unions in Philadelphia in joining with us to present a united front in the fight for repeal of this tax.

"Petitions for a referendum for repeal of the wage tax will be circulated while the Wage Tax Protest League will continue its fight in Congress for the pending legislation to exempt federal employes living outside Philadelphia from the tax," Owen said. Workers said they proposed to stay out only one day.

ALLOWS GERMANS TO FORM UNIONS

BERLIN, Aug. 6.—(AP)—Gen. Eisenhower told Germans in the U. S. Occupation zone today that they may form local unions and engage in local political activities with the aim of helping prepare for the coming winter, which he predicted will be hard.

LIST OF MINERS IN ARMY REQUESTED

WASHINGTON, Aug. 6 — (AP) — The Solid Fuels Administration has asked coal mine owners for identification of miners now in military service, it was learned today. The action was taken in line with demands by Solid Fuels Administrator Ickes for release of 30,000 men to stave off what Ickes said might be a "disastrous" fuel year.

The SFA has instructed mine operators to supply by tomorrow the serial numbers and the branch of service of their employes now in uniform. Earlier they had sought the names of the men. Ickes said release of the miners is necessary if coal is to be shipped to Europe and he has emphasized his belief that coal is needed in Europe to prevent "anarchy." Of the goal of 6,000,000 tons for overseas shipment, at least 700,000 tons is on its way.

CHERRY TREE BLOOMS

A cherry tree is in bloom for the second time this year in the yard at the home of Mrs. Edward Staley, Ironville.

Faint Idea of New Bomb

NEW YORK, Aug. 6—(AP)—A faint idea of the power within the atomic bomb: On June 6, 1917, a munitions ship blew up in a collision in Halifax, N. S., harbor; 1,500 persons were killed, 4,000 injured, 20,000 made homeless, two and one-half square miles of the city devastated.

That munitions ship carried 3,000 tons of TNT—about one-seventh of the equivalent of the new bomb.

WASHINGTON, Aug. 6—(AP)—The atomic bomb packs a punch equivalent to that normally delivered by 2,000 B29s.

The President said the missile has an explosive force equal to 20,000 tons—40,000,000 pounds—of TNT. Assuming a B29 carried a bomb load of 10 tons of TNT, four 500-plane raids by the world's biggest bombers would be necessary to equal in destructive power the exploding fury of one atomic bomb.

The atomic bomb dwarfs by 2,000 times the blast power of the British "grand slam"

WEATHER
Eastern Pennsylvania: Sunny And Pleasant With Moderate Temperatures And Rather Low Humidity Thursday And Friday, Clear And Cool Thursday Night.

Intelligencer Journal.

The Leading Newspaper in the Garden Spot of America, Home Owned for Home Folks Since 1794

ATOMIC BOMBS
May Win the War
But Your Waste
PAPER IS NEEDED
To Ship Supplies
OVERSEAS

152nd Year.—No. 46. | Entered as second class matter August 9, 1944 at the Post Office at Lancaster, Pa., under the Act of March 3, 1879. Reg. U. S. Pat. Off. | LANCASTER, PA., THURSDAY MORNING, AUGUST 9, 1945 | CITY | EIGHTEEN PAGES. | 20c PER WEEK—4c Per Copy

RUSSIA OPENS WAR ON JAPAN

2ND ATOMIC BOMB DROPPED

HOT HAY FIRES BIG BARN NEAR GORDONVILLE

Ellis Denlinger Suffers Loss Of Between $15,000 And $20,000; Crops Destroyed

Alarge barn on the farm of H. E. Denlinger, Gordonville R1, together with all of the season's crops, was completely destroyed about 10 p. m. Wednesday night. The loss was estimated at between $15,000 and $20,000, partially covered by insurance, by Ellis Denlinger, son of the owner. Combustion of hot hay was given as the cause of the blaze.

Besides the barn itself, a 70 by 90-foot structure, five calves, 700 bales (12 tons) of straw, 13 acres of hay, 420 bushels of wheat, two silos, a corn planter and a hay rake and loader were destroyed. Firemen saved a $3,000 incubator of 10,000-egg capacity.

Wednesday afternoon Denlinger smelled hot hay and upon investigation, thought it was dangerous. The family kept some watch on the hay, but about 10 p. m. the hay mow suddenly burst into flames.

6 FIRE COMPANIES CALLED

Denlinger summoned the Intercourse Fire Company. Other fire companies responding were: Paradise, Gap, Gordonville, Bird-in-Hand, Kinzer and Lafayette. Water was pumped out of a cistern into a relay tank at the house and 300 feet of hose was laid to the Pequea Creek for water supply.

Four calves were saved by Ellis Denlinger, son of the owner, and cows and horses were turned into the meadow. A tractor was saved, also.

Amos Brackbill, assistant chief of the Intercourse Fire Company, said that his firemen would stay all night at the scene of the fire in case the wind would get up and blow the sparks toward the house and garage. The latter building was saved by the firemen, although it is only 10 feet from the barn.

"We Lead All The Rest"

FARM CORNER

By The Farm Editor

1,000 AT FARMERS' FIELD DAY MEETING

Miles Horst, state secretary of agriculture, Dr. E. L. Nixon and Dr. I. O. Pepper, of State College, and F. S. Bucher, county farm agent, lead the discussions following the demonstrations and display at the Farmers' Field Day on the H. H. Haverstick farm Wednesday afternoon.

Attendance was estimated at over a thousand.

New ideas in farm machinery some representing inventions of Lancaster County farmers, and a display of a wide variety of implements kept the attention of all in attendance.

COW TEST REPORTS

The Garden Spot Cow Testing Association reported 104 cows in milk for the month of July and nineteen dry, with 63 producing over 1000 pounds of milk, and 36 producing over forty pounds of butterfat. Four cows each produced over a ton of milk during the month, two in the herd of Warren L. Eby, and one each in the

More of FARM CORNER on Page 6

Weather Calendar

COMPARATIVE TEMPERATURES

Station	High	Low
Water Works	81	56
Ephrata	78	58
Official High for Year, June 30		97
Official Low for Year, Jan. 25		—1
Character of Day		Clear

SUN
Rises—6:09 a. m. Sets—8:09 p. m.

MOON
Sets—9:31 p. m. First Quarter, Aug. 15

STARS
Morning—Mars-Venus-Saturn
Evening—Jupiter-Mercury

NEARBY FORECASTS
Maryland, Delaware, New Jersey: Sunny and pleasant with moderate temperatures and rather low humidity Thursday and Friday; clear and cool Thursday night.

SAVE THIS NEWSPAPER
Make this newspaper do double work — give it to your paper-salvage drive.

Nagasaki Target Of Missile, Spaatz Reveals At Guam

Crew Members Radio That Results Were Good; Japs Say Dead At Hiroshima "Are Too Numerous To Be Counted"

Guam (Thursday)—(AP)—Nagasaki was attacked with the world's second atomic bomb at noon today.

Crew members reported good results. No further details will be available until the mission returns, General Spaatz announced in a special communique.

The first atomic bomb fell on Hiroshima Monday and wiped out 60 per cent of that city of 343,000.

Nagasaki, Japan's 12th largest city, is on Kyushu. It was raided first by B-29s on Aug. 10 last year and was hit only July 31 and again next day by Far East Air Force bombers and fighters from Okinawa.

This was the first time it was attacked by Marianas-based B-29s.

Nagasaki, although only two-thirds as large as Hiroshima in population, is considered more important industrially. With a population now estimated at 255,000, its 12 square miles are jam-packed with eave to eave buildings which won it the name of "Sea of Roofs."

It was vitally important as a port for trans-shipment of military supplies and the embarkation of troops in support of Japan's operations in China, Formosa, Southeast Asia and the Southwest Pacific. It was highly important as a major shipbuilding and repair center for both naval and merchantmen.

The city also included industrial suburbs of Inase and Akunoura on the western side of the harbor and Urakami. The combined area is nearly double Hiroshima's.

Japs Report Horror Scenes In Hiroshima

San Francisco—(AP)—Destruction of "practically all living things" in atom shattered Hiroshima, city of 343,000, was reported by Japan Wednesday in broadcasts picturing such confusion that a definite check on casualties was impossible.

Persons outdoors were "burned to death while those indoors were killed by the indescribable pressure and heat" generated by the atomic bomb dropped on the city in Monday's historic raid, one broadcast said.

While "authorized quarters" charged America with violation of International Law in using the bomb, a special meeting of government officials considered a report on the "disastrous ruin" that befell Hiroshima.

Tokyo's reports, monitored by the FCC, said of the stricken city: "Practically all living things,

More of BOMB on Page 6

AUTO BREAKS DOWN LIGHT STANDARD ON WEST KING STREET

Driver Slightly Hurt But Four Companions Escape Injury In Crash

The driver of an automobile which tore down a street light standard at 44 W. King St., was slightly hurt while her four companions escaped injury at 10 p. m. Wednesday. The accident attracted several hundred persons as sparks from several electric wires sputtered and city firemen were called to the scene by police.

The driver, Elizabeth Gerlach, twenty-five, 630 N. Market St., suffered a nose bleed, according to attendants at the Lancaster General Hospital where she was taken by police. The woman refused to be admitted to the hospital for observation, and signed her own release, attendants said.

City Policeman John Ehleiter, who witnessed the accident, said the woman was driving south on Prince Street and while making a left turn to go east on King Street, stalled the motor of her car in the intersection. She started the motor and proceeded east on King Street, suddenly running over the curb on the south side and striking the lamp post.

The automobile knocked the post to the pavement, and then ran over the prone pole. Policeman Ehleiter, who assisted the in-

More of ACCIDENTS on Page 6

REGISTRATION BOOKS CLOSE SEPTEMBER 17

The registration books at the Court House will be closed Monday, September 17, instead of Saturday, October 6, it became known Wednesday.

The State Democratic committee called attention to the change in a letter from Harrisburg telling of an amendment to the registration law enacted at the recent session of the legislature.

Previously the books closed 30 days before an election. Under the new law, they will close 50 days before an election.

RECAPTURE ESCAPED POW AT HIGHSPIRE

Middletown, Pa. —(AP)— Joseph Mohr, twenty-two, a German prisoner of war, was recaptured Wednesday night at nearby Highspire by a civilian worker at the Middletown Air Technical Service Command depot.

Army authorities said Ray L. Kennedy, the worker, found Mohr in a field back of his home. Mohr escaped from a box reclamation plant opposite the depot Tuesday afternoon.

Kennedy and a neighbor turned Mohr over to Army authorities at the depot.

Master Plan For Mass Trial Of German War Criminals Approved

London—(AP)—A master plan for the mass trial of Germany's arch war criminals before an international military tribunal was signed Wednesday by the legal representatives of the United States, Great Britain, Russian and France.

The historic document, setting legal and military precedents, gives the high tribunal sweeping powers to punish by death, deprive the convicted of stolen property, disregard "technical rules of evidence" in the interests of speed and take strict measures to prevent delays.

Under the agreement the permanent seat of the tribunal is to be established in Berlin, but the first trial will be held at Nuernberg, long the seat and meeting place of the Nazi party.

The tribunal itself is to consist of four members, each with an alternate, representing the four big powers. Before this body will be arraigned such Nazi bigwigs as Reichsmarshal Hermann Goering, former Foreign Minister von Rib-

More of WAR TRIALS on Page 13

Red Move Completes Ring About Japs

Map locates Russian territory (shaded areas) bordering Japan and Jap-held areas on the north as Soviet declaration of war on Japan Wednesday completed the Allied ring around the Japs. Distance is from Vladivostok area bases to Tokyo, now under threat from the north as well as the south. Black areas are Jap-held. (AP Wirephoto.)

Third Fleet, British Carrier Planes Smack Japan's Main Home Island In Heavy Attack

(By The Associated Press)

As Russia threw its mighty strength into the fight against Japan today, the U. S. Third Fleet and British carrier aircraft punctuated the Soviets' war declaration with a heavy dawn attack on northern Honshu, Nippon's main home island.

Admiral Nimitz said the attacks on northern Honshu shipping, inland installations and other targets by planes of Admiral Halsey's Third Fleet and British carrier aircraft — "are continuing now," but he did not name specific land points hit.

It was a return engagement of the powerful Allied naval force which had pounded Japan's ships and shores from July 10 to 31, before retiring under threat of a typhoon.

OTHER AIR ATTACKS

Nimitz also announced Army and Navy plane attacks Wednesday in the Kuriles, including the Kataoka naval base on Shimushu, and on the same day a U. S. battleship and smaller units bombarded Japanese antiaircraft emplacements, ammunition dumps and buildings on Wake.

Nipponese shipping totaling 5,500 tons was sunk or damaged by U. S. Navy Privateer aircraft in Tsushimu Straits, between Korea and Japan, and off Honshu.

Marianas-based Superforts pounded four Japanese mainland target cities Wednesday, and General MacArthur announced Thursday that American and Allied planes in more than 400 sorties Sunday and Monday sank or damaged 59 more Nipponese vessels.

The aerial attacks announced by MacArthur took far east Air Forces and other Allied planes from Korea to Malaya and the East Indies. Only four Japanese planes rose in any interception efforts, and all were shot down.

In other attacks of the day more than 50 Superforts struck the Nakajima Musinotama aircraft plant in the Tokyo area while a smaller force simultaneously bombed the Tokyo arsenal. More than 100 B-29s on another mission hit Fukuyama, chemical and aircraft parts producing center 42 miles north-

More of FLEET on Page 6

WALLET, $80 STOLEN

Jesse L. Fisher, Ronks R1, reported to State Police the theft of his wallet, containing $80 in cash and his "A" gasoline ration book Wednesday. The theft occurred at Haverstick's Garden Spot farm, Lincoln Highway west, where Fisher was working. He told police he had changed clothing before starting to work, and left the wallet in his trousers, which he placed in the tobacco barn. The theft occurred between noon and 5 p. m.

SAILOR AND FLIER DECLARED DEAD; MARINE WOUNDED

Death Of Paul B. Martin And Earl F. Flick Verified; Dale E. Wilkinson Wounded

WAR CASUALTIES

Combat casualties reported Wednesday among Lancaster county men in the armed forces:

KILLED

Paul B. Martin, fireman first class, 530 E. Ross St., in the Pacific area. Previously reported missing.

Staff Sgt. Earl F. Flick, Columbia, over Germany. Previously reported missing.

WOUNDED

Pfc. Dale E. Wilkinson, Maytown, on Okinawa.

Two Lancaster county service men, one a sailor and the other a flier, previously reported missing in action, were declared killed according to word recieved by their families. In addition, a Maytown marine was listed as wounded on Okinawa.

Paul B. Martin, fireman first class, son of Mr. and Mrs. Clayton R. Martin, 530 E. Ross St., who was reported missing in action in May, 1942, was killed June 3, 1942, according to a Navy Department telegram received by his parents.

Paul B. Martin

The 19-year-old sailor was serving aboard the gunboat Tulsa in the Manila Bay area. He was one of the first Lancaster men to be reported missing in action. He enlisted at the age of eighteen, and served in Hawaii before being transferred to the gunboat in August, 1941. No explanation for the long delay was given by the Navy Department, but the telegram stated that his death

More of SAILOR on Page 13

PACIFIC FLEET TO GIVE RUSSIA FULL ASSISTANCE

Guam, (Thursday) — (AP) — The United States Pacific Fleet will give full assistance to the Russian effort against Japan, Admiral Nimitz said today in welcoming entry of the Soviets into the war. The commander-in-chief of the Pacific Fleet issued a statement.

Nimitz had been awakened during Wednesday night to be informed of the momentous news.

"We welcome Russia as a powerful partner in the war against Japan," the admiral said.

"Russia's brave and battle-tested armies, in the advantageously geopraphical position which they held in relation to Japan, arrayed with the already overwhelming force of other United Nations, will help hasten defeat of the Japanese.

"The Pacific Fleet will in turn give assistance to the Russian effort."

AMERICA COUNTS ON EARLY DOOM OF ENEMY IN PACIFIC

Byrnes Says "But Little Time" Remains For Japs, Truman Reveals Red Declaration

Washington—(AP)—Mighty Russia, battle-toughened in victory over Germany, went to war Wednesday night against Axis Japan.

America and her Allies applauded, and counted on the early doom of the enemy of the Pacific.

Russia declared war at the request of the United States, Britain,

More of AMERICA on Page 6

WGAL TO CARRY REPORT OF PRESIDENT TRUMAN

Washington — (AP) — President Truman will report to the nation Thursday night in a 30-minute address at 10 p. m. Eastern War Time over all radio networks. The address was expected originally to cover primarily Potsdam conference results. Now it is deemed likely the President will give a full appraisal of revised conditions growing out of Russia's war declaration.

The address will be carried by Radio Station WGAL.

Attack On Eastern Manchukuo Border Reported By Tokyo

Russian Aircraft Start Bombing Jap Targets; Molotov Discloses Action Against Nipponese To Speed "Universal Peace"

New York—(AP)—The Tokyo radio said Wednesday night that the Soviet Army suddenly launched an attack against Japanese forces on the eastern Soviet Manchukuo border early Thursday morning, Japanese time.

According to a communique released by Kwantung Army headquarters at 3:30 a. m. Thursday, Japanese time, the broadcast said, the Soviet Army suddenly opened the attack against Japanese forces with its ground forces.

Simultaneously, the broadcast said the communique added, a small number of Soviet aircraft started bombing attacks on Manchukuo territory.

There was no indication of the exact location of the attacks.

The eastern border of the Jap puppet territory lies within about thirty airline miles, at the nearest point, of the great Soviet Pacific base at Vladivostok. The eastern Manchukuo border area also includes the Changkufeng area, near the northern tip of Korea, where the Jap Kwantung army was defeated in a "vest pocket" undeclared war with Soviet Far Eastern forces before the war in Europe began.

Molotov Says Nation Went To War As Loyal Duty To Her Allies

Moscow—(AP)—Long columns of singing Red Army men tramped through the heart of Moscow Thursday, 45 minutes after the Soviet radio announced to the people of Russia that the nation would be at war with Japan at one second after midnight.

People piled out of buildings and apartments to cheer the marching soldiers of the Red Army, whose force was being turned against the Japanese, the Soviet government said, at the request of the Allies to speed "universal peace."

Foreign Commissar Vyacheslav Molotov disclosed that Emperor Hirohito had asked the Soviet Union to mediate "about mid-July" in the war in the Pacific, but added that Tokyo's rejection of the Potsdam unconditional surrender ultimatum caused the proposals to "lose all significance."

Molotov said the Emperor's request was transmitted through a special Japanese mission in the Soviet capital.

The Foreign Commissar said President Truman, Winston Churchill, then Prime Minister, and Clement Attlee, who succeeded Churchill, had been informed.

A high foreign diplomatic source said Wednesday night this was one of two such moves the Japanese had made.

The streets of Moscow were fairly full of civilians and soldiers when the news broke, but many citizens chose to stick close by their radios in anticipation of word of the first action by Soviet forces against the enemy in the Pacific.

Russia gave the Japanese seven hours warning she meant to strike. Molotov handed Russia's declaration of war to Japanese Ambassador to Russia, Naotake Sato, at 5 p. m., Russian time. Three hours later, the Moscow radio broadcast the news to the world, and at 8:30 p. m., Molotov called in correspondents.

IN JOVIAL MOOD

In a jovial mood, he leaned across a birch table, lighted up a long Russian cigarette and made his announcement. He was perfectly informal as he asked permission to read the text of the declaration.

Russia went to war as her "loyal allied duty" after she was asked to do so by the United States, Britain and China and had rejected Tokyo's suggestions she mediate the war, Molotov said.

Immediately Russia made her decision the Ambassadors of the three great Allied countries warring with the Japanese were informed. They expressed "satisfaction."

Molotov had summoned Japanese Envoy Sato to the Kremlin and read him the declaration of war, which Sato was to relay to Tokyo. The declaration said Russia would

More of RUSSIAN on Page 6

KURILES VOLCANO REPORTED ERUPTING

Adak, Aleutians—(AP)—Long dormant Chikura Dake volcano on Paramushiro in Japan's Kurile islands was reported by Army and Navy pilots Wednesday to be erupting 20,000 feet in the air.

The mile-high peak is three miles from Kakumbatsu airfield on Paramushiro and within 15 miles of two other airfields, but the pilots did not disclose whether lava was rolling down on any of the enemy installations.

There are two other volcanoes on the island, one of which is active.

EXTRA!! **Intelligencer Journal.** EXTRA!!

The Leading Newspaper in the Garden Spot of America, Home Owned for Home Folks Since 1794

152nd Year.—No. 51. Entered as second class matter August 9, 1944 at the Post Office at Lancaster, Pa., under the Act of March 3, 1879. Reg. U. S. Pat. Off. LANCASTER, PA., WEDNESDAY MORNING, AUGUST 15, 1945. FOUR PAGES. 20c PER WEEK—4c Per Copy

JAPAN QUITS!

Washington—(AP)—President Truman announced at 7:00 P. M. EWT Tuesday night Japanese acceptance of surrender terms.

They will be accepted by General Douglas MacArthur when arrangements can be completed.

Mr. Truman read the formal message relayed from Emperor Hirohito through the Swiss government in which the Japanese ruler pledged the surrender on the terms laid down by the Big Three Conference at Potsdam.

ISSUES STATEMENT

President Truman made this statement:

"I have received this afternoon a message from the Japanese government in reply to the message forwarded to that government by the Secretary of State on August 11.

"I deem this reply a full acceptance of the Potsdam declaration which specifies the unconditional surrender of Japan.

"In this reply there is no qualification.

"Arrangements are now being made for the formal signing of surrender terms at the earliest possible moment.

"General Douglas MacArthur has been appointed the Supreme Allied Commander to receive the Japanese surrender.

"Great Britain, Russia and China will be represented by high ranking officers.

"Meantime, the Allied armed forces have been ordered to suspend offensive action.

"The proclamation of V-J Day must wait terms by Japan."

Simultaneously Mr. Truman disclosed that Selective Service is taking immediate steps to slash inductions from 80,000 to 50,000 a month.

Henceforth, Mr. Truman said, only those men under 26 will be drafted for the reduced quotas.

The White House made public the Japanese government's message accepting that ended the war which started December 7, 1941.

The text of their message which was delivered by the Swiss Charge d'Affaires follows:

"Communication of the Japanese government of August 14, 1945, addressed to the governments of the United States, Great Britain, the Soviet Union, and China:

"With reference to the Japanese government's note of August 10 regarding their acceptance of the provisions of the Potsdam declaration and the reply of the governments of the United States, Great Britain, the Soviet Union and China sent by American Secretary of State Byrnes under the date of August 11, the Japanese government have the honor to communicate to the governments of the four powers as follows:

"1. His Majesty the Emperor has issued an imperial rescript regarding Japan's acceptance of the provisions of the Potsdam declaration.

"2. His Majesty the Emperor is prepared to authorize and insure the signature by his government and the imperial general headquarters of necessary terms for carrying out the provisions of the Potsdam declaration. His Majesty is also prepared to issue his commands to all military, naval, and air authorities of Japan and all the forces under their control wherever located to cease active operations, to surrender arms, and to issue such other orders as may be required by the Supreme Commander of the Allied forces for the execution of the above mentioned terms."

The President made the historic announcement to a huge crowd of reporters who had been virtually living in the White House for days in anticipation of just such a development.

PRESIDENT SMILING

Smiling and surrounded by his staff, the President told the press that the Japanese had decided to accept unconditional surrender and mentioned that the reporters would not have to take any notes.

Mr. Truman said prepared statements would be available as they left and three were issued, one detailing MacArthur's appointment and containing the Japanese note, a second disclosing the immediate cutback in the draft and the third in which Mr. Truman congratulated "one of the hardest working groups of war workers"—the federal employees who were on the job for the past four years.

The President said they were entitled to a holiday Wednesday and Thursday with pay and only skeleton forces would be maintained.

Literally beaming with pleasure, close associates of the President around his desk when the announcement was made included Admiral of the Fleet William D. Leahy, personal Chief of Staff; Secretary of State Byrnes, Commodore James Vardaman, the President's Naval Aide; Brig. Gen. Harry Vaughan, his Military Aide; Secretary of the Navy James V. Forrestal; Secretary of the Treasury Fred M. Vinson; Leo T. Crowley, Foreign Economic Administrator; David K. Niles, special assistant; Maj. Gen. Philip B. Fleming, Public Works Administrator; Mathew Connelly, private secretary.

Byrnes, who played a major part in working out the surrender, sat at the President's right.

Newsreel cameras buzzed to record the momentous occasion, and flashlight bulbs flickered.

Attlee, Moscow Radio Announce Surrender Of Japanese

London (Wednesday) — (AP) — Prime Minister Attlee announced Japan had surrendered.

London (Wednesday) — (AP) — The Moscow radio announced at midnight (7 p. m. EWT) the unconditional surrender of Japan.

Orders Taprooms Closed

Harrisburg—(AP)—Governor Edward Martin Tuesday night ordered the immediate closing of all State Liquor Stores and licensed establishments under the Board's supervision until further notice with President Truman's announcement of the Japanese surrender. a

PREDICTS 5,000,000 TO LEAVE ARMY

Washington — (AP) — President Truman Tuesday night forecast that 5,000,000 to 5,500,000 men now in the Army may be returned to civilian life within the next 12 to 18 months.

To Receive Jap Surrender

General Douglas A. MacArthur has been designated supreme Allied commander to receive the surrender of the Japanese, President Truman announced tonight in Washington.

As Peace Week Began—To Be Ended Today With Prayers

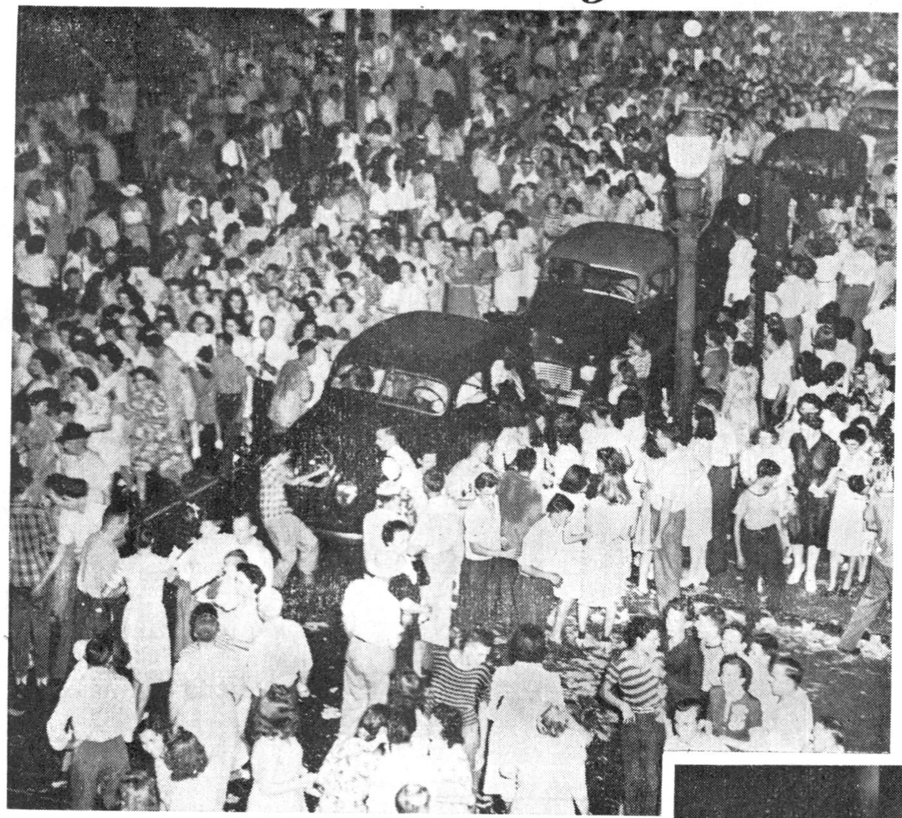

VICTORY WEEK rolled in on the yells of thousands as Lancaster crowded downtown streets for an all-night salute to the end of World War II.

CHURCH SERVICES were held all over the area, some previously prepared, others hurriedly assembled. They were a prelude to the services which will be held today, a Day of Prayer set aside by President Truman.

COUNTY TOWNS, like New Holland, held brief formal programs. This is a Community Prayer service sponsored by the borough churches and the American Legion, Tuesday night.

MIDSUMMER NIGHT'S DREAM of victory had its Puck. He was perched for hours on the forbidden precincts of a firebox, adding his shill whistle to the general discord of joy.

METROPOLITAN SNOW STORM over Penn Square in this picture, preceded the mounting roar as the hours went on. This photo and the one above will mark the historic moment for Lancaster families for years to come.

NOBODY EVER SAW HORNS of as many different noises and shapes, nor listened more eagerly. This trumpet had it all over the ordinary tin kind, with plenty of young lungpower behind it.

THIS ONE SPEAKS for itself, if prematurely. Other signs were equally expressive if hurriedly made.

LAST WAR-END JAMBOREE, if the charter makes good, gave Lancaster a chance to put in everything it had for past and future as thousands blew the lid off four years of pent up nerves. It was Hallowe'en, Christmas, July 4th and Thanksgiving all in one. It was three days of celebration as of 1918 all packed into one night in 1945.

ROCKETS RED GLARE put firey tinsel on the deep curtain of the night—and smoked up nobody knows how many faces. But who cared? Sparks dropped like Very flares under the wobbling sticks. It was a shower of golden good fortune—but hot!

BUT DON'T STOP NOW, we've still got to save tin and paper until we've been adjusted to peacetime production. Wind up your celebration by plunking those tin cans and paper packs in the salvage bin. It's still there, yawning and scrap-happy.

WEATHER

Eastern Pennsylvania: Some Cloudiness Wednesday And Thursday. Warmer Wednesday.

Intelligencer Journal.

The Leading Newspaper in the Garden Spot of America, Home Owned for Home Folks Since 1794

Are You Registered? Last Day September 15

152nd Year.—No. 63. Entered as second class matter August 8, 1944 at the Post Office at Lancaster, Pa., under the Act of March 3, 1879. Reg. U. S. Pat. Off. LANCASTER, PA., WEDNESDAY MORNING, AUGUST 29, 1945 CITY FOURTEEN PAGES. 20c PER WEEK—4c Per Copy

HALSEY IN TOKYO BAY ON MISSOURI

$40,000 FIRE AT STOCKYARDS HERE

Two Persons Hurt Fighting Blaze In East Cattle Pens

10 Fire Companies Battle Spectacular Blaze Which Destroys An Acre Of Sheds Used By PRR To Feed And Water Livestock In Transit

Two persons were injured fighting a brief but spectacular fire which swept a portion of the Union Stock Yards at 5:15 p. m. Tuesday, causing damage estimated by firemen at between $30,000 and $40,000.

Immediately after the fire, investigations were started by State Police, firemen and the Pennsylvania Railroad Company, owners of the property, into the cause of the blaze. Chief Elmer Lipp, of the Eden Fire Company said boys had been seen playing around the sheds a short time before the fire was discovered.

The injured were:

George Lander, forty-nine, 827 Reservoir St., of Company No. 3, this city, who was overcome by smoke. He was treated at the Lancaster General Hospital and after being detained an hour for observation was discharged.

Titus Denlinger, twenty-four, Ronks, R1, a spectator, who was assisting city firemen, was burned on the upper right arm when he fell against a hot iron side of a burning box car. He was treated in the same hospital.

The fire, occurring at the time stores and industrial plants were closing, attracted a huge crowd of spectators, as dense clouds of smoke billowed upwards from the burning sheds. State Police assisted city police in rerouting traffic from the vicinity and keeping the area cleared for firemen.

10 FIRE COMPANIES RESPOND

Three city companies and seven county companies responded to alarms sounded after the fire looked as though it might sweep across the tracks of the Pennsylvania Railroad and ignite the main portion of the stock yards.

The fire burned out a triangular section of sheds along the south side of the Pennsylvania Railroad Company main line east of the Lititz Pike. Four cattle cars were burned, five badly scorched and ten escaped damage from the flames. These cars were loaded with cattle for shipment when the fire started, but employes of the Union Stock Yards herded them from the cars and drove some of them into pens at the east end of the yards, out of reach of the flames, and the balance were driven through an underpass under the tracks to the main yards.

WOMAN DISCOVERED FIRE

The fire was discovered by Mrs. Laura Shimp 1053 Lititz Ave., who resides next to the yards. She said the fire was in the central part of the sheds, which cover approximately an acre of ground.

Before the arrival of firemen, the flames had gained considerable headway and, feeding on the creosote-soaked itmbers, had swept through the sheds, aided by a slight west wind. Employes of the yards saw the smoke about the time the alarm was sounded and drove the cattle from the cars to safety.

Assistant Chief Frank Deen and Pumper Companies No. 3 and 6 and Truck A, responded to the alarm. Chief Harry Miller, who was not on duty at the time, also responded.

Calls were sent for additional apparatus and firemen from Eden, the two Neffsville companies, Bird-in-Hand, Witmer, East Petersburg and the Lafayette Fire Company responded.

City firemen laid three pumper streams, using 2400 feet of hose,

More Of FIRE On Page 9

"We Lead All The Rest"

FARM CORNER

By The Farm Editor

BRIGHTER OUTLOOK FOR TOBACCO CROP AFTER LATE START

County Growers See Prospects Of First Class Harvest Despite "Breaks"

Despite a late start, due to an acute shortage of plants in early Spring and weeks of wet weather which followed after the crop was once started in late May and June, prospects of a first class quality crop of Lancaster county tobacco this year have greatly improved recently, tobacco men said Tuesday.

The Lancaster County Tobacco Growers' Cooperative association this week sent five experienced tobacco men into the field to check conditions and their first reports are the 1945 crop looks "much better" since the rain Saturday night, which followed two weeks of sunshine.

A long drawn out season of tobacco cutting is seen, however, as a result of the variable growing weather and widely separated planting dates. A few growers started cutting tobacco here as

More Of FARM CORNER On Page 9

Weather Calendar

COMPARATIVE TEMPERATURES

Station	High	Low
Water Works	76	49
Ephrata	88	52
Last Year (Ephrata)	78	50
Official High for Year, June 30		97
Official Low for Year, Jan. 25		—1
Character of Day		Clear

SUN

Rises—6:28 a. m. Sets—7:41 p. m.

MOON

Rises—11:48 Last Quarter Aug. 29

STARS

Morning—Mars, Venus, Saturn.
Evening—Jupiter, Mercury.

NEARBY FORECASTS

New Jersey: Some cloudiness Wednesday and Thursday. Warmer Wednesday.

Maryland and Delaware: Fair Wednesday and Thursday. A little warmer Wednesday.

EXTENDED WEATHER FORECAST

Extended forecast for period Wednesday through Sunday: Fair except scattered showers Thursday over northern section, and Thursday night or Friday over southern section; rising temperature followed by cooler Thursday over north portion and on Friday over south portion.

SAVE THIS NEWSPAPER

Make this newspaper do double work — give it to your paper-salvage drive.

WOMAN FATALLY BURNED AS APRON CATCHES FIRE

Mrs. Elizabeth Breneman, 66, Landisville, Dies In Hospital Here

Burns sustained when her apron caught fire while making jelly at her home at Landisville Tuesday morning, caused the death of Mrs. Elizabeth Breneman, sixty-six, at St. Joseph's Hospital, at 4:30 p. m. Tuesday.

The Landisville woman, wife of Amos Breneman, was alone in the kitchen at her home about 8:30 a. m., when the accident occurred. Just a few minutes before, her daughter, Mrs. Elmer Leaman, who was working in the kitchen with her, had gone outdoors to buy meat from Robert Edwards, a meat dealer.

The first intimation of the trag-

More Of WOMAN On Page 9

Furloughed Vet Finds Fishing Here Is Still Fine

Sgt. Harry Carson, just back from the battlefields of Europe, found the fishing as good if not better than ever before.

Fishing at the Safe Harbor dam, the sergeant landed a six-pound salmon that measured 25 and a quarter inches.

What is more, he took his limit of salmon—six.

The bait was minnows.

Sergeant Carson is spending a 30-day furlough at home. He lives at 427 N. Cherry St.

Columns Of Smoke Billow Upward At Stockyards

A spectacular photograph taken at the height of the fire which destroyed the east yard at the Union Stock Yards, Lititz Pike, shows the clouds of smoke and flame which attracted hundreds of persons to the scene of the blaze Tuesday afternoon. The photograph, taken from the Lititz Pike bridge, looking southeast, shows the fire as it burned away the pens in a triangular section on the south side of the Pennsylvania Railroad tracks. In the foreground can be seen the main line tracks of the Pennsylvania Railroad, with the ties smouldering. The cattle in cars along the loading platform in left foreground had been removed to a place of safety. (Photo by Alfred Weaver)

Charred embers and damaged cattle cars are all that remain after firemen extinguished flames which gutted a triangular section of pens of the East Yards of the Union Stock Yards, Tuesday afternoon. The above view, taken from the Lititz Pike Bridge, looking east, reveals the extent of the damage caused by the brief fire which, feeding on creosote-soaked timbers, completely gutted the pens. On both sides of the pens can be seen the livestock cars damaged by the flames. These cars were filled with cattle when the fire was first discovered, but the animals were driven to safety by stock yard employes before they were injured. (Intell Photo)

ELEVEN SHIPS DUE WITH 10,596 MEN FROM ETO TODAY

Eleven transports are scheduled to arrive at three east coast ports Wednesday with a total of 10,596 troops from the European Theater of Operations.

Seven of the vessels are headed towards New York with 6,951 men, three to Boston with 3,544 and one to Newport News, Va., with 101.

LANCASTRIANS ABOARD

Among Lancastrians scheduled to be on their way home are:

Aboard the New York City Victory, due Wednesday at New York: Pfc. Paul L. Hoover, Lancaster. Technician Fourth Grade Victor E. Wissler, Lancaster.

More Of REDEPLOYMENT Page 9

Job Opportunities Here Still Varied And Plentiful

(By CHARLES W. FITZKEE)

Job opportunities in the Lancaster county area are as plentiful and as varied as they were before the surrender of Japan two weeks ago, and new openings are being announced faster than applicants for them can be found.

The strange situation of jobs going begging while an estimated 3,700 Lancaster county men and women were laid off due to cancellation of war contracts was revealed Tuesday in an independent survey.

The figures stack up in this fashion: The War Manpower Commission estimates that 3,700 men

More Of JOB On Page 9

275 Additional Jobs Created At Armstrong Cork

The Armstrong Cork Company announced Tuesday that 275 additional jobs had been created at the floor plant of the company through increases in usage quotas of linseed oil and rosin granted by government agencies since the surrender of Japan.

When the surrender of Japan

More of 275 on Page 9

POINT SYSTEM OF ARMY REVISED TO SPEED DISCHARGES

Washington —(AP)— The Army reported Tuesday it was revising its point system to speed up discharges and would reduce its strength from 8,000,000 to 2,500,000 men by next July 1.

War Department officials, testifying before the House Military committee, nevertheless supported President Truman's proposal to keep on drafting men for military service. They made no specific mention however, of the Chief Executive's suggestion that only men 18 to 25 years old be drafted, for terms limited to two years.

During their appearance before

More Of POINT On Page 9

MacArthur Flying North From Manila For Entry Thursday

With Admiral Halsey Off Yokohama (Wednesday)—(AP)—Big warships of the Third Fleet, headed by Halsey's flagship, the Missouri, anchored today off Yokohama—bomb-shattered port of Tokyo.

In the distance appeared the shapes of buildings which presumably were those of Tokyo itself, approximately 20 miles from the anchorages by the large ships.

Manila (Wednesday)—(AP)—Powerful warships of the Third Fleet led by Admiral Halsey aboard the 45,000 ton battleship Missouri began a triumphal penetration of Tokyo Bay today as General MacArthur flew north from Manila for his entry into Japan Thursday.

The Missouri was followed by another 45,000-ton battleship the Iowa, Admiral Nimitz' flagship, the battleship South Dakota, and the British battleship Duke of York to pave the way for the landing of 10,000 Marines and Blue Jackets tomorrow at Yokosuka.

(Norman Paige, American Broadcasting Company correspondent, said the Yokosuka landings were scheduled for 10 a. m. Thursday—9 p. m. Wednesday Eastern War Time).)

The mighty display of American naval power, moving through Uraga strait into the bay, occurred as the United States flag flew for the first time in victory over conquered Nippon—within 18 miles of the Emperor's palace in Tokyo.

Followed by other warships, Halsey rode the battlewagon into the bay at 7:08 a. m. (6:08 p. m. Tuesday Eastern War Time) as great sea and airborne forces were poised for large scale occupation landings, backed by warships massing from as far away as the Aleutians.

General MacArthur left Manila today by plane for Okinawa on his way to his triumphal entry of Japan.

MASTER PLAN

The unfolding of his master plan for the powerful occupation pointed toward the historic surrender signing Sept. 2 aboard the battleship Missouri in Tokyo Bay.

Airborne troops raised the Stars and Stripes at Atsugi airfield, southwest of Tokyo, which they are preparing for the arrival Thursday of MacArthur and thousands of troops in air transports from Okinawa.

While Third Fleet units rode at anchor in Tokyo Bay, a pending

More Of SURRENDER On Page 9

300 SURVIVORS OF OLD HEAVY CRUISER HOUSTON LOCATED

American Officer Declares Group Held In Japanese Prison Camp

Washington —(AP)— An American officer brought word out of Thailand jungles Tuesday that some 300 survivors of the old heavy cruiser Houston, which vanished in 1942, are in a Japanese prison camp.

The Houston was part of an Allied naval force that tried to halt Japan's march through the Pacific islands and took a licking in the battle of the Java Sea on Feb. 27, 1942. The cruiser disappeared the next night while trying to run Soenda Strait, between Java and Sumatra.

OFFICIAL REPORT

The first official report that some of her crew had been picked up came Tuesday from Lt. Col. Nicol Smith, who operated with underground forces in Thailand for the Office of Strategic Services. The number of survivors is approximate, Smith said, but "anyone having relatives on the crew of the

More Of 300 On Page 9

FISHERMEN FINED FOR BAIT VIOLATIONS

Two fishermen who ran afoul of the law in dipping bait fish were fined $10 and costs each Tuesday.

They are Frank Kendig, 234 Coral St., and G. H. Reisinger, 258 N. 3rd St., Columbia.

Fish Warden Robert Greener charged Kendig with having 106 bait fish when the law allows only 35 to a fisherman.

He charged that Reisinger used suckers, which he caught in a net, for bait fish.

The charges were preferred before Alderman J. Edward Wetzel.

WAINWRIGHT WILL WITNESS FORMAL JAPS' SURRENDER

U. S. Hero Imprisoned By Japs Since Corregidor Accepts M'Arthur Invitation

Manila (Wednesday) —(AP)— Lt. Gen. Jonathan Wainwright, American hero imprisoned by the Japanese since he surrendered Corregidor, today accepted an invitation of General MacArthur to witness Japan's formal surrender in Tokyo Bay Sunday.

The presence of Wainwright aboard the battleship Missouri in Tokyo bay for the ceremony would offer a dramatic contrast to his grim experience in being forced to sign the capitulation of American forces in the Philippines early in 1942.

The invitation also was extended to Wainwright's chief of staff, Brig. Gen. Lewis C. Beebe, aides, Lt. Col. John Pugh and Maj. Thomas Dooley, and orderly and chauffeur, Sgt. John Carroll. All were captured with the General at Corregidor.

MacArthur said he also hoped the British commander who signed the surrender at Singapore could be present.

The supreme commander of the

More Of WAINWRIGHT On Page 9

VACANCIES IN FIRE DEPT. REACH 19

The number of vacancies in the City Fire Department will reach 19 Saturday when the resignation of William Ansel, 531 Green St., becomes effective.

Of the 19, eight are reported by city officials to be men in the armed forces whose places are being kept for them. A civil service list of aspirants for jobs who have passed all mental and physical tests, as well as other qualifications, has not yet been acted upon, it was said Tuesday.

Commissioner Frank J. Sekinger Tuesday asked Council to approve the resignation of Ansel who plans to enter business. The resignation was accepted. A member of the department for seven years, he was stationed at Station 3, E. King St.

Council also adopted the resolution introduced two weeks ago by Commissioner E. W. Bowman to remove from the City Plan an unopened alley running from Schuylkill to Delaware Sts. between S. Marshall and S. Franklin Sts. The land is part of the Riverview Cemetery.

FREE ADS TO HELP VETS SECURE JOBS

Service men with medical or honorable discharges, seeking positions may place a 7-time Want-ad in the Help Offered columns of the Lancaster Newspapers. This service is extended by the newspapers to facilitate readjustment of servicemen to civilian life.

The Weather
Eastern Pennsylvania: Partly Cloudy And Cooler With Scattered Afternoon Showers Sunday; Monday Fair And Cool.

SUNDAY NEWS

3 A. M. Edition
The Sunday News carries the full report of world wide news services—LATEST NEWS by Associated Press, International News Service and Complete Local News.

VOL. 22—NO. 51 | Entered as second class matter September 21, 1923 at the Post Office at Lancaster Pa., under the Act of March 3, 1879. | LANCASTER, PA., SUNDAY, SEPTEMBER 2, 1945 | 30 PAGES—230 COLUMNS—EIGHT CENTS

JAPS SIGN SURRENDER; TODAY SET AS V-J DAY

Strike Seen Halting Buses For Weekend

Union Spokesman Says No Action Possible Before Tuesday; Streets Bare of Public Conveyances

Lancaster's streets were still bare of public buses and trolleys Saturday night with no action on the situation possible before Tuesday, according to a spokesman for 200 striking operators.

The spokesman, Anthony Flick, secretary of Local 1241, Amalgamated Association of Street, Electric Railway, and Motor Coach Employes (AFL), said that is the earliest officials could be reassembled for possible negotiations.

He emphasized, however, that the union was "sitting tight" and the first step "will have to be made by the Conestoga Transportation Co."

Hold Progress Meeting

Flick reported that a meeting held at 4 p. m. Saturday by members of the union "was of no major importance" and that its purpose was merely to receive a progress report on the strike.

The union voted its work stoppage after the company refused to agree to a contract which would contain a "perpetual" clause.

The union wants a contract, which, it claims, will do away the necessity of renewal each year and permit negotiation on specific clauses without terminating the entire contract.

The company has stated that it cannot grant a contract which would have the essence of "recognizing the existing employe union for all time, regardless of changing employe preferences and company conditions."

Downtown Traffic Drops

As Lancaster apparently headed toward a "busless and trolleyless" Labor Day, effects of the transportation halt felt here all day Sat-

STRIKE—Page 7

Truman Hails New Security

Text on Page 14

Washington, Sept. 1—(INS)—President Truman tonight proclaimed tomorrow V-J Day to signalize victory of liberty over tyranny and retribution for the infamy of Pearl Harbor.

The President addressed the world from the White House by radio. His triumphant speech was part of a program in which America's war chiefs who accepted Japan's unconditional surrender aboard the 45,000-ton battleship Missouri in Tokyo bay also participated.

Sees New Security

Mr. Truman said that from this day of supreme American victory the nation must move forward to a "new era of security at home," and keep faith with her heroic battle dead to build a better world of peace and happiness.

Sternly he warned that the United States never would forget the Japanese sneak attack on Pearl Harbor. He asserted that "the evil done by the Japanese war lords can never be repaired or forgotten."

"But," the President said, "their power to destroy and kill has been taken from them.

"Their armies and what is left of their navy are now impotent."

Tribute To Fighters

Mr. Truman paid tribute to the armed forces who fought through to victory. He will address American service men directly by radio tomorrow at approximately 9:19 p. m. EWT.

"As President of the United States," the chief executive stated, "I proclaim Sunday, September second, 1945, to be V-J Day—the day of formal surrender by Japan.

"It is not yet the day for the formal proclamation of the end of the war or of the cessation of hostilities.

"But it is a day which we Americans shall always remember as a day of retribution—as we remember that other day of infamy (Pearl Harbor).

"From this day we move forward. We move toward a new era

TRUMAN—Page 6

MacARTHUR LOOKS ON AS SHIGEMITSU SIGNS — Japan's Foreign Minister, Mamoru Shigemitsu (right seated), signs unconditional surrender papers aboard the U.S.S. Missouri in Tokyo Bay as General MacArthur (left at mike) and Lieut. Gen. Richard Sutherland, his chief of staff (center) witness the historic moment. (AP Wirephoto via Navy Radiophoto, from the U.S.S. Iowa in Tokyo Bay.)

20 Min. Ceremony On Missouri Ends Dreams Of Empire

Text of surrender documents on Page 14.

U. S. S. Missouri, Tokyo Bay, Sunday, Sept. 2—(AP)—Two nervous Japanese formally and unconditionally surrendered all remnants of their smashed empire to the Allies today, restoring peace to a war-battered world.

Surrender hour was cool and cloudy, but the sun broke through the overcast 20 minutes later as General MacArthur intoned "these proceedings are closed."

Foreign Minister Mamoru Shigemitsu, who signed for the Japanese government, doffed his top hat and nervously fingered his fountain pen before he firmly signed the two copies of the surrender document—one for Japan, one for the Allies. Shigemitsu penned his name in English on one document.

Gen. Yoshijiro Umezu, for the Imperial Staff, also nervous, signed hurriedly; quickly stepped aside. A Japanese colonel wiped his eyes. All of the Nipponese presente were tense and drawn.

Then MacArthur signed, deliberately, using five pens. The first two-silverplated especially for the occasion—he handed in turn to Lt. Gen. Jonathon M. Wainwright and to British Gen. Arthur Ernest Percival, who were forced to surrender Corregidor and Singapore, respectively, in the war's darkest hours.

Wainwright and Percival smiled; saluted snappily. They had been rescued only a few days ago from Japanese prisoner of war camps.

"It is my earnest hope and indeed the hope of all mankind that from this solemn occasion a better world shall emerge out of the blood and carnage of the past," MacArthur said.

The historic signing took place on a long table on the gallery deck.

Will Not Forget Pearl Harbor

Minutes later, from the White House, where Japanese warlords once asserted they would dictate their own peace terms, President Truman broadcast:

"We shall not forget Pearl Harbor. The Japanese militarists will not forget the U.S.S. Missouri."

The 45,000-ton Missouri, which less than a month ago was blasting Japanese war industries with her 16-inch guns, had those rifles pointed skyward and her bow pointed toward the heart of Japan for the ceremony.

Once there was a slight delay when it appeared someone had signed on the wrong line.

All Allied representatives were sober-faced, but obviously glad it's over. Soldiers, sailors and Marines some of whom had fought their way across the Pacific, hardly could hide a trace of exuberance on their serious faces.

MacArthur's hand shook slightly as he reached "Dou – – –" in his first signature. His face twitched but his voice was strong although he appeared to be under great emotional strain.

After the Japanese signed, he said dramatically, "will General Wainwright and General Percival step forward while I sign?"

Wainwright, by his own request, was accompanied by his chief of staff, Brig. Gen. Lewis Beebe; his aides, Col. John Pugh and Lt. Col. Thomas Dooley, and his orderly-chauffeur, Sgt. Herbert Carroll. Percival was accompanied by his orderly.

Among United States naval officers present were Admiral Nimitz, who signed for his country; his chief of staff, Vice Adm. Forrest C. Sherman; Admiral Halsey; Vice Admiral John A. Towers, commander of naval air in the Pacific; Vice Adm. Theodore C. Wilkinson, who directed many amphibious landings under both Halsey and Adm. Thomas C. Kinkaid, commander of the

SURRENDER CEREMONY—Page 6

BYRNES PLEDGES DRASTIC CHANGE IN JAP POLITICS

Allies Will Judge Whether New Government Will Bring Peace, He Warns

Washington, Sept. 1—(AP)—Secretary of State Byrnes tonight promised revolutionary political changes in Japan to allow the eventual development, by the Japanese people themselves, of a peacefully-inclined government.

He said that "we expect" to see such a government emerge eventually but he sternly added:

"We and our Allies shall be the judges as to whether the government which does emerge will or will not contribute to the peace and security of the world. We shall judge that government by its deeds, not by its words."

Byrnes made the assertion in a 400-word statement on the formal surrender of the Japanese aboard the battleship Missouri off Tokyo tonight. Along with this, the State Department released V-J Day statements also by two former Secretaries of State and a former Undersecretary. They said:

Depends On Human Race

Former Secretary Cordell Hull: "The very survival of the human race now depends upon its ability to build a system of organized relations among men and among nations, in which our newly-found powers will be made to serve the ends of human welfare."

Former Secretary E. R. Stettinius, Jr., designated as chief American delegate to the United Nations: "The destructive force of modern methods of warfare which has been made so terribly evident by the atomic bomb, makes it all too clear that civilization cannot survive another war. x x x The world cannot permit the new (United Nations)

BYRNES—Page 7

'We Shall Not Forget'—Truman

Washington, Sept. 1—President Truman attributed this four-fold significance to V-J Day:

1. For This Country—A day for "renewed consecration to the principles which have made us the strongest nation on earth and which, in this war, we have striven so mightily to preserve."
2. For Japan—An end of "power to destroy and kill."
3. For The World—A bright new era of hope for "peace and international goodwill and cooperation."
4. For History—"The day of formal surrender by Japan."

"We shall not forget Pearl Harbor," he said.

"The Japanese militarists will not forget the U. S. S. Missouri.

"The evil done by the Japanese war lords can never be repaired or forgotten. But their power to destroy and kill has been taken from them. Their armies and what is left of their navy are now impotent."

LABOR TRIBUTE PAID BY TRUMAN

Says Nation Recognizes Dignity And Importance Of Those In Nation Who Work

Washington, Sept. 1—(AP)—President Truman said tonight in a Labor Day statement that the nation recognizes the importance and dignity of labor and the right of every American to a wage which will permit a decent living standard.

The President's comment was echoed by other leaders in the country, as the United States prepared to celebrate the Labor Day holiday.

Concern was voiced by some leaders, however, lest the process of reconversion and attendant unemployment might not be promptly solved.

Told To Have Fun

Meanwhile the nation's war workers, who have been urged since the start of the war to regard Labor Day as just another working day,

LABOR—Page 7

MacArthur Demands Japs Obey Quickly

Tokyo, Sept. 2—(Sunday)—(INS)—Under pain of "drastic and summary punishment," Imperial Japan today was commanded by Gen. Douglas MacArthur to speed up surrender of warriors, liberate prisoners, and disarm quickly and completely.

The Supreme Allied Commander dictated his crisp and stern instructions through imperial headquarters in his "General Order No. 1"—a document which has few parallels for the crushing thoroughness with which it reduces a formerly great power to military impotence.

Speedily carrying out his promise of firm treatment for Nippon, made at surrender ceremonies today aboard the U.S.S. Missouri, Gen. MacArthur also ordered the Japs to cooperate fully as the Allied occupation gets under way.

Pending their liberation, the prisoners and internees must be well cared for—in contrast to the horrible treatment those already delivered have reported—and they must be given self-government at once.

If all the orders are not obeyed "scrupulously and promptly", the first general order said, those who fail in their responsibility "will incur drastic and summary punishment at the hands of Allied military authorities and the Japanese government."

Provisions of Order

Provisions of the order included:

I—Japs in all fields were ordered to "cease hostilities at once," "remain in their present locations," "surrender unconditionally to commanders" representing the United Nations, and carry out the victors' instructions "completely

MAC ARTHUR—Page 6

2 ELECTROCUTED NEAR LEBANON

Lebanon, Sept. 1—Two men were electrocuted shortly before 11 p. m. Saturday by a live wire which they were attempting to clear from the highway 10 miles north of here.

The dead were reported as Elmer Planken, Annville R2, and Salvadore DiGiorgio, New York City.

First accounts were that an electric storm blew an electric pole and wires on the road in front of a truck operated by DiGiorgio. Planken, a passing motorist, was said to have stopped to help clear away the wires.

State police were investigating.

Holiday Travel Soars To Four-Year High

Highway, train, and through bus travel to and from Lancaster soared to a four-year high Saturday as the city plunged into what was expected to be its biggest week-end since Pearl Harbor, marked by official V-J Day today and a "full-dress" observance of Labor Day tomorrow.

Huge crowds, preparing to celebrate and take advantag of what is predicted will be ideal weekend weather, thronged to bus and train ticket windows and waiting rooms throughout the day or climbed into family automobiles, rejuvenated by full tanks of gasoline, to roar out on the highways.

For the first time since end of the war terminated many travel restrictions, "extra" trains and buses, their aisles filled with standees, were available for local travelers.

A heavy electrical storm, accompanied by rain, struck some sections of the county late Saturday night.

Their capacity for victory celebration exhausted by previous displays, Lancastrians received the formal V-J proclamation quietly last night, and no special observance was planned for today except V-J prayer in individual city churches.

There was only one negative factor in Lancaster's Labor Day weekend—but that was a big one. The transportation strike was expected to cut severely attendance at local parks and swimming pools.

Labor Day tomorrow will find practically all business activity halted here. Banks, government agencies, stores, and offices will be closed. In addition, all local factories will give their employes

TRAVEL—Page 7

Japs' Document Bound In Black

U. S. S. Missouri, Tokyo Bay, Sunday, Sept. 2—(AP)—The surrender document handed the Japanese signatories was bound in black—traditional color for mourning.

The copy retained by General MacArthur for the Allies was bound in green—traditional color of new life and new hope.

First 2 Holiday Motor Casualties

An 18-year-old Peach Bottom youth and an 11-year-old city boy were the first local casualties from holiday weekend motor accidents.

Roy Eller, Peach Bottom, was admitted to St. Joseph's Hospital shortly after 8 p. m. Saturday, suffering from contusions of the left shoulder, arm, and chest, sustained two hours earlier when he reportedly lost control of his truck and it went off the road on the Quarryville-Peach Bottom Road.

George Gertz, 20 W. Lemon St., suffered a right foot injury when he ran into a slow-moving car, operated by Edward L. Gochenauer 233 N. Queen St., on Market St. Saturday afternoon.

Lightning Fires 12-Room Dwelling and Warehouse

Fire, apparently set by lightning during Saturday night's electric storm, destroyed a large frame house at Manheim R1, inflicting estimated $15,000 damage and simultaneously set ablaze a potato warehouse a short distance away.

Firemen from four county companies were forced to lay hose for a mile into Manheim to fight the blaze which completely gutted a 12-room property tenanted by the Oliver Rohrer family on the Manheim Pike, one and one-half miles south of Manheim.

At least four firemen from the Landisville company were reported overcome by smoke while fighting the fire at the Lancaster Junction warehouse which was continuing into the early morning hours. Manheim equipment also was fighting the warehouse blaze. The property is known as the Cassell Warehouse.

The house fire routed three persons from their beds, and when it was discovered that the fire had burned out the telephone wire, Rufus Rohrer, twenty, son of the tenant, drove into Manheim to give the alarm.

The fire was discovered by his father shortly after 11:15 p. m. when he was awakened by the smell of smoke. Rohrer investigated and found the south side of the attic of the house on fire.

Assisted by neighbors, he carried most of the first floor furniture to safety, but furniture and clothing in the rest of the house was a total loss.

Draws 600 To Scene

Fire companies present were from Manheim, E. Petersburg, Mt.

LIGHTNING—Page 7

City Man Listed Among Liberated Crew Of "Houston"

A city sailor was listed by the Navy Department Saturday night as one of the enlisted men of the Houston crew who were liberated and are now in Calcutta, India.

The local man is Robert Leon Hanley, S2-c, USNR, son of Mr. and Mrs. Howard M. Hanley, 230 W. Strawberry St.

It was officially reported that 92 officers and enlisted men of the Cruiser Houston, which disappeared Feb. 28, 1942, have been liberated. All of them, with the exception of two Chinese mess attendants, had previously been listed as prisoners of war. There was no indication as to exactly where this group had been held prisoners. The Navy stated that an officer and an enlisted man, also have been liberated in Thailand.

There was no immediate explanation as to what happened to the cruiser, which disappeared after reporting that it had made contact with a force of Japanese ships. The Houston had 982 officers and men aboard when she disappeared. The Navy listed 94 liberated survivors; 108 identified dead; 179 prisoners of war; 594 in missing status and seven whose status is in doubt.

German Prisoner Flees Middletown

Middletown, Pa., Sept. 1—(AP)—Walter Richter, 19, a German prisoner of war, escaped from barracks at the Middletown Air Technical Service Command last night, Army authorities announced today.

The prisoner, who is six feet tall, weighs 140 pounds, has blue eyes, fair skin and brown hair, was last seen at 9:25 p. m. last night but was missing at 7 a. m. check-up today.

Declaration And Terms That Japs Agreed To Do

(By the Associated Press)

The Potsdam ultimatum, to whose terms the Japanese bowed at the surrender ceremonies in Tokyo Bay, calls for the elimination "for all time" of the authority and influence of those who led Japan into the war and stern justice for war criminals.

Others of the terms laid down by President Truman and Prime Minister Clement Attlee of Britain call for:

Occupation of Japanese territory until the Allies feel the peace of the world is assured;

Limitation of Japanese sovereignty to the main Japanese islands of Honshu, Hokkaido, Kyushu, Shikoku and a few minor islands, stripping Japan of all her conquests;

Complete disarmament of Japanese armed forces;

Removal by the Japanese of all obstacles to a revival of freedom of speech, religion and thought.

What Japs Agreed To

Article by article here is what Japan agreed to do under the terms of surrender:

1. **Accept all provisions of the Potsdam declaration.**
2. **Surrender unconditionally all armed forces.**
3. **Cease hostilities forthwith and preserve and save from damage all ships, aircraft and military and civil property.**
4. **Command imperial general headquarters to issue orders to all field commanders everywhere to surrender their forces unconditionally.**
5. **See that all civil, military and naval officials obey and**

DECLARATION—Page 7

ALP Ban Refused By Supreme Court

Philadelphia, Sept. 1—(AP)—The Pennsylvania Supreme Court today rejected five different appeals to bar American Labor Party candidates from the ballot in the coming general elections.

The court declined, by a vote of 3 to 2, to take original jurisdiction in an appeal against the city of Philadelphia, but voted unanimously against two appeals against the Commonwealth of Pennsylvania and two Dauphin county suits against John M. Morrison as Secretary of the Commonwealth.

School Bell Sounds Call To Classes And Era Of Peace

FIFTY-YEAR-OLD CHART from the archives of St. Mary's parochial school familar to older generations who learned their spelling without complications is being demonstrated at the Model School, Millersville, Miss Daisy E. Hoffmeier, supervisor. Below, the "Big Book" combines spelling and "social consciousness."

BAREFOOT SCHOOL DAYS preserve the oldest American tradition as Stumptown's one-room school begins first peacetime classes in four years. Furnace in rear is all set for wintry months. Teacher, Hazel McKay, ten.

BACK TO SCHOOL brought out thousands of Lancaster city and county children to begin a new epoch of education and peace in the community's wide variety of classrooms. A glance at the pictures here suggests that you might still read the whole history of American education and travel no more than ten miles either way from the county seat. There are the old school pumps competing with modern water systems, furnaces in the classroom, fancy air-conditioning apparatus, barefoot pupils and pupils in the newest styles, old equipment and ultra modern gadgets preserved and developed steadily through years of war and peace until they have become as much a part of our personal backgrounds as the three Rs themselves. This year although the attendance is under previous records due to normal fluctuations, the slogan "Back to School" is showing results in this area. The story is as new as 1945, and as old as the first schools 100 years ago.

THE "BIG BOOK" adds a touch of color, gears the big pictures with the little pictures in the primers, and helps to emphasize the family unit. The cat is not only the cat, but the mother of the little cats, there is a house, etc. Miss Mary Lovette, instructing at the Model School, Millersville.

AARON AT THE PUMP tries out his muscles for those drinks which will be in demand at recess. He is Aaron Beiler at the Stumptown school.

MAKING IT COUNT are Elizabeth Becker and William Caci, second day at St. Mary's using an old now aided in modern education by small sticks and abacus which has taught generations of Lancastrians, charts.

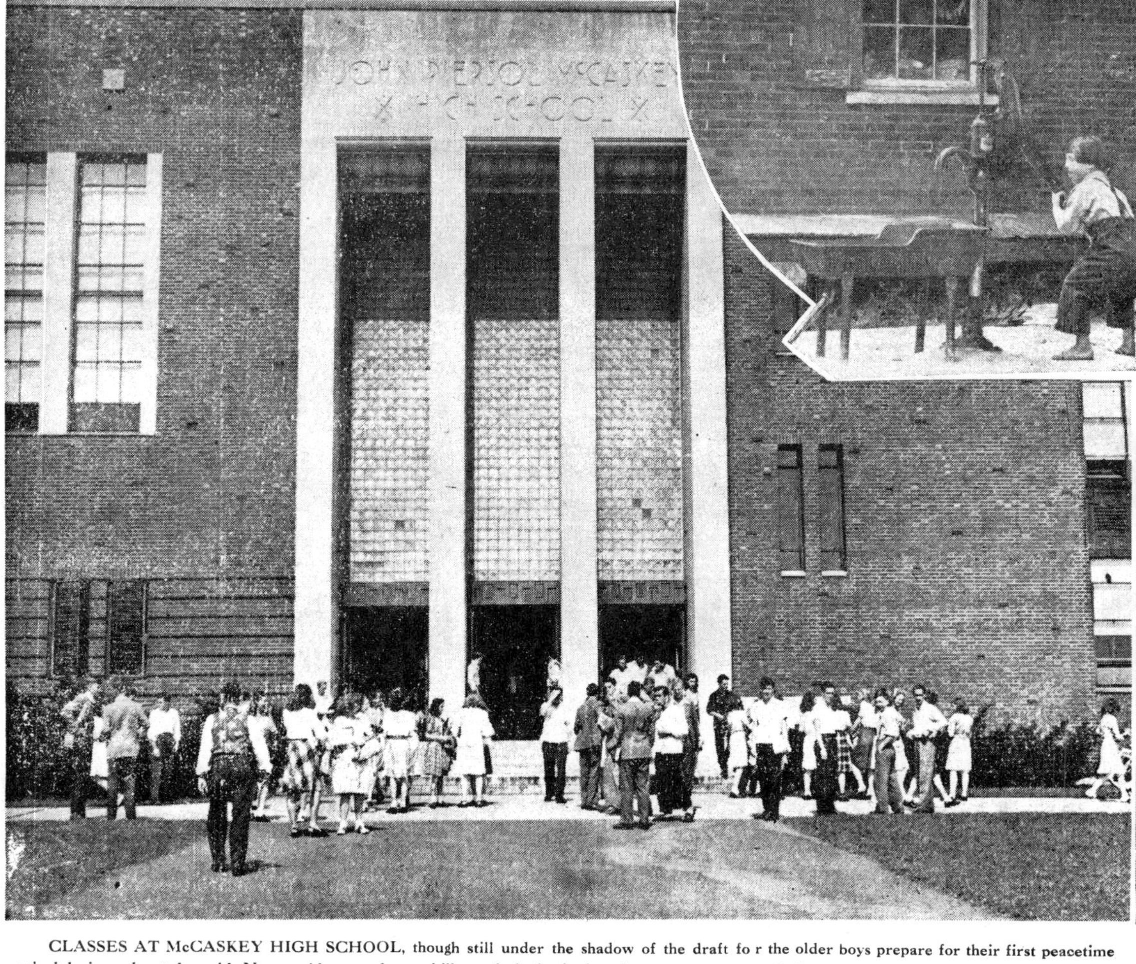

CLASSES AT McCASKEY HIGH SCHOOL, though still under the shadow of the draft fo r the older boys prepare for their first peacetime schedule in a changed world. New problems and new skills mark the beginning of a new postwar generation.

YOUNGEST FRY at Nathan C. Schaeffer school, Manheim twp., begin their first day under the eye of Mrs. Gladys Martin Fret, in a kindergarten which in the modern system synchronizes subjects with higher classes. They move to first grade next year.

One Defense Dept. Is Called Blunder
See Lawrence — Editorial Page

LANCASTER NEW ERA

WEATHER
Fair and a little colder tonight; Saturday increasing cloudiness and continued cold.

69th Year—No. 21,279 | Entered as second class matter January 31, 1924, at the Post Office at Lancaster, Pa., under the Act of March 3, 1879, Reg. U. S. Pat. Off. | LANCASTER, PA., FRIDAY, DECEMBER 21, 1945 | CITY EDITION | 22 PAGES | 20c PER WEEK—4c Per Copy

Gen. Patton Dies As Crash Injuries Weaken Heart

GEN. GEORGE S. PATTON, JR.

Led 3rd Army Across Europe; Wife Is at Side

HEIDELBERG, Germany, Dec. 21—(AP)—Gen. George S. Patton, Jr., who led the victorious U. S. Third Army from the beaches of Normandy into Czechoslovakia, died at 5:50 P. M. (11:50 A. M. EST) today a dozen days after his neck was broken in a traffic accident.

The general's stout old fighting heart weakened during the day from effects of pulmonary complications which had beset his apparent recovery from the broken neck and partial paralysis.

Mrs. Patton was with him.

The announcement of the general's death was made by Brig. Gen. John M. Willen of the U. S. Seventh Army.

60 Years Old Nov. 11

The general was 60 last Nov. 11. He was commander of the U. S. 15th Army at the time of his death. He had served briefly as acting commander of all American forces in the European theater a few days before his automobile and an army truck collided near Mannheim on Sunday, Dec. 9.

Patton himself, when his condition was critical after the motor car accident, described it as "a hell of a way to die."

Heidelberg, an old university town, was one of the thousands of places which the Third Army captured in his rough ride over Germany.

Sketch of Gen. Patton's life appears on Page 6.

Unscratched In Battle

By an ironic twist, Patton had gone unscratched through all his campaigns of the war. The peacetime accident left him paralyzed from the shoulders down.

Gen. Joseph T. McNarney, U. S. Commander in the European theater, commented that it was his "painful duty to announce the death of a great fighter and a great man."

The official announcement said: "Gen. Patton died at 5:50 tonight it was announced by Brig. Gen. John M. Willen, chief of staff of the Seventh Army. The general died peacefully."

The expert at armored warfare who campaigned brilliantly in Africa, Sicily, France, Belgium, Germany, Austria and Czechoslovakia in Allied drives that staggered Germany to her knees last Spring had been making an amazing recovery until yesterday.

Heart Became Affected

It was then that the respiratory condition developed. By morning today, doctors were gravely worried about the deterioration in his condition. As Patton's life ebbed away, his heart became affected.

Shortly before his death, Maj. Gen. A. W. Kenner, Chief of Army Surgeons in Europe, left European headquarters in Frankfurt for Patton's bedside.

Only two minutes before the General died, the 130th Station Hospital issued this bulletin on his condition:

"General Patton's condition is considered serious. There has been a pulmonary complication which has resulted in an accumulation of secretions in the lungs thus embarrassing respiration. Paralysis of

(See GEN. PATTON—Page 6)

116 STORES READY FOR SEMI-ANNUAL SALES DAY TODAY

Hour More Of Shopping To Be Provided At 37th Such Event

This is Lancaster Sales Day, the semi-annual event eagerly waited by thousands of consumers in the Lancaster trade area.

After thirty-six such sales, experienced shoppers need no assurance that this sale, the thirty-seventh, will be well worth while. Those who plan to visit Lancaster for the first time Wednesday (today) are sure to be delighted with the great assortment of merchandise from which they can select bargains.

STORES OPEN EARLY

One hundred and sixteen participating stores are ready to open at 8:30 a. m. a half hour earlier than usual. Stores will remain open an extra half-hour in the afternoon —until 5:30—thus giving buyers an extra hour for shopping.

Each of the 116 stores has made careful preparation for the event. Windows have been newly decorated (and incidentally, in the window of each participating store is a large, green and white sales day banner as a means of identification); stocks have been replenished; extra salespeople have been employed to take care of the expected crowds. Merchandise values and services will be excellent, making this an event worth planning to attend. Those who have not already made plans to come to Lancaster Wednesday may still do so to take advantage of this opportunity to fill personal and household needs at the reductions in effect for this one day only. Bargains will be available to the late afternoon shopper as well as to those who are on hand early in the morning.

AID TO ALLIES DRIVE LITERATURE ARRIVES

Local Unit of Committee To Defend America Also Has Buttons To Distribute At Headquarters

Buttons and literature relative to the newly organized Women's Division of the Committee to Defend America by Aiding the Allies are available at the local committee's headquarters, 117 East King street, it was announced Tuesday by Mrs. John F. Steinman, chairman of the local committee. The committee members are busy circulating petitions which are being sent to President Franklin D. Roosevelt and Congress asking them to aid those who are fighting against dictators of Europe. These buttons and literature are free and may be obtained at the headquarters.

Intelligencer Journal Weather Calendar

COMPARATIVE TEMPERATURES

Station	High	Low
Intell Journal	95	72
Water Works	98	70
Ephrata	101	73
Last Year (Ephrata)	93	72
Official High for Year, July 26		102.5
Official Low for Year, Jan. 20		2
Character of Day		Clear

HOURLY TEMPERATURES

(Tuesday)			
8 a. m.	77	9 p. m.	77
11 a. m.	84	10 p. m.	77
2 p. m.	92	11 p. m.	77
5 p. m.	94	Midnight	75
6 p. m.	79	(Wednesday)	
7 p. m.	78	1 a. m.	74
8 p. m.	79	2 a. m.	74
		3 a. m.	74

HUMIDITY

8 a. m.—84 11 a. m.—64 2 p. m.—50
5 p. m.—54 8 p. m.—79 11 p. m.—79
Average Humidity 69
Dew Point, 11 p. m. 71

More of WEATHER on Page 7

DAYLIGHT TIME IN INTELL
All time mentioned in The Intelligencer Journal is Daylight Time unless otherwise noted.

Oregon Man Jailed In Theft of Scarce Foods

Harold Z. White, forty-five, Oregon, convicted on charges of larceny and receiving stolen goods by a jury in the last case tried at the December term of Criminal Court, was jailed for eight months and fined $50 and costs by Judge Wissler this morning.

Herbert R. Harvey, forty, Paradise, the alleged ringleader of a gang involved in wholesale thefts of scarce foodstuffs from the Miller and Hartman warehouse, previously received 1 1-2 to 3 years, and a 17-year-old employe accomplice was placed on probation. The fourth and final member of the

(See COURT—Page 19)

FOOD STOLEN FROM FREEZING LOCKERS

State Police have received a number of complaints of foodstuff thefts from storage lockers at the Lancaster Ice Mfg. Co., Engleside.

The latest theft involved a 19-pound ham and other items from the locker of Martin Lefever, Millersville. Lefever told police the ham, which he was storing for a friend, was to be used at a Christmas party.

Last month, H. B. Johnson, of Lititz, reported the theft of 20 chickens and between 20 and 25 pounds of beef from his locker and previously police received complaints of other thefts of meat and poultry from the Engleside plant.

Mayor Invites the UNO To Establish Capital Here

Some of Requirements for World Peace Center Include 1 Sq. Acre Land, 1200 Year-Around Hotel Rooms, Big Auditoriums, etc.

Mayor Cary today sent a cable to the United Nations Preparatory Commission now meeting in London inviting the organization to consider Lancaster as a possible site for the proposed permanent World Capital.

The mayor sent the cablegram following an announcement by the commission that it favors a site in a small city on the eastern seaboard of the United States. The text of the mayor's message cabled to London today was as follows:

"United Nations Preparatory Commission,
London, England.

"Lancaster, Pa., invites the United Nations Preparatory Commission to consider our city as site for the World Capital of the UNO. We are a community of 110,000 population situated centrally among the major cities of New York, Philadelphia and Washington, D. C. We are on the main line of the largest railroad in the United States and have adequare airport facilities. Lancaster was founded in the 18th century by English immigrants and is rich in historical heritage and scenic beauty. Most of our people are descendants of original settlers, making for a conservative and truly patriotic atmosphere.

DALE E. CARY, Mayor."

Some Of Requirements

Some of the requirements for the UNO capital, as previously announced, are:

The community that gets the capital or some individual must donate to the UNO not less than one square mile of land.

The community must provide a hotel of not less than 1,200 rooms to operate the year around.

An auditorium and conference rooms to accommodate several thousand persons must be provided.

Adequate housing in homes built to the specifications provided by the UNO must be provided by the community.

The community that gets the capital also must have adequate railroad and air travel facilities and an airport that can accommodate the biggest and newest planes.

The policy on who pays for the capital buildings on the square

(See UNO CAPITAL—Page 6)

Needy to Get Yule Cheer —Also 100 Lbs. of Butter

The first peacetime Christmas here in five years is being observed with the annual distribution of food and other Yule needs to the underprivileged by civic, fraternal, and religious organizations.

The round of children's Christmas parties also is in full swing and will continue over the weekend and through Christmas Day and the holiday season.

Approximately 100 pounds of Christmas butter—count them—will be distributed by the Elks' Club with its annual Yule baskets for the needy next Monday afternoon.

Each basket will contain one pound of butter and they will be distributed to about 100 families by truck between 1 and 3 p. m. The baskets also will contain ham, lard, scrapple, and canned goods.

J. A. Butler is chairman of the club's charity committee in charge of the project. Wilbert Starr is in charge of filling the baskets and distributing them.

Complete Holiday Meal

The Water Street Mission will distribute 50 Yule food baskets to needy families tomorrow. The baskets will contain the ingredients of a complete holiday meal—one peck of potatoes, one head of cabbage, two pounds of beans, two cans of corn, two loaves of bread, turnips, one jar of peanut butter, one pound of margarine, one pound of lard, and cash certificates for meat and sugar.

The Mission also will serve its annual Christmas dinner to approximately 500 persons, starting at 11 a. m. Monday.

Food Orders For 130

The Salvation Army is distributing food orders this week to 130 needy families. The orders are being substituted for the usual Salvation Army Christmas baskets.

In addition, 500 "sunshine baskets" will be distributed at the County and Long Homes and the city hospitals, and 200 gifts are ready for distribution to servicemen at the Penn Square canteen.

The annual Salvation Army Christmas party for children will be held at the headquarters next Wednesday at 7:30 p. m.

Rounding out local activities are the projects of the Family Bureau

(See CHRISTMAS—Page 19)

FEW TIRES AFTER RATIONING ENDS

May Be Scarce Here For All of 1946

ONLY SUGAR LEFT ON RATION LIST; THE END IS NOT IN SIGHT

Termination of tire rationing New Year's Day will leave only sugar on the national ration list.

The list once included meats, canned foods, gasoline, automobiles, shoes, fuel oil, coffee and several other commodities.

No early end to sugar rationing is in sight.

In Pennsylvania, whisky also is still rationed.

Tire rationing ends January 1 after four years of thin treads, but it will be many months before passenger car operators can get the tires they need, according to opinions expressed today by local distributors.

The decision of OPA and civilian production administration to lift controls is based on their "considered opinion" that there no longer is any danger of a transportation breakdown.

Both agencies emphasized, however, that despite a big increase in tire production, all motorists will not be able to walk in and buy new casings for some time.

May Be Scarce All of '46

"A plentiful supply of tires is not in sight for several months, perhaps all of 1946," said CPA Administrator John D. Small.

OPA Chief Chester Bowles cautioned that "many motorists will have to wait for tires." He urged dealers not to sell complete sets "to those who can get along with one or two tires during the next several months."

Hundreds of Unfilled Orders

One local tire dealer said that he has a "fist full" of Ration Board

(See TIRES—Page 19)

Ford's Next-door Neighbor Is Found Slain In His Auto

HOLLAND, Mich., Dec. 21—(AP)—The body of Ray Gordon Beh, 34, a next-door neighbor of Henry Ford II in Grosse Pointe Farms, Mich., was found this morning in a snow covered car at a side of a main highway north of Holland, a bullet wound in his right side.

Police said Beh had been dead since Thursday. A sales representative for an eastern airplane firm, Beh called his wife Wednesday night from a Chicago hotel and told her he would be in Muskegon, Mich., Thursday and would return to the exclusive Detroit suburb Friday.

Mrs. Beh said her husband was in the habit of picking up hitch-hikers and that he "always" gave lifts to men in uniform. No gun was found in Beh's car.

GALES FIRE MINES ON ENGLISH COAST

DOVER, England, Dec. 21—(AP)—Wintry gales swept a new and menacing series of floating mines today among shipping and near towns on the English channel coast.

Repeated explosions shook the Straits of Dover as demolition crews in sweepers exploded loose mines. Other mines blew up when they hit the Goodwin sands. Heavy seas brought the worst floods in 50 years to Cork, Eire.

20,000 GI Brides To Come to States--"If, When and But"

LONDON, Dec. 21.— (AP) —A U. S. Navy spokesman said today thousands of brides of servicemen and their babies could start sailing for the United States between Jan. 10-20 if sufficient shipping was provided and if President Truman signs a bill allowing them to enter as non-quota immigrant.

The American embassy expects by Jan. 1 to have 6,500 applications for visas, the maximum quota allotment. The pending bill would allow from 15,000 to 20,000 dependents of service men to enter the United States each month.

Four hospital ships have been assigned tentatively to begin transporting some 25,000 wives and 20,000 infants of servicemen. To do the job quickly, we will need larger ships like the Europa.

MARSHALL MEETS CHIANGS IN NANKING

NANKING, Dec. 21—(AP)—Gen. George C. Marshall, President Truman's special envoy to China, arrived here by plane today and was met at the airfield by Generalissimo Chiang Kai-Shek and Madame Chiang.

The two men saluted and clasped hands on the dusty, windswept Nanking airfield. Lt. Gen. Albert C. Wedemeyer, commanding American forces in China, accompanied Marshall to Nanking.

The party drove to the Generalissimo's residence to begin the historic conferences.

SUFFRAGE!

CHEHALIS, Wash., Dec. 21 —(AP) —The Lewis County Women's Republican Club finally have let the bars down.

They're letting men join but only as associated members.

NEW HOUSING PLAN GOES IN EFFECT JAN. 15

Many of 400,000 Homes Planned for '46 Will Rent for Under $80

WASHINGTON, Dec. 21—(AP)—The government's program to spur home construction will go into effect Jan. 15, John D. Small announced today.

The chief of the Civilian Production Administration ordered that dwellings costing $10,000 or less be offered first to veterans and told a news conference that the top rent on these dwellings will be $80 a month.

400,000 Homes In '46

Small estimated that at least 400,000 homes will be built under the program in 1946.

"We expect," he added, "that a substantial number of these will sell at considerably less than $10,000."

This means, Small said, that a great many of the new dwellings will rent for under $80 a month.

The CPA chief outlined a new regulation restoring 10 kinds of critically scarce building materials to a priority system and announced that the Federal Housing Administration will handle applications for these through its 52 field offices.

Priority On Materials

Beginning Jan. 15, home builders who qualify will be assigned a so-called "H.H." rating for these materials.

Ratings will be awarded either to individual veterans who wish to build for themselves, or to builders desiring to erect one or more buildings.

Housing already underway may be brought within the program, Small said, if it meets the $10,000 price limit, is offered first to veterans, and meets other standards outlined in the regulation.

Vets Given Choice

All applicants for priorities assistance in obtaining materials must agree to make the housing available to veterans during the period of construction and for 30 days thereafter.

At the conclusion of that period it may be sold or rented to a non-veteran at the same sale price or rental applicable to veterans.

Building materials covered by the new regulation are:

Common and face brick, clay sewer pipe, structural tile, gypsum board, gypsum lath, cast iron soil pipe and fittings, cast iron radiation equipment, bath tubs, lumber and millwork.

M'ARTHUR DENIES THREAT TO QUIT

Also Spikes Report Of Friction With Soviets

TOKYO, Dec. 21.—(AP)—Gen MacArthur today denied a broadcast report that his headquarters had become embroiled in arguments with the Russians over assignment of Soviet occupation troops to Japan and that MacArthur had threatened to resign.

"I am here to serve and not to hinder or obstruct American government," the Supreme Commander of the Allied Powers said in a statement issued by his office.

"It is my full purpose to see the thing through. The question of Russian participation in the occupation is a matter for other decision than my own."

The statement said that the broadcast report, "purported to have been made by Larry Tighe of the American Broadcasting Corporation, has absolutely no basis in fact."

It concluded:

"If Tighe made the statement he is alleged to have broadcast from Tokyo, someone must have been feeding him a funny type of 'hooch' being peddled around Tokyo on the black market."

(Taking to the air after issuance of the statement, Tighe said "I reaffirm the story which I previously broadcast that the express desire of the commander of this area is that the Russian troops not be allowed to take over the Japanese island of Hokkaido.")

NAZI BROADCASTER TO DIE IN ENGLAND

LONDON, Dec. 21—(AP)—Walter Purdy, 27, former royal naval officer, was sentenced to death for high treason today after a jury at Old Bailey agreed on a verdict of guilty in 17 minutes.

Purdy was charged with broadcasting and preparing leaflets for the Nazis after he had been made a prisoner of war.

Auto Safety Hints

The State Police say:

Signs bearing the legend, "Slippery when wet" have become familiar to Pennsylvania motorists. They are erected only at places along the highways where it is known that the surface of the roadway becomes slippery during rainy weather, and these warning signs should never be ignored.

Don't be the one to test the accuracy of the warning signs —obey them.

'FACT' GROUPS GET RIGHT TO URGE RAISES

New Directive Allows Hikes Regardless Of Result On Prices

WASHINGTON, Dec. 21—(AP)—The Administration laid down specific rules and policies today giving the government Fact Finding Boards broad authority to recommend wage increases which may or may not result in price increases.

At the same time, the boards were cautioned that, in proposing any wage increases, any individual Fact Finding panel must "satisfy itself" that employers could or could not absorb the additional cost at prevailing prices.

Must Find "Ability To Pay"

In reaching its decision, the "panel must necessarily inquire into the issue of the employer's ability to pay," the fact finders were told. However, the policy statement pointed out, "ability to pay is a limitation on and does not necessarily constitute a measure of the amount of fair increase."

Shortly after the statement was issued by Secretary of Labor Schwellenbach, the oil-wage fact finding board announced its adjournment until Jan. 7 at the request of several of the oil companies involved.

The recess was taken to allow the companies and the CIO Oil Workers union to resume collective bargaining, on a plant-by-plant basis, over the 30 per cent wage increase demanded by the union. Attorneys for Socony-Vacuum, Standard Oil of Ohio, and the Atlantic Refining Co., said they would use the time to bargain with the union and that in some cases the negotiations already were underway.

Blue Print For Others

Although the Schwellenbach fact-finding rules and policies were given direct to the Oil Board, they were considered a blueprint for all federal fact-finding.

On the basis, they would apply to the Presidentially-appointed boards in the General Motors strike and steel wage disputes.

Official interpretations of the exact scope of the fact finding authority were not immediately available. However, the panels were given specific permission to recommend either wage increases which employers could absorb without increasing prices or, when necessary, increases which might result in price advances.

Further, the fact finders will be allowed to suggest a broadening of wage-price stabilization standards now in force so as to extend possible price relief in specific cases.

On the subject of introduction of company books, which President

(See LABOR—Page 6)

YULE GIFTS BURN, TREE IS SAVED

Fire Damages Home Near Mount Joy

Fire, which damaged their parents' home to the extent of $1,500, at the same time put a damper on the Christmas plans of Fandler, aged three, and his brother, nine-months, sons of Mr. and Mrs. Robert J. Torma, Mt. Joy.

Originating from an overheated furnace, the flames broke into the Forma living room, where a decorated Christmas tree had already been set up, and destroyed most of the toys surrounding it.

The tree, however, was undamaged.

The blaze was discovered by Mrs. Torma about 8 a. m. It spread through the partitions of the frame farmhouse, damaging the walls from the cellar to the attic, and broke out into the living room on the first floor where the Christmas tree and presents were ready.

Firemen of the Mount Joy Co. had to detour the two engines through the fields because of drifted roads. Ray Myers, fire chief, said the men laid over 300 feet of hose to a small run on the farm in order to get water, and it took them over two hours to get the blaze under control.

CHRISTMAS COOKIES, HAM ARE SCARCE

Crowds of pre-holiday shoppers thronged city markets today buying up the main course and "fixings" for their Christmas dinners.

There still was a plentiful supply of poultry, but many butchers reported they were sold out of all turkeys under 10 pounds. Chickens also were selling fast.

Two other holiday standbys were hard to get. The scarce sugar supply cut down on Christmas cookies, star-shaped, confectionery Santa Clauses etc. Ham also was limited in supply. Most markets will have a special holiday session on Monday.

YORK CONTEST HOLDS UP COUNT

HARRISBURG, Dec. 21.— (AP) — An election contest in York County that must be settled by the courts, is holding up the compilation by the State Elections Bureau of the official state-wide vote in the 1945 election of two Superior Court judges.

The Bureau reported that the York County Commissioners informed the State that the returns from the county will be withheld until the contest is settled.

Says Kimmel Didn't Carry Out "Entirely Clear" Order

WASHINGTON, Dec. 21—(AP)—Adm. R. K. Turner asserted today that Adm. Husband E. Kimmel did not comply with "entirely clear" orders and expressed the opinion that if Kimmel had done so losses at Pearl Harbor would have been cut "materially."

Turner also told a Senate-House committee investigating the Dec. 7, 1941, disaster that the Pacific Fleet under Kimmel had been prepared for "just such an attack" and was "ready for war."

The Navy Department, Turner said, had given Kimmel "perfectly specific and entirely clear" orders to take the necessary measures against a Japanese attack.

"Did Kimmel comply, in your opinion?" asked Vice Chairman Cooper (D-Tenn).

"He did not, in my opinion," said Turner.

Prepared "War Warning"

Turner, as Chief of the Navy War Plans division had prepared a Nov. 27, 1941 "war warning" message for Pacific commanders.

If Kimmel had complied, pursued Cooper, "would the disastrous effects not have occurred or have been materially reduced?"

"I think they would have been materially reduced," Turner replied, "and there was a good chance we could have inflicted considerable damage on the Japanese fleet."

"We know now from experience," Turner added, "that a carrier based attack is difficult to stop, and a considerable portion of the attack might have gotten in. But it could have been broken up and have had considerably less effect.

(The Japanese bombers and torpedo bombers sank or badly damaged all the major units in the fleet at Pearl Harbor.)

Saw War Inevitable

Answering a series of questions by Cooper, Turner testified:

1. That the fleet had undergone "many months of preparation for just such an attack as the Japanese made."

2. That "within the limits of the materials program I felt confident the fleet was prepared and ready for war."

3. That he, Adm. Harold R. Stark, then Chief of Naval Oper-

(See PEARL HARBOR—Page 6)

2nd Armored Div., "Hell on Wheels," Starts for Home

PARIS, Dec. 21—(AP)—The famous Second Armored (Hell on Wheels) Division has started home, the Army announced today. An advance party reached Marseille to prepare for the unit's embarkation for the United States.

The 82nd Airborne Division was still shuttling from Le Havre to England, when the troops will sail for home.

The 80th Infantry Division was in Le Havre, from which 7,500 will shuttle to England for re-embarkation and the rest will sail directly to the United States.

The redeployment status of other units: Major portion at home, rest at sea—79th Division; at sea—26th, 36th, 89th and 90th Divisions; first elements at Marseille staging area —100th Division; first elements moving to Bremerhaven—29th Division. Alerted for shipment—84th and 94th Divisions and 22nd Corps Headquarters.

17 DIE IN CRASH

OSLO, Norway, Dec. 21—(AP)—Seventeen passengers and crewmen of a C-47 transport plane operated by the RAF Transport Command were killed when the plane crashed near Oslo Tuesday.

Among the passengers injured was First Lt. A. Neilsen of the U. S. Army. Four Canadians were among those killed.

MARRIED WOMAN AND VET SLAIN

Her Husband Questioned by Allentown Police

ALLENTOWN, Dec. 21.— (AP) — A gunman in a slouch hat shot and killed a 22-year-old discharged air corps lieutenant and his woman companion, witnesses told police today.

A couple, whose names were not disclosed, were quoted by police chief Wayne Elliott as saying they drove Benjamin Clifford Bowman, Jr., of Williamsport, Pa., and Mrs. Madeline Barnak, 21, of Allentown, to Mrs. Barnak's home last midnight. Driving away, they heard two shots and saw the gunman flee.

Elliott said they could not identify him further then as "a man in a slouch hat."

Freshman At Lehigh

The couple, Elliott related, told him Bowman, a freshman at Lehigh College in Bethlehem, met Mrs. Barnak at a Bethlehem night club. Mrs. Barnak, they said, had accompanied them to the night club.

The girl's husband, John Barnak, 30, an employe of the Bethlehem Steel Corporation, was held without charge for questioning. Elliott said adding Barnak denied knowledge of the deaths.

Father Heard Shots

Charles Schiffner, the girl's father, with whom she lived, told Elliott he heard the shots and hurried to the scene. The couple died almost instantly, a coroner's report disclosed.

Coroner Alexander M. Peters of Lehigh County said Mrs. Barnak died of hemorrhage due to a wound in the right chest inflicted by a bullet from a .32-caliber automatic and that Bowman died of hemorrhage and shock from a bullet wound in the right temple inflicted by the same gun.

Bowman's father, Maj. B. Clifford Bowman, is stationed with the air corps in Italy. His grandfather,

(See SLAYING—Page 19)

Says Germany Unable To Live As Democracy

PHILADELPHIA, Dec. 21.— (AP) —Germany is not capable of setting up and living under a democratic government, says Brig. Gen. Eric Fisher Wood, a member of Gen. Dwight D. Eisenhower's staff during World War II.

Wood, a native of Bedford County, Pa., told Penn Athletic Club members yesterday that democratic elements had fled Germany or had been eliminated.

120,000 Stymied Veterans Hit "Hurry Up and Wait"

SAN FRANCISCO, Dec. 21 —(AP)— "It's the same old Army," said Corporal R. A. Holzman, of Long Island, N. Y. "Hurry up and wait."

Holzman was one of nearly 100,000 veterans from the Pacific who today appeared likely to be stranded at West coast ports on Christmas Day because of lack of transportation.

Nearly 120,000 veterans were stymied at the ports today, and ships were scheduled to dump an additional 15,000 more daily on harrassed Army and Navy transportation officials, a far larger number than they expected to have transportation for.

Just Hoped and Hoped

"We had hopes of getting home by Christmas," said Pfc. Julius P. Brenner, of Hudson, N. Y. "Nobody promised us we would. We just hoped we would. I've been overseas only 25 months. Lots of these fellows have been over a lot longer."

Brenner sent a telegram to his parents:

"Living aboard ship because of transportation tieup. Have no idea

(See TROOPS—Page 6)

GALE DELAYING 6,700

ABOARD THE USS RANDOLPH, Dec. 20.—(Delayed)—(AP)—Buffeted by mountainous seas and 70-mile winds, this converted aircraft carrier is striving valiantly to get 6,700 returning veterans of the Italian campaign home for Christmas.

Originally scheduled to dock in New York on Sunday morning, the Randolph will now be lucky to make it by Christmas Day.